SHELLY CASHMAN SERIES®

Microsoft® Office 365™
OFFICE 2016

INTERMEDIATE

SHELLY CASHMAN SERIES®

Microsoft® Office 365™
OFFICE 2016

INTERMEDIATE

Steven M. Freund

Corinne L. Hoisington

Mary Z. Last

Philip J. Pratt

Susan L. Sebok

Joy L. Starks

Misty E. Vermaat

CENGAGE
Learning·

Australia • Brazil • Japan • Korea • Mexico • Singapore • Spain • United Kingdom • United States

CENGAGE
Learning®

Microsoft® Office 2016: Intermediate
Steven M. Freund, Corinne L. Hoisington,
Mary Z. Last, Philip J. Pratt, Susan L. Sebok,
Joy L. Starks, Misty E. Vermaat

SVP, GM Skills & Global Product Management:
Dawn Gerrain

Product Director: Kathleen McMahon

Senior Product Team Manager: Lauren Murphy

Product Team Manager: Andrea Topping

Senior Director, Development: Marah
Bellegarde

Product Development Manager: Leigh Hefferon

Managing Content Developer: Emma F.
Newsom

Developmental Editors: Amanda Brodkin, Deb
Kaufmann, Lyn Markowicz, Lisa Ruffolo,
Karen Stevens

Product Assistant: Erica Chapman

Manuscript Quality Assurance: Jeffrey
Schwartz, John Freitas, Serge Palladino,
Susan Pedicini, Danielle Shaw

Senior Production Director: Wendy Troeger

Production Director: Patty Stephan

Senior Content Project Manager: Matthew
Hutchinson

Manufacturing Planner: Julio Esperas

Designer: Diana Graham

Text Designer: Joel Sadagursky

Cover Template Designer: Diana Graham

Cover image(s): karawan/Shutterstock.com;
Mrs. Opossum/Shutterstock.com

Compositor: Lumina Datamatics, Inc.

Vice President, Marketing: Brian Joyner

Marketing Director: Michele McTighe

Marketing Manager: Stephanie Albracht

The material in this book was written using Microsoft Office 2016 and was
Quality Assurance tested before the publication date. As Microsoft continually updates Office 2016 and Office 365, your software experience may vary
slightly from what is seen in the printed text.

Mac users: If you're working through this product using a Mac, some of the
steps may vary. Additional information for Mac users is included with the data
files for this product.

For product information and technology assistance, contact us at
Cengage Learning Customer & Sales Support, 1-800-354-9706

For permission to use material from this text or product,
submit all requests online at **www.cengage.com/permissions**.
Further permissions questions can be e-mailed to
permissionrequest@cengage.com

Library of Congress Control Number: 2016935646

ISBN: 978-1-305-87038-3

ISBN: 978-1-305-87039-0 (hardcover, spiral-bound)

Cengage Learning
20 Channel Center Street
Boston, MA 02210
USA

Cengage Learning is a leading provider of customized learning solutions with
employees residing in nearly 40 different countries and sales in more than 125
countries around the world. Find your local representative at **www.cengage.
com.**

Cengage Learning products are represented in Canada by Nelson Education, Ltd.

To learn more about Cengage Learning, visit **www.cengage.com**

Purchase any of our products at your local college store or at our preferred
online store **www.cengagebrain.com**

Printed in the United States of America
Print Number: 02   Print Year: 2017

Microsoft® Office 365™
OFFICE 2016

INTERMEDIATE

Contents

Microsoft PowerPoint 2016

Microsoft **Excel 2016**

Microsoft **Access 2016**

Microsoft **Outlook 2016**

MODULE THREE
Managing Contacts and Personal Contact Information with Outlook

Productivity Apps for School and Work

Corinne Hoisington

Lochlan keeps track of his class notes, football plays, and internship meetings with OneNote.

Zoe is using the annotation features of Microsoft Edge to take and save web notes for her research paper.

Nori is creating a Sway site to highlight this year's activities for the Student Government Association.

Hunter is adding interactive videos and screen recordings to his PowerPoint resume.

© Rawpixel/Shutterstock.com

Being computer literate no longer means mastery of only Word, Excel, PowerPoint, Outlook, and Access. To become technology power users, Hunter, Nori, Zoe, and Lochlan are exploring Microsoft OneNote, Sway, Mix, and Edge in Office 2016 and Windows 10.

Learn to use productivity apps!
Links to companion **Sways**, featuring **videos** with hands-on instructions, are located on www.cengagebrain.com.

Introduction to OneNote 2016

notebook | section tab | To Do tag | screen clipping | note | template | Microsoft OneNote Mobile app | sync | drawing canvas | inked handwriting | Ink to Text

As you glance around any classroom, you invariably see paper notebooks and notepads on each desk. Because deciphering and sharing handwritten notes can be a challenge, Microsoft OneNote 2016 replaces physical notebooks, binders, and paper notes with a searchable, digital notebook. OneNote captures your ideas and schoolwork on any device so you can stay organized, share notes, and work with others on projects. Whether you are a student taking class notes as shown in **Figure 1** or an employee taking notes in company meetings, OneNote is the one place to keep notes for all of your projects.

Figure 1: OneNote 2016 notebook

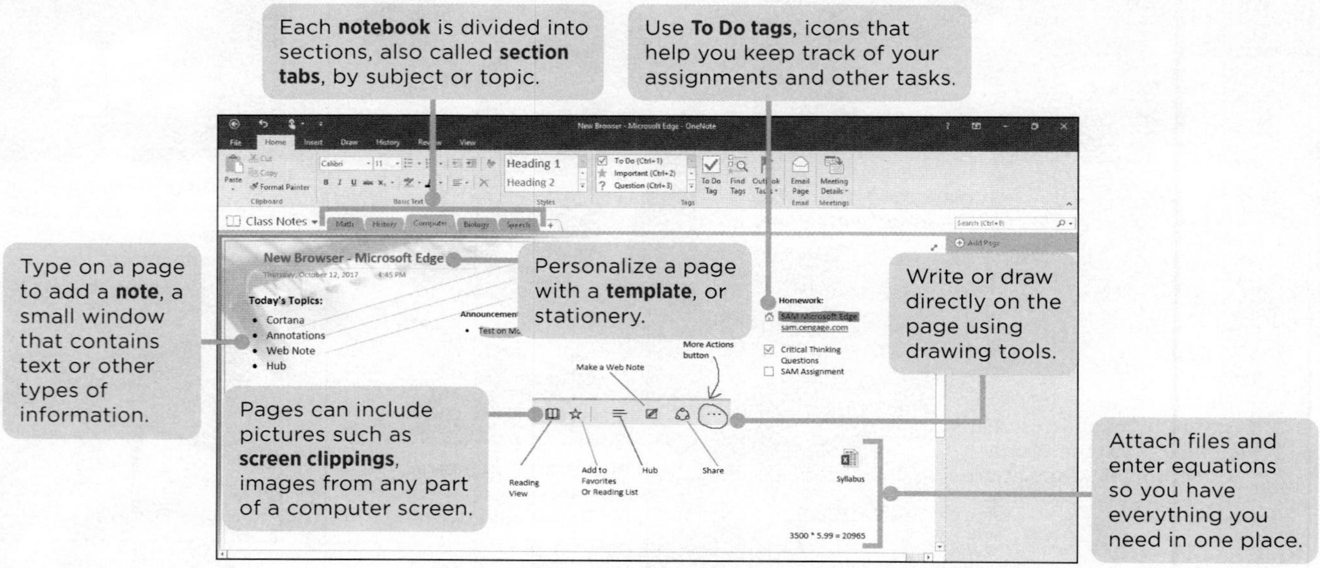

Each **notebook** is divided into sections, also called **section tabs**, by subject or topic.

Use **To Do tags**, icons that help you keep track of your assignments and other tasks.

Type on a page to add a **note**, a small window that contains text or other types of information.

Personalize a page with a **template**, or stationery.

Write or draw directly on the page using drawing tools.

Pages can include pictures such as **screen clippings**, images from any part of a computer screen.

Attach files and enter equations so you have everything you need in one place.

Creating a OneNote Notebook

OneNote is divided into sections similar to those in a spiral-bound notebook. Each OneNote notebook contains sections, pages, and other notebooks. You can use One-Note for school, business, and personal projects. Store information for each type of project in different notebooks to keep your tasks separate, or use any other organization that suits you. OneNote is flexible enough to adapt to the way you want to work.

When you create a notebook, it contains a blank page with a plain white background by default, though you can use templates, or stationery, to apply designs in categories such as Academic, Business, Decorative, and Planners. Start typing or use the buttons on the Insert tab to insert notes, which are small resizable windows that can contain text, equations, tables, on-screen writing, images, audio and video recordings, to-do lists, file attachments, and file printouts. Add as many notes as you need to each page.

Syncing a Notebook to the Cloud

OneNote saves your notes every time you make a change in a notebook. To make sure you can access your notebooks with a laptop, tablet, or smartphone wherever you are, OneNote uses cloud-based storage, such as OneDrive or SharePoint. **Microsoft OneNote Mobile app**, a lightweight version of OneNote 2016 shown in **Figure 2**, is available for free in the Windows Store, Google Play for Android devices, and the AppStore for iOS devices.

If you have a Microsoft account, OneNote saves your notes on OneDrive automatically for all your mobile devices and computers, which is called **syncing**. For example, you can use OneNote to take notes on your laptop during class, and then open OneNote on your phone to study later. To use a notebook stored on your computer with your OneNote Mobile app, move the notebook to OneDrive. You can quickly share notebook content with other people using OneDrive.

Figure 2: Microsoft OneNote Mobile app

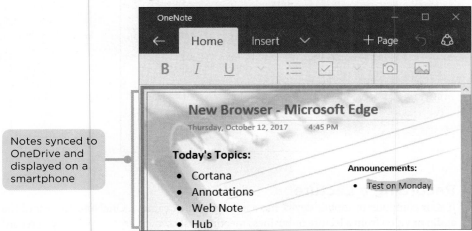

Notes synced to OneDrive and displayed on a smartphone

Taking Notes

Use OneNote pages to organize your notes by class and topic or lecture. Beyond simple typed notes, OneNote stores drawings, converts handwriting to searchable text and mathematical sketches to equations, and records audio and video.

OneNote includes drawing tools that let you sketch freehand drawings such as biological cell diagrams and financial supply-and-demand charts. As shown in **Figure 3**, the Draw tab on the ribbon provides these drawing tools along with shapes so you can insert diagrams and other illustrations to represent your ideas. When you draw on a page, OneNote creates a **drawing canvas**, which is a container for shapes and lines.

On the Job Now

OneNote is ideal for taking notes during meetings, whether you are recording minutes, documenting a discussion, sketching product diagrams, or listing follow-up items. Use a meeting template to add pages with content appropriate for meetings.

Figure 3: Tools on the Draw tab

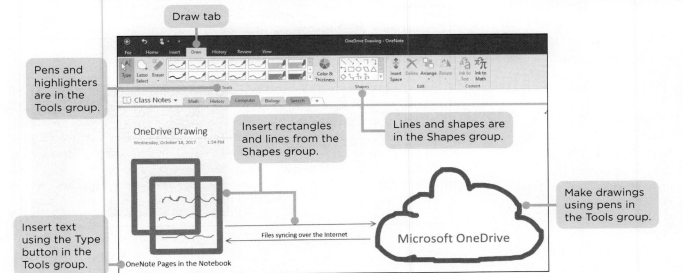

Draw tab

Pens and highlighters are in the Tools group.

Insert rectangles and lines from the Shapes group.

Lines and shapes are in the Shapes group.

Make drawings using pens in the Tools group.

Insert text using the Type button in the Tools group.

Converting Handwriting to Text

When you use a pen tool to write on a notebook page, the text you enter is called **inked handwriting**. OneNote can convert inked handwriting to typed text when you use the **Ink to Text** button in the Convert group on the Draw tab, as shown in **Figure 4**. After OneNote converts the handwriting to text, you can use the Search box to find terms in the converted text or any other note in your notebooks.

Figure 4: Converting handwriting to text

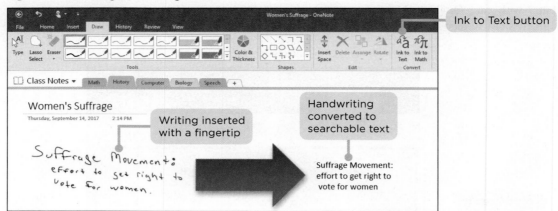

On the Job Now

Use OneNote as a place to brainstorm ongoing work projects. If a notebook contains sensitive material, you can password-protect some or all of the notebook so that only certain people can open it.

Recording a Lecture

If your computer or mobile device has a microphone or camera, OneNote can record the audio or video from a lecture or business meeting as shown in **Figure 5**. When you record a lecture (with your instructor's permission), you can follow along, take regular notes at your own pace, and review the video recording later. You can control the start, pause, and stop motions of the recording when you play back the recording of your notes.

Figure 5: Video inserted in a notebook

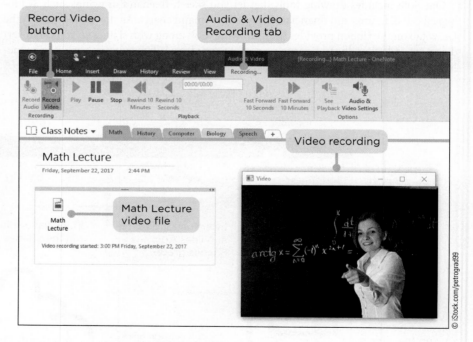

Try This Now

1: Taking Notes for a Week

Learn to use OneNote!
Links to companion **Sways**, featuring **videos** with hands-on instructions, are located on www.cengagebrain.com.

As a student, you can get organized by using OneNote to take detailed notes in your classes. Perform the following tasks:

    a. Create a new OneNote notebook on your Microsoft OneDrive account (the default location for new notebooks). Name the notebook with your first name followed by "Notes," as in **Caleb Notes**.

    b. Create four section tabs, each with a different class name.

    c. Take detailed notes in those classes for one week. Be sure to include notes, drawings, and other types of content.

    d. Sync your notes with your OneDrive. Submit your assignment in the format specified by your instructor.

2: Using OneNote to Organize a Research Paper

You have a research paper due on the topic of three habits of successful students. Use OneNote to organize your research. Perform the following tasks:

    a. Create a new OneNote notebook on your Microsoft OneDrive account. Name the notebook **Success Research**.

    b. Create three section tabs with the following names:

- **Take Detailed Notes**
- **Be Respectful in Class**
- **Come to Class Prepared**

    c. On the web, research the topics and find three sources for each section. Copy a sentence from each source and paste the sentence into the appropriate section. When you paste the sentence, OneNote inserts it in a note with a link to the source.

    d. Sync your notes with your OneDrive. Submit your assignment in the format specified by your instructor.

3: Planning Your Career

Note: This activity requires a webcam or built-in video camera on any type of device.

    Consider an occupation that interests you. Using OneNote, examine the responsibilities, education requirements, potential salary, and employment outlook of a specific career. Perform the following tasks:

    a. Create a new OneNote notebook on your Microsoft OneDrive account. Name the notebook with your first name followed by a career title, such as **Kara - App Developer**.

    b. Create four section tabs with the names **Responsibilities, Education Requirements, Median Salary**, and **Employment Outlook**.

    c. Research the responsibilities of your career path. Using OneNote, record a short video (approximately 30 seconds) of yourself explaining the responsibilities of your career path. Place the video in the Responsibilities section.

    d. On the web, research the educational requirements for your career path and find two appropriate sources. Copy a paragraph from each source and paste them into the appropriate section. When you paste a paragraph, OneNote inserts it in a note with a link to the source.

    e. Research the median salary for a single year for this career. Create a mathematical equation in the Median Salary section that multiplies the amount of the median salary times 20 years to calculate how much you will possibly earn.

    f. For the Employment Outlook section, research the outlook for your career path. Take at least four notes about what you find when researching the topic.

    g. Sync your notes with your OneDrive. Submit your assignment in the format specified by your instructor.

Introduction to Sway

Sway site | responsive design | Storyline | card | Creative Commons license | animation emphasis effects | Docs.com

Expressing your ideas in a presentation typically means creating PowerPoint slides or a Word document. Microsoft Sway gives you another way to engage an audience. Sway is a free Microsoft tool available at Sway.com or as an app in Office 365. Using Sway, you can combine text, images, videos, and social media in a website called a **Sway site** that you can share and display on any device. To get started, you create a digital story on a web-based canvas without borders, slides, cells, or page breaks. A Sway site organizes the text, images, and video into a **responsive design**, which means your content adapts perfectly to any screen size as shown in **Figure 6**. You store a Sway site in the cloud on OneDrive using a free Microsoft account.

Figure 6: Sway site with responsive design

You can display a Sway presentation in a web browser.

Sway uses responsive design to make sure pages fit perfectly on any device.

Creating a Sway Presentation

You can use Sway to build a digital flyer, a club newsletter, a vacation blog, an informational site, a digital art portfolio, or a new product rollout. After you select your topic and sign into Sway with your Microsoft account, a **Storyline** opens, providing tools and a work area for composing your digital story. See **Figure 7**. Each story can include text, images, and videos. You create a Sway by adding text and media content into a Storyline section, or **card**. To add pictures, videos, or documents, select a card in the left pane and then select the Insert Content button. The first card in a Sway presentation contains a title and background image.

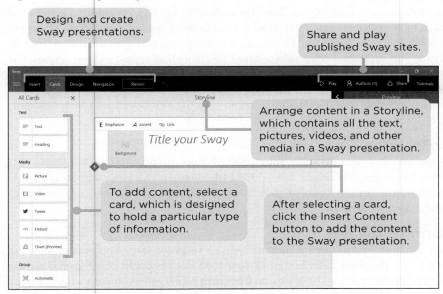

Adding Content to Build a Story

As you work, Sway searches the Internet to help you find relevant images, videos, tweets, and other content from online sources such as Bing, YouTube, Twitter, and Facebook. You can drag content from the search results right into the Storyline. In addition, you can upload your own images and videos directly in the presentation. For example, if you are creating a Sway presentation about the market for commercial drones, Sway suggests content to incorporate into the presentation by displaying it in the left pane as search results. The search results include drone images tagged with a **Creative Commons license** at online sources as shown in **Figure 8**. A Creative Commons license is a public copyright license that allows the free distribution of an otherwise copyrighted work. In addition, you can specify the source of the media. For example, you can add your own Facebook or OneNote pictures and videos in Sway without leaving the app.

On the Job Now

If you have a Microsoft Word document containing an outline of your business content, drag the outline into Sway to create a card for each topic.

Figure 8: Images in Sway search results

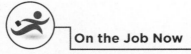

On the Job Now

If your project team wants to collaborate on a Sway presentation, click the Authors button on the navigation bar to invite others to edit the presentation.

Designing a Sway

Sway professionally designs your Storyline content by resizing background images and fonts to fit your display, and by floating text, animating media, embedding video, and removing images as a page scrolls out of view. Sway also evaluates the images in your Storyline and suggests a color palette based on colors that appear in your photos. Use the Design button to display tools including color palettes, font choices, **animation emphasis effects**, and style templates to provide a personality for a Sway presentation. Instead of creating your own design, you can click the Remix button, which randomly selects unique designs for your Sway site.

Publishing a Sway

Use the Play button to display your finished Sway presentation as a website. The Address bar includes a unique web address where others can view your Sway site. As the author, you can edit a published Sway site by clicking the Edit button (pencil icon) on the Sway toolbar.

Sharing a Sway

When you are ready to share your Sway website, you have several options as shown in **Figure 9**. Use the Share slider button to share the Sway site publically or keep it private. If you add the Sway site to the Microsoft **Docs.com** public gallery, anyone worldwide can use Bing, Google, or other search engines to find, view, and share your Sway site. You can also share your Sway site using Facebook, Twitter, Google+, Yammer, and other social media sites. Link your presentation to any webpage or email the link to your audience. Sway can also generate a code for embedding the link within another webpage.

Figure 9: Sharing a Sway site

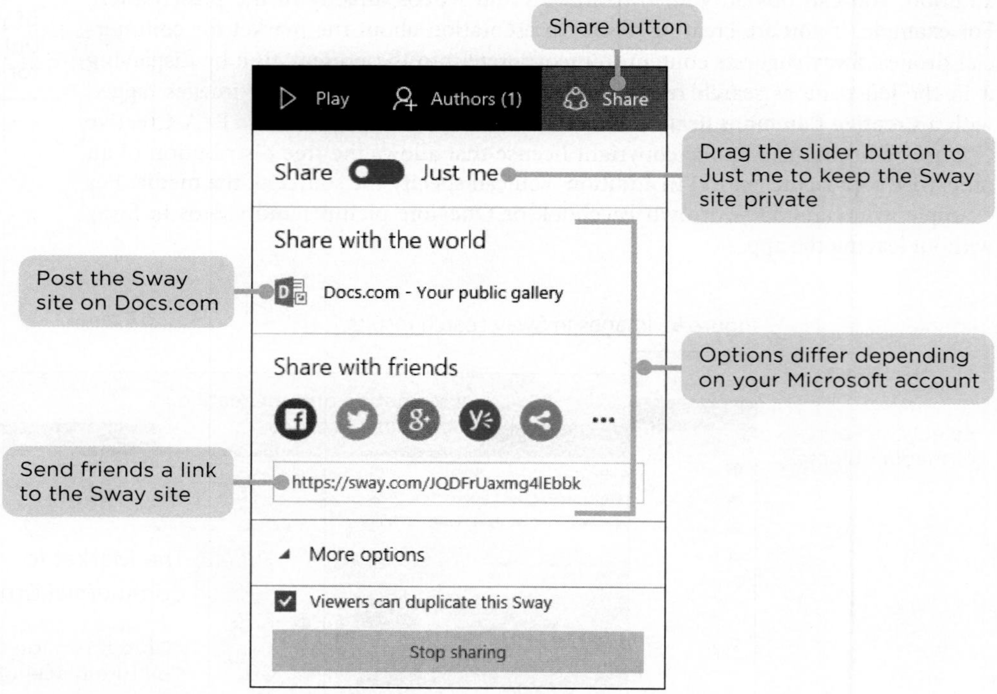

Share button

Play   Authors (1)   Share

Share ⬤ Just me — Drag the slider button to Just me to keep the Sway site private

Share with the world

Post the Sway site on Docs.com — Docs.com - Your public gallery

Share with friends — Options differ depending on your Microsoft account

Send friends a link to the Sway site — https://sway.com/JQDFrUaxmg4lEbbk

◢ More options

☑ Viewers can duplicate this Sway

Stop sharing

Try This Now

Learn to use Sway!
Links to companion **Sways**, featuring **videos** with hands-on instructions, are located on www.cengagebrain.com.

1: Creating a Sway Resume

Sway is a digital storytelling app. Create a Sway resume to share the skills, job experiences, and achievements you have that match the requirements of a future job interest. Perform the following tasks:

a. Create a new presentation in Sway to use as a digital resume. Title the Sway Storyline with your full name and then select a background image.
b. Create three separate sections titled **Academic Background, Work Experience**, and **Skills**, and insert text, a picture, and a paragraph or bulleted points in each section. Be sure to include your own picture.
c. Add a fourth section that includes a video about your school that you find online.
d. Customize the design of your presentation.
e. Submit your assignment link in the format specified by your instructor.

2: Creating an Online Sway Newsletter

Newsletters are designed to capture the attention of their target audience. Using Sway, create a newsletter for a club, organization, or your favorite music group. Perform the following tasks:

a. Create a new presentation in Sway to use as a digital newsletter for a club, organization, or your favorite music group. Provide a title for the Sway Storyline and select an appropriate background image.
b. Select three separate sections with appropriate titles, such as Upcoming Events. In each section, insert text, a picture, and a paragraph or bulleted points.
c. Add a fourth section that includes a video about your selected topic.
d. Customize the design of your presentation.
e. Submit your assignment link in the format specified by your instructor.

3: Creating and Sharing a Technology Presentation

To place a Sway presentation in the hands of your entire audience, you can share a link to the Sway presentation. Create a Sway presentation on a new technology and share it with your class. Perform the following tasks:

a. Create a new presentation in Sway about a cutting-edge technology topic. Provide a title for the Sway Storyline and select a background image.
b. Create four separate sections about your topic, and include text, a picture, and a paragraph in each section.
c. Add a fifth section that includes a video about your topic.
d. Customize the design of your presentation.
e. Share the link to your Sway with your classmates and submit your assignment link in the format specified by your instructor.

Introduction to Office Mix

add-in | clip | slide recording | Slide Notes | screen recording | free-response quiz

Bottom Line
- Office Mix is a free PowerPoint add-in from Microsoft that adds features to PowerPoint.
- The Mix tab on the PowerPoint ribbon provides tools for creating screen recordings, videos, interactive quizzes, and live webpages.

To enliven business meetings and lectures, Microsoft adds a new dimension to presentations with a powerful toolset called Office Mix, a free add-in for PowerPoint. (An **add-in** is software that works with an installed app to extend its features.) Using Office Mix, you can record yourself on video, capture still and moving images on your desktop, and insert interactive elements such as quizzes and live webpages directly into PowerPoint slides. When you post the finished presentation to OneDrive, Office Mix provides a link you can share with friends and colleagues. Anyone with an Internet connection and a web browser can watch a published Office Mix presentation, such as the one in **Figure 10**, on a computer or mobile device.

Figure 10: Office Mix presentation

Adding Office Mix to PowerPoint

To get started, you create an Office Mix account at the website mix.office.com using an email address or a Facebook or Google account. Next, you download and install the Office Mix add-in (see **Figure 11**). Office Mix appears as a new tab named Mix on the PowerPoint ribbon in versions of Office 2013 and Office 2016 running on personal computers (PCs).

Learn to use Office Mix!
Links to companion **Sways**, featuring **videos** with hands-on instructions, are located on www.cengagebrain.com.

Figure 11: Getting started with Office Mix

Capturing Video Clips

A **clip** is a short segment of audio, such as music, or video. After finishing the content on a PowerPoint slide, you can use Office Mix to add a video clip to animate or illustrate the content. Office Mix creates video clips in two ways: by recording live action on a webcam and by capturing screen images and movements. If your computer has a webcam, you can record yourself and annotate the slide to create a **slide recording** as shown in **Figure 12**.

Figure 12: Making a slide recording

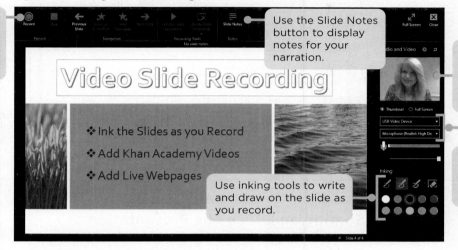

Record your voice; also record video if your computer has a camera.

Use the Slide Notes button to display notes for your narration.

For best results, look directly at your webcam while recording video.

Choose a video and audio device to record images and sound.

Use inking tools to write and draw on the slide as you record.

When you are making a slide recording, you can record your spoken narration at the same time. The **Slide Notes** feature works like a teleprompter to help you focus on your presentation content instead of memorizing your narration. Use the Inking tools to make annotations or add highlighting using different pen types and colors. After finishing a recording, edit the video in PowerPoint to trim the length or set playback options.

The second way to create a video is to capture on-screen images and actions with or without a voiceover. This method is ideal if you want to show how to use your favorite website or demonstrate an app such as OneNote. To share your screen with an audience, select the part of the screen you want to show in the video. Office Mix captures everything that happens in that area to create a **screen recording**, as shown in **Figure 13**. Office Mix inserts the screen recording as a video in the slide.

Figure 13: Making a screen recording

Record the action on the screen within the red dashed outline.

Select Area button

Record audio while capturing your on-screen actions.

Inserting Quizzes, Live Webpages, and Apps

To enhance and assess audience understanding, make your slides interactive by adding quizzes, live webpages, and apps. Quizzes give immediate feedback to the user as shown in **Figure 14**. Office Mix supports several quiz formats, including a **free-response quiz** similar to a short answer quiz, and true/false, multiple-choice, and multiple-response formats.

Figure 14: Creating an interactive quiz

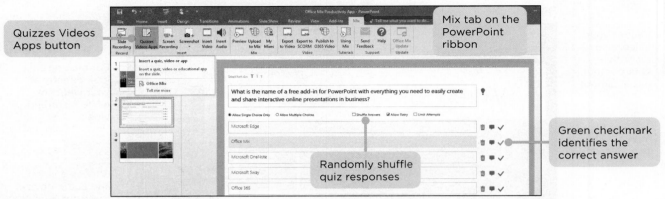

Sharing an Office Mix Presentation

When you complete your work with Office Mix, upload the presentation to your personal Office Mix dashboard as shown in **Figure 15**. Users of PCs, Macs, iOS devices, and Android devices can access and play Office Mix presentations. The Office Mix dashboard displays built-in analytics that include the quiz results and how much time viewers spent on each slide. You can play completed Office Mix presentations online or download them as movies.

Figure 15: Sharing an Office Mix presentation

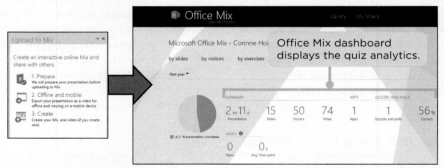

Try This Now

Learn to use Office Mix!
Links to companion **Sways**, featuring **videos** with hands-on instructions, are located on www.cengagebrain.com.

1: Creating an Office Mix Tutorial for OneNote

Note: This activity requires a microphone on your computer.

Office Mix makes it easy to record screens and their contents. Create PowerPoint slides with an Office Mix screen recording to show OneNote 2016 features. Perform the following tasks:

a. Create a PowerPoint presentation with the Ion Boardroom template. Create an opening slide with the title **My Favorite OneNote Features** and enter your name in the subtitle.

b. Create three additional slides, each titled with a new feature of OneNote. Open OneNote and use the Mix tab in PowerPoint to capture three separate screen recordings that teach your favorite features.

c. Add a fifth slide that quizzes the user with a multiple-choice question about OneNote and includes four responses. Be sure to insert a checkmark indicating the correct response.

d. Upload the completed presentation to your Office Mix dashboard and share the link with your instructor.

e. Submit your assignment link in the format specified by your instructor.

2: Teaching Augmented Reality with Office Mix

Note: This activity requires a webcam or built-in video camera on your computer.

A local elementary school has asked you to teach augmented reality to its students using Office Mix. Perform the following tasks:

a. Research augmented reality using your favorite online search tools.

b. Create a PowerPoint presentation with the Frame template. Create an opening slide with the title **Augmented Reality** and enter your name in the subtitle.

c. Create a slide with four bullets summarizing your research of augmented reality. Create a 20-second slide recording of yourself providing a quick overview of augmented reality.

d. Create another slide with a 30-second screen recording of a video about augmented reality from a site such as YouTube or another video-sharing site.

e. Add a final slide that quizzes the user with a true/false question about augmented reality. Be sure to insert a checkmark indicating the correct response.

f. Upload the completed presentation to your Office Mix dashboard and share the link with your instructor.

g. Submit your assignment link in the format specified by your instructor.

3: Marketing a Travel Destination with Office Mix

Note: This activity requires a webcam or built-in video camera on your computer.

To convince your audience to travel to a particular city, create a slide presentation marketing any city in the world using a slide recording, screen recording, and a quiz. Perform the following tasks:

a. Create a PowerPoint presentation with any template. Create an opening slide with the title of the city you are marketing as a travel destination and your name in the subtitle.

b. Create a slide with four bullets about the featured city. Create a 30-second slide recording of yourself explaining why this city is the perfect vacation destination.

c. Create another slide with a 20-second screen recording of a travel video about the city from a site such as YouTube or another video-sharing site.

d. Add a final slide that quizzes the user with a multiple-choice question about the featured city with five responses. Be sure to include a checkmark indicating the correct response.

e. Upload the completed presentation to your Office Mix dashboard and share your link with your instructor.

f. Submit your assignment link in the format specified by your instructor.

Introduction to Microsoft Edge

Reading view | Hub | Cortana | Web Note | Inking | sandbox

Microsoft Edge is the default web browser developed for the Windows 10 operating system as a replacement for Internet Explorer. Unlike its predecessor, Edge lets you write on webpages, read webpages without advertisements and other distractions, and search for information using a virtual personal assistant. The Edge interface is clean and basic, as shown in **Figure 16**, meaning you can pay more attention to the webpage content.

Figure 16: Microsoft Edge tools

Forward button · New tab button · Web address in the Address bar · Add to favorites or reading list button · Reading view button · Back button · More button · Share Web Note button · Refresh (F5) button · Hub (Favorites, reading list, history, and downloads) button · Make a Web Note button

Browsing the Web with Microsoft Edge

One of the fastest browsers available, Edge allows you to type search text directly in the Address bar. As you view the resulting webpage, you can switch to **Reading view**, which is available for most news and research sites, to eliminate distracting advertisements. For example, if you are catching up on technology news online, the webpage might be difficult to read due to a busy layout cluttered with ads. Switch to Reading view to refresh the page and remove the original page formatting, ads, and menu sidebars to read the article distraction-free.

Consider the **Hub** in Microsoft Edge as providing one-stop access to all the things you collect on the web, such as your favorite websites, reading list, surfing history, and downloaded files.

Locating Information with Cortana

Cortana, the Windows 10 virtual assistant, plays an important role in Microsoft Edge. After you turn on Cortana, it appears as an animated circle in the Address bar when you might need assistance, as shown in the restaurant website in **Figure 17**. When you click the Cortana icon, a pane slides in from the right of the browser window to display detailed information about the restaurant, including maps and reviews. Cortana can also assist you in defining words, finding the weather, suggesting coupons for shopping, updating stock market information, and calculating math.

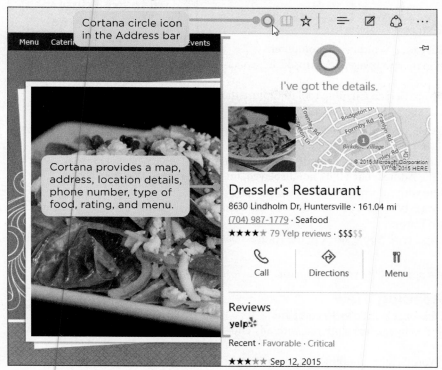

Annotating Webpages

One of the most impressive Microsoft Edge features are the **Web Note** tools, which you use to write on a webpage or to highlight text. When you click the Make a Web Note button, an **Inking** toolbar appears, as shown in **Figure 18**, that provides writing and drawing tools. These tools include an eraser, a pen, and a highlighter with different colors. You can also insert a typed note and copy a screen image (called a screen clipping). You can draw with a pointing device, fingertip, or stylus using different pen colors. Whether you add notes to a recipe, annotate sources for a research paper, or select a product while shopping online, the Web Note tools can enhance your productivity. After you complete your notes, click the Save button to save the annotations to OneNote, your Favorites list, or your Reading list. You can share the inked page with others using the Share Web Note button.

On the Job Now

To enhance security, Microsoft Edge runs in a partial sandbox, an arrangement that prevents attackers from gaining control of your computer. Browsing within the **sandbox** protects computer resources and information from hackers.

Figure 18: Web Note tools in Microsoft Edge

Try This Now

Learn to use Edge!
Links to companion **Sways**, featuring **videos** with hands-on instructions, are located on www.cengagebrain.com.

1: Using Cortana in Microsoft Edge

Note: This activity requires using Microsoft Edge on a Windows 10 computer.

Cortana can assist you in finding information on a webpage in Microsoft Edge. Perform the following tasks:

a. Create a Word document using the Word Screen Clipping tool to capture the following screenshots.

- Screenshot A—Using Microsoft Edge, open a webpage with a technology news article. Right-click a term in the article and ask Cortana to define it.
- Screenshot B—Using Microsoft Edge, open the website of a fancy restaurant in a city near you. Make sure the Cortana circle icon is displayed in the Address bar. (If it's not displayed, find a different restaurant website.) Click the Cortana circle icon to display a pane with information about the restaurant.
- Screenshot C—Using Microsoft Edge, type **10 USD to Euros** in the Address bar without pressing the Enter key. Cortana converts the U.S. dollars to Euros.
- Screenshot D—Using Microsoft Edge, type **Apple stock** in the Address bar without pressing the Enter key. Cortana displays the current stock quote.

b. Submit your assignment in the format specified by your instructor.

2: Viewing Online News with Reading View

Note: This activity requires using Microsoft Edge on a Windows 10 computer.

Reading view in Microsoft Edge can make a webpage less cluttered with ads and other distractions. Perform the following tasks:

a. Create a Word document using the Word Screen Clipping tool to capture the following screenshots.

- Screenshot A—Using Microsoft Edge, open the website **mashable.com**. Open a technology article. Click the Reading view button to display an ad-free page that uses only basic text formatting.
- Screenshot B—Using Microsoft Edge, open the website **bbc.com**. Open any news article. Click the Reading view button to display an ad-free page that uses only basic text formatting.
- Screenshot C—Make three types of annotations (Pen, Highlighter, and Add a typed note) on the BBC article page displayed in Reading view.

b. Submit your assignment in the format specified by your instructor.

3: Inking with Microsoft Edge

Note: This activity requires using Microsoft Edge on a Windows 10 computer.

Microsoft Edge provides many annotation options to record your ideas. Perform the following tasks:

a. Open the website **wolframalpha.com** in the Microsoft Edge browser. Wolfram Alpha is a well-respected academic search engine. Type **US$100 1965 dollars in 2015** in the Wolfram Alpha search text box and press the Enter key.

b. Click the Make a Web Note button to display the Web Note tools. Using the Pen tool, draw a circle around the result on the webpage. Save the page to OneNote.

c. In the Wolfram Alpha search text box, type the name of the city closest to where you live and press the Enter key. Using the Highlighter tool, highlight at least three interesting results. Add a note and then type a sentence about what you learned about this city. Save the page to OneNote. Share your OneNote notebook with your instructor.

d. Submit your assignment link in the format specified by your instructor.

4 Creating a Document with a Title Page, Lists, Tables, and a Watermark

Objectives

You will have mastered the material in this module when you can:

- Border a paragraph
- Change paragraph indentation
- Insert and format a SmartArt graphic
- Apply character effects
- Insert a section break
- Insert a Word document in an open document
- Insert formatted headers and footers

- Sort paragraphs and tables
- Use the format painter
- Add picture bullets to a list
- Create a multilevel list
- Modify and format Word tables
- Sum columns in a table
- Create a watermark
- Change theme fonts

Introduction

During the course of your business and personal endeavors, you may want or need to provide a recommendation to a person or group of people for their consideration. You might suggest they purchase a product, such as a vehicle or books, or contract a service, such as designing their webpage or remodeling their house. Or, you might try to convince an audience to take an action, such as signing a petition, joining a club, visiting an establishment, or donating to a cause. You may be asked to request funds for a new program or activity or to promote an idea, such as a benefits package to company employees or a budget plan to upper management. To present these types of recommendations, you may find yourself writing a proposal.

A proposal generally is one of three types: sales, research, or planning. A **sales proposal** sells an idea, a product, or a service. A **research proposal** usually requests funding for a research project. A **planning proposal** offers solutions to a problem or improvement to a situation.

Project — Sales Proposal

Sales proposals describe the features and value of products and services being offered, with the intent of eliciting a positive response from the reader. Desired outcomes include the reader accepting ideas, purchasing products, contracting services, volunteering time, contributing to a cause, or taking an action. A well-written proposal can be the key to obtaining the desired results.

The project in this module follows generally accepted guidelines for writing short sales proposals and uses Word to create the sales proposal shown in Figure 4–1. The sales proposal in this module is designed to persuade readers to patronize an animal clinic. The proposal has a colorful title page to attract readers' attention. To add impact, the sales proposal has a watermark consisting of animal paw prints, positioned behind the content on each page. It also uses lists and tables to summarize and highlight important data.

In this module, you will learn how to create the sales proposal shown in Figure 4–1. The following roadmap identifies general activities you will perform as you progress through this module:

1. CREATE a TITLE PAGE for the proposal.
2. INSERT an EXISTING Word DOCUMENT in the proposal.
3. CREATE a HEADER AND FOOTER in the proposal.
4. EDIT AND FORMAT LISTS in the proposal.
5. EDIT AND FORMAT TABLES in the proposal.
6. CREATE a WATERMARK in the proposal.

To Run Word and Change Word Settings

If you are using a computer to step through the project in this module and you want your screens to match the figures in this book, you should change your screen's resolution to 1366 × 768.

The following steps run Word, display formatting marks, and change the zoom to page width.

1 Run Word and create a blank document in the Word window. If necessary, maximize the Word window.

2 If the Print Layout button on the status bar is not selected (shown in Figure 4–2), click it so that your screen is in Print Layout view.

3 If the 'Show/Hide ¶' button (Home tab | Paragraph group) is not selected already, click it to display formatting marks on the screen.

4 To display the page the same width as the document window, if necessary, click the Page Width button (View tab | Zoom group).

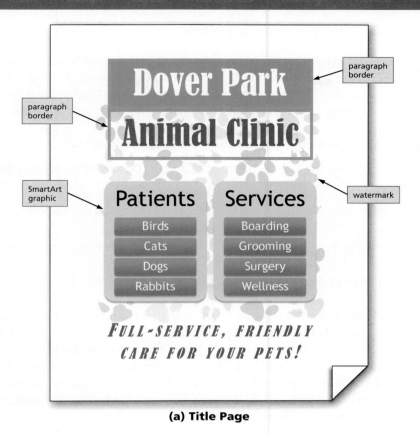

paragraph border

paragraph border

SmartArt graphic

watermark

(a) Title Page

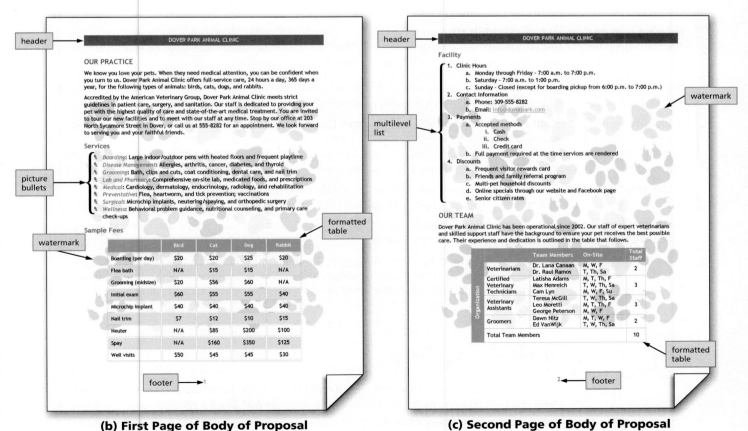

header

OUR PRACTICE

picture bullets

watermark

formatted table

footer

(b) First Page of Body of Proposal

header

multilevel list

watermark

OUR TEAM

formatted table

footer

(c) Second Page of Body of Proposal

Figure 4–1

To Change Theme Colors

Recall that Word provides document themes, which contain a variety of color schemes and other effects. You should select a theme that includes colors that reflect the goals of a sales proposal. This proposal uses the Celestial document theme. The following steps change the document theme.

1 Click Design on the ribbon to display the Design tab.

2 Click the Themes button (Design tab | Document Formatting group) to display the Themes gallery.

3 Click Celestial in the Themes gallery to change the document theme to the selected theme.

Creating a Title Page

A **title page** is a separate cover page that contains, at a minimum, the title of a document. For a sales proposal, the title page usually is the first page of the document. Solicited proposals often have a specific format for the title page. Guidelines for the title page of a solicited proposal may stipulate the margins, spacing, layout, and required contents, such as title, sponsor name, author name, date, etc. With an unsolicited proposal, by contrast, you can design the title page in a way that best presents its message.

CONSIDER THIS

How do you design an eye-catching title page?
The title page is the first section a reader sees on a sales proposal. Thus, it is important that the title page appropriately reflects the goal of the sales proposal. When designing the title page, consider its text and graphics.

- **Use concise, descriptive text.** The title page should contain a short, descriptive title that accurately reflects the message of the sales proposal. The title page also may include a theme or slogan. Do not place a page number on the title page.

- **Identify appropriate fonts, font sizes, and colors for the text.** Use fonts that are easy to read. Avoid using more than three different fonts because too many fonts can make the title page visually confusing. Use larger font sizes to add impact to the title page. To give the title more emphasis, its font size should be larger than any other text on the title page. Use colors that complement one another and convey the meaning of the proposal.

- **Use graphics to reinforce the goal.** Select simple graphics that clearly communicate the fundamental nature of the proposal. Possible graphics include shapes, pictures, and logos.

- **Use colors that complement text colors.** Be aware that too many graphics and colors can be distracting. Arrange graphics with the text so that the title page is attractive and uncluttered.

The title page of the sales proposal in this module (shown in Figure 4–1a) contains a colorful title that is surrounded by a border with some shading, an artistic graphic with text, a colorful slogan, and the faded paw prints image in the background. The steps in the next several sections create this title page. The faded image of the paw prints is added to all pages at the end of this module.

To Format Characters

The title in the sales proposal should use a large font size and an easy-to-read font, and should be the focal point on the page. *Why? To give the title more emphasis, its font size should be larger than any other text on the title page.* The following steps enter the title, Dover Park Animal Clinic, with the first two words centered on the first line and the second two words centered on the second line.

1 Click Home on the ribbon to display the Home tab.

2 Click the Center button (Home tab | Paragraph group) to center the paragraph that will contain the title.

3 Click the Font arrow (Home tab | Font group). Scroll to and then click 'Bernard MT Condensed' (or a similar font) in the Font gallery, so that the text you type will use the selected font.

4 Click the Font Size arrow (Home tab | Font group) and then click 72 in the Font Size gallery, so that the text you type will use the selected font size.

5 Type **Dover Park** and then press the ENTER key to enter the first line of the title.

6 Click the Font Color arrow (Home tab | Font group) and then click 'Purple, Accent 1' (fifth color, first row) in the Font Color gallery, so that the text you type will use the selected font color.

7 Type **Animal Clinic** as the second line of the title (shown in Figure 4–2).

BTW

The Ribbon and Screen Resolution
Word may change how the groups and buttons within the groups appear on the ribbon, depending on the computer or mobile device's screen resolution. Thus, your ribbon may look different from the ones in this book if you are using a screen resolution other than 1366 × 768.

To Border a Paragraph

1 CREATE TITLE PAGE | 2 INSERT EXISTING DOCUMENT | 3 CREATE HEADER & FOOTER
4 EDIT & FORMAT LISTS | 5 EDIT & FORMAT TABLES | 6 CREATE WATERMARK

If you click the Borders button (Home tab | Paragraph group), Word applies the most recently defined border, or, if one has not been defined, it applies the default border to the current paragraph. To specify a border different from the most recently defined border, you click the Borders arrow (Home tab | Paragraph group).

In this project, the first line of the title in the sales proposal (Dover Park) has a 6-point olive green border around it. *Why? You want the title to stand out more than the rest of the text on the title page.* The following steps add a border to all edges of a paragraph.

1
- Position the insertion point in the paragraph to border, in this case, the first line of the document.
- Click the Borders arrow (Home tab | Paragraph group) to display the Borders gallery (Figure 4–2).

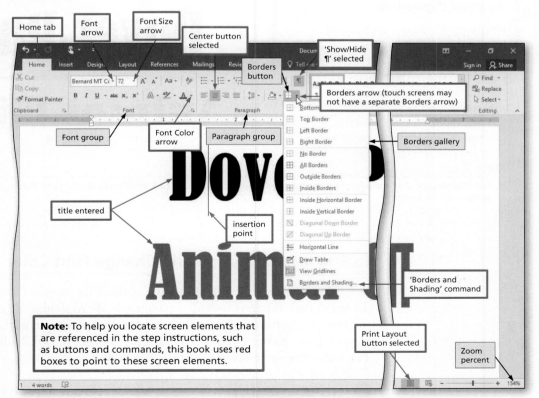

Figure 4–2

②

- Click Borders and Shading in the Borders gallery to display the Borders and Shading dialog box.
- Click Box in the Setting area (Borders and Shading dialog box), which will place a border on each edge of the current paragraph.
- Click the Color arrow and then click 'Olive Green, Accent 4' (eighth color, first row) in the Color palette to specify the border color.
- Click the Width arrow and then click 6 pt to specify the thickness of the border (Figure 4–3).

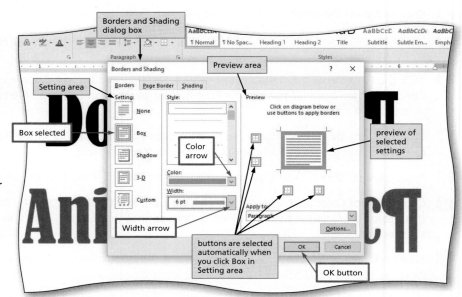

Q&A

For what purpose are the buttons in the Preview area used?

They are toggles that display and remove the top, bottom, left, and right borders from the diagram in the Preview area.

Figure 4–3

③

- Click the OK button (Borders and Shading dialog box) to place the border shown in the preview area of the dialog box around the current paragraph in the document (Figure 4–4).

Q&A

How would I remove an existing border from a paragraph?

Click the Borders arrow (Home tab | Paragraph group) and then click the border in the Borders gallery that identifies the border you wish to remove, or click No Border to remove all borders.

Figure 4–4

Other Ways

1. Click 'Borders and Shading' button (Design tab | Page Background group), click Borders tab (Borders and Shading dialog box), select desired border, click OK button

To Shade a Paragraph and Change Font Color

To make the first line of the title of the sales proposal more eye-catching, it is shaded in teal. When you shade a paragraph, Word shades the rectangular area behind any text or graphics in the paragraph from the left margin of the paragraph to the right margin. If the paragraph is surrounded by a border, Word shades inside the border. The following steps shade a paragraph and change font color.

① With the insertion point in the paragraph to shade, the first line in this case (shown in Figure 4–4), click the Shading arrow (Home tab | Paragraph group) to display the Shading gallery.

2 Click 'Teal, Accent 3' (seventh color, first row) in the Shading gallery to shade the current paragraph (shown in Figure 4–5).

3 Drag through the words, Dover Park, in the first line of the title to select the text.

4 Click the Font Color arrow (Home tab | Font group) to display the Font Color gallery and then click 'White, Background 1' (first color, first row) to change the color of the selected text (shown in Figure 4–5).

To Border Another Paragraph

To make the second line of the title of the sales proposal (Animal Clinic) more eye-catching, it has a 6-point gold border around it. The following steps add a border to all edges of a paragraph.

1 Position the insertion point in the paragraph to border (in this case, the second paragraph containing the text, Animal Clinic).

2 Click the Borders arrow (Home tab | Paragraph group) to display the Borders gallery and then click 'Borders and Shading' in the Border gallery to display the Borders and Shading dialog box.

3 Click Box in the Setting area (Borders and Shading dialog box), which will place a border on each edge of the current paragraph.

4 Click the Color arrow and then click 'Gold, Accent 5' (ninth color, first row) in the Color palette to specify the border color.

5 If necessary, click the Width arrow and then click 6 pt to specify the thickness of the border.

6 Click the OK button to place the defined border shown around the current paragraph in the document (Figure 4–5).

BTW
Touch Screen Differences
The Office and Windows interfaces may vary if you are using a touch screen. For this reason, you might notice that the function or appearance of your touch screen differs slightly from this module's presentation.

Figure 4–5

To Change Spacing after a Paragraph

Currently, a small amount of blank space exists between the two paragraph borders because Word automatically places 8 points of blank space below paragraphs (shown in Figure 4–5). The following steps remove the blank space below the first paragraph.

1 Position the insertion point in the paragraph to be adjusted (in this case, the paragraph containing the text, Dover Park).

2 Display the Layout tab. Click the Spacing After down arrow (Layout tab | Paragraph group) as many times as necessary until 0 pt is displayed in the Spacing After box to remove the space below the current paragraph (shown in Figure 4–6).

Q&A What if I am using a touch screen?
Tap the Spacing After box (Layout tab | Paragraph group) and then type 0 to change the spacing below the paragraph.

To Change Left and Right Paragraph Indent

1 CREATE TITLE PAGE | 2 INSERT EXISTING DOCUMENT | 3 CREATE HEADER & FOOTER
4 EDIT & FORMAT LISTS | 5 EDIT & FORMAT TABLES | 6 CREATE WATERMARK

The borders around the first and second paragraphs and the shading in the first paragraph currently extend from the left margin to the right margin (shown in Figure 4–5). In this project, the edges of the border and shading are closer to the text in the title. **Why?** *You do not want such a large gap between the edge of the text and the border.* If you want the border and shading to start and end at a location different from the margin, you change the left and right paragraph indent.

The Increase Indent and Decrease Indent buttons (Home tab | Paragraph group) change the left indent by ½-inch, respectively. In this case, however, you cannot use these buttons because you want to change both the left and right indent. The following steps change the left and right paragraph indent.

1

- Be sure the insertion point is positioned in the paragraph to indent (the first paragraph, in this case). Click the Indent Left up arrow (Layout tab | Paragraph group) five times so that 0.5" is displayed in the Indent Left box because you want to adjust the paragraph left indent by this amount (or, if using touch, tap the Indent Left box (Layout tab | Paragraph group) and then type 0.5 to change the left indent).
- Click the Indent Right up arrow (Layout tab | Paragraph group) five times so that 0.5" is displayed in the Indent Right box because you want to adjust the paragraph right indent by this amount (or, if using touch, tap the Indent Right box (Layout tab | Paragraph group) and then type 0.5 to change the right indent) (Figure 4–6).

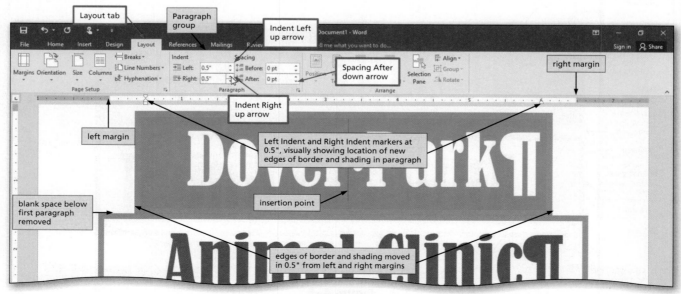

Figure 4–6

Experiment

- Repeatedly click the Indent Right and Indent Left up and down arrows (Layout tab | Paragraph group) and watch the left and right edges of the current paragraph change in the document window. When you have finished experimenting, set the left and right indent each to 0.5".

②

- Repeat Step 1 for the second paragraph, so that the paragraph containing the words, Animal Clinic, also has a left and right indent of 0.5" (shown in Figure 4–7).

Other Ways

1. Drag Left Indent and Right Indent markers on ruler	2. Click Paragraph Settings Dialog Box Launcher (Home tab | Paragraph group), click Indents and Spacing tab (Paragraph dialog box), set indentation values, click OK button	3. Right-click paragraph (or, if using touch, tap 'Show Context Menu' button on mini toolbar), click Paragraph on shortcut menu, click Indents and Spacing tab (Paragraph dialog box), set indentation values, click OK button

To Clear Formatting

The title is finished. When you press the ENTER key to advance the insertion point from the end of the second line to the beginning of the third line on the title page, the border will be carried forward to line 3, and any text you type will be a 72-point Bernard MT Condensed Purple, Accent 1 font. The paragraphs and characters on line 3 should not have the same paragraph and character formatting as line 2. Instead, they should be formatted using the Normal style. The following steps clear formatting, which applies the Normal style formats to the location of the insertion point.

① If necessary, press the END key to position the insertion point at the end of line 2, that is, after the c in Clinic.

② Press the ENTER key.

③ Display the Home tab. Click the 'Clear All Formatting' button (Home tab | Font group) to apply the Normal style to the location of the insertion point (Figure 4–7).

Q&A Could I have clicked Normal in the Styles gallery instead of the Clear All Formatting button?
Yes.

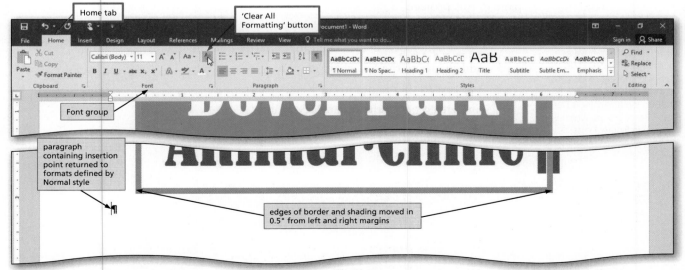

Figure 4–7

4 Save the title page on your hard drive, OneDrive, or other storage location using the file name, Animal Clinic Title Page.

Q&A | Why should I save the title page at this time?
You have performed many tasks while creating this title page and do not want to risk losing work completed thus far.

SmartArt Graphics

Microsoft Office 2016 includes **SmartArt graphics**, which are visual representations of information. Many different types of SmartArt graphics are available, allowing you to choose one that illustrates your message best. Table 4–1 identifies the purpose of some of the more popular types of SmartArt graphics. Within each type, Office provides numerous layouts. For example, you can select from 40 different layouts of the list type.

Table 4–1 SmartArt Graphic Types	
Type	**Purpose**
List	Shows nonsequential or grouped blocks of information.
Process	Shows progression, timeline, or sequential steps in a process or workflow.
Cycle	Shows continuous sequence of steps or events.
Hierarchy	Illustrates organization charts, decision trees, and hierarchical relationships.
Relationship	Compares or contrasts connections between concepts.
Matrix	Shows relationships of parts to a whole.
Picture	Uses images to present a message.
Pyramid	Shows proportional or interconnected relationships with the largest component at the top or bottom.

SmartArt graphics contain shapes. You can add text or pictures to shapes, add more shapes, or delete shapes. You also can modify the appearance of a SmartArt graphic by applying styles and changing its colors. The next several sections demonstrate the following general tasks to create the SmartArt graphic on the title page in this project:

1. Insert a SmartArt graphic.
2. Delete unneeded shapes from the SmartArt graphic.
3. Add shapes to the SmartArt graphic.
4. Add text to the shapes in the SmartArt graphic.
5. Change colors of the SmartArt graphic.
6. Apply a style to the SmartArt graphic.

BTW

Resetting Graphics
If you want to remove all formats from a SmartArt graphic and start over, you would click the Reset Graphic button (SmartArt Tools Design tab | Reset group), which is shown in Figure 4–15.

To Insert a SmartArt Graphic

Below the title on the title page is a grouped list SmartArt graphic. *Why?* *The Grouped List SmartArt graphic allows you to place multiple lists side by side on the document, which works well for the content on this title page. The following steps insert a SmartArt graphic centered below the title on the title page.*

1

- With the insertion point on the blank paragraph below the title (shown in Figure 4–7), click the Center button (Home tab | Paragraph group) so that the inserted SmartArt graphic will be centered below the title.
- Display the Insert tab.
- Click the 'Insert a SmartArt Graphic' button (Insert tab | Illustrations group) to display the Choose a SmartArt Graphic dialog box (Figure 4–8).

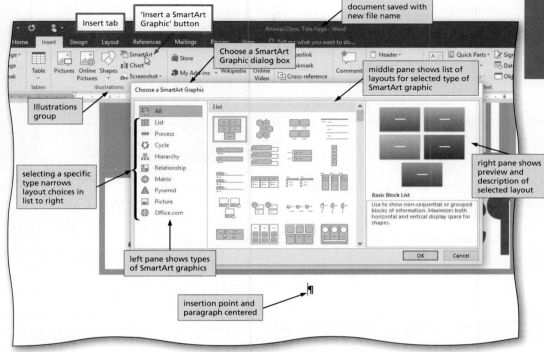

Figure 4–8

🔍 **Experiment**

- Click various SmartArt graphic types in the left pane of the dialog box and watch the related layout choices appear in the middle pane.

- Click various layouts in the list of layouts in the middle pane to see the preview and description of the layout appear in the right pane of the dialog box.

2

- Click List in the left pane (Choose a SmartArt Graphic dialog box) to display the layout choices related to the selected SmartArt graphic type.
- Click Grouped List in the middle pane, which displays a preview and description of the selected layout in the right pane (Figure 4–9).

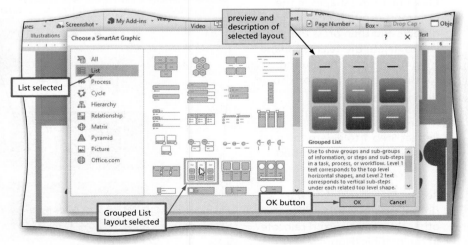

Figure 4–9

● Click the OK button
to insert the selected
SmartArt graphic
in the document
at the location of
the insertion point
(Figure 4–10).

<table>
<tr><td rowspan="6" style="writing-mode: vertical-lr;">**Q&A**</td></tr>
</table>

What if the Text
Pane appears next
to the SmartArt
graphic?
Close the Text Pane
by clicking its Close
button or clicking
the Text Pane
button (SmartArt
Tools Design tab |
Create Graphic
group).

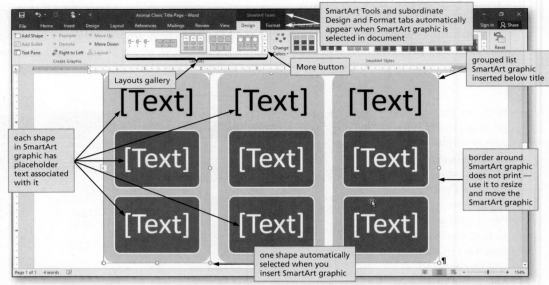

Figure 4–10

Can I change the layout of the inserted SmartArt graphic?
Yes. Click the More button in the Layouts gallery (SmartArt Tools Design tab | Layouts group) to display the list of
layouts and then select the desired layout.

To Delete Shapes from a SmartArt Graphic

1 CREATE TITLE PAGE | 2 INSERT EXISTING DOCUMENT | 3 CREATE HEADER & FOOTER
4 EDIT & FORMAT LISTS | 5 EDIT & FORMAT TABLES | 6 CREATE WATERMARK

The Grouped List SmartArt graphic initially has three outer groups that consist of nine different shapes
(shown in Figure 4–10). Notice that each shape in the SmartArt graphic initially shows **placeholder text**, which
indicates where text can be typed in a shape. The next step in this project is to delete one entire group. *Why? The
SmartArt graphic in this project consists of only two major groups (Patients and Services).* The following steps delete
one entire group, or three shapes, in the SmartArt graphic.

①

● Click one of the shapes in the
rightmost group in the SmartArt
graphic and then press the DELETE
key to delete the selected shape
from the graphic (or, if using
touch, tap the Cut button (Home
tab | Clipboard group)).

②

● Repeat Step 1 to delete the next
shape in the rightmost group.

③

● Repeat Step 1 to delete the
rightmost group and notice the
other shapes resize and relocate
in the graphic (Figure 4–11).

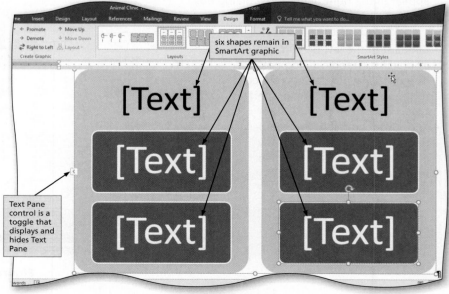

Figure 4–11

Other Ways

1. Click Cut button (Home tab | Clipboard group)   2. Right-click selected shape, click Cut on shortcut menu

To Add Text to Shapes in a SmartArt Graphic

The placeholder text in a shape indicates where text can be typed in the shape. The following steps add text to the three shapes in the first group via their placeholder text. **Why?** *After entering the text in these three shapes, you will need to add two more shapes to finish the content in the group.*

- Click the top-left shape to select it and then type `Patients` to replace the placeholder text, [Text], with the entered text.

Q&A

How do I edit placeholder text if I make a mistake?
Click the placeholder text to select it and then correct the entry.

What if my typed text is longer than the shape?
The font size of the text may be adjusted or the text may wordwrap within the shape.

- Click the middle-left shape to select it and then type `Birds` as the new text.

- Click the lower-left shape to select it and then type `Cats` as the new text (Figure 4–12).

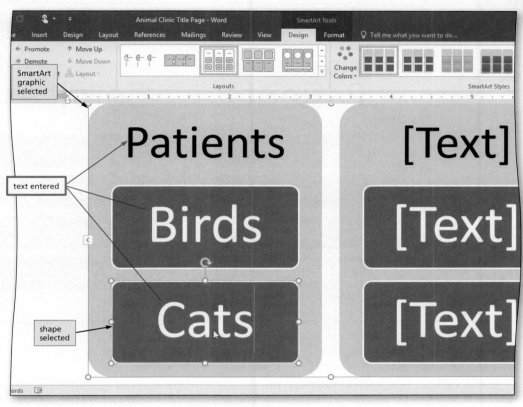

Figure 4–12

Other Ways

1. Click Text Pane control, enter text in Text Pane, close Text Pane

2. Click Text Pane button (SmartArt Tools Design tab | Create Graphic group), enter text in Text Pane, click Text Pane button again

3. Right-click shape (or, if using touch, tap Edit Text button on mini toolbar), click Exit Edit Text on shortcut menu, enter text

To Add Shapes to a SmartArt Graphic

The following steps add shapes to the SmartArt graphic. **Why?** *Each group in this project has four subordinate items, which means two shapes need to be added to each group.*

- Click the Add Shape button (SmartArt Tools Design tab | Create Graphic group) to add a shape to the SmartArt graphic (or, if using touch, tap the Add Shape button (SmartArt Tools Design tab | Create Graphic group) and then tap 'Add Shape After').

- Repeat Step 1 to add the final shape to the group.

❸
- Click a subordinate shape on the right (one of the purple shapes) to select it.
- Repeat Steps 1 and 2 so that the same number of shapes appear on the right and left sides of the SmartArt graphic.

❹
- Enter the text in the shapes as shown in Figure 4–13.

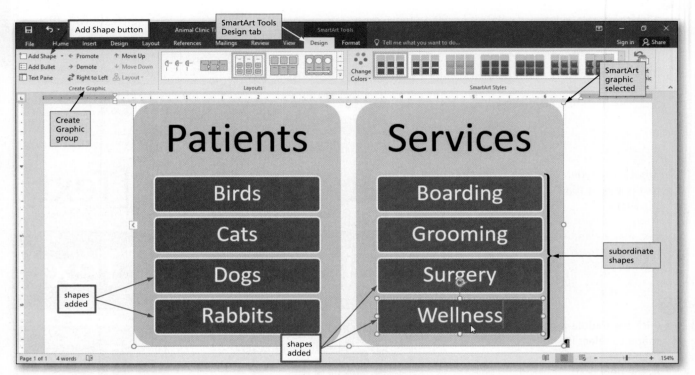

Figure 4–13

Other Ways

1. Click Add Shape arrow (SmartArt Tools Design tab), click desired shape position

2. Right-click paragraph (or, if using touch, tap 'Show Context Menu' button on mini toolbar), point to Add Shape on shortcut menu, click desired shape position

To Change Colors of a SmartArt Graphic

1 CREATE TITLE PAGE | 2 INSERT EXISTING DOCUMENT | 3 CREATE HEADER & FOOTER
4 EDIT & FORMAT LISTS | 5 EDIT & FORMAT TABLES | 6 CREATE WATERMARK

Word provides a variety of colors for a SmartArt graphic and the shapes in the graphic. In this project, the inside shapes are green, instead of purple. **Why?** *The current dark purple color competes with the title, so you want a softer color for the shapes.* The following steps change the colors of a SmartArt graphic.

- With the SmartArt graphic selected (shown in Figure 4–13), click the Change Colors button (SmartArt Tools Design tab | SmartArt Styles group) to display the Change Colors gallery.

Q&A What if the SmartArt graphic is not selected?
Click the SmartArt graphic to select it.

- Point to 'Colorful Range - Accent Colors 3 to 4' in the Change Colors gallery to display a live preview of the selected color applied to the SmartArt graphic in the document (Figure 4–14).

 Experiment

- Point to various colors in the Change Colors gallery and watch the colors of the graphic change in the document window.

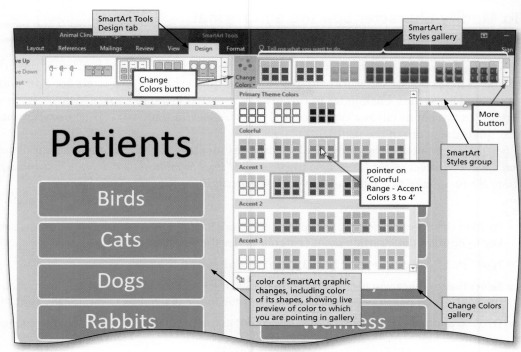

Figure 4–14

❷
- Click 'Colorful Range - Accent Colors 3 to 4' in the Change Colors gallery to apply the selected color to the SmartArt graphic.

To Apply a SmartArt Style

1 CREATE TITLE PAGE | 2 INSERT EXISTING DOCUMENT | 3 CREATE HEADER & FOOTER
4 EDIT & FORMAT LISTS | 5 EDIT & FORMAT TABLES | 6 CREATE WATERMARK

The next step is to apply a SmartArt style to the SmartArt graphic. **Why?** *Word provides a SmartArt Styles gallery, allowing you to change the SmartArt graphic's format to a more visually appealing style.* The following steps apply a SmartArt style to a SmartArt graphic.

❶
- With the SmartArt graphic still selected, click the More button in the SmartArt Styles gallery (shown in Figure 4–14) to expand the SmartArt Styles gallery.

- Point to Moderate Effect in the SmartArt Styles gallery to display a live preview of that style applied to the graphic in the document (Figure 4–15).

 Experiment

- Point to various SmartArt styles in the SmartArt Styles gallery and watch the style of the graphic change in the document window.

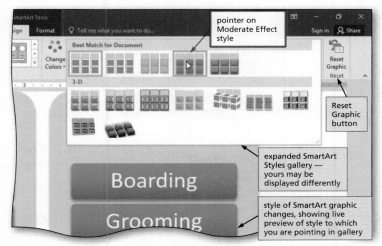

❷
- Click Moderate Effect in the SmartArt Styles gallery to apply the selected style to the SmartArt graphic.

Figure 4–15

To Modify Character Spacing and Format Characters Using the Font Dialog Box

In this project, the next step is to enter and format the text at the bottom of the title page. This text is the theme of the proposal and is formatted so that it is noticeable. Its characters are a 36-point, italic, purple Bernard MT Condensed font. Each letter in this text is formatted in **small caps**, which are letters that look like capital letters but are not as tall as a typical capital letter. Also, you want extra space between each character so that the text spans the width of the page.

Thus, the next steps apply all of the formats mentioned above using the Font dialog box. *Why? Although you could use buttons on the Home tab to apply some of these formats, the small caps effect and expanded spacing are applied using the Font dialog box. Thus, you apply all the formats using the Font dialog box.*

- Position the insertion point on the paragraph mark to the right of the SmartArt graphic and then press the ENTER key to position the insertion point centered below the SmartArt graphic.

- Type `Full-service, friendly care for your pets!`

- Select the sentence you just typed and then click the Font Dialog Box Launcher (Home tab | Font group) to display the Font dialog box. If necessary, click the Font tab in the dialog box to display the Font sheet.

- Scroll to and then click 'Bernard MT Condensed' in the Font list (Font dialog box) to change the font of the selected text.

- Click Italic in the Font style list to italicize the selected text.

- Scroll through the Size list and then click 36 to change the font size of the selected text.

- Click the Font color arrow and then click 'Purple, Accent 1' (fifth color, first row) in the Font color palette to change the color of the selected text.

- Click the Small caps check box in the Effects area so that each character is displayed as a small capital letter (Figure 4–16).

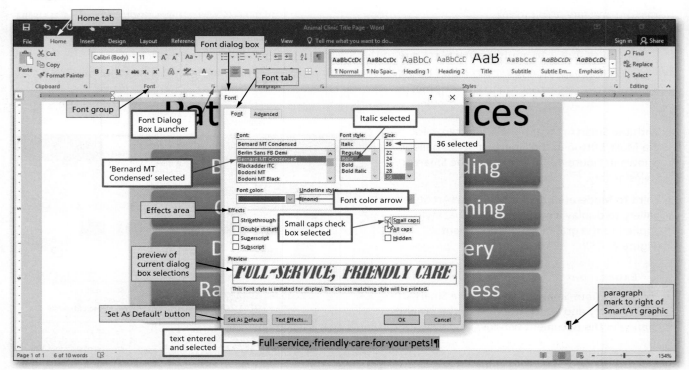

Figure 4–16

2

- Click the Advanced tab (Font dialog box) to display the Advanced sheet in the Font dialog box.
- Click the Spacing arrow and then click Expanded to increase the amount of space between characters by 1 pt, which is the default.
- Double-click the value in the Spacing By box to select it and then type **7** because you want this amount of blank space to be displayed between each character.
- Click in any box in the dialog box for the change to take effect and display a preview of the entered value in the Preview area (Figure 4–17).

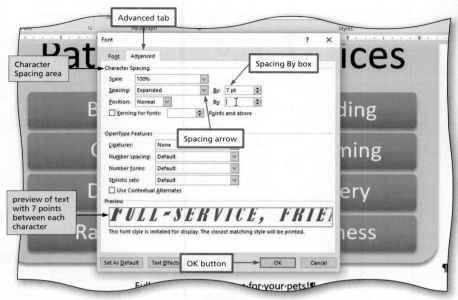

Figure 4–17

Can I click the Spacing By arrows instead of typing a value in the box? Yes.

3

- Click the OK button to apply font changes to the selected text. If necessary, scroll so that the selected text is displayed completely in the document window.
- Click to remove the selection from the text (Figure 4–18).

36-point italic purple Bernard MT Condensed font in small caps and expanded

Figure 4–18

Other Ways

1. Right-click selected text (or, if using touch, tap 'Show Context Menu' button on mini toolbar), click Font on shortcut menu, select formats (Font dialog box), click OK button
2. Press CTRL+D, select formats (Font dialog box), click OK button

To Zoom One Page, Change Spacing before and after a Paragraph, and Set Zoom Level

The final step in creating the title page is to adjust spacing above and below the SmartArt graphic. You want to see the entire page while adjusting the spacing. Thus, the following steps zoom one page, increase spacing before and after the paragraph containing the SmartArt graphic, and then set the zoom level back to page width because you will be finished with the title page.

1 Display the View tab. Click the One Page button (View tab | Zoom group) to display the entire page as large as possible centered in the document window.

2 Position the insertion point in the paragraph to adjust, in this case, on the paragraph mark to the right of the SmartArt graphic.

3 Display the Layout tab. Click the Spacing Before up arrow (Layout tab | Paragraph group) as many times as necessary until 42 pt is displayed in the Spacing Before box because you want to increase the space above the graphic (or, if using touch, tap the Spacing After box (Layout tab | Paragraph group) and then type   42   to change the spacing below the paragraph).

4 Click the Spacing After up arrow (Layout tab | Paragraph group) as many times as necessary until 30 pt is displayed in the Spacing After box because you want to increase the space below the graphic (or, if using touch, tap the Spacing After box (Layout tab | Paragraph group) and then type   30   to change the spacing below the paragraph) (Figure 4–19).

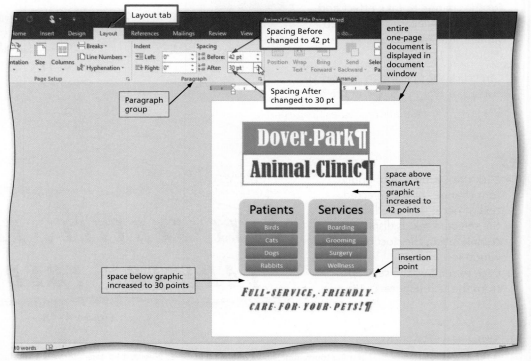

Figure 4–19

Q&A What if the document spills to two pages?

Decrease the spacing above or below the SmartArt graphic until the title page contents fit on a single page.

5 Display the View tab. Click the Page Width button (View tab | Zoom group) to change the zoom to page width.

6 Save the title page again on the same storage location with the same file name.

Break Point: If you wish to take a break, this is a good place to do so. You can exit Word now. To resume at a later time, run Word, open the file called Animal Clinic Title Page, and continue following the steps from this location forward.

Inserting an Existing Document in an Open Document

Assume you already have prepared a draft of the body of the proposal and saved it with the file name, Animal Clinic Draft. You would like the draft to be displayed on a separate page following the title page.

In the following sections, you will insert the draft of the proposal below the title page and then edit the draft by deleting a page break and applying styles.

To Save an Open Document with a New File Name

The current file name on the title bar is Animal Clinic Title Page, yet the document you will work on from this point forward in the module will contain both the title page and the body of the sales proposal. To keep the title page as a separate document called Animal Clinic Title Page, you should save the open document with a new file name. If you save the open document by using the Save button on the Quick Access Toolbar, Word will assign it the current file name. You want the open document to have a new file name. The following step saves the open document with a new file name.

 Save the title page on your hard drive, OneDrive, or other storage location using the file name, Animal Clinic Sales Proposal.

Sections

All Word documents have at least one section. A Word document can be divided into any number of sections. During the course of creating a document, you will create a new **section** if you need to change the top margin, bottom margin, page alignment, paper size, page orientation, page number position, or contents or position of headers, footers, or footnotes in just a portion of the document.

The pages in the body of the sales proposal require page formatting different from that of the title page. The title page will not have a header or footer; the next two pages will have a header and footer. When you want to change page formatting for a portion of a document, you create a new section in the document. Each section then may be formatted differently from the others. Thus, the title page formatted with no header or footer will be in one section, and the next two pages of the proposal, which will have a header and footer, will be in another section.

To Insert a Next Page Section Break

1 CREATE TITLE PAGE | **2 INSERT EXISTING DOCUMENT** | **3 CREATE HEADER & FOOTER**
4 EDIT & FORMAT LISTS | 5 EDIT & FORMAT TABLES | 6 CREATE WATERMARK

When you insert a section break, you specify whether the new section should begin on a new page. *Why?* *Sometimes you want a page break to occur with a section break, as in this project. Other times, you do not want a page break to occur with a section break (which will be illustrated in a later module).* In this project, the title page is separate from the next two pages. Thus, the section break should contain a page break. The following steps insert a next page section break, which instructs Word to begin the new section on a new page in the document.

- Position the insertion point at the end of the title page (following the exclamation point), which is the location where you want to insert the next page section break.

• Display the Layout tab. Click the 'Insert Page and Section Breaks' button (Layout tab | Page Setup group) to display the Insert Page and Section Breaks gallery (Figure 4–20).

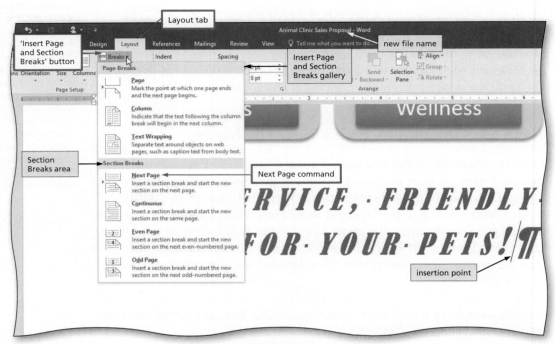

Figure 4–20

❷

• Click Next Page in the Section Breaks area of the Insert Page and Section Breaks gallery to insert a next page section break in the document at the location of the insertion point. If necessary, scroll so that your screen matches Figure 4–21.

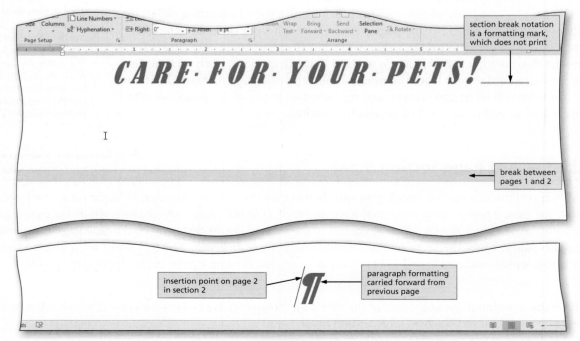

Figure 4–21

TO DELETE A SECTION BREAK

Word stores all section formatting in the section break. If you wanted to delete a section break and all associated section formatting, you would perform the following tasks.

1. Select the section break notation by dragging through it.
2. Right-click the selection to display a mini toolbar or shortcut menu and then click Cut on the mini toolbar or shortcut menu to delete the selection.

or

1. Position the insertion point immediately to the left or right of the section break notation.
2. Press the DELETE key to delete a section break to the right of the insertion point or press the BACKSPACE key to delete a section break to the left of the insertion point.

To Clear Formatting

When you create a section break, Word carries forward any formatting at the location of the insertion point to the next section. Thus, the current paragraph is formatted the same as the last line of the title page. In this project, the paragraphs and characters on the second page should be returned to the Normal style. Thus, the following step clears formatting.

1 Display the Home tab. With the insertion point positioned on the paragraph mark on the second page, click the 'Clear All Formatting' button (Home tab | Font group) to apply the Normal style to the location of the insertion point (shown in Figure 4–22).

BTW

Sections
To see the formatting associated with a section, double-click the section break notation, or click the Page Setup Dialog Box Launcher (Layout tab | Page Setup group) to display the Page Setup dialog box. You can change margin settings and page orientation for a section in the Margins sheet. To change paper sizes for a section, click the Paper tab (Page Setup dialog box). The Layout tab (Page Setup dialog box) allows you to change header and footer specifications and vertical alignment for the section. To add a border to a section, click the Borders button in the Layout sheet.

To Insert a Word Document in an Open Document

1 CREATE TITLE PAGE | 2 INSERT EXISTING DOCUMENT | **3 CREATE HEADER & FOOTER**
4 EDIT & FORMAT LISTS | 5 EDIT & FORMAT TABLES | 6 CREATE WATERMARK

The next step is to insert the draft of the sales proposal at the top of the second page of the document. *Why? You will modify a draft of the body of the proposal, which is located on the Data Files. Please contact your instructor for information about accessing the Data Files.* The following steps insert an existing Word document in an open document.

- Be sure the insertion point is positioned on the paragraph mark at the top of page 2, which is the location where you want to insert the contents of the Word document.

- Display the Insert tab.

- Click the Object arrow (Insert tab | Text group) to display the Object menu (Figure 4–22).

Q&A What if I click the Object button by mistake?
Click the Cancel button (Object dialog box) and then repeat this step.

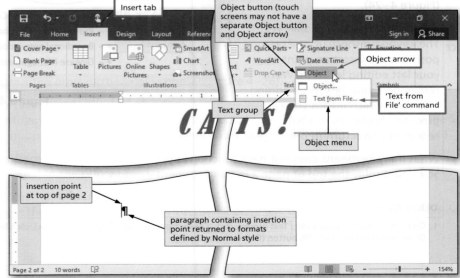

Figure 4–22

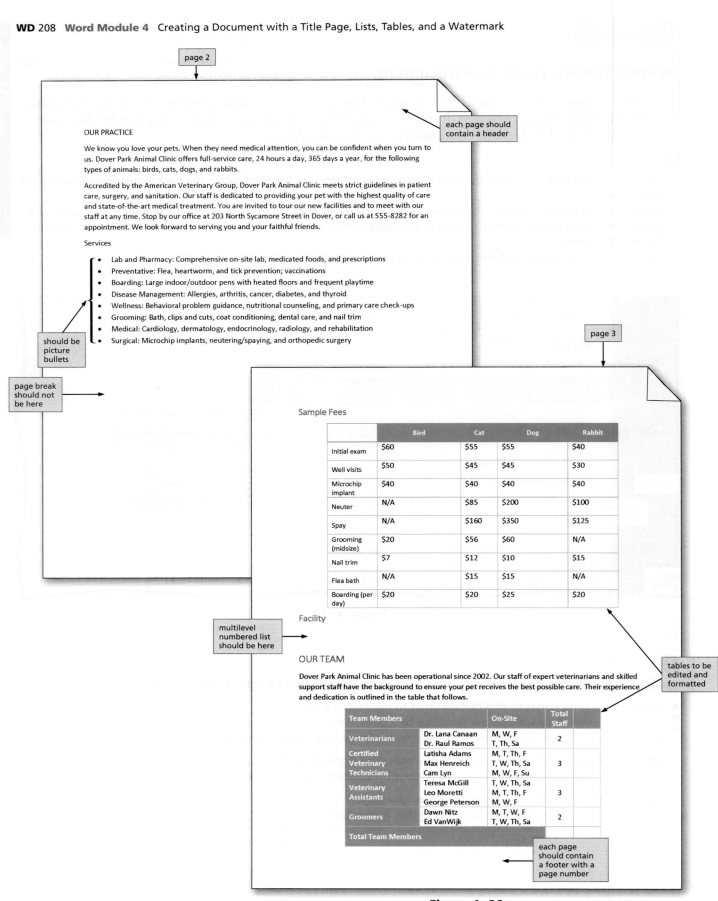

Figure 4–26

What elements should the body of a sales proposal contain?

Be sure to include basic elements in your sales proposals:

- **Include an introduction, body, and conclusion.** The introduction could contain the subject, purpose, statement of problem, need, background, or scope. The body may include costs, benefits, supporting documentation, available or required facilities, feasibility, methods, timetable, materials, or equipment. The conclusion summarizes key points or requests an action.

- **Use headers and footers.** Headers and footers help to identify every page. A page number should be in either the header or footer. If the sales proposal should become disassembled, the reader can use the page numbers in the headers or footers to determine the order and pieces of your proposal.

To Delete a Page Break

1 CREATE TITLE PAGE | 2 INSERT EXISTING DOCUMENT | 3 CREATE HEADER & FOOTER
4 EDIT & FORMAT LISTS | 5 EDIT & FORMAT TABLES | 6 CREATE WATERMARK

After reviewing the draft in Figure 4–26, you notice it contains a page break below the bulleted list. The following steps delete a page break. *Why? This page break below the bulleted list should not be in the proposal.*

1

- Scroll to display the page break notation.
- To select the page break notation, double-click it (Figure 4–27).

2

- Press the DELETE key to remove the page break from the document.

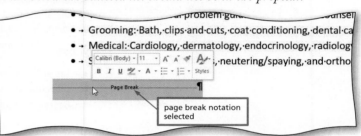

page break notation selected

Figure 4–27

Other Ways
1. With page break notation selected, click Cut button (Home tab | Clipboard group)   2. With page break notation selected, right-click selection and then click Cut on mini toolbar or shortcut menu   3. With the insertion point to the left or right of the page break notation, press DELETE or BACKSPACE, respectively

To Apply Heading Styles

Word has many built-in, or predefined, styles that you can use to format text. Three of the Styles shown in the Styles gallery in Figure 4–28 are for headings: Heading 1 for the major headings and Heading 2 and Heading 3 for minor headings. In the Animal Clinic Draft, all headings except for the first two were formatted using heading styles.

The following steps apply the Heading 1 style to the paragraph containing the text, OUR PRACTICE, and the Heading 2 style to the paragraph containing the text, Services.

1 Position the insertion point in the paragraph to be formatted to the Heading 1 style, in this case, the first line on the second page with the text, OUR PRACTICE.

2 Click Heading 1 in the Style gallery (Home tab | Styles group) to apply the selected style to the paragraph containing the insertion point.

Q&A Why did a square appear on the screen near the left edge of the paragraph formatted with the Heading 1 style?

The square is a nonprinting character, like the paragraph mark, that indicates text to its right has a special paragraph format applied to it.

3 Position the insertion point in the paragraph to be formatted to the Heading 2 style, in this case, the line above the bulleted list with the text, Services.

4 Click Heading 2 in the Style gallery (Home tab | Styles group) to apply the selected style to the paragraph containing the insertion point (Figure 4–28).

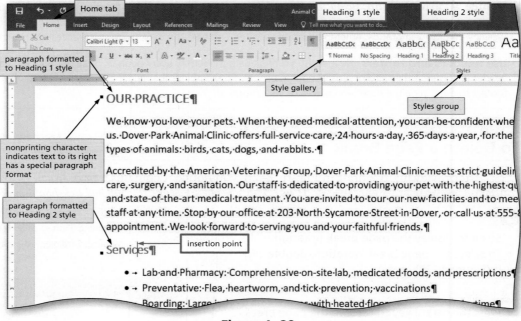

Figure 4–28

To Change Spacing before and after a Paragraph

The next step is to adjust spacing above and below the current paragraph, that is, the heading above the bulleted list. This paragraph is formatted using the Heading 2 style, which places no space above the paragraph and 8 points below the paragraph. You would like this paragraph, and all other paragraphs formatted using the Heading 2 style, to have 12 points of space above them and 6 points of space below them. Thus, the following steps adjust the spacing before and after a paragraph.

1 Display the Layout tab. Position the insertion point as shown in Figure 4–29. Click the Spacing Before up arrow (Layout tab | Paragraph group) as many times as necessary so that 12 pt is displayed in the Spacing Before box (or, if using touch, tap the Spacing Before box (Layout tab | Paragraph group) and then type **12** to change the spacing above the paragraph).

2 If necessary, click the Spacing After up arrow (Layout tab | Paragraph group) so that 6 pt is displayed in the Spacing After box (or, if using touch, tap the Spacing After box (Layout tab | Paragraph group) and then type **6** to change the spacing below the paragraph).

To Update a Style to Match a Selection

You want all paragraphs formatted in the Heading 2 style in the proposal to use this adjusted spacing. Thus, the following steps update the Heading 2 style so that this adjusted spacing is applied to all Heading 2 paragraphs in the document.

1 If necessary, position the insertion point in the paragraph containing the style to be updated.

2   Display the Home tab. Right-click Heading 2 in the Styles gallery (Home tab | Styles group) to display a shortcut menu (Figure 4–29).

3   Click 'Update Heading 2 to Match Selection' on the shortcut menu to update the Heading 2 style to reflect the settings at the location of the insertion point.

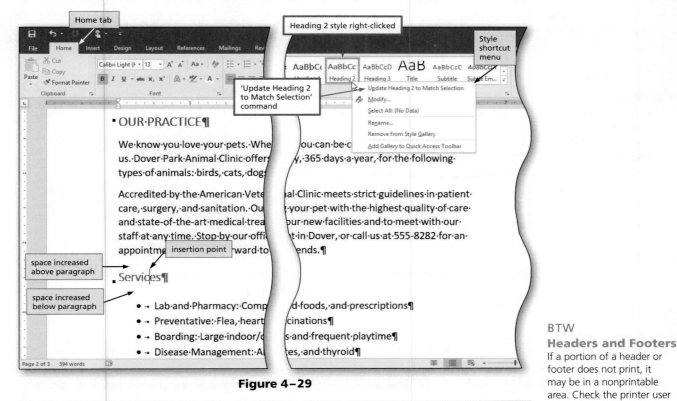

Figure 4–29

Creating Headers and Footers

A header is text that prints at the top of each page in the document. A footer is text that prints at the bottom of each page. In this proposal, you want the header and footer to appear on each page after the title page; that is, you do not want the header and footer on the title page. Recall that the title page is in a separate section from the rest of the sales proposal. Thus, the header and footer should not be in section 1, but they should be in section 2. The steps in the following sections explain how to create a header and footer in section 2 only.

To Insert a Formatted Header Different from the Previous Header

1 CREATE TITLE PAGE | 2 INSERT EXISTING DOCUMENT | **3 CREATE HEADER & FOOTER**
4 EDIT & FORMAT LISTS | 5 EDIT & FORMAT TABLES | 6 CREATE WATERMARK

Word provides several built-in preformatted header designs for you to insert in documents. The following steps insert a formatted header in section 2 of the sales proposal that is different from the previous header. *Why?* *You do not want the header to appear on the title page, so you will instruct Word to not place the header in the previous section. Recall that the title page is in section 1 and the body of the proposal is in section 2.*

1

- Display the Insert tab. Click the 'Add a Header' button (Insert tab | Header & Footer group) and then click Edit Header in the Header gallery to switch to the header for section 2.
- If the 'Link to Previous' button (Header & Footer Tools Design tab | Navigation group) is selected, click it to deselect the button because you do not want the header in this section to be copied to the previous section (that is, the header should not be on the title page).

BTW

Headers and Footers
If a portion of a header or footer does not print, it may be in a nonprintable area. Check the printer user instructions to see how close the printer can print to the edge of the paper. Then, click the Page Setup Dialog Box Launcher (Layout tab | Page Setup group), click the Layout tab (Page Setup dialog box), adjust the From edge text box to a value that is larger than the printer's minimum margin setting, click the OK button, and then print the document again.

- Click the 'Add a Header' button (Header & Footer Tools Design tab | Header & Footer group) to display the Add a Header gallery (Figure 4–30).

 Experiment

- Scroll through the list of built-in headers to see the variety of available formatted header designs.

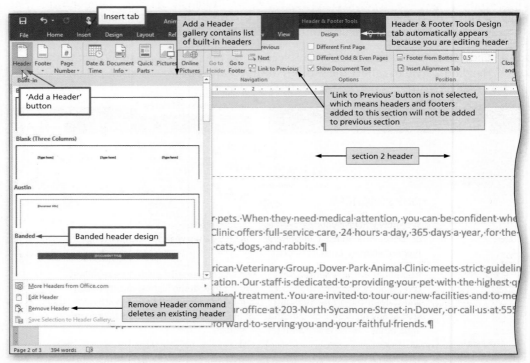

Figure 4–30

2

- If necessary, scroll to and then click the Banded header design in the Add a Header gallery to insert the formatted header in the header of section 2, which contains a content control (Figure 4–31).

Figure 4–31

Q&A

What is a content control?

A **content control** is an object that contains sample text or instructions for filling in text and graphics.

3

- Click the content control, [DOCUMENT TITLE], to select it and then type **Dover Park Animal Clinic** in the content control (Figure 4–32).

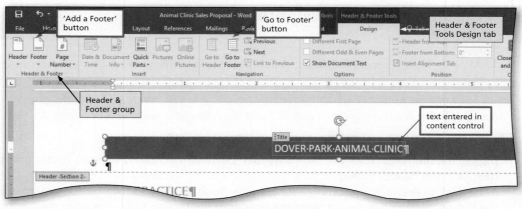

Figure 4–32

If requested by your instructor, enter your name instead of the clinic name shown in Figure 4–32.

Q&A How would I delete a header?
You would click Remove Header in the Header gallery.

Other Ways

1. Click 'Add a Header' button (Insert tab | Header & Footer group), select desired header in list

2. Click 'Explore Quick Parts' button (Insert tab | Text group), click 'Building Blocks Organizer' on Quick Parts menu, select desired header (Building Blocks Organizer dialog box), click Insert button

To Insert a Formatted Footer

BTW
Page Numbers
If Word displays {PAGE} instead of the actual page number, press ALT+F9 to turn off field codes. If Word prints {PAGE} instead of the page number, open the Backstage view, click the Options tab to display the Word Options dialog box, click Advanced in the left pane (Word Options dialog box), scroll to the Print area, remove the check mark from the 'Print field codes instead of their values' check box, and then click the OK button.

The next step is to insert the footer. Word provides the same built-in preformatted footer designs as header designs. The footer design that corresponds to the header just inserted contains a centered page number. The following steps insert a formatted footer in section 2 of the sales proposal that corresponds to the header just inserted.

1 Click the 'Go to Footer' button (shown in Figure 4–32) (Header & Footer Tools Design tab | Navigation group) to display the footer for section 2.

2 If the 'Link to Previous' button (Header & Footer Tools Design tab | Navigation group) is selected, click it to deselect the button because you do not want the footer in this section to be copied to the previous section (that is, the footer should not be on the title page).

3 Click the 'Add a Footer' button (shown in Figure 4–32) (Header & Footer Tools Design tab | Header & Footer group) to display the Add a Footer gallery.

4 Click the Banded footer design to insert the formatted footer in the footer of section 2 (shown in Figure 4–33).

Q&A Why is the page number a 2?
The page number is 2 because, by default, Word begins numbering pages from the beginning of the document.

To Format Page Numbers to Start at a Different Number

1 CREATE TITLE PAGE | 2 INSERT EXISTING DOCUMENT | 3 CREATE HEADER & FOOTER
4 EDIT & FORMAT LISTS | 5 EDIT & FORMAT TABLES | 6 CREATE WATERMARK

On the page after the title page in the proposal, you want to begin numbering with a number 1, instead of a 2 as shown in Figure 4–33. *Why? Word begins numbering pages from the beginning of the document, and you want it to begin numbering from the first page of the body of the proposal. Thus, you need to instruct Word to begin numbering the pages in section 2 with the number 1.* The following steps format the page numbers so that they start at a different number.

- Click the 'Add Page Numbers' button (Header & Footer Tools Design tab | Header & Footer group) to display the Add Page Numbers menu (Figure 4–33).

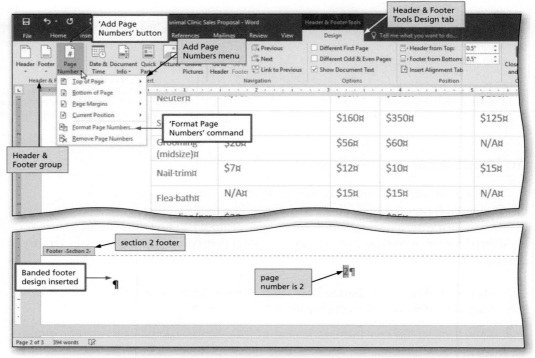

Figure 4–33

- Click 'Format Page Numbers' on the Add Page Numbers menu to display the Page Number Format dialog box.

- Click Start at in the Page numbering area (Page Number Format dialog box), which displays a 1 by default as the starting page number (Figure 4–34).

Q&A Can I also change the look of the page number?
Yes. Click the Number format arrow (Page Number Format dialog box) for a list of page number variations.

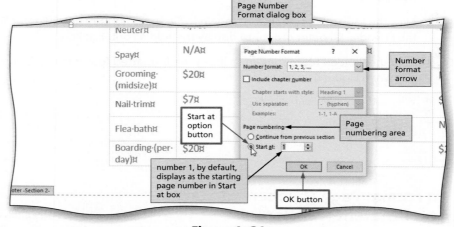

Figure 4–34

- Click the OK button to change the starting page number for section 2 to the number 1 (Figure 4–35).

- Click the 'Close Header and Footer' button (Header & Footer Tools Design tab | Close group) to close the header and footer.

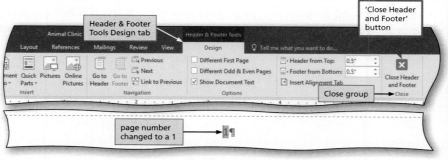

Figure 4–35

Other Ways

1. Click 'Add Page Numbers' button (Insert tab | Header & Footer group), click 'Format Page Numbers' on Add Page Numbers menu, set page formats (Page Number Format dialog box), click OK button

Editing and Formatting Lists

The finished sales proposal in this module has two lists: a bulleted list and a numbered list (shown in Figures 4–1b and 4–1c at the beginning of this module). The bulleted list is in alphabetical (sorted) order, the first word of each list item is emphasized, and the bullets are graphical instead of simple round dots. The numbered list has multiple levels for each numbered item. The following sections illustrate steps used to edit and format the lists in the proposal:

1. Sort a list of paragraphs.
2. Format text in the first list item and then copy the format to text in each of the remaining list items.
3. Customize bullets in a list of paragraphs.
4. Create a multilevel numbered list.

To Sort Paragraphs

1 CREATE TITLE PAGE | 2 INSERT EXISTING DOCUMENT | 3 CREATE HEADER & FOOTER
4 EDIT & FORMAT LISTS | 5 EDIT & FORMAT TABLES | 6 CREATE WATERMARK

The next step is to alphabetize the paragraphs in the bulleted list. ***Why? It is easier for readers to locate information in lists that are in alphabetical order.*** In Word, you can arrange paragraphs in alphabetic, numeric, or date order based on the first character in each paragraph. Ordering characters in this manner is called **sorting**. The following steps sort paragraphs.

- If necessary, scroll to display the paragraphs to be sorted.
- Drag through the paragraphs to be sorted, in this case, the bulleted list.
- Click the Sort button (Home tab | Paragraph group) to display the Sort Text dialog box (Figure 4–36).

Q&A

What does ascending mean? Ascending means to sort in alphabetic, numeric, or earliest-to-latest date order.

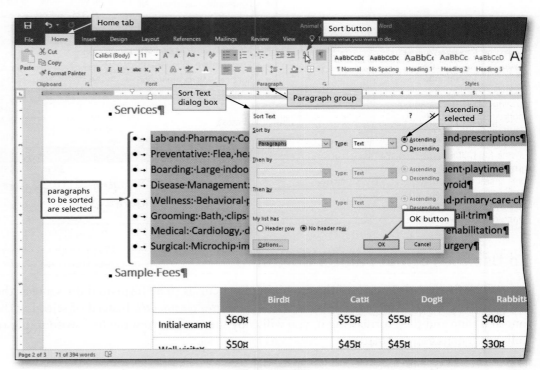

Figure 4–36

- Click the OK button (Sort Text dialog box) to instruct Word to alphabetize the selected paragraphs (shown in Figure 4–37).
- Click anywhere to remove the selection from the text.

To Apply a Style Using the Mini Toolbar

The text up to the colon in each list item is to be formatted in italic with the color purple. Although you could apply formatting using buttons in the Font group on the ribbon, it is more efficient to use the Intense Emphasis style. If you use a style and decide at a later time that you want to modify the formatting, you simply modify the style and Word will apply the changes to all text formatted with that style. Thus, the following steps format text using a style.

1 Select the text to be formatted (in this case, the text, Boarding, in the first list item).

2 Click the Styles button on the mini toolbar to display the Styles gallery (Figure 4–37).

3 Click Intense Emphasis in the Styles gallery to apply the selected style to the selected text.

Q&A Could I use the Styles gallery on the Home tab instead of the mini toolbar?
Yes.

BTW

Format Painter

If you also want to copy paragraph formatting, such as alignment and line spacing, select the paragraph mark at the end of the paragraph prior to clicking the Format Painter button (Home tab | Clipboard group). If you want to copy only character formatting, such as fonts and font sizes, do not include the paragraph mark in your selected text.

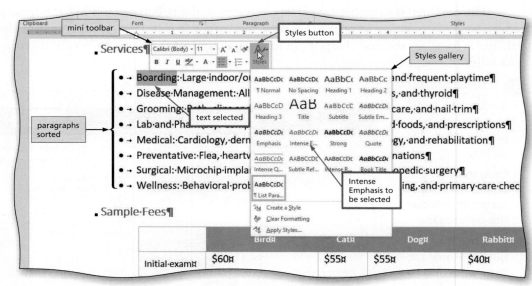

Figure 4–37

To Use the Format Painter Button

1 CREATE TITLE PAGE | 2 INSERT EXISTING DOCUMENT | 3 CREATE HEADER & FOOTER
4 EDIT & FORMAT LISTS | 5 EDIT & FORMAT TABLES | 6 CREATE WATERMARK

The first words in each of the remaining list items is to be formatted the same as the first words in the first list item. **Why?** *You would like the lists to be formatted consistently.* Instead of selecting the text in each list item one at a time and then formatting it, you will copy the format from the first word to the remaining words. The following steps copy formatting.

1

• Position the insertion point in the text that contains the formatting you wish to copy (the text, Boarding, in this case).

• Double-click the Format Painter button (Home tab | Clipboard group) to turn on the format painter.

Q&A Why double-click the Format Painter button?
To copy formats to only one other location, click the Format Painter button (Home tab | Clipboard group) once. If you want to copy formatting to multiple locations, however, double-click the Format Painter button so that the format painter remains active until you turn it off.

- Move the pointer to where you want to copy the formatting (the text, Disease Management, in this case) and notice that the format painter is active (Figure 4–38).

Q&A How can I tell if the format painter is active?
The pointer has a paintbrush attached to it when the format painter is active.

2

- Select the text in the next list item (the text, Disease Management, in this case) to paste the copied format to the selected text.

Q&A What if the Format Painter button no longer is selected?
Repeat Step 1.

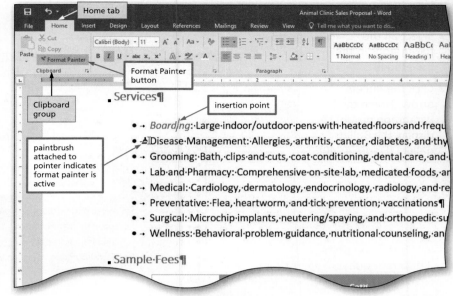

Figure 4–38

3

- Repeat Step 2 for the remaining the list items, selecting text up to the colon in Grooming, Lab and Pharmacy, Medical, Preventative, Surgical, and Wellness.
- Click the Format Painter button (Home tab | Clipboard group) to turn off the format painter (Figure 4–39).

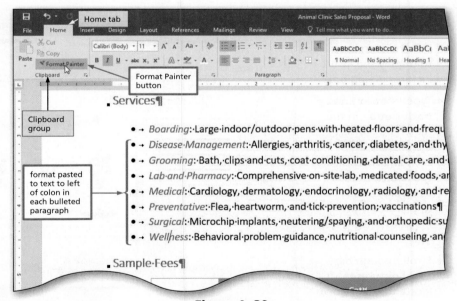

Figure 4–39

To Customize Bullets in a List

1 CREATE TITLE PAGE | 2 INSERT EXISTING DOCUMENT | 3 CREATE HEADER & FOOTER
4 EDIT & FORMAT LISTS | 5 EDIT & FORMAT TABLES | 6 CREATE WATERMARK

The bulleted list in the sales proposal draft uses default bullet characters, that is, the dot symbol. The following steps change the bullets in a list from the default to picture bullets. *Why? You want to use a more visually appealing bullet that looks like a veterinary caduceus. Word refers to graphical bullets as picture bullets.*

1

- Select all the paragraphs in the bulleted list.
- Click the Bullets arrow (Home tab | Paragraph group) to display the Bullets gallery (Figure 4–40).

Q&A
Can I select any of the bullet characters in the Bullet Library area of the Bullets gallery?
Yes, but if you prefer a different bullet character, follow the rest of these steps.

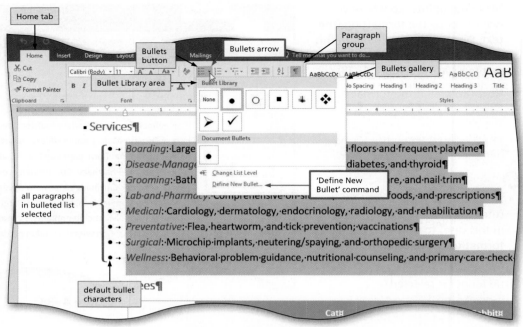

Figure 4–40

2

- Click 'Define New Bullet' in the Bullets gallery to display the Define New Bullet dialog box.

- Click the Picture button (Define New Bullet dialog box) to display the Insert Pictures dialog box.

- Type **veterinary caduceus** in the search box (Insert Pictures dialog box) and then click the Search button to display a list of pictures that matches the entered search text.

- Scroll through the list of pictures to locate the one shown in Figure 4–41, or a similar image. (If necessary, click the 'Show all web results' button to display more images that match the search text.)

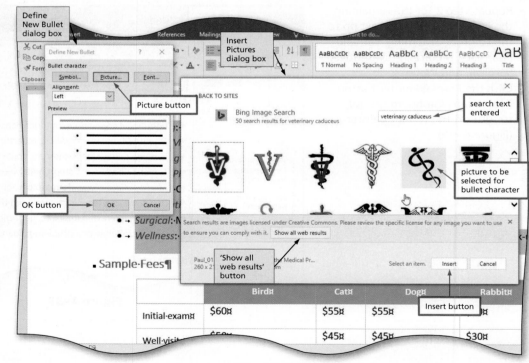

Figure 4–41

Q&A
What if I cannot locate the image in Figure 4-41, and I would like to use that exact image?
The image is located on the Data Files. You can click the Cancel button, click the 'Browse from a file' link in the Insert Pictures dialog box, navigate to the file called aesculab-stab-2400px.png in the Data Files, select the file, and then click the Insert button (Insert Picture dialog box) to show a preview of the selected picture bullet in the Define New Bullet dialog box. Proceed to Step 4.

● Click the desired picture to select it.

● Click the Insert button (Insert Pictures dialog box) to download the image, close the dialog box, and show a preview of the selected picture bullet in the Define New Bullet dialog box.

● Click the OK button (Define New Bullet dialog box) to change the bullets in the selected list to picture bullets.

● When the Word window is visible again, click in the selected list to remove the selection (Figure 4–42).

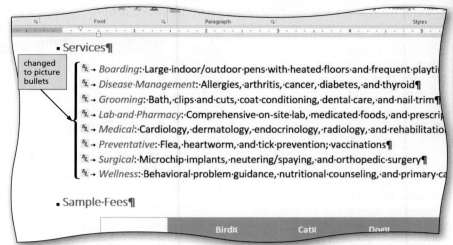

Figure 4–42

To Create a Multilevel Numbered List

1 CREATE TITLE PAGE | 2 INSERT EXISTING DOCUMENT | 3 CREATE HEADER & FOOTER
4 EDIT & FORMAT LISTS | 5 EDIT & FORMAT TABLES | 6 CREATE WATERMARK

The next step is to create a multilevel numbered list below the Facility heading on the last page of the sales proposal in this module (shown in Figure 4–1c at the beginning of this module). *Why? You would like to list the team members and their hours at the clinic.*

A **multilevel list** is a list that contains several levels of list items, with each lower level displaying a different numeric, alphabetic, or bullet character. In a multilevel list, the first level is displayed at the left edge of the list and subsequent levels are indented; that is, the second level is indented below the first, the third level is indented below the second level, and so on. The list is referred to as a numbered list if the first level contains numbers or letters and is referred to as a bulleted list if the first level contains a character other than a number or letter.

For the list in this project, the first level uses numbers (i.e., 1., 2., 3.), the second level uses lowercase letters (a., b., c.), and the third level uses lowercase Roman numerals (for example, i., ii., iii.). The following steps create a multilevel numbered list.

● Position the insertion point at the location for the multilevel numbered list, which in this case is the blank line below the Facility heading on the last page of the sales proposal.

● Click the Multilevel List button (Home tab | Paragraph group) to display the Multilevel List gallery (Figure 4–43).

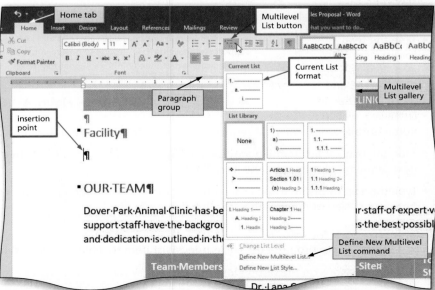

Figure 4–43

2

- Click the Current List format in the Multilevel List gallery to display the current paragraph as a multilevel list item using the current number format, which in this case is an indented 1 followed by a period.

 What if I wanted a different number format?
You would click the Multilevel List button (Home tab | Paragraph group) and then select the desired format in the Multilevel List gallery, or click Define New Multilevel List in the Multilevel List gallery (shown in Figure 4-43) to define your own format.

- Type **Clinic Hours** as a first-level list item and then press the ENTER key, which automatically places the next sequential number for the current level at the beginning of the next line (in this case, 2.) (Figure 4–44).

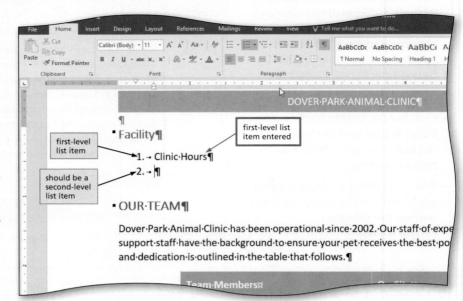

Figure 4–44

3

- Press the TAB key to demote the current list item (the 2.) to the next lower level, which is indented below the higher-level list item (in this case, converting 2. to a.).

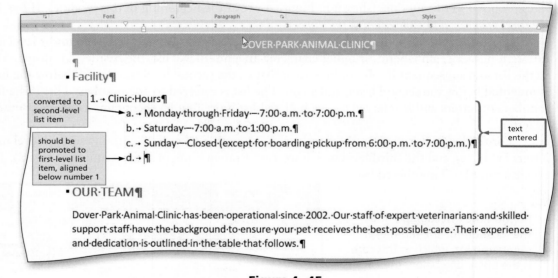

Figure 4–45

4

- Type the text for list item 1-a as shown in Figure 4–45 and then press the ENTER key, which automatically places the next sequential list item for the current level on the next line (in this case, b.).

- Type the text for list item 1-b as shown in Figure 4–45 and then press the ENTER key, which automatically places the next sequential list item on the next line (in this case, c.).

- Type the text for list item 1-c as shown in Figure 4–45 and then press the ENTER key, which automatically places the next sequential list item on the next line (Figure 4–45).

5

- Press SHIFT+TAB to promote the current-level list item to a higher-level list item (in this case, converting d. to 2.).

 Can I use buttons on the ribbon instead of pressing TAB or SHIFT+TAB to promote and demote list items?
Yes. With the insertion point in the item to adjust, you can click the Increase Indent or Decrease Indent button (Home tab | Paragraph group) or right-click the list item and then click the desired command on the shortcut menu.

6

- Type **Contact Information** as a first-level list item and then press the ENTER key.

- Press the TAB key to demote the current level list item to a lower-level list item (in this case, converting 3. to a.).

- Type **Phone: 309-555-8282** and then press the ENTER key.

- Type **Email: info@ doverpark.com** and then press the ENTER key.

- Press SHIFT+TAB to promote the current-level list item to a higher-level list item (in this case, converting c. to 3.).

- Type **Payments** as a first-level list item, press the ENTER key, and then press the TAB key to demote the current-level list item to a lower-level list item (in this case, converting 4. to a.).

- Type **Accepted methods** and then press the ENTER key (Figure 4-46).

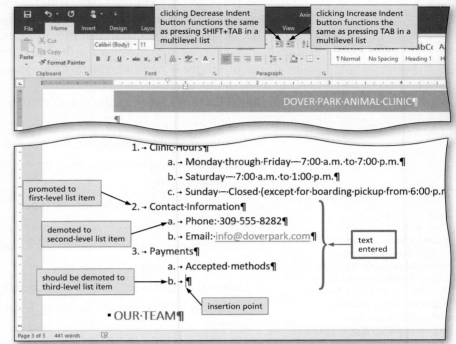

Figure 4–46

7

- Press the TAB key to demote the current-level list item to a lower-level list item (in this case, converting b. to i.).

- Type **Cash** and then press the ENTER key.

- Type **Check** and then press the ENTER key.

- Type **Credit card** and then press the ENTER key.

- Press SHIFT+TAB to promote the current-level list item to a higher-level list item (in this case, converting iii. to b.).

- Type the text for list item 3-b as shown in Figure 4–47 and then press the ENTER key.

- Press SHIFT+TAB to promote the current-level list item to a higher-level list item (in this case, converting c. to 4.).

- Finish entering the list as shown in Figure 4–47.

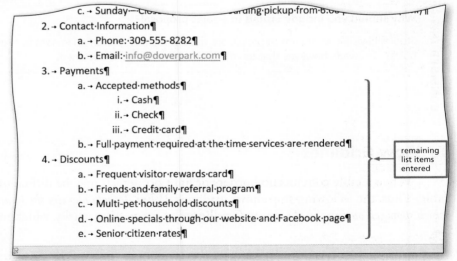

Figure 4–47

- Save the proposal again on the same storage location with the same file name.

Other Ways

1. Type **1.,** press SPACEBAR, type numbered list, pressing ENTER key at end of each item in list

Break Point: If you wish to take a break, this is a good place to do so. You can exit Word now. To resume at a later time, run Word, open the file called Animal Clinic Sales Proposal, and continue following the steps from this location forward.

Editing and Formatting Tables

The sales proposal draft contains two Word tables: the sample fees table and the team members table (shown earlier in the module in Figure 4–26). The sample fees table shows the sample fees for a variety of patient types, and the team members table shows details about various staff members at the clinic. In this section, you will make several modifications to these two tables so that they appear as shown in Figure 4–1 at the beginning of this module.

The following pages explain how to modify the tables in the sales proposal draft:

1. Sample fees table
   a. Change the column width for the column containing the type of services.
   b. Change row heights so that they are not so tall.
   c. Shade table cells.
   d. Sort the table contents by service type.
   e. Change cell spacing.
   f. Change the column width of columns containing costs.

2. Team members table
   a. Delete the extra column on the right edge of the table.
   b. Split table cells so that the heading, Team Members, is above the second column.
   c. Display text in a cell vertically to the left of the table.
   d. Remove cell shading from the table.
   e. Add borders to the table.
   f. Sum columns in the table.

BTW

Table Wrapping
If you want text to wrap around a table, instead of displaying above and below the table, do the following: either right-click the table and then click Table Properties on the shortcut menu, or click the Table Properties button (Table Tools Layout tab | Table group), click the Table tab (Table Properties dialog box), click Around in the Text wrapping area, and then click the OK button.

CONSIDER THIS

Why should you include visuals in a sales proposal?

Studies have shown that most people are visually oriented, preferring images to text. Use tables to clarify ideas and illustrate points. Be aware, however, that too many visuals can clutter a document.

To Show Gridlines

1 CREATE TITLE PAGE | 2 INSERT EXISTING DOCUMENT | 3 CREATE HEADER & FOOTER
4 EDIT & FORMAT LISTS | 5 EDIT & FORMAT TABLES | 6 CREATE **WATERMARK**

When a table contains no borders or light borders, it may be difficult to see the individual cells in the table. Thus, the following step shows gridlines. *Why? To help identify the location of cells, you can display gridlines, which show cell outlines on the screen.* **Gridlines** are formatting marks, which means the gridlines do not print.

- Display the table to be edited in the document window (in this case, the sample fees table).
- Position the insertion point in any cell in the table.
- Display the Table Tools Layout tab.

- If gridlines are not displayed on the screen, click the 'View Table Gridlines' button (Table Tools Layout tab | Table group) to show gridlines in the table (Figure 4–48).

Q&A How do I turn off table gridlines?
Click the 'View Table Gridlines' button again.

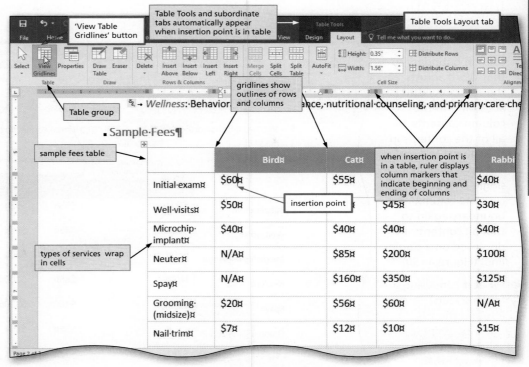

Figure 4–48

To Change Column Width

1 CREATE TITLE PAGE | 2 INSERT EXISTING DOCUMENT | 3 CREATE HEADER & FOOTER
4 EDIT & FORMAT LISTS | 5 EDIT & FORMAT TABLES | 6 CREATE WATERMARK

Notice in Figure 4–48 that the leftmost column containing the types of services is not wide enough to fit the contents; that is, some of the services wrap in the cells. Thus, you will change the column width of just this single column. **Why?** *In this proposal, the services should appear on a single line that is just wide enough to accommodate the types of services.*

You can change a column width by entering a specific value on the ribbon or in a dialog box, or by using a marker on the ruler or the column boundary. The following steps change column width by using a column's boundary.

1

- Position the pointer on the column boundary to the right of the column to adjust (in this case, to the right of the first column) so that the pointer changes to a double-headed arrow split by two vertical bars (Figure 4–49).

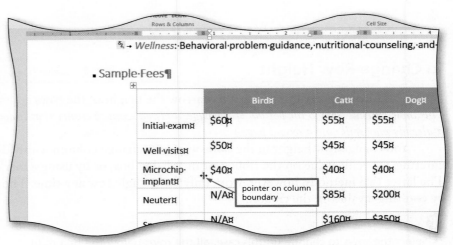

Figure 4–49

2

- Double-click the column boundary so that Word adjusts the column width according to the column contents. (If all of the contents in the column still are not displayed on a single line, double-click the column boundary again so that all contents are displayed on a single line) (Figure 4–50).

Q&A What if I am using a touch screen?

Position the insertion point in the column to adjust, tap the AutoFit button (Table Tools Layout tab | Cell Size group), and then tap AutoFit Contents on the AutoFit menu.

Figure 4–50

Experiment

- Practice changing this column's width using other techniques: drag the 'Move Table Column' marker on the horizontal ruler to the right and then to the left. Click the 'Table Column Width' box up and down arrows (Table Tools Layout tab | Cell Size group). When you have finished experimenting, type **1.34** in the 'Table Column Width' box (Table Tools Layout tab | Cell Size group).

Other Ways

1. Drag 'Move Table Column' marker on horizontal ruler to desired width	2. Enter desired value in 'Table Column Width' box (Table Tools Layout tab | Cell Size group)	3. Click Table Properties button (Table Tools Layout tab | Table group), click Column tab (Table Properties dialog box), enter width, click OK button

To Change Row Height

1 CREATE TITLE PAGE | 2 INSERT EXISTING DOCUMENT | 3 CREATE HEADER & FOOTER
4 EDIT & FORMAT LISTS | 5 EDIT & FORMAT TABLES | 6 CREATE WATERMARK

The next step in this project is to narrow the height of the rows containing the services and fees. *Why? This table extends close to the bottom of the page, and you want to ensure that it does not spill onto the next page. (Note that it already may spill onto a second page.)*

You change row height in the same ways you change column width. That is, you can change row height by entering a specific value on the ribbon or in a dialog box, or by using a marker on the ruler or the row boundary. The latter two methods, however, work only for a single row at a time. The following steps change row height by entering a value on the ribbon.

1

- Select the rows to change (in this case, all the rows below the first row).

Q&A How do I select rows?

Point to the left of the first row and then drag downward when the pointer changes to a right-pointing arrow (or, if using touch, drag through the rows).

②

- Click the 'Table Row Height' box up or down arrows (Table Tools Layout tab | Cell Size group) as many times as necessary until the box displays 0.3" to change the row height to this value (or, if using touch, enter **0.3** in the 'Table Row Height' box (Table Tools Layout tab | Cell Size group) (Figure 4–51).

- Click anywhere to remove the selection from the table.

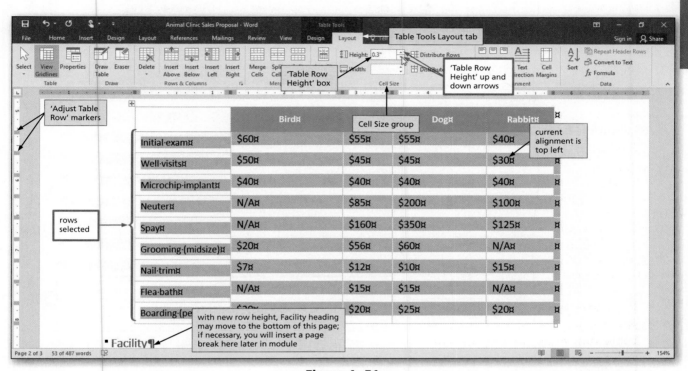

Figure 4–51

Other Ways

1. Click Table Properties button (Table Tools Layout tab | Table group), click Row tab (Table Properties dialog box), enter row height, click OK button	2. Right-click selected row (or, if using touch, tap 'Show Context Menu' button on mini toolbar), click Table Properties on shortcut menu, click Row tab, enter row height (Table Properties dialog box), click OK button	3. For a single row, drag row boundary (horizontal gridline at bottom of row in table) to desired height	4. Drag 'Adjust Table Row' marker on vertical ruler to desired height

To Align Data in Cells

The next step is to change the alignment of the data in cells that contain the dollar amounts. Recall that, in addition to aligning text horizontally in a cell (left, center, or right), you can align it vertically within a cell (top, center, or bottom). Currently, the dollar amounts have a top left alignment (shown in Figure 4–51). In this project, they should be aligned center so that they are more centered within the row height and width. The following steps change the alignment of data in cells.

① Select the cells containing dollar amounts, as shown in Figure 4–52.

◁ | How do I select a series of cells?
Q&A | Drag through the cells.

2 Click the Align Center button (Table Tools Layout tab | Alignment group) to center the contents of the selected cells (Figure 4–52).

3 Click anywhere to remove the selection from the table.

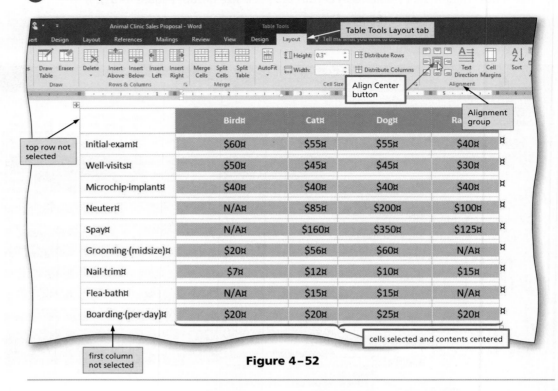

Figure 4–52

To Shade a Table Cell

1 CREATE TITLE PAGE | 2 INSERT EXISTING DOCUMENT | 3 CREATE HEADER & FOOTER
4 EDIT & FORMAT LISTS | 5 EDIT & FORMAT TABLES | 6 CREATE WATERMARK

In this table, the cell in the upper-left corner of the table is to be shaded teal. *Why? You want all cells in the top row shaded the same color.* The following steps shade a cell.

1

• Position the insertion point in the cell to shade (in this case, the cell in the upper-left corner of the table).

• Display the Table Tools Design tab.

• Click the Shading arrow (Table Tools Design tab | Table Styles group) to display the Shading gallery (Figure 4–53).

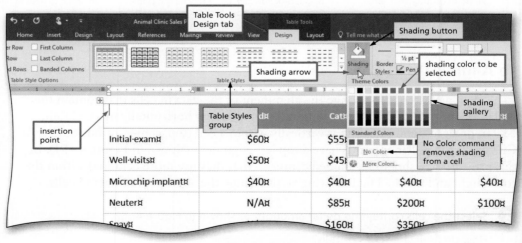

Figure 4–53

Experiment

• Point to various colors in the Shading gallery and watch the shading color of the current cell change.

- Click 'Teal, Accent 3' (seventh color, first row) in the Shading gallery to apply the selected shading color to the current cell (shown in Figure 4-54).

Q&A | How do I remove shading from a cell?
Click the Shading arrow (Table Tools Design tab | Table Styles group) and then click No Color in the Shading gallery.

To Sort a Table

1 CREATE TITLE PAGE | 2 INSERT EXISTING DOCUMENT | 3 CREATE HEADER & FOOTER
4 EDIT & FORMAT LISTS | 5 EDIT & FORMAT TABLES | **6 CREATE WATERMARK**

The next task is to sort rows in the table. ***Why? The services should be listed in alphabetical order.*** The following steps sort rows in a table.

- Select the rows to be sorted (in this case, all the rows below the first row).

Q&A | What if I want to sort all rows in the table?
Place the insertion point anywhere in the table instead of selecting the rows.

- Display the Table Tools Layout tab.
- Click the Sort button (Table Tools Layout tab | Data group) to display the Sort dialog box (Figure 4–54).

Q&A | What is the purpose of the Then by area (Sort dialog box)?
If you have multiple values for a particular column, you can sort by columns within columns. For example, if the table had a city column and a last name column, you could sort by last names within cities.

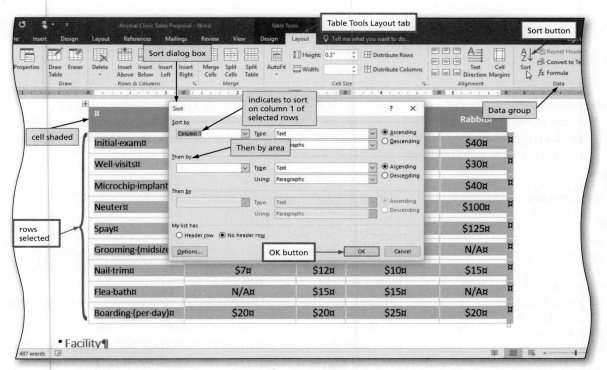

Figure 4–54

- Click the OK button (Sort dialog box) to instruct Word to alphabetize the selected rows.
- Click anywhere to remove the selection from the text (Figure 4–55).

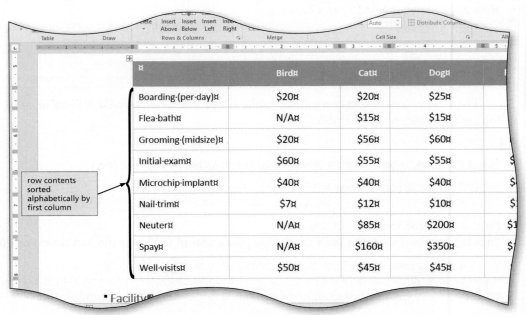

row contents sorted alphabetically by first column

	Bird¤	Cat¤	Dog¤	
Boarding·(per·day)¤	$20¤	$20¤	$25¤	
Flea·bath¤	N/A¤	$15¤	$15¤	
Grooming·(midsize)¤	$20¤	$56¤	$60¤	
Initial·exam¤	$60¤	$55¤	$55¤	$
Microchip·implant¤	$40¤	$40¤	$40¤	$
Nail·trim¤	$7¤	$12¤	$10¤	$
Neuter¤	N/A¤	$85¤	$200¤	$1
Spay¤	N/A¤	$160¤	$350¤	$
Well·visits¤	$50¤	$45¤	$45¤	

·Facility¶

Figure 4–55

To Select Nonadjacent Items

1 CREATE TITLE PAGE | 2 INSERT EXISTING DOCUMENT | 3 CREATE HEADER & FOOTER
4 EDIT & FORMAT LISTS | 5 EDIT & FORMAT TABLES | 6 CREATE WATERMARK

The next step is to select every other row in the table and shade it light teal. ***Why?*** *You feel that using shading on alternating rows will make it easier to read across individual rows.* Word provides a method of selecting nonadjacent items, which are items such as text, cells, or graphics that are not next to each other, that is, not to the immediate right, left, top, or bottom. When you select nonadjacent items, you can format all occurrences of the items at once. The following steps select nonadjacent cells.

- Select the first row to format (in this case, the row containing the Flea bath service).

- While holding down the CTRL key, select the next row to format (in this case, the row containing the Initial exam service) to select the nonadjacent row.

- While holding down the CTRL key, select the remaining nonadjacent rows (that is, the rows containing the Nail trim and Spay services), as shown in Figure 4–56.

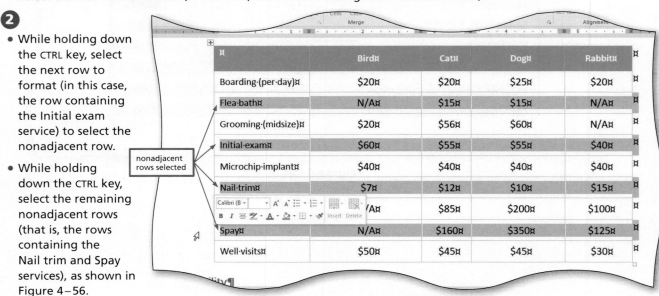

nonadjacent rows selected

	Bird¤	Cat¤	Dog¤	Rabbit¤	¤
Boarding·(per·day)¤	$20¤	$20¤	$25¤	$20¤	¤
Flea·bath¤	N/A¤	$15¤	$15¤	N/A¤	¤
Grooming·(midsize)¤	$20¤	$56¤	$60¤	N/A¤	¤
Initial·exam¤	$60¤	$55¤	$55¤	$40¤	¤
Microchip·implant¤	$40¤	$40¤	$40¤	$40¤	¤
Nail·trim¤	$7¤	$12¤	$10¤	$15¤	¤
	/A¤	$85¤	$200¤	$100¤	¤
Spay¤	N/A¤	$160¤	$350¤	$125¤	¤
Well·visits¤	$50¤	$45¤	$45¤	$30¤	¤

Figure 4–56

Q&A Do I follow the same procedure to select any nonadjacent item?
Yes. Select the first item and then hold down the CTRL key while selecting the remaining items.

What if my keyboard does not have a CTRL key?
You will need to format each row individually, one at a time.

To Shade Selected Cells

With the alternating rows selected, the next step is to shade them light teal. The following steps shade selected cells.

1 Display the Table Tools Design tab.

2 With the rows selected, click the Shading arrow (Table Tools Design tab | Table Styles group) to display the Shading gallery and then click 'Teal, Accent 3, Lighter 80%' (seventh color, second row) in the Shading gallery to shade the selected rows with the selected color.

3 Click anywhere to remove the selection from the table (Figure 4–57).

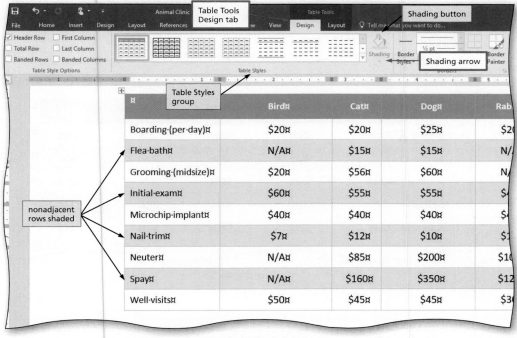

BTW

Table Headings
If a table continues on the next page, you can instruct Word to repeat the table headings at the top of the subsequent page(s) containing the table. To do this, select the first row in the table and then click the 'Repeat Header Rows' button (Table Tools Layout tab | Data group).

Figure 4–57

To Change Cell Spacing

1 CREATE TITLE PAGE | 2 INSERT EXISTING DOCUMENT | 3 CREATE HEADER & FOOTER
4 EDIT & FORMAT LISTS | 5 EDIT & FORMAT TABLES | **6 CREATE WATERMARK**

The next step in formatting the sample fees table is to place a small amount of white space between every cell in the table. *Why? You feel the table would be easier to read with white space surrounding each cell.* The following steps change spacing between cells.

1
- Display the Table Tools Layout tab.
- Position the insertion point somewhere in the table and then click the Cell Margins button (Table Tools Layout tab | Alignment group) to display the Table Options dialog box.

- Place a check mark in the 'Allow spacing between cells' check box and then click the up arrow once so that 0.02" is displayed in this box, because you want to increase space between cells by this value (Figure 4–58).

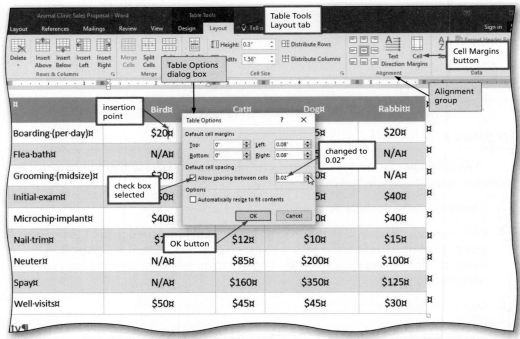

Figure 4–58

2

- Click the OK button (Table Options dialog box) to apply the cell spacing changes to the current table (Figure 4–59).

Q&A

Why are the column dividers in the first row wavy?

Gridlines are still showing, which causes a wavy appearance of the lines. When you hide gridlines later in the project, the wavy lines will disappear.

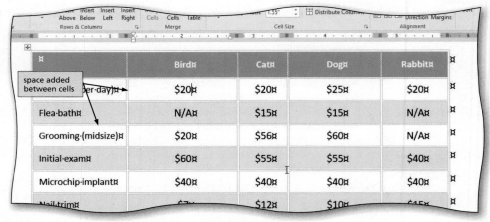

Figure 4–59

Other Ways

1. Click Table Properties button (Table Tools Layout tab | Table group), click Table tab (Table Properties dialog box), click Options button, select desired options (Table Options dialog box), click OK button in each dialog box

2. Right-click table (or, if using touch, tap 'Show Context Menu' button on mini toolbar), click Table Properties on shortcut menu, click Table tab (Table Properties dialog box), click Options button, select desired options (Table Options dialog box), click OK button in each dialog box

To Change Column Width

In reviewing the sample fees table, you notice that the columns containing the fees are different widths. Thus, the final step in formatting the sample fees table is to change the column widths because you want the columns containing the rates to all be the same width, specifically .95". The following steps change column widths by specifying a value on the ribbon.

1 Select the columns to be resized, in this case, all columns except the first.

2 Click the 'Table Column Width' box (Table Tools Layout tab | Cell Size group) to select it.

3 Type `.95` in the 'Table Column Width' box and then press the ENTER key to change the width of the selected table columns (Figure 4–60).

4 Click anywhere to remove the selection from the table.

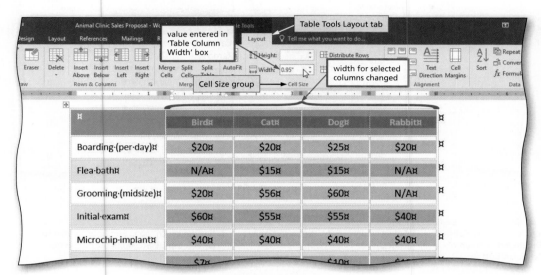

Figure 4–60

To Page Break Manually

If the Facility heading appears at the bottom of the page below the sample fees table, insert a page break immediately to its left so that this heading appears at the top of the last page of the proposal (as shown in Figure 4–1 at the beginning of this module). The following steps insert a manual page break, if necessary.

1 If the Facility heading is not on the last page of the proposal, position the insertion point immediately to the left of the F in Facility.

2 Display the Insert tab.

3 Click the 'Insert a Page Break' button (Insert tab | Pages group) to insert a manual page break at the location of the insertion point, which will move the Facility heading to the last page of the proposal.

To Delete a Column

1 CREATE TITLE PAGE | 2 INSERT EXISTING DOCUMENT | 3 CREATE HEADER & FOOTER
4 EDIT & FORMAT LISTS | **5 EDIT & FORMAT TABLES** | **6 CREATE WATERMARK**

With the service fees table finished, the next task is to format the team members table. The following steps delete a column from a table. **Why?** *The table in the draft of the proposal contains a blank column that should be deleted.*

- Scroll to display the team members table in the document window.
- Position the insertion point in the column to be deleted (in this case, the rightmost column).

- Click the Delete Table button (Table Tools Layout tab | Rows & Columns group) to display the Delete Table menu (Figure 4–61).

- Click Delete Columns on the Delete Table menu to delete the column containing the insertion point (shown in Figure 4–62).

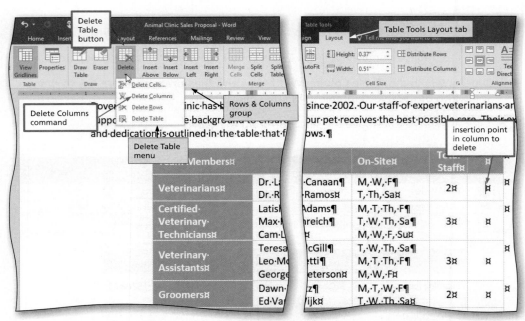

Figure 4–61

Other Ways

1. Right-click column to delete, click Delete Cells on shortcut menu, click 'Delete entire column' (Delete Cells dialog box), click OK button

2. Select column, right-click selection, click Delete Columns on shortcut menu

3. If using touch, press and hold column to delete, tap Delete Table button on mini toolbar, tap Delete Columns

TO DELETE A ROW

If you wanted to delete a row, you would perform the following tasks.

1. Position the insertion point in the row to be deleted; click the Delete Table button (Table Tools Layout tab | Rows & Columns group) and then click Delete Rows on the Delete Table menu.

or

2. If using touch, press and hold row to delete, tap Delete Table button on mini toolbar, tap Delete Rows.

or

3. Right-click the row to delete, click Delete Cells on the shortcut menu, click 'Delete entire row' (Delete Cells dialog box), and then click the OK button.

or

4. Select the row to be deleted, right-click the selected row, and then click Delete Rows on the shortcut menu.

To Split Cells

1 CREATE TITLE PAGE | 2 INSERT EXISTING DOCUMENT | 3 CREATE HEADER & FOOTER
4 EDIT & FORMAT LISTS | 5 EDIT & FORMAT TABLES | 6 CREATE WATERMARK

The top, left cell of the table contains the text, Team Members. In the draft of the sales proposal, this row is above the first two columns in the table (the job titles and employee name). This heading, Team Members, should be above the descriptions of the employee names, that is, above the second column. Thus, you will split the cell into two cells. **Why?** *With the cell split, you can reposition the heading, Team Members, above the second column.* The following steps split a single cell into two separate cells.

- Position the insertion point in the cell to split, in this case the top left cell as shown in Figure 4–62.
- Click the Split Cells button (Table Tools Layout tab | Merge group) to display the Split Cells dialog box (Figure 4–62).

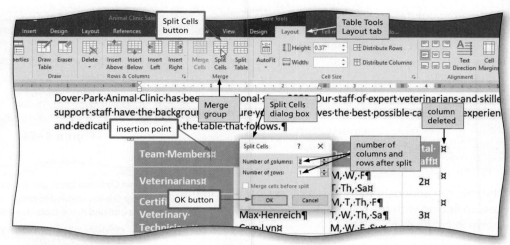

Figure 4–62

- Verify the number of columns and rows into which you want the cell split, in this case, 2 columns and 1 row.
- Click the OK button (Split Cells dialog box) to split the one cell into two columns (Figure 4–63).

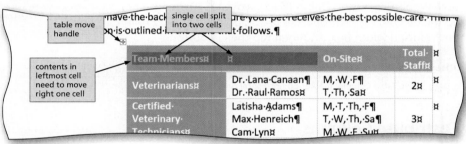

Figure 4–63

Other Ways

1. Right-click cell, click Split Cells on shortcut menu (or, if using touch, tap 'Show Context Menu' button on mini toolbar)

To Move Cell Contents

When you split a cell into two cells, Word places the contents of the original cell in the leftmost cell after the split. In this case, the contents (Team Members) should be in the right cell. Thus, the following steps move cell contents.

1. Select the cell contents to be moved (in this case, Team Members).

2. Drag the cell contents to the desired location (in this case, the second cell in the first row) (shown in Figure 4–64).

Q&A What if I cannot drag the cell contents properly?
Use the Cut and Paste commands.

BTW

Moving Tables
If you wanted to move a table to a new location, you would click in the table to display the table move handle in the upper-left corner of the table (shown in Figure 4–63) and then drag the table move handle to move the entire table to a new location.

1 CREATE TITLE PAGE | 2 INSERT EXISTING DOCUMENT | 3 CREATE HEADER & FOOTER
4 EDIT & FORMAT LISTS | 5 EDIT & FORMAT TABLES | 6 CREATE WATERMARK

To Move a Cell Boundary

Notice in Figure 4–64 that the cell boundary to the left of the Team Members label does not line up with the boundary to the right of the job titles. *Why not? This is because when you split a cell, Word divides the cell into evenly sized cells.* If you want the boundary to line up with other column boundaries, drag it to the desired location. The following steps move a cell boundary.

- Position the pointer on the cell boundary you wish to move so that the pointer changes to a double-headed arrow split by two vertical bars (Figure 4–64).

Q&A What if I cannot see the cell boundary?
Be sure that table gridlines are showing: View Table Gridlines button (Table Tools Layout tab | Table group).

Figure 4–64

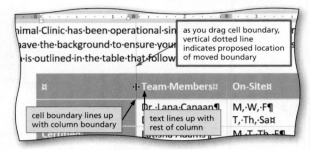

- Drag the cell boundary to the desired new location, in this case, to line up with the column boundary to its right, as shown in Figure 4–65.

Q&A What if I am using a touch screen?
Position the insertion point in the upper-left cell, tap the Table Properties button (Table Tools Layout tab | Table group), tap the Cell tab (Table Properties dialog box), type 1.27 in the Preferred width box, and then tap the OK button.

Figure 4–65

Other Ways

1. Drag 'Move Table Column' marker on horizontal ruler to desired width

To Distribute Columns

1 CREATE TITLE PAGE | 2 INSERT EXISTING DOCUMENT | 3 CREATE HEADER & FOOTER
4 EDIT & FORMAT LISTS | 5 EDIT & FORMAT TABLES | 6 **CREATE WATERMARK**

The next step in formatting the team members table is to make the width of the first three columns uniform, that is, the same width. The following step distributes selected columns. *Why? Instead of checking and adjusting the width of each column individually, you can make all columns uniform at the same time.*

1

- Select the columns to format, in this case, the three leftmost columns.
- Click the Distribute Columns button (Table Tools Layout tab | Cell Size group) to make the width of the selected columns uniform (Figure 4–66).

Q&A How would I make all columns in the table uniform?
Simply place the insertion point somewhere in the table before clicking the Distribute Columns button.

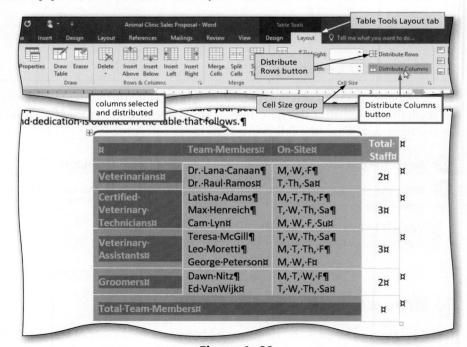

Figure 4–66

Other Ways

1. Right-click selected columns, click 'Distribute Columns Evenly' on shortcut menu (or, if using touch, tap 'Show Context Menu' button on mini toolbar)

TO DISTRIBUTE ROWS

If you wanted to make rows the same height, you would perform the following tasks.

1. Select the rows to format.
2. Click the Distribute Rows button (Table Tools Layout tab | Cell Size group) (shown in Figure 4-66) to make the width of the selected rows uniform.

or

1. Right-click selected columns and then click 'Distribute Rows Evenly' on the shortcut menu (or, if using touch, tap the 'Show Context Menu' button on the mini toolbar).

To Insert a Column

In this project, the left edge of the team members table has a column that displays the label, Organization. Thus, the following steps insert a column at the left edge of the table.

1 Position the insertion point somewhere in the first column of the table.

2 Click the 'Insert Columns to the Left' button (Table Tools Layout tab | Rows & Columns group) to insert a column to the left of the column containing the insertion point (Figure 4–67).

3 Click anywhere in the table to remove the selection.

BTW
Draw Table
If you want to draw the boundary, rows, and columns of a table, click the 'Add a Table' button (Insert tab | Tables group) and then click Draw Table in the Add a Table gallery. Use the pencil-shaped pointer to draw the perimeter of the table and the inside rows and columns. Use the Table Eraser button (Table Tools Design tab | Draw group) to erase lines in the table. To continue drawing, click the Draw Table button (Table Tools Design tab | Draw group).

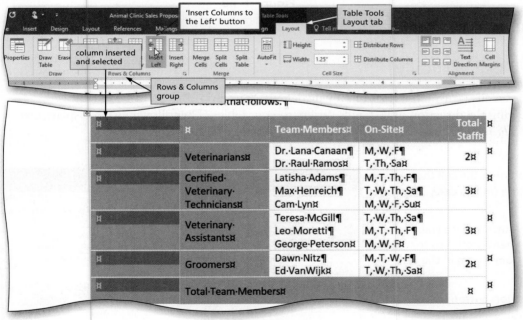

Figure 4–67

To Merge Cells and Enter Text

The label, Organization, is to be displayed vertically to the left of the bottom five rows in the table. To display this text, the five cells should be merged into a single cell. The following steps merge cells and then enter text in the merged cell.

1 Select the cells to merge, in this case, the bottom five cells in the first column of the table.

2 Click the Merge Cells button (Table Tools Layout tab | Merge group) to merge the five selected cells into one cell.

3 Type **Organization** in the merged cell.

4 If necessary, center the entered text (Figure 4–68).

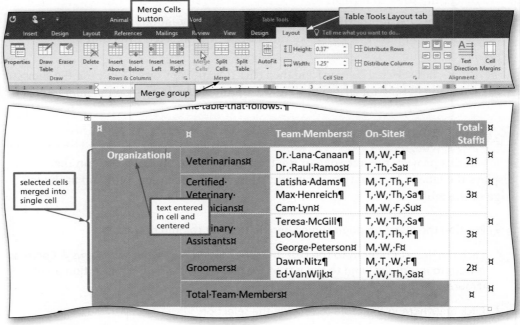

Figure 4–68

To Display Text in a Cell Vertically

1 CREATE TITLE PAGE | 2 INSERT EXISTING DOCUMENT | 3 CREATE HEADER & FOOTER
4 EDIT & FORMAT LISTS | 5 EDIT & FORMAT TABLES | 6 CREATE WATERMARK

The data you enter in cells is displayed horizontally by default. You can rotate the text so that it is displayed vertically. Changing the direction of text adds variety to your tables. The following step displays text vertically in a cell. *Why? The label, Organization, is displayed vertically at the left edge of the table.*

1

- Position the insertion point in the cell that contains the text to rotate (in this case, Organization).

- Click the Text Direction button twice (Table Tools Layout tab | Alignment group) so that the text reads from bottom to top in the cell (Figure 4–69).

Q&A Why click the Text Direction button twice? The first time you click the Text Direction button (Table Tools Layout tab | Alignment group), the text in the cell reads from top to bottom. The second time you click it, the text is displayed so that it reads from bottom to top (Figure 4–69). If you were to click the button a third time, the text would be displayed horizontally again.

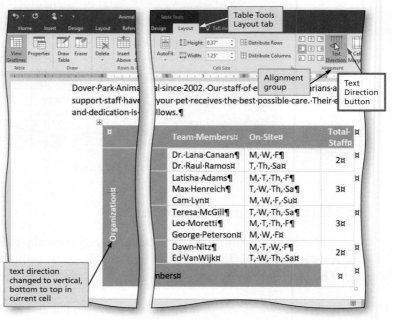

Figure 4–69

To Change Column Width

The cell containing the vertical text is too wide. Thus, the next step is to change the width of that column. The following step changes column width using the ruler.

1 Drag the column's boundary inward, as shown in Figure 4–70, to resize the column.

Q&A What if I am using a touch screen?

Position the insertion point in the column to adjust. Tap the 'Table Column Width' box (Table Tools Layout tab | Cell Size group), type `.35` as the column width, and then press the ENTER key.

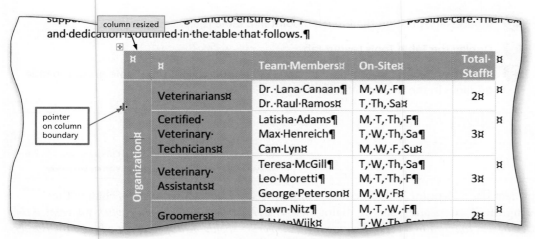

Figure 4–70

To Remove Cell Shading

In this table, only the first row and first column should have shading. Thus, the following steps remove shading from table cells.

1 Select the cells that should not contain shading (in this case, all of the cells below the first row and to the right of the first column).

2 Display the Table Tools Design tab. Click the Shading arrow (Table Tools Design tab | Table Styles group) to display the Shading gallery (Figure 4–71).

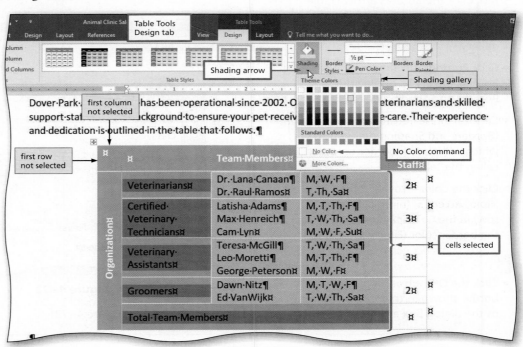

Figure 4–71

3 Click No Color in the Shading gallery to remove the shading from the selected cells (shown in Figure 4–72).

4 Click anywhere in the table to remove the selection.

To Hide Gridlines

You no longer need to see the gridlines in the table. Thus, you can hide the gridlines. The following steps hide gridlines.

1 If necessary, position the insertion point in a table cell.

2 Display the Table Tools Layout tab.

3 Click the 'View Table Gridlines' button (Table Tools Layout tab | Table group) to hide gridlines in the table on the screen.

To Border a Table

1 CREATE TITLE PAGE | 2 INSERT EXISTING DOCUMENT | 3 CREATE HEADER & FOOTER
4 EDIT & FORMAT LISTS | 5 EDIT & FORMAT TABLES | 6 **CREATE WATERMARK**

The table in this project has a ½-point, gold border around all cells. The following steps change the border color in a table using the Borders and Shading dialog box. **Why?** *Earlier in this module when you created the title page, the border line weight was changed to 6 point. Because the table border should be ½ point, you will use the Borders and Shading dialog box to change the line weight before adding the border to the table.*

1

- Position the insertion point somewhere in the table.

- Display the Table Tools Design tab. Click the Borders arrow (Table Tools Design tab | Table Styles group) to display the Borders gallery.

- Click Borders and Shading in the Borders gallery to display the Borders and Shading dialog box.

- Click All in the Setting area (Borders and Shading dialog box), which will place a border on every cell in the table.

- Click the Color arrow and then click 'Gold, Accent 5' (ninth color, first row) in the Color palette to specify the border color (Figure 4–72).

2

- Click the OK button to place the border shown in the preview area
of the dialog box around the table cells in the document (shown in Figure 4–73).

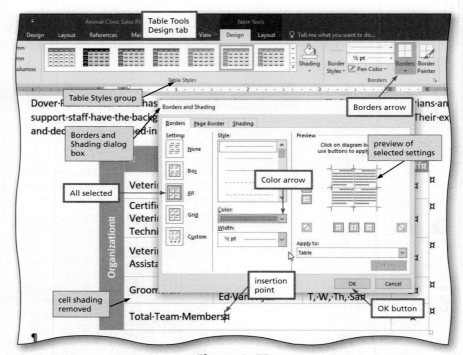

Figure 4–72

To Sum Columns in a Table

Word can calculate the totals of rows and columns. You also can specify the format for how the totals will be displayed. The following steps sum a column in the table. *Why? In this project, the last row should display the sum (total) of the values in the last column: Total Staff.*

- Position the insertion point in the cell to contain the sum (last row, Total Staff column).

2

- Display the Table Tools Layout tab.

- Click the Formula button (Table Tools Layout tab | Data group) to display the Formula dialog box (Figure 4–73).

Q&A What is the formula that shows in the Formula box, and can I change it?
Word places a default formula in the Formula box, depending on the location of the

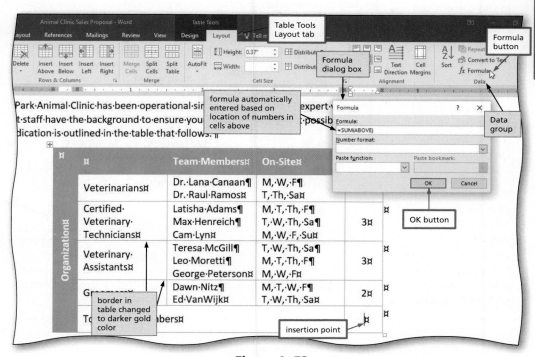

Figure 4–73

numbers in surrounding cells. In this case, because numbers are above the current cell, Word displays a formula that will add the numbers above the current cell. You can change the formula that Word proposes, or type a different formula. For example, instead of summing numbers you can multiply them.

3

- Click the Number format arrow (Formula dialog box) and then click the desired format for the result of the computation, in this case, the format with the numeral 0 (Figure 4–74).

Q&A Why select the format with the numeral 0?
You want the result to be displayed as a whole number, so you select the numeral 0. If you

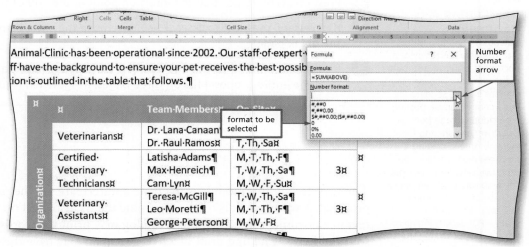

Figure 4–74

wanted the result to display with cents, you would select the format #,##0.00 (the # symbol means to display a blank if the number has a value of zero).

- Click the OK button (Formula dialog box) to place the sum of the numbers using the specified format in the current cell (Figure 4–75).

Q&A

Can I sum a row instead of a column? Yes. You would position the insertion point in an empty cell at the right edge of the row before clicking the Formula button.

If I make a change to a number in a table, does Word automatically recalculate the sum? No. You will need to update the field by right-clicking it and then clicking Update Field on the shortcut menu or by selecting the field and then pressing the F9 key.

er·Park·Animal·Clinic·has·been·operational·since·2002.·Our·staff·of·expert·veterinarians·and·skilled·
port·staff·have·the·background·to·ensure·your·pet·receives·the·best·possible·care.·Their·experience·
dedication·is·outlined·in·the·table·that·follows.¶

Organization¤	¤	Team·Members¤	On-Site¤	Total·Staff¤
	Veterinarians¤	Dr.·Lana·Canaan¶ Dr.·Raul·Ramos¤	M,·W,·F¶ T,·Th,·Sa¤	2¤
	Certified· Veterinary· Technicians¤	Latisha·Adams¶ Max·Henreich¶ Cam·Lyn¤	M,·T,·Th,·F¶ T,·W,·Th,·Sa¶ M,·W,·F,·Su¤	3¤
	Veterinary· Assistants¤	Teresa·McGill¶ Leo·Moretti¶ George·Peterson¤	T,·W,·Th,·Sa¶ M,·T,·Th,·F¶ M,·W,·F¤	3¤
	Groomers¤	Dawn·Nitz¶ Ed·VanWijk¤	M,·T,·W,·F¶ T,·W,·Th,·Sa¤	2¤
	Total·Team·Members¤			10¤

sums calculated and entered

Figure 4–75

update the field by right-clicking it and then clicking Update Field on the shortcut menu or by selecting the field and then pressing the F9 key.

To Delete a Blank Paragraph

If you notice an extra paragraph mark below the team member table that it is causing an extra blank page in the document, you should delete the blank paragraph. If necessary, the following steps delete a blank paragraph.

1 Press CTRL+END to position the insertion point at the end of the document.

2 If necessary, press the BACKSPACE key to remove the extra blank paragraph and delete the blank page.

3 If text spills onto a fourth page, remove space above paragraphs in the sales proposal until the entire proposal fits on three pages, as shown in Figure 4–1.

BTW
Distributing a Document
Instead of printing and distributing a hard copy of a document, you can distribute the document electronically. Options include sending the document via email; posting it on cloud storage (such as OneDrive) and sharing the file with others; posting it on social media, a blog, or other website; and sharing a link associated with an online location of the document. You also can create and share a PDF or XPS image of the document, so that users can view the file in Acrobat Reader or XPS Viewer instead of in Word.

Creating a Watermark

The final task in this module is to create a watermark for the pages of the sales proposal. A **watermark** is text or a graphic that is displayed on top of or behind the text in a document. For example, a catalog may print the words, Sold Out, on top of sold-out items. The first draft of a five-year-plan may have the word, Draft, printed behind the text of the document. Some companies use their logos or other graphics as watermarks to add visual appeal to their documents.

To Zoom Multiple Pages

The following steps display multiple pages in their entirety in the document window as large as possible, so that you can see the position of the watermark as you create it.

 Press CTRL+HOME to position the insertion point at the beginning of the document.

 Display the View tab. Click the Multiple Pages button (View tab | Zoom group) to display all three pages in the document window as large as possible.

To Create a Watermark

1 CREATE TITLE PAGE | 2 INSERT EXISTING DOCUMENT | 3 CREATE HEADER & FOOTER
4 EDIT & FORMAT LISTS | 5 EDIT & FORMAT TABLES | **6 CREATE WATERMARK**

In this project, the image of paw prints is displayed behind all content in the proposal as a watermark. *Why? The graphic adds visual appeal to the document, enticing readers to look at its contents.* The following steps create a watermark.

• Display the Design tab.

• Click the Watermark button (Design tab | Page Background group) to display the Watermark gallery (Figure 4–76).

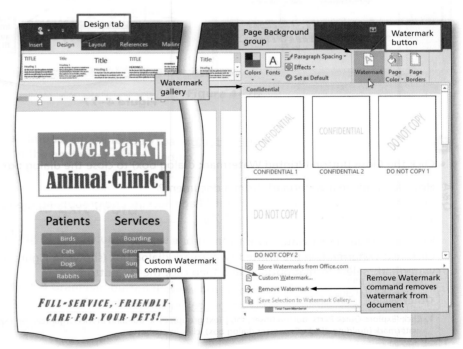

Figure 4–76

• Click Custom Watermark in the Watermark gallery to display the Printed Watermark dialog box.

• Click the Picture watermark option button to select it (Printed Watermark dialog box), which enables you to select an image for the watermark.

• Click the Select Picture button to display the Insert Pictures dialog box.

• Type **paw prints** in the Search box and then click the Search button. Click the paw prints image shown in Figure 4–1, or a similar image, and then click the Insert button to download the image and close the dialog box. (Or, you can click the 'Browse from a file' link in the Insert Pictures dialog box, navigate to the file called Colorful-Paw-Prints-Pattern-Background-2400px.png in the Data Files, select the file, and then click the Insert button (Insert Picture dialog box)).

What decisions will you need to make when creating your next proposal?
Use these guidelines as you complete the assignments in this module and create your own proposals outside of this class.

1. Identify the nature of the proposal.
   a) If someone else requests that you develop the proposal, it is solicited. Be sure to include all requested information in a **solicited proposal**.
   b) When you write a proposal because you recognize a need, the proposal is unsolicited. With an **unsolicited proposal**, you must gather information you believe will be relevant and of interest to the intended audience.

2. Design an eye-catching title page.
   a) The title page should convey the overall message of the sales proposal.
   b) Use text, graphics, formats, and colors that reflect the goals of the sales proposal.
   c) Be sure to include a title.

3. Compose the text of the sales proposal.
   a) Sales proposals vary in length, style, and formality, but all should be designed to elicit acceptance from the reader.
   b) The sales proposal should have a neat, organized appearance.
   c) A successful sales proposal uses succinct wording and includes lists for textual messages.
   d) Write text using active voice, instead of passive voice.
   e) Assume that readers of unsolicited sales proposals have no previous knowledge about the topic.
   f) Be sure the goal of the proposal is clear.
   g) Establish a theme and carry it throughout the proposal.

4. Enhance the sales proposal with appropriate visuals.
   a) Use visuals to add interest, clarify ideas, and illustrate points.
   b) Visuals include tables, charts, and graphical images (i.e., photos, etc.).

5. Proofread and edit the proposal.
   a) Carefully review the sales proposal to be sure it contains no spelling, grammar, mathematical, or other errors.
   b) Check that transitions between sentences and paragraphs are smooth. Ensure that the purpose of the proposal is stated clearly.
   c) Ask others to review the proposal and give you suggestions for improvements.

Apply Your Knowledge

Reinforce the skills and apply the concepts you learned in this module.

Working with a Table

Note: To complete this assignment, you will be required to use the Data Files. Please contact your instructor for information about accessing the Data Files.

Instructions: Run Word. Open the document called Apply 4–1 Projected College Expenses Draft located on the Data Files. The document contains a Word table that you are to modify. The modified table is shown in Figure 4–79.

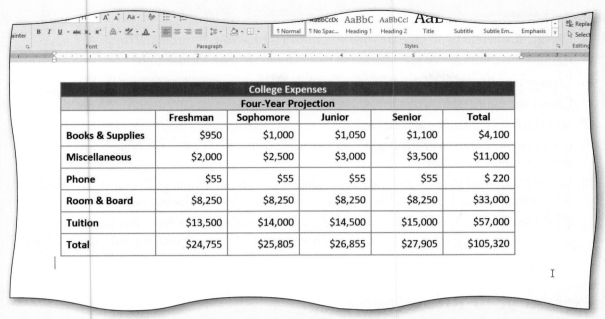

College Expenses					
Four-Year Projection					
	Freshman	Sophomore	Junior	Senior	Total
Books & Supplies	$950	$1,000	$1,050	$1,100	$4,100
Miscellaneous	$2,000	$2,500	$3,000	$3,500	$11,000
Phone	$55	$55	$55	$55	$ 220
Room & Board	$8,250	$8,250	$8,250	$8,250	$33,000
Tuition	$13,500	$14,000	$14,500	$15,000	$57,000
Total	$24,755	$25,805	$26,855	$27,905	$105,320

Figure 4–79

Perform the following tasks:

1. Show gridlines.
2. Delete the blank column between the Junior and Senior columns.
3. Use the Distribute Rows command to evenly space all the rows in the table.
4. Use the Distribute Columns command to make the Freshman, Sophomore, Junior, Senior, and Total columns evenly spaced.
5. Change the width of the Freshman, Sophomore, Junior, Senior, and Total columns to 1".
6. Use the Formula button (Table Tools Layout tab | Data group) to place totals in the bottom row for the Freshman, Sophomore, Junior, and Senior columns. The totals should be formatted to display dollar signs (no cents). *Hint*: You will need to edit the formula and remove the .00 from the end of it.
7. Use the Formula button (Table Tools Layout tab | Data group) to place totals in the right column, also formatted to display dollar signs (no cents). Start in the bottom-right cell and work your way up the column.
8. Add a row to the top of the table. Merge all cells in the first row into a single cell. Enter the title, College Expenses, as the table title. Change the alignment to Align Top Center.
9. Split the cell in the first row into two rows (one column). In the new cell below the title, enter the text, Four-Year Projection, as the subtitle.
10. Shade the first row Purple, Accent 4, Darker 25%. Change the font color of text in the first row to White, Background 1. Shade the second row Purple, Accent 4, Lighter 80%.
11. Add a 1 pt, White, Background 1, Darker 50% border to all cells in the table.
12. Hide gridlines.
13. Change the height of the row containing the year-in-college headings (row 3) to 0.1". Change the alignment of these headings to Align Top Center.

Continued >

STUDENT ASSIGNMENTS

Apply Your Knowledge *continued*

14. Change the height of all expense rows and the total row (rows 4 through 9) to 0.3".

15. Change the alignment of the cells in the first column to Align Center Left.

16. Change the alignment of the cells containing dollar amounts to Align Center Right.

17. Center the entire table across the width of the page.

18. Sort the rows containing the expenses.

19. If requested by your instructor, add your last name to the first row of the table before the words, College Expenses.

20. Save the modified file with the file name, Apply 4–1 Projected College Expenses Modified, and submit it (shown in Figure 4–79) in the format specified by your instructor.

21. ✳ Which number format did you use in the Formula dialog box in #6 in this exercise? Why do some totals have a space after the dollar sign and others do not? Which formula appeared in #7?

Extend Your Knowledge

Extend the skills you learned in this module and experiment with new skills. You may need to use Help to complete the assignment.

Using Word's Draw Table Feature
Instructions: Run Word. You will use Word's Draw Table feature to draw a table.

Perform the following tasks:

1. Use Help to learn about Draw Table and text watermarks.

2. Draw the table shown in Figure 4–80. That is, use the Draw Table button to create the blank table.

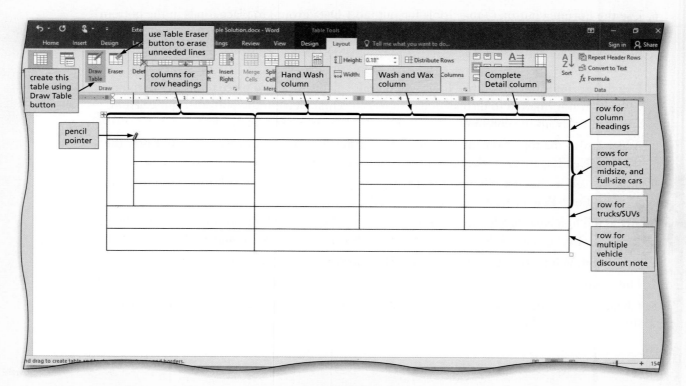

Figure 4–80

3. In the top row, enter these headings in the columns: Type of Vehicle, Hand Wash, Wash and Wax, and Complete Detail.

4. In the leftmost column of the table, enter the text, Car, so that it displays vertically in the cell.

5. In the second column of the table, enter these labels in the second, third, and fourth rows (to the right of the vertical text, Car): Compact, Midsize, and Full-size. Enter these labels in the bottom two leftmost rows: Truck/SUV and Multiple vehicle discount.

6. For the Hand Wash column, enter $50 in the cell to the right of the Compact, Midsize, and Full-size rows.

7. For the Wash and Wax column, use this data for the table: Compact – $100, Midsize - $115, Full-size - $120, and Truck/SUV - $150.

8. For the Complete Detail column, use this data for the table: Compact – $225, Midsize - $250, Full-size - $300, and Truck/SUV - $375.

9. Enter the text, $20 savings per vehicle serviced in a single month!, in the rightmost bottom row.

10. Align and shade table cells, along with any other relevant enhancements, as you deem appropriate (alignment, shading, etc.).

11. If requested by your instructor, enter your name below the table.

12. Save the revised document using the file name, Extend 4–1 Car Wash Table, and then submit it in the format specified by your instructor.

13. ✸ Which alignment and shading for the table cells did you choose and why?

Expand Your World

Create a solution that uses cloud or web technologies by learning and investigating on your own from general guidance.

Using Word Online to Create a Table

Instructions: You are using a mobile device or computer at school that does not have Word but has Internet access. To make use of time between classes, you use Word Online to create a table showing your volunteer service (Figure 4–81).

Perform the following tasks:

1. Run a browser. Search for the text, Word Online, using a search engine. Visit several websites to learn about Word Online. Navigate to the Office Online website. You will need to sign in to your OneDrive account.

2. Create a new blank Word document using Word Online. Name the document Expand 4–1 Volunteer Services. Change the zoom to page width.

3. Enter and format the table, as shown in Figure 4–81.

4. Apply a table style to the table (any style).

5. Change colors of the table to a color other than blue.

6. Remove the First Column shading (Table Tools Layout tab | Table Style Options group).

Continued >

Expand Your World *continued*

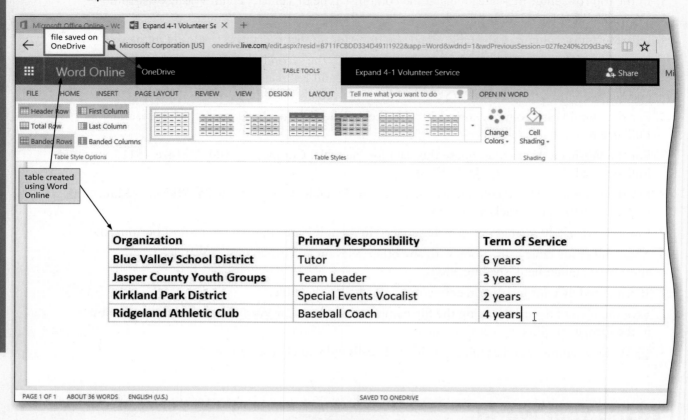

Figure 4–81

7. Narrow the width of the last column to fit the contents better and then change the cell alignment in this column to Align Top Center. How did you adjust the column width?

8. Add a row to the bottom of the table that identifies volunteer service you have performed.

9. Save the document again.

10. Submit the Expand 4–1 Volunteer Service document in the format requested by your instructor. Sign out of your OneDrive account.

11. ✳ Which table features that are covered in the module are not available in Word Online? Answer the question posed in #7.

In the Labs

Design, create, modify, and/or use a document following the guidelines, concepts, and skills presented in this module. Labs 1 and 2, which increase in difficulty, require you to create solutions based on what you learned in the module; Lab 3 requires you to apply your creative thinking and problem-solving skills to design and implement a solution.

Lab 1: **Creating a Proposal with a SmartArt Graphic, a Bulleted List, and a Table**

Note: To complete this assignment, you will be required to use the Data Files. Please contact your instructor for information about accessing the Data Files.

Problem: The owner of Java Junction has hired you to prepare a sales proposal for her coffee shop (Figure 4–82).

Perform the following tasks:

1. Change the document theme to Retrospect.
2. Change the theme fonts to the Tw Cen MT-Rockwell font set.
3. Create the title page as shown in Figure 4–82a. Be sure to do the following:
   a. Insert the SmartArt graphic, add text to it, and bold the text. Change the colors and style of the SmartArt graphic as shown. Change the spacing above the SmartArt graphic to 42 points and the spacing after the graphic to 54 points.
   b. Change the fonts, font sizes, and font colors as specified in the figure. Add the paragraph border. Indent the left and right edges of the title paragraph by 0.25 inches and the left and right edges of the paragraph below the SmartArt graphic by 0.5 inches. Expand the characters in the sentence at the bottom of the page by 7 points.
4. At the bottom of the title page, insert a next page section break. Clear formatting.
5. Create the second page of the proposal as shown in Figure 4–82b.
   a. Format the Heading 1 style as shown and update the Heading 1 style accordingly.
   b. Enter the multilevel list as shown.
   c. Create the table as shown. Border the table as specified. Distribute rows so that they are all the same height. Change the row height to 0.21 inches. Center the table between the margins. Change the first column's alignment to Align Top Left the text, and all other text in the table to Align Top Center. Shade the table cells as specified. Change cell spacing to 0.04 inches between cells.
   d. Insert the formatted footer using the Blank (Three Columns) design. The footer should appear only on the second page (section) of the proposal. Enter the footer text as shown.
   e. If requested by your instructor, change the phone number in the footer to your phone number.
6. Add a picture watermark of the coffee beans. The picture is located on the Data Files. Scale the picture to 50% in the Printed Watermark dialog box.
7. Adjust the spacing above and below paragraphs as necessary to fit all content as shown in the figure.
8. Check the spelling. Save the document with Lab 4–1 Coffee House Proposal as the file name.
9. ✷ This proposal contains a multilevel numbered list. How would you change the font size of the numbers and letters at the beginning of each list item?

Continued >

In the Labs *continued*

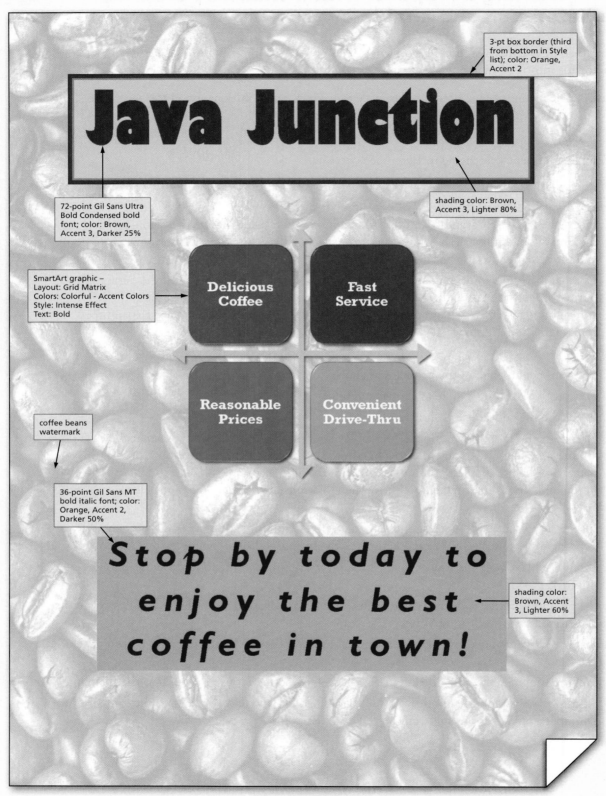

Figure 4–82 (a)

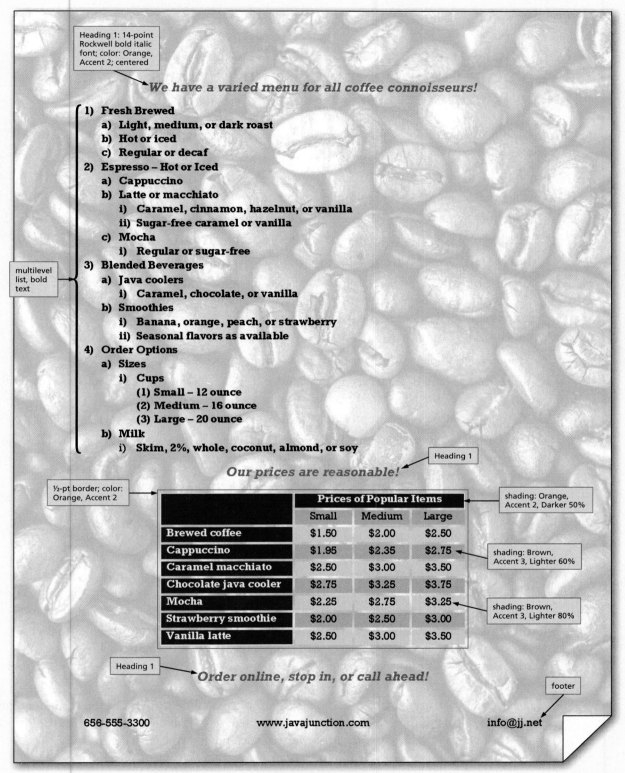

Heading 1: 14-point Rockwell bold italic font; color: Orange, Accent 2; centered

We have a varied menu for all coffee connoisseurs!

multilevel list, bold text

1) **Fresh Brewed**
   a) **Light, medium, or dark roast**
   b) **Hot or iced**
   c) **Regular or decaf**
2) **Espresso – Hot or Iced**
   a) **Cappuccino**
   b) **Latte or macchiato**
      i) **Caramel, cinnamon, hazelnut, or vanilla**
      ii) **Sugar-free caramel or vanilla**
   c) **Mocha**
      i) **Regular or sugar-free**
3) **Blended Beverages**
   a) **Java coolers**
      i) **Caramel, chocolate, or vanilla**
   b) **Smoothies**
      i) **Banana, orange, peach, or strawberry**
      ii) **Seasonal flavors as available**
4) **Order Options**
   a) **Sizes**
      i) **Cups**
         (1) **Small – 12 ounce**
         (2) **Medium – 16 ounce**
         (3) **Large – 20 ounce**
   b) **Milk**
      i) **Skim, 2%, whole, coconut, almond, or soy**

Our prices are reasonable! Heading 1

½-pt border; color: Orange, Accent 2

shading: Orange, Accent 2, Darker 50%

shading: Brown, Accent 3, Lighter 60%

shading: Brown, Accent 3, Lighter 80%

	Prices of Popular Items		
	Small	Medium	Large
Brewed coffee	$1.50	$2.00	$2.50
Cappuccino	$1.95	$2.35	$2.75
Caramel macchiato	$2.50	$3.00	$3.50
Chocolate java cooler	$2.75	$3.25	$3.75
Mocha	$2.25	$2.75	$3.25
Strawberry smoothie	$2.00	$2.50	$3.00
Vanilla latte	$2.50	$3.00	$3.50

Heading 1 *Order online, stop in, or call ahead!*

footer

656-555-3300   www.javajunction.com   info@jj.net

Figure 4–82 (b)

Continued >

In the Labs *continued*

Lab 2: Creating a Proposal with a SmartArt Graphic, a Complex Table, Picture Bullets, and a Numbered List

Problem: The owner of the A-Plus Tutoring has hired you to prepare a sales proposal that describes the center (Figure 4–83).

Perform the following tasks:
1. Change the document theme to the Facet theme.
2. Change the theme fonts to the Franklin Gothic font set.
3. Create the title page as shown in Figure 4–83a. Be sure to do the following:
   a. Insert the Vertical Equation SmartArt graphic, located in the Relationship category.
   b. Change the fonts, font sizes, font colors, and shading as indicated in the figure. Indent the left and right edges of the title paragraph by 0.5 inches. Expand the characters in the sentence at the bottom of the page by 7 points.
4. At the bottom of the title page, insert a next page section break. Clear formatting.
5. Create the second page of the proposal as shown in Figure 4–83b.
   a. Insert the formatted header using the Banded design. The header should appear only on the second page of the proposal. Enter the header text as shown.
   b. If requested by your instructor, add your name to the header.
   c. Format the headings using the heading styles specified. Adjust spacing before the Heading 1 style to 18 point and after to 6 point, and before the Heading 2 style to 12 point and after to 6 point. Update both heading styles.
   d. Create the bulleted list using the picture bullets shown (search for the keyword, star, or use the image on the Data Files).
   e. Create the multilevel numbered list as shown.
   f. Create the table as shown. Distribute rows so that they are all the same height (about 0.29"). Align center all text except the row headings, which should be set to Align Center Left. Center the table. Change the direction of the Weekdays heading as shown. Shade the table cells as indicated in the figure.
6. Create a text watermark of 10 occurrences of the text, A+, with each occurrence separated by a space. In the Printed Watermark dialog box, change the watermark to 48-point Verdana with a semitransparent color of Blue-Gray, Text 2, Lighter 60%. The layout should be diagonal.
7. If necessary, adjust spacing above and below paragraphs to fit all content as shown in the figure. Check the spelling of the proposal. Save the document with Lab 4–2 Tutoring Center Proposal as the file name and then submit it in the format specified by your instructor.
8. ✺ This proposal contains a text watermark, which is semitransparent by default. For what type of text would you want to remove the check mark from the semitransparent check box?

Figure 4–83 (a)

Continued >

In the Labs *continued*

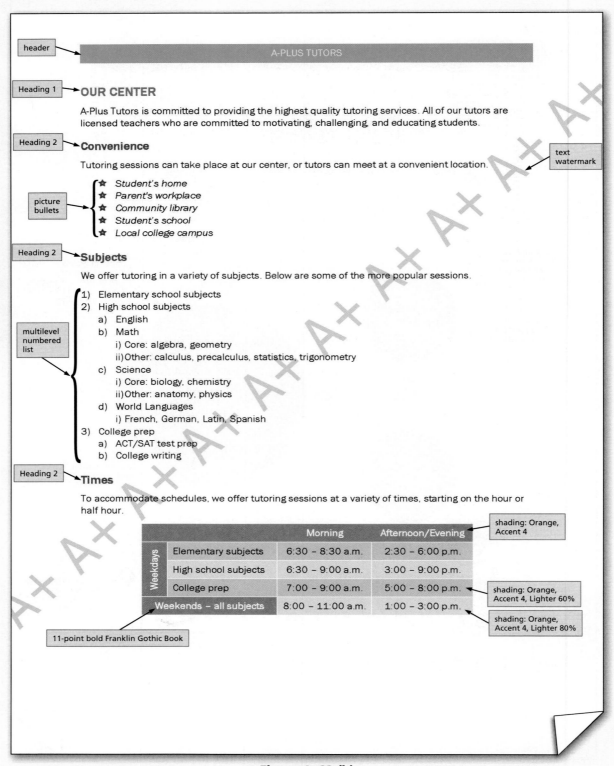

Figure 4–83 (b)

Lab 3: **Consider This: Your Turn**

Create a Proposal for a Small Business

Note: To complete this assignment, you will be required to use the Data Files. Please contact your instructor for information about accessing the Data Files.

Problem: As a part-time employee at a local deli, you have been asked to design a multipage sales proposal that can be distributed in the community.

Part 1:   The proposal should contain a title page, followed by a page of information about the deli. The title page is to contain the deli name, Deli Delicious, formatted with a border and shading. Include an appropriate SmartArt graphic that contains these words, at a minimum: fresh ingredients, reasonable prices, fast service, and dine in or carry out. Include this text on the title page: Stop by, call ahead, or order online!

The source content for the second page of the proposal is in a file called Lab 4–3 Consider This Your Turn Deli Draft. Use the concepts and techniques presented in this module to create and format the sales proposal. Include an appropriate watermark. Be sure to check the spelling and grammar of the finished document. Submit your assignment in the format specified by your instructor.

Part 2:   ☀ You made several decisions while creating the sales proposal in this assignment: how to organize and format the title page (fonts, font sizes, colors, shading, styles, etc.), which SmartArt graphic to use on the title page, and how to organize and format the tables and lists. What was the rationale behind each of these decisions? When you proofread the document, what further revisions did you make and why?

5 | Using a Template to Create a Resume and Sharing a Finished Document

Objectives

You will have mastered the material in this module when you can:

- Use a template to create a document
- Change document margins
- Personalize a document template
- Indent a paragraph
- Customize theme fonts
- Create and modify a style
- Insert a building block
- Save a Word document as a PDF file and edit a PDF file
- Run the compatibility checker
- Enable others to access a document on OneDrive
- Send a Word document using email
- Save a Word document as a webpage
- Format text as a hyperlink
- Change a style set

Introduction

Some people prefer to use their own creative skills to design and compose Word documents. Using Word, for example, you can develop the content and decide the location of each item in a document. On occasion, however, you may have difficulty composing a particular type of document. To assist with the task of creating certain types of documents, such as resumes and letters, Word provides templates. A **template** is similar to a form with prewritten text; that is, Word prepares the requested document with text and/or formatting common to all documents of this nature. After Word creates a document from a template, you fill in the blanks or replace prewritten words in the document.

Once you have created a document, such as a resume, you often share it with others electronically via email, webpages, or links.

Project — Resume

At some time, you will prepare a resume to send to prospective employers. In addition to some personal information, a **resume** usually contains the applicant's educational background and job experience. Employers review many resumes for each vacant position. Thus, you should design your resume carefully so that it presents you as the best candidate for the job.

The project in this module follows generally accepted guidelines for creating resumes and uses Word to create the resume shown in Figure 5–1. The resume for Nina Tamaya Yazzie, an upcoming graduate of a journalism program, uses a Word template to present relevant information to a potential employer.

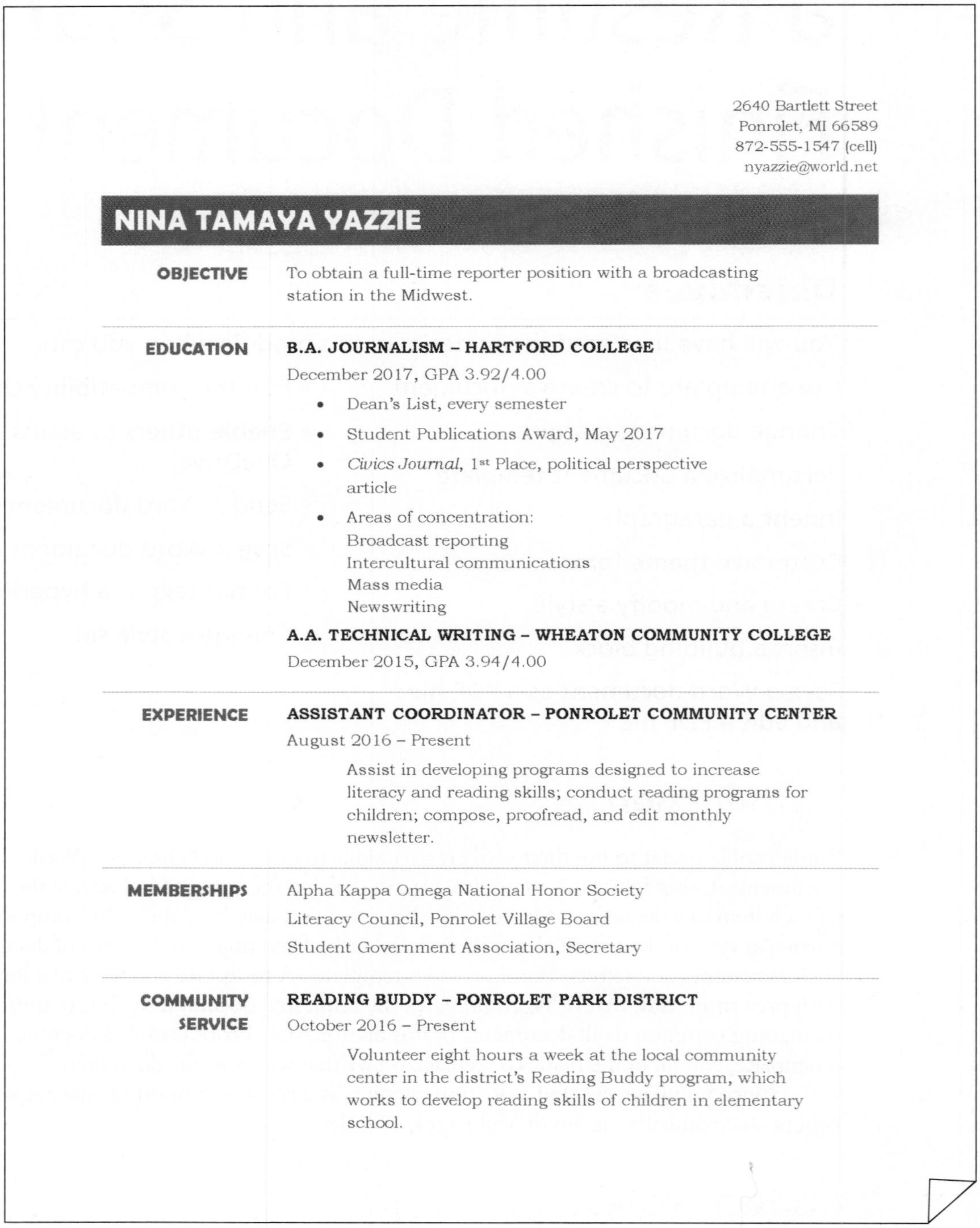

2640 Bartlett Street
Ponrolet, MI 66589
872-555-1547 (cell)
nyazzie@world.net

NINA TAMAYA YAZZIE

OBJECTIVE To obtain a full-time reporter position with a broadcasting station in the Midwest.

EDUCATION **B.A. JOURNALISM – HARTFORD COLLEGE**
December 2017, GPA 3.92/4.00

- Dean's List, every semester
- Student Publications Award, May 2017
- *Civics Journal*, 1st Place, political perspective article
- Areas of concentration:
  Broadcast reporting
  Intercultural communications
  Mass media
  Newswriting

A.A. TECHNICAL WRITING – WHEATON COMMUNITY COLLEGE
December 2015, GPA 3.94/4.00

EXPERIENCE **ASSISTANT COORDINATOR – PONROLET COMMUNITY CENTER**
August 2016 – Present

Assist in developing programs designed to increase literacy and reading skills; conduct reading programs for children; compose, proofread, and edit monthly newsletter.

MEMBERSHIPS Alpha Kappa Omega National Honor Society

Literacy Council, Ponrolet Village Board

Student Government Association, Secretary

COMMUNITY SERVICE **READING BUDDY – PONROLET PARK DISTRICT**
October 2016 – Present

Volunteer eight hours a week at the local community center in the district's Reading Buddy program, which works to develop reading skills of children in elementary school.

Figure 5–1

In this module, you will learn how to create the resume shown in Figure 5–1. The following roadmap identifies general activities you will perform as you progress through this module:

1. CREATE a new resume DOCUMENT FROM a Word TEMPLATE.

2. MODIFY AND FORMAT the resume TEMPLATE.

3. SAVE the resume DOCUMENT IN OTHER FORMATS so that you can share it with others.

4. MAKE the resume DOCUMENT AVAILABLE ONLINE so that others can access it.

5. CREATE a WEBPAGE FROM the resume WORD DOCUMENT.

6. FORMAT the resume WEBPAGE.

To Run Word and Change Word Settings

If you are using a computer to step through the project in this module and you want your screens to match the figures in this book, you should change your screen's resolution to 1366 × 768. The following steps run Word, display formatting marks, and change the zoom to page width.

1 Run Word and create a blank document in the Word window. If necessary, maximize the Word window.

2 If the Print Layout button on the status bar is not selected (shown in Figure 5–4), click it so that your screen is in Print Layout view.

3 If the 'Show/Hide ¶' button (Home tab | Paragraph group) is not selected already, click it to display formatting marks on the screen.

4 To display the page the same width as the document window, if necessary, click the Page Width button (View tab | Zoom group).

BTW
Touch Screen Differences
The Office and Windows interfaces may vary if you are using a touch screen. For this reason, you might notice that the function or appearance of your touch screen differs slightly from this module's presentation.

Using a Template to Create a Resume

Although you could compose a resume in a blank document window, this module shows how to use a template instead, where Word formats the resume with appropriate headings and spacing. You then customize the resume that the template generated by filling in blanks and by selecting and replacing text.

To Create a New Document from an Online Template

1 CREATE DOCUMENT FROM TEMPLATE | 2 MODIFY & FORMAT TEMPLATE | 3 SAVE DOCUMENT IN OTHER FORMATS
4 MAKE DOCUMENT AVAILABLE ONLINE | 5 CREATE WEBPAGE FROM WORD DOCUMENT | 6 FORMAT WEBPAGE

Word has a variety of templates available online to assist you with creating documents. Available online templates include agendas, award certificates, calendars, expense reports, greeting cards, invitations, invoices, letters, meeting minutes, memos, resumes, and statements. When you select an online template, Word downloads (or copies) it from the Office.com website to your computer or mobile device. Many of the templates use the same design or style. *Why? If you create related documents, such as a resume and a cover letter, you can use the same template design or style so that the documents complement one another.* The following steps create a resume using the Basic resume (Timeless design) template.

1

- Click File on the ribbon to open the Backstage view and then click the New tab in the Backstage view to display the New gallery, which initially lists several featured templates.

- Type **resume** in the 'Search for online templates' box and then click the Start searching button to display a list of online resume templates.

- If necessary, scroll through the list of templates to display the Basic resume (Timeless design) thumbnail (Figure 5–2).

Q&A

Can I select a template from the Word start screen that appears when I initially run Word?
Yes, instead of selecting Blank document from the Word start screen, you can select any of the available templates.

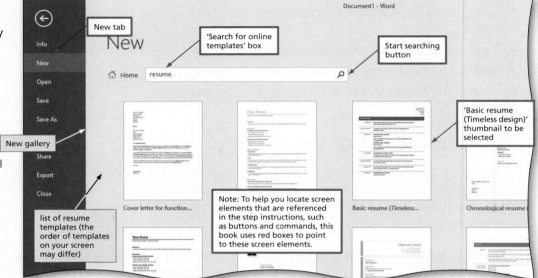

Figure 5–2

2

- Click the 'Basic resume (Timeless design)' thumbnail to select the template and display it in a preview window (Figure 5–3).

🔍 **Experiment**

- Click the Back and Forward buttons on the sides of the preview window to view previews of other templates. When finished, display the 'Basic resume (Timeless design)' thumbnail in the preview window.

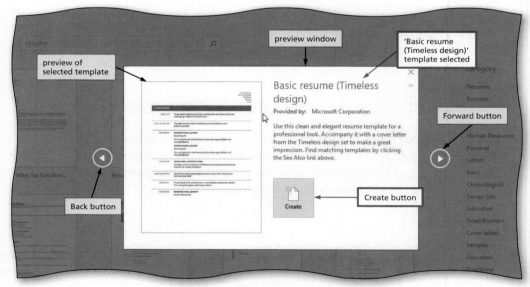

Figure 5–3

Q&A

What if I cannot locate the Basic resume (Timeless design) template?
Exit the Backstage view and then proceed to the steps called To Open a Document Created from a Template that are shaded yellow and immediately follow these steps.

3

- Click the Create button to create a new document based on the selected template (Figure 5–4).

- If the resume template displays your name instead of the text, YOUR NAME, as shown in Figure 5–4, click the Undo button on the Quick Access Toolbar to reset the content control (content controls are discussed in the next section).

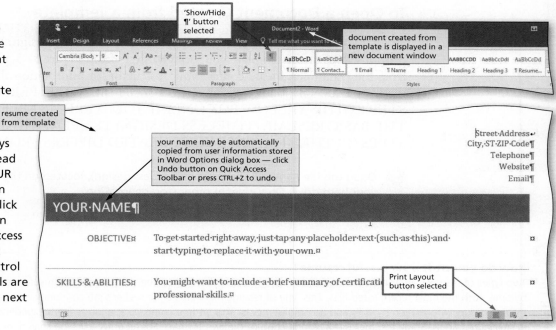

Figure 5–4

4

- If requested by your instructor, print the resume template so that you can see the entire resume created by the resume template using the Basic resume (Timeless design) (Figure 5–5).

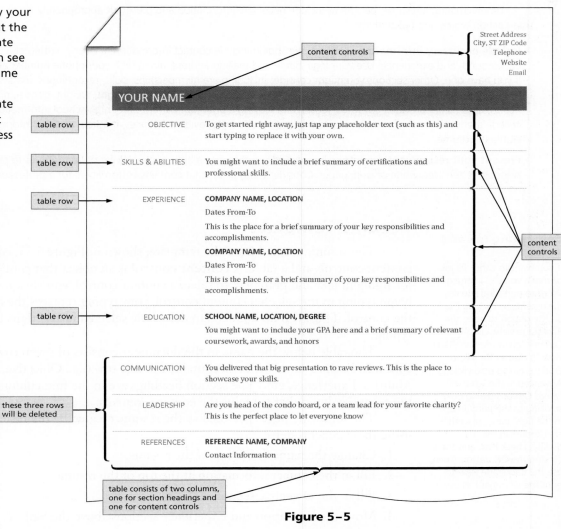

Figure 5–5

To Open a Document Created from a Template

If you are unable to locate the Basic resume (Timeless design) template in the previous steps or the template you located differs from Figure 5–5, you can open it from the Data Files. Please contact your instructor for information about accessing the Data Files. The following step opens a document. NOTE: PERFORM THE STEP IN THIS YELLOW BOX ONLY IF YOU WERE UNABLE TO LOCATE THE BASIC RESUME (TIMELESS DESIGN) TEMPLATE IN THE PREVIOUS STEPS OR THE TEMPLATE YOU LOCATED DIFFERS FROM FIGURE 5–5.

1 Open the file named Basic resume (Timeless design), located on the Data Files, from your hard drive, OneDrive, or other storage location.

CONSIDER THIS

How do you craft a successful resume?

Two types of resumes are the chronological resume and the functional resume. A chronological resume sequences information by time, with the most recent listed first. This type of resume highlights a job seeker's job continuity and growth. A functional resume groups information by skills and accomplishments. This resume emphasizes a job seeker's experience and qualifications in specialized areas. Some resumes use a combination of the two formats. For an entry-level job search, experts recommend a chronological resume or a combination of the two types of resumes.

When creating a resume, be sure to include necessary information and present it appropriately. Keep descriptions concise, using action words and bulleted lists.

- **Include necessary information.** Your resume should include contact information, a clearly written objective, educational background, and experience. Use your legal name and mailing address, along with your phone number and email address, if you have one. Other sections you might consider including are memberships, skills, recognitions and awards, and/or community service. Do not include your Social Security number, marital status, age, height, weight, gender, physical appearance, health, citizenship, previous pay rates, reasons for leaving a prior job, current date, high-school information (if you are a college graduate), and references. Employers assume you will provide references, if asked, and this information simply clutters a resume.

- **Present your resume appropriately.** For printed resumes, use a high-quality ink-jet or laser printer to print your resume on standard letter-sized white or ivory paper. Consider using paper that contains cotton fibers for a professional look.

BTW
Conserving Ink and Toner
If you want to conserve ink or toner, you can instruct Word to print draft quality documents by clicking File on the ribbon to open the Backstage view, clicking the Options tab in the Backstage view to display the Word Options dialog box, clicking Advanced in the left pane (Word Options dialog box), scrolling to the Print area in the right pane, placing a check mark in the 'Use draft quality' check box, and then clicking the OK button. Then, use the Backstage view to print the document as usual.

Resume Template

The resume created from the template, shown in Figure 5–5, contains several content controls and a table. A **content control** is an object that contains instructions for filling in text and graphics. To select a content control, you click it. As soon as you begin typing in the selected content control, your typing replaces the instructions in the control. Thus, you do not need to delete the selected instructions before you begin typing.

The table below the name in the document consists of seven rows and two columns. Each resume section is contained in one row (i.e., Objective, Skills & Abilities, Experience, etc.) The section headings are in the first column, followed by the second column that contains the content controls.

The following pages personalize the resume created by the resume template using these general steps:

1. Change the name at the top of the resume.
2. Fill in the contact information at the top of the resume.
3. Fill in the Objective section.
4. Move the Education and Experience sections above the Skills & Abilities section.

5. Fill in the Education and Experience sections.

6. Change the Skills & Abilities heading to Memberships and fill in this section.

7. Add a row for the Community Service section and fill in this section.

8. Delete the last three unused rows.

To Change Theme Colors

Recall that Word provides document themes, which contain a variety of color schemes and other effects. This resume uses the Aspect theme colors. The following steps change the theme colors.

1 Click Design on the ribbon to display the Design tab.

2 Click the Themes Colors button (Design tab | Document Formatting group) to display the Theme Colors gallery.

3 Scroll to and then click Aspect in the Theme Colors gallery to change the theme colors to the selected theme.

BTW
The Ribbon and Screen Resolution
Word may change how the groups and buttons within the groups appear on the ribbon, depending on the computer or mobile device's screen resolution. Thus, your ribbon may look different from the ones in this book if you are using a screen resolution other than 1366 x 768.

To Set Custom Margins

1 CREATE DOCUMENT FROM TEMPLATE | 2 MODIFY & FORMAT TEMPLATE | 3 SAVE DOCUMENT IN OTHER FORMATS
4 MAKE DOCUMENT AVAILABLE ONLINE | 5 CREATE WEBPAGE FROM WORD DOCUMENT | 6 FORMAT WEBPAGE

The resume template selected in this project uses .75-inch top, bottom, left, and right margins. You prefer slightly wider margins for the top, left, and right edges of the resume and a smaller bottom margin. *Why? You do not want the text to run so close to the top edge and sides of the page and do not want the resume to spill to a second page.* In earlier modules, you changed the margins by selecting predefined settings in the Margins gallery. The margins you will use for the resume in this module, however, are not predefined. Thus, the next steps set custom margins.

1

• Display the Layout tab.

• Click the Adjust Margins button (Layout tab | Page Setup group) to display the Margins gallery (Figure 5–6).

Q&A What is the difference between the Custom Margins setting and the Custom Margins command?
The Custom Margins setting applies the most recent custom margins to the current document, whereas the Custom Margins command displays the Custom Margins dialog box so that you can specify new margin settings.

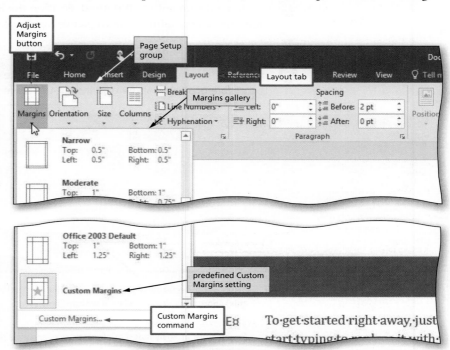

Figure 5–6

- Click Custom Margins in the Margins gallery to display the Page Setup dialog box. If necessary, click the Margins tab (Page Setup dialog box) to display the Margins sheet.

- Type 1 in the Top box to change the top margin setting and then press the TAB key to position the insertion point in the Bottom box.

- Type .5 in the Bottom box to change the bottom margin setting and then press the TAB key to position the insertion point in the Left box.

- Type 1 in the Left box to change the left margin setting and then press the TAB key to position the insertion point in the Right box.

- Type 1 in the Right box to change the right margin setting (Figure 5–7).

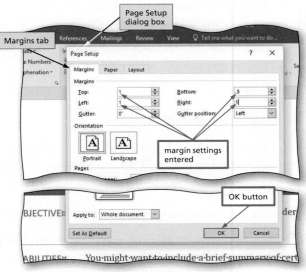

Figure 5–7

- Click the OK button to set the custom margins for this document.

Other Ways

1. Drag margin boundaries on ruler

To View Gridlines

When tables contain no borders, such as those in this resume, it can be difficult to see the individual cells in the table. To help identify the location of cells, you can display gridlines, which show cell outlines on the screen. The following steps show gridlines.

1. Scroll the document up, if desired. Position the insertion point in any table cell (in this case, the cell containing the Objective heading).

2. Display the Table Tools Layout tab.

3. If it is not selected already, click the 'View Table Gridlines' button (Table Tools Layout tab | Table group) to show gridlines in the table (Figure 5–8).

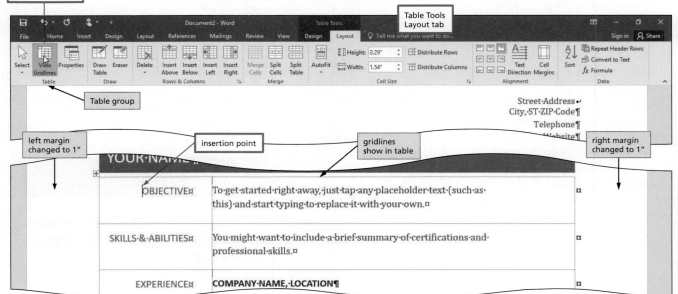

Figure 5–8

To Modify a Content Control and Replace Its Placeholder Text

The next step is to select the Your Name content control that the template inserted in the resume, increase its font size slightly, and replace its placeholder text with the job seeker's name. Word uses **placeholder text** to indicate where text can be typed. To replace placeholder text in a content control, you select the content control and then type.

The Your Name content control on your resume may already contain your name. ***Why?*** *Word copies the user name from the Word Options dialog box and places it in the Your Name content control. Note that if your name appears instead of the text, YOUR NAME, the following steps may execute differently.* The next steps modify a content control and replace its placeholder text.

- Click the content control to be modified (in this case, the Your Name content control) to select it.

 How can I tell if a content control is selected?

The appearance of selected content controls varies. When you select some content controls, they are surrounded by a rectangle. Selected content controls also may have a name that is attached to the top, and/or a tag that is attached to its upper-left corner. You can drag a tag to move a content control from one location to another. With other content controls, the text inside the content control appears selected as shown in Figure 5–9.

- If necessary, click the content control name (in this case, the words Your Name) to select the contents of the content control (Figure 5–9).

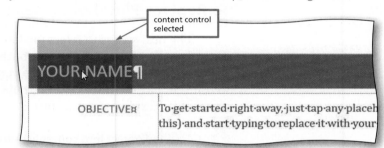

Figure 5–9

- Click the 'Increase Font Size' button (Home tab | Font group) to increase the font size of the text in the selected content control to the next font size (Figure 5–10).

 What if my font size does not change?
You may need to modify the style: right-click the Name style in the Styles gallery, click Modify on the shortcut menu, change the font size to 18 (Modify Style dialog box), and then click the OK button.

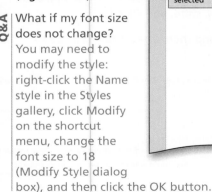

Figure 5–10

3

- Type **Nina Tamaya Yazzie** to replace the content control with the job seeker's name (Figure 5–11).

  If requested by your instructor, enter your name instead of the job seeker's name shown in Figure 5–11.

Q&A

Why does the text appear in uppercase letters even though I type in lowercase letters?
This content control includes formatting that displays the text in uppercase letters.

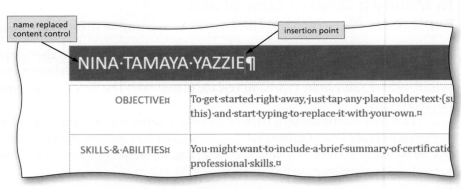

Figure 5–11

To Replace Placeholder Text in More Content Controls

The next step is to select the Contact Info, Telephone, and Email content controls in the upper-right corner of the resume and replace their placeholder text with personal information. Because you do not have a website, you will leave the website contact control as is and delete it in later steps. The following steps replace the placeholder text in content controls.

1 Click the Contact Info content control to select it (Figure 5–12).

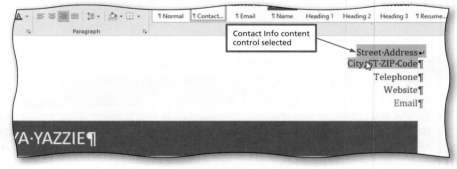

Figure 5–12

BTW
Selecting Rows
To move table rows (discussed in the next section), you must select them first. To do this, point to the left of the first row to select and then drag downward or upward when the pointer changes to a right-pointing block arrow. If you are using a touch screen, drag the selection handles to select the rows.

2 Type **2640 Bartlett Street** as the street address, press the ENTER key, and then type **Ponrolet, MI 66589** as the city, state, and ZIP code.

3 Click the Telephone content control to select it and then type **872-555-1547 (cell)** as the cell phone number.

4 Click the Email content control to select it and then type **nyazzie@world.net** as the email address.

To Delete a Content Control

1 CREATE DOCUMENT FROM TEMPLATE | 2 MODIFY & FORMAT TEMPLATE | 3 SAVE DOCUMENT IN OTHER FORMATS
4 MAKE DOCUMENT AVAILABLE ONLINE | 5 CREATE WEBPAGE FROM WORD DOCUMENT | 6 FORMAT WEBPAGE

The following steps delete the Website content control. *Why?* You do not have a website.

- Click the Website content control to select it.

- Right-click the selected content control to display a shortcut menu (Figure 5–13).

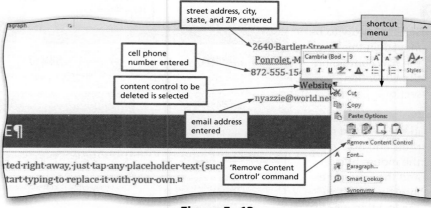

Figure 5–13

- Click 'Remove Content Control' on the shortcut menu to delete the selected content control, which also deletes the placeholder text contained in the content control.

- Press the DELETE key to remove the blank line between the phone number and the email address (Figure 5–14).

- Save the title page on your hard drive, OneDrive, or other storage location using the file name, Yazzie Resume.

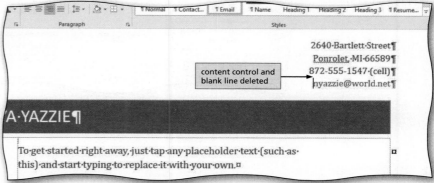

Figure 5–14

Q&A Why should I save the resume at this time?
You have performed many tasks while creating this resume and do not want to risk losing work completed thus far.

Other Ways

1. With content control selected, click Cut button (Home tab | Clipboard group)

2. With content control selected, press CTRL+X or DELETE or BACKSPACE

To Move Table Rows

1 CREATE DOCUMENT FROM TEMPLATE | 2 MODIFY & FORMAT TEMPLATE | 3 SAVE DOCUMENT IN OTHER FORMATS
4 MAKE DOCUMENT AVAILABLE ONLINE | 5 CREATE WEBPAGE FROM WORD DOCUMENT | 6 FORMAT WEBPAGE

In the resume, you would like the Education and Experience sections immediately below the Objective section, in that order. *Why? You want to emphasize your educational background and experience.* Thus, the next step is to move rows in the resume. Each row contains a separate section in the resume. You will move the row containing the Education section below the row containing the Objective section. Then, you will move the row containing the Experience section so that it is below the moved row containing the Education section.

You use the same procedure to move table rows as to move text. That is, select the rows to move and then drag them to the desired location. The following steps use drag-and-drop editing to move table rows.

- Display the View tab. Click the 100% button (View tab | Zoom group) to display the resume at 100 percent zoom in the document window.

- Scroll so that the Objective, Experience, and Education sections appear in the document window at the same time.

● Select the row to be moved, in this case, the row containing the Education section.

● Position the pointer in the selected row, press and hold down the mouse button and then drag the insertion point to the location where the selected row is to be moved (Figure 5–15).

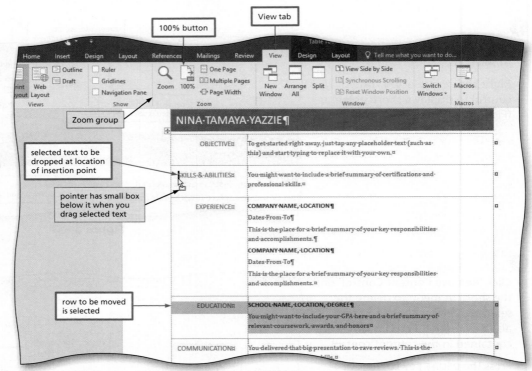

Figure 5–15

● Release the mouse button to move the selected row to the location of the insertion point (Figure 5–16).

Q&A

What if I accidentally drag text to the wrong location?
Click the Undo button on the Quick Access Toolbar and try again.

What if I am using a touch screen?
If you have a stylus,

Figure 5–16

you can follow Steps 1 through 3 using the stylus. If you are using your finger, you will need to use the cut-and-paste technique: tap to position the insertion point in the row to be moved, tap the Select Table button (Table Tools Layout tab | Table group), and then tap Select Row; press the selection to display the mini toolbar and then tap the Cut button on the mini toolbar to remove the row; tap to position the insertion point at the location where you want to move the row; display the Home tab and then tap the Paste button (Home tab | Clipboard group) to place the row at the location of the insertion point.

- Repeat Steps 2 and 3 to move the row containing the Experience section so that it is positioned below the row containing the Education section (Figure 5–17).

- Click anywhere to remove the selection.

- Change the zoom to page width.

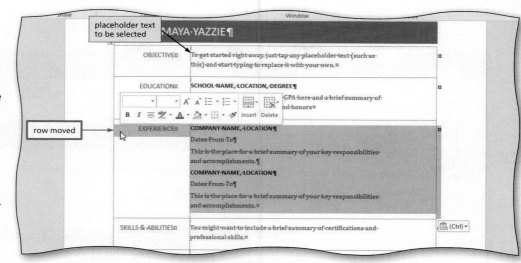

Figure 5–17

Other Ways

1. Click Cut button (Home tab | Clipboard group), click where text or object is to be pasted, click Paste button (Home tab | Clipboard group)

2. Right-click selected text, click Cut on shortcut menu or mini toolbar, right-click where text or object is to be pasted, click 'Keep Source Formatting' on shortcut menu (or, if using touch, tap Paste on mini toolbar)

3. Press CTRL+X, position insertion point where text or object is to be pasted, press CTRL+V

To Modify Text in a Content Control

The following steps select the Objective content control in the resume and then replace its placeholder text with personal information.

1 If necessary, scroll to display the Objective section of the resume in the document window.

2 In the Objective section of the resume, click the placeholder text that begins, 'To get started…', in the Objective content control (shown in Figure 5–17) to select it.

3 Type the objective: **To obtain a full-time reporter position with a broadcasting station in the Midwest.**

BTW

Insert Controls
The content controls in some templates contain an Insert Control, which allows you to duplicate text in the control. Because the template used in the module does not contain an Insert Control, you copy and paste items to duplicate them. Lab 2 in the student assignments at the end of this module uses a template that contains an Insert Control.

To Copy and Paste Items in a Table Cell

1 CREATE DOCUMENT FROM TEMPLATE | 2 MODIFY & FORMAT TEMPLATE | 3 SAVE DOCUMENT IN OTHER FORMATS

4 MAKE DOCUMENT AVAILABLE ONLINE | 5 CREATE WEBPAGE FROM WORD DOCUMENT | 6 FORMAT WEBPAGE

In the resume, you copy the school name information in the Education section so that it appears twice in the table cell containing the Education content control. **Why?** *You would like to add two degrees to the resume.* The following steps copy and paste text in a cell.

1

- Select the text to be copied (in this case, all of the text in the Education content control).

- Display the Home tab.

- Click the Copy button (Home tab | Clipboard group) to copy the selected item in the table cell to the Office Clipboard (Figure 5–18).

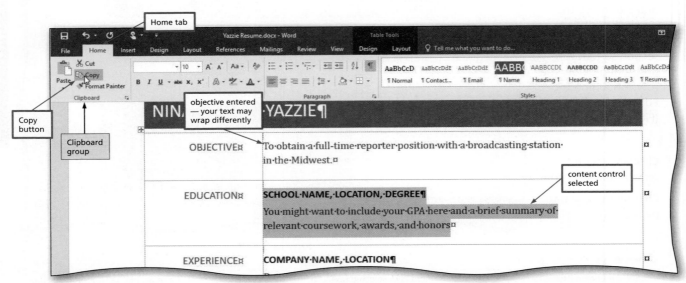

Figure 5–18

2

- Position the insertion point at the end of the text in the Education content control (that is, after the s in honors) and then press the ENTER key to place the insertion point at the location where the copied item should be pasted.

- Click the Paste button (Home tab | Clipboard group) to paste the copied item in the document at the location of the insertion point (Figure 5–19).

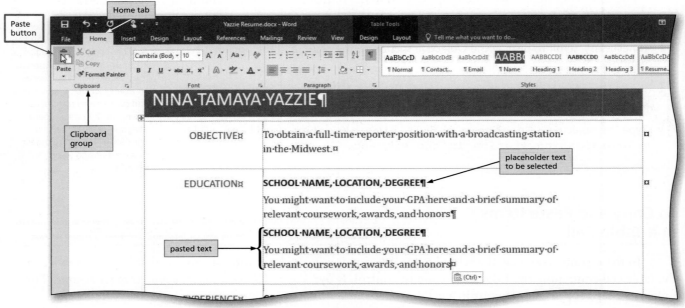

Figure 5–19

Q&A What if I click the Paste arrow by mistake?

Click the Paste arrow again to remove the Paste menu and repeat Step 2.

Other Ways

1. Click Copy on shortcut menu (or, if using touch, tap Copy on mini toolbar), right-click where item is to be pasted, click 'Keep Source Formatting' in Paste Options area on shortcut menu (or, if using touch, tap Paste on mini toolbar)

2. Select item, press CTRL+C, position insertion point at paste location, press CTRL+V

To Replace Placeholder Text in a Content Control

The next step is to begin to enter text in the Education section of the resume. The following step replaces placeholder text.

 In the Education section of the resume, select the placeholder text, SCHOOL NAME, LOCATION, DEGREE, in the first content control (shown in Figure 5–19) and then type **B.A. JOURNALISM - HARTFORD COLLEGE** as the degree and school name (shown in Figure 5–20).

To Use AutoComplete

1 CREATE DOCUMENT FROM TEMPLATE | 2 MODIFY & FORMAT TEMPLATE | 3 SAVE DOCUMENT IN OTHER FORMATS
4 MAKE DOCUMENT AVAILABLE ONLINE | 5 CREATE WEBPAGE FROM WORD DOCUMENT | 6 FORMAT WEBPAGE

As you begin typing, Word may display a ScreenTip that presents a suggestion for the rest of the word or phrase you are typing. **Why?** *With its **AutoComplete** feature, Word predicts the word or phrase you are typing and displays its prediction in a ScreenTip.* If the AutoComplete prediction is correct, you can instruct Word to finish your typing with its prediction, or you can ignore Word's prediction. Word draws its AutoComplete suggestions from its dictionary and from AutoText entries you create and save in the Normal template.

The following steps use the AutoComplete feature as you type the graduation date in the Education section of the resume.

- In the Education section of the resume, click the placeholder text that begins, 'You might want to…', in the first content control and then type **Dece** and notice the AutoComplete ScreenTip that appears on the screen (Figure 5–20).

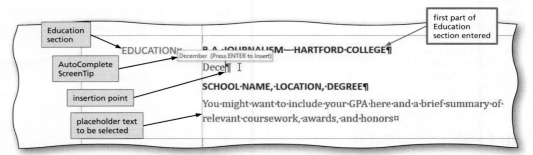

Figure 5–20

Q&A Why would my screen not display the AutoComplete ScreenTip?
Depending on previous Word entries, you may need to type more characters in order for Word to predict a particular word or phrase accurately. Or, you may need to turn on AutoComplete by clicking File on the ribbon to open the Backstage view, clicking the Options tab in the Backstage view to display the Word Options dialog box, clicking Advanced in the left pane (Word Options dialog box), placing a check mark in the 'Show AutoComplete suggestions' check box, and then clicking the OK button.

- Press the ENTER key to instruct Word to finish your typing with the word or phrase that appeared in the AutoComplete ScreenTip.

Q&A What if I do not want to use the text proposed in the AutoComplete ScreenTip?
Simply continue typing and the AutoComplete ScreenTip will disappear from the screen.

❸

- Press the SPACEBAR. Type **2017, GPA 3.92/4.00** and then press the ENTER key (Figure 5–21).

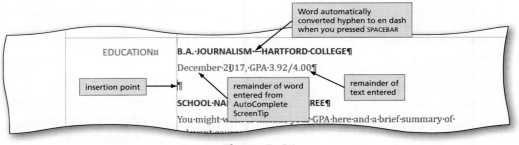

Figure 5–21

To Enter More Text

The following steps continue entering text in the Education section of the resume.

1 Type **Dean's List, every semester** and then press the ENTER key.

2 Type **Student Publications Award, May 2017** and then press the ENTER key.

3 Type **Civics Journal, 1st Place, political perspective article** and then italicize the journal title.

4 Bullet the three paragraphs just entered (Figure 5–22).

BTW
AutoFormat
Word automatically formats quotation marks, dashes, lists, fractions, ordinals, and other items, depending on your typing and settings. To check if an AutoFormat option is enabled, click File on the ribbon to open the Backstage view, click the Options tab in the Backstage view, click Proofing in the left pane (Word Options dialog box), click the AutoCorrect Options button, click the 'AutoFormat As You Type' tab (AutoCorrect dialog box), select the appropriate check boxes, and then click the OK button in each open dialog box.

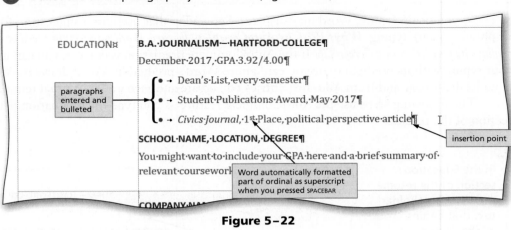

Figure 5–22

To Enter a Line Break

1 CREATE DOCUMENT FROM TEMPLATE | 2 MODIFY & FORMAT TEMPLATE | 3 SAVE DOCUMENT IN OTHER FORMATS
4 MAKE DOCUMENT AVAILABLE ONLINE | 5 CREATE WEBPAGE FROM WORD DOCUMENT | 6 FORMAT WEBPAGE

The next step in personalizing the resume is to enter the areas of concentration in the Education section. You want only the first line, which says, Areas of concentration:, to begin with a bullet. If you press the ENTER key on subsequent lines, Word automatically will carry forward the paragraph formatting, which includes the bullet. Thus, you will not press the ENTER key between each line. Instead, you will create a line break. **Why?** *A line break advances the insertion point to the beginning of the next physical line, ignoring any paragraph formatting.* The following steps enter the areas of concentration using a line break, instead of a paragraph break, between each line.

• With the insertion point positioned as shown in Figure 5–22, press the ENTER key.

• If necessary, turn off italics. Type **Areas of concentration:** and then press SHIFT+ENTER to insert a line break character and move the insertion point to the beginning of the next physical line (Figure 5–23).

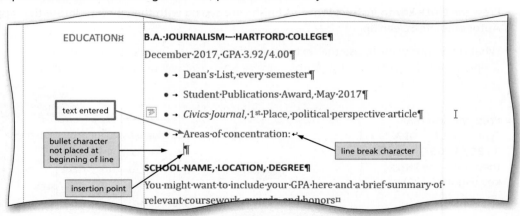

Figure 5–23

2

- Type **Broadcast reporting** and then press SHIFT+ENTER.

- Type **Intercultural communications** and then press SHIFT+ENTER.

- Type **Mass media** and then press SHIFT+ENTER.

- Type **Newswriting** as the last entry. Do not press SHIFT+ENTER at the end of this line (Figure 5–24).

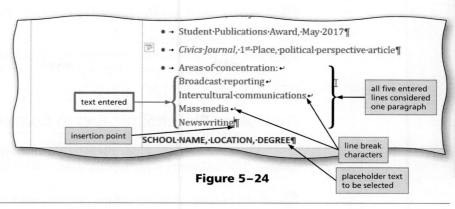

Figure 5–24

To Replace Placeholder Text in Content Controls

The next step is to enter the information for the second degree in the Education section of the resume. The following steps replace placeholder text.

1 In the Education section of the resume, select the placeholder text, SCHOOL NAME, LOCATION, DEGREE, in the second content control (shown in Figure 5–24) and then type **A.A. TECHNICAL WRITING – WHEATON COMMUNITY COLLEGE** as the degree and school name.

2 Select the placeholder text that begins, 'You might want to…', in the second content control and then type **December 2015, GPA 3.94/4.00** (Figure 5–25).

BTW
Line Break Characters
A line break character is a formatting mark that indicates a line break at the end of the line. Like paragraph marks, tab characters, and other formatting marks, line break characters do not print.

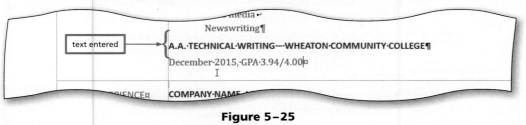

Figure 5–25

To Delete Text

The following steps delete text from the Experience content control. *Why? You have only one job experience entry for the resume.*

1 Select the text to delete (in this case, the entire second job experience entry in the Experience section) (Figure 5–26).

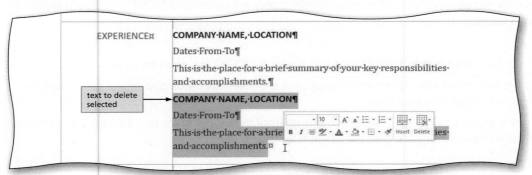

Figure 5–26

2 Press the DELETE key to delete the second job experience entry from the content control.

3 Press the BACKSPACE key to remove the blank line below the remaining item in the content control (shown in Figure 5–27).

To Replace Placeholder Text in Content Controls

The next step is to enter the job information for the Experience section of the resume. The following steps replace placeholder text.

1 In the Experience section of the resume, select the placeholder text, COMPANY NAME, LOCATION, in the content control and then type **ASSISTANT COORDINATOR – PONROLET COMMUNITY CENTER** as the job title and company name.

2 Select the placeholder text that begins 'Dates From…' in the content control and then type **August 2016 – Present** as the dates. Press the SPACEBAR so that the hyphen changes to an en dash.

3 Select the placeholder text that begins 'This is the place…' in the content control and then type this text (Figure 5–27): **Assist in developing programs designed to increase literacy and reading skills; conduct reading programs for children; compose, proofread, and edit monthly newsletter.**

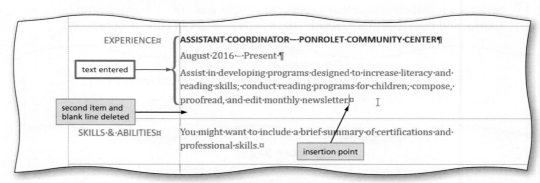

Figure 5–27

1 CREATE DOCUMENT FROM TEMPLATE | 2 MODIFY & FORMAT TEMPLATE | 3 SAVE DOCUMENT IN OTHER FORMATS
4 MAKE DOCUMENT AVAILABLE ONLINE | 5 CREATE WEBPAGE FROM WORD DOCUMENT | 6 FORMAT WEBPAGE

To Indent a Paragraph

In the resume, the lines below the job start date and end date that contain the job responsibilities are to be indented. *Why? You believe the responsibilities would be easier to read if they are indented.* The following step indents the left and right edges of a paragraph.

- With the insertion point in the paragraph to indent (shown in Figure 5–27), display the Layout tab.
- Click the Indent Left up arrow (Layout tab | Paragraph group) until the Indent Left box displays 0.5" to indent the left margin of the current paragraph one-half inch.
- Click the Indent Right down arrow (Layout tab | Paragraph group) until the Indent Right box displays 0.5" to indent the right margin of the current paragraph one-half inch (Figure 5–28).

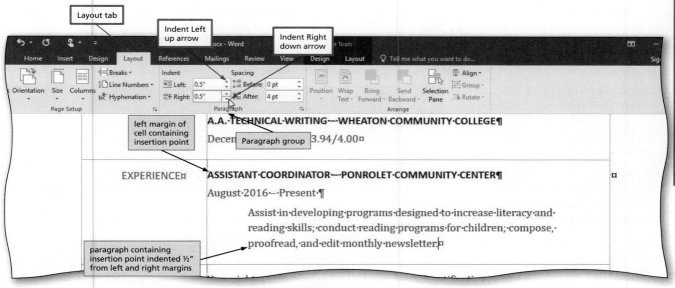

Figure 5-28

Other Ways

1. Drag Left Indent/Right Indent marker on horizontal ruler

2. For left margin, click Increase Indent button (Home tab | Paragraph group)

3. Click Paragraph Dialog Box Launcher (Home tab | Paragraph group), click Indents and Spacing tab (Paragraph dialog box), set indentation in Left/Right boxes, click OK button

4. Right-click text (or, if using touch, tap 'Show Context Menu' button on mini toolbar), click Paragraph on shortcut menu, click Indents and Spacing tab (Paragraph dialog box), set indentation in Left/Right boxes, click OK button

5. For left margin, press CTRL+M

To Replace Placeholder Text in Content Controls

The next step is to enter the membership information. You will replace the text in the Skills & Abilities section with membership information. The following steps replace placeholder text.

1 Select the text, SKILLS & ABILITIES, and then type **MEMBERSHIPS** as the new section heading.

2 In the Memberships section, select the placeholder text that begins, 'You might want…', in the content control and then type **Alpha Kappa Omega National Honor Society** and then press the ENTER key.

3 Type **Literacy Council, Ponrolet Village Board** and then press the ENTER key.

4 Type **Student Government Association, Secretary** as the final item in this section (shown in Figure 5-29).

To Copy and Paste a Table Item

1 CREATE DOCUMENT FROM TEMPLATE | 2 MODIFY & FORMAT TEMPLATE | 3 SAVE DOCUMENT IN OTHER FORMATS
4 MAKE DOCUMENT AVAILABLE ONLINE | 5 CREATE WEBPAGE FROM WORD DOCUMENT | 6 FORMAT WEBPAGE

The next section of the resume in this module is the Community Service section, which is organized exactly like the Experience section. Thus, you copy the Experience section and paste it below the Memberships section. *Why? It will be easier to edit the Experience section rather than format the Community Service section from scratch.*

You use the same procedure to copy table rows that you use to copy text. That is, select the rows to copy and then paste them at the desired location. The following steps copy table rows.

- Display the View tab. Click the 100% button (View tab | Zoom group) to display the resume at 100 percent zoom in the document window.

- If necessary, scroll so that the Experience and Memberships sections appear in the document window at the same time.

- Select the row to be copied, in this case, the row containing the Experience section in the resume.

- Display the Home tab.

- Click the Copy button (Home tab | Clipboard group) to copy the selected row in the document to the Office Clipboard (Figure 5–29).

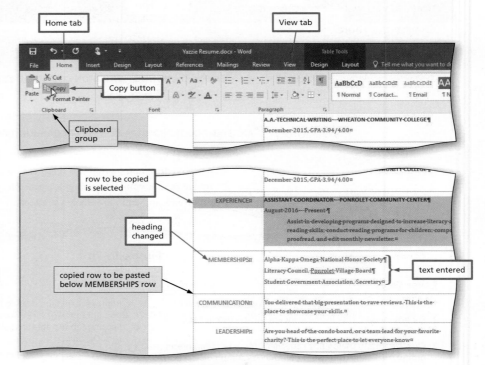

Figure 5–29

- Position the insertion point at the location where the copied row should be pasted, in this case, to the left of the M in the Memberships heading.

- Click the Paste arrow (Home tab | Clipboard group) to display the Paste gallery.

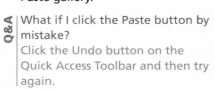

Q&A What if I click the Paste button by mistake?
Click the Undo button on the Quick Access Toolbar and then try again.

- Point to the 'Insert as New Rows' button in the Paste gallery to display a live preview of that paste option applied to the row in the table (Figure 5–30).

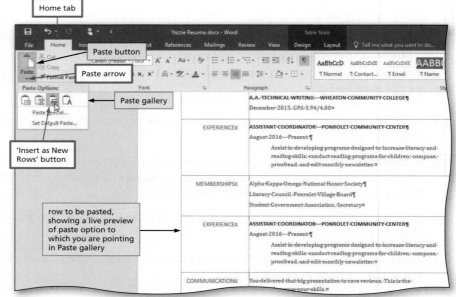

Figure 5–30

Experiment

- Point to the four options in the Paste gallery and watch the format of the pasted row change in the document window.

- Click the 'Insert as New Rows' button in the Paste gallery to apply the selected option to the pasted table row because you want the pasted row to use the same formatting as the copied row.

- Change the zoom to page width.

Other Ways
1. Right-click selected item, click Copy on mini toolbar or shortcut menu, right-click where item is to be pasted, click desired option in Paste Options area on shortcut menu   2. Select item, press CTRL+C, position insertion point at paste location, press CTRL+V

To Delete Rows and Edit Text

Because you will not be using the last three rows of the resume template, the next step is to delete them and then enter the remainder of the text in the resume, that is, the Community Service section. The following steps delete rows and edit text.

1 If necessary, display the Table Tools Layout tab.

2 Select the last three rows of the table (Communication, Leadership, and References), which might appear on a second page, click the Delete Table button (Table Tools Layout tab | Rows & Columns group), and then click Delete Rows on the Delete Table menu.

3 Below the Memberships heading, select the text, EXPERIENCE, and then type **COMMUNITY SERVICE** as the new section heading.

4 In the Community Service section of the resume, select the text, ASSISTANT COORDINATOR, and then type **READING BUDDY** to replace the text.

5 Select the text, COMMUNITY CENTER, and then type **PARK DISTRICT** to replace the text.

6 Select the text, August, and then type **October** to replace the month.

7 Select the indented paragraph of text and then type this text (Figure 5–31): **Volunteer eight hours a week at the local community center in the district's Reading Buddy program, which works to develop reading skills of children in elementary school.**

8 Save the resume again on the same storage location with the same file name.

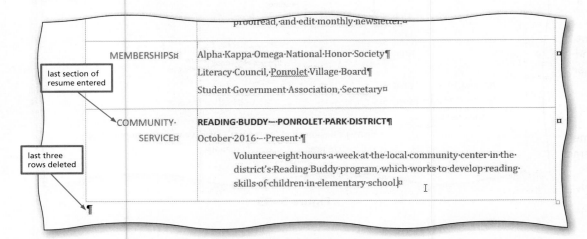

Figure 5–31

To Customize Theme Fonts

Recall that a font set defines one font for headings in a document and another font for body text. This resume currently uses the Calibri-Cambria font set, which specifies the Calibri font for the headings and the Cambria font for body text. The resume in this module creates a customized font set (theme font). **Why?** *You want the headings to use the Berlin Sans FB Demi font and the body text to use the Bookman Old Style font.* The following steps create a customized theme font set with the name, Resume Text.

- Display the Design tab.
- Click the Theme Fonts button (Design tab | Document Formatting group) to display the Theme Fonts gallery (Figure 5–32).

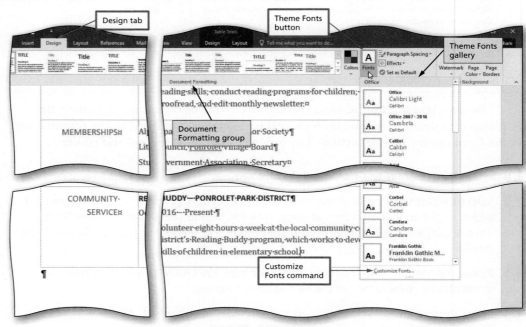

Figure 5–32

- Click Customize Fonts in the Theme Fonts gallery to display the Create New Theme Fonts dialog box.
- Click the Heading font arrow (Create New Theme Fonts dialog box); scroll to and then click 'Berlin Sans FB Demi' (or a similar font).
- Click the Body font arrow; scroll to and then click 'Bookman Old Style' (or a similar font).
- Type **Resume Text** in the Name text box as the name for the new theme font (Figure 5–33).

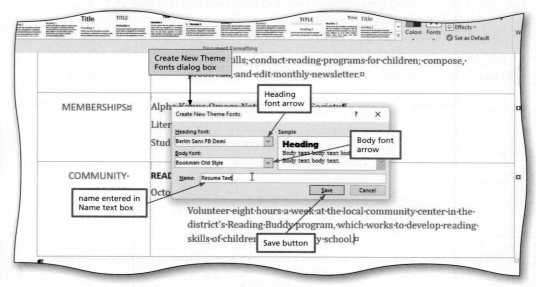

Figure 5–33

• Click the Save button (Create New Theme Fonts dialog box) to create the customized theme font with the entered name (Resume Text, in this case) and apply the new heading fonts to the current document (Figure 5–34).

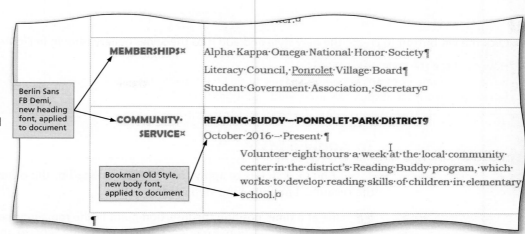

Figure 5–34

To Create a Style

1 CREATE DOCUMENT FROM TEMPLATE | 2 MODIFY & FORMAT TEMPLATE | 3 SAVE DOCUMENT IN OTHER FORMATS
4 MAKE DOCUMENT AVAILABLE ONLINE | 5 CREATE WEBPAGE FROM WORD DOCUMENT | 6 FORMAT WEBPAGE

Recall that a style is a predefined set of formats that appears in the Styles gallery. You have used styles in the Styles gallery to apply formats to text and have updated existing styles. You also can create your own styles.

The next task in this project is to create a style for the section headings in the resume. *Why? To illustrate creating a style, you will increase the font size of a section heading and save the new format as a style. Then, you will apply the newly defined style to the remaining section headings.* The following steps format text and then create a style based on the formats in the selected paragraph.

• Position the insertion point in the Memberships heading, display the Home tab, and then click the 'Increase Font Size' button (Home tab | Font group) to increase the font size of the heading.

• Click the More button (shown in Figure 5–36) in the Styles gallery (Home tab | Styles group) to expand the gallery (Figure 5–35).

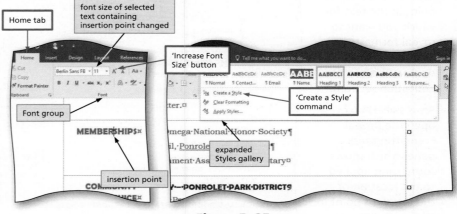

Figure 5–35

• Click 'Create a Style' in the Styles gallery to display the Create New Style from Formatting dialog box.

• Type **Resume Headings** in the Name text box (Create New Style from Formatting dialog box) (Figure 5–36).

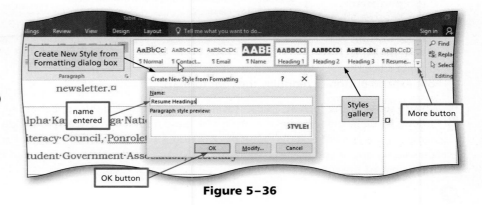

Figure 5–36

• Click the OK button to create the new style and add it to the Styles gallery (shown in Figure 5–37).

Q&A
How can I see the style just created?

If the style name does not appear in the in-ribbon Styles gallery, click the More button in the Styles gallery (Home tab | Styles group) to display the expanded Styles gallery.

To Apply a Style

The next step is to apply the style just created to the other section headings in the resume. The following step applies a style.

1 One at a time, position the insertion point in the remaining section headings (Objective, Education, Experience, and Community Service) and then click Resume Headings in the Styles gallery to apply the selected style to each heading.

To Reveal Formatting

1 CREATE DOCUMENT FROM TEMPLATE | 2 MODIFY & FORMAT TEMPLATE | 3 SAVE DOCUMENT IN OTHER FORMATS
4 MAKE DOCUMENT AVAILABLE ONLINE | 5 CREATE WEBPAGE FROM WORD DOCUMENT | 6 FORMAT WEBPAGE

Sometimes, you want to know what formats were applied to certain text items in a document. *Why? For example, you may wonder which font, font size, font color, and other effects were applied to the degree and job titles in the resume.* To display formatting applied to text, use the Reveal Formatting task pane. The following steps open and then close the Reveal Formatting task pane.

1

• Position the insertion point in the text for which you want to reveal formatting (in this case, the degree name in the Education section).

• Press SHIFT+F1 to open the Reveal Formatting task pane, which shows formatting applied to the location of the insertion point in (Figure 5–37).

 Experiment

• Click the Font collapse button to hide the Font formats. Click the Font expand button to redisplay the Font formats.

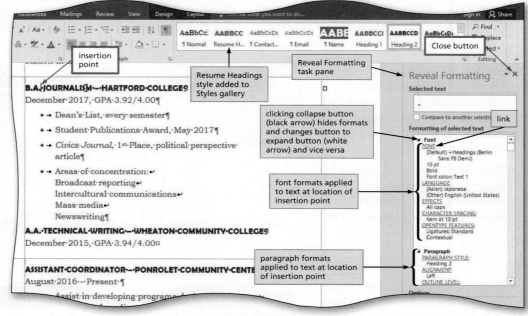

Figure 5–37

Q&A
Why do some of the formats in the Reveal Formatting task pane appear as links?

Clicking a link in the Reveal Formatting task pane displays an associated dialog box, allowing you to change the format of the current text. For example, clicking the Font link in the Reveal Formatting task pane would display the Font dialog box. If you made changes in the Font dialog box and then clicked the OK button, Word would change the format of the current text.

2

• Close the Reveal Formatting task pane by clicking its Close button.

To Modify a Style Using the Styles Dialog Box

The next step is to modify the Heading 2 style. *Why? The degree and job names in the resume currently have a different font than the other text in the resume. You prefer that all text in the resume use the same font.* Thus, the following steps modify a style.

- Right-click the style name to modify in the Styles gallery (Heading 2 in this case) (Home tab | Styles group) to display a shortcut menu (Figure 5–38).

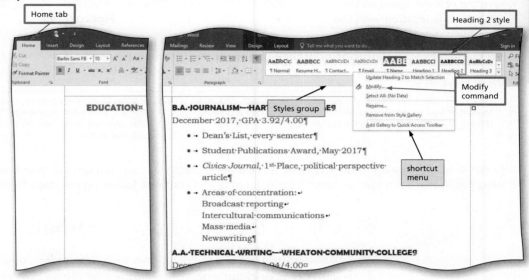

Figure 5–38

- Click Modify on the shortcut menu to display the Modify Style dialog box.

- Click the Font arrow (Modify Style dialog box) and then click Bookman Old Style in the Font gallery to change the font of the current style.

- Place a check mark in the Automatically update check box so that any future changes you make to the style in the document will update the current style automatically (Figure 5–39).

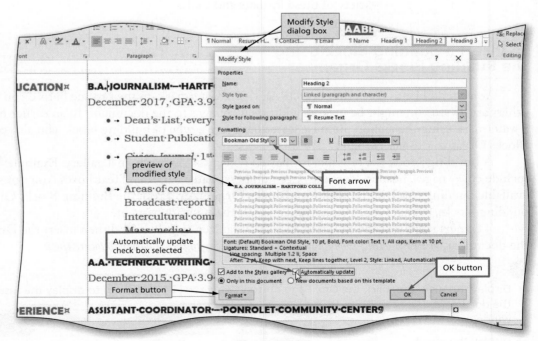

Figure 5–39

Q&A   What is the purpose of the Format button in the Modify Style dialog box?

If the formatting you wish to change for the style is not available in the Modify Style dialog box, you can click the Format button and then select the desired command after you click the Format button to display a dialog box that contains additional formatting options.

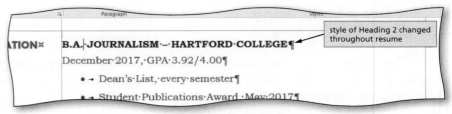

3

- Click the OK button to close the dialog box and apply the style changes to the paragraphs in the document (Figure 5–40).

- Save the resume again on the same storage location with the same file name.

Figure 5–40

- If requested by your instructor, print the finished resume (shown in Figure 5–1).

Other Ways

1. Click Styles Dialog Box Launcher (Home tab | Styles group), click arrow to right of style to modify, click Modify on menu, change settings (Modify Style dialog box), click OK button

2. Click Styles Dialog Box Launcher, click Manage Styles button, scroll to style and then select it (Manage Styles dialog box), click Modify button, change settings (Modify Style dialog box), click OK button in each dialog box

Break Point: If you wish to take a break, this is a good place to do so. You can exit Word now. To resume at a later time, run Word, open the file called Yazzie Resume, and continue following the steps from this location forward.

Sharing a Document with Others

You may want to share Word documents with others electronically, such as via email, USB flash drive, or cloud storage. To ensure that others can read and/or open the files successfully, Word provides a variety of formats and tools to assist with sharing documents. This section uses the Yazzie Resume created in this module to present a variety of these formats and tools.

To Insert a Building Block Using the Building Blocks Organizer

1 CREATE DOCUMENT FROM TEMPLATE | 2 MODIFY & FORMAT TEMPLATE | **3 SAVE DOCUMENT IN OTHER FORMATS**
4 MAKE DOCUMENT AVAILABLE ONLINE | 5 CREATE WEBPAGE FROM WORD DOCUMENT | 6 FORMAT WEBPAGE

You would like to place the text, DRAFT, as a watermark on the resume before you share it, so that others are aware you might be making additional changes to the document. In an earlier module, you inserted a watermark using the ribbon. Because watermarks are a type of building block, you also can use the Building Blocks Organizer to insert them.

A **building block** is a reusable formatted object that is stored in a gallery. Examples of building blocks include cover pages, headers, footers, page numbers, watermarks, and text boxes. You can see a list of every available building block in the **Building Blocks Organizer**. From the Building Blocks Organizer, you can sort building blocks, change their properties, or insert them in a document.

The next steps sort the Building Blocks Organizer by gallery and then insert the Draft 1 building block in the document. **Why?** *Sorting the building blocks by gallery makes it easier to locate them.*

- Display the View tab. Click the One Page button (View tab | Zoom group) to display the resume in its entirety in the document window.

- Display the Insert tab.

- Click the 'Explore Quick Parts' button (Insert tab | Text group) to display the Explore Quick Parts menu (Figure 5–41).

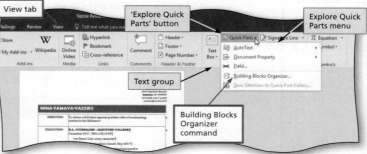

Figure 5–41

2

- Click 'Building Blocks Organizer' on the Explore Quick Parts menu to display the Building Blocks Organizer dialog box.

Experiment

- Drag the scroll bars in the Building Blocks Organizer so that you can look at all the columns and rows in the dialog box.

- Click the Gallery heading (Building Blocks Organizer dialog box) in the building blocks list to sort the building blocks by gallery (Figure 5–42).

Experiment

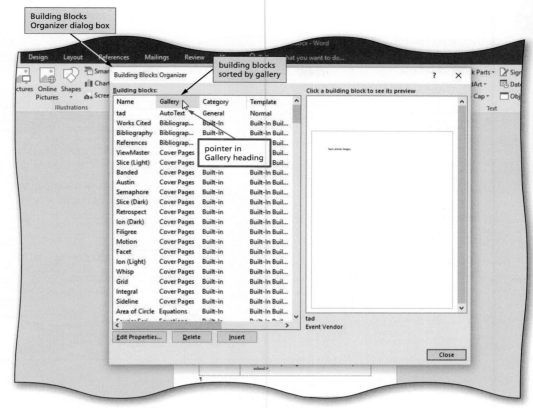

Figure 5–42

- Click various names in the building blocks list and notice that a preview of the selected building block appears in the dialog box.

3

- Scroll through the building blocks list to the Watermarks group in the Gallery column and then click DRAFT 1 to select this building block (Figure 5–43).

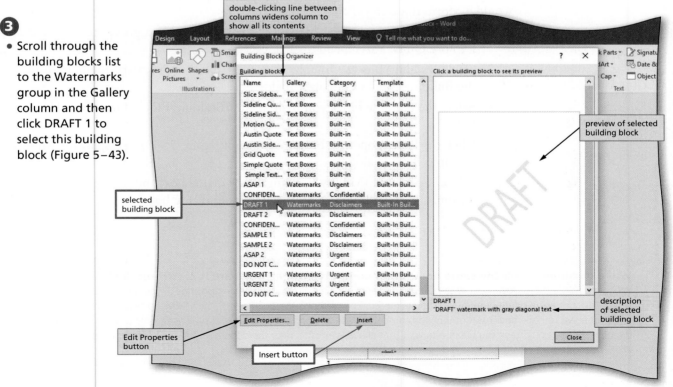

Figure 5–43

4

- Click the Insert button to insert the selected building block in the document (Figure 5–44).

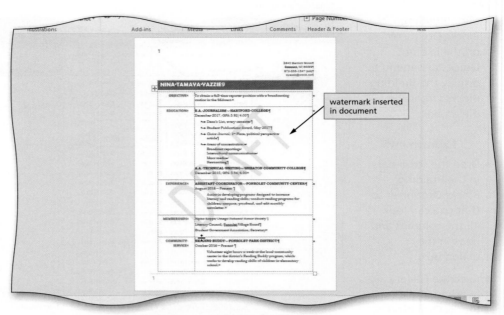

watermark inserted in document

Figure 5–44

To Edit Properties of Building Block Elements

Properties of a building block include its name, gallery, category, description, location where it is saved, and how it is inserted in the document. If you wanted to change any of these building block properties for a particular building block, you would perform these steps.

1. Click the 'Explore Quick Parts' button (Insert tab | Text group) to display the Explore Quick Parts menu.
2. Click 'Building Blocks Organizer' on the Explore Quick Parts menu to display the Building Blocks Organizer dialog box.
3. Select the building block you wish to edit (Building Blocks Organizer dialog box).
4. Click the Edit Properties button (shown in Figure 5–43) to display the Modify Building Block dialog box.
5. Edit any property (Modify Building Block dialog box) and then click the OK button. Close the Building Blocks Organizer dialog box.

CONSIDER THIS

Will a document look the same on another computer when you share it electronically?

When sharing a Word document with others, you cannot be certain that it will look or print the same on their computers or mobile devices as on your computer or mobile device. For example, the document may wordwrap text differently on others' computers and mobile devices. If others do not need to edit the document (that is, if they need only to view and/or print the document), you could save the file in a format that allows others to view the document as you see it. Two popular such formats are PDF and XPS.

To Save a Word Document as a PDF File and View the PDF File in Adobe Reader

1 CREATE DOCUMENT FROM TEMPLATE | 2 MODIFY & FORMAT TEMPLATE | 3 SAVE DOCUMENT IN OTHER FORMATS
4 MAKE DOCUMENT AVAILABLE ONLINE | 5 CREATE WEBPAGE FROM WORD DOCUMENT | 6 FORMAT WEBPAGE

PDF, which stands for Portable Document Format, is a file format created by Adobe Systems that shows all elements of a printed document as an electronic image. Users can view a PDF file without the software that created the original document. Thus, the PDF format enables users to share documents with others easily. To view, navigate, and print a PDF file, you use an application called **Adobe Reader**, which can be downloaded free from Adobe's website.

When you save a Word document as a PDF file, the original Word document remains intact; that is, Word creates a copy of the file in the PDF format. The following steps save the Yazzie Resume Word document as a PDF file and then open the Yazzie Resume PDF file in Adobe Reader. *Why? You want to share the resume with others but want to ensure it looks the same on their computer or mobile device as it does on yours.*

1

- Open the Backstage view and then click the Export tab in the Backstage view to display the Export gallery.

- If necessary, click 'Create PDF/ XPS Document' in the left pane of the Export gallery to display information about creating PDF/ XPS documents in the right pane (Figure 5–45).

Q&A Why does the left pane of my Export gallery have an additional command related to creating an Adobe PDF?
Depending on your installation settings in Adobe, you may have an additional tab on your ribbon and/or additional commands in galleries, etc., related to Adobe functionality.

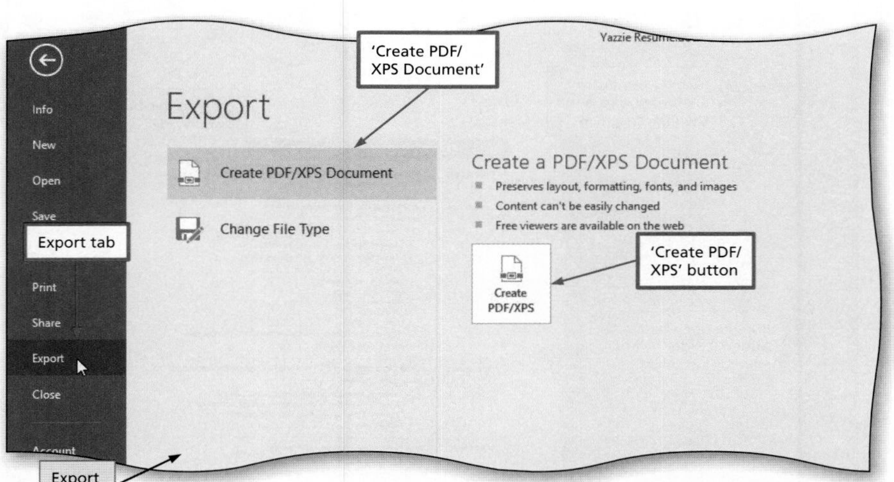

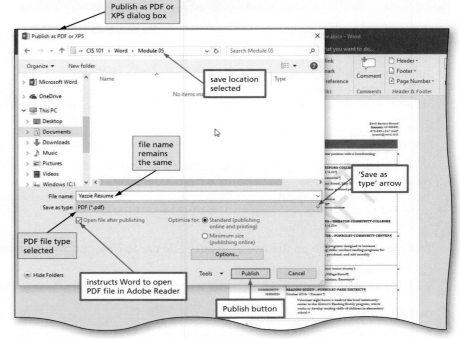

Figure 5–45

2

- Click the 'Create PDF/XPS' button in the right pane to display the Publish as PDF or XPS dialog box.

- Navigate to the desired save location (Publish as PDF or XPS dialog box).

Q&A Can the file name be the same for the Word document and the PDF file?
Yes. The file names can be the same because the file types are different: one is a Word document and the other is a PDF file.

- If necessary, click the 'Save as type' arrow and then click PDF.

- If necessary, place a check mark in the 'Open file after publishing' check box so that Word will display the resulting PDF file in Adobe Reader (Figure 5–46).

Figure 5–46

Why is my 'Open file after publishing' check box dimmed?

You do not have Adobe Reader installed on your computer. Use a search engine, such as Google, to search for the text, get adobe reader. Then, click the link in the search results to download Adobe Reader and follow the on-screen instructions to install the program. After installing Adobe Reader, repeat these steps.

3

- Click the Publish button to create the PDF file from the Word document and then, because the check box was selected, open the resulting PDF file in Adobe Reader.

- If necessary, click the Maximize button in the Adobe Reader window to maximize the window (Figure 5–47).

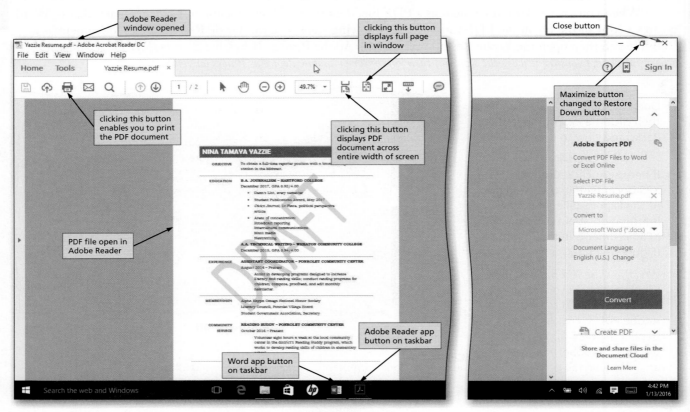

Figure 5–47

Do I have to display the resulting PDF file in Adobe Reader?

No. If you do not want to display the document in Adobe Reader, you would not place a check mark in the 'Open file after publishing' check box in the Publish as PDF or XPS dialog box (shown in Figure 5–46).

Is the Yazzie Resume Word document still open?

Yes. Word still is running with the Yazzie Resume document opened.

What if a blank screen appears instead of Adobe Reader or if the document appears in a different program?

You may not have Adobe Reader installed. Press the Start key on the keyboard to redisplay the Start screen and then navigate back to Word, or close the program in which the document opened.

4

- Click the Close button on the Adobe Reader title bar to close the Yazzie Resume.pdf file and exit Adobe Reader.

Can I edit documents in Adobe Reader?

No, you need Adobe Acrobat or some other program that enables editing of PDF files.

Other Ways

1. Press F12, click 'Save as type' box arrow (Save As dialog box), select PDF in list, click Save button

To Open a PDF File from Word

When you use Word to open a PDF file, Word converts it to an editable document. *Why? You may want to change the contents of a PDF file.* The editable PDF file that Word creates from the PDF file may appear slightly different from the PDF due to the conversion process. To illustrate this feature, the next steps open the PDF file just saved.

1

- Open the Backstage view and then click the Open tab in the Backstage view to display the Open gallery.

- Click OneDrive, This PC, or another location in the left pane that references the location of the saved PDF file, click the Browse button, and then navigate to the location of the PDF file to be opened.

- If necessary, click the File Types arrow to display a list of file types that can be opened by Word (Figure 5–48).

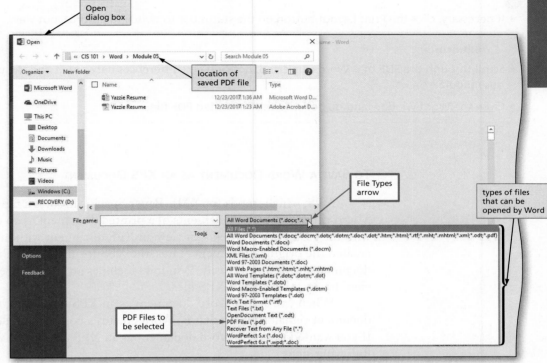

Figure 5–48

Q&A Why does the PDF file already appear in my list?

If the file type is All Word Documents, Word displays all file types that it can open in the file list.

2

- Click PDF Files in the File Types list, so that Word displays PDF file names in the dialog box.

- Click Yazzie Resume to select the PDF file to be opened (Figure 5–49).

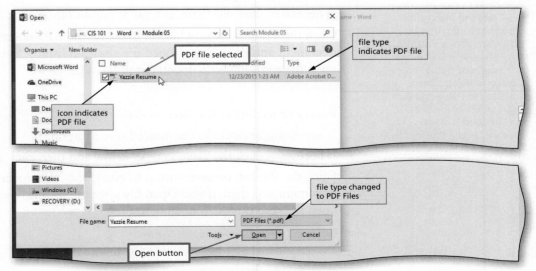

Figure 5–49

3

- Click the Open button (Open dialog box) to open the selected file and display the opened document in the Word window.
- If Word displays a dialog box indicating it will begin converting the document, click its OK button.

4

- If necessary, click the Print Layout button on the status bar to switch to Print Layout view.

Experiment

- Scroll through the PDF that Word converted, noticing any differences between it and the original resume created in this module.
- Close the Word window and do not save this converted PDF file.

TO SAVE A WORD DOCUMENT AS AN XPS DOCUMENT

XPS, which stands for XML Paper Specification, is a file format created by Microsoft that shows all elements of a printed document as an electronic image. As with the PDF format, users can view an XPS document without the software that created the original document. Thus, the XPS format also enables users to share documents with others easily. Windows includes an XPS Viewer, which enables you to view, navigate, and print XPS files.

When you save a Word document as an XPS document, the original Word document remains intact; that is, Word creates a copy of the file in the XPS format. If you wanted to save a Word document as an XPS document, you would perform the following steps.

1. Open the Backstage view and then click the Export tab in the Backstage view to display the Export gallery.
2. Click 'Create PDF/XPS Document' in the left pane of the Export gallery to display information about PDF/XPS documents in the right pane and then click the 'Create PDF/XPS' button to display the Publish as PDF or XPS dialog box.
3. If necessary, navigate to the desired save location.
4. If necessary, click the 'Save as type' arrow and then click XPS Document.
5. Click the Publish or Save button to create the XPS document from the Word document and then, if the 'Open file after publishing' check box was selected, open the resulting XPS document in the XPS Viewer.

or

1. Press F12 to display the Save As dialog box.
2. If necessary, navigate to the desired save location.
3. If necessary, click the 'Save as type' arrow and then click XPS Document.
4. Click the Publish or Save button to create the XPS document from the Word document and then, if the 'Open file after publishing' check box was selected, open the resulting XPS document in the XPS Viewer.

Q&A | What if I do not have an XPS Viewer?
The document will open in a browser window.

5. If necessary, exit the XPS Viewer.

BTW
Distributing a Document
Instead of printing and distributing a hard copy of a document, you can distribute the document electronically. Options include sending the document via email; posting it on cloud storage (such as OneDrive) and sharing the file with others; posting it on social media, a blog, or other website; and sharing a link associated with an online location of the document. You also can create and share a PDF or XPS image of the document, so that users can view the file in Adobe Reader or XPS Viewer instead of in Word.

To Run the Compatibility Checker

Word 2016 enables you to determine if a document is compatible (will work with) with earlier versions of Microsoft Word. *Why? If you would like to save a document, such as your resume, in the Word 97-2003 format so that it can be opened by users with earlier versions of Microsoft Word, you want to ensure that all of its elements (such as building blocks, content controls, and graphics) are compatible with earlier versions of Word.* The following steps run the compatibility checker.

1

- Open the Backstage view and then, if necessary, click the Info tab in the Backstage view to display the Info gallery.

- Click the 'Check for Issues' button in the Info gallery to display the Check for Issues menu (Figure 5–50).

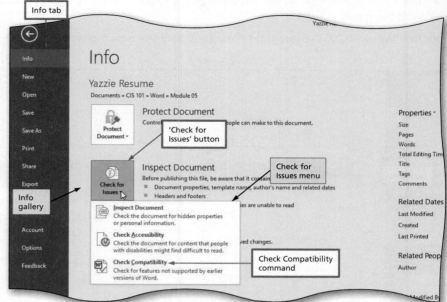

Figure 5–50

2

- Click Check Compatibility on the Check for Issues menu to display the Microsoft Word Compatibility Checker dialog box, which shows any content that may not be supported by earlier versions of Word (Figure 5–51).

3

- Click the OK button (Microsoft Word Compatibility Checker dialog box) to close the dialog box.

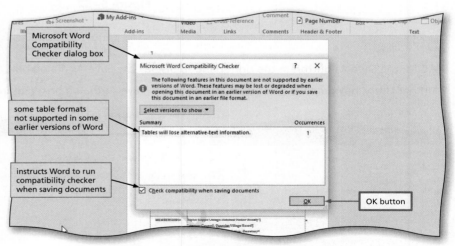

Figure 5–51

To Save a Word 2016 Document in an Earlier Word Format

If you send a document created in Word 2016 to users who have a version of Word earlier than Word 2007, they will not be able to open the Word 2016 document. *Why? Word 2016 saves documents in a format that is not backward compatible with versions earlier than Word 2007. Word 2016 documents have a file type of .docx, and versions prior to Word 2007 have a .doc file type.* To ensure that all Word users can open your Word 2016 document, you should save the document in a Word 97-2003 format. The following steps save the Word 2016 format of the Yazzie Resume document in the Word 97-2003 format.

①

- Open the Backstage view and then click the Export tab in the Backstage view to display the Export gallery.
- Click 'Change File Type' in the left pane of the Export gallery to display information in the right pane about various Word file types.
- Click 'Word 97-2003' in the right pane to specify the new file type (Figure 5–52).

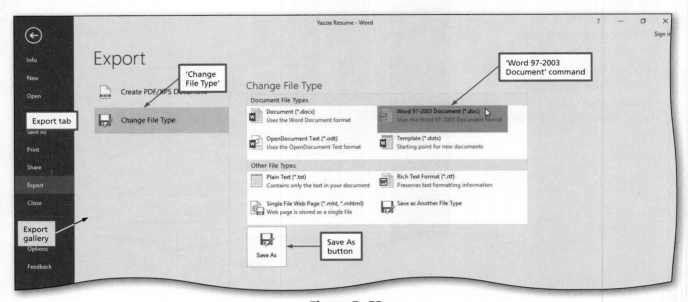

Figure 5–52

②

- Click the Save As button in the right pane to display the Save As dialog box.
- If necessary, navigate to the desired save location (Save As dialog box) (Figure 5–53).

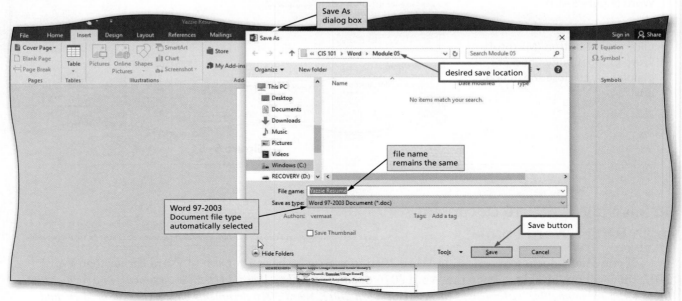

Figure 5–53

Word Module 5

Q&A Can the file name be the same for the Word 2016 document and the Word 97-2003 document?
Yes. The file names can be the same because the file types are different: one is a Word document with a .docx extension, and the other is a Word document with a .doc extension. The next section discusses file types and extensions.

3

- Click the Save button, which may display the Microsoft Word Compatibility Checker dialog box before saving the document (Figure 5–54).

Q&A My screen did not display the Microsoft Word Compatibility Checker dialog box. Why not?
If the 'Check compatibility when saving documents' check box is not selected (as shown in Figure 5–51), Word will not check compatibility when saving a document.

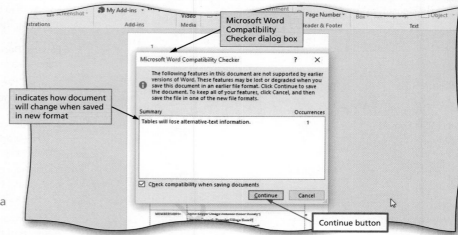

Microsoft Word Compatibility Checker dialog box

indicates how document will change when saved in new format

Continue button

Figure 5–54

Compatibility Mode notation on title bar indicates that document has been saved in a format different from Word 2016 format

4

- If the Microsoft Word Compatibility Checker dialog box is displayed, click its Continue button to save the document on the selected drive with the current file name in the specified format (Figure 5–55).

Q&A Is the Word 2016 format of the Yazzie Resume document still open?
No. Word closed the original document (the Word 2016 format of the Yazzie Resume).

Can I use Word 2016 to open a document created in an earlier version of Word?
Yes, but you may notice that the appearance of the document differs when opened in Word 2016.

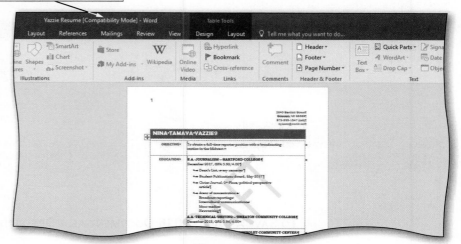

Figure 5–55

- Because you are finished with the Word 97-2003 format of the Yazzie Resume, close the document.

Other Ways

1. Press F12, click 'Save as type' arrow (Save As dialog box), select 'Word 97-2003 Document' in list, click Save button

File Types

When saving documents in Word, you can select from a variety of file types that can be opened in Word using the Export gallery in the Backstage view (shown in Figure 5–52) or by clicking the 'Save as type' arrow in the Save As dialog box. To save in these varied formats (Table 5–1), you follow the same basic steps as just illustrated.

Table 5–1 File Types			
File Type	**File Extension**	**File Explorer Image**	**Description**
OpenDocument Text	.odt		Format used by other word processing programs, such as Google Docs and OpenOffice.org
PDF	.pdf		Portable Document Format, which can be opened in Adobe Reader
Plain Text	.txt		Format where all or most formatting is removed from the document
Rich Text Format	.rtf		Format designed to ensure file can be opened and read in many programs; some formatting may be lost to ensure compatibility
Single File Web Page	.mht		HTML (Hypertext Markup Language) format that can be opened in a browser; all elements of the webpage are saved in a single file
Web Page	.htm		HTML format that can be opened in a browser; various elements of the webpage, such as graphics, saved in separate files and folders
Word 97-2003 Document	.doc		Format used for documents created in versions of Word from Word 97 to Word 2003
Word 97-2003 Template	.dot		Format used for templates created in versions of Word from Word 97 and Word 2003
Word Document	.docx		Format used for Word 2016, Word 2013, Word 2010, or Word 2007 documents
Word Template	.dotx		Format used for Word 2016, Word 2013, Word 2010, or Word 2007 templates
XPS	.xps		XML (Extensible Markup Language) Paper Specification, which can be opened in the XPS Viewer

TO SAVE A WORD 2016 DOCUMENT AS A DIFFERENT FILE TYPE

To save a Word 2016 document as a different file type, you would follow these steps.

1. Open the Backstage view and then click the Export tab in the Backstage view to display the Export gallery.
2. Click 'Change File Type' in the Export gallery to display information in the right pane about various file types that can be opened in Word.
3. Click the desired file type in the right pane and then click the Save As button to display the Save As dialog box.
4. Navigate to the desired save location (Save As dialog box) and then click the Save button in the dialog box.
5. If the Microsoft Word Compatibility Checker dialog box appears and you agree with the changes that will be made to the document, click the Continue button (Microsoft Word Compatibility Checker dialog box) to save the document on the selected drive with the current file name in the specified format.

Note: The steps in the next several sections require that you have a Microsoft account and an Internet connection. If you do not have a Microsoft account or an Internet connection, read the steps without performing them.

To Invite Others to View or Edit
a Document

If you have a OneDrive account, you can share a Word document saved on OneDrive with others through email message invitations. **Why?** *Invited users can click a link in an email message that displays a webpage enabling them to view or edit the document on OneDrive.* The following steps invite a user to view the Yazzie Resume document. If you do not have a Microsoft account or an Internet connection, read these steps without performing them.

- If necessary, run Word. Open the Word 2016 format of the Yazzie Resume and then save the Yazzie Resume on OneDrive.

- Click the Share button in the upper-right corner of the ribbon to open the Share pane (Figure 5–56).

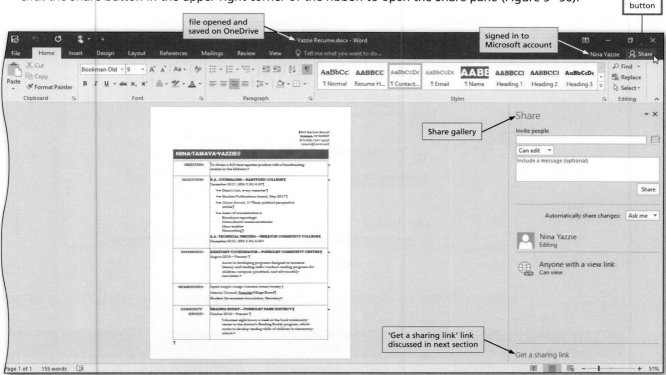

Figure 5–56

Why does my screen display a 'Save to Cloud' button in the Share pane?
The document has not been saved on OneDrive and/or you are not signed in to your Microsoft account.

- In the Share pane, type the email address(es) of the person(s) with whom you want to share the document, click the box arrow so that you can specify Can edit, if necessary, and then type a message to the recipient(s) (Figure 5–57).

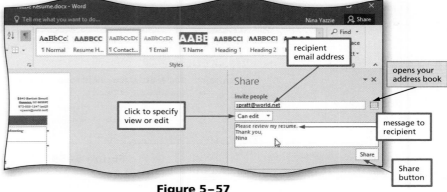

Figure 5–57

3

- Click the Share button in the Share pane to send the message along with a link to the document on OneDrive to the listed recipient(s).

Other Ways

1. Open Backstage view, click Share tab, click 'Share with People' in left pane in Share gallery, enter email address and message in Share pane, click Share button in Share pane

How does a recipient access the shared document?

The recipient receives an email message that indicates it contains a link to a shared document (Figure 5–58). When the recipient clicks the link in the email message, the document opens in Word Online on OneDrive (Figure 5–59).

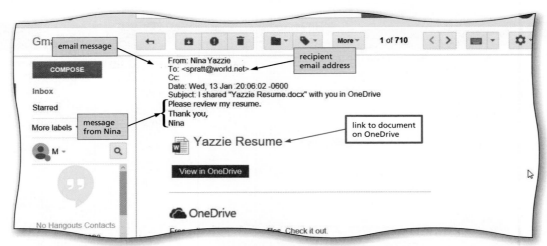

Figure 5–58

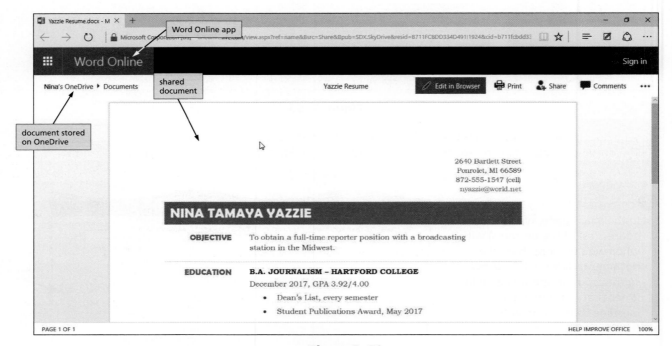

Figure 5–59

To Get a Sharing Link

Why share a link? Instead of inviting people to view or edit a document, you can create a link to the document's location on OneDrive and then send others the link via an email message or text message, post it on a website or online social network, or communicate it via some other means. The following steps get a sharing link. If you do not have a Microsoft account or an Internet connection, read these steps without performing them.

1

- If necessary, click Share button in the upper-right corner of the ribbon to open the Share pane and then click 'Get a sharing link' at the bottom of the Share pane (shown in Figure 5–56) to display options for obtaining a link to a document on OneDrive in the right pane (Figure 5–60).

Q&A Why does my screen display a 'Save to Cloud' button in the right pane?
The document has not been saved on OneDrive and/or you are not signed in to your Microsoft account.

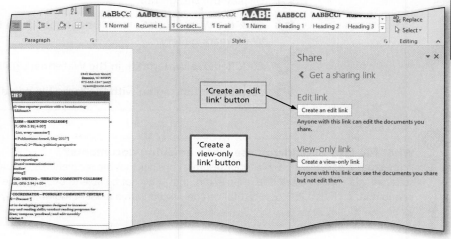

Figure 5–60

2

- Click the 'Create a view-only link' button in the Share pane to create the link associated with the file on OneDrive (Figure 5–61).

Q&A What do I do with the link?
You can copy and paste the link in an email or text message, on a webpage, or some other location.

What is the difference between a view link and an edit link?
A view link enables others to read the document but not modify it, while an edit link enables others to both view and edit the document.

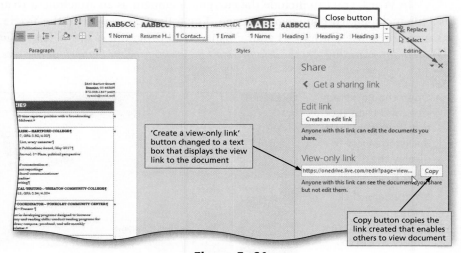

Figure 5–61

3

- Click the Close button in the upper-right corner of the Share pane to close the pane.

Other Ways

1. Open Backstage view, click Share tab, click 'Share with People' in right pane in Share gallery, enter email address and message in Share pane, click 'Get a sharing link' in Share pane

To Remove a Watermark

The following steps remove the DRAFT watermark from the resume in the document window, if it was saved with the document, because you now consider the document final and would like to distribute it to potential employers.

1 If necessary, open the Yazzie Resume (Word 2016 format).

2 Display the Design tab.

3 Click the Watermark button (Design tab | Page Background group) to display the Watermark gallery.

4 Click Remove Watermark in the Watermark gallery to remove the watermark.

5 Save the resume again with the same file name.

CONSIDER THIS

What file type should you use when emailing documents?

If you email a document, such as your resume, consider that the recipient, such as a potential employer, may not have the same software you used to create the resume and, thus, may not be able to open the file. As an alternative, you could save the file in a format, such as a PDF or XPS, that can be viewed with a reader program. Many job seekers also post their resumes on the web.

To Send a Document Using Email

1 CREATE DOCUMENT FROM TEMPLATE | 2 MODIFY & FORMAT TEMPLATE | 3 SAVE DOCUMENT IN OTHER FORMATS
4 MAKE DOCUMENT AVAILABLE ONLINE | 5 CREATE WEBPAGE FROM WORD DOCUMENT | 6 FORMAT WEBPAGE

In Word, you can include the current document as an attachment to an email message. An attachment is a file included with an email message. The following steps send the Yazzie Resume as an email attachment, assuming you use Outlook as your default email program. *Why? When you attach an email document from within Word, it automatically uses the default email program, which is Outlook in this case.*

1

- Open the Backstage view and then click the Share tab in the Backstage view to display the Share gallery.

- If necessary, click Email in the left pane of the Share gallery to display information in the right pane about various ways to send a document via email from within Word (Figure 5–62).

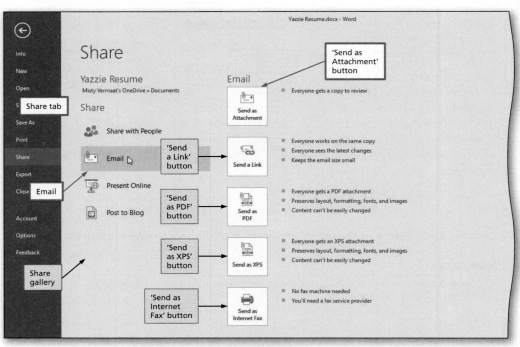

Figure 5–62

Q&A

Why is my list of share options in the Share gallery shorter?
You have not saved the document previously on OneDrive.

What are the purpose of the 'Send as PDF' and 'Send as XPS' buttons?
Depending on which button you click, Word converts the current document either to the PDF or XPS format and then attaches the PDF or XPS document to the email message.

Why is my 'Send a Link' button dimmed?
You have not saved the document previously on OneDrive.

2

- Click the 'Send as Attachment' button to run your default email program (Outlook, in this case), which automatically attaches the active Word document to the email message.

- Fill in the To text box with the recipient's email address.

- Fill in the message text (Figure 5–63).

3

- Click the Send button to send the email message along with its attachment to the recipient named in the To text box and then close the email window.

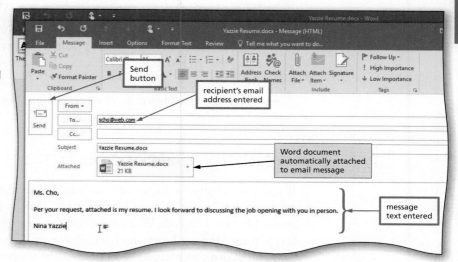

Figure 5–63

- Because you are finished working with the Yazzie Resume on OneDrive, you can sign out of your Microsoft Account, if you wish to do so.

TO USE THE DOCUMENT INSPECTOR

Word includes a Document Inspector that checks a document for content you might not want to share with others, such as personal information. Before sharing a document with others, you may want to check for this type of content. If you wanted to use the Document Inspector, you would do the following:

1. Open the Backstage view and, if necessary, click the Info tab in the Backstage view to display the Info gallery.

2. Click the 'Check for Issues' button in the Info gallery to display the Check for Issues menu.

3. Click Inspect Document on the Check for Issues menu to display the Document Inspector dialog box.

4. Click the Inspect button (Document Inspector dialog box) to instruct Word to inspect the document.

5. Review the results (Document Inspector dialog box) and then click the Remove All button(s) for any item that you do not want to be saved with the document.

6. When finished removing information, click the Close button to close the dialog box.

TO CUSTOMIZE HOW WORD OPENS EMAIL ATTACHMENTS

When a user sends you an email message that contains a Word document as an attachment, Word may display the document in Read mode. This view is designed to

BTW
Internet Fax
If you do not have a standalone fax machine, you can send and receive faxes in Word by clicking the 'Send as Internet Fax' button in the Backstage view (shown in Figure 5–62). To send or receive faxes using Word, you first must sign up with a fax service provider by clicking the OK button in the Microsoft Office dialog box that appears the first time you click the 'Send as Internet Fax' button, which displays an Available Fax Services webpage. You also may need to install either the Windows Fax printer driver or Windows Fax Services component on your computer. When sending a fax, Word converts the document to an image file and attaches it to an email message where you enter the recipient's fax number, name, subject, and message for the cover sheet, and then click a Send button to deliver the fax.

increase the readability and legibility of an on-screen document. Read mode, however, does not represent how the document will look when it is printed. For this reason, many users prefer working in Print Layout view to read documents. To exit Read mode, press the ESC key.

If you wanted to customize how Word opens email attachments, you would do the following.

1. Open the Backstage view and then click the Options tab in the Backstage view to display the Word Options dialog box.

2. If necessary, click General in the left pane (Word Options dialog box).

3. If you want email attachments to open in Read mode, place a check mark in the 'Open e-mail attachments and other uneditable files in reading view' check box; otherwise, remove the check mark to open email attachments in Print Layout view.

4. Click the OK button to close the dialog box.

Creating a Webpage from a Word Document

If you have created a document, such as a resume, using Word, you can save it in a format that can be opened by a browser, such as Internet Explorer. When you save a file as a webpage, Word converts the contents of the document into **HTML** (Hypertext Markup Language), which is a set of codes that browsers can interpret. Some of Word's formatting features are not supported by webpages. Thus, your webpage may look slightly different from the original Word document.

When saving a document as a webpage, Word provides you with three choices:

- The **single file web page format** saves all of the components of the webpage in a single file that has a **.mht** extension. This format is particularly useful for sending documents via email in HTML format.

- The **web page format** saves some of the components of the webpage in a folder, separate from the webpage. This format is useful if you need access to the individual components, such as images, that make up the webpage.

- The **filtered web page format** saves the file in webpage format and then reduces the size of the file by removing specific Microsoft Office formats. This format is useful if you want to speed up the time it takes to download a webpage that contains graphics, video, audio, or animations.

The webpage created in this section uses the single file web page format.

To Save a Word Document as a Webpage

1 CREATE DOCUMENT FROM TEMPLATE | 2 MODIFY & FORMAT TEMPLATE | 3 SAVE DOCUMENT IN OTHER FORMATS
4 MAKE DOCUMENT AVAILABLE ONLINE | 5 CREATE WEBPAGE FROM WORD DOCUMENT | 6 FORMAT WEBPAGE

The following steps save the Yazzie Resume created earlier in this module as a webpage. *Why? You intend to post your resume online.*

- If necessary, open the Word 2016 format of the resume file. Open the Backstage view and then click the Export tab in the Backstage view to display the Export gallery.

- Click 'Change File Type' in the left pane of the Export gallery to display information in the right pane about various file types that are supported by Word.

- Click 'Single File Web Page' in the right pane to specify a new file type (Figure 5–64).

What if I wanted to save the document as a web page instead of a single file web page?
You would click 'Save as Another File Type' in the Change File Type area, click the Save As button, click the 'Save as type' arrow in the Save As dialog box, and then click Web Page in the Save as type list.

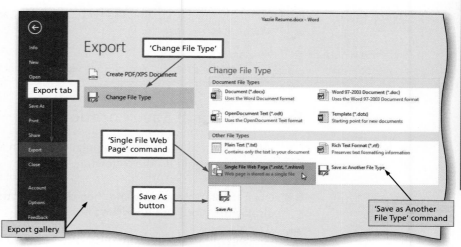

Figure 5–64

2

- Click the Save As button in the right pane to display the Save As dialog box.

- If necessary, navigate to the desired save location (Save As dialog box).

- If necessary, type **Yazzie Resume** in the File name box to change the file name.

- Click the Change Title button to display the Enter Text dialog box.

- Type **Yazzie Resume** in the Page title text box (Enter Text dialog box) (Figure 5–65).

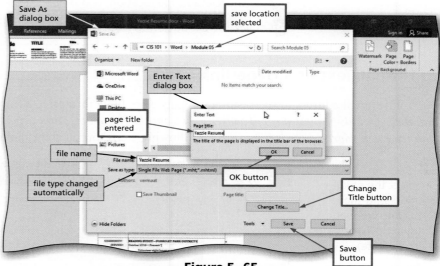

Figure 5–65

3

- Click the OK button (Enter Text dialog box) to close the dialog box.

- Click the Save button (Save As dialog box) to save the resume as a webpage and then display it in the document window in Web Layout view.

- If necessary, change the zoom to 100% (Figure 5–66).

- If the Microsoft Word Compatibility Checker dialog box appears, click its Continue button.

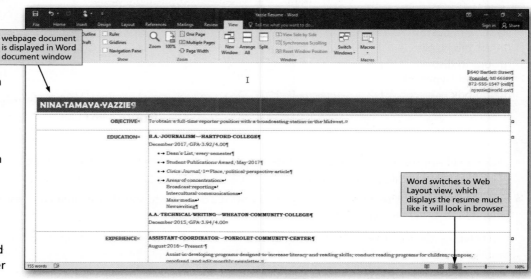

Figure 5–66

Q&A
Can I switch to Web Layout view at any time by clicking the Web Layout button on the taskbar?
Yes.

Can I save the webpage to a web server?
If you have access to a web server, you can save the webpage from Word directly to the web server.

To Set a Default Save Location

If you wanted to change the default location that Word uses when it saves a document, you would do the following.

1 Open the Backstage view and then click the Options tab in the Backstage view to display the Word Options dialog box.

2 Click Save in the left pane (Word Options dialog box) to display options for saving documents in the right pane.

3 In the 'Default file location' text box, type the new desired save location.

4 Click the OK button to close the dialog box.

To Format Text as a Hyperlink

1 CREATE DOCUMENT FROM TEMPLATE | 2 MODIFY & FORMAT TEMPLATE | 3 SAVE DOCUMENT IN OTHER FORMATS
4 MAKE DOCUMENT AVAILABLE ONLINE | 5 CREATE WEBPAGE FROM WORD DOCUMENT | **6 FORMAT WEBPAGE**

The email address in the resume webpage should be formatted as a hyperlink. **Why?** *When webpage visitors click the hyperlink-formatted email address, you want their email program to run automatically and open an email window with the email address already filled in.* The following steps format the email address as a hyperlink.

- Select the email address in the resume webpage (nyazzie@world.net, in this case).

- Display the Insert tab.

- Click the 'Add a Hyperlink' button (Insert tab | Links group) to display the Insert Hyperlink dialog box (Figure 5–67).

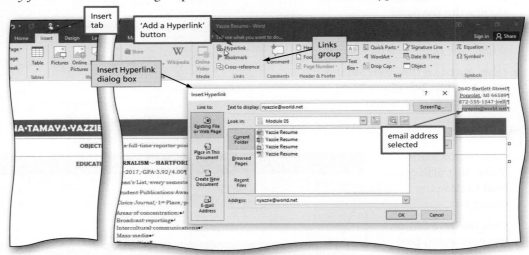

Figure 5–67

2

- Click E-mail Address in the Link to bar (Insert Hyperlink dialog box) so that the dialog box displays email address settings instead of webpage settings.

- In the E-mail address text box, type **nyazzie@world.net** to specify the email address that the browser uses when a user clicks the hyperlink.

Can I change the text that automatically appeared in the 'Text to display' text box?
Yes. Word assumes that the hyperlink text should be the same as the email address, so as soon as you enter the email address, the same text is entered in the 'Text to display' text box.

- If the email address in the 'Text to display' text box is preceded by the text, mailto:, delete this leading text because you want only the email address to appear in the document.

- Click the ScreenTip button to display the Set Hyperlink ScreenTip dialog box.

- Type `Send email message to Nina Yazzie.` in the 'ScreenTip text' text box (Set Hyperlink ScreenTip dialog box) to specify the text that will be displayed when a user points to the hyperlink (Figure 5–68).

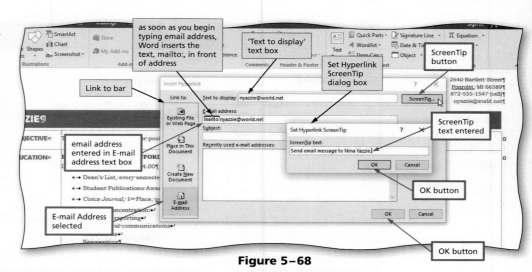

Figure 5–68

3

- Click the OK button in each dialog box to format the email address as a hyperlink (Figure 5–69).

Q&A

How do I know if the hyperlink works?
In Word, you can test the hyperlink by holding down the CTRL key while clicking the hyperlink. In this case, CTRL+clicking the email address should open an email window.

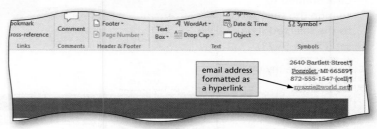

Figure 5–69

Other Ways

1. Right-click selected text, click Hyperlink on shortcut menu   2. Select text, press CTRL+K

TO EDIT A HYPERLINK

If you needed to edit a hyperlink, for example, to change its ScreenTip or its link, you would follow these steps.

1. Position the insertion point in the hyperlink.
2. Click the 'Add a Hyperlink' button (Insert tab | Links group) or press CTRL+K to display the Edit Hyperlink dialog box.

or

1. Right-click the hyperlink to display a shortcut menu.
2. Click Edit Hyperlink on the shortcut menu to display the Edit Hyperlink dialog box.

To Change the Style Set

1 CREATE DOCUMENT FROM TEMPLATE | 2 MODIFY & FORMAT TEMPLATE | 3 SAVE DOCUMENT IN OTHER FORMATS
4 MAKE DOCUMENT AVAILABLE ONLINE | 5 CREATE WEBPAGE FROM WORD DOCUMENT | **6 FORMAT WEBPAGE**

Word provides several built-in style sets to help you quickly change the look of an entire document. *Why? A style set contains formats for fonts and paragraphs.* The following steps change the style set to the Shaded style set.

- Display the Design tab.

- Click the More button (Design tab | Document Formatting group) (shown in Figure 5–71) to display the expanded Style Set gallery (Figure 5–70).

Experiment

• Point to various style sets in the Style Set gallery and watch the font and paragraph formatting change in the document window.

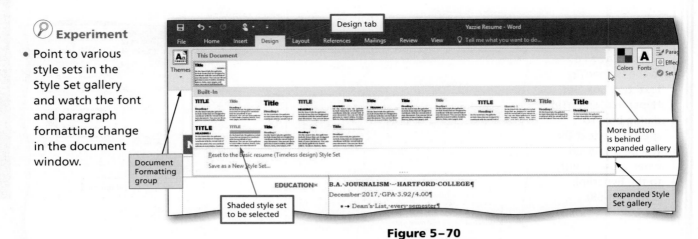

Figure 5–70

2

• Click Shaded to change the style set to the selected style set (Figure 5–71).

Q&A Can I create my own style sets?
Yes. Modify the fonts and other formats as desired, click 'Save as a New Style Set' in the expanded Style Set gallery (shown in Figure 5–70), enter the name for the style set (Save as a New Style Set dialog box), and then click the Save button to create the custom style set. You then can access the custom style set through the Style Set gallery.

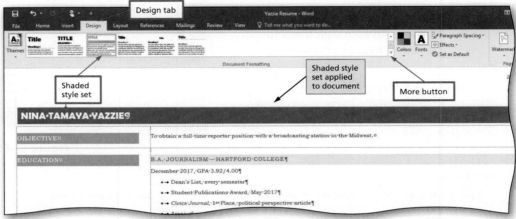

Figure 5–71

• Save the resume webpage again on the same storage location with the same file name and then exit Word.

To Test a Webpage in a Browser

1 CREATE DOCUMENT FROM TEMPLATE | 2 MODIFY & FORMAT TEMPLATE | 3 SAVE DOCUMENT IN OTHER FORMATS
4 MAKE DOCUMENT AVAILABLE ONLINE | 5 CREATE WEBPAGE FROM WORD DOCUMENT | 6 FORMAT WEBPAGE

After creating and saving a webpage, you should test it in at least one browser. *Why? You want to be sure it looks and works the way you intended.* The following steps use File Explorer to display the resume webpage in the Microsoft Edge browser.

1

• Click the File Explorer button on the Windows taskbar to open the File Explorer window.

• Navigate to the location of the saved resume webpage file (Figure 5–72).

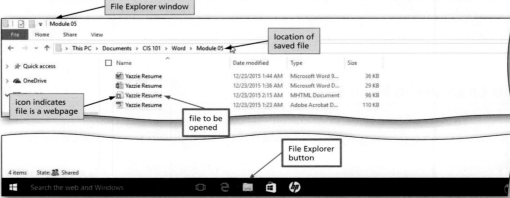

Figure 5–72

2

- Double-click the webpage file name, Yazzie Resume, to run Microsoft Edge and display the webpage file in the browser window (Figure 5–73).

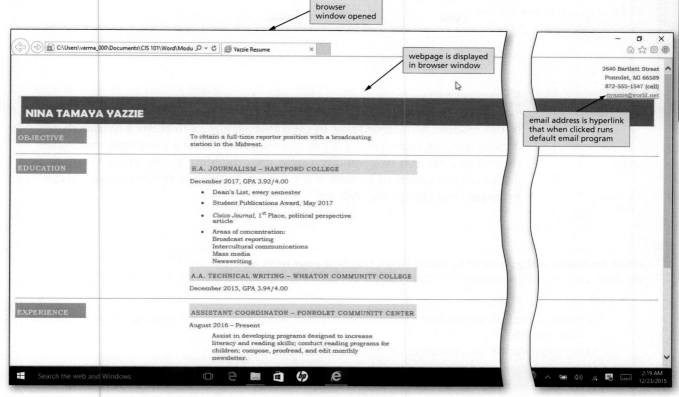

Figure 5–73

3

- With the webpage document displayed in the browser, click the email address link to run the email program with the email address displayed in the email window (Figure 5–74).

- If Microsoft Edge displays a security dialog box, click its Allow button.

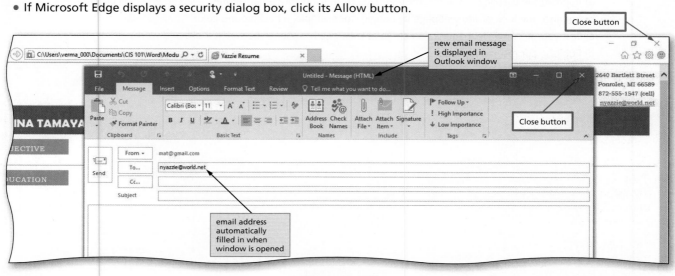

Figure 5–74

4

- Exit all running apps.

How do you publish a webpage?

Once you have created a webpage, you can publish it. **Publishing** is the process of making a webpage available to others on a network, such as the Internet or a company's intranet. Many Internet service providers (ISPs) offer storage space on their web servers at no cost to their subscribers.

Summary

In this module, you learned how to use a Word template to create a document, set custom margins, personalize a document template, indent a paragraph, customize theme fonts, create a style, modify a style, insert building blocks, save a Word document in a variety of formats, share a document online via OneDrive, insert a hyperlink, and change the style set.

What decisions will you need to make when creating your next resume?

Use these guidelines as you complete the assignments in this module and create your own resumes outside of this class.

1. Craft a successful resume.

   a) Include necessary information (at a minimum, your contact information, objective, educational background, and work experience).

   b) Honestly present all your positive points.

   c) Organize information appropriately.

   d) Ensure the resume is error free.

2. For electronic distribution, ensure the document is in the proper format.

   a) Save the resume in a format that can be shared with others.

   b) Ensure that others will be able to open the resume using software on their computers or mobile devices and that the look of the resume will remain intact when recipients open the resume.

3. If desired, create a resume webpage from your resume Word document.

   a) Improve the usability of the resume webpage by making your email address a link to an email program.

   b) Enhance the look of the webpage by adding, for example, a background color.

   c) Test your finished webpage document in at least one browser to be sure it looks and works as intended.

   d) Publish your resume webpage.

Apply Your Knowledge

Reinforce the skills and apply the concepts you learned in this module.

Saving a Word Document in a Variety of Formats

Note: To complete this assignment, you will be required to use the Data Files. Please contact your instructor for information about accessing the Data Files.

Instructions: Run Word. Open the document, Apply 5 – 1 Protect Your Hearing, from the Data Files. You are to save the document as a single file web page (Figure 5 – 75), a PDF document, an XPS document, and in the Word 97-2003 format.

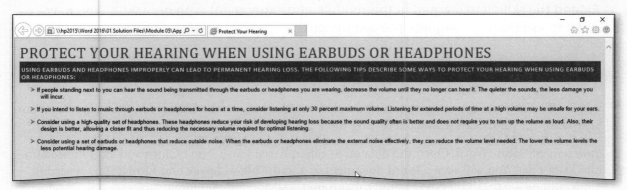

Figure 5 – 75

Perform the following tasks:

1. Save the document as a single file web page using the file name, Apply 5 – 1 Protect Your Hearing Webpage. In the Save As dialog box, click the Change Title button and change the webpage title to Protect Your Hearing. If necessary, increase the zoom percentage so that the document is readable on your screen.

2. If requested by your instructor, add another bullet point with a personal suggestion about protecting hearing when using earbuds or headphones followed by your name in parentheses.

3. Add the background color Orange, Accent 2, Lighter 80% to the webpage document.

4. Change the style set to Shaded. Save the file again.

5. Use Microsoft Edge or another browser to view the webpage (shown in Figure 5 – 75). If requested by your instructor, print the webpage. What differences do you notice between the Word document format and the single file web page format? Exit the browser and then close the webpage document in Word.

6. Open the original Apply 5 – 1 Protect Your Hearing document. If requested by your instructor, perform Step 2 again. Save the document as a PDF document and then view the PDF document in Adobe Reader. Submit the document as specified by your instructor. Exit Adobe Reader. In Word, open the PDF document just created. What differences do you notice between the Word document format and the PDF format? Close the converted PDF document without saving it.

7. If necessary, open the original Apply 5 – 1 Protect Your Hearing document. If requested by your instructor, perform Step 2 again. Save the document as an XPS Document and then view the XPS document in the XPS Viewer. Submit the document as specified by your instructor. What differences do you notice between the Word document format and the XPS format? Exit the XPS Viewer.

Continued >

Apply Your Knowledge *continued*

8. If necessary, open the original Apply 5–1 Protect Your Hearing document. Run the compatibility checker. What issue(s) were identified by the compatibility checker? Save the document in the Word 97-2003 format. Submit the document as specified by your instructor.

9. If your instructor allows, email the document saved in #8 to his or her email account.

10. ✳ Answer the questions posed in #5, #6, #7, and #8. If you wanted to email this document to others, which format would you choose and why?

Extend Your Knowledge

Extend the skills you learned in this module and experiment with new skills. You may need to use Help to complete the assignment.

Creating a Multi-File Webpage, Applying a Fill Effect and Highlights, and Inserting Screen Shots

Note: To complete this assignment, you will be required to use the Data Files. Please contact your instructor for information about accessing the Data Files.

Instructions: Run Word. Open the document called Extend 5–1 NFC Chips and Tags located on the Data Files. You will save a Word document as a multi-file webpage and format it by inserting links, adding a pattern fill effect as the background, and applying highlights to text. Then, you will create a new document that contains screen shots of the webpage and files created for the webpage.

Perform the following tasks:

1. Use Help to learn about saving as a webpage (not a single file web page), hyperlinks, pattern fill effects, text highlight color, and screen shots.

2. If requested by your instructor, add your name on a separate line at the end of the document.

3. Save the Extend 5–1 NFC Chips and Tags file in the web page format (not as a single file web page) using the file name, Extend 5–1 NFC Chips and Tags Webpage.

4. Using a browser, search for a website that lists phones with NFC technology. At the end of the document, type a line of text that directs the reader to that web address for a list of phones with NFC technology. Format the web address in the document as a hyperlink so that when a user clicks the web address, the associated webpage is displayed in the browser window.

5. Add a page color of your choice to the document. Add a pattern fill effect of your choice to the page color.

6. Apply a text highlight color of your choice to at least five words in the document.

7. Save the document again. Test the webpage by double-clicking its file name in File Explorer. Test the web address link on the webpage. Leave this window open so that you can include its screen shot in the next step.

8. Redisplay the Word window. Create a new Word document. Use Word to insert a screen shot of the webpage displaying in the File Explorer window. Below the screen shot of the webpage, insert a screen shot(s) of File Explorer that shows all the files and folders created by saving the document as a webpage. Insert callout shapes with text that points to and identifies the files and folders created by saving the document as a webpage (Figure 5–76). Save the document with the file name, Extend 5–1 NFC Chips and Tags Screen Shots.

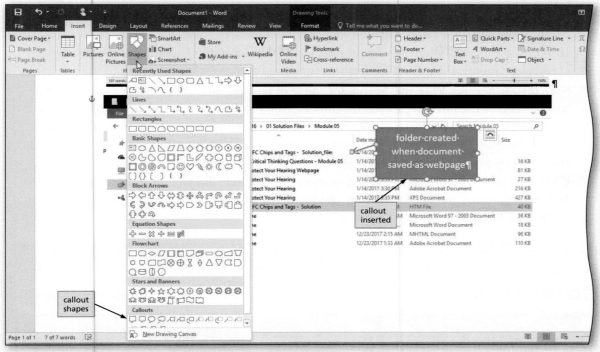

Figure 5–76

9. Close all open windows. Submit the files in the format specified by your instructor.

10. ✸ Why would you add a pattern fill effect to a background?

Expand Your World

Create a solution that uses cloud or web technologies by learning and investigating on your own from general guidance.

Sharing a Resume Online

Notes:

- You will use OneDrive and a job sharing website account, which you can create at no cost, to complete this assignment. If you do not have these accounts and do not want to create them, read this assignment without performing the instructions.

- To complete this assignment, you will be required to use the Data Files. Please contact your instructor for information about accessing the Data Files.

Instructions: You are a marketing management graduate from Mockingbird College. You have prepared a resume and are ready to share it with potential employers. You will save it on your OneDrive account, invite others to view it, get a sharing link, send it via email, and post it on a job sharing website (Figure 5–77).

Perform the following tasks:

1. In Word, open the document, Expand 5–1 Cucci Resume, from the Data Files. Look through the resume so that you are familiar with its contents and formats.

2. If requested by your instructor, change the name at the top of the resume to your name.

3. Save the resume on your OneDrive account.

Continued >

Expand Your World *continued*

4. In Word, invite at least one of your classmates to view your resume document. If requested, include your instructor in the invitation.

5. In Word, get a sharing link for the resume. Email the sharing link to at least one of your classmates. Submit the link in the format requested by your instructor.

6. Save the resume as a PDF file. Search for the text, post resume online, using a search engine. Visit several of the job search websites and determine on which one you would like to post a resume. If requested, create an account or profile, fill in the requested information, and then upload the PDF format of the resume (Figure 5–77). Submit the posting in the format requested by your instructor. Delete the posted resume from the job search website.

7. ✳ Which job search websites did you evaluate? Which one did you select to use and why? What would cause the file size of your resume to be too large to upload (post)? How can you reduce the file size?

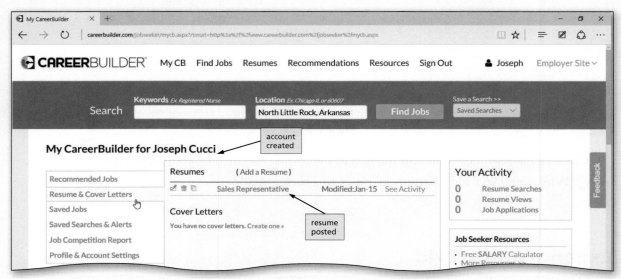

Figure 5–77

In the Labs

Design, create, modify, and/or use a document following the guidelines, concepts, and skills presented in this module. Labs 1 and 2, which increase in difficulty, require you to create solutions based on what you learned in the module; Lab 3 requires you to apply your creative thinking and problem-solving skills to design and implement a solution.

Lab 1: Creating a Resume from a Template (same template as in this module's project)

Problem: You are psychology student at Olympia State College. As graduation quickly is approaching, you prepare the resume shown in Figure 5–78 using one of Word's resume templates.

Perform the following tasks:

1. Use the Basic resume (Timeless design) template to create a resume. If you cannot locate this template or if the template you locate differs from Figure 5–5 shown at the beginning of this module, open the file called Basic resume (Timeless design) from the Data Files.

2. Change the document theme to Headlines.

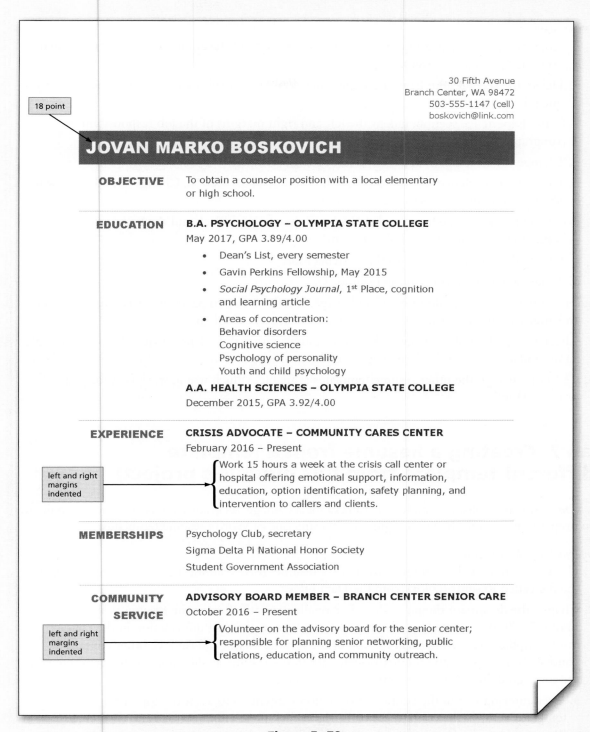

18 point

30 Fifth Avenue
Branch Center, WA 98472
503-555-1147 (cell)
boskovich@link.com

JOVAN MARKO BOSKOVICH

OBJECTIVE   To obtain a counselor position with a local elementary
or high school.

EDUCATION   **B.A. PSYCHOLOGY – OLYMPIA STATE COLLEGE**
May 2017, GPA 3.89/4.00

- Dean's List, every semester
- Gavin Perkins Fellowship, May 2015
- *Social Psychology Journal*, 1st Place, cognition
  and learning article
- Areas of concentration:
  Behavior disorders
  Cognitive science
  Psychology of personality
  Youth and child psychology

A.A. HEALTH SCIENCES – OLYMPIA STATE COLLEGE
December 2015, GPA 3.92/4.00

EXPERIENCE   **CRISIS ADVOCATE – COMMUNITY CARES CENTER**
February 2016 – Present

left and right margins indented

Work 15 hours a week at the crisis call center or
hospital offering emotional support, information,
education, option identification, safety planning, and
intervention to callers and clients.

MEMBERSHIPS   Psychology Club, secretary
Sigma Delta Pi National Honor Society
Student Government Association

COMMUNITY SERVICE   **ADVISORY BOARD MEMBER – BRANCH CENTER SENIOR CARE**
October 2016 – Present

left and right margins indented

Volunteer on the advisory board for the senior center;
responsible for planning senior networking, public
relations, education, and community outreach.

Figure 5–78

3. Personalize the resume as shown in Figure 5–78. Following are some guidelines for some sections of the resume:

   a. Change the margins to 1" on the top, left, and right, and .5" on the bottom.

   b. If requested by your instructor, use your own name and contact information in the content controls. Delete the line containing the Website content control.

   c. Move the Education and Experience rows so that they appear as shown in Figure 5–78. Insert line breaks in the areas of concentration section of the education information.

Continued >

In the Labs *continued*

    d. Copy and paste the text in the table cell containing the Education content control so that you can enter both degrees.

    e. Delete the second item from the Experience content control because the resume lists only one job.

    f. In the Experience section, indent the left and right margins of the job responsibilities paragraphs one-half inch.

    g. Change the heading, Skill & Abilities, to Memberships.

    h. Copy the Experience section to below the Memberships section. Change the added row to show the community service information.

    i. Customize the theme fonts so that the headings are Arial Black and the body text is Verdana. Name the customized font Lab 1 Resume.

    j. Modify the Heading 2 style to the Verdana font.

    k. Delete any unused rows in the resume.

4. The entire resume should fit on a single page. If it flows to two pages, decrease spacing before and after paragraphs until the entire resume text fits on a single page.

5. Check the spelling of the resume. Save the resume with Lab 5–1 Boskovich Resume as the file name, and submit it in the format specified by your instructor.

6. ✳ Look through the other resume templates available. Which would work best for your resume? Why?

Lab 2: Creating a Resume from a Template (different template from this module's project)

Problem: You are a business student at Eureka Falls College. As graduation is approaching quickly, you prepare the resume shown in Figure 5–79 using one of Word's resume templates.

Perform the following tasks:

1. Use the Resume (color) template to create a resume. If you cannot locate this template, open the file called Resume (color) from the Data Files.

2. Change the document theme to slate. Personalize, modify, format the resume as shown in Figure 5–79. If requested by your instructor, use your personal information in the contact information content controls at the top of the resume. Insert and remove other content controls, as necessary, and modify placeholder in the resume as shown in the figure. Following are some guidelines for some sections of the resume:

    a. After entering text in the contact information content controls at the top of the resume template, remove the content controls (right-click the content control and then click 'Remove Content Control' on the shortcut menu so that your text remains but the content control is deleted). When you selected the contact information content controls, they appeared on the screen different from the template used in this module. How did they differ?

    b. To add the third job in the Experience section, click the bottom job experience control to select it and then click the Insert Control at the bottom right edge of the selected control. After entering the text in the content control, remove the content control so that text remains but the content control is deleted. Note that the resume template in this module's project did not contain an Insert Control. Describe the appearance of the Insert Control.

    c. Create a customized theme font set that uses Rockwell for headings and Arial for body text. Save the theme font with the name, Lab 2 Resume.

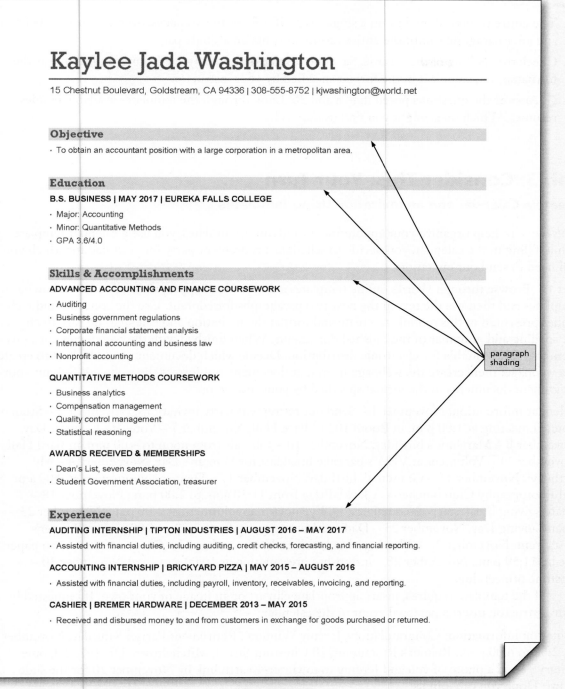

Figure 5–79

d. Modify the Section style to contain paragraph shading of Gray 80%, Text 2, Lighter 90%. Update the style so that it applies to the entire resume.

e. Increase the font size of the name to 28 point and the street address control to 10 point. Create a style called Contact Info using the format in the street address. Apply the Contact Info style to the city, state, ZIP code, phone number, and email address (the vertical bars before and after the phone number should remain at 9 point).

Continued >

In the Labs *continued*

3. The entire resume should fit on a single page. If it flows to two pages, decrease spacing before and after paragraphs until the entire resume text fits on a single page.

4. Check the spelling of the resume. Save the resume with Lab 5–2 Washington Resume as the file name, and submit it in the format specified by your instructor.

5. ✺ Answer the questions posed in #2a and 2b. Look through the templates available besides resumes. Which ones might you find useful? Why?

Lab 3: **Consider This: Your Turn**

Create a Calendar and an Invitation Using Templates

Problem: To help organize your appointments and important dates, you use a calendar template. While filling in the calendar, you decide to schedule a retirement party for your dad for which you will need to send out invitations.

Part 1:   Browse through Word's online templates and download appropriate calendar and invitation templates and then use the text in the next two paragraphs for content. Use the concepts and techniques presented in this module to create and format the invitation and calendar. Be sure to check the spelling and grammar of the finished documents. When finished with the two documents, save them in a form suitable for electronic distribution. Decide which document would be best to create as a webpage; then, create the webpage from that document and format the webpage. Submit your assignment documents in the format specified by your instructor.

Calendar information: November 1 – Send out retirement party invitations, November 2 – Student Council meeting at 1:00 p.m. in Room 103 in Pace Hall, November 7 – Vote! It's Election Day, November 8 – Marianne's birthday, November 10 – Job Fair from noon to 4:00 p.m. in Bard Hall, November 11 – Volunteer at VFW's pancake breakfast for Veteran's Day, November 14 – My birthday!, November 15 – Grandma's birthday, November 17 – Dentist appointment at 9:00 a.m. and Photography Club luncheon at Jack's Pizza from 11:30 a.m. to 2:00 p.m., November 18 – Thanksgiving break starts, November 20 – Eye doctor appointment at 1:00 p.m., November 23 – Thanksgiving Day, November 25 – Dad's retirement party from 2:00 to 6:00 p.m. at Reimer's Restaurant, November 26 – Thanksgiving break ends, November 27 – Corporate Law term paper due by 11:59 p.m., November 28 – internship presentation at 10:00 a.m., and November 30 – capstone project due.

If the template requires, insert appropriate clip art or an image of your own. If requested by your instructor, insert a personal event in the calendar.

Invitation information: Congratulations Jeremy Winters!; Retirement Party!; Saturday, November 26, 2:00 to 6:00 p.m.; Reimer's Restaurant, 10 Chestnut Street, Mitcheltown, DE 19722; Come hungry!; Send a photo of you and Jeremy to mwinters@earth.link by November 20 for the slide show!; Hope you can join us!

If the template requires, insert appropriate clip art or an image of your own. If requested by your instructor, use your name and contact information instead of the information listed here.

Part 2:   ✺ You made several decisions while creating the calendar and invitation in this assignment: which template to use, where to position elements, how to format elements, which graphic(s) to use, in which format to save the documents for electronic distribution, which document to create as a webpage, and how to format the webpage. What was the rationale behind each of these decisions?

6 | Generating Form Letters, Mailing Labels, and a Directory

Objectives

You will have mastered the material in this module when you can:

- Explain the merge process
- Use the Mail Merge task pane and the Mailings tab on the ribbon
- Use a letter template as the main document for a mail merge
- Create and edit a data source
- Insert merge fields in a main document
- Use an IF field in a main document
- Merge form letters

- Select records to merge
- Sort data records
- Address and print mailing labels and envelopes
- Change page orientation
- Merge all data records to a directory
- Convert text to a table

Introduction

People are more likely to open and read a personalized letter than a letter addressed as Dear Sir, Dear Madam, or To Whom It May Concern. Creating individual personalized letters, though, can be a time-consuming task. Thus, Word provides the capability of creating a form letter, which is an easy way to generate mass mailings of personalized letters. The basic content of a group of form letters is similar. Items such as name and address, however, vary from one letter to the next. With Word, you easily can address and print mailing labels or envelopes for the form letters.

Project — Form Letters, Mailing Labels, and a Directory

Both businesses and individuals regularly use form letters to communicate with groups of people via the postal service or email. Types of form letter correspondence include announcements of sales to customers, notices of benefits to employees, invitations to the public to participate in a sweepstakes giveaway, and job application letters to potential employers.

The project in this module follows generally accepted guidelines for writing form letters and uses Word to create the form letters shown in Figure 6–1. The form letters inform potential employers of your interest in a job opening at their organization. Each form letter states the potential employer's name and address, available job position, and whether the job is at a radio or television station.

To generate form letters, such as the ones shown in Figure 6–1, you create a main document for the form letter (Figure 6–1a), create or specify a data source (Figure 6–1b), and then **merge**, or blend, the main document with the data source to generate a series of individual letters (Figure 6–1c). In Figure 6–1a, the main document represents the portion of the form letter that is repeated from one merged letter to the next. In Figure 6–1b, the data source contains the individual's and organization's name and address, available position, and type of broadcast station for various potential employers. To personalize each letter, you merge the potential employer data in the data source with the main document for the form letter, which generates or prints an individual letter for each potential employer listed in the data source.

Word provides two methods of merging documents: the Mail Merge task pane and the Mailings tab on the ribbon. The Mail Merge task pane displays a wizard, which is a step-by-step progression that guides you through the merging process. The Mailings tab provides buttons and boxes you use to merge documents. This module illustrates both techniques.

In this module, you will learn how to create the form letters shown in Figure 6–1. The following roadmap identifies general activities you will perform as you progress through this module:

1. IDENTIFY the MAIN DOCUMENT for the form letters.

2. CREATE a DATA SOURCE.

3. COMPOSE the MAIN DOCUMENT for the form letters.

4. MERGE the DATA SOURCE with the main document.

5. ADDRESS the MAILING LABELS.

6. MERGE all data records TO a DIRECTORY.

To Run Word and Change Word Settings

If you are using a computer to step through the project in this module and you want your screens to match the figures in this book, you should change your screen's resolution to 1366 × 768. The following steps run Word, display formatting marks, and change the zoom to page width.

1 Run Word and create a blank document in the Word window. If necessary, maximize the Word window.

2 If the Print Layout button on the status bar is not selected, click it so that your screen is in Print Layout view.

(a) Main Document for the Form Letter

(b) Data Source

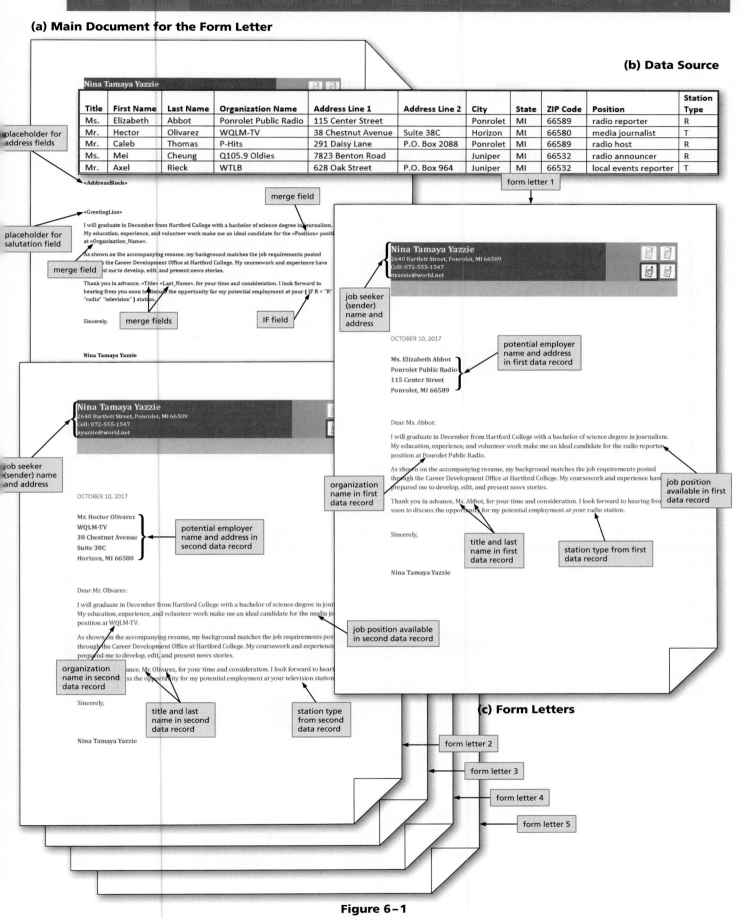

placeholder for address fields

placeholder for salutation field

merge field

merge field

merge fields

IF field

Title	First Name	Last Name	Organization Name	Address Line 1	Address Line 2	City	State	ZIP Code	Position	Station Type
Ms.	Elizabeth	Abbot	Ponrolet Public Radio	115 Center Street		Ponrolet	MI	66589	radio reporter	R
Mr.	Hector	Olivarez	WQLM-TV	38 Chestnut Avenue	Suite 38C	Horizon	MI	66580	media journalist	T
Mr.	Caleb	Thomas	P-Hits	291 Daisy Lane	P.O. Box 2088	Ponrolet	MI	66589	radio host	R
Ms.	Mei	Cheung	Q105.9 Oldies	7823 Benton Road		Juniper	MI	66532	radio announcer	R
Mr.	Axel	Rieck	WTLB	628 Oak Street	P.O. Box 964	Juniper	MI	66532	local events reporter	T

form letter 1

job seeker (sender) name and address

potential employer name and address in first data record

organization name in first data record

job position available in first data record

title and last name in first data record

station type from first data record

(c) Form Letters

job seeker (sender) name and address

potential employer name and address in second data record

job position available in second data record

organization name in second data record

title and last name in second data record

station type from second data record

form letter 2

form letter 3

form letter 4

form letter 5

Figure 6–1

3 If the 'Show/Hide ¶' button (Home tab | Paragraph group) is not selected already, click it to display formatting marks on the screen.

4 To display the page the same width as the document window, if necessary, click the Page Width button (View tab | Zoom group).

Identifying the Main Document for Form Letters

The first step in the mail merge process is to identify the type of document you are creating for the main document. Typical installations of Word support five types of main documents: letters, email messages, envelopes, labels, and a directory. In this section of the module, you create letters as the main document. Later in this module, you will specify labels and a directory as the main document.

CONSIDER THIS

How should you create the letter for the main document?

When creating form letters, you either can type the letter for the main document from scratch in a blank document window or use a letter template. If you enter the contents of the main document from scratch, you can compose it according to the block, modified block, or semi-block letter style, formatted appropriately with business letter spacing. Alternatively, you can use a letter template to save time because Word prepares a letter with text and/or formatting common to all letters. Then, you customize the resulting letter by selecting and replacing prewritten text.

To Identify the Main Document for the Form Letter Using the Mail Merge Task Pane

1 IDENTIFY MAIN DOCUMENT | 2 CREATE DATA SOURCE | 3 COMPOSE MAIN DOCUMENT
4 MERGE DATA SOURCE | 5 ADDRESS MAILING LABELS | 6 MERGE TO DIRECTORY

This module uses a template for the main document for the form letter, where you select predefined content controls and placeholder text and replace them with personalized content, adjusting formats as necessary. *Why? You use the same style that you used with the resume in the previous module so that the two documents complement one another.* The following steps use the Mail Merge task pane to identify the Timeless letter template as the main document for a form letter.

1

- Click Mailings on the ribbon to display the Mailings tab.

- Click the 'Start Mail Merge' button (Mailings tab | Start Mail Merge group) to display the Start Mail Merge menu (Figure 6–2).

What is the function of the E-mail Messages command?

Instead of sending individual letters, you can send individual email messages using email addresses in the data source or using a Microsoft Outlook Contacts list.

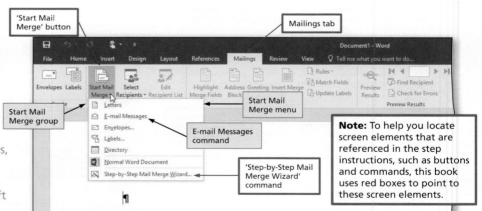

Figure 6–2

2

- Click 'Step-by-Step Mail Merge Wizard' on the Start Mail Merge menu to display Step 1 of the Mail Merge wizard in the Mail Merge task pane (Figure 6–3).

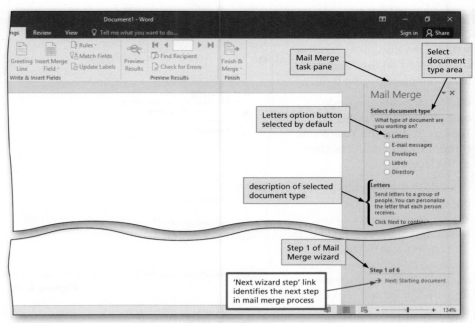

Figure 6–3

3

- Click the 'Next wizard step' link at the bottom of the Mail Merge task pane to display Step 2 of the Mail Merge wizard, which requests you select a starting document.

- Click 'Start from a template' in the Select starting document area and then click the 'Select mail merge template' link to display the Select Template dialog box.

Q&A Why does the link name in the step differ from the name displayed in the Mail Merge task pane?

As with buttons and boxes, the text that appears on the screen may vary, depending on your screen resolution. The name that appears in the ScreenTip (when you point to the link), however, never changes. For this reason, this book uses the name that appears in the ScreenTip to identify links, buttons, boxes, and other on-screen elements.

- Click the Letters tab (Select Template dialog box) to display the Letters sheet and then click Timeless letter, which shows a preview of the selected template in the Preview area (Figure 6–4).

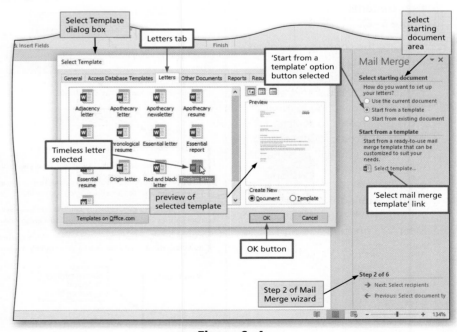

Figure 6–4

Experiment

- Click various Letter templates in the Letters sheet and watch the preview change in the right pane of the dialog box. When you are finished experimenting, click the Timeless letter template to select it.

Q&A What if I cannot locate the Timeless letter template?

Skip the remainder of these steps and proceed to the steps called To Start a Mail Merge from an Existing Document that are shaded yellow, which immediately follow this set of steps.

4

- Click the OK button to display a letter in the document window that is based on the Timeless letter template (Figure 6–5).

- If necessary, click the Undo button on the Quick Access Toolbar to reset the Your Name content control at the bottom of the letter.

Q&A
Can I close the Mail Merge task pane?
Yes, you can close the Mail Merge task pane at any time by clicking its Close button. When you want to continue with the merge process, you repeat these steps and Word will resume the merge process at the correct step in the Mail Merge wizard.

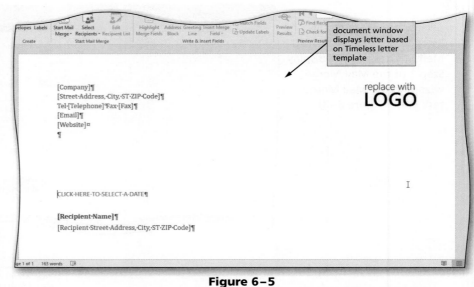

Figure 6–5

5

- Print the document shown on the screen so that you easily can see the entire letter contents (Figure 6–6).

Q&A
What are the content controls in the document?
Recall that a content control contains placeholder text and instructions for filling in areas of the document. To select a content control, click it. Later in this module, you will personalize the placeholder text and content controls. You also will remove the content controls as you are finished adding text to them.

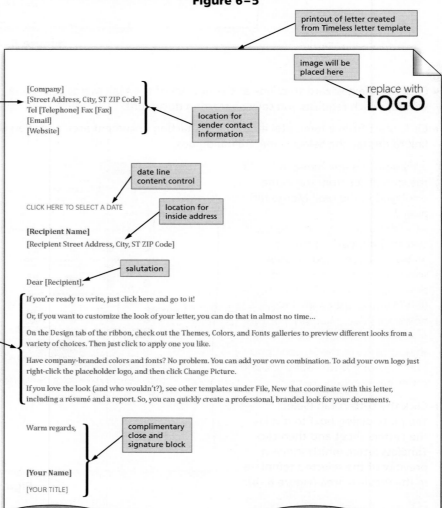

Figure 6–6

Other Ways

1. Open Backstage view, click New tab, type `letters` in 'Search for online templates' box, click Start searching button, click desired letter template, click Create button

To Start a Mail Merge from an Existing Document

If you are unable to locate the Timeless letter template in the previous steps or if your template differs from the one shown in Figure 6–6, you can open the template from the Data Files. Please contact your instructor for information about accessing the Data Files. The following steps open a document. NOTE: PERFORM THE STEPS IN THIS YELLOW BOX ONLY IF YOU WERE UNABLE TO LOCATE THE TIMELESS LETTER TEMPLATE IN THE PREVIOUS STEPS.

1 Click the 'Start from existing document' option button in the Mail Merge task pane to display options for opening a document in the task pane.

2 Click the Open button that appears in the Mail Merge task pane to display the Open dialog box.

3 Navigate to the location of the Timeless letter file to be opened. Click the Timeless letter file to select it.

4 Click the Open button (Open dialog box) to open the selected file.

TO CHANGE THE USER NAME AND INITIALS

If you wanted to change the user name and initials associated with your copy of Microsoft Word, you would perform the following steps.

1. Open the Backstage view and then click the Options tab to display the Word Options dialog box.

2. If necessary, click General in the left pane (Word Options dialog box).

3. Enter your name in the User name text box.

4. Enter your initials in the Initials text box.

5. Click the OK button.

To Change Theme Colors

Recall that Word provides document themes, which contain a variety of color schemes and other effects. This cover letter uses the Aspect theme colors to match the theme colors used in the resume. The following steps change the theme colors.

1 Click Design on the ribbon to display the Design tab.

2 Click the Theme Colors button (Design tab | Document Formatting group) to display the Theme Colors gallery.

3 Scroll to and then click Aspect in the Theme Colors gallery to change the theme colors to the selected theme.

To Enter and Format the Sender Information

The next step is to enter the sender's contact information at the top of the letter. You will use the [Company] placeholder text for the sender's name. You will delete the [Fax] and [Website] placeholder text because this sender does not have a fax or website.

Then, you will change the font size of the text. The following steps enter and format the sender information.

1 Select the placeholder text, [Company], and then type **Nina Tamaya Yazzie** as the sender name.

If requested by your instructor, enter your name instead of the job seeker's name.

2 Select the placeholder text, [Street Address, City, ST ZIP Code], and then type **2640 Bartlett Street, Ponrolet, MI 66589** as the sender's address.

3 Select the text, Tel, and then type **Cell:** as the label. Select the placeholder text, [Telephone], and then type **872-555-1547** as the sender's cell phone number.

4 Delete the Fax label and [Fax] placeholder text.

5 Select the placeholder text, [Email], and then type **nyazzie@world.net** as the sender's email address.

6 Delete the [Website] placeholder text and then press the BACKSPACE key to delete the blank line.

7 Increase the font size of the name to 14 point, and decrease the font size of the street address, cell phone, and email address to 9 point.

8 Select the name and all contact information. Bold the text (shown in Figure 6–7).

BTW
The Ribbon and Screen Resolution
Word may change how the groups and buttons within the groups appear on the ribbon, depending on the computer or mobile device's screen resolution. Thus, your ribbon may look different from the ones in this book if you are using a screen resolution other than 1366 × 768.

To Change a Picture and Format It

The current picture in the letter contains the text, replace with LOGO, which is a placeholder for a picture. The following steps change a picture.

1 Right-click the picture to be changed (in this case, the picture placeholder with the text, replace with LOGO) to display a shortcut menu (Figure 6–7).

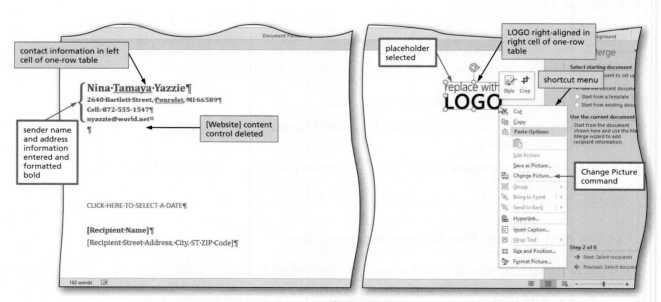

Figure 6–7

2 Click Change Picture on the shortcut menu to display the Insert Pictures dialog box.

Q&A Can I use the Change Picture button (Picture Tools Format tab | Adjust group) instead of the shortcut menu to display the Insert Pictures dialog box?
Yes.

3 Type **notepad** in the Search box (Insert Pictures dialog box) and then click the Search button to display a list of images that matches the entered search text.

4 Scroll through the list of images to locate the one shown in Figure 6–8 (or a similar image), click the image to select it, and then click the Insert button (Insert Picture dialog box) to download the image, close the dialog box, and replace the selected placeholder with the new picture file (shown in Figure 6–8).

Q&A What if I cannot locate the same image?
Click the Cancel button and then click the From File button (Insert tab | Illustrations group), navigate to the Notepad-Icons-2400px.png file on the Data Files, and then click the Insert button (Insert Picture dialog box) to insert the picture.

5 Use the Shape Height and Shape Width boxes (Picture Tools Format tab | Size group) to change the picture height to approximately .8" and width to .79".

To Shade Cells and a Shape

In the letter in this module, the left and right cells of the table containing the contact information and picture are shaded different colors. These two cells are contained in a rectangular shape, which extends below these two cells. By shading the cells in the table and the rectangular shape each a separate color, you create a letterhead with three different colors. The following steps shade table cells and a shape.

1 Position the insertion point in the contact information (upper-left cell of table). Display the Table Tools Layout tab and then, if necessary, click the 'View Table Gridlines' button (Table Tools Layout tab | Table group) to show table gridlines.

Q&A Why show table gridlines?
With table gridlines showing, the cells are easier to see.

2 Display the Table Tools Design tab. With the insertion point in the left cell, click the Shading arrow (Table Tools Design tab | Table Styles group) and then click 'Orange, Accent 1, Darker 25%' (fifth color, fifth row) to shade the current cell with the selected color.

3 Select the contact information in the left cell and change its font color to 'White, Background 1' (first color, first row).

4 Position the insertion point in the cell with the picture, click the Shading arrow (Table Tools Design tab | Table Styles group) and then click 'Tan, Background 2, Darker 25%' (third color, third row) to shade the current cell with the selected color.

5 Position the insertion point on the paragraph mark below the shaded cell to select the rectangle drawing object. Display the Drawing Tools Format tab. Click the Shape Fill arrow (Drawing Tools Format tab | Shape Styles group) to display the Shape Fill gallery (Figure 6–8) and then click 'Orange, Accent 1, Lighter 40%' (fifth color, fourth row) to shade the selected shape with the selected color.

6 Hide table gridlines.

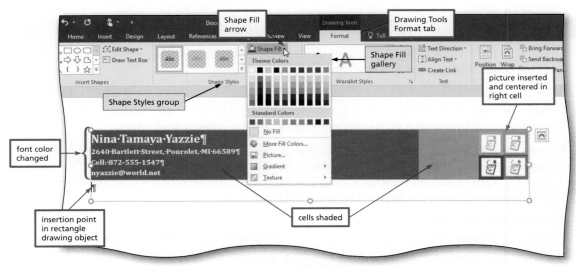

Figure 6–8

To Change Margin Settings

The Timeless letter template uses 1.9-inch top and .75-inch bottom, left, and right margins. You want the form letter to use 1-inch top and bottom margins and 1.25-inch left and right margins. The following steps change the margin settings.

1 Click the Date content control to deselect the drawing object.

2 Display the Layout tab. Click the Adjust Margins button (Layout tab | Page Setup group) to display the Margins gallery and then click Custom Margins at the bottom of the gallery to display the Page Setup dialog box.

3 Change the values in the Top, Bottom, Left, and Right boxes (Page Setup dialog box) to 1", 1", 1.25", and 1.25", respectively (Figure 6–9).

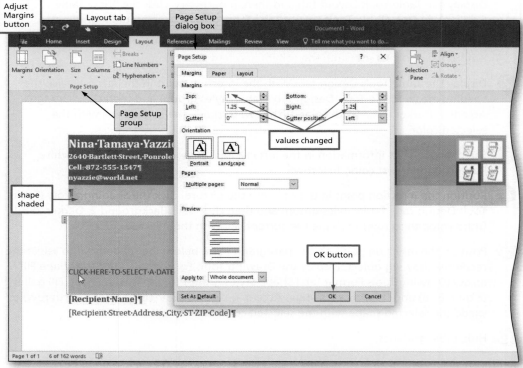

Figure 6–9

④ Click the OK button to change the margin values.

Q&A Why is the top margin unchanged?
The template specifies that the rectangle shape be positioned a certain distance from the top of the page, regardless of margin settings. The next steps change the position of the shape.

To Specify the Position of a Graphic

1 IDENTIFY MAIN DOCUMENT | **2 CREATE DATA SOURCE** | **3 COMPOSE MAIN DOCUMENT**
4 MERGE DATA SOURCE | **5 ADDRESS MAILING LABELS** | **6 MERGE TO DIRECTORY**

The next step is to change the distance between the shape and the top of the page. *Why? You want a one-inch space above the shape.* The following steps specify the position of a graphic.

①

• Click the rectangle shape to select it.

• Click the Layout Options button attached to the shape to display the Layout Options gallery (Figure 6–10).

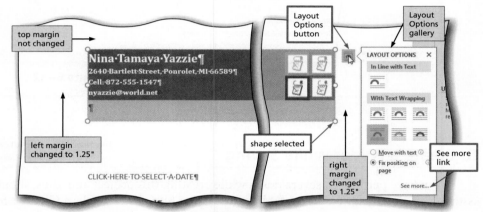

Figure 6–10

②

• Click the See more link (Layout Options gallery) to display the Position tab in the Layout dialog box.

• Click Absolute position in the Vertical area (Layout dialog box), select the value in the Absolute position box, and then type 1 to specify the distance in inches from the top of the page.

• If necessary, click the below arrow and select Page (Figure 6–11).

Q&A What is the difference between the specifications in the Horizontal and Vertical areas? Horizontal settings specify the graphic's position left to right on the page, whereas vertical settings specify the graphic's position top to bottom on the page.

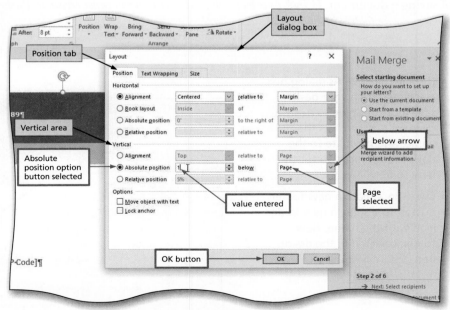

Figure 6–11

• Click the OK button to change the position of the selected graphic (Figure 6–12).

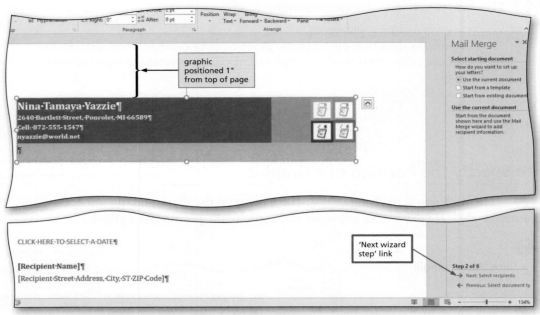

Figure 6–12

To Create a Folder while Saving

1 IDENTIFY MAIN DOCUMENT | 2 CREATE DATA SOURCE | 3 COMPOSE MAIN DOCUMENT | 4 MERGE DATA SOURCE | 5 ADDRESS MAILING LABELS | 6 MERGE TO DIRECTORY

You have performed several tasks while creating this project and, thus, should save it. The following steps assume you already have created folders for storing files, for example, a CIS 101 folder (for your class) that contains a Word folder and module folders. You want to save this and all other documents created in this module in a folder called Job Hunting folder in the Word folder. The following steps create a folder during the process of saving a document. *Why? This folder does not exist, so you must create it. Rather than creating the folder in Windows, you can create folders in Word.*

• Display the Save As dialog box associated with your desired save location, type **Yazzie Cover Letter** as the file name, and navigate to the desired save location for the new folder.

• Click the 'Create a new folder' button to display a new folder icon with the name, New folder, selected in the dialog box (Figure 6–13).

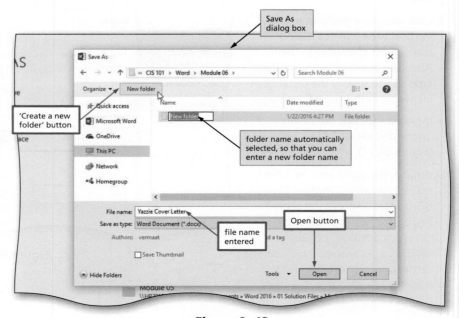

Figure 6–13

2

- Type **Job Hunting** as the new folder name and then press the ENTER key to create the new folder.

- Click the Open button to open the selected folder, in this case, the Job Hunting folder (Figure 6–14).

3

- Click the Save button (Save As dialog box) to save the current document in the selected folder on the selected drive.

Q&A Can I create a folder in any other dialog box?
Yes. Any dialog box that displays a File list, such as the Open and Insert File dialog boxes, also has the 'Create a new folder' button, allowing you to create a new folder in Word instead of using Windows for this task.

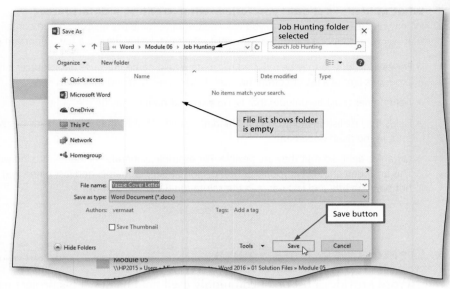

Figure 6–14

Creating a Data Source

The **data source** is a file that contains the variable, or changing, values from one merged document to the next. A data source can be an Access database table, an Outlook contacts list, or an Excel worksheet. If the necessary and properly organized data already exists in one of these Office programs, you can instruct Word to use the existing file as the data source for the mail merge. Otherwise, you can create a new data source using one of these programs.

As shown in Figure 6–15, a data source often is shown as a table that consists of a series of rows and columns. Each row is called a **record**. The first row of a data source is called the **header record** because it identifies the name of each column. Each row below the header row is called a data record. A **data record** contains the text that varies in each occurrence of the merged document. The data source for the project in this module contains five data records. In this project, each data record identifies a different potential employer. Thus, five form letters will be generated from this data source.

Each column in the data source is called a **data field**. A data field represents a group of similar data. Each data field must be identified uniquely with a name, called a **field name**. For example, Position is the name of the data field (column) that contains the available job position. In this module, the data source contains 11 data fields with the following field names: Title, First Name, Last Name, Organization Name, Address Line 1, Address Line 2, City, State, ZIP Code, Position, and Station Type.

BTW
Fields and Records
Field and record are terms that originate from the software development field. Do not be intimidated by these terms. A field is simply a column in a table, and a record is a row. Instead of as a field, some software developers identify a column of data as a variable or an attribute. All three terms (field, variable, and attribute) have the same meaning.

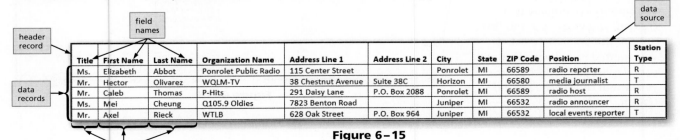

Title	First Name	Last Name	Organization Name	Address Line 1	Address Line 2	City	State	ZIP Code	Position	Station Type
Ms.	Elizabeth	Abbot	Ponrolet Public Radio	115 Center Street		Ponrolet	MI	66589	radio reporter	R
Mr.	Hector	Olivarez	WQLM-TV	38 Chestnut Avenue	Suite 38C	Horizon	MI	66580	media journalist	T
Mr.	Caleb	Thomas	P-Hits	291 Daisy Lane	P.O. Box 2088	Ponrolet	MI	66589	radio host	R
Ms.	Mei	Cheung	Q105.9 Oldies	7823 Benton Road		Juniper	MI	66532	radio announcer	R
Mr.	Axel	Rieck	WTLB	628 Oak Street	P.O. Box 964	Juniper	MI	66532	local events reporter	T

Figure 6–15

What guidelines should you follow when creating a data source?

When you create a data source, you will need to determine the fields it should contain. That is, you will need to identify the data that will vary from one merged document to the next. Following are a few important points about fields:

• For each field, you may be required to create a field name. Because data sources often contain the same fields, some programs create a list of commonly used field names that you may use.

• Field names must be unique; that is, no two field names may be the same.

• Fields may be listed in any order in the data source. That is, the order of fields has no effect on the order in which they will print in the main document.

• Organize fields so that they are flexible. For example, separate the name into individual fields: title, first name, and last name. This arrangement allows you to print a person's title, first name, and last name (e.g., Ms. Elizabeth Abbot) in the inside address but only the title and last name in the salutation (Dear Ms. Abbot).

To Create a New Data Source

1 IDENTIFY MAIN DOCUMENT | 2 CREATE DATA SOURCE | 3 COMPOSE MAIN DOCUMENT
4 MERGE DATA SOURCE | 5 ADDRESS MAILING LABELS | 6 MERGE TO DIRECTORY

Word provides a list of 13 commonly used field names. This project uses 9 of the 13 field names supplied by Word: Title, First Name, Last Name, Company Name, Address Line 1, Address Line 2, City, State, and ZIP Code. This project does not use the other four field names supplied by Word: Country or Region, Home Phone, Work Phone, and E-mail Address. Thus, you will delete these four field names. Then, you will change the Company Name field name to Organization Name. *Why? The term, organization, better describes the potential employers in this project.* You also will add two new field names (Position and Station Type) to the data source. *Why? You want to reference the available position, as well as the station type, in the form letter.* The next steps create a new data source for a mail merge.

1

• Click the 'Next wizard step' link at the bottom of the Mail Merge task pane (shown in Figure 6–12) to display Step 3 of the Mail Merge wizard, which requests you select recipients.

• Click 'Type a new list' in the Select recipients area, which displays the Type a new list area.

• Click the 'Create new recipient list' link to display the New Address List dialog box (Figure 6–16).

Q&A

When would I use the other two option buttons in the Select recipients area?

If a data source already was created, you would use the first option: Use an existing list. If you wanted to use your Outlook contacts list as the data source, you would choose the second option.

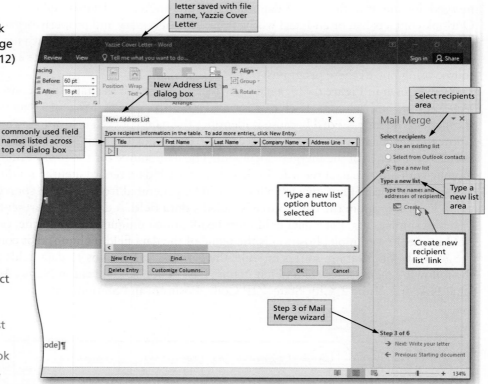

Figure 6–16

2

- Click the Customize Columns button (New Address List dialog box) to display the Customize Address List dialog box (Figure 6–17).

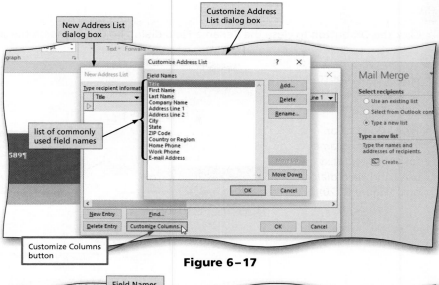

Figure 6–17

3

- Click 'Country or Region' in the Field Names list (Customize Address List dialog box) to select the field to be deleted and then click the Delete button to display a dialog box asking if you are sure you want to delete the selected field (Figure 6–18).

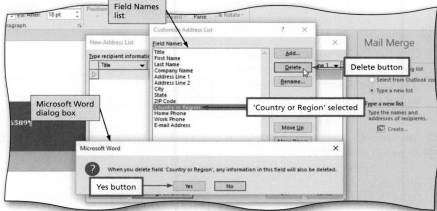

Figure 6–18

4

- Click the Yes button (Microsoft Word dialog box) to delete the field.

- Click Home Phone in the Field Names list to select the field. Click the Delete button (Customize Address List dialog box) and then click the Yes button (Microsoft Word dialog box) to delete the field.

- Use this same procedure to delete the Work Phone and E-mail Address fields.

5

- Click Company Name in the Field Names list to select the field to be renamed.

- Click the Rename button to display the Rename Field dialog box.

- Type **Organization Name** in the To text box (Rename Field dialog box) (Figure 6–19).

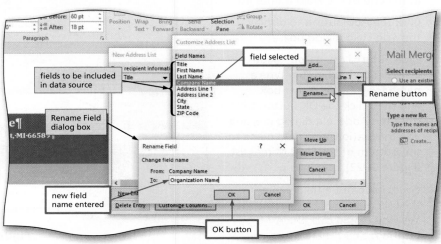

Figure 6–19

6

- Click the OK button to close the Rename Field dialog box and rename the selected field.

7

- Click the Add button to display the Add Field dialog box.

- Type **Position** in the 'Type a name for your field' text box (Add Field dialog box) (Figure 6–20).

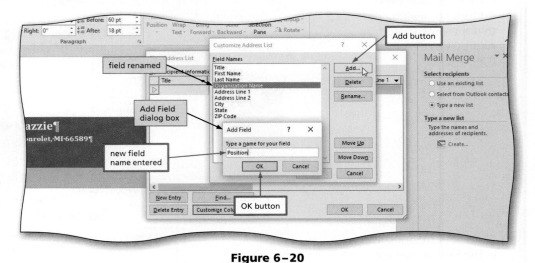

Figure 6–20

8

- Click the OK button to close the Add Field dialog box and add the Position field name to the Field Names list immediately below the selected field (Figure 6–21).

Q&A Can I change the order of the field names in the Field Names list?
Yes. Select the field name and then click the Move Up or Move Down button (Customize Address List dialog box) to move the selected field in the direction of the button name.

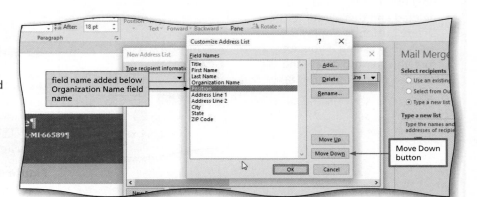

Figure 6–21

9

- With the Position field selected, click the Move Down button five times to position the selected field at the end of the Field Names list.

- Click the Add button to display the Add Field dialog box.

- Type **Station Type** (Add Field dialog box) in the 'Type a name for your field' text box and then click the OK button to close the Add Field dialog box and add the Station Type field name to the bottom of the Field Names list (Figure 6–22).

Q&A Could I add more field names to the list?
Yes. You would click the Add button for each field name you want to add.

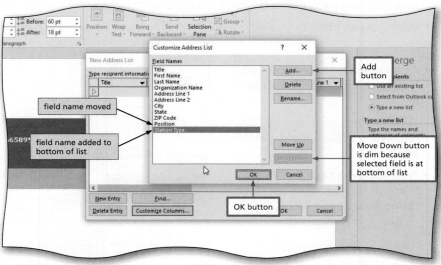

Figure 6–22

- Click the OK button to close the Customize Address List dialog box, which positions the insertion point in the Title text box for the first record (row) in the New Address List dialog box (Figure 6–23).

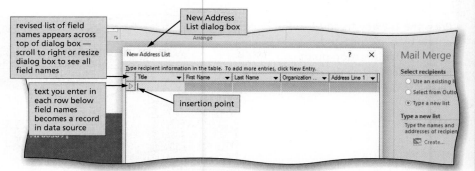

Figure 6–23

- Type **Ms.** and then press the TAB key to enter the title for the first data record.

- Type **Elizabeth** and then press the TAB key to enter the first name.

- Type **Abbot** and then press the TAB key to enter the last name.

- Type **Ponrolet Public Radio** and then press the TAB key to enter the organization name.

- Type **115 Center Street** to enter the first address line (Figure 6–24).

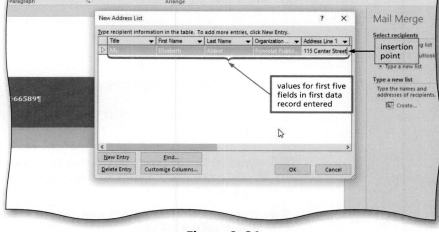

Figure 6–24

Q&A What if I notice an error in an entry?

Click the entry and then correct the error as you would in the document window.

What happened to the rest of the Organization Name entry?

It is stored in the field, but you cannot see the entire entry because it is longer than the display area.

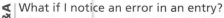

- Press the TAB key twice to leave the second address line empty.

- Type **Ponrolet** and then press the TAB key to enter the city.

- Type **MI** and then press the TAB key to enter the state code.

- Type **66589** and then press the TAB key to enter the ZIP code.

- Type **radio reporter** and then press the TAB key to enter the position.

- Type **R** to enter the code for the station type (Figure 6–25).

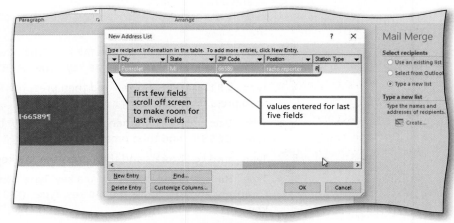

Figure 6–25

Q&A What does the R mean in the station type?

You decide to enter R for radio station and T for television station to minimize the amount of redundant typing for these records.

- Press the TAB key to add a new blank record and position the insertion point in the Title field of the new record (Figure 6–26).

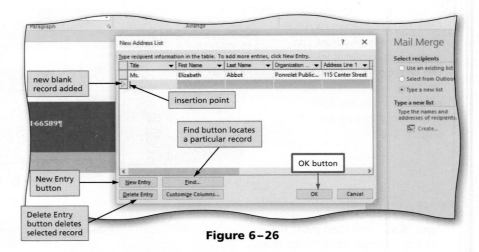

Figure 6–26

Other Ways

1. Click Select Recipients button (Mailings tab | Start Mail Merge group)

To Enter More Records

The following steps enter the remaining four records in the New Address List dialog box.

1 Type **Mr.** and then press the TAB key. Type **Hector** and then press the TAB key. Type **Olivarez** and then press the TAB key. Type **WQLM-TV** and then press the TAB key.

2 Type **38 Chestnut Avenue** and then press the TAB key. Type **Suite 38C** and then press the TAB key.

3 Type **Horizon** and then press the TAB key. Type **MI** and then press the TAB key. Type **66580** and then press the TAB key.

4 Type **media journalist** and then press the TAB key. Type **T** and then press the TAB key.

Q&A Instead of pressing the TAB key, can I click the New Entry button at the end of one row to add a new blank record?

Yes. Clicking the New Entry button at the end of a row has the same effect as pressing the TAB key.

5 Type **Mr.** and then press the TAB key. Type **Caleb** and then press the TAB key. Type **Thomas** and then press the TAB key. Type **P-Hits** and then press the TAB key.

6 Type **291 Daisy Lane** and then press the TAB key. Type **P.O. Box 2088** and then press the TAB key.

7 Type **Ponrolet** and then press the TAB key. Type **MI** and then press the TAB key. Type **66589** and then press the TAB key.

8 Type **radio host** and then press the TAB key. Type **R** and then press the TAB key.

9 Type **Ms.** and then press the TAB key. Type **Mei** and then press the TAB key. Type **Cheung** and then press the TAB key. Type **Q105.9 Oldies** and then press the TAB key.

10 Type **7823 Benton Road** and then press the TAB key twice. Type **Juniper** and then press the TAB key. Type **MI** and then press the TAB key. Type **66532** and then press the TAB key.

11 Type **radio announcer** and then press the TAB key. Type **R** and then press the TAB key.

Type **Mr.** and then press the TAB key. Type **Axel** and then press the TAB key. Type **Rieck** and then press the TAB key. Type **WTLB** and then press the TAB key.

⑬ Type **628 Oak Street** and then press the TAB key. Type **P.O. Box 694** and then press the TAB key.

⑭ Type **Juniper** and then press the TAB key. Type **MI** and then press the TAB key. Type **66532** and then press the TAB key.

⑮ Type **local events reporter** and then press the TAB key. Type **T** and then click the OK button (shown in Figure 6–26), which displays the Save Address List dialog box (shown in Figure 6–27).

BTW

Saving Data Sources
Word, by default, saves a data source in the My Data Sources folder on your computer or mobile device's default storage location. Likewise, when you open a data source, Word initially looks in the My Data Sources folder for the file. Because the data source files you create in Word are saved as Microsoft Access database file types, you can open and view these files in Access if you are familiar with Microsoft Access.

To Save a Data Source when Prompted by Word

1 IDENTIFY MAIN DOCUMENT | 2 **CREATE DATA SOURCE** | 3 COMPOSE MAIN DOCUMENT
4 MERGE DATA SOURCE | 5 ADDRESS MAILING LABELS | 6 MERGE TO DIRECTORY

When you click the OK button in the New Address List dialog box, Word displays the Save Address List dialog box. *Why? You immediately save the data source so that you do not lose any entered information.* By default, the save location is the My Data Sources folder on your computer's hard drive. In this module, you save the data source to the Job Hunting folder created earlier in this module. The following steps save the data source.

1

- Type **Yazzie Prospective Employers** in the File name box (Save Address List dialog box) as the name for the data source. Do not press the ENTER key after typing the file name because you do not want to close the dialog box at this time.

- Navigate to the desired save location for the data source (for example, the Job Hunting folder) (Figure 6–27).

Q&A What is a Microsoft Office Address Lists file type?
It is a Microsoft Access database file. If you are familiar with Microsoft Access, you can open the Yazzie Prospective Employers file in Access. You do not have to be familiar with Access or have

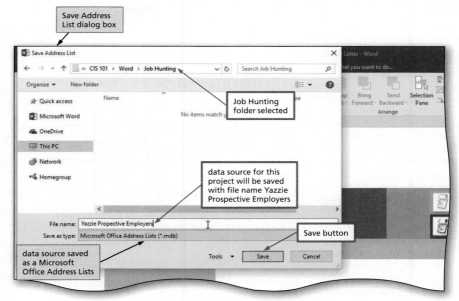

Figure 6–27

Access installed on your computer, however, to continue with this mail merge process. Word simply stores a data source as an Access table because it is an efficient method of storing a data source.

2

- Click the Save button (Save Address List dialog box) to save the data source in the selected folder using the entered file name and then display the Mail Merge Recipients dialog box (Figure 6–28).

Q&A What if the fields in my Mail Merge Recipients list are in a different order?
The order of fields in the Mail Merge Recipients list has no effect on the mail merge process. If Word rearranges the order, you can leave them in the revised order.

3

- Click the OK button to close the Mail Merge Recipients dialog box.

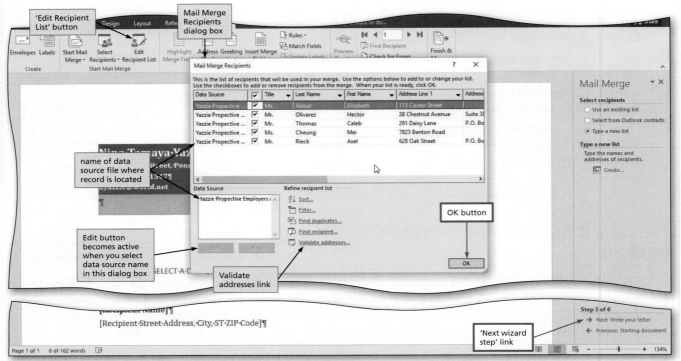

Figure 6–28

BTW
Validating Addresses
If you have installed address validation software, you can click the Validate addresses link (shown in Figure 6–28) in the Mail Merge Recipients dialog box to validate your recipients' addresses. If you have not yet installed address validation software and would like information about doing so, click the Validate addresses link in the Mail Merge Recipients dialog box and then click the Yes button in the Microsoft Word dialog box to display a related Microsoft Office webpage.

Editing Records in the Data Source

All of the data records have been entered in the data source and saved with the file name, Yazzie Prospective Employers. To add or edit data records in the data source, you would click the 'Edit Recipient List' button (Mailings tab | Start Mail Merge group) to display the Mail Merge Recipients dialog box (shown in Figure 6–28). Click the data source name in the Data Source list and then click the Edit button (Mail Merge Recipients dialog box) to display the data records in a dialog box similar to the one shown in Figure 6–26. Then, add or edit records as described in the previous steps. If you want to edit a particular record and the list of data records is long, you can click the Find button to locate an item, such as a last name, quickly in the list.

To delete a record, select it using the same procedure described in the previous paragraph. Then, click the Delete Entry button in the dialog box (shown in Figure 6–26).

Using an Existing Data Source

Instead of creating a new data source, you can use an existing Microsoft Outlook Contacts list, an Access database table, or an Excel table as a data source in a mail merge. To use an existing data source, select the appropriate option in the Select recipients area in the Mail Merge task pane or click the Select Recipients button (Mailings tab | Start Mail Merge group) and then click the desired option on the Select Recipients menu.

For a Microsoft Outlook Contacts list, click 'Select from Outlook contacts' in the Mail Merge task pane or 'Choose from Outlook Contacts' on the Select Recipients menu to display the Select Contacts dialog box. Next, select the contact folder you wish to import (Select Contacts dialog box) and then click the OK button.

For other existing data source types, such as an Access database table or an Excel worksheet, click 'Use an existing list' in the Mail Merge task pane or on the Select Recipients menu to display the Select Data Source dialog box. Next, select the file name of the data source you wish to use and then click the Open button (Select Data Source dialog box).

With Access, you can use any field in the database in the main document. (Later in this module you use an existing Access database table as the data source.) For the merge to work correctly with an Excel table, you must ensure data is arranged properly and that the table is the only element in the file. The first row of the table should contain unique field names, and the table cannot contain any blank rows.

Composing the Main Document for the Form Letters

The next step in this project is to enter and format the text and fields in the main document for the form letters (shown in Figure 6–1a at the beginning of this module). A **main document** contains the constant, or unchanging, text, punctuation, spaces, and graphics, as well as references to the data in the data source. You will follow these steps to compose the main document for the form letter.

1. Enter the date.
2. Enter the address block.
3. Enter the greeting line (salutation).
4. Enter text and insert a merge field.
5. Enter additional text and merge fields.
6. Insert an IF field.
7. Enter the remainder of the letter.
8. Merge the letters.

CONSIDER THIS

What guidelines should you follow when composing the main document for a form letter?
The finished main document letter should look like a symmetrically framed picture with evenly spaced margins, all balanced below an attractive letterhead or return address. The content of the main document for the form letter should contain proper grammar, correct spelling, logically constructed sentences, flowing paragraphs, and sound ideas; it also should reference the data in the data source properly.

Be sure the main document for the form letter includes all essential business letter elements. All business letters should contain a date line, inside address, message, and signature block. Many business letters contain additional items, such as a special mailing notation(s), an attention line, a salutation, a subject line, a complimentary close, reference initials, and an enclosure notation. When finished, proofread your letter carefully.

To Display the Next Step in the Mail Merge Wizard

The following step displays the next step in the Mail Merge wizard, which is to write the letter.

1 Click the 'Next wizard step' link at the bottom of the Mail Merge task pane (shown in Figure 6–28) to display Step 4 of the Mail Merge wizard in the Mail Merge task pane (shown in Figure 6–29).

To Enter the Date

The next step is to enter the date in the letter. *Why? All business letters should contain a date, which usually is positioned below the letterhead or return address.* You can click the date content control and type the correct date, or you can click the arrow and select the date from a calendar. The following steps use the calendar to select the date.

❶

- Click the Date content control to select it and then click its arrow to display a calendar.

- Scroll through the calendar months until the desired month appears, October 2017, in this case (Figure 6–29).

❷

- Click 10 in the calendar to display the selected month, day, and year in the date line of the form letter (shown in Figure 6–30).

- Click outside the content control to deselect it.

- Right-click the date to display a shortcut menu and then click 'Remove Content Control' on the shortcut menu so that your text (the selected date) remains but the content control is deleted.

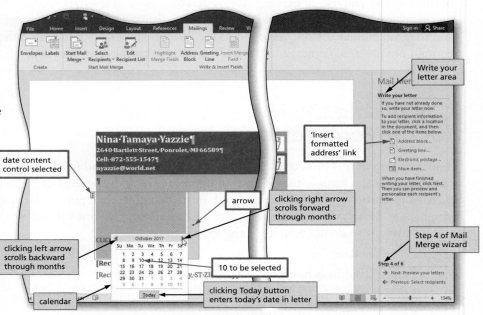

Figure 6–29

Q&A
Why delete the content control?
You no longer need the content control because you already selected the date.

Other Ways

1. Type date in Date content control	2. Click 'Insert Date & Time' button (Insert tab | Text group)

Merge Fields

In this form letter, the inside address appears below the date line, and the salutation is placed below the inside address. The contents of the inside address and salutation are located in the data source. To link the data source to the main document, you insert the field names from the data source in the main document.

In the main document, field names linked to the data source are called **merge fields** because they merge, or combine, the main document with the contents of the data source. When a merge field is inserted in the main document, Word surrounds the field name with **merge field characters**, which are chevrons (« ») that mark the beginning and ending of a merge field. Merge field characters are not on the keyboard; therefore, you cannot type them directly in the document. Word automatically displays them when a merge field is inserted in the main document.

Most letters contain an address and salutation. For this reason, Word provides an AddressBlock merge field and a GreetingLine merge field. The **AddressBlock merge field** contains several fields related to an address: Title, First Name, Middle Name, Last Name, Suffix, Company, Street Address 1, Street Address 2, City, State, and ZIP Code. When Word uses the AddressBlock merge field, it automatically looks for any fields in the associated data source that are related to an address and then formats the address block properly when you merge the data source with the main document. For example, if your inside address does not use a middle name, suffix, or company, Word omits these items from the inside address and adjusts the spacing so that the address prints correctly.

To Insert the AddressBlock Merge Field

1 IDENTIFY MAIN DOCUMENT | 2 CREATE DATA SOURCE | 3 COMPOSE MAIN DOCUMENT
4 MERGE DATA SOURCE | 5 ADDRESS MAILING LABELS | 6 MERGE TO DIRECTORY

The default format for the AddressBlock merge field is the first name and last name on one line, followed by the street address on the next line, and then the city, state, and postal code on the next line. In this letter, you want the potential employer's title (i.e., Ms.) to appear to the left of the first name. **Why?** *You want to address the potential employers formally.* You also want the organization name to appear above the street address, if it does not already. The following steps insert the AddressBlock merge field in this format.

1

- Delete the content control that contains placeholder text for the recipient's address and then press the DELETE key to delete the blank paragraph.

- Delete the [Recipient Name] placeholder text but leave the paragraph mark; position the insertion point to the left of the paragraph mark because you will insert the AddressBlock merge field in that location.

- Click the 'Insert formatted address' link in the Mail Merge task pane (shown in Figure 6–29) to display the Insert Address Block dialog box.

- Scroll through the list of recipient name formats (Insert Address Block dialog box) and then click the format 'Mr. Joshua Randall Jr.' in this list, because that format places the title to the left of the first name and last name.

Experiment

- Click various recipient name formats and watch the preview change in the dialog box. When finished experimenting, click 'Mr. Joshua Randall Jr.' for the format.

Q&A Why is the 'Insert company name' check box dimmed?
The data source does not have a match to the Company Name in the AddressBlock merge field so this check box will be dimmed. Recall that earlier in this project the Company Name field was renamed as Organization Name, which causes the fields to be unmatched. The next step shows how to match the fields. If the Organization Name already appears in your AddressBlock merge field, proceed to Step 4.

- Click the Match Fields button (Insert Address Block dialog box) to display the Match Fields dialog box (Figure 6–30).

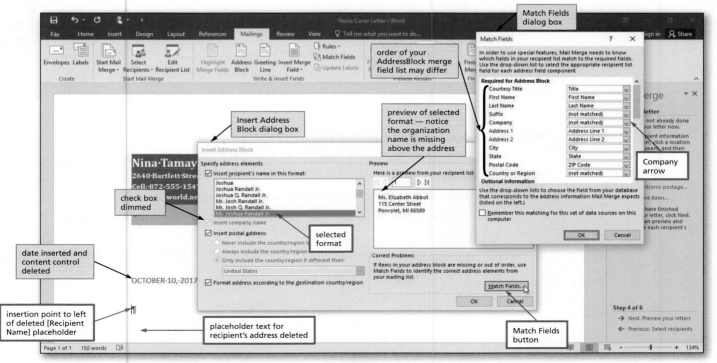

Figure 6–30

• Click the Company arrow (Match Fields dialog box) to display a list of fields in the data source and then click Organization Name to place that selected field as the match field (Figure 6–31).

• Click the OK button (Match Fields dialog box) to close the dialog box, and notice the 'Insert company name' check box no longer is dimmed (Insert Address Block dialog box) because the Company field now has a matched field in the data source.

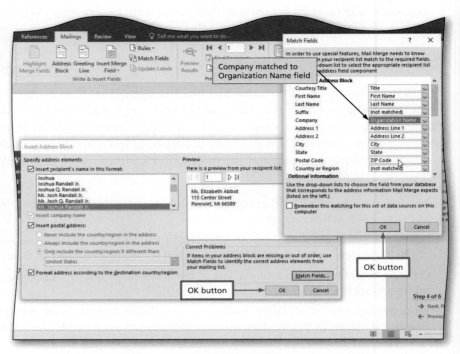

Figure 6–31

• Click the OK button (Insert Address Block dialog box) to insert the AddressBlock merge field at the location of the insertion point (Figure 6–32).

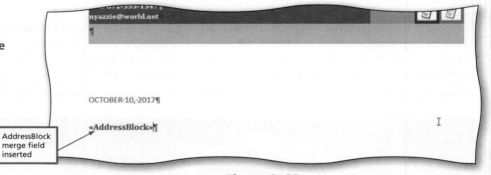

Figure 6–32

TO EDIT THE ADDRESSBLOCK MERGE FIELD

If you wanted to change the format of or match fields in the AddressBlock merge field, you would perform the following steps.

1. Right-click the AddressBlock merge field to display a shortcut menu.

2. Click 'Edit Address Block' on the shortcut menu to display the Modify Address Block dialog box.

3. Make necessary changes and then click the OK button (Modify Address Block dialog box).

To View Merged Data in the Main Document

Instead of displaying merge fields, you can display merged data. *Why? One way to see how fields, such as the AddressBlock fields, will look in the merged letter, is to view merged data.* The following step views merged data.

- Click the 'View Merged Data' button (Mailings tab | Preview Results group) to display the values in the current data record, instead of the merge fields.

- Scroll up, if necessary, to view the address fields (Figure 6–33).

Q&A How can I tell which record is showing?
The current record number is displayed in the Preview Results group.

Why is the spacing in my address different from Figure 6–33?
You may have inserted the AddressBlock field on the line in the template that contained the recipient's address, instead of the line that contained the recipient's name. To fix the address spacing, select the entire address and then change the spacing before and after to 2 pt (Layout tab | Paragraph group).

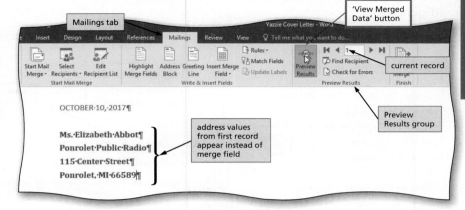

Figure 6–33

To Insert the GreetingLine Merge Field

The **GreetingLine merge field** contains text and fields related to a salutation. The default greeting for the salutation is in the format, Dear Elizabeth, followed by a comma. In this letter, you want the salutation to be followed by a colon. *Why? Business letters use a more formal salutation (Dear Ms. Abbot:) in the cover letter.* The following steps insert the GreetingLine merge field.

- Delete the word, Dear, the [Recipient] placeholder text, and the comma in the salutation but leave the paragraph mark; position the insertion point to the left of the paragraph mark because you will insert the GreetingLine merge field in that location.

- Click the 'Insert formatted salutation' link in the Mail Merge task pane to display the Insert Greeting Line dialog box.

- If necessary, click the middle arrow in the Greeting line format area (Insert Greeting Line dialog box); scroll to and then click the format, Mr. Randall, in this list because you want the title followed by the last name format.

- If necessary, click the rightmost arrow in the Greeting line format area and then click the colon (:) in the list (Figure 6–34).

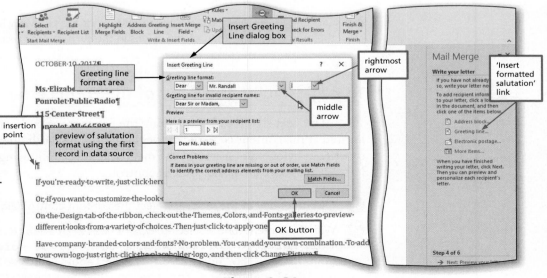

Figure 6–34

2

- Click the OK button (Insert Greeting Line dialog box) to insert the GreetingLine merge field at the location of the insertion point (Figure 6–35).

Q&A Why are the values for the title and last name displayed instead of the merge field names?
With the 'View Merged Data' button (Mailings tab | Preview Results group) still selected, the field values are displayed instead of the field names.

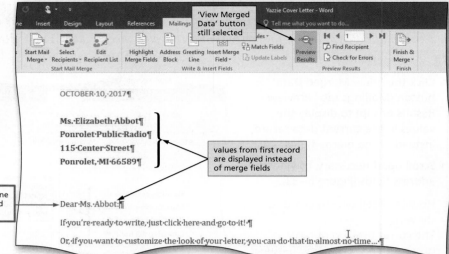

Figure 6–35

To Edit the GreetingLine Merge Field

If you wanted to change the format of or match fields in the GreetingLine merge field, you would perform the following steps.

1. Right-click the GreetingLine merge field to display a shortcut menu.
2. Click 'Edit Greeting Line' on the shortcut menu to display the Modify Greeting Line dialog box.
3. Make the necessary changes and then click the OK button (Modify Greeting Line dialog box).

To View Merge Fields in the Main Document

Because you will be entering merge fields in the document next, you wish to display the merge fields instead of the merged data. The following step views merge fields instead of merged data.

1 Click the 'View Merged Data' button (Mailings tab | Preview Results group) to display the merge fields instead of the values in the current data record (shown in Figure 6–36).

To Begin Typing the Body of the Form Letter

The next step is to begin typing the message, or body of the letter, which is located at the content control that begins with the placeholder text, If you're ready to write..., below the GreetingLine merge field. The following steps begin typing the letter at the location of the content control.

1 Click the body of the letter to select the content control (Figure 6–36).

2 With the content control selected, type **I will graduate in December from Hartford College with a bachelor of science degree in journalism. My education, experience, and volunteer work make me an ideal candidate for the** and then press the SPACEBAR (shown in Figure 6–37).

Q&A Why is the text, bachelor of science, in all lowercase letters?

This book uses the *Chicago Manual of Style* for grammar and punctuation rules, which specifies that degree names should be written in all lowercase letters.

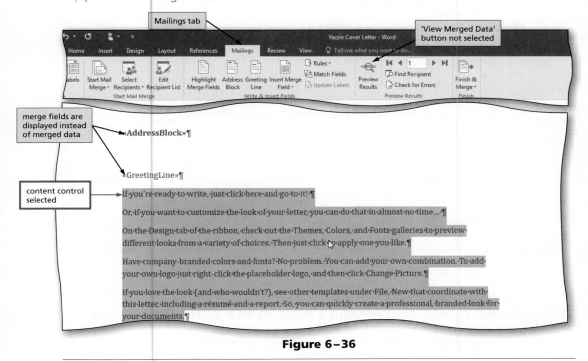

Figure 6–36

BTW

'Insert Merge Field' Button

If you click the 'Insert Merge Field' button instead of the 'Insert Merge Field' arrow (Figure 6–37), Word displays the Insert Merge Field dialog box instead of the Insert Merge Field menu. To insert fields from the dialog box, click the field name and then click the Insert button. The dialog box remains open so that you can insert multiple fields, if necessary. When you have finished inserting fields, click the Close button in the dialog box.

To Insert a Merge Field in the Main Document

1 IDENTIFY MAIN DOCUMENT | 2 CREATE DATA SOURCE | 3 COMPOSE MAIN DOCUMENT
4 MERGE DATA SOURCE | 5 ADDRESS MAILING LABELS | 6 MERGE TO DIRECTORY

The next step is to insert the Position merge field into the main document. **Why?** *The first sentence in the first paragraph of the letter identifies the advertised job position, which is a merge field.* To instruct Word to use data fields from the data source, you insert merge fields in the main document for the form letter. The following steps insert a merge field at the location of the insertion point.

1

- Click the 'Insert Merge Field' arrow (Mailings tab | Write & Insert Fields group) to display the Insert Merge Field menu (Figure 6–37).

Q&A What if I accidentally click the 'Insert Merge Field' button instead of the arrow?
Click the Cancel button in the Insert Merge Field dialog box and repeat Step 1.

Why is the underscore character in some of the field names?
Word places an underscore character in place of the space in merge fields.

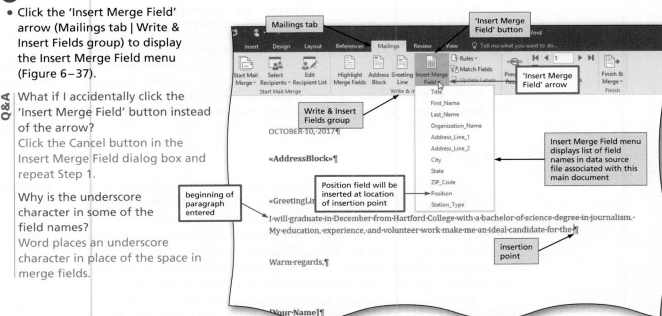

Figure 6–37

2

- Click Position on the Insert Merge Field menu to insert the selected merge field in the document at the location of the insertion point (Figure 6–38).

◄ **Q&A** | Will the word, Position, and the chevron characters print when I merge the form letters?
No. When you merge the data source with the main document, the value in the Position field (e.g., radio reporter) will print at the location of the merge field, Position.

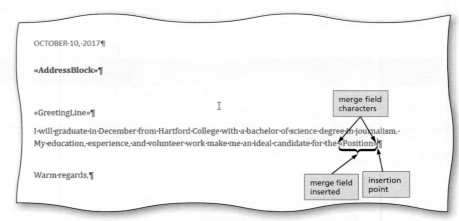

Figure 6–38

Other Ways

1. Click 'Insert Merge Field' button (Mailings tab | Write & Insert fields group), click desired field (Insert Merge Field dialog box), click Insert button, click Close button

---

BTW

Merge Fields
When you insert fields in a document, the displayed fields may be surrounded by braces instead of chevrons, and extra instructions may appear between the braces. If this occurs, then field codes have been turned on. To turn off field codes so that they are not displayed, press ALT+F9.

To Enter More Text and Merge Fields in the Main Document

The following steps enter more text and merge fields into the form letter.

1 With the insertion point at the location shown in Figure 6–38, press the SPACEBAR, type `position at` and then press the SPACEBAR again.

2 Click the 'Insert Merge Field' arrow (Mailings tab | Write & Insert Fields group) and then click Organization_Name on the Insert Merge Field menu to insert the selected merge field in the document. Press the PERIOD key.

3 Press the ENTER key. Type `As shown on the accompanying resume, my background matches the job requirements posted through the Career Development Office at Hartford College. My coursework and experience have prepared me to develop, edit, and present news stories.` and then press the ENTER key.

4 Type `Thank you in advance,` and then press the SPACEBAR. Insert the Title merge field, press the SPACEBAR, and then insert the Last Name merge field. Type `, for your time and consideration. I look forward to hearing from you soon to discuss the opportunity for my potential employment at your` and then press the SPACEBAR (shown in Figure 6–39).

IF Fields

In addition to merge fields, you can insert Word fields that are designed specifically for a mail merge. An **IF field** is an example of a Word field. One form of the IF field is called an **If...Then:** If a condition is true, then perform an action. For example, if Mary owns a house, then send her information about homeowner's insurance. Another form of the IF field is called an **If...Then...Else**: if a condition is true, then perform an action; else perform a different action. For example, if John has an email address, then send him an email message; else send him the message via the postal service.

In this project, the form letter checks the station type and displays text associated with the station type. If the station type is R, then the form letter should print the text, radio; else if the station type is T, then the form letter should print the text, television. Thus, you will use an If...Then...Else: IF the Station_Type is equal to R, then insert radio; else insert television.

The phrase that appears after the word If is called a rule, or condition. A **condition** consists of an expression, followed by a comparison operator, followed by a final expression.

Expression   The expression in a condition can be a merge field, a number, a series of characters, or a mathematical formula. Word surrounds a series of characters with quotation marks ("). To indicate an empty, or null, expression, Word places two quotation marks together ("").

Comparison Operator   The comparison operator in a condition must be one of six characters: = (equal to or matches the text), <> (not equal to or does not match text), < (less than), <= (less than or equal to), > (greater than), or >= (greater than or equal to).

If the result of a condition is true, then Word evaluates the **true text**. If the result of the condition is false, Word evaluates the **false text** if it exists. In this project, the first expression in the condition is a merge field (Station_Type); the comparison operator is equal to (=); and the second expression is the text "R". The true text is "radio". The false text is "television". The complete IF field is as follows:

BTW

IF Fields
The phrase, IF field, originates from computer programming. Do not be intimidated by the terminology. An IF field simply specifies a decision. Some software developers refer to it as an IF statement. Complex IF statements include one or more nested IF fields. A nested IF field is a second IF field inside the true or false text of the first IF field.

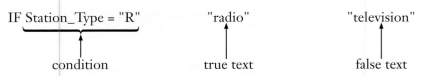

IF Station_Type = "R"	"radio"	"television"
condition	true text	false text

To Insert an IF Field in the Main Document

1 IDENTIFY MAIN DOCUMENT | 2 CREATE DATA SOURCE | 3 COMPOSE MAIN DOCUMENT
4 MERGE DATA SOURCE | 5 ADDRESS MAILING LABELS | 6 MERGE TO DIRECTORY

The next step is to insert an IF field in the main document. ***Why?*** *You want to print the station type in the letter.* The following steps insert this IF field in the form letter: If the Station_Type is equal to R, then insert radio, else insert television.

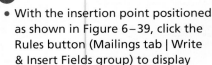

- With the insertion point positioned as shown in Figure 6–39, click the Rules button (Mailings tab | Write & Insert Fields group) to display the Rules menu (Figure 6–39).

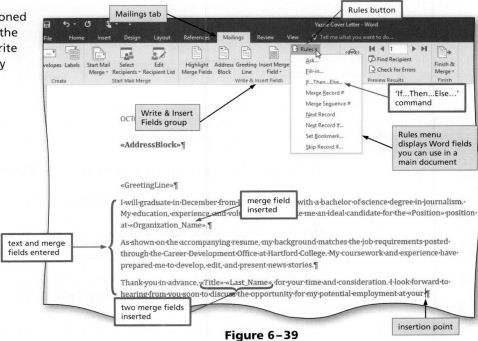

Figure 6–39

2

- Click 'If...Then...Else...' on the Rules menu to display the Insert Word Field: IF dialog box, which is where you enter the components of the IF field (Figure 6–40).

Figure 6–40

3

- Click the Field name arrow (Insert Word Field: IF dialog box) to display the list of fields in the data source.

- Scroll through the list of fields in the Field name list and then click Station_Type to select the field.

- Position the insertion point in the Compare to text box and then type **R** as the comparison text.

- Press the TAB key and then type **radio** as the true text.

- Press the TAB key and then type **television** as the false text (Figure 6–41).

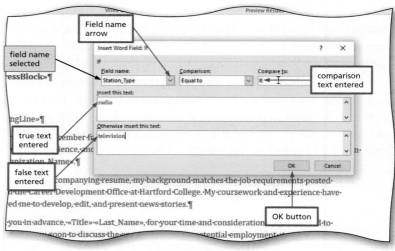

Figure 6–41

Q&A Does the capitalization matter in the comparison text?

Yes. The text, R, is different from the text, r, in a comparison. Be sure to enter the text exactly as you entered it in the data source.

4

- Click the OK button (Insert Word Field: IF dialog box) to insert the IF field at the location of the insertion point (Figure 6–42).

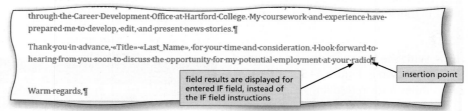

Figure 6–42

Q&A Why does the main document display the text, radio, instead of the IF field instructions?

The text, radio, is displayed because the first record in the data source has a station type equal to R. Word, by default, evaluates the IF field using the current record and displays the results, called the **field results**, in the main document instead of displaying the IF field instructions. Later in the module, you will view the IF field instructions.

To Enter the Remaining Text in the Main Document

The following steps enter the remainder of the text into the form letter.

1 Press the SPACEBAR. Type **station** and then press the PERIOD key.

2 Change the closing to the word, Sincerely.

3 Change the placeholder text in the Your Name content control to Nina Tamaya Yazzie. If necessary, delete the content control so that the name remains but the content control is deleted.

If requested by your instructor, enter your name instead of the job seeker's name.

4 Delete the Your Title content control (Figure 6–43).

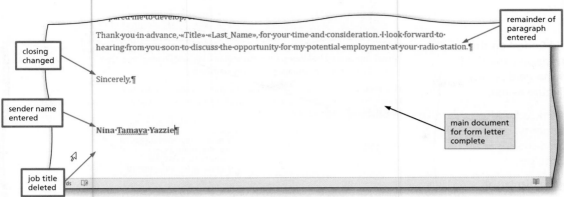

closing changed

sender name entered

job title deleted

remainder of paragraph entered

Thank·you·in·advance,·«Title»·«Last_Name»,·for·your·time·and·consideration.·I·look·forward·to· hearing·from·you·soon·to·discuss·the·opportunity·for·my·potential·employment·at·your·radio·station.¶

Sincerely,¶

Nina·Tamaya·Yazzie¶

main document for form letter complete

Figure 6–43

5 Make any additional adjustments to spacing, formats, etc., so that your main document looks like Figure 5–1 shown at the beginning of this module.

To Highlight Merge Fields

If you wanted to highlight all the merge fields in a document so that you could identify them quickly, you would perform the following steps.

1. Click the 'Highlight Merge Fields' button (Mailings tab | Write & Insert Fields group) to highlight the merge fields in the document.

2. When finished viewing merge fields, click the 'Highlight Merge Fields' button (Mailings tab | Write & Insert Fields group) again to remove the highlight from the merge fields in the document.

BTW
Word Fields
In addition to the IF field, Word provides other fields that may be used in form letters. For example, the ASK and FILLIN fields prompt the user to enter data for each record in the data source. The SKIP RECORD IF field instructs the mail merge not to generate a form letter for a data record if a specific condition is met.

To Display a Field Code

1 IDENTIFY MAIN DOCUMENT | 2 CREATE DATA SOURCE | 3 COMPOSE MAIN DOCUMENT
4 MERGE DATA SOURCE | 5 ADDRESS MAILING LABELS | 6 MERGE TO DIRECTORY

The instructions in the IF field are not displayed in the document; instead, the field results are displayed for the current record (shown in Figure 6–42). The instructions of an IF field are called **field codes**, and the default for Word is for field codes not to be displayed. Thus, field codes do not print or show on the screen unless you turn them on. You use one procedure to show field codes on the screen and a different procedure to print them on a hard copy.

The following steps show a field code on the screen. *Why? You might want to turn on a field code to verify its accuracy or to modify it. Field codes tend to clutter the screen. Thus, most Word users turn them off after viewing them.*

1

- If necessary, scroll to display the last paragraph of the letter in the document window.

- Right-click the field results showing the text, radio, to display a shortcut menu (Figure 6–44).

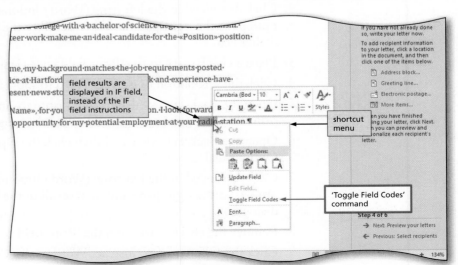

field results are displayed in IF field, instead of the IF field instructions

shortcut menu

'Toggle Field Codes' command

Figure 6–44

2

- Click 'Toggle Field Codes' on the shortcut menu to display the field codes instead of the field results for the IF field (Figure 6–45).

Q&A

Will displaying field codes affect the merged documents?
No. Displaying field codes has no effect on the merge process.

What if I wanted to display all field codes in a document?
You would press ALT+F9. Then, to hide all the field codes, press ALT+F9 again.

Why does the IF field turn gray?
Word, by default, shades a field in gray when the field is selected. The shading displays on the screen to help you identify fields; the shading does not print on a hard copy.

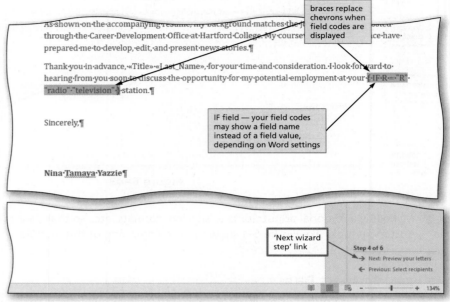

Figure 6–45

- Save the main document for the form letter again on the same storage location with the same file name.

Other Ways

1. With insertion point in field, press SHIFT+F9

TO PRINT FIELD CODES IN THE MAIN DOCUMENT

When you merge or print a document, Word automatically converts field codes that show on the screen to field results. You may want to print the field codes version of the form letter, however, so that you have a hard copy of the field codes for future reference. When you print field codes, you must remember to turn off the field codes option so that merged documents print field results instead of field codes. If you wanted to print the field codes in the main document, you would perform the following steps.

1. Open the Backstage view and then click the Options tab to display the Word Options dialog box.
2. Click Advanced in the left pane (Word Options dialog box) to display advanced options in the right pane and then scroll to the Print area in the right pane of the dialog box.
3. Place a check mark in the 'Print field codes instead of their values' check box.
4. Click the OK button to instruct Word to show field codes when the document prints.
5. Open the Backstage view, click the Print tab, and then click the Print button to print the document with all field codes showing.
6. Open the Backstage view and then click the Options tab to display the Word Options dialog box.
7. Click Advanced in the left pane (Word Options dialog box) to display advanced options in the right pane and then scroll to the Print area in the right pane of the dialog box.
8. Remove the check mark from the 'Print field codes instead of their values' check box.
9. Click the OK button to instruct Word to show field results the next time you print the document.

Opening a Main Document

You open a main document the same as you open any other Word document (i.e., clicking Open in the Backstage view). If Word displays a dialog box indicating it will run an SQL command, click the Yes button (Figure 6–46).

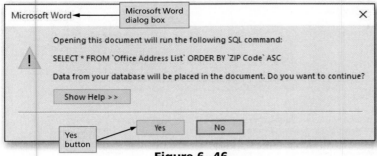

Figure 6–46

When you open a main document, Word attempts to open the associated data source file, too. If the data source is not in exactly the same location (i.e., drive and folder) as when it originally was saved, Word displays a dialog box indicating that it could not find the data source (Figure 6–47). When this occurs, click the 'Find Data Source' button to display the Open Data Source dialog box, which allows you to locate the data source file. (Word may display several dialog boxes requiring you to click an OK (or similar) button until the one shown in Figure 6–47 appears.)

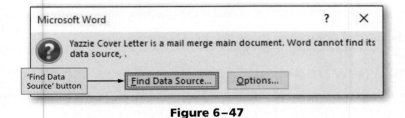

Figure 6–47

BTW

Data Source and Main Document Files
When you open a main document, if Word cannot locate the associated data source file or it does not display a dialog box with the 'Find Data Source' button, then the data source may not be associated with the main document. To associate the data source with the main document, click the Select Recipients button (Mailings tab | Start Mail Merge group), click 'Use an Existing List' on the Select Recipients menu, and then locate the data source file. When you save the main document, Word will associate the data source with the main document.

Break Point: If you wish to take a break, this is a good place to do so. You can exit Word now. To resume at a later time, run Word, open the file called Yazzie Cover Letter, and continue following the steps from this location forward.

Merging the Data Source with the Main Document to Generate Form Letters

The next step in this project is to merge the data source with the main document to generate the form letters (shown in Figure 6–1c at the beginning of this module). **Merging** is the process of combining the contents of a data source with a main document.

You can merge the form letters to a new document, which you can edit, or merge them directly to a printer. You also have the option of merging all data in a data source or merging just a portion of it. The following sections discuss various ways to merge.

To Preview the Merged Letters Using the Mail Merge Task Pane

1 IDENTIFY MAIN DOCUMENT | 2 CREATE DATA SOURCE | 3 COMPOSE MAIN DOCUMENT
4 MERGE DATA SOURCE | 5 ADDRESS MAILING LABELS | 6 MERGE TO DIRECTORY

Earlier in this module, you previewed the data in the letters using a button on the ribbon. The following step uses the Mail Merge wizard to preview the letters. *Why? The next wizard step previews the letters so that you can verify the content is accurate before performing the merge.*

1

- Click the 'Next wizard step' link at the bottom of the Mail Merge task pane (shown in Figure 6–45) to display Step 5 of the Mail Merge wizard in the Mail Merge task pane (Figure 6–48).

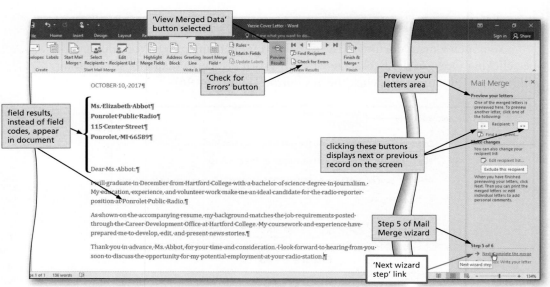

Figure 6–48

To Check for Errors

Before merging documents, you can instruct Word to check for errors that might occur during the merge process. If you wanted to check for errors, you would perform the following steps.

1. Click the 'Check for Errors' button (Mailings tab | Preview Results group) (shown in Figure 6–48) or press ALT+SHIFT+K to display the Checking and Reporting Errors dialog box.

2. Select the desired option and then click the OK button.

To Merge the Form Letters to a New Document Using the Mail Merge Task Pane

With the data source and main document for the form letter complete, the next step is to merge them to generate the individual form letters. You can merge the letters to the printer or to a new document. *Why? If you merge the documents to a new document, you can save the merged documents in a file and then print them later, review the merged documents for accuracy and edit them as needed, or you can add personal messages to individual merged letters.* The following steps merge the form letters to a new document.

1

- Click the 'Next wizard step' link at the bottom of the Mail Merge task pane (shown in Figure 6–48) to display Step 6 of the Mail Merge wizard in the Mail Merge task pane.

- Click the 'Merge to new document' link in the Mail Merge task pane to display the Merge to New Document dialog box (Figure 6–49).

Q&A

What if I wanted to print the merged letters immediately instead of reviewing them first in a new document window?

You would click the 'Merge to printer' link instead of the 'Merge to new document' link.

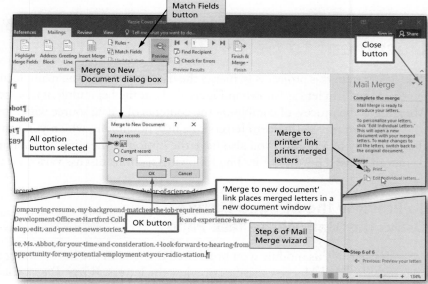

Figure 6–49

- If necessary, click All (Merge to New Document dialog box) so that all records in the data source are merged.

Q&A

Do I have to merge all records?

No. Through this dialog box, you can merge the current record or a range of record numbers.

- Click the OK button to merge the letters to a new document, in this case, five individual letters — one for each potential employer in the data source. (If Word displays a dialog box containing a message about locked fields, click its OK button.)

- Display the View tab and then click the Multiple Pages button (View tab | Zoom group) so that you can see miniature versions of all five letters in the document window at once (Figure 6–50).

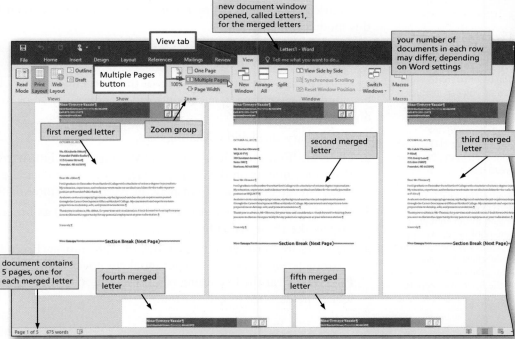

Figure 6–50

- Change the zoom back to page width.

Experiment

- Scroll through the merged documents so that you can read all five letters.

Q&A

Why does my screen show an extra blank page at the end?

You might have a blank record in the data source, or the spacing may cause an overflow to a blank page.

Can I edit the merged letters?

Yes, you can edit the letters as you edit any other Word document. Always proofread the merged letters for accuracy before distributing them.

- Save the merged letters in the Job Hunting folder on your hard drive, OneDrive, or other storage location using the file name, Yazzie Merged Cover Letters. If requested by your instructor, print the merged letters. Close the document window containing the merged letters.

Q&A

Do I have to save the document containing the merged letters?

No. You can close the document without saving it.

- Click the Close button on the Mail Merge task pane title bar (shown in Figure 6–49) because you are finished with the Mail Merge wizard.

- If necessary, click the 'View Merged Data' button to show field codes instead of merged data.

Other Ways

1. Click 'Finish & Merge' button (Mailings tab | Finish group), click 'Edit Individual Documents'

Correcting Merge Field Errors in Merged Documents

If the wrong field results appear, Word may be mapping the fields incorrectly. To view fields, click the Match Fields button (Mailings tab | Write & Insert Fields group) (shown in Figure 6–49). Then, review the fields in the list. For example, Last Name should map to the Last Name field in the data source. If it does not, click the arrow to change the name of the data source field.

If the fields are mapped incorrectly, the data in the data source may be incorrect. For a discussion about editing records in the data source, refer to that section earlier in this module.

BTW

Conserving Ink and Toner

If you want to conserve ink or toner, you can instruct Word to print draft quality documents by clicking File on the ribbon to open the Backstage view, clicking the Options tab in the Backstage view to display the Word Options dialog box, clicking Advanced in the left pane (Word Options dialog box), scrolling to the Print area in the right pane, placing a check mark in the 'Use draft quality' check box, and then clicking the OK button. Then, use the Backstage view to print the document as usual.

TO MERGE THE FORM LETTERS TO A PRINTER

If you are certain the contents of the merged letters will be correct and do not need individual editing, you can perform the following steps to merge the form letters directly to the printer.

1. If necessary, display the Mailings tab.
2. Click the 'Finish & Merge' button (Mailings tab | Finish group) and then click Print Documents on the Finish & Merge menu, or click the 'Merge to printer' link (Mail Merge task pane), to display the Merge to Printer dialog box.
3. If necessary, click All (Merge to Printer dialog box) and then click the OK button to display the Print dialog box.
4. Select desired printer settings. Click the OK button (Print dialog box) to print five separate letters, one for each potential employer in the data source, as shown in Figure 6–1c at the beginning of this module. (If Word displays a message about locked fields, click its OK button.)

To Select Records to Merge

1 IDENTIFY MAIN DOCUMENT | 2 CREATE DATA SOURCE | 3 COMPOSE MAIN DOCUMENT
4 MERGE DATA SOURCE | 5 ADDRESS MAILING LABELS | 6 MERGE TO DIRECTORY

Instead of merging all of the records in the data source, you can choose which records to merge, based on a condition you specify. The dialog box in Figure 6–49 allows you to specify by record number which records to merge. Often, though, you want to merge based on the contents of a specific field. The following steps select records for a merge. *Why? You want to merge just those potential employers who are television stations.*

- Click the 'Edit Recipient List' button (Mailings tab | Start Mail Merge group) to display the Mail Merge Recipients dialog box (Figure 6–51).

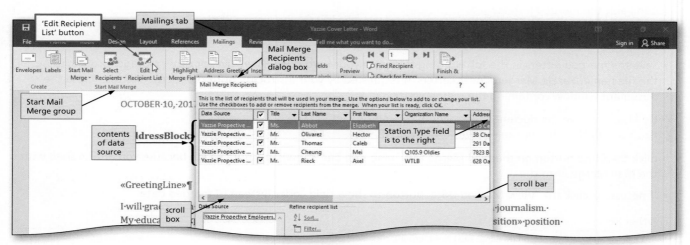

Figure 6–51

2

- Drag the scroll box to the right edge of the scroll bar (Mail Merge Recipients dialog box) so that the Station Type field appears in the dialog box.

- Click the arrow to the right of the field name, Station Type, to display sort and filter criteria for the selected field (Figure 6–52).

Q&A
What are the filter criteria in the parentheses?
The (All) option clears any previously set filter criteria. The (Blanks) option selects records that contain blanks in that field, and the (Nonblanks) option selects records that do not contain blanks in that field. The (Advanced) option displays the Filter and Sort dialog box, which allows you to perform more advanced record selection operations.

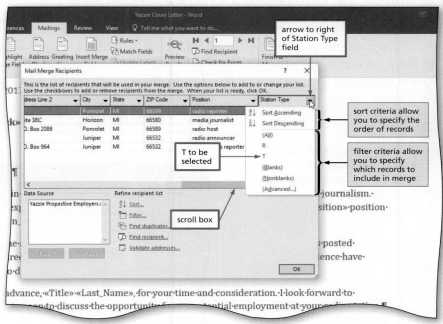

Figure 6–52

3

- Click T to reduce the number of data records displayed (Mail Merge Recipients dialog box) to two, because two potential employers are television stations (Figure 6–53).

Q&A
What happened to the other three records that did not meet the criteria?
They still are part of the data source; they just are not appearing in the Mail Merge Recipients dialog box. When you clear the filter, all records will reappear.

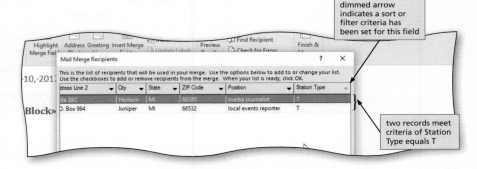

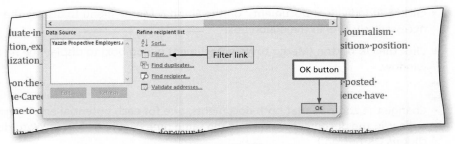

Figure 6–53

4

- Click the OK button to close the Mail Merge Recipients dialog box.

Other Ways

1. Click Filter link (Mail Merge Recipients dialog box), click Filter Records tab (Sort and Filter dialog box), enter filter criteria, click OK button

To Merge the Form Letters to a New Document Using the Ribbon

The next step is to merge the selected records. To do this, you follow the same steps described earlier. The difference is that Word will merge only those records that meet the criteria specified, that is, just those with a station type equal to T (for television). The following steps merge the filtered records to a new document using the ribbon.

- Click the 'Finish & Merge' button (Mailings tab | Finish group) to display the Finish & Merge menu (Figure 6–54).

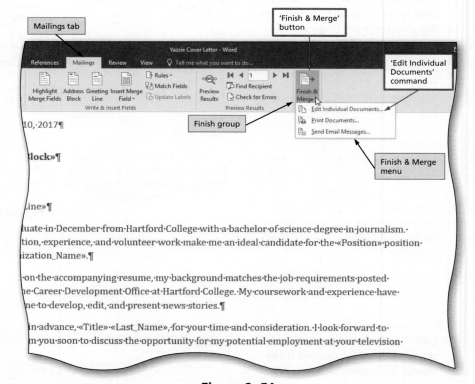

Figure 6–54

- Click 'Edit Individual Documents' on the Finish & Merge menu to display the Merge to New Document dialog box. If necessary, click All in the dialog box.
- Click the OK button (Merge to New Document dialog box) to display the merged documents in a new document window.

- Change the zoom so that both documents, one for each potential employer whose station type field equals T, appear in the document window at the same time (Figure 6–55). (If Word displays a message about locked fields, click its OK button.)

- Close the window. Do not save the merged documents.

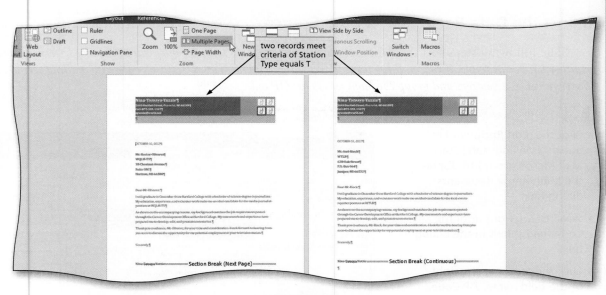

Figure 6–55

To Remove a Merge Condition

1 IDENTIFY MAIN DOCUMENT | 2 CREATE DATA SOURCE | 3 COMPOSE MAIN DOCUMENT
4 MERGE DATA SOURCE | 5 ADDRESS MAILING LABELS | 6 MERGE TO DIRECTORY

The next step is to remove the merge condition. *Why? You do not want future merges be restricted to potential employers with a station type equal to T.* The following steps remove a merge condition.

1

- Click the 'Edit Recipient List' button (Mailings tab | Start Mail Merge group) to display the Mail Merge Recipients dialog box.

2

- Click the Filter link (Mail Merge Recipients dialog box) to display the Filter and Sort dialog box.

- If necessary, click the Filter Records tab to display the Filter Records sheet (Figure 6–56).

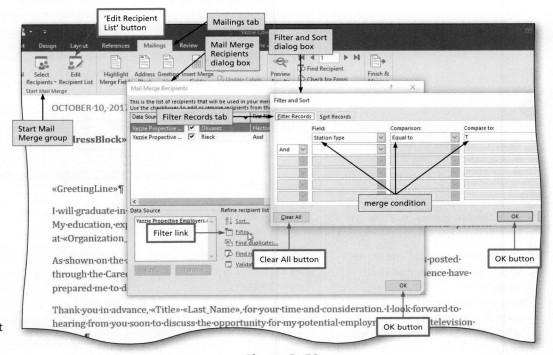

Figure 6–56

 Can I specify a merge condition in this dialog box instead of using the box arrow in the Mail Merge Recipients dialog box?
Yes.

3

- Click the Clear All button (Filter and Sort dialog box) to remove the merge condition from the dialog box.
- Click the OK button in each of the two open dialog boxes to close the dialog boxes.

To Sort the Data Records in a Data Source

The following steps sort the data records by ZIP code. *Why? You may want the form letters printed in a certain order. For example, if you mail the form letters using the U.S. Postal Service's bulk rate mailing service, the post office requires that you sort and group the form letters by ZIP code.*

- Click the 'Edit Recipient List' button (Mailings tab | Start Mail Merge group) to display the Mail Merge Recipients dialog box.

- Scroll to the right until the ZIP Code field shows in the dialog box.

- Click the arrow to the right of the field name, ZIP Code, to display a menu of sort and filter criteria (Figure 6–57).

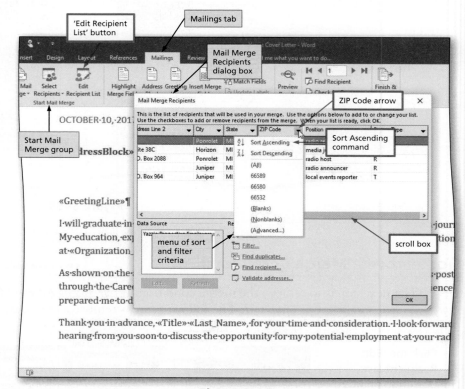

Figure 6–57

- Click Sort Ascending on the menu to sort the data source records in ascending (smallest to largest) order by ZIP Code (Figure 6–58).

- Click the OK button to close the Mail Merge Recipients dialog box.

Q&A

In what order would the form letters print if I merged them again now?

Word would merge them in ZIP code order; that is, the records with ZIP code 66532 would appear first, and the records with ZIP code 66589 would appear last.

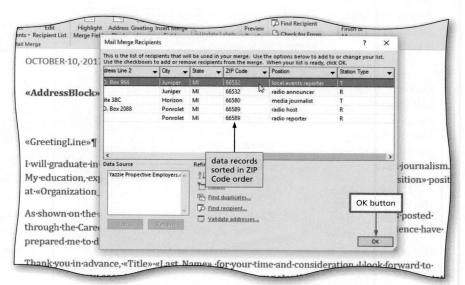

Figure 6–58

Other Ways

1. Click Sort link (Mail Merge Recipients dialog box), enter sort criteria (Sort and Filter dialog box), click OK button

To Find and Display Data

Why? *If you wanted to find a particular record in the data source and display that record's data in the main document on the screen, you can search for a field value.* The following steps find Cheung, which is a last name in the data source, and display that record's values in the form letter currently displaying on the screen.

- If necessary, click the 'View Merged Data' button (Mailings tab | Preview Results group) to show field results instead of merged fields on the screen.

- Click the Find Recipient button (Mailings tab | Preview Results group) to display the Find Entry dialog box.

- Type **Cheung** in the Find text box (Find Entry dialog box) as the search text.

- Click the Find Next button to display the record containing the entered text (Figure 6–59).

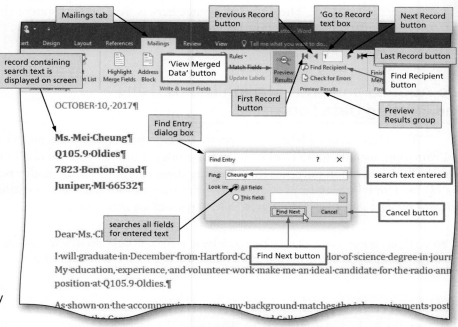

Figure 6–59

- Click the Cancel button (Find Entry dialog box) to close the dialog box.

- Close the open document. If a Microsoft Word dialog box is displayed, click the Save button to save the changes.

Displaying Data Source Records in the Main Document

When you are viewing merged data in the main document (shown in Figure 6–59) — that is, the 'View Merged Data' button (Mailings tab | Preview Results group) is selected — you can click buttons and boxes in the Preview Results group on the Mailings tab to display different results and values. For example, click the Last Record button to display the values from the last record in the data source, the First Record button to display the values in record one, the Next Record button to display the values in the next consecutive record number, or the Previous Record button to display the values from the previous record number. You also can display a specific record by clicking the 'Go to Record' text box, typing the record number you would like to be displayed in the main document, and then pressing the ENTER key.

BTW
Closing Main Document Files
Word always asks if you want to save changes when you close a main document, even if you just saved the document. If you are sure that no additional changes were made to the document, click the Don't Save button; otherwise, click the Save button — just to be safe.

Addressing Mailing Labels and Envelopes

Now that you have merged and printed the form letters, the next step is to print addresses on mailing labels to be affixed to envelopes for the form letters. The mailing labels will use the same data source as the form letter, Yazzie Prospective Employers. The format and content of the mailing labels will be exactly the same as the inside address in the main document for the form letter. That is, the first line will contain the title and first name followed by the last name. The second line will contain the organization name, and so on. Thus, you will use the AddressBlock merge field in the mailing labels.

You follow the same basic steps to create the main document for the mailing labels as you did to create the main document for the form letters. That is, determine the appropriate data source, create the label main document, and then merge the main document with the data source to generate the mailing labels and envelopes. The major difference here is that the data source already exists because you created it earlier in this module.

To Address and Print Mailing Labels Using an Existing Data Source

1 IDENTIFY MAIN DOCUMENT | 2 CREATE DATA SOURCE | 3 COMPOSE MAIN DOCUMENT
4 MERGE DATA SOURCE | 5 ADDRESS MAILING LABELS | 6 MERGE TO DIRECTORY

To address mailing labels, you specify the type of labels you intend to use. Word will request the label information, including the label vendor and product number. You can obtain this information from the box of labels. For illustration purposes in addressing these labels, the label vendor is Avery and the product number is J8158. The following steps address and print mailing labels using an existing data source. *Why? You already created the data source earlier in this module, so you will use that data source.*

Note: If your printer does not have the capability of printing mailing labels, read these steps without performing them. If you are in a laboratory environment, ask your instructor if you should perform these steps or read them without performing them.

- Open the Backstage view. Click the New tab in the Backstage view to display the New gallery. Click the Blank document thumbnail to open a new blank document window.
- If necessary, change the zoom to page width.
- Display the Mailings tab. Click the 'Start Mail Merge' button (Mailings tab | Start Mail Merge group) and then click 'Step-by-Step Mail Merge Wizard' on the Start Mail Merge menu to display Step 1 of the Mail Merge wizard in the Mail Merge task pane.
- Click Labels in the Select document type area to specify labels as the main document type (Figure 6–60).

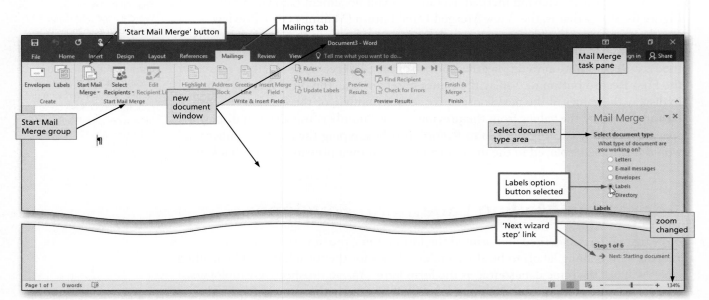

Figure 6–60

2

- Click the 'Next wizard step' link at the bottom of the Mail Merge task pane to display Step 2 of the Mail Merge wizard.

- In the Mail Merge task pane, click the 'Select label size' link to display the Label Options dialog box.

- Select the label vendor and product number (in this case, Avery A4/A5 and J8158), as shown in Figure 6–61.

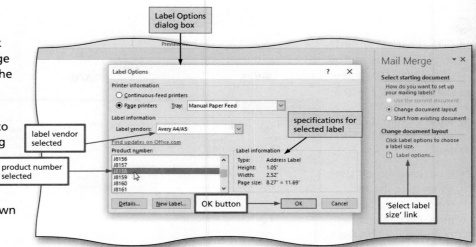

Figure 6–61

3

- Click the OK button (Label Options dialog box) to display the selected label layout as the main document (Figure 6–62).

- If gridlines are not displayed, click the 'View Table Gridlines' button (Table Tools Layout tab | Table group) to show gridlines.

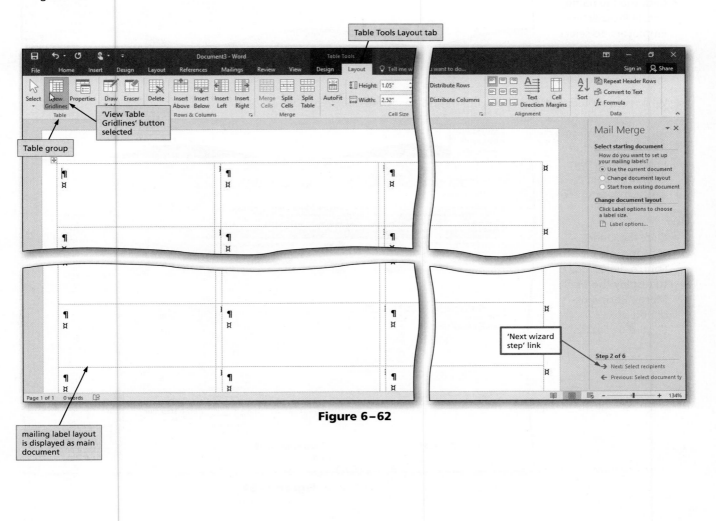

Figure 6–62

4

- Click the 'Next wizard step' link at the bottom of the Mail Merge task pane to display Step 3 of the Mail Merge wizard, which allows you to select the data source.

- If necessary, click 'Use an existing list' in the Select recipients area. Click the 'Select recipient list file' link to display the Select Data Source dialog box.

- If necessary, navigate to the location of the data source (in this case, the Job Hunting folder).

- Click the file name, Yazzie Prospective Employers, to select the data source you created earlier in the module (Figure 6–63).

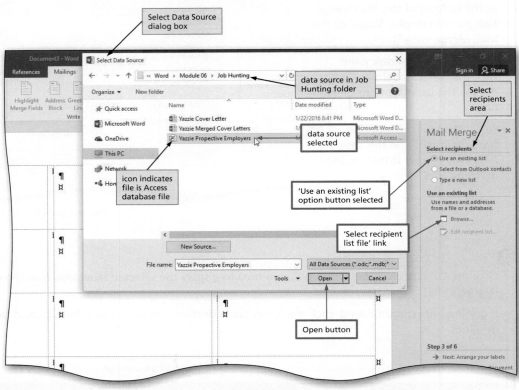

Figure 6–63

Q&A What is the folder initially displayed in the Select Data Source dialog box?

It is the default folder for storing data source files. Word looks in that folder, by default, for an existing data source.

5

- Click the Open button (Select Data Source dialog box) to display the Mail Merge Recipients dialog box (Figure 6–64).

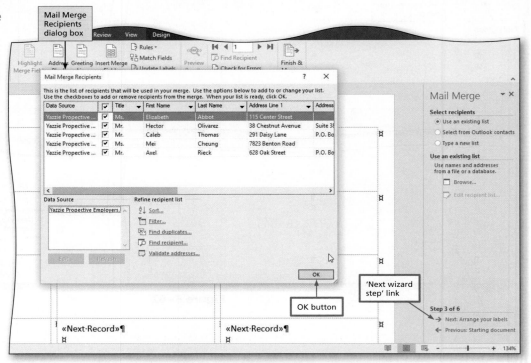

Figure 6–64

6

- Click the OK button (Mail Merge Recipients dialog box) to close the dialog box.

- At the bottom of the Mail Merge task pane, click the 'Next wizard step' link to display Step 4 of the Mail Merge wizard in the Mail Merge task pane.

- In the Mail Merge task pane, click the 'Insert formatted address' link to display the Insert Address Block dialog box (Figure 6–65).

- If necessary, match the company name to the Organization

Name field by clicking the Match Fields button (Insert Address Block dialog box), clicking the Company box arrow (Match Fields dialog box), clicking Organization Name in the list, and then clicking the OK button (Match Fields dialog box).

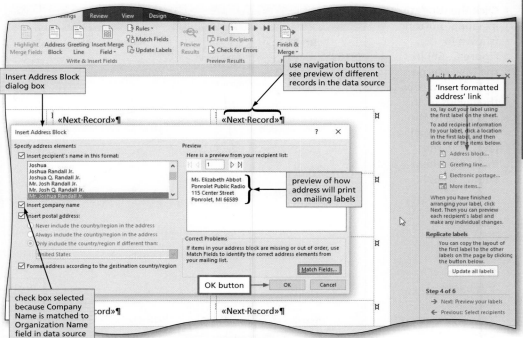

Figure 6–65

7

- Click the OK button to close the dialog box and insert the AddressBlock merge field in the first label of the main document (Figure 6–66).

Q&A Do I have to use the AddressBlock merge field?

No. You can click the Insert Merge Field button (Mailings tab | Write & Insert Fields group) and then select the preferred fields for the mailing labels, organizing the fields as desired.

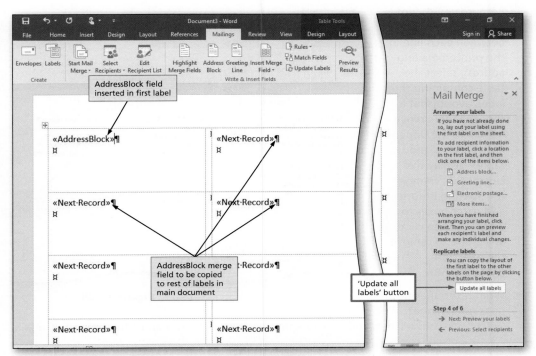

Figure 6–66

8

- Click the 'Update all labels' button (shown in Figure 6–66) in the Mail Merge task pane to copy the layout of the first label to the remaining label layouts in the main document (Figure 6–67).

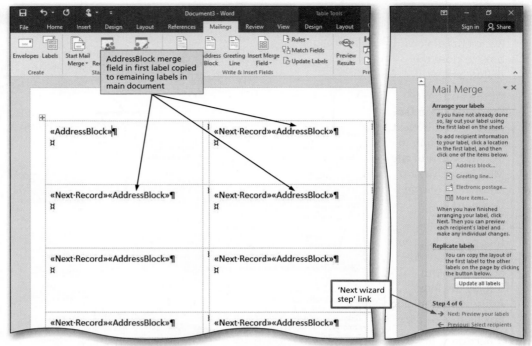

Figure 6–67

9

- Click the 'Next wizard step' link at the bottom of the Mail Merge task pane to display Step 5 of the Mail Merge wizard, which shows a preview of the mailing labels in the document window.

- Because you do not want a blank space between each line in the printed mailing address, select the table containing the label layout (that is, click the table move handle in the upper-left corner of the table), display the Layout tab, change the Spacing Before and After boxes to 0 pt, and then click anywhere to remove the selection (Figure 6–68).

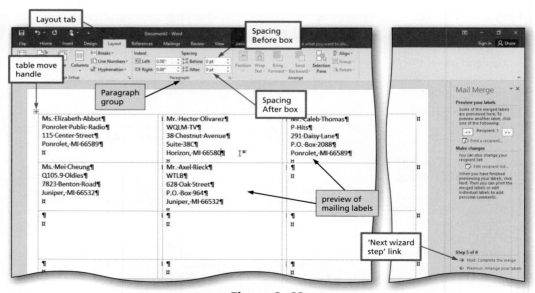

Figure 6–68

Q&A What if the spacing does not change?

Drag through the labels and try changing the Spacing Before and After boxes to 0 again.

10

- Click the 'Next wizard step' link at the bottom of the Mail Merge task pane to display Step 6 of the Mail Merge wizard.

- Click the 'Merge to a new document' link to display the Merge to New Document dialog box.

- If necessary, click All (Merge to New Document dialog box) so that all records in the data source will be included in the merge (Figure 6–69).

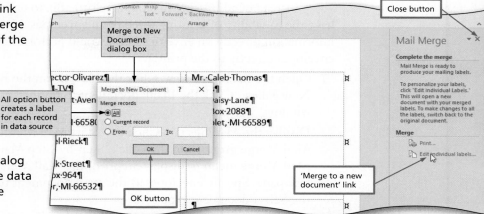

Figure 6–69

11

- If necessary, insert a sheet of blank mailing labels in the printer.

- Click the OK button (Merge to New Document dialog box) to merge the mailing labels to a new document.

- Save the merged mailing labels in the Job Hunting folder on your hard drive, OneDrive, or other storage location using the file name, Yazzie Merged Mailing Labels. If requested by your instructor, print the merged labels (Figure 6–70).

12

- Close the document window containing the merged labels.

- Click the Close button at the right edge of the Mail Merge task pane.

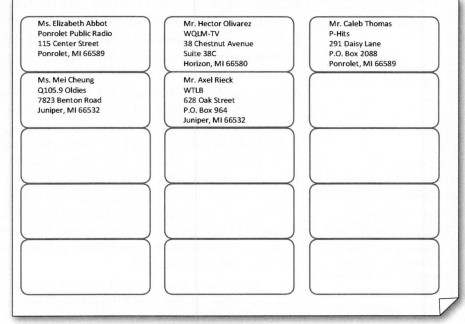

Figure 6–70

- Click the 'View Merged Data' button to show field codes instead of merged data on the labels.

- Save the mailing label main document in the Job Hunting folder on your hard drive, OneDrive, or other storage location using the file name, Yazzie Mailing Labels.

- Close the mailing label main document.

How should you position addresses on an envelope?
An envelope should contain the sender's full name and address in the upper-left corner of the envelope. It also should contain the addressee's full name and address, positioned approximately in the vertical and horizontal center of the envelope. The address can be printed directly on the envelope or on a mailing label that is affixed to the envelope.

CONSIDER THIS

To Address and Print Envelopes

Instead of addressing mailing labels to affix to envelopes, your printer may have the capability of printing directly on envelopes. If you wanted to print address information directly on envelopes, you would perform the following steps to merge the envelopes directly to the printer.

1. Open the Backstage view. Click the New tab in the Backstage view to display the New gallery. Click the Blank document thumbnail to open a new blank document window.

2. Display the Mailings tab. Click the 'Start Mail Merge' button (Mailings tab | Start Mail Merge group) and then click 'Step-by-Step Mail Merge Wizard' on the Start Mail Merge menu to display Step 1 of the Mail Merge wizard in the Mail Merge task pane. Specify envelopes as the main document type by clicking Envelopes in the Select document type area.

3. Click the 'Next wizard step' link at the bottom of the Mail Merge task pane to display Step 2 of the Mail Merge wizard. In the Mail Merge task pane, click the 'Set Envelope Options' link to display the Envelope Options dialog box.

4. Select the envelope size and then click the OK button (Envelope Options dialog box), which displays the selected envelope layout as the main document.

5. If your envelope does not have a preprinted return address, position the insertion point in the upper-left corner of the envelope layout and then type a return address.

6. Click the 'Next wizard step' link at the bottom of the Mail Merge task pane to display Step 3 of the Mail Merge wizard, which allows you to select the data source. Select an existing data source or create a new one. At the bottom of the Mail Merge task pane, click the 'Next wizard step' link to display Step 4 of the Mail Merge wizard in the Mail Merge task pane.

7. Position the insertion point in the middle of the envelope. In the Mail Merge task pane, click the 'Insert formatted address' link to display the Insert Address Block dialog box. Select desired settings and then click the OK button to close the dialog box and insert the AddressBlock merge field in the envelope layout of the main document. If necessary, match fields so that the Company is matched to the Organization_Name field.

8. Click the 'Next wizard step' link at the bottom of the Mail Merge task pane to display Step 5 of the Mail Merge wizard, which shows a preview of an envelope in the document window.

9. Click the 'Next wizard step' link at the bottom of the Mail Merge task pane to display Step 6 of the Mail Merge wizard. In the Mail Merge task pane, click the 'Merge to printer' link to display the Merge to Printer dialog box. If necessary, click All (Merge to Printer dialog box) so that all records in the data source will be included in the merge.

10. If necessary, insert blank envelopes in the printer. Click the OK button to display the Print dialog box. Click the OK button (Print dialog box) to print the addresses on the envelopes. Close the Mail Merge task pane.

BTW

AddressBlock Merge Field
Another way to insert the AddressBlock merge field in a document is to click the Address Block button (Mailings tab | Write & Insert Fields group).

Merging All Data Records to a Directory

You may want to print the data records in the data source. Recall that the data source is saved as a Microsoft Access database table. Thus, you cannot open the data source in Word. To view the data source, you click the 'Edit Recipient List' button

(Mailings tab | Start Mail Merge group), which displays the Mail Merge Recipients dialog box. This dialog box, however, does not have a Print button.

One way to print the contents of the data source is to merge all data records in the data source into a single document, called a directory. A **directory** is a listing from the contents of the data source. A directory does not merge each data record to a separate document; instead, a directory lists all records together in a single document. When you merge to a directory, the default organization of a directory places each record one after the next, similar to the look of entries in a telephone book.

To create a directory, follow the same process as for the form letters. That is, determine the appropriate data source, create the directory main document, and then merge the main document with the data source to create the directory.

The directory in this module is more organized with the rows and columns divided and field names placed above each column (shown in Figure 6–83). To accomplish this look, the following steps are required:

1. Change the page orientation from portrait to landscape, so that each record fits on a single row.

2. Create a directory layout, placing a separating character between each merge field.

3. Merge the directory to a new document, which creates a list of all records in the data source.

4. Convert the directory to a table, using the separator character as the identifier for each new column.

5. Format the table containing the directory.

6. Sort the table by organization name within city, so that it is easy to locate a particular record.

BTW

Converting Main Document Files
If you wanted to convert a mail merge main document to a regular Word document, you would open the main document, click the 'Start Mail Merge' button (Mailings tab | Start Mail Merge group), and then click 'Normal Word Document' on the Start Mail Merge menu (shown in Figure 6–72).

To Change Page Orientation

1 IDENTIFY MAIN DOCUMENT | 2 CREATE DATA SOURCE | 3 COMPOSE MAIN DOCUMENT
4 MERGE DATA SOURCE | 5 ADDRESS MAILING LABELS | 6 MERGE TO DIRECTORY

When a document is in **portrait orientation**, the short edge of the paper is the top of the document. You can instruct Word to lay out a document in **landscape orientation**, so that the long edge of the paper is the top of the document. The following steps change the orientation of the document from portrait to landscape. *Why? You want an entire record to fit on a single line in the directory.*

1

- If necessary, create a new blank document in the Word window and change the zoom to page width.

- Display the Layout tab.

- Click the 'Change Page Orientation' button (Layout tab | Page Setup group) to display the Change Page Orientation gallery (Figure 6–71).

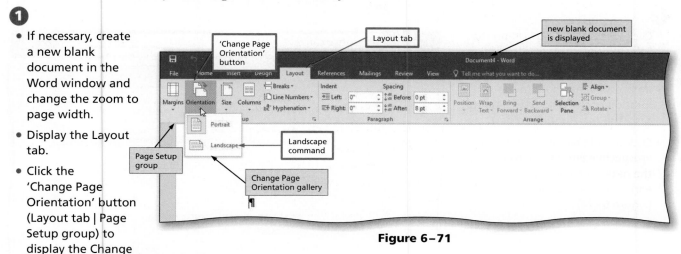

Figure 6–71

2

- Click Landscape in the Change Page Orientation gallery to change the page orientation to landscape.

- If necessary, change the zoom to page width again so that both the left and right edges of the page are visible in the document window.

To Merge to a Directory

The next steps merge the data records in the data source to a directory. *Why? You would like a listing of all records in the data source.* For illustration purposes, the following steps use the buttons on the Mailings tab rather than using the Mail Merge task pane to merge to a directory.

1

- Display the Mailings tab.
- Click the 'Start Mail Merge' button (Mailings tab | Start Mail Merge group) to display the Start Mail Merge menu (Figure 6–72).

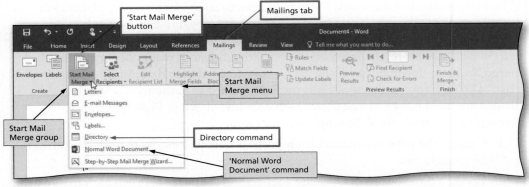

Figure 6–72

2

- Click Directory on the Start Mail Merge menu to select the main document type.

3

- Click the Select Recipients button (Mailings tab | Start Mail Merge group) to display the Select Recipients menu (Figure 6–73).

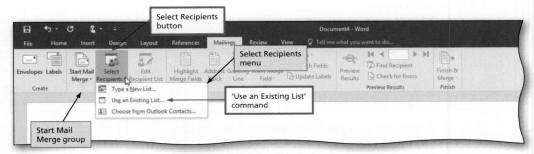

Figure 6–73

4

- Click 'Use an Existing List' on the Select Recipients menu to display the Select Data Source dialog box.
- If necessary, navigate to the location of the data source (in this case, the Job Hunting folder).
- Click the file name, Yazzie Prospective Employers, to select the data source you created earlier in the module (Figure 6–74).

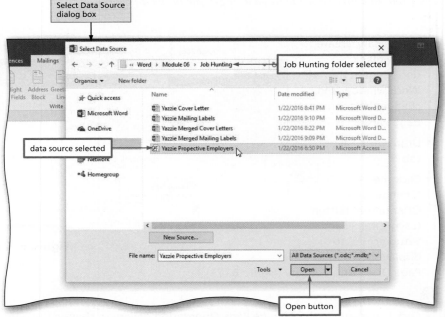

Figure 6–74

- Click the Open button (Select Data Source dialog box) to associate the selected data source with the current main document.

- Click the 'Insert Merge Field' arrow (Mailings tab | Write & Insert Fields group) to display the Insert Merge Field menu (Figure 6–75).

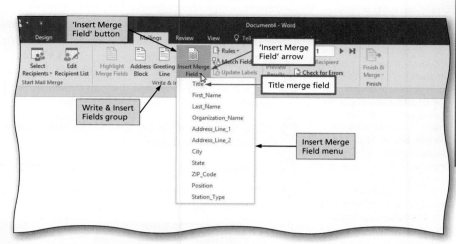

Figure 6–75

- Click Title on the Insert Merge Field menu to insert the selected merge field in the document.

- Press the COMMA (,) key to place a comma after the inserted merge field.

Q&A Why insert a comma after the merge field?

In the next steps, you will convert the entered merge fields to a table format with the records in rows and the fields in columns. To do this, Word divides the columns based on a character separating each field. In this case, you use the comma to separate the merge fields.

- Repeat Steps 6 and 7 for the First_Name, Last_Name, Organization_Name, Address_Line_1, Address_Line_2, City, State, and ZIP_Code fields on the Insert Merge Field menu, so that these fields in the data source appear in the main document separated by a comma, except do not type a comma after the last field (ZIP_Code).

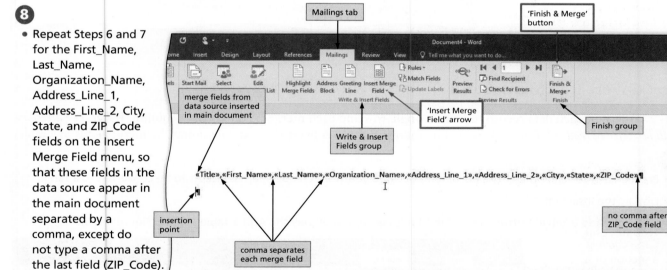

- Press the ENTER key (Figure 6–76).

Figure 6–76

Q&A Why press the ENTER key after entering the merge fields names?

This will place the first field in each record at the beginning of a new line.

Why are the Position and Station_Type fields not included in the directory?

You just want the directory listing to show the contact information for each potential employer.

- Save the directory main document in the Job Hunting folder on your hard drive, OneDrive, or other storage location using the file name, Yazzie Potential Employer Directory.

BTW
**Distributing a
Document**
Instead of printing and
distributing a hard copy of a
document, you can distribute
the document electronically.
Options include sending the
document via email; posting
it on cloud storage (such as
OneDrive) and sharing the
file with others; posting it
on social media, a blog, or
other website; and sharing a
link associated with an online
location of the document.
You also can create and share
a PDF or XPS image of the
document, so that users can
view the file in Adobe Reader
or XPS Viewer instead of in
Word.

To Merge to a New Document

The next step is to merge the data source and the directory main document to a new document, so that you can edit the resulting document. The following steps merge to a new document.

1 Click the 'Finish & Merge' button (Mailings tab | Finish group) to display the Finish & Merge menu.

2 Click 'Edit Individual Documents' on the Finish & Merge menu to display the Merge to New Document dialog box.

3 If necessary, click All (Merge to New Document dialog box).

4 Click the OK button to merge the data records to a directory in a new document window (Figure 6–77).

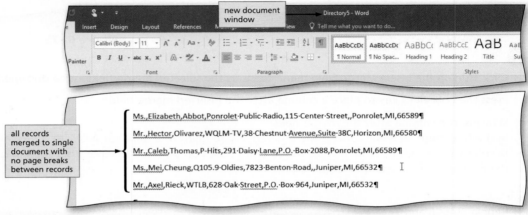

Figure 6–77

To Convert Text to a Table

1 IDENTIFY MAIN DOCUMENT | 2 CREATE DATA SOURCE | 3 COMPOSE MAIN DOCUMENT
4 MERGE DATA SOURCE | 5 ADDRESS MAILING LABELS | **6 MERGE TO DIRECTORY**

You want each data record to be in a single row and each merge field to be in a column. *Why? The directory will be easier to read if it is in table form.* The following steps convert the text containing the merge fields to a table.

1

• Press CTRL+A to select the entire document, because you want all document contents to be converted to a table.

• Display the Insert tab.

• Click the 'Add a Table' button (Insert tab | Tables group) to display the Add a Table gallery (Figure 6–78).

Q&A | Can I convert
a section of a
document to a
table?
Yes, simply select
the characters,
lines, or paragraphs
to be converted
before displaying
the Convert Text to
Table dialog box.

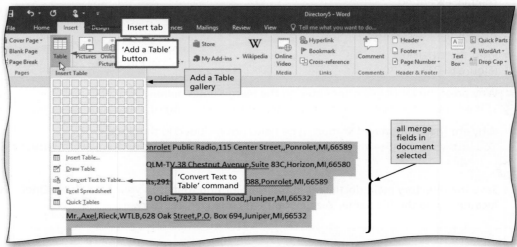

Figure 6–78

2

- Click 'Convert Text to Table' in the Add a Table gallery to display the Convert Text to Table dialog box.

- If necessary, type 9 in the 'Number of columns' box (Convert Text to Table dialog box) to specify the number of columns for the resulting table.

- Click 'AutoFit to window', which instructs Word to fit the table and its contents to the width of the window.

- If necessary, click Commas to specify the character that separates the merge fields in the document (Figure 6–79).

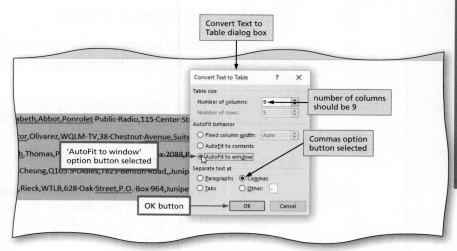

Figure 6–79

3

- Click the OK button to convert the selected text to a table and then, if necessary, click to remove the selection from the table (Figure 6–80).

Q&A Can I format the table?

Yes. You can use any of the commands on the Table Tools Design and Table Tools Layout tabs to change the look of the table.

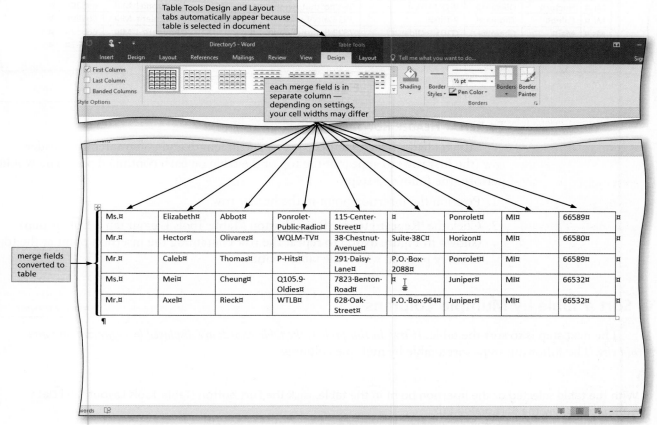

Ms.¤	Elizabeth¤	Abbot¤	Ponrolet· Public·Radio¤	115·Center· Street¤	¤	Ponrolet¤	MI¤	66589¤	¤
Mr.¤	Hector¤	Olivarez¤	WQLM-TV¤	38·Chestnut· Avenue¤	Suite·38C¤	Horizon¤	MI¤	66580¤	¤
Mr.¤	Caleb¤	Thomas¤	P-Hits¤	291·Daisy· Lane¤	P.O.·Box· 2088¤	Ponrolet¤	MI¤	66589¤	¤
Ms.¤	Mei¤	Cheung¤	Q105.9· Oldies¤	7823·Benton· Road¤	¤	Juniper¤	MI¤	66532¤	¤
Mr.¤	Axel¤	Rieck¤	WTLB¤	628·Oak· Street¤	P.O.·Box·964¤	Juniper¤	MI¤	66532¤	¤

Figure 6–80

To Modify and Format a Table

The table would be more descriptive if the field names were displayed in a row above the actual data. The following steps add a row to the top of a table and format the data in the new row.

1 Add a row to the top of the table by positioning the insertion point in the first row of the table and then clicking the 'Insert Rows Above' button (Table Tools Layout tab | Rows & Columns group).

2 Click in the first (leftmost) cell of the new row. Type `Title` and then press the TAB key. Type `First Name` and then press the TAB key. Type `Last Name` and then press the TAB key. Type `Organization Name` and then press the TAB key. Type `Address Line 1` and then press the TAB key. Type `Address Line 2` and then press the TAB key. Type `City` and then press the TAB key. Type `State` and then press the TAB key. Type `ZIP Code` as the last entry in the row.

3 Bold the contents of the first row.

4 Use the AutoFit Contents command on the ribbon or the shortcut menu to make all columns as wide as their contents. If necessary, adjust individual column widths so that the table looks like Figure 6–81.

5 Center the table between the margins (Figure 6–81).

header row added and bold

Title¤	First·Name¤	Last·Name¤	Organization·Name¤	Address·Line·1¤	Address·Line·2¤	City¤	State¤	ZIP·Code¤	¤
Ms.¤	Elizabeth¤	Abbot¤	Ponrolet·Public·Radio¤	115·Center·Street¤	¤	Ponrolet¤	MI¤	66589¤	¤
Mr.¤	Hector¤	Olivarez¤	WQLM-TV¤	38·Chestnut·Avenue¤	Suite·38C¤	Horizon¤	MI¤	66580¤	¤
Mr.¤	Caleb¤	Thomas¤	P-Hits¤	291·Daisy·Lane¤	P.O.·Box·2088¤	Ponrolet¤	MI¤	66589¤	¤
Ms.¤	Mei¤	Cheung¤	Q105.9·Oldies¤	7823·Benton·Road¤	¤	Juniper¤	MI¤	66532¤	¤
Mr.¤	Axel¤	Rieck¤	WTLB¤	628·Oak·Street¤	P.O.·Box·964¤	Juniper¤	MI¤	66532¤	¤

Figure 6–81

TO REPEAT HEADER ROWS

If you had a table that exceeded a page in length and you wanted the header row (the first row) to appear at the top of the table on each continued page, you would perform the following steps.

1. Position the insertion point in the header row.

2. Click the 'Repeat Header Rows' button (Table Tools Layout tab | Data group) (shown in Figure 6–82) to repeat the row containing the insertion point at the top of every page on which the table continues.

To Sort a Table by Multiple Columns

1 IDENTIFY MAIN DOCUMENT | 2 CREATE DATA SOURCE | 3 COMPOSE MAIN DOCUMENT
4 MERGE DATA SOURCE | 5 ADDRESS MAILING LABELS | **6 MERGE TO DIRECTORY**

The next step is to sort the table. *Why? In this project, the table records are displayed by organization name within city.* The following steps sort a table by multiple columns.

1

- With the table selected or the insertion point in the table, click the Sort button (Table Tools Layout tab | Data group) to display the Sort dialog box.

- Click the Sort by arrow (Sort dialog box); scroll to and then click City in the list.

- Click the first Then by arrow and then click Organization Name in the list.

- If necessary, click Header row so that the first row remains in its current location when the table is sorted (Figure 6–82).

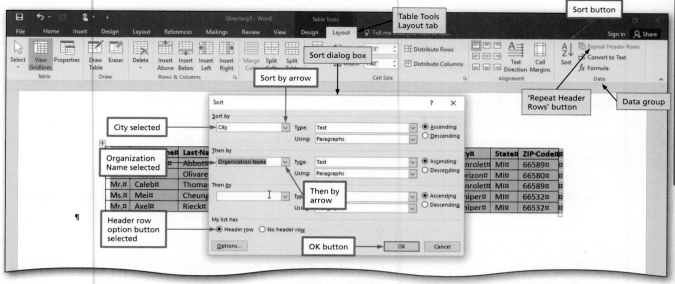

Figure 6–82

2

- Click the OK button to sort the records in the table in ascending Organization Name order within ascending City order (Figure 6–83).

- If necessary, click to deselect the table.

- Save the merged directory in the Job Hunting folder on your hard drive, OneDrive, or other storage location using the file name, Yazzie Merged Potential Employer Directory.

- If requested by your instructor, print the merged directory.

Q&A | If Microsoft Access is installed on my computer, can I use that to print the data source?
As an alternative to merging to a directory and printing the results, if you are familiar with Microsoft Access and it is installed on your computer, you can open and print the data source in Access.

- Exit Word.

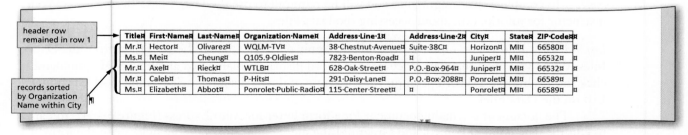

Figure 6–83

Summary

In this module, you learned how to create and print form letters, work with merge fields and an IF field, open a main document, create and edit a data source, address mailing labels and envelopes from a data source, change page orientation, merge to a directory, and convert text to a table.

What decisions will you need to make when creating your next form letter?

Use these guidelines as you complete the assignments in this module and create your own form letters outside of this class.

1. Identify the main document for the form letter.

   a) Determine whether to type the letter from scratch in a blank document window or use a letter template.

2. Create or specify the data source.

   a) Determine if the data exists already in an Access database table, an Outlook contacts list, or an Excel worksheet.

   b) If you cannot use an existing data source, create a new one using appropriate field names.

3. Compose the main document for the form letter.

   a) Ensure the letter contains all essential business letter elements and is visually appealing.

   b) Be sure the letter contains proper grammar, correct spelling, logically constructed sentences, flowing paragraphs, and sound ideas.

   c) Properly reference the data in the data source.

4. Merge the main document with the data source to create the form letters.

   a) Determine the destination for the merge (i.e., a new document, the printer, etc.).

   b) Determine which records to merge (all of them or a portion of them).

5. Determine whether to generate mailing labels or envelopes.

   a) Create or specify the data source.

   b) Ensure the mailing label or envelope contains all necessary information.

6. Create a directory of the data source.

   a) Create or specify the data source.

   b) If necessary, format the directory appropriately.

Apply Your Knowledge

Reinforce the skills and apply the concepts you learned in this module.

Editing, Printing, and Merging a Form Letter and Its Data Source

Note: To complete this assignment, you will be required to use the Data Files. Please contact your instructor for information about accessing the Data Files.

Instructions: Run Word. Open the document, Apply 6–1 Oil Change Letter Draft, from the Data Files. When you open the main document, if Word displays a dialog box about an SQL command, click the Yes button. If Word prompts for the name of the data source, select Apply 6–1 Customer List on the Data Files.

The document is a main document for a form letter for Auto Express (Figure 6–84). You are to edit the date content control and GreetingLine merge field, add a merge field, print the form letter, add a record to the data source, and merge the form letters to a file.

Perform the following tasks:

1. Edit the date content control so that it contains the date 10/30/2017.

2. Edit the GreetingLine merge field so that the salutation ends with a comma (,).

3. At the end of the last paragraph of the letter, insert the Vehicle_Type merge field between the word, your, and the exclamation point (shown in Figure 6–84).

4. Save the modified main document for the form letter with the file name, Apply 6–1 Oil Change Letter Modified.

5. Highlight the merge fields in the document. How many were highlighted? Remove the highlight from the merge fields.

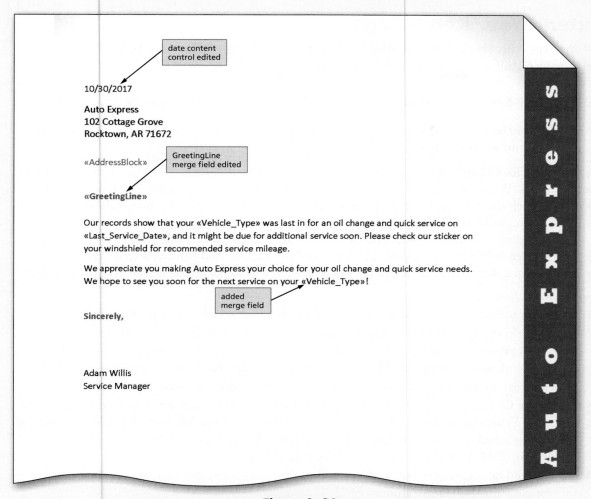

Figure 6–84

6. View merged data in the document. Use the navigation buttons in the Preview Results group to display merged data from various records in the data source. What is the last name shown in the first record? The third record? The fifth record? View merge fields (that is, turn off the view merged data).

7. Print the main document for the form letter (shown in Figure 6–84). If requested by your instructor, save the main document as a PDF.

8. If requested by your instructor, add a record to the data source that contains your personal information. Type **7/14/2016** in the Last_Service_Date field, and add the type of vehicle you own (or would like to own) in the Vehicle_Type field.

9. In the data source, change Kimberly Johnson's last name to Holloway.

10. Sort the data source by the Last Name field.

11. Save the main document for the form letter again.

12. Merge the form letters to a new document. Save the new document with the file name, Apply 6–1 Oil Change Merged Letters.

13. If requested by your instructor, merge the form letters directly to the printer.

14. Submit the saved documents in the format specified by your instructor.

15. ✷ Answer the questions posed in #5 and #6. The form letter used in this assignment was based on one of Word's online mail merge letter templates called Adjacency letter. What other online mail merge letter templates are available through Word? Which template do you like best and why?

Extend Your Knowledge

Extend the skills you learned in this module and experiment with new skills. You may need to use Help to complete the assignment.

Editing an IF Field, Inserting a Fill-In Field, and Merging Using Outlook and Access

Note: To complete this assignment, you will be required to use the Data Files. Please contact your instructor for information about accessing the Data Files.

Instructions: Run Word. Open the document called Extend 6–1 Donation Letter Draft located on the Data Files. When you open the main document, if Word displays a dialog box about an SQL command, click the Yes button. If Word prompts for the name of the data source, select Extend 6–1 Donor List on the Data Files.

The document is a main document for a form letter thanking and inviting a donor to a pancake breakfast (Figure 6–85). You will modify an IF field, and add a Fill-in field, print field codes, create envelopes for records in the data source, use an Access database file as a data source, and merge to email addresses.

Perform the following tasks:

1. Use Help to learn about mail merge, IF fields, Fill-in fields, and merging to email addresses.
2. The IF field in the draft file has the true and false text reversed. Edit the IF field so that donations greater than or equal to $25 may bring two guests and all others may bring one guest. *Hint*: Use the 'Toggle Field Codes' command on the shortcut menu (right-click the IF field code in the document window) and edit the IF field directly in the document.
3. Above the GreetingLine merge field (shown in Figure 6–85), insert a Fill-in field that asks this question: What date will you be mailing these letters? Select the Ask once check box so that the question is asked only once, instead of for each letter. When merging the letters, use a date in October of 2017. What is the purpose of the Fill-in field?
4. If requested by your instructor, add a record to the data source that contains your personal information and a donation amount of 25.
5. Save the modified letter with the file name, Extend 6–1 Donation Letter Modified.
6. Merge the letters to a new document. Save the merged letters using the file name, Extend 6–1 Donation Merged Letters. On the letter with the donation of $100, add an extra sentence of thanks at the end of the first paragraph.
7. Print the main document for the form letter. If requested by your instructor, save the main document as a PDF.
8. Print the form letter with field codes showing; that is, print it with the 'Print field codes instead of their values' check box selected in the Word Options dialog box. Be sure to deselect this check box after printing the field codes version of the letter. How does this printout differ from the one printed in #7?
9. Submit the main document and merged letters in the format specified by your instructor.
10. If your instructor requests, create envelopes for each letter in the data source. Submit the merged envelopes in the format specified by your instructor.
11. If Access is installed on your computer or mobile device, and if you are familiar with Access and your instructor requests it, create the data source included with the assignment in Access and then open the main document with the Access database file as the data source.
12. If your instructor requests, display your personal record on the screen and merge the form letter to an email message, specifying that only the current receives the message. Submit the merged email message in the format specified by your instructor.
13. ✳ Answer the questions posed in #3 and #8. If you choose to merge to email addresses, what is the purpose of the various email formats?

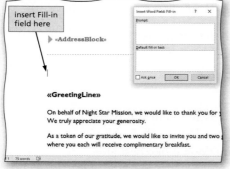

Figure 6–85

Expand Your World

Create a solution that uses cloud or web technologies by learning and investigating on your own from general guidance.

Exploring Add-Ins for Office Apps

Instructions: You regularly use apps on your phone and tablet to look up a variety of information. In Office apps, you can use add-ins, which essentially are apps that work with Word and the other Office apps. You would like to investigate some of the add-ins available for Word to determine which ones would be helpful for you to use.

Note: You will be required to use your Microsoft account to complete this assignment. If you do not have a Microsoft account and do not want to create one, read this assignment without performing the instructions.

Perform the following tasks:
1. Use Help to learn about Office add-ins. If necessary, sign in to your Windows account.

2. If you are not signed in already, sign in to your Microsoft Account in Word.

3. Display the Insert tab and then click the 'Insert an Add-in' button (Insert tab | Add-ins group) to display the Office Add-ins dialog box. (If a menu is displayed, click the See All link to display the Office Add-ins dialog box.) Click the Office Store button or the STORE tab (Office Add-ins dialog box) to visit the online Office Store.

4. Scroll through add-ins in the various categories (Figure 6–86). Locate a free add-in that you feel would be helpful to you while you use Word, click the Add button, and then follow the instructions to add the add-in to Word.

5. In Word, click the 'Insert an Add-in' button again to display the Office Add-ins dialog box. Click the add-in you added and then click the Insert button to use the add-in. Click the 'Insert an Add-in' arrow to see the added add-in in the list.

6. Practice using the add-in. Does the add-in work as you intended? Would you recommend the add-in to others?

7. ✻ Which add-ins, if any, were already on your computer or mobile device? Which add-in did you download and why? Answer the questions in #6.

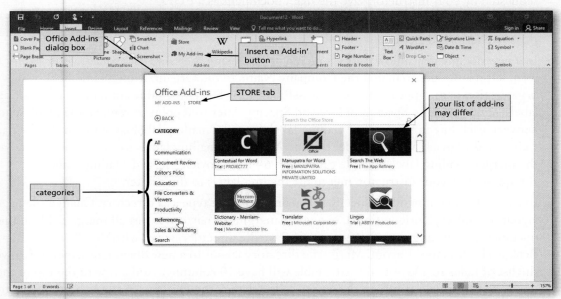

Figure 6–86

In the Labs

Design, create, modify, and/or use a document following the guidelines, concepts, and skills presented in this module. Labs 1 and 2, which increase in difficulty, require you to create solutions based on what you learned in the module; Lab 3 requires you to apply your creative thinking and problem-solving skills to design and implement a solution.

Lab 1: Creating a Form Letter Using a Template, a Data Source, Mailing Labels, and a Directory

Problem: You are graduating this May and have prepared your resume (shown in Figure 5–78 in Module 5). You decide to create a cover letter for your resume as a form letter that you will send to potential employers. The main document for the form letter is shown in Figure 6–87a.

Perform the following tasks:

1. Use the Timeless letter template to begin creating the main document for the form letter. If you cannot locate this template, open the file called Timeless letter from the Data Files. If necessary, change the document theme to Headlines (or a similar theme). Customize the theme fonts to match the resume (that is, headings Arial Black and body text Verdana). Save the main document for the form letter with the file name, Lab 6–1 Boskovich Cover Letter.

2. Type a new data source using the data shown in Figure 6–87b. Delete the field names not used and add one field name: Position. Rename the Company_Name field to Organization_Name. If requested by your instructor, add a record to the data source that contains your personal information. Save the data source with the file name, Lab 6–1 Boskovich Potential Employers.

3. Save the main document for the form letter again. Enter the text, image, merge fields, and formats as shown in the figure. Insert the AddressBlock and GreetingLine merge fields according to the sample formats shown in the figure. (Be sure to match the Company Name to the Organization_Name field so that the organization name appears in the AddressBlock field. *Hint:* Use the Insert Address Block dialog box, or click the Match Fields button (Mailings tab | Write & Insert Fields group). Change the top and bottom margins to 1 inch and the left and right margins to 1.25 inches. Specify the position of the rectangle graphic to 1 inch from the top of the page. Reduce the space above the paragraph containing the date to 36 point. If requested by your instructor, save the main document as a PDF.

4. Merge the form letters to a new document. Save the merged letters in a file called Lab 6–1 Boskovich Merged Letters.

5. In a new document window, address mailing labels using the same data source you used for the form letters. Be sure to match the Company Name to the Organization_Name field so that the organization name appears in the AddressBlock field. Select the table containing the mailing labels and change the Spacing Before and Spacing After to 0 point to remove the blank space between each line in the printed mailing label. Save the mailing label layout with the file name, Lab 6–1 Boskovich Mailing Label Layout. Merge the mailing labels to a new document. Save the merged mailing labels in a file called Lab 6–1 Boskovich Merged Mailing Labels. If requested by your instructor, merge the mailing labels to the printer.

6. In a new document window, specify the main document type as a directory. Change the page layout to landscape orientation. Change the margins to narrow. Insert all merge fields in the document, separating each with a comma. Save the directory layout with the file name, Lab 6–1 Boskovich Directory Layout. Merge the directory layout to a new document window. Convert the list of fields to a Word table (the table will have 10 columns). Add a row to the top of the table and insert field names in the empty cells. Change the font size of all text in the table to 9 point. Apply the List Table 3 - Accent 3 table style (remove formatting from the first column).

Resize the table columns so that the table looks like Figure 6–87b. Center the table. Sort the table in the directory listing by the Last Name field. Save the merged directory with the file name, Lab 6–1 Boskovich Merged Sorted Directory Listing.

7. Submit all documents in the format specified by your instructor.

8. ✸ If you did not want to use the AddressBlock and Greeting Line fields, how would you enter the address and salutation so that the letters printed the correct fields from each record?

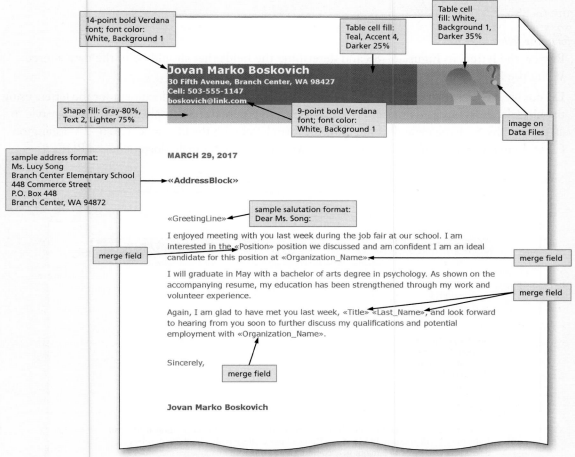

(a) Main Document for Form Letter

Figure 6–87

Title	First Name	Last Name	Organization Name	Address Line 1
Ms.	Lucy	Song	Branch Center Elementary School	448 Commerce Street
Mr.	Miguel	Arroyo	Johnston Elementary	829 Placid Boulevard
Mr.	Dashuan	Titus	Delman High School	17 South Street
Ms.	LaToya	Carrothers	Harrust High School	85 Windmill Lane
Mr.	Matthew	Mason	Squire Elementary	200 Eaton Parkway

Address Line 2	City	State	ZIP Code	Position
P.O. Box 448	Branch Center	WA	98472	counselor
	Sandfly	WA	98420	school counselor
P.O Box 17	Delman	WA	98404	high school counselor
	Harrust	WA	98496	student services counselor
	Mitcheltown	WA	98461	school counselor

(b) Data Source

Figure 6–87

Continued >

In the Labs *continued*

Lab 2: Designing a Data Source, Form Letter, and Directory from Sample Letters

Problem: You are graduating this May and have prepared your resume (shown in Figure 5–79 in Module 5). You decide to create a cover letter for your resume as a form letter that you will send to potential employers. Sample drafted letters for the cover letter are shown in Figure 6–88a and Figure 6–88b.

Perform the following tasks:

1. Review the letters in Figure 6–88 and determine the fields that should be in the data source. Write the field names on a piece of paper.

2. Do not use a template to create this form letter. In Word, create a main document for the letters using the block letter style. Create the letterhead as shown in Figure 6–88a. Apply the No Spacing style to all paragraphs. Save the main document for the form letter with the file name, Lab 6–2 Washington Cover Letter. If requested by your instructor, save the cover letter main document as a PDF.

Kaylee Jada Washington
15 Chestnut Boulevard, Goldstream, CA 94336 • Phone: 308-555-8752 • Email: kjwashington@world.com

letterhead

April 19, 2017

Ms. Lana Canaan
Morgan Industries
22 Chambers Lane
P.O. Box 22
Goldstream, CA 94336

Dear Ms. Canaan:

I am writing in response to your advertisement for the staff accountant position at Morgan Industries. I will graduate in May from Eureka Falls College with a bachelor of science degree in business, with a major in accounting and a minor in quantitative methods.

My coursework and experience make me an ideal candidate for this full-time position. As shown on my accompanying resume, I have firsthand experience with many financial duties, including payroll, inventory, receivables, invoicing, reporting, auditing, credit checks, and forecasting.

I am confident I will be a valuable asset to your staff. I look forward to the opportunity to meet with you, Ms. Canaan, to discuss my qualifications and potential employment with Morgan Industries.

Sincerely,

Kaylee Washington

(a) Sample First Letter
Figure 6–88

3. Create a data source containing five records, consisting of data from the two letters shown in Figure 6–88 and then add three more records with your own data. If requested by your instructor, add a record to the data source that contains your personal information. Save the data source with the file name, Lab 6–2 Washington Potential Employers.

4. Enter the text and merge fields into the letter. The letter requires one IF field that displays the text, full-time, if the available job position is for a full-time employee; otherwise, it displays the words, part-time, if the available job position is for a part-time employee. Merge the form letters to a new document. Save the merged letters with the file name, Lab 6–2 Washington Merged Letters. Submit the merged letters in the format specified by your instructor.

5. Merge the data source to a directory. Convert it to a Word table. Add an attractive border to the table and apply any other formatting you feel necessary. Submit the directory in the format specified by your instructor.

6. ✳ Which fields did you use in your data source?

Kaylee Jada Washington

15 Chestnut Boulevard, Goldstream, CA 94336 • Phone: 308-555-8752 • Email: kjwashington@world.com

April 19, 2017

Mr. Raul Ramos
Bartlett Insurance
104 Michigan Street
P.O. Box 104
Goldstream, CA 94336

Dear Mr. Ramos:

I am writing in response to your advertisement for the accounting analyst position at Bartlett Insurance. I will graduate in May from Eureka Falls College with a bachelor of science degree in business, with a major in accounting and a minor in quantitative methods.

My coursework and experience make me an ideal candidate for this part-time position. As shown on my accompanying resume, I have firsthand experience with many financial duties, including payroll, inventory, receivables, invoicing, reporting, auditing, credit checks, and forecasting.

I am confident I will be a valuable asset to your staff. I look forward to the opportunity to meet with you, Mr. Ramos, to discuss my qualifications and potential employment with Bartlett Insurance.

Sincerely,

Kaylee Washington

(b) Sample Second Letter
Figure 6–88

Continued >

In the Labs *continued*

Lab 3: **Consider This: Your Turn**

Create Thank You Form Letters

Problem: As owner of Pine Valley Campground, you would like to send form letters to recent guests, thanking them for their stay.

Part 1:   Pine Valley Campground is located at 8754 Wilderness Lane, Harpville, KY 42194; website is www.pinevalley.com; email address is info@pinevalley.com. In the form letters, thank guests for their recent stay — identifying the starting date of their stay, the type of campsite in which they stayed, and the length of their stay. Mention you hope they enjoyed their stay and look forward to seeing them again. Also mention that they will receive a 10 percent discount on any future stays this season if they bring this letter to check-in.

Use the concepts and techniques presented in this module to create and format this form letter. Use your name and phone number in the sender information in the main document. The merge fields for the data source are shown in Table 6–1. All merge fields in the data source should be used at least once in the form letter. Merge all records and use a filter to merge just those guests who stayed at tent sites. Be sure to check the spelling and grammar of the finished documents. Create a directory of the data source records. Address and print accompanying labels or envelopes for the form letters. Submit your assignment in the format specified by your instructor.

Table 6–1											
Title	First Name	Last Name	Address Line 1	Address Line 2	City	State	ZIP Code	Site Type	Reservation Date	Length of Stay
Mr.	Jonah	Weinberg	35009 Clark Street	Apt. D3	Harpville	KY	42194	tent	September 8	two nights
Ms.	Shannon	O'Malley	13292 Cherry Street		Hill City	KY	42002	full hookup	September 12	four nights
Mr.	Tyrone	Davis	908 Wilson Court	P.O. Box 77	Harpville	KY	42194	water and electric	September 7	three nights
Ms.	Louella	Drake	172 East Park Street	Apt. 132	Blackburg	KY	42392	full hookup	September 8	two nights
Ms.	Roberta	Jeffries	201 Timmons Place	Unit 20C	Horizon	KY	42509	tent	September 10	two nights

Part 2:   ☀ You made several decisions while creating the form letter, data source, and directory in this assignment: whether to use a template or create the letter from scratch, wording to use, where to position text and merge fields in the letter, how to format elements, how to set up the data source, and how to format the directory. What was the rationale behind each of these decisions?

7 | Creating a Newsletter with a Pull-Quote and Graphics

Objectives

You will have mastered the material in this module when you can:

- Insert and format WordArt
- Set custom tab stops
- Crop a graphic
- Rotate a graphic
- Format a document in multiple columns
- Justify a paragraph
- Hyphenate a document
- Format a character as a drop cap

- Insert a column break
- Insert and format a text box
- Copy and paste using a split window
- Balance columns
- Modify and format a SmartArt graphic
- Copy and paste using the Office Clipboard
- Add an art page border

Introduction

Professional-looking documents, such as newsletters and brochures, often are created using desktop publishing software. With desktop publishing software, you can divide a document in multiple columns, wrap text around diagrams and other graphical images, change fonts and font sizes, add color and lines, and so on, to create an attention-grabbing document. Desktop publishing software, such as Microsoft Publisher, Adobe PageMaker, or QuarkXpress, enables you to open an existing word processing document and enhance it through formatting tools not provided in your word processing software. Word, however, provides many of the formatting features that you would find in a desktop publishing program. Thus, you can use Word to create eye-catching newsletters and brochures.

Project — Newsletter

A newsletter is a publication geared for a specific audience that is created on a recurring basis, such as weekly, monthly, or quarterly. The audience may be subscribers, club members, employees, customers, patrons, students, etc.

The project in this module uses Word to produce the two-page newsletter shown in Figure 7–1. The newsletter is a monthly publication called *Security Trends*. Each issue of *Security Trends* contains a feature article and announcements. This month's feature article discusses biometrics. The feature article spans the first two columns of the first page of the newsletter and then continues on the second page. The announcements, which are located in the third column of the first page, inform subscribers about discounts and an upcoming webinar and announce the topic of the next issue's feature article.

The *Security Trends* newsletter in this module incorporates the desktop publishing features of Word. The body of each page of the newsletter is divided in three columns. A variety of fonts, font sizes, and colors add visual appeal to the document. The first page has text wrapped around a pull-quote, and the second page has text wrapped around a graphic. Horizontal and vertical lines separate distinct areas of the newsletter, including a page border around the perimeter of each page.

The project in this module involves several steps requiring you to drag and drop. If you drag to the wrong location, you may want to cancel an action. Remember that you always can click the Undo button on the Quick Access Toolbar or press CTRL+Z to cancel your most recent action.

In this module, you will learn how to create the newsletter shown in Figure 7–1. The following roadmap identifies general activities you will perform as you progress through this module:

1. CREATE the NAMEPLATE FOR the FIRST PAGE of the newsletter.
2. FORMAT the FIRST PAGE of the body of the newsletter.
3. CREATE a PULL-QUOTE on the first page of the newsletter.
4. CREATE the NAMEPLATE FOR the SECOND PAGE of the newsletter.
5. FORMAT the SECOND PAGE of the body of the newsletter.
6. ADD a PAGE BORDER to the newsletter.

Desktop Publishing Terminology

As you create professional-looking newsletters and brochures, you should be familiar with several desktop publishing terms. Figure 7–1 identifies these terms:

- A **nameplate**, or **banner**, is the portion of a newsletter that contains the title of the newsletter and usually an issue information line.
- The **issue information line** identifies the specific publication.
- A **ruling line**, usually identified by its direction as a **horizontal rule** or **vertical rule**, is a line that separates areas of the newsletter.
- A **subhead** is a heading within the body of the newsletter.
- A **pull-quote** is text that is *pulled*, or copied, from the text of the document and given graphical emphasis.

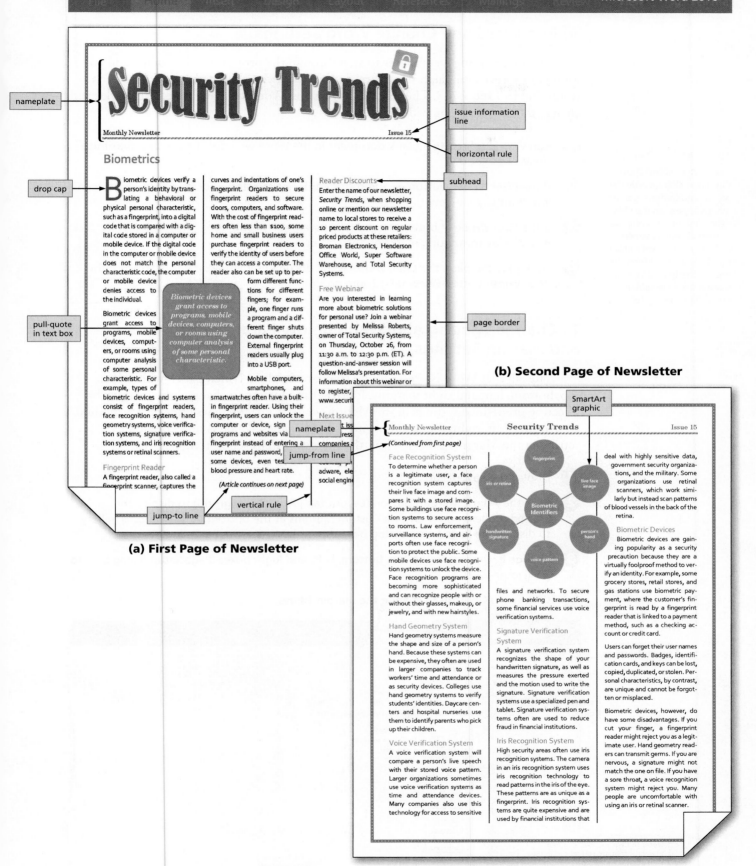

nameplate

issue information line

horizontal rule

drop cap

subhead

pull-quote in text box

page border

(b) Second Page of Newsletter

SmartArt graphic

nameplate

jump-from line

vertical rule

jump-to line

(a) First Page of Newsletter

Figure 7–1

To Run Word and Change Word Settings

If you are using a computer to step through the project in this module and you want your screens to match the figures in this book, you should change your screen's resolution to 1366 × 768. The following steps run Word, display formatting marks, and change the zoom to page width.

BTW

The Ribbon and Screen Resolution
Word may change how the groups and buttons within the groups appear on the ribbon, depending on the computer or mobile device's screen resolution. Thus, your ribbon may look different from the ones in this book if you are using a screen resolution other than 1366 × 768.

1 Run Word and create a blank document in the Word window. If necessary, maximize the Word window.

2 If the Print Layout button on the status bar is not selected, click it so that your screen is in Print Layout view.

3 If the 'Show/Hide ¶' button (Home tab | Paragraph group) is not selected already, click it to display formatting marks on the screen.

4 To display the page the same width as the document window, if necessary, click the Page Width button (View tab | Zoom group).

To Change Spacing above and below Paragraphs and Margin Settings

Recall that Word is preset to use standard 8.5-by-11-inch paper, with 1-inch top, bottom, left, and right margins. In earlier modules, you changed the margins by selecting predefined settings in the Margins gallery. For the newsletter in this module, all margins (left, right, top, and bottom) are .75 inches, which is not a predefined setting in the Margins gallery. Thus, the following steps set custom margins.

1 Display the Layout tab.

2 Click the Adjust Margins button (Layout tab | Page Setup group) to display the Margins gallery and then click Custom Margins at the bottom of the Margins gallery to display the Page Setup dialog box.

3 Change each value in the Top, Bottom, Left, and Right boxes (Page Setup dialog box) to .75 (Figure 7–2).

4 Click the OK button to change the margin values.

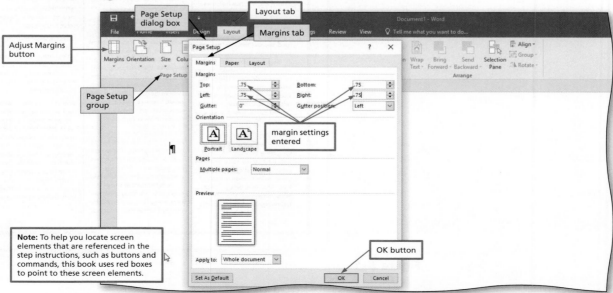

Figure 7–2

To Change Theme Colors

The newsletter in this module uses the Frame theme. The following steps change the theme to Frame.

1 Display the Design tab.

2 Click the Themes button (Design tab | Document Formatting group) and then click Frame in the Themes gallery to change the document theme.

BTW
Touch Screen Differences
The Office and Windows interfaces may vary if you are using a touch screen. For this reason, you might notice that the function or appearance of your touch screen differs slightly from this module's presentation.

Creating the Nameplate

The nameplate on the first page of this newsletter consists of the information above the multiple columns (shown in Figure 7–1a at the beginning of this module). In this project, the nameplate includes the newsletter title, Security Trends, an image of a lock, and the issue information line.

The following sections use the steps outlined below to create the nameplate for the first page of the newsletter in this module.

1. Enter and format the newsletter title using WordArt.

2. Set custom tab stops for the issue information line.

3. Enter text in the issue information line.

4. Add a horizontal rule below the issue information line.

5. Insert and format the image.

How should you design a nameplate?

A nameplate visually identifies a newsletter. It should catch the attention of readers, enticing them to read a newsletter. Usually, the nameplate is positioned horizontally across the top of the newsletter, although some nameplates are vertical. The nameplate typically consists of the title of the newsletter and the issue information line. Some also include a subtitle, a slogan, and a graphical image or logo.

Guidelines for the newsletter title and other elements in the nameplate are as follows:

• Compose a title that is short, yet conveys the contents of the newsletter. In the newsletter title, eliminate unnecessary words such as these: the, newsletter. Use a decorative font in as large a font size as possible so that the title stands out on the page.

• Other elements on the nameplate should not compete in size with the title. Use colors that complement the title. Select easy-to-read fonts.

• Arrange the elements of the nameplate so that it does not have a cluttered appearance. If necessary, use ruling lines to visually separate areas of the nameplate.

CONSIDER THIS

To Insert WordArt

1 CREATE NAMEPLATE FOR FIRST PAGE | 2 FORMAT FIRST PAGE | 3 CREATE PULL-QUOTE
4 CREATE NAMEPLATE FOR SECOND PAGE | 5 FORMAT SECOND PAGE | 6 ADD PAGE BORDER

In Module 3, you inserted a shape drawing object in a document. Recall that a drawing object is a graphic you create using Word. Another type of drawing object, called **WordArt**, enables you to create text with special effects, such as shadowed, rotated, stretched, skewed, and wavy effects.

This project uses WordArt for the newsletter title, Security Trends. ***Why?*** *A title created with WordArt is likely to draw the reader's attention.* The following steps insert WordArt.

- Display the Insert tab.

- Click the Insert WordArt button (Insert tab | Text group) to display the Insert WordArt gallery (Figure 7–3).

Q&A Once I select a WordArt style, can I customize its appearance?
Yes. The next steps customize the WordArt style selected here.

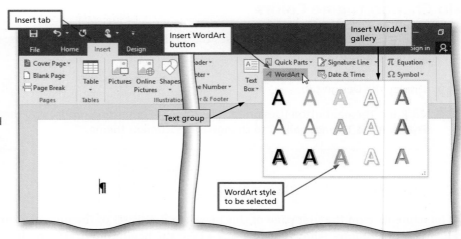

Figure 7–3

- Click 'Fill - Teal, Accent 1, Outline - Background 1, Hard Shadow - Accent 1' in the WordArt gallery (third WordArt style in last row) to insert a drawing object in the document that is formatted according to the selected WordArt style, which contains the placeholder text, Your text here (Figure 7–4).

- Type **Security Trends** to replace the selected placeholder text in the WordArt drawing object (shown in Figure 7–5).

Q&A What if my placeholder text no longer is selected?
Drag through it to select it.

How do I correct a mistake in the WordArt text?
You correct WordArt text using the same techniques you use to correct document text.

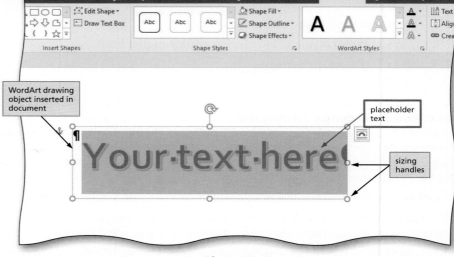

Figure 7–4

To Resize WordArt

You resize WordArt the same way you resize any other graphic. That is, you can drag its sizing handles or enter values in the Shape Height and Shape Width boxes. The next steps resize the WordArt drawing object.

1 With the WordArt drawing object selected, if necessary, display the Drawing Tools Format tab.

2 Change the value in the Shape Height box to 1.44 and the value in the Shape Width box to 7 (Figure 7–5).

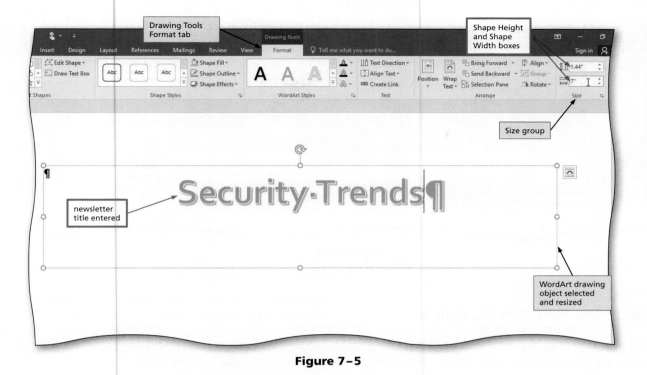

Figure 7-5

To Change the Font and Font Size of WordArt Text

You change the font and font size of WordArt text the same way you change the font and font size of any other text. That is, you select the text and then change its font and font size. The following steps change the font and font size of WordArt text.

1 Select the WordArt text, in this case, Security Trends.

2 Change the font of the selected text to Bernard MT Condensed (or a similar font).

3 Change the font size of the selected text to 72 point (shown in Figure 7-6).

To Change an Object's Text Wrapping

When you insert a drawing object in a Word document, the default text wrapping is Square, which means text will wrap around the object in the shape of a square. Because you want the nameplate above the rest of the newsletter, you change the text wrapping for the drawing object to Top and Bottom. The following steps change a drawing object's text wrapping.

1 With the WordArt drawing object selected, click the Layout Options button that is attached to the WordArt drawing object to display the Layout Options gallery.

2 Click 'Top and Bottom' in the Layout Options gallery so that the WordArt drawing object will not cover the document text; in this case, the paragraph mark moves below the WordArt drawing object (Figure 7-6).

3 Close the Layout Options gallery.

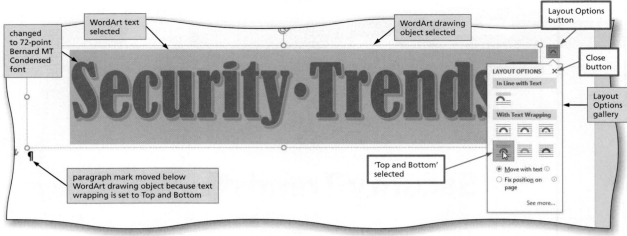

Figure 7–6

To Change the WordArt Fill Color

The next step is to change the color of the WordArt text so that it displays a teal and orange gradient fill color. **Gradient** means the colors blend into one another. Word includes several built-in gradient fill colors, or you can customize one for use in drawing objects. The following steps change the fill color of the WordArt drawing object to a built-in gradient fill color and then customize the selected fill color. *Why? Using a gradient fill color will add interest to the title.*

1

- With the WordArt drawing object selected, click the Text Fill arrow (Drawing Tools Format tab | WordArt Styles group) to display the Text Fill gallery.

Q&A

The Text Fill gallery did not appear. Why not?
Be sure you click the Text Fill arrow, which is to the right of the Text Fill button. If you mistakenly click the Text Fill button, Word places a default fill in the selected WordArt instead of displaying the Text Fill gallery.

2

- Point to Gradient in the Text Fill gallery to display the Gradient gallery (Figure 7–7).

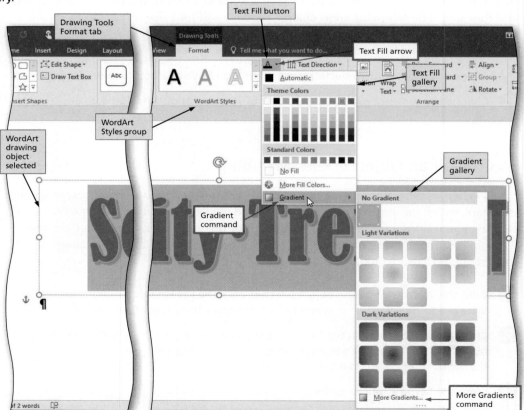

Figure 7–7

3

- Click More Gradients in the Gradient gallery to open the Format Shape task pane. If necessary, click the Text Options tab in the Format Shape task pane and then, if necessary, click the 'Text Fill & Outline' button. If necessary, expand the Text Fill section.

- Click Gradient fill in the Text Fill section to display options related to gradient colors in the task pane (Figure 7–8).

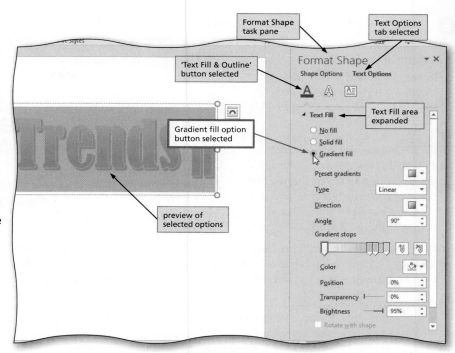

Figure 7–8

4

- Click the Preset gradients button in the Format Shape task pane to display a palette of built-in gradient fill colors (Figure 7–9).

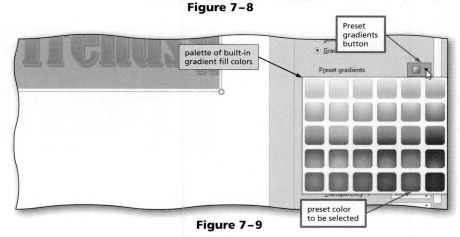

Figure 7–9

5

- Click 'Radial Gradient - Accent 5' (bottom row, fifth column) in the Preset gradients palette to select the built-in gradient color, which shows a preview in the Gradient stops area (Figure 7–10).

Q&A What is a gradient stop?
A gradient stop is the location where two colors blend. You can change the color of a stop so that Word changes the color of the blend. You also can add or delete stops, with a minimum of two stops and a maximum of ten stops per gradient fill color.

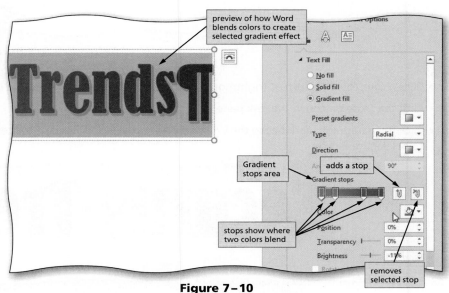

Figure 7–10

- Click the second gradient stop to select it and then click the Color button to display a Color palette, from which you can select a color for the selected stop (Figure 7–11).

7

- Click 'Orange, Accent 4, Darker 25%' (fifth row, eighth column) in the Color palette to change the color of the selected stop and the gradient between the selected stop and the next stop.

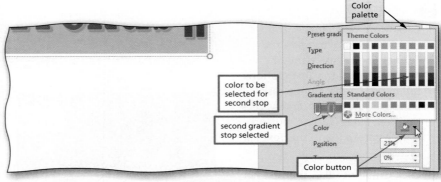

Figure 7–11

- Click the rightmost gradient stop to select it and then click the Color button to display a Color palette. Click 'Orange, Accent 4, Darker 25%' (fifth row, eighth column) in the Color palette to change the color of the selected stop and the gradient between the selected stop and the previous stop.

Q&A

Can I move a gradient stop?

Yes. You can drag a stop to any location along the color bar. You also can adjust the position, brightness, and transparency of any selected stop.

8

- Click the Direction button to display a gallery that shows a variety of directions for the gradient colors (Figure 7–12).

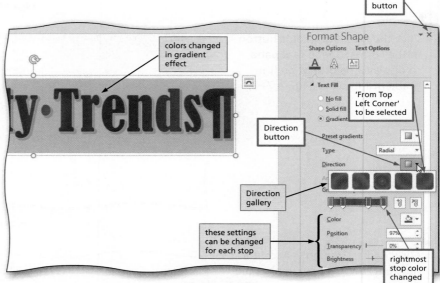

Figure 7–12

9

- Click 'From Top Left Corner' (rightmost direction) in the Direction gallery to specify the direction to blend the colors.
- Click the Close button in the task pane.
- Click the paragraph mark below the WordArt drawing object to deselect the text so that you can see its gradient fill colors (Figure 7–13).

Figure 7–13

To Change the WordArt Shape

1 CREATE NAMEPLATE FOR FIRST PAGE | 2 FORMAT FIRST PAGE | 3 CREATE PULL-QUOTE

4 CREATE NAMEPLATE FOR SECOND PAGE | 5 FORMAT SECOND PAGE | 6 ADD PAGE BORDER

Word provides a variety of shapes to make your WordArt more interesting. The following steps change the WordArt shape. **Why?** *The WordArt in this newsletter has a wavy appearance.*

- Click the WordArt drawing object to select it.

- If necessary, display the Drawing Tools Format tab.

- Click the Text Effects button (Drawing Tools Format tab | WordArt Styles group) to display the Text Effects gallery.

- Point to Transform in the Text Effects gallery to display the Transform gallery.

- Point to 'Double Wave 1' (third effect, fifth row in Warp area) in the Transform gallery to display a live preview of the selected transform effect applied to the selected drawing object (Figure 7–14).

🔎 **Experiment**

- Point to various text effects in the Transform gallery and watch the selected drawing object conform to that transform effect.

Figure 7–14

- Click 'Double Wave 1' in the Transform gallery to change the shape of the WordArt drawing object.

To Set Custom Tab Stops Using the Tabs Dialog Box

1 CREATE NAMEPLATE FOR FIRST PAGE | 2 FORMAT FIRST PAGE | 3 CREATE PULL-QUOTE

4 CREATE NAMEPLATE FOR SECOND PAGE | 5 FORMAT SECOND PAGE | 6 ADD PAGE BORDER

The issue information line in this newsletter contains the text, Monthly Newsletter, at the left margin and the issue number at the right margin (shown in Figure 7–1a at the beginning of this module). In Word, a paragraph cannot be both left-aligned and right-aligned. **Why?** *If you click the 'Align Text Right' button (Home tab | Paragraph group), for example, all text will be right-aligned.* To place text at the right margin of a left-aligned paragraph, you set a tab stop at the right margin.

One method of setting custom tab stops is to click the ruler at the desired location of the tab stop, which you learned in an earlier module. You cannot click, however, at the right margin location. Thus, the following steps use the Tabs dialog box to set a custom tab stop.

1

- If necessary, display the Home tab.

- Position the insertion point on the paragraph mark below the WordArt drawing object, which is the paragraph to be formatted with the custom tab stops.

- Click the Paragraph Settings Dialog Box Launcher to display the Paragraph dialog box (Figure 7–15).

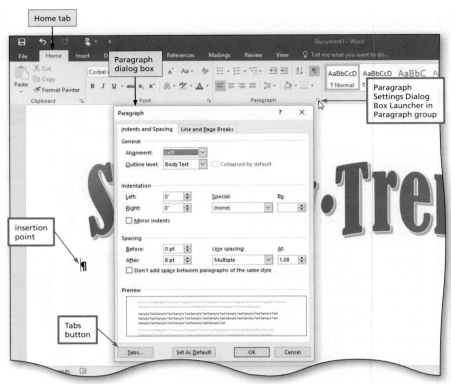

Figure 7–15

2

- Click the Tabs button (Paragraph dialog box) to display the Tabs dialog box.

- Type 7 in the 'Tab stop position' text box (Tabs dialog box).

- Click Right in the Alignment area to specify alignment for text at the tab stop (Figure 7–16).

3

- Click the Set button (Tabs dialog box) to set a right-aligned custom tab stop at the specified position.

- Click the OK button to set the defined tab stops.

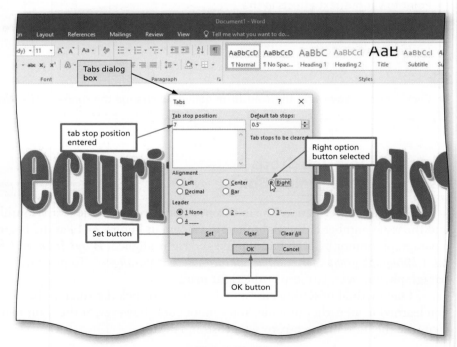

Figure 7–16

Other Ways

1. Click desired tab stop on ruler

2. Right-click paragraph (or, if using touch, tap 'Show Context Menu' button on mini toolbar), click Paragraph on shortcut menu, click Tabs button (Paragraph dialog box), enter desired settings, click OK button

To Enter Text

The following steps enter the issue information line text.

1 With the insertion point on the paragraph below the WordArt, change the font to Century Schoolbook (or a similar font) and the font size to 10 point.

2 Type **Monthly Newsletter** on line 2 of the newsletter.

If requested by your instructor, enter your name instead of the word, Monthly.

3 Press the TAB key and then type **Issue 15** to complete the issue information line (Figure 7–17).

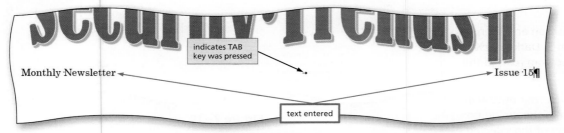

Monthly Newsletter

indicates TAB key was pressed

Issue 15¶

text entered

Figure 7–17

 Q&A The nameplate does not appear to extend to the right margin. Why not?

If you have formatting marks displaying, the paragraph mark consumes space at the right margin. To see how the nameplate will print, turn off formatting marks.

To Border One Edge of a Paragraph

1 CREATE NAMEPLATE FOR FIRST PAGE | 2 FORMAT FIRST PAGE | 3 CREATE PULL-QUOTE
4 CREATE NAMEPLATE FOR SECOND PAGE | 5 FORMAT SECOND PAGE | 6 ADD PAGE BORDER

In Word, you use borders to create ruling lines. As discussed in previous modules, Word can place borders on any edge of a paragraph; that is, Word can place a border on the top, bottom, left, and right edges of a paragraph.

One method of bordering paragraphs is by clicking the desired border in the Borders gallery, which you learned in an earlier module. If you want to specify a particular border, for example, one with color, you use the Borders and Shading dialog box. The following steps use the Borders and Shading dialog box to place a border below a paragraph. *Why? In this newsletter, the issue information line has a 3-point diagonally striped teal border below it.*

1

- Click the Borders arrow (Home tab | Paragraph group) to display the Borders gallery (Figure 7–18).

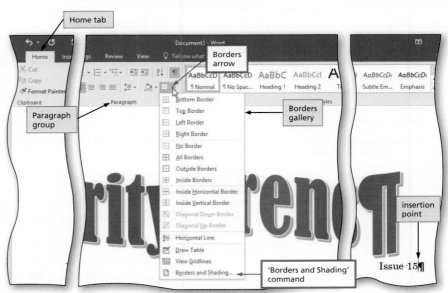

Figure 7–18

2

- Click 'Borders and Shading' in the Borders gallery to display the Borders and Shading dialog box.

- Click Custom in the Setting area (Borders and Shading dialog box) because you are setting just a bottom border.

- Scroll through the Style list and click the style shown in Figure 7–19, which is a diagonally striped line for the border.

- Click the Color button and then click 'Teal, Accent 5, Darker 50%' (ninth column, bottom row) in the Color gallery.

- Click the Bottom Border button in the Preview area of the dialog box to show a preview of the selected border style (Figure 7–19).

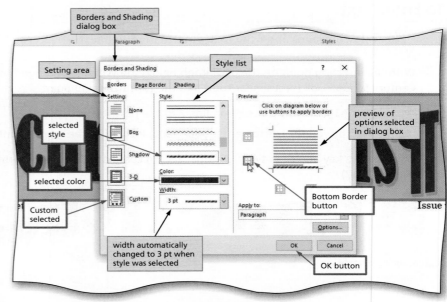

Figure 7–19

Q&A What is the purpose of the buttons in the Preview area?
They are toggles that display and remove the top, bottom, left, and right borders from the diagram in the Preview area.

3

- Click the OK button to place the defined border on the paragraph containing the insertion point (Figure 7–20).

Figure 7–20

Q&A How would I change an existing border?
You first remove the existing border by clicking the Borders arrow (Home tab | Paragraph group) and then clicking the border in the Borders gallery that identifies the border you wish to remove. Then, add a new border as described in these steps.

Other Ways

1. Click 'Borders and Shading' button (Design tab | Page Background group), click Borders tab (Borders and Shading dialog box), select desired border, click OK button

To Insert a Picture

The next steps insert an image of locks in the nameplate.

1 Display the Insert tab.

2 Click the Online Pictures button (Insert tab | Illustrations group) to display the Insert Pictures dialog box.

③ Type `locks` in the Search box (Insert Pictures dialog box) to specify the search text and then click the Search button to display a list of images that match the entered search text.

④ Scroll through the list of images to locate the one shown in Figure 7–21 (or a similar image), click the image to select it, and then click the Insert button (Insert Picture dialog box) to download the image, close the dialog box, and insert the selected image at the location of the insertion point in the document.

Q&A

What if I cannot locate the same image as in Figure 7–21?
Click the Cancel button to close the dialog box and then click the From File button (Insert tab | Illustrations group) to display the Insert Picture dialog box, navigate to and select the 1383900176-2400px.png file on the Data Files, and then click the Insert button (Insert Picture dialog box) to insert the picture.

What if my inserted image is not in the same location as in Figure 7–21?
The image may be in a different location, depending on the position of the insertion point when you inserted the image. In a later section, you will move the image to a different location.

To Change the Color of a Graphic

The following steps change the color of the graphic (the locks) to a shade of gold.

① With the graphic still selected, click the Color button (Picture Tools Format tab | Adjust group) to display the Color gallery (Figure 7–21).

② Click 'Gold, Accent color 2 Light' (third color, bottom row) in the Recolor area in the Color gallery to change the color of the selected graphic.

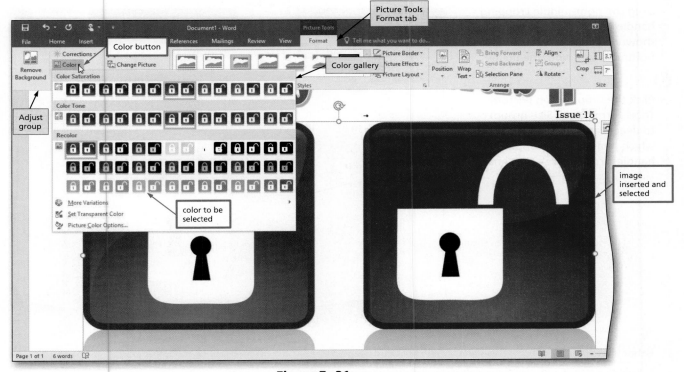

Figure 7–21

To Crop a Graphic

The next step is to format the image just inserted. You would like to remove the rightmost lock from the image. *Why? You want just one lock to appear in the newsletter.* Word allows you to **crop**, or remove edges from, a graphic. The following steps crop a graphic.

1

- With the graphic selected, click the Crop button (Picture Tools Format tab | Size group), which places cropping handles on the image in the document.

Q&A What if I mistakenly click the Crop arrow?
Click the Crop button.

- Position the pointer on the right-middle cropping handle so that it looks like a sideways letter T (Figure 7–22).

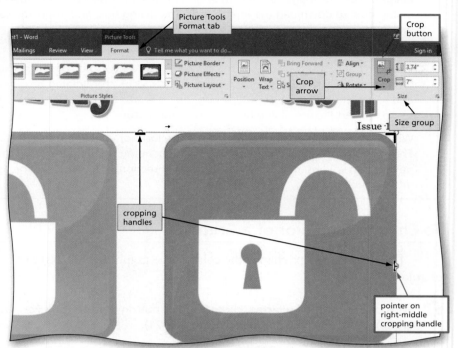

Figure 7–22

2

- Drag the right-middle cropping handle inward to the location shown in Figure 7–23 to crop the rightmost lock from the image.

3

- Click the Crop button (Picture Tools Format tab | Size group) to deactivate the cropping tool, which removes the cropping handles from the selected image.

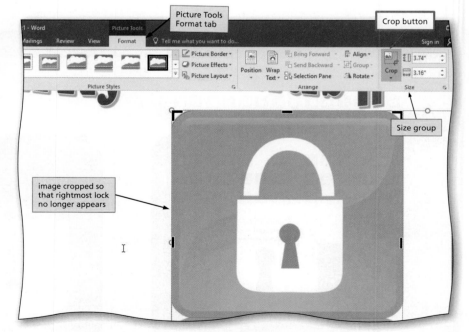

Figure 7–23

Other Ways

1. Right-click graphic, click Crop button on mini toolbar, drag cropping handles, click Crop button

To Change an Object's Text Wrapping and Size

When you insert an object (image) in a Word document, the default text wrapping is In Line with Text, which means the object is part of the current paragraph. Because you want the lock image behind the newsletter title, you change the text wrapping for the image to Behind Text. The next steps change a drawing object's text wrapping and also change its size.

1 With the lock graphic selected, click the Layout Options button attached to the graphic to display the Layout Options gallery.

2 Click Behind Text in the Layout Options gallery so that the image is positioned behind text in the document.

3 Close the Layout Options gallery.

4 Change the values in the Shape Height and Shape Width boxes (Picture Tools Format tab | Size group) to .6" and .51", respectively.

To Move a Graphic

The clip art image needs to be moved up so that the bottom of the lock is on the s in the word, Trends, in the newsletter title. The following steps move a graphic.

1 Hide formatting marks so that you can see exactly where the letter s ends.

2 Drag the graphic to the location shown in Figure 7–24.

Figure 7–24

To Use the Selection Task Pane

1 CREATE NAMEPLATE FOR FIRST PAGE | 2 FORMAT FIRST PAGE | 3 CREATE PULL-QUOTE
4 CREATE NAMEPLATE FOR SECOND PAGE | 5 FORMAT SECOND PAGE | 6 ADD PAGE BORDER

The next step is to rotate the lock image, but because it is positioned behind the text, it may be difficult to select it. The following step opens the Selection task pane. *Why? The Selection task pane enables you easily to select items on the screen that are layered behind other objects.*

1

- If necessary, click in the graphic to display the Picture Tools Format tab.

- Click the 'Display the Selection Pane' button (Picture Tools Format tab | Arrange group) to open the Selection task pane (Figure 7–25).

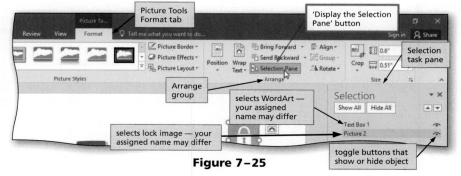

Figure 7–25

Experiment

- Click Text Box 1 in the Selection task pane to select the WordArt drawing object. Click Picture 2 in the Selection task pane to select the lock image.

Q&A What are the displayed names in the Selection task pane?
Word assigns names to each object in the document. The names displayed on your screen may differ.

To Rotate a Graphic

1 CREATE NAMEPLATE FOR FIRST PAGE | 2 FORMAT FIRST PAGE | 3 CREATE PULL-QUOTE
4 CREATE NAMEPLATE FOR SECOND PAGE | 5 FORMAT SECOND PAGE | 6 ADD PAGE BORDER

The following steps rotate a graphic. *Why?* *You would like the lock image angled inward a bit more.*

1

- If necessary, click Picture 2 in the Selection task pane to select the lock image.
- Position the pointer on the graphic's rotate handle (Figure 7–26).

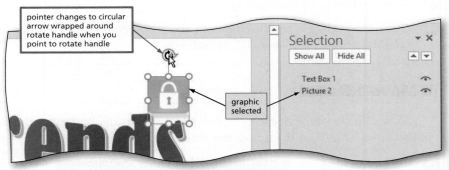

Figure 7–26

2

- Drag the rotate handle rightward and outward to rotate the graphic slightly as shown in Figure 7–27. (You may need to rotate the graphic a few times to position it in the desired location.)

Q&A Can I drag the rotate handle in any direction?
You can drag the rotate handle clockwise or counterclockwise.

Figure 7–27

What if I am using a touch screen?
Because the rotate handle is not available on a touch screen, you enter the degree of rotation in the Size dialog box. Tap the Rotate Objects button (Picture Tools Format tab | Arrange group) to display the Rotate Objects menu, tap 'More Rotation Options' on the Rotate Objects menu to display the Size sheet in the Layout dialog box, change the Rotation value to 14, and then tap the OK button.

3

- Click the Close button on the Selection task pane to close the task pane.
- Click somewhere in the issue information line to deselect the graphic.
- Save the title page on your hard drive, OneDrive, or other storage location using the file name, Security Trends Newsletter.

Break Point: If you wish to take a break, this is a good place to do so. You can exit Word now. To resume at a later time, run Word, open the file called Security Trends Newsletter, and continue following the steps from this location forward.

Formatting the First Page of the Body of the Newsletter

The next step is to format the first page of the body of the newsletter. The body of the newsletter in this module is divided in three columns (shown in Figure 7–1a at the beginning of this module). The first two columns contain the feature article, and the third column contains announcements. The characters in the paragraphs are aligned on both the right and left edges — similar to newspaper columns. The first letter in the first paragraph is much larger than the rest of the characters in the paragraph. A vertical rule separates the columns. The steps in the following sections format the first page of the body of the newsletter using these desktop publishing features.

What guidelines should you follow when creating the body of a newsletter?
While content and subject matter of newsletters may vary, the procedures used to create newsletters are similar:

- **Write the body copy.** Newsletters should contain articles of interest and relevance to readers. Some share information, while others promote a product or service. Use active voice in body copy, which is more engaging than passive voice. Proofread the body copy to be sure it is error free. Check all facts for accuracy.

- **Organize body copy in columns.** Most newsletters arrange body copy in columns. The body copy in columns, often called **snaking columns** or newspaper-style columns, flows from the bottom of one column to the top of the next column.

- **Format the body copy.** Begin the feature article on the first page of the newsletter. If the article spans multiple pages, use a continuation line, called a jump or jump line, to guide the reader to the remainder of the article. The message at the end of the article on the first page of the newsletter is called a **jump-to line**, and a **jump-from line** marks the beginning of the continuation, which is usually on a subsequent page.

- **Maintain consistency.** Be consistent with placement of body copy elements in newsletter editions. If the newsletter contains announcements, for example, position them in the same location in each edition so that readers easily can find them.

- **Maximize white space.** Allow plenty of space between lines, paragraphs, and columns. Tightly packed text is difficult to read. Separate the text adequately from graphics, borders, and headings.

- **Incorporate color.** Use colors that complement those in the nameplate. Be careful not to overuse color. Restrict color below the nameplate to drop caps, subheads, graphics, and ruling lines. If you do not have a color printer, still change the colors because the colors will print in shades of black and gray, which add variety to the newsletter.

- **Select and format subheads.** Develop subheads with as few words as possible. Readers should be able to identify content of the next topic by glancing at a subhead. Subheads should be emphasized in the newsletter but should not compete with text in the nameplate. Use a larger, bold, or otherwise contrasting font for subheads so that they stand apart from the body copy. Use this same format for all subheads for consistency. Leave a space above subheads to visually separate their content from the previous topic. Be consistent with spacing above and below subheads throughout the newsletter.

- **Divide sections with vertical rules.** Use vertical rules to guide the reader through the newsletter.

- **Enhance the document with visuals.** Add energy to the newsletter and emphasis to important points with graphics, pull-quotes, and other visuals, such as drop caps, to mark beginning of an article. Use these elements sparingly, however, so that the newsletter does not have a crowded appearance. Fewer, large visuals are more effective than several smaller ones. If you use a graphic that you did not create, be sure to obtain permission to use it in the newsletter and give necessary credit to the creator of the graphic.

To Clear Formatting

The next step is to enter the title of the feature article below the horizontal rule. To do this, position the insertion point at the end of the issue information line (after the 5 in Issue 15) and then press the ENTER key. Recall that the issue information line has a bottom border. When you press the ENTER key in a bordered paragraph, Word carries forward any borders to the next paragraph. Thus, after you press the ENTER key, you should clear formatting to format the new paragraph as the Normal style. The following steps clear formatting.

1 Click at the end of line 2 (the issue information line) so that the insertion point is immediately after the 5 in Issue 15. Press the ENTER key to advance the insertion point to the next line, which also moves the border down one line.

2 If necessary, display the Home tab. Click the 'Clear All Formatting' button (Home tab | Font group) to apply the Normal style to the location of the insertion point, which in this case moves the new paragraph below the border on the issue information line.

To Format Text as a Heading Style, Modify a Heading Style, and Adjust Spacing before and after the Paragraph

Below the bottom border in the nameplate is the title of the feature article, Biometrics. The following steps apply the Heading 1 style to this paragraph, modify the style, and adjust the paragraph spacing.

1 If necessary, display formatting marks.

2 With the insertion point on the paragraph mark below the border, click Heading 1 (Home tab | Styles group) to apply the Heading 1 style to the paragraph containing the insertion point.

3 Increase the font size 20 point. Bold the paragraph. Update the Heading 1 style to reflect these changes.

4 Type **Biometrics** as the title of the feature article.

5 Display the Layout tab. Change the Spacing Before box to 18 pt and the Spacing After box to 12 pt (Figure 7–28).

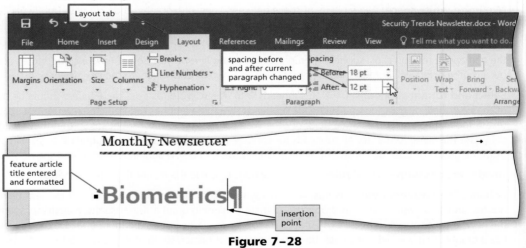

Figure 7–28

Columns

When you begin a document in Word, it has one column. You can divide a portion of a document or the entire document in multiple columns. Within each column, you can type, modify, or format text.

To divide a portion of a document in multiple columns, you use section breaks. Word requires that a new section be created each time you alter the number of columns in a document. Thus, if a document has a nameplate (one column) followed by an article of three columns followed by an article of two columns, the document would be divided in three separate sections.

How should you organize the body copy in columns?

Be consistent from page to page with the number of columns. Narrow columns generally are easier to read than wide ones. Columns, however, can be too narrow. A two- or three-column layout generally is appealing and offers a flexible design. Try to have between five and fifteen words per line. To do this, you may need to adjust the column width, the font size, or the leading (line spacing). Font size of text in columns should be no larger than 12 point but not so small that readers must strain to read the text.

To Insert a Continuous Section Break

1 CREATE NAMEPLATE FOR FIRST PAGE | 2 FORMAT FIRST PAGE | 3 CREATE PULL-QUOTE
4 CREATE NAMEPLATE FOR SECOND PAGE | 5 FORMAT SECOND PAGE | 6 ADD PAGE BORDER

The next step is to insert a continuous section break below the nameplate. ***Why?*** *In this module, the nameplate is one column and the body of the newsletter is three columns.* The term, continuous, means the new section should be on the same page as the previous section, which, in this case, means that the three columns of body copy will be positioned directly below the nameplate on the first page of the newsletter. The following steps insert a continuous section break.

1

- With the insertion point at the end of the feature article title (shown in Figure 7–28), press the ENTER key to position the insertion point below the article title.

- Click the 'Insert Page and Section Breaks' button (Layout tab | Page Setup group) to display the Insert Page and Section Breaks gallery (Figure 7–29).

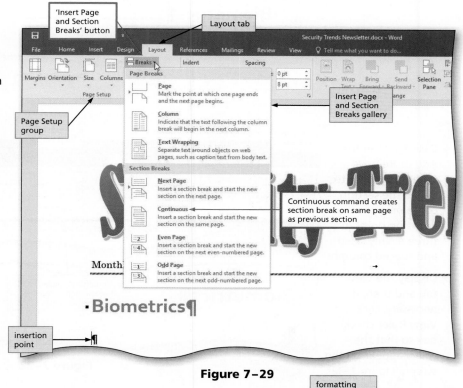

Figure 7–29

2

- Click Continuous in the Insert Page and Section Breaks gallery to insert a continuous section break above the insertion point (Figure 7–30).

Figure 7–30

To Change the Number of Columns

1 CREATE NAMEPLATE FOR FIRST PAGE | 2 FORMAT FIRST PAGE | 3 CREATE PULL-QUOTE
4 CREATE NAMEPLATE FOR SECOND PAGE | 5 FORMAT SECOND PAGE | 6 ADD PAGE BORDER

The document now has two sections. The nameplate is in the first section, and the insertion point is in the second section. The second section should be formatted to three columns. ***Why?*** *The feature article and announcements appear in three columns that snake across the page.* Thus, the following steps format the second section in the document as three columns.

1

- Click the 'Add or Remove Columns' button (Layout tab | Page Setup group) to display the Add or Remove Columns gallery (Figure 7–31).

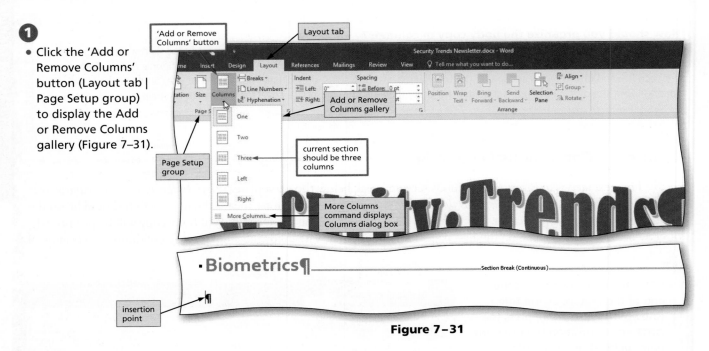

Figure 7–31

2

- Click Three in the Add or Remove Columns gallery to divide the section containing the insertion point in three evenly sized and spaced columns

- Display the View tab and then, if necessary, click the View Ruler check box so that the rulers appear on the screen (Figure 7–32).

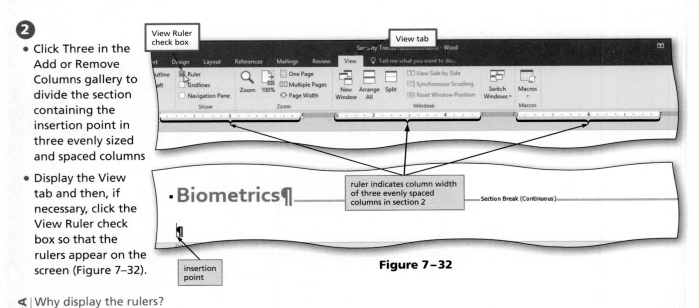

Figure 7–32

Q&A

Why display the rulers?
You want to see the column widths on the ruler.

What if I want columns of different widths?
You would click More Columns in the Add or Remove Columns gallery, which displays the Columns dialog box. In this dialog box, you can specify varying column widths and spacing.

To Justify a Paragraph

1 CREATE NAMEPLATE FOR FIRST PAGE | 2 FORMAT FIRST PAGE | 3 CREATE PULL-QUOTE
4 CREATE NAMEPLATE FOR SECOND PAGE | 5 FORMAT SECOND PAGE | 6 ADD PAGE BORDER

The following step enters the first paragraph of the feature article using justified alignment. *Why? The text in the paragraphs of the body of the newsletter is **justified**, which means that the left and right margins are aligned, like the edges of newspaper columns.*

1

- Display the Home tab.

- Click the Justify button (Home tab | Paragraph group) so that Word aligns both the left and right margins of typed text.

- Type the first paragraph of the feature article (Figure 7–33): `Biometric devices verify a person's identity by translating a behavioral or physical personal characteristic, such as a fingerprint, into a digital code that is compared with a digital code stored in a computer or mobile device. If the digital code in the computer or mobile device does not match the personal characteristic code, the computer or mobile device denies access to the individual.` and then press the ENTER key.

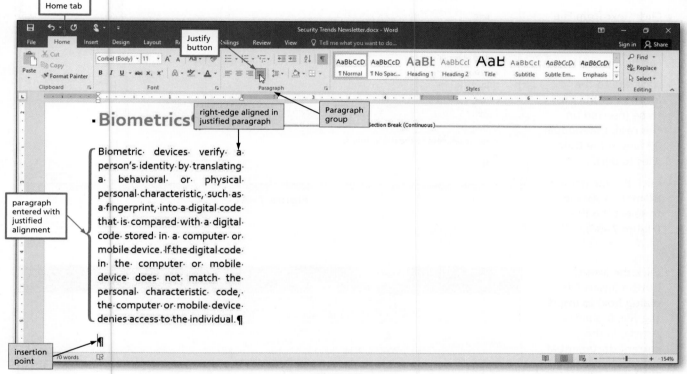

Figure 7–33

Q&A

Why do some words have extra space between them?

When a paragraph is formatted to justified alignment, Word places extra space between words so that the left and right edges of the paragraph are aligned. To remedy big gaps, sometimes called rivers, you can add or rearrange words, change the column width, change the font size, and so on.

Other Ways

1. Right-click paragraph (or, if using touch, tap 'Show Context Menu' button on mini toolbar), click Paragraph on shortcut menu, click 'Indents and Spacing' tab (Paragraph dialog box), click Alignment arrow, click Justified, click OK button

2. Click Paragraph Settings Dialog Box Launcher (Home tab or Layout tab | Paragraph group), click Indents and Spacing tab (Paragraph dialog box), click Alignment arrow, click Justified, click OK button

3. Press CTRL+J

To Insert a File in a Column of the Newsletter

1 CREATE NAMEPLATE FOR FIRST PAGE | 2 FORMAT FIRST PAGE | 3 CREATE PULL-QUOTE
4 CREATE NAMEPLATE FOR SECOND PAGE | 5 FORMAT SECOND PAGE | 6 ADD PAGE BORDER

The next step is to insert a file named Biometrics Article in the newsletter. *Why? To save you time typing, the rest of the feature article is located on the Data Files.* Please contact your instructor for information about accessing the Data Files. The following steps insert the Biometrics Article file in a column of the newsletter.

1

- Display the Insert tab.

- With the insertion point positioned in the left column as shown in Figure 7–33, click the Object arrow (Insert tab | Text group) to display the Object menu.

- Click 'Text from File' on the Object menu to display the Insert File dialog box.

- Navigate to the location of the file to be inserted (in this case, the Module 07 files in the Data Files folder).

- Click the file named Biometrics Article to select the file (Figure 7–34).

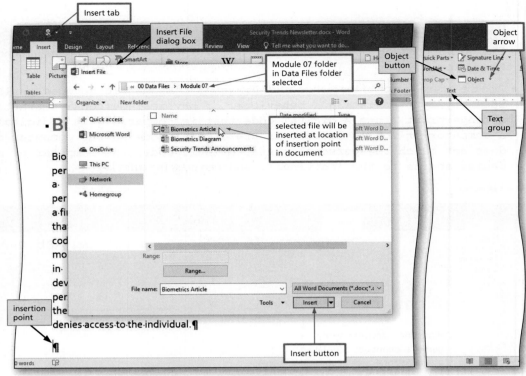

Figure 7–34

2

- Click the Insert button (Insert File dialog box) to insert the file, Biometrics Article, in the current document at the location of the insertion point.

- So that you can see the entire inserted article, display multiple pages on the screen by clicking the Multiple Pages button (View tab | Zoom group) (Figure 7–35).

3

- When you are finished viewing the document, change the zoom to page width so that the newsletter content is larger on the screen.

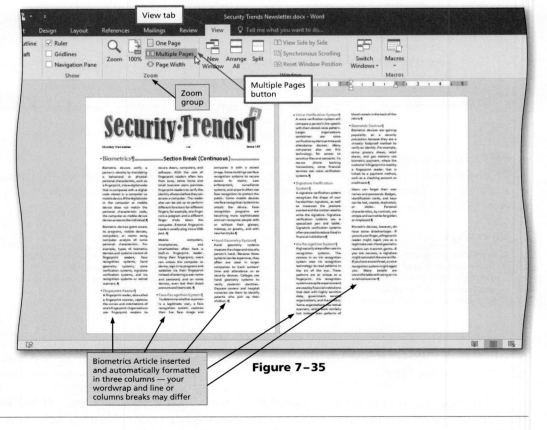

Figure 7–35

To Increase Column Width and Place a Vertical Rule between Columns

1 CREATE NAMEPLATE FOR FIRST PAGE | 2 FORMAT FIRST PAGE | 3 CREATE PULL-QUOTE
4 CREATE NAMEPLATE FOR SECOND PAGE | 5 FORMAT SECOND PAGE | 6 ADD PAGE BORDER

The columns in the newsletter currently contain many rivers. *Why? The justified alignment in the narrow column width often causes large gaps between words.* To eliminate some of the rivers, you increase the size of the columns slightly in this newsletter. In newsletters, you often see a vertical rule separating columns. Through the Columns dialog box, you can change column width and add vertical rules. The following steps increase column widths and add vertical rules between columns.

1

- Position the insertion point somewhere in the feature article text.
- Display the Layout tab.
- Click the 'Add or Remove Columns' button (Layout tab | Page Setup group) to display the Add or Remove Columns gallery (Figure 7–36).

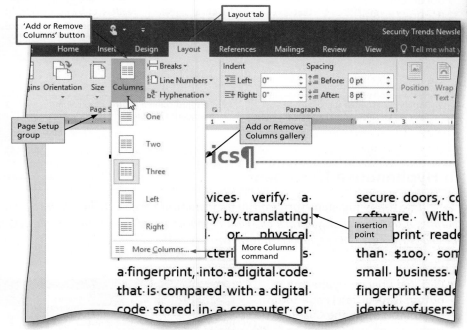

Figure 7–36

2

- Click More Columns in the Add or Remove Columns gallery to display the Columns dialog box.
- If necessary, in the Width and spacing area (Columns dialog box), click the Width up arrow until the Width box reads 2.1".

 Q&A How would I make the columns different widths?
You would remove the check mark from the 'Equal column width' check box and then set the individual column widths in the dialog box.

- Place a check mark in the Line between check box to select the check box (Figure 7–37).

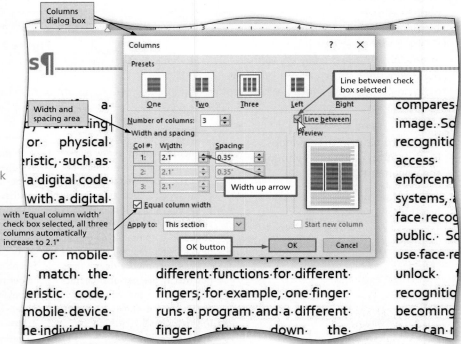

Figure 7–37

- Click the OK button to make the columns slightly wider and place a line (vertical rule) between each column in the document (Figure 7–38).

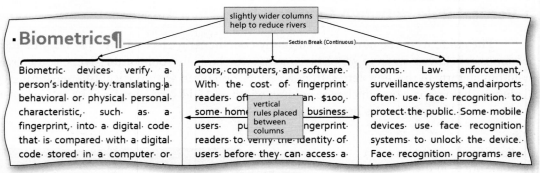

Figure 7–38

Other Ways

1. Double-click shaded space between columns on ruler, enter settings (Columns dialog box), click OK button

2. To adjust column widths, drag column boundaries on ruler

3. To insert single rule, click Borders arrow (Home tab | Paragraph group)

To Hyphenate a Document

1 CREATE NAMEPLATE FOR FIRST PAGE | 2 FORMAT FIRST PAGE | 3 CREATE PULL-QUOTE
4 CREATE NAMEPLATE FOR SECOND PAGE | 5 FORMAT SECOND PAGE | 6 ADD PAGE BORDER

The following steps turn on the hyphenation feature. *Why? To further eliminate some of the rivers in the columns of the newsletter, you turn on Word's hyphenation feature so that words with multiple syllables are hyphenated at the end of lines instead of wrapped in their entirety to the next line.*

- Click the Change Hyphenation button (Layout tab | Page Setup group) to display the Change Hyphenation gallery (Figure 7–39).

Q&A

What is the difference between Automatic and Manual hyphenation?

Automatic hyphenation places hyphens wherever words can break at a syllable in the document. With manual hyphenation, Word displays a dialog box for each word it could hyphenate, enabling you to accept or reject the proposed hyphenation.

Figure 7–39

- Click Automatic in the Change Hyphenation gallery to hyphenate the document (Figure 7–40).

Q&A

What if I do not want a particular word hyphenated?

You can reword text, and Word will redo the hyphenation automatically.

Biometric· devices· verify· a· per-son's·identity·by·translating·a·be-havioral· or· physical· personal· characteristic,· such· as· a· finger-print,· into· a· digital· code· that· is· compared· with· a· digital· code· stored· in· a· computer· or· mobile· device.·If·the·digital·code·in·the· computer· or· mobile· device· does· not· match· the· personal· charac-teristic· code,· the· computer· or· mobile· device· denies· access· to· the·individual.¶

With·the·cost·of·fingerprint·read-ers· often·[several words hyphenated in document] $100,· some· home· ar[...]ness· users· purchase· fingerprint· readers· to· verify·the·identity·of·users·before· they·can·access·a·computer.·The· reader·also·can·be·set·up·to·per-form· different· functions· for· dif-ferent·fingers;·for·example,·one· finger·runs·a·program·and·a·dif-ferent·finger·shuts·down·the·com-puter.· External· fingerprint· read-ers·usually·plug·into·a·USB·port.·¶

and·airports·o[...] nition·to·prot[...] mobile·devic[...] tion·systems·[...] Face· recogni[...] becoming· m[...] and·can·recog[...] without·their·[...] jewelry,·and·v[...]

▪ Hand·Geon[...]
Hand·geome[...] the·shape·an[...] hand.·Because[...]

Figure 7–40

To Format a Character as a Drop Cap

The first character in the feature article in this newsletter; that is, the capital letter B, is formatted as a drop cap. **Why?** *To add interest to an article, you often see a* **drop cap**, *which is a capital letter whose font size is larger than the rest of the characters in the paragraph.* In Word, the drop cap can sink into the first few lines of text, or it can extend into the left margin, which often is called a stick-up cap. In this newsletter, the paragraph text wraps around the drop cap.

The following steps create a drop cap in the first paragraph of the feature article in the newsletter.

1

- Position the insertion point somewhere in the first paragraph of the feature article.

- Display the Insert tab.

- Click the 'Add a Drop Cap' button (Insert tab | Text group) to display the Add a Drop Cap gallery (Figure 7–41).

🔍 **Experiment**

- Point to various commands in the Add a Drop Cap gallery to see a live preview of the drop cap formats in the document.

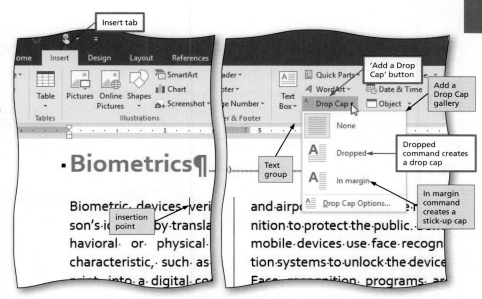

Figure 7–41

2

- Click Dropped in the Add a Drop Cap gallery to format the first letter in the paragraph containing the insertion point (the B in Biometric, in this case) as a drop cap and wrap subsequent text in the paragraph around the drop cap (Figure 7–42).

Q&A What is the outline around the drop cap in the document? When you format a letter as a drop cap, Word places a frame around it. A **frame** is a container for text that allows you to position the text anywhere on the page. Word formats a frame for the drop cap so that text wraps around it. The frame also contains a paragraph mark nonprinting character to the right of the drop cap, which may or may not be visible on your screen.

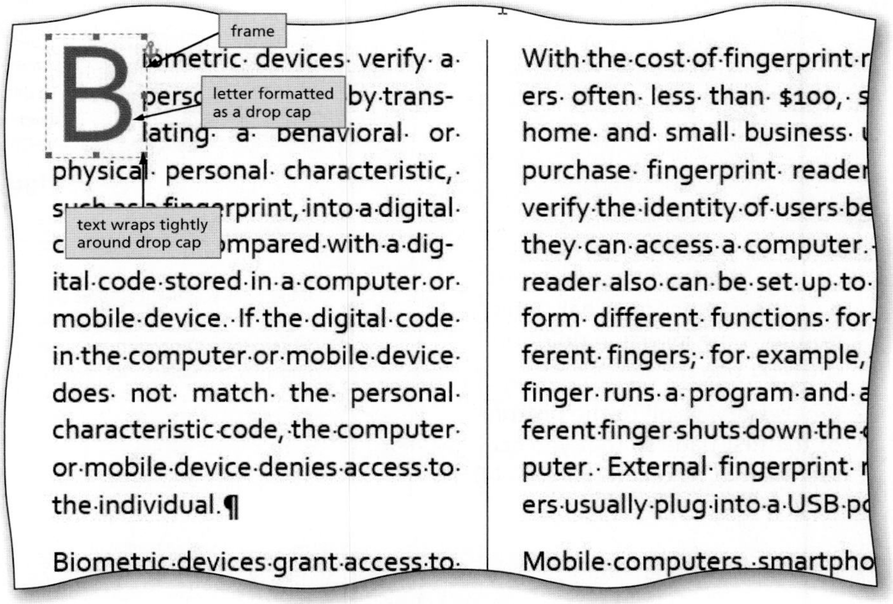

Figure 7–42

To Format the Drop Cap

The following step changes the font color of the drop cap.

1 With the drop cap selected, display the Home tab and then change the font color of the drop cap to 'Orange, Accent 4, Darker 25%' (eighth color, fifth row) in Font Color gallery (shown in Figure 7-1a at the beginning of this module).

Q&A What if my frame no longer is displayed?
Click the drop cap to select it. Then, click the blue selection rectangle to display the frame.

To Insert a Next Page Section Break

1 CREATE NAMEPLATE FOR FIRST PAGE | 2 FORMAT FIRST PAGE | 3 CREATE PULL-QUOTE
4 CREATE NAMEPLATE FOR SECOND PAGE | 5 FORMAT SECOND PAGE | 6 ADD PAGE BORDER

The third column on the first page of the newsletter is not a continuation of the feature article. ***Why not?*** *The third column, instead, contains several reader announcements. The feature article continues on the second page of the newsletter (shown in Figure 7–1b at the beginning of this module).* Thus, you must insert a next page section break, which is a section break that also contains a page break, at the bottom of the second column so that the remainder of the feature article moves to the second page. The following steps insert a next page section break in the second column.

1

• Position the insertion point at the location for the section break, in this case, to the left of the F in the Face Recognition System heading.

• Display the Layout tab.

• Click the 'Insert Page and Section Breaks' button (Layout tab | Page Setup group) to display the Insert Page and Section Breaks gallery (Figure 7–43).

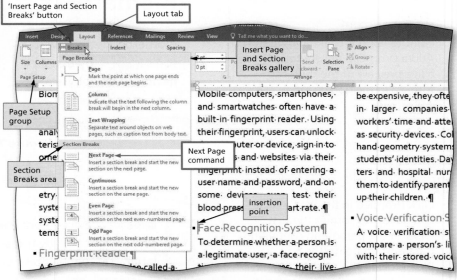

Figure 7–43

2

• In the Section Breaks area in the gallery, click Next Page to insert a next page section break, which positions the insertion point on the next page.

• If necessary, scroll to the bottom of the first page so that you can see the moved text (Figure 7–44).

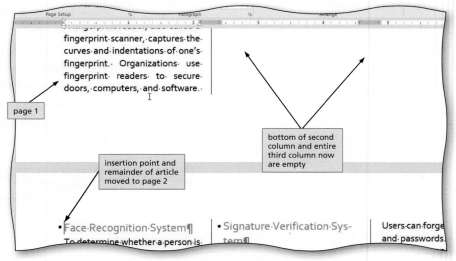

Figure 7–44

To Enter Text

The next step is to insert a jump-to line at the end of the second column, informing the reader where to look for the rest of the feature article. The following steps insert a jump-to line at the end of the text in the second column on the first page of the newsletter.

1 Scroll to display the end of the text in the second column of the first page of the newsletter and then position the insertion point to the left the paragraph mark that is to the left of the section break notation.

2 Press the ENTER key twice to insert a blank line for the jump-to text above the section break notation.

3 Press the UP ARROW key to position the insertion point on the blank line. If the blank line is formatted in the Heading 1 style, click the 'Clear All Formatting' button (Home tab | Font group) so that the entered text follows the Normal style.

4 Press CTRL+R to right align the paragraph mark. Press CTRL+I to turn on the italic format. Type **(Article continues on next page)** as the jump-to text and then press CTRL+I again to turn off the italic format.

To Insert a Column Break

1 CREATE NAMEPLATE FOR FIRST PAGE | 2 FORMAT FIRST PAGE | 3 CREATE PULL-QUOTE
4 CREATE NAMEPLATE FOR SECOND PAGE | 5 FORMAT SECOND PAGE | 6 ADD PAGE BORDER

In the *Security Trends* newsletters, for consistency, the reader announcements always begin at the top of the third column. If you insert the Security Trends Announcements at the current location of the insertion point, however, they will begin at the bottom of the second column. ***Why?*** *The insertion point currently is at the bottom of the second column.*

For the reader announcements to be displayed in the third column, you insert a **column break** at the bottom of the second column, which places the insertion point at the top of the next column. Thus, the following steps insert a column break at the bottom of the second column.

- Position the insertion point to the left of the paragraph mark on the line containing the next page section break, which is the location where the column break should be inserted.

- If necessary, display the Layout tab.

- Click the 'Insert Page and Section Breaks' button (Layout tab | Page Setup group) to display the Insert Page and Section Breaks gallery (Figure 7–45).

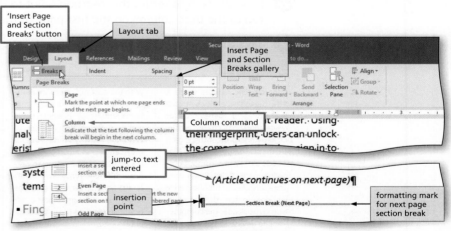

Figure 7–45

- Click Column in the Insert Page and Section Breaks gallery to insert a column break at the location of the insertion point and move the insertion point to the top of the next column (Figure 7–46).

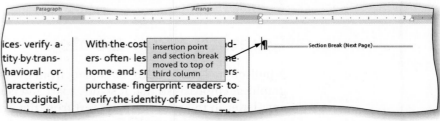

Figure 7–46

What if I wanted to remove a column break?
You would double-click it to select it and then click the Cut button (Home tab | Clipboard group) or press the DELETE key.

Other Ways

1. Press CTRL+SHIFT+ENTER

To Insert a File in a Column of the Newsletter

So that you do not have to enter the entire third column of announcements in the newsletter, the next step in the project is to insert the file named Security Trends Announcements in the third column of the newsletter. This file contains the three announcements: the first about reader discounts, the second about an upcoming webinar, and the third about the topic of the next newsletter issue.

The Security Trends Announcements file is located on the Data Files. Please contact your instructor for information about accessing the Data Files. The following steps insert a file in a column of the newsletter.

1 With the insertion point at the top of the third column, display the Insert tab.

2 Click the Object arrow (Insert tab | Text group) to display the Object menu and then click 'Text from File' on the Object menu to display the Insert File dialog box.

3 Navigate to the location of the file to be inserted (in this case, the Data Files folder).

4 Click Security Trends Announcements to select the file.

5 Click the Insert button (Insert File dialog box) to insert the file, Security Trends Announcements, in the document at the location of the insertion point.

Q&A What if text from the announcements column spills onto the second page of the newsletter?
You will format text in the announcements column so that all of its text fits in the third column of the first page.

6 Press SHIFT+F5 to return the insertion point to the last editing location, in this case, the top of the third column on the first page of the newsletter (Figure 7–47).

7 Save the newsletter again on the same storage location with the same file name.

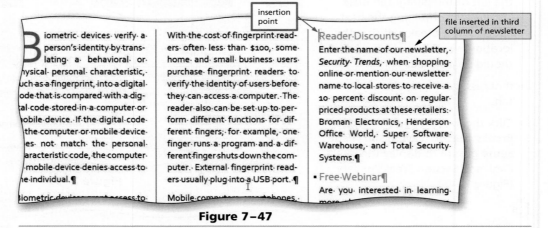

Figure 7–47

Creating a Pull-Quote

A pull-quote is text pulled, or copied, from the text of the document and given graphical emphasis so that it stands apart and commands the reader's attention. The newsletter in this project copies text from the first page of the newsletter and places it in a pull-quote, also on the first page between the first and second columns (shown in Figure 7–1a at the beginning of this module).

What guidelines should you follow when using pull-quotes?

Because of their bold emphasis, pull-quotes should be used sparingly in a newsletter. Pull-quotes are useful for breaking the monotony of long columns of text. Typically, quotation marks are used only if you are quoting someone directly. If you use quotation marks, use curly (or smart) quotation marks instead of straight quotation marks.

To create the pull-quote in this newsletter, follow this general procedure:

1. Create a **text box**, which is a container for text that allows you to position the text anywhere on the page.

2. Copy the text from the existing document to the Office Clipboard and then paste the text from the Office Clipboard to the text box.

3. Resize and format the text box.

4. Move the text box to the desired location.

To Insert a Text Box

1 CREATE NAMEPLATE FOR FIRST PAGE | 2 FORMAT FIRST PAGE | 3 CREATE PULL-QUOTE
4 CREATE NAMEPLATE FOR SECOND PAGE | 5 FORMAT SECOND PAGE | 6 ADD PAGE BORDER

The first step in creating the pull-quote is to insert a text box. A text box is like a frame; the difference is that a text box has more graphical formatting options than does a frame. The following steps insert a built-in text box. **Why?** *Word provides a variety of built-in text boxes, saving you the time of formatting the text box.*

- Click the 'Choose a Text Box' button (Insert tab | Text group) to display the Choose a Text Box gallery.

Experiment

- Scroll through the Choose a Text Box gallery to see the variety of available text box styles.

- Scroll to display Simple Quote in the Choose a Text Box gallery (Figure 7–48).

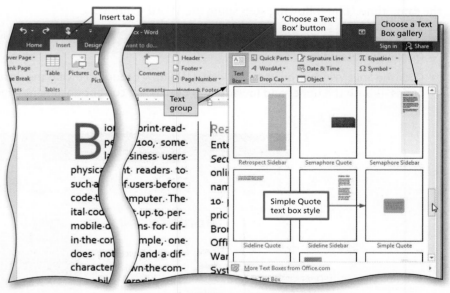

Figure 7–48

- Click Simple Quote in the Choose a Text Box gallery to insert that style of text box in the document.

- If necessary, drag the text box to the approximate location shown in Figure 7–49.

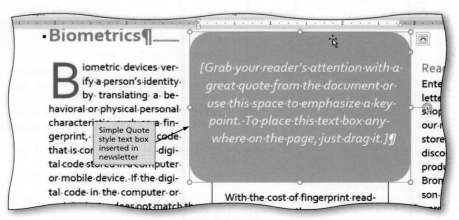

Figure 7–49

Q&A Does my text box need to be in the exact same location as in Figure 7–49?
No. You will move the text box later.

The layout of the first page is not correct because of the text box. What do I do?
You will enter text in the text box and then position it in the correct location. At that time, the layout of the first page will be fixed.

Other Ways

1. Click 'Explore Quick Parts' button (Insert tab | Text group), click 'Building Blocks Organizer' on Explore Quick Parts menu, select desired text box name in Building blocks list, click Insert button

1 CREATE NAMEPLATE FOR FIRST PAGE | 2 FORMAT FIRST PAGE | 3 CREATE PULL-QUOTE
4 CREATE NAMEPLATE FOR SECOND PAGE | 5 FORMAT SECOND PAGE | 6 ADD PAGE BORDER

To Split the Window

The text that you will copy for the pull-quote is in the middle of the first page on the newsletter and the pull-quote (text box) is near the top of the first page of the newsletter. Thus, the next step is to copy the pull-quote text from the middle of the first page and then paste it in the pull-quote at the top of the first page. You would like to view the pull-quote and the text to be copied on the screen at the same time. *Why? Viewing both simultaneously will simplify the copying and pasting process.*

Word allows you to split the window in two separate panes, each containing the current document and having its own scroll bar. This enables you to scroll to and view two different portions of the same document at the same time. The following step splits the Word window.

- Display the View tab.

- Click the Split Window button (View tab | Window group) to divide the document window in two separate panes — both the upper and lower panes display the current document (Figure 7–50).

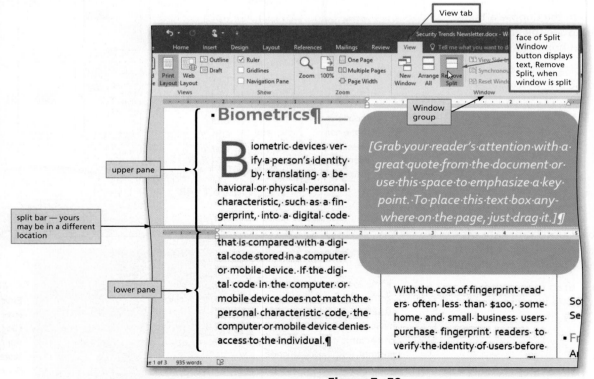

Figure 7–50

Other Ways

1. Press ALT+CTRL+S

TO ARRANGE ALL OPEN WORD DOCUMENTS ON THE SCREEN

If you have multiple Word documents open and want to view all of them at the same time on the screen, you can instruct Word to arrange all the open documents on the screen from top to bottom. If you wanted to arrange all open Word documents on the same screen, you would perform the following steps.

1. Click the Arrange All button (View tab | Window group) to display each open Word document on the screen.

2. To make one of the arranged documents fill the entire screen again, maximize the window by clicking its Maximize button or double-clicking its title bar.

To Copy and Paste Using Split Windows

1 CREATE NAMEPLATE FOR FIRST PAGE | 2 FORMAT FIRST PAGE | 3 CREATE PULL-QUOTE
4 CREATE NAMEPLATE FOR SECOND PAGE | 5 FORMAT SECOND PAGE | 6 ADD PAGE BORDER

The following steps copy text from the middle of the first page of the newsletter to the Clipboard (the source) and then paste the text into the text box (the destination) at the top of the newsletter. **Why?** *The item being copied is called the* **source**. *The location to which you are pasting is called the* **destination**.

- In the upper pane, scroll so that all placeholder text in the text box is visible, as shown in Figure 7–51.

- In the lower pane, scroll to display the text to be copied, as shown in Figure 7–51, and then select the text to be copied: Biometric devices grant access to programs, mobile devices, computers, or rooms using computer analysis of some personal characteristic.

- Display the Home tab.

- Click the Copy button (Home tab | Clipboard group) to copy the selected text to the Clipboard (Figure 7–51).

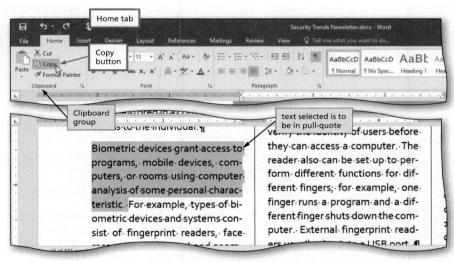

Figure 7–51

- In the upper pane, if necessary, scroll to display the text in the text box. Click the text in the text box to select it.

- Click the Paste arrow (Home tab | Clipboard group) to display the Paste menu.

Q&A What if I click the Paste button by mistake?
Click the Paste Options button to the right of the pasted text in the text box to display the Paste Options menu.

- Point to the Merge Formatting button on the Paste menu and notice the text box shows a live preview of the selected paste option (Figure 7–52).

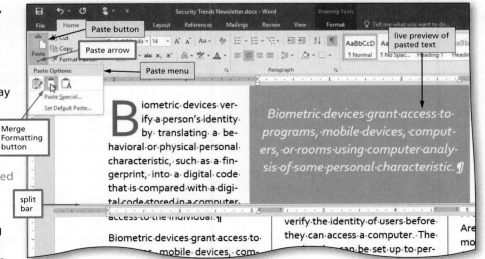

Figure 7–52

Q&A Why select the Merge Formatting button on the Paste menu?
You want the pasted text to use the formats that were in the text box (the destination) instead of the formats of the copied text (the source).

• Click the Merge Formatting button on the Paste menu to paste the copied text into the text box.

Q&A Why does a hyphen appear in the source?
Word may have hyphenated the word automatically. You will format the pull-quote text next.

Other Ways

1. Click copy on shortcut menu (or, if using touch, tap Copy on mini toolbar), right-click where item is to be pasted, click 'Keep Source Formatting' in Paste Options area on shortcut menu (or, if using touch, tap Paste on mini toolbar)

2. Select text to copy, press CTRL+C; select destination for pasted text, press CTRL+V

To Remove a Split Window

The next step is to remove the split window so that you can position the pull-quote. The following step removes a split window.

1 Double-click the split bar (shown in Figure 7–52), or click the Split Window button again (View tab | Window group), or press ALT+SHIFT+C, to remove the split window and return to a single Word window on the screen.

To Format Text in the Text Box

The next steps format text in the pull-quote.

BTW
Rotating Text Box Text
To rotate text in a text box, select the text box, click the Text Direction button (Drawing Tools Format tab | Text group), and then click the desired direction on the Text Direction menu.

1 If necessary, scroll to display the text box in the document window.

2 Select all the text in the text box, change its font to Century Schoolbook (or a similar font), bold the text, and change its font size to 11 point. If necessary, center this paragraph.

3 Click in the text box to deselect the text, but leave the text box selected (shown in Figure 7–53).

To Resize a Text Box

The next step in formatting the pull-quote is to resize the text box. You resize a text box the same way as any other object. That is, you drag its sizing handles or enter values in the height and width boxes through the Size button (Drawing Tools Format tab | Size group). The following steps resize the text box and insert line break characters.

1 Drag the sizing handles so that the pull-quote looks about the same size as Figure 7–53.

2 Verify the pull-quote dimensions in the Shape Height and Shape Width boxes (Drawing Tools Format tab | Size group) and, if necessary, change the value in the Shape Height box to 1.75 and the Shape Width box to 2.08.

Q&A What if some of the words in the text box are hyphenated?
Insert line break characters to eliminate any hyphenated words in the text box; that is, position the insertion point to the left of the first letter in the hyphenated word and then press SHIFT+ENTER to insert a line break character, which places the entire word on the next line and removes the hyphen.

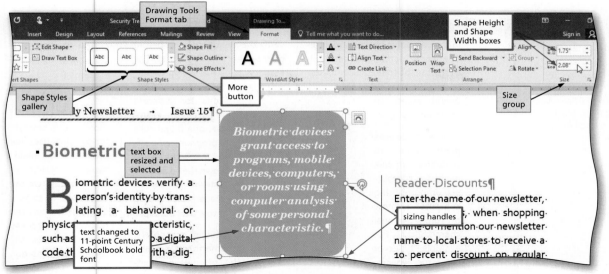

Figure 7–53

To Apply a Shape Style to a Text Box

The next step in formatting the pull-quote is to apply a shape style to the text box to coordinate its colors with the rest of the newsletter. The following steps apply a shape style to a text box.

1 With the text box still selected, click the More button (shown in Figure 7–53) in the Shape Styles gallery (Drawing Tools Format tab | Shape Styles group) to expand the gallery.

2 Point to 'Colored Fill - Orange, Accent 4' (fifth style, second row) in the Shape Styles gallery to display a live preview of that style applied to the text box (Figure 7–54).

3 Click 'Colored Fill - Orange, Accent 4' in the Shape Styles gallery to apply the selected style to the shape.

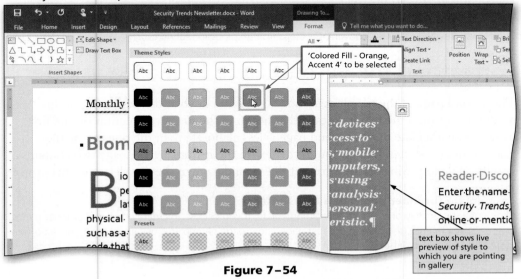

Figure 7–54

To Position a Text Box

The following steps move the text box to the desired location in the newsletter.

1 With the text box still selected, drag the text box to its new location (Figure 7–55). You may need to drag and/or resize the text box a couple of times so that it looks similar to this figure.

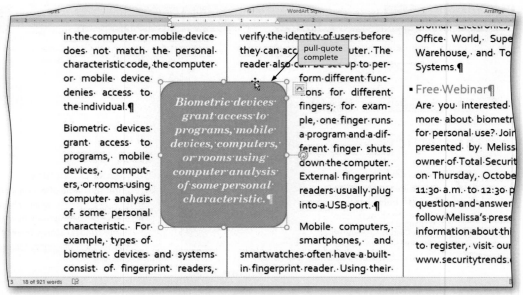

Figure 7–55

2 Click outside the text box to remove the selection.

Q&A   Why does my text wrap differently around the text box?
Differences in wordwrap often relate to the printer used by your computer. Thus, your document may wordwrap around the text box differently.

3 If the jump-to line, which is supposed to appear at the bottom of the second column (shown in Figure 7–56), moved to the top of the third column, position the insertion point in the article title (Biometrics) and decrease the spacing before and after (Layout tab) until the jump-to line moves back to the bottom of the second column.

4 Save the newsletter again on the same storage location with the same file name.

Break Point: If you wish to take a break, this is a good place to do so. You can exit Word now. To resume at a later time, run Word, open the file called Security Trends Newsletter, and continue following the steps from this location forward.

Formatting the Second Page of the Newsletter

The second page of the newsletter (shown in Figure 7–1b at the beginning of this module) continues the feature article that began in the first two columns on the first page. The nameplate on the second page is less elaborate than the one on the first page of the newsletter. In addition to the text in the feature article, page two contains a graphic. The following sections format the second page of the newsletter in this project.

How do you create a nameplate for inner pages of a newsletter?
The top of the inner pages of a newsletter may or may not have a nameplate. If you choose to create one for your inner pages, it should not be the same as, or compete with, the one on the first page. Inner page nameplates usually contain only a portion of the nameplate from the first page of a newsletter.

1 CREATE NAMEPLATE FOR FIRST PAGE | 2 FORMAT FIRST PAGE | 3 CREATE PULL-QUOTE
4 CREATE NAMEPLATE FOR SECOND PAGE | 5 FORMAT SECOND PAGE | 6 ADD PAGE BORDER

To Change Column Formatting

The document currently is formatted in three columns. The nameplate at the top of the second page, however, should be in a single column. ***Why?** The nameplate should span across the top of the three columns below it.* The next step, then, is to change the number of columns at the top of the second page from three to one.

As discussed earlier in this project, Word requires a new section each time you change the number of columns in a document. Thus, you first must insert a continuous section break and then format the section to one column so that the nameplate can be entered on the second page of the newsletter. The following steps insert a continuous section break and then change the column format.

1

- If you have a blank page between the first and second pages of the newsletter, position the insertion point to the left of the paragraph mark at the end of the third column on the first page of the newsletter and then press the DELETE key as many times as necessary to delete the blank line causing the overflow.

- Position the insertion point at the upper-left corner of the second page of the newsletter (to the left of F in Face).

- Display the Layout tab.

- Click the 'Insert Page and Section Breaks' button (Layout tab | Page Setup group) to display the Insert Page and Section Breaks gallery (Figure 7–56).

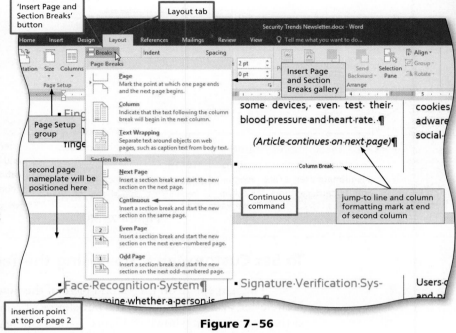

Figure 7–56

2

- Click Continuous in the Insert Page and Section Breaks gallery to insert a continuous section break above the insertion point.

- Press the UP ARROW key to position the insertion point to the left of the continuous section break just inserted.

- Click the 'Add or Remove Columns' button (Layout tab | Page Setup group) to display the Add or Remove Columns gallery (Figure 7–57).

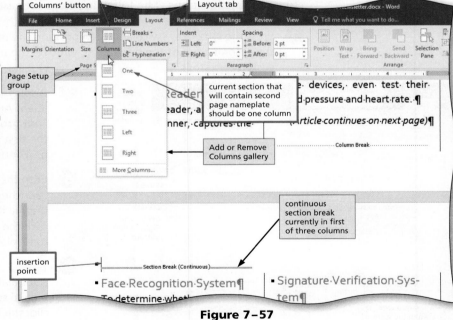

Figure 7–57

3

- Click One in the Add or Remove Columns gallery to format the current section to one column, which now is ready for the second page nameplate.

- If necessary, scroll to display the bottom of the first page and the top of the second page, so that you can see the varying columns in the newsletter (Figure 7–58).

Q&A Can I change the column format of existing text?

Yes. If you already have typed text and would like it to be formatted in a different number of columns, select the text, click the 'Add or Remove Columns' button (Layout tab | Page Setup group), and then click the number of columns desired in the Add or Remove Columns gallery. Word automatically creates a new section for the newly formatted columns.

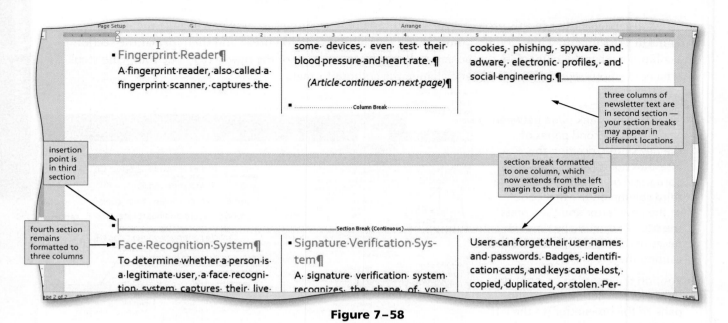

Figure 7–58

To Set Custom Tab Stops Using the Tabs Dialog Box

The nameplate on the second page of the newsletter contains the text, Monthly Newsletter, at the left margin, the newsletter title in the center, and the issue number at the right margin (shown in Figure 7–1a at the beginning of this module). To properly align the text in the center and at the right margin, you will set custom tab stops at these locations. The following steps set custom tab stops.

1 Press the ENTER key twice and then position the insertion point on the first line of the second page of the newsletter, which is the paragraph to be formatted with the custom tab stops.

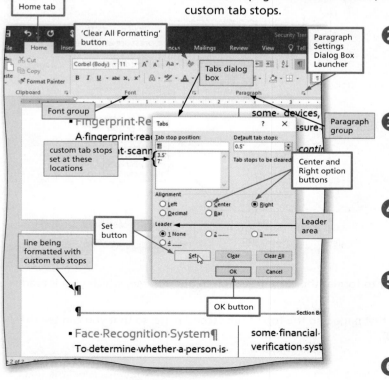

2 Display the Home tab and then click the 'Clear All Formatting' button (Home tab | Font group) to apply the Normal style to the first line on the second page of the newsletter.

3 Click the Paragraph Settings Dialog Box Launcher (Home tab | Paragraph group) to display the Paragraph dialog box and then click the Tabs button (Paragraph dialog box) to display the Tabs dialog box.

4 Type **3.5** in the Tab stop position text box (Tabs dialog box), click Center in the Alignment area to specify the tab stop alignment, and then click the Set button to set the custom tab stop.

5 Type **7** in the Tab stop position text box (Tabs dialog box), click Right in the Alignment area to specify the tab stop alignment, and then click the Set button to set the custom tab stop (Figure 7–59).

6 Click the OK button to set custom tab stops using the specified alignments.

Figure 7–59

To Format and Enter Text and Add a Border

The following steps enter the newsletter title at the top of the second page in the third section.

1 With the insertion point on the first line of the second page of the newsletter, click the Font Color arrow and then change the font color of the current text to 'Teal, Accent 5, Darker 50%' (ninth column, bottom row). Change the font to Century Schoolbook (or a similar font) and then type **Monthly Newsletter** at the left margin.

If requested by your instructor, enter your name instead of the word, Monthly.

2 Press the TAB key to advance the insertion point to the centered tab stop. Increase the font size to 14 point and then click the Bold button (Home tab | Font group) to bold the text. Type **Security Trends** at the centered tab stop.

3 Press the TAB key to advance the insertion point to the right-aligned tab stop. Reduce the font size to 11 point and then click the Bold button (Home tab | Font group) to turn off the bold format. Type **Issue 15** at the right-aligned tab stop.

4 Click the Borders button (Home tab | Paragraph group) to add a bottom border (shown in Figure 7–60).

◄ | Why is the border formatted already?
Q&A | When you define a custom border, Word uses that custom border the next time you click the Borders button in the Borders gallery.

BTW
Leader Characters
Leader characters, such as a series of dots, often are used in a table of contents to precede page numbers. Four types of leader characters, which Word places in the space occupied by a tab character, are available in the Leader area of the Tabs dialog box (shown in Figure 7–59).

To Enter Text

The second page of the feature article on the second page of this newsletter begins with a jump-from line (the continued message) immediately below the nameplate. The next steps enter the jump-from line.

1 Position the insertion point on the blank line above the heading, Face Recognition System, to the left of the paragraph mark.

2 Click the 'Clear All Formatting' button (Home tab | Font group) to apply the Normal style to the location of the insertion point.

3 Press CTRL+I to turn on the italic format.

4 Type **(Continued from first page)** and then press CTRL+I to turn off the italic format (Figure 7–60).

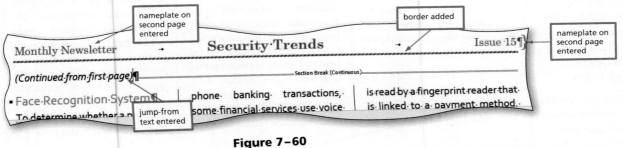

Figure 7–60

To Balance Columns

Currently, the text on the second page of the newsletter completely fills up the first and second columns and almost fills the third column. The text in the three columns should consume the same amount of vertical space. *Why? Typically, the text in columns of a newsletter is balanced.* To balance columns, you insert a continuous section break at the end of the text. The following steps balance columns.

1

- Scroll to the bottom of the text in the third column on the second page of the newsletter and then position the insertion point at the end of the text.

- If an extra paragraph mark is below the last line of text, press the DELETE key to remove the extra paragraph mark.

- Display the Layout tab.

- Click the 'Insert Page and Section Breaks' button (Layout tab | Page Setup group) to display the Insert Page and Section Breaks gallery (Figure 7–61).

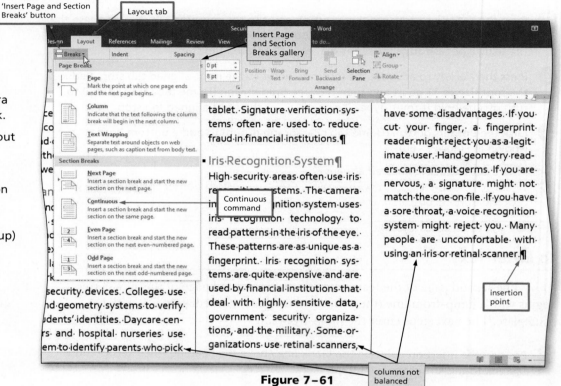

Figure 7–61

2

- Click Continuous in the Insert Page and Section Breaks gallery to insert a continuous section break, which balances the columns on the second page of the newsletter (Figure 7–62).

- Save the newsletter again on the same storage location with the same file name.

be expensive, they often are used in larger companies to track workers' time and attendance or as security devices. Colleges use hand geometry systems to verify students' identities. Daycare centers and hospital nurseries use them to identify parents who pick up their children. ¶

▪ Voice Verification System¶
A voice verification system will compare a person's live speech with their stored voice pattern.

¶

▪ Iris Recognition System¶
High security areas often use iris recognition systems. The camera in an iris recognition system uses iris recognition technology to read patterns in the iris of the eye. These patterns are as unique as a fingerprint. Iris recognition systems are quite expensive and are used by financial institutions that deal with highly sensitive data, government security organizations, and the military. Some organizations use retinal scanners,

are unique and cannot be forgotten or misplaced.¶

Biometric devices, however, do have some disadvantages. If you cut your finger, a fingerprint reader might reject you as a legitimate user. Hand geometry readers can transmit germs. If you are nervous, a signature might not match the one on file. If you have a sore throat, a voice recognition system might reject you. Many people are uncomfortable with using an iris or retinal scanner.____

[columns balanced]

Figure 7–62

Modifying and Formatting a SmartArt Graphic

Recall from Module 4 that Microsoft Office includes **SmartArt graphics**, which are visual representations of ideas. Many different types of SmartArt graphics are available, allowing you to choose one that illustrates your message best.

In this newsletter, a SmartArt graphic is positioned on the second page, at the top of the second column. Because the columns are small in the newsletter, it is best to work with a SmartArt graphic in a separate document window so that you easily can see all of its components. When finished editing the graphic, you can copy and paste it in the newsletter. You will follow these steps for the SmartArt graphic in this newsletter:

1. Open the document that contains the SmartArt graphic for the newsletter.
2. Modify the layout of the graphic.
3. Add a shape and text to the graphic.
4. Format a shape and the graphic.
5. Copy and paste the graphic in the newsletter.
6. Resize the graphic and position it in the desired location.

To Open a Document from Word

The first draft of the SmartArt graphic is in a file called Biometrics Diagram on the Data Files. Please contact your instructor for information about accessing the Data Files. The following steps open the Biometrics Diagram file.

1 Navigate to the location of the Data Files on your hard drive, OneDrive, or other storage location.

2 Open the file named Biometrics Diagram on the Data Files.

3 Click the graphic to select it and display the SmartArt Tools Design and Format tabs (Figure 7–63).

Q&A Is the *Security Trends* Newsletter file still open?
Yes. Leave it open because you will copy the modified diagram to the second page of the newsletter.

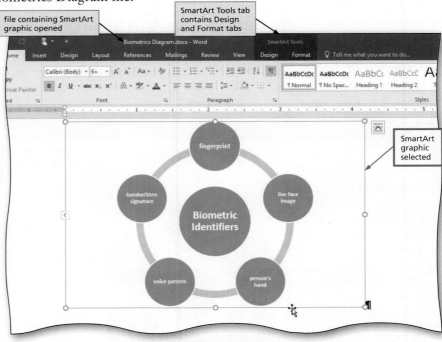

Figure 7–63

1 CREATE NAMEPLATE FOR FIRST PAGE | 2 FORMAT FIRST PAGE | 3 CREATE PULL-QUOTE |
4 CREATE NAMEPLATE FOR SECOND PAGE | 5 FORMAT SECOND PAGE | 6 ADD PAGE BORDER

To Change the Layout of a SmartArt Graphic

The following step changes the layout of an existing SmartArt graphic. *Why? The SmartArt graphic currently uses the Radial Cycle layout, and this newsletter uses the Basic Radial layout.*

1

- If necessary, display the SmartArt Tools Design tab.

- Scroll through the layouts in the Layouts gallery until Basic Radial appears, if necessary, and then click Basic Radial to change the layout of the SmartArt graphic (Figure 7–64).

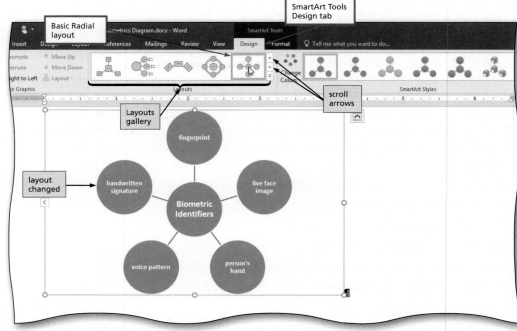

Figure 7–64

Other Ways

1. Right-click the selected graphic, click Layout button on mini toolbar and select desired layout, or click Change Layout on shortcut menu, select desired layout, click OK button

To Add a Shape to a SmartArt Graphic

The current SmartArt graphic has five perimeter shapes. This newsletter has a sixth shape. The following step adds a shape to a SmartArt graphic.

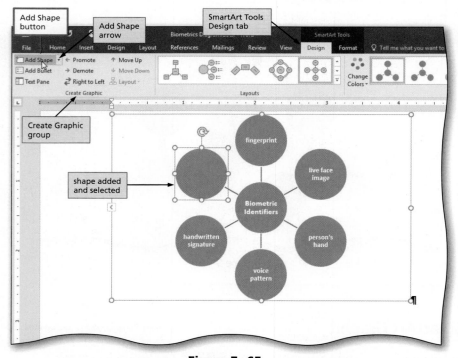

Figure 7–65

1 With the diagram selected, click the Add Shape button (SmartArt Tools Design tab | Create Graphic group) to add a shape to the SmartArt graphic (Figure 7–65).

Q&A

Why did my screen display a menu instead of adding a shape?
You clicked the Add Shape arrow instead of the Add Shape button. Clicking the Add Shape button adds the shape automatically; clicking the Add Shape arrow displays a menu allowing you to specify the location of the shape.

How do I delete a shape?
Select the shape by clicking it and then press the DELETE key, or right-click the shape and then click Cut on the mini toolbar or shortcut menu.

To Add Text to a SmartArt Graphic through the Text Pane

In Module 4, you added text directly to the shapes in a SmartArt graphic. In this project, you enter the text through the Text Pane. *Why? Some users prefer to enter text in the Text Pane instead of in the shape.* The following steps use the Text Pane to add text to a shape.

1
- Click the Text Pane control, which is on the left side of the SmartArt graphic, to display the Text Pane to the left of the SmartArt graphic.

2
- In the Text Pane, if necessary, position the insertion point to the right of the bullet that has no text to its right.
- Type **iris or retina** as the text for the shape (Figure 7–66).

3
- Click the Close button in the Text Pane to close the Text Pane.

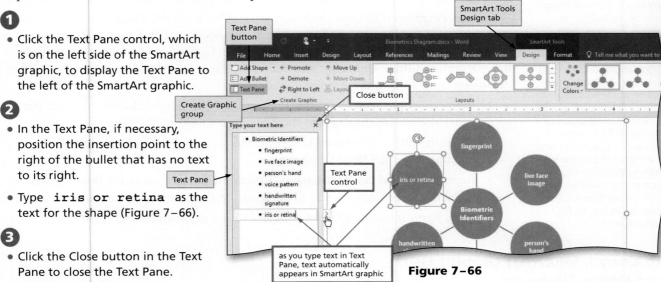

Figure 7–66

Q&A Can I instead close the Text Pane by clicking the Text Pane button (SmartArt Tools Design tab | Create Graphic group)?
Yes.

- Save the file containing the SmartArt graphic with a new file name on your hard drive, OneDrive, or other storage location using Biometrics Diagram Modified as the file name.

Other Ways

1. Click Text Pane button (SmartArt Tools Design tab | Create Graphic group)

To Format SmartArt Graphic Text

To format text in an entire SmartArt graphic, select the graphic and then apply the format. The following steps bold the text in the SmartArt graphic.

1 If necessary, click the shape just added to select it.

2 Display the Home tab. Click the Bold button (Home tab | Font group) to bold the text in the SmartArt graphic (shown in Figure 7–67).

TO MODIFY THEME EFFECTS

If you wanted to change the look of graphics, such as SmartArt graphics, you would perform the following steps to change the theme effects.

1. Click the Theme Effects button (Design tab | Document Formatting group).

2. Click the desired effect in the Theme Effects gallery.

TO SAVE CUSTOMIZED THEMES

When you modify the theme effects, theme colors, or theme fonts, you can save the modified theme for future use. If you wanted to save a customized theme, you would perform the following steps.

1. Click the Themes button (Design tab | Document Formatting group) to display the Themes gallery.

BTW
Demoting Text Pane Text
Instead of pressing the TAB key in the Text Pane, you could click the Demote Selection button (SmartArt Tools Design tab | Create Graphic group) to increase (or move to the right) the indent for a bulleted item. You also can click the Promote Selection button (SmartArt Tools Design tab | Create Graphic group) to decrease (or move to the left) the indent for a bulleted item.

BTW
Clipboard Task Pane and Icon
You can control when the Clipboard task pane appears on the Word screen and the Office Clipboard icon appears in the notification area on the taskbar. To do this, first display the Clipboard task pane by clicking the Clipboard Dialog Box Launcher on the Home tab. Next, click the Options button at the bottom of the Clipboard task pane and then click the desired option on the menu. For example, if you want to be able to open the Clipboard task pane by clicking the Office Clipboard icon on the Windows taskbar, click 'Show Office Clipboard Icon on Taskbar' on the Options menu.

2. Click 'Save Current Theme' in the Themes gallery.

3. Enter a theme name in the File name box (Save Current Theme dialog box).

4. Click the Save button to add the saved theme to the Themes gallery.

Copying and Pasting

The next step is to copy the SmartArt graphic from this document window and then paste it in the newsletter. To copy from one document and paste into another, you can use the Office Clipboard. Through the Office Clipboard, you can copy multiple items from any Office document and then paste them into the same or another Office document by following these general guidelines:

1. Items are copied *from* a **source document**. If the source document is not the active document, display it in the document window.

2. Open the Office Clipboard task pane and then copy items from the source document to the Office Clipboard.

3. Items are copied *to* a **destination document**. If the destination document is not the active document, display the destination document in the document window.

4. Paste items from the Office Clipboard to the destination document.

To Copy a SmartArt Graphic Using the Office Clipboard

1 CREATE NAMEPLATE FOR FIRST PAGE | 2 FORMAT FIRST PAGE | 3 CREATE PULL-QUOTE
4 CREATE NAMEPLATE FOR SECOND PAGE | 5 FORMAT SECOND PAGE | 6 ADD PAGE BORDER

The following step copies the SmartArt graphic to the Office Clipboard. **Why?** *Sometimes you want to copy multiple items to the Office Clipboard through the Clipboard task pane and then paste them later.*

1

- Click the Clipboard Dialog Box Launcher (Home tab | Clipboard group) to open the Clipboard task pane.

- If the Office Clipboard in the Clipboard task pane is not empty, click the Clear All button in the Clipboard task pane.

- With the SmartArt graphic selected in the document window, click the Copy button (Home tab | Clipboard group) to copy the selected text to the Clipboard (Figure 7–67).

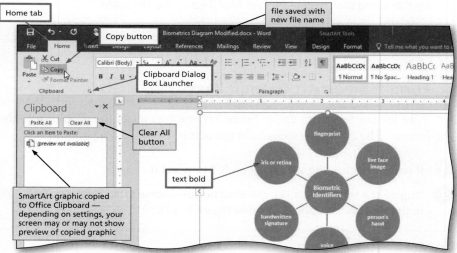

Figure 7–67

Other Ways
1. With Clipboard task pane open, right-click selected item, click Copy on mini toolbar or shortcut menu	2. With Clipboard task pane open and item to copy selected, press CTRL+C

To Switch from One Open Document to Another

1 CREATE NAMEPLATE FOR FIRST PAGE | 2 FORMAT FIRST PAGE | 3 CREATE PULL-QUOTE
4 CREATE NAMEPLATE FOR SECOND PAGE | 5 FORMAT SECOND PAGE | 6 ADD PAGE BORDER

The following steps switch from the open Biometrics Diagram Modified document (the source document) to the open Security Trends Newsletter document (the destination document). **Why?** *You want to paste the copied diagram into the newsletter document.*

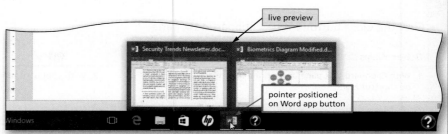

1

- Point to the Word app button on the taskbar to display a live preview of the open documents or window titles of the open documents, depending on your computer's configuration (Figure 7–68).

live preview

pointer positioned on Word app button

Figure 7–68

2

- Click the live preview of the Security Trends Newsletter on the Windows taskbar to display the selected document in the document window (shown in Figure 7–69).

Other Ways

1. Click Switch Windows button (View tab | Window group), click document name

2. Press ALT+TAB

To Paste from the Office Clipboard

1 CREATE NAMEPLATE FOR FIRST PAGE | 2 FORMAT FIRST PAGE | 3 CREATE PULL-QUOTE
4 CREATE NAMEPLATE FOR SECOND PAGE | 5 FORMAT SECOND PAGE | 6 ADD PAGE BORDER

The following steps paste from the Office Clipboard. *Why? You want to paste the copied SmartArt graphic into the destination document, in this case, the newsletter document.*

1

- Position the insertion point at the end of the first paragraph at the top of the second column on the second page of the newsletter.

- If the Clipboard task pane is not open on the screen, display the Home tab and then click the Clipboard Dialog Box Launcher (Home tab | Clipboard group) to open the Clipboard task pane.

- Click the SmartArt graphic entry in the Office Clipboard to paste it in the document at the location of the insertion point (Figure 7–69).

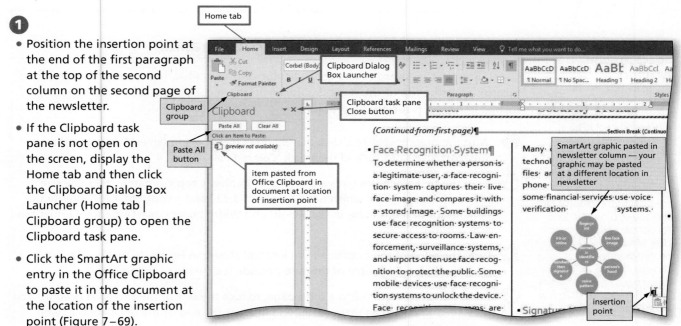

Home tab

Clipboard Dialog Box Launcher

Clipboard task pane Close button

Clipboard group

Paste All button

item pasted from Office Clipboard in document at location of insertion point

SmartArt graphic pasted in newsletter column — your graphic may be pasted at a different location in newsletter

insertion point

Figure 7–69

Q&A

What if my pasted graphic is in a different location?
The location of your graphic may differ. You will move the graphic in the next steps.

Does the destination document have to be a different document?
No. The source and destination documents can be the same document.

What is the function of the Paste All button?
If you have multiple items on the Office Clipboard, it pastes all items in a row, without any characters between them, at the location of the insertion point or selection.

• Click the Close button in the Clipboard task pane.

Other Ways
1. With Clipboard task pane open, right-click selected item, click Paste on shortcut menu   2. With Clipboard task pane open, press CTRL+V

To Format a Graphic as Floating

The text in the newsletter should wrap tightly around the graphic; that is, the text should conform to the graphic's shape. Thus, the next step is to change the graphic from inline to floating with a wrapping style of tight. The following steps format the graphic as floating with tight wrapping.

1 Click the SmartArt graphic to select it.

2 With the SmartArt graphic selected, click the Layout Options button that is attached to the graphic to display the Layout Options gallery.

3 Click Tight in the Layout Options gallery to change the graphic from inline to floating with tight wrapping.

4 Close the Layout Options gallery.

To Format and Position the SmartArt Graphic

The next tasks are to change the color of the graphic, increase its size, and then position it at the top of the second column on the second page. The following steps format and then position the graphic.

1 With the graphic selected, click the Change Colors button (SmartArt Design tab | SmartArt Styles group) and then click 'Colored Fill - Accent 4'.

2 Drag the sizing handles outward until the graphic is approximately the same size as shown in Figure 7–70, which has a height of 3.32" and a width of 4.25". (Verify the dimensions of the graphic in the Height and Width boxes (SmartArt Tools Format tab | Size group)).

3 Drag the edge of the graphic to the location shown in Figure 7–70. You may have to drag the graphic a couple of times to position it similarly to the figure.

4 If the newsletter spills onto a third page, reduce the size of the SmartArt graphic. You may need to delete an extra paragraph mark at the end of the document, as well.

BTW
Space around Graphics
The space between a graphic and the text, which sometimes is called the run-around, should be at least 1/8" and should be the same for all graphics in a document. Adjust the run-around of a selected floating graphic by doing the following: click the Wrap Text button (SmartArt Tools Format tab | Arrange group), click 'More Layout Options' on the Wrap Text menu, click the Position tab (Layout dialog box), adjust the values in the Horizontal and Vertical boxes, and then click the OK button.

TO LAYER THE SMARTART GRAPHIC IN FRONT OF TEXT

In Word, you can layer objects on top of or behind other objects. If you wanted to layer the SmartArt graphic on top of all text, you would perform the following steps.

1. Click the SmartArt graphic to select it. Click the Bring Forward arrow (SmartArt Tools Format tab | Arrange group) to display the Bring Forward menu.

2. Click 'Bring in Front of Text' on the Bring Forward menu to position the selected object on top of all text.

To Edit Wrap Points in an Object

In Word, you can change how text wraps around an object, called editing wrap points. The following steps edit the wrap points in the SmartArt diagram at the top of the second page of the newsletter. *Why? You want to ensure that text starts on a complete line below the bottom of the graphic.*

1

- If necessary, click the SmartArt graphic to select it. Click the Wrap Text button (SmartArt Tools Format tab | Arrange group) to display the Wrap Text menu (Figure 7–70).

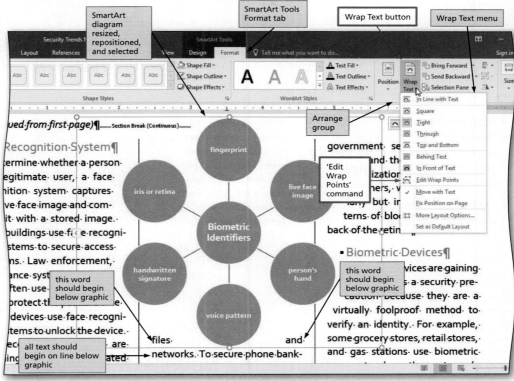

Figure 7–70

2

- Click 'Edit Wrap Points' on the Wrap Text menu to display wrap points around the graphic.

- Position the pointer on the black wrap point to the lower-left of the shape in the diagram containing the text, voice pattern, as shown in Figure 7–71, so that the pointer changes to a four-headed dot.

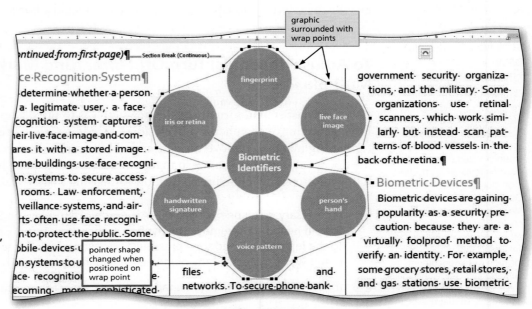

Figure 7–71

● Drag the black wrap point to the lower-left of the graphic as shown in Figure 7–72, so that the text (the word, files, in this case) will appear on a complete line below the shape.

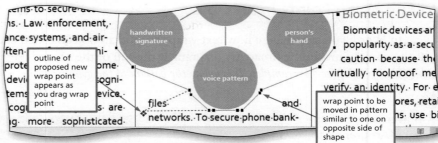

Figure 7–72

● Drag the black wrap point to the lower-right of the graphic as shown in Figure 7–73, so that the text begins on a complete line below the graphic.

● Click outside the graphic so that it no longer is selected.

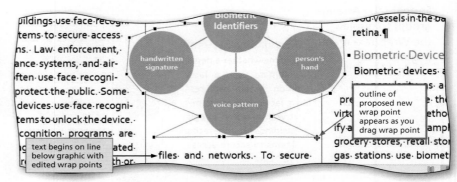

Figure 7–73

Finishing the Newsletter

With the text and graphics in the newsletter entered and formatted, the next step is to view the newsletter as a whole and determine if it looks finished in its current state. To give the newsletter a finished appearance, you will add a border to its edges.

BTW
Distributing a Document
Instead of printing and distributing a hard copy of a document, you can distribute the document electronically. Options include sending the document via email; posting it on cloud storage (such as OneDrive) and sharing the file with others; posting it on social media, a blog, or other website; and sharing a link associated with an online location of the document. You also can create and share a PDF or XPS image of the document, so that users can view the file in Adobe Reader or XPS Viewer instead of in Word.

To Adjust Headings, Turn Off Formatting Marks, and Zoom Multiple Pages

The last step in formatting the newsletter is to place a border around its edges. First, you remove a hyphen from a heading by adding a line break. Then, you turn off formatting marks to remove the clutter from the screen, and you place both pages in the document window at once so that you can see all the page borders applied. The following steps add a line break, turn off formatting marks, and zoom multiple pages.

1 If necessary, scroll below the SmartArt graphic to display the Signature Verification System heading. To remove the hyphen in the word, System, place the insertion point to the left of the S and then press SHIFT+ENTER to create a line break and move the entire word, System, to the next line (shown in Figure 7–74).

2 If necessary, display the Home tab and then turn off formatting marks.

3 Display the View tab and then display multiple pages on the screen. You may need to increase the zoom slightly so that the borders in the nameplates appear.

To Add an Art Page Border

The following steps add a page border around the pages of the newsletter. *Why? This newsletter has a teal art border around the perimeter of each page.*

- Display the Design tab.

- Click the 'Borders and Shading' button (Design tab | Page Background group) to display the Borders and Shading dialog box. If necessary, click the Page Border tab.

Q&A What if I cannot select the 'Borders and Shading' button because it is dimmed?
Click somewhere in the newsletter to make the newsletter the active document and then repeat Step 1.

- Click Box in the Setting area (Borders and Shading dialog box) to specify a border on all four sides of the page.

- Click the Art arrow, scroll to and then click the art border shown in Figure 7–74.

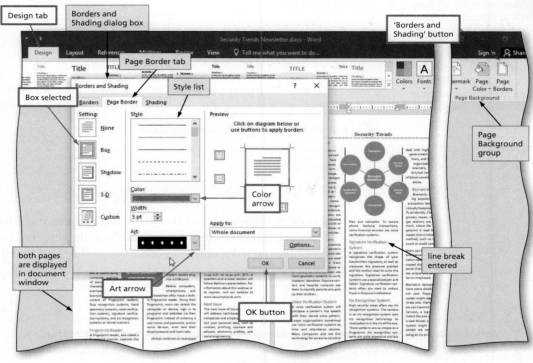

Figure 7–74

- Click the Color arrow and then click 'Teal, Accent 5, Darker 50%' (bottom row, ninth column) on the palette (Figure 7–74).

- Click the OK button to place the defined border on each page of the newsletter (Figure 7–75).

Figure 7–75

To Save, Print, and Exit Word

The newsletter now is complete. You should save the document, print it, and then exit Word.

1 Save the newsletter again on the same storage location with the same file name.

2 If desired, print the newsletter (shown in Figure 7–1 at the beginning of this module).

Q&A

What if an error message appears about margins?
Depending on the printer you are using, you may need to set the margins differently for this project.

What if one or more of the borders do not print?
Click the 'Borders and Shading' button (Design tab | Page Background group), click the Options button (Borders and Shading dialog box), click the Measure from arrow and click Text, change the four text boxes to 15 pt, and then click the OK button in each dialog box. Try printing the document again. If the borders still do not print, adjust the text boxes in the dialog box to a number smaller than 15 pt.

3 Exit Word, closing all open documents.

Summary

In this module, you have learned how to create a professional-looking newsletter using Word's desktop publishing features such as the following: inserting and modifying WordArt, organizing a document in columns, adding horizontal and vertical rules, inserting and formatting pull-quotes, inserting and formatting graphics, and adding an art page border.

CONSIDER THIS: PLAN AHEAD

What decisions will you need to make when creating your next newsletter?
Use these guidelines as you complete the assignments in this module and create your own newsletters outside of this class.

1. Create the nameplate.

   a) Determine the location of the nameplate.

   b) Determine content, formats, and arrangement of text and graphics.

   c) If appropriate, use ruling lines.

2. Determine content for the body of the newsletter.

   a) Write the body copy.

   b) Organize the body copy in columns.

   c) Format the body copy and subheads.

   d) Incorporate color.

   e) Divide sections with vertical rules.

   f) Enhance with visuals.

3. Bind and distribute the newsletter.

   a) Determine if newsletters should be printed, posted on bulletin boards, sent as an email message, or posted on websites.

   b) For multipage newsletters that will be printed, determine the appropriate method of binding the pages.

   c) For online newsletters, select a format that most users will be able to open.

Apply Your Knowledge

Reinforce the skills and apply the concepts you learned in this module.

Working with Desktop Publishing Elements of a Newsletter

Note: To complete this assignment, you will be required to use the Data Files. Please contact your instructor for information about accessing the Data Files.

Instructions: Run Word. Open the document named Apply 7–1 Energy Saver Newsletter Draft from the Data Files. The document contains a newsletter that you are to modify so that it appears as shown in Figure 7–76.

Perform the following tasks:

1. Change the WordArt shape to Chevron Down.
2. Turn on automatic hyphenation.
3. Change the column width of the columns in the body of the newsletter to 1.9".
4. Add a vertical rule (line) between each column.
5. Change the style of the pull-quote (text box) to 'Light 1 Outline, Colored Fill - Dark Green, Accent 3' (Drawing Tools Format tab | Shape Styles group).
6. Format the first paragraph with a drop cap.
7. Change the alignment of the paragraph containing the drop cap from left-aligned to justified.
8. Change the layout of the SmartArt graphic to Converging Radial.
9. Use the Text Pane to add the text, Building Automation, to the empty shape in the SmartArt graphic. Verify that the font size of text in the top and bottom shapes is 14 point and 11 point, respectively.
10. If necessary, move the SmartArt graphic and the pull-quote so that they are positioned similarly to the ones in Figure 7–76.
11. Change the color of the page border to Orange, Accent 5, Lighter 40%.
12. If requested by your instructor, add your name to the left of the text, Weekly Newsletter, in the issue information line.
13. If the newsletter flows to two pages, reduce the size of elements such as WordArt or pull-quote, or adjust spacing above or below paragraphs so that the newsletter fits on a single page. Make any other necessary adjustments to the newsletter.
14. Save the modified file with the file name, Apply 7–1 Energy Saver Newsletter Modified.
15. Submit the revised newsletter in the format specified by your instructor.
16. ☀ When you use hyphenation to divide words at the end of a line, what are the accepted guidelines for dividing the words? *Hint:* Use a search engine to search the text, end of line hyphenation.

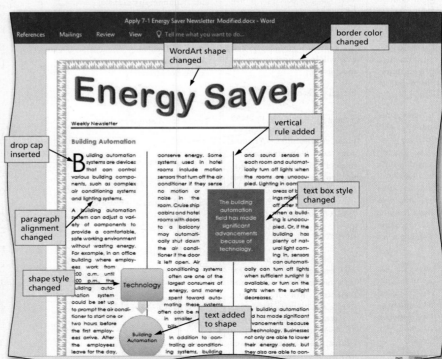

Figure 7–76

Extend Your Knowledge

Extend the skills you learned in this module and experiment with new skills. You may need to use Help to complete the assignment.

Adding Equations to a Newsletter and Enhancing a Nameplate

Note: To complete this assignment, you will be required to use the Data Files. Please contact your instructor for information about accessing the Data Files.

Instructions: Run Word. Open the document, Extend 7–1 Frosh Tips Newsletter Draft, from the Data Files. You will add equations to the newsletter, change the format of the WordArt, format the drop cap, adjust the hyphenation rules, move the page border closer to the text, clear tabs, and insert leader characters.

Perform the following tasks:

1. Use Help to learn about equations, WordArt options, borders, hyphenation, and tabs.

2. Insert the equations shown in Figure 7–77 in the newsletter in their appropriate locations. *Hint:* Use the 'Insert an Equation' arrow or 'Insert an Equation' button (Insert tab | Symbols group).

3. Change the WordArt by adding at least two WordArt style text effects. Change the color of the WordArt text outline. Change the color of the WordArt text fill color.

4. Add a shape fill color to the text box surrounding the WordArt.

5. Add a drop cap to the first paragraph in the body of the newsletter. Change the number of lines to drop from three to four lines. Change the distance from the text to 0.1".

6. Change the hyphenation rules to limit consecutive hyphens to two.

7. Change the page border so that the border is closer to the text.

8. If the newsletter flows to two pages, reduce the size of elements, such as WordArt or the pull-quote or the table, or adjust spacing above or below paragraphs so that the newsletter fits on a single page. Make any other necessary adjustments to the newsletter.

9. Clear the tabs in the issue information line in the nameplate. Use the Tabs dialog box to insert a right-aligned tab stop at the 7" mark. Fill the tab space with a leader character of your choice.

10. If requested by your instructor, change the word, Freshman, in the issue information line to your last name.

11. Submit the revised newsletter in the format specified by your instructor.

12. ✹ Which equations are predefined in Word? Which structures are available on the Equation Tools Design tab? How do you change the alignment of an equation?

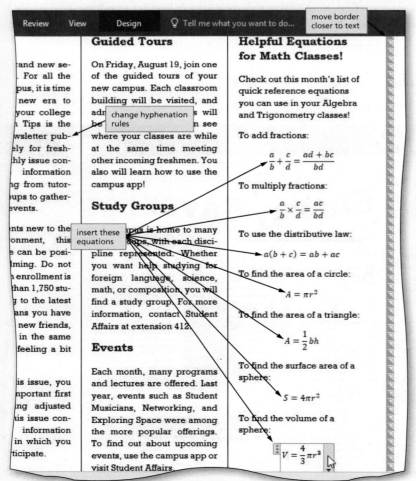

Figure 7–77

Expand Your World

Create a solution that uses cloud or web technologies by learning and investigating on your own from general guidance.

Using Windows Essentials

Instructions: You have heard that Windows Essentials includes some useful programs, so you decide to learn about it, download it, and use its programs.

Note: You may be required to use your Microsoft account to complete this assignment. If you do not have a Microsoft account and do not want to create one, read the assignment without performing the instructions.

Perform the following tasks:

1. Run a browser. Search for the text, Windows Essentials, using a search engine. Click a link to learn about Windows Essentials.

2. Navigate to the website to download Windows Essentials (Figure 7–78) and then follow the instructions to download Windows Essentials.

3. One at a time, run each program included with Windows Essentials. Browse through the features and functions of each program.

4. ✳ What programs are included with Windows Essentials? What is the purpose of each program? Which programs will you use and why?

Figure 7–78

In the Labs

Design, create, modify, and/or use a document following the guidelines, concepts, and skills presented in this module. Labs 1 and 2, which increase in difficulty, require you to create solutions based on what you learned in the module; Lab 3 requires you to apply your creative thinking and problem-solving skills to design and implement a solution.

Lab 1: Creating a Newsletter with a Pull-Quote (Text Box) and an Article on File

Note: To complete this assignment, you will be required to use the Data Files. Please contact your instructor for information about accessing the Data Files.

Problem: You are an editor of the newsletter, *Vintage Living*. The next edition is due out in one week (Figure 7–79). The text for the articles in the newsletter is in a file on the Data Files. You need to create the nameplate and the text box for the pull-quote.

Perform the following tasks:

1. Change all margins to .75 inches. Depending on your printer, you may need different margin settings. Change the theme to Retrospect.

2. Create the nameplate using the formats identified in Figure 7–79. Create the title using WordArt. Set the WordArt wrapping to 'Top and Bottom'. If necessary, drag the bottom of the WordArt up to shorten the image. Dimensions of WordArt should be approximately 1.41" x 7.06". Set a right-aligned custom tab stop at the right margin.

Continued >

In the Labs continued

3. Below the nameplate, enter the heading, Purchasing an Old House: Part 1, as shown in the figure. Format the heading using the Heading 1 style. Change the spacing above this paragraph to 24 pt and the spacing after to 12 pt.

4. Create a continuous section break below the heading, Purchasing an Old House: Part 1.

5. Format section 2 to three columns.

6. Insert the Lab 7–1 Purchasing an Old House - Part 1 Article file, which is located on the Data Files, in section 2 below the nameplate.

7. Format the newsletter according to Figure 7–79. Insert a column break before the heading, Brick and Stone. Columns should have a width of 2.1" with spacing of 0.35". Place a vertical rule between the columns.

8. If necessary, insert a continuous section break at the end of the document to balance the columns.

9. Format the subheads using the Heading 2 style.

10. Insert a text box using the Retrospect Quote built-in text box. The text for the pull-quote is in the Paint section of the article. Split the window. Use the split window to copy the text and then paste it in the text box. Remove the split window. Change the fill color (shape fill) of the text box to Brown, Accent 4. Change the font to 12-point Bookman Old Style. Resize the text box so that it is similar in size to Figure 7–79. Position the text box as shown in Figure 7–79.

11. Add the page border as shown in the figure.

12. If the document does not fit on a single page, adjust spacing above and below paragraphs.

13. If requested by your instructor, change the word, Weekly, in the issue information line to your name.

14. Save the document with Lab 7–1 Vintage Living Newsletter as the file name and then submit it in the format specified by your instructor.

15. ☀ This newsletter used a pull-quote. What other text in the newsletter could appear in the pull-quote?

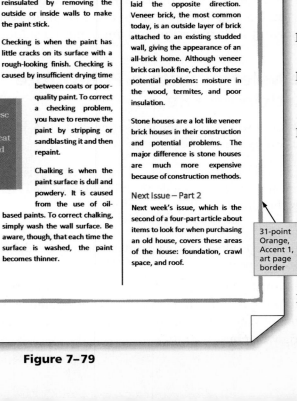

Figure 7–79

Lab 2: **Creating a Newsletter with a SmartArt Graphic and an Article on File**

Note: To complete this assignment, you will be required to use the Data Files. Please contact your instructor for information about accessing the Data Files.

Problem: You are responsible for the monthly preparation of the newsletter called *Health Check*. The next edition discusses technology-related repetitive strain injuries (Figure 7–80). This article already has been prepared and is on the Data Files. You need to create the nameplate, the SmartArt graphic, and the section at the bottom of the newsletter.

Perform the following tasks:

1. Change all margins to .75 inches. Depending on your printer, you may need different margin settings. Change the document theme to Droplet.

2. Create the nameplate using the formats identified in Figure 7–80. Create the title using WordArt. Set a right-aligned custom tab stop at the right margin. Set the WordArt wrapping to Top and Bottom. If necessary, drag the bottom of the Word Art up to shorten the image. Search for and insert an image of a check mark, similar to the one shown in the figure (the exact image is located on the Data Files). Resize and rotate the image as shown in the figure. Format the image as Behind Text and position the image as shown.

3. Below the nameplate, enter the heading, Technology-Related Repetitive Strain Injuries, as shown in the figure.

4. Create a continuous section break below the heading.

5. Format section 2 to two columns.

6. Insert the Lab 7–2 Health Risks for Technology Users Article file, which is located on the Data Files, in section 2 below the nameplate.

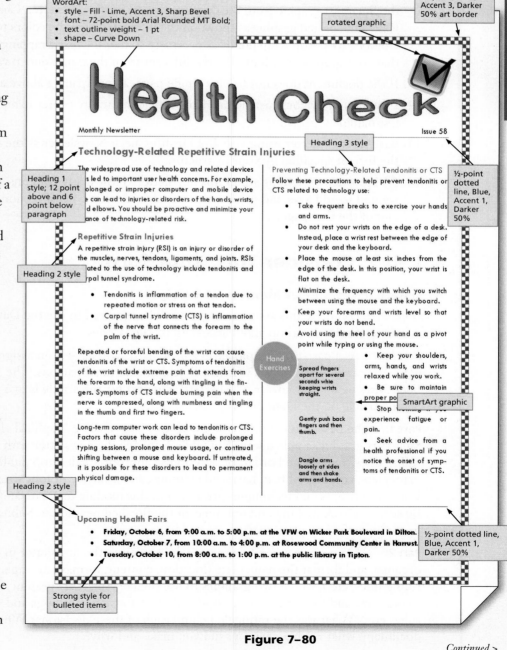

Figure 7–80

Continued >

STUDENT ASSIGNMENTS

In the Labs *continued*

7. Format the newsletter according to Figure 7–80. Columns should have a width of 3.33" with spacing of 0.35". Place a vertical rule between the columns.

8. Use Word's automatic hyphenation feature to hyphenate the document.

9. Insert a continuous section break at the end of the last bulleted item in the second column to balance the columns.

10. In the next section, change the number of columns from two to one. Enter the text shown at the bottom of the newsletter.

11. Add the page border as shown in the figure.

12. Open a new document window and create the SmartArt graphic shown in Figure 7–80. Use the Stacked List layout. Because this newsletter has only one list, delete the shapes for the second list. Add the text shown in the figure (you will need to add shapes to this list). Resize the border of the SmartArt graphic to the edges of the list shapes. Use the Office Clipboard to copy and paste the SmartArt graphic from the current window to the newsletter. Change the wrapping to tight. Resize the pasted graphic as shown in the figure. Change the colors to Colorful Range - Accent Colors 3 to 4. Edit wrap points as necessary so that the text wrapping is similar to the figure. Note that your graphic may look slightly different from the figure due to variations in the shape size.

13. If the document does not fit on a single page, adjust spacing above and below paragraphs.

14. If requested by your instructor, change the community center name from Rosewood to your last name.

15. Save the newsletter using Lab 7–2 Health Check Newsletter as the file name and submit it in the format specified by your instructor.

16. ✳ How many sections are in this newsletter? How many columns are in each section? If you wanted to add a second page to this newsletter, what type of section break would appear at the end of the first page?

Lab 3: **Consider This: Your Turn**

Create a Newsletter about ATM Safety

Note: To complete this assignment, you will be required to use the Data Files. Please contact your instructor for information about accessing the Data Files.

Problem: As a part-time employee at a local bank, you have been assigned the task of creating a newsletter called *Bank News*, which will be available to all patrons. The article in Issue 28 of the *Bank News* newsletter covers ATM safety. The text for the article is in a file called Lab 7–3 ATM Safety Article on the Data Files.

Part 1:   The newsletter should contain at least two of these graphical elements: an image, a SmartArt graphic, a pull-quote, or a table. Enhance the newsletter with a drop cap, WordArt, color, ruling lines, and a page border. Be sure to use appropriate desktop publishing elements, including a nameplate, columns of text, balanced columns, and a variety of font sizes, font colors, and shading. Use the concepts and techniques presented in this module to create and format the newsletter. Be sure to check spelling and grammar of the finished newsletter. Submit your assignment in the format specified by your instructor.

Part 2:   ✳ You made several decisions while creating the newsletter in this assignment: how to organize and format the nameplate (location, content, formats, arrangement of text and graphics, ruling lines, etc.), which two graphics to use (image, SmartArt graphic, text box, or table), and how to organize and format the body copy (columns, formats, headings and subheads, color, vertical rules, etc.). What was the rationale behind each of these decisions? When you proofread the document, what further revisions did you make and why?

4 Creating and Formatting Information Graphics

Objectives

You will have mastered the material in this module when you can:

- Insert a SmartArt graphic
- Insert images from a file into a SmartArt graphic
- Format a SmartArt graphic
- Convert text to a SmartArt graphic
- Create and format a chart
- Rotate a chart

- Change the chart title and legend
- Separate a pie chart slice
- Create and format a table
- Insert a symbol in a table
- Change table text alignment and orientation
- Add an image to a table

Introduction

Audiences generally focus first on the visual elements displayed on a slide. Graphical elements increase **visual literacy**, which is the ability to examine and assess these images. They can be divided into two categories: images and information graphics. Images are the illustrations and photos you have used in Modules 1, 2, and 3, and information graphics are tables, charts, graphs, and diagrams. Both sets of visuals help audience members interpret and retain material, so they should be designed and presented with care.

Project — Presentation with SmartArt, a Chart, and a Table

On average, a person generates more than four pounds of trash every day. This waste includes aluminum cans, plastic and glass bottles, and various metals. Recycling efforts are increasing as communities provide dedicated areas for collecting materials, but the U.S. Environmental Protection Agency estimates that only 30 percent of recyclable materials actually make their way to recycling bins instead of landfills. Your community has three areas in town where residents can drop off cans, bottles, and metals, and you want to prepare a presentation that publicizes these locations and the need for everyone to take action. The project in this module follows visual content guidelines and uses PowerPoint to create the presentation shown in Figure 4–1. The slide show

BTW
Information Graphics Increase Retention
When audience members view graphics and listen to a speaker, they become engaged in the presentation. They tune out distractions and recall more material during a presentation when clear graphics, including SmartArt, charts, and tables, are displayed visually and then explained verbally.

uses several visual elements to help audience members understand how recycling benefits the environment and where products can be recycled. The first two slides are enhanced with SmartArt graphics and pictures. The three-dimensional pie chart on Slide 3 depicts the amount of glass, metal, paper, and plastic recycled in your town, and the five-column table on Slide 4 lists the locations of three recycling centers and the types of materials accepted at each site.

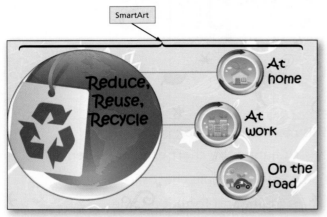

(a) Slide 1 (Title Slide with SmartArt Enhanced with Photos)

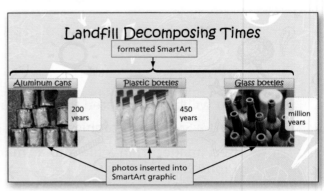

(b) Slide 2 (SmartArt Enhanced with Photos)

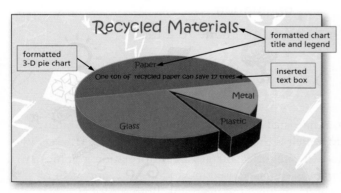

(c) Slide 3 (3-D Chart)

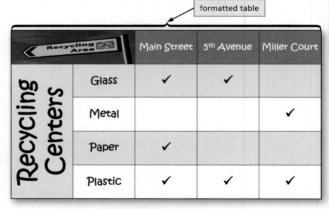

(d) Slide 4 (Five-column Chart)

Figure 4–1

In this module, you will learn how to create the slides shown in Figure 4–1. The following roadmap identifies general activities you will perform as you progress through this module:

1. INSERT and MODIFY a SMARTART graphic.
2. ADD SMARTART STYLES and EFFECTS.
3. CONVERT TEXT TO a SMARTART graphic and FORMAT the content.
4. CREATE a CHART to show proportions.
5. FORMAT a CHART by changing style and layout.
6. CREATE a TABLE to compare and contrast data.
7. CHANGE TABLE content STYLE and ALIGNMENT.

Creating and Formatting a SmartArt Graphic

An illustration often can help convey relationships between key points in your presentation. Microsoft Office 2016 includes **SmartArt graphics**, which are visual representations of your ideas. The SmartArt layouts have a variety of shapes, arrows, and lines to correspond to the major points you want your audience to remember.

BTW
Updated Layouts
Some of the items in the SmartArt Styles gallery may be updates; Microsoft periodically adds layouts to the Office. com and corresponding categories.

You can create a SmartArt graphic in two ways: Select a SmartArt graphic type and then add text and pictures, or convert text or pictures already present on a slide to a SmartArt graphic. Once the SmartArt graphic is present, you can customize its look. Table 4–1 lists the SmartArt types and their uses.

Table 4–1 SmartArt Graphic Layout Types and Purposes	
Type	**Purpose**
List	Show nonsequential information
Process	Show steps in a process or timeline
Cycle	Show a continual process
Hierarchy	Create an organizational chart
Relationship	Illustrate connections
Matrix	Show how parts relate to a whole
Pyramid	Show proportional relationships with the largest component at the top or bottom
Picture	Include a placeholder for pictures within the graphic
Office.com	Use addition layouts available from Office.com

To Insert a SmartArt Graphic

1 INSERT & MODIFY SMARTART | 2 ADD SMARTART STYLES & EFFECTS | 3 CONVERT TEXT TO SMARTART & FORMAT
4 CREATE CHART | 5 FORMAT CHART | 6 CREATE TABLE | 7 CHANGE TABLE STYLE & ALIGNMENT

Several SmartArt layouts have placeholders for one or more pictures, and they are grouped in the Picture category. The 'Circular Picture Callout' graphic is appropriate for this presentation. *Why? It has one large area for a picture and three other areas for smaller pictures. These images would allow you to insert pictures of recycling possibilities, which should create interest among community residents considering participating in these efforts.* The following steps open the Recycling presentation, save the file with a new name, and then insert the 'Circular Picture Callout' SmartArt graphic on Slide 1.

1

- Run PowerPoint and then open the presentation, Recycling, from the Data Files.

- Save the presentation using the file name, Area Recycling.

- With Slide 1 selected, display the Insert tab and then click the SmartArt button (Insert tab | Illustrations group) to display the Choose a SmartArt Graphic dialog box.

- Click Picture in the left pane to display the Picture gallery.

- Click the 'Circular Picture Callout' graphic (second graphic in first row) to display a preview of this layout in the right pane (Figure 4–2).

 Experiment

- Click various categories and graphics in the SmartArt Styles gallery and view the various layouts.

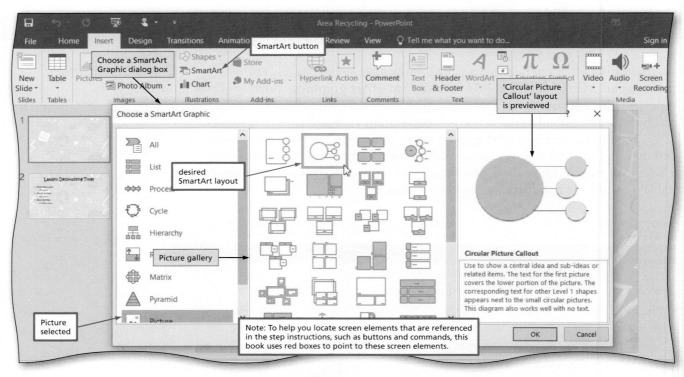

Figure 4–2

2

- Click the OK button to insert this SmartArt layout on Slide 1.

- If necessary, click the Text Pane button (SmartArt Tools Design tab | Create Graphic group) or the arrow icon in the center-left edge of the graphic to open the Text Pane if it does not display automatically (Figure 4–3).

Q&A Can I click either the Text Pane button or the arrow icon to close the Text Pane? Yes.

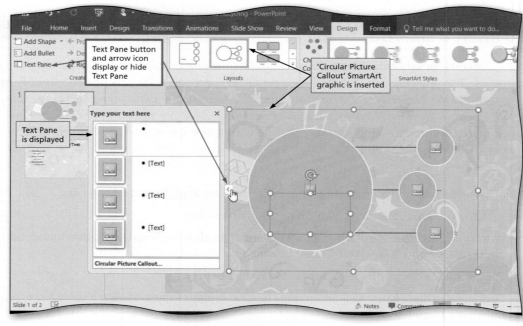

Figure 4–3

Other Ways

1. Click 'Insert a SmartArt graphic' icon in placeholder

Text Pane

The **Text Pane** assists you in creating a graphic because you can direct your attention to developing and editing the message without being concerned with the actual graphic. The Text Pane consists of two areas: The top portion has the text that will appear in the SmartArt layout and the bottom portion gives the name of the graphic and suggestions of what type of information is best suited for this type of visual. Each SmartArt graphic has an associated Text Pane with bullets that function as an outline and map directly to the image. You can create new lines of bulleted text and then indent and demote these lines. You also can check spelling. Table 4–2 shows the keyboard shortcuts you can use with the Text Pane.

Table 4–2 Text Pane Keyboard Shortcuts

Activity	Shortcut
Indent text	TAB or ALT+SHIFT+RIGHT ARROW
Demote text	SHIFT+TAB or ALT+SHIFT+LEFT ARROW
Add a tab character	CTRL+TAB
Create a new line of text	ENTER
Check spelling	F7
Merge two lines of text	DELETE at the end of the first text line
Display the shortcut menu	SHIFT+F10
Switch between the SmartArt drawing canvas and the Text Pane	CTRL+SHIFT+F2
Close the Text Pane	ALT+F4
Switch the focus from the Text Pane to the SmartArt graphic border	ESC

BTW
Touch Screen Differences
The Office and Windows interfaces may vary if you are using a touch screen. For this reason, you might notice that the function or appearance of your touch screen differs slightly from this module's presentation.

To Enter Text in a SmartArt Graphic

1 INSERT & MODIFY SMARTART | 2 ADD SMARTART STYLES & EFFECTS | 3 CONVERT TEXT TO SMARTART & FORMAT
4 CREATE CHART | 5 FORMAT CHART | 6 CREATE TABLE | 7 CHANGE TABLE STYLE & ALIGNMENT

Why? *You want to add text that shows the topic of the presentation and labels the images you will add on this slide.* The 'Circular Picture Callout' graphic has placeholders for text that can supplement the visuals. The following steps insert four lines of text in the Text Pane and in the corresponding SmartArt shapes on Slide 1.

- If necessary, position the insertion point beside the first bullet in the Text Pane. Type **Reduce, Reuse, Recycle** in the first bullet paragraph and then click the second bullet line or press the DOWN ARROW key to move the insertion point to the second bullet paragraph (Figure 4–4).

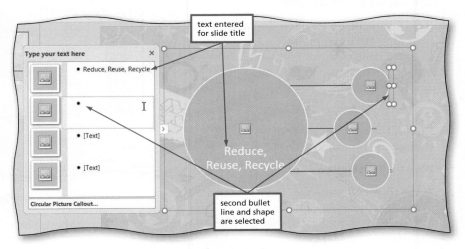

Figure 4–4

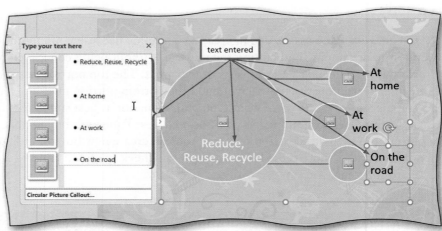

Figure 4–5

- Type **At home** in the second bullet paragraph and then click the third bullet line or press the DOWN ARROW key to move the insertion point to the third bullet paragraph.

- Type **At work** in the third bullet paragraph and then click the fourth bullet line or press the DOWN ARROW key to move the insertion point to the fourth bullet paragraph.

- Type **On the road** in the fourth bullet paragraph. Do not press the DOWN ARROW or ENTER keys (Figure 4–5).

Q&A I mistakenly pressed the DOWN ARROW or ENTER key. How can I delete the bullet paragraph I just added?
Press the BACKSPACE key to delete the paragraph.

When I mistakenly pressed the TAB key to move to the next paragraph, the current paragraph's level is changed. How can I fix it?
Press SHIFT+TAB to return to the previous level.

Other Ways

1. Right-click SmartArt graphic, click Show Text Pane on shortcut menu, enter text in Text Pane

To Format Text Pane Characters

1 INSERT & MODIFY SMARTART | 2 ADD SMARTART STYLES & EFFECTS | 3 CONVERT TEXT TO SMARTART & FORMAT
4 CREATE CHART | 5 FORMAT CHART | 6 CREATE TABLE | 7 CHANGE TABLE STYLE & ALIGNMENT

Once the desired characters are entered in the Text Pane, you can change the font size and apply formatting features, such as bold, italic, and underlined text. **Why?** *Changing the font and adding effects can help draw the audience members to the varied slide content and coordinate with the visual content.* The following steps format the text by changing the font and bolding the letters.

- With the Text Pane open, drag through all four bullet paragraphs to select the text and display the mini toolbar.

Q&A If my Text Pane no longer is displayed, how can I get it to appear?
Click the control, which is the tab with a left-pointing arrow, on the left side of the SmartArt graphic.

- Display the Font gallery and change the font to Kristen ITC.

- Bold the text (Figure 4–6).

Q&A These formatting changes did not appear in the Text Pane. Why?
Not all the formatting changes are evident in the Text Pane, but they appear in the corresponding shape.

Figure 4–6

- Click the Close button in the SmartArt Text Pane so that it no longer is displayed.

To Insert a Picture from a File into a SmartArt Graphic

The picture icons in the middle of the four circles in the 'Circular Picture Callout' SmartArt layout indicate that the shapes are designed to hold images. These images can add a personalized touch to your presentation. *Why? The purpose of this presentation is to show the wide variety of recycling possibilities, and audience members would be familiar with the three topics shown in these SmartArt circles.* You can select files from the Internet or from images you have obtained from other sources, such as a photograph taken with your digital camera. The following steps insert images located in the Data Files into the large SmartArt circle.

1

- Click the 'Insert Picture from File' icon in the SmartArt large circle picture placeholder (shown in Figure 4–6) to display the Insert Picture dialog box.

- Click the Browse button in the From a file area to display the Insert Picture dialog box.

- If necessary, navigate to the desired picture location (in this case, the Module 04 folder in the Data Files folder) and then click Globe to select the file (Figure 4–7).

Q&A What if the illustration is not in the Data Files folder?
Use the same process, but be certain to select the location containing the picture in the file list.

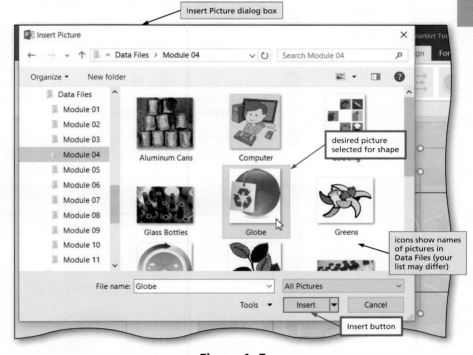

Figure 4–7

2

- Click the Insert button (Insert Picture dialog box) to insert the Globe picture into the SmartArt large circle picture placeholder (Figure 4–8).

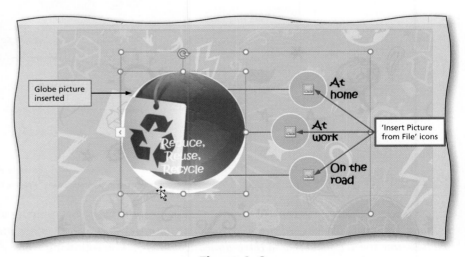

Figure 4–8

Other Ways

1. Click Shape Fill button (SmartArt Tools Format tab | Shape Styles group), click Picture

2. Right-click SmartArt shape, click Fill button, click Picture

BTW
**The Ribbon and
Screen Resolution**
PowerPoint may change
how the groups and buttons
within the groups appear
on the ribbon, depending
on the computer or mobile
device's screen resolution.
Thus, your ribbon may look
different from the ones in
this book if you are using a
screen resolution other than
1366 x 768.

To Insert Additional Pictures from a File into a SmartArt Graphic

The Globe illustration fills the left shape in the SmartArt graphic, and you want to insert additional recycling photos in the three circles in the right portion of the graphic. These images are located in the Data Files. The following steps insert photos into the three smaller SmartArt graphic circles.

1 Click the 'Insert Picture from File' icon in the top circle to the left of the words, At home, to display the Insert Pictures dialog box.

2 Click the Browse button in the 'From a file' area, scroll down and then click Home in the list of picture files, and then click the Insert button (Insert Picture dialog box) to insert the photo into the top-right SmartArt circle picture placeholder.

3 Click the center 'Insert Picture from File' icon to the left of the words, At work, click the Browse button in the Insert Pictures dialog box, and then insert the photo with the file name, Work, into the placeholder.

4 Click the bottom 'Insert Picture from File' icon to the left of the words, On the road, and then insert the photo with the file name, Road, into the placeholder (Figure 4–9).

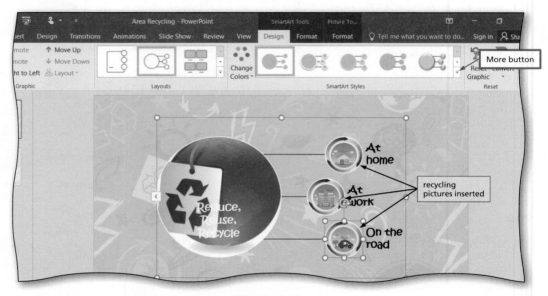

Figure 4–9

To Apply a SmartArt Style

1 INSERT & MODIFY SMARTART | 2 ADD SMARTART STYLES & EFFECTS | 3 CONVERT TEXT TO SMARTART & FORMAT
4 CREATE CHART | 5 FORMAT CHART | 6 CREATE TABLE | 7 CHANGE TABLE STYLE & ALIGNMENT

You can change the look of your SmartArt graphic easily by applying a **SmartArt style**. *Why? You can use these professionally designed effects to customize the appearance of your presentation with a variety of shape fills, edges, shadows, line styles, gradients, and three-dimensional styles.* The following steps add the Cartoon style to the 'Circular Picture Callout' SmartArt graphic.

1

- With the SmartArt graphic still selected, click the SmartArt Styles More button (SmartArt Tools Design tab | SmartArt Styles group) (shown in Figure 4–9) to expand the SmartArt Styles gallery (Figure 4–10)

Q&A How do I select the graphic if it no longer is selected?
Click the graphic anywhere except the pictures you just added.

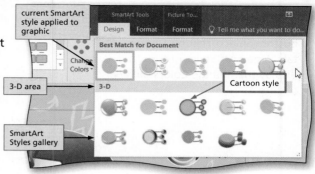

Figure 4–10

2

- Point to the Cartoon style in the 3-D area (third style in first 3-D row) in the SmartArt Styles gallery to display a live preview of this style (Figure 4–11).

🔍 **Experiment**

- Point to various styles in the SmartArt Styles gallery and watch the 'Circular Picture Callout' graphic change styles.

3

- Click Cartoon to apply this style to the graphic.

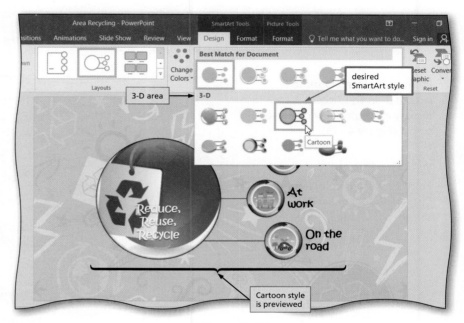

Figure 4–11

Other Ways

1. Right-click SmartArt graphic in an area other than a picture, click Style button

To Change SmartArt Color

1 INSERT & MODIFY SMARTART | 2 ADD SMARTART STYLES & EFFECTS | 3 CONVERT TEXT TO SMARTART & FORMAT
4 CREATE CHART | 5 FORMAT CHART | 6 CREATE TABLE | 7 CHANGE TABLE STYLE & ALIGNMENT

Another modification you can make to your SmartArt graphic is to change its color. As with the WordArt Style gallery, PowerPoint provides a gallery of color options you can preview and evaluate. The following steps change the SmartArt graphic color to a Colorful range. *Why? The styles in the Colorful range have different colors for the text and other slide elements. The images in your SmartArt have green accents and the globe land and oceans are dark green and blue, so you want SmartArt elements that coordinate and are visible with these colors.*

1

- With the SmartArt graphic still selected, click the Change Colors button (SmartArt Tools Design tab | SmartArt Styles group) to display the Change Colors gallery (Figure 4–12).

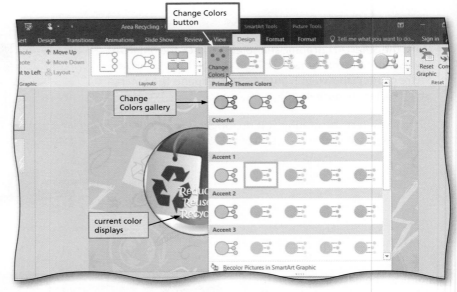

Figure 4–12

2

- Point to 'Colored Outline – Accent 3' in the Accent 3 area to display a live preview of these colors (Figure 4–13).

Experiment

- Point to various colors in the Change Colors gallery and watch the shapes change colors.

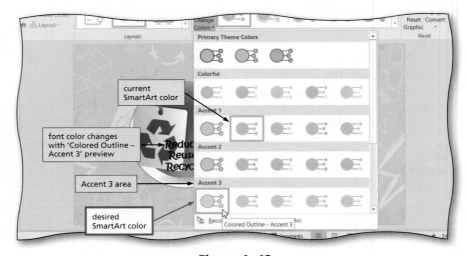

Figure 4–13

3

- Click 'Colored Outline – Accent 3' to apply this color variation to the graphic (Figure 4–14).

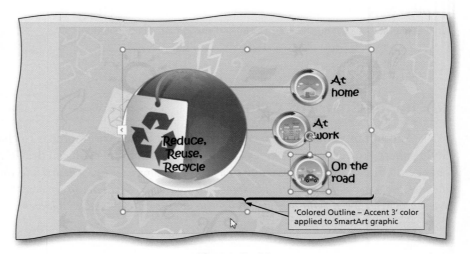

Figure 4–14

Other Ways

1. Right-click SmartArt graphic in an area other than a picture, click Color button

To Resize a SmartArt Graphic

When you view the completed graphic, you may decide that individual shapes or the entire piece of art needs to be enlarged or reduced. If you change the size of one shape, the other shapes also may change size to maintain proportions. Likewise, the font size may change in all the shapes if you increase or decrease the font size of one shape. On Slide 1, you want to change the SmartArt graphic size. *Why? A larger graphic size will fill the empty space on the slide and add readability.* All the shapes will enlarge proportionally when you adjust the graphic's height and width. The following step resizes the SmartArt graphic.

- With the SmartArt graphic still selected, drag the upper-left sizing handle to the upper-left corner of the slide.
- Drag the lower-right sizing handle to the lower-right corner of the slide, as shown in Figure 4–15.

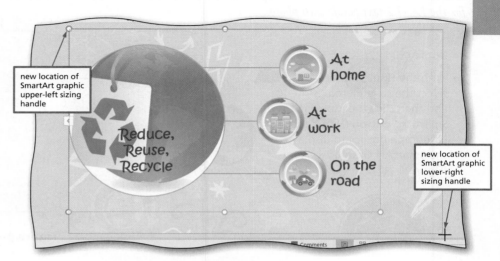

Figure 4–15

Other Ways

1. Right-click SmartArt graphic, click Size and Position on shortcut menu

To Change the Font Size and Move a Text Box

Why? The text box in the large SmartArt circle is covering the recycling tag. The letters would be more readable if they were displayed in the dark blue and green areas of the globe and enlarged slightly. The following steps increase the font size and then move the text box.

- Select the three words in the large SmartArt circle text box and then click the 'Increase Font Size' button on the mini toolbar menu twice to increase the font size to 48 point.

- Click any of the letters in the large SmartArt circle to select the text box.
- Drag the text box upward to the location shown in Figure 4–16.

Figure 4–16

To Convert Text to a SmartArt Graphic

You quickly can convert small amounts of slide text and pictures into a SmartArt graphic. Once you determine the type of graphic, such as process or cycle, you then have a wide variety of styles from which to choose in the SmartArt Graphics gallery. As with other galleries, you can point to the samples and view a live preview if you are using a mouse. The following steps convert the six bulleted text paragraphs on Slide 2 to the 'Titled Picture Blocks' graphic, which is part of the Picture category. *Why? This SmartArt style is a good match for the content of Slide 2. It has three large areas for photos, placeholders for the Level 1 text above each photo, and placeholders for the Level 2 text beside each photo.*

1

- Display Slide 2.

- With the Home tab displayed, select the six bulleted list items and then click the 'Convert to SmartArt' button (Home tab | Paragraph group) to display the SmartArt Graphics gallery (Figure 4–17).

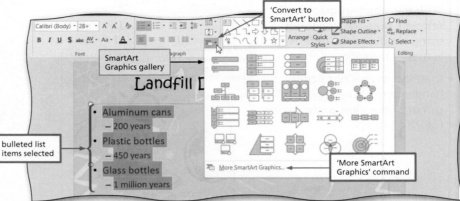

Figure 4–17

2

- Click 'More SmartArt Graphics' in the SmartArt Graphics gallery to display the Choose a SmartArt Graphic dialog box.

- Click Picture in the left pane to display the Picture gallery.

- Click the 'Titled Picture Blocks' graphic (first graphic in fourth row) to display a preview of this graphic in the right pane (Figure 4–18).

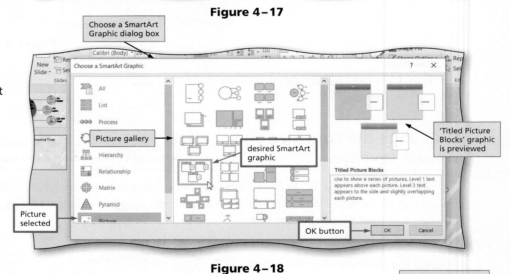

Figure 4–18

3

- Click the OK button (Choose a SmartArt Graphic dialog box) to apply this shape and convert the text (Figure 4–19).

 How can I edit the text that displays in the three shapes?
You can click the text and then make the desired changes. Also, if you display the Text Pane on the left side of the graphic, you can click the text you want to change and make your edits.

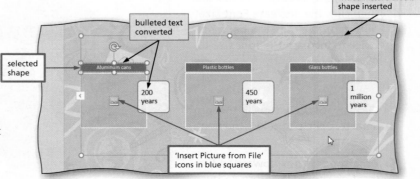

Figure 4–19

Other Ways

1. Select text, click 'Convert to SmartArt' on shortcut menu

To Insert Pictures from a File into a SmartArt Graphic

The picture icon in each of the three blue boxes in the SmartArt graphic indicates the shape is designed to hold an image. In this presentation, you will add images located in the Data Files. The following steps insert photos into the SmartArt graphic.

① Click the 'Insert Picture from File' icon in the left blue box under the words, Aluminum cans, to display the Insert Pictures dialog box.

② Click the Browse button in the 'From a file' area, click the Aluminum Cans icon in the list of picture files, and then click the Insert button (Insert Picture dialog box) to insert the picture into the left SmartArt square picture placeholder.

③ Click the 'Insert Picture from File' icon in the center blue box under the words, Plastic bottles, to display the Insert Picture dialog box, click the Browse button to display the Insert Picture dialog box, and then insert the picture with the file name, Plastic Bottles, into the placeholder.

④ Click the 'Insert Picture from File' icon in the right blue box under the words, Glass bottles, and then insert the picture with the file name, Glass Bottles, into the placeholder (Figure 4–20).

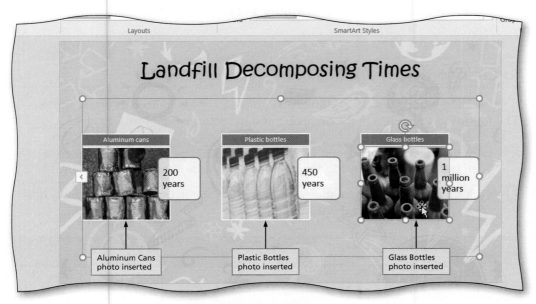

Figure 4–20

To Add a SmartArt Style to the Graphic

To enhance the appearance of the group of squares, you can add a three-dimensional style. The following steps add the Subtle Effect to the 'Titled Picture Blocks' graphic.

① With the SmartArt graphic still selected, if necessary, display the SmartArt Tools Design tab and then click the SmartArt Styles More button (SmartArt Tools Design tab | SmartArt Styles) to expand the SmartArt Styles gallery.

BTW
Building Speaker Confidence
As you rehearse your speech, keep in mind that your audience will be studying the visual elements during your actual presentation and will not be focusing on you. Using information graphics in a presentation should give you confidence as a presenter because they support your verbal message and help reinforce the message you are trying to convey.

2 Click Subtle Effect in the Best Match for Document area (third graphic) to apply this style to the graphic (Figure 4–21).

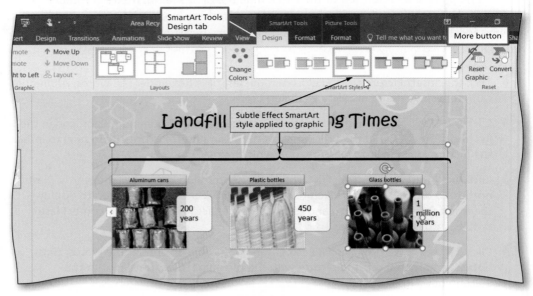

Figure 4–21

To Change the SmartArt Color

Adding more colors to the SmartArt graphic would enhance its visual appeal. The following steps change the SmartArt graphic color to a Colorful range.

1 With the SmartArt graphic still selected, click the Change Colors button (SmartArt Tools Design tab | SmartArt Styles group) to display the Change Colors gallery.

2 Click 'Colorful Range – Accent Colors 5 to 6' (last color in Colorful row) to apply this color variation to the graphic (Figure 4–22).

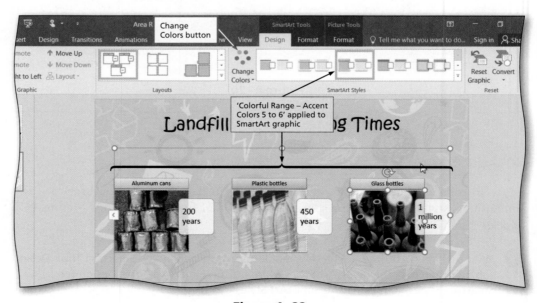

Figure 4–22

To Resize a SmartArt Graphic

Although white space on a slide generally is good to have, Slide 2 has sufficient space to allow the SmartArt graphic size to increase slightly. When you adjust the graphic's height and width, all the squares will enlarge proportionally. The following step resizes the SmartArt graphic.

1 With the SmartArt graphic still selected, drag the top-left sizing handle diagonally upward to the left edge of the slide and below the title text placeholder. Then drag the bottom-right sizing handle diagonally to the bottom-right edge of the slide, as shown in Figure 4–23.

Q&A Can I drag other sizing handles to resize the graphic?
You can drag the upper-right and lower-left sizing handles. If you drag the middle-left handle, however, you will display the Text Pane.

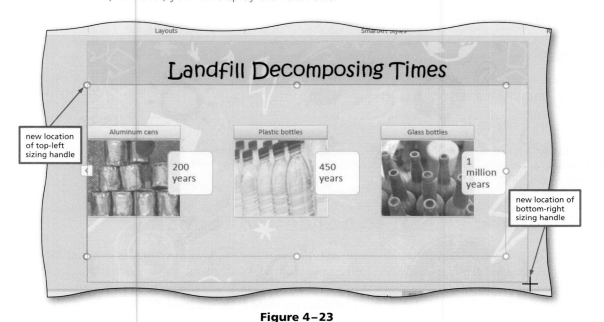

Figure 4–23

To Format SmartArt Graphic Text

1 INSERT & MODIFY SMARTART | 2 ADD SMARTART STYLES & EFFECTS | **3 CONVERT TEXT TO SMARTART & FORMAT**
4 CREATE CHART | 5 FORMAT CHART | 6 CREATE TABLE | 7 CHANGE TABLE STYLE & ALIGNMENT

The text in the three rectangles above the photos can be reformatted. You can select all three rectangles and then change the text. **Why?** *Changing the size, color, and other aspects will make the text more readable.* For consistency and efficiency, it is best to format the same items on a slide simultaneously. These rectangles are separate items in the SmartArt graphic. Select these objects by selecting one rectangle, pressing and holding down the SHIFT key, and then selecting the second and third rectangles. The following steps simultaneously bold and underline the rectangle text, change the font color to Dark Blue, increase the font size, and change the font.

1

• Click the rectangle labeled Aluminum cans to select it. Press and hold down the SHIFT key and then click the Plastic bottles and Glass bottles rectangles (Figure 4–24).

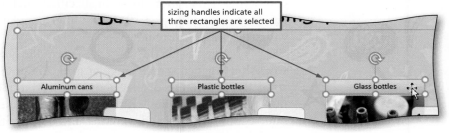

Figure 4–24

2

- Display the Home tab and then click the Bold button (Home tab | Font group).

- Click the Underline button (Home tab | Font group) to add an underline to the text.

- Click the Font Color arrow and then click Dark Blue (ninth color in Standard Colors row) to change the font color to Dark Blue.

- Click the 'Increase Font Size' button several times to increase the font size to 24 point.

- Change the font to Kristen ITC (Figure 4–25).

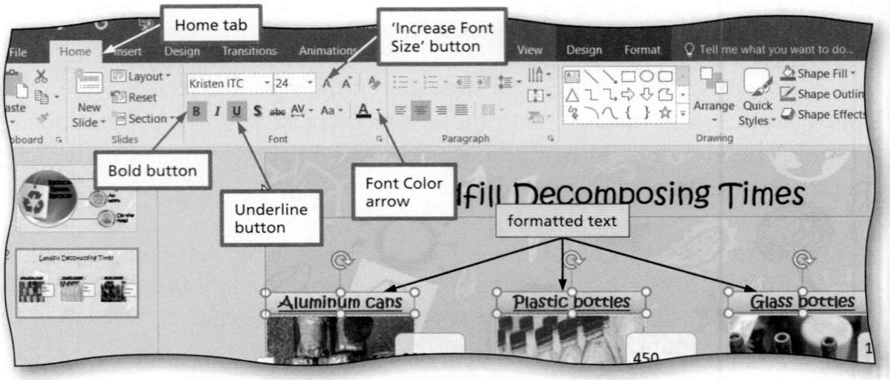

Figure 4–25

Q&A Can I make other formatting changes to the graphics' text?
Yes. You can format the text by making any of the modifications in the Font group.

If I am using a touch screen, can I modify all three rectangles simultaneously?
No. You need to repeat Step 2 for each of the rectangles.

Break Point: If you wish to take a break, this is a good place to do so. Be sure to save the Area Recycling file again and then you can exit PowerPoint. To resume at a later time, run PowerPoint, open the file called Area Recycling, and continue following the steps from this location forward.

BTW
Applying a Chart Style
Each chart type has a variety of styles that can change the look of the chart. To apply a style, select the entire chart area, click a white space near the chart, click the More button (Chart Tools Design tab | Chart Styles group) to display the Chart Styles gallery, and then select a style.

Adding a Chart to a Slide and Formatting

On average, people discard three pounds of garbage each day. Much of this material can be recycled and can be divided into four categories: glass, metal, paper, and plastic. Some communities offer curbside recycling, and many schools and offices have recycling programs, particularly for paper. The chart on Slide 3, shown in earlier in Figure 4–1c, shows the proportion of the four categories of materials that commonly are recycled.

Microsoft Excel and Microsoft Graph

PowerPoint uses one of two programs to develop a chart. It opens Microsoft Excel if that software is installed on your system. If Excel is not installed, PowerPoint opens Microsoft Graph and displays a chart with its associated data in a table called a datasheet. Microsoft Graph does not have the advanced features found in Excel. In this module, the assumption is made that Excel has been installed. When you start to create a chart, Excel opens and displays a chart in the PowerPoint slide. The default chart type is a **Clustered Column chart**. The Clustered Column chart is appropriate when comparing two or more items in specified intervals, such as comparing how inflation has risen during the past 10 years. Other popular chart types are line, bar, and pie. You will use a pie chart in Slide 3.

The figures for the chart are entered in a corresponding **Microsoft Excel worksheet**, which is a rectangular grid containing vertical columns and horizontal rows. Column letters display above the grid to identify particular **columns**, and row numbers display on the left side of the grid to identify particular **rows**. **Cells** are the intersections of rows and columns, and they are the locations for the chart data and text labels. For example, cell A1 is the intersection of column A and row 1. Numeric and text data are entered in the **active cell**, which is the one cell surrounded by a heavy border. You will replace the sample data in the worksheet by typing entries in the cells, but you also can import data from a text file, import an Excel worksheet or chart, or paste data obtained from another program. Once you have entered the data, you can modify the appearance of the chart using menus and commands.

In the following pages, you will perform these tasks:

1. Insert a chart and then replace the sample data.

2. Change the line and shape outline weights.

3. Change the chart layout.

4. Resize the chart and then change the title and legend font size.

5. Rotate the chart.

6. Separate a pie slice.

7. Insert a text box and format text.

How can I choose an appropriate chart type?

General adult audiences are familiar with bar and pie charts, so those chart types are good choices. Specialized audiences, such as engineers and architects, are comfortable reading scatter and bubble charts.

Common chart types and their purposes are as follows:

• Column — Vertical bars compare values over a period of time.

• Bar — Horizontal bars compare two or more values to show how the proportions relate to each other.

• Line — A line or lines show trends, increases and decreases, levels, and costs during a continuous period of time.

• Pie — A pie chart divides a single total into parts to illustrate how the segments differ from each other and the whole.

• Scatter — A scatterplot displays the effect on one variable when another variable changes.

In general, three-dimensional charts are more difficult to comprehend than two-dimensional charts. The added design elements in a three-dimensional chart add clutter and take up space. A chart may include a **legend**, which is a box that identifies each slice of the pie chart and coordinates with the colors assigned to the slice categories. A legend may help to unclutter the chart, so consider using one prominently on the slide.

CONSIDER THIS

To Insert a Chart

1 INSERT & MODIFY SMARTART | 2 ADD SMARTART STYLES & EFFECTS | 3 CONVERT TEXT TO SMARTART & FORMAT
4 CREATE CHART | 5 FORMAT CHART | 6 CREATE TABLE | 7 CHANGE TABLE STYLE & ALIGNMENT

The next step in developing the presentation is to insert a pie chart. *Why? The pie chart is a useful tool to show proportional amounts. In this presentation, you want to show how much content is recycled, and the slices of pie will show that paper is the most commonly recovered material.* The following steps insert a chart with sample data into Slide 3.

• Click the New Slide button (Home tab | Slides group) to add Slide 3 to the presentation (Figure 4–26).

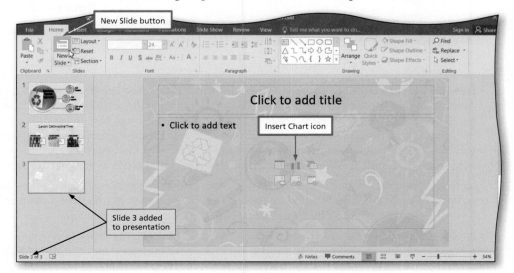

Figure 4–26

- Click the Insert Chart icon in the content placeholder to display the Insert Chart dialog box.
- Click Pie in the left pane to display the Pie gallery and then click the 3-D Pie button (second chart) to select that chart type (Figure 4–27).

Experiment

- Point to the 3-D Pie chart to see a large preview of this type.

Q&A Can I change the chart type after I have inserted a chart?
Yes. Click the 'Change Chart Type' button in the Type group on the Chart Tools Design tab to display the Change Chart Type dialog box and then make another selection.

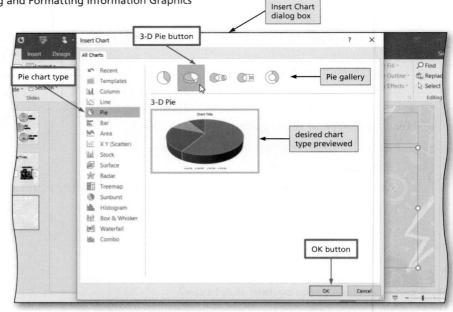

Figure 4–27

- Click the OK button (Insert Chart dialog box) to start the Microsoft Excel program and open a worksheet on the top of the Area Recycling presentation (Figure 4–28).

Q&A What do the numbers in the worksheet and the chart represent?
Excel places sample data in the worksheet and charts the sample data in the default chart type.

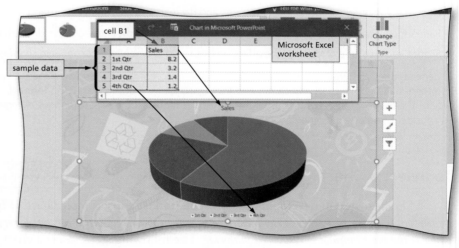

Figure 4–28

Other Ways

1. Click Chart button (Insert tab | Illustrations group)

How do I locate credible sources to obtain information for the graphic?

At times, you are familiar with the data for your chart or table because you have conducted in-the-field, or primary, research by interviewing experts or taking measurements. Other times, however, you must gather the data from secondary sources, such as magazine articles, newspaper articles, or websites. General circulation magazines and newspapers, such as *Newsweek* and the *Wall Street Journal*, use experienced journalists and editors to verify their information. Also, online databases, such as EBSCO-host, OCLC FirstSearch, LexisNexis Academic, and NewsBank contain articles from credible sources.

Some sources have particular biases, however, and they present information that supports their causes. Political, religious, and social publications and websites often are designed for specific audiences who share a common point of view. You should, therefore, recognize that data from these sources can be skewed.

If you did not conduct the research yourself, you should give credit to the source of your information. You are acknowledging that someone else provided the data and giving your audience the opportunity to obtain the same materials you used. Type the source at the bottom of your chart or table, especially if you are distributing handouts of your slides. At the very least, state the source during the body of your speech.

To Replace Sample Data

The next step in creating the chart is to replace the sample data, which will redraw the chart. *Why? The worksheet displays sample data in two columns and five rows, but you want to change this data to show the specific recycling categories and the amount of material recovered.* The first row and left column contain text labels and will be used to create the chart title and legend. The other cells contain numbers that are used to determine the size of the pie slices. The steps on the next page replace the sample data in the worksheet.

- Click cell B1, which is the intersection of column B and row 1, to select it.

Q&A Why did my pointer change shape?
The pointer changes to a block plus sign to indicate a cell is selected.

- Type **Recycled Materials** in cell B1 to replace the sample chart title (Figure 4–29).

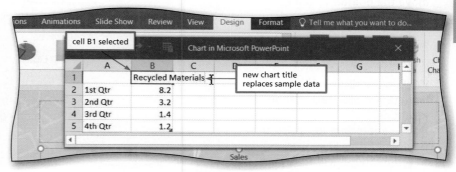

Figure 4–29

②

- Click cell A2 to select that cell.

- Type **Glass** in cell A2 (Figure 4–30).

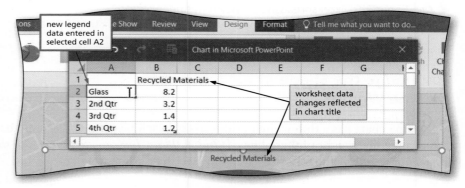

Figure 4–30

- Move the pointer to cell A3.

- Type **Paper** in cell A3 and then move the pointer to cell A4.

- Type **Metal** in cell A4 and then move the pointer to cell A5.

- Type **Plastic** in cell A5 (Figure 4–31).

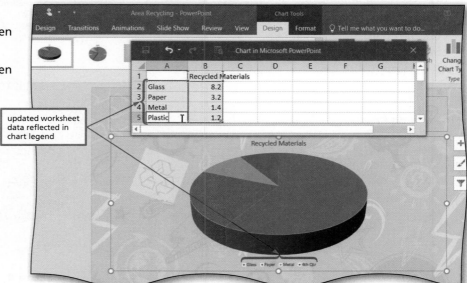

Figure 4–31

4

- Click cell B2, type 24 in that cell, and then move the pointer to cell B3.

- Type 40 in cell B3 and then move the pointer to cell B4.

- Type 10 in cell B4 and then move the pointer to cell B5.

- Type 6 in cell B5.

- Press the ENTER key to move the pointer to cell B6 (Figure 4–32).

Q&A Why do the slices in the PowerPoint pie chart change locations?
As you enter data in the Excel worksheet, the chart slices rotate to reflect these new figures.

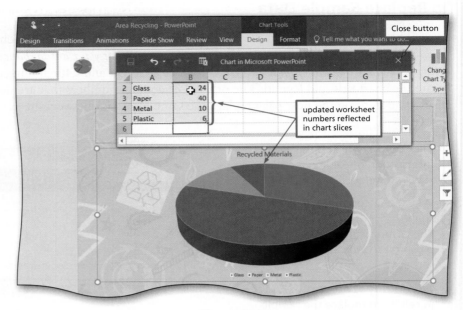

Figure 4–32

5

- Close Excel by clicking its Close button.

Q&A Can I open the Excel spreadsheet once it has been closed?
Yes. Click the chart to select it and then click the Edit Data button (Chart Tools Design tab | Data group).

To Change the Shape Outline Weight

1 INSERT & MODIFY SMARTART | 2 ADD SMARTART STYLES & EFFECTS | 3 CONVERT TEXT TO SMARTART & FORMAT
4 CREATE CHART | **5 FORMAT CHART** | 6 CREATE TABLE | 7 CHANGE TABLE STYLE & ALIGNMENT

The chart has a thin white outline around each pie slice and around each color square in the legend. You can change the weight of these lines. ***Why?*** *A thicker line can accentuate each slice and add another strong visual element to the slide.* The following steps change the outline weight.

1

- Click the center of the pie chart to select it and display the sizing handles around each slice.

- Click the Chart Tools Format tab to display the Chart Tools Format ribbon (Figure 4–33).

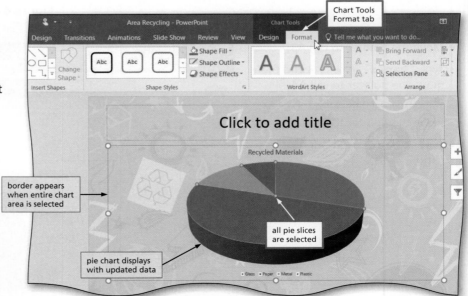

Figure 4–33

- Click the Shape Outline arrow (Chart Tools Format tab | Shape Styles group) to display the Shape Outline gallery.
- Point to Weight in the Shape Outline gallery to display the Weight gallery.
- Point to 4½ pt to display a live preview of this outline line weight (Figure 4–34).

Experiment

- Point to various weights on the submenu and watch the border weights on the pie slices change.

- Click 4½ pt to increase the border around each slice to that width.

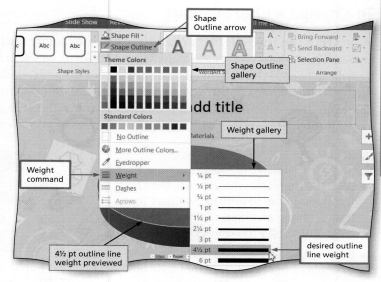

Figure 4–34

Other Ways

1. Right-click chart, click Outline button, click Weight

To Change the Shape Outline Color

1 INSERT & MODIFY SMARTART | 2 ADD SMARTART STYLES & EFFECTS | 3 CONVERT TEXT TO SMARTART & FORMAT
4 CREATE CHART | 5 FORMAT CHART | 6 CREATE TABLE | 7 CHANGE TABLE STYLE & ALIGNMENT

Why? *At this point, it is difficult to see the borders around the legend squares and around each pie slice because they are white.* You can change this color to add contrast to each slice and legend color square. The following steps change the border color.

- With the pie chart selected, click the Shape Outline arrow (Chart Tools Format tab | Shape Styles group) to display the Shape Outline gallery.
- Point to Green (sixth color in Standard Colors row) to display a live preview of that border color on the pie slice shapes and legend squares (Figure 4–35).

Experiment

- Point to various colors in the Shape Outline gallery and watch the border colors on the pie slices change.

- Click Green to add green borders around each slice and also around the color squares in the legend.

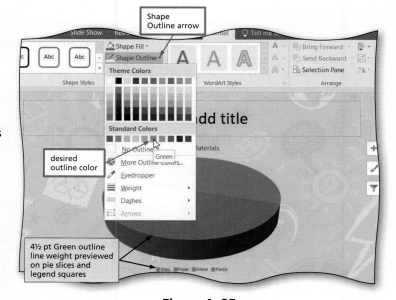

Figure 4–35

Other Ways

1. Right-click chart, click Outline button, click desired color

To Change a Chart Layout

Once you have selected a chart type, you can modify the look of the chart elements by changing its layout. The various layouts move the legend above or below the chart, or they move some or all of the legend data directly onto the individual chart pieces. For example, in the pie chart type, seven different layouts display various combinations of percentages and identifying information on the chart, and show or do not show the chart title. The following steps apply a chart layout with a title and legend that displays on the pie slices. *Why?* *Your data consists of category names and percentages, so you need a layout that shows the proportion of each category along with a chart title.*

- With the chart still selected, click the Chart Tools Design tab to display the Chart Tools Design ribbon and then click the Quick Layout button to display the Quick Layout gallery.

- Point to Layout 5 (second chart in second row) to display a live preview of that style on the pie slice shapes (Figure 4–36).

🔎 Experiment

- Point to various layouts in the Quick Layout gallery and watch the layouts on the chart change.

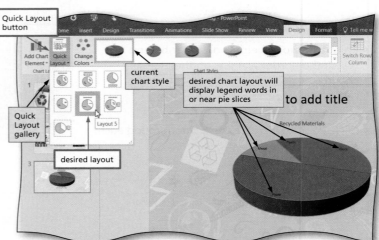

Figure 4–36

- Click Layout 5 in the Quick Layout gallery to apply the selected layout to the chart.

To Resize a Chart

You resize a chart the same way you resize a SmartArt graphic or any other graphical object. When designing a slide, you may want to delete the slide title text placeholder. *Why?* *Removing the title text placeholder increases the white space on the slide, so you are able to enlarge the chart and aid readability. In addition, the chart layout displays a title that provides sufficient information to describe the chart's purpose.* The following steps delete the title text placeholder and resize the chart to fill Slide 3.

- Click a border of the title text placeholder so that it displays as a solid line and then press the DELETE key to remove the placeholder.

Q&A
If I am using a touch screen, how do I delete the placeholder?
Press and hold on a border of the title text placeholder and then tap Delete on the shortcut menu to remove the placeholder.

- Select the chart and then drag the upper-left sizing handle to the upper-left corner of the slide.

- Drag the lower-right sizing handle to the lower-right corner of the slide, as shown in Figure 4–37.

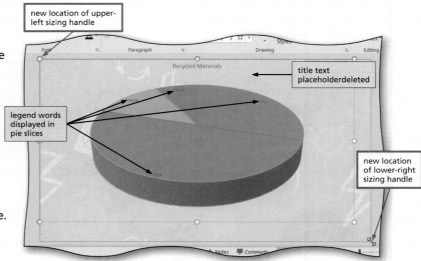

Figure 4–37

To Change the Title and Legend Font and Font Size

1 INSERT & MODIFY SMARTART | 2 ADD SMARTART STYLES & EFFECTS | 3 CONVERT TEXT TO SMARTART & FORMAT
4 CREATE CHART | 5 FORMAT CHART | 6 CREATE TABLE | 7 CHANGE TABLE STYLE & ALIGNMENT

Depending upon the complexity of the chart and the overall slide, you may want to increase the font size of the chart title and legend. *Why? The larger font size increases readability.* The following steps change the font size of both of these chart elements.

- Click the chart title, Recycled Materials, to select the text box.

- Click the 'Increase Font Size' button (Home tab | Font group) repeatedly until the font size is 48 point.

- Change the font of the chart title to Kristen ITC (Figure 4–38).

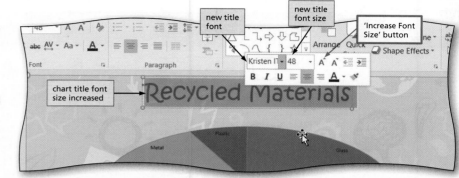

Figure 4–38

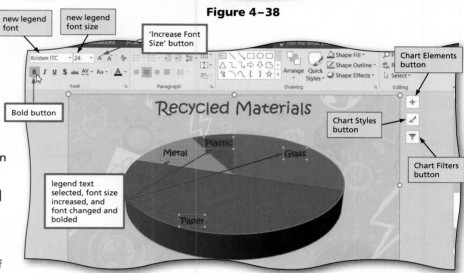

- Click one of the legends to select all the legends simultaneously.

- Click the 'Increase Font Size' button (Home tab | Font group) repeatedly until the font size of the legend text is 24 point.

- Change the legend font to Kristen ITC.

- Click the Bold button (Home tab | Font group) to bold the legend text (Figure 4–39).

Q&A What are the functions of the three buttons on the right side of the slide?

The Chart Elements button allows you to display the chart title, data labels, and legends; the Chart Styles button shows chart styles and color options; the Chart Filters button allows you to show, hide, edit, or rearrange data.

Figure 4–39

To Rotate a Chart

1 INSERT & MODIFY SMARTART | 2 ADD SMARTART STYLES & EFFECTS | 3 CONVERT TEXT TO SMARTART & FORMAT
4 CREATE CHART | 5 FORMAT CHART | 6 CREATE TABLE | 7 CHANGE TABLE STYLE & ALIGNMENT

Excel determines where each slice of pie is positioned in the chart. You may desire to have a specific slice display in a different location, such as at the top or bottom of the circle. You can rotate the entire chart clockwise until a particular part of the chart displays where you desire. A circle's circumference is 360 degrees, so if you want to move a slice from the top of the chart to the bottom, you would rotate it halfway around the circle, or 180 degrees. Similarly, if you a want a slice to move one-quarter of the way around the slide, you would rotate it either 90 degrees or 270 degrees. The steps on the next page rotate the chart so that the purple Plastic slice displays at the bottom of the chart. *Why? Consumers use many plastic products, so you want to call attention to the fact that this material should be recycled.*

1

- Click the purple Plastic slice of the pie chart to select it. Click the Chart Tools Format tab to display the Chart Tools Format ribbon.

- Click the Format Selection button (Chart Tools Format tab | Current Selection group) to display the Format Data Point pane (Figure 4–40).

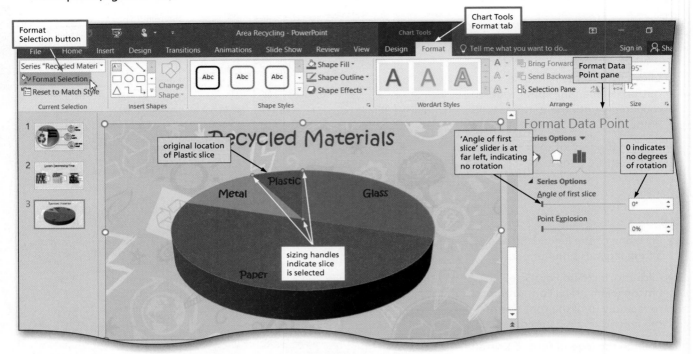

Figure 4–40

2

- Click the 'Angle of first slice' slider and drag it to the right until 150 is displayed in the 'Angle of first slice' box to rotate the Plastic slice 150 degrees to the right (Figure 4–41).

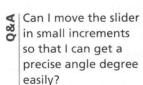 Can I move the slider in small increments so that I can get a precise angle degree easily?
Yes. Click the up or down arrows in the

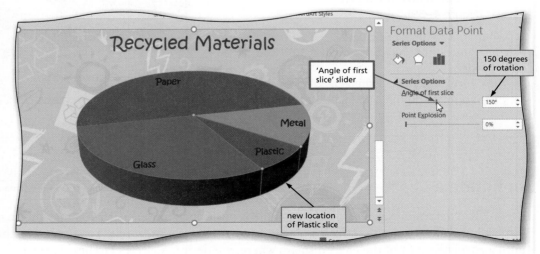

Figure 4–41

'Angle of first slice' box to move the slider in one-degree increments or select the box and type the desired degree.

Other Ways

1. Right-click selection, click 'Format Data Point' on shortcut menu

To Separate a Pie Slice

Why? *At times, you may desire to draw the viewers' attention to a particular area of the pie chart. To add this emphasis, you can separate, or explode, one or more slices.* For example, you can separate the purple Plastic slice of the chart to stress that it is important to recycle this material. The following steps separate a chart slice.

1

- Click the Point Explosion slider and drag it to the right until 15 is displayed in the Point Explosion box to separate the slice from the pie chart (Figure 4–42).

Q&A Can I move the slider in small increments so that I can get a precise percentage easily?

Yes. Click the up or down arrows in the Point Explosion box to move the slider in one-percent increments or select the box and type the desired percentage.

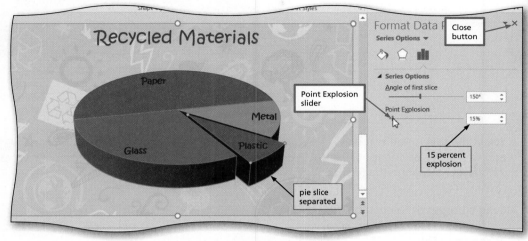

Figure 4–42

2

- Click the Close button in the Format Data Point pane to close the pane.

Q&A Can I specify a precise position where the chart will display on the slide?

Yes. Right-click the edge of the chart, click 'Format Chart Area' on the shortcut menu, click 'Size & Properties' in Format Chart Area task pane, enter measurements in the Position section, and then specify from the Top Left Corner or the Center of the slide.

Other Ways

1. Right-click selection, click 'Format Data Point' on shortcut menu, set Point Explosion percentage

To Insert a Text Box and Format Text

A text box can contain information that is separate from the title or content placeholders. You can place this slide element anywhere on the slide and format the letters using any style and effect. You also can change the text box shape by moving the sizing handles. The steps on the next page insert a text box, add text, and then format these characters. *Why?* *You want to add an interesting fact about recycling paper.*

1

- Display the Insert tab, click the Text Box button (Insert tab | Text group), and then click below the Paper label (Figure 4–43).

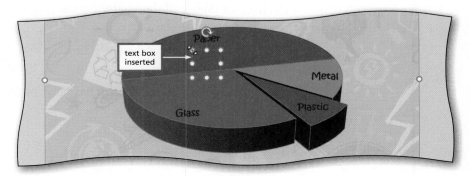

Figure 4–43

• If necessary, click the text box and then type **One ton of recycled paper can save 17 trees** in the text box (Figure 4–44).

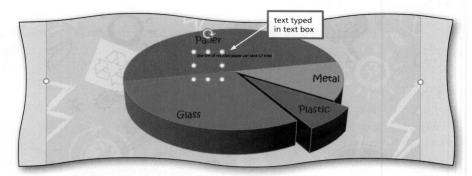

Figure 4–44

• Select the text in the text box and then increase the font size to 20 point and change the font to Kristen ITC.

• Drag a border of the text box to center the text in the Paper slice, as shown in Figure 4–45.

Q&A Can I change the shape of the text box?
Yes. Drag the sizing handles to the desired dimensions.

• Click outside the pie chart to deselect the text.

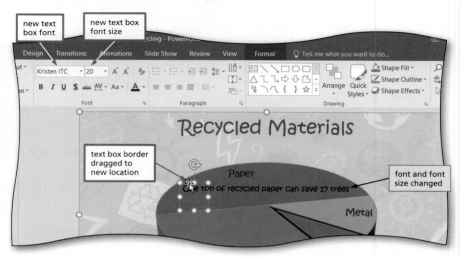

Figure 4–45

Break Point: If you wish to take a break, this is a good place to do so. Be sure to save the Area Recycling file again and then you can exit PowerPoint. To resume at a later time, run PowerPoint, open the file called Area Recycling, and continue following the steps from this location forward.

Adding a Table to a Slide and Formatting

One effective method of organizing information on a slide is to use a **table**, which is a grid consisting of rows and columns. You can enhance a table with formatting, including adding colors, lines, and backgrounds, and changing fonts.

In the following pages, you will perform these tasks:

1. Insert a table and then enter data and symbols.
2. Apply a table style.
3. Add table borders and an effect.
4. Resize the table.
5. Merge table cells and then display text in the cell vertically.
6. Add an image.
7. Align text in cells.
8. Format table data.

Tables

The table on Slide 4 (shown earlier in Figure 4–1d) contains information about the three recycling centers in the community and the types of materials accepted at each location. This data is listed in five columns and five rows.

To begin developing this table, you first must create an empty table and insert it into the slide. You must specify the table's **dimension**, which is the total number of rows and columns. This table will have a 5 × 5 dimension: the first number indicates the number of columns and the second specifies the number of rows. You will fill the cells with data pertaining to the types of materials permitted. Then you will format the table using a table style.

To Insert an Empty Table

1 INSERT & MODIFY SMARTART | 2 ADD SMARTART STYLES & EFFECTS | 3 CONVERT TEXT TO SMARTART & FORMAT
4 CREATE CHART | 5 FORMAT CHART | 6 CREATE TABLE | 7 CHANGE TABLE STYLE & ALIGNMENT

The following steps insert an empty table with five columns and five rows into Slide 4. *Why? The first row will contain the column headings, and the additional rows will have information about four recycling categories. The five columns will contain the table title and the locations of the recycling centers.*

- Add a new slide to the presentation (Figure 4–46).

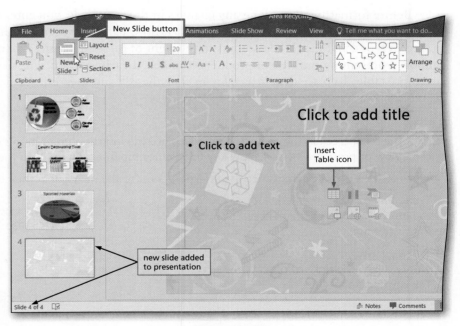

Figure 4–46

- Click the Insert Table icon in the content placeholder to display the Insert Table dialog box.

- Click the up arrow to the right of the 'Number of rows' box three times so that the number 5 appears in the box (Figure 4–47).

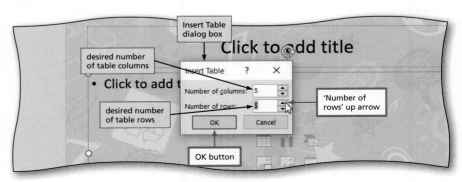

Figure 4–47

• Click the OK button (Insert table dialog box) to insert the table into Slide 4 (Figure 4–48).

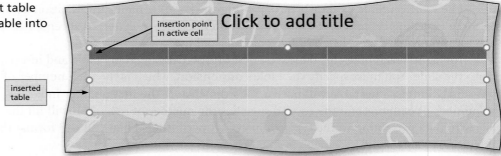

Figure 4–48

Other Ways
1. Click Table button (Insert tab | Tables group), drag to select columns and rows, click or press ENTER

To Enter Data in a Table

1 INSERT & MODIFY SMARTART | 2 ADD SMARTART STYLES & EFFECTS | 3 CONVERT TEXT TO SMARTART & FORMAT
4 CREATE CHART | 5 FORMAT CHART | 6 CREATE TABLE | 7 CHANGE TABLE STYLE & ALIGNMENT

Before formatting or making any changes in the table style, you enter the data in the table. *Why? It is easier to see formatting and style changes applied to existing data.* The second column will have the four material categories types, and the three columns to the right of these categories will contain data with check mark symbols representing the type of products accepted at each location. The next step is to enter data in the cells of the empty table. To place data in a cell, you click the cell and then type text. The following steps enter the data in the table.

• Click the second cell in the second column to place the insertion point in this cell. Type **Glass** and then click the cell below or press the DOWN ARROW key to advance the insertion point to the next cell in this column.

• Type **Metal** and then advance the insertion point to the next cell in this column.

• Type **Paper** and then advance the insertion point to the next cell in this column.

• Type **Plastic** and click the empty cell to the right or press the TAB key (Figure 4–49).

Q&A

What if I pressed the ENTER key after filling in the last cell?
Press the BACKSPACE key.

How would I add more rows to the table?
Press the TAB key when the insertion point is positioned in the bottom-right cell.

If I am using a touch screen, how do I add rows to the table?
Press and hold the bottom-right cell, tap Insert on the shortcut menu, and then tap Insert Rows Below.

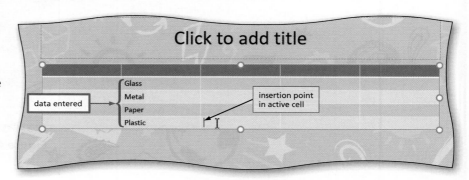

Figure 4–49

2

- Click the third cell in the first row to place the insertion point in this cell. Type **Main Street** and then advance the insertion point to the adjacent right cell in this row.

- Type **5th Avenue** and then advance the insertion point to the adjacent right cell.

- Type **Miller Court** as the cell content (Figure 4–50).

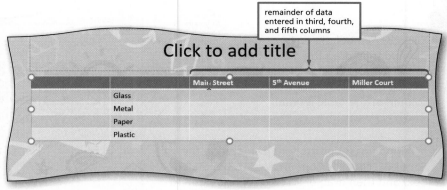

remainder of data entered in third, fourth, and fifth columns

Figure 4–50

- If requested by your instructor, type the name of the street you grew up on instead of the name, Miller Court.

Q&A How do I correct cell contents if I make a mistake?
Click the cell and then correct the text.

To Insert a Symbol

1 INSERT & MODIFY SMARTART | 2 ADD SMARTART STYLES & EFFECTS | 3 CONVERT TEXT TO SMARTART & FORMAT
4 CREATE CHART | 5 FORMAT CHART | **6 CREATE TABLE** | **7 CHANGE TABLE STYLE & ALIGNMENT**

The data in tables frequently consists of words. At times, however, the cells can contain characters and pictures that depict specific meanings. ***Why?*** *Audience members easily can identify these images, such as mathematical symbols and geometric shapes.* You can add illustrations and photos to the table cells and also can insert special symbols. Many symbols are found in the Webding and Wingding fonts. You insert symbols, such as mathematical characters and dots, by changing the font using the Symbol dialog box. The following steps insert a check mark symbol in several table cells.

1

- Click the second cell in the third column to place the insertion point in this cell.

- Display the Insert tab.

- Click the Symbol button (Insert tab | Symbols group) to display the Symbol dialog box (Figure 4–51).

Q&A What if the symbol I want to insert already appears in the Symbol dialog box?
You can click any symbol shown in the dialog box to insert it in the slide.

Figure 4–51

Why does my 'Recently used symbols' list display different symbols from those shown in Figure 4–51?
As you insert symbols, PowerPoint places them in the 'Recently used symbols' list.

- Click the Symbol dialog box title bar and then drag the dialog box to the lower-left edge of the slide so that the some of the second column of the table is visible.

- If Wingdings is not the font displayed in the Font box, click the Font arrow (Symbol dialog box) and then drag or scroll to Wingdings and click this font.

- Drag or scroll down until the last row of this font is visible.

- Click the check mark symbol as shown in Figure 4–52.

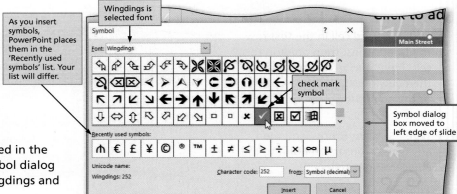

Figure 4–52

- Click the Insert button (Symbol dialog box) to place the check mark symbol in the selected table cell (Figure 4–53).

Q&A Why is the Symbol dialog box still open?
The Symbol dialog box remains open, allowing you to insert additional symbols in the selected cell.

- Click the Close button (Symbol dialog box).

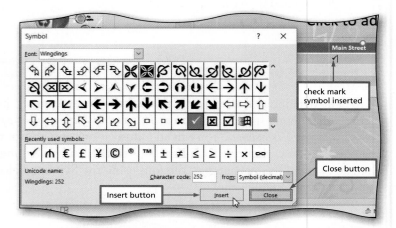

Figure 4–53

To Copy a Symbol

1 INSERT & MODIFY SMARTART | 2 ADD SMARTART STYLES & EFFECTS | 3 CONVERT TEXT TO SMARTART & FORMAT
4 CREATE CHART | 5 FORMAT CHART | **6 CREATE TABLE** | **7 CHANGE TABLE STYLE & ALIGNMENT**

The Recycling Centers chart will contain check marks for the types of material accepted. To add the check marks to specific cells, you would need to repeat the process you used to insert the first check mark. Rather than inserting this symbol from the Symbol dialog box, you can copy the symbol and then paste it in the appropriate cells. **Why?** *This process can be accomplished more quickly with copy and paste when using the same symbol multiple times.* The following steps copy the check mark symbol to cells in the Slide 4 table.

1

- Select the check mark symbol in the table, display the Home tab, and then click the Copy button (Home tab | Clipboard group) to copy the check mark symbol to the Office Clipboard (Figure 4–54).

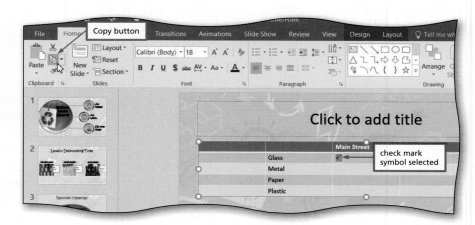

Figure 4–54

- Click the third cell in the third column to place the insertion point in this cell and then click the Paste button (Home tab | Clipboard group) (Figure 4–55).

- Press the BACKSPACE key to delete the extra row that is displayed in the cell when the symbol is pasted.

Q&A If I am using a touch screen, how do I delete the extra row?
Display the onscreen keyboard and then press the BACKSPACE key.

Figure 4–55

- Using Figure 4–56 as a guide, continue pasting the check mark symbols in the table cells.

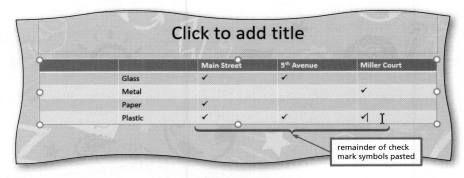

Figure 4–56

To Apply a Table Style

1 INSERT & MODIFY SMARTART | 2 ADD SMARTART STYLES & EFFECTS | 3 CONVERT TEXT TO SMARTART & FORMAT
4 CREATE CHART | 5 FORMAT CHART | 6 CREATE TABLE | **7 CHANGE TABLE STYLE & ALIGNMENT**

When you inserted the table, PowerPoint automatically applied a style. Thumbnails of this style and others are displayed in the Table Styles gallery. These styles use a variety of colors and shading and are grouped in the categories of Best Match for Document, Light, Medium, and Dark. The following steps apply a table style in the Best Match for Document area to the Slide 4 table. *Why? The styles in the Best Match for Document use the theme colors applied to the presentation, so they coordinate nicely with the colors you have been using in the first three slides in this presentation.*

- With the insertion point in the table, display the Table Tools Design tab (Figure 4–57).

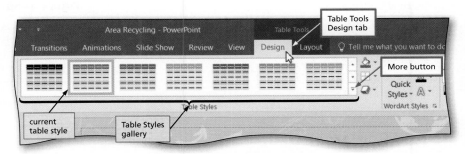

Figure 4–57

- Click the More button in the Table Styles gallery (Table Tools Design tab | Tables Styles group) to expand the Table Styles gallery.
- Scroll down and then point to 'Medium Style 3 – Accent 1' in the Medium area (second style in third Medium row) to display a live preview of that style applied to the table (Figure 4–58).

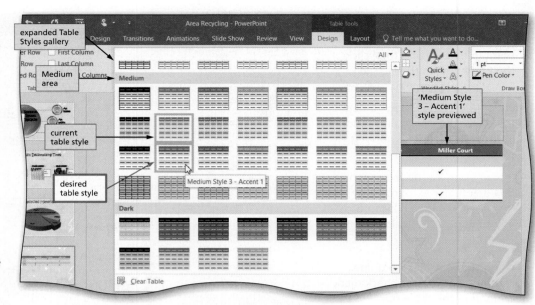

Figure 4–58

 Experiment

- Point to various styles in the Table Styles gallery and watch the colors and format change on the table.

- Click 'Medium Style 3 – Accent 1' in the Table Styles gallery to apply the selected style to the table (Figure 4–59).

Q&A Can I resize the columns and rows or the entire table? Yes. To resize columns or rows, drag a **column boundary** (the border to the right of a column) or the **row boundary** (the border at the bottom of a row) until the column or row is the desired width or height. To resize the entire table, drag a **table sizing handle**.

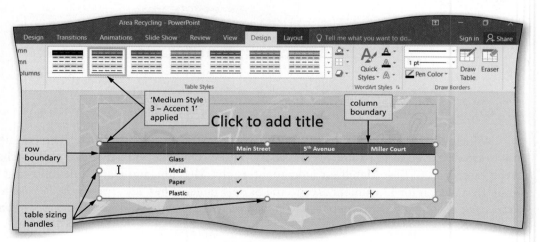

Figure 4–59

To Add Borders to a Table

1 INSERT & MODIFY SMARTART | 2 ADD SMARTART STYLES & EFFECTS | 3 CONVERT TEXT TO SMARTART & FORMAT
4 CREATE CHART | 5 FORMAT CHART | 6 CREATE TABLE | **7 CHANGE TABLE STYLE & ALIGNMENT**

The Slide 4 table does not have borders around the entire table or between the cells. The following steps add borders to the entire table. *Why? These details will give the chart some dimension and add to its visual appeal.*

1

- Click the edge of the table so that the insertion point does not appear in any cell.

- Click the Borders arrow (Table Tools Design tab | Table Styles group) to display the Borders gallery (Figure 4–60).

Q&A Why is the button called No Border in the ScreenTip and Borders on the ribbon?
The ScreenTip name for the button will change based on the type of border, if any, present in the table. Currently no borders are applied.

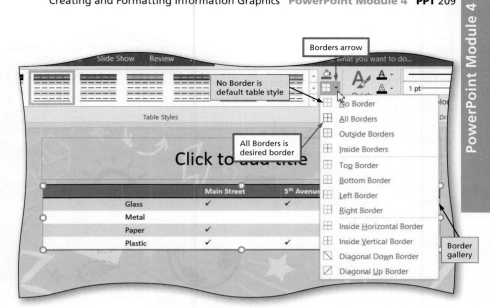

Figure 4–60

2

- Click All Borders in the Borders gallery to add borders around the entire table and to each table cell (Figure 4–61).

Q&A Why is the border color black?
PowerPoint's default border color is black. This color is displayed on the Pen Color button (Table Tools Design tab | Draw Borders group).

Can I apply any of the border options in the Border gallery?
Yes. You can vary the look of your table by applying borders only to the cells, around the table, to the top, bottom, left or right edges, or a combination of these areas.

Figure 4–61

To Add an Effect to a Table

1 INSERT & MODIFY SMARTART | 2 ADD SMARTART STYLES & EFFECTS | 3 CONVERT TEXT TO SMARTART & FORMAT
4 CREATE CHART | 5 FORMAT CHART | 6 CREATE TABLE | **7 CHANGE TABLE STYLE & ALIGNMENT**

Why? *Adding an effect will enhance the table design.* PowerPoint gives you the option of applying a bevel to specified cells so they have a three-dimensional appearance. You also can add a shadow or reflection to the entire table. The following steps add a shadow and give a three-dimensional appearance to the entire table.

1

- With the table selected, click the Effects button (Table Tools Design tab | Table Styles group) to display the Effects menu.

Q&A What is the difference between a shadow and a reflection?
A shadow gives the appearance that light is falling on the table, which causes a shadow behind the graphic. A reflection gives the appearance that the table is shiny, so a mirror image appears below the actual graphic.

2

- Point to Shadow to display the Shadow gallery (Figure 4–62).

Q&A How do the shadows differ in the Outer, Inner, and Perspective categories?

The Outer shadows are displayed on the outside of the table, whereas the Inner shadows are displayed in the interior cells. The Perspective shadows give the illusion that a light is shining from the right or left side of the table or from above, and the table is casting a shadow.

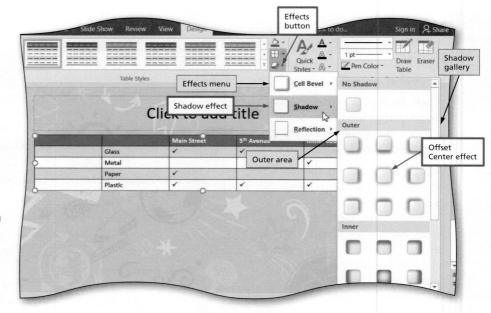

Figure 4–62

3

- Point to Offset Center in the Outer category (second shadow in second row) to display a live preview of this shadow (Figure 4–63).

Experiment

- Point to the various shadows in the Shadow gallery and watch the shadows change in the table.

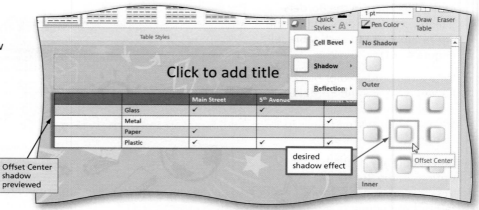

Figure 4–63

4

- Click Offset Center to apply this shadow to the table.
- Click outside the table so it no longer is selected (Figure 4–64).

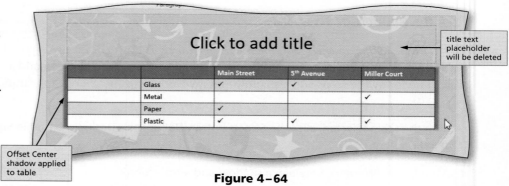

Figure 4–64

To Resize a Table

Why? *On Slide 4, you can remove the title text placeholder because the table will have the title, Recycling Centers, in the first column. If you resize the table to fill the slide it will be more readable.* You resize a table the same way you resize a chart, a SmartArt graphic, or any other graphical object. The following steps resize the table to fill Slide 4.

1

- Click a border of the title text placeholder so that it displays as a solid line and then press the DELETE key to remove the placeholder (Figure 4–65).

Q&A If I am using a touch screen, how do I remove the placeholder?

Press and hold a border of the title text placeholder and then tap Delete on the shortcut menu.

Figure 4–65

2

- Select the table and then drag the upper-left sizing handle diagonally to the upper-left corner of the slide.

- Drag the lower-right sizing handle diagonally to the lower-right corner of the slide, as shown in Figure 4–66.

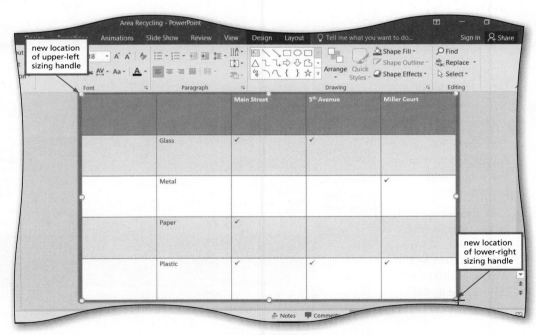

Figure 4–66

To Merge Cells

You want to insert a photo of a recycling sign in the area where the first two cells reside in the first row, so you need to make room for this picture. In addition, you want to merge cells in the first column to fit a chart title. *Why? To provide space for graphics and text, you can merge two or more cells to create one large cell.* The Slide 4 table title will display vertically in the first column. The following steps merge two cells in the first table row into a single cell and merge four cells in the first column into a single cell.

- Drag through the first and second column cells in the first table row to select these two cells (Figure 4–67).

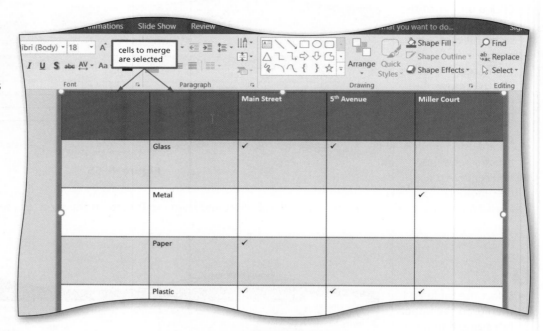

Figure 4–67

- Click the Table Tools Layout tab to display the Table Tools Layout ribbon.
- Click the Merge Cells button (Table Tools Layout tab | Merge group) to merge the two cells into one cell (Figure 4–68).

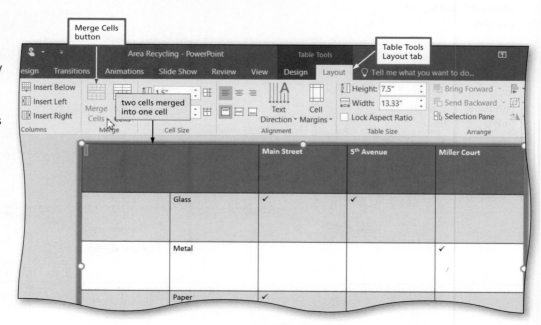

Figure 4–68

3

- Drag through the second, third, fourth, and fifth cells in the first table column to select these cells (Figure 4–69).

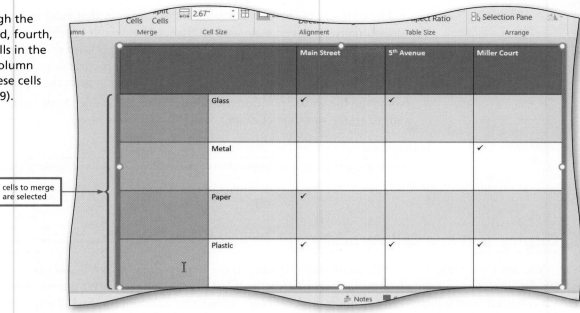

cells to merge are selected

Figure 4–69

4

- Click the Merge Cells button to merge these cells (Figure 4–70).

Q&A Could I have merged the four cells in the first column before merging the two cells in the first row? Yes.

Merge Cells button

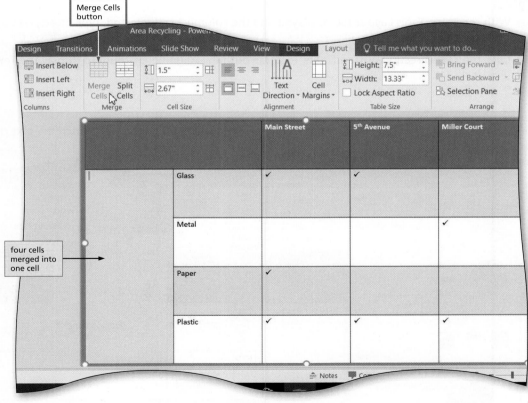

four cells merged into one cell

Figure 4–70

Other Ways

1. Right-click selected cells, click Merge Cells on shortcut menu

To Change Table Column Height and Width

The font size of the text in a table cell determines that cell's minimum height. You occasionally, however, may need to change the default height or width of a table column or row. To resize a column or row, you would perform the following steps.

1. Select the table. To change the height, position the pointer over the inside border of the column you want to resize and then drag the column to the right or left.

2. To change the width, position the pointer over the inside border of the row you want to resize and then click and drag the row up or down.

Other Ways

1. Enter desired measurements in Height and Width boxes (Table Tools Layout tab | Cell Size group)

To Display Text in a Cell Vertically

1 INSERT & MODIFY SMARTART | 2 ADD SMARTART STYLES & EFFECTS | 3 CONVERT TEXT TO SMARTART & FORMAT
4 CREATE CHART | 5 FORMAT CHART | 6 CREATE TABLE | **7 CHANGE TABLE STYLE & ALIGNMENT**

You want the Slide 4 table title to display vertically in the first column. ***Why?*** *To add variety to your slides, you can display text in a nonstandard manner.* By rotating text 270 degrees, you call attention to these letters. The default orientation of table cell text is horizontal. You can change this direction to stack the letters so they display above and below each other, or you can rotate the direction in 90-degree increments. The following steps rotate the text in the first column cell.

- With the Table Tools Layout tab displayed and the column 1 cell selected, type **Recycling Centers** in the table cell.

- Click the Text Direction button (Table Tools Layout tab | Alignment group) to display the Text Direction gallery (Figure 4–71).

Experiment

- Point to the three other direction options in the Text Direction gallery and watch the text change in the cell.

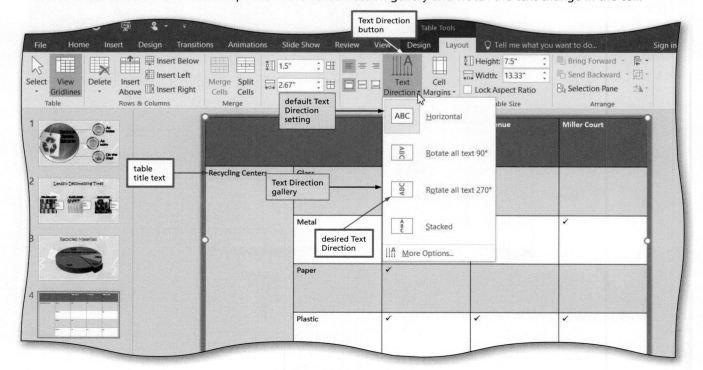

Figure 4–71

2

- Click 'Rotate all text 270°' to rotate the text in the cell (Figure 4–72).

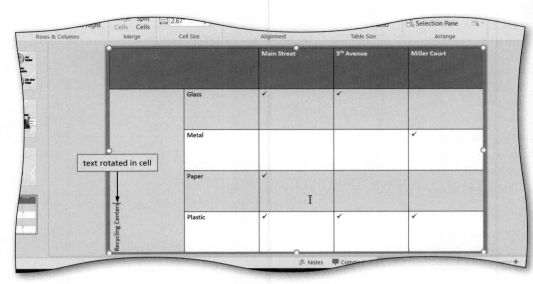

text rotated in cell

Figure 4–72

Other Ways

1. Right-click selected cells, click Format Shape on shortcut menu, click Text Options tab, click Textbox icon, click Text direction arrow

To Add an Image to a Table and Change the Transparency

1 INSERT & MODIFY SMARTART | 2 ADD SMARTART STYLES & EFFECTS | 3 CONVERT TEXT TO SMARTART & FORMAT
4 CREATE CHART | 5 FORMAT CHART | 6 CREATE TABLE | **7 CHANGE TABLE STYLE & ALIGNMENT**

Another table enhancement you can make is to add a photo or illustration to a table cell. The following steps add a picture of a recycling center sign to the upper-left table cell and then decrease the transparency so the picture is displayed with the full color intensity. ***Why?*** *This illustration is another graphical element that reinforces the purpose of the table.*

1

- Right-click the first cell in the first row to display the shortcut menu and mini toolbar (Figure 4–73).

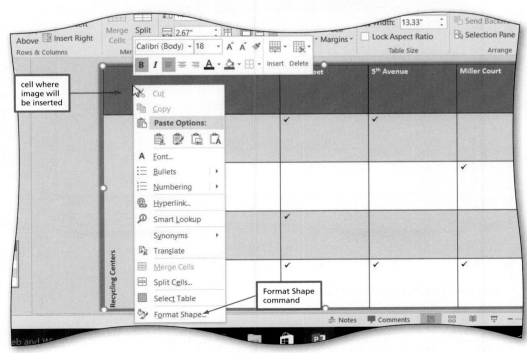

cell where image will be inserted

Format Shape command

Figure 4–73

- Click Format Shape to display the Format Shape pane and then, if necessary, click Fill to expand the Fill section.
- Click 'Picture or texture fill' to select this option (Figure 4–74).

- Click the File button to display the Insert Picture dialog box.
- Click the Recycling Sign picture located in the Data Files and then click the Insert

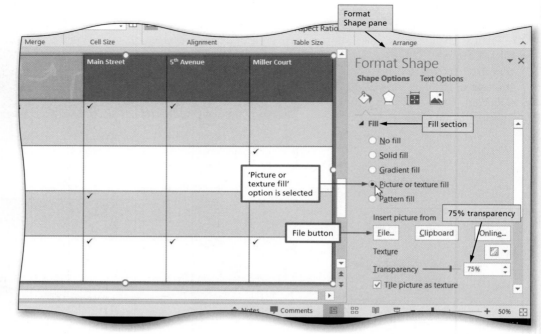

button (Insert Picture dialog box) to insert the Recycling Sign picture into the table cell.

Figure 4–74

- If the Transparency is more than 0%, drag slider to the left until 0% is displayed in the Transparency text box (Figure 4–75).

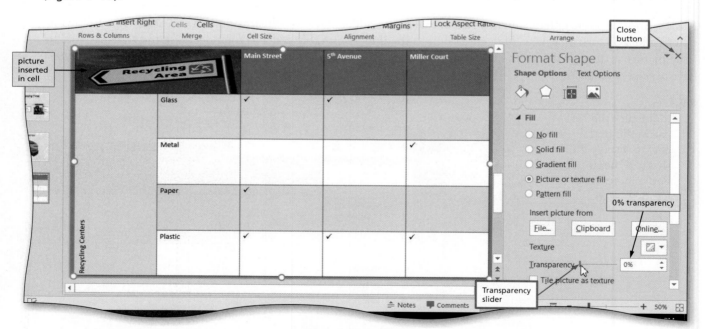

Figure 4–75

- Click the Close button (Format Shape pane).

Other Ways
1. Right-click selected cell, click Shape Fill arrow on mini toolbar, click Picture

To Align Text in Cells

The data in each cell can be aligned horizontally and vertically. You change the horizontal alignment of each cell in a similar manner as you center, left-align, or right-align text in a placeholder. You also can change the vertical alignment so that the data displays at the top, middle, or bottom of each cell. The following steps center the text both horizontally and vertically in each table cell. *Why?* *Having the text centered vertically and horizontally helps balance the cells by distributing the empty space evenly around the cell contents.*

1
- Click the Select button (Table Tools Layout tab |Table group) to display the Select menu (Figure 4–76).

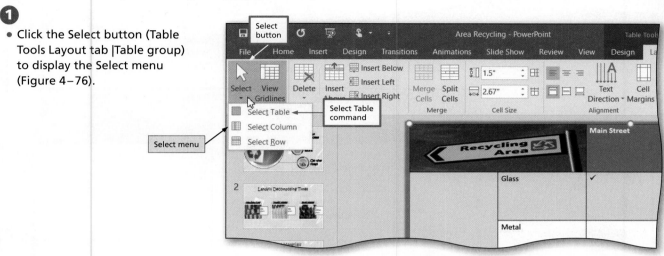

Figure 4–76

2
- Click Select Table in the Select menu to select the entire table.
- Click the Center button (Table Tools Layout tab | Alignment group) to center the text between the left and right borders of each cell in the table (Figure 4–77).

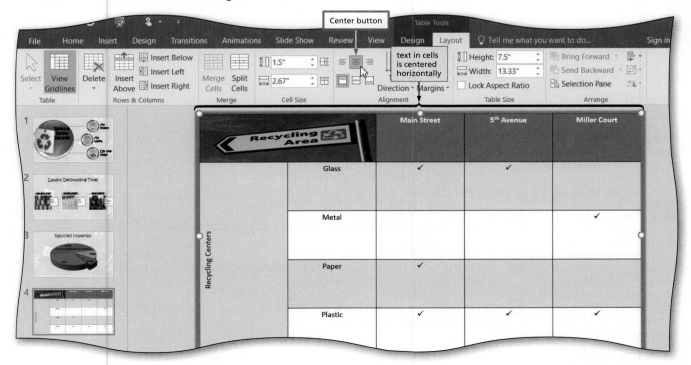

Figure 4–77

❸

- Click the Center Vertically button (Table Tools Layout tab | Alignment group) to center the text between the top and bottom borders of each cell in the table (Figure 4–78).

Q&A | Must I center all the table cells, or can I center only specific cells?
You can center as many cells as you desire at one time by selecting one or more cells.

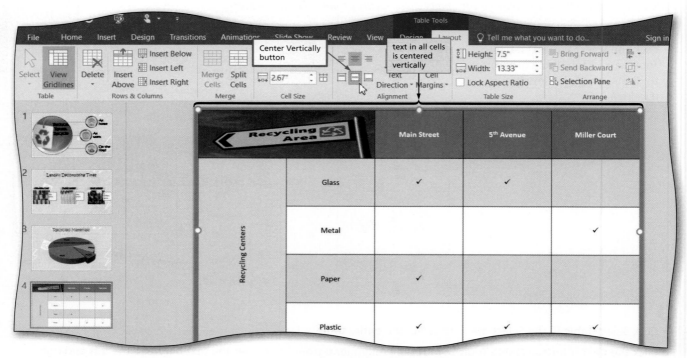

Figure 4–78

Other Ways

1. Right-click selected cells, click Format Shape on shortcut menu, click Text Options tab, click Textbox icon, click Vertical alignment arrow

---

BTW
Clearing Table Formatting
The table you create on Slide 4 has five columns and five rows. Many times, however, you may need to create larger tables and then enter data into many cells. In these cases, experienced PowerPoint designers recommend clearing all formatting from the table so that you can concentrate on the numbers and letters and not be distracted by the colors and borders. To clear formatting, click the Clear Table command at the bottom of the Table Styles gallery (Table Tools Design tab | Table Styles group). Then, add a table style once you have verified that all table data is correct.

To Format Table Data

The final table enhancement is to bold the text in all cells and increase the font size of the title and the symbols. The entire table is selected, so you can bold all text simultaneously. The title and symbols will have different font sizes. The following steps format the data.

❶ Display the Home tab and then click the Bold button (Home tab | Font group) to bold all text in the table.

❷ Select the table title text in the first column and then increase the font size to 72 point and change the font to Kristen ITC.

❸ Select the three column headings and then increase the font size to 28 point and change the font to Kristen ITC.

④ Select the four cells with the recycling category names in the second column and then increase the font size to 32 point and change the font to Kristen ITC.

⑤ Select all the table cells below the column headings and then increase the font size of the check marks to 40 point (Figure 4–79).

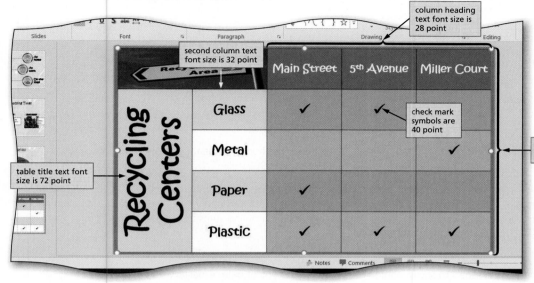

Figure 4–79

To Add a Transition between Slides

A final enhancement you will make in this presentation is to apply the Crush transition in the Exciting category to all slides and change the transition duration to 3.00. The following steps apply this transition to the presentation.

① Apply the Crush transition in the Exciting category (Transitions tab | Transition to This Slide group) to all four slides in the presentation.

② Change the transition duration from 02.00 to 03.00 for all slides.

To Save and Print the Presentation

With the presentation completed, you should save the file and print handouts for your audience. The following steps save the file and then print a presentation handout with two slides per page.

① Save the presentation again in the same storage location with the same file name.

② Open the Backstage view, click the Print tab, click 'Full Page Slides' in the Settings area, click 2 Slides in the Handouts area to display a preview of the handout, and then click the Print button in the Print gallery to print the presentation.

③ Because the project now is complete, you can exit PowerPoint.

BTW
Printing Document Properties
PowerPoint 2016 does not allow you to print document properties. This feature, however, is available in other Office 2016 apps, including Word and Excel.

BTW
Conserving Ink and Toner
If you want to conserve ink or toner, you can instruct PowerPoint to print draft quality documents by clicking File on the ribbon to open the Backstage view, clicking the Options tab in the Backstage view to display the PowerPoint Options dialog box, clicking Advanced in the left pane (PowerPoint Options dialog box), scrolling to the Print area in the right pane, not placing a check mark in the High quality check box, and then clicking the OK button. Then, use the Backstage view to print the document as usual.

BTW
Distributing a Document
Instead of printing and distributing a hard copy of a document, you can distribute the document electronically. Options include sending the document via email; posting it on cloud storage (such as OneDrive) and sharing the file with others; posting it on social media, a blog, or other website; and sharing a link associated with an online location of the document. You also can create and share a PDF or XPS image of the document, so that users can view the file in Acrobat Reader or XPS Viewer instead of in PowerPoint.

Summary

In this module you have learned how to insert a SmartArt graphic and then add pictures and text, convert text to a SmartArt graphic, create and format a chart and a table, change table text alignment and orientation, and insert symbols.

CONSIDER THIS: PLAN AHEAD

What decisions will you need to make when creating your next presentation?

Use these guidelines as you complete the assignments in this module and create your own slide show decks outside of this class.

1. Audiences recall visual concepts more quickly and accurately than when viewing text alone, so consider using graphics in your presentation.

   a) Decide the precise message you want to convey to your audience.

   b) Determine if a SmartArt graphic, chart, or table is the better method of presenting the information.

2. Choose an appropriate SmartArt layout.

   a) Determine which layout best represents the concept you are attempting to present. Some of the layouts, such as Matrix, Pyramid, and Relationship, offer outstanding methods of showing how ideas are connected to each other, while other layouts, such as Cycle, List, and Process, are best at showing steps to complete a task.

   b) Use Table 4–1 to help you select a layout.

3. Choose an appropriate chart type.

   a) Charts are excellent visuals to show relationships between groups of data, especially numbers.

   b) Decide which chart type best conveys the points you are attempting to make in your presentation. PowerPoint provides a wide variety of styles within each category of chart, so determine which one is most effective in showing the relationships.

4. Obtain information for the graphic from credible sources.

   a) Text or numbers should be current and correct.

   b) Verify the sources of the information.

   c) Be certain you have typed the data correctly.

   d) Acknowledge the source of the information on the slide or during your presentation.

5. Test your visual elements.

   a) Show your slides to several friends or colleagues and ask them to interpret what they see.

   b) Have your test audience summarize the information they perceive on the tables and charts and compare their analyses to what you are attempting to convey.

Apply Your Knowledge

Reinforce the skills and apply the concepts you learned in this module.

Converting Text to a SmartArt Graphic

Note: To complete this assignment, you will be required to use the Data Files. Please contact your instructor for information about accessing the Data Files.

Instructions: Run PowerPoint. Open the presentation called Apply 4–1 Camping, which is located in the Data Files.

The slide in the presentation presents information about tent or RV camping or renting a cabin at a campground. The document you open is a partially formatted presentation. You are to convert the list to SmartArt and format the graphic so the slide looks like Figure 4–80.

Perform the following tasks:

1. Select the WordArt title, Camp Bullfrog, and increase the font size to 60 point. Also change the font case to UPPERCASE, and then add the 'Orange, 18 pt glow, Accent color 1' glow text effect (in Glow Variations area), as shown in Figure 4–80.

2. Convert the list to SmartArt by applying the Vertical Box List layout (in List category). Change the colors to 'Colorful Range – Accent Colors 5 to 6'. Apply the Cartoon 3-D Style.

3. Resize this SmartArt graphic to approximately 3.52" × 8".

4. With the Text Pane open, select the three Level 1 bullet paragraphs, change the font to Arial, increase the font size to 24 point, change the font color to 'Black, Text 1' (in first Theme Colors row), and then bold this text.

5. With the Text Pane open, select the four Level 2 bullet paragraphs, change the font to Arial and increase the font size to 20 point.

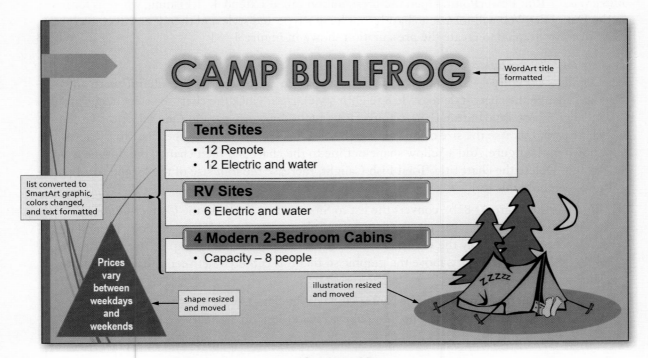

Figure 4–80

Continued >

Apply Your Knowledge *continued*

6. Increase the size of the camping illustration to approximately 3.42" × 4.72" and then move the illustration to the lower-right corner of the slide, as shown in the figure. Adjust the size of the triangle shape to approximately 2.67" × 2.49" and then move this shape to the lower-left corner of the slide, as shown.

7. If requested by your instructor, add your grandfather's first name after the word, people, on the last line of the Level 2 bullet paragraph.

8. Apply the Window transition in the Dynamic Content category to the slide. Change the duration to 4.00 seconds.

9. View the presentation and then save the file using the file name, Apply 4–1 Camp Bullfrog.

10. Submit the revised document in the format specified by your instructor.

11. ✺ In Step 2, you chose the Vertical Box List and changed the colors of the SmartArt graphic. How did this style improve the slide and increase the audience's attention to the content?

Extend Your Knowledge

Extend the skills you learned in this module and experiment with new skills. You may need to use Help to complete the assignment.

Changing the Chart Type and Style and Formatting a SmartArt Graphic

Note: To complete this assignment, you will be required to use the Data Files. Please contact your instructor for information about accessing the Data Files.

Instructions: Run PowerPoint. Open the presentation called Extend 4–1 Fishing, which is located in the Data Files. You will format a chart by applying a type and style and then you will convert text to a SmartArt graphic to create the presentation shown in Figure 4–81.

Perform the following tasks:

1. On Slide 1 (Figure 4–81a), change the chart type from a Line chart to a Column chart, and then change the chart style to Style 8 (eighth style). *Hint:* Click the chart to select it, click the Change Chart Type button (Chart Tools Design tab | Type group), and then select the Column chart type. Increase the size of the chart to 5.56" × 7.4" and then move the chart to the location shown in the figure. Add a Yellow shape outline to the chart and then change the outline weight to 3 pt. Delete the chart title, Total Fish Caught. Increase the font size of the legend to 14 point and then bold this text.

2. On Slide 2 (Figure 4–81b), convert the list to SmartArt by applying the Converging Radial graphic (in Relationship category). Change the colors to 'Colored Fill - Accent 2', located in the Accent 2 area. Apply the Polished 3-D style. Resize the SmartArt graphic to approximately 4.84" × 7.97". If necessary, move the graphic so that it is centered between the left edge of the slide and the angler.

3. On Slide 2, increase the size of the center circle of the SmartArt graphic to approximately 2.75" × 2.75" and then change the font color to Dark Blue (in Standard Colors).

(a) Slide 1

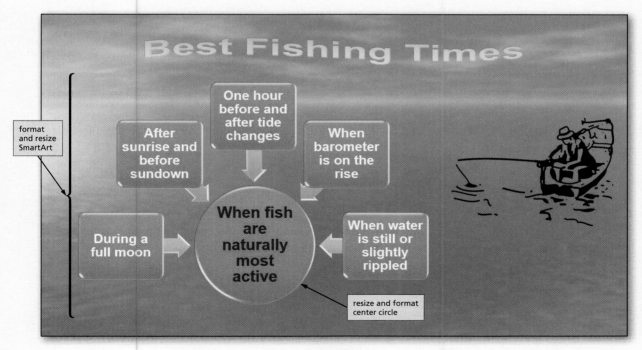

(b) Slide 2
Figure 4–81 (Continued)

Continued >

Extend Your Knowledge *continued*

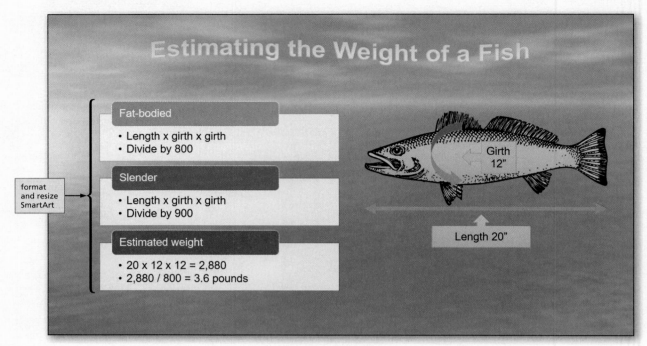

(c) Slide 3
Figure 4–81

4. On Slide 3 (Figure 4–81c), convert the list to SmartArt by applying the Vertical Box List graphic (in List category). Change the colors to 'Colorful Range - Accent Colors 3 to 4'. Apply the Brick Scene 3-D style. Select the text in the three colored rectangle shapes in the SmartArt graphic and then increase the font size to 22 point and bold this text.

5. If requested by your instructor, insert a text box on Slide 2 in the lower-right area of the slide and add the name of the first school you attended.

6. Apply the Ripple transition in the Exciting category to all slides and then change the duration to 3.00 seconds.

7. View the presentation and then save the file using the file name, Extend 4–1 Best Fishing Times.

8. Submit the revised document in the format specified by your instructor.

9. ✳ In this assignment, you changed the chart style on Slide 1 and changed the text to SmartArt graphics on Slides 2 and 3. How did these edits enhance the presentation?

Expand Your World

Create a solution that uses cloud or web technologies by learning and investigating on your own from general guidance.

Creating Charts and Graphs Using Websites

Instructions: PowerPoint presents a wide variety of chart and table layouts, and you must decide which one is effective in presenting the relationships between data and indicating important trends.

Several websites offer opportunities to create graphics that help explain concepts to your audience. Many of these websites are easy to use and allow you to save the chart or graph you create and then import it into your PowerPoint presentation.

Perform the following tasks:

1. Visit one of the following websites, or locate other websites that help you create a chart or graph: ChartGo (chartgo.com), Chartle (chartle.net), Rich Chart Live (richchartlive.com), Online Charts Builder (charts.hohli.com), or Lucidchart (lucidchart.com).

2. Create a chart using the same data supplied for Slide 3 in the Area Recycling presentation.

3. Save the new chart and then insert it into a new Slide 3 in the Area Recycling presentation. Delete the original Slide 3 in the presentation.

4. If requested to do so by your instructor, add your grandmother's first name to the chart title.

5. Save the presentation using the file name, Expand 4–1 Area Recycling.

6. Submit the assignment in the format specified by your instructor.

7. ✺ Which features do the websites offer that help you create charts and graphs? How does the graphic you created online compare to the chart you created using PowerPoint? How do the websites allow you to share your graphics using social networks?

In the Labs

Design, create, modify, and/or use a presentation following the guidelines, concepts, and skills presented in this module. Labs 1 and 2, which increase in difficulty, require you to create solutions based on what you learned in the module; Lab 3 requires you to apply your creative thinking and problem-solving skills to design and implement a solution.

Lab 1: Inserting and Formatting SmartArt and Formatting a Table

Note: To complete this assignment, you will be required to use the Data Files. Please contact your instructor for information about accessing the Data Files.

Problem: You have an interest in composting and thought this topic would be appropriate for an informative speech assignment in your communication class. Create the slides shown in Figure 4–82.

Perform the following tasks:

1. Run PowerPoint. Open the presentation called Lab 4–1 Compost, which is located in the Data Files. On Slide 1 (Figure 4–82a), insert the Hexagon Cluster SmartArt graphic (in seventh Picture row).

2. In the SmartArt Text Pane, type **Browns** as the first Level 1 text that will appear in the lower-left hexagon shape. Type **Greens** as the second Level 1 text that will appear to the right of the first hexagon shape on the right, **Air** as the third Level 1 text for the upper left hexagon shape, and **Water** as the fourth Level 1 text for the fourth hexagon shape, as shown in the figure.

Continued >

In the Labs *continued*

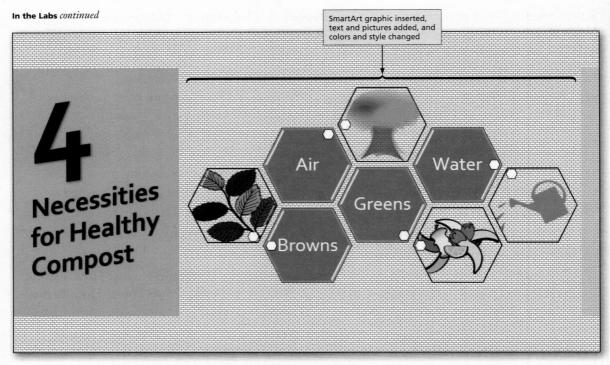

(a) Slide 1

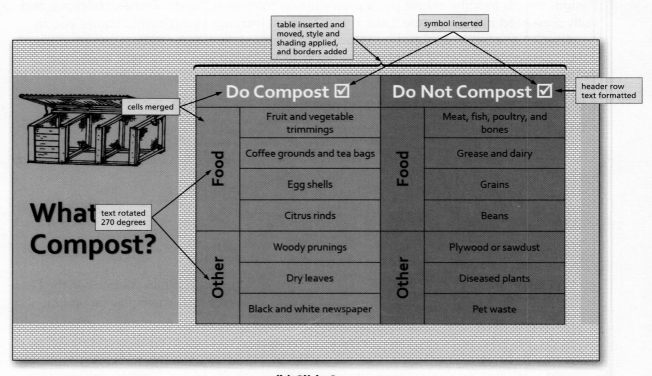

(b) Slide 2
Figure 4–82

3. Insert the picture called Leaves, which is available in the Data Files, in the left hexagon shape. Insert the picture called Tree, which is available in the Data Files, in the top hexagon shape. Insert the picture called Water, which is available in the Data Files, in the right hexagon shape. Insert the picture called Greens, which is available in the Data files, in the bottom hexagon shape.

4. Change the colors of the SmartArt graphic to 'Colored Fill - Accent 6' (second color in Accent 6 row). Apply the Cartoon 3-D style. Adjust the size of the SmartArt graphic to approximately 6.58" × 8.84" and then move it to the area shown in the figure.

5. On Slide 2 (Figure 4–82b), insert a table with 4 columns and 8 rows. Increase the size of the table to 5.82" × 8.5" and then move the table to the area shown in the figure. In row 1, merge cells 1 and 2 and then merge cells 3 and 4. In column 1, select rows 2, 3, 4, and 5 and then merge them. In column 3, select rows 2, 3, 4, and 5 and then merge them. In column 1, select rows 6, 7, and 8 and then merge them. In column 3, select rows 6, 7, and 8 and then merge them.

6. Change the width of the two vertically merged cells in column 1 to 1" by typing **1** in the Table Column Width text box (Table Tools Layout tab | Cell Size). Repeat this process to change the width of the two vertically merged cells in column 3.

7. Change the width of rows 2 through 8 in column 2 to 3.2". Repeat this process for rows 2 through 8 in column 4.

8. Enter the data in the table shown in Table 4–3 What to Compost?

Table 4–3 What to Compost?			
Do Compost		**Do Not Compost**	
Food	Fruit and vegetable trimmings	Food	Meat, fish, poultry, and bones
	Coffee grounds and tea bags		Grease and dairy
	Egg shells		Grains
	Citrus rinds		Beans
Other	Woody prunings	Other	Plywood or sawdust
	Dry leaves		Diseased plants
	Black and white newspaper		Pet waste

9. Change the font size for the words, Food, and Other, in both columns 1 and 3 to 28 point and then bold this text. Rotate these four words 270°. Select the table, center the table text, and then center the text vertically, as shown in the figure.

10. Change the font size of the table header text to 32 point and then center this text. Insert the Wingdings 254 symbol (checked box in the last row of the gallery) after the text, Do Compost. Copy this symbol after the text, Do Not Compost, as shown in the figure.

Continued >

In the Labs *continued*

11. Apply the 'Themed Style 1 – Accent 5' (in first Best Match for Document row) to the table. Change the shading of the left side of the table under the heading, Do Compost, to 'Brown, Accent 4' (first Theme Colors row). Change the shading of the right side of the table under the heading, Do Not Compost, to 'Orange, Accent 6' (first Theme Colors row).

12. Add borders to all table cells.

13. If requested by your instructor, insert a text box with the name of your grade school under the SmartArt diagram on Slide 1.

14. Apply the Fade transition in the Subtle category to both slides and then change the duration to 2.25 seconds.

15. View the presentation and then save the file using the file name, Lab 4–1 Compost Necessities.

16. Submit the document in the format specified by your instructor.

17. ✷ On Slide 1, you used the Hexagon Cluster SmartArt graphic. Is this style appropriate for this presentation content? Why? Why did you select the style of the table on Slide 2?

Lab 2: **Creating a Presentation with SmartArt, a Chart, and a Table**

Note: To complete this assignment, you will be required to use the Data Files. Please contact your instructor for information about accessing the Data Files.

Problem: For a special project, you surveyed students attending your culinary school about searching for recipes on the Internet. You had a positive response and decided to share the results of your study with school administrators and fellow students by creating the slides shown in Figure 4–83.

Perform the following tasks:

1. Run PowerPoint. Open the presentation called Lab 4–2 Recipes, which is located in the Data Files.

2. On Slide 1 (Figure 4–83a), insert the Pyramid List SmartArt graphic (in List group). Enter the text shown in the figure and then bold this text. Change the colors of the graphic to 'Gradient Loop – Accent 2' (Accent 2 row) and then change the style to Inset (first 3-D row). Send the graphic backward and move it to the right so the illustration will display as shown in the figure.

3. On Slide 2, insert a 3-D Pie chart, as shown in Figure 4–83b. Use the data in Table 4–4 Important Features to replace the sample data in the worksheet. Change the Quick Layout to Layout 1. Change the chart style to Style 3. Select the chart title text, Column 1, and then press the DELETE key to delete this text.

4. Increase the legend font size to 20 point and then bold this text. Select the chart, and then rotate it approximately 75 degrees so that the Fresh ingredients slice is at the bottom-right. Separate the Fresh ingredients slice 20%, add a 6 pt border to this slice, and then change its border color to Light Green (Standard Colors row).

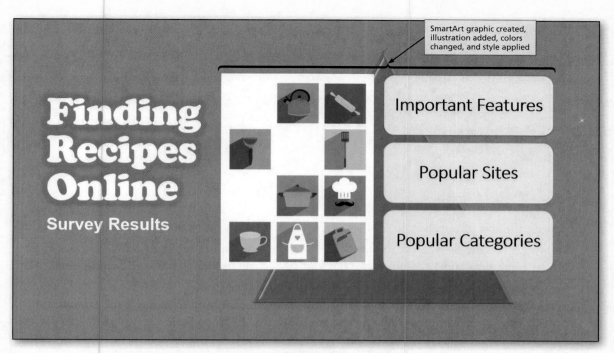

(a) Slide 1

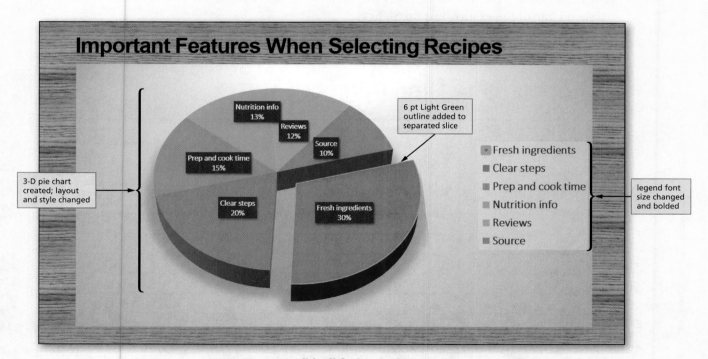

(b) Slide 2
Figure 4–83 (Continued)

Continued >

In the Labs *continued*

Table 4–4 Important Features	
Fresh ingredients	30%
Clear steps	20%
Prep and cook time	15%
Nutrition info	13%
Reviews	12%
Source	10%

5. Increase the size of the chart to 6.11" × 11.76" and then move it to the location shown on Slide 2.

6. On Slide 3 (Figure 4–82c), in the header row of the table, split the upper-left and upper-right cells to 2 columns and 1 row. Increase the font size of the header row text to 36 point and then bold this text.

7. Increase the size of the table to approximately 5.31" × 12.06" and then move the table to the location shown in the figure. Change the table style to 'Themed Style 2 - Accent 1' (second row in Best Match for Document area). Change the borders to All Borders. Insert the picture called Computer, which is located in the Data Files, in the second cell of the table's first row. Insert the picture called Cooking, which is located in the Data Files, in the fourth cell of the table's first row.

8. If requested by your instructor, enter the name of the last TV program you watched as the second line of the subtitle text on Slide 1.

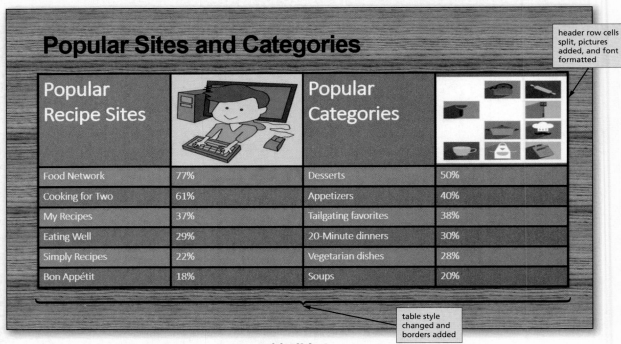

(c) Slide 3
Figure 4–83

9. Apply the Uncover transition in the Subtle category to all slides and then change the duration to 3.25 seconds.

10. View the presentation and then save the file using the file name, Lab 4–2 Recipes Online Survey.

11. Submit the revised document in the format specified by your instructor.

12. ✷ How did adding a SmartArt graphic to the title slide enhance the presentation?

Lab 3: **Consider This: Your Turn**

Design and Create a Presentation about Recycling Materials

Note: To complete this assignment, you will be required to use the Data Files. Please contact your instructor for information about accessing the Data Files.

Part 1:   The Area Recycling presentation you created in this module addresses issues community residents may have regarding the types of materials consumers can recycle, how long these products take to decompose in landfills, and where recycling centers are located in town. Questions may remain, however, on which materials are safe to recycle and which should be placed in trash receptacles. Aluminum cans, for example, are fine for recycling, but aluminum foil, metal coat hangers, and scrap metal are not. Plastic bottles are allowed, but their caps, lids, and sprayers must be removed. Newspapers, magazines, and brown paper bags are fine, but saturated pizza boxes, waxy ice cream containers, and paper towel rolls are not. Finally, glass food containers can be recycled, but window glass, dishware, and ceramics cannot. Open the Area Recycling file you created and then use the concepts and techniques presented in this module to add a new Slide 5 with a table containing information regarding products that can and cannot be recycled. Review websites for additional recycling guidelines. Apply a table style, add borders, an effect, and a symbol, change colors where appropriate, and add a recycling icon. Review and revise your presentation as needed and then save the file using the file name, Lab 4–3 Recycling Materials. Submit your assignment in the format specified by your instructor.

Part 2:   ✷ You made several decisions while creating the presentation in this assignment: applying a table style, adding borders and an effect, changing the table colors, and adding a picture and symbol. What was the rationale behind each of these decisions? When you reviewed the document, what further revisions did you make and why? Where would you recommend showing this slide show?

5 | Collaborating on and Delivering a Presentation

Objectives

You will have mastered the material in this module when you can:

- Combine PowerPoint files
- Accept and reject a reviewer's proposed changes
- Delete, reply to, and insert comments
- Reuse slides from an existing presentation
- Insert slide footer content
- Set slide size and presentation resolution

- Save files as a PowerPoint show
- Package a presentation for storage on a compact disc
- Save a presentation in a previous PowerPoint format
- Inspect and protect files
- Use presentation tools to navigate and annotate slide shows

BTW
Review Cycle Value
The review cycle plays an important role in developing an effective PowerPoint presentation. Your reviewers may raise issues and make comments about your material, and their concerns may help enhance your final slides. Terms and graphics that seem clear to you may raise questions among people viewing your material. Audience members may have diverse technical skills and educational levels, so it is important to understand how they may interpret your slides.

Introduction

Often presentations are enhanced when individuals collaborate to fine-tune text, visuals, and design elements on the slides. A **review cycle** occurs when a slide show designer shares a file with multiple reviewers so they can make comments and changes to their copies of the slides and then return the file to the designer. A **comment** is a description that normally does not display as part of the slide show. It can be used to clarify information that may be difficult to understand, to pose questions, or to communicate suggestions. The designer then can display the comments, modify their content, and ask the reviewers to again review the presentation, and continue this process until the slides are satisfactory. Once the presentation is complete, the designer can protect the file so no one can open it without a password, remove comments and other information, and assure that slide content has not been altered. The designer also can save the presentation to a CD, DVD, or flash drive, or as a PowerPoint show that will run without opening PowerPoint. In addition, a presenter can use PowerPoint's variety of tools to run the show effectively and emphasize various elements on the screen.

Project — Presentation with Comments, Inserted Slides, Protection, and Annotation

BTW

Pixels
Screen resolution specifies the amount of pixels displayed on your screen. The word, pixel, combines pix (for "pictures") and el (for "element").

The seven slides in the Chicago presentation (Figure 5–1) give information and provide images of that Midwestern city's skyline, famous building, and attractions. All slides in the presentation were developed using versions of PowerPoint used prior to the current PowerPoint 2016. In these previous versions, the slides used a 4:3 width-to-height ratio, which was the standard proportion of computer monitors at that time. Today, however, most people use PowerPoint 2016's default 16:9 ratio, which is the proportion of most widescreen monitors today. You will change the slide size in your Chicago presentation after all the slides are created.

When you are developing a presentation, it often is advantageous to ask a variety of people to review your work in progress. These individuals can evaluate the wording, art, and design, and experts in the subject can check the slides for accuracy. They can add comments to the slides in specific areas, such as a paragraph, a graphic, or a table. You then can review their comments and use them to modify and enhance your work. You also can insert slides from other presentations into your presentation.

Once you develop the final set of slides, you can complete the file by removing any comments and personal information, adding a password so that unauthorized people cannot see the file contents without your permission, saving the file as a PowerPoint show so it runs automatically when you open a file, and saving the file to a CD, DVD, or flash drive.

When running your presentation, you may decide to show the slides nonsequentially. For example, you may need to review a slide you discussed already, or you may want to skip some slides and jump forward. You also may want to emphasize, or **annotate**, material on the slides by highlighting text or writing on the slides. You can save your annotations to review during or after the presentation.

In this module, you will learn how to create the slides shown in Figure 5–1. The following roadmap identifies general activities you will perform as you progress through this module:

1. COLLABORATE on a presentation by using comments.

2. FORMAT SLIDES and SET SLIDE SHOW RESOLUTION.

3. SAVE and PACKAGE a PRESENTATION.

4. PROTECT and SECURE a PRESENTATION.

5. USE PRESENTATION TOOLS to navigate and annotate slides during a presentation.

CONSIDER THIS

What are some tips for collaborating successfully?

Working with your classmates can yield numerous benefits. Your peers can assist in brainstorming, developing key ideas, revising your project, and keeping you on track so that your presentation meets the assignment goals.

The first step when collaborating with peers is to define success. What, ultimately, is the goal? For example, are you developing a persuasive presentation to school administrators in an effort to fund a new club? Next, you can set short-term and long-term goals that help lead you to completing the project successfully. These goals can be weekly tasks to accomplish, such as interviewing content experts, conducting online research, or compiling an annotated bibliography. After that, you can develop a plan to finish the project by outlining subtasks that each member must accomplish. Each collaborator should inform the group members when the task is complete or if problems are delaying progress. When collaborators meet, whether in person or online, they should establish an agenda and have one member keep notes of topics discussed.

theme changed to Headlines

WordArt from reviewer

subtitle text from reviewer

(a) Slide 1 (Title Slide Enhanced from Reviewer)

screen clipping from another presentation

SmartArt graphic created by reviewer

date added

footer text

(b) Slide 2 (SmartArt from Reviewer)

layout changed by reviewer

(c) Slide 3 (Enhanced from Reviewer)

(d) Slide 4 (Reused from Existing Presentation)

picture formatting changed

original theme retained

(e) Slide 5 (Reused from Existing Presentation)

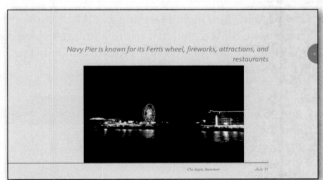

(f) Slide 6 (Inserted from Reviewer's Presentation)

(g) Slide 7 (Inserted from Reviewer's Presentation)

Figure 5–1

BTW
The Ribbon and Screen Resolution
PowerPoint may change how the groups and buttons within the groups appear on the ribbon, depending on the computer or mobile device's screen resolution. Thus, your ribbon may look different from the ones in this book if you are using a screen resolution other than 1366 x 768.

BTW
Touch Screen Differences
The Office and Windows interfaces may vary if you are using a touch screen. For this reason, you might notice that the function or appearance of your touch screen differs slightly from this module's presentation.

Collaborating on a Presentation

PowerPoint provides several methods to collaborate with friends or coworkers who can view your slide show and then provide feedback. When you **collaborate**, you work together on a document with other PowerPoint users who are cooperating jointly and assisting willingly with the endeavor. You can distribute your slide show physically to others by exchanging a compact disc or a flash drive. You also can share your presentation through the Internet by sending the file as an email attachment or saving the file to a storage location, such as Microsoft OneDrive or Microsoft Office SharePoint.

In the following pages, you will follow these general steps to collaborate with Bernie Halen, who has analyzed a presentation you created after visiting Chicago for a weekend this past summer:

1. Combine (merge) presentations.
2. Print slides and comments.
3. Review and accept or reject changes.
4. Reply to a comment.
5. Insert a comment.
6. Delete a comment.

To Merge a Presentation

1 COLLABORATE | 2 FORMAT SLIDES & SET SLIDE SHOW RESOLUTION | 3 SAVE & PACKAGE A PRESENTATION
4 PROTECT & SECURE PRESENTATION | 5 USE PRESENTATION TOOLS

Why? *Bernie Halen reviewed your Chicago presentation and made several comments, so you want to combine (merge) his changes with your file to see if they improve the original design and slide content.* Bernie's changes to the initial presentation include adding a subtitle, converting the Slide 1 title and subtitle text to WordArt, and changing the Slide 2 bulleted list to a SmartArt graphic. A transition is added to all slides, the theme is changed, paragraphs are edited, and two slides are added. The following steps merge this reviewer's file with your Chicago Final presentation.

- Run PowerPoint and then open the presentation, Chicago, from the Data Files.

- Save the presentation using the file name, Chicago Final.

- Display the Review tab (Figure 5–2).

Q&A Why do the slides have a different size than the slides I have seen in previous presentations?
The slides in the Chicago presentation use a

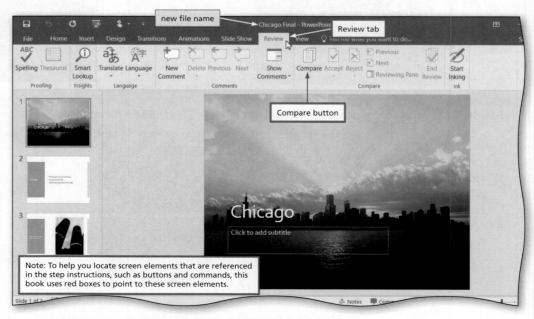

Figure 5–2

4:3 ratio, which was the default setting in PowerPoint versions prior to PowerPoint 2013.

2

- Click the Compare button (Review tab | Compare group) to display the Choose File to Merge with Current Presentation dialog box.

- With the list of your Data Files displaying, click Chicago - Bernie to select the file name (Figure 5–3).

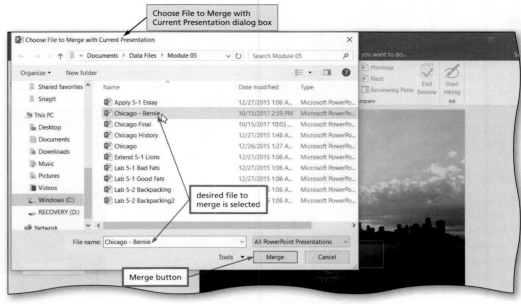

Figure 5–3

3

- Click the Merge button (Choose File to Merge with Current Presentation dialog box) to merge Bernie Halen's presentation with the Chicago presentation and to display the Revisions pane.

- If necessary, click the Show Comments button (Review tab | Comments group) to display the Comments pane (Figure 5–4).

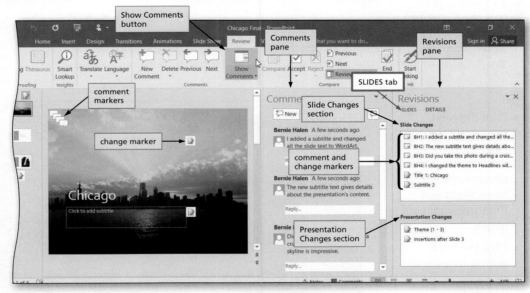

Figure 5–4

Q&A

When does the Comments pane display automatically?
It displays when left open during a previous PowerPoint session. Clicking the Show Comments button or the Comments button on the status bar displays or hides the Comments pane.

How do I display the Revisions pane if it does not display automatically?
Click the Reviewing Pane button (Review tab | Compare group) to display the Revisions pane.

If several reviewers have made comments and suggestions, can I merge their files, too?
Yes. Repeat Steps 1, 2, and 3. Each reviewer's initials display in a color-coded comment box.

To Print Comments

1 COLLABORATE | 2 FORMAT SLIDES & SET SLIDE SHOW RESOLUTION | 3 SAVE & PACKAGE A PRESENTATION
4 PROTECT & SECURE PRESENTATION | 5 USE PRESENTATION TOOLS

You can print each slide and the comments a reviewer has made before you begin to accept and reject each suggestion. *Why? As owner of the original presentation, you want to review the comments and modifications on a hard copy before making decisions about whether to accept these suggestions.* PowerPoint can print these slides and comments on individual pages. The following steps print the slides with comments.

1

- Open the Backstage view and then click the Print tab to display the Print gallery.

- Click 'Full Page Slides' in the Print gallery to display print layouts.

- If necessary, click 'Print Comments and Ink Markup' to place a check mark by this option and turn on printing comment pages (Figure 5–5).

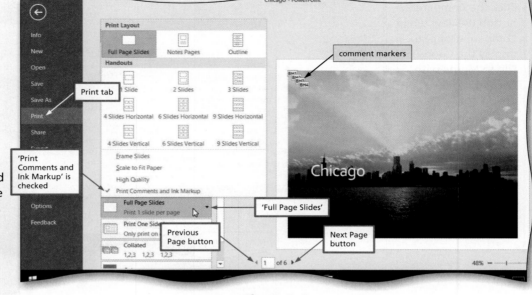

Figure 5–5

Q&A If I want to print only the slides and not the comments, would I click 'Print Comments and Ink Markup' to remove the check mark?
Yes. Tapping or clicking the command turns on and turns off printing the notes pages.

2

- Click the Next Page and Previous Page buttons to scroll through the previews of the three slides and the three comment pages.

- Click the Print button to print the six pages (Figure 5–6).

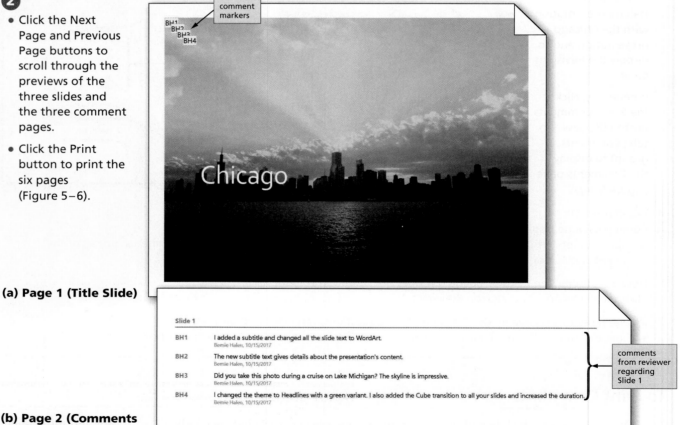

(a) Page 1 (Title Slide)

(b) Page 2 (Comments from Reviewer)

Figure 5–6 (Continued)

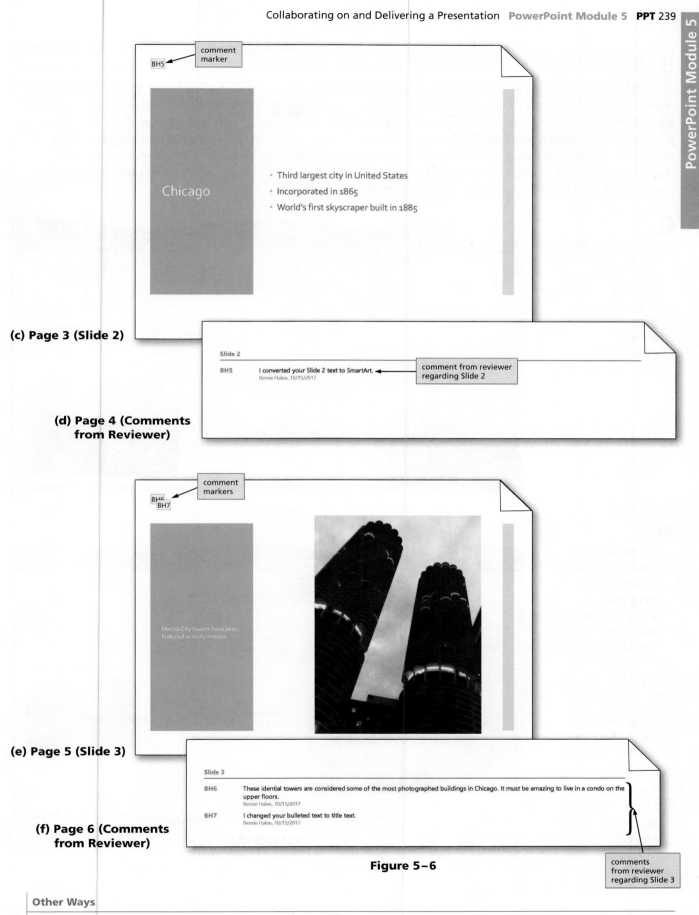

(c) Page 3 (Slide 2)

(d) Page 4 (Comments from Reviewer)

(e) Page 5 (Slide 3)

(f) Page 6 (Comments from Reviewer)

Figure 5–6

Other Ways

1. Press CTRL+P, click 'Full Page Slides' in the Print gallery, if necessary check 'Print Comments and Ink Markup', click Print button

To Preview the Presentation Changes

The reviewer made several changes to the overall presentation and then edited your three slides. You can preview his modifications to obtain an overview of his suggestions. *Why? Seeing his edits now can help you decide later whether to accept or reject each change as you step through each revision.* The changes that apply to the entire presentation are displayed in the Presentation Changes section of the Revisions pane, and changes to each individual slide are displayed in the Slide Changes section of this pane. Vertical rectangular icons indicate change markers, and horizontal rectangular icons represent comment markers. Each reviewer's revisions are color-coded. The following steps preview the merged presentation.

- If necessary, display the Review tab. With Slide 1 displaying, click the SLIDES tab in the Revisions pane to display a thumbnail of merged Slide 1 (Figure 5–7).

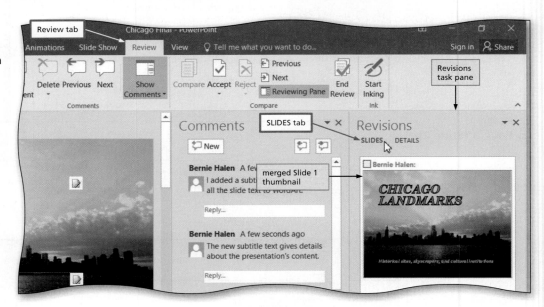

Figure 5–7

- Click the Bernie Halen check box above the Slide 1 thumbnail (Revisions pane) to view the proposed text changes in the main slide pane (Figure 5–8).

- Click the Bernie Halen check box again to undo the changes.

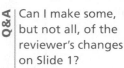
Can I make some, but not all, of the reviewer's changes on Slide 1?

Yes. PowerPoint allows you to view each proposed change individually and then either accept or reject the modification.

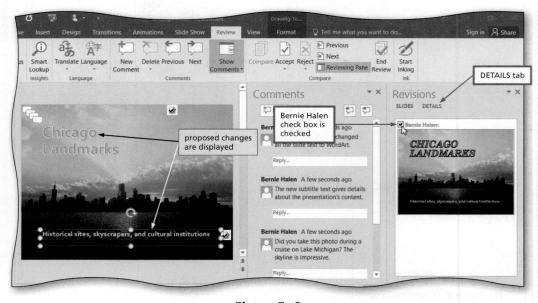

Figure 5–8

How do I accept and evaluate criticism positively?

Receiving feedback from others ultimately should enhance your presentation. If several of your reviewers make similar comments, such as too much text appears on one slide or that a chart would help present your concept, then you should heed their criticism and modify your slides. Criticism from a variety of people, particularly if they are from different cultures or vary in age, gives a wide range of viewpoints. Some reviewers might focus on the font size, others on color and design choices, while others might single out the overall message. These individuals should evaluate and comment on your work, such as saying that the overall presentation is good or that a particular paragraph is confusing, and then give specific information of what elements are effective or how you can edit the paragraph.

When you receive these comments, do not get defensive. Ask yourself why your reviewers would have made these comments. Perhaps they lack a background in the subject matter. Or they may have a particular interest in this topic and can add their expertise.

To Review, Accept, and Reject Presentation Changes

1 COLLABORATE | 2 FORMAT SLIDES & SET SLIDE SHOW RESOLUTION | 3 SAVE & PACKAGE A PRESENTATION
4 PROTECT & SECURE PRESENTATION | 5 USE PRESENTATION TOOLS

Changes that affect the entire presentation are indicated in the Presentation Changes section of the Revisions pane. These changes can include transitions, color schemes, fonts, and backgrounds. They also can include slide insertions. Bernie inserted three slides in his review; two have identical text and different photos of the city's popular tourist attraction, Navy Pier. After inserting these slides in the presentation, you can view each slide and then delete, or reject, a slide insertion. The following steps display and accept the reviewer's three slides and then delete one of the inserted slides. *Why? You want to see all the slides and then evaluate how they add value to the presentation. Two of the slides have similar photos of Navy Pier, and you want to use the slide that shows the most buildings and attractions on that structure.*

- Click the DETAILS tab in the Revisions pane.

- Click the first presentation change marker, Theme (1 - 3), in the Presentation Changes section of the Revisions pane to display the Theme box with an explanation of the proposed change for all slides in the presentation (Figure 5–9).

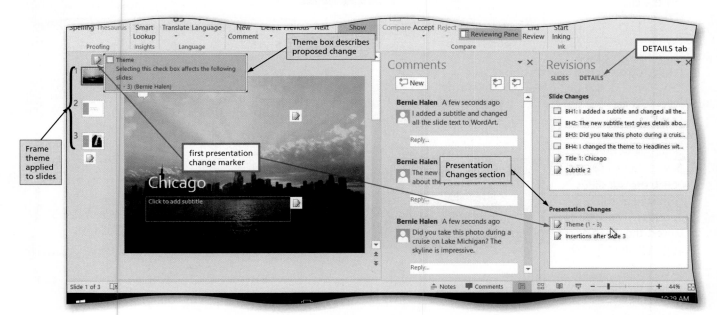

Figure 5–9

2

- Click the Theme check box to view the new Headlines theme on all slides (Figure 5–10).

Q&A Can I also apply the change by tapping or clicking the Accept Change button (Review tab | Compare group)?
Yes. Either method applies the Headlines theme.

If I decide to not apply the new theme, can I reverse this change?
Yes. Click the Reject Change button (Review tab | Compare group) or click the check box to remove the check and reject the reviewer's theme modification.

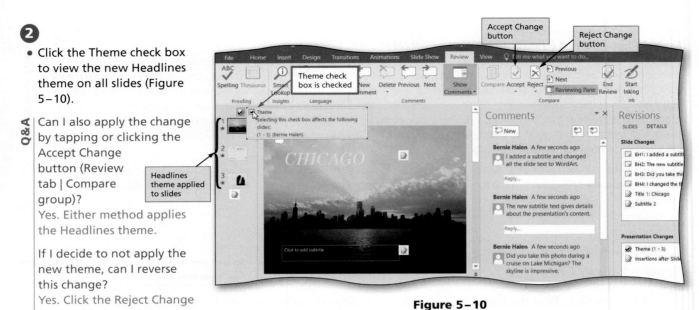

Figure 5–10

3

- Click the second presentation change marker, Insertions after Slide 3, in the Presentation Changes section to display an insertion box with a list of the three proposed new slides to insert into the presentation, two with no title text and one with the title text, 'Evening cruises offer spectacular views of the city' (Figure 5–11).

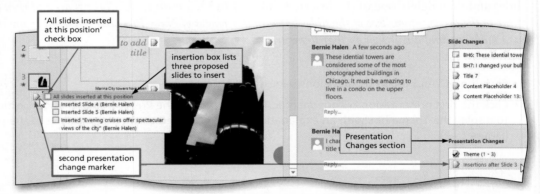

Figure 5–11

Q&A What is the significance of the check boxes in the insertion box?
You can click the first check box to insert all three slides in your presentation. You can elect to insert one or two slides by clicking the check mark to the left of each slide title.

4

- Click the 'All slides inserted at this position' check box to insert the three new slides (Figure 5–12).

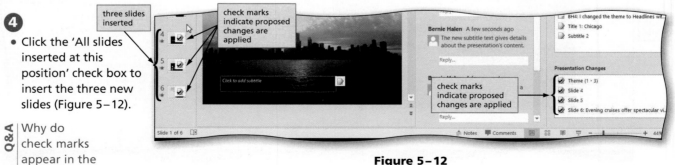

Figure 5–12

Q&A Why do check marks appear in the Slides 4, 5, and 6 thumbnails in the Slides tab and in the Presentation Changes section?
The check marks indicate you have applied the proposed change.

5

- Display Slide 4 and review the slide contents. Then, display Slide 5 and compare the photo on this slide to the photo on Slide 4.

- Display Slide 4 again and then read the comment Bernie made about Slides 4 and 5 (Figure 5–13).

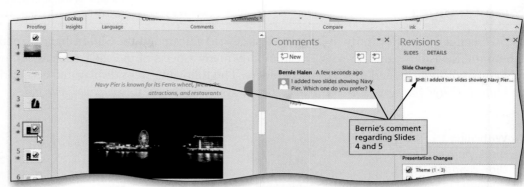

Figure 5–13

6

- Display Slide 5 and then click the change marker on the Slide 5 thumbnail to display the insertion box (Figure 5–14).

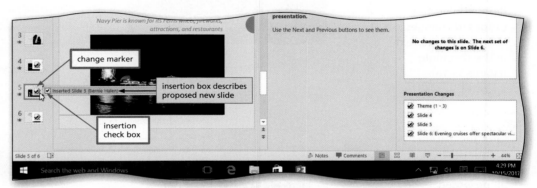

Figure 5–14

7

- Click the 'Inserted Slide 5' check box to clear this check box and delete Slide 5 from the presentation (Figure 5–15).

Q&A If I decide to insert the original Slide 5, how can I perform this task?
Click the change marker above the current Slide 5 to insert the slide you deleted.

Figure 5–15

Other Ways

1. Click Next Change or Previous Change button (Review tab | Compare group), click Accept Change button or Reject Change button

2. Right-click proposed change, click Accept Change or Reject Change on shortcut menu

To Review, Accept, and Reject Slide Changes

1 COLLABORATE | 2 FORMAT SLIDES & SET SLIDE SHOW RESOLUTION | 3 SAVE & PACKAGE A PRESENTATION
4 PROTECT & SECURE PRESENTATION | 5 USE PRESENTATION TOOLS

Changes that affect only the displayed slide are indicated in the Slide Changes section of the DETAILS tab on the Revisions pane. A reviewer can modify many aspects of the slide, such as adding and deleting pictures and clips, editing text, and moving placeholders. The following steps display and accept the reviewer's revisions to Slide 1. *Why? You agree with the changes Bernie suggested because they enhance your slides.*

1

- With Slide 1 displaying, click the slide change, 'Title 1: Chicago,' in the Slide Changes section of the Revisions pane to display the Title 1 box with Bernie Halen's five proposed changes for the Chicago text in the rectangle (Figure 5–16).

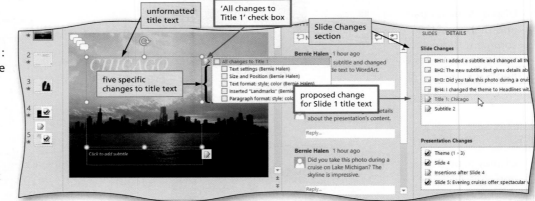

Figure 5–16

2

- Click the 'All changes to Title 1' check box to preview all proposed changes to the Chicago text (Figure 5–17).

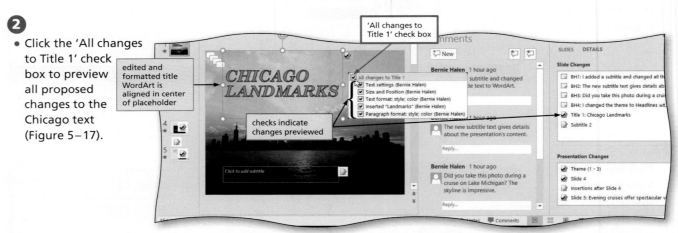

Figure 5–17

3

- Click to uncheck the Text settings check box to preview only the other changes to the title text, not the alignment of the title SmartArt (Figure 5–18).

Q&A

Can I select any combination of the check boxes to modify the text in the rectangle?
Yes. You can click the individual check boxes to preview the reviewer's modifications.

Figure 5–18

- Click the slide change, Subtitle 2, in the Slide Changes section to display the insertion box showing the changes to the Slide 2 subtitle.
- Click the 'All changes to Subtitle 2' check box to view the proposed changes (Figure 5–19).

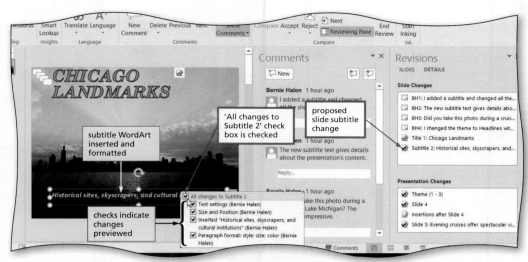

Figure 5–19

Other Ways

1. Click Next Change or Previous Change button (Review tab | Compare group), click Accept Change button or Reject Change button

2. Right-click proposed change, click Accept Change or Reject Change on shortcut menu

To Review Comments

1 COLLABORATE | 2 FORMAT SLIDES & SET SLIDE SHOW RESOLUTION | 3 SAVE & PACKAGE A PRESENTATION
4 PROTECT & SECURE PRESENTATION | 5 USE PRESENTATION TOOLS

Why? *You want to look at each comment before deciding to accept or reject the changes.* The Comments pane displays the reviewer's name above each comment, and an associated comment marker is displayed on the slide and in the Slide Changes section of the Revisions pane. The following steps review comments for Slide 1.

- Click the BH1 comment in the Slide Changes section to select the comment and the associated comment marker on the slide (Figure 5–20).

Q&A Why does the number 1 display after the commenter's initials in the Slide Changes section of the Revisions pane? The number indicates it is the first comment the reviewer inserted.

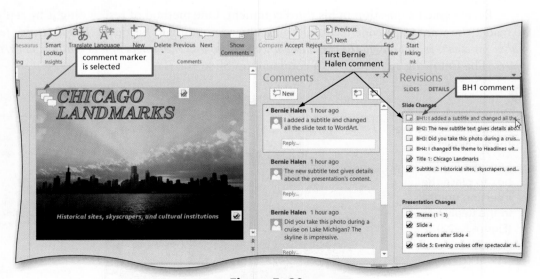

Figure 5–20

2

- Read the comment and then click the Next button in the Comments pane to select the second comment and the associated comment marker on the slide (Figure 5–21).

Q&A Can I click the buttons on the Review tab instead of the buttons in the Comments pane? Yes. Either method allows you to review comments.

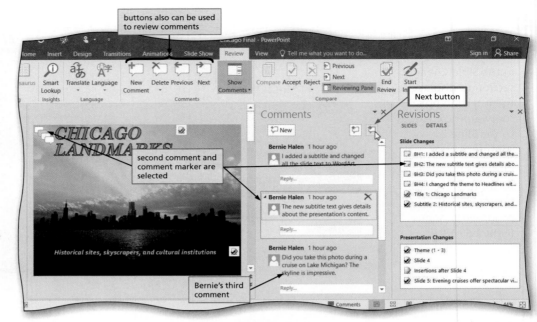

Figure 5–21

3

- Click the Next button to review the third comment and click it again to review the fourth comment.

Other Ways

1. Click Next button or Previous button (Review tab | Comments group)

To Reply to a Comment

1 COLLABORATE | 2 FORMAT SLIDES & SET SLIDE SHOW RESOLUTION | 3 SAVE & PACKAGE A PRESENTATION
4 PROTECT & SECURE PRESENTATION | 5 USE PRESENTATION TOOLS

Bernie asked a question in his third comment. One method of responding is by replying to the comment he made. You want to provide feedback to him by responding to his query. *Why? Giving feedback helps the reviewer realize his efforts in improving the presentation were useful and encourages him to continue to participate in collaboration efforts.* The following steps reply to a comment on Slide 1.

1

- With Slide 1 displaying, select the third comment.

- Click the Reply box to place the insertion point in the Reply box (Figure 5–22).

Figure 5–22

2

- Type **When I was in Chicago this past summer, I took a sightseeing cruise that began on the Chicago River and then went out on Lake Michigan.** in the Reply box and then press the ENTER key (Figure 5–23).

Q&A Why does my name differ from that shown in the figure, which is Marianne?
The name reflects the information that was entered when Microsoft Office 2016 was installed on your computer.

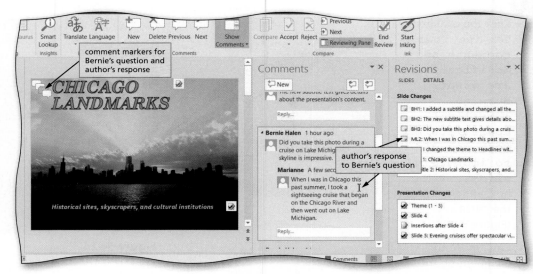

Figure 5–23

To Insert a Comment

1 COLLABORATE | 2 FORMAT SLIDES & SET SLIDE SHOW RESOLUTION | 3 SAVE & PACKAGE A PRESENTATION
4 PROTECT & SECURE PRESENTATION | 5 USE PRESENTATION TOOLS

Bernie Halen's comments and changes greatly enhanced your slide show, and you would like to thank him for taking the time to review your original slides and to respond to his questions. *Why? He will be able to see what modifications you accepted.* The following steps insert a comment on Slide 1.

1

- With Slide 1 displaying, click the Insert Comment button, which has the label New (Comments pane), to open a comment box in the Comments pane (Figure 5–24).

Q&A Why is my comment box displayed at the top of the Comments pane?
Depending upon your computer, PowerPoint will display the new box either at the beginning or the end of the list of comments in the Comments pane.

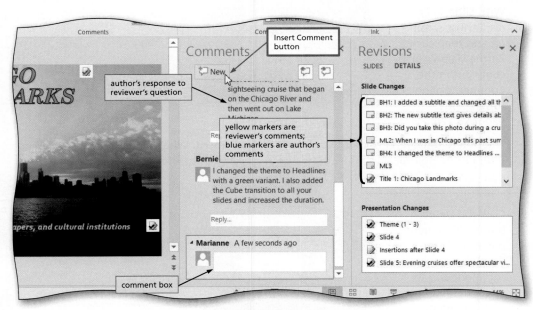

Figure 5–24

- Click the comment box, type **Your comments and modifications are great, Bernie. I really appreciate the work you did to improve my slides.** in the box, and then press the ENTER key (Figure 5–25).

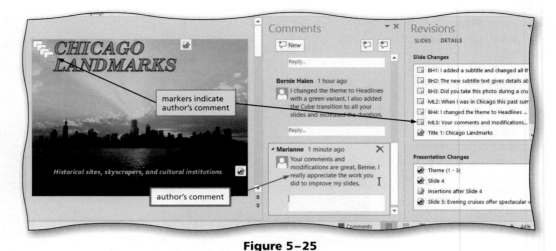

Figure 5–25

Q&A Can I move the comment on the slide?
Yes. Select the comment icon on the slide and then drag it to another location on the slide.

Other Ways

1. Click New Comment button (Review tab | Comments group)

To Delete a Comment

1 COLLABORATE | 2 FORMAT SLIDES & SET SLIDE SHOW RESOLUTION | 3 SAVE & PACKAGE A PRESENTATION
4 PROTECT & SECURE PRESENTATION | 5 USE PRESENTATION TOOLS

Once you have reviewed comments, you may no longer want them to be a part of your slides. You can delete comments that you have read and considered as you are preparing your slides. The following steps delete three of Bernie's comments. **Why?** *They are not necessary now because you have incorporated the changes into your initial presentation.*

- With Slide 1 displaying, scroll up and then click Bernie Halen's first comment in the Comments pane to select it (Figure 5–26).

Figure 5–26

Q&A The Delete button is not displayed in this first comment. What should I do?
Position the pointer up slightly beside Bernie's comment so that it appears as an I-beam.

- Click the Delete button (Comments pane) to delete Bernie's first comment and to select the new first comment, which previously was the second comment in the list (Figure 5–27).

Figure 5–27

3

- Delete the selected comment about the new subtitle.

- Skip the next comment.

- Select the last Bernie Halen comment regarding the theme, variant, and transition and then delete this comment (Figure 5–28).

Figure 5–28

Other Ways

1. Click Delete Comment button (Review tab | Comments group)   2. Right-click comment, click Delete Comment on shortcut menu

To Review and Accept Slide Changes on the Remaining Slides

You have accepted most of Bernie Halen's presentation and Slide 1 changes. He also inserted comments in and made changes to other slides. The following steps review his comments and accept his modifications.

1 Click the Next button (Comments pane) several times until Slide 2 displays.

2 Read the comment labeled BH5 and then delete this comment.

3 Click the SLIDES tab in the Revisions pane to show a thumbnail of Slide 2 in the Revisions pane.

4 Click the check box above the Slide 2 thumbnail (Revisions pane) to display a preview of the Slide 2 revisions.

5 Click the Next button (Comments pane) to display Slide 3. Read and then delete the two comments on this slide.

6 Click the check box above the Slide 3 thumbnail (Revisions pane) to display a preview of the Slide 3 revisions.

7 Click the Next button (Comments pane) to display Slide 4. Read the comment and then type **I chose Slide 4 because it displayed more buildings and attractions.** as a reply.

8 Click the Next button to display Slide 5 (Figure 5–29).

BTW
**Reviewers'
Technology
Limitations**
People who receive copies of your presentation to review may not be able to open a PowerPoint 2016 file saved in the default .pptx format because they have a previous version of this software or may not have Internet access available readily. For these reasons, you need to know their software and hardware limitations and distribute your file or handouts accordingly.

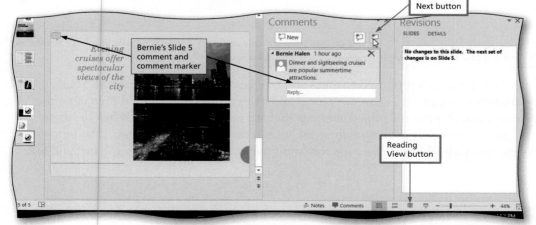

Figure 5–29

To Run the Revised Presentation in Reading View

Bernie's changes modified the original presentation substantially, so it is a good idea to review the new presentation. The following steps review the slides in Reading view. *Why? This view helps you see large images of the slides so you can evaluate their content without needing to start Slide Show view.*

- Display Slide 1 and then click the Reading View button on the status bar to display Slide 1 in this view (Figure 5–30).

- Click the Next and Previous buttons to review the changes on each slide.
- Click the black 'End of slide show' screen to end the slide show and return to Normal view.

Figure 5–30

Other Ways

1. Click Reading View button (View tab | Presentation Views group)

How should I give constructive criticism when I am reviewing a presentation?
If you are asked to critique a presentation, begin and end with positive comments. Give specific details about a few key areas that can be improved. Be honest, but be tactful. Avoid using the word, you. For example, instead of writing, "You need to give some statistics to support your viewpoint," write "I had difficulty understanding which departments' sales have increased in the past six months. Perhaps a chart with specific figures would help depict how dramatically revenues have improved."

To End the Review and Hide Markup

You have analyzed all of the reviewer's proposed changes and replied to some of his questions. Your review of the merged presentation is complete, so you can accept and apply all the changes and then close the Comments and Revisions panes. You also can hide the comments that are present on Slide 1. *Why? You do not need to see the comments when you are developing the remainder of the presentation, so you can hide them.* The following steps end the review of the merged slides (which closes the Revisions pane), close the Comments pane, and hide the comment markers.

• Click the End Review button (Review tab | Compare group) to display the Microsoft PowerPoint dialog box (Figure 5–31).

Figure 5–31

2

• Click the Yes button (Microsoft PowerPoint dialog box) to apply the changes you accepted and discard the changes you rejected.

Q&A

Which changes are discarded?
You did not apply the aligned WordArt on Slide 1 and did not insert Bernie's proposed Slide 5.

• Click the Show Comments arrow (Review tab | Comments group) to display the Show Comments menu (Figure 5–32).

Figure 5–32

3

• Click Comments Pane in the menu to remove the check mark and close the Comments pane.

Q&A

Can I also close the Comments pane by tapping or clicking the Close button in that pane?
Yes.

• Click the Show Comments arrow to display the Show Comments menu again (Figure 5–33).

Figure 5–33

4

• Click Show Markup in the menu to hide comments on the slide.

SharePoint

In a business environment, PowerPoint presentations can be stored on a centrally located Slide Library that resides on a server running Office SharePoint. These slide shows can be shared, reused, and accessed by many individuals who then can copy materials into their individual presentations. The Slide Library functions in much the same manner as your community library, for SharePoint time stamps when an individual has borrowed a particular slide or presentation and then time stamps the slide or presentation when it is returned. If a particular slide in the Library has been updated, anyone who has borrowed that slide is notified that the content has changed. In this manner, people creating PowerPoint presentations can track the changes to presentations, locate the latest versions of slides, and check for slide updates.

Reusing Slides from an Existing Presentation

Occasionally you may want to insert a slide from another presentation into your presentation. PowerPoint offers two methods of obtaining these slides. One way is to open the second presentation and then copy and paste the desired slides. The second method is to use the Reuse Slides pane to view and then select the desired slides.

The PowerPoint presentation with the file name, Chicago History, has colorful pictures and useful text. It contains three slides, and you would like to insert two of these slides, shown in Figure 5–34, into your Chicago Final presentation. You would also like to use a part of one of the Chicago History slides in Slide 2 of your presentation.

(a) Slide 1 (Insert and Use Headlines Formatting)

(b) Slide 2 (Insert and Keep Original Theme)

(c) Slide 3 (Snip Part of Graphic)

Figure 5–34

To Reuse Slides from an Existing Presentation

You want to insert two slides from the Chicago History presentation in the Chicago Final presentation directly after Slide 3. PowerPoint converts inserted slides to the theme and styles of the current presentation, so the inserted slides will inherit the styles of the current Headlines theme and Chicago Final presentation. However, you want the second slide to keep the source formatting of the Chicago History presentation, which uses the Wisp theme. ***Why?*** *The Wisp theme has a plant in the background and uses earthy colors.* You also will need to add the Cube transition to the second slide because you are not applying the Chicago Final formatting. The Chicago History presentation is in your Data Files. The following steps add these two slides to your presentation, and specify that the second slide keep its original (source) formatting.

- Display Slide 3 and then display the Home tab.

- Click the New Slide arrow (Slides group) to display the Headlines layout gallery (Figure 5–35).

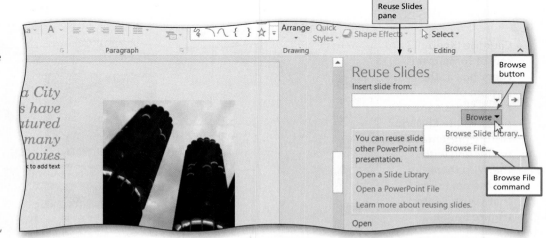

Figure 5–35

- Click Reuse Slides in the Headlines layout gallery to display the Reuse Slides pane.

- Click the Browse button (Reuse Slides pane) (Figure 5–36).

Q&A What are the two Browse options shown?
If the desired slides are in a Slide Library on Office SharePoint, then you would click Browse Slide Library. The slides you need, however, are in your Data Files, so you need to click Browse File.

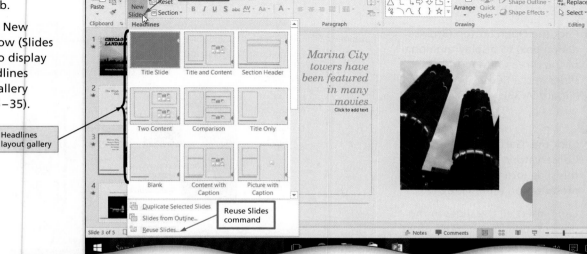

Figure 5–36

3

- Click Browse File to display the Browse dialog box.

- If necessary, navigate to the location of your Data Files and then click Chicago History to select the file (Figure 5–37).

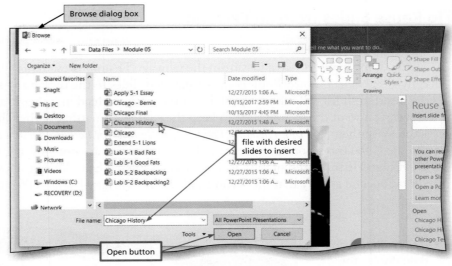

Figure 5–37

4

- Click the Open button (Browse dialog box) to display thumbnails of the three Chicago History slides in the Reuse Slides pane (Figure 5–38).

5

- Click the 'Garfield Park Conservatory' thumbnail to insert this slide into the Chicago Final presentation after Slide 3.

Q&A Can I insert all the slides in the presentation in one step instead of selecting each one individually?
Yes. Right-click any thumbnail and then click 'Insert All Slides'.

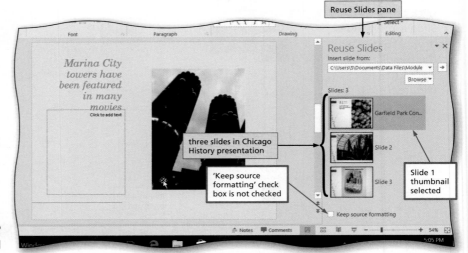

Figure 5–38

6

- Click the 'Keep source formatting' check box at the bottom of the Reuse Slides pane to preserve the Chicago History presentation formatting with the Wisp theme for the next slide that you will insert (Figure 5–39).

Q&A What would happen if I did not check this box?
PowerPoint would change the formatting to the characteristics found in the Headlines theme.

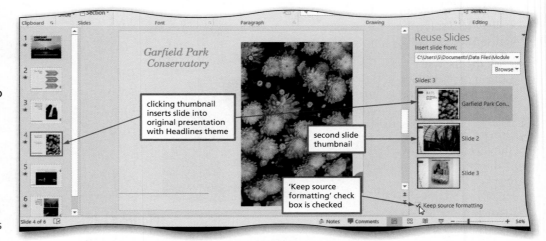

Figure 5–39

- Click the Slide 2 thumbnail (Reuse Slides pane) to insert this slide into the presentation as the new Slide 5 in the Chicago Final presentation with the Wisp theme retained (Figure 5–40).

- Click the Close button in the Reuse Slides pane so that it no longer is displayed.

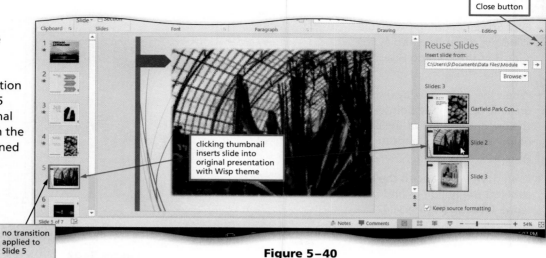

Figure 5–40

- Apply the Cube transition (in the Exciting category) to Slide 5 and change the duration to 2.50.

To Capture Part of a Screen Using Screen Clipping

1 COLLABORATE | 2 FORMAT SLIDES & SET SLIDE SHOW RESOLUTION | 3 SAVE & PACKAGE A PRESENTATION
4 PROTECT & SECURE PRESENTATION | 5 USE PRESENTATION TOOLS

At times you may be developing a presentation and need a portion of a clip or picture in another presentation. You can capture, or **snip**, part of an object on a slide in another presentation that is open. PowerPoint refers to this presentation as being available. The following steps snip part of an image on Slide 3 of the Chicago History presentation and paste it on Slide 2 in the Chicago Final presentation. *Why? This portion of the vintage American Airlines poster has buildings and the word, Chicago, and you desire to place this snip on Slide 2 to reinforce Chicago's rich history.*

- Open the Chicago History file from your Data Files and then display Slide 3 of this presentation.

- Display Slide 2 of the Chicago Final presentation.

- Display the Insert tab and then click the Screenshot button (Insert tab | Images group) to display the Available Windows gallery (Figure 5–41).

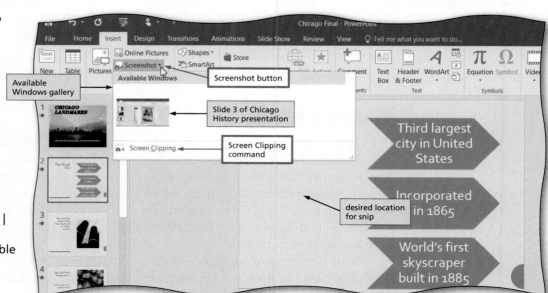

Figure 5–41

- Click Screen Clipping (Available Windows gallery) to display Slide 3 of the Chicago History presentation.

- When the white overlay displays on Slide 3, move the pointer to the upper-left edge of the poster below the words, American Airlines.

- Drag downward and to the right to select the buildings and the word, Chicago (Figure 5–42).

Figure 5–42

- Release the mouse button.

- When the snip displays on Slide 2 of the Chicago Final presentation, drag the snip below the title text, The Windy City, using the vertical and horizontal guides to help with positioning (Figure 5–43).

Q&A My clip is a different size than the one shown in Figure 5–43. What should I do?
You can resize the clip in the same manner that you resize pictures.

Figure 5–43

- Close the Chicago History presentation.

Q&A Why should I close this file?
You no longer need the Chicago History presentation because you have inserted the slides and the screen clip.

Adding a Footer

Slides can contain information at the top or bottom. The area at the top of a slide is called a **header**, and the area at the bottom is called a **footer**. In general, footer content displays along the lower edge of a slide, but the theme determines where these elements are placed. As a default, no information is displayed in the header or footer. You can choose to apply only a header, only a footer, or both a header and footer. In addition, you can elect to have the header or footer display on single slides, all slides, or all slides except the title slide.

Slide numbers are one footer element. They help a presenter organize a talk. While few audience members are cognizant of this aspect of a slide, the presenter can glance at the number and know which slide contains particular information. If an audience member asks a question pertaining to information contained on a slide that had been displayed previously or is on a slide that has not been viewed yet, the presenter can jump to that slide in an effort to answer the question. In addition, the slide number helps pace the slide show. For example, a speaker could have the presentation timed so that Slide 4 is displaying three minutes into the talk.

PowerPoint gives the option of displaying the current date and time obtained from the system or a fixed date and time that you specify. In addition, you can add relevant information, such as your name, your school or business name, or the purpose of your presentation in the Footer area.

To Add a Footer with Fixed Information

To reinforce the fact that you visited Chicago, also called Chi-town, in July, you can add this information in the Footer area. You also can add a slide number. The following steps add this text to all slides in the presentation except the title slide. ***Why?*** *In general, the footer text should not display on the title slide. In addition, the title slide has a large photo in the background, so you do not want the footer text to overlap this content.*

- Display the Insert tab.

- Click the 'Header & Footer' button (Insert tab | Text group) to display the Header and Footer dialog box.

- If necessary, click the Slide tab to display the Slide sheet (Figure 5–44).

Q&A Can I use this dialog box to add a header?
The slide theme determines the location of the placeholders at the top or bottom of the slide. The footer elements generally are displayed along the lower edge of the slide. Some themes, however, have the footer elements along the top edge, so they are considered header text.

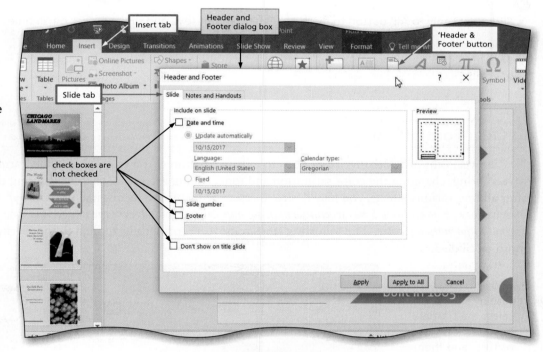

Figure 5–44

- Click 'Date and time' to select this check box.
- Click Fixed to select this option. Select the existing date and then type `July 31` in the Fixed box.
- Click Slide number to select this check box.
- Click Footer to select this check box.
- Type `Chi-town Summer` in the Footer box.
- If requested by your instructor, type the name of your grade school instead of the word, Summer.

- Click the 'Don't show on title slide' check box to select the box (Figure 5–45).

What are the black boxes in the Preview section?

The black box in the lower-left placeholder indicates where the footer text and fixed date will appear on the slide; the small black box in the bottom-right placeholder indicates where the page number will appear.

What if I want the current date and time to appear?

Click Update automatically in the 'Date and time' section.

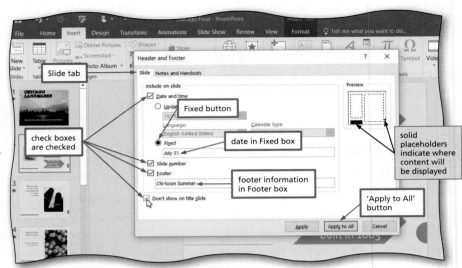

Figure 5–45

❸

- Click the 'Apply to All' button to display the date, footer text, and slide number on all slides except Slide 1.

When would I click the Apply button instead of the 'Apply to All' button?

Click the Apply button when you want the header and footer information to appear only on the slide currently selected.

To Clear Formatting

PowerPoint provides myriad options to enhance pictures. You can, for example, format the images by recoloring, changing the color saturation and tone, adding artistic effects, and altering the picture style. After adding various effects, you may desire to reset the picture to its original state. *Why? The Garfield Park Conservatory photo on Slide 5 has several formatting adjustments that obscure the image, and now you want to see the original unformatted picture.* The following steps remove all formatting applied to the Garfield Park Conservatory photo on Slide 5.

❶

- Display Slide 5, select the Garfield Park Conservatory picture, and then display the Picture Tools Format tab (Figure 5–46).

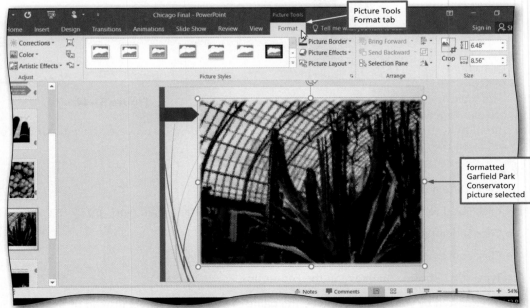

Figure 5–46

2

- Click the Reset Picture button (Format tab | Adjust group) to remove all formatting from the picture (Figure 5–47).

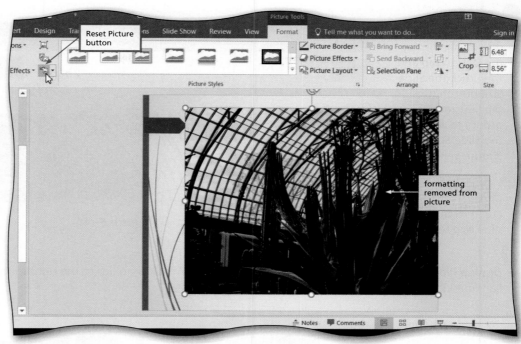

Figure 5–47

Other Ways

1. Right-click picture, click Format Picture, click Picture icon (Format Picture pane), click Picture Corrections, click Reset

Break Point: If you wish to take a break, this is a good place to do so. Be sure to save the Chicago Final file again and then you can exit PowerPoint. To resume at a later time, run PowerPoint, open the file called Chicago Final, and continue following the steps from this location forward.

Changing Slide Size and Slide Show Resolution

Today's technology presents several options you should consider when developing your presentation. The on-screen show ratio determines the height and width proportions. The screen resolution affects the slides' clarity.

To Set Slide Size

1 COLLABORATE | 2 FORMAT SLIDES & SET SLIDE SHOW RESOLUTION | 3 SAVE & PACKAGE A PRESENTATION

4 PROTECT & SECURE PRESENTATION | 5 USE PRESENTATION TOOLS

Prior to PowerPoint 2013, PowerPoint set slides in a 4:3 size ratio, which is the proportion found on a standard monitor that is not widescreen. If you know your presentation will be viewed on a wide screen or you are using a widescreen display, you can change the slide size to optimize the proportions. The following steps change the default setting to 16:9 and then adjust the bulleted paragraphs on Slides 4 and 6. *Why? This 16:9 dimension is the proportion of most widescreen displays. When the slide width is changed, some of the words in the paragraphs are not spaced evenly. A good design principle is to keep all words in a prepositional phrase together on one line.*

- With Slide 5 displaying, display the Design tab and then click the Slide Size button (Design tab | Customize group) to display the Slide Size gallery (Figure 5–48).

- Click Widescreen (16:9) to change the slide size setting.

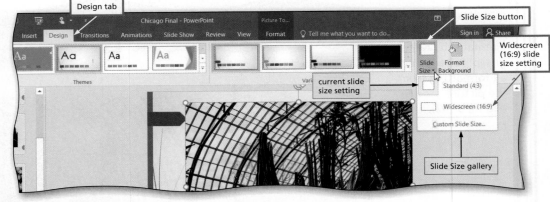

Figure 5–48

- Display Slide 1 and then drag the right edge of the WordArt placeholder to the right so that the word, Landmarks, is displayed on one line.

- Adjust the size of the Slide 3 photo so that it is approximately 5.21" x 6.97" and then use the vertical and horizontal guides to help with position it to the location shown in Figure 5–49.

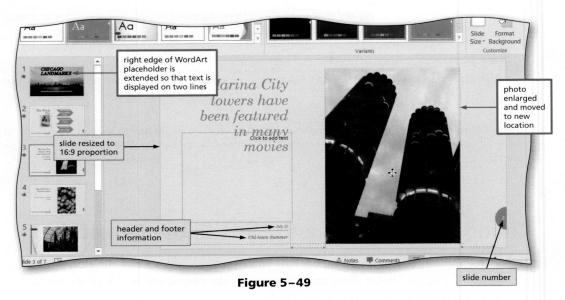

Figure 5–49

To Set Presentation Resolution

1 COLLABORATE | 2 FORMAT SLIDES & SET SLIDE SHOW RESOLUTION | 3 SAVE & PACKAGE A PRESENTATION
4 PROTECT & SECURE PRESENTATION | 5 USE PRESENTATION TOOLS

Screen, or presentation, resolution affects the number of pixels that are displayed on your screen. When screen resolution is increased, more information is displayed, but it is decreased in size. Conversely, when screen resolution is decreased, less information is displayed, but that information is increased in size. Throughout this book, the screen resolution has been set to 1366 x 768. The following steps change the presentation resolution to 800 x 600. **Why?** *You may need to run your presentation on a monitor that has a different resolution.*

- Display the Slide Show tab and then click the 'Set Up Slide Show' button (Slide Show tab | Set Up group) to display the Set Up Show dialog box.

- If necessary, click the Slide show monitor arrow in the Multiple monitors section and then choose Primary Monitor.

- Click the Resolution arrow in the Multiple monitors section to display the Resolution list (Figure 5–50).

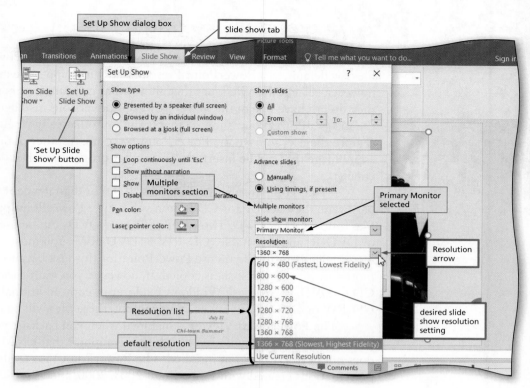

Figure 5–50

- Click 800 x 600 to change the slide show resolution setting.

- If necessary, click the 'Use Presenter View' check box to clear the check box (Figure 5–51).

Q&A What is Presenter view?
When you use Presenter view, you control the slide show using one screen only you can see, but your audience views the slides on another main screen.

4

- Click the OK button to close the Set Up Show dialog box and apply the new resolution to the slides.

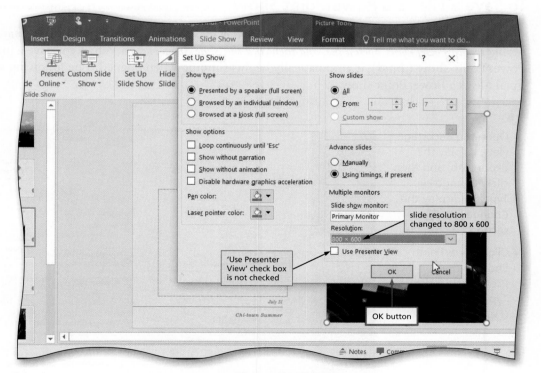

Figure 5–51

Saving and Packaging a Presentation

PowerPoint 2016, PowerPoint 2013, PowerPoint 2010, and PowerPoint 2007 save files, by default, as a PowerPoint Presentation with a .pptx file extension. You can, however, select other file types that allow other computer users to view your slides if they do not have one of the newer PowerPoint versions installed. You also can save the file as a PowerPoint show so that it runs automatically when opened and does not require the user to have the PowerPoint program. Another option is to save one slide as an image that can be inserted into another program, such as Microsoft Word, or emailed.

If your computer has compact disc (CD) or digital video disc (DVD) burning hardware, the Package for CD option will copy a PowerPoint presentation and linked files onto a CD or DVD. Two types of CDs or DVDs can be used: recordable (CD-R or DVD-R) and rewritable (CD-RW or DVD-RW). You must copy all the desired files in a single operation if you use PowerPoint for this task because you cannot add any more files after the first set is copied. If, however, you want to add more files to the CD or DVD, you can use Windows Explorer to copy additional files. If you are using a CD-RW or DVD-RW with existing content, these files will be overwritten.

The **PowerPoint Viewer** is included when you package your presentation so you can show the presentation on another computer that has Microsoft Windows but does not have PowerPoint installed. The PowerPoint Viewer also allows users to view presentations created with PowerPoint 2003, 2000, and 97.

To Save a File as a PowerPoint Show

1 COLLABORATE | 2 FORMAT SLIDES & SET SLIDE SHOW RESOLUTION | 3 SAVE & PACKAGE A PRESENTATION
4 PROTECT & SECURE PRESENTATION | 5 USE PRESENTATION TOOLS

Why? *To simplify giving a presentation in front of an audience, you may want to start your slide show without having to run PowerPoint, open a file, and then click the Slide Show button.* When you save a presentation as a **PowerPoint show (.ppsx)**, it automatically begins running when opened. The following steps save the Chicago Final file as a PowerPoint show.

- Open the Backstage view, display the Export tab, and then click 'Change File Type' to display the Change File Type section.

- Click PowerPoint Show in the Presentation File Types section (Figure 5–52).

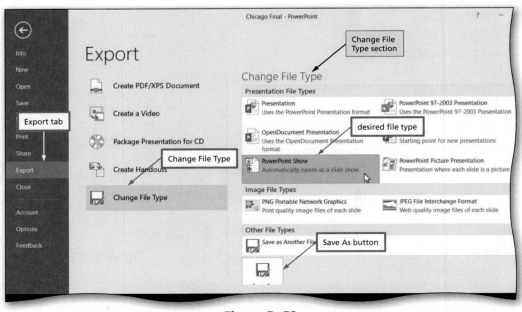

Figure 5–52

- Click the Save As button to display the Save As dialog box.

- Type **Chicago Final Show** in the File name box (Figure 5–53).

- Click the Save button to close the Save As dialog box.

- Close the current Chicago Final Show presentation.

Why do I want to close the current Chicago Final Show file?
It is best to use the more current version of the presentation to complete the remaining tasks in this module.

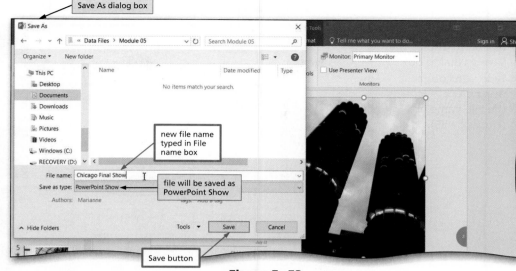

Figure 5–53

Other Ways

1. Click File on ribbon, click Save As in Backstage view, click Browse button to locate save location, click 'Save as type' arrow, select PowerPoint Show, click Save button

To Save a Slide as an Image

1 COLLABORATE | 2 FORMAT SLIDES & SET SLIDE SHOW RESOLUTION | 3 SAVE & PACKAGE A PRESENTATION
4 PROTECT & SECURE PRESENTATION | 5 USE PRESENTATION TOOLS

To create visually interesting slides, you insert pictures, clips, and video files into your presentation. Conversely, you may want to insert a PowerPoint slide into another document, such as a file you created in Microsoft Word. *Why? A slide may have information that you want to share with an audience and include with other material that is not part of the PowerPoint presentation.* You can save one slide as an image and then insert this file into another document. The following steps save Slide 2 as a JPEG File Interchange Format image.

- Open the Chicago Final presentation and then display Slide 2.

- Open the Backstage view, display the Export tab, and then click 'Change File Type' to display the Change File Type section.

- Click 'JPEG File Interchange Format' in the Image File Types section (Figure 5–54).

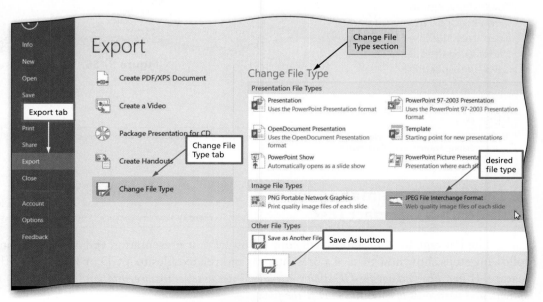

Figure 5–54

- Click the Save As button to display the Save As dialog box.
- Type **Chicago SmartArt** in the File name box (Figure 5–55).

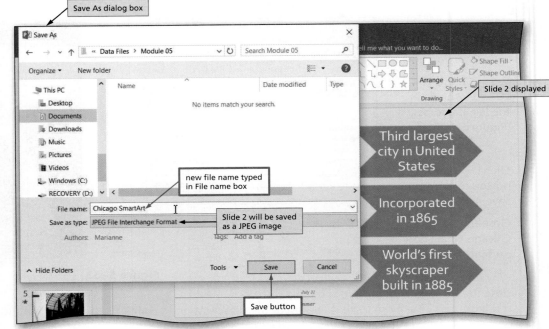

Figure 5–55

- Click the Save button (Save As dialog box) to display the Microsoft PowerPoint dialog box (Figure 5–56).

- Click the 'Just This One' button to save only Slide 2 as a file in JPEG (.jpg) format.

Q&A What would happen if I clicked All Slides? PowerPoint would save each slide as a separate file in a folder with the file name you specified.

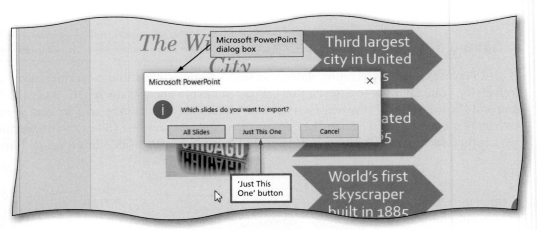

Figure 5–56

Other Ways

1. Click File on ribbon, click Save As in Backstage view, click Browse button to locate save location, click 'Save as type' arrow, select JPEG File Interchange Format, click Save button

---

To Package a Presentation for Storage on a Compact Disc

1 COLLABORATE | 2 FORMAT SLIDES & SET SLIDE SHOW RESOLUTION | 3 SAVE & PACKAGE A PRESENTATION
4 PROTECT & SECURE PRESENTATION | 5 USE PRESENTATION TOOLS

The Package for CD option will copy a PowerPoint presentation and linked files onto a CD or DVD. The following steps show how to save a presentation and related files to a CD or DVD using the Package for CD feature. *Why? The Package for CD dialog box allows you to select the presentation files to copy, linking and embedding options, and passwords to open and modify the files.*

- Insert a CD-RW or DVD-RW or a blank CD-R or DVD-R into your CD or DVD drive.
- Open the Backstage view, display the Export tab, and then click 'Package Presentation for CD' (Figure 5–57).

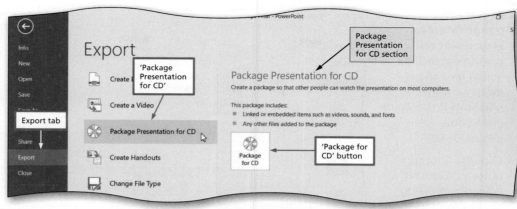

Figure 5–57

2

- Click the 'Package for CD' button in the Package Presentation for CD section to display the Package for CD dialog box.
- Delete the text in the 'Name the CD' box and then type **Chicago** in the box (Figure 5–58).

Q&A What if I want to add more files to the CD?
Click the Add button and then locate the files you want to add to the CD.

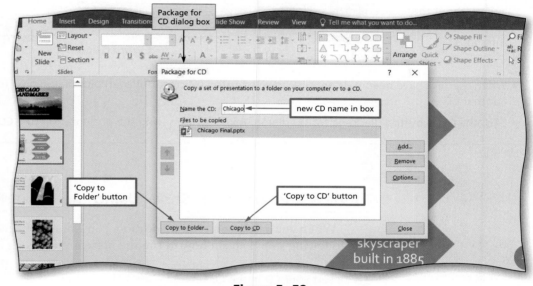

Figure 5–58

3

- Click the 'Copy to CD' button to begin packaging the presentation files and to display the Microsoft PowerPoint dialog box (Figure 5–59).

Q&A When would I copy the files to a folder instead of a CD?
If you want to copy your presentation to a network or to a storage medium other than a CD or DVD, such as a USB flash drive, click the 'Copy to Folder' button, enter a folder name and location, and then click the OK button.

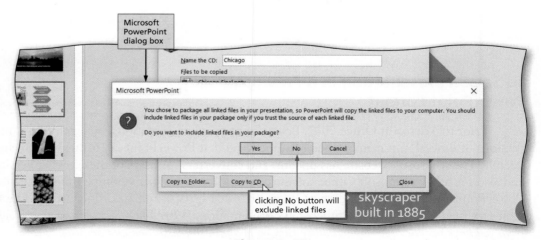

Figure 5–59

• Click the No button (Microsoft PowerPoint dialog box) to not include linked files and to display another Microsoft PowerPoint dialog box (Figure 5-60).

• Click the Continue button (Microsoft PowerPoint dialog box) to continue copying the presentation to a CD without the comments added to the slides.

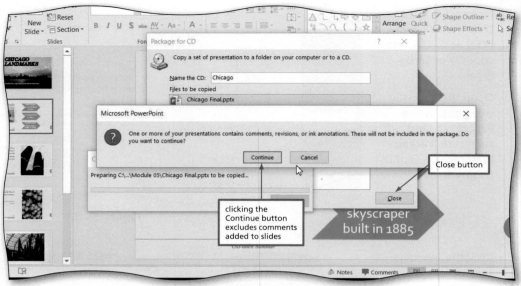

Figure 5-60

• When the files have been written, click the No button (Microsoft PowerPoint dialog box) to not copy the files to another CD.

• Click the Close button (Package for CD dialog box) to finish saving the presentation to a CD.

To View a PowerPoint Show Using the PowerPoint Viewer

When you arrive at a remote location, you will run the packaged presentation. The following steps explain how to run the presentation using the PowerPoint Viewer.

1 Insert your CD in the CD drive.

2 Accept the licensing agreement for the PowerPoint Viewer to open and run the slide show.

To Save a Presentation in a Previous PowerPoint Format

1 COLLABORATE | 2 FORMAT SLIDES & SET SLIDE SHOW RESOLUTION | 3 SAVE & PACKAGE A PRESENTATION
4 PROTECT & SECURE PRESENTATION | 5 USE PRESENTATION TOOLS

Prior to Microsoft Office 2007, PowerPoint saved presentations, by default, as a .ppt file type. The earlier versions of PowerPoint cannot open the .pptx type that PowerPoint 2016, 2013, 2010, and 2007 creates by default. The Microsoft website has updates and converters for users of these earlier versions of the program and also for other Microsoft Office software. The Microsoft Office Compatibility Pack for Word, Excel, and PowerPoint will open, edit, and save Office 2016, 2013, 2010, and 2007 documents. The following steps save the Chicago Final file as PowerPoint 97-2003 Presentation. *Why? You cannot assume that people who obtain a .pptx file from you have installed the Compatibility Pack, so to diminish frustration and confusion you can save a presentation as a .ppt type that will open with earlier versions of PowerPoint.*

- Open the Backstage view, display the Export tab, and then click 'Change File Type'.
- Click 'PowerPoint 97-2003 Presentation' in the Presentation File Types section (Figure 5–61).

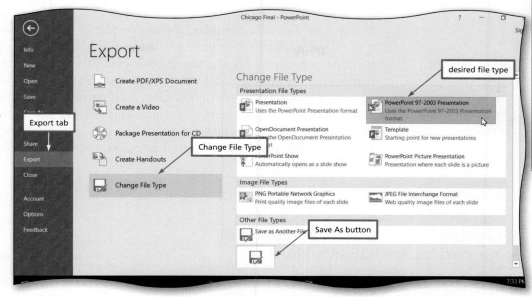

Figure 5–61

- Click the Save As button to display the Save As dialog box.
- Type **Chicago Final Previous Version** in the File name box (Figure 5–62).

- Click the Save button (Save As dialog box) to save the Chicago Final presentation as a .ppt type and display the Microsoft PowerPoint Compatibility Checker.

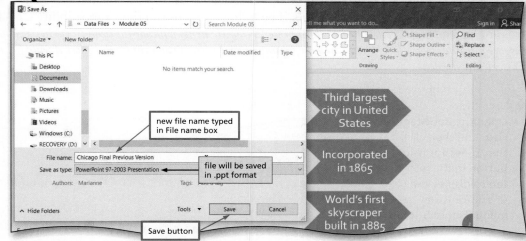

Figure 5–62

Q&A Why does this Compatibility Checker dialog box display?
PowerPoint is alerting you that the older file version will not keep some of the features used in the presentation. You will learn more about the Compatibility Checker in the next section of this module.

- Click the Continue button (Microsoft PowerPoint Compatibility Checker) to continue to save the presentation.

5

- Close the current PowerPoint file and then open your Chicago Final presentation.

Q&A Why do I want to open this presentation instead of using the current file?
The current file is saved in a previous version of PowerPoint, so some features are not available when you run the final version of the slide show. It is best to use the more current version of the presentation to complete the remaining tasks in this module.

Other Ways

1. Click File on ribbon, click Save As in Backstage view, click Browse button to locate save location, click 'Save as type' arrow, select 'PowerPoint 97-2003 Presentation', click Save button

Protecting and Securing a Presentation

When your slides are complete, you can perform additional functions to finalize the file and prepare it for distributing to other users or running on a computer other than the one used to develop the file. For example, the **Compatibility Checker** reviews the file for any feature that will not work properly or display on computers running a previous PowerPoint version. In addition, the Document Inspector locates inappropriate information, such as comments, in a file and allows you to delete these slide elements. You also can set passwords so only authorized people can distribute, view, or modify your slides. When the review process is complete, you can indicate this file is the final version.

To Identify Presentation Features Not Supported by Previous Versions

1 COLLABORATE | 2 FORMAT SLIDES & SET SLIDE SHOW RESOLUTION | 3 SAVE & PACKAGE A PRESENTATION
4 PROTECT & SECURE PRESENTATION | 5 USE PRESENTATION TOOLS

PowerPoint 2016 has many new features not found in some previous versions of PowerPoint, especially versions older than PowerPoint 2007. For example, WordArt formatted with Quick Styles is an enhancement found only in PowerPoint 2016, 2013, 2010, and 2007. If you give your file to people who have a previous PowerPoint version installed on their computers, they will be able to open the file but may not be able to see or edit some special features and effects. The following steps run the Compatibility Checker. *Why? You can use the Compatibility Checker to see which presentation elements will not function in earlier versions of PowerPoint and display a summary of the elements in your Chicago Final presentation that will be lost if your file is opened in some earlier PowerPoint versions.*

1

• Open the Backstage view and then click the 'Check for Issues' button in the Info tab to display the Check for Issues menu (Figure 5–63).

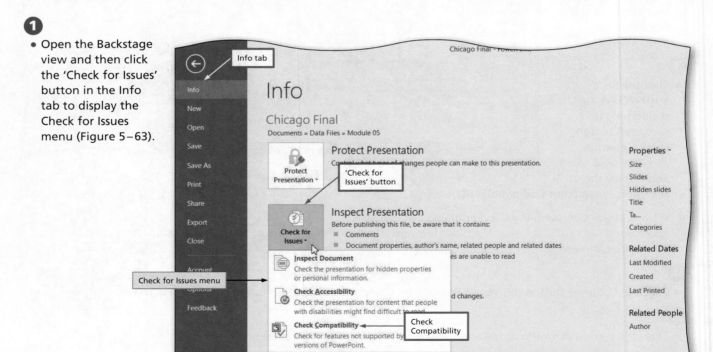

Figure 5–63

2

- Click Check Compatibility to display the Microsoft PowerPoint Compatibility Checker dialog box.

- View the comments in the Summary section regarding the five features that are not supported by earlier versions of PowerPoint (Figure 5–64).

Q&A

Why do the numbers 2, 1, 11, 4, and 2 display in the Occurrences column in the right side of the Summary section?
The numbers indicate the number of times incompatible elements, such as the SmartArt graphic, appear in the presentation.

What happens if I click the Help links in the Summary section?
PowerPoint will provide additional information about the particular incompatible slide element.

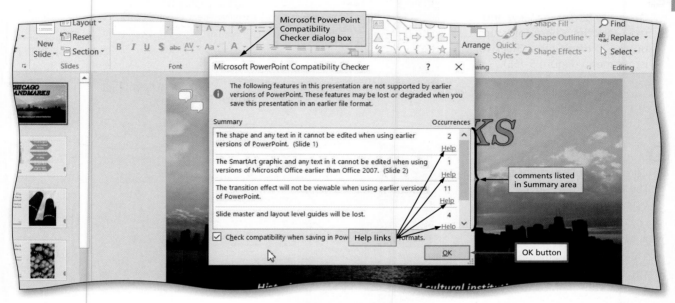

Figure 5–64

3

- Click the OK button (Microsoft PowerPoint Compatibility Checker dialog box) to close the dialog box and return to the presentation.

To Remove Inappropriate Information

1 COLLABORATE | 2 FORMAT SLIDES & SET SLIDE SHOW RESOLUTION | 3 SAVE & PACKAGE A PRESENTATION
4 PROTECT & SECURE PRESENTATION | 5 USE PRESENTATION TOOLS

As you work on your presentation, you might add information meant only for you to see. For example, you might write comments to yourself or put confidential information in the Notes pane. You would not want other people to access this information if you give a copy of the presentation file to them. You also added a comment and replied to Bernie Halen's questions, and you may not want anyone other than him to view this information. The Document Inspector provides a quick and efficient method of searching for and deleting inappropriate information.

It is a good idea to make a duplicate copy of your file and then inspect this new second copy. *Why? If you tell the Document Inspector to delete content, such as personal information, comments, invisible slide content, or notes, and then decide you need to see those slide elements, quite possibly you will be unable to retrieve the information by using the Undo command.* The following steps save a duplicate copy of your Chicago Final presentation, run the Document Inspector on this new file, and then delete comments.

①

- Open the Backstage view, click the Save As tab, and then click the Browse button to open the Save As dialog box.

- Type **Chicago Final Duplicate** in the File name box.

- Click the Save button to change the file name and save another copy of this presentation.

②

- Open the Backstage view and then click the 'Check for Issues' button to display the Check for Issues menu (Figure 5–65).

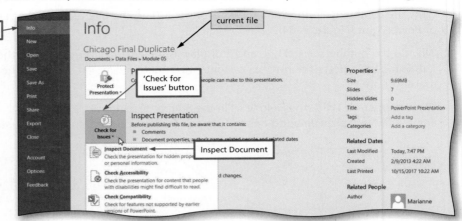

Figure 5–65

③

- Click Inspect Document to display the Document Inspector dialog box (Figure 5–66).

Q&A What information does the Document Inspector check?
This information includes text in the Document Information Panel, such as your name and company. Other information includes details of when the file was last saved, objects formatted as invisible, graphics and text you dragged off a slide, presentation notes, and email headers.

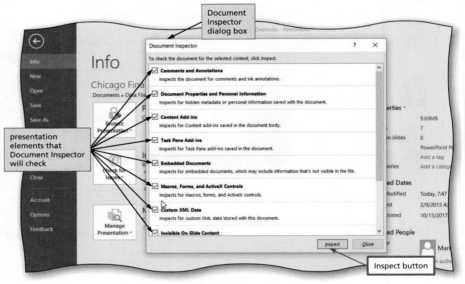

Figure 5–66

④

- Click the Inspect button to check the document and display the inspection results (Figure 5–67).

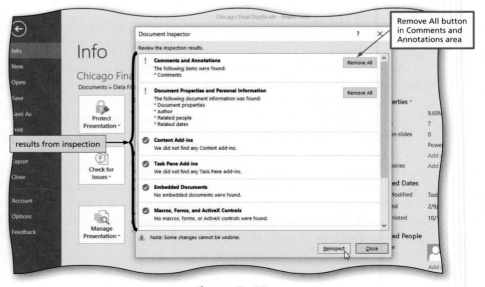

Figure 5–67

5

- Click the Remove All button in the Comments and Annotations section of the inspection results to remove the comments from the presentation (Figure 5–68).

Q&A Should I also remove the document properties and personal information?
You might want to delete this information so that no identifying information, such as your name, is saved.

6

- Click the Close button (Document Inspector dialog box) to close the dialog box.

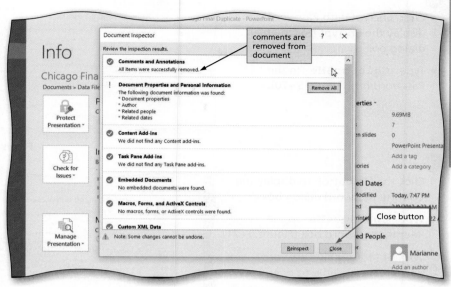

Figure 5–68

What types of passwords are best for security?
A password should be at least six characters and contain a combination of letters and numbers. Using both uppercase and lowercase letters is advised. Do not use a password that someone could guess, such as your first or last name, spouse's or child's name, telephone number, birth date, street address, license plate number, or Social Security number.

Once you develop this password, write it down in a secure place. Underneath your keyboard is not a secure place, nor is your middle desk drawer.

To Set a Password

1 COLLABORATE | 2 FORMAT SLIDES & SET SLIDE SHOW RESOLUTION | 3 SAVE & PACKAGE A PRESENTATION
4 PROTECT & SECURE PRESENTATION | 5 USE PRESENTATION TOOLS

Why? *You can protect your slide content by using a password.* You can prohibit a user from modifying a file without entering the password. The following steps set a password for the Chicago Final Duplicate file.

1

- With Backstage view open and the Info tab displaying, click the Protect Presentation button to display the Protect Presentation menu (Figure 5–69).

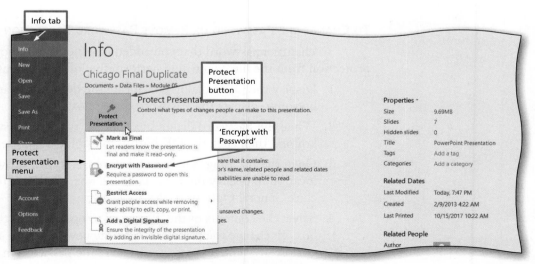

Figure 5–69

- Click 'Encrypt with Password' to display the Encrypt Document dialog box.
- Type **Chicago4Me** in the Password box (Figure 5–70).

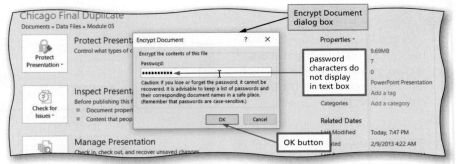

Figure 5–70

- Click the OK button to display the Confirm Password dialog box.
- Type **Chicago4Me** in the Reenter password box (Figure 5–71).

Q&A | What if I forget my password?
You will not be able to open your file. For security reasons, Microsoft or other companies cannot retrieve a lost password.

Figure 5–71

4
- Click the OK button in the Confirm Password dialog box.

Q&A | When does the password take effect?
You will need to enter your password the next time you open your presentation.

To Open a Presentation with a Password

To open a file that has been protected with a password, you would perform the following steps.

1. Display the Open dialog box, locate the desired file, and then click the Open button to display the Password dialog box.
2. When the Password dialog box appears, type the password in the Password box and then click the OK button to display the presentation.

To Change the Password or Remove Password Protection

To change a password that you added to a file or to remove all password protection from the file, you would perform the following steps.

1. Display the Open dialog box, locate the desired file, and then click the Open button to display the Password dialog box.
2. When the Password dialog box appears, type the password in the Password box and then click the OK button to display the presentation.
3. Open the Backstage view, click Save As, and then browse to the desired Save location to display the Save As dialog box. Click the Tools button and then click General Options in the Tools list.
4. Select the contents of the 'Password to open' box or the 'Password to modify' box. To change the password, type the new password and then click the OK button. To remove a password, delete the password in the box. If prompted, retype your password to reconfirm it, and then click the OK button.
5. Click the Save button and then click the Yes button to resave the presentation.

To Mark a Presentation as Final

Why? *When your slides are completed, you may want to prevent others or yourself from accidentally changing the slide content or features.* If you use the **Mark as Final** command, the presentation becomes a read-only document. The following steps mark the presentation as a final (read-only) document.

1

• With Backstage view open and the Info tab displaying for the Chicago Final Duplicate file, click the Protect Presentation button to display the Protect Presentation menu again (Figure 5–72).

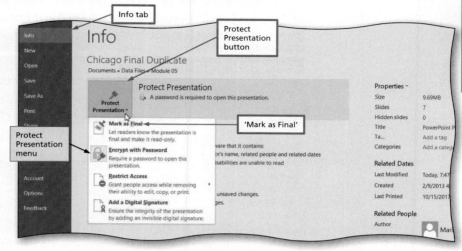

Figure 5–72

2

• Click 'Mark as Final' to display the Microsoft PowerPoint dialog box indicating that the presentation will be saved as a final document (Figure 5–73).

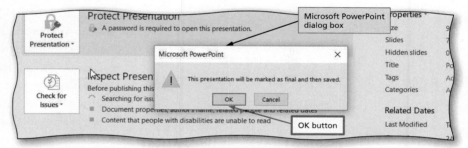

Figure 5–73

3

• Click the OK button (Microsoft PowerPoint dialog box) to save the file and to display another Microsoft PowerPoint dialog box with information about a final version of a document and indicating that the presentation is final (Figure 5–74).

 Can I turn off this read-only status so that I can edit the file?
Yes. Click Mark as Final in the Protect Presentation menu to toggle off the read-only status.

Figure 5–74

4

• Click the OK button (Microsoft PowerPoint dialog box). If an Information bar is displayed above the slide, click the Edit Anyway button to allow changes to be made to the presentation.

5

• Close the Chicago Final Duplicate file and then open the original Chicago Final presentation.

Using Presentation Tools

When you display a particular slide and view the information, you may want to return to one of the other slides in the presentation. Jumping to particular slides in a presentation is called **navigating**. A set of keyboard shortcuts can help you navigate to various slides during the slide show. When running a slide show, you can press the F1 key to see a list of these keyboard controls. These navigational features are listed in Table 5–1.

Table 5–1 Slide Show Shortcuts

Keyboard Shortcut	Purpose
N ENTER SPACEBAR PAGE DOWN RIGHT ARROW DOWN ARROW	Perform the next animation or advance to the next slide
P BACKSPACE LEFT ARROW UP ARROW PAGE UP	Perform the previous animation or return to the previous slide
NUMBER FOLLOWED BY ENTER	Go to a specific slide number
B	Display a blank black slide
W	Display a blank white slide
S	Stop or restart an automatic presentation
ESC	End a presentation
E	Erase on-screen annotations
H	Go to the next slide if the next slide is hidden
T	Set new timings while rehearsing
R	Rerecord slide narration and timing
CTRL+P	Change the pointer to a pen
CTRL+A	Change the pointer to an arrow
CTRL+E	Change the pointer to an eraser
CTRL+M	Show or hide ink markup

Delivering and Navigating a Presentation Using the Control Bar

When you begin running a presentation in full screen mode and move the pointer, a control bar is displayed with buttons that allow you to navigate to the next slide or previous slide, mark up the current slide, display slide thumbnails, zoom, or change the current display. When you move the mouse, the control bar is displayed in the lower-left corner of the slide; it disappears after the mouse has not been moved for three seconds. Table 5–2 describes the buttons on the control bar.

Table 5–2 Slide Show Control Bar Buttons

Description	Function
Previous	Previous slide or previous animated element on the slide
Next	Next slide or next animated element on the slide
Pen and laser pointer tools	Shortcut menu for laser pointer, pen, highlighter, and eraser
See all slides	View thumbnails of all slides in presentation
Zoom into the slide	Zoom in on specific slide area
Options	Shortcut menu for slide navigation and screen displays. Also displays Presenter View on a single monitor.

To Highlight Items on a Slide

You click the arrow buttons on the left side of the control bar to navigate backward or forward through the slide show. The 'Pen and laser pointer tools' button has a variety of functions, most often to emphasize aspects of slides or to make handwritten notes. The following steps highlight an item on a slide in Slide Show view. *Why? You want to call attention to the presentation's featured city.*

- If necessary, display Slide 1 and then run the slide show.

- If the control bar is not visible in the lower-left corner of the slide, move the pointer on the slide.

- Click the 'Pen and laser pointer tools' button on the control bar to display a menu (Figure 5–75).

Q&A Why is the slide displaying smaller than normal?
You changed the resolution to 800 x 600, so the slide size is reduced.

Figure 5–75

- Click Highlighter and then drag over the word, Chicago, several times until all the letters are highlighted (Figure 5–76).

Figure 5–76

To Change Ink Color

Instead of Highlighter, you also can click Pen to draw or write notes on the slides. *Why? The Pen tool is much thinner than the Highlighter, so you can write words or draw fine lines on the slides.* When the presentation ends, PowerPoint will prompt you to keep or discard the ink annotations. The following steps change the pointer to a pen and then change the color of ink during the presentation.

- Click the Next button to display Slide 2. Click the 'Pen and laser pointer tools' button on the control bar and then click Pen on the menu.

- Click the 'Pen and laser pointer tools' button on the control bar and then point to the color Blue (Figure 5–77).

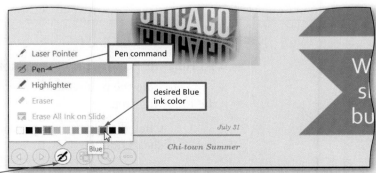

Figure 5–77

2

- Click the color Blue.

- Drag the pointer around the title text to draw a circle around the word, Windy (Figure 5–78).

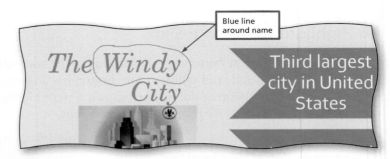

Figure 5–78

3

- Right-click the slide to display the shortcut menu and then point to End Show (Figure 5–79).

Figure 5–79

4

- Click End Show to display the Microsoft PowerPoint dialog box (Figure 5–80).

5

- Click the Discard button (Microsoft PowerPoint dialog box) to end the presentation without saving the annotations.

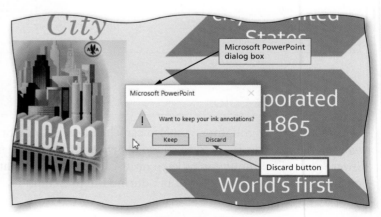

Figure 5–80

To Hide the Pointer and Slide Show Control Bar

To hide the pointer and the control bar during the slide show, you would perform the following step.

1. Click the Options button on the control bar, click Arrow Options, and then click Hidden.

TO CONSTANTLY DISPLAY THE POINTER AND SLIDE SHOW CONTROL BAR

By default, the pointer and control bar are set at Automatic, which means they are hidden after three seconds of no movement. After you hide the pointer and control bar, they remain hidden until you choose one of the other commands on the Options menu. They are displayed again when you move the mouse.

To keep the pointer and control bar displayed at all times during a slide show, you would perform the following step.

1. Click the Options button on the control bar, click Arrow Options, and then click Visible.

To Save, Reset the Resolution, and Print the Presentation

With the presentation completed, you should save the file and print handouts for your audience. The following steps reset the resolution to 1366 x 768, save the file, and then print a presentation handout.

1 Click the 'Set Up Slide Show' button (Slide Show tab | Set Up group), click the Resolution arrow (Set Up Show dialog box), select 1366 x 768, and then click the OK button.

2 Save the presentation again in the same storage location with the same file name.

3 Print the slides as a handout using the 4 Slides Horizontal layout. If necessary, click 'Print Comments and Ink Markup' on the Print menu to deactivate the command and turn off printing comment pages (Figure 5–81).

4 Because the project now is complete, you can exit PowerPoint, closing all open documents.

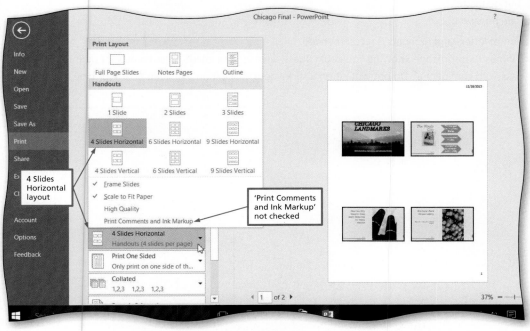

Figure 5–81

BTW

Conserving Ink and Toner

If you want to conserve ink or toner, you can instruct PowerPoint to print draft quality documents by clicking File on the ribbon to open the Backstage view, clicking the Options tab in the Backstage view to display the PowerPoint Options dialog box, clicking Advanced in the left pane (PowerPoint Options dialog box), scrolling to the Print area in the right pane, placing a check mark in the 'Use draft quality' check box, and then clicking the OK button. Then, use the Backstage view to print the document as usual.

BTW

Printing Document Properties

PowerPoint 2016 does not allow you to print document properties. This feature, however, is available in other Office 2016 apps, including Word and Excel.

BTW

Distributing a Document

Instead of printing and distributing a hard copy of a document, you can distribute the document electronically. Options include sending the document via email; posting it on cloud storage (such as OneDrive) and sharing the file with others; posting it on social media, a blog, or other website; and sharing a link associated with an online location of the document. You also can create and share a PDF or XPS image of the document, so that users can view the file in Acrobat Reader or XPS Viewer instead of in PowerPoint.

Summary

In this module you have learned how to merge presentations, review a reviewer's comments, and then review, accept, and reject proposed changes, as well as reply to and insert comments. You reused slides from another presentation, added a footer, cleared formatting from a photo, and changed the slide size and presentation resolution. You also protected and secured the file with a password, checked compatibility, and removed inappropriate information. You then saved the presentation as a PowerPoint show, in a previous PowerPoint format, and packaged on a compact disc. Finally, you ran the presentation and annotated the slides with a highlighter and pen.

CONSIDER THIS: PLAN AHEAD

What decisions will you need to make when creating your next presentation?
Use these guidelines as you complete the assignments in this module and create your own slide show decks outside of this class.

1. Develop a collaboration plan for group members to follow.

    a) Set an overall group goal.

    b) Set long-term and short-term goals.

    c) Identify subtasks that must be completed.

    d) Set a schedule.

2. Accept both positive and negative feedback.

    a) Realize that this criticism helps you to improve yourself and your work.

    b) Oral and written comments from others can help reinforce positive aspects and identify flaws.

    c) Seek comments from a variety of people who genuinely want to help you develop an effective presentation.

3. Give constructive criticism when asked to critique a presentation.

    a) Begin and end with positive comments.

    b) Give specific details about a few areas that can be improved.

    c) Be honest, but be tactful.

4. Select an appropriate password.

    a) A combination of letters and numbers is recommended.

    b) Avoid using words that someone knowing you could guess, such as your child's, best friend's, or pet's name.

    c) Keep your password confidential. Do not write it on a sticky note, place it on a bulletin board, or hide it under your keyboard.

Apply Your Knowledge

Reinforce the skills and apply the concepts you learned in this module.

Inserting and Deleting Comments, Adding a Footer, Saving as a Previous Version, Inspecting a Document, and Marking as Final

Note: To complete this assignment, you will be required to use the Data Files. Please contact your instructor for information about accessing the Data Files.

Instructions: Run PowerPoint. Open the presentation called Apply 5 – 1 Essay, which is located in the Data Files.

The slides in the presentation present information about steps for writing an essay. The document you open is a partially formatted presentation. You are to insert and reply to comments, add a footer, inspect the document, mark the presentation as final, and save it as a previous Power-Point version. Your presentation should look like Figure 5 – 82.

Perform the following tasks:

1. On Slide 1 (Figure 5 – 82a), insert a comment and then type: `I suggest changing the title to: Essay Writing about Nature.` as the text. In the Reply box, type: `That is a good idea. I will edit the slide.` as a reply to the comment.

2. On Slide 2 (Figure 5 – 82b), select the bulleted list, insert a new comment, and then type `I suggest converting this bulleted list to the Vertical Bullet List SmartArt graphic.` as the text. In the Reply box type `I agree. I will create this graphic.` as a reply to the comment.

3. On Slide 2, convert the bulleted list to the Vertical Bullet List SmartArt graphic (in List area). Change the color to 'Colorful Range - Accent Colors 2 to 3' (in Colorful row) and then change the style to Cartoon (in first 3-D row). Resize the SmartArt graphic to approximately 4.22" × 5.14", as shown in Figure 5 – 82b.

4. Display the Header and Footer dialog box and then add the slide number and the automatic date and time to only Slide 2. Type your name as the footer text (Figure 5 – 82a).

5. If requested by your instructor, add your current or previous pet's name in the subtitle placeholder on Slide 1.

6. Apply the Wind transition in the Exciting category to both slides. Change the duration to 3.25 seconds.

7. Save the presentation using the file name, Apply 5 – 1 Essay Writing. Inspect the document and remove all document properties and personal information. (Do not remove comments and annotations.) Mark the presentation as final.

8. Save the presentation again as a PowerPoint 97-2003 (.ppt) document using the name Apply 5 – 1 Nature Writing. Submit both presentations in the format specified by your instructor.

9. ✻ In Step 3, you converted the bulleted list to a SmartArt graphic and changed the colors and style of the graphic. How did this improve the presentation?

Continued >

Apply Your Knowledge *continued*

(a) Slide 1

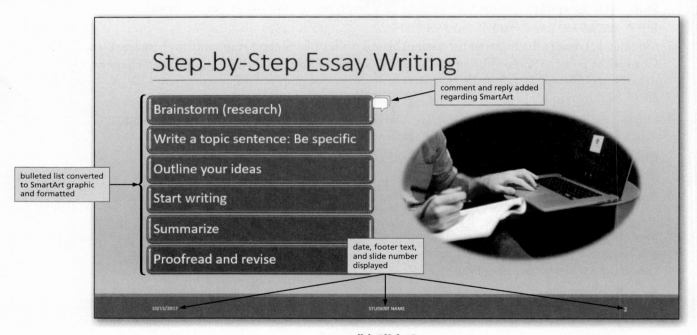

(b) Slide 2

Figure 5–82

Extend Your Knowledge

Extend the skills you learned in this module and experiment with new skills. You may need to use Help to complete the assignment.

Changing Headers and Footers on Slides and Handouts, Inserting and Editing a Comment, and Saving a Slide as an Image

Note: To complete this assignment, you will be required to use the Data Files. Please contact your instructor for information about accessing the Data Files.

Instructions: Run PowerPoint. Open the presentation called Extend 5–1 Lions, which is located in the Data Files. You will change and add information to a footer on a slide and handout. You also will add and change comments and save the slide as an image.

Perform the following tasks:

1. Display the Header and Footer dialog box and then add your next birthday as the fixed date footer text. Type your school's name followed by the words, `Zoology Club – meets every Monday at noon` as the footer text. This footer text will be displayed in the area shown in Figure 5–83.

2. Display the Notes and Handouts tab in the Header and Footer dialog box and then add the text, `Roaring Lions`, as the header text and `Zoology 101` as the footer text.

3. Increase the font size of the footer text to 16 point, bold and italicize this text, and then change the font color to Dark Red (in Standard Colors). *Hint:* Select the footer text boxes and then make the required font changes.

4. Insert a comment on the slide to remind yourself to ask the Zoology Club president if you can post this slide on the organization's website.

5. Edit the existing comment about World Lion Day on the slide by adding this sentence, `This event was founded by Big Cat Rescue, an animal sanctuary in Florida.` to the end of the comment.

6. If requested by your instructor, add the name of your home town after the words, Zoology Club, in the slide footer.

7. Apply the Window transition in the Dynamic Content category to the slide and then change the duration to 2.25 seconds.

8. Save the presentation using the file name, Extend 5–1 Roaring Lions.

9. Save the slide as a .jpg image with the file name, Extend 5–1 Roaring Lions Photo.

10. Submit the revised document in the format specified by your instructor.

11. ✹ In this assignment, you changed the font size and color of the footer text on the slide. How did these changes enhance the slide? You saved the slide as an image. Where could you display this slide other than on the Zoology Club website?

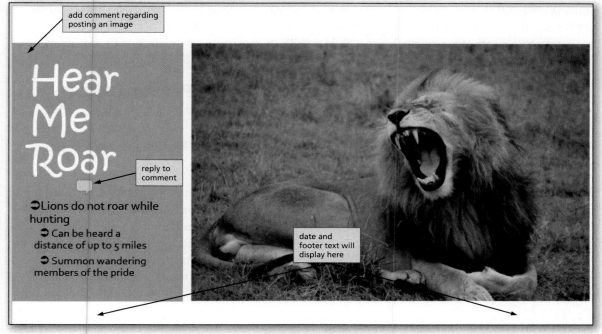

Figure 5–83

Expand Your World

Create a solution that uses cloud or web technologies by learning and investigating on your own from general guidance.

Researching Online Travel Websites

Instructions: You can obtain information about attractions and events worldwide by visiting websites that focus on travel and tourism. Many cities and states have comprehensive websites to promote adventures, events, geography, itineraries, and activities. In this module you learned about a few landmarks in Chicago, and several websites feature detailed information about these and other attractions, tours, and events in this town.

Perform the following tasks:
1. Visit one of the following websites, or locate other websites that contain information about Chicago: Choose Chicago (choosechicago.com), Chicago Traveler (chicagotraveler.com), Chicago Attractions (chicago.org/things-to-do/attraction), or Navy Pier (navypier.com).
2. Locate information on the sites displayed in your Chicago Final slides, tours, attractions, events, sports, architecture, or other activities.
3. Create at least two new slides and then insert them into your Chicago Final presentation. Use SmartArt or WordArt where appropriate.
4. If requested to do so by your instructor, replace the words, Chi-town Summer, in the footer with your high school mascot's name.
5. Save the presentation using the file name, Expand 5 – 1 Chicago Final Travel.
6. Submit the assignment in the format specified by your instructor.
7. ✹ Which features do the websites offer that help you develop content for the two new slides? Who would you ask to review and comment on your revised presentation?

In the Labs

Design, create, modify, and/or use a presentation following the guidelines, concepts, and skills presented in this module. Labs 1 and 2, which increase in difficulty, require you to create solutions based on what you learned in the module; Lab 3 requires you to apply your creative thinking and problem-solving skills to design and implement a solution.

Lab 1: Adding Comments, Protecting a Presentation, and Reusing a Slide

Note: To complete this assignment, you will be required to use the Data Files. Please contact your instructor for information about accessing the Data Files.

Problem: The health food store in your town is planning a series of nutritional seminars, and the first topic concerns choosing products that contain healthy fats. The manager has begun developing PowerPoint slides in two separate files: one regarding beneficial fats and another discussing harmful fats. You agree to help her complete the project by editing the files and then combining slides from both files and creating one presentation. You add a comment and protect the final presentation with a password before sending it to her for approval. When you run the presentation, you add annotations. The annotated slides are shown in Figures 5 – 84a and 5 – 84b. Create the slides shown in Figure 5 – 84.

Perform the following tasks:

1. Run PowerPoint. Open the presentation called Lab 5 – 1 Good Fats, which is located in the Data Files.

2. On Slide 1 (Figure 5 – 84a), add a comment on the cookie illustration and then type `You show a cookie, which probably contains bad fats, on this slide. I suggest you add some information about bad fats to this presentation.` as the text.

3. Open the presentation called Lab 5 – 1 Bad Fats, which is located in the Data Files. Set the slide size to Widescreen (16:9) and then change the slide show resolution to 1366 x 768.

4. On Slide 2 (Figure 5 – 84b), clear the formatting from the fried food picture. Then, apply the 'Reflected Bevel, Black' picture style to this photo.

5. Save the Lab 5 – 1 Bad Fats file with the file name, Lab 5 – 1 Bad Fats Revised, and then close this file.

6. With the Lab 5 – 1 Good Fats file open, insert Slide 2 from the Lab 5 – 1 Bad Fats Revised file, keeping the source formatting.

7. On Slide 1, change the title text to, Fats in Our Diet.

8. Run the Compatibility Checker to identify the presentation features not supported in previous PowerPoint versions. Summarize these features in a comment placed on Slide 1.

9. Protect the presentation with the password, fats.

10. If requested by your instructor, add the name of the city in which you were born as the subtitle text on Slide 1.

11. Apply the Peel Off transition in the Exciting category to all slides and then change the duration to 2.50 seconds.

12. Save the presentation using the file name, Lab 5 – 1 Fats in our Diet.

13. Run the presentation. On Slide 1, use the Pen tool and Blue ink to draw a circle around the word, Fats. When Slide 3 (Figure 5 – 84c) is displayed, use the Highlighter tool and Light Green ink to highlight the text, Lowers LDL, in both middle boxes, as shown in the figure. Click the Next button to reach the end of the slide show. Save the annotations.

(a) Slide 1
Figure 5 – 84 (Continued)

Continued >

In the Labs *continued*

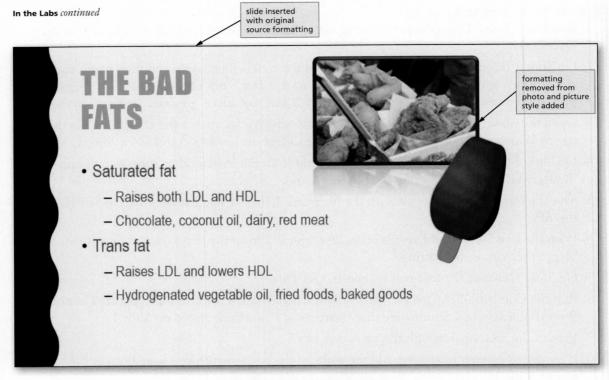

(b) **Slide 2 (Inserted Slide)**

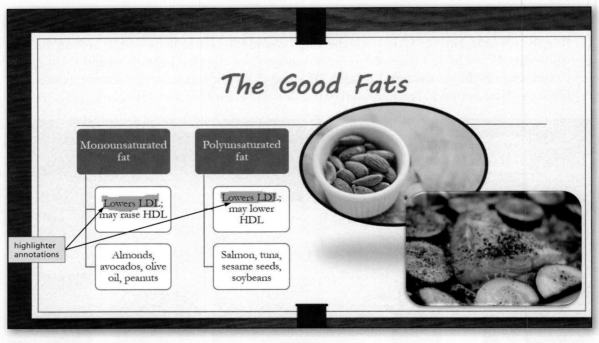

(c) **Slide 3**

Figure 5–84

14. Submit the document in the format specified by your instructor.

15. ✳ You reused one slide from another presentation. How did combining the slides from the two files help make the presentation more effective for the store manager?

Lab 2: **Reviewing and Accepting Comments in a Protected Presentation, Merging Presentations, Using Screen Clipping, and Packaging the Presentation for Storage on a Compact Disc**

Note: To complete this assignment, you will be required to use the Data Files. Please contact your instructor for information about accessing the required files.

Problem: Backpackers of all ages and abilities explore the world's exceptional wilderness. They travel on their own, with experienced guides, or with friends and family. Your local sporting goods store is forming a hiking club, and the owner has asked you to help generate interest in the sport. You develop four slides and then ask the owner to review the content. Use her input to create the presentation shown in Figure 5–85. In addition, use the Package for CD feature to distribute the presentation to potential backpacking club members.

Perform the following tasks:

1. Run PowerPoint. Open the presentation called Lab 5–2 Backpacking, which is located in the Data Files. The password is Backpacking.

2. Merge the owner's revised file, Lab 5–2 Backpacking2, located in the Data Files. Accept the theme presentation change so that the transition is added to all slides. Review all of her comments on all four slides. Preview the slides and then print the slides and the comments.

3. On Slide 1 (Figure 5–85a), accept all changes except for the subtitle font color modification.

4. On Slide 2 (Figure 5–85b), accept all the changes.

5. On Slide 3 (Figure 5–85c), accept all the changes.

6. On Slide 4 (Figure 5–85d), accept all changes except for the Text Placeholder 20: National Park Destinations.

7. Search the Internet for National Park Service backpacking guidelines. Insert a screenshot of one of these webpages on Slide 4. You may need to reduce the size of the screenshot on your slide.

8. On Slide 1, enhance the photo by applying the Bevel Perspective Left, White Picture style (in last row).

9. On Slide 4, enhance the photo by applying the Moderate Frame, Black Picture style (in second row).

10. Inspect the document and then remove all document properties and personal information.

11. If requested by your instructor, enter the name of the last TV program you watched as the fourth subtitle paragraph on Slide 1.

12. End the review and hide markup.

13. Save the presentation using the file name, Lab 5–2 Backpacking Basics.

14. Mark the presentation as final.

15. Save the presentation using the Package for CD feature. Name the CD Lab 5–2 Trail Blazers. Submit the revised document and the CD in the format specified by your instructor.

16. ✻ Why would you accept the reviewer's granite texture to the title font on Slide 1? How did converting the bulleted list on Slide 2 to a SmartArt graphic improve the presentation?

Continued >

In the Labs *continued*

(a) Slide 1

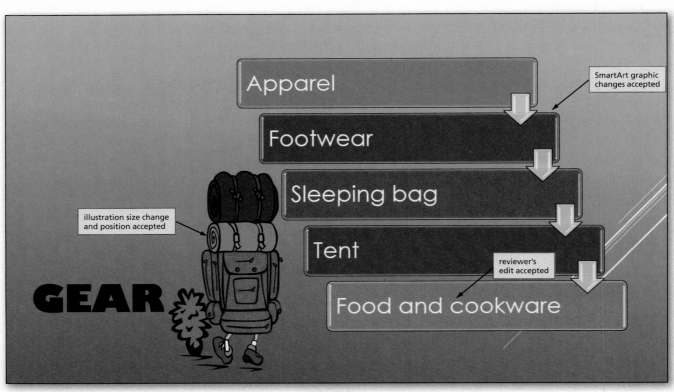

(b) Slide 2
Figure 5–85 (Continued)

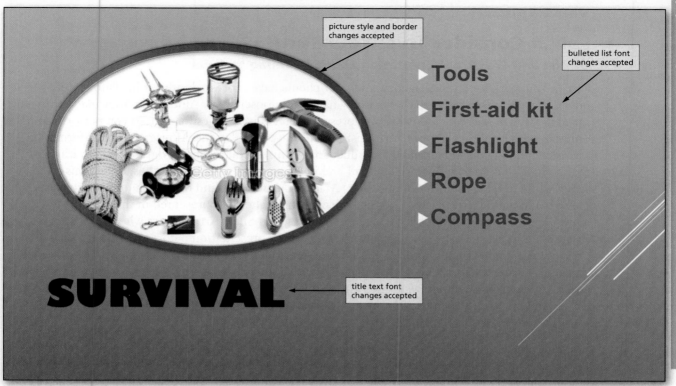

(c) Slide 3

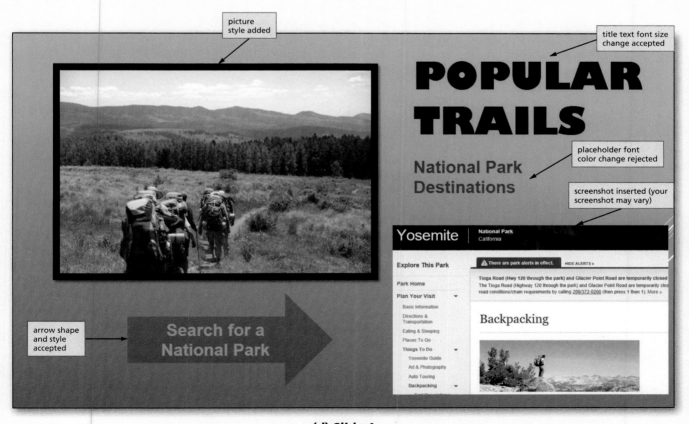

(d) Slide 4

Figure 5–85

Continued >

In the Labs *continued*

Lab 3: **Consider This: Your Turn**

Design and Create a Presentation about Traveling to Cuba

Part 1: You work for a travel agency, and your clients have expressed interest in visiting Cuba now that travel restrictions to that country have been loosened for Americans. Your manager has asked if you would create a PowerPoint presentation about this destination, so you perform some online research to learn about Cuban history and travel regulations. After gathering information, you recommend your travel agency conduct an organized educational program with an itinerary that includes lectures on Spanish colonial architecture, tours to artists' studios, excursions to sandy white beaches and the rolling Sierra Maestra Mountains, and brief community projects in Havana and Santiago de Cuba. Use the concepts and techniques presented in this module to create a presentation. Select a suitable theme, use WordArt and SmartArt graphics where appropriate, insert comments, and ask your manager to review your presentation before you make it final. The presentation could contain photos, illustrations, and videos. The Data Files contains illustrations and a photo called Cuba Flag, Cuba Coat of Arms, Cuba Provinces, and Cuba Coffee Cup. Review and revise your presentation as needed and then save the file using the file name, Lab 5–3 Cuba Travel. Submit your assignment in the format specified by your instructor.

Part 2: ✳ You made several decisions while creating the presentation in this assignment: where to place text, how to format the text (such as font and font size), which graphical image(s) to use, which styles and effects to apply, where to position the graphical images, and which shapes to use to add interest to the presentation. What was the rationale behind each of these decisions? When you reviewed the document, what further revisions did you make and why? Where would you recommend showing this slide show?

6 Navigating Presentations Using Hyperlinks and Action Buttons

Objectives

You will have mastered the material in this module when you can:

- Create a presentation from a Microsoft Word outline
- Add hyperlinks to slides and objects
- Hyperlink to other Microsoft Office documents
- Add action buttons and action settings
- Display guides to position slide elements
- Align placeholder text
- Create columns in a placeholder
- Change paragraph line spacing
- Format bullet size and color
- Change bullet characters to pictures and numbers
- Hide slides

BTW
Developing Outlines
A formal outline can help you arrange slide content in multiple levels of major and supporting details. Before you can create this outline, however, you may attempt to develop your ideas by using a scratch outline, which is a rough sketch of the possible major points you would like to showcase and the order in which they might appear.

Introduction

Many writers begin composing reports and documents by creating an outline. Others review their papers for consistency by saving the document with a new file name, removing all text except the topic headings, and then saving the file again. An outline created in Microsoft Word or another word-processing program works well as a shell for a PowerPoint presentation. Instead of typing text in PowerPoint, as you did in previous projects, you can import this outline, add visual elements such as clip art, photos, and graphical bullets, and ultimately create an impressive slide show. When delivering the presentation, you can navigate forward and backward through the slides using hyperlinks and action buttons to emphasize particular points, to review material, or to address audience concerns.

Project — Presentation with Action Buttons, Hyperlinks, and Formatted Bullet Characters

Speakers may elect to begin creating their presentations with an outline (Figure 6–1a) and then add formatted bullets and columns. When presenting these slides during a speaking engagement, they can run their PowerPoint slides nonsequentially depending

BTW
Defining Outline Levels
Imported outlines can have a maximum of nine outline levels, whereas PowerPoint outlines are limited to six levels (one for the title text and five for body paragraph text.) When you import an outline, all text in outline levels six through nine is treated as a fifth-level paragraph.

upon the audience's needs and comprehension. Each of the three pictures on the Conquer Your Clutter title slide (Figure 6–1b) branches, or hyperlinks, to another slide in the presentation. Action buttons and hyperlinks on Slides 2, 3, and 4 (Figures 6–1c through 6–1e) allow the presenter to jump to Slide 5 (Figure 6–1f), slides in another presentation (Figures 6–1g and 6–1h), or a Microsoft Word document (Figure 6–1i). The four resources on Slide 5 are hyperlinks that, when clicked during a presentation, display webpages of organizations that accept donations of household goods. The slides in the presentation have a variety of embellishments, including a two-column list on Slide 4 that provides tips on organizing a kitchen, formatted graphical bullets on Slides 2 and 5 of a sad face and a question mark, and a numbered list on Slide 3.

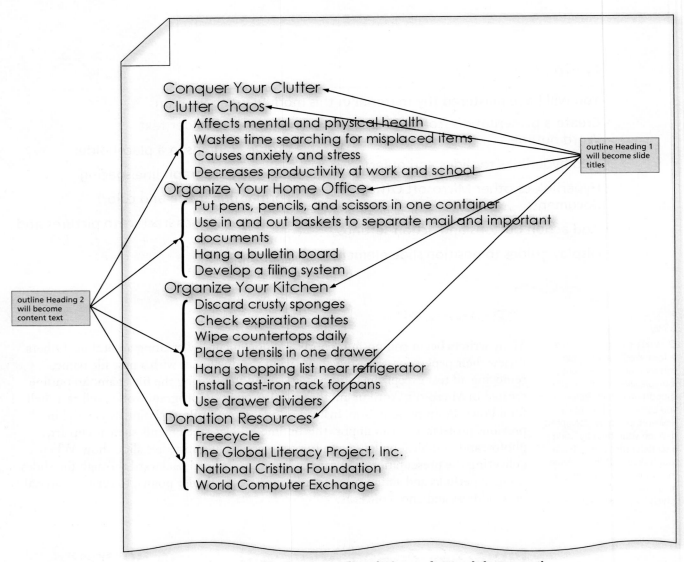

(a) Clutter Outline (Microsoft Word document)

Figure 6–1 (Continued)

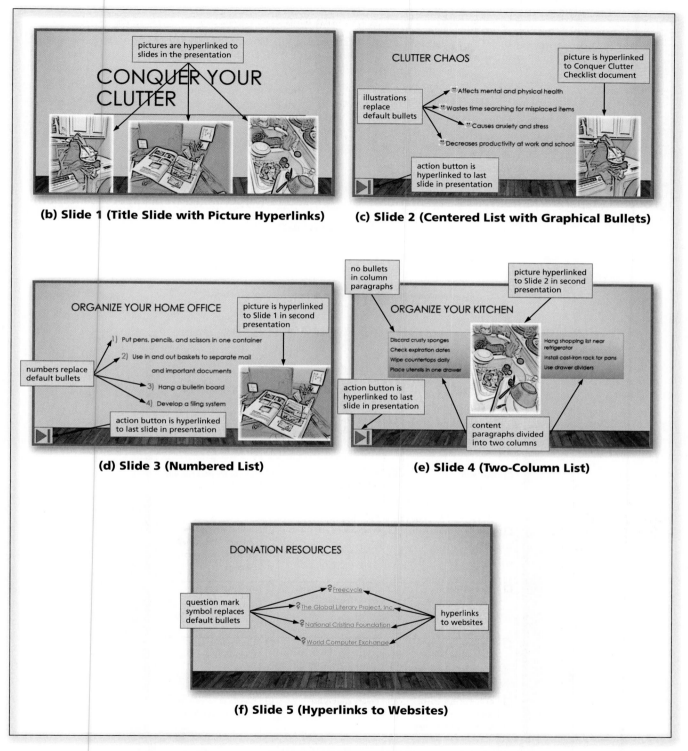

(b) Slide 1 (Title Slide with Picture Hyperlinks)

(c) Slide 2 (Centered List with Graphical Bullets)

(d) Slide 3 (Numbered List)

(e) Slide 4 (Two-Column List)

(f) Slide 5 (Hyperlinks to Websites)

Figure 6–1 (Continued)

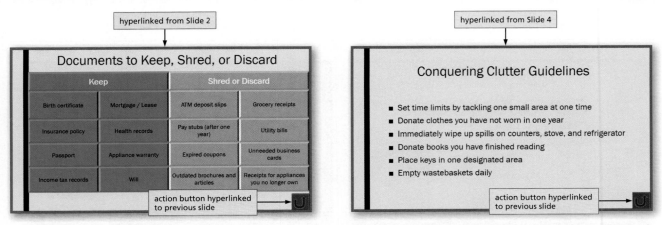

(g) Slide 1 (Hyperlinked from First Presentation)   **(h) Slide 2 (Hyperlinked from First Presentation)**

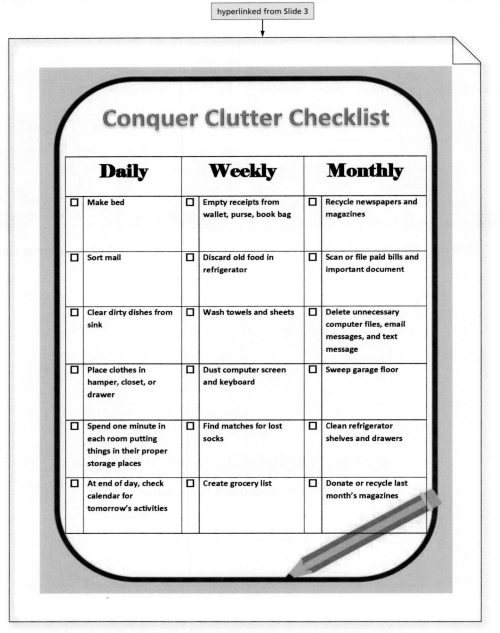

(i) Conquer Clutter Checklist (Microsoft Word document)

Figure 6–1

In this module, you will learn how to create the slides shown in Figure 6–1. The following roadmap identifies general activities you will perform as you progress through this module:

1. OPEN a Microsoft Word OUTLINE.
2. ADD PICTURE and TEXT HYPERLINKS.
3. ADD ACTION BUTTONS and HYPERLINKS.
4. POSITION PICTURES in content placeholders.
5. ALIGN PLACEHOLDER TEXT.
6. CONVERT and FORMAT BULLETS.

Creating a Presentation from a Microsoft Word Outline

An outline created in Microsoft Word or another word-processing program works well as a shell for a PowerPoint presentation. Instead of typing text in PowerPoint, you can import this outline, add visual elements such as pictures and graphical bullets, and ultimately create an impressive slide show.

In the following pages, you will follow these general steps to create a presentation from a Microsoft Word outline:

1. Add hyperlinks to pictures and paragraphs.
2. Insert action buttons and then link them to other slides and files.
3. Align pictures and text.
4. Create columns.
5. Change and format bullet characters.

Converting Documents for Use in PowerPoint

PowerPoint can produce slides based on an outline created in Microsoft Word, another word-processing program, or a webpage if the text was saved in a format that PowerPoint can recognize. Microsoft Word 2016, 2013, 2010, and 2007 files use the **.docx** file extension in their file names. Text originating in other word-processing programs for later use with PowerPoint should be saved in Rich Text Format (.rtf) or plain text (.txt). Webpage documents that use an HTML extension (.htm or .html) also can be imported.

PowerPoint automatically opens Microsoft Office files, and many other types of files, in the PowerPoint format. The **Rich Text Format (.rtf)** file type is used to transfer formatted documents between applications, even if the programs are running on different platforms, such as Windows and Mac OS. When you insert a Word or Rich Text Format document into a presentation, PowerPoint creates an outline structure based on heading styles in the document. A Heading 1 in a source document becomes a slide title in PowerPoint, a Heading 2 becomes the first level of content text on the slide, a Heading 3 becomes the second level of text on the slide, and so on.

If the original document contains no heading styles, PowerPoint creates an outline based on paragraphs. For example, in a .docx or .rtf file, for several lines of text styled as Normal and broken into paragraphs, PowerPoint turns each paragraph into a slide title.

BTW
The Ribbon and Screen Resolution
PowerPoint may change how the groups and buttons within the groups appear on the ribbon, depending on the computer or mobile device's screen resolution. Thus, your ribbon may look different from the ones in this book if you are using a screen resolution other than 1366 × 768.

To Open a Microsoft Word Outline as a Presentation

Why? *Instead of typing text for each of the five PowerPoint slides, you can open a Microsoft Word outline and have PowerPoint create the slides automatically.* The text for the Conquer Your Clutter presentation is contained in a Word file that is saved in the Rich Text Format (.rtf). The following steps open this Microsoft Word outline located in the Data Files as a presentation in PowerPoint.

- Run PowerPoint. If necessary, maximize the PowerPoint window.

- Apply the Blank Presentation theme.

- Open the Backstage view, display the Open dialog box, and then navigate to the Data Files so that you can open the Clutter Outline file in that location.

- Click the File Type arrow to display the File Type list (Figure 6–2).

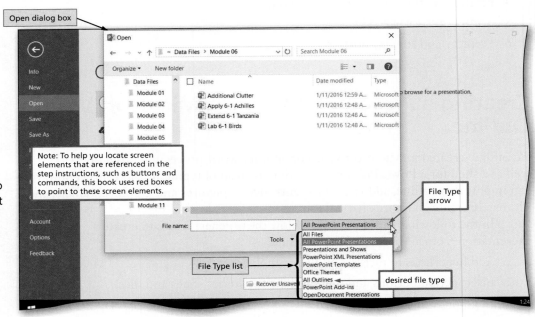

Figure 6–2

❷

- Click All Outlines to select this file type.

- Click Clutter Outline to select the file (Figure 6–3).

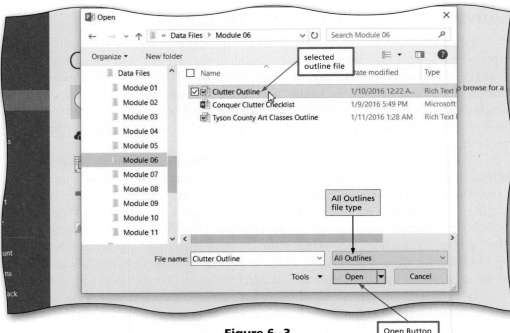

Figure 6–3

3

- Click the Open button to create the five slides in your presentation (Figure 6–4).

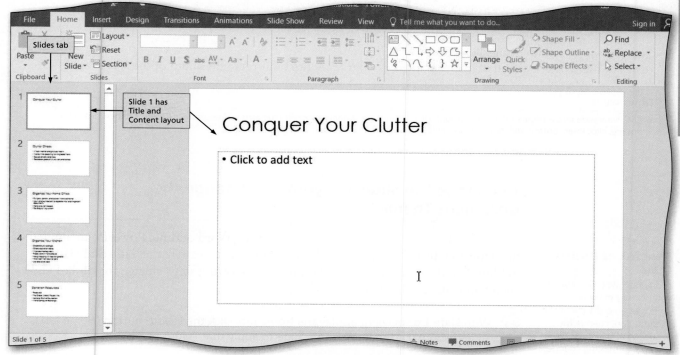

Figure 6–4

4

- Display the View tab and then click the Outline View button (View tab | Presentation Views group) to view the outline in the Slides tab (Figure 6–5).

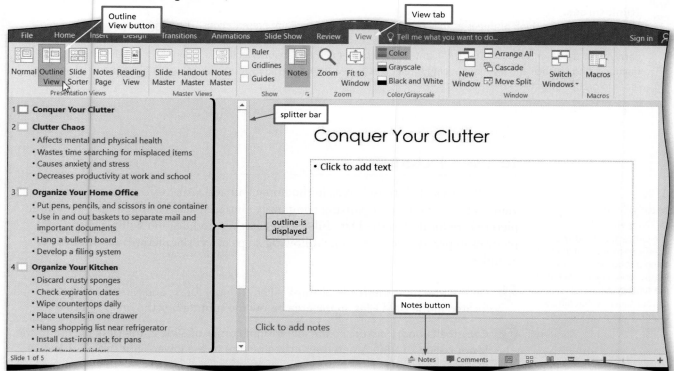

Figure 6–5

Q&A

Do I need to see the text as an outline in the Slides tab now?

No, but sometimes it is helpful to view the content of your presentation in this view before looking at individual slides.

Do I need to change to Normal view to navigate between slides?

No, you can click the slide number in Outline view to navigate to slides.

Can I change the width of the Slides tab?

Yes. Click the splitter bar and drag it to the left or right to reduce or increase the width of the Slides tab.

Other Ways

1. Click New Slide arrow (Home tab | Slides group), click Slides from Outline, click File Type arrow, if necessary click All Outlines, click desired outline, click Insert button, delete first blank slide

---

To Change the Slide 1 Layout and Change the Document Theme

BTW

Benefits of Outline View

Work in Outline view when you want to make global edits, get an overview of the presentation, change the sequence of bullets or slides, or apply formatting changes.

When you created the new slides from the Word outline, PowerPoint applied the Title and Text slide layout to all slides. You want to apply the Title Slide layout to Slide 1 to introduce the presentation. The following steps change the Slide 1 slide layout and change the theme to Gallery.

1 With Slide 1 displaying, display the Home tab, click the Layout button (Home tab | Slides group), and then click Title Slide to apply that layout to Slide 1.

2 Apply the Gallery document theme (shown in Figure 6–6).

3 If necessary, click the Notes button on the status bar to close the Notes pane.

CONSIDER THIS

Think threes.

Speechwriters often think of threes as they plan their talks and PowerPoint presentations. The number three is considered a symbol of balance, as in an equilateral triangle that has three 60-degree angles, the three meals we eat daily, or the three parts of our day — morning, noon, and night. A speech generally has an introduction, a body, and a conclusion. Audience members find balance and harmony seeing three objects on a slide, so whenever possible, plan visual components on your slides in groups of three.

To Insert Pictures

BTW

Touch Screen Differences

The Office and Windows interfaces may vary if you are using a touch screen. For this reason, you might notice that the function or appearance of your touch screen differs slightly from this module's presentation.

Pictures of cluttered areas in the home will add visual interest and cue the viewers to the topic of organizing commonly cluttered areas of the home. The three pictures are located in the Data Files. Later in this module, you will position the pictures in precise locations. The following steps insert the pictures on Slides 1, 2, 3, and 4.

1 On the title slide, insert the pictures called Laundry, Desk, and Kitchen, which are located in the Data Files, in the area below the subtitle box shown in Figure 6–6.

2 Copy the Laundry picture to the lower-right corner of Slide 2, the Desk picture to the lower-center of Slide 3, and the Kitchen picture to the lower-right corner of Slide 4.

3 Save the presentation using Conquer Your Clutter as the file name.

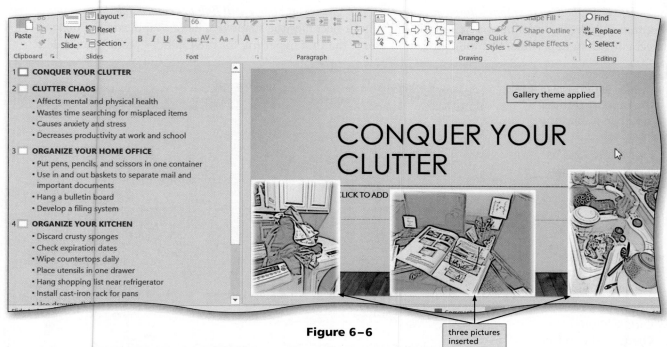

Gallery theme applied

CONQUER YOUR CLUTTER

CLICK TO ADD

Figure 6–6

three pictures inserted

Choose outstanding hyperlink images or text.

Good speakers are aware of their audiences and know their speech material well. They have rehearsed their presentations and know where the hypertext is displayed on the slides. During a presentation, however, they sometimes need to divert from their planned material. Audience members may interrupt with questions, the room may not have optimal acoustics or lighting, or the timing may be short or long. It is helpful, therefore, to make the slide hyperlinks as large and noticeable to speakers as possible. The presenters can glance at the slide and receive a visual cue that it contains a hyperlink. They then can decide whether to click the hyperlink to display a webpage.

Adding Hyperlinks and Action Buttons

Speakers sometimes skip from one slide to another in a presentation in response to audience needs or timing issues. In addition, if Internet access is available, they may desire to display a webpage during a slide show to add depth to the presented material and to enhance the overall message. When presenting the Conquer Your Clutter slide show and discussing the information on Slides 1, 2, 3, or 4, a speaker might want to skip to the last slide in the presentation and then access a website for a specific group that accepts donated technology, books, clothes, and other household items. Or the presenter may be discussing information on Slide 5 and want to display Slide 1 to begin discussing a new topic.

One method of jumping nonsequentially to slides is by clicking a hyperlink or an action button on a slide. A **hyperlink**, also called a **link**, connects one slide to a webpage, another slide, a custom show consisting of specific slides in a presentation, an email address, or a file. A hyperlink can be any element of a slide. This includes a single letter, a word, a paragraph, or any graphical image such as a picture, shape, or graph.

BTW
Customizing ScreenTips
You can create a custom ScreenTip that displays when you hover your mouse over a hyperlink. Click the ScreenTip button (Insert Hyperlink dialog box), type the desired ScreenTip text (Set Hyperlink ScreenTip dialog box), and then click the OK button.

To Add a Hyperlink to a Picture

Why? *In the Conquer Your Clutter presentation, each picture on Slide 1 will link to another slide in the same presentation.* When you point to a hyperlink, the pointer becomes the shape of a hand to indicate the text or object contains a hyperlink. The following steps create the first hyperlink for the Laundry picture on Slide 1.

1

- Display Slide 1, select the Laundry picture, and then display the Insert tab.

- Click the Hyperlink button (Insert tab | Links group) to display the Insert Hyperlink dialog box.

- If necessary, click the 'Place in This Document' button in the Link to area.

- Click '2. Clutter Chaos' in the 'Select a place in this document' area (Insert Hyperlink dialog box) to select and display a preview of this slide (Figure 6–7).

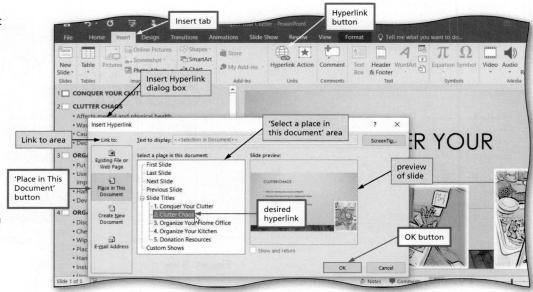

Figure 6–7

Q&A Could I also have selected the Next Slide link in the 'Select a place in this document' area?
Yes. Either action would create the hyperlink to Slide 2.

2

- Click the OK button (Insert Hyperlink dialog box) to insert the hyperlink.

Q&A I clicked the Laundry picture, but Slide 2 did not display. Why?
Hyperlinks are active only when you run the presentation or are in Reading view, not when you are creating it in Normal or Slide Sorter view.

Other Ways

1. Right-click text or object, click Hyperlink, select slide, click OK button   2. Select text or object, press CTRL+K, select slide, press ENTER

To Add Hyperlinks to the Remaining Slide 1 Pictures

The hyperlink for the Laundry picture is complete. The next task is to create the hyperlinks for the other two pictures on Slide 1.

1 On Slide 1, click the Desk picture.

2 Click the Hyperlink button, if necessary click 'Place in This Document', and then click '3. Organize Your Home Office' to select this slide as the hyperlink. Click the OK button.

3 Click the Kitchen picture, click the Hyperlink button, and then click '4. Organize Your Kitchen'. Click the OK button.

To Add a Hyperlink to a Paragraph

If you are connected to the Internet when you run the presentation, you can click each hyperlinked paragraph, and your browser will open a new window and display the corresponding webpage for each hyperlink. By default, hyperlinked text is displayed with an underline and in a color that is part of the color scheme. The following steps create a hyperlink for the first paragraph on Slide 5. *Why? Each second-level paragraph will be a hyperlink to webpage for an organization that accepts donated household and technology products.*

- Display Slide 5 and then select the second-level paragraph that appears first, Freecycle, to select the text.

- Display the Insert Hyperlink dialog box and then click the 'Existing File or Web Page' button in the Link to area (Figure 6–8).

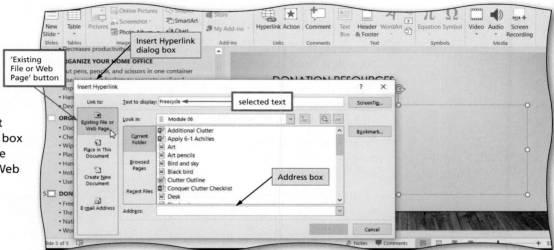

Figure 6–8

- If necessary, delete the text in the Address text box and then type **www .freecycle.org** in the Address box (Figure 6–9).

Q&A | Why does http:// appear before the address I typed?
PowerPoint automatically adds this protocol identifier before web addresses.

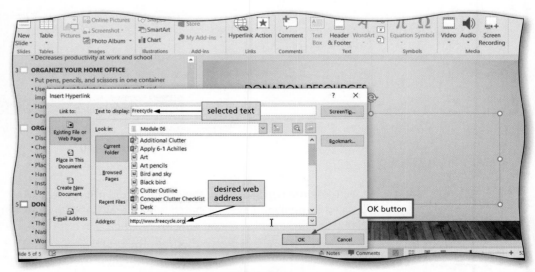

Figure 6–9

- Click the OK button to insert the hyperlink.

Q&A | Why is this paragraph now underlined and displaying a new font color?
The default style for hyperlinks is underlined text. The Gallery built-in theme hyperlink color is red, so PowerPoint formatted the paragraph to that color automatically.

Other Ways

1. Right-click selected text, click Hyperlink, click 'Existing File or Web Page', type address, click OK button

2. Select text, press CTRL+K, click 'Existing File or Web Page', type address, press ENTER key

To Add Hyperlinks to the Remaining Slide 5 Paragraphs

The hyperlink for the second-level paragraph that appears first is complete. The next task is to create the hyperlinks for the other second-level paragraphs on Slide 5.

1 Select The Global Literary Project, Inc., which is the second-level paragraph that appears second.

2 Display the Insert Hyperlink dialog box and then type `www.glpinc.org` in the Address box. Click the OK button.

3 Select the third paragraph, National Cristina Foundation, display the Insert Hyperlink dialog box, type `www.cristina.org` in the Address box, and then click the OK button.

4 Select the fourth paragraph, World Computer Exchange, display the Insert Hyperlink dialog box, type `www.worldcomputerexchange.org` in the Address box, and then click the OK button (Figure 6–10).

If requested by your instructor, add a fifth bulleted paragraph with the city or county in which you were born.

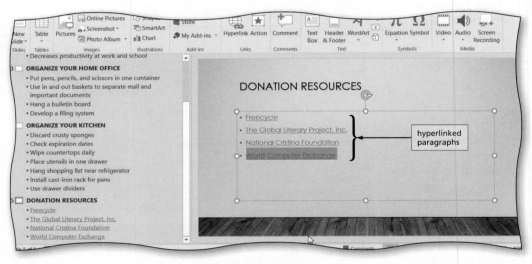

Figure 6–10

Q&A I clicked the hyperlink, but the webpage did not display. Why?
As with the hyperlinks associated with the pictures on Slide 1, hyperlinks associated with text are active only in Reading view or when you run the presentation.

Action Buttons

PowerPoint provides 12 built-in action buttons. An **action button** is a particular type of hyperlink that has a built-in function. Each action button performs a specific task, such as displaying the next slide, providing help, giving information, or playing a sound. In addition, the action button can activate a hyperlink that allows users to jump to a specific slide in the presentation. The picture on the action button indicates the type of function it performs. For example, the button with the house icon represents the home slide, or Slide 1. To achieve a personalized look, you can customize an action button with a photograph, piece of clip art, logo, text, or any graphic you desire. Table 6–1 describes each of the built-in action buttons.

Button Name	Image	Description
Table 6–1 Built-In Action Buttons		
Back or Previous	◁	Returns to the previous slide displayed in the same presentation.
Forward or Next	▷	Jumps to the next slide in the presentation.
Beginning	◁	Jumps to Slide 1. This button performs the same function as the Home button.
End	▷	Jumps to the last slide in the presentation.
Home	🏠	Jumps to Slide 1. This button performs the same function as the Beginning button.
Information	ⓘ	Does not have any predefined function. Use it to direct a user to a slide with details or facts.
Return	↩	Returns to the previous slide displayed in any presentation. For example, you can place it on a hidden slide or on a slide in a custom slide show and then return to the previous slide.
Movie	🎬	Does not have any predefined function. You generally would use this button to jump to a slide with an inserted video clip.
Document	🗎	Opens a program other than PowerPoint. For example, you can open Microsoft Word or Microsoft Excel and display a page or worksheet.
Sound	🔊	Does not have any predefined function. You generally would use this button to jump to a slide with an inserted audio clip.
Help	❓	Does not have any predefined function. Use it to direct a user to a slide with instructions or contact information.
Custom	☐	Does not have any predefined function. You can add a clip, picture, graphic, or text and then specify a unique purpose.

Customize action buttons for a unique look.

PowerPoint's built-in action buttons have icons that give the presenter an indication of their function. Designers frequently customize these buttons with images related to the presentation. For example, in a grocery store presentation, the action buttons may have images of a coupon, dollar sign, and question mark to indicate links to in-store coupons, sale items, and the customer service counter. Be creative when you develop your own presentations and attempt to develop buttons that have specific meanings for your intended audience.

CONSIDER THIS

To Insert an Action Button

1 OPEN OUTLINE | 2 ADD PICTURE & TEXT HYPERLINKS | **3 ADD ACTION BUTTONS & HYPERLINKS**
4 POSITION PICTURES | 5 ALIGN PLACEHOLDER TEXT | 6 CONVERT & FORMAT BULLETS

In the Conquer Your Clutter slide show, the action buttons on Slides 2, 3, and 4 hyperlink to the last slide, Slide 5. You will insert and format the action button shape on Slide 2 and copy it to Slides 3 and 4, and then create a link to Slide 5. *Why? You will be able to display Slide 5 at any point in the presentation by clicking the action button.* When you click the action button, a sound will play. This sound will vary depending upon which slide is displayed. The following steps insert an action button on Slide 2 and link it to Slide 5.

- Display Slide 2 and then click the Shapes button (Insert tab | Illustrations group) to display the Shapes gallery.

- Scroll down and then point to the 'Action Button: End' shape in the Action Buttons area (fourth image) (Figure 6–11).

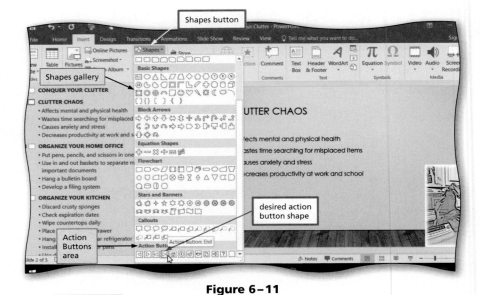

Figure 6–11

- Click the 'Action Button: End' shape.

- Click the lower-left corner of the slide to insert the action button and to display the Action Settings dialog box.

- If necessary, click the Mouse Click tab (Action Settings dialog box) (Figure 6–12).

Q&A | Why is Last Slide the default hyperlink setting?
The End shape establishes a hyperlink to the last slide in a presentation.

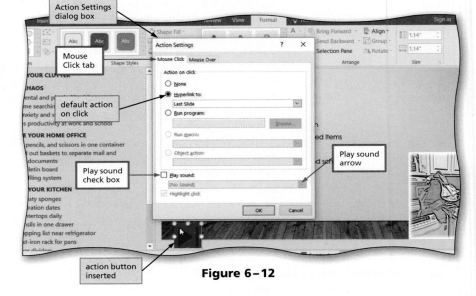

Figure 6–12

- Click the Play sound check box and then click the Play sound arrow to display the Play sound list (Figure 6–13).

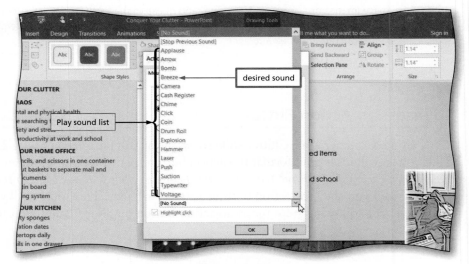

Figure 6–13

4

- Click Breeze in the Play sound list to select that sound (Figure 6–14).

Q&A I did not hear the sound when I selected it. Why not?
The Breeze sound will play when you run the slide show and click the action button.

5

- Click the OK button to apply the hyperlink setting and sound to the action button and to close the Action Settings dialog box.

Figure 6–14

To Size an Action Button

The action button size can be decreased to make it less obvious on the slide. The following step resizes the selected action button.

1 With the action button still selected and the Drawing Tools Format tab displaying, size the action button so that it is 0.8" x 0.9". If necessary, move the action button to the lower-left corner of the slide, as shown in Figure 6–15.

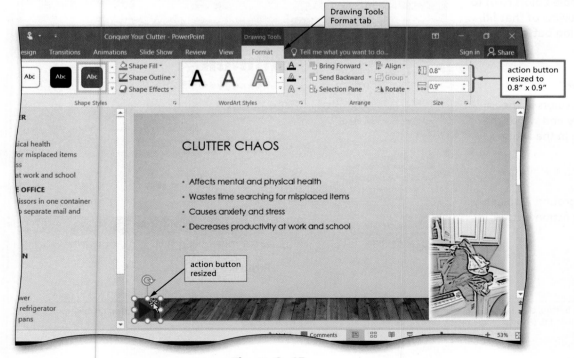

Figure 6–15

To Change an Action Button Fill Color

You can select a new action button fill color to coordinate with slide elements. The following steps change the fill color from Red to Tan. *Why? The action button's red interior color does not coordinate well with the wooden floor on the slide. A tan color will blend with the slide background and complement the dark brown floor.*

1

• With the action button still selected, click the Shape Fill arrow (Drawing Tools Format tab | Shape Styles gallery) to display the Shape Fill gallery (Figure 6–16).

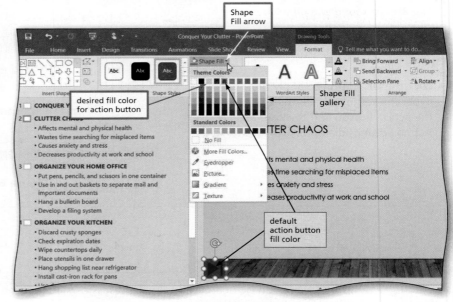

Figure 6–16

2

• Point to 'Tan, Background 2' (third color in first Theme Colors row) to display a live preview of that fill color on the action button (Figure 6–17).

 **Experiment**

• Point to various colors in the Shape Fill gallery and watch the fill color change in the action button.

3

• Click 'Tan, Background 2' to apply this color to the action button.

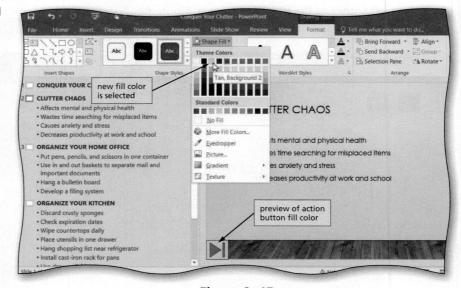

Figure 6–17

Other Ways

1. Right-click action button, click Format Shape on shortcut menu, click Fill on Shape Options tab (Format Shape pane), click Fill Color button, click desired color

2. Right-click action button, click Shape Fill button on mini toolbar, click desired color

To Copy an Action Button

The Slide 2 action button is formatted and positioned correctly. You can copy this shape to Slides 3 and 4. ***Why?*** *Copying the formatted shape saves time and ensures consistency.* The following steps copy the Slide 2 action button to the next two slides in the presentation.

- Right-click the action button on Slide 2 to display a shortcut menu (Figure 6–18).

Q&A Why does my shortcut menu have different commands?
Depending upon where you pressed or right-clicked, you might see a different shortcut menu. As long as this menu displays the Copy command, you can use it. If the Copy command is not visible, right-click the slide again to display another shortcut menu.

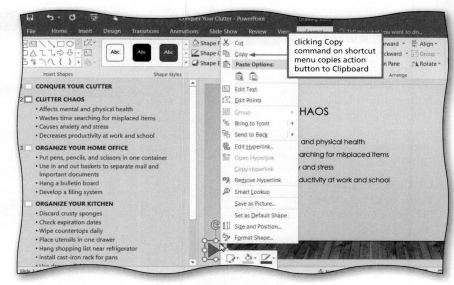

Figure 6–18

- Click Copy on the shortcut menu to copy the action button to the Clipboard.
- Display Slide 3 and then click the Paste button (Home tab | Clipboard group) to paste the action button in the lower-left corner of Slide 3 (Figure 6–19).

❸

- Display Slide 4 and then click the Paste button to paste the action button in the lower-left corner of Slide 4.

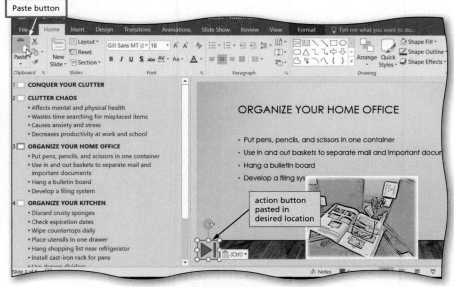

Figure 6–19

Other Ways

1. Copy button (Home tab | Clipboard group), Paste button (Home tab | Clipboard group)

2. CTRL+C to copy, CTRL+V to paste

To Edit an Action Button Setting

When you copied the action button, PowerPoint retained the settings to hyperlink to the last slide and to play the Breeze sound. The following steps edit the Slide 3 and Slide 4 hyperlink sound settings. *Why? For variety, you want to change the sounds that play for the Slide 3 and Slide 4 action buttons.*

1

- With the action button still selected on Slide 4, display the Insert tab and then click the Action button (Insert tab | Links group) shown in Figure 6–21 to display the Action Settings dialog box.

- Click the Play sound arrow to display the Play sound menu (Figure 6–20).

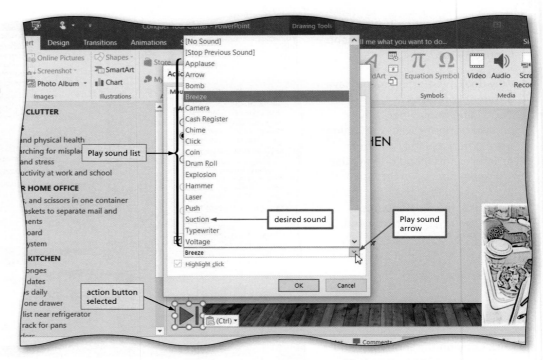

Figure 6–20

2

- Click Suction in the Play sound list to select the Suction sound to play when the action button is clicked (Figure 6–21).

- Click the OK button (Action Settings dialog box) to apply the new sound setting to the Slide 4 action button.

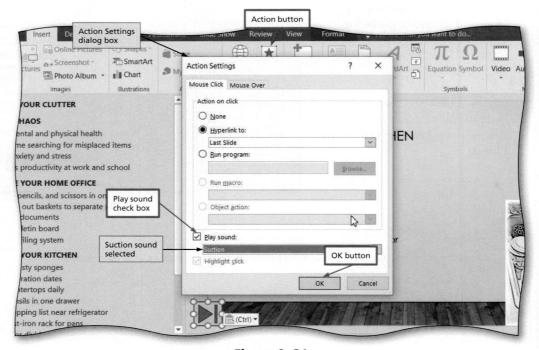

Figure 6–21

- Display Slide 3, select the action button, and then click the Action button (Insert tab | Links group) to display the Action Settings dialog box.

- Click the Play sound arrow to display the Play sound menu.

- Click Typewriter in the Play sound list (Figure 6–22).

- Click the OK button (Action Settings dialog box) to apply the new sound setting to the Slide 3 action button.

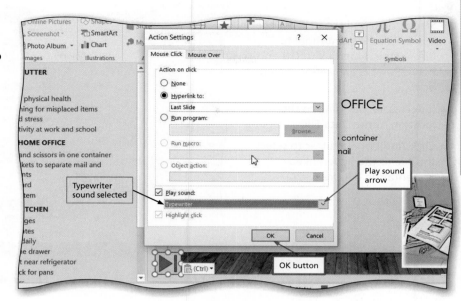

Figure 6–22

To Hyperlink to Another PowerPoint File

1 OPEN OUTLINE | 2 ADD PICTURE & TEXT HYPERLINKS | 3 ADD ACTION BUTTONS & HYPERLINKS
4 POSITION PICTURES | 5 ALIGN PLACEHOLDER TEXT | 6 CONVERT & FORMAT BULLETS

While hyperlinks are convenient tools to navigate through the current PowerPoint presentation or to webpages, they also allow you to open a second PowerPoint presentation and display a particular slide in that file. Much clutter can arise when paper files are piled on work surfaces and on the floor, so you desire to show your audience some useful information about retaining and disposing paper documents. The first slide in another presentation, Additional Clutter, has a table listing documents to keep and others to shred or discard. The following steps hyperlink the Desk picture on Slide 3 to the first slide in the second presentation. *Why? The hyperlink offers a convenient method of moving from one presentation to another. A speaker has the discretion to use the hyperlink depending upon the audience's interest in the topic and time considerations.*

- Display Slide 3 and then select the Desk picture.

- Display the Insert tab and then click the Action button (Insert tab | Links group) to display the Action Settings dialog box.

- Click Hyperlink to in the 'Action on click' area and then click the Hyperlink to arrow to display the Hyperlink to menu (Figure 6–23).

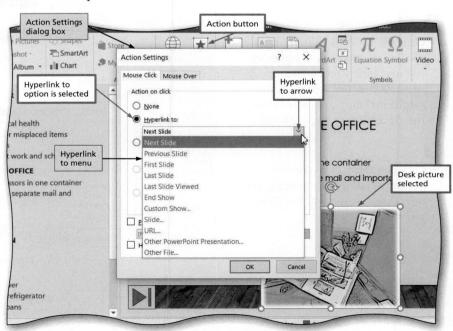

Figure 6–23

2

- Scroll down and then click 'Other PowerPoint Presentation' to display the Hyperlink to Other PowerPoint Presentation dialog box.

- If necessary, navigate to the location of the Data Files.

- Click Additional Clutter to select this file as the hyperlinked presentation (Figure 6–24).

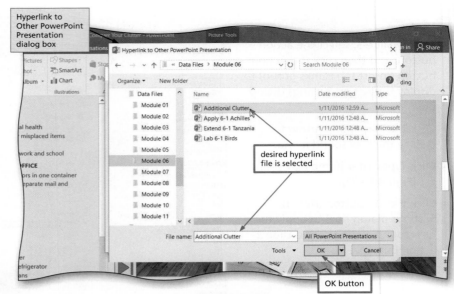

Figure 6–24

3

- Click the OK button to display the Hyperlink to Slide dialog box (Figure 6–25).

Q&A What are the two items listed in the Slide title area?
They are the title text of the two slides in the Additional Clutter presentation.

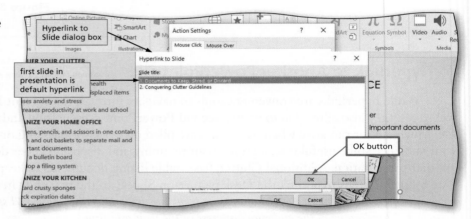

Figure 6–25

4

- Click the OK button (Hyperlink to Slide dialog box) to hyperlink the first slide (Documents to Keep, Shred, or Discard) in the Additional Clutter presentation to the Desk picture (Figure 6–26).

5

- Click the OK button (Action Settings dialog box) to apply the new action setting to the Slide 3 picture.

Figure 6–26

Other Ways

1. Select picture, click Hyperlink button (Insert menu | Links group), click 'Existing File or Web Page' (Link to: area), browse to and select desired file, click OK button

2. Right-click picture, click Hyperlink on shortcut menu, click 'Existing File or Web Page' (Link to: area), browse to and select desired file, click OK button

To Hyperlink to a Second Slide in Another PowerPoint File

Another slide in the Additional Clutter presentation gives specific tips on how to begin decluttering a home. This slide might be useful to display during a presentation when a speaker is discussing the information on Slide 4, which describes organizing a kitchen. At this point in the presentation, audience members may be eager to begin the process of organizing, so the techniques shown on this slide could provide a good starting point. If the speaker has time to discuss the material and the audience wants to know these tips, he could click the Kitchen picture on Slide 4 and then hyperlink to Slide 2 in the second presentation. The following steps hyperlink Slide 4 to the second slide in the Additional Clutter presentation.

1 Display Slide 4, select the Kitchen picture, and then click the Action button (Insert tab | Links group) to display the Action Settings dialog box.

2 Click Hyperlink to in the 'Action on click' area, click the Hyperlink to arrow, and then click 'Other PowerPoint Presentation' in the Hyperlink to menu.

3 Click Additional Clutter in the Hyperlink to Other PowerPoint Presentation dialog box to select this file as the hyperlinked presentation and then click the OK button.

4 Click '2. Conquering Clutter Guidelines' (Hyperlink to Slide dialog box) (Figure 6–27).

5 Click the OK button (Hyperlink to Slide dialog box) to hyperlink the second slide in the Additional Clutter presentation to the Kitchen picture.

6 Click the OK button (Action Settings dialog box) to apply the new action setting to the Slide 4 picture.

BTW

Verifying Hyperlinks
Always test your hyperlinks prior to giving a presentation. Web addresses change frequently, so if your hyperlinks are to websites, be certain your Internet connection is working, the websites are active, and that the content on these pages is appropriate for your viewers. If your hyperlinks direct PowerPoint to display specific slides and to open files, click the hyperlinks to verify your desired actions are followed and that the files exist.

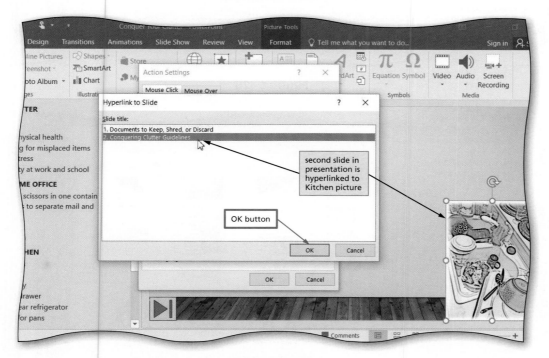

Figure 6–27

To Hyperlink to a Microsoft Word File

Slide 2 in your presentation provides information about problems that can arise from disorganization in the home. Professional organizers recommend keeping a list of reoccurring tasks that should be completed daily, weekly, and monthly. A convenient form for recording these details is located in the Data Files. The file, Conquer Clutter Checklist, was created using Microsoft Word, and it would be useful to display this document when discussing the information on Slide 2 of your presentation. *Why? The checklist can serve as a reminder of which organization tasks have been completed and which need to be done.* PowerPoint allows a speaker to hyperlink to other Microsoft Office documents in a similar manner as linking to another PowerPoint file. The following steps hyperlink the Laundry picture on Slide 2 to the Microsoft Word document with the file name, Conquer Clutter Checklist.

- Display Slide 2, select the Laundry picture, and then click the Action button (Insert tab | Links group) to display the Action Settings dialog box.

- Click Hyperlink to, click the Hyperlink to arrow to display the Hyperlink to menu, and then point to Other File at the end of the Hyperlink to list (Figure 6–28).

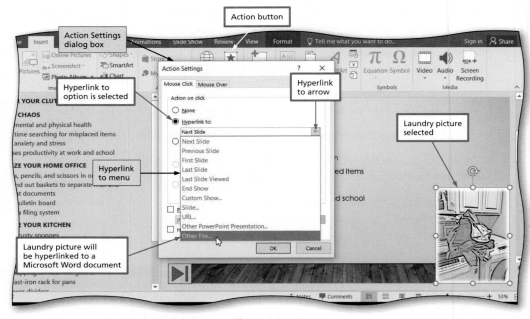

Figure 6–28

- Click Other File to display the Hyperlink to Other File dialog box, scroll down, and then click Conquer Clutter Checklist to select this file as the hyperlinked document (Figure 6–29).

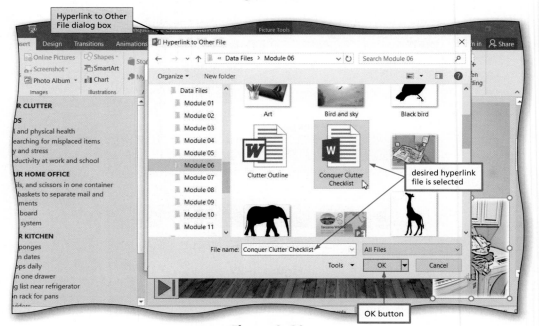

Figure 6–29

3

- Click the OK button (Hyperlink to Other File dialog box) to hyperlink this file to the Laundry picture action button (Figure 6–30).

4

- Click the OK button (Action Settings dialog box) to apply the new action setting to the Slide 2 picture.

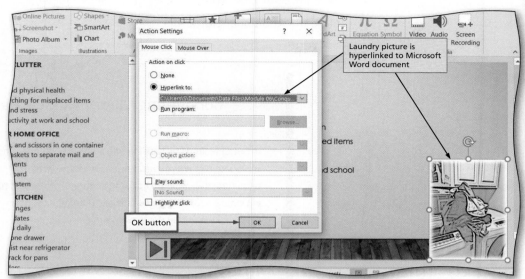

Figure 6–30

To Insert and Format Action Buttons on the Hyperlinked File

The pictures on Slide 3 and Slide 4 hyperlink to slides in the Additional Clutter file. While running the main presentation, if you click an action button or picture link that opens and then displays a slide from another presentation, you may need to review this slide and then return to the previous slide displayed in the first presentation. The Return action button performs this function. The following steps open the Additional Clutter file and then insert and format the Return action button on both slides.

1 In the Backstage view, click the Open command to display the Open pane, navigate to the location of the Data Files, click the File Type arrow to display the File Type list, and then click 'All PowerPoint Presentations' to select this file type.

2 Open the Additional Clutter file located on the Data Files.

3 With Slide 1 displaying, click the Shapes button (Insert tab | Illustrations group) and then scroll down and click the 'Action Button: Return' shape (seventh image).

4 Insert the action button in the lower-right corner of the slide.

5 When the Action Settings dialog box is displayed, select 'Hyperlink to Other PowerPoint Presentation' in the Hyperlink to area to hyperlink the action button to Slide 3 (Organize Your Home Office) in the Conquer Your Clutter presentation.

6 Size the action button so that it is 0.8" x 0.8" and, if necessary, move it to the lower-right corner of the slide.

7 Change the action button fill color to Purple (last color in Standard Colors row).

8 Copy the action button to the same location on Slide 2 (Figure 6–31). Display the Action Settings dialog box and then hyperlink this action button to Slide 4 (Organize Your Kitchen) in the Conquer Your Clutter presentation.

BTW
Showing a Range of Slides
If your presentation consists of many slides, you may want to show only a portion of them in your slide show. For example, if your 30-slide presentation is designed to accompany a 30-minute speech and you are given only 10 minutes to present, you may elect to display only the first 10 slides. Rather than have the show end abruptly after Slide 10, you can elect to show a range of slides. To specify this range, display the Slide Show tab, click the Set Up Slide Show button, and then specify the starting and ending slide numbers in the From and To boxes in the Show slides area (Set Up Show dialog box).

⑨ Save the Additional Clutter file using the same file name.

⑩ Close the Additional Clutter file.

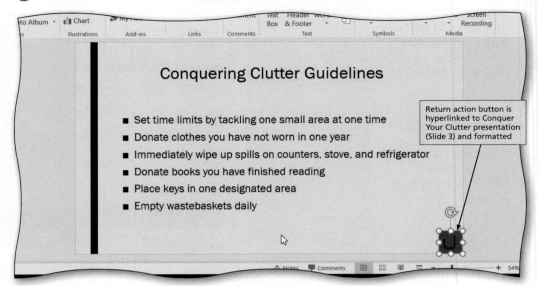

Figure 6–31

Break Point: If you wish to take a break, this is a good place to do so. Be sure to save the Conquer Your Clutter file again and then you can quit PowerPoint. To resume at a later time, start PowerPoint, open the file called Conquer Your Clutter, and continue following the steps from this location forward.

Positioning Slide Elements

BTW
Measurement System
The vertical and horizontal rulers display the units of measurement in inches by default. This measurement system is determined by the settings in Microsoft Windows. You can change the measurement system to centimeters by customizing the numbers format in the 'Clock, Language, and Region' area of the Control Panel. Click Region, click Additional Settings, and then choose the desired measurement system.

At times you may desire to arrange slide elements in precise locations. PowerPoint provides useful tools to help you position shapes and objects on slides. **Drawing guides** are two straight dotted lines, one horizontal and one vertical. When an object is close to a guide, its corner or its center (whichever is closer) **snaps**, or aligns precisely, on top of the guide. You can drag a guide to a new location to meet your alignment requirements. Another tool is the vertical or horizontal **ruler**, which can help you drag an object to a precise location on the slide. The center of a slide is 0.00 on both the vertical and the horizontal rulers.

Aligning and Distributing Objects

If you display multiple objects, PowerPoint can **align** them above and below each other (vertically) or side by side (horizontally). The objects, such as SmartArt graphics, clip art, shapes, boxes, and WordArt, can be aligned relative to the slide so that they display along the top, left, right, or bottom borders or in the center or middle of the slide. They also can be aligned relative to each other, meaning that you position either the first or last object in the desired location and then command PowerPoint to move the remaining objects in the series above, below, or beside it. Depending on the alignment option that you click, objects will move straight up, down, left, or right, and might cover an object already located on the slide. Table 6–2 describes alignment options.

Table 6–2 Alignment Options

Alignment	Action
Left	Aligns the edges of the objects to the left
Center	Aligns the objects vertically through the centers of the objects
Right	Aligns the edges of the objects to the right
Top	Aligns the top edges of the objects
Middle	Aligns the objects horizontally through the middles of the objects
Bottom	Aligns the bottom edges of the objects
to Slide	Aligns one object to the slide

One object remains stationary when you align objects relative to each other by their edges. For example, Align Left aligns the left edges of all selected objects with the left edge of the leftmost object. The leftmost object remains stationary, and the other objects are aligned relative to it. Objects aligned to a SmartArt graphic are aligned to the leftmost edge of the SmartArt graphic, not to the leftmost shape in the SmartArt graphic. Objects aligned relative to each other by their middles or centers are aligned along a horizontal or vertical line that represents the average of their original positions. All of the objects might move.

Smart Guides appear automatically when two or more shapes are in spatial alignment with each other, even if the shapes vary in size. To evenly space multiple objects horizontally or vertically, you **distribute** them. PowerPoint determines the total length between either the outermost edges of the first and last selected object or the edges of the entire slide. It then inserts equal spacing among the items in the series. You also can distribute spacing by using the Size and Position dialog box, but the Distribute command automates this task.

BTW
Displaying Slides
The slides in this presentation have important information about home organization. Your audience needs time to read and contemplate the advice you are providing in the content placeholders, so you must display the slides for a sufficient amount of time. Some public speaking experts recommend each slide in a presentation should display for at least one minute so that audience members can look at the material, focus on the speaker, and then refer to the slide again.

To Display Slide Thumbnails in the Slides Tab

The major slide elements are inserted on all slides, and you next will arrange these essential features. It is easier to move and align these elements when the main Slide pane is large. The following step changes the view from Outline view to Normal view.

1 Display the View tab and then click the Normal button (View tab | Presentation Views group) to display the slide thumbnails in the Slides tab.

2 If the Notes pane is displayed, click the Notes button on the status bar to close the Notes pane.

To Display the Drawing Guides

1 OPEN OUTLINE | 2 ADD PICTURE & TEXT HYPERLINKS | 3 ADD ACTION BUTTONS & HYPERLINKS
4 POSITION PICTURES | 5 ALIGN PLACEHOLDER TEXT | 6 CONVERT & FORMAT BULLETS

Why? *Guides help you align objects on slides.* Using a mouse, when you point to a guide and then press and hold the mouse button, PowerPoint displays a box containing the exact position of the guide on the slide in inches. An arrow is displayed below the guide position to indicate the vertical guide either left or right of center. An arrow also is displayed to the right of the guide position to indicate the horizontal guide either above or below center. The following step displays the guides.

● Display Slide 2 of the Conquer Your Clutter presentation and then click the Guides check box (View tab | Show group) to display the horizontal and vertical guides (Figure 6–32).

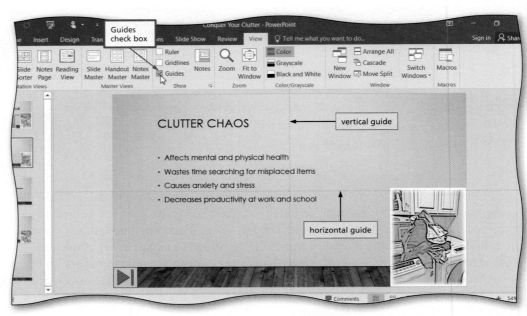

Figure 6–32

Other Ways

1. Right-click area of slide other than a placeholder or object, point to 'Grid and Guides' on shortcut menu, click Guides

2. Press ALT+F9 to toggle guides on/off

To Position a Picture Using Guides

1 OPEN OUTLINE | 2 ADD PICTURE & TEXT HYPERLINKS | 3 ADD ACTION BUTTONS & HYPERLINKS
4 POSITION PICTURES | 5 ALIGN PLACEHOLDER TEXT | 6 CONVERT & FORMAT BULLETS

The upper edge of the three pictures on Slides 2, 3, and 4 should be displayed in precisely the same location, as should the left edge of the pictures on Slides 2 and 4. *Why? They will appear static as you transition from one slide to the next during the slide show.* The following steps position the picture on Slide 2.

● Position the pointer on the horizontal guide in a blank area of the slide so that the pointer changes to a double-headed arrow and then drag the horizontal guide to 0.25 inches below the center. Do not release the mouse button (Figure 6–33).

◄ | Why does 0.25
Q&A | display when I hold down the mouse button?
The ScreenTip

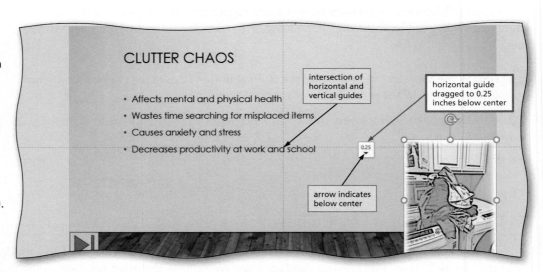

Figure 6–33

displays the horizontal guide's position. A 0.00 setting means that the guide is precisely in the middle of the slide and is not above or below the center, so a .25 setting indicates the guide is 1/4-inch below the center line.

2

- Release the mouse button to position the horizontal guide at 0.25, which is the intended location of the picture's top border.

- Position the pointer on the vertical guide in a blank area of the slide so that the pointer changes to a double-headed arrow and then drag the vertical guide to 2.50 inches right of the center to position the vertical guide.

- Drag the picture so the upper-left corner touches the intersection of the vertical and horizontal guides to position the picture in the desired location (Figure 6–34).

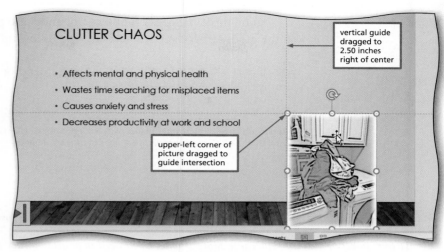

Figure 6–34

Q&A Can I add guides to help me align multiple objects?
Yes. Position the pointer over one guide and then press the CTRL key. When you drag your pointer, a second guide appears.

To Position the Slide 4 and Slide 3 Pictures

The pictures on Slide 4 and Slide 3 should be positioned in the same location as the Slide 2 picture. The guides will display in the same location as you display each slide, so you easily can align similar objects on multiple slides. The following steps position the pictures on Slide 4 and Slide 3.

1 Display Slide 4 and then drag the picture so the upper-left corner of the Kitchen picture touches the intersection of the guides.

2 Display Slide 3 and use the guides to position the Desk picture (Figure 6–35).

BTW
Drawing Guides and Touch Screens
If you are using a touch screen, you may not be able to change the position of the drawing guides. In addition, the measurements indicating the position of the guides are not displayed.

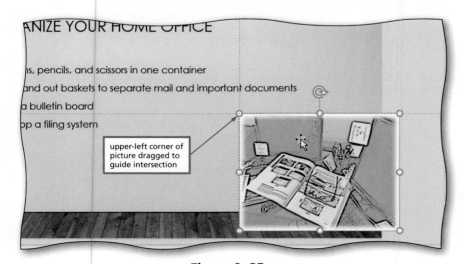

Figure 6–35

To Hide Guides

The three pictures on Slides 2, 3, and 4 are positioned in the desired locations, so the guides no longer are needed. The following step hides the guides.

1 If necessary, display the View tab and then click the Guides check box (View tab | Show group) to clear the check mark.

Other Ways

1. Right-click area of slide other than a placeholder or object, click Grid and Guides on shortcut menu, click Guides to turn off Guides
2. Press ALT+F9 to toggle guides on/off

To Display the Rulers

1 OPEN OUTLINE | 2 ADD PICTURE & TEXT HYPERLINKS | 3 ADD ACTION BUTTONS & HYPERLINKS
4 POSITION PICTURES | 5 ALIGN PLACEHOLDER TEXT | 6 CONVERT & FORMAT BULLETS

Why? *To begin aligning the three Slide 1 objects, you need to position either the left or the right object.* The vertical or horizontal **ruler** can help you drag an object to a precise location on the slide. The center of a slide is 0.00 on both the vertical and the horizontal rulers. The following step displays the rulers.

1

• If necessary, display the View tab and then click the Ruler check box (View tab | Show group) to display the vertical and horizontal rulers (Figure 6–36).

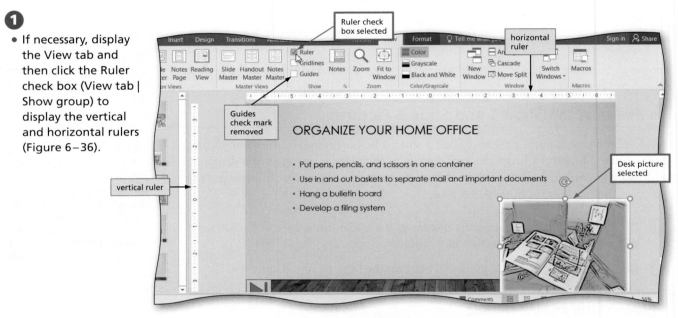

Figure 6–36

Other Ways

1. Right-click area of slide other than a placeholder or object, click Ruler
2. Press SHIFT+ALT+F9 to toggle ruler on/off

To Align Pictures

1 OPEN OUTLINE | 2 ADD PICTURE & TEXT HYPERLINKS | 3 ADD ACTION BUTTONS & HYPERLINKS
4 POSITION PICTURES | 5 ALIGN PLACEHOLDER TEXT | 6 CONVERT & FORMAT BULLETS

Why? *The three pictures on Slide 1 will look balanced if the bottom edges are aligned.* One method of creating this orderly appearance is by dragging the borders to a guide. Another method that is useful when you have multiple objects is to use one of PowerPoint's align commands. On Slide 1, you will position the far left picture of the Laundry and then align its bottom edge with those of the Desk and Kitchen pictures. The following steps align the Slide 1 pictures.

- Display Slide 1 and then position the pointer over the clothes pile in the Laundry picture.

- Drag the picture so that the center of the clothes pile is positioned approximately 5½ inches left of the center and approximately 2 inches below the center so that the bottom of the picture aligns with the bottom of the slide (Figure 6–37).

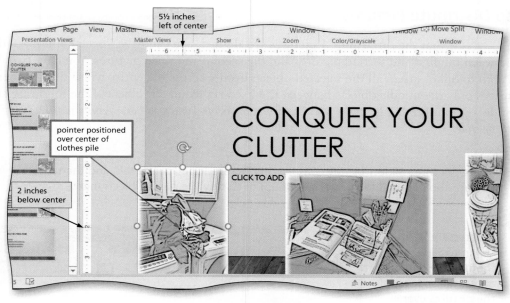

Figure 6–37

- Position the pointer over the pencils in the Desk picture.

- Drag the Desk picture so the pencils are positioned approximately 1 inch right of the center and approximately 1½ inches below the center so that the bottom of the picture aligns with the bottom of the slide and the Laundry picture (Figure 6–38).

Figure 6–38

- Position the pointer over the faucet in the Kitchen picture.

- Drag the Kitchen picture so the faucet is positioned approximately 5 inches right of the center and approximately 3/4 inch below the center bottom of the picture aligns with the bottom of the slide and the other pictures (Figure 6–39).

Figure 6–39

To Distribute Pictures

Now that the three Slide 1 pictures are aligned, you can have PowerPoint place the same amount of space between the first and second pictures and the second and third pictures. You have two distribution options: 'Align to Slide' spaces all the selected objects evenly across the entire width of the slide; 'Align Selected Objects' spaces only the middle objects between the fixed right and left objects. The following steps use the 'Align to Slide' option. *Why? This option will distribute the Slide 1 pictures horizontally to fill some of the space along the bottom of the slide.*

1
- Select the three Slide 1 pictures, display the Picture Tools Format tab, and then click the Align Objects button (Picture Tools Format tab | Arrange group) to display the Align Objects menu.

2
- If necessary, click 'Align to Slide' so that PowerPoint will adjust the spacing of the pictures evenly between the slide edges and then click the Align button to display the Align menu again (Figure 6–40).

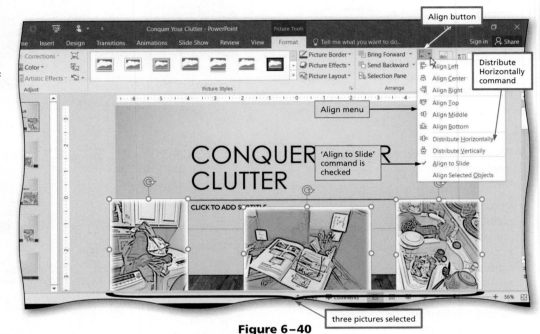

Figure 6–40

3
- Click Distribute Horizontally to adjust the spacing (Figure 6–41).

Figure 6–41

To Hide Rulers

The three pictures on Slide 1 are positioned in the desired locations, so the rulers no longer need to display. The following step hides the rulers.

1 Display the View tab and then click the Ruler check box (View tab | Show group) to remove the check mark.

Other Ways
1. Right-click area of slide other than a placeholder or object, click Ruler
2. Press SHIFT+ALT+F9 to toggle ruler on/off

Hiding a Slide

Slides 2, 3, and 4 present a variety of organizing information with hyperlinks. Depending on the audience's needs and the time constraints, you may decide not to display one or more of these slides. If need be, you can use the **Hide Slide** command to hide a slide from the audience during the normal running of a slide show. When you want to display the hidden slide, press the H key. No visible indicator displays to show that a hidden slide exists. You must be aware of the content of the presentation to know where the hidden slide is located.

When you run your presentation, the hidden slide does not display unless you press the H key when the slide preceding the hidden slide is displaying. For example, if you choose to hide Slide 4, then Slide 4 will not display unless you press the H key when Slide 3 displays in Slide Show view.

To Hide a Slide

1 OPEN OUTLINE | 2 ADD PICTURE & TEXT HYPERLINKS | 3 ADD ACTION BUTTONS & HYPERLINKS
4 POSITION PICTURES | 5 ALIGN PLACEHOLDER TEXT | 6 CONVERT & FORMAT BULLETS

Slide 4 discusses tips for organizing a kitchen. As the presenter, you decide whether to show Slide 4. *Why? If time permits, or if the audience requires information on this subject, you can display Slide 4.* When you hide a slide in Slide Sorter view, a slash appears through the slide number, which indicates the slide is hidden. The following steps hide Slide 4.

1

• Click the Slide Sorter view button on the status bar to display the slide thumbnails.

• Click Slide Show on the ribbon to display the Slide Show tab and then click the Slide 4 thumbnail to select it (Figure 6–42).

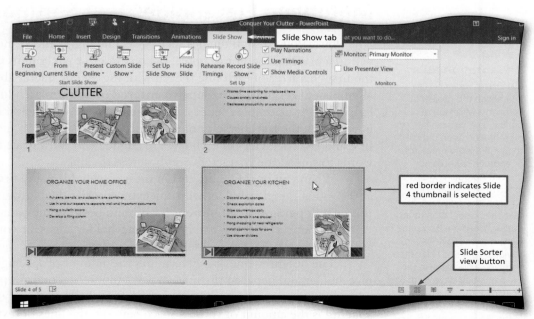

Figure 6–42

- Click the Hide Slide
  button (Slide Show
  tab | Set Up group)
  to hide Slide 4
  (Figure 6–43).

Q&A

How do I know that
Slide 4 is hidden?
The slide number has
a slash through it to
indicate Slide 4 is a
hidden slide.

What if I decide I no
longer want to hide
a slide?
Repeat Step 2. The
Hide Slide button is
a toggle; it either
hides or displays a
slide.

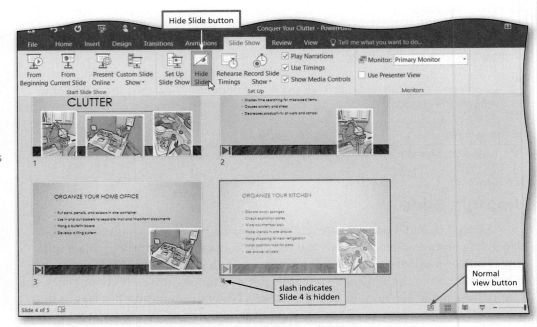

Figure 6–43

❸
- Click the Normal view button to display Slide 4.

Other Ways

1. Right-click desired slide in Slide Sorter view or Normal view on Slides tab, click Hide Slide on shortcut menu

---

Break Point: If you wish to take a break, this is a good place to do so. Be sure to save the Conquer Your Clutter file again and then you can quit PowerPoint. To resume at a later time, start PowerPoint, open the file called Conquer Your Clutter, and continue following the steps from this location forward.

Modifying Placeholder Text Settings

The PowerPoint design themes specify default alignment of and spacing for text within a placeholder. For example, the text in most paragraphs is **left-aligned**, so the first character of each line is even with the first character above or below it. Text alignment also can be horizontally **centered** to position each line evenly between the left and right placeholder edges; **right-aligned**, so that the last character of each line is even with the last character of each line above or below it; and **justified**, where the first and last characters of each line are aligned and extra space is inserted between words to spread the characters evenly across the line.

When you begin typing text in most placeholders, the first paragraph is aligned at the top of the placeholder with any extra space at the bottom. You can change this default **paragraph alignment** location to position the paragraph lines centered vertically between the top and bottom placeholder edges, or you can place the last line at the bottom of the placeholder so that any extra space is at the top.

The design theme also determines the amount of spacing around the sides of the placeholder and between the lines of text. An internal **margin** provides a cushion of space between text and the top, bottom, left, and right sides of the placeholder. **Line spacing** is the amount of vertical space between the lines of text in a paragraph, and **paragraph spacing** is the amount of space above and below a paragraph. PowerPoint adjusts the line spacing and paragraph spacing automatically to accommodate various font sizes within the placeholder.

Long lists of items can be divided into several **columns** to fill the placeholder width and maximize the slide space. Once you have created columns, you can adjust the amount of space between the columns to enhance readability.

To Center Placeholder Text

1 OPEN OUTLINE | 2 ADD PICTURE & TEXT HYPERLINKS | 3 ADD ACTION BUTTONS & HYPERLINKS
4 POSITION PICTURES | 5 ALIGN PLACEHOLDER TEXT | 6 CONVERT & FORMAT BULLETS

By default, all placeholder text in the Gallery document theme is left-aligned. You want the text to be centered, or placed with equal space horizontally between the left and right placeholder edges, on some slides. *Why? Changing the alignment adds variety to the slide deck.* The following steps center the text in the content placeholders on Slides 2, 3, and 5.

- Display Slide 2 and then select the four paragraphs in the content placeholder (Figure 6–44).

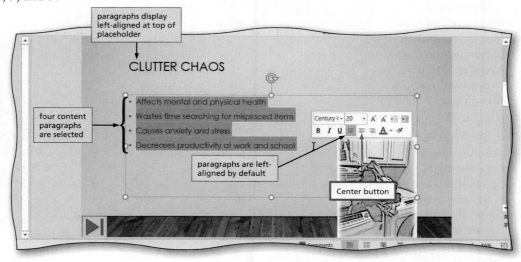

Figure 6–44

- Click the Center button on the mini toolbar (shown in Figure 6–44) to center these paragraphs (Figure 6–45).

- Repeat Steps 1 and 2 to center the paragraph text in the content placeholders on Slides 3 and 5. Do not center the paragraph text on Slide 4.

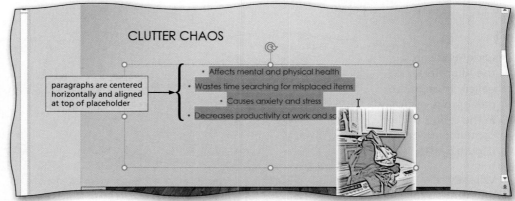

Figure 6–45

Q&A Why is the Slide 4 text not centered?
Later in this project you will split this text into two columns.

Other Ways			
1. Click Center button (Home tab | Paragraph group)	2. Right-click selected text, click Paragraph on shortcut menu, click Alignment arrow (Paragraph dialog box), click Centered, click OK button	3. Click Paragraph Dialog Box Launcher (Home tab | Paragraph group), click Alignment arrow (Paragraph dialog box), click Centered, click OK button	4. Press CTRL+E

To Align Placeholder Text

The Gallery document theme aligns the text paragraphs at the top of the content placeholders. This default setting can be changed easily so that the paragraphs are aligned in the center or at the bottom of the placeholder. The following steps align the paragraphs vertically in the center of the content placeholders on Slides 4 and 5. *Why? The slides have a large amount of blank space, so centering the paragraphs vertically will fill some of this area and increase readability.*

1
- With the Slide 5 paragraphs still selected, display the Home tab and then click the Align Text button (Home tab | Paragraph group) to display the Align Text gallery.

- Point to Middle in the Align Text gallery to display a live preview of the paragraphs aligned in the center of the content placeholder (Figure 6–46).

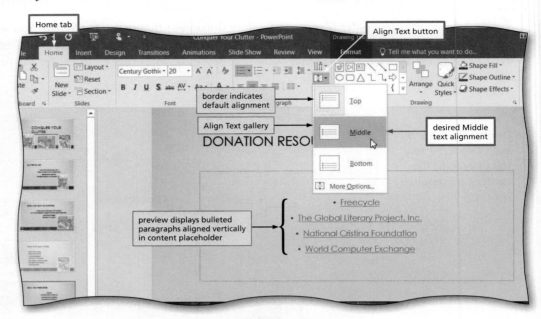

Figure 6–46

Experiment
- Point to the Bottom option in the gallery to see a preview of that alignment.

2
- Click Middle in the Align Text gallery to align the paragraphs vertically in the center of the content placeholder (Figure 6–47).

Q&A What is the difference between centering the paragraphs in the placeholder and centering the text? Clicking the Align Text button and then clicking Middle moves the paragraphs up or down so that the first and last paragraphs are equal distances from the top and bottom placeholder borders. The Center button, on the other hand, moves the paragraphs left or right so that the first and last words in each line are equal distances from the left and right box borders.

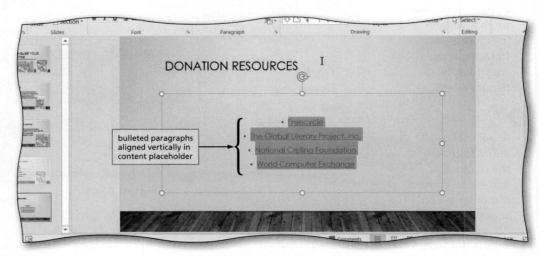

Figure 6–47

- Repeat Steps 1 and 2 to center the paragraph text in the middle of the content placeholder on Slide 4.

To Change Paragraph Line Spacing

The vertical space between lines of text is called **line spacing**. PowerPoint adjusts the amount of space based on font size. Default line spacing is 1.0, which is considered single spacing. Other preset options are 1.5, 2.0 (double spacing), 2.5, and 3.0 (triple spacing). You can specify precise line spacing intervals between, before, and after paragraphs in the Indents and Spacing tab of the Paragraph dialog box. The following steps increase the line spacing of the content paragraphs from single (1.0) to double (2.0) on Slides 2, 3, and 5. *Why?* *The additional space helps fill some of the area on the slide and also helps your audience read the paragraph text more easily.*

1
- With the Home tab displayed, display Slide 2 and select the four content paragraphs.
- Click the Line Spacing button (Home tab | Paragraph group) to display the Line Spacing gallery.
- Point to 2.0 in the Line Spacing gallery to display a live preview of this line spacing (Figure 6–48).

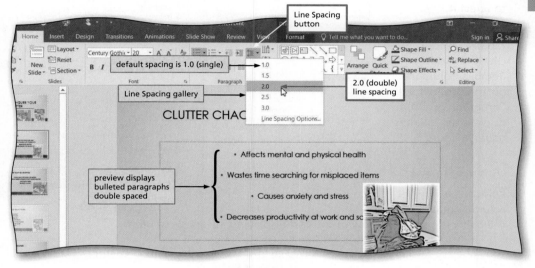

Figure 6–48

Experiment
- Point to each of the line spacing options in the gallery to see a preview of that line spacing.

2
- Click 2.0 in the Line Spacing gallery to change the line spacing to double.

3
- Repeat Steps 1 and 2 to change the line spacing to 2.0 for the paragraph text in the content placeholders on Slides 3 and 5. Do not change the line spacing on Slide 4.

Q&A | Why is the line spacing not changing on Slide 4?
These content placeholder paragraphs will be changed into columns, so spacing is not a design concern at this time.

4
- Move the Laundry picture on Slide 2 to the right so that it does not overlap the text in the last bulleted paragraph.

Other Ways

1. Right-click selected text, click Paragraph on shortcut menu, click Line Spacing arrow (Paragraph dialog box), click Double, click OK button

2. Click Paragraph Dialog Box Launcher (Home tab | Paragraph group), click Line Spacing arrow (Paragraph dialog box), click Double, click OK button

To Create Columns in a Placeholder

Why? The list of organizing tips in the Slide 4 placeholder is lengthy and lacks visual appeal. You can change these items into two, three, or more columns and then adjust the column widths. The following steps change the placeholder elements into columns.

- Display Slide 4 and then click the content placeholder to select it.

- With the Home tab displayed, click the 'Add or Remove Columns' button (Home tab | Paragraph group) to display the Columns gallery (Figure 6–49).

 Experiment

- Point to each of the column options in the gallery to see a preview of the text displaying in various columns.

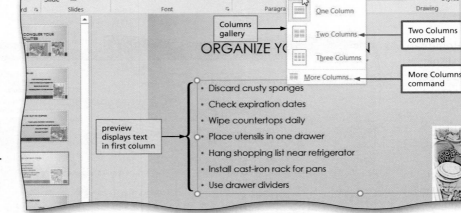

Figure 6–49

Q&A Why doesn't the content display in two columns if I pointed to two columns?
Because all the text fits in the first column in the placeholder.

- Click Two Columns to create two columns of text.

- Drag the bottom sizing handle up to the location shown in Figure 6–50.

Q&A Why is the bottom sizing handle between the fourth and fifth paragraphs?
Seven organization tips are listed in the content placeholder, so dividing the paragraphs in two groups will help balance the layout.

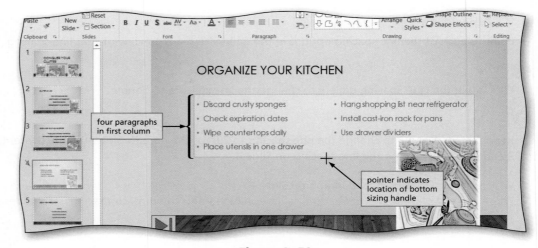

Figure 6–50

- Release the mouse button to resize the content placeholder and create the two columns of text.

Other Ways

1. Right-click placeholder, click Format Shape, click Text Options (Format Shape pane), click Textbox button, click Columns button, enter number of columns in Number box

To Adjust Column Spacing

1 OPEN OUTLINE | 2 ADD PICTURE & TEXT HYPERLINKS | 3 ADD ACTION BUTTONS & HYPERLINKS
4 POSITION PICTURES | 5 ALIGN PLACEHOLDER TEXT | 6 CONVERT & FORMAT BULLETS

Why? *The space between the columns in the placeholder can be increased to make room for the Kitchen picture, which you want to move between the columns.* The following steps increase the spacing between the columns.

 1

- With the placeholder selected, click the 'Add or Remove Columns' button and then click More Columns.

- Click the Spacing box up arrow (Columns dialog box) until 3.5" is displayed (Figure 6–51).

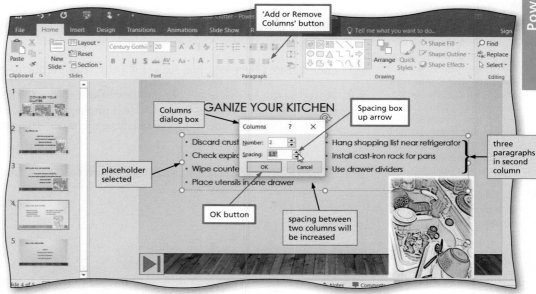

Figure 6–51

 2

- Click the OK button to increase the spacing between the columns (Figure 6–52).

Q&A Why did the font size decrease when I increased the spacing between columns?
PowerPoint automatically adjusts placeholder text to fit in columns with specified spacing.

Can I change the paragraphs back to one column easily?
Yes. Click the Columns button and then click One Column.

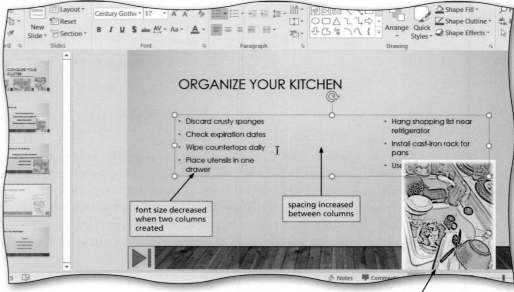

Figure 6–52

Other Ways

1. Right-click placeholder, click Format Shape, click Text Options (Format Shape pane), click Textbox, click Columns button, enter space between columns in Spacing box

To Format the Content Placeholder

BTW

Conserving Ink and Toner

If you want to conserve ink or toner, you can instruct PowerPoint to print draft quality documents by clicking File on the ribbon to open the Backstage view, clicking the Options tab in the Backstage view to display the PowerPoint Options dialog box, clicking Advanced in the left pane (PowerPoint Options dialog box), scrolling to the Print area in the right pane, placing a check mark in the 'Use draft quality' check box, and then clicking the OK button. Then, use the Backstage view to print the document as usual.

To add interest to the Slide 4 content placeholder, apply a Quick Style and then move the Kitchen picture from the lower-right corner to the space between the columns. The following steps apply a purple Subtle Effect style to the placeholder and then change the picture location.

1 With the placeholder selected, click the Quick Styles button (Home tab | Drawing group) to display the Quick Styles gallery.

2 Click 'Subtle Effect – Purple, Accent 4' (fifth style in fourth row).

3 Move the Kitchen picture from the lower-right corner to the area between the two columns so that a vertical Smart Guide is displayed in the center of the picture and a horizontal Smart Guide is displayed below the picture (Figure 6–53).

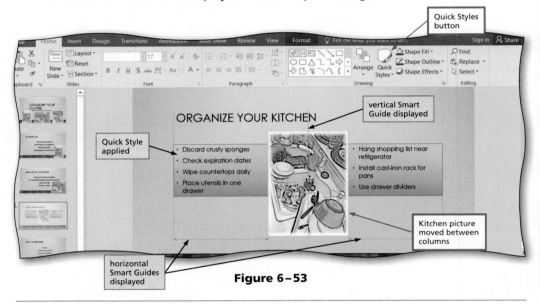

Figure 6–53

To Enter a Line Break

1 OPEN OUTLINE | 2 ADD PICTURE & TEXT HYPERLINKS | 3 ADD ACTION BUTTONS & HYPERLINKS
4 POSITION PICTURES | 5 ALIGN PLACEHOLDER TEXT | 6 CONVERT & FORMAT BULLETS

Why? *The second paragraph in Slide 3 in your presentation is lengthy and extends above the Desk picture. Separating the paragraph after the word, mail, can emphasize the fact that baskets serve two separate functions: one for mail and documents that need attention, and the other for items that have been addressed.* If you press the ENTER key at the end of a line, PowerPoint automatically applies paragraph formatting, which could include indents and bullets. To prevent this formatting from occurring, you can press SHIFT+ENTER to place a **line break** at the end of the line, which moves the insertion point to the beginning of the next line. The following steps place a line break before the word, and, on Slide 3.

1

• Display Slide 3 and then place the insertion point before the word, and, (after the word, mail) in the second paragraph (Figure 6–54).

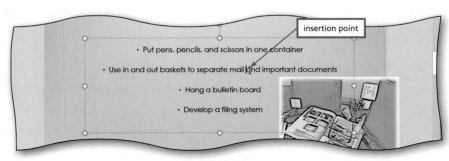

Figure 6–54

- Press SHIFT+ENTER to insert a line break character and move the words, and important documents, to the third line in the placeholder (Figure 6–55).

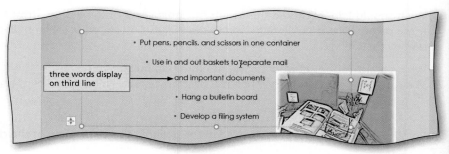

Figure 6–55

Modifying Bullets

PowerPoint allows you to change the default appearance of bullets in a slide show. The document themes determine the bullet character. A **bullet character** is a symbol, traditionally a closed circle, that sets off items in a list. It can be a predefined style, a variety of fonts and characters displayed in the Symbol gallery, or a picture from a file or from Office.com. You may want to change a bullet character to add visual interest and variety. Once you change the bullet character, you also can change its size and color.

If desired, you can change every bullet in a presentation to a unique character. If your presentation has many bulleted slides, however, you would want to have a consistent look on all slides by making the bullets a similar color and size.

To customize your presentation, you can change the default slide layout bullets to numbers by changing the bulleted list to a numbered list. PowerPoint provides a variety of numbering options, including Arabic and Roman numerals. These numbers can be sized and recolored, and the starting number can be something other than 1 or I. In addition, PowerPoint's numbering options include upper- and lower-case letters.

BTW
Printing Document Properties
PowerPoint 2016 does not allow you to print document properties. This feature, however, is available in other Office 2016 apps, including Word and Excel.

To Change a Bullet Character to a Picture

1 OPEN OUTLINE | 2 ADD PICTURE & TEXT HYPERLINKS | 3 ADD ACTION BUTTONS & HYPERLINKS
4 POSITION PICTURES | 5 ALIGN PLACEHOLDER TEXT | **6 CONVERT & FORMAT BULLETS**

Why? *The plain bullet characters for the Gallery document theme do not add much visual interest and do not relate to the topic of chaos that can result from disorganization.* One method of modifying these bullets is to use a relevant picture. The following steps change the first paragraph bullet character to the Sad Face picture, which is located in the Data Files.

- Display Slide 2. With the Home tab still displaying, select all four content placeholder paragraphs.

Q&A
Can I insert a different bullet character in each paragraph?
Yes. Select only a paragraph and then perform the steps below for each paragraph.

- Click the Bullets arrow (Home tab | Paragraph group) to display the Bullets gallery (Figure 6–56).

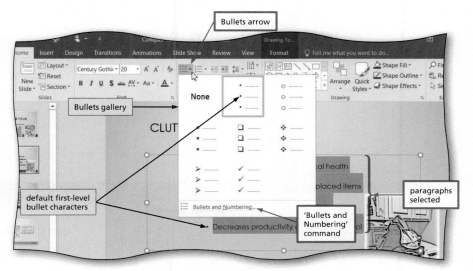

Figure 6–56

What should I do if I clicked the Bullets button instead of the Bullets arrow?
If the paragraphs are bulleted, clicking the Bullets button removes the bullets. Click the Bullets button again to display the bullets.

Why is a gray box displayed around the three characters?
They are the default first-level bullet characters for the Gallery document theme.

Experiment

● Point to each of the bullets displayed in the gallery to see a preview of the characters.

2

● Click 'Bullets and Numbering' to display the Bullets and Numbering dialog box (Figure 6–57).

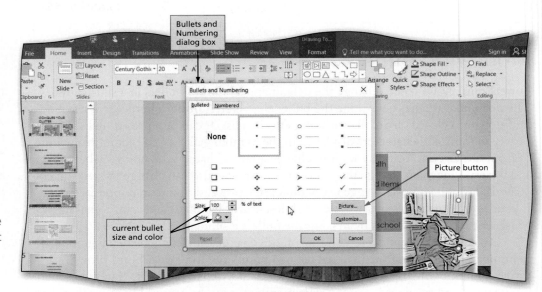 Why are my bullets different from those displayed in Figure 6–57?
The bullets most recently inserted are displayed as the first items in the dialog box.

Figure 6–57

3

● Click the Picture button (Bullets and Numbering dialog box) to display the Insert Pictures dialog box (Figure 6–58).

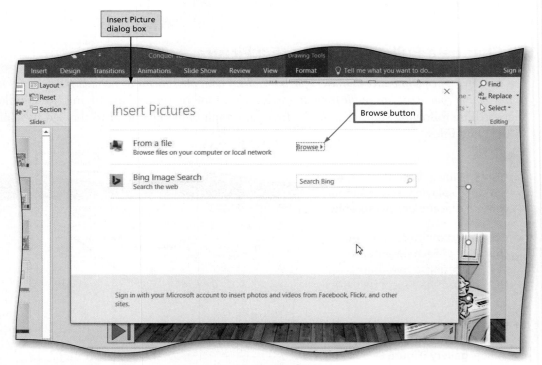

Figure 6–58

- Click the Browse button in the 'From a file' area (Insert Pictures dialog box) to display the Insert Picture dialog box.

- If necessary, navigate to the location of the Data Files.

- Scroll down and then click Sad Face to select the file (Figure 6–59).

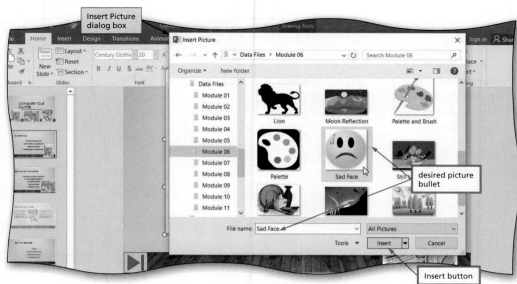

Figure 6–59

- Click the Insert button (Insert Picture dialog box) to insert the Sad Face picture as the paragraph bullet character (Figure 6–60).

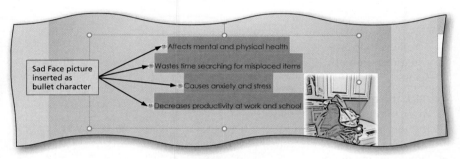

Figure 6–60

Other Ways

1. Right-click paragraph, point to Bullets on shortcut menu, click 'Bullets and Numbering'

To Change a Bullet Character to a Symbol

1 OPEN OUTLINE | 2 ADD PICTURE & TEXT HYPERLINKS | 3 ADD ACTION BUTTONS & HYPERLINKS
4 POSITION PICTURES | 5 ALIGN PLACEHOLDER TEXT | 6 CONVERT & FORMAT BULLETS

Why? *For variety and to add a unique characteristic to the presentation, another bullet change you can make is to insert a symbol as the character.* Symbols are found in several fonts, including Webdings, Wingdings, Wingdings 2, and Wingdings 3. These fonts are available when slides have themes other than the Office theme. The following steps change the bullet character on Slide 5 to a question mark symbol.

1

- Display Slide 5, select all four hyperlinked paragraphs, click the Bullets arrow (Home tab | Paragraph group), and then click 'Bullets and Numbering' to display the Bullets and Numbering dialog box (Figure 6–61).

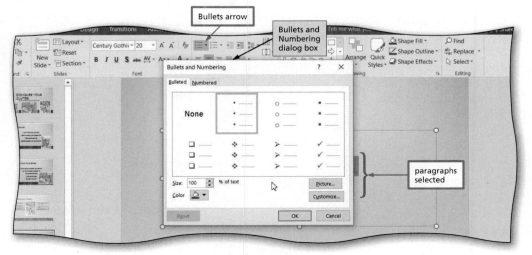

Figure 6–61

2

- Click the Customize button (Bullets and Numbering dialog box) to display the Symbol dialog box (Figure 6–62).

Q&A Why is a symbol selected?
That symbol is the default bullet for the first-level paragraphs in the Gallery document theme.

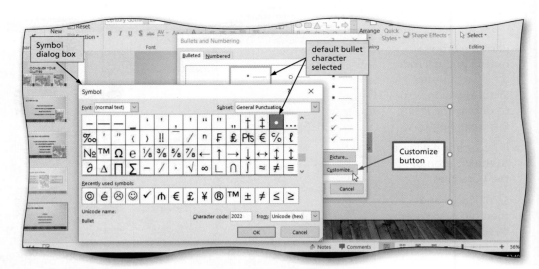

Figure 6–62

3

- Scroll up to locate the question mark symbol.

- Click the question mark symbol to select it (Figure 6–63).

Q&A Why does my dialog box have more rows of symbols and different fonts from which to choose?
The rows and fonts displayed depend upon how PowerPoint was installed on your system and the screen you are viewing.

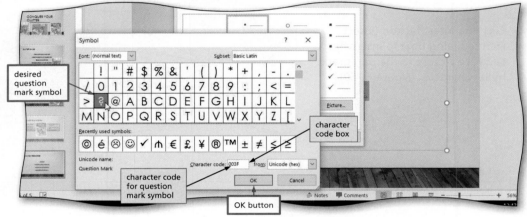

Figure 6–63

What is the character code that is displayed in the Symbol dialog box?
Each character in each font has a unique code. If you know the character code, you can type the number in the Character code box to display that symbol. The character code for the question mark symbol is 003F.

4

- Click the OK button (Symbol dialog box) to display the question mark bullet in the Bullets and Numbering dialog box (Figure 6–64).

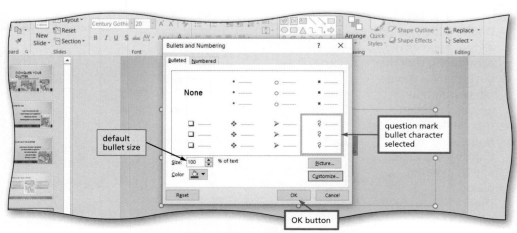

Figure 6–64

- Click the OK button (Bullets and Numbering dialog box) to insert the question mark symbol as the paragraph bullet (Figure 6–65).

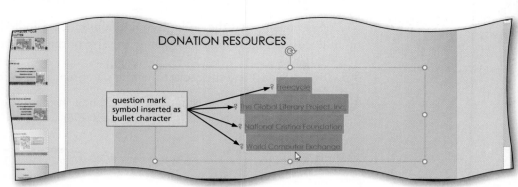

Figure 6–65

To Change Bullet Size

1 OPEN OUTLINE | 2 ADD PICTURE & TEXT HYPERLINKS | 3 ADD ACTION BUTTONS & HYPERLINKS
4 POSITION PICTURES | 5 ALIGN PLACEHOLDER TEXT | 6 CONVERT & FORMAT BULLETS

Bullets have a default size determined by the document theme. **Bullet size** is measured as a percentage of the text size and can range from 25 to 400 percent. The following steps change the question mark symbol size. *Why? It is difficult to see the symbol, so increasing its size draws attention to the visual element.*

- With the Slide 5 paragraphs still selected, click the Bullets arrow (Home tab | Paragraph group) and then click 'Bullets and Numbering' in the Bullets gallery to display the Bullets and Numbering dialog box.

- Set the size in the Size box to 150 (Figure 6–66).

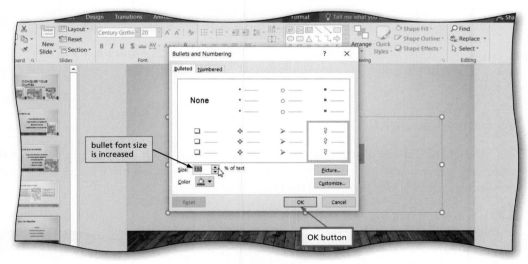

Figure 6–66

- Click the OK button to increase the question mark bullet size to 150 percent of its original size (Figure 6–67).

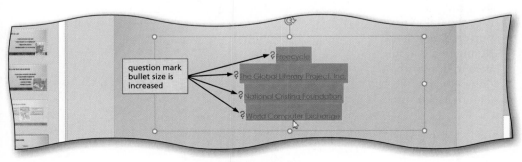

Figure 6–67

To Change the Size of Other Bullet Characters

For consistency, the bullet character on Slide 2 should have a similar size as that on Slide 5. The following steps change the size of the Sad Face bullets.

1 Display Slide 2 and then select the four paragraphs in the content placeholder.

2 Display the Bullets and Numbering dialog box, increase the bullet size to 150% of text size, and then click the OK button (Figure 6–68).

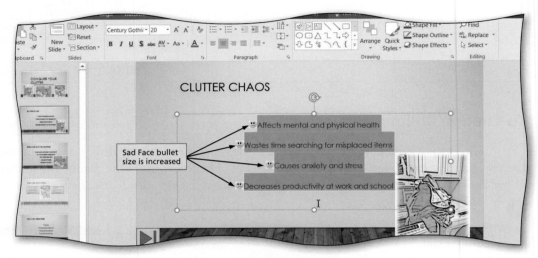

Figure 6–68

To Format Bullet Color

1 OPEN OUTLINE | 2 ADD PICTURE & TEXT HYPERLINKS | 3 ADD ACTION BUTTONS & HYPERLINKS
4 POSITION PICTURES | 5 ALIGN PLACEHOLDER TEXT | 6 CONVERT & FORMAT BULLETS

A default **bullet color** is based on the eight colors in the design theme. Additional standard and custom colors also are available. The following steps change the question mark bullet color to Purple. *Why? This color coordinates with the action buttons and the Quick Style on Slide 4.*

1

• Display Slide 5, select the four hyperlinked paragraphs, display the Bullets and Numbering dialog box, and then click the Color button (Bullets and Numbering dialog box) to display the Color gallery (Figure 6–69).

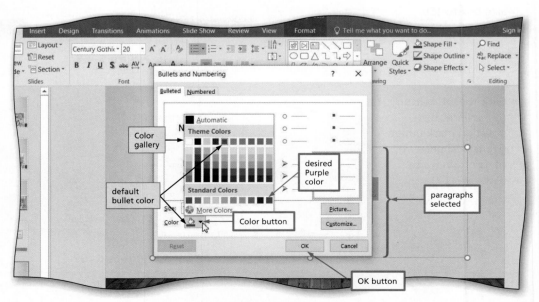

Figure 6–69

- Click the color Purple in the Standard Colors area to change the bullet color to Purple (last color in Standard Colors row) (Figure 6–70).

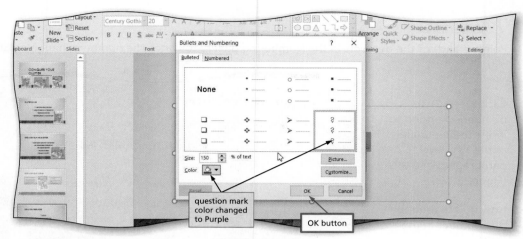

Figure 6–70

- Click the OK button (Bullets and Numbering dialog box) to apply the color Purple to the question mark bullets (Figure 6–71).

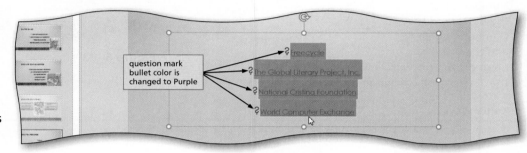

Figure 6–71

Other Ways

1. Right-click paragraph, point to Bullets on shortcut menu, click Bullets and Numbering, select color

To Change a Bullet Character to a Number

1 OPEN OUTLINE | 2 ADD PICTURE & TEXT HYPERLINKS | 3 ADD ACTION BUTTONS & HYPERLINKS
4 POSITION PICTURES | 5 ALIGN PLACEHOLDER TEXT | **6 CONVERT & FORMAT BULLETS**

PowerPoint allows you to change the default bullets to numbers. The process of changing the bullet characters is similar to the process of adding bullets to paragraphs. The following steps change the first-level paragraph bullet characters on Slide 3 to numbers. *Why? Numbers help to show steps in a sequence and also help guide a speaker during the presentation when referring to specific information in the paragraphs.*

- Display Slide 3 and then select all content paragraphs.

- With the Home tab still displaying, click the Numbering arrow (Home tab | Paragraph group) to display the Numbering gallery.

- Point to the 1) 2) 3) numbering option in the Numbering gallery to display a live preview of these numbers (Figure 6–72).

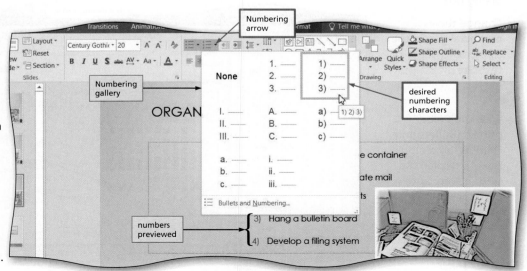

Figure 6–72

Experiment

- Point to each of the numbers in the Numbering gallery to watch the numbers change on Slide 3.

2

- Click the 1) 2) 3) numbering option to insert these numbers as the first-level paragraph characters (Figure 6–73).

 How do I change the first number in the list?
Click 'Bullets and Numbering' at the bottom of the Numbering gallery and then click the up or down arrow in the Start at box to change the number.

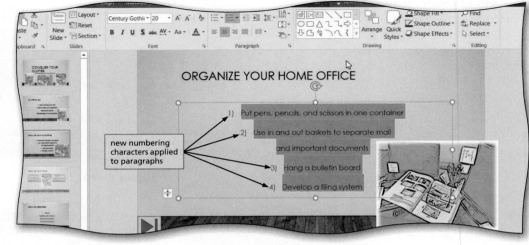

Figure 6–73

Other Ways

1. Right-click paragraph, point to Numbering on shortcut menu, select numbering characters

To Format a Numbered List

1 OPEN OUTLINE | 2 ADD PICTURE & TEXT HYPERLINKS | 3 ADD ACTION BUTTONS & HYPERLINKS
4 POSITION PICTURES | 5 ALIGN PLACEHOLDER TEXT | 6 CONVERT & FORMAT BULLETS

Why? *To add emphasis, you can increase the size of the new numbers inserted in Slide 3.* As with bullets, numbering characters are measured as a percentage of the text size and can range from 25 to 400 percent. The color of these numbers also can change. The original color is based on the eight colors in the design theme. Additional standard and custom colors are available. The following steps change the size and color of the numbers to 125 percent and Purple, respectively.

1

- With the Slide 3 content paragraphs still selected, click the Numbering arrow (Home tab | Paragraph group) to display the Numbering gallery and then click 'Bullets and Numbering' to display the Bullets and Numbering dialog box.

- Change the numbers' size in the Size box to 125% of text size.

2

- Click the Color button (Bullets and Numbering dialog box) to display the color gallery and then click Purple to change the numbers' font color (Figure 6–74).

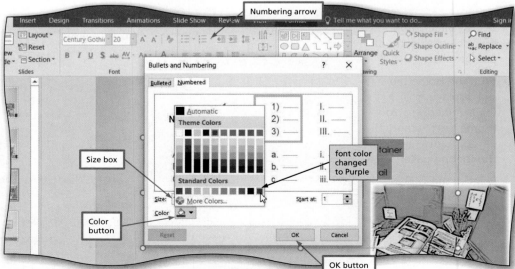

Figure 6–74

- Click the OK button (Bullets and Numbering dialog box) to apply the new numbers' font size and color.

Other Ways

1. Right-click paragraph, point to Numbering on shortcut menu, click 'Bullets and Numbering', click up or down Size arrow until desired size is displayed, click Color button, select color, click OK button

To Remove Bullet Characters

1 OPEN OUTLINE | 2 ADD PICTURE & TEXT HYPERLINKS | 3 ADD ACTION BUTTONS & HYPERLINKS
4 POSITION PICTURES | 5 ALIGN PLACEHOLDER TEXT | 6 CONVERT & FORMAT BULLETS

The organization tips listed in the two Slide 4 columns are preceded by a bullet character. The following steps remove the bullet characters from the items in the two columns on Slide 4. *Why? The slide may appear less cluttered if you remove the bullets.*

- Display Slide 4, select all the text in the two columns, and then click the Bullets arrow (Home tab | Paragraph group).

- Point to the None option in the Bullets gallery to display a live preview of how the slide will appear without bullets (Figure 6–75).

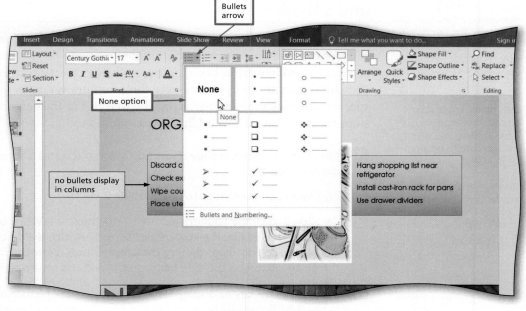

- Click the None option to remove the bullet characters on Slide 4.

Figure 6–75

Q&A
Would I use the same technique to remove numbers from a list?
Yes. The None option also is available in the Numbering gallery.

Other Ways

1. Select bulleted text, click Bullets button to toggle bullets off

---

Consider the audience's interests.
As audience members start to view your presentation, they often think about their personal needs and wonder, "How will this presentation benefit me?" As you may have learned in your psychology classes, Maslow's hierarchy of needs drives much of your behavior, starting with basic sustenance and moving on to safety, belonging, ego-status, and self-actualization. Audience members cannot move to the next higher level of needs until their current level is satisfied. For example, an individual must first satisfy his needs of hunger and thirst before he can consider partaking in leisure time activities. Your presentations must meet the requirements of your audience members; otherwise, these people will not consider your talk as benefiting their needs. Having hyperlinks and action buttons can help you tailor a presentation to fulfill the audience's satisfaction level.

CONSIDER THIS

Running a Slide Show with Hyperlinks and Action Buttons

The Conquer Your Clutter presentation contains a variety of useful features that provide value to an audience. The graphics should help viewers understand and recall the information being presented. The hyperlinks on Slide 5 show useful websites of organizations that accept donations of household goods and technology. In addition, the action button allows a presenter to jump to Slide 5 while Slides 2, 3, or 4 are being displayed. If an audience member asks a question or if the presenter needs to answer specific questions regarding kitchen organization when Slide 3 is displaying, the information on the hidden Slide 4 can be accessed immediately by pressing the H key.

To Run a Slide Show with Hyperlinks, Action Buttons, and a Hidden Slide

Running a slide show that contains hyperlinks and action buttons is an interactive experience. A presenter has the option to display slides in a predetermined sequence or to improvise based on the audience's reaction and questions. When a presentation contains hyperlinks and the computer is connected to the Internet, the speaker can click the links to display the websites in the default browser. The following steps run the Conquer Your Clutter presentation.

1 Click Slide 1. Click the Slide Show button on the status bar to run the slide show and display Slide 1.

2 Click the Laundry picture to display Slide 2.

3 On Slide 2, click the Laundry picture to run Microsoft Word and open the Conquer Clutter Checklist file. If a PowerPoint Security Notice dialog box is displayed, click the Yes button to continue running the presentation. View the information and then click the Close button on the title bar to exit Word and return to Slide 2.

4 Press the ENTER key to display Slide 3. Click the Desk picture to link to the first slide in the Additional Clutter presentation. If a PowerPoint Security Notice dialog box is displayed, click the Yes button to continue running the presentation.

5 Click the Return action button on the first slide to return to Slide 3 in the Conquer Your Clutter presentation. If a PowerPoint Security Notice dialog box is displayed, click the Yes button to continue running the presentation.

6 Press the H key to display Slide 4. Click the Kitchen picture to link to the second slide, Conquering Clutter Guidelines, in the Additional Clutter presentation. If a PowerPoint Security Notice dialog box is displayed, click the Yes button to continue running the presentation. Click the Return action button on the second slide to return to Slide 4 in the Conquer Your Clutter presentation.

7 Press the ENTER key to display Slide 5. Click the first hyperlink to start your browser and access the Freecycle webpage. If necessary, maximize the webpage window when the page is displayed. Click the Close button on the webpage title bar to close the browser.

8 Continue using the hyperlinks and action buttons and then end both presentations.

BTW
Distributing a Document
Instead of printing and distributing a hard copy of a document, you can distribute the document electronically. Options include sending the document via email; posting it on cloud storage (such as OneDrive) and sharing the file with others; posting it on social media, a blog, or other website; and sharing a link associated with an online location of the document. You also can create and share a PDF or XPS image of the document, so that users can view the file in Acrobat Reader or XPS Viewer instead of in PowerPoint.

To Save, Print, and Exit PowerPoint

The presentation now is complete. You should save the slides, print a handout, and then exit PowerPoint.

1 Save the Conquer Your Clutter presentation again in the same storage location with the same file name.

2 Print the slides as a handout with two slides per page.

3 Exit PowerPoint, closing all open documents.

Summary

In this module you have learned how to open a Microsoft Word outline as a PowerPoint presentation, develop slides with hyperlinks and action buttons, position slide elements using the drawing guides and rulers, align and distribute pictures, center and align placeholder text, and create columns and then adjust the width. You also learned to change a bullet character to a picture or a symbol and then change its size and color, and to format a numbered list. Finally, you ran the presentation using the action buttons and hyperlinks.

What decisions will you need to make when creating your next presentation?
Use these guidelines as you complete the assignments in this module and create your own slide show decks outside of this class.

1. Many aspects of our lives are grouped in threes: sun, moon, stars; reduce, reuse, recycle; breakfast, lunch, dinner. Your presentation and accompanying presentation likewise can be grouped in threes: introduction, body, and conclusion.

2. Make the hypertext graphics or letters large so a speaker is prompted to click them easily during a speaking engagement.

3. Customize action buttons for a unique look. Add pictures and other graphic elements to add interest or make the buttons less obvious to your viewers.

4. Audience members desire to hear speeches and view presentations that benefit them in some way based on their personal needs. A presenter, in turn, must determine the audience's physical and psychological needs and then tailor the presentation to fit each speaking engagement.

Consider This: Plan Ahead

Apply Your Knowledge

Reinforce the skills and apply the concepts you learned in this module.

Aligning Placeholder Text, Changing Paragraph Line Spacing, Revising a Presentation with Action Buttons, Creating Columns in a Placeholder, and Hiding Slides

Note: To complete this assignment, you will be required to use the Data Files. Please contact your instructor for information about accessing the Data Files.

Instructions: Run PowerPoint. Open the presentation called Apply 6–1 Achilles, which is located in the Data Files.

The slides in the presentation present information about the Achilles tendon. The document you open is a partially formatted presentation. You are to change the theme variant, insert action buttons, and hide slides. Your presentation should look like Figure 6–76.

Perform the following tasks:

1. Change the Berlin theme variant from green to blue (the second color variant).

2. On Slide 1 (Figure 6–76a), change the title font to Matura MT Script Capitals and apply the WordArt style, 'Fill - White, Text 1, Outline - Background 1, Hard Shadow - Background 1' (first style in third row), to the title text. Align the title text in the middle of the placeholder and then center the text in the placeholder as shown in the figure. Change the line spacing of the three paragraphs in the black placeholder to 1.0 and then center these paragraphs.

3. On Slide 2 (Figure 6–76b), create a hyperlink for the text, Sports participation, to Slide 5 (Figure 6–76e). On Slide 5, insert a Back or Previous action button in the lower-right corner of the slide to hyperlink to Last Slide Viewed and play the Click sound. Change the color of the action button to 'Black, Background 1'. Size the button so that it is approximately 0.75" × 0.75". Copy and paste this action button to the lower-right corner of Slide 6.

4. On Slide 2 (Figure 6–76b), create a hyperlink for the text, High heels, to Slide 6 (Figure 6–76f).

5. On Slides 2, 3 (Figure 6–76c), and 4 (Figure 6–76d), increase the size of the foot bullets to 125% of text size. Remove the bullet characters on Slide 5.

6. On Slide 4, create two columns in the text placeholder, adjust the column spacing to 1.00", and then adjust the height of the box so that the columns appear as shown in Figure 6–76d.

7. Hide Slides 5 and 6.

8. If requested by your instructor, add the street you grew up on in the subtitle placeholder on Slide 1.

9. Add the Blinds transition for all slides. Change the duration to 2.75 seconds.

10. Run the presentation and verify the links and action buttons are correct. Save the presentation using the file name, Apply 6–1 Achilles Tendon.

11. Submit the revised document in the format specified by your instructor.

12. ✸ In this presentation, you used action buttons between the text on Slide 2 and Slides 5 and 6. Why? When would a presenter want to hide Slides 5 and 6 and when would a presenter want to display them?

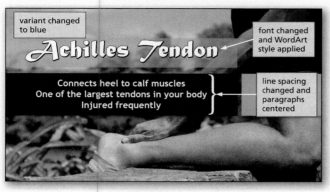

(a) Slide 1

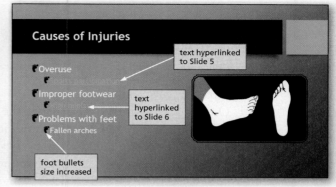

(b) Slide 2

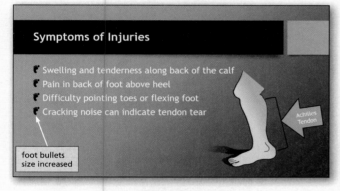

(c) Slide 3

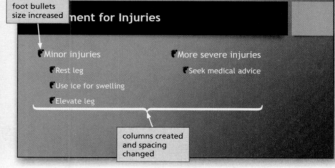

(d) Slide 4

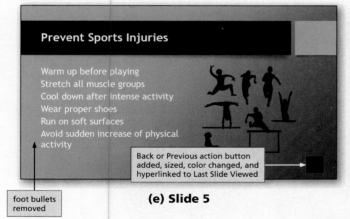

(e) Slide 5

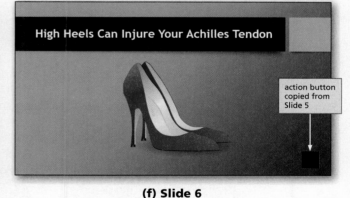

(f) Slide 6

Figure 6–76

Extend Your Knowledge

Extend the skills you learned in this module and experiment with new skills. You may need to use Help to complete the assignment.

Inserting a Photo into an Action Button and Changing a Bullet Character to a Picture

Note: To complete this assignment, you will be required to use the Data Files. Please contact your instructor for information about accessing the Data Files.

Continued >

Extend Your Knowledge *continued*

Instructions: Run PowerPoint. Open the presentation called Extend 6-1 Tanzania, which is located in the Data Files. You will insert hyperlinks on Slide 1, insert action buttons on Slides 2, 3, and 4, and change the bullet characters to pictures on Slides 2, 3, and 4, as shown in Figure 6–77.

Perform the following tasks:

1. On Slide 1 (Figure 6–77a), change the title text font to AR DARLING and then increase the font size to 72 point. Change the subtitle text paragraph alignment to Justified by selecting the text, displaying the Home tab, clicking the Paragraph Dialog Box Launcher (Home tab | Paragraph group), clicking the Alignment arrow in the General area (Paragraph dialog box), and then clicking Justified. Also, change the line spacing to Exactly 40 point by clicking the

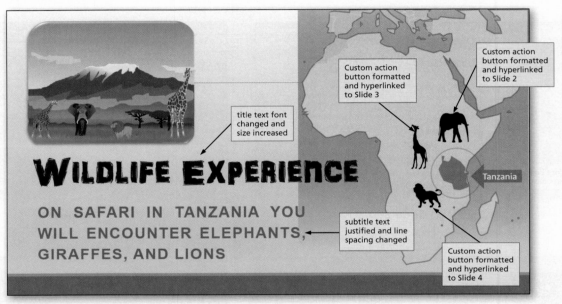

(a) Slide 1

(b) Slide 2

Figure 6–77 (Continued)

Line Spacing arrow in the Spacing area (Paragraph dialog box), clicking Exactly, and then increasing the line spacing in the At box.

2. On Slide 1, insert three Custom action buttons (last button in Action Buttons area) on the Africa map. Format these shapes by inserting the pictures called Elephant, Giraffe, and Lion, which are located in the Data Files. Change the size of the elephant shape to approximately 0.8" × 0.8", the giraffe shape to approximately 1.21" × 0.96", and the lion shape to approximately 0.64" × 0.73", and then move the three action buttons to the location shown in the figure. Also remove the shape outline from each action button.

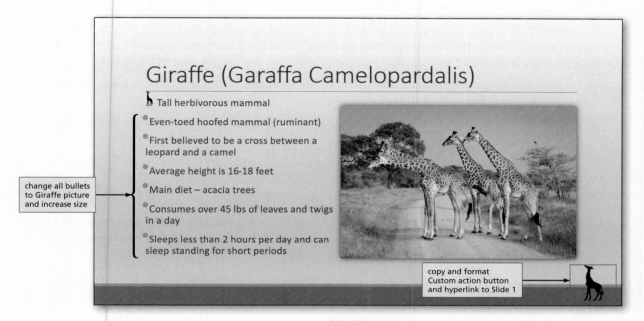

change all bullets to Giraffe picture and increase size

copy and format Custom action button and hyperlink to Slide 1

(c) Slide 3

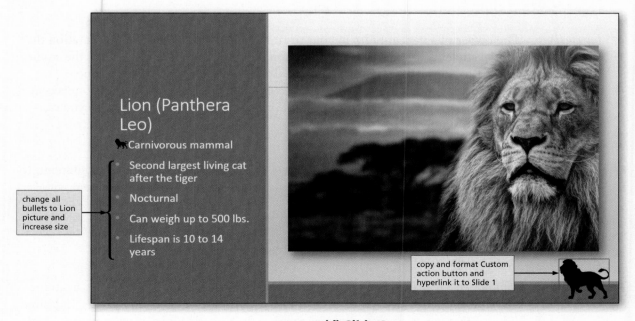

change all bullets to Lion picture and increase size

copy and format Custom action button and hyperlink it to Slide 1

(d) Slide 4

Figure 6–77 (Continued)

Continued >

Extend Your Knowledge *continued*

3. Hyperlink each picture on Slide 1 to the corresponding slide. For example, the elephant picture should hyperlink to Slide 2 (Figure 6–77b). The other two pictures should hyperlink to Slides 3 and 4 (Figures 6–77c and 6–77d), respectively.

4. On Slide 2 (Figure 6–77b), insert a Custom action button in the lower-right area of the slide and then hyperlink it to Slide 1. Change the size to approximately .75" × .75". Format this shape by inserting the picture called Elephant, which is located in the Data Files. Adjust the transparency of the photo to 80%. Copy and paste this action button on Slides 3 and 4. Change the picture to Giraffe on Slide 3 and Lion on Slide 4.

5. On Slides 2, 3, and 4, change the bullet characters for the paragraphs using the Elephant picture on Slide 2, the Giraffe picture on Slide 3, and the Lion picture on Slide 4. Increase the size of the bullets to 130% for the elephant, 200% for the giraffe, and 118% for the lion.

6. If requested by your instructor, add the year you graduated from high school after the word, Lions, in the subtitle placeholder on Slide 1.

7. Apply the Vortex transition in the Exciting category to all slides and then change the duration to 3.50 seconds.

8. Run the presentation and verify the hyperlinks and action buttons are correct. Save the presentation using the file name, Extend 6-1 Wildlife Experience.

9. Submit the revised document in the format specified by your instructor.

10. ✸ In Step 1, you changed the look of the title and subtitle fonts by changing the font and line spacing. How did this enhance your title slide? How did adding action buttons improve the presentation?

Expand Your World

Create a solution that uses cloud or web technologies by learning and investigating on your own from general guidance.

Using Google Slides to Upload and Edit Files

Instructions: The owner of a dance studio in your town has asked you to create a presentation that encourages potential students to register for lessons. You began working on the slides at the studio but did not have time to finish the slides there and need to complete the slide deck at home. Although you do not have PowerPoint on your home computer, you have an Internet connection and a Google account. You uploaded your PowerPoint presentation to Google Drive so you can view and edit it later from home.

Notes:
- You will use a Google account, which you can create at no cost, to complete this assignment. If you do not have a Google account and do not want to create one, read this assignment without performing the instructions.
- To complete this assignment, you will be required to use the Data Files. Please contact your instructor for information about accessing the Data Files.

Perform the following tasks:

1. In PowerPoint, open the presentation, Expand 6-1 Dancing Lessons in PowerPoint, from the Data Files. Review the slides so that you are familiar with their contents and formats. If desired, print the slides so that you easily can compare them to the Google Slides converted file. Close the presentation.

2. Run a browser. Search for the text, Google Slides, using a search engine. Visit several websites to learn about Google Slides and Google Drive. Navigate to the Google website. If you do not have a Google account and you want to create one, click the Get Started button and follow the instructions. If you do not have a Google account and you do not want to create one, read the remaining instructions without performing them. If you have a Google account, sign in to your account.

3. If necessary, click Drive to display Google Drive. Click the New button, click the File upload, or similar, button, and then follow the instructions to navigate to the location of the file, Expand 6-1 Dancing Lessons in PowerPoint, and upload the file.

4. Rename the file on Google Drive to Expand 6-1 Dancing Lessons in Google. Open the file in Google Slides (Figure 6–78). What differences do you see between the PowerPoint document and the Google Slides converted document? Modify the document in Google Slides so that it looks appealing. If requested by your instructor, replace the name, Stephanie, on Slide 1 with the name of your favorite grade school teacher. Download the revised document to your local storage medium. Submit the document in the format requested by your instructor.

5. What is Google Drive? What is Google Slides? Answer the question posed in #4. If you have an Android smartphone, download the Google Slides app and edit the Expand 6-1 Dancing Lessons file. Do you prefer using Google Slides or PowerPoint? Why?

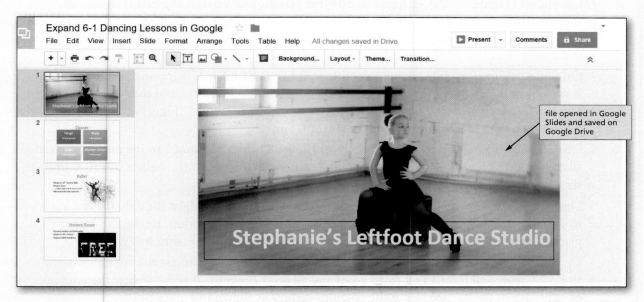

Figure 6–78

In the Labs

Design, create, modify, and/or use a presentation following the guidelines, concepts, and skills presented in this module. Labs 1 and 2, which increase in difficulty, require you to create solutions based on what you learned in the module; Lab 3 requires you to apply your creative thinking and problem-solving skills to design and implement a solution.

Continued >

In the Labs *continued*

Lab 1: Creating Columns in a Box, Increasing the Size of Bullets, Inserting Hyperlinks, Using Guides, and Formatting Bullets

Note: To complete this assignment, you will be required to use the Data Files. Please contact your instructor for information about accessing the Data Files.

Problem: As a member of the Audubon Society, you have enjoyed observing and taking photos of birds. You recently started studying ornithology and would like to share some interesting character- istics you have discovered about our feathered friends with other members of your local Audubon Society chapter. Create the slides shown in Figure 6–79.

Perform the following tasks:

1. Run PowerPoint. Open the presentation called Lab 6-1 Birds, which is located in the Data Files.

2. Create a background for Slides 2 through 5 by inserting the photo called Bird and Sky, which is located in the Data Files. Change the transparency to 50%, as shown in Figures 6–79b through 6–79e.

3. On Slide 1 (Figure 6–79a), change the title text placeholder vertical alignment to Middle. Increase the title text size to 80 point, change the color to Dark Blue (in Standard Colors), and then bold this text. Change the subtitle text placeholder vertical alignment to Middle, increase the subtitle text size to 32 point, and then italicize this text.

4. On Slide 2 (Figure 6–79b), change the title font to AR BLANCA, increase the title text font size to 44 point, change the color to Dark Blue (in Standard Colors), and then bold this text. Use the Format Painter to format the title text on Slides 3, 4, and 5 (Figures 6–79c, 6–79d, and 6–79e) with the same features as the title text on Slide 2.

5. Change the bullet characters for all the level 1 text on Slides 2, 3, and 5 to the illustration called Black Bird, which is available in the Data Files. Increase the size of the bullets to 150% of text size, as shown in Figures 6–79b and 6–79c.

6. On Slide 2, create two columns in the text placeholder and then adjust the column spacing to 1". Change all level 1 text to 32 point and all level 2 text to 24 point. Resize the content placeholder so the paragraphs in the columns display as shown in Figure 6–79b.

7. On Slide 3, create three columns in the text placeholder and then adjust the column spacing to 1.5". Change all level 1 text to 28 point and all level 2 text to 24 point. Resize the content placeholder so the paragraphs in the columns display as shown in Figure 6–79c.

8. On Slide 3, create hyperlinks for the three words in the box, Mantle, Coverts, and Tertials, to Slide 4. (If spell check prompts you to correct the spelling of these three words, ignore the options shown.)

9. On Slide 4, change the color of the shape fill of the 11 callout shapes to Light Blue (in Standard Colors), as shown in Figure 6–79d. Display rulers and guides. With the 11 callout shapes and the bird illustration selected, move these objects so they are centered horizontally and vertically on the slide. Turn off rulers and guides.

10. Insert a Return action button in the lower-right corner of Slide 4 and then hyperlink the button to the Previous Slide, which will be Slide 3 when you run the presentation. Change the color of this action button to 'Gold, Accent 4' (first Theme Colors row) and then change the transparency to 50%, as shown in Figure 6–79d.

(a) Slide 1

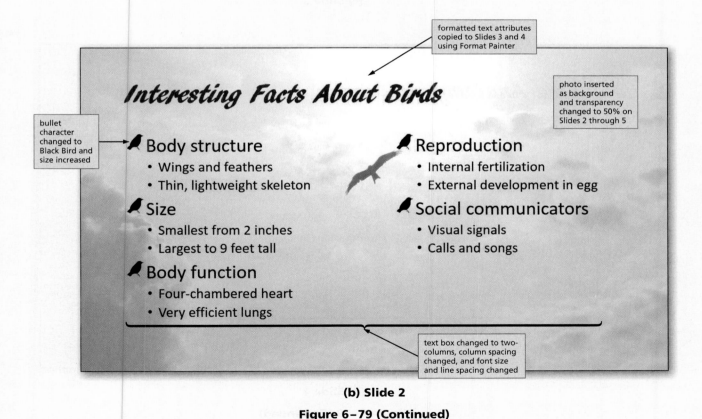

(b) Slide 2

Figure 6–79 (Continued)

11. On Slide 5, increase the size of the title text to 44 point so it appears on two lines, as shown in Figure 6–79e. Increase the size of the photo to 5.76" × 7.3", apply the 'Beveled Oval, Black' picture style, add the Glow Diffused artistic effect (fourth effect in second row), and then move the photo to the location shown in the figure.

Continued >

In the Labs *continued*

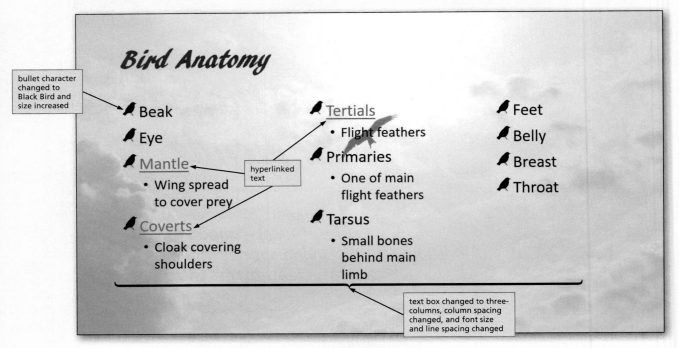

(c) Slide 3

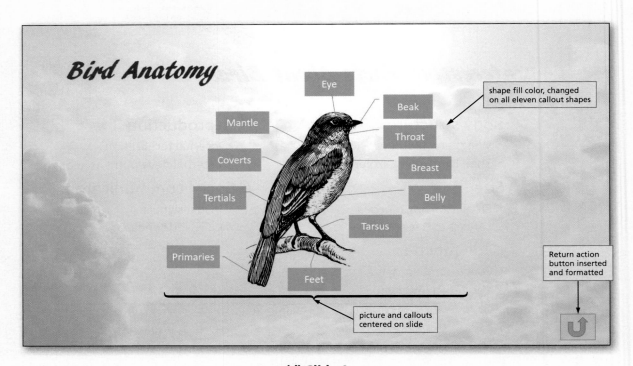

(d) Slide 4

Figure 6–79 (Continued)

12. Create hyperlinks for the three ornithologists shown on Slide 5. Type `www.audubon.org /content/john-james-audubon` for John James Audubon, `www.wilsonsociety .org/society/awilsoninfo.html` for Alexander Wilson, and `www.britannica .com/biography/John-Gould` for John Gould.

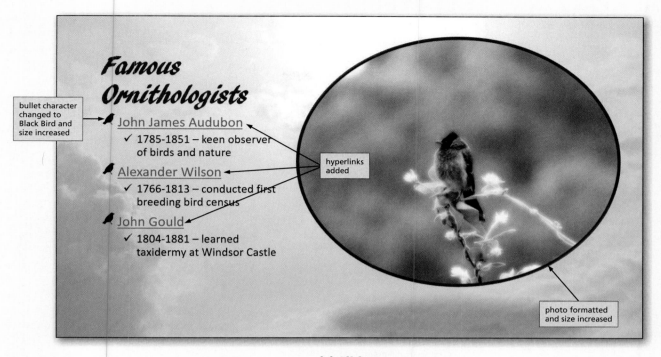

(e) Slide 5

Figure 6–79

13. If requested by your instructor, add your high school mascot as the last line of the subtitle text on Slide 5.

14. Apply the Origami transition in the Exciting Content category to all slides and then change the duration to 3.50 seconds.

15. Run the presentation and verify the hyperlinks and action buttons are correct. Save the presentation using the file name, Lab 6-1 Our Feathered Friends.

16. Submit the document in the format specified by your instructor.

17. ✹ In Step 8, you added hyperlinks to three of the bird anatomy paragraphs on Slide 3 and linked them to Slide 4. Why would a speaker desire to use these hyperlinks? In Step 12, you added hyperlinks to the names of famous ornithologists and linked them to websites. How would a speaker use these hyperlinks during a presentation?

Lab 2: Opening a Microsoft Word Outline as a Presentation, Inserting a Hyperlink to Another Office Document, Using Rulers and Guides, Entering Line Breaks, and Formatting Bullets

Note: To complete this assignment, you will be required to use the Data Files. Please contact your instructor for information about accessing the Data Files.

Problem: Your community center is offering painting classes beginning in January. You received a document outlining the classes that will be offered and a Microsoft Excel file that gives detailed information about the painting classes, schedule, and costs. To help promote the classes, you create the five slides shown in Figures 6–80b through 6–80f.

Continued >

In the Labs *continued*

Tyson County Art Classes
Class Sessions
 Taught in a casual and fun atmosphere
 Experience traditional and non-traditional techniques
 Develop your personal style
 Learn a variety of styles and techniques
Oils
 Three landscape options
  Moon Reflection
  Sunset
  Tree and Birds
Acrylics
 Two still life options
  Pottery
  Birds
Required Art Supplies
 Smock
 Sketch book
 Colored pencils

(a) Tyson County Art Classes Outline (Microsoft Word Document)

(b) Slide 1

Figure 6–80 (Continued)

	Tyson County Adult Painting Classes Beginning in January				
Class and Teacher	**Project**	**Canvas Size**	**Day and Time**	**Duration**	**Cost including all supplies**
Oils by Erick	Moon Reflection	16 x 20	M,W,F 9 a.m.	6 weeks	$195
Oils by Erick	Moon Reflection	8 x 10	Tue & Thur 9 a.m.	5 weeks	$165
Oils by Erick	Sunset	16 x 20	M,W,F 2 p.m.	6 weeks	$195
Oils by Erick	Sunset	8 x 10	Tue & Thur 2 p.m.	5 weeks	$165
Oils by Erick	Trees and Birds	16 x 20	M,W,F 7 p.m.	6 weeks	$195
Oils by Erick	Trees and Birds	8 x 10	Tue & Thur 7 p.m.	5 weeks	$165
Acrylics by Sandy	Still Life Pottery	11 x 14	Mon & Wed 11 a.m.	6 weeks	$150
Acrylics by Sandy	Still Life Pottery	8 x 10	Tue & Fri 2 p.m.	6 weeks	$130
Acrylics by Sandy	Still Life Birds	11 x 14	Mon & Thur 2 p.m.	5 weeks	$150
Acrylics by Sandy	Still Life Birds	8 x 10	Mon & Thur 7 p.m.	5 weeks	$130

(c) Tyson County Art Classes (Microsoft Excel file)

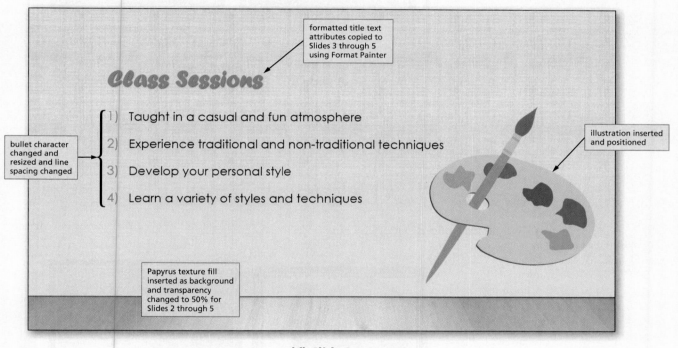

(d) Slide 2

Figure 6–80 (Continued)

Perform the following tasks:

1. Run PowerPoint. Open the Microsoft Word outline, Lab 6-2 Tyson County Art Classes Outline (Figure 6–80a), which is located in the Data Files, as a presentation.

2. Change the Slide 1 layout to Title Slide (Figure 6–80b). Change the title font to Forte and then apply a text shadow to this text. Enter a line break before the word, Art. Change the line spacing for the title to 1.0.

3. Change the theme to Gallery and then select the gold variant. Create a background on Slide 1 only using the illustration called Art, which is located in the Data Files, and then change the transparency to 35%.

Continued >

In the Labs *continued*

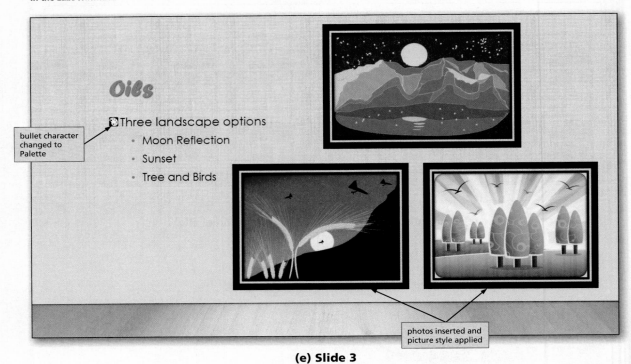

(e) Slide 3

(f) Slide 4

Figure 6–80 (Continued)

4. On Slide 1, move the subtitle placeholder to the upper-right corner of the slide, type **January Schedule**, bold and right-align this text, and then change the color to Green (in Standard colors). Create a hyperlink for this text to the Excel document called Tyson County Art Classes (Figure 6–80c), which is located in the Data Files.

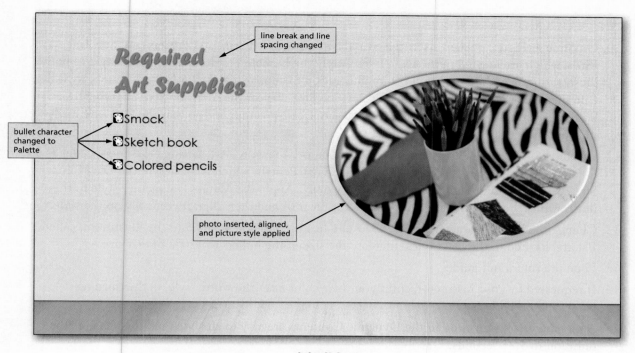

line break and line spacing changed

bullet character changed to Palette

photo inserted, aligned, and picture style applied

Required
Art Supplies

Smock
Sketch book
Colored pencils

(g) Slide 5

Figure 6–80

5. On Slides 2 through 5, change the background to the Papyrus texture fill (first texture in first row) and then change the transparency to 50%. Display the rulers and guides. Move the horizontal guide to 2.67" below the center and move the vertical guide to 5.75" left of the center. To add a second vertical guide, right-click a blank area of the slide, select Grid and Guides, and then click Add Vertical Guide. Move the new vertical guide to 6.21" right of the center.

6. On Slide 2 (Figure 6-80d), insert the illustration called Pallet and Brush, which is located in the Data Files. Size this illustration to approximately 4.16" × 3.84" and then align it with the horizontal and vertical guides on the right.

7. Change the line spacing to 1.5 for the placeholder text on Slide 2, change the bullet characters to the 1) 2) 3) numbered bullets, increase the bullet size to 110% of text size, and then change the color to Green (in Standard Colors).

8. On Slide 3 (Figure 6–80e), insert the three illustrations called Moon Reflection, Sunset, and Tree and Birds, which are located in the Data Files. Apply the 'Double Frame, Black' picture style to the three illustrations. Size the Moon Reflection illustration to approximately 2.41" × 4", the Sunset illustration to approximately 2.43" × 3.5", and the Tree and Birds illustration to approximately 2.43" × 3.47". Select the Align Bottom alignment for the Sunset and Tree and Birds illustrations and then position them at 2.67" below center and so that the Tree and Birds is against the right guide at 6.21". Center the Moon Reflection illustration above the other two illustrations, as shown in the figure.

9. On Slide 2, change the title font to Forte, increase the font size to 40 point, change the font color to Green (sixth color in Standard colors), and then apply a text shadow to the text. Use the Format Painter to format the title text on Slides 3, 4, and 5 with the same features as the title text on Slide 2.

Continued >

In the Labs *continued*

10. On Slide 4 (Figure 6–80f), insert the two illustrations called Still Life Pottery and Still Life Birds, which are located in the Data Files. Apply the Double Frame, Black picture style to both illustrations. Size the Still Life Pottery illustration to approximately 2.59" × 3.47" and the Still Life Birds illustration to approximately 2.75" × 3.89". Select the Align Bottom alignment for both illustrations and then position them at 2.67" below center and so that the Still Life Birds illustration is against the right guide at 6.21".

11. On Slide 5 (Figure 6–80g), insert a line break before the word, Art. Change the line spacing for the title to 1.0. Insert the illustration called Art Pencils, which is located in the Data Files. Size the illustration to approximately 4.01" × 6.02". Apply the Metal Oval picture style to the illustration. Align the left edge of the illustration at 0" and then align it vertically on the slide.

12. Change the bullet character for all the level 1 text on Slides 3, 4, and 5 to the illustration called Palette, located in the Data Files. Increase the size of the bullets to 120% of text size.

13. Hide the rulers and guides.

14. If requested by your instructor, enter your hair color after the word, style, in the third text paragraph on Slide 2.

15. Apply the Orbit transition in the Dynamic Content category to all slides and then change the duration to 3.25 seconds.

16. Run the presentation and verify the hyperlinks and action buttons are correct. Save the presentation using the file name, Lab 6-2 Tyson County Art Classes.

17. Submit the document in the format specified by your instructor.

18. ✸ Why did you add the art illustration as a background on Slide 1? Did changing the bullet characters to pictures add interest to the presentation?

Lab 3: **Consider This: Your Turn**

Design and Create a Presentation about Interior Design

Part 1: In the project for this module, you developed slides with guidelines for organizing a home, including specific information about arranging items in an office and a kitchen. Once areas of your home are organized, you can create rooms that fit your personality and your budget. One method of beginning a room design from scratch is to look at photos online and in magazines. Lighting, upholstered pieces, wooden cabinets, and accessories help influence the room's style. You want to start shopping for furniture and decide to create a PowerPoint presentation to show to interior decorators at the stores. Use the concepts and techniques presented in this module to create this presentation. Begin by developing a Microsoft Word outline with information about your style preferences and budget. Then, open this outline as a PowerPoint presentation, select a suitable theme, and include hyperlinks to websites that show rooms you admire. Change the bullet characters on at least one slide to a picture or a symbol. You may want to use one or more of the five photos called Lighting, Office, Living Room, Drawers and Ottoman in the Data Files, and you can include your own photos if they are appropriate for this topic. Review and revise your presentation as needed and then save the file using the file name, Lab 6-3 Interior Design. Submit your assignment in the format specified by your instructor.

Part 2: ✸ You made several decisions while creating the presentation in this assignment: where to place text, how to format the text (such as font, font size, and colors), which image(s) to use, formatting bullets, and inserting hyperlinks to add interest to the presentation. What was the rationale behind each of these decisions? When you reviewed the document, what further revisions did you make and why?

7 | Creating a Self-Running Presentation Containing Animation

Objectives

You will have mastered the material in this module when you can:

- Remove a photo background
- Crop and compress a photo
- Animate slide content with entrance, emphasis, and exit effects
- Add and adjust motion paths for animations
- Reorder animation sequences
- Associate sounds with animations

- Control animation timing
- Animate SmartArt graphics and charts
- Insert and animate a text box
- Animate bulleted lists
- Rehearse timings
- Set slide show timings manually

Introduction

BTW
Animation Types
The transitions you have been applying between slides in a presentation are one type of PowerPoint animations. In this module you will use another type of animation to move or change elements on the slide. Animation is effective in adding interest to slide content and to call attention to important content. As a caution, however, resist the urge to add animation simply for the sake of animation when it does not have a purpose on a particular slide.

One method used for disseminating information is a **kiosk**. This freestanding, self-service structure is equipped with computer hardware and software and is used to provide information or reference materials to the public. Some have a touch screen or keyboard that serves as an input device and allows users to select various options so they can browse or find specific information. Advanced kiosks allow customers to place orders, make payments, and access the Internet. Many kiosks have multimedia devices for playing sound and video clips.

Various elements on PowerPoint slides can have movement to direct the audience's attention to the point being made. For example, each paragraph in a bulleted list can fade or disappear after being displayed for a set period of time. Each SmartArt graphic component can appear in sequence. A picture can grow, shrink, bounce, or spin, depending upon its relationship to other slide content. PowerPoint's myriad animation effects allow you to use your creativity to design imaginative and distinctive presentations.

Project — Presentation with Adjusted Pictures, Animated Content, and Slide Timings

Drones are becoming commonplace for personal, commercial, and private ventures. These pilotless aerial vehicles are guided by remote control and can be equipped with such items as cameras, supplies, radar, and sensors. The title slide (Figure 7–1a) has animated title text and a drone that moves and turns in the sky. The second slide (Figure 7–1b) shows drones that are flying across a field. The third slide (Figure 7–1c) uses animated SmartArt to explain the process the Federal Aviation Administration has developed to govern drone registrations. The next slide is an animated chart that shows some of the general drone applications (Figure 7–1d). More specific uses of drones are shown in the last slide (Figure 7–1e).

(a) Slide 1 (Title Slide with Animated WordArt and Photo)

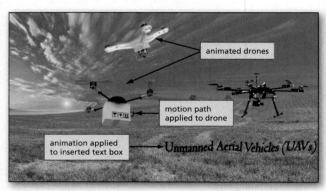

(b) Slide 2 (Animated Photos with Motion Path and Sound)

(c) Slide 3 (Animated SmartArt)

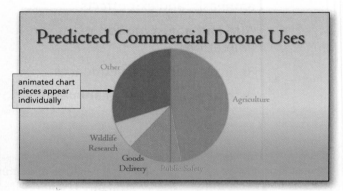

(d) Slide 4 (Animated Chart)

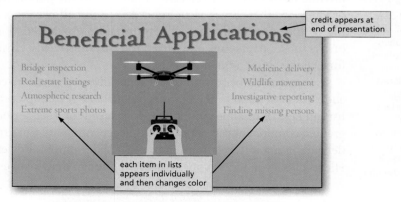

(e) Slide 5 (Animated Lists and Credit)

Figure 7–1

In this module, you will learn how to create the slides shown in Figure 7–1. The following roadmap identifies general activities you will perform as you progress through this module:

1. MODIFY PHOTOS by removing the background, cropping, and compressing.
2. ADD ENTRANCE, EMPHASIS, and EXIT ANIMATIONS to photos and text.
3. ANIMATE BOXES, SMARTART, and CHARTS.
4. CHANGE ANIMATION EFFECTS.
5. SET slide show TIMINGS.

BTW

The Ribbon and Screen Resolution
PowerPoint may change how the groups and buttons within the groups appear on the ribbon, depending on the computer or mobile device's screen resolution. Thus, your ribbon may look different from the ones in this book if you are using a screen resolution other than 1366×768.

Adjusting and Cropping a Photo

At times you may desire to emphasize one section of a photo and eliminate distracting background content. PowerPoint includes formatting tools that allow you to edit photos. The **Remove Background** command isolates the foreground from the background, and the **Crop** command removes content along the top, bottom, left, or right edges. Once you format the photo to include only the desired content, you can **compress** the image to reduce the file size.

To Remove a Background

1 MODIFY PHOTOS | 2 ADD ENTRANCE, EMPHASIS, & EXIT ANIMATIONS
3 ANIMATE BOXES, SMARTART, & CHARTS | 4 CHANGE ANIMATION EFFECTS | 5 SET TIMINGS

The title slide in the Animated Drones presentation has a photo of a yellow drone hovering over a road. You want to eliminate the road and other background from the image. *Why? To direct the viewers' attention to the drone.* The PowerPoint Background Removal feature makes it easy to eliminate extraneous aspects. When you click the Remove Background button, PowerPoint attempts to select the foreground of the photo and overlay a magenta marquee selection on this area. You then can adjust the marquee shape and size to contain all foreground photo components you want to keep. The following steps remove the background from the drone photo.

- Run PowerPoint. If necessary, maximize the PowerPoint window.
- Open the presentation, Drones, located in the Data Files.
- Save the presentation using the file name, Animated Drones.

- With the title slide displaying, click the drone photo to select it and then click the Picture Tools Format tab (Figure 7–2).

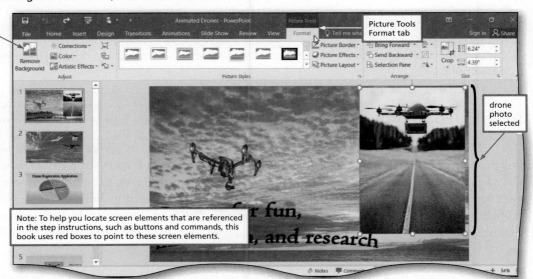

Figure 7–2

- Click the Remove Background button (Picture Tools Format tab | Adjust group) to display the Background Removal tab and a marquee selection area.

- Click and drag the center handle on the bottom of the background removal lines toward the box under the drone and then drag the center handles on the left and right background removal lines outward so that the entire drone is displayed in the marquee selection area.

- Zoom the slide to 150%. Use the vertical and horizontal scroll bars to adjust the slide so the entire yellow drone photo is visible (Figure 7–3).

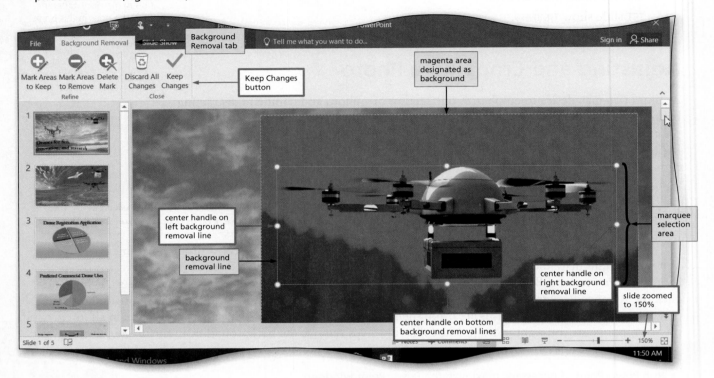

Figure 7–3

Q&A | How does PowerPoint determine the area to display within the marquee?
Microsoft Research software engineers developed the algorithms that determine the portions of the photo in the foreground.

- Click the Keep Changes button (Background Removal tab | Close group) to discard the unwanted photo background.

To Refine Background Removal

1 MODIFY PHOTOS | 2 ADD ENTRANCE, EMPHASIS, & EXIT ANIMATIONS
3 ANIMATE BOXES, SMARTART, & CHARTS | 4 CHANGE ANIMATION EFFECTS | 5 SET TIMINGS

Why? In many cases, the Remove Background command discards all the undesired photo components. When the background is integrated closely with the foreground photo, however, some undesired pieces occasionally remain and other desired pieces are discarded. In the title slide drone photo, part of the white background was not removed, so it is displayed under the right propeller. In contrast, some parts of the propellers were deleted, most notably the left propeller, along with the background. Tools on the Background Removal tab allow you to mark specific areas to remove and to keep. The following steps mark an area to discard and three propeller blades to areas to keep.

- Click the Remove Background button to display the Background Removal tab and the marquee selection area.

- Click the 'Mark Areas to Remove' button (Background Removal tab | Refine group) and then position the pointer in the white area below the right propeller (Figure 7–4).

Figure 7–4

Q&A What if different areas were kept/removed in my photo?
Read the steps to Keep or Discard areas of a photo, and keep or remove as appropriate to show just the drone against the sky.

Why did my pointer change shape?
The pointer changed to a pencil to indicate you are about to draw on a precise area of the photo.

I am using a touch screen and am having difficulty positioning the pointer. What should I do?
Zoom your screen to increase the level of detail you need. Using a mouse also might help with this task.

②

- Click and then drag the pointer across the white area to indicate the portion of the photo to discard (Figure 7–5).

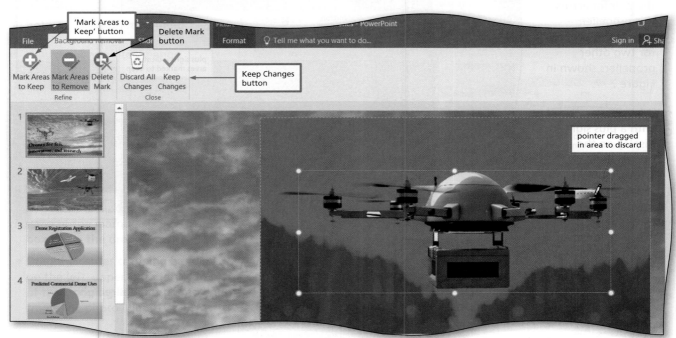

Figure 7–5

Q&A | Does cropping actually cut the photo's edges?
No. Although you cannot see the cropped edges, they exist until you save the file.

Can I crop a picture to exact dimensions?
Yes. Right-click the picture and then click Format Picture on the shortcut menu. On the Crop pane, under Picture position, enter the measurements in the Width and Height boxes.

❸

- Click the Crop button again to crop the edges.

Q&A | Can I press the ESC key to crop the edges?
Yes.

Can I change the crop lines?
If you have not saved the file, you can undo your crops by clicking the Undo button on the Quick Access Toolbar, or clicking the Reset Picture button (Picture Tools Format tab | Adjust group), or pressing CTRL+Z. If you have saved the file, you cannot undo the crop.

Other Ways

1. Right-click photo, click Crop on shortcut menu

BTW
Simultaneous Cropping on Two or Four Sides
To crop equally on two sides simultaneously, press the CTRL key while dragging the center cropping handle on either side inward. To crop all four sides equally, press the CTRL key while dragging a corner cropping handle inward.

TO CROP A PICTURE TO A SHAPE

In addition to cropping a picture, you can change the shape of a picture by cropping it to a specific shape. The picture's proportions are maintained, and it automatically is trimmed to fill the shape's geometry. To crop to a specific shape, you would perform the following steps.

1. Select the picture you want to crop.
2. Display the Picture Tools Format tab and then click the Crop arrow (Picture Tools Format tab | Size group) to display the Crop menu.
3. Point to 'Crop to Shape' and then click the desired shape in the Shape gallery.

---

1 MODIFY PHOTOS | 2 ADD ENTRANCE, EMPHASIS, & EXIT ANIMATIONS
3 ANIMATE BOXES, SMARTART, & CHARTS | 4 CHANGE ANIMATION EFFECTS | 5 SET TIMINGS

To Compress a Photo

Photos inserted into slides greatly increase the total PowerPoint file size. PowerPoint automatically compresses photo files inserted into slides by eliminating details, generally with no visible loss of quality. You can increase the compression and, in turn, decrease the file size if you instruct PowerPoint to compress a photo you have cropped so you can save space on a storage medium such as a hard disk, USB flash drive, or optical disk. Although these storage devices generally have a large storage capacity, you might want to reduce the file size. *Why? A smaller size reduces the download time from an FTP server or website. Also, some Internet service providers restrict an attachment's file size.*

The photo on the title slide is cropped and displays only the drone. You will not need any of the invisible portions of the photo, so you can delete them permanently and reduce the photo file size. The following steps compress the size of the title slide drone photo.

❶

- With the drone photo selected, click the Compress Pictures button (Picture Tools Format tab | Adjust group) to display the Compress Pictures dialog box (Figure 7–10).

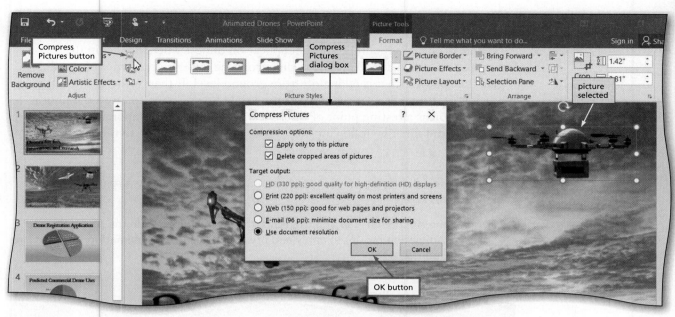

Figure 7–10

Q&A If I want to add an artistic effect, should I apply the effect prior to or after compressing a picture?

Compress a picture and then apply the artistic effect.

2

- Click the OK button (Compress Pictures dialog box) to delete the cropped portions of this photo and compress the image.

Q&A Can I undo the compression?

Yes, as long as you have not saved the file after compressing the photo.

Animating Slide Content

The Slide 1 background photo shows a drone in the sunset sky. When the presentation begins, the audience will view this scene and then see another drone enter from the lower-right corner, move across the slide, pulse slightly at the center of the slide, and then continue moving upward. To create this animation on the slide, you will use entrance, emphasis, and exit effects.

    If you need to move objects on a slide once they are displayed, you can define a **motion path**. This predefined movement determines where an object will be displayed and then travel. Motion paths are grouped into the Basic, Lines & Curves, and Special categories. You can draw a **custom path** if none of the predefined paths meets your needs.

BTW
Touch Screen Differences
The Office and Windows interfaces may vary if you are using a touch screen. For this reason, you might notice that the function or appearance of your touch screen differs slightly from this module's presentation.

Use animation sparingly.
PowerPoint audience members usually take notice the first time an animation is displayed on the screen. When the same animation effect is applied throughout a presentation, the viewers generally become desensitized to the effect unless it is highly unusual or annoying. Resist the urge to use animation effects simply because PowerPoint provides the tools to do so. You have options to decide how text or a slide element enters and exits a slide and how it is displayed once it is present on the slide; your goal, however, is to use these options wisely. Audiences soon tire of a presentation riddled with animations, causing them to quickly lose their impact.

 CONSIDER THIS

BTW
Icon Colors for Animation Effects
Using a traffic signal analogy may help you remember the sequence of events as you apply animation effects to control how objects enter, move on, and exit slides. Green icons indicate when the animation effect starts on the slide. Yellow icons represent the object's motion; use them with caution so they do not distract from the message you are conveying to your audience. Red icons indicate when the object stops appearing on a slide.

To Animate a Photo Using an Entrance Effect

The drone you modified will not appear on Slide 1 when you begin the presentation. Instead, it will enter the slide from the lower-right corner of the slide to give the appearance it is taking off from ground level. It then will continue moving upward until it reaches near the center of the slide, so you need to move the photo to this location as a resting point of where it will stop moving temporarily, as if it is hovering in mid-air. The following steps apply an entrance effect to the drone photo.

1 With Slide 1 displaying, zoom to 55% and then move the yellow drone photo above the word, research.

2 Display the Animations tab and then click the Fly In animation in the Animation gallery (Animation group) to apply and preview this entrance animation for the drone photo (Figure 7–11).

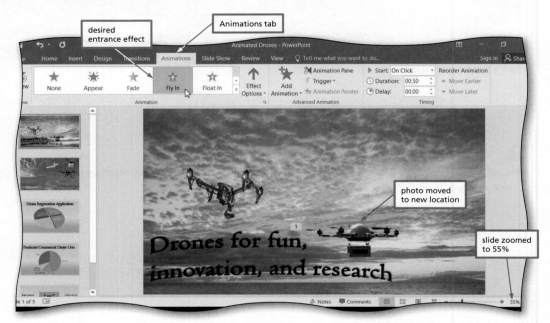

Figure 7–11

To Change Animation Direction

By default, the photo appears on the slide by entering from the bottom edge. You can modify this direction and specify that it enters from another side or from a corner. The following steps change the drone photo entrance animation direction to the bottom-right corner.

BTW
Numbered Animation Effects
A number is displayed next to an object you animate. Each time you assign an animation effect to an object, a new number is displayed. These effects are numbered in the sequence you apply the animations.

1 Click the Effect Options button (Animations tab | Animation group) to display the Direction gallery (Figure 7–12).

2 Click the 'From Bottom-Right' arrow in the Direction gallery to apply this direction to the entrance animation and show a preview.

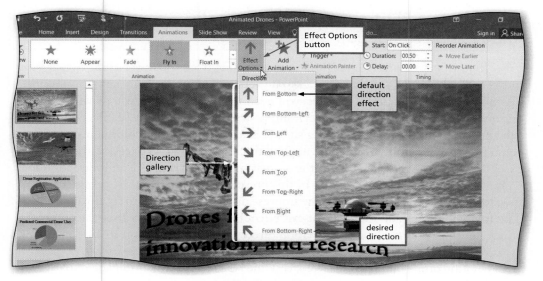

Figure 7–12

To Animate a Photo Using an Emphasis Effect

The drone will enter the slide from the lower-right corner and stop in the center of the slide. You then want it to fade out and in, or pulse, slightly to give the impression that it is hovering over the water. PowerPoint provides several effects that you can apply to a picture once it appears on a slide. These movements are categorized as emphasis effects, and they are colored yellow in the Animation gallery. You already have applied an entrance effect to the drone photo, so you want to add another animation to this photo. The following steps apply an emphasis effect to the drone photo after the entrance effect.

1 With the drone photo still selected, click the Add Animation button (Animations tab | Advanced Animation group) to expand the Animation gallery (Figure 7–13).

2 Click Pulse in the Emphasis section to apply this emphasis effect to the drone photo.

BTW
Effects for Objects with Text
Some entrance and exit effects (such as Flip, Drop, and Whip) and some emphasis effects (such as Brush Color, Shimmer, and Wave) are available only for objects that contain text. If you want to apply an animation effect that is not available for this reason, add a space inside your object.

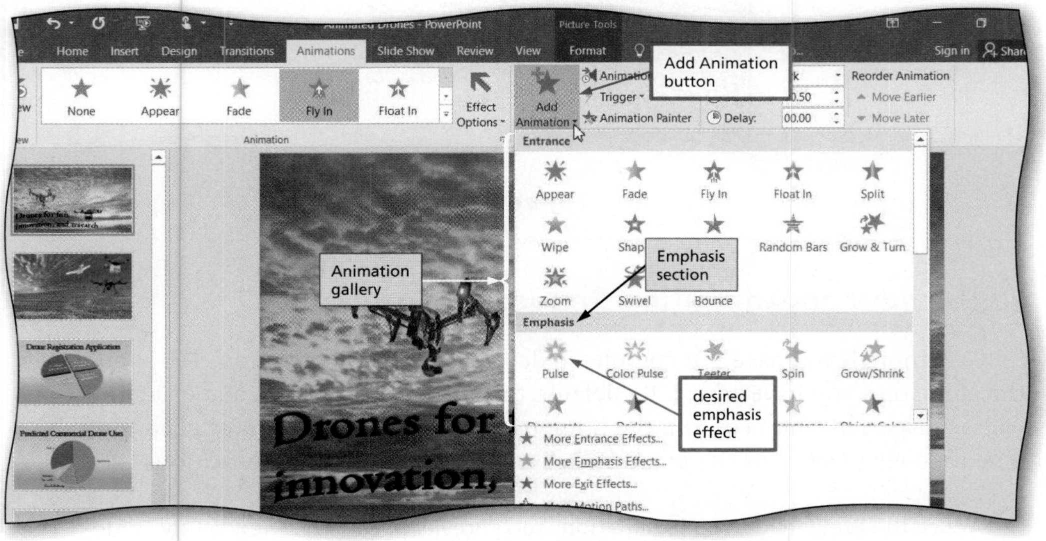

Figure 7–13

To Animate a Photo Using an Exit Effect and Change Animation Direction

The animated drone photo will enter the slide from the lower-right corner, stop in the center of the slide, and then pulse. It then will continue flying straight upward. To continue this animation sequence, you need to apply an exit effect. As with the entrance and emphasis effects, PowerPoint provides a wide variety of effects that you can apply to remove a picture from a slide. These exit effects are colored red in the Animation gallery. You already have applied the Fly In entrance effect, so the Fly Out exit effect would give continuity to the animation sequence. The default direction for a photo to exit a slide is To Bottom. In this presentation, you want the drone to exit toward the top of the slide to give the impression it is continuing to fly through the air. The following steps add the Fly Out exit effect to the drone photo after the emphasis effect and then change the exit animation direction from To Bottom to To Top.

1 With the drone photo still selected, click the Add Animation button again to expand the Animation gallery. Scroll down to display the Exit section (Figure 7–14).

2 Click Fly Out in the Exit section to add this exit effect to the sequence of drone photo animations.

3 Click the Effect Options button to display the Direction gallery and then click the To Top arrow to apply this direction to the exit animation effect.

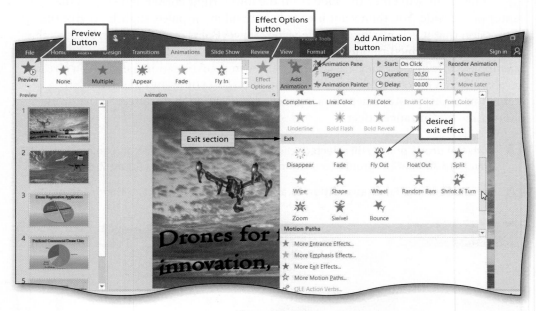

Figure 7–14

To Preview an Animation Sequence

Although you have not completed developing the presentation, you should view the animation you have added. By default, the entrance, emphasis, and exit animations will be displayed when you run the presentation and tap the screen or click the mouse. The following step runs the presentation and displays the three animations.

1 Click the Preview button (Animations tab | Preview group) to view all the Slide 1 animation.

To Modify Entrance Animation Timing

The three animation effects are displayed quickly. To create a dramatic effect, you can change the timing so that the background photo displays and then, a few seconds later, the drone starts to fly through the sky slowly. The default setting is to start each animation with a mouse click, but you can change this setting so that the entrance effect is delayed until a specified number of seconds has passed. The following steps modify the start, delay, and duration settings for the entrance animation.

1 Click the 1 numbered tag on the left side of the drone photo and then click the Start arrow (Animations tab | Timing group) to display the start timing menu.

2 Click After Previous to change the start timing setting.

3 Click the Duration up arrow (Animations tab | Timing group) several times to increase the time from 00.50 second to 03.00 seconds.

4 Click the Delay up arrow (Animations tab | Timing group) several times to increase the time from 00.00 second to 02.00 seconds (Figure 7–15).

5 Click the Preview button to view the animations.

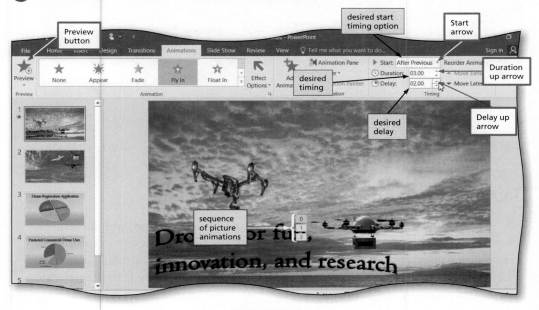

Figure 7–15

To Modify Emphasis and Exit Timings

Now that the entrance animation settings have been modified, you can change the emphasis and exit effects for the drone photo. The emphasis effect can occur once the entrance effect has concluded, and then the exit effect can commence. You will increase the duration of the exit effect compared with the duration of the entrance effect. The animation sequence should flow without stopping, so you will not change the default delay timing of 00.00 second. The following steps modify the start and duration settings for the emphasis and exit animations.

1 Click the 1 sequence number, which now represents the emphasis effect, on the left side of the drone photo, click the Start arrow, and then click After Previous to change the start timing option setting.

BTW
Developing Animations
You can add the parts of the animation in any order and then change the sequence. Many slide designers, however, develop the animation using the sequence in which the elements will display on the slide in an effort to save time and help organize the animation sequence.

2 Increase the duration time to 04.00 seconds.

3 Click the 1 sequence number, which now represents the exit effect, and then change the start timing to After Previous.

4 Increase the duration time to 06.00 seconds (Figure 7–16).

5 Preview the Slide 1 animations.

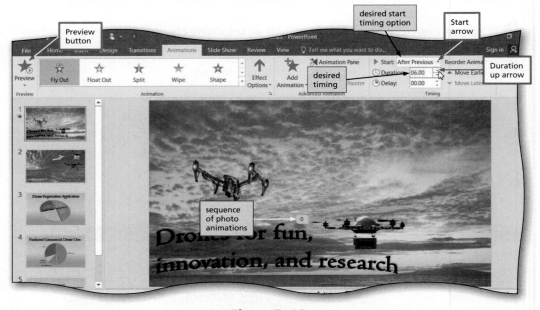

Figure 7–16

BTW
Selecting Paragraph Text Animation Options
Multi-level bulleted list paragraphs can have animation effects that help direct the audience's attention. For example, you can animate the second-level paragraphs so they are displayed individually along with any associated third-level paragraphs. To specify a text animation option, display the Animation Pane, click an animation you want to manipulate in the list, click this animation's list arrow to display a menu, click Effect Options in the list, and then click the Text Animation tab in the dialog box. If desired, you can click the Group Text arrow and select a paragraph level, such as 2nd level, in the list. Click the Automatically after check box and enter a time if you want the next bulleted paragraph to appear after a specific number of seconds. In addition, click the 'In reverse order' check box to build the paragraphs from the bottom to the top of the slide.

To Animate Title Text Placeholder Paragraphs

The drone photo on Slide 1 has one entrance, one emphasis, and one exit animation, and you can add similar animations to the Slide 1 title text placeholder. For a special effect, you can add several emphasis animations to one slide element. The following steps add one entrance and two emphasis animations to the title text paragraph.

1 Click the Slide 1 title text placeholder to select it.

2 Click the border so that it displays as a solid line.

3 Click the More button in the Animation gallery (Animations tab | Animation group) to expand the Animation gallery.

4 Click the Float In entrance effect in the Animation gallery to add this animation.

5 Change the start timing option to With Previous.

6 Change the duration time to 02.00 seconds.

7 Click the Add Animation button and then click the Font Color Emphasis animation effect.

8 Change the start timing option to After Previous.

9 Click the Add Animation button and then click the Wave emphasis animation effect.

⑩ Change the start timing option to With Previous (Figure 7–17).

Figure 7–17

BTW
Animating Text by Word or by Letter
One animation effect you can use is having each word or each letter in a paragraph display individually instead of having the entire paragraph display at once. To apply this animation effect, display the Animation Pane, click an animation you want to change in the list, click this animation's list arrow to display a menu, click Effect Options in the list, and then click the Effect tab in the dialog box. In the Enhancements area, click the Animate Text arrow and then click By word or By letter in the list. You then can specify the amount of delay that should occur between each word or each letter by adjusting the figure in the '% delay between words' or '% delay between letters' box.

To Change Animation Order

1 MODIFY PHOTOS | 2 ADD ENTRANCE, EMPHASIS, & EXIT ANIMATIONS
3 ANIMATE BOXES, SMARTART, & CHARTS | 4 CHANGE ANIMATION EFFECTS | 5 SET TIMINGS

Two title slide elements have animations: the drone photo and the title text placeholder. PowerPoint applies the animations in the order you created them, so on this slide the drone photo animations will appear first and then the title text placeholder animation will follow. You can reorder animation elements. *Why? You may decide one set of animations should appear before another set or you also can reorder individual animation elements within an animation group.* In this presentation, you decide to display the title text placeholder animation first, and then you decide that the Wave emphasis effect should appear before the Font Color emphasis effect. The following steps reorder the two animation groups on the slide and then reorder the Font Color and Wave emphasis effects.

❶

- If necessary, click the Slide 1 title text placeholder border so that it displays as a solid line. Click the Animation Pane button (Animations tab | Advanced Animation group) to display the Animation Pane (Figure 7–18).

Q&A Why are the three Rectangle effects shaded in the Animation Pane?
The shading corresponds to the three animation effects that you applied to the title text placeholder. The green star indicates the entrance effect, the A with the multicolor underline indicates the Font Color emphasis effect, and the gold star indicates the Wave emphasis effect.

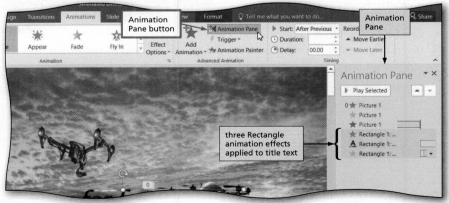

Figure 7–18

Why do I see a different number after the Rectangle label?
PowerPoint numbers slide elements consecutively, so you may see a different number if you have added and deleted photos, text, and other graphics. You will rename these labels in a later set of steps.

2

- Click the up button in the Animation Pane three times to move the three Rectangle animations above the Picture animations (Figure 7–19).

- Click the Play Selected button (Animation Pane) to see the reordered animations.

Q&A Can I click the Move Earlier button (Animations tab | Timing group) on the ribbon instead of the up button in the Animation Pane? Yes. Either button will change the animation order.

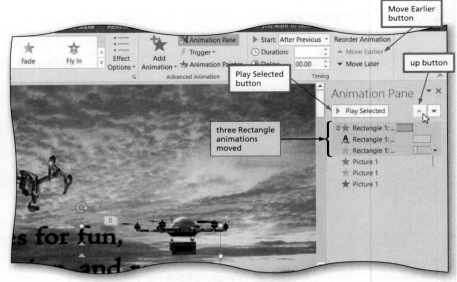

Figure 7–19

3

- In the Animation Pane, click the second Rectangle label representing the Font Color animation to select it and then click the down button to move this animation below the Rectangle label representing the Wave animation (Figure 7–20).

- Click the Play From button (Animation Pane) to see the reordered text placeholder animations beginning with the font color change and the drone animations.

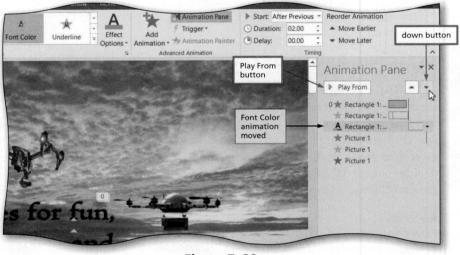

Figure 7–20

Q&A Can I click the Move Later button (Animations tab | Timing group) on the ribbon instead of the down button in the Animation Pane? Yes. Either button will change the animation order.

Can I view the Animation Pane at any time when I am adding and adjusting animation effects? Yes. Click the Animation Pane button (Animations tab | Advanced Animation group) to display the Animation Pane.

To Rename Slide Objects

1 MODIFY PHOTOS | 2 ADD ENTRANCE, EMPHASIS, & EXIT ANIMATIONS
3 ANIMATE BOXES, SMARTART, & CHARTS | 4 CHANGE ANIMATION EFFECTS | 5 SET TIMINGS

The two animated title slide elements are listed in the Animation Pane as Rectangle and Picture. You can give these objects meaningful names. *Why? So that you can identify them in the animation sequence.* The following steps rename the animated Slide 1 objects.

- Display the Home tab and then click the Select button (Home tab | Editing group) to display the Select menu (Figure 7–21).

- Click Selection Pane in the Select menu to display the Selection pane.

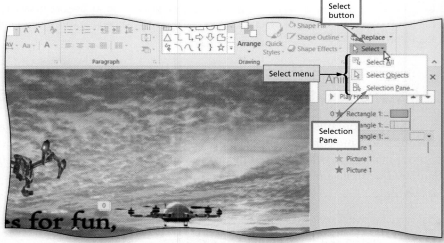

Figure 7–21

- Click the Picture label in the Selection pane and then click the label again to place the insertion point in the box (Figure 7–22).

Q&A What does the Picture label represent on three animations? It indicates that the green entry, yellow emphasis, and red exit animations are applied to a picture, in this case the drone photo.

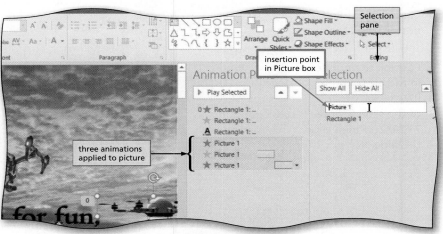

Figure 7–22

- Delete the text and then type **Drone** in the Picture box.

- Click the Rectangle label in the Selection pane, click the label again, delete the text, and then type **Title Text** in the Rectangle box (Figure 7–23).

Q&A What does the Rectangle label represent on three animations? It indicates that the green entry and two emphasis animations are applied to the title text placeholder.

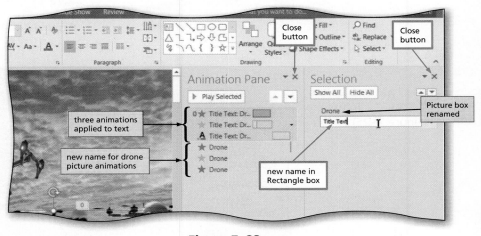

Figure 7–23

- Click the Close button on the Selection pane.

- Click the Close button on the Animation pane.

Break Point: If you wish to take a break, this is a good place to do so. Be sure to save the Animated Drones file again and then you can exit PowerPoint. To resume at a later time, run PowerPoint, open the file called Animated Drones, and continue following the steps from this location forward.

To Insert a Text Box and Format Text

1 MODIFY PHOTOS | 2 ADD ENTRANCE, EMPHASIS, & EXIT ANIMATIONS
3 ANIMATE BOXES, SMARTART, & CHARTS | 4 CHANGE ANIMATION EFFECTS | 5 SET TIMINGS

Slide 2 contains three elements that you will animate. First, you will add a text box, format and animate text, and add a motion path and sound. Next, you will add an entrance effect and custom motion path to a drone photo. Finally, you will animate one drone and copy the animations to the other drones using the Animation Painter. The first sequence will be a text box in the lower-left corner of the slide. The following steps add a text box to Slide 2.

- Display Slide 2 and then display the Insert tab.

- Click the Text Box button (Insert tab | Text group).

- Position the pointer in the grass in the lower-left corner of the slide (Figure 7–24) and then click the slide.

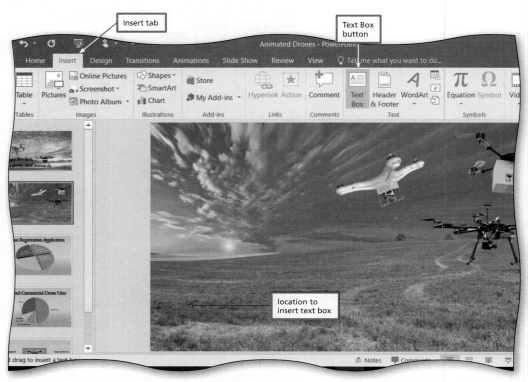

Figure 7–24

- Type **Unmanned Aerial Vehicles (UAVs)** in the box (Figure 7–25).

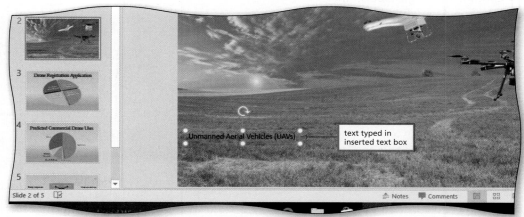

Figure 7–25

- Display Slide 1, position the pointer in the second line of the title text placeholder, and then double-click the Format Painter button (Home tab | Clipboard group) (Figure 7–26).

I am using a touch screen and cannot use the Format Painter for this task. What should I do?
You may need to change the formatting manually.

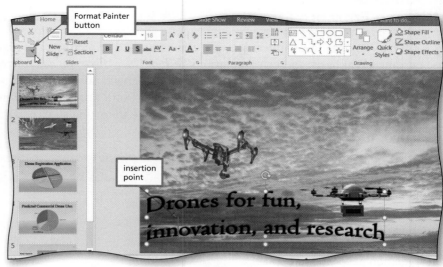

Figure 7–26

- Display Slide 2 and then triple-click the inserted box to apply the Slide 1 title text format to the text in the box.

- Press the ESC key to turn off the Format Painter feature.

- Change the font size to 36 point (Figure 7–27).

Figure 7–27

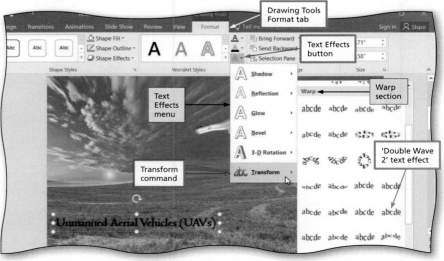

- Display the Drawing Tools Format tab, click the Text Effects button (Drawing Tools Format tab | WordArt Styles group), point to Transform in the Text Effects menu, and then apply the 'Double Wave 2' WordArt text effect (last effect in fifth row of Warp section) to the words in the box (Figure 7–28).

Figure 7–28

To Animate a Text Box
Using an Entrance Effect

Boxes can have the same animation effects applied to pictures and placeholders, and slide designers often use entrance, emphasis, and exit animations. *Why? These effects can add interest to slides, and the default timings can be changed to synchronize with the slide content.* The 13 effects shown in the Entrance section of the Animation gallery are some of the more popular choices; PowerPoint provides many more effects that are divided into the Basic, Subtle, Moderate, and Exciting categories. The following steps add an entrance effect to the text box.

- If necessary, click the text box to select it and then display the Animations tab.

- Click the More button in the Animation gallery (Animations tab | Animation group) to expand the Animation gallery (Figure 7–29).

- Click More Entrance Effects in the Animation gallery to display the Change Entrance Effect dialog box.

Experiment

- Click some of the entrance effects in the various areas and watch the effect preview in the box on Slide 2.

Can I move the dialog box so that I can see the effect preview?
Yes. Drag the dialog box title bar so that the dialog box does not cover the box.

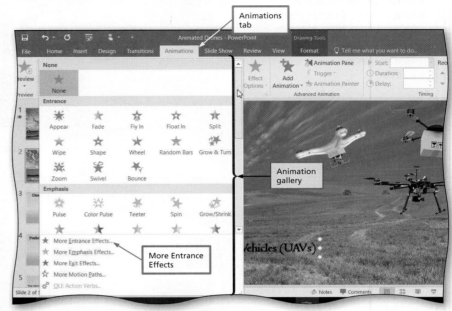

Figure 7–29

- Click Expand in the Subtle section (Figure 7–30).

Why do I see a preview of the effects when I click their names?
The Preview Effect box is selected. If you do not want to see previews, click the box to deselect it.

Figure 7–30

4

- Click the OK button (Change Entrance Effect dialog box) to apply the Expand entrance effect to the text.

- Change the start timing option to With Previous.

- Change the duration to 03.00 seconds (Figure 7–31).

Q&A Can I remove an animation?
Yes. Click None (Animations tab | Animation group). You may need to click the More button to see None.

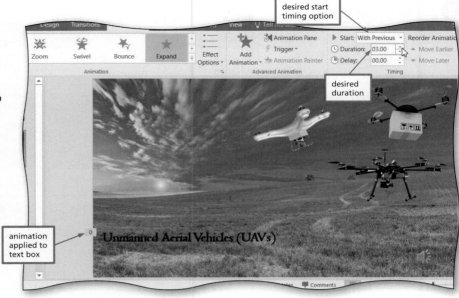

Figure 7–31

To Animate a Text Box by Applying a Motion Path

1 MODIFY PHOTOS | 2 ADD ENTRANCE, EMPHASIS, & EXIT ANIMATIONS

3 ANIMATE BOXES, SMARTART, & CHARTS | **4 CHANGE ANIMATION EFFECTS** | **5 SET TIMINGS**

Why? *One of the more effective methods of animating slide objects is to use a motion path to predetermine the route the object will follow.* In your presentation, the text box will move from the left side of the slide to the right side in an upward curving motion that simulates a drone's flight through the sky. The following steps apply a motion path to the Slide 2 text box and then reverse the direction of the arc.

1

- With the Slide 2 text box still selected, click the Add Animation button (Animations tab | Advanced Animation group) to expand the Animation gallery.

- Scroll down until the Motion Paths section is visible (Figure 7–32).

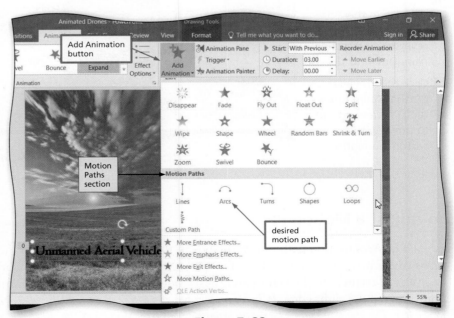

Figure 7–32

2

- Click the Arcs motion path to apply the animation to the box.

- Change the start timing option to After Previous.

- Change the duration to 05.00 seconds (Figure 7–33).

 Q&A Are more motion paths available in addition to those shown in the Animation gallery? Yes. To see additional motion paths, click More Motion Paths in the lower portion of the Animation gallery. The motion paths are arranged in the Basic, Lines & Curves, and Special categories.

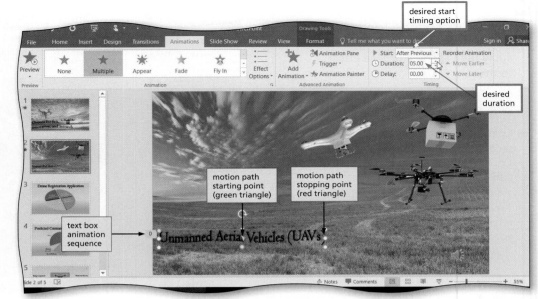

Figure 7–33

3

- Click the Effect Options button (Animations tab | Animation group) to display the Effect Options gallery (Figure 7–34).

4

- Click Up in the Direction section to reverse the direction from Down to Up.

- Click the Preview button (Animations tab | Preview group) to preview the custom animation.

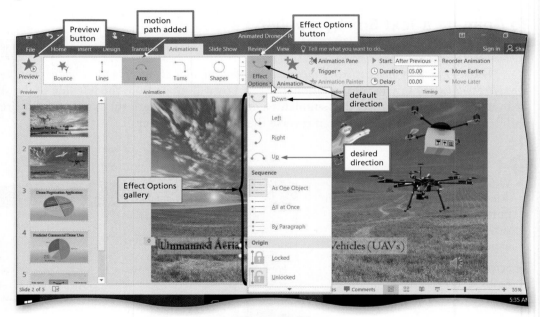

Figure 7–34

To Adjust a Motion Path

1 MODIFY PHOTOS | 2 ADD ENTRANCE, EMPHASIS, & EXIT ANIMATIONS
3 ANIMATE BOXES, SMARTART, & CHARTS | 4 CHANGE ANIMATION EFFECTS | 5 SET TIMINGS

The Arcs motion path moves the box in the correct directions, but the path can be extended to move across the entire width of the slide. The green triangle at the end of the word, Aerial, indicates the starting point, and the red triangle in the right parenthesis indicates the stopping point. You would like to move the stopping point toward the right edge. **Why?** *The text box is positioned on the left side of the slide, so it does not need to be moved to the left. The stopping point, however, is positioned in the middle of the slide, so it can be moved to the right to increase the distance and provide the maximum animation effect on the slide.* The following steps move the stopping point on the Slide 2 text box animation.

1

- Click the text box to select it. Drag the red stopping point to the location shown in Figure 7–35.

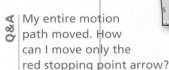

Q&A My entire motion path moved. How can I move only the red stopping point arrow?
Be certain your pointer is a two-headed arrow and not a four-headed arrow.

If I wanted to move the starting point, what would I do?
Drag the green starting point to the desired location.

Figure 7–35

2

- Preview the custom animation.

- Click the slide to clear the selected text and view the motion path (Figure 7–36).

Q&A I do not see the motion path on my slide. Where is it?
The white motion path is difficult to see against the green grass. If you look carefully, however, you can see the white line overlaying the first few letters of the word, Vehicles.

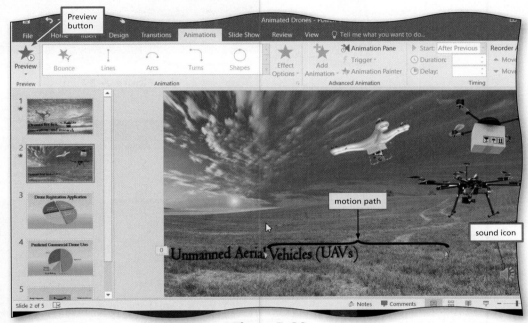

Figure 7–36

My animation is not exactly like the path shown in Figure 7–36. Can I change the path?
Yes. Continue adjusting the starting and stopping points and playing the animation until you are satisfied with the effect.

To Associate a Sound with an Animation

1 MODIFY PHOTOS | 2 ADD ENTRANCE, EMPHASIS, & EXIT ANIMATIONS
3 ANIMATE BOXES, SMARTART, & CHARTS | 4 CHANGE ANIMATION EFFECTS | 5 SET TIMINGS

Why? *Sounds can enhance a presentation if used properly, and they can be linked to other animations on the slide.* Slide 2 already has an inserted drone sound. The following step associates the sound with the box on Slide 2.

1

- Move the pointer to the location where the sound icon is located on Slide 2 (shown in Figure 7–36) and then click the sound icon to display the sizing handles for the sound icon.

- Click the Play button (Animations tab | Animation group).

- Change the start timing option to With Previous (Figure 7–37).

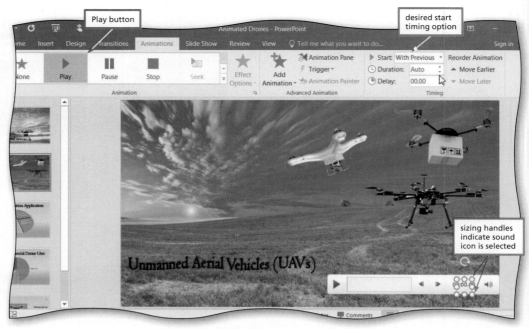

Figure 7–37

2

- Click the location where the sound icon is located and then display the Audio Tools Playback tab.

- Click 'Loop until Stopped' (Audio Tools Playback tab | Audio Options group) to select the check box (Figure 7–38).

Q&A How do I know animation has been added to the drone sound?
The 0 in the numbered tag indicates an animation is applied.

Figure 7–38

To Draw a Custom Motion Path

1 MODIFY PHOTOS | 2 ADD ENTRANCE, EMPHASIS, & EXIT ANIMATIONS

3 ANIMATE BOXES, SMARTART, & CHARTS | 4 CHANGE ANIMATION EFFECTS | 5 SET TIMINGS

Why? *Although PowerPoint supplies a wide variety of motion paths, at times they may not fit the precise animations your presentation requires. In that situation, you can draw a custom path that specifies the unique movement your slide element should make.* Slide 2 has clips of several drones. You can animate a drone to fly to several areas in the sky. No preset motion path presents the exact motion you want to display, so you will draw your own custom path.

Drawing a custom path requires some practice and patience. A mouse is required to perform this task, and you click the mouse to begin drawing the line. If you want the line to change direction, such as to curve, you click again. When you have completed drawing the path, you double-click to end the line. The following steps draw a custom motion path.

- Select the drone carrying a box photo in the upper-right corner of the slide (shown in Figure 7–38). Apply the Fade entrance effect and then change the start timing option to After Previous.

- Click the Add Animation button and then scroll down until the entire Motion Paths section is visible (Figure 7–39).

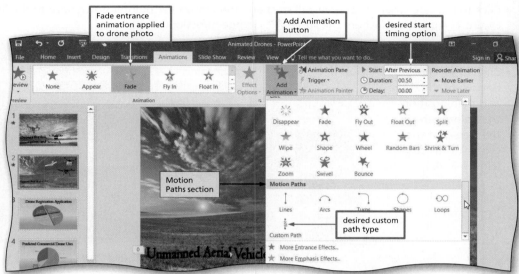

Figure 7–39

Q&A Can I draw a custom motion path when using a touch screen?
No. You must use a mouse to perform this task.

- Click Custom Path in the Motion Paths gallery to add this animation.

- Click the Effect Options button (Animations tab | Animation group) to display the Type gallery (Figure 7–40).

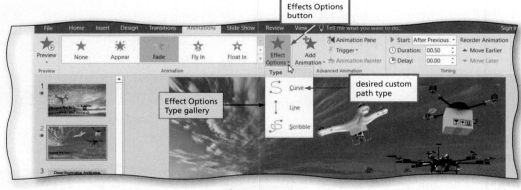

Figure 7–40

❸

- Click Curve in the Type gallery and then position the pointer directly on top of the drone's box.

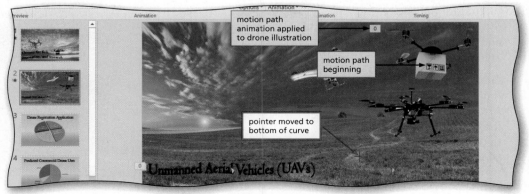

Figure 7–41

Why did I need to change the option from Scribble to Curve?

Your custom motion path will select particular locations on the slide, and the Curve type will create rounded edges to connect the lines you draw. The Scribble option would draw only straight lines, so the drone would not have smooth turns as it flew from one location to the next.

- Click to indicate where the curve will start and then move the pointer downward to the location shown in Figure 7–41, which is where the curve will change direction.

- Click to set the bottom of the curve and then position the pointer above the tree near the center of the slide (Figure 7–42).

Figure 7–42

- Click to set the location above the tree where the drone will change direction. Position the pointer on the left side of the white drone, as shown in Figure 7–43, and then click to set the top of the curve in this direction of travel.

Figure 7–43

- Position the pointer on the horizon, as shown in Figure 7–44, and then double-click to indicate the end of the motion path and preview this animation.

- Change the start timing option to After Previous and the duration setting to 07.00 seconds (Figure 7–44).

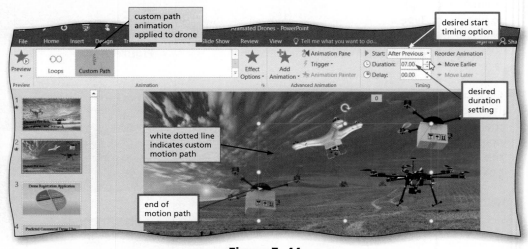

Figure 7–44

If my curve is not correct, can I delete it?

Yes. Select the motion path, press the DELETE key, and then repeat the previous steps.

To Use the Animation Painter to Animate a Picture

At times, you may desire to apply the same animation effects to several objects on a slide. On Slide 2, for example, you want to animate the three drones with identical entrance, emphasis, and exit effects. As with the Format Painter that is used to duplicate font and paragraph attributes, the Animation Painter copies animation effects. Using the Animation Painter can save time. *Why? It duplicates numerous animations quickly and consistently.* The following steps animate one drone and then use the Animation Painter to copy these effects to two other drones.

- Select the white drone that is located near the center of the slide and then apply the Fly In entrance effect.

- Click the Effect Options button and then change the direction to 'From Top-Left'.

- Change the start timing option to After Previous and the duration to 06.00 seconds (Figure 7–45).

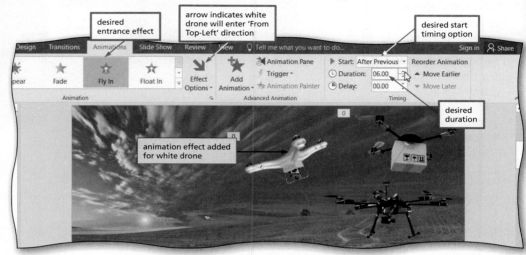

Figure 7–45

- Select the white drone, add the Pulse emphasis effect, change the start timing option to After Previous, and then change the duration to 02.00 seconds (Figure 7–46).

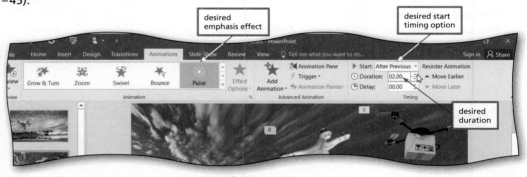

Figure 7–46

- With the white drone still selected, add the Fade exit effect, change the start timing option to After Previous, and then change the duration to 03.00 seconds (Figure 7–47).

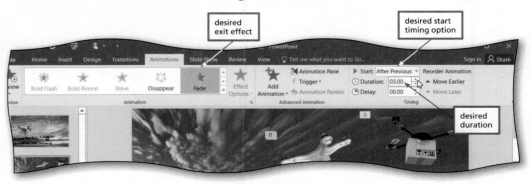

Figure 7–47

Q&A | Can I copy the animation to an object on another slide?
Yes. Once you establish the desired animation effects, you can copy them to any object that can be animated on any slide.

4

- Click the drone with the box, which has the motion path and other animation effects, to select it and then click the Animation Painter button (Animations tab | Advanced Animation group).

- Position the pointer over the black drone with the camera, which is located beneath the drone with the box (Figure 7–48).

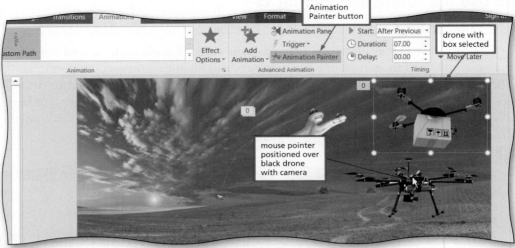

Figure 7–48

Q&A Why did my pointer change shape?
The pointer changed shape by displaying a paintbrush to indicate that the Animation Painter function is active.

5

- Click the black drone to apply the same entrance, emphasis, and exit animation effects as those added to the drone with the box (Figure 7–49).

- Preview the animation effects.

Q&A Can I copy the animations to more than one object simultaneously?
Yes. Double-click the Animation Painter button and then apply it to multiple items. The Animation Painter functions in a similar manner as the Format Painter.

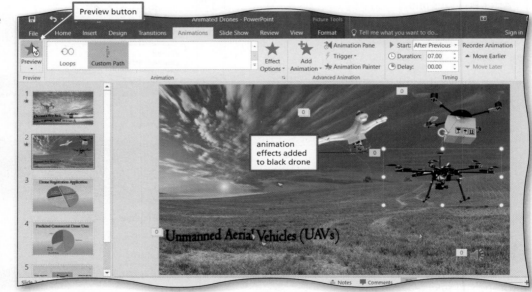

Figure 7–49

Other Ways

1. Select animated object, press ALT+SHIFT+C, click target object to copy animation

---

Break Point: If you wish to take a break, this is a good place to do so. Be sure to save the Animated Drones file again and then you can exit PowerPoint. To resume at a later time, run PowerPoint, open the file called Animated Drones, and continue following the steps from this location forward.

To Animate a SmartArt Graphic

The Federal Aviation Administration (FAA) requires every person who owns a drone weighing more than .55 pounds to file a Drone Registration Application. This online form has four registration components, and they are shown in the Slide 3 SmartArt graphic. You want to add animation to each SmartArt shape. *Why? This animation emphasizes each step in the registration process and helps the audience concentrate on each component.* While you can add a custom animation to each shape in the cycle, you also can use one of PowerPoint's built-in animations to simplify the animation procedure. The following steps apply an entrance animation effect to the Segmented Cycle diagram.

1

- Display Slide 3, select the SmartArt graphic, and then display the Animation gallery (Figure 7–50).

2

- Select the Zoom entrance effect.

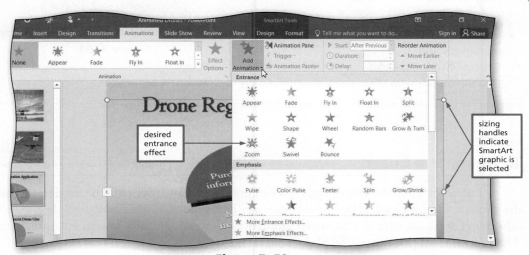

Figure 7–50

To Change a SmartArt Graphic Animation Sequence

By default, all SmartArt graphic components enter the slide simultaneously. You can modify this entrance sequence setting. *Why? Each element will enter one at a time and build a clockwise sequence.* The following steps change the sequence for the SmartArt animation to One by One.

1

- Click the Effect Options button to display the Effect Options gallery (Figure 7–51).

Q&A Can I reverse the order of individual shapes in the SmartArt sequence? No. You can reverse the order of the entire SmartArt graphic but not individual shapes within the sequence.

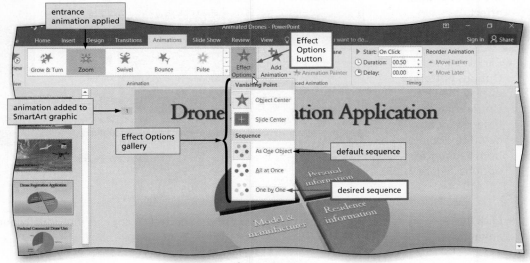

Figure 7–51

2

- Click 'One by One' in the Sequence section to change the animation order.

- Change the start timing option to After Previous, the duration to 04.00 seconds, and the delay to 01.00 second (Figure 7–52).

- Preview the animations and watch the four SmartArt graphic components enter the slide individually in a clockwise sequence.

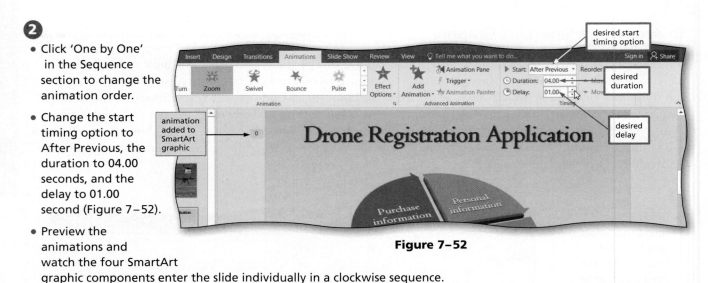

Figure 7–52

To Animate a Chart

1 MODIFY PHOTOS | 2 ADD ENTRANCE, EMPHASIS, & EXIT ANIMATIONS

3 ANIMATE BOXES, SMARTART, & CHARTS | 4 CHANGE ANIMATION EFFECTS | 5 SET TIMINGS

The chart on Slide 4 shows general categories of how drones will be used in the future. You can animate the slices of the pie chart. *Why? So that each slice enters the slide individually and the audience's attention is drawn to each type of drone.* As with the SmartArt animation, PowerPoint gives you many options to animate the chart data. The following steps animate the Slide 4 chart slices.

1

- Display Slide 4 and then click an area outside of the chart so that the frame is displayed.

- Display the Animation gallery and then apply the Fly In entrance effect.

2

- Click the Effect Options button to display the Effect Options gallery. If necessary, scroll down to display both Sequence options (Figure 7–53).

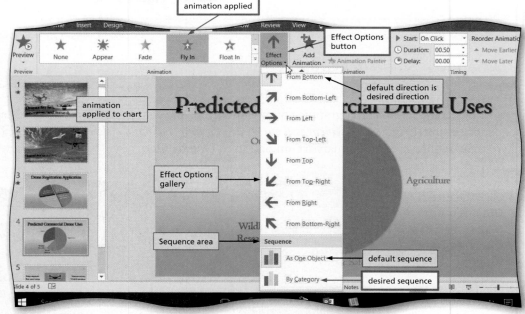

Figure 7–53

3

- Click By Category to change the chart animation so that each slice appears individually and to preview the animations.

- Change the start timing option to After Previous, change the duration to 02.00 seconds, and change the delay to 01.50 seconds (Figure 7–54).

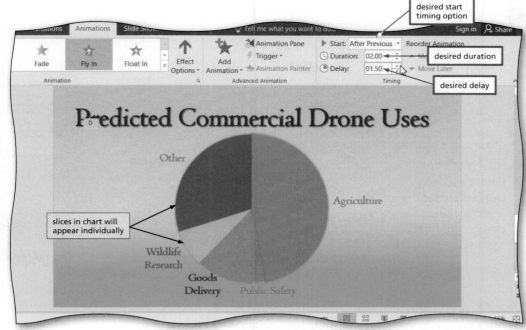

Figure 7–54

To Animate a List

1 MODIFY PHOTOS | 2 ADD ENTRANCE, EMPHASIS, & EXIT ANIMATIONS

3 ANIMATE BOXES, SMARTART, & CHARTS | 4 CHANGE ANIMATION EFFECTS | 5 SET TIMINGS

The two lists on Slide 5 give specific applications where drone use has benefited the general public or commercial interests. Each item in the placeholder is a separate paragraph. You can have each paragraph in the left list enter the slide individually. **Why?** *To add interest during a presentation.* When the entire list has displayed, the list can disappear and then each paragraph in the right list can appear. The following steps animate the Slide 5 paragraph lists.

- Display Slide 5 and then select the left text placeholder.

- Apply the Shape entrance animation effect, change the start timing option to After Previous, change the duration to 03.00 seconds, and then change the delay to 01.50 seconds (Figure 7–55).

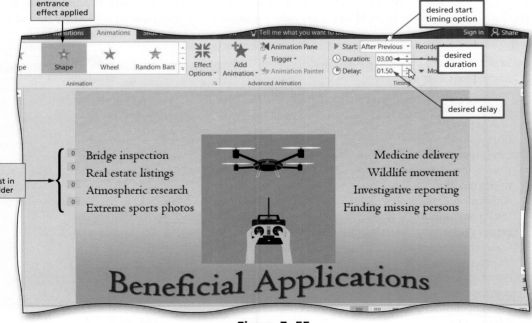

Figure 7–55

• Click the Effect Options button to display the Effect Options gallery (Figure 7–56).

• Change the Shapes from Circle to Box.

• Click the Effect Options button again and then change the Direction to Out.

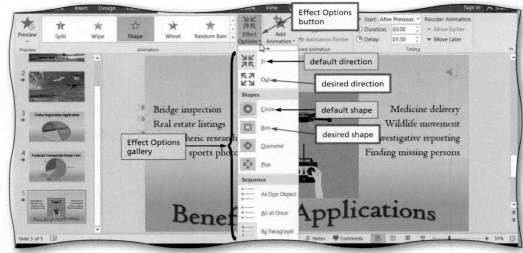

Figure 7–56

CONSIDER THIS

Select colors for dimming text.

After paragraphs of text are displayed, you can change the color, or dim the text, to direct the audience's attention to another area of the slide. Choose the dimming colors carefully. For example, use cool colors, such as blue, purple, and turquoise, as backgrounds so that the audience focuses on the next brighter, contrasting color on the slide. Be certain the color you choose can be seen against the background. In addition, use a maximum of three colors unless you have a compelling need to present more variety.

To Dim Text after Animation

1 MODIFY PHOTOS | 2 ADD ENTRANCE, EMPHASIS, & EXIT ANIMATIONS
3 ANIMATE BOXES, SMARTART, & CHARTS | 4 CHANGE ANIMATION EFFECTS | 5 SET TIMINGS

As each item in the list is displayed, you may desire to have the previous item removed from the screen or to have the font color change, or **dim**. PowerPoint provides several options for you to alter this text by specifying an After Animation effect. The following steps dim each item in the left placeholder list by changing the font color to light blue. ***Why?*** *That color is similar to the blue color on the remote control in the illustration.*

• Select the four paragraphs in the left placeholder and then click the Animation Pane button (Animations tab | Advanced Animation group) to display the Animation Pane. Click the double arrow under Content Placeholder to expand the contents and display the four left placeholder paragraphs.

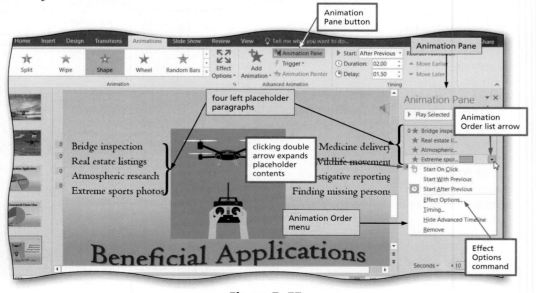

Figure 7–57

• Click 'Extreme sports photos' in the list and then click the Animation Order list arrow to the right of 'Extreme sports photos' to display the Animation Order menu (Figure 7–57).

Q&A Do I need to click the Bridge inspection paragraph, or could I click any of the four paragraphs?
Clicking any of the paragraphs will display the Animation Order menu. When you click the last item, you can see all the paragraphs listed above it.

2
- Click Effect Options in the Animation Order menu to display the Box dialog box.
- Click the After animation arrow to display the After animation menu (Figure 7–58).

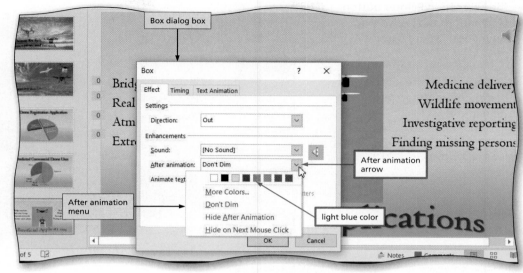

Figure 7–58

3
- Click the color light blue (fifth color in row of colors) to select this color for the dim effect (Figure 7–59).

4
- Click the OK button (Box dialog box) to apply the dim effect to the four items in the left placeholder on Slide 5.

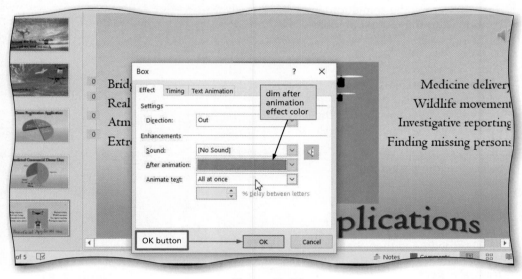

Figure 7–59

To Use the Animation Painter to Animate Text

1 MODIFY PHOTOS | 2 ADD ENTRANCE, EMPHASIS, & EXIT ANIMATIONS
3 ANIMATE BOXES, SMARTART, & CHARTS | 4 CHANGE ANIMATION EFFECTS | 5 SET TIMINGS

All animations have been applied to the left placeholder paragraphs. You now can copy these animations to the four items in the right text placeholder. The following steps use the Animation Painter to copy the animations. **Why?** *Copying the animations saves time and ensures consistency between the left and right paragraphs.*

1

- Click the word, Bridge, in the left text placeholder and then click the Animation Painter button (Animations tab | Advanced Animation group) (Figure 7–60).

Q&A Can I place the insertion point in any word in the left text placeholder instead of the first item in the list?
Yes. All the paragraphs have the same animation effects applied, so you can click any word in the list.

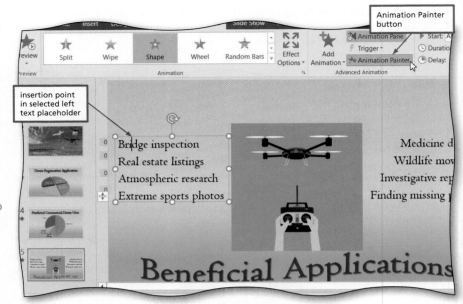

Figure 7–60

2

- Click the word, Medicine, in the right list to copy the animations in the left list to the four paragraphs in the right list.

Q&A Can I click any word in the right text placeholder instead of the first item in the list?
Yes. You can click any word in the list to copy the animation effects to all words.

- Select the four paragraphs in the list in the right placeholder, click the Start arrow and change the start timing option to After Previous, change the duration to 03.00 seconds, and then change the delay to 01.50 seconds (Figure 7–61).

- Close the Animation Pane.

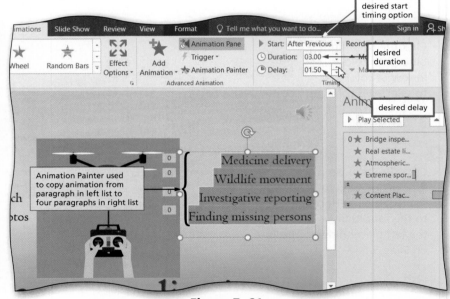

Figure 7–61

To Create Credits

1 MODIFY PHOTOS | 2 ADD ENTRANCE, EMPHASIS, & EXIT ANIMATIONS
3 ANIMATE BOXES, SMARTART, & CHARTS | 4 CHANGE ANIMATION EFFECTS | 5 SET TIMINGS

Many motion pictures use production credits at the end of the movie to acknowledge the people who were involved in the filmmaking process or to provide additional information about the actors or setting. You, too, can use a credit or closing statement at the end of your presentation. *Why? You can use credits to thank individuals or companies who helped you develop your slide show or to leave your audience with a final thought.* The following steps display text as an ascending credit line on Slide 5.

- With Slide 5 displaying, click the placeholder with the words, Beneficial Applications, at the bottom of the slide to select it.

- Display the Animation gallery and then click More Entrance Effects to display the Add Entrance Effect dialog box.

- Scroll down to display the Exciting section (Figure 7–62).

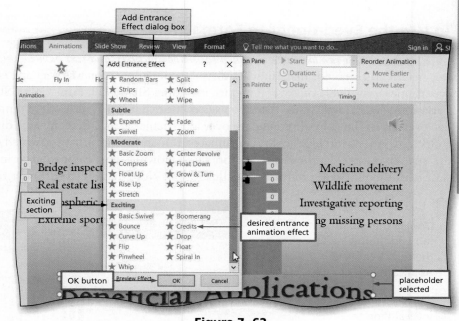

Figure 7–62

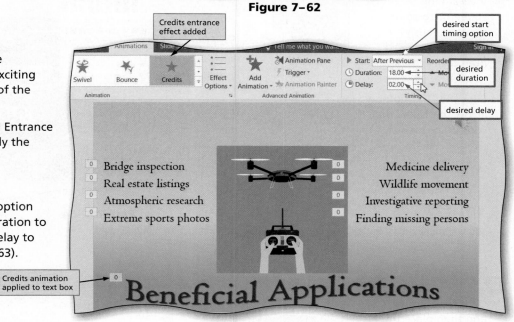

Figure 7–63

- Click the Credits entrance animation effect in the Exciting section to see a preview of the animation effect.

- Click the OK button (Add Entrance Effect dialog box) to apply the effect.

- Change the start timing option to After Previous, the duration to 18.00 seconds, and the delay to 02.00 seconds (Figure 7–63).

- Preview the animation.

TO REPEAT CREDITS

To have the credits display more than one time, you would perform the following steps.

1. Display the Animation Pane, click the Animation Order list arrow to the right of the slide element used for the credits, and then click Effect Options in the Animation Order menu.

2. When the Credits dialog box appears, click the Timing tab.

3. Click the Repeat arrow and then select the number of times you desire to have the credits repeat.

To Use the Eyedropper to Format Text

Why? *A slide can look cohesive when the shapes, pictures, and text have identical colors.* The eyedropper tool can ensure precise color matching. The eyedropper allows you to select any color on the slide to match. The eyedropper is available on several menus, including Shape Fill, Font Color, Shape Outline, Text Outline, Picture Variations, and Glow Colors. After you select the eyedropper, move the pointer to any area of the slide to see a live preview of the color. If you hover over a particular area, a ScreenTip is displayed with the color name and its RGB (red, green, and blue) color coordinates. If many colors are intertwined on the slide, press the ENTER key or the SPACEBAR to select the desired color. The following steps color the text in the text box at the bottom of the slide with the pink color in the drone illustration. Note that the eyedropper tool is not available on touch screens.

1

- Display the Home tab and then select the text, Beneficial Applications.

Q&A Can I select several slide elements to color simultaneously?
Yes. Press CTRL and then click the objects you desire to color.

- Click the Font Color arrow to display the Font Color menu (Figure 7–64).

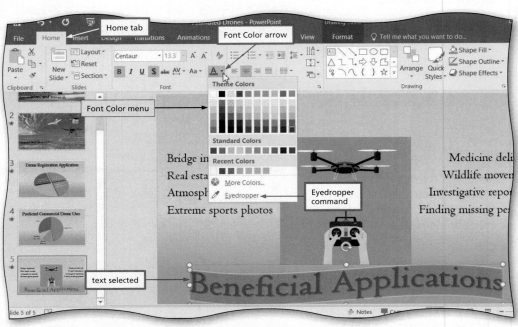

Figure 7–64

2

- Click Eyedropper and then place the pointer over the Pink area of the drone (Figure 7–65).

Q&A Can I cancel using the eyedropper without selecting a color?
Yes. Press the ESC key.

3

- Click the drone to apply the Pink color to the selected text box text.

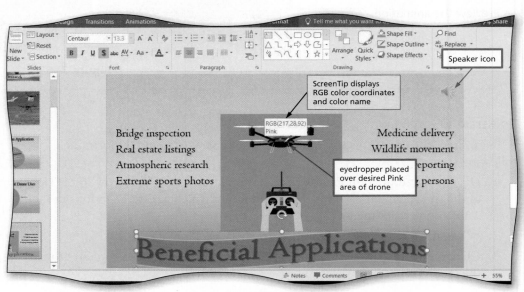

Figure 7–65

To Trigger an Animation Effect

If you select the On Click start timing option and run the slide show, PowerPoint starts the animation when you click any part of the slide or press the SPACEBAR. You may, however, want the option to play an animation in a particular circumstance. *Why? You may have an animated sequence ready to show if time permits or if you believe your audience needs time to understand a process and would understand the concept more readily if you revealed one part of a SmartArt graphic at a time.* A **trigger** specifies when an animation or other action should occur. It is linked to a particular component of a slide so that the action occurs only when you click this slide element. For example, you can trigger an animation effect to start when you click a shape or other object that has the animation applied, or you can trigger an animation effect to begin playing at the start of, or sometime during, an audio or video clip. If you click any other part of the slide, PowerPoint will display the next slide in the presentation. The following steps set the drone illustration on Slide 5 as the trigger to play music, which is an audio clip identified as Closing Music.

- Display the Animations tab and then click the speaker icon (shown in Figure 7–65) in the upper-right corner of the slide.

- Click the Play button (Animations tab | Animation group), click the Trigger button (Animations tab | Advanced Animation group) to display the Trigger menu, and then point to 'On Click of' to display the list of Slide 5 elements (Figure 7–66).

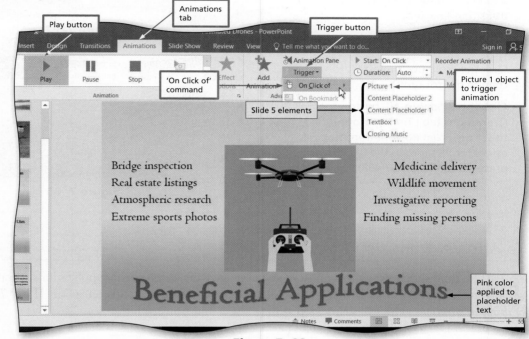

Figure 7–66

2

- Click Picture 1, which is the drone illustration, as the object that will trigger the animation when clicked.

Q&A | How do I know the trigger animation has been added to the Closing Music file?
The tag, with a symbol resembling a lightning bolt, indicates the trigger animation is applied.

To Modify a Transition Effect

The Box transition will be applied to the five slides in this presentation. The default rotation is From Right, so the current slide turns to the left while the new slide appears from the right side of the screen. You can change the Box rotation so that the current slide moves to the top of the screen and the new slide appears from the bottom. *Why? You want the transition effect to emulate a drone taking off from the ground and flying upward.* The following steps apply the Box transition and then modify the transition effect for all slides in the presentation.

- Display the Transitions tab and then apply the Box transition (in Exciting category) to all slides in the presentation.

- Click the Effect Options button (Transitions tab | Transition to This Slide group) to display the Effect Options gallery (Figure 7–67).

Q&A
Are the same four effects available for all transitions?
No. The transition effects vary depending upon the particular transition selected.

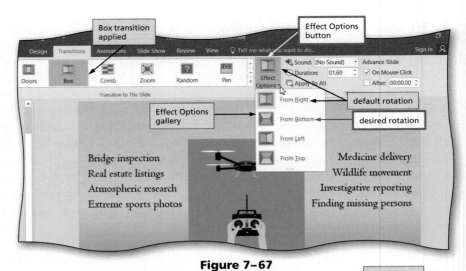

Figure 7–67

- Click the From Bottom effect to change the rotation.

- Click the 'Apply To All' button (Transitions tab | Timing group) to set the From Bottom transition effect for all slides in the presentation (Figure 7–68).

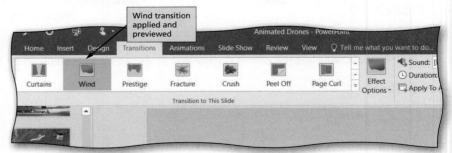

Figure 7–68

To Apply a Transition to a Single Slide

1 MODIFY PHOTOS | 2 ADD ENTRANCE, EMPHASIS, & EXIT ANIMATIONS
3 ANIMATE BOXES, SMARTART, & CHARTS | 4 CHANGE ANIMATION EFFECTS | 5 SET TIMINGS

The final slide in the presentation acquaints viewers with specific applications where drones can benefit society and commercial interests. You can change the transition for this one slide. **Why?** *To emphasize the variety of drone applications.* The following step applies the Wind transition to Slide 5.

- With Slide 5 and the Transitions tab displaying, display the Transitions gallery and then click the Wind transition (in Exciting category) to select this effect for Slide 5 and to see a preview (Figure 7–69).

Figure 7–69

To Run an Animated Slide Show

All changes are complete. You now can view the Animated Drones presentation. The following steps run the slide show.

1 Click the 'Start From Beginning' button in the Quick Access Toolbar to start the presentation and display the title slide.

2 Display each slide, and review the information.

3 When Slide 5 is displayed, click the drone illustration to trigger the music to play while the list of drone applications is displayed.

4 Save the Animated Drones presentation again with the same file name.

Preparing for a Self-Running Presentation

In previous slide shows, you clicked to advance from one slide to the next. Because all animations have been added to the slides in the presentation, you now can set the time each slide is displayed on the screen. You can set these times in one of two ways. The first method is to specify each slide's display time manually. The second method is to use PowerPoint's **rehearsal feature**, which allows you to advance through the slides at your own pace, and the amount of time you view each slide is recorded. You will use the second technique in this module and then adjust the fourth slide's timing manually.

When you begin rehearsing a presentation, the Rehearsal toolbar is displayed. The **Rehearsal toolbar** contains buttons that allow you to start, pause, and repeat viewing the slides in the slide show and to view the times for each slide as well as the elapsed time. Table 7–1 describes the buttons on the Rehearsal toolbar.

Table 7–1 Rehearsal Toolbar Buttons		
Button Name	**Image**	**Description**
Next	➡	Displays the next slide or next animated element on the slide.
Pause Recording	❚❚	Stops the timer. Tap or click the Next or Pause Recording button to resume timing.
Slide Time	0:00:00	Indicates the length of time a slide has been displayed. You can enter a slide time directly in the Slide Time box.
Repeat	↺	Clears the Slide Time box and resets the timer to 0:00:00.
Elapsed Time	0:00:00	Indicates slide show total time.

Give your audience sufficient time to view a slide.
The presentation in this module is designed to run continuously at a kiosk without a speaker's physical presence. Your audience, therefore, must read or view each slide and absorb the information without your help as a narrator. Be certain to give them time to read the slide and grasp the concept you are presenting. They will become frustrated if the slide changes before they have finished viewing and assimilating the material. As you set the slide timings, read each slide aloud and note the amount of time that elapses. Add a few seconds to this time and use this amount for the total time the slide is displayed.

To Rehearse Timings

1 MODIFY PHOTOS | 2 ADD ENTRANCE, EMPHASIS, & EXIT ANIMATIONS
3 ANIMATE BOXES, SMARTART, & CHARTS | 4 CHANGE ANIMATION EFFECTS | 5 SET TIMINGS

You need to determine the length of time each slide should be displayed. *Why? Audience members need sufficient time to read the text and watch the animations.* Table 7–2 indicates the desired timings for the five slides in the Drones presentation. Slide 1 is displayed and then the title text and animated drone photo appear for 25 seconds. The Slide 2 title text, sound, and clip are displayed for 1:05. Slide 3 has the animated SmartArt, and it takes 45 seconds for the elements to display. The slices in the Slide 4 pie chart can display in 40 seconds, and the two lists and rolling credit on Slide 5 display for one minute, ten seconds.

Table 7–2 Slide Rehearsal Timings		
Slide Number	**Display Time**	**Elapsed Time**
1	0:00	0:25
2	1:05	1:15
3	0:45	2:15
4	0:40	2:50
5	1:10	3:45

BTW
Using the Morph Transition
The Morph transition is a new PowerPoint 2016 feature that helps you animate, move, and emphasize objects smoothly across your slides. To use this transition, you need two consecutive slides with at least one object in common. Place the object on one slide and apply the morph transition to this slide. Then, move the object to a new location on the second slide. When you run the slide show, the object will appear to move seamlessly from one location to the other.

BTW
Conserving Ink and Toner
If you want to conserve ink or toner, you can instruct PowerPoint to print draft quality documents by clicking File on the ribbon to open the Backstage view, clicking the Options tab in the Backstage view to display the PowerPoint Options dialog box, clicking Advanced in the left pane (PowerPoint Options dialog box), scrolling to the Print area in the right pane, placing a check mark in the 'Use draft quality' check box, and then clicking the OK button. Then, use the Backstage view to print the document as usual.

CONSIDER THIS

BTW
Discarding Slide Timings
To remove the slide timings, display the Slide Show tab, click the 'Record Slide Show' arrow (Slide Show tab | Set Up group), point to Clear, and then click 'Clear Timings on All Slides'.

The following steps add slide timings to the slide show.

1

- Display Slide 1 and then click Slide Show on the ribbon to display the Slide Show tab (Figure 7–70).

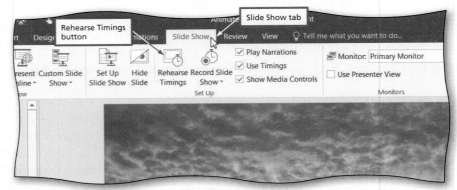

Figure 7–70

2

- Click the Rehearse Timings button (Slide Show tab | Set Up group) to start the slide show and the counter (Figure 7–71).

Figure 7–71

3

- When the Elapsed Time displays 00:25, click the Next button to display Slide 2.

- When the Elapsed Time displays 01:15, click the Next button to display Slide 3.

- When the Elapsed Time displays 02:15, click the Next button to display Slide 4.

- When the Elapsed Time displays 02:50, click the Next button to display Slide 5.

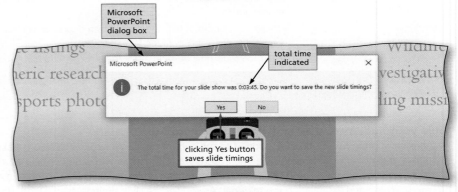

Figure 7–72

- When the Elapsed Time displays 03:45, click the Next button to display the Microsoft PowerPoint dialog box (Figure 7–72).

4

- Click the Yes button to keep the new slide timings with an elapsed time of 03:45.

- Click the Slide Sorter view button and then, if necessary, zoom the view to display all five thumbnails. Review the timings displayed in the lower-right corner of each slide (Figure 7–73).

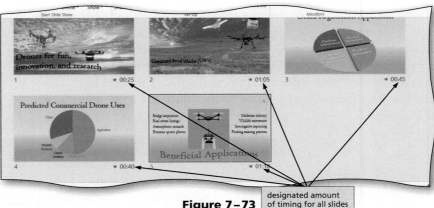

Figure 7–73

To Adjust Timings Manually

Why? *If the slide timings need adjustment, you manually can change the length of time each slide is displayed.* In this presentation, you decide to display Slide 4 for 45 seconds instead of 40 seconds. The following step increases the Slide 4 timing.

1

- In Slide Sorter view, display the Transitions tab and then select Slide 4.

- Change the 'Advance Slide After' setting (Transitions tab | Timing group) to 00:45.00 (Figure 7–74).

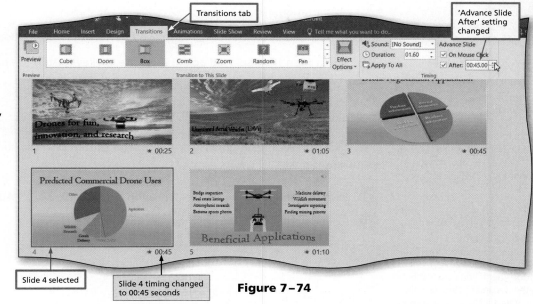

Figure 7–74

To Create a Self-Running Presentation

Why? *The Drones presentation can accompany a speech, but it also can run unattended at hobby shops.* When the last slide in the presentation is displayed, the slide show **loops**, or restarts, at Slide 1. PowerPoint has the option of running continuously until the user presses the ESC key. The following steps set the slide show to run in this manner.

1

- Display the Slide Show tab and then click the 'Set Up Slide Show' button (Slide Show tab | Set Up group) to display the Set Up Show dialog box.

- Click 'Browsed at a kiosk (full screen)' in the Show type section (Figure 7–75).

2

- Click the OK button to apply this show type.

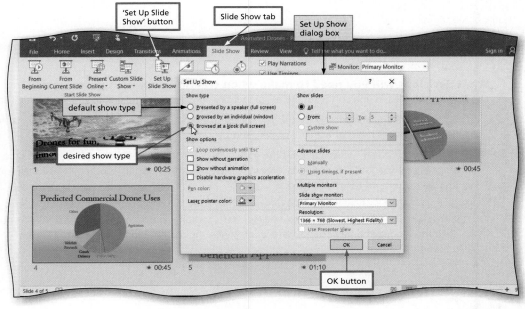

Figure 7–75

To Run an Animated Slide Show

All changes are complete. You now can view the presentation. The following steps run the slide show.

1 Click the From Beginning button (Slide Show tab | Start Slide Show group) to start the presentation.

2 As each slide automatically is displayed, review the information.

3 When Slide 1 is displayed again, press the ESC key to stop the presentation.

To Save and Exit PowerPoint

The presentation now is complete. You should save the slides with a new file name and then exit PowerPoint.

1 Save the Animated Drones presentation with the file name, Automatic Drones.

2 Exit PowerPoint, closing all open documents.

Summary

In this module you have learned how to remove a background from a photo and then crop and compress the image. You then applied entrance, emphasis, and exit effects to slide content and created a custom animation using a motion path. Also, you inserted and animated a text box and associated a sound with this text. You animated a SmartArt graphic, a chart, and two lists. Then, you set slide timings and created a slide show that runs automatically.

CONSIDER THIS: PLAN AHEAD

What decisions will you need to make when creating your next presentation?
Use these guidelines as you complete the assignments in this module and create your own slide show decks outside of this class.

1. Do not use animation merely for the sake of using animation. Prior to using an animation effect, think about why you need it and how it will affect your presentation.

2. The dimming effect, which changes the color of text paragraphs after they display on a slide, can be used effectively to emphasize important points and to draw the audience's attention to another area of the slide. Select dimming colors that suit the purpose of the presentation.

3. On average, an audience member will spend only eight seconds viewing a basic slide with a simple graphic or a few words. They need much more time to view charts, graphs, and SmartArt graphics. When you are setting slide timings, keep this length of time in mind, particularly when the presentation is viewed at a kiosk without a speaker's physical presence.

Apply Your Knowledge

Reinforce the skills and apply the concepts you learned in this module.

Applying Entrance and Emphasis Effects, Animating a SmartArt Graphic, Renaming a Slide Object, Animating a Text Box by Applying a Motion Path, and Adjusting a Motion Path

Note: To complete this assignment, you will be required to use the Data Files. Please contact your instructor for information about accessing the Data Files.

Instructions: Run PowerPoint. Open the presentation called Apply 7–1 Dogs, which is located in the Data Files. The slides in this presentation present information about your dog walking service. The document you open is a partially formatted presentation. You are to add entrance and emphasis effects to text, an illustration, and a SmartArt graphic. You will adjust a custom motion path, and animate a text box by applying a motion path. Your slides should look like Figure 7–76.

Perform the following tasks:

1. On Slide 1 (Figure 7–76a), increase the size of the dog illustration in the lower-left corner of the slide to 1.75" × 2.21" and remove the 'Simple Frame - Black' picture style from the dog illustration *Hint:* Click the Reset Picture button (Picture Tools Format tab | Adjust group), and then move the picture to the location shown in the figure.

2. Apply the Fly In, From Left entrance effect to the dog illustration, change the start timing option from On Click to After Previous, and then change the duration to 1.75 seconds. Rename the dog illustration from Picture 3 to Dog1.

3. Convert the bulleted text on Slide 1 to the Radial Venn SmartArt graphic (first graphic in fourth Cycle row). Change the font to Arial. Decrease the size of the center circle of the SmartArt graphic to approximately 1.5" × 1.5" and then change the size of the four outer circles of the SmartArt graphic to 1" × 1". Move the four outer circles so they touch the center circle of the SmartArt graphic and then move the graphic to the location shown in the figure. (*Hint:* If needed, use the arrow keys to move the circles in smaller increments and use the guides, if necessary, to keep the circles aligned.) Change the color to 'Transparent Gradient Range - Accent 1' (fifth color in Accent 1 row) and then apply the Cartoon 3-D style (third style in first 3-D row).

4. Apply the 'Grow & Turn' entrance effect to the SmartArt graphic. Add the 'One by One' effect option, change the start timing option to After Previous, and then change the duration to 1.50 seconds.

5. Insert a text box in the center of the Slide 1 and then type   `Call 555-555-1234 for more information`   in the text box. Change the font to Arial, bold the text, and then change the font color to 'White, Background 1' (first color in first Theme Colors row). If necessary, change the size of the text box so that the text is all on one line. Move the text box to the lower-left corner of the slide. Apply an Arc Up motion path to the text box, change the Start timing option to After Previous, and then change the duration to 2.50 seconds. Adjust the motion path of the text box so that it ends in the lower-right corner of the slide.

6. Open the Animation Pane, select the Dog1 animation object, and then move it down so that it is the last animation on Slide 1. Preview the Slide 1 animations.

7. On Slide 2 (Figure 7–76b), select the title and apply the Random Bars entrance effect, and then change the direction to vertical. Change the start timing option from On Click to After Previous and then change the duration to 2.50 seconds.

Continued >

Apply Your Knowledge *continued*

8. Apply the Bold Reveal emphasis effect to the three paragraphs in the content placeholder. Select the paragraphs, display the Animation Pane, click the Animation Order list arrow to the right of one of the paragraphs, click Effect Options in the Animation Order list, and then click the Animate text arrow in the Bold Reveal dialog box. Choose the By word effect option and then change the delay to 0.5 seconds between words. Click OK to close the Bold Reveal dialog box. Change the start timing option to After Previous and then change the duration to 1.25 seconds.

(a) Slide 1

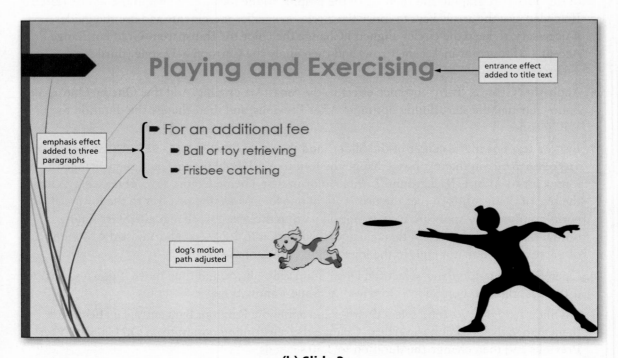

(b) Slide 2

Figure 7–76

9. On Slide 2, adjust the custom motion path for the dog by moving the stopping point (red triangle) to the left edge of the slide. Also, to make the dog jump higher, move the middle sizing handle of the custom motion path box up below the third paragraph of the content placeholder.

10. Open the Animation Pane, and select the title object, and move it up to the first position in the animation. Also, select the Picture 3 object and move it down so it is the last animation on the slide. Close the Animation Pane. Preview the Slide 2 animations.

11. If requested by your instructor, add your grandmother's first name in the lower-left text box after the word, Call, on Slide 1.

12. Run the slide show and then save the presentation using the file name, Apply 7–1 Dog Walking Service.

13. Submit the revised document in the format specified by your instructor.

14. ✳ In this presentation, you converted text to a SmartArt graphic on Slide 1. How will adding this animation to the graphic help focus the audience's attention on this content when you give this presentation?

Extend Your Knowledge

Extend the skills you learned in this module and experiment with new skills. You may need to use Help to complete the assignment.

Changing Animation, Adding Sound to Animation, Copying Animation Using the Animation Painter, Compressing a Photo, and Cropping a Photo to a Shape

Note: To complete this assignment, you will be required to use the Data Files. Please contact your instructor for information about accessing the Data Files.

Instructions: Run PowerPoint. Open the presentation called Extend 7–1 Walking Club, which is located in the Data Files. You will change, reorder, and add sound to animation, copy animations using the Animation Painter, and crop a photo to a shape, as shown in Figure 7–77.

Perform the following tasks:

1. On Slide 1 (Figure 7–77a), add the 'Double Wave 1' Transform text effect (third effect in fifth Warp row) to the title WordArt and then change the color of the text to White, Text 1 (second color in first Theme Colors row). Apply the Wipe entrance effect with the From Left effect option to the title. Change the effect option to By word and then increase the delay between words to 50%. Change the start timing option to After Previous and the duration to 3.00 seconds.

2. Change the Zoom entrance effect on the Explosion 2 shape in the lower right corner of Slide 1 to the 'Grow & Turn' entrance effect. Change the effect option to By word. Change the start timing option to After Previous, change the duration to 3.50 seconds, and then add the Click sound that is included with PowerPoint. (*Hint*: In the Animation Pane, select the Explosion 2 shape, display the Animation Order menu, click Effect Options on the Animation Order menu to display the Grow & Turn dialog box, display the Sound list in the Enhancements section, and then select the sound.) Reorder this entrance effect animation, Explosion 2, so that it follows the title animation. Preview the Slide 1 animation.

3. On Slide 2 (Figure 7–77b), apply the Transparency emphasis effect with the 25% effect option to the SmartArt graphic. Change the sequence to 'One by One'. Change the start timing option to After Previous and then change the duration to 1.50 seconds.

4. Select the female walker illustration on Slide 2 and apply the Fade entrance effect. Change the start timing option to After Previous and then change the duration to 3.75 seconds. Preview the Slide 2 animations.

Continued >

Extend Your Knowledge *continued*

5. On Slide 3 (Figure 7–77c), select the Moonlight walk photo in the upper right corner of the slide and compress it. Crop the picture to fill an oval shape. (Hint: With the picture selected, display the Picture Tools Format tab, click the Crop button arrow, point to 'Crop to Shape', and then click the Oval shape in the Basic Shapes area.) Adjust the size of the shape to approximately 3.25" × 3.43". Change the weight of the border to 3 pt and then change the border color to Orange (third color in Standard Colors).

(a) Slide 1

(b) Slide 2

Figure 7–77 (Continued)

Continued >

6. In the orange rectangular text placeholder on Slide 3, select the text 'New Trail Open' and then apply the Fly In, From Right entrance effect. Change the start timing option to After Previous and the duration to 3.00 seconds. Use the Animation Painter to apply same animations to the text 'Join us for a'. Select the text 'Moonlight walk' and then apply the Fly In, From Bottom entrance effect. Change the start timing option to After Previous and the duration to 3.25 seconds. Change the color to green after animation. (*Hint*: In the Fly In dialog box, click the arrow in the After animation box and then select More Colors. In the Colors dialog box, select a

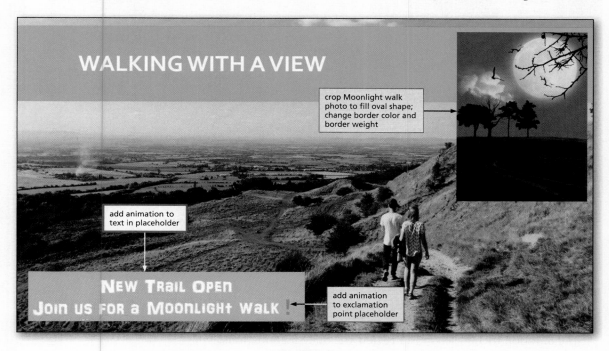

(c) Slide 3

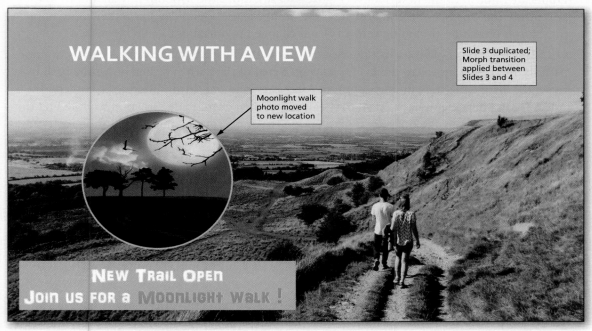

(d) Slide 4

Figure 7–77 (Continued)

Continued >

Extend Your Knowledge *continued*

(e) Slide 5

Figure 7–77

green color from the left side of the color chart.) Select the text box with the exclamation point and then add the Bounce entrance effect. Change the start timing option to After Previous and the duration to 3.00 seconds. Preview the Slide 3 animations.

7. Duplicate Slide 3. In the new Slide 4 (Figure 7–77d), move the Moonlight walk photo to the area above the words, New Trail Open, in the orange text placeholder. On Slide 4 only, apply the Morph transition (in Subtle category) and change the duration to 3.00 seconds.

8. On Slide 5 (Figure 7–77e), select the person silhouette illustration and draw a custom motion path so the person moves to the front and center area of the path and then down the path to the end. Change the start timing option to After Previous and the duration to 3.25 seconds. Add a Grow/Shrink emphasis effect to the man and then change the direction to Both and the Amount to Tiny. Change the start timing option to After Previous and the duration to 1.50 seconds. Add a Disappear exit effect to the person. Change the start timing option to After Previous and the duration to 1.50 seconds. Preview the Slide 4 animations.

9. On Slide 5, select the three paragraphs in the placeholder, increase the font size to 24 point, underline the text, and then change the line spacing to 3.0. Move the placeholder to the bottom of the slide, apply the Credits entrance effect, hide after animation, and add the Chime sound (chimes.wav). Change the start timing option to After Previous, and the duration to 16.00 seconds. Repeat the credits 2 times. (*Hint*: Display the Animation Pane, click the Animation Order list arrow to the right of 'Register now…', click Effect Options in the Animation Order menu, click the Timing tab, click the Repeat arrow, and then click 2.)

10. If requested by your instructor, add the name of your current or previous pet as the fourth paragraph of the credits on Slide 5.

11. Run the presentation and then save the file using the file name, Extend 7–1 Four Seasons Walking Club.

12. Submit the revised document in the format specified by your instructor.

13. ✳ In Step 2, you changed the entrance effect for the explosion shape. Is this new entrance effect more effective? Why or why not? In Step 7, did adding the Disappear exit effect to the illustration add visual interest to the slide? Why? Is the Morph transition a beneficial addition to PowerPoint 2016?

Expand Your World

Create a solution that uses cloud or web technologies by learning and investigating on your own from general guidance.

Locating and Inserting Animated GIF Files

Instructions: In this module you animated photos, a SmartArt object, a chart, and text. Some objects, however, already have animation applied when inserted into a PowerPoint slide or other file, such as a website. These animated GIF files generally are simple pictures with a limited number of colors. As noted in this module, animated GIFs cannot be cropped.

GIF, or Graphics Interchange Format, images were introduced in 1987 and are used frequently. They may or may not be animated. Many websites provide a variety of free and low-cost animated GIFs, and some offer information about creating animated GIF files. Care must be taken, however, to visit and download files from reputable sources so that malware is not embedded in the image. You can use a search engine or another search tool to locate recommended or popular resources.

Perform the following tasks:
1. Visit one of the following websites, or locate other websites that contain animated GIFs: Gifs.net, GIFanimations, Giphy, or Animation Factory.
2. Locate files that could enhance your Animated Drones presentation. Some websites have collections of hobbies that could be useful.
3. Download at least two animated GIFs and then insert them into your Animated Drones presentation.
4. If requested to do so by your instructor, insert the name of your favorite grade school teacher in the footer.
5. Save the presentation using the file name, Expand 7 – 1 GIF Animated Drones.
6. Submit the assignment in the format specified by your instructor.
7. ✳ Why did you select these particular images for your slides? Do the animated GIF images enhance or detract from your presentation? Where might you use GIF files other than in PowerPoint slides?

In the Labs

Design, create, modify, and/or use a presentation following the guidelines, concepts, and skills presented in this module. Labs 1 and 2, which increase in difficulty, require you to create solutions based on what you learned in the module; Lab 3 requires you to apply your creative thinking and problem-solving skills to design and implement a solution.

Continued >

In the Labs *continued*

Lab 1: Adding Sound to Animation, Using the Eyedropper to Match Colors, Cropping a Photo, and Animating a SmartArt Graphic

Note: To complete this assignment, you will be required to use the Data Files. Please contact your instructor for information about accessing the Data Files.

Problem: You work as a dietician. In addition to meeting one-on-one with clients, you give group presentations about healthy eating. When you meet with new clients, you use PowerPoint presentations to supplement the nutritional information you discuss. Many of your clients are unfamiliar with the pomegranate, a super food that has many health benefits, so you decide to create a new presentation on that topic. You located a presentation about pomegranates, and now you want to update it by removing and adding animations, adding sounds to an animation, using the eyedropper to match colors, and cropping a photo. You create the slides shown in Figure 7–78.

Perform the following tasks:

1. Run PowerPoint. Open the presentation, Lab 7–1 Pomegranate, from the Data Files.

2. Change the Slice theme variant from green to red (third color variant).

3. On Slide 1 (Figure 7–78a), change the title font text to Arial Black, increase the size to 72 point, center the text, and have it appear on three lines. Decrease the width of the title placeholder to 5.18". Apply the 'Isometric Right Up' 3-D Rotation text effect (second in Parallel group) to the title text. Apply the Fly In, 'From Bottom Right' entrance effect to the text. Change the start timing option to After Previous and then change the duration to 2.50. Add the Laser audio sound. Animate text By word with 50% delay between words. With the title text still selected, use the eyedropper to match the green leaf color in the pomegranate picture.

4. Select the subtitle text on Slide 1 and remove the Swivel entrance effect from the subtitle text. Change the font to Rockwell Extra Bold, increase the size to 54 point, change the line spacing to exactly 40 point, and then align the subtitle in the bottom of the placeholder.

5. On Slide 1, crop the pomegranate picture on the left side to the farthest-left leaf and on the bottom to just below the pomegranate, as shown in Figure 7–78a. Increase the size of the pomegranate picture to approximately 5.77" × 6.71", apply the 'Bevel Perspective Left, White' picture style to the picture, and then if necessary, move it to the location shown in Figure 7–78a.

6. On Slide 2 (Figure 7–78b), change the title text font to Rockwell Extra Bold, increase the font size to 40 point and then change the color to the same color you created with the eyedropper for the title on Slide 1 (Green color in Recent Colors). Add the Zoom entrance effect to the Slide 2 title text, change the start timing option to After Previous, and then change the duration to 2.00 seconds. Animate text By word and then change the delay between words to 100%. Use the Format Painter and Animation Painter to apply these same attributes to the title text on Slide 3.

7. Select the five bulleted paragraphs on Slide 2 and then apply the Pulse emphasis effect. Change the start timing option to After Previous and then change the duration to 2.25 seconds. Change the After animation color to Black, animate text By word, and then add the Suction sound.

8. On Slide 3 (Figure 7–78c), select the four shapes surrounding the pomegranate illustration, apply the Bounce entrance effect, keep the start timing option to On Click, and then change the duration to 2.50 seconds.

9. On the Slide 4 title (Figure 7–78d), change the word, ONE, to the numeral 1. Change the word, GLASS, to SERVING. Change the title text font to Rockwell Extra Bold and then increase the size to 36 point. Increase the size of the numeral 1 to 88 point.

10. Convert the bulleted text on Slide 4 to the Nested Target SmartArt graphic. Change the color to 'Gradient Range - Accent 4' (third in Accent 4 row) and then apply the Cartoon 3-D style (third style in the first 3-D row) to the SmartArt graphic. Change the transparency of the background picture to 25%.

(a) Slide 1

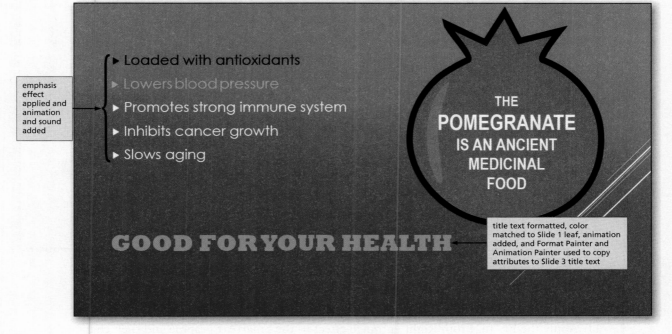

(b) Slide 2

Figure 7–78 (Continued)

Continued >

In the Labs *continued*

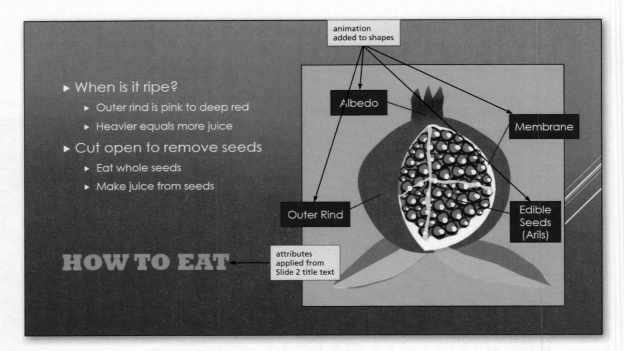

(c) Slide 3

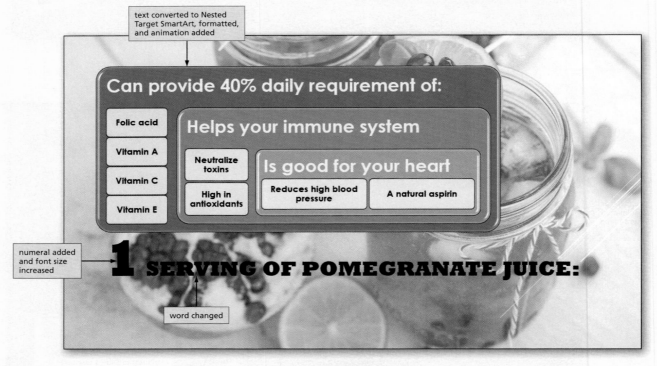

(d) Slide 4

Figure 7–78

11. Apply the Fly In, From Right entrance effect to the SmartArt graphic and then change the sequence to One by One. Change the start timing option to After Previous, change the duration to 0.50 seconds, and then add the chime sound.

12. If requested by your instructor, add the city or county in which you were born as the sixth bulleted paragraph on Slide 2.

13. Run the presentation and then save the file using the file name, Lab 7 – 1 Super Pomegranate.

14. Submit the document in the format specified by your instructor.

15. ✳ Why did you remove the Swivel entrance effect from the subtitle text on Slide 1? Why did you crop the pomegranate picture on Slide 1? How did using the eyedropper tool to match colors help improve the presentation?

Lab 2: Animating a Photo, List, SmartArt, and Chart, Applying a Transition to a Single Slide, and Creating a Self-Running Presentation

Note: To complete this assignment, you will be required to use the Data Files. Please contact your instructor for information about accessing the Data Files.

Problem: Many students have difficulty attempting to find balance in their lives. When juggling the demands of school, family, and work, they feel overwhelmed and exhausted. Your school's Student Life office is offering a seminar with tips for bringing balance to a daily routine, and the director has asked you to develop slides to accompany the presenter, plus a presentation that can be shown at a kiosk. Create the four slides shown in Figure 7 – 79.

Perform the following tasks:

1. Run PowerPoint. Open the presentation, Lab 7–2 Balance, which is located in the Data Files. Add the Berlin theme with the green variant.

2. On Slide 1 (Figure 7 – 79a), increase the size of the title text placeholder to approximately 3" × 8.6", change the font size to 44 pt, and then center the text. Apply the WordArt style, 'Fill – White, Outline - Accent 1, Shadow' (fourth style in first row). Apply the Glow text effect, 'Lime, 11 pt glow, Accent color 1' (first effect in third Glow Variations row), to this text. Apply the Teeter emphasis effect to the WordArt title. Change the start timing option to After Previous and then change the duration to 4.00 seconds.

3. Remove the background from the key picture, change its size to 4.3" × 4.3", and then move it to the location shown in Figure 7 – 79a. Apply the Float In entrance effect to this picture with a direction of Float Down. Change the start timing option to After Previous and then change the duration to 2.00 seconds. Open the Animation pane and the Selection pane. Change the name of this picture to Key in the Selection pane. Trigger the key picture to appear on the click of the Subtitle. Close both the Animation and Selection panes.

4. Change the subtitle font size to 36 point and then change the color to Light Blue (seventh color in Standard colors). Apply the Stretch entrance effect (in the Moderate area) to the subtitle. Change the start timing option to After Previous and then change the duration to 1.50 seconds.

5. On Slide 2 (Figure 7 – 79b), change the title text font size to 40 point, change the font color to Light Blue, and then bold this text. Use the Format Painter to apply these same attributes to the title text on Slides 3 and 4.

6. Remove the background from the scale picture, increase its size to approximately 4.5" × 8.31", and then move it to the location shown in Figure 7 – 79b. Apply the Fade entrance effect to the photo. Change the start timing option to After Previous, change the duration to 3.25 seconds, and then change the delay to 1.00 seconds.

7. Apply the 'Fill - White, Text 1, Outline - Background 1, Hard Shadow - Background 1' WordArt style (first style in third row) to the word, Work, and the word, Life. Add a Turns motion path for the Work text box so that it curves to the right down to the scale's left tray. To

Continued >

In the Labs *continued*

adjust the motion path, drag the bottom-right sizing handle to the desired location. Change the start timing option to After Previous and change the duration to 2.50 seconds.

8. Add a Turns motion path for the Life text box so that it curves to the left down to the scale's right tray. Change the start timing option to After Previous, change the duration to 2.50 seconds, and then change the delay to 2.00 seconds.

9. On Slide 3 (Figure 7–79c), apply the Float In entrance effect to the photo. Change the start timing option to After Previous and then change the duration to 2.00 seconds.

10. If requested by your instructor, replace the fifth bulleted paragraph on Slide 3 with the name of the last movie you saw.

11. Apply the Fly In, From Top entrance effect to the bulleted text. Change the start timing option to After Previous and then change the duration to 2.00 seconds.

12. On Slide 4, change the chart style to Style 2 and then change the chart color to Color 4 (last row in Colorful area), as shown in Figure 7–79d. Display the Format Data Labels task pane, display the Label Options sheet, and then display only the Category Name labels. Center these labels and then increase the font size to 24 point. Apply the Shape entrance effect to the chart, change the direction to In, and then change the shape to Box. Change the sequence to By Category. Change the timing option to After Previous and then change the duration to 1.50 seconds.

13. Apply the Cube transition in the Exciting section to Slide 4 only, select the From Left effect option, and then change the duration to 1.50 seconds.

14. Run the presentation and then save the file using the file name, Lab 7–2 Balance Life.

15. Rehearse the presentation and then set the slide timings to 15 seconds for Slide 1, 20 seconds for Slides 2 and 3, and 25 seconds for Slide 4. Set the show type as 'Browsed at a kiosk.'

16. Save the presentation again using the file name, Lab 7–2 Balance Life Timings.

(a) Slide 1

17. Submit the document in the format specified by your instructor.

18. ✳ Did you have difficulty removing the background from the key and scale pictures on Slides 1 and 2? How did removing the backgrounds enhance these two slides? Where would you run the presentation with the slide timings?

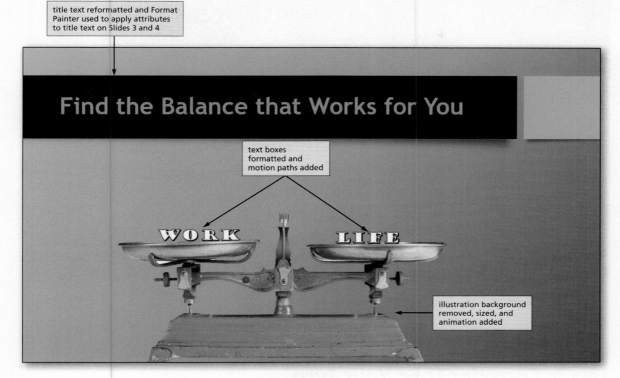

title text reformatted and Format Painter used to apply attributes to title text on Slides 3 and 4

text boxes formatted and motion paths added

illustration background removed, sized, and animation added

(b) Slide 2

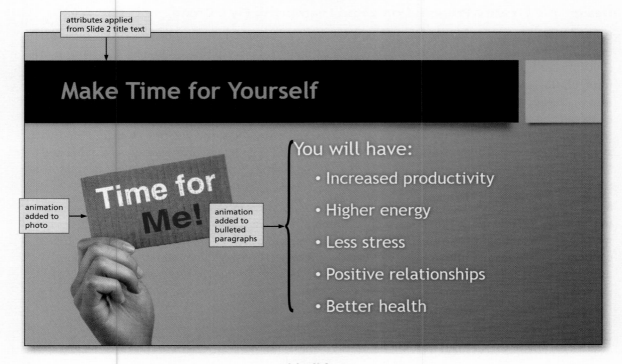

attributes applied from Slide 2 title text

animation added to photo

animation added to bulleted paragraphs

(c) Slide 3

Continued >

In the Labs *continued*

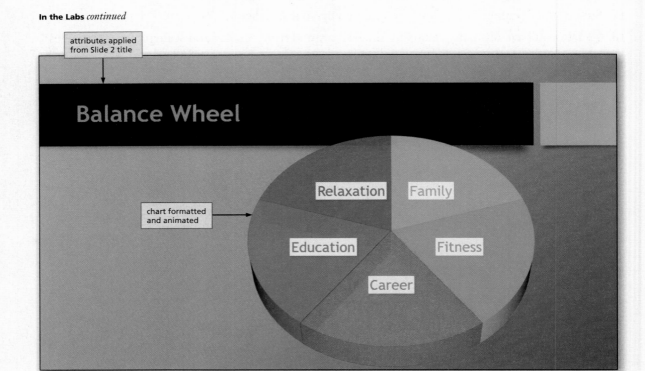

(d) Slide 4

Figure 7–79

Lab 3: Consider This: Your Turn

Design and Create a Presentation about Learning to Fly a Drone

Part 1: The project in this module presents the topic of drones. Learning to fly a drone takes practice, skill, and a knowledge of basic aeronautical principles. Pilots of these unmanned aerial vehicles (UAVs) need to understand how the four aerodynamic forces — lift, gravity, thrust, and drag — interact. Review some websites to learn about the physics involved in flight. Also, research the factors to consider when buying a drone, such as cost, weight, size, battery, and materials. Use the concepts and techniques presented in this module to create a presentation. Select a suitable theme and animate slide content with entrance, emphasis, and exit effects. Include one animated SmartArt graphic showing the four aerodynamic forces. Review and revise your presentation as needed and then save the file using the file name, Lab 7–3 Drone Flying. Submit your assignment in the format specified by your instructor.

Part 2: ✳ You made several decisions while creating the presentation in this assignment: where to place text, how to format the text (such as font and font size), which graphical image(s) to use, where to crop and remove backgrounds from pictures, and which animations to use for graphic elements. What was the rationale behind each of these decisions? When you reviewed the document, what further revisions did you make and why? Where would you recommend showing this slide show?

4 Financial Functions, Data Tables, and Amortization Schedules

Objectives

You will have mastered the material in this module when you can:

- Assign a name to a cell and refer to the cell in a formula using the assigned name
- Determine the monthly payment of a loan using the financial function PMT
- Understand the financial functions PV (present value) and FV (future value)
- Create a data table to analyze data in a worksheet
- Create an amortization schedule
- Control the color and thickness of outlines and borders

- Add a pointer to a data table
- Analyze worksheet data by changing values
- Use range names and print sections of a worksheet
- Set print options
- Protect and unprotect cells in a worksheet
- Hide and unhide worksheets and workbooks
- Use the formula checking features of Excel

Introduction

Two of the more powerful aspects of Excel are its wide array of functions and its capability of organizing answers to what-if questions. In this module, you will learn about financial functions such as the PMT function, which allows you to determine a monthly payment for a loan, and the PV function, which allows you to determine the present value of an investment.

In earlier modules, you learned how to analyze data by using Excel's recalculation feature and goal seeking. This module introduces an additional what-if analysis tool, called a **data table**. You use a data table to automate data analyses and organize the results returned by Excel. Another important loan analysis tool is an amortization schedule. An **amortization schedule** shows the beginning and ending balances of a loan and the amount of payment that is applied to the principal and interest during each payment period.

In previous modules, you learned how to print in a variety of ways. In this module, you will learn additional methods of printing using range names and a print area.

Finally, this module introduces you to cell protection; hiding and unhiding worksheets and workbooks; and formula checking. **Cell protection** ensures that users do not inadvertently change values that are critical to the worksheet. Hiding portions of a workbook lets you show only the parts of the workbook that the user needs to see. The **formula checker** examines the formulas in a workbook in a manner similar to the way the spelling checker examines a workbook for misspelled words.

Project — Mortgage Payment Calculator with Data Table and Amortization Schedule

The project in this module follows proper design guidelines and uses Excel to create the worksheet shown in Figure 4–1. NCU, a credit union, provides mortgages (loans) for homes and other types of property. The credit union's chief financial officer has asked for a workbook that loan officers and customers can use to calculate mortgage payment information, review an amortization schedule, and compare mortgage payments for varying annual interest rates. To ensure that the loan officers and customers do not delete the formulas in the worksheet, she has asked that cells in the worksheet be protected so that they cannot be changed accidentally.

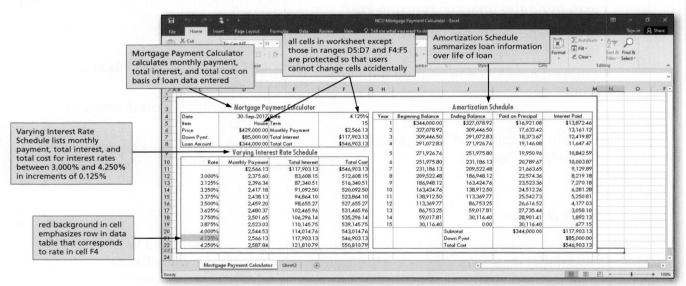

Figure 4–1

The requirements document for the NCU Mortgage Payment Calculator worksheet is shown in Figure 4–2. It includes the needs, source of data, summary of calculations, and special requirements.

File   Home   Insert   Page Layout   Formulas   Data   Review   View

Worksheet Title	NCU Mortgage Payment Calculator
Needs	An easy-to-read worksheet that 1. Determines the monthly payment, total interest, and total cost for a mortgage. 2. Shows a data table that answers what-if questions based on changing interest rates. 3. Highlights the rate in the data table that matches the actual interest rate. 4. Shows an amortization schedule that lists annual summaries of interest paid, principal paid, and balance on principal.
Source of data	Data supplied by the credit union includes interest rate and term of mortgage. Data supplied by the customer includes item to be purchased, price, down payment. All other data is calculated or created in Excel.

Calculations	1. The following calculations must be made for each mortgage:
	  a. Mortgage Amount = Price − Down Payment
	  b. Monthly Payment = PMT function
	  c. Total Interest = 12 × Term × Monthly Payment − Loan Amount
	  d. Total Cost = 12 × Term × Monthly Payment + Down Payment
	2. The Amortization Schedule involves the following calculations:
	  a. Beginning Balance = Loan Amount
	  b. Ending Balance = PV function or zero
	  c. Paid on Principal = Beginning Balance − Ending Balance
	  d. Interest Paid = 12 × Monthly Payment − Paid on Principal or 0
	  e. Paid on Principal Subtotal = SUM function
	  f. Interest Paid Subtotal = SUM function

Special Requirements	1. Assign names to the ranges of the three major worksheet components separately and together to allow the worksheet components to be printed separately or together easily. 2. Use locked cells and worksheet protection to prevent loan officers and customers from inadvertently making changes to formulas and functions contained in the worksheet.

Figure 4–2

In addition, using a sketch of the worksheet can help you visualize its design. The sketch of the worksheet consists of titles, column and cell headings, the location of data values, and a general idea of the desired formatting (Figure 4–3).

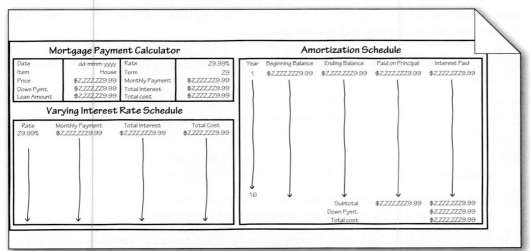

Figure 4–3

BTW
Good Worksheet Design
Consider creating worksheets with an eye towards reusing them in the future. Carefully design worksheets as if they will be on display and evaluated by your fellow workers. Smart worksheet design starts with visualizing the results you need. A well-designed worksheet often is used for many years.

As shown in the worksheet sketch in Figure 4–3, the three basic sections of the worksheet are the Mortgage Payment Calculator on the upper-left side, the Varying Interest Rate Schedule data table on the lower-left side, and the Amortization Schedule on the right side. The worksheet will be created in this order.

With a good understanding of the requirements document, an understanding of the necessary decisions, and a sketch of the worksheet, the next step is to use Excel to create the worksheet.

In this module, you will learn how to create and use the workbook shown in Figure 4–1. The following roadmap identifies general activities you will perform as you progress through this module:

1. CREATE the MORTGAGE PAYMENT CALCULATOR in the worksheet.

2. CREATE a DATA TABLE in the worksheet.

3. CREATE the AMORTIZATION SCHEDULE in the worksheet.

4. FORMAT the WORKSHEET.

5. CREATE PRINT AREAS in the worksheet.

6. PROTECT CELLS in the worksheet.

7. CHECK FORMULAS of the worksheet.

BTW

The Ribbon and Screen Resolution

Excel may change how the groups and buttons within the groups appear on the ribbon, depending on the computer's screen resolution. Thus, your ribbon may look different from the ones in this book if you are using a screen resolution other than 1366 x 768.

To Apply a Theme to the Worksheet

The following steps apply the Integral theme to the workbook.

1 Run Excel and create a blank workbook in the Excel window.

2 Apply the Integral theme to the workbook.

BTW

Global Formatting

To assign formats to all the cells in all the worksheets in a workbook, click the Select All button, right-click a sheet tab, and click 'Select All Sheets' on the shortcut menu. Next, assign the formats. To deselect the worksheets, hold down the SHIFT key and click the Sheet1 tab or select Ungroup sheets on the shortcut menu. You also can select a cell or a range of cells and then select all worksheets to assign formats to that cell or a range of cells on all worksheets in a workbook.

To Enter the Section and Row Titles and System Date

The next step is to enter the Mortgage Payment Calculator section title, row titles, and system date. The Mortgage Payment Calculator section title also will be changed to the Title cell style and vertically middle-aligned. The following steps enter the section title, row titles, and system date.

1 Select cell C3 and then type **Mortgage Payment Calculator** as the section title.

Q&A Why did I not begin creating the worksheet in cell A1?
Two rows at the top of the worksheet and two columns on the left of the worksheet will be left blank to provide a border around the worksheet.

2 Select the range C3:F3 and then click the 'Merge & Center' button (Home tab | Alignment group) to merge and center the section title in the selected range.

3 Click the Cell Styles button (Home tab | Styles group) and then click Title cell style in the Cell Styles gallery to apply the selected style to the active cell.

4 Click the Middle Align button (Home tab | Alignment group) to vertically center the text in the selected cell.

⑤ Select cell C4, type `Date` as the row title, and then press the TAB key to complete the entry in the cell and select the cell to the right.

⑥ With cell D4 selected, type `=NOW()` and then click the Enter button to add a function to the cell that displays today's date.

⑦ Right-click cell D4 to open a shortcut menu and then click Format Cells on the shortcut menu to display the Format Cells dialog box. Click the Number tab to display the Number sheet, click Date in the Category list, scroll down in the Type list, and then click 14–Mar–2012 to select a date format.

⑧ Click the OK button (Format Cells dialog box) to close the Format Cells dialog box.

⑨ Enter the following text in the indicated cells:

Cell	Text	Cell	Text
		E4	Rate
C5	Item	E5	Term
C6	Price	E6	Monthly Payment
C7	Down Pymt.	E7	Total Interest
C8	Loan Amount	E8	Total Cost

BTW
Touch Screen Differences
The Office and Windows interfaces may vary if you are using a touch screen. For this reason, you might notice that the function or appearance of your touch screen differs slightly from this module's presentation.

To Adjust the Column Widths and Row Heights

To make the worksheet easier to read, the width of columns A and B will be decreased and used as a separator between the left edge of the worksheet and the row headings. Using a column(s) as a separator between sections on a worksheet is a technique used by spreadsheet specialists. The width of columns C through F will be increased so that the intended values fit. The height of row 3, which contains the title, will be increased so that it stands out. The height of rows 1 and 2 will be decreased to act as visual separators for the top of the calculator.

① Click column heading A and then drag through column heading B to select both columns. Position the pointer on the right boundary of column heading B and then drag to the left until the ScreenTip indicates Width: .92 (12 pixels) to change the width of both columns.

② Position the pointer on the right boundary of column heading C and then drag to the right until the ScreenTip indicates Width: 12.00 (101 pixels) to change the column width.

③ Click column heading D to select it and then drag through column headings E and F to select multiple columns. Position the pointer on the right boundary of column heading F and then drag until the ScreenTip indicates Width: 16.00 (133 pixels) to change multiple column widths.

④ Click row heading 1 to select it and then drag through row heading 2 to select both rows. Position the pointer on the bottom boundary of row heading 2 and then drag until the ScreenTip indicates Height: 9.00 (12 pixels).

5 Select an empty cell to deselect the selected columns (Figure 4–4).

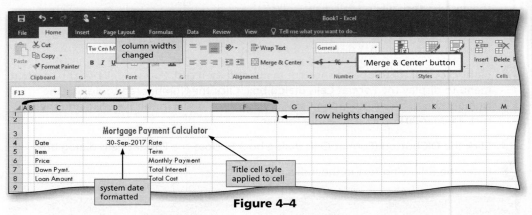

Figure 4–4

To Change the Sheet Tab Name

The following steps change the Sheet1 sheet tab name to a descriptive name and then save the workbook.

1 Double-click the Sheet1 tab and then enter `Mortgage Payment Calculator` as the sheet tab name.

2 Save the workbook on your hard drive, OneDrive, or other storage location using `NCU Mortgage Payment Calculator` as the file name.

Q&A Why should I save the workbook at this time?
You have performed many tasks while creating this workbook and do not want to risk losing work completed thus far.

BTW
Cell References in Formulas
Are you tired of writing formulas that are difficult to decipher because of cell references? The Name Manager can help add clarity to your formulas by allowing you to assign names to cells. You then can use the names, such as Rate, rather than the cell reference, such as D2, in the formulas you create. To access the Name Manager, click the Name Manager button (Formulas tab | Defined Names group).

Creating Cell Names

Worksheets often have column titles at the top of each column and row titles to the left of each row that describe the data within the worksheet. You can use these titles within formulas when you want to refer to the related data by name. A **cell name** often is created from column and row titles. You also can define descriptive names that are not column titles or row titles to represent cells, ranges of cells, formulas, or constants. Names are global to the workbook. That is, a name assigned to a cell or cell range on one worksheet in a workbook can be used on other worksheets in the same workbook to reference the named cell or range. Assigning names to a cell or range of cells allows you to select them quickly using the Name box (shown in Figure 4–7). Clicking the name will select the corresponding cell or range, and highlight the cell or range on the worksheet.

To Format Cells before Entering Values

While you usually format cells after you enter values, Excel also allows you to format cells before you enter the values. The following steps assign the currency style format with a floating dollar sign to the ranges D6:D8 and F6:F8 before the values are entered.

1 Select the range D6:D8 and, while holding down the CTRL key, select the nonadjacent range F6:F8.

2 Right-click one of the selected ranges to display a shortcut menu and then click Format Cells on the shortcut menu to display the Format Cells dialog box.

3 If necessary, click the Number tab (Format Cells dialog box) to display the Number sheet, select Currency in the Category list, and then select the second format, $1,234.10 (red font color), in the Negative numbers list.

4 Click the OK button (Format Cells dialog box) to assign the currency style format with a floating dollar sign to the selected ranges, D6:D8 and F6:F8 in this case.

Q&A What will happen when I enter values in these cells?
As you enter numbers into these cells, Excel will display the numbers using the currency style format. You also could have selected the range C6:F8 rather than the nonadjacent ranges and assigned the currency style format to this range, which includes text. The currency style format has no impact on text in a cell.

To Enter the Loan Data

As shown in the Source of Data section of the requirements document in Figure 4–2, five items make up the loan data in the worksheet: the item to be purchased, the price of the item, the down payment, the interest rate, and the term (number of years) over which the loan is paid back. The following steps enter the loan data.

1 Select cell D5. Type **House** and then click the Enter button in the formula bar to enter text in the selected cell.

2 With cell D5 still active, click the Align Right button (Home tab | Alignment group) to right-align the text in the selected cell.

3 Select cell D6 and then enter **429000** for the price of the house.

4 Select cell D7 and then enter **85000** for the down payment.

5 Select cell F4 and then enter **4.125%** for the interest rate.

6 Click the Enter button in the formula bar to complete the entry of the interest rate, and then click the Increase Decimal button (Home tab | Number group) once to increase the number of decimal places to three.

7 Select cell F5 and then enter **15** for the number of years.

8 Click the Enter button in the formula bar to complete the entry of data in the worksheet (Figure 4–5).

BTW
When to Format
Excel lets you format cells (1) before you enter data; (2) when you enter data, through the use of format symbols; (3) incrementally after entering sections of data; and (4) after you enter all the data. Experienced users usually format a worksheet in increments as they build the worksheet, but occasions do exist when it makes sense to format cells before you enter any data.

BTW
Entering Percentages
When you format a cell to display percentages, Excel assumes that whatever you enter into that cell in the future will be a percentage. Thus, if you enter the number .5, Excel translates the value as 50%. A potential problem arises, however, when you start to enter numbers greater than or equal to one. For instance, if you enter the number 25, do you mean 25% or 2500%? If you want Excel to treat the number 25 as 25% instead of 2500% and Excel interprets the number 25 as 2500%, then click Options in the Backstage view. When the Excel Options dialog box appears, click Advanced in the left pane, and make sure the 'Enable automatic percent entry' check box in the right pane is selected.

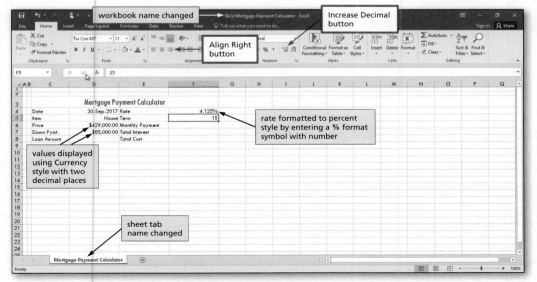

Figure 4–5

BTW
Entering Interest Rates
An alternative to requiring the user to enter an interest rate as a percentage, such as 4.125%, is to allow the user to enter the interest rate as a number without a percent sign (4.125) and then divide the interest rate by 1200, rather than 12.

Q&A Why are the entered values already formatted?

The values in cells D6 and D7 in Figure 4–5 are formatted using the currency style with two decimal places because this format was assigned to the cells prior to entering the values. Because the percent sign (%) was appended to 4.125 when it was entered in cell F4, Excel formats the interest rate using the percentage style with two decimal places (thus, the value appears as 4.13). Using the Increase Decimal button increased the number of visible decimal places to three.

To Create Names Based on Row Titles

1 CREATE MORTGAGE PAYMENT CALCULATOR | 2 CREATE DATA TABLE | 3 CREATE AMORTIZATION SCHEDULE
4 FORMAT WORKSHEET | 5 CREATE PRINT AREAS | 6 PROTECT CELLS | 7 CHECK FORMULAS

Why? *Naming a cell that you plan to reference in a formula helps make the formula easier to read and remember.* For example, the loan amount in cell D8 is equal to the price in cell D6 minus the down payment in cell D7. According to what you learned in earlier modules, you can enter the loan amount formula in cell D8 as =D6 – D7. By naming cells D6 and D7 using the corresponding row titles in cells C6 and C7, however, you can enter the loan amount formula as =Price – Down_Pymt., which is clearer and easier to understand than =D6 – D7. In addition to assigning a name to a single cell, you can follow the same steps to assign a name to a range of cells. The following steps assign the row titles in the range C6:C8 to their adjacent cell in column D and assign the row titles in the range E4:E8 to their adjacent cell in column F.

1

- Select the range C6:D8.

- Display the Formulas tab.

- Click the 'Create from Selection' button (Formulas tab | Defined Names group) to display the Create Names from Selection dialog box (Figure 4–6).

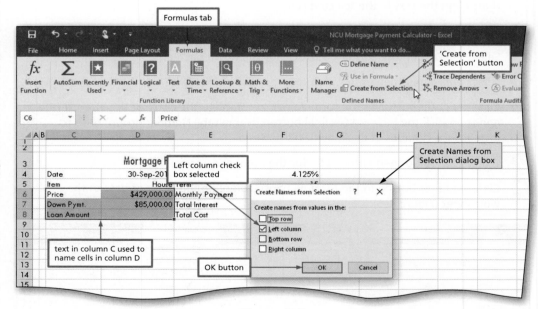

Figure 4–6

2

- Click the OK button (Create Names from Selection dialog box) to name the cells selected in the right column of the selection, D6:D8 in this case.

- Select the range E4:F8 and then click the 'Create from Selection' button (Formulas tab | Defined Names group) to display the Create Names from Selection dialog box.

- Click the OK button (Create Names from Selection dialog box) to assign names to the cells selected in the right column of the selection, F4:F8 in this case.

Q&A Are names absolute or relative cell references?

Names are absolute cell references. This is important to remember if you plan to copy formulas that contain names rather than cell references.

- Deselect the selected range and then click the Name box arrow in the formula bar to view the created names (Figure 4–7).

Q&A

Is a cell name valid when it contains a period, as with the Down_Pymt. cell name?
Yes. Periods and underscore characters are allowed in cell names. A cell name may not begin with a period or an underscore, however.

Are there any limitations on cell names?
Names may not be longer than 255 characters.

What if I make a mistake creating a cell name?
Click the Name Manager button (Formulas tab | Defined Names group) to display the Name Manager dialog box. Select the range to edit or delete, and then click the appropriate button to edit or delete the selected range.

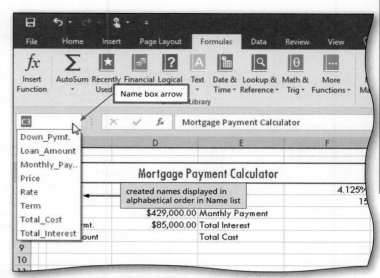

Figure 4–7

Other Ways

1. Select cell or range, type name in Name box, press ENTER key

2. Select cell or range, click Define Name button (Formulas tab | Defined Names group), type name, click OK button (New Name dialog box)

3. Select cell or range, click Name Manager button (Formulas tab | Defined Names group), click New (Name Manager dialog box), type name, click OK button (New Name dialog box), click Close button (Name Manager dialog box)

4. Select range, press CTRL+SHIFT+F3

What do you do if a cell you want to name does not have a text item in an adjacent cell?
If you want to assign a name that does not appear as a text item in an adjacent cell, use the Define Name button (Formulas tab | Defined Names group) or select the cell or range and then type the name in the Name box in the formula bar.

What do I need to consider when naming cells, and how can I use named cells?
You can use the assigned names in formulas to reference cells in the ranges D6:D8 or F4:F8. Excel is not case sensitive with respect to names of cells. You can enter the cell names in formulas in either uppercase or lowercase letters. To use a name that consists of two or more words in a formula, you should replace any space with the underscore character (_), as this is a commonly used standard for creating cell names. For example, the name, Down Pymt., can be written as down_pymt. or Down_Pymt. when you want to reference the adjacent cell D7. The Name Manager dialog box appears when you click the Name Manager button. The Name Manager dialog box allows you to create new names and edit or delete existing names.

CONSIDER THIS

To Enter the Loan Amount Formula Using Names

1 CREATE MORTGAGE PAYMENT CALCULATOR | 2 CREATE DATA TABLE | 3 CREATE AMORTIZATION SCHEDULE
4 FORMAT WORKSHEET | 5 CREATE PRINT AREAS | 6 PROTECT CELLS | 7 CHECK FORMULAS

Why? Once you have created names, you can use them instead of cell references in formulas. To determine the loan amount, enter the formula =Price – Down_Pymt. in cell D8. The following steps enter the formula using names.

1

- Select cell D8.

- Type **=p** and then scroll down the Formula AutoComplete list until you see the Price entry (Figure 4–8).

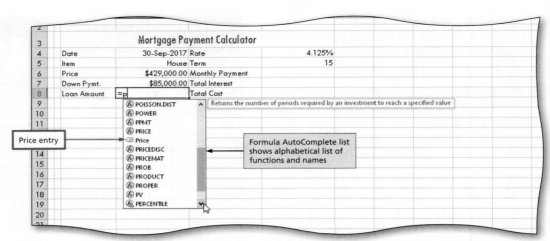

Figure 4–8

2

- Double-click Price to enter it in cell D8.

- Type **−d**.

- Double-click Down_Pymt. in the Formula AutoComplete list to select it and display the formula in both cell D8 and the formula bar using the cell names instead of the cell references (Figure 4–9).

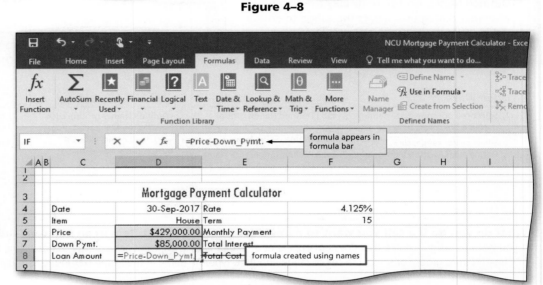

Figure 4–9

3

- Click the Enter button to assign the formula to the selected cell, =Price – Down_Pymt. to cell D8 (Figure 4–10).

Q&A What happens if I enter my formula using Point mode instead of using names?
If you enter a formula using Point mode and click a cell that has an assigned name, Excel will insert the name of the cell rather than the cell reference.

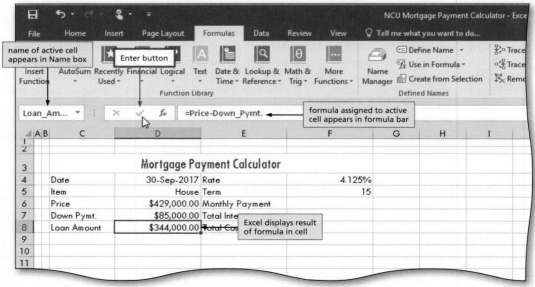

Figure 4–10

The PMT Function

You can use Excel's PMT function to determine the monthly payment. The **PMT function** calculates the payment for a loan based on constant payments and a constant interest rate. The PMT function has three arguments: rate, periods, and loan amount. Its general form is as follows:

=PMT (rate, periods, loan amount)

where rate is the interest rate per payment period, periods is the number of payments over the life of the loan, and loan amount is the amount of the loan.

In the worksheet shown in Figure 4–10, Excel displays the annual interest rate in cell F4. Financial institutions, however, usually calculate interest on a monthly basis. The rate value in the PMT function is, therefore, Rate / 12 (cell F4 divided by 12), rather than just Rate (cell F4). The periods (or number of payments) in the PMT function is 12 * Term (12 times cell F5) because each year includes 12 months, or 12 payments.

Excel considers the value returned by the PMT function to be a debit and, therefore, returns a negative number as the monthly payment. To display the monthly payment as a positive number, begin the function with a negative sign instead of an equal sign. The PMT function for cell F6 is:

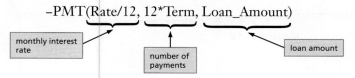

To Enter the PMT Function

1 CREATE MORTGAGE PAYMENT CALCULATOR | 2 CREATE DATA TABLE | 3 CREATE AMORTIZATION SCHEDULE
4 FORMAT WORKSHEET | 5 CREATE PRINT AREAS | 6 PROTECT CELLS | 7 CHECK FORMULAS

Why? *The next step in building the mortgage payment calculator is to determine the monthly payment for the mortgage.* The following steps use the keyboard, rather than Point mode or the Insert Function dialog box, to enter the PMT function to determine the monthly payment in cell F6.

- Select cell F6.

- Type the function
  `–pmt(Rate/12,`
  `12*Term,`
  `Loan_Amount` in
  cell F6, which also
  displays in the
  formula bar
  (Figure 4–11).

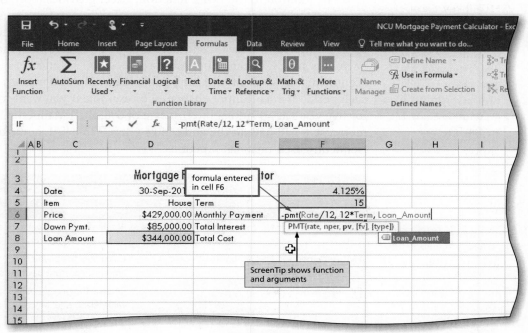

Figure 4–11

Q&A

What happens as I begin to enter the function?
The ScreenTip shows the general form of the PMT function (after you type the opening parenthesis). The arguments in brackets in the ScreenTip are optional and not required for the computation required in this project. The Formula AutoComplete list (Figure 4–8) shows functions and cell names that match the letters that you type on the keyboard. You can type the complete cell name, such as Loan_Amount, or double-click the cell name in the list. When you have completed entering the function and click the Enter button or press the ENTER key, Excel will add the closing parenthesis to the function. Excel also may scroll the worksheet to the right in order to accommodate the ScreenTip.

2

• Click the Enter button in the formula bar to complete the function (Figure 4–12).

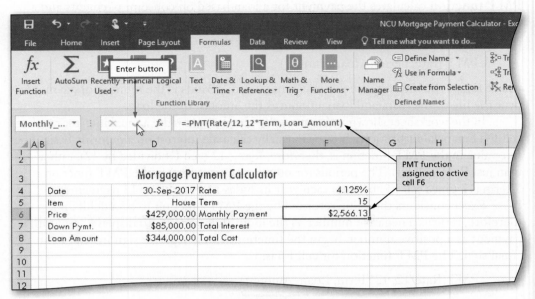

Figure 4–12

Other Ways

1. Click Financial button (Formulas tab | Function Library group), select PMT function, enter arguments, click OK button

2. Click Insert Function button in formula bar, select Financial category, select PMT function, click OK button, enter arguments, click OK button (Function Arguments dialog box)

Other Financial Functions

In addition to the PMT function, Excel provides more than 50 financial functions to help you solve the most complex finance problems. These functions save you from entering long, complicated formulas to obtain needed results. For example, the **FV function** returns the future value of an investment based on scheduled payments and an unchanging interest rate. The FV function requires the following arguments: the interest rate per period, the number of periods, and the payment made each period (which cannot change). For example if you want to invest $200 per month for five years at an annual interest rate of 6%, the FV function will calculate how much money you will have at the end of five years. Table 4–1 summarizes three of the more frequently used financial functions.

Table 4–1 Frequently Used Financial Functions	
Function	**Description**
FV (rate, periods, payment)	Returns the future value of an investment based on periodic, constant payments and a constant interest rate.
PMT (rate, periods, loan amount)	Calculates the payment for a loan based on the loan amount, constant payments, and a constant interest rate.
PV (rate, periods, payment)	Returns the present value of an investment. The present value is the total amount that a series of future payments now is worth.

To Determine the Total Interest and Total Cost

The next step is to determine the total interest the borrower will pay on the loan (the lending institution's gross profit on the loan) and the total cost the borrower will pay for the item being purchased. The total interest (cell F7) is equal to the number of payments times the monthly payment, minus the loan amount:

$$=12*Term*Monthly\_Payment-Loan\_Amount$$

The total cost of the item to be purchased (cell F8) is equal to the price plus the total interest:

$$=Price+Total\_Interest$$

The following steps enter formulas to determine the total interest and total cost using names.

1 Select cell F7, use the keyboard to enter the formula `=12 * term * monthly_ payment - loan_amount` to determine the total interest, and then click the Enter button.

2 Select cell F8 and then use the keyboard to enter the formula `=price + total_ interest` to determine the total cost.

3 Select an empty cell to deselect cell F8 (Figure 4–13).

4 Save the workbook again on the same storage location with the same file name.

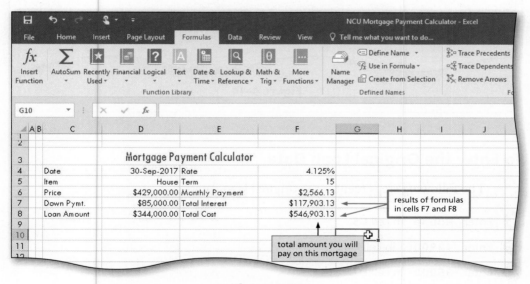

Figure 4–13

BTW

Range Finder

Remember to check all your formulas carefully. You can double-click a cell containing a formula and Excel will use Range Finder to highlight the cells that provide data for that formula. While Range Finder is active, you can drag the outlines from one cell to another to change the cells referenced in the formula, provided the cells have not been named.

BTW

Testing a Worksheet

It is good practice to test the formulas in a worksheet repeatedly until you are confident they are correct. Use data that tests the limits of the formulas. For example, you should enter negative numbers, zero, and large positive numbers when test ing formulas.

To Enter New Loan Data

Assume you want to purchase a condominium for $185,900.00. You have $45,000 for a down payment and you want the loan for a term of 10 years. NCU currently is charging 3.625% interest for a 10–year loan. The following steps enter the new loan data.

1 Enter `Condominium` in cell D5.

2 Enter `185900` in cell D6.

3 Enter **45000** in cell D7.

4 Enter **3.625%** in cell F4.

5 Enter 10 in cell F5, and then select an empty cell to recalculate the loan information in cells D8, F6, F7, and F8 (Figure 4–14).

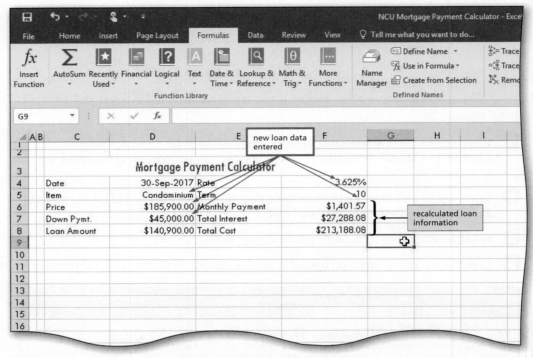

Figure 4–14

To Enter the Original Loan Data

The following steps reenter the original loan data.

1 Enter **House** in cell D5.

2 Enter **429000** in cell D6.

3 Enter **85000** in cell D7.

4 Enter **4.125** in cell F4.

5 Enter 15 in cell F5 and then select cell C10 to complete the entry of the original loan data.

Q&A What is happening on the worksheet as I enter the original data?
Excel instantaneously recalculates all formulas in the worksheet each time you enter a value. Once you have re-entered all the initial data, Excel displays the original loan information, as shown in Figure 4–13.

Can the Undo button on the Quick Access Toolbar be used to change back to the original data?
Yes. The Undo button must be clicked five times, once for each data item. You also can click the Undo arrow and drag through the first five entries in the Undo list.

BTW

Expanding Data Tables

The data table created in this module is relatively small. You can continue the series of percentages to the bottom of the worksheet and insert additional formulas in columns to create as large of a data table as you want.

Using a Data Table to Analyze Worksheet Data

You already have seen that if you change a value in a cell, Excel immediately recalculates any formulas that reference the cell directly or indirectly. But what if you want to compare the results of the formula for several different values? Writing down or trying to remember all the answers to the what-if questions would be unwieldy. If you use a data table, however, Excel will organize the answers in the worksheet for you.

A **data table** is a range of cells that shows answers generated by formulas in which different values have been substituted. Data tables must be built in an unused area of the worksheet (in this case, the range C9:F22). Figure 4–15a illustrates the content needed for the Data Table command. With a **one-input data table**, you can vary the value in one cell (in this worksheet, cell F4, the interest rate). Excel then calculates the results of one or more formulas and fills the data table with the results, as shown in Figure 4–15b.

The interest rates that will be used to analyze the loan formulas in this project range from 3.000% to 4.250%, increasing in increments of 0.125%. The one-input data table shown in Figure 4–15b illustrates the impact of varying the interest rate on three formulas: the monthly payment (cell F6), total interest paid (cell F7), and the total cost of the item to be purchased (cell F8). The series of interest rates in column C are called input values.

BTW

Data Tables
Data tables have one purpose: to organize the answers to what-if questions. You can create two kinds of data tables. The first type involves changing one input value to see the resulting effect on one or more formulas. The second type involves changing two input values to see the resulting effect on one formula.

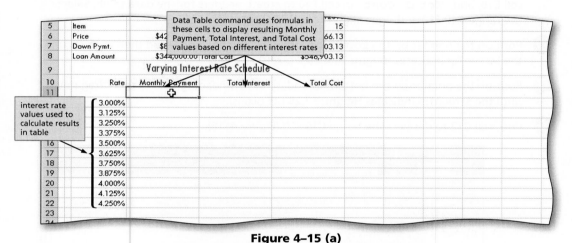

Figure 4–15 (a)

Figure 4–15 (b)

Can you use a data table when you need to vary the values in two cells rather than one?
An alternative to a one-input table is a two-input data table. A **two-input data table** allows you to vary the values in two cells. For example, you can use a two-input data table to see how your monthly mortgage payment will be affected by changing both the interest rate and the term of the loan.

To Enter the Data Table Title and Column Titles

The first step in constructing the data table shown in Figure 4–15b is to enter the data table section title and column titles in the range C9:F10 and adjust the heights of rows 9 and 10.

1 Select cell C9 and then type `Varying Interest Rate Schedule` as the data table section title.

2 Select cell C3 and then click the Format Painter button (Home tab | Clipboard group) to copy the format of the cell. Click cell C9 to apply the copied format to the cell.

3 Type `Rate` In cell C10, `Monthly Payment` in cell D10, `Total Interest` in cell E10, and `Total Cost` in cell F10 to create headers for the data table. Select the range C10:F10 and right-align the column titles.

4 Position the pointer on the bottom boundary of row heading 9 and then drag up until the ScreenTip indicates Height: 20.25 (27 pixels).

5 Position the pointer on the bottom boundary of row heading 10 and then drag down until the ScreenTip indicates Height: 17.25 (23 pixels).

6 Click cell C12 to deselect the range C10:F10 (Figure 4–16).

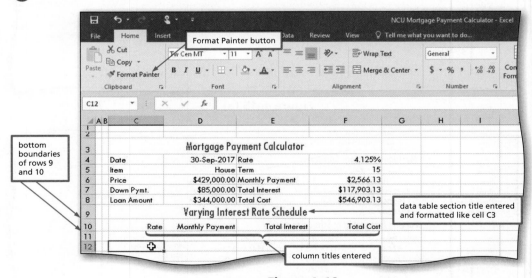

Figure 4–16

To Create a Percentage Series Using the Fill Handle

1 CREATE MORTGAGE PAYMENT CALCULATOR | 2 CREATE DATA TABLE | 3 CREATE AMORTIZATION SCHEDULE
4 FORMAT WORKSHEET | 5 CREATE PRINT AREAS | 6 PROTECT CELLS | 7 CHECK FORMULAS

Why? *These percentages will serve as the input data for the data table.* The following steps create the percentage series in column C using the fill handle.

1

- With cell C12 selected, type **3.0%** as the first number in the series.

- Select cell C13 and then type **3.125%** as the second number in the series.

- Select the range C12:C13.

- Drag the fill handle through cell C22 to create the border of the fill area as indicated by the shaded border (Figure 4–17). Do not lift your finger or release the mouse button.

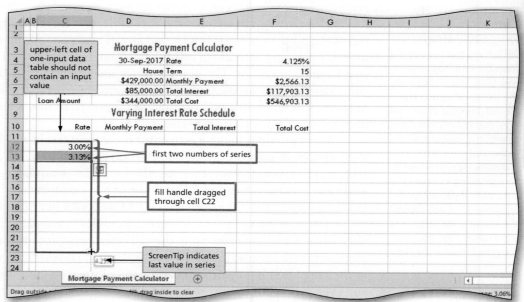

Figure 4–17

2

- Lift your finger or release the mouse button to generate the percentage series, in this case from 3.00% to 4.25%.

- Click the Increase Decimal button (Home tab | Number group) to increase the number of decimal places shown to 3.

- Click cell D11 to deselect the selected range, C12:C22 in this case (Figure 4–18).

What is the purpose of the percentages in column C?

The percentages in column C represent different annual interest rates, which will be used when calculating the data table. The series begins in cell C12, not cell C11, because the cell immediately to the upper-left of the formulas in a one-input data table should not include an input value.

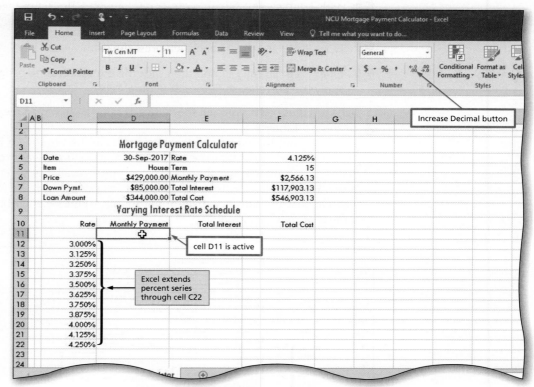

Figure 4–18

Other Ways

1. Right-drag fill handle in direction to fill, click Fill Series on shortcut menu

BTW
Formulas in Data Tables
Any experienced Excel user will tell you that to enter the formulas at the top of the data table, you should enter the cell reference or name of the cell preceded by an equal sign. This ensures that if you change the original formula in the worksheet, Excel automatically will change the corresponding formula in the data table. If you use a cell reference, Excel also copies the format to the cell. If you use a name, Excel does not copy the format to the cell.

To Enter the Formulas in the Data Table

The next step in creating the data table is to enter the three formulas at the top of the table in cells D11, E11, and F11. The three formulas are the same as the monthly payment formula in cell F6, the total interest formula in cell F7, and the total cost formula in cell F8. The number of formulas you place at the top of a one-input data table depends on the purpose of the table. Some one-input data tables will have only one formula, while others might have several. In this case, three formulas are affected when the interest rate changes.

Excel provides four ways to enter these formulas in the data table: (1) retype the formulas in cells D11, E11, and F11; (2) copy cells F6, F7, and F8 to cells D11, E11, and F11, respectively; (3) enter the formulas `=monthly_payment` in cell D11, `=total_interest` in cell E11, and `=total_cost` in cell F11; or (4) enter the formulas `=F6` in cell D11, `=F7` in cell E11, and `=F8` in cell F11.

The best alternative to define the formulas in the data table is the fourth alternative, which involves using the cell references preceded by an equal sign. This method is best because (1) it is easier to enter; (2) if you change any of the formulas in the range F6:F8, the formulas at the top of the data table are immediately updated; and (3) Excel automatically will assign the format of the cell reference (currency style format) to the cell. Using the third alternative, which involves using cell names, is nearly as good an alternative, but Excel will not assign formatting to the cells when you use cell names. The following steps enter the formulas of the data table in row 11.

1 With cell D11 active, type   `=f6`   and then press the RIGHT ARROW key to enter the first parameter of the function to be used in the data table.

2 Type   `=f7`   in cell E11 and then press the RIGHT ARROW key.

3 Type   `=f8`   in cell F11 and then click the Enter button to assign the formulas and apply the Currency style format (Figure 4–19).

Q&A Why are these cells assigned the values of cells in the Mortgage Payment Calculator area of the worksheet?

It is important to understand that the entries in the top row of the data table (row 11) refer to the formulas that the loan officer and customer want to evaluate using the series of percentages in column C. Furthermore, recall that when you assign a formula to a cell, Excel applies the format of the first cell reference in the formula to the cell. Thus, Excel applies the currency style format to cells D11, E11, and F11 because that is the format of cells F6, F7, and F8.

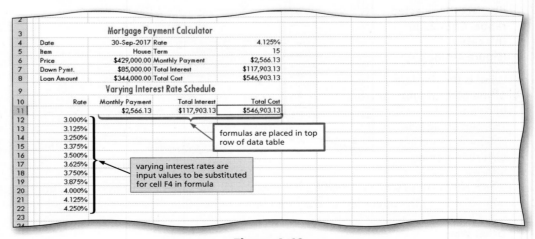

Figure 4–19

To Define a Range as a Data Table

After creating the interest rate series in column C and entering the formulas in row 11, the next step is to define the range C11:F22 as a data table. Cell F4 is the input cell for the data table, which means cell F4 is the cell in which values from column C in the data table are substituted in the formulas in row 11. **Why?** *You want Excel to generate the monthly payment, monthly interest, and total cost for the various interest rates.*

- Select the range C11:F22 as the range in which to create the data table.

- Display the Data tab and then click the 'What-If Analysis' button (Data tab | Forecast group) to display the What-If Analysis menu (Figure 4–20).

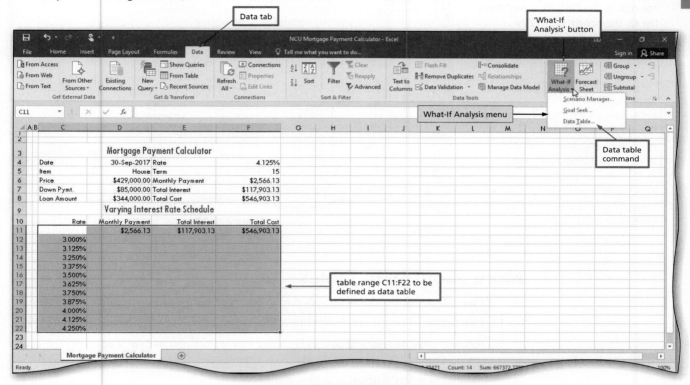

Figure 4–20

- Click Data Table on the What-If Analysis menu to display the Data Table dialog box.

- Click the 'Column input cell' box (Data Table dialog box) and then click cell F4 in the Mortgage Payment Calculator section of the spreadsheet to select the input cell for the data table (Figure 4–21).

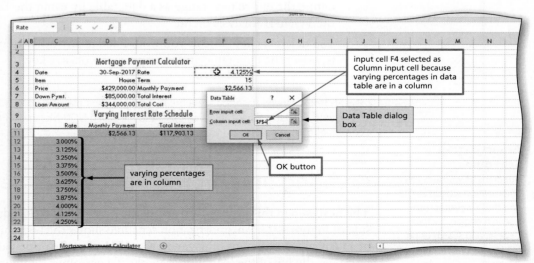

Figure 4–21

Q&A What is the purpose of clicking cell F4?

The purpose of clicking cell F4 is to select it for the Column input cell. A marquee surrounds the selected cell F4, indicating it will be the input cell in which values from column C in the data table are substituted in the formulas in row 11. $F$4 now appears in the 'Column input cell' box in the Data Table dialog box.

3

- Click the OK button (Data Table dialog box) to create the data table.
- Apply the currency style with no currency symbol and the second format in the Negative numbers list to the range D12:F22.
- Deselect the selected range, D11:F22 in this case (Figure 4–22).

Q&A How does Excel create the data table?

Excel calculates the results of the three formulas in row 11 for each interest rate in column C and immediately fills columns D, E, and F of the data table. The resulting values for each interest rate are displayed in the corresponding rows.

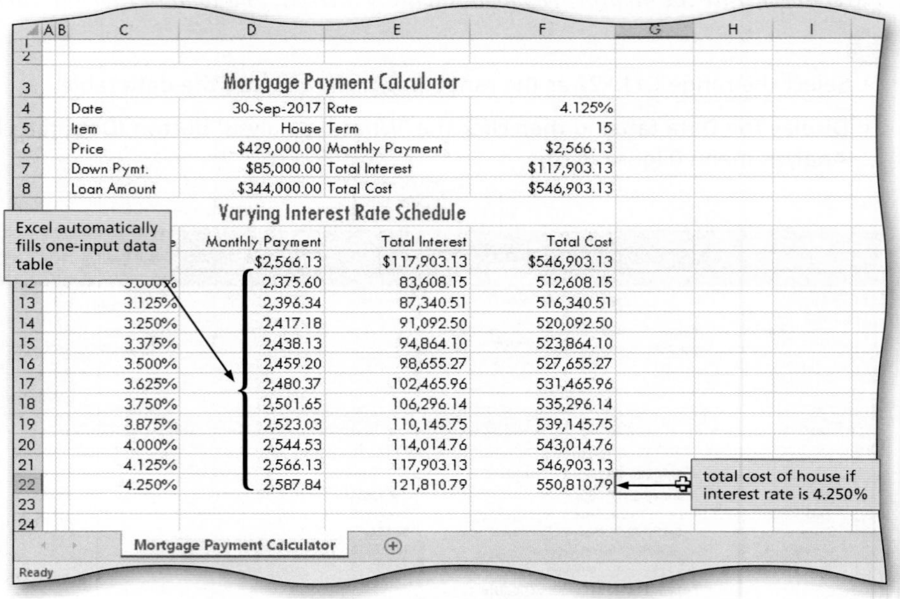

Row	C	D	E	F
3		Mortgage Payment Calculator		
4	Date	30-Sep-2017	Rate	4.125%
5	Item	House	Term	15
6	Price	$429,000.00	Monthly Payment	$2,566.13
7	Down Pymt.	$85,000.00	Total Interest	$117,903.13
8	Loan Amount	$344,000.00	Total Cost	$546,903.13
9		Varying Interest Rate Schedule		
10		Monthly Payment	Total Interest	Total Cost
11		$2,566.13	$117,903.13	$546,903.13
12	3.000%	2,375.60	83,608.15	512,608.15
13	3.125%	2,396.34	87,340.51	516,340.51
14	3.250%	2,417.18	91,092.50	520,092.50
15	3.375%	2,438.13	94,864.10	523,864.10
16	3.500%	2,459.20	98,655.27	527,655.27
17	3.625%	2,480.37	102,465.96	531,465.96
18	3.750%	2,501.65	106,296.14	535,296.14
19	3.875%	2,523.03	110,145.75	539,145.75
20	4.000%	2,544.53	114,014.76	543,014.76
21	4.125%	2,566.13	117,903.13	546,903.13
22	4.250%	2,587.84	121,810.79	550,810.79

Figure 4–22

More about Data Tables

The following list details important points you should know about data tables:

1. The formula(s) you are analyzing must include a cell reference to the input cell.
2. You can have as many active data tables in a worksheet as you want.
3. While only one value can vary in a one-input data table, the data table can analyze as many formulas as you want.
4. To include additional formulas in a one-input data table, enter them in adjacent cells in the same row as the current formulas (row 11 in Figure 4–22) and then define the entire new range as a data table by using the Data Table command on the What-If Analysis menu.
5. You delete a data table as you would delete any other item on a worksheet. That is, select the data table and then press the DELETE key.

Break Point: If you wish to take a break, this is a good place to do so. You can exit Excel now. To resume at a later time, run Excel, open the file called NCU Mortgage Payment Calculator, and continue following the steps from this location forward.

BTW
Amortization Schedules
Hundreds of websites offer amortization schedules. To find these websites, use a search engine, such as Google, and search using the keywords, amortization schedule.

Creating an Amortization Schedule

The next step in this project is to create the Amortization Schedule section on the right side of Figure 4–23. An amortization schedule shows the beginning and ending balances of a loan and the amount of payment that applies to the principal and interest for each year over the life of the loan. For example, if a customer wanted to pay off the loan after six years, the Amortization Schedule section would tell the loan officer what the payoff would be (cell J10 in Figure 4–23). The Amortization Schedule section shown in Figure 4–23 will work only for loans of up to 15 years; however, you could extend the table to any number of years. The Amortization Schedule section also contains summaries in rows 20, 21, and 22. These summaries should agree exactly with the corresponding amounts in the Mortgage Payment Calculator section in the range C3:F8.

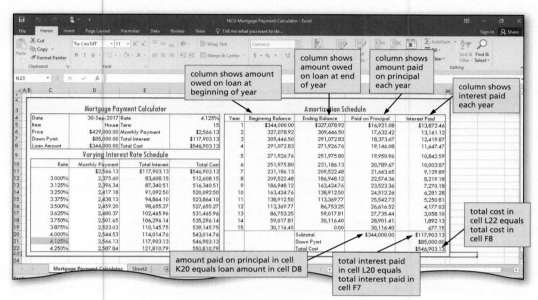

Figure 4–23

To Change Column Widths and Enter Titles

The first step in creating the Amortization Schedule section is to adjust the column widths and enter the section title and column titles. The following steps adjust column widths and enter column titles for the Amortization Schedule section.

1 Position the pointer on the right boundary of column heading G and then drag to the left until the ScreenTip shows Width: .92 (12 pixels) to change the column width.

2 Position the pointer on the right boundary of column heading H and then drag to the left until the ScreenTip shows Width: 6.00 (53 pixels) to change the column width.

3 Drag through column headings I through L to select them. Position the pointer on the right boundary of column heading L and then drag to the right until the ScreenTip shows Width: 16.00 (133 pixels) to change the column widths.

4 Select cell H3. Type **Amortization Schedule** and then press the ENTER key to enter the section title.

5 Select cell C3, click the Format Painter button (Home tab | Clipboard group) to activate the format painter, and then click cell H3 to copy the format of cell C3.

6 Click the 'Merge & Center' button (Home tab | Alignment group) to split the selected cell, cell H3 in this case. Select the range H3:L3 and then click the 'Merge & Center' button (Home tab | Alignment group) to merge and center the section title over the selected range.

7 Enter the following column headings in row 4: **Year** in cell H4, **Beginning Balance** in cell I4, **Ending Balance** in cell J4, **Paid on Principal** in cell K4, and **Interest Paid** in cell L4. Select the range H4:L4 and then click the Center button (Home tab | Alignment group) to center the column headings.

8   Select cell H5 to display the centered section title and column headings (Figure 4–24).

Q&A Why was cell H3 split, or unmerged, in Step 6?
After using the format painter, Excel attempted to merge and center the text in cell H3 because the source of the format, cell C3, is merged and centered across four columns. The Amortization Schedule section, however, includes five columns. Splitting cell H3 changed cell H3 back to being one column instead of including four columns. Next, the section heading was merged and centered across five columns as required by the design of the worksheet.

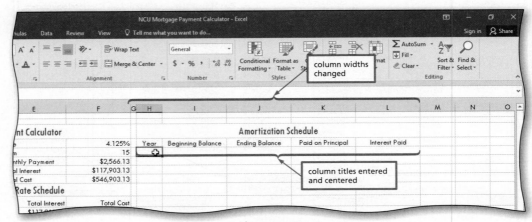

Figure 4–24

To Create a Series of Integers Using the Fill Handle

The next step is to use the fill handle to create a series of numbers that represent the years during the life of the loan. The series begins with 1 (year 1) and ends with 15 (year 15). The following steps create a series of years in the range H5:H19.

1   With cell H5 active, type **1** as the initial year. Select cell H6 and then type **2** to represent the next year.

2   Select the range H5:H6 and then drag the fill handle through cell H19 to complete the creation of a series of integers, 1 through 15 in the range H5:H19 in this case (Figure 4–25).

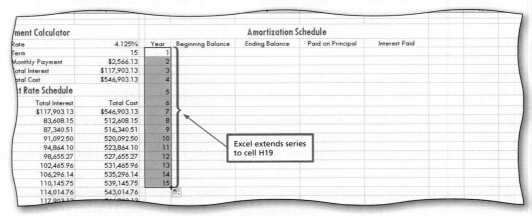

Figure 4–25

Q&A Why is year 5 of the amortization schedule larger than the other rows in the amortization schedule?

The design of the worksheet called for a large font size for the varying interest rate schedule section of the worksheet, which is in row 9 of the worksheet. To accommodate the larger font size, the height of row 9 was increased. Year 5 of the worksheet is in the taller row 9 and, therefore, is taller than the other years in the amortization schedule.

Formulas in the Amortization Schedule

Four formulas form the basis of the amortization schedule. These formulas are found in row 5. Later, these formulas will be copied through row 19. The formulas are summarized in Table 4–2.

Table 4–2 Formulas for the Amortization Schedule			
Cell	**Column Heading**	**Formula**	**Example**
I5	Beginning Balance	=D8	The beginning balance (the balance at the end of a year) is the initial loan amount in cell D8.
J5	Ending Balance	=IF(H5<=$F$5, PV($F$4/12, 12*($F$5–H5), –$F$6), 0)	The ending balance (the balance at the end of a year) is equal to the present value of the payments paid over the remaining life of the loan. (This formula is fully explained in the following text.)
K5	Paid on Principal	=I5–J5	The amount paid on the principal at the end of the year is equal to the beginning balance (cell I5) minus the ending balance (cell J5).
L5	Interest Paid	=IF(I5>0, 12*$F$6–K5, 0)	The interest paid during the year is equal to 12 times the monthly payment (cell F6) minus the amount paid on the principal (cell K5).

Of the four formulas in Table 4–2, perhaps the most difficult to understand is the PV function that will be assigned to cell J5. The **PV function** returns the present value of an annuity. An **annuity** is a series of fixed payments (such as the monthly payment in cell F6) made at the end of each of a fixed number of periods (months) at a fixed interest rate. You can use the PV function to determine the amount the borrower still owes on the loan at the end of each year. The PV function has three arguments: rate, number of periods, and payment amount per period. Its general form is as follows:

$$=PV(rate, period, payment)$$

where rate is the interest rate per payment period, period is the number of payments remaining in the life of the loan, and payment is the amount of the monthly payment.

The PV function is used to determine the ending balance after the first year (cell J5) by using a term equal to the number of months for which the borrower still must make payments. For example, if the loan is for 15 years (180 months), then the borrower still owes 168 payments after the first year (180 months–12 months). The number of payments outstanding can be determined from the formula 12*($F$5–H5) or 12*(15–1), which equals 168. Recall that column H contains integers that represent the years of the loan. After the second year, the number of payments remaining is 156, and so on.

If you assign the PV function as shown in Table 4–2 to cell J5 and then copy it to the range J6:J19, the ending balances for each year will be displayed properly. However, if the loan is for fewer than 15 years, any ending balances for the years beyond the term of the loan are invalid. For example, if a loan is taken out for 5 years, then the rows representing years 6 through 15 in the amortization schedule should be zero. The PV function, however, will display negative numbers for those years even though the loan already has been paid off.

To avoid displaying negative ending balances, the worksheet should include a formula that assigns the PV function to the range I5:I19 as long as the corresponding year in column H is less than or equal to the number of years in the term (cell F5). If the corresponding year in column H is greater than the number of years in cell F5, then the ending balance for that year and the remaining years should be zero. The following IF function causes either the value of the PV function or zero to be displayed in cell J5, depending on whether the corresponding value in column H is greater than — or less than or equal to — the number of years in cell F5. Recall that the dollar signs within the cell references indicate the cell references are absolute and, therefore, will not change as you copy the function downward.

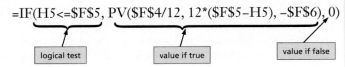

$$=IF(H5<=\$F\$5, \ PV(\$F\$4/12, \ 12*(\$F\$5-H5), \ -\$F\$6), \ 0)$$

logical test   value if true   value if false

In the preceding formula, the logical test determines if the year in column H is less than or equal to the term of the loan in cell F5. If the logical test is true, then the IF function assigns the PV function to the cell. If the logical test is false, then the IF function assigns zero (0) to the cell. You also could use two double-quote symbols (" ") to indicate to Excel to leave the cell blank if the logical test is false.

The PV function in the IF function includes absolute cell references (cell references with dollar signs) to ensure that the references to cells in column F do not change when the IF function later is copied down the column.

To Enter the Formulas in the Amortization Schedule

1 CREATE MORTGAGE PAYMENT CALCULATOR | 2 CREATE DATA TABLE | 3 CREATE AMORTIZATION SCHEDULE
4 FORMAT WORKSHEET | 5 CREATE PRINT AREAS | 6 PROTECT CELLS | 7 CHECK FORMULAS

Why? Creating an amortization schedule allows you to see the costs of a mortgage and the balance still owed for any year in the term of the loan. This information can be very helpful when making financial decisions. The following steps enter the four formulas shown in Table 4–2 into row 5. Row 5 represents year 1 of the loan.

• Select cell I5 and then enter **=d8** as the beginning balance of the loan.

• Select cell J5 and then type **=if(h5<=f5, pv(f4/12, 12*(f5-h5), -f6), 0)** as the entry (Figure 4–26).

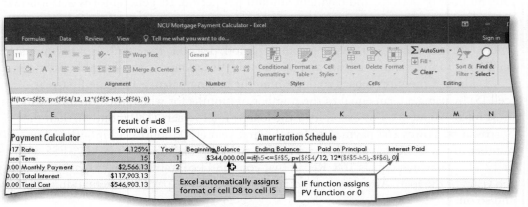

Figure 4–26

• Click the Enter button in the formula bar to insert the formula in the selected cell (Figure 4–27).

Q&A What happens when the Enter button is clicked?
Excel evaluates the IF function in cell J5 and displays the result of the PV function (327078.9227), because the value in cell H5 (1) is less than the term of the loan in cell F5 (15). With cell J5 active, Excel also displays the formula in the formula bar. If the borrower wanted to pay off the loan after one year, the cost would be $327,078.92.

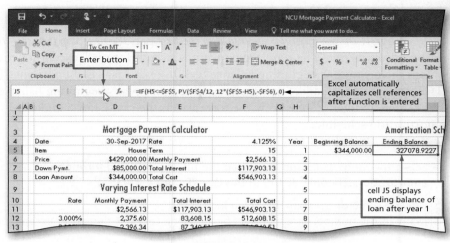

Figure 4–27

3

• Select cell K5. Enter the formula `=i5 – j5` and then press the RIGHT ARROW key to complete the entry and select cell L5.

• Enter the formula `=if(i5 > 0, 12 * $f$6 – k5, 0)` in cell L5 (Figure 4–28).

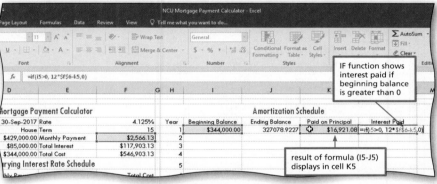

Figure 4–28

4

• Click the Enter button in the formula bar to complete the entry of the formula (Figure 4–29).

Q&A Why are some of the cells in the range I5:L5 not formatted?
When you enter a formula in a cell, Excel assigns the cell the same format as the first cell reference in the formula. For example, when you enter =d8 in cell I5, Excel assigns the format in cell D8 to cell I5. The same applies to cell K5. Although this method of formatting also works for most functions, it does not work for the IF function. Thus, the results of the IF functions in cells J5 and L5 are formatted using the general style format, which is the default format when you open a new workbook.

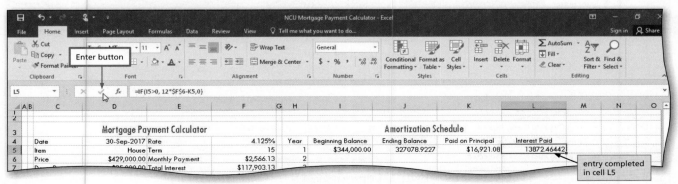

Figure 4–29

To Copy the Formulas to Fill the Amortization Schedule

Why? *With the formulas entered into the first row, the next step is to copy them to the remaining rows in the amortization schedule.* The required copying is straightforward, except for the beginning balance column. To obtain the next year's beginning balance (cell I6), last year's ending balance (cell J5) must be used. After cell J5 (last year's ending balance) is copied to cell I6 (next year's beginning balance), then I6 can be copied to the range I7:I19. The following steps copy the formulas in the range J5:L5 and cell I6 through to the remainder of the amortization schedule.

• Select the range J5:L5 and then drag the fill handle down through row 19 to copy the formulas through the amortization schedule, J6:L19 in this case (Figure 4–30).

Q&A Why do some of the numbers seem incorrect?
Many of the numbers are incorrect because the cells in column I — except for cell I5 — do not yet contain values.

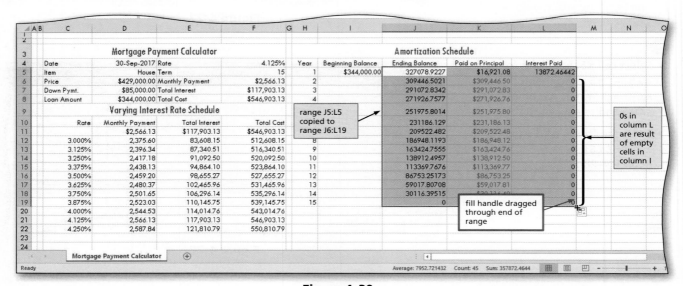

Figure 4–30

• Select cell I6, type =j5 as the cell entry, and then click the Enter button in the formula bar to display the ending balance (327078.9227) for year 1 as the beginning balance for year 2 (Figure 4–31).

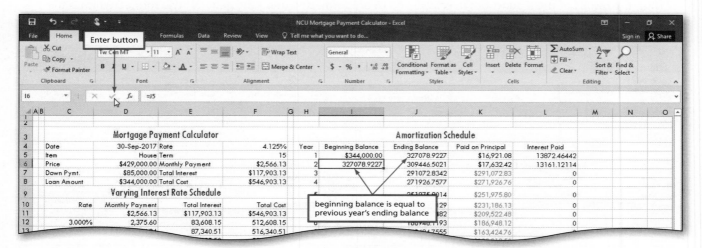

Figure 4–31

- With cell I6 active, drag the fill handle down through row 19 to copy the formula in cell I6 (=J5) to the range I7:I19 (Figure 4–32).

Q&A

What happens after the fill operation is complete?

Because the cell reference J5 is relative, Excel adjusts the row portion of the cell reference as it is copied downward. Thus, each new beginning balance in column I is equal to the ending balance of the previous year.

E	F	G	H	I	J	K	L	M	N	O
Calculator					Amortization Schedule					
	4.125%		Year	Beginning Balance	Ending Balance	Paid on Principal	Interest Paid			
	15		1	$344,000.00	327078.9227	$16,921.08	13872.46442			
Payment	$2,566.13		2	327078.9227	309446.5021	$17,632.42	13161.12114			
terest	$117,903.13		3	309446.5021	291072.8342	$18,373.67	12419.87378			
Cost	$546,903.13		4	291072.8342	271926.7577	$19,146.08	11647.4652			
ate Schedule			5	271926.7577	251975.8014	$19,950.96	10842.58543			
Total Interest	Total Cost		6	251975.8014	231186.129	$20,789.67	10003.8694			
$117,903.13	$546,903.13		7	231186.129	209522.482	$21,663.65	9129.894684		Paid on Principal and Interest Paid values now are correct	
83,608.15	cell copied through range I6 to I19		8	209522.482	186948.1193	$22,574.36	8219.179042			
87,340.51			9	186948.1193	163424.7555	$23,523.36	7270.177927			
91,092.50	520,092.50		10	163424.7555	138912.4957	$24,512.26	6281.28186			
94,864.10	523,864.10		11	138912.4957	113369.7676	$25,542.73	5250.813702			
98,655.27	527,655.27		12	113369.7676	86753.25173	$26,616.52	4177.025807			
102,465.96	531,465.96		13	86753.25173	59017.80708	$27,735.44	3058.097064			
106,296.14	535,296.14		14	59017.80708	30116.39515	$28,901.41	1892.129799			
110,145.75	539,145.75		15	30116.39515	0	$30,116.40	677.1465667			
114,014.76	543,014.76									
117,903.13	546,903.13			fill handle dragged through destination range						
121,810.79	550,810.79									

Figure 4–32

Other Ways

1. Select cells containing formulas to copy, click Copy (Home tab | Clipboard group), select destination cell or range, click Paste (Home tab | Clipboard group)

To Enter the Total Formulas in the Amortization Schedule

The next step is to determine the amortization schedule totals in rows 20 through 22. These totals should agree with the corresponding totals in the Mortgage Payment Calculator section (range F7:F8). The following steps enter the total formulas in the amortization schedule.

1 Select cell J20 and then enter **Subtotal** as the row title.

2 Select the range K20:L20 and then click the Sum button (Home tab | Editing group) to sum the selected range.

3 Select cell J21 and then enter **Down Pymt.** as the row title.

4 Select cell L21 and then enter **=d7** to copy the down payment to the selected cell.

5 Select cell J22 and then enter **Total Cost** as the row title.

6 Select cell L22, type `=K20 + L20 + L21` as the total cost, and then click the Enter button in the formula bar to complete the amortization schedule totals (Figure 4–33).

Q&A

What was accomplished in the previous steps?

The formula assigned to cell L22 (=K20+L20+L21) sums the total amount paid on the principal (cell K20), the total interest paid (cell L20), and the down payment (cell L21). Excel assigns cell K20 the same format as cell K5 because cell K5 is the first cell reference in =SUM(K5:K19). Furthermore, because cell K20 was selected first when the range K20:L20 was selected to determine the sum, Excel assigned cell L20 the same format it assigned to cell K20. Finally, cell L21 was assigned the currency style format, because cell L21 was assigned the formula =d7, and cell D7 has a currency style format. For the same reason, the value in cell L22 appears with the currency style format.

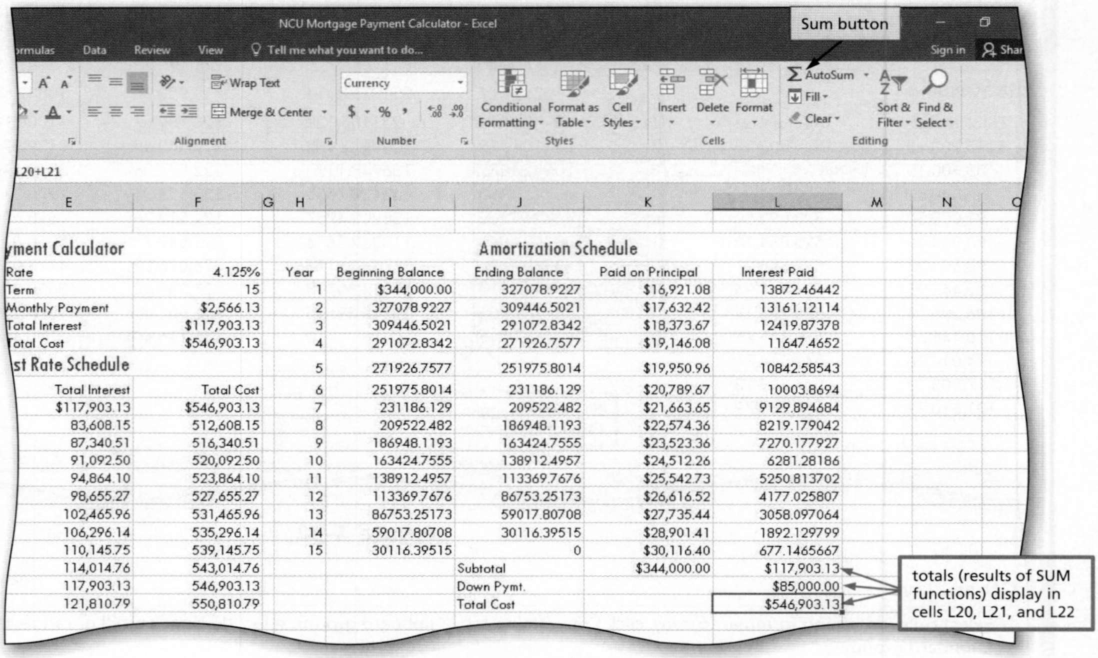

Figure 4–33

To Format the Numbers in the Amortization Schedule

The next step in creating the amortization schedule is to format it so that it is easier to read. When the beginning balance formula (=d8) was entered earlier into cell I5, Excel copied the currency style format along with the value from cell D8 to cell I5. The following steps copy the currency style format from cell I5 to the range J5:L5. The comma style format then will be assigned to the range I6:L19.

1 Select cell I5 and then click the Format Painter button (Home tab | Clipboard group) to turn on the format painter. Drag through the range J5:L5 to assign the currency style format to the cells.

2 Select the range I6:L19 and then right-click the selected range to display a shortcut menu. Click Format Cells on the shortcut menu to display the Format Cells dialog box and then, if necessary, click the Number tab (Format Cells dialog box) to display the Number sheet.

③ Select Currency in the Category list to select a currency format, select None in the Symbol list to choose no currency symbol, and then click the second format, 1,234.10, in the Negative numbers list to create a currency format.

④ Click the OK button (Format Cells dialog box) to apply the currency format to the selected range.

⑤ Deselect the range I6:L19 and display the numbers in the amortization schedule, as shown in Figure 4–34.

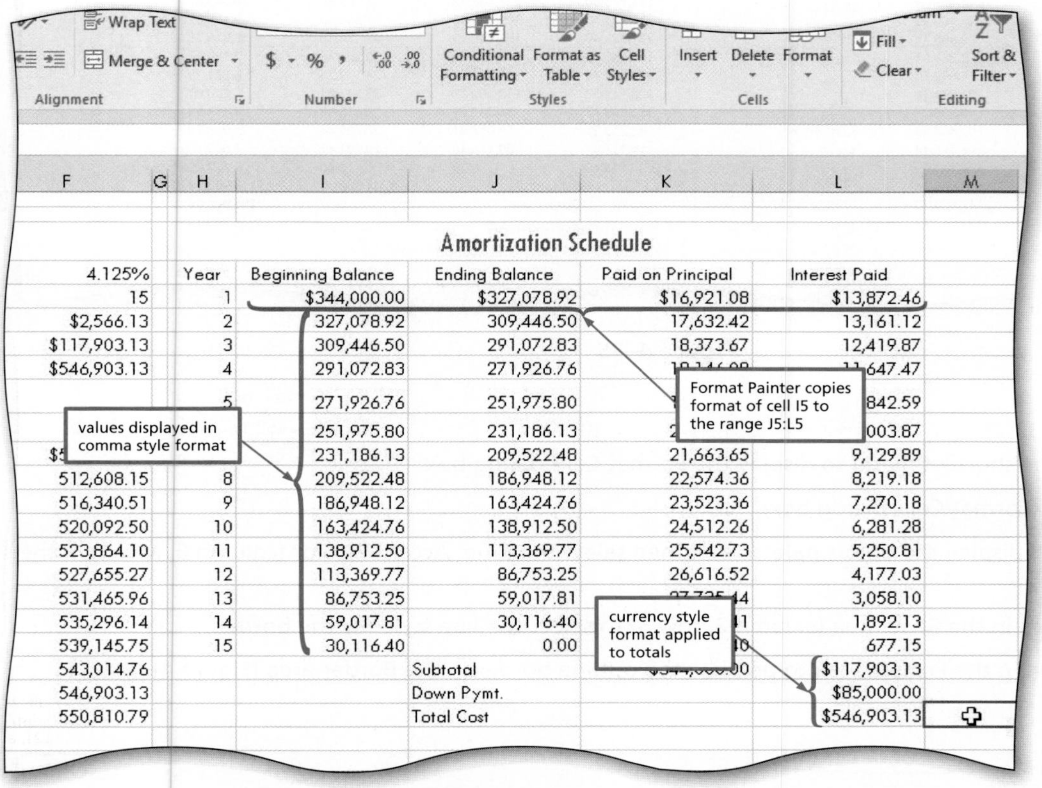

BTW
Round-Off Errors
If you manually add the numbers in column L (range L5:L19) and compare it to the sum in cell L20, you will notice that the total interest paid is $0.01 off. This round-off error is due to the fact that some of the numbers involved in the computations have additional decimal places that do not appear in the cells. You can use the ROUND function on the formula entered into cell L5 to ensure the total is exactly correct. For information on the ROUND function, click the Insert Function button in the formula bar, click 'Math & Trig' in the 'Or select a category' list, scroll down in the 'Select a function' list, and then click ROUND.

BTW
Undoing Formats
If you began assigning formats to a range and then realize you made a mistake and want to start over, select the range, click the Cell Styles button (Home tab | Styles group), and then click Normal in the Cell Styles gallery.

Figure 4–34

Formatting the Worksheet

Previous modules introduced you to outlining a range using cell borders or cell background colors to differentiate portions of a worksheet. The Borders button (Home tab | Font group), however, offers only a limited selection of border thicknesses. To control the color and thickness, Excel requires that you use the Border sheet in the Format Cells dialog box.

To Add Custom Borders to a Range

1 CREATE MORTGAGE PAYMENT CALCULATOR | 2 CREATE DATA TABLE | 3 CREATE AMORTIZATION SCHEDULE
4 FORMAT WORKSHEET | 5 CREATE PRINT AREAS | 6 PROTECT CELLS | 7 CHECK FORMULAS

Why? *Borders can be used to distinguish the different functional parts of a worksheet.* The following steps add a medium blue border to the Mortgage Payment Calculator section. To subdivide the row titles and numbers further, light borders also are added within the section, as shown in Figure 4–1.

- Select the range C4:F8 and then right-click to display a shortcut menu and mini toolbar (Figure 4–35).

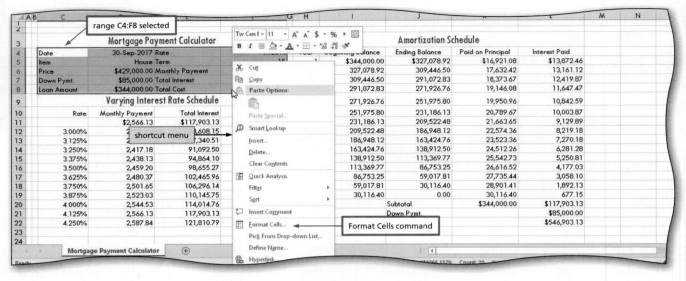

Figure 4–35

- Click Format Cells on the shortcut menu to display the Format Cells dialog box.

- Display the Border tab (Format Cells dialog box).

- Click the Color arrow to display the Colors palette and then select the Blue, Accent 2 color (column 6, row 1) in the Theme Colors area.

- Click the medium border in the Style area (column 2, row 5) to select the line style for the border.

- Click the Outline button in the Presets area to preview the outline border in the Border area (Figure 4–36).

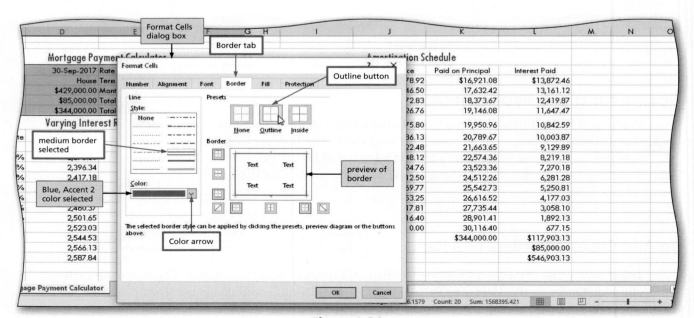

Figure 4–36

❸

- Click the light border in the Style area (column 1, row 7) and then click the Vertical Line button in the Border area to preview the blue vertical border in the Border area (Figure 4–37).

Q&A How do I create a border?

As shown in Figure 4–37, you can add a variety of borders with different colors to a cell or range of cells. It is important that you select border characteristics in the order specified in the steps; that is, (1) choose the border color, (2) choose the border line style, and then (3) choose the border type. This order first defines the border characteristics and then applies those characteristics. If you do these steps in any other order, you may not end up with the borders you intended.

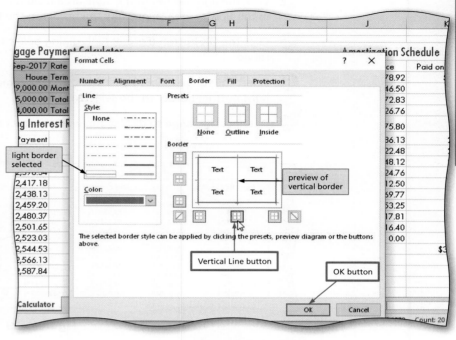

Figure 4–37

❹

- Click the OK button to add a blue outline with vertical borders to the right side of each column in the selected range, C4:F8 in this case (Figure 4–38).

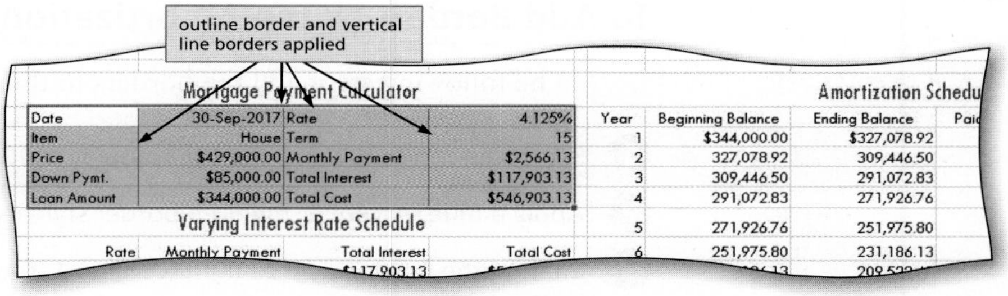

Figure 4–38

Other Ways

1. Click More Borders button arrow (Home tab | Font group), click More Borders, select border options, click OK

2. Click Format button (Home tab | Cells group), click Format Cells, click Border tab, select border options, click OK

To Add Borders to the Varying Interest Rate Schedule

The following steps add the same borders you applied to the Mortgage Payment Calculator to the Varying Interest Rate Schedule.

❶ Select the range C10:F22. Right-click the selected range to display a shortcut menu and then click Format Cells on the shortcut menu to display the Format Cells dialog box.

❷ If necessary, click the Border tab (Format Cells dialog box) to display the Border sheet. Click the Color arrow to display the Colors palette and then click Blue, Accent 2 (column 6, row 1) in the Theme Colors area to change the border color.

❸ Click the medium border in the Style area (column 2, row 5). Click the Outline button in the Presets area to preview the border in the Border area.

④ Click the light border in the Style area (column 1, row 7). Click the Vertical Line button in the Border area to preview the border in the Border area.

⑤ Click the OK button (Format Cells dialog box) to apply custom borders to the selected range.

⑥ Select the range C10:F10 and then use the Format Cells dialog box to apply a blue, light bottom border to the selected range.

⑦ Deselect the range to display the worksheet, as shown in Figure 4–39.

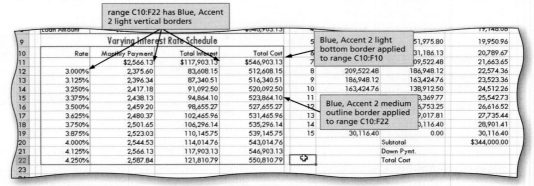

Figure 4–39

To Add Borders to the Amortization Schedule

The following steps add the borders to the Amortization Schedule.

① Select the range H4:L22, and then display the Format Cells dialog box.

② Apply a Blue, Accent 2, medium border style using the Outline preset.

③ Change the border style to light (column 1, row 7) and then click the Vertical Line button in the Border area to preview the border in the Border area.

④ Click the OK button to apply custom borders to the selected range.

⑤ Select the range H5:L19 and then use the Format Cells dialog box to apply a blue, light upper border and a blue, light bottom border to the selected range.

⑥ Deselect the range to display the worksheet, as shown in Figure 4–40.

ent Calculator		Amortization Schedule				
te	4.125%	Year	Beginning Balance	Ending Balance	Paid on Principal	Interest Paid
m	15	1	$344,000.00	$327,078.92	$16,921.08	$13,872.46
nthly Payment	$2,566.13	2	327,078.92	309,446.50	17,632.42	13,161.12
tal Interest	$117,903.13	3	309,446.50	291,072.83	18,373.67	12,419.87
tal Cost	$546,903.13	4	291,072.83	271,926.76	19,146.08	11,647.47
st [borders applied to amortization schedule]		5	271,926.76	251,975.80	19,950.96	10,842.59
tal Cost		6	251,975.80	231,186.13	20,789.67	10,003.87
$117,903.13	$546,903.13	7	231,186.13	209,522.48	21,663.65	9,129.89
83,608.15	512,608.15	8	209,522.48	186,948.12	22,574.36	8,219.18
87,340.51	516,340.51	9	186,948.12	163,424.76	23,523.36	7,270.18
91,092.50	520,092.50	10	163,424.76	138,912.50	24,512.26	6,281.28
94,864.10	523,864.10	11	138,912.50	113,369.77	25,542.73	5,250.81
98,655.27	527,655.27	12	113,369.77	86,753.25	26,616.52	4,177.03
102,465.96	531,465.96	13	86,753.25	59,017.81	27,735.44	3,058.10
106,296.14	535,296.14	14	59,017.81	30,116.40	28,901.41	1,892.13
110,145.75	539,145.75	15	30,116.40	0.00	30,116.40	677.15
114,014.76	543,014.76			Subtotal	$344,000.00	$117,903.13
117,903.13	546,903.13			Down Pymt.		$85,000.00
121,810.79	550,810.79			Total Cost		$546,903.13

Figure 4–40

To Use Borders and Fill Color to Visually Define and Group the Financial Tools

The following steps add a border and fill color to the entire group of financial tools on the worksheet.

1 Change the height of row 23 to 9.0 (12 pixels).

2 Change the width of column M to .92 (12 pixels).

3 Select the range B2:M23.

4 Add a Dark Green, Accent 5, (column 9, row 1) heavy style (column 2, row 6) Outline border to the selected range.

5 With the range B2:M23 still selected, click the Fill Color arrow (Home tab | Font group) and apply a fill color of White, Background 1 (column 1, row 1) to the selected range. Deselect the range (Figure 4–41).

6 Save the workbook again on the same storage location with the same file name.

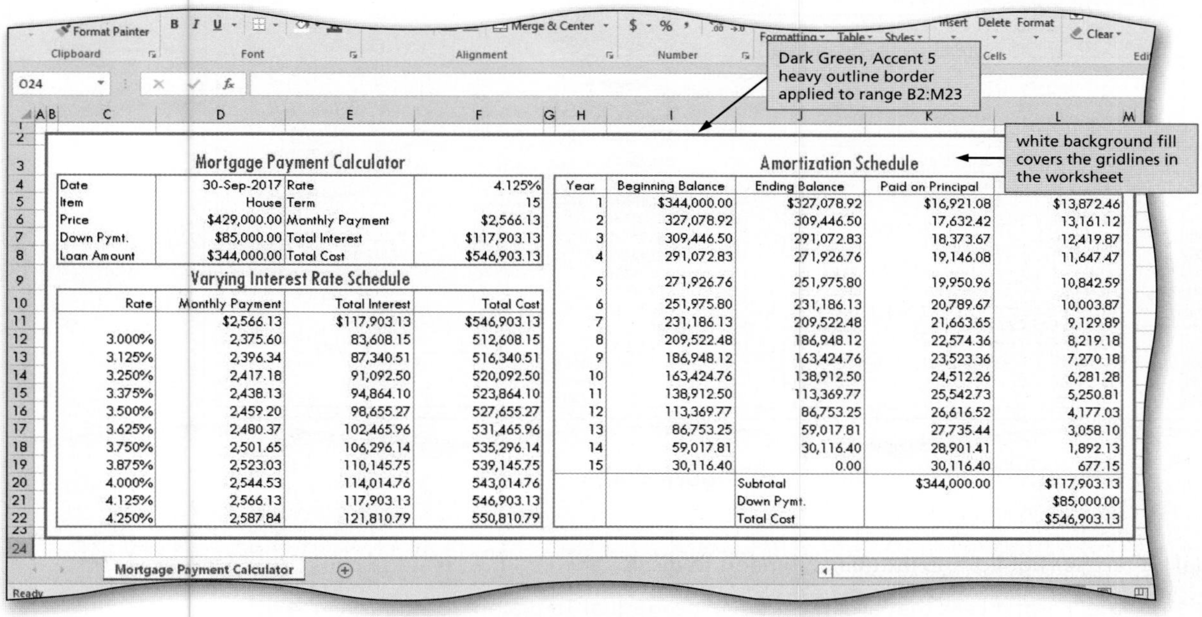

Figure 4–41

Highlighting Cells in the Data Table Using Conditional Formatting

If the interest rate in cell F4 is between 3.000% and 4.250% and its decimal portion is a multiple of 0.125 (such as 4.125%), then one of the rows in the data table agrees exactly with the monthly payment, interest paid, and total cost in the range F6:F8. For example, in Figure 4–41 row 21 (4.125%) in the data table agrees with the results in the range F6:F8, because the interest rate in cell C21 is the same as the interest rate in cell F4. Analysts often look for the row in the data table that agrees with the input cell results. You can use conditional formatting to highlight a row, or a single cell in the row.

BTW
Conditional Formatting
You can add as many conditional formats to a range as you like. After adding the first condition, click the Conditional Formatting button (Home tab | Styles group) and then click New Rule to add more conditions. If more than one condition is true for a cell, then Excel applies the formats of each condition, beginning with the first.

To Add a Pointer to the Data Table Using Conditional Formatting

Why? *To make the row with the active interest rate stand out, you can add formatting that serves as a pointer to that row.* To add a pointer, you can use conditional formatting to highlight the cell in column C that agrees with the input cell (cell F4). The following steps apply conditional formatting to column C in the data table.

- Select the range C12:C22 and then click the Conditional Formatting button (Home tab | Styles group) to display the Conditional Formatting gallery.

- Point to 'Highlight Cells Rules' to display the submenu (Figure 4–42).

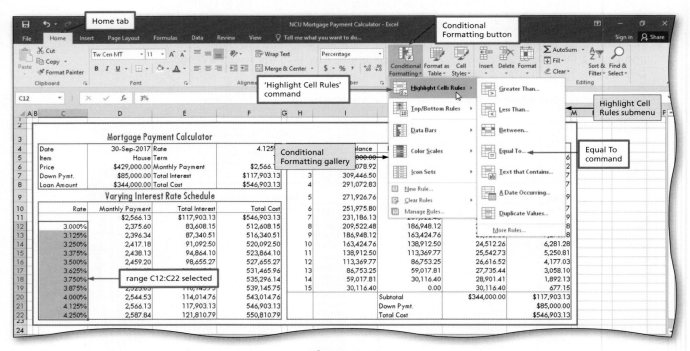

Figure 4–42

- Click Equal To on the Highlight Cells Rules submenu to display the Equal To dialog box.

- Type **=$F$4** in the 'Format cells that are EQUAL TO:' box (Equal To dialog box) (Figure 4–43).

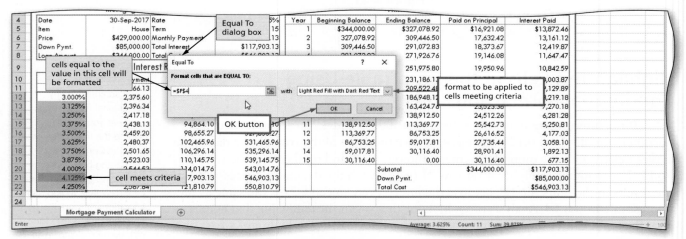

Figure 4–43

- Click the OK button to apply the conditional formatting rule.

- Deselect the range (Figure 4–44).

Q&A How does Excel apply the conditional formatting? Cell C21 in the data table, which contains the value, 4.125%, appears with a red background and dark red text, because the value 4.125% is the same as the interest rate value in cell F4.

Mortgage Payment Calculator

Date	30-Sep-2017	Rate	4.125%
Item	House	Term	15
Price	$429,000.00	Monthly Payment	$2,566.13
Down Pymt.	$85,000.00	Total Interest	$117,903.13
Loan Amount	$344,000.00	Total Cost	$546,903.13

Varying Interest Rate Schedule

Rate	Monthly Payment	Total Interest	Total Cost
	$2,566.13	$117,903.13	$546,903.13
3.000%	2,375.60	83,608.15	512,608.15
3.125%	2,396.34	87,340.51	516,340.51
3.250%	2,417.18	91,092.50	520,092.50
3.375%	2,438.13	94,864.10	523,864.10
3.500%			655.27
3.625%	2	cell entry has a light red background and dark red text because the value in cell C21 equals the value in cell F4	1,465.96
3.750%	2		5,296.14
3.875%	2		9,145.75
4.000%	2		3,014.76
4.125%	2,566.13	117,903.13	546,903.13
4.250%	2,587.84	121,810.79	550,810.79

Amortization Schedule

Year	Beginning Balance	Ending Balance	Paid on Principal
1	$344,000.00	$327,078.92	$16,921.08
2	327,078.92	309,446.50	17,632.42
3	309,446.50	291,072.83	18,373.67
4	291,072.83	271,926.76	19,146.08
5	271,926.76	251,975.80	19,950.96
6	251,975.80	231,186.13	20,789.67
7	231,186.13	209,522.48	21,663.65
8	209,522.48	186,948.12	22,574.36
9	186,948.12	163,424.76	23,523.36
10	163,424.76	138,912.50	24,512.26
11	138,912.50	113,369.77	25,542.73
12	113,369.77	86,753.25	26,616.52
13	86,753.25	59,017.81	27,735.44
14	59,017.81	30,116.40	28,901.41
15	30,116.40	0.00	30,116.40
		Subtotal	$344,000.00
		Down Pymt.	
		Total Cost	

Figure 4–44

- Select cell F4 and then enter **4.000** as the interest rate (Figure 4–45).

Mortgage Payment Calculator

Date	30-Sep-2017	Rate	4.000%
Item	House	Term	15
Price	$429,000.00	Monthly Payment	$2,544.53
Down Pymt.	$85,000.00	Total Interest	$114,014.76
Loan Amount	$344,000.00	Total Cost	$543,014.76

Varying Interest Rate Schedule

Rate	Monthly Payment	Total Interest	Total Cost
	$2,544.53	$114,014.76	$543,014.76
3.000%	2,375.60	83,608.15	512,608.15
3.125%	2,396.34	87,340.51	516,340.51
3.250%	2,417.18	91,092.50	520,092.50
3.375%		new cell formatted with light red background and dark red text because value in cell F4 changed	23,864.10
3.500%			27,655.27
3.625%			31,465.96
3.750%			35,296.14
3.875%			39,145.75
4.000%	2,544.53	114,014.76	543,014.76
4.125%	2,566.13	117,903.13	546,903.13
4.250%	2,587.84	121,810.79	550,810.79

Amortization Schedule

Year	Beginning Balance	Paid on Principal	Interest Paid
1	$344,000.00	$17,085.29	$13,449.03
2	326,914.71	309,133.34	17,781.37	12,752.95
3	309,133.34	290,627.53	18,505.81	12,028.51
4	290,627.53	271,367.76	19,259.77	11,274.55
5	271,367.76	251,323.32	20,044.44	10,489.88
6	251,323.32	230,462.24	20,861.08	9,673.24
7	230,462.24	208,751.25	21,710.99	8,823.32
8	208,751.25	186,155.72	22,595.53	7,938.79
9	186,155.72	162,639.61	23,516.11	7,018.21
10	162,639.61	138,165.42	24,474.19	6,060.13
11	138,165.42	112,694.11	25,471.31	5,063.01
12	112,694.11	86,185.06	26,509.05	4,025.27
13	86,185.06	58,595.99	27,589.07	2,945.25
14	58,595.99	29,882.90	28,713.09	1,821.23
15	29,882.90	0.00	29,882.90	651.41
	Subtotal	$344,000.00	$114,014.76
	Down Pymt.		$85,000.00
	Total Cost		$543,014.76

value changed in cell F4

Figure 4–45

⑤

- Enter **4.125** in cell F4 to return the Mortgage Payment Calculator, Varying Interest Rate Schedule, and Amortization Schedule sections to their original states.

Q&A What happened when I changed the interest rate from 4.125% to 4.000%?

The cell containing the new rate received a red background and dark red text, while the original cell (cell C21) reverted to its original formatting (Figure 4–45). The red background and dark red text serve as a pointer in the data table to indicate which row agrees with the input cell (cell F4). When the loan officer using this worksheet enters a new percentage in cell F4, the pointer will move or disappear. The formatting will disappear if the interest rate in cell F4 falls outside the range of the data table or does not appear in the data table, for example, if the interest rate is 5.000% or 4.100%.

To Enter New Loan Data

With the Mortgage Payment Calculator, Varying Interest Rate Schedule, and Amortization Schedule sections of the worksheet complete, you can use them to generate new loan information. For example, assume you want to purchase land for $125,000.00. You have $30,000.00 for a down payment and want a seven-year loan. NCU currently is charging 3.625% interest for a seven-year loan on land. The following steps enter the new loan data.

1 Enter **Land** in cell D5.

2 Enter **125000** in cell D6.

3 Enter **30000** in cell D7.

4 Enter **3.625** in cell F4.

5 Enter **7** in cell F5 and then press the DOWN ARROW key to calculate the loan data.

6 Click on an empty cell to display the worksheet, as shown in Figure 4–46.

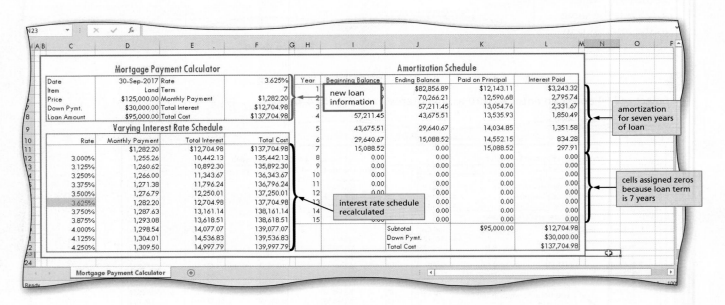

Figure 4–46

To Enter the Original Loan Data

The following steps reenter the original loan data.

1 Enter **House** in cell D5.

2 Enter **429000** in cell D6.

3 Enter **85000** in cell D7.

4 Enter **4.125** in cell F4.

5 Enter **15** in cell F5.

Printing Sections of the Worksheet

In Module 2, you learned how to print a section of a worksheet by first selecting it and then using the Selection option in the Print dialog box. If you find yourself continually selecting the same range in a worksheet to print, you can set a specific range to print each time you print the worksheet. When you set a range to print, Excel will continue to print only that range until you clear it.

To Set Up a Worksheet to Print

1 CREATE MORTGAGE PAYMENT CALCULATOR | 2 CREATE DATA TABLE | 3 CREATE AMORTIZATION SCHEDULE
4 FORMAT WORKSHEET | 5 CREATE PRINT AREAS | 6 PROTECT CELLS | 7 CHECK FORMULAS

Why? Specifying print options allows you to conserve paper and toner and to customize the layout of your worksheet on the printed page. This section describes print options available in the Page and Sheet tabs in the Page Setup dialog box (Figure 4–47). These print options affect the way the worksheet will appear in the printed copy or when previewed. One important print option is the capability of printing in black and white, even when your printer is a color printer. Printing in black and white not only speeds up the printing process but also saves ink. The following steps ensure any printed copy fits on one page and prints in black and white.

- Display the Page Layout tab and then click the Page Setup Dialog Box Launcher (Page Layout tab | Page Setup group) to display the Page Setup dialog box.

- If necessary, click the Page tab (Page Setup dialog box) to display the Page sheet and then click Fit to in the Scaling area to set the worksheet to print on one page (Figure 4–47).

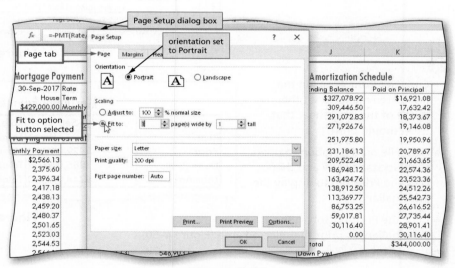

Figure 4–47

- Click the Sheet tab (Page Setup dialog box) and then click 'Black and white' in the Print area to select the check box (Figure 4–48).

- Click the OK button (Page Setup dialog box) to close the dialog box.

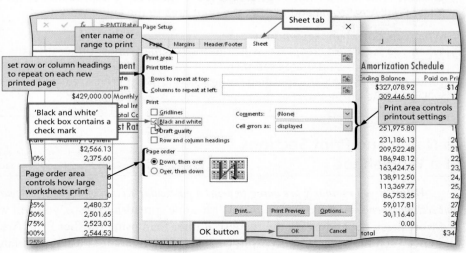

Figure 4–48

Other Ways

1. Click File tab, click Print tab, click Page Setup link, select options

To Set the Print Area

Why? *If you do not need to print the entire worksheet, setting the print area allows you easily to specify the section you want to print.* The following steps print only the Mortgage Payment Calculator section by setting the print area to the range C3:F8.

1

- Select the range C3:F8 and then click the Print Area button (Page Layout tab | Page Setup group) to display the Print Area menu (Figure 4–49).

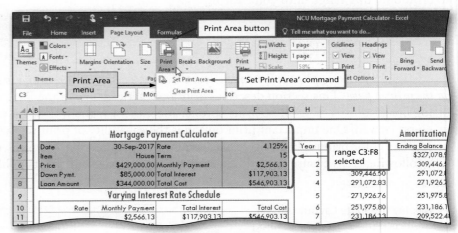

Figure 4–49

2

- Click 'Set Print Area' on the Print Area menu to set the range of the worksheet that Excel should print.

- Click File on the ribbon to open the Backstage view and then click the Print tab to display the Print gallery.

- Click the Print button in the Print gallery to print the selected area (Figure 4–50).

Mortgage Payment Calculator

Date	30-Sep-2017	Rate	4.125%
Item	House	Term	15
Price	$429,000.00	Monthly Payment	$2,566.13
Down Pymt.	$85,000.00	Total Interest	$117,903.13
Loan Amount	$344,000.00	Total Cost	$546,903.13

Figure 4–50

3

- Click the Print Area button (Page Layout tab | Page Setup group) to display the Print Area menu and then click the 'Clear Print Area' command to reset the print area to the entire worksheet.

Q&A What happens when I set a print area?

When you set a print area, Excel will print the specified range, rather than the entire worksheet. If you save the workbook with the print area set, then Excel will remember the settings the next time you open the workbook and continue to print only the specified range. Clicking 'Clear Print Area' on the Print Area menu, as described in Step 3, will revert the settings so that the entire workbook will print.

To Name and Print Sections of a Worksheet

Why? *If you regularly are going to print a particular section of a worksheet, naming the section allows you to specify that section whenever you need to print it.* With some spreadsheet apps, you will want to print several different areas of a worksheet, depending on the request. Rather than using the 'Set Print Area' command or manually selecting the range each time you want to print, you can name the ranges using the Name box in the formula bar. You then can use one of the names to select an area before using the 'Set Print Area' command or Print Selection option. The following steps name the Mortgage Payment Calculator, the Varying Interest Rate Schedule, the Amortization Schedule sections, as well as the entire worksheet, and then print each section.

- Click the Page Setup Dialog Box Launcher (Page Layout tab | Page Setup group) to display the Page Setup dialog box, click the Sheet tab and then click 'Black and white' to remove the check mark and ensure that Excel prints in color on color printers.

- Click the OK button to close the Page Setup dialog box.

- If necessary, select the range C3:F8, click the Name box in the formula bar, and then type **Mortgage_Payment** to name the range (Figure 4–51). *Hint:* Remember to include the underscore between Mortgage and Payment.

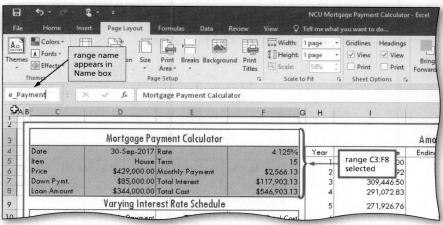

Figure 4–51

- Press the ENTER key to create the range name.

- Select the range C9:F22, click the Name box in the formula bar, type **Interest_Schedule** as the name of the range, and then press the ENTER key to create a range name.

- Select the range H3:L22, click the Name box in the formula bar, type **Amortization_Schedule** as the name of the range, and then press the ENTER key to create a range name.

- Select the range B2:M23, click the Name box in the formula bar, type **Financial_Tools** as the name of the range, and then press the ENTER key to create a range name.

- Select an empty cell and then click the Name box arrow in the formula bar to display the Name box list with the new range names (Figure 4–52).

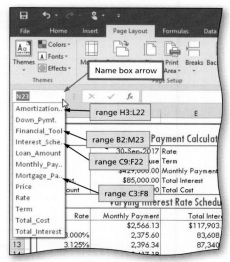

Figure 4–52

- Click Mortgage_Payment in the Name list to select the range associated with the name, C3:F8 in this case.

- Click File on the ribbon to open the Backstage view and then click the Print tab in the Backstage view to display the Print gallery.

- Click the 'Print Active Sheets' button in the Settings area and then click Print Selection to select the desired item to print (Figure 4–53).

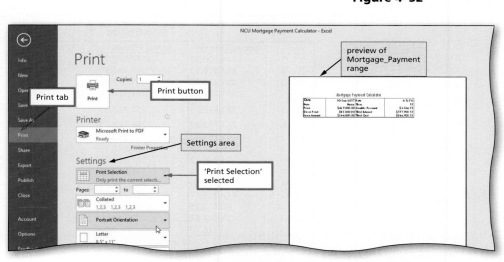

Figure 4–53

4

- Click the Print button in the Print gallery to print the selected named range, Mortgage_Payment in this case.

- One at a time, use the Name box to select the names Interest_Schedule, Amortization_Schedule, and Financial_Tools, and then print them following the instructions in Step 3 to print the remaining named ranges (Figure 4–54).

5

- Save the workbook again on the same storage location with the same file name.

Mortgage_Payment range printout

Mortgage Payment Calculator

Date	30-Sep-2017	Rate	4.125%
Item	House	Term	15
Price	$429,000.00	Monthly Payment	$2,566.13
Down Pymt.	$85,000.00	Total Interest	$117,903.13
Loan Amount	$344,000.00	Total Cost	$546,903.13

Figure 4–54a

Interest_Schedule range printout

Varying Interest Rate Schedule

Rate	Monthly Payment	Total Interest	Total Cost
	$2,566.13	$117,903.13	$546,903.13
3.000%	2,375.60	83,608.15	512,608.15
3.125%	2,396.34	87,340.51	516,340.51
3.250%	2,417.18	91,092.50	520,092.50
3.375%	2,438.13	94,864.10	523,864.10
3.500%	2,459.20	98,655.27	527,655.27
3.625%	2,480.37	102,465.96	531,465.96
3.750%	2,501.65	106,296.14	535,296.14
3.875%	2,523.03	110,145.75	539,145.75
4.000%	2,544.53	114,014.76	543,014.76
4.125%	2,566.13	117,903.13	546,903.13
4.250%	2,587.84	121,810.79	550,810.79

Figure 4–54b

Amortization_Schedule range printout

Amortization Schedule

Year	Beginning Balance	Ending Balance	Paid on Principal	Interest Paid
1	$344,000.00	$327,078.92	$16,921.08	$13,872.46
2	327,078.92	309,446.50	17,632.42	13,161.12
3	309,446.50	291,072.83	18,373.67	12,419.87
4	291,072.83	271,926.76	19,146.08	11,647.47
5	271,926.76	251,975.80	19,950.96	10,842.59
6	251,975.80	231,186.13	20,789.67	10,003.87
7	231,186.13	209,522.48	21,663.65	9,129.89
8	209,522.48	186,948.12	22,574.36	8,219.18
9	186,948.12	163,424.76	23,523.36	7,270.18
10	163,424.76	138,912.50	24,512.26	6,281.28
11	138,912.50	113,369.77	25,542.73	5,250.81
12	113,369.77	86,753.25	26,616.52	4,177.03
13	86,753.25	59,017.81	27,735.44	3,058.10
14	59,017.81	30,116.40	28,901.41	1,892.13
15	30,116.40	0.00	30,116.40	677.15
		Subtotal	$344,000.00	$117,903.13
		Down Pymt.		$85,000.00
		Total Cost		$546,903.13

Figure 4–54c

Q&A

Why does the Financial_Tools range print on one page? Recall that the Fit to option was selected earlier (Figure 4–47). This selection ensures that each of the printouts fits across the page in portrait orientation.

Financial_Tools range printout

Mortgage Payment Calculator

Date	30-Sep-2017	Rate	4.125%
Item	House	Term	15
Price	$429,000.00	Monthly Payment	$2,566.13
Down Pymt.	$85,000.00	Total Interest	$117,903.13
Loan Amount	$344,000.00	Total Cost	$546,903.13

Varying Interest Rate Schedule

Rate	Monthly Payment	Total Interest	Total Cost
	$2,566.13	$117,903.13	$546,903.13
3.000%	2,375.60	83,608.15	512,608.15
3.125%	2,396.34	87,340.51	516,340.51
3.250%	2,417.18	91,092.50	520,092.50
3.375%	2,438.13	94,864.10	523,864.10
3.500%	2,459.20	98,655.27	527,655.27
3.625%	2,480.37	102,465.96	531,465.96
3.750%	2,501.65	106,296.14	535,296.14
3.875%	2,523.03	110,145.75	539,145.75
4.000%	2,544.53	114,014.76	543,014.76
4.125%	2,566.13	117,903.13	546,903.13
4.250%	2,587.84	121,810.79	550,810.79

Amortization Schedule

Year	Beginning Balance	Ending Balance	Paid on Principal	Interest Paid
1	$344,000.00	$327,078.92	$16,921.08	$13,872.46
2	327,078.92	309,446.50	17,632.42	13,161.12
3	309,446.50	291,072.83	18,373.67	12,419.87
4	291,072.83	271,926.76	19,146.08	11,647.47
5	271,926.76	251,975.80	19,950.96	10,842.59
6	251,975.80	231,186.13	20,789.67	10,003.87
7	231,186.13	209,522.48	21,663.65	9,129.89
8	209,522.48	186,948.12	22,574.36	8,219.18
9	186,948.12	163,424.76	23,523.36	7,270.18
10	163,424.76	138,912.50	24,512.26	6,281.28
11	138,912.50	113,369.77	25,542.73	5,250.81
12	113,369.77	86,753.25	26,616.52	4,177.03
13	86,753.25	59,017.81	27,735.44	3,058.10
14	59,017.81	30,116.40	28,901.41	1,892.13
15	30,116.40	0.00	30,116.40	677.15
	Subtotal		$344,000.00	$117,903.13
	Down Pymt.			$85,000.00
	Total Cost			$546,903.13

Figure 4–54d

Other Ways

1. Select cell or range, click Define Name button (Formulas tab | Defined Names group), type name, click OK button (New Name dialog box)

2. Select cell or range, click Name Manager button (Formulas tab | Defined Names group), click New button, type name, click OK button (New Name dialog box), click Close button (Name Manager dialog box)

3. Select cell or range, press CTRL+F3

Break Point: If you wish to take a break, this is a good place to do so. You can exit Excel now. To resume at a later time, run Excel, open the file called NCU Mortgage Payment Calculator, and continue following the steps from this location forward.

Protecting and Hiding Worksheets and Workbooks

When building a worksheet for novice users, you should protect the cells in the worksheet that you do not want changed, such as cells that contain text or formulas. Doing so prevents users from making changes to text and formulas in cells.

When you create a new worksheet, all the cells are assigned a locked status, but the lock is not engaged, which leaves cells unprotected. **Unprotected cells** are cells whose values you can change at any time. **Protected cells** are cells that you cannot change.

CONSIDER THIS

How do you determine which cells to protect in a worksheet?

Deciding which cells to protect often depends upon the audience for your worksheet. In general, the highest level of security would be to protect all cells except those that require an entry by the user of the worksheet. This level of protection might be recommended for novice users, clients, or customers. A lesser safeguard would be to protect any cells containing formulas, so that users of the worksheet cannot modify the formulas. Finally, if you are creating a worksheet for your boss or a trusted team member, you might want to leave the cells unprotected, in case he or she needs to edit the worksheet. In any case, you should protect cells only after the worksheet has been tested fully and the correct results appear. Protecting a worksheet is a two-step process:

1. Select the cells you want to leave unprotected and then change their cell protection settings to an unlocked status.

2. Protect the entire worksheet.

At first glance, these steps may appear to be backwards. However, once you protect the entire worksheet, you cannot change anything, including the locked status of individual cells.

To Protect a Worksheet

Why? *Protecting a worksheet allows you to determine which cells a user can modify.* In the Mortgage Payment Calculator worksheet, the user should be able to make changes to only five cells: the item in cell D5, the price in cell D6, the down payment in cell D7, the interest rate in cell F4, and the term in cell F5 (Figure 4–55). These cells must remain unprotected so that the user can enter data. The remaining cells in the worksheet can be protected so that the user cannot change them. The following steps protect the NCU Mortgage Payment Calculator worksheet.

- Select the range D5:D7 and then while holding down the CTRL key, select the nonadjacent range F4:F5.

- Right-click one of the selected ranges to display a shortcut menu and mini toolbar (Figure 4–55).

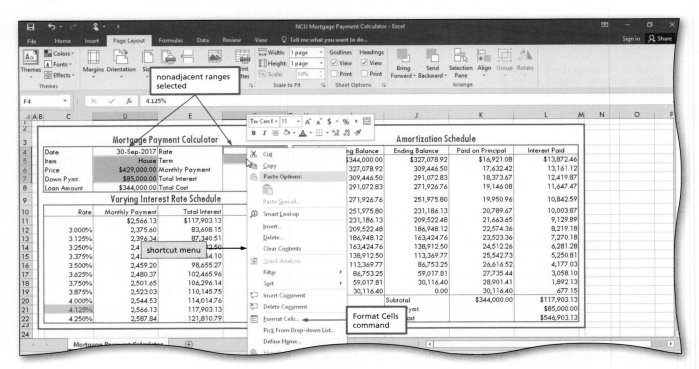

Figure 4–55

2

- Click Format Cells on the shortcut menu to display the Format Cells dialog box.

- Click the Protection tab (Format Cells dialog box) and then click Locked to remove the check mark (Figure 4–56).

Q&A What happens when I remove the check mark from Locked check box?

Removing the check mark from Locked check box allows users to modify the selected cells (D5:D7 and F4:F5) after the Protect Sheet command is invoked.

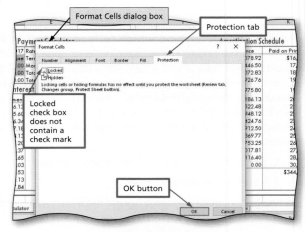

Figure 4–56

- Click the OK button to close the Format Cells dialog box.

- Deselect the ranges, and display the Review tab (Figure 4–57).

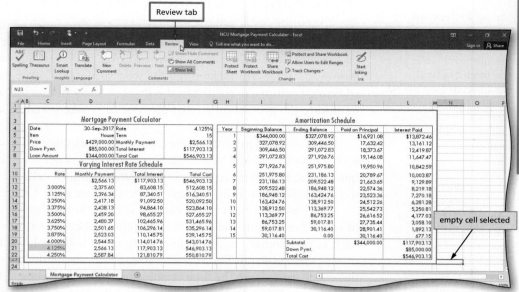

Figure 4–57

- Click the Protect Sheet button (Review tab | Changes group) to display the Protect Sheet dialog box.

- Verify that the 'Protect worksheet and contents of locked cells' check box (at the top of the Protect Sheet dialog box) and the first two check boxes in the list contain check marks so that the user of the worksheet can select both locked and unlocked cells (Figure 4–58).

Q&A What do the three checked settings mean?

With all three check boxes selected, the worksheet (except for the cells left unlocked) is protected from modification. The two check boxes in the list allow users to select any cell on the worksheet, but they only can change unlocked cells.

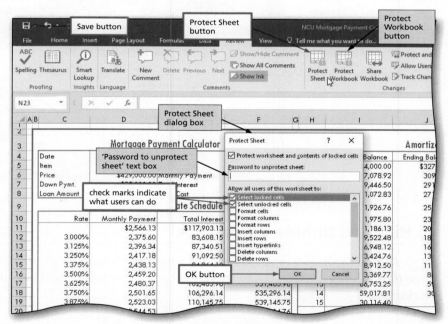

Figure 4–58

- Click the OK button (Protect Sheet dialog box) to close the Protect Sheet dialog box.

- Save the workbook again on the same storage location with the same file name.

Other Ways

1. Click Format Cells Dialog Box Launcher (Home tab | Font, Alignment, or Number group), click Protection tab, remove check mark from Locked check box, click OK button

2. Click File tab, click Info tab, click Protect Workbook, click Protect Current Sheet, select options, click OK

BTW
**Using Protected
Worksheets**
You can move from one
unprotected cell to another
unprotected cell in a
worksheet by using the TAB
and SHIFT+TAB keys. This is
especially useful when the
cells are not adjacent to one
another.

BTW
Hiding Worksheets
When sharing workbooks
with others, you may not
want them to see some of
your worksheets. Hiding
worksheets obscures the
worksheets from casual
inspection; however, it is not
only for hiding worksheets
from others' eyes. Sometimes,
you have several worksheets
that include data that you
rarely require or that you use
only as a reference. To clean
up the list of sheet tabs, you
can hide worksheets that
you do not need on a regular
basis.

More about Worksheet Protection

Now all of the cells in the worksheet, except for the ranges D5:D7 and F4:F5, are protected. The Protect Sheet dialog box, shown in Figure 4–58, enables you to protect the worksheet using a password. You can create a password when you want to prevent others from changing the worksheet from protected to unprotected. The additional settings in the list in the Protect Sheet dialog box also give you the option to modify the protection so that the user can make certain changes, such as formatting cells or inserting hyperlinks.

If you want to protect more than one worksheet in a workbook, either select each worksheet before you begin the protection process or click the Protect Workbook button, shown in Figure 4–58. If you want to unlock cells for specific users, you can use the 'Allow Users to Edit Ranges' button (Review tab | Changes group).

When this protected worksheet is made available to users, they will be able to enter data in only the unprotected cells. If they try to change any protected cell, such as the monthly payment in cell F6, Excel will display a dialog box with an error message, as shown in Figure 4–59. You can eliminate this error message by removing the check mark from the 'Select unlocked cells' check box in the Protect Sheet dialog box (Figure 4–58). With the check mark removed, users cannot select a locked cell.

To unprotect the worksheet so that you can change all cells in the worksheet, click the Unprotect Sheet button (Review tab | Changes group).

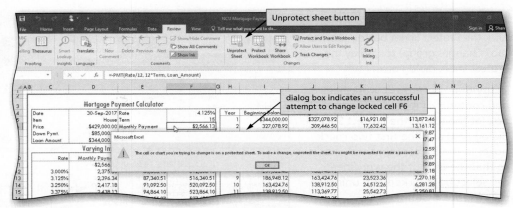

Figure 4–59

To Hide and Unhide a Worksheet

1 CREATE MORTGAGE PAYMENT CALCULATOR | 2 CREATE DATA TABLE | 3 CREATE AMORTIZATION SCHEDULE
4 FORMAT WORKSHEET | 5 CREATE PRINT AREAS | 6 PROTECT CELLS | 7 CHECK FORMULAS

Why? *You can hide rows, columns, and worksheets that contain sensitive data. Afterwards, when you need to access these hidden rows, columns, and worksheets, you can unhide them.* The following steps hide and then unhide a worksheet.

- Click the New sheet button to insert a new worksheet in the workbook.
- Right-click the Mortgage Payment Calculator sheet tab to display a shortcut menu (Figure 4–60).

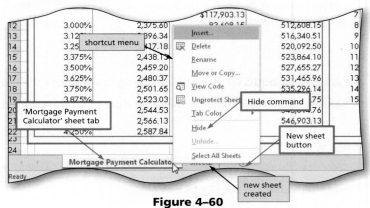

Figure 4–60

Why insert a new worksheet?
Workbooks must contain at least one visible worksheet. In order to hide the Mortgage Payment Calculator worksheet, there must be another visible worksheet in the workbook.

Why does the Unhide command on the shortcut menu appear dimmed?
The Unhide command appears dimmed when it is unavailable; because no worksheets are hidden, the command is unavailable.

②

- Click Hide on the shortcut menu to hide the Mortgage Payment Calculator worksheet.

- Right-click any sheet tab to display a shortcut menu.

- Click Unhide on the shortcut menu to display the Unhide dialog box.

- If necessary, click Mortgage Payment Calculator in the Unhide sheet list (Unhide dialog box) to select the worksheet to unhide (Figure 4–61).

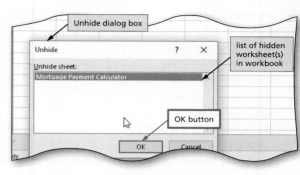

Figure 4–61

 Why should I hide a worksheet?
Hiding worksheets in a workbook is a common approach when working with complex workbooks that contain one worksheet with the results users need to see and one or more worksheets with essential data that, while important to the functionality of the workbook, is unimportant to users of the workbook. Thus, these data worksheets often are hidden from view. Although the worksheets are hidden, the data and formulas on the hidden worksheets remain available for use by other worksheets in the workbook. This same logic applies to hidden rows and columns.

③

- Click the OK button (Unhide dialog box) to reveal the hidden worksheet.

To Hide and Unhide a Workbook

1 CREATE MORTGAGE PAYMENT CALCULATOR | 2 CREATE DATA TABLE | 3 CREATE AMORTIZATION SCHEDULE
4 FORMAT WORKSHEET | 5 CREATE PRINT AREAS | 6 PROTECT CELLS | 7 CHECK FORMULAS

In addition to hiding worksheets, you also can hide an entire workbook. *Why? This feature is useful when you have several workbooks open simultaneously and want the user to be able to view only one of them. Also, some users hide the entire workbook when the computer is unattended and they do not want others to be able to see the workbook.* The following steps hide and unhide a workbook.

①

- Display the View tab (Figure 4–62).

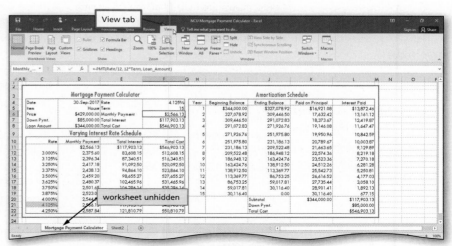

Figure 4–62

2

- Click the Hide Window button (View tab | Window group) to hide the NCU Mortgage Payment Calculator workbook.

- Click the Unhide Window button (View tab | Window group) to display the Unhide dialog box.

- If necessary, click NCU Mortgage Payment Calculator in the Unhide workbook list (Unhide dialog box) to select a workbook to unhide (Figure 4–63).

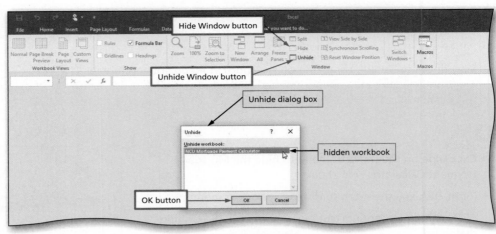

Figure 4–63

3

- Click the OK button (Unhide dialog box) to unhide the selected hidden workbook and display the workbook in the same state as it was in when it was hidden.

Formula Checking

Similar to the spelling checker, Excel has a formula checker that checks formulas in a worksheet for rule violations. You invoke the formula checker by clicking the Error Checking button (Formulas tab | Formula Auditing group). Each time Excel encounters a cell containing a formula that violates one of its rules, it displays a dialog box containing information about the formula and a suggestion about how to fix the formula. Table 4–3 lists Excel's error checking rules. You can choose which rules you want Excel to use by enabling and disabling them in the Formulas pane in the Excel Options dialog box shown in Figure 4–64.

Table 4–3 Error Checking Rules

Rule	Description
Cells containing formulas that result in an error	The cell contains a formula that does not use the expected syntax, arguments, or data types.
Inconsistent calculated column formula in tables	The cell contains formulas or values that are inconsistent with the column formula or tables.
Cells containing years represented as 2 digits	The cell contains a text date with a two-digit year that can be misinterpreted as the wrong century.
Numbers formatted as text or preceded by an apostrophe	The cell contains numbers stored as text.
Formulas inconsistent with other formulas in the region	The cell contains a formula that does not match the pattern of the formulas around it.
Formulas which omit cells in a region	The cell contains a formula that does not include a correct cell or range reference.
Unlocked cells containing formulas	The cell with a formula is unlocked in a protected worksheet.
Formulas referring to empty cells	The cells referenced in a formula are empty.
Data entered in a table is invalid	The cell has a data validation error.

To Enable Background Formula Checking

Through the Excel Options dialog box, you can enable background formula checking. *Why? You want Excel to continually review the workbook for errors in formulas as you create or manipulate data, formulas, and functions.* The following steps enable background formula checking.

- Click File on the ribbon to open the Backstage view and then click the Options tab to display the Excel Options dialog box.

- Click Formulas in the left pane (Excel Options dialog box) to display options related to formula calculation, performance, and error handling in the right pane.

- Click any check box in the 'Error checking rules' area that does not contain a check mark so that all error checking rules are enabled (Figure 4–64). As you add check marks, click the 'Reset Ignored Errors' button to reset error checking.

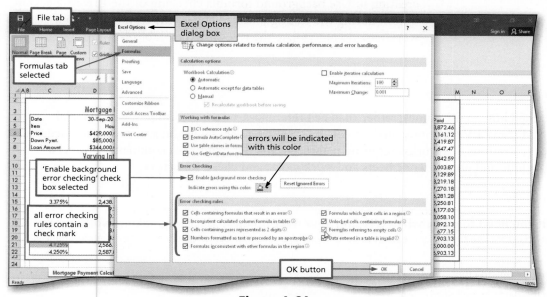

Figure 4–64

- Click the OK button (Excel Options dialog box) to close the Excel Options dialog box.

- If desired, sign out of your Microsoft account.

- Exit Excel.

More about Background Formula Checking

When background formula checking is enabled and a formula fails to pass one of the rules, Excel adds a small green triangle to the upper-left corner of the cell.

Assume, for example, that background formula checking is enabled and that cell F6, which contains the PMT function in the NCU Mortgage Payment Calculator workbook, is unlocked. Because one of the error checking rules, shown in Table 4–3, stipulates that a cell containing a formula must be locked, Excel displays a green triangle in the upper-left corner of cell F6.

When you select the cell with the green triangle, a Trace Error button appears next to the cell. If you click the Trace Error button, Excel displays the Trace Error menu (Figure 4–65). The first item in the menu identifies the error (Unprotected

BTW
Distributing a Workbook
Instead of printing and distributing a hard copy of a workbook, you can distribute the workbook electronically. Options include sending the workbook via email; posting it on cloud storage (such as OneDrive) and sharing the file with others; posting it on social media, a blog, or other website; and sharing a link associated with an online location of the workbook. You also can create and share a PDF or XPS image of the workbook, so that users can view the file in Acrobat Reader or XPS Viewer instead of in Excel.

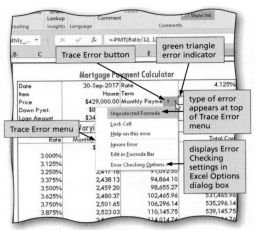

Figure 4–65

Formula). The remainder of the menu lists commands from which you can choose. The first command locks the cell. Invoking the Lock Cell command fixes the problem so that the formula no longer violates the rule. Selecting the 'Error Checking Options' command displays the Excel Options dialog box with the Formulas tab active, as shown in Figure 4–64.

The background formula checker can become annoying when you are creating worksheets that may violate the formula rules until referenced cells contain data. You often can end up with green triangles in cells throughout your worksheet. If this is the case, then disable background formula checking by removing the check mark from the 'Enable background error checking' check box (Figure 4–64) and use the Error Checking button (Formulas tab | Formula Auditing group) to check your worksheet once you have finished creating it. Use background formula checking or the Error Checking button during the testing phase to ensure the formulas in your workbook do not violate the rules listed in Table 4–3.

Summary

In this module, you learned how to use names, rather than cell references, to enter formulas; use financial functions, such as the PMT and PV functions; analyze data by creating a data table and amortization schedule; set print options and print sections of a worksheet using names and the Set Print Area command; protect a worksheet or workbook; hide and unhide worksheets and workbooks; and check for errors.

What decisions will you need to make when creating your next financial decision-making worksheet?
Use these guidelines as you complete the assignments in this module and create your own worksheets for evaluating financial scenarios.

1. Determine the worksheet structure.

   a) Determine the data you will need.

   b) Determine the layout of your data.

   c) Determine the layout of the financial calculator.

   d) Determine the layout of any data tables.

2. Create the worksheet.

   a) Enter titles, subtitles, and headings.

   b) Enter data, functions, and formulas.

   c) Assign names to cells and cell ranges.

   d) Create data tables.

3. Format the worksheet.

   a) Format the titles, subtitles, and headings.

   b) Format the numbers as necessary.

   c) Format the text.

4. Perform what-if analyses.

   a) Adjust values in the assumptions table to review scenarios of interest.

5. Secure the cell contents.

   a) Lock and unlock cells as necessary.

   b) Protect the worksheet.

Apply Your Knowledge

Reinforce the skills and apply the concepts you learned in this module.

Loan Payment Calculator

Note: To complete this assignment, you will be required to use the Data Files. Please contact your instructor for information about accessing the Data Files.

Instructions: Run Excel. Open the workbook Apply 4–1 Loan Payment Calculator. You will re-create the Loan Payment Calculator pictured in Figure 4–66. You will be instructed to print several times in this assignment. If requested or allowed by your instructor, consider saving paper by printing to a PDF file.

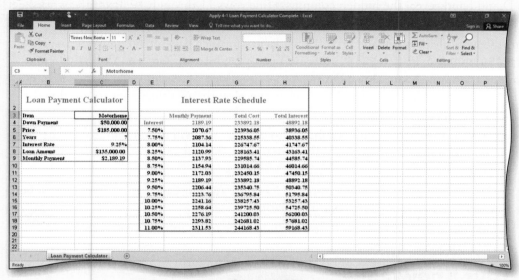

Figure 4–66

Perform the following tasks:

1. Select the range B4:C9. Use the 'Create from Selection' button (Formulas tab | Defined Names group) to create names for cells in the range C4:C9 using the row titles in the range B4:B9.

2. Enter the formulas shown in Table 4–4.

Table 4–4 Loan Payment Calculator and Interest Rate Schedule Formulas	
Cell	**Formula**
C8	=Price–Down_Payment
C9	=-PMT(Interest_Rate/12, 12*Years, Loan_Amount)
F4	=Monthly_Payment
G4	=12*Monthly_Payment*Years+Down_Payment
H4	=G4–Price

3. Use the Data Table button in the What-If Analysis gallery (Data tab | Forecast group) to define the range E4:H19 as a one-input data table. Use the Interest Rate in the Loan Payment Calculator as the column input cell.

4. Use the Page Setup dialog box to select the Fit to and 'Black and white' options. Select the range B2:C9 and then use the 'Set Print Area' command to set a print area. Use the Print button in the Print gallery in the Backstage view to print the worksheet. Use the 'Clear Print Area' command to clear the print area.

Continued >

Apply Your Knowledge *continued*

5. Name the following ranges: B2:C9 – **Calculator**; E2:H19 – **Rate_Schedule**; and B2:H19 – **All_Sections**. Print each range by selecting the name in the Name box and using the Print Selection option on the Print tab in the Backstage view.

6. Unlock the range C3:C7. Protect the worksheet so that the user can select only unlocked cells.

7. Press CTRL+` and then print the formulas version in landscape orientation. Press CTRL+` again to return to the values version.

8. Hide and then unhide the Loan Payment Calculator worksheet. Hide and then unhide the workbook. Delete the extra worksheet you made so that you could hide the Loan Payment Calculator worksheet. Unprotect the worksheet and then hide columns E through H. Select columns D and I and reveal the hidden columns. Hide rows 11 through 19. Print the worksheet. Select rows 10 and 20 and unhide rows 11 through 19. Protect the worksheet.

9. Determine the monthly payment and print the worksheet for each data set: (a) Item = **Home**; Down Payment = **$50,000.00**; Price = **$244,900.00**; Years = **15**; Interest Rate = **4.125%**; (b) Item = **Debt Consolidation Loan**; Down Payment = **$0.00**; Price = **$25,000.00**; Years = **5**; Interest Rate = **11.75%**. Set the values in cells C3:C7 back to the Motorhome values after completing the above calculations.

10. If requested by your instructor, add your initials to cell E3. You will need to unprotect the worksheet and unlock the cell to do so. Make sure to lock the cell and protect the worksheet after adding your initials.

11. Save the workbook using the file name, Apply 4–1 Loan Payment Calculator Complete. Submit the revised workbook as specified by your instructor.

12. ✳ How would you revise the Interest Rate Schedule to be more informative to the user?

Extend Your Knowledge

Extend the skills you learned in this module and experiment with new skills. You may need to use Help to complete the assignment.

Retirement Planning

Note: To complete this assignment, you will be required to use the Data Files. Please contact your instructor for information about accessing the Data Files.

Instructions: Run Excel. Open the workbook Extend 4–1 403B Planning Sheet. The data file contains a financial calculator for a 403(b) retirement plan. You will create a two-input data table that will help employees understand the impact that the amount they invest and the rate of return will have on their retirement earnings (Figure 4-67). Recall from the module that a two-input data table allows for two variables (amount invested and rate of return, in this case) in a formula.

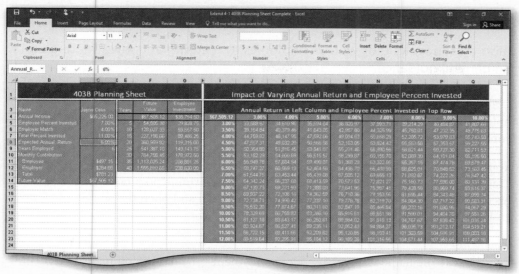

Figure 4–67

Perform the following tasks:

1. Type **Impact of Varying Annual Return and Employee Percent Invested** in cell I1. Type **Annual Return in Left Column and Employee Percent Invested in Top Row** in cell I3.

2. Save the workbook using the file name, Extend 4–1 403B Planning Sheet Complete.

3. Change the width of column H to 0.67 (8 pixels). Merge and center the titles in cells I1 and I3 over columns I through Q. Format the titles using the Title cell style for both the title and subtitle, a font size of 18 for the title, and a font size of 14 for the subtitle. Change the column widths of columns I through Q to 13.00 (96 pixels). Format cells I1 and I3 to match the fill and font color in cell B1.

4. For a two-input data table, the formula you are analyzing must be assigned to the upper-left cell in the range of the data table. Because cell C14 contains the future value formula to be analyzed, enter **=c14** in cell I4.

5. Use the fill handle to create two lists of percentages: (a) 3.00% through 12.00% in increments of 0.50% in the range I5:I23 and (b) 3.00% through 10.00% in increments of 1.00% in the range J4:Q4.

6. Use the Data Table button in the What-If Analysis gallery (Data tab | Forecast group) to define the range I4:Q23 as a two-input data table. Enter **C8** in the 'Row input cell' box and **C5** in the 'Column input cell' box (Data Table dialog box). Click the OK button to populate the table.

7. Format the two-input data table using a white font color and the fill color used in cells B3:G12. Bold ranges I4:Q4 and I5:I23. Format cells J5:Q23 to match the number format used in cells F5:G12. Place a light border around the range I3:Q23, light borders between columns in that same range, and a bottom border on the range I4:Q4.

8. Protect the worksheet so that the user can select only unlocked cells (C3:C6 and C8:C9).

9. If necessary, change the print orientation to landscape. Print the worksheet using the Fit to option. Print the formulas version of the worksheet.

10. If requested by your instructor, change the name in cell C3 to your name.

11. Save your changes to the workbook and submit the revised workbook as specified by your instructor.

12. ❄ How could you improve the design of the worksheet to make the impact of various combinations of Employee Investment and Expected Annual Return more easily identified?

Expand Your World

Create a solution that uses cloud or web technologies by learning and investigating on your own from general guidance.

Down Payment Options for a Home

Note: To complete this assignment, you will be required to use the Data Files. Please contact your instructor for information about accessing the Data Files.

Instructions: You are planning to buy a home as soon as you can save enough to make a 20% down payment. Your task is to create a calculator that you can use to determine possible savings options, and to share this calculator with family using OneDrive. Run Excel and open the workbook, Expand 4–1 Down Payment Calculator.

Perform the following tasks:
1. Save the file using the file name Expand 4–1 Down Payment Calculator Complete.
2. Identify a home for sale in your local housing market that you would consider buying. Use the asking price for that home as the current value of the house, or use an online tool such as Zillow.com to find the current estimated value of the home. Enter this value in your Down Payment Calculator, and calculate the needed down payment.
3. Determine the amount you consider reasonable as a monthly savings toward a down payment, and enter this in your down payment calculator.
4. Use the Future Value function to calculate how much you could save, using the rate of return and years to save in the worksheet. Remember to use a minus sign before the function so that the calculation will appear positive.
5. Create a two-input data table that calculates the future value of savings. You can decide which two inputs you would like to use for your data table.
6. Format the worksheet using techniques you have learned to present the worksheet content in a visually appealing form.
7. If requested by your instructor, save the file on OneDrive.
8. Use Excel Online to create two charts showing the relationship between the future value of savings and the two inputs from your data table.
9. Submit the workbook as specified by your instructor.
10. ✳ Why did you select the two inputs used in your data table? How useful are they for evaluating down payment savings options?

In the Labs

Design, create, modify and/or use a workbook following the guidelines, concepts, and skills presented in this module. Labs 1 and 2, which increase in difficulty, require you to create solutions based on what you learned in the module; Lab 3 requires you to apply your creative thinking and problem-solving skills to design and implement a solution.

Lab 1: Analyzing Education Savings

Problem: You have been asked by the employee relations and resource department to develop an education planning worksheet that will allow each current employee to see the effect (dollar accumulation) of investing a percentage of his or her monthly salary in a 529(c) Education Savings plan over a period of years (Figure 4–68). Employees can contribute up to $15,000 per year per child to plans. The employee relations and resource department wants a one-input data table to show the future value of the investment for different years. The final worksheet is shown in Figure 4–68.

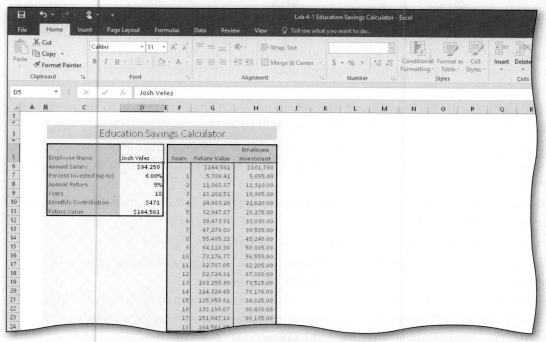

Figure 4–68

Perform the following tasks:

1. Run Excel. Apply the Retrospect theme to the worksheet. Change the column widths to the following: A and F = 6.57 (51 pixels); B, E, and I = 0.75 (9 pixels); C = 22.14 (160 pixels); D, G, and H = 12.71 (94 pixels). Change the heights of rows 2, 4, and 25 to 8.25 (11 pixels).

2. In cell C3, enter **Education Savings Calculator** as the worksheet title. Merge and center cell C3 across columns C through H. Apply the Title cell style to cell C3. Change the background color of C3 to Olive Green, Text 2, Lighter 80% and change its font color to Brown, Accent 3, Darker 25%.

3. Enter **Employee Name** in cell C5, **Annual Salary** in cell C6, **Percent Invested (up to)** in cell C7, **Annual Return** in cell C8, **Years** in cell C9, **Monthly Contribution** in cell C10, and **Future Value** in cell C11. Add the data in Table 4–5 to column D. Use the currency and percent style formats to format the numbers in the range D6:D8.

Table 4–5 Education Savings Employee Data	
Row Title	**Data**
Employee Name	Josh Velez
Annual Salary	$94,250
Percent Invested	6.00%
Annual Return	5%
Years	18

4. Use the Create from Selection button (Formulas tab | Defined Names group) to assign the row titles in column C (range C6:C11) as cell names for the adjacent cells in column D. Use these newly created names to assign formulas to cells in the range D10:D11.

Continued >

In the Labs *continued*

    a. Employee Monthly Contribution (cell D10) = IF(Percent_Invested__up_to * Annual_Salary < 15000, Percent_Invested__up_to * Annual_Salary / 12, 15000 / 12)

    b. Future Value (cell D11) = –FV(Annual_Return/12, Years*12, Monthly_Contribution)

       The Future Value function (FV) returns to the cell the future value of the investment. The future value of an investment is its value at some point in the future based on a series of payments of equal amounts made over a number of periods while earning a constant rate of return.

    c. If necessary, use the Format Painter button (Home tab | Clipboard group) to assign the currency style format in cell D6 to the range D10:D11.

5. Add the background color Orange, Accent 1, Lighter 60%, and the font color Olive Green, Text 2 to cells C5:C11, and a medium outside border to the range C5:D11, as shown in Figure 4–68.

6. Use the concepts and techniques developed in this module to add the data table in Figure 4–68 to the range F5:H24 as follows:

    a. Enter and format the table column titles in row 5 as shown in Figure 4–68.

    b. Use the fill handle to create the series of years beginning with 1 and ending with 18 in increments of 1 in column F, beginning in cell F7.

    c. In cell G6, enter `=D11` as the formula. In cell H6, enter `=12 * D10 * D9` as the formula (recall that using cell references in the formulas means Excel will copy the formats).

    d. Use the Data Table command to define the range F6:H24 as a one-input data table. Use cell D9 as the column input cell.

    e. Format the numbers in the range G7:H24 using the comma style format. Add the background color Orange, Accent 1, Lighter 60%, the font color Olive Green, Text 2, and a light bottom border to cells F5:H5. Add light vertical borders to cells F6:H24, and a medium outside border to the range F5:H24, as shown in Figure 4–68.

7. Add a fill pattern with the pattern color Tan, Accent 5, Lighter 60% and the pattern style 12.5% Gray to the range B2:I25. *Hint:* Look on the Fill sheet in the Format Cells dialog box. Change the sheet tab name to **Education Savings Calculator** and color to Orange, Accent 1, Lighter 60%, as shown in Figure 4–68.

8. Remove gridlines by removing the check mark from the View Gridlines check box (Page Layout tab | Sheet Options group).

9. If requested by your instructor, change the Employee Name in cell D5 to your name.

10. Unlock the cells in the range D5:D9. Protect the worksheet. Allow users to select only unlocked cells.

11. Save the workbook using the file name, Lab 4–1 Education Savings Calculator. Submit the workbook as requested by your instructor.

Lab 2: **Consumer Debt Analysis and Interest Comparison Table**

Problem: As part of an ongoing program to educate incoming students about the financial realities of credit cards, you have been asked to create a consumer debt analysis worksheet including an interest comparison table, as shown in Figure 4–69. This worksheet, which will be distributed during freshman orientation as part of the electronic orientation package, also should demonstrate the goal-seeking capabilities of Excel.

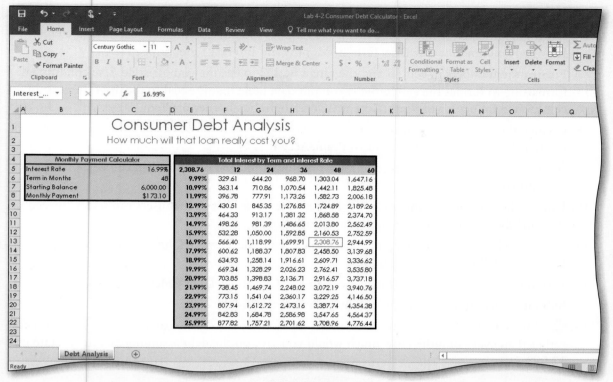

Figure 4–69

Perform the following tasks:

1. Run Excel. Apply the Ion Boardroom theme to a new worksheet. Change the width of columns A and D to .85 (11 pixels), columns B:C to 21.25 (175 pixels), and columns E:J to 9.50 (81 pixels).

2. Enter the worksheet title, **Consumer Debt Analysis**, in cell B1, apply the Title cell style, change its font size to 28–point and font color to Plum, Accent 1. Enter the worksheet subtitle, **How much will that loan really cost you?**, in cell B2, and apply the Title cell style, and change its font color to Plum, Accent 1. One at a time, merge and center cells B1 and B2 across columns B through J.

3. Type **Monthly Payment Calculator** in cell B4, and merge and center the range B4:C4. Type **Total Interest by Term and Interest Rate** in cell E4, and then merge and center the range E4:J4. Bold the text in cells B4 and E4. Type **Interest Rate** in cell B5, **Term in Months** in cell B6, **Starting Balance** in cell B7, and **Monthly Payment** in cell B8. Create the series shown in E6:E22 (enter **9.99%** in cell E6, **10.99%** in cell E7, and then use the Fill Handle to fill the remaining percentages through cell E22) and F5:J5 (enter **12, 24, 36, 48,** and **60** in the cells, respectively). Use the Create from Selection button (Formulas tab | Defined Names group) to assign the row titles in the ranges B5:B8 to the adjacent cells in ranges C5:C8.

4. Enter **16.99%** in cell C5, **48** in cell C6, and **6000** in cell C7. Apply the comma style format to cell C7. Determine the monthly payment amount by entering the PMT function in cell C8. (*Hint:* Unlike the module project, in this example the term is expressed in months, not years. The interest rate remains an annual rate, however. Adjust your use of the function accordingly.)

5. Enter a formula for total interest paid in cell E5. Total interest is determined by calculating the total of all monthly payments for the term, and then subtracting the starting balance from that total.

Continued >

In the Labs *continued*

6. Create the interest comparison table in the range E5:J22 by creating a two-input data table. Row and column inputs will be Term in Months and Interest Rate, respectively.

7. Format the numbers in cell E5 and the range F6:J22 to use the comma style. Use conditional formatting to format the cell in the two-input data table that is equal to the Total Interest in cell E5 to a font color of Plum, Accent 1, and a light box border of Plum, Accent 1.

8. Change the colors and draw the borders as shown in Figure 4–69. Change the sheet tab name to Debt Analysis and the tab color to Plum, Accent 1.

9. If requested by your instructor, add the word, for, at the end of the title in cell B1, followed by your initials.

10. Unlock the cells in the ranges C5:C7. Protect the worksheet so that users can select any cell in the worksheet, but can change only the unlocked cells.

11. Remove gridlines by removing the check mark from the View Gridlines check box (Page Layout tab | Sheet Options group).

12. Save the workbook using the file name, Lab 4–2 Consumer Debt Calculator.

13. Submit the assignment as requested by your instructor.

14. ✸ How would you adjust your calculations if you wanted to make payments every two weeks rather than every month? How much would you save on the debt assuming an interest rate of 12.99%?

Lab 3: **Consider This: Your Turn**

Apply your creative thinking and problem-solving skills to design and implement a solution.

Determining the Break-Even Point

Part 1:   You have been hired by Alison Chang, owner of a small start-up company, to create a data table that analyzes the break-even point for a new product she is developing. She would like you to analyze the break-even point for prices ranging from $12.99 to $17.99 per unit, in $0.50 increments. You can calculate the number of units she must sell to break even (break-even point) if you know the fixed expenses, the price per unit, and the expense (cost) per unit. The following formula determines the break-even point:

Break-Even Point = Fixed Expenses / (Price per Unit – Expense per Unit)

Assume Fixed Expenses = $7,000; Price per Unit = $14.99; and Expense per Unit = $8.00.

Use the concepts and techniques presented in this module to determine the break-even point and then create the data table. Use the Price per Unit as the input cell and the break-even value as the result. Protect the worksheet so that only cells with data can be selected. Submit your assignment in the format specified by your instructor.

You can calculate additional break-even points by using a two-way table and varying Fixed Expenses or Expense per Unit in addition to Price per Unit. Which of the following provides the owner with a wider range of break-even points: varying Fixed Expenses between $6500 and $7000 in increments of $250 or varying Expense per Unit between $7.60 and $8.00 in increments of $0.20?

Part 2:   ✸ You made several decisions while creating the worksheet for this assignment. How did you set up the worksheet? How did you decide how to create the data table? What additional break-even points did you calculate, and why?

5 | Working with Multiple Worksheets and Workbooks

Objectives

You will have mastered the material in this module when you can:

- Format a consolidated worksheet
- Fill using a linear series
- Use date, time, and rounding functions
- Apply a custom format code
- Create a new cell style
- Copy a worksheet
- Drill to add data to multiple worksheets at the same time
- Select and deselect sheet combinations

- Enter formulas that use 3-D cell references
- Use the Paste gallery
- Format a 3-D pie chart with an exploded slice and lead lines
- Save individual worksheets as separate workbook files
- View and hide multiple workbooks
- Consolidate data by linking separate workbooks

Introduction

Typically, an organization will need to store data unique to various areas, departments, locations, or regions. If you enter each department's data, for example, on a different worksheet in a single workbook, you can use the sheet tabs at the bottom of the Excel window to move from worksheet to worksheet or department to department. Note, however, that many business applications require data from several worksheets to be summarized on one worksheet. To facilitate this summarization, you can create a cumulative worksheet, entering formulas and functions that reference cells from the other worksheets. The process of summarizing data gathered from multiple worksheets onto one worksheet is called **consolidation**.

Another important concept presented in this module is the use of custom format codes and cell styles. Custom format codes allow you to specify, in detail, how a cell entry will appear. For example, you can create a custom format code to indicate how positive numbers, negative numbers, zeros, and text are displayed in a cell. Custom cell styles store specific font formatting for repeated use.

As you learn how to work with multiple worksheets and workbooks, you also will learn about Excel's many formatting features for pie charts, such as exploding slices and adding lead lines.

Project — Consolidated Expenses Worksheet

The project in the module follows proper design guidelines and uses Excel to create the worksheets shown in Figure 5–1. Twelve-Tone Concert Venues manages three different small venues for concerts and shows, each with seating for approximately one thousand people. The management wants to project consolidated expenses for the next two years, along with separate worksheets for each venue. The first worksheet shows the actual expenses for 2017, the projected percentage change, and the resulting expenses for 2018 and 2019. The 2017 expenses — consolidated from the three venues — will be highlighted in a 3-D pie chart. These expenses do not include talent expenses as that is handled by booking and ticket agencies.

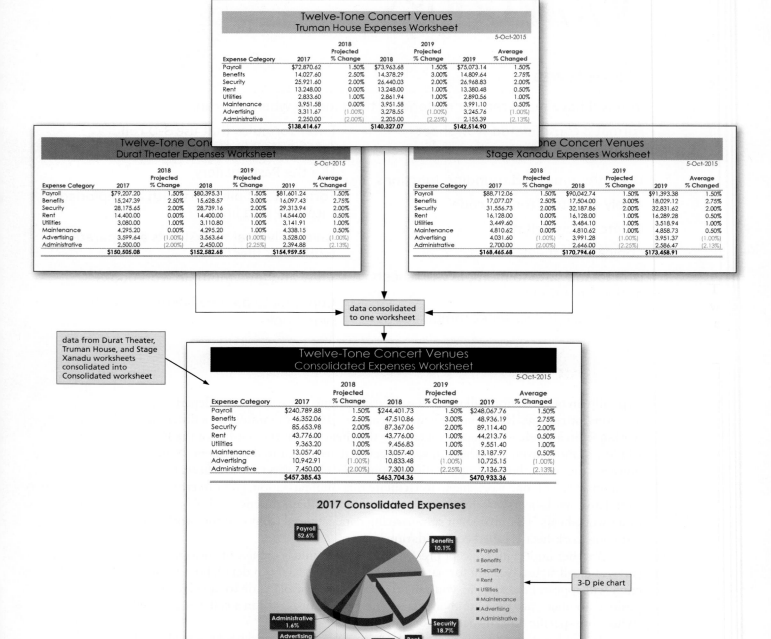

Figure 5–1

The requirements document for the Concert Venues Consolidated Workbook is shown in Table 5–1. It includes the needs, source of data, summary of calculations, and other facts about its development.

Table 5–1 Requirements Document	
Worksheet Title	**Twelve-Tone Concert Venues**
Needs	The needs are as follows: 1. Create a workbook containing three worksheets (one for each of the three venues), one worksheet to consolidate the expenses, and a pie chart. 2. Each worksheet should be identical in structure and allow for display of the current expenses and projected expenses for the next two years. 3. The worksheets should print with a common header and footer. 4. The chart should show the 2017 consolidated expenses and draw attention to the largest expense after payroll.
Source of Data	Twelve-Tone Concert Venues will provide the data for each of the three venues. Projection assumptions also will be provided by Twelve-Tone Concert Venues.
Calculations	The following formulas should be included: a. 2018 Expenses = 2017 Expenses + (2017 Expenses * 2018 % Change) b. 2019 Expenses = 2018 Expenses + (2018 Expenses * 2019 % Change) c. Average % Change = (2018 % Change + 2019 % Change) / 2 d. Use the SUM function to determine totals Note: Use dummy data in the consolidated worksheet to verify the formulas. Round the percentages. Format other numbers using standard accounting rules, which require a dollar sign only on the first and last numbers in a currency column.
Other Tasks	Investigate a method the company can use to consolidate data from multiple workbooks into a new workbook.

In addition, using a sketch of the worksheet can help you visualize its design. The sketch of the consolidated worksheet (the first of the four worksheets in this workbook) consists of titles, column and row headings, the location of data values, and a general idea of the desired formatting, as shown in Figure 5–2.

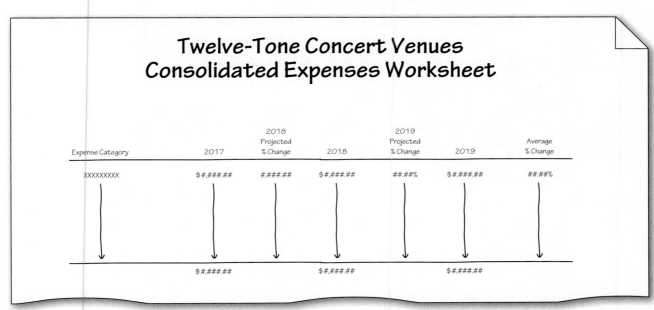

Figure 5–2

The following roadmap identifies general activities you will perform as you progress through this module:

1. Create and FORMAT the consolidated WORKSHEET.
2. FILL using a LINEAR SERIES.
3. USE DATE and ROUND FUNCTIONS.
4. APPLY a CUSTOM FORMAT CODE.
5. CREATE CELL STYLES.
6. Add and POPULATE WORKSHEETS.
7. INSERT a 3-D Pie CHART.
8. LINK WORKBOOKS.

BTW
The Ribbon and Screen Resolution
Excel may change how the groups and buttons within the groups appear on the ribbon, depending on the computer's screen resolution. Thus, your ribbon may look different from the ones in this book if you are using a screen resolution other than 1366 × 768.

Creating the Consolidated Worksheet

The first step in creating the workbook is to create the first worksheet shown in Figure 5–1. This worksheet eventually will contain consolidated data with titles, column and row headings, formulas, and formatting. It also represents the format used on each of the individual locations, which will be copied to the three other worksheets. You will create sample data first, to verify formats and formulas.

To Apply a Theme

1 FORMAT WORKSHEET | 2 FILL LINEAR SERIES | 3 USE DATE & ROUND FUNCTIONS | 4 APPLY CUSTOM FORMAT CODE
5 CREATE CELL STYLES | 6 POPULATE WORKSHEETS | 7 INSERT CHART | 8 LINK WORKBOOKS

The following steps apply a theme to the worksheet.

1 Run Excel and create a blank workbook in the Excel window. Maximize the Excel window and the worksheet, if necessary.

2 Zoom to approximately 120%.

3 Display the Page Layout tab, click the Themes button (Page Layout tab | Themes group), and then scroll to display the Mesh theme (Figure 5–3).

4 Click the Mesh theme to apply it to the workbook.

Q&A | What is the best way to zoom?
You can use the Zoom In and Zoom Out buttons on the taskbar, or drag the Zoom slider. Some users like using CTRL+WHEEL to zoom. The View tab also has some useful zoom tools.

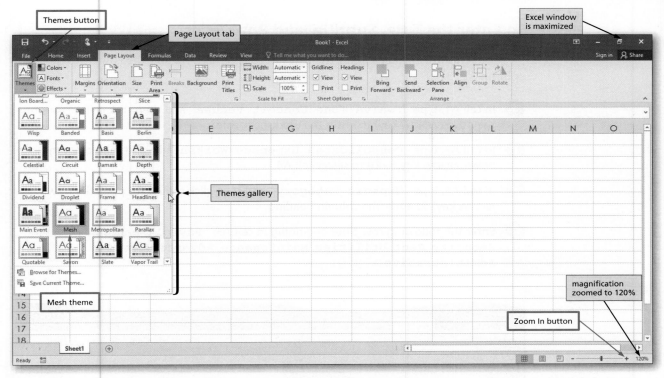

Figure 5–3

To Format the Worksheet

The following steps format the cells in the consolidated worksheet. The row heights and column widths need to be changed to accommodate the data in the worksheet.

① Drag the bottom boundary of row heading 4 down until the row height is 51.00 (68 pixels) to change the row height.

② Drag the right boundary of column heading A to the right until the column width is 18.00 (149 pixels) to change the column width.

③ Click the heading for column B and then SHIFT+CLICK the heading for column G to select all the columns in the range.

④ Drag the right boundary of column heading G to 12.00 (101 pixels) to change the width of multiple columns.

⑤ Click cell A1 to deselect the columns (Figure 5–4).

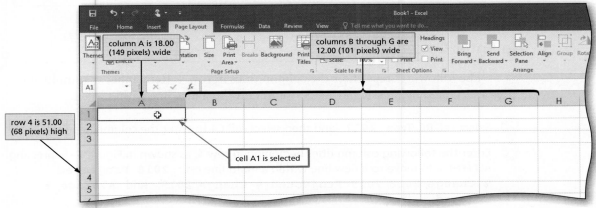

Figure 5–4

To Enter the Title, Subtitle, and Row Titles

The following steps enter the titles in cells A1 and A2 and the row titles in column A.

1 In cell A1, type `Twelve-Tone Concert Venues` and then click cell A2 (or press the DOWN ARROW key) to enter the worksheet title.

2 In cell A2, type `Consolidated Expenses Worksheet` and then press the DOWN ARROW key twice to select cell A4.

3 In cell A4, type `Expense Category` and then click cell A5 (or press the DOWN ARROW key) to enter the column heading.

4 Enter the following row titles beginning in cell A5: `Payroll, Benefits, Security, Rent, Utilities, Maintenance, Advertising,` and `Administrative`.

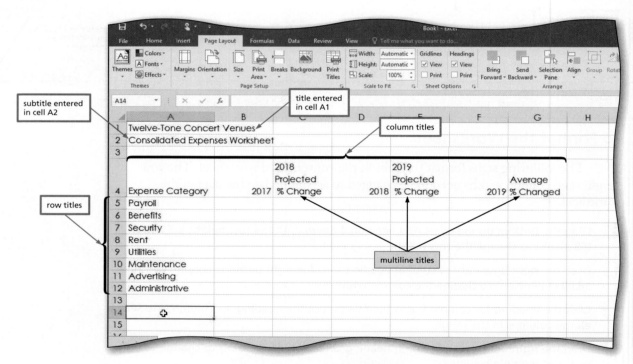

Figure 5–5

To Enter Column Titles

The following steps enter the column titles in row 4. Remember that multi-line titles are created by pressing ALT+ENTER to move to a new line within a cell.

1 Select cell B4. Type `2017` and then select cell C4 to enter the column heading.

2 Enter the following column titles beginning in row 4, as shown in Figure 5–5, pressing ALT+ENTER to move to a new line within a multi-line cell: `2018 Projected % Change, 2018, 2019 Projected % Change, 2019,` and `Average % Changed`.

Fill Series

In previous modules, you used the fill handle to create a numerical series. By entering the first two numbers in a series, Excel determined the increment amount, and filled the cells accordingly. There are other kinds of series, however, including a **date series** (Jan, Feb, Mar, etc.), an **auto fill series** (1, 1, 1, etc.), a **linear series** (1, 2, 3, etc. or 2, 4, 6, etc.), and a **growth series** that multiplies values by a constant factor. For these precise series, you can use the Fill button and the Series dialog box.

To Create Linear Series

1 FORMAT WORKSHEET | **2 FILL LINEAR SERIES** | 3 USE DATE & ROUND FUNCTIONS | 4 APPLY CUSTOM FORMAT CODE
5 CREATE CELL STYLES | 6 POPULATE WORKSHEETS | 7 INSERT CHART | 8 LINK WORKBOOKS

While creating the consolidated worksheet in this module, sample data is used for the 2017 expenditures, the 2018 projected % change, and the 2019 projected % change values. *Why? Entering sample data creates placeholder content and assists in the layout of the consolidated worksheet.*

You will use the fill handle to create a series of integers in column B. Normally you would enter the first two numbers in a series so that Excel can determine the increment amount; however, if your series is incremented by 1, you do not have to enter two numbers. You can CTRL+drag the fill handle to increment by 1 across cells.

If you want to increment by a different value, you can use the Series dialog box. In the Series dialog box, you can choose to increment by any step value, including positive and negative decimals, again by entering only a single value. The following steps create sample data in the consolidated worksheet.

- Select cell B5.
- Type **1** and then click the Enter button in the formula bar to enter the first value in the series.
- CTRL+drag the fill handle down through cell B12 to create a fill series incremented by 1 (Figure 5–6).

Q&A

How do I use the fill handle, if I am using a touch screen?
Press and hold the selected cell to display the mini toolbar, tap AutoFill on the mini toolbar, and then drag the AutoFill icon.

What would happen if I did not use the CTRL key?
If you drag without the CTRL key, the cells would be filled with the number, 1.

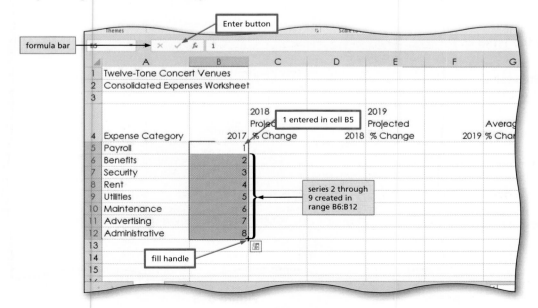

Figure 5–6

2

- Select cell C5 and then type **2%** to enter a percentage in this column.

- Display the Home tab.

- Select the range C5:C12 and then click the Fill button (Home tab | Editing group) to display the Fill gallery (Figure 5–7).

Q&A How are the directional commands in the Fill gallery used?
Those commands are alternatives to using the fill handle. Select an empty cell or cells adjacent to the cell that contains the data that you want to use. You then can fill the selection using the Fill button and the appropriate directional command.

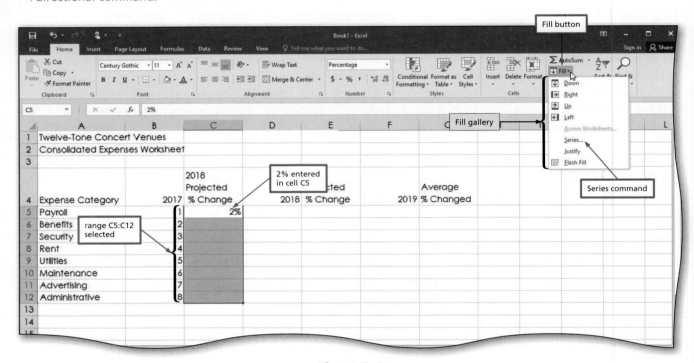

Figure 5–7

3

- Click Series to display the Series dialog box.

- Type **.021** in the Step value box to increment by a decimal number (Figure 5–8).

Q&A Why am I using an increment of .021?
You are generating random placeholder numbers. You can use any increment step; however, since this column will eventually be percentages, a decimal may be appropriate.

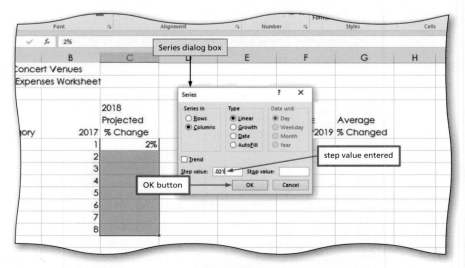

Figure 5–8

4

- Click the OK button (Series dialog box) to fill the series.

- Click the Increase Decimal button (Home tab | Number group) twice, to display two decimal places.

- Repeat Steps 2, 3, and 4 to create a linear series beginning with `3%` and incrementing by `.01` in the range E5:E12.

- Click an empty cell to remove the selection (Figure 5–9).

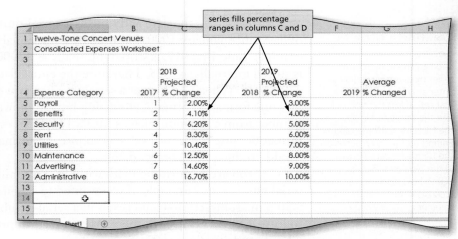

series fills percentage ranges in columns C and D

Figure 5–9

Other Ways

1. To increment by 1, enter first number; select original cell and blank adjacent cell, drag fill handle through range

Date, Time, and Round Functions

Entering dates in Excel can be as easy as typing the parts of the date separated by slashes, such as 6/14/2017. However, when you want a date that automatically updates, or you want to access part of the current date for a variety of reasons, Excel has many date and time functions, including those shown in Table 5–2. Use Excel Help to search for more information about these and other date and time functions.

BTW
Creating Customized Formats
Each format symbol within the format code has special meaning. Table 5–2 summarizes the more frequently used format symbols and their meanings.

Table 5–2 Functions Related to Date and Time					
	Function	**Definition**	**Syntax**	**Example**	**Sample Result**
Date Functions	DATE	Returns the formatted date based on the month, day, and year	DATE(year, month, day)	=DATE(117,6,14)	6/14/2017
	DATEVALUE	Converts a date that is stored as text to a serial number for calculations	DATEVALUE(date_text)	=DATEVALUE("6/14/2017")	42900
	DAY	Returns the day value from a serial date	DAY(serial_number)	=DAY(42900)	14
	MONTH	Returns the month value from a serial date	MONTH(serial_number)	=MONTH(42900)	6
	TODAY	Returns the current date	TODAY()	=TODAY()	6/14/2017
	WEEKDAY	Returns the day of the week from a serial date, with a second option for starting the week on Sunday (1) or Monday (2)	WEEKDAY(serial_number,return_type)	=WEEKDAY(42900,1)	4 (Wednesday)
	YEAR	Returns the year value from a serial date	YEAR(serial_number)	=YEAR(42900)	2017
Time Functions	HOUR	Returns the hour value from a serial date	HOUR(serial_number)	=HOUR(0.33605324)	8
	MINUTE	Returns the minute value from a serial date	MINUTES(serial_number)	=MINUTE(0.33605324)	3
	SECOND	Returns the second value from a serial date	SECOND(serial_number)	=SECOND(0.33605324)	55
	TIME	Returns the formatted date based on the hour, minute, and second	TIME(hour, minute, second)	=TIME(8,3,55)	8:03 AM
	TIMEVALUE	Converts a time that is stored as text to a serial number for calculations	TIMEVALUE(time_text)	=TIMEVALUE("8:03:55 am")	0.33605324
Other Functions	NOW	Returns both date and time	NOW()	=NOW()	6/14/2017 8:03

BTW
Creating a Growth Series
You can create a growth series by doing the following: enter an initial value in the first cell, select the first cell and the range to fill, click the Fill button (Home tab | Editing group), click Series on the Fill menu, click Growth in the Type area (Series dialog box), and then enter a constant factor in the Step value box.

BTW
Updating the TODAY function
If the TODAY function does not update the date when you expect it to, you might need to change the settings that control when the worksheet recalculates. On the File tab, click Options, and then in the Formulas category under Calculation options, make sure that Automatic is selected.

BTW
Copying
To copy the contents of a cell to the cell directly below it, click in the target cell and press CTRL+D.

Excel stores the date and time as a **serial number** representing the number of days since January 1900, followed by a fractional portion of a 24-hour day. For example, June 14, 2017, is stored internally as 42900. The time, for example 3:00 p.m., is stored internally as .625. Therefore the entire date and time would be stored as 42900.625. When you format a serial number, you can use the Short Date, Long Date, or Time formats (Format Cells dialog box). If, however, you have generated the serial number from a function such as MONTH, DAY, or YEAR, you must use the Number format because the return value is an integer; formatting it with a date or time format would produce an incorrect date.

If you are performing math with dates and times, your answer will result in a serial number. For example, if you wanted to calculate elapsed time from 9:00 a.m. to 3:30 p.m., subtraction would result in a serial number, 0.2708. You then would need to format the number with the TIME format (h:mm), which would result in 6:30 or 6 hours and 30 minutes (Figure 5–10).

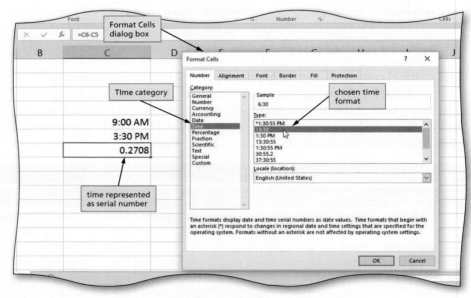

Figure 5–10

Another set of useful functions have to do with rounding. Rounding numbers off, especially for dollars and cents, prevents formulas from creating awkward answers with long decimal notations. Table 5–3 displays some of the more popular round functions.

Table 5–3 Rounding Functions

Function	Definition	Syntax	Example	Sample Result
ROUND	Rounds a number to a specified number of decimal places	ROUND(number, num_digits)	=ROUND(833.77,0)	834
ROUNDDOWN	Rounds a number down, toward zero	ROUNDDOWN(number, num_digits)	=ROUNDDOWN(833.77,0)	833
ROUNDUP	Rounds a number up, away from zero	ROUNDUP(number, num_digits)	=ROUNDUP(833.77,0)	834
MROUND	Returns a number rounded to the desired multiple	MROUND(number, multiple)	=MROUND(833.77,5)	835

CONSIDER THIS

When should you use the ROUND function?

When you multiply or divide decimal numbers, the answer may contain more decimal places than the format allows. If this happens, you run the risk of the column totals being off by a penny or so; resulting values of calculations could include fractions of a penny beyond the two decimal places that currency formats usually display. For example, as shown in the worksheet sketch in Figure 5–2, columns C, E, and G use the currency and comma style formats with two decimal places; however, the formulas used to calculate values for these columns result in several additional decimal places that Excel maintains for computation purposes. For this reason, it is recommended that you use the ROUND function on formulas that potentially can result in more decimal places than the applied format displays in a given cell.

To Use the TODAY Function

1 FORMAT WORKSHEET | 2 FILL LINEAR SERIES | 3 USE DATE & ROUND FUNCTIONS | 4 APPLY CUSTOM FORMAT CODE

5 CREATE CELL STYLES | 6 POPULATE WORKSHEETS | 7 INSERT CHART | 8 LINK WORKBOOKS

Recall that you have used the NOW function to access the system date and time. You also can use the **TODAY function**, which returns only the date. Both functions are designed to update each time the worksheet is opened. The function takes no arguments but accesses the internal clock on your computer and displays the current date. As with the NOW function, you can format the date in a variety of styles.

The TODAY function also is useful for calculating intervals. For example, if you want to calculate an age, you can subtract the birth year from the TODAY function to find that person's age as of this year's birthday. The following steps use the TODAY function to enter the system date into the worksheet. *Why? The TODAY function will update each time the worksheet is opened.*

1

- Select cell G3, type **=today()**, and then click the Enter button to enter the system date (Figure 5–11).

Q&A Should I use lowercase or uppercase on functions? Either one will work. To delineate functions in the text passages of this book, they are displayed in all caps.

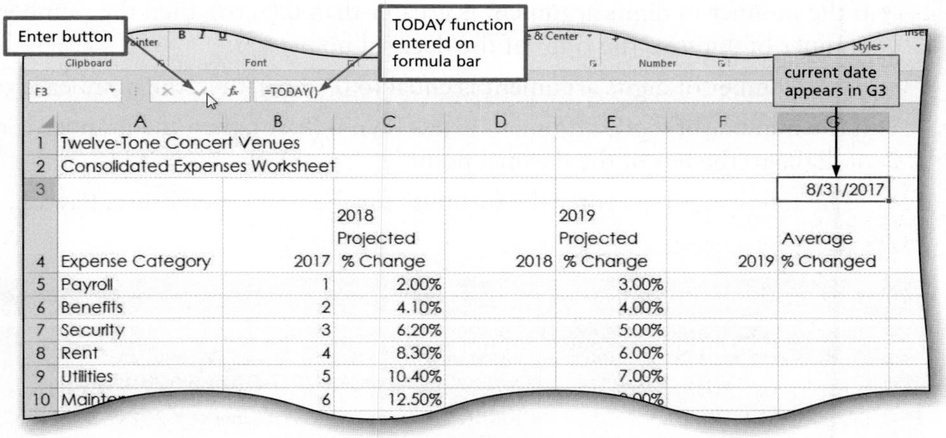

Figure 5–11

2

- Right-click cell G3 and then click Format Cells on the shortcut menu.

- If necessary, click Date in the Category list (Format Cells dialog box).

- Click 14-Mar-12 in the Type list to format the date (Figure 5–12).

Q&A Why change the format of the date? The date might be displayed as a series of number signs if the date, as initially formatted by Excel, does not fit in the width of the cell.

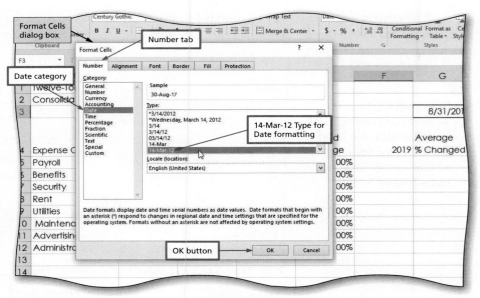

Figure 5–12

- Click the OK button (Format Cells dialog box) to close the dialog box.
- Click an empty cell to deselect the previous cell.

Other Ways

1. Select cell, click Date & Time button (Formulas tab | Function Library group), click TODAY, click OK button (Function Arguments dialog box)

To Enter Formulas Using the ROUND Function

1 FORMAT WORKSHEET | 2 FILL LINEAR SERIES | 3 USE DATE & ROUND FUNCTIONS | 4 APPLY CUSTOM FORMAT CODE
5 CREATE CELL STYLES | 6 POPULATE WORKSHEETS | 7 INSERT CHART | 8 LINK WORKBOOKS

The **ROUND function** in Excel is used to round numbers to a specified number of decimal places. The general form of the ROUND function is

=ROUND (number, number of digits)

where the number argument can be a number, a cell reference that contains a number, or a formula that results in a number; and the number of digits argument can be any positive or negative number used to determine the number of places to which the number will be rounded. Positive numbers round to the right of the decimal point; for example, 18.257 formatted for 1 decimal place would display 18.3. Negative numbers round to the left of the decimal point; for example, 18.257 formatted for -1 decimal place would display 20.

The following is true about the ROUND function:

- If the number of digits argument is greater than 0 (zero), then the number is rounded to the specified number of digits to the right of the decimal point.
- If the number of digits argument is equal to 0 (zero), then the number is rounded to the nearest integer.
- If the number of digits argument is less than 0 (zero), then the number is rounded to the specified number of digits to the left of the decimal point.

The following steps enter the formulas for the first expenditure, Payroll, in cells D5, F5, and G5. (See Table 5–4.)

Table 5–4 Formulas for cells D5, F5, and G5			
Cell	**Description**	**Formula**	**Entry**
D5	2018 Expense	ROUND(2017 Expense + 2017 Expense * 2018 % Change, 2)	=ROUND(B5 + B5 * C5, 2)
F5	2019 Expense	ROUND(2018 Expense + 2018 Expense * 2019 % Change, 2)	=ROUND(D5 + D5 * E5, 2)
G5	Average % Change	ROUND((2018 % Change + 2019 % Change) / 2, 4)	=ROUND((C5 + E5) / 2, 4)

The projected expenses will be rounded to two decimal places, while the average will be rounded to four decimal places. *Why? Because the averages are very small at this point in the process, using four decimal digits provides the most representative results.*

- Select cell D5, type `=round(b5+b5*c5,2)`, and then click the Enter button in the formula bar to display the resulting value (Figure 5–13).

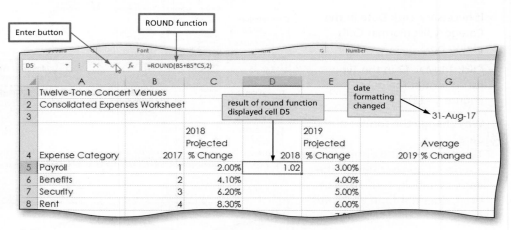

Figure 5–13

2

- Drag the fill handle on cell D5 down to copy the formula to cells D6:D12.

- Select cell F5, type
=round(d5+d5*e5,2),
and then click the Enter button to display the resulting value
(Figure 5–14).

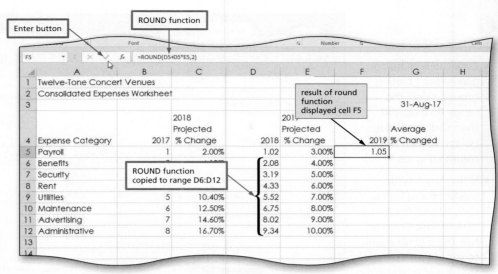

Figure 5–14

3

- Select cell G5, type
=round((c5+e5)/2,4),
and then click the Enter button to display the resulting value
(Figure 5–15).

Q&A Do I need to use two sets of parentheses in the function?
Yes, the outer set of parentheses are for the function and the inner set is to force Excel to add the two values before dividing to calculate the average.
Recall that Excel follows the order of operations and performs multiplication and division before addition and subtraction, unless you use parentheses.

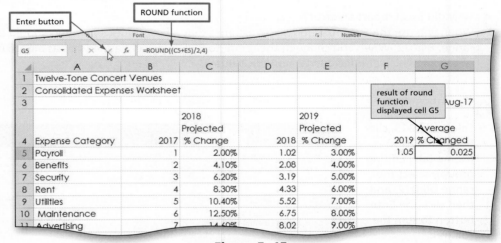

Figure 5–15

4

- Select cells F5:G5.

- Drag the fill handle down through cells F12:G12 to copy both formulas down to the selected range (Figure 5–16).

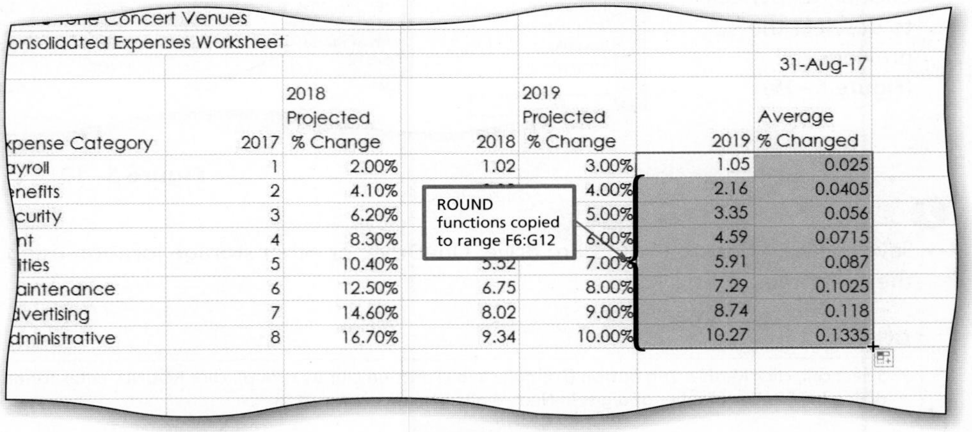

Q&A Are the values in column G supposed to display all four decimal places?
Yes, because you entered a 4 at the end of the function, Excel rounds to four decimal places; however, a default setting in Excel is to ignore zeroes at the end of decimal places, because they are not significant. You will change that default setting later in the module.

Figure 5–16

5

- Select cell B13.
- Click the Sum button (Home tab | Editing group), select the range B5:B12, and then click the Enter button to sum the column (Figure 5–17).
- If the Trace Error button is displayed, click it, and then click Ignore Error on the Trace Error menu to ignore an error that Excel mistakenly reported.

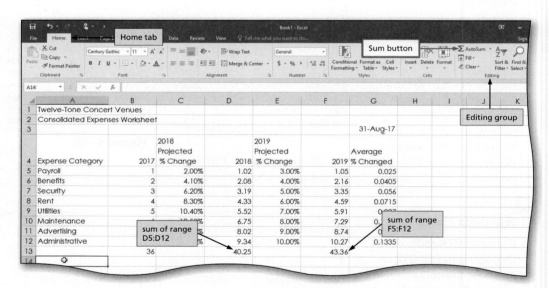

Figure 5–17

Q&A Why did Excel report an error?

When you use the SUM function, Excel assumes that all contiguous numbers should be summed, in this case the range, B4:B12. When you changed the range to B5:B12, Excel flagged this as a potential error, due to the exclusion of cell B4, which also included a numeric value.

6

- Select cell D13, click the Sum button (Home tab | Editing group), select the range D5:D12, and then click the Enter button to sum the column.
- In cell F13, calculate the sum for the range F5:F12.
- Click an empty cell to deselect the previous cell (Figure 5–18).

Figure 5–18

7

- Save the workbook on your hard drive, OneDrive, or other storage location using Concert Venues Consolidated as the file name.

Other Ways

1. Select cell, click Math & Trig button (Formulas tab | Function Library group), click ROUND, enter formula in Number box (Formula Arguments dialog box), enter number of digits in Num_digits box, click OK button

Break Point: If you wish to take a break, this is a good place to do so. You can exit Excel. To resume at a later time, run Excel, open the file called Concert Venues Consolidated, and continue following the steps from this location forward.

To Format the Title and Subtitle

The following steps format the worksheet title and subtitle to change the font size, to center both titles across columns A through G, to change the background color, and to change the font color. You will choose colors from the Mesh theme.

1 Select the range A1:A2, click the Cell Styles button (Home tab | Styles group), and then click the Title style to apply the style to the range. Recall that pointing to a style will cause Excel to display the name of the style in a ScreenTip.

2 Select cell A1 and change the font size to 20.

3 Select the range A1:G1 and then click the 'Merge & Center' button (Home tab | Alignment group) to merge and center the text in the selected range.

4 Select cell A2 and change the font size to 18.

5 Select the range A2:G2 and then click the 'Merge & Center' button (Home tab | Alignment group) to merge and center the text in the selected range.

6 Select the range A1:A2, click the Fill Color arrow (Home tab | Font group), and then click 'Black, Text 1' in the Fill Color gallery to change the fill color.

7 Click the Font Color arrow (Home tab | Font group) and then click 'Orange, Accent 6, Lighter 60%' (column 10, row 3) in the Font Color gallery to change the font color.

To Format the Column Titles and Total Row

The following steps center and underline the column titles, and create borders on the total row.

1 Select the range B4:G4 and then click the Center button (Home tab | Alignment group) to center the text in the cells.

2 CTRL+click cell A4 to add it to the selected range, and then use the Cell Styles button (Home tab | Styles group) to apply the Heading 3 cell style.

3 Select the range A13:G13 and then assign the Total cell style to the range.

4 Click an empty cell to deselect the range (Figure 5–19).

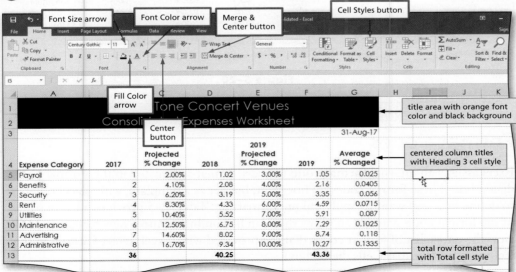

Figure 5–19

To Format with a Floating Dollar Sign

The consolidated worksheet for this module contains floating dollar signs in the first row of numbers and in the totals. The following steps use the Format Cells dialog box to assign a currency style with a floating dollar sign and two decimal places to the appropriate cells. Recall that a floating dollar sign always appears immediately to the left of the first significant digit in the cell, while the Accounting Number Format button (Home tab | Number group) creates a fixed dollar sign.

1 Select cell B5. While holding down the CTRL key, select the nonadjacent cells D5, F5, B13, D13, and F13. Right-click any selected cell to display the shortcut menu.

2 Click Format Cells on the shortcut menu to display the Format Cells dialog box. If necessary, click the Number tab (Format Cells dialog box) to display the Number sheet.

3 Click Currency in the Category list. If necessary, click the Symbol button and then click $ in the list.

4 Click the red ($1,234.10) in the Negative numbers list to select a currency format that displays negative numbers in red with parentheses and a floating dollar sign.

5 Click the OK button (Format Cells dialog box) to assign the Currency style.

6 Click an empty cell to deselect the previous cells (Figure 5–20).

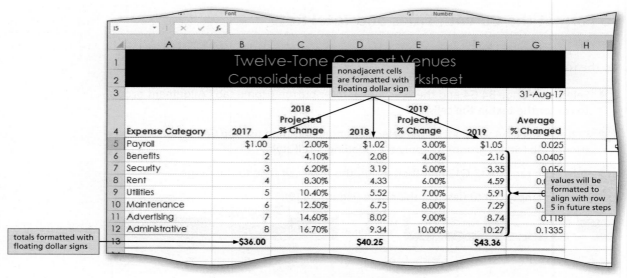

Figure 5–20

Format Codes

Excel assigns an internal **format code** to every format style listed in the Format Cells dialog box. These format codes do not print, but act as a template, with placeholders to define how you want to apply unique formatting. Table 5–5 provides a list of some of the format code symbols and how they can be combined into a new format code. To view the entire list of format codes that are provided with Excel, select Custom in the Category list (Format Cells dialog box).

Table 5–5 Format Symbols in Format Codes

Format Symbol	Example of Symbol in Code	Description
# (number sign)	###.##	Serves as a digit placeholder. If the value in a cell has more digits to the right of the decimal point than number signs in the format, Excel rounds the number. All digits to the left of the decimal point are displayed.
0 (zero)	0.00	Works like a number sign (#), except that if the number is less than 1, Excel displays a 0 in the ones' place.
. (period)	#0.00	Ensures Excel will display a decimal point in the number. The placement of zeros determines how many digits appear to the left and right of the decimal point.
% (percent)	0.00%	Displays numbers as percentages of 100. Excel multiplies the value of the cell by 100 and displays a percent sign after the number.
, (comma)	#,##0.00	Displays a comma as a thousands' separator.
( )	#0.00;(#0.00)	Displays parentheses around negative numbers.
$, +, or –	$#,##0.00; ($#,##0.00)	Displays a floating sign ($, +, or –).
* (asterisk)	$*##0.00	Displays a fixed sign ($, +, or –) to the left, followed by spaces until the first significant digit.
[color]	#.##;[Red]#.##	Displays the characters in the cell in the designated color. In the example, positive numbers appear in the default color, and negative numbers appear in red.
" " (quotation marks)	$0.00 "Surplus"; $-0.00 "Shortage"	Displays text along with numbers entered in a cell.
_ (underscore)	#,##0.00_)	Adds a space. When followed by a parentheses, positive numbers will align correctly with parenthetical negative numbers.

BTW

Sample Data
As you develop more sophisticated workbooks, it will become increasingly important that you create good test data to ensure your workbooks are free of errors. The more you test a workbook, the more confident you will be in the results generated. Always take the time to select sample data that tests the limits of the formulas.

Before you create custom format codes or modify existing codes, you should understand their makeup. A format code can have up to four sections: the desired format for positive numbers, the desired format for negative numbers, how zeros should be treated, and any desired format for text. Each section is separated by a semicolon. For example, the following format code would produce results similar to the sample values shown.

$* #,##0.00; [Magenta]$(#,##0.00); * "-"??; "The answer is "@

$ 15.75 $(1,238.99)   –   The answer is yes

A format code need not have all four sections. For most applications, a format code will have a positive section and possibly a negative section. If you omit the zero formatting section, zero values will use the positive number formatting.

BTW

Summing a Row or Column
You can reference an entire column or an entire row in a function argument by listing only the column or only the row. For example, = sum(a:a) sums all the values in all the cells in column A, and = sum(1:1) sums all the values in all the cells in row 1. You can verify this by entering = sum(a:a) in cell C1 and then begin entering numbers in a few of the cells in column A. Excel will respond by showing the sum of the numbers in cell C1.

To Create a Custom Format Code

1 FORMAT WORKSHEET | 2 FILL LINEAR SERIES | 3 USE DATE & ROUND FUNCTIONS | 4 APPLY CUSTOM FORMAT CODE
5 CREATE CELL STYLES | 6 POPULATE WORKSHEETS | 7 INSERT CHART | 8 LINK WORKBOOKS

The following steps create and assign a custom format code to the ranges that contain percentages. *Why?* *A workbook may call for a visual presentation of data that cannot be accomplished with Excel's existing format codes.* In this case, the format code will display percentages with two decimal places to the right of the decimal point and also display negative percentages in magenta with parentheses.

1

- CTRL+drag to select the ranges C5:C12, E5:E12, and G5:G12, right-click any of the selected ranges to display the shortcut menu, and then click Format Cells to display the Format Cells dialog box.

- If necessary, click the Number tab (Format Cells dialog box) and then click Custom in the Category list.

- Delete the word General in the Type box (Format Cells dialog box) and then type `0.00%;[Magenta](0.00%)` to enter a custom format code (Figure 5–21).

Q&A What does the custom format mean?

The custom format has been modified to show percentages with two decimal places and to show negative percentages in magenta with parentheses. A zero value will display as 0.00%. In the Sample area, Excel displays a sample of the custom format assigned to the first number in the selected ranges.

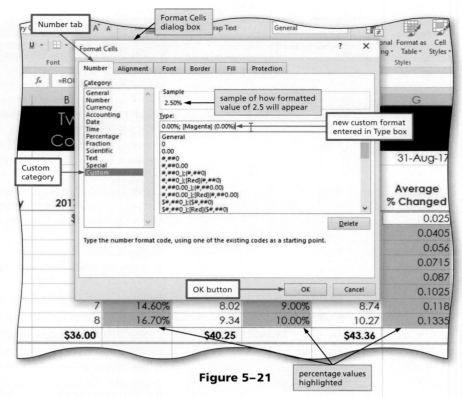

Figure 5–21

2

- Click the OK button (Format Cells dialog box) to display the numbers using the custom format code (Figure 5–22).

Q&A Can I reuse the custom format code?

Yes. When you create a new custom format code, Excel adds it to the bottom of the Type list on the Number sheet (Format Cells dialog box) to make it available for future use.

fx | =ROUND((C5+E5)/2,4)

Twelve-Tone Concert Venues
Consolidated Expenses Worksheet

31-Aug-17

2017	2018 Projected % Change	2018	2019 Projected % Change	2019	Average % Changed
$1.00	2.00%	$1.02	3.00%	$1.05	2.50%
2	4.10%	2.08	4.00%	2.16	4.05%
3	6.20%	3.19	5.00%	3.35	5.60%
4	8.30%	4.33	6.00%	4.59	7.15%
5	10.40%	5.52	7.00%	5.91	8.70%
6	12.50%	6.75	8.00%	7.29	10.25%
7	14.60%	8.02	9.00%	8.74	11.80%
8	16.70%	9.34	10.00%	10.27	13.35%
$36.00		$40.25		$43.36	

Figure 5–22

Other Ways

1. Select range or ranges, click Number Format Dialog Box Launcher (Home tab | Number group), click Custom in Category list (Format Cells dialog box | Number tab), enter format code in Type box, click OK button

To Format with the Comma Style

The following steps format the numbers other than the first row or totals with the comma style.

1 Select the ranges B6:B12, D6:D12, and F6:F12.

2 Click the Comma Style button (Home tab | Number group) to display the numbers in the selected ranges using the comma style.

3 Select an empty cell to deselect the range.

Q&A Why is the comma style used for numbers that are not large enough to display commas?
The comma style allows the values in the cells to align properly with the values in row 5, which are formatted with the currency style with floating dollar signs and parentheses for negative numbers.

Creating a Cell Style

Recall that a cell style is a group of built-in format specifications, such as font, font style, color, size, alignment, borders, and shading. A cell style also may contain information regarding nonvisual characteristics, such as cell protection. Earlier you used the Title cell style to format the worksheet headings. Now you will learn how to create a custom cell style. In addition to those styles listed in the Cell Styles gallery, Excel makes several cell styles available with all workbooks and themes, such as currency, comma, and percent, listed in the Number group (Home tab).

BTW

Accuracy
The result of an arithmetic operation, such as multiplication or division, is accurate to the factor with the least number of decimal places.

Tips to remember when creating a new style

• When you are creating a cell style, pay close attention to the Style Includes area of the Style dialog box (Figure 5–24). A style affects the format of a cell or range of cells only if the corresponding check box is selected. For example, if the Font check box is not selected in the Style dialog box, then the cell maintains the font format it had before the style was assigned.

• If you assign two different styles to a cell or range of cells, Excel adds the second style to the first, rather than replacing it. If the two cell styles include different settings for an attribute, such as fill color, then Excel applies the setting for the second style.

• You can merge styles from another workbook into the active workbook by using the Merge Styles command in the Cell Styles gallery (Home tab | Styles group). Before you use the Merge Styles command, however, you must open the workbook that contains the desired styles.

• The six check boxes in the Style dialog box are identical to the six tabs in the Format Cells dialog box (Figure 5–24).

CONSIDER THIS

Once created, new cell styles appear at the top of the Cell Styles gallery, and are saved for the current workbook. By right-clicking the style in the Cell Styles gallery, you can delete, modify, or duplicate the style. Create a new style in a workbook or merge styles when you plan to use a group of format specifications over and over.

It is easy to confuse cell styles and format codes. While they overlap slightly in some areas, cell styles have more to do with words, fonts and borders, while format codes have more to do with values, decimal places, and special characters.

BTW

Normal Style
The Normal style is the format style that Excel initially assigns to all cells in a workbook. If you change the Normal style, Excel applies the new format specifications to all cells that are not assigned another style.

To Create a New Cell Style

The following steps create a new style called 4-Digit Year by modifying the existing Normal style. *Why? Creating a new style allows you to group a number of cell formats together for ease, reuse, and consistency of application.* The **Normal style** is the default style that is applied to all cells when you start Excel. The Normal style includes characteristics such as font, border, alignment, and other settings. You will create a new style to include a date and alignment format, along with other characteristics of the Normal style. The new style will use dark orange text and be centered within the cell.

- Click the Cell Styles button (Home tab | Styles group) to display the Cell Styles gallery (Figure 5–23).

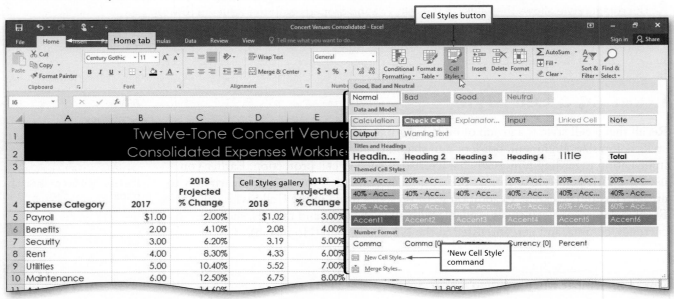

Figure 5–23

2

- Click 'New Cell Style' in the Cell Styles gallery to display the Style dialog box.
- In the Style name text box, type **4-Digit Year** to name the new style (Figure 5–24).

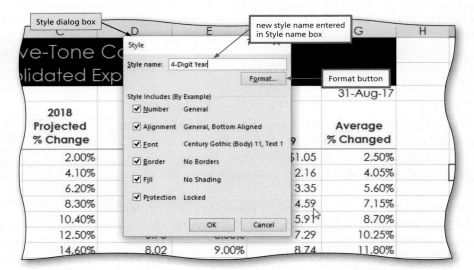

Figure 5–24

3

- Click the Format button (Style dialog box) to display the Format Cells dialog box.

- If necessary, click the Number tab (Format Cells dialog box), click Date in the Category list, and then click '14-Mar-2012' in the Type list to define the new style as a date style (Figure 5–25).

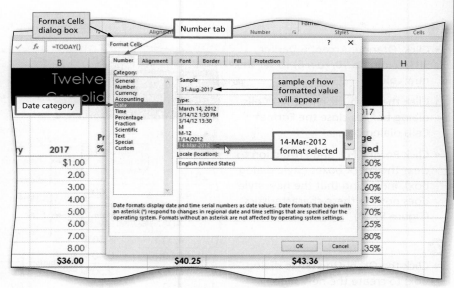

Figure 5–25

4

- Click the Alignment tab (Format Cells dialog box) to display the Alignment sheet. Click the Horizontal button, and then click Center to define the alignment of the new style (Figure 5–26).

Q&A What is the difference between the text alignment options here and the ones on the Home tab?
Many of them are the same; however, in this dialog box, you can make adjustments that are more precise. Keep in mind that you cannot use the buttons on the Home tab when you are creating a new style.

Figure 5–26

5

- Click the Font tab (Format Cells dialog box) and then click the Color button to display the Color gallery (Figure 5–27).

Q&A What are superscript and subscript on the Font sheet?
A **superscript** is a small number placed above the normal text line to indicate exponentiation. A **subscript** is a small number placed below the normal text line such as those used in scientific and chemical notations.

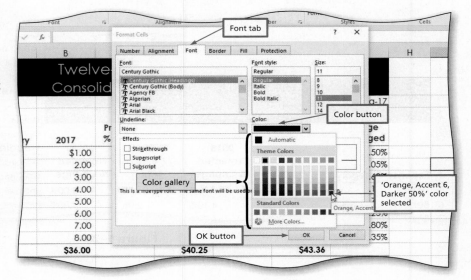

Figure 5–27

- Click 'Orange, Accent 6 Darker 50%' (column 10, row 6) to set the new color.

- Click the OK button (Format Cells dialog box) to close the Format Cells dialog box.

- Click Border, Fill, and Protection to clear the check boxes (Style dialog box), indicating that the new style does not use these characteristics (Figure 5–28).

- Click the OK button (Style dialog box) to create the new style.

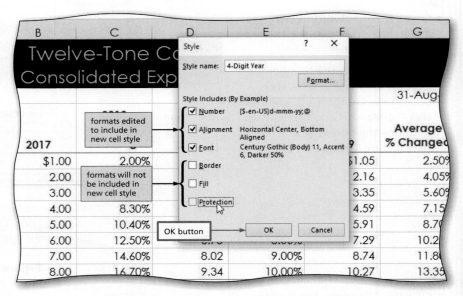

Figure 5–28

To Apply a New Style

1 FORMAT WORKSHEET | 2 FILL LINEAR SERIES | 3 USE DATE & ROUND FUNCTIONS | 4 APPLY CUSTOM FORMAT CODE
5 CREATE CELL STYLES | 6 POPULATE WORKSHEETS | 7 INSERT CHART | 8 LINK WORKBOOKS

In earlier steps, cell G3 was assigned the system date using the TODAY function. The following steps assign cell G3 the new 4-Digit Year style, which centers the content of the cell and assigns it the date format dd-mmm-yyyy in orange. *Why? Using a style ensures a consistent application of formatting instructions.*

- Select cell G3 and then click the Cell Styles button (Home tab | Styles group) to display the Cell Styles gallery (Figure 5–29).

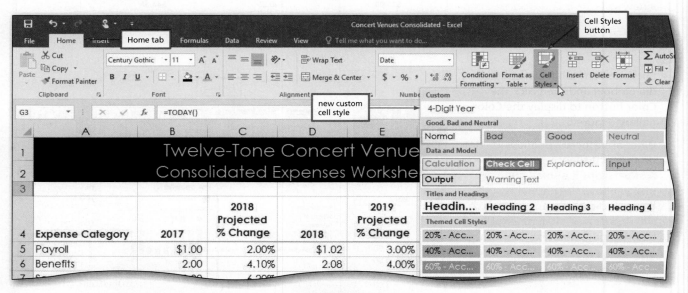

Figure 5–29

2

- Click the 4-Digit Year style to assign the new style to the selected cell (Figure 5–30).

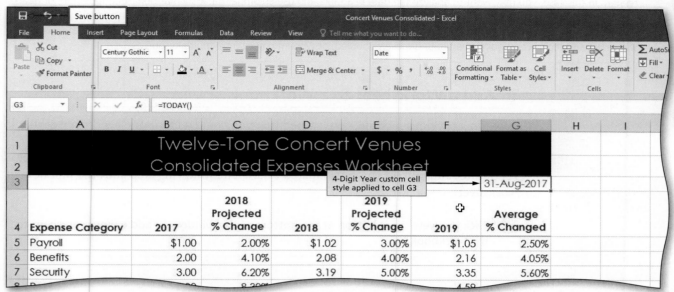

Figure 5–30

To Use the Spelling Checker

The formatting is complete. The following steps use the spelling checker to check the spelling in the worksheet, and then save the consolidated worksheet.

1 Select cell B2, click the Review tab, and then click the Spelling button (Review tab | Proofing group) to check the spelling in the workbook. Correct any misspelled words.

2 Click the Save button on the Quick Access Toolbar to save the workbook.

Break Point: If you wish to take a break, this is a good place to do so. You can exit Excel. To resume at a later time, run Excel, open the file called Concert Venues Consolidated, and continue following the steps from this location forward.

Working with Multiple Worksheets

A workbook contains one worksheet by default. You can add more worksheets, limited only by the amount of memory in your computer. When working with multiple worksheets, you should name and color the sheet tabs so that you can identify them easily. With the consolidated worksheet complete, the next steps are to insert and populate worksheets in the workbook, by copying the data from the consolidated worksheet to the location worksheets, and adjusting the formatting and values. You will learn three different ways to copy data across worksheets.

BTW
Default Number of Worksheets
An alternative to adding worksheets is to change the default number of worksheets before you open a new workbook. To change the default number of worksheets in a blank workbook, click Options in the Backstage view and then change the number in the 'Include this many sheets' box in the 'When creating new workbooks' area (Excel Options dialog box).

How do I determine how many worksheets to add to a workbook?

Excel provides three basic choices when you consider how to organize data. Use a single worksheet when the data is tightly related. In this case, you may want to analyze the data in a table and use columnar data, such as department, region, or quarter, to identify groups. Use multiple worksheets when data is related but can stand alone on its own. For example, each region, department, or quarter may contain enough detailed information that you may want to analyze the data in separate worksheets. Use multiple workbooks when data is loosely coupled, or when it comes from multiple sources.

To Add a Worksheet to a Workbook

In a previous module, you learned that you could add a worksheet to a workbook by clicking the New sheet button at the bottom of the workbook. The Concert Venues Consolidated workbook requires four worksheets — one for each of the three venue sites and one for the consolidated totals. The following step adds the first new worksheet.

1 Click the New sheet button at the bottom of the window to add a new worksheet to the workbook.

To Copy and Paste from One Worksheet to Another

1 FORMAT WORKSHEET | 2 FILL LINEAR SERIES | 3 USE DATE & ROUND FUNCTIONS | 4 APPLY CUSTOM FORMAT CODE
5 CREATE CELL STYLES | 6 POPULATE WORKSHEETS | 7 INSERT CHART | 8 LINK WORKBOOKS

With two worksheets in the workbook, the next step is to copy the contents of Sheet1 to Sheet2. *Why? When the desired content of the new worksheet mirrors or closely follows that of an existing worksheet, copying the existing content minimizes the chances of introducing errors.* Sheet1 eventually will be used as the Consolidated worksheet with consolidated data. Sheet2 will be used for one of the three venue site worksheets.

In the process of copying, you must first select the populated cells. You can press CTRL+A to select the rectangular range that contains populated cells. You can press CTRL+A twice to select all of the rows and columns in the worksheet, you can drag around the cells to create a selection, or you can click the Select All button located just below the Name box at the intersection of the row and column headings. The manner in which you select all of the data depends on where you are in the worksheet and your personal preference of using the mouse versus the keyboard. The following steps copy the content of one worksheet to another using the Select All button.

1

- Click the Sheet1 sheet tab to display the worksheet.

- Click the Select All button to select the entire worksheet.

- Click the Copy button (Home tab | Clipboard group) to copy the contents of the worksheet (Figure 5–31).

Q&A
Can I use the shortcut keys, CTRL+C and CTRL+V, to copy and paste?
Yes. In addition, you can use the shortcut menu to copy and paste.

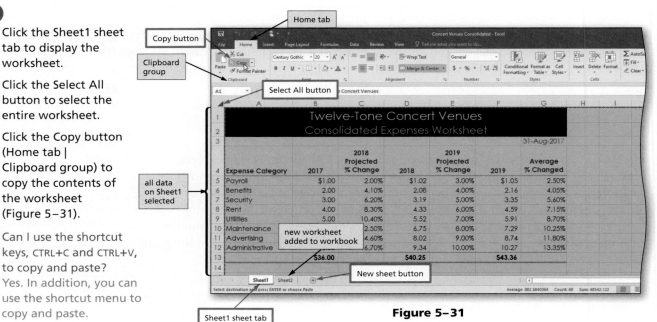

Figure 5–31

2

- Click the Sheet2 sheet tab at the bottom of the worksheet to display Sheet2.

- Press the ENTER key to copy the data from the Office Clipboard to the selected sheet.

- Zoom to approximately 120% (Figure 5–32).

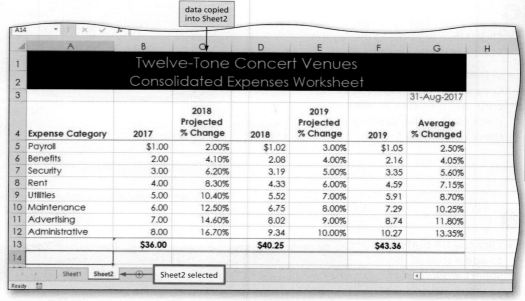

Figure 5–32

Q&A Can I use the Paste button (Home tab | Clipboard group) to paste the data?
Yes. Recall that if you complete a paste operation using the ENTER key however, the marquee disappears and the Office Clipboard is cleared, as it no longer contains the copied data following the action.

Other Ways

1. Select cells, press CTRL+C, select destination cell press CTRL+V
2. Select cells, press CTRL+C, select destination cell, press ENTER
3. Right-click selected cells, click Copy, right-click destination cell, click appropriate Paste button

To Copy a Worksheet Using a Shortcut Menu

1 FORMAT WORKSHEET | 2 FILL LINEAR SERIES | 3 USE DATE & ROUND FUNCTIONS | 4 APPLY CUSTOM FORMAT CODE
5 CREATE CELL STYLES | 6 POPULATE WORKSHEETS | 7 INSERT CHART | 8 LINK WORKBOOKS

The following steps create a worksheet using the shortcut menu that appears when you right-click a sheet tab. *Why? The shortcut menu and resulting dialog box allow you more flexibility in exactly where and how to move and copy.*

1

- Right-click the Sheet1 sheet tab to display the shortcut menu (Figure 5–33).

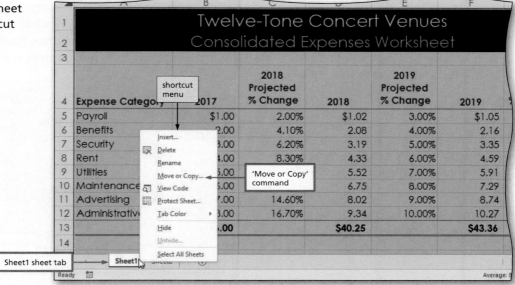

Figure 5–33

2

- Click 'Move or Copy' to display the Move or Copy dialog box.

- In the Before sheet list (Move or Copy dialog box), click '(move to end)' and then click to place a check mark in the 'Create a copy' check box (Figure 5–34).

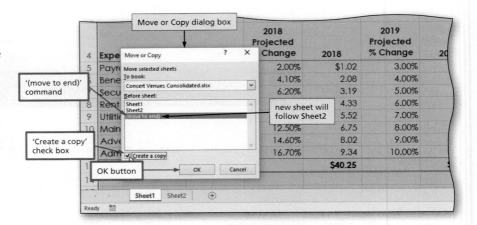

Figure 5–34

3

- Click the OK button to add a copy of the Sheet1 worksheet to the workbook (Figure 5–35).

Q&A
Why is it named Sheet1 (2) instead of Sheet3?
Excel indicates that it is a copy by referring to the original sheet.

	Twelve-Tone Concert Venues Consolidated Expenses Worksheet						
3							31-Aug-2017
4	Expense Category	2017	2018 Projected % Change	2018	2019 Projected % Change	2019	Average % Changed
5	Payroll	$1.00	2.00%	$1.02	3.00%	$1.05	2.50%
6	Benefits	2.00	4.10%	2.08	4.00%	2.16	4.05%
7	Security	3.00	6.20%	3.19	5.00%	3.35	5.60%
8	Rent	4.00	8.30%	4.33	6.00%	4.59	7.15%
9	Utilities	5.00	10.40%	5.52	7.00%	5.91	8.70%
10	Maintenance	6.00	12.50%	6.75	8.00%	7.29	10.25%
11	Advertising	7.00	14.60%	8.02	9.00%	8.74	11.80%
12	Administrative	8.00	16.70%	9.34	10.00%	10.27	13.35%
13		$36.00		$40.25		$43.36	
14							

Figure 5–35

To Copy a Worksheet Using the CTRL Key

1 FORMAT WORKSHEET | 2 FILL LINEAR SERIES | 3 USE DATE & ROUND FUNCTIONS | 4 APPLY CUSTOM FORMAT CODE

5 CREATE CELL STYLES | 6 POPULATE WORKSHEETS | 7 INSERT CHART | 8 LINK WORKBOOKS

Another way to create a copy of a worksheet is by pressing the CTRL key while you drag the sheet tab. *Why? Using the CTRL key is faster than selecting and copying, then pasting.* As you drag, Excel will display a small triangular arrow to show the destination location of your copy. The following steps create a third copy, for a total of four worksheets in the workbook.

1

- Select Sheet1.

- CTRL+drag the Sheet1 sheet tab to a location to the right of the other sheet tabs. Do not release the drag (Figure 5–36).

2

- Release the drag to create the worksheet copy named Sheet1 (3).

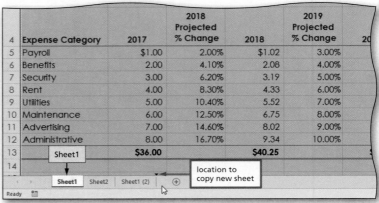

Figure 5–36

To Drill an Entry through Worksheets

1 FORMAT WORKSHEET | 2 FILL LINEAR SERIES | 3 USE DATE & ROUND FUNCTIONS | 4 APPLY CUSTOM FORMAT CODE
5 CREATE CELL STYLES | 6 POPULATE WORKSHEETS | 7 INSERT CHART | 8 LINK WORKBOOKS

The next step is to replace the sample numbers for the 2018 and 2019 projected percentage change. The percentage changes are identical on all four sheets. For example, the 2018 % change for payroll in cell D6 is 1.50% on all four sheets.

To speed data entry, Excel allows you to enter a number in the same cell through all selected worksheets. This technique is referred to as **drilling an entry**. *Why drill an entry? In cases where multiple worksheets have the same layout and the same calculations performed on data, drilling entries of data or formulas ensures consistency across the worksheets.* When you drill, all affected sheets must be selected. Table 5–6 contains the new figures for cells C5:C12 and E5:E12.

Table 5–6 Projected % Change Values for 2018 and 2019				
Category	Cell	2018 Projected % Change	Cell	2019 Projected % Change
Payroll	C5	1.5	E5	1.5
Benefits	C6	2.5	E6	3
Security	C7	2	E7	2
Rent	C8	0	E8	1
Utilities	C9	1	E9	1
Maintenance	C10	0	E10	1
Advertising	C11	−1	E11	−1
Administrative	C12	−2	E12	−2.25

The following steps select all sheets, drill the 2018 and 2019 projected percentage change entries from Table 5–6 through all four worksheets, and then ungroup the selection.

1

- Right-click Sheet1 and then click 'Select All Sheets' on the shortcut menu.

- Select cell C5. Type **1.5** and then press the DOWN ARROW key to change sample data in the selected cell to the actual value.

- Enter the 15 remaining 2018 and 2019 values from Table 5–6 to the appropriate cells to display the actual percentages (Figure 5–37).

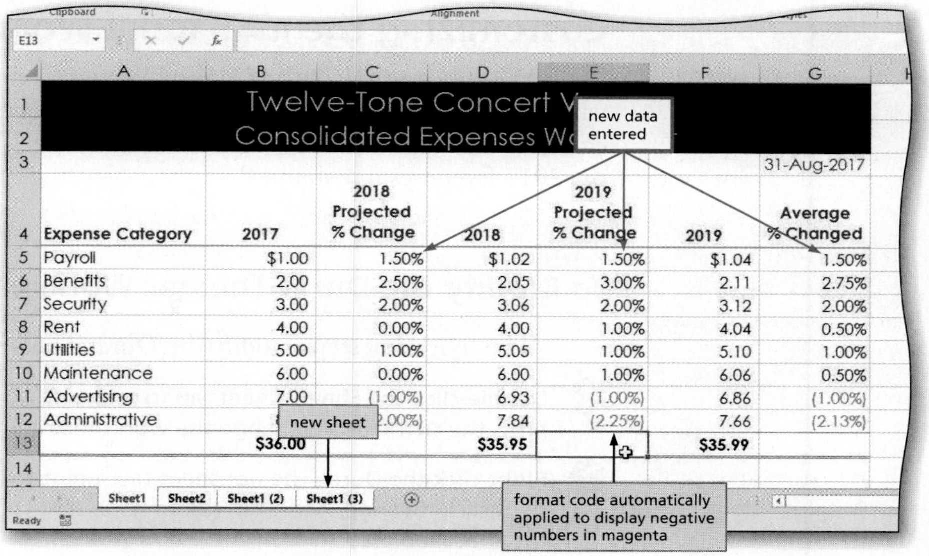

Q&A What is the benefit of drilling data through worksheets?
In these steps, 16 new numbers were entered on one worksheet. By drilling the entries through the other worksheets, 64 new numbers now appear, 16 on each of the worksheets. Excel's capability of drilling data through selected worksheets is an efficient way to enter data that is common among worksheets.

Figure 5–37

2

- Right-click Sheet1 and then click Ungroup Sheets on the shortcut menu.

🔎 **Experiment**

- One at a time, click the Sheet2 sheet tab, the Sheet1 (2) sheet tab, and the Sheet1 (3) sheet tab to verify that all four worksheets are identical.

BTW
Deleting Worksheets
Recall from Module 4 that you can delete a worksheet by right-clicking the sheet tab of the worksheet you want to delete, and then clicking Delete on the shortcut menu.

Selecting and Deselecting Sheets

Beginning Excel users sometimes have difficulty trying to select and deselect sheets. Table 5–7 summarizes how to select and deselect multiple sheets using a mouse and keyboard.

BTW
Selecting Multiple Worksheets
When multiple worksheets are selected, the Excel title bar reflects the selection by adding the notation, [Group]. All of the sheet tabs also are highlighted.

Table 5–7 Summary of How to Select and Deselect Sheets

Task	How to Carry Out the Task
Select individual sheet	Click sheet tab.
Select all sheets	Right-click any sheet tab, click 'Select All Sheets' on shortcut menu.
Select adjacent sheets	Select the first sheet by clicking its tab, and then hold down the SHIFT key and click the sheet tab at the other end of the list of adjacent sheet tabs.
Select nonadjacent sheets	Select the first sheet by clicking its tab, then hold down the CTRL key and click the sheet tabs of the remaining sheets you want to select.
Deselect all sheets	Right-click any sheet tab, click Ungroup Sheets on shortcut menu or click the individual sheet tab that you wish to select.
Deselect one of many sheets	CTRL+click the sheet tab you want to deselect.

Customizing the Individual Worksheets

With the outline of the Concert Venues Consolidated workbook created, you will modify the individual worksheets by changing the worksheet name, sheet tab color, and worksheet subtitle. You also will change the color of the title area and enter the 2017 Expenses in column B.

To Modify the Durat Theater Worksheet

The following steps modify the Durat Theater worksheet (Sheet2).

1 Double-click the Sheet2 sheet tab to select it. Type **Durat Theater** and then press the ENTER key to change the worksheet name.

2 Right-click the Durat Theater sheet tab, point to Tab Color on the shortcut menu, and then click 'Orange, Accent 6' (column 10, row 1) in the Theme Colors area to change the sheet tab color.

3 Double-click cell A2. Drag through the word, Consolidated, to select the text, and then type **Durat Theater** to change the worksheet subtitle.

4 Select the range A1:A2. Click the Fill Color arrow (Home tab | Font group) and then click 'Orange, Accent 6' (column 10, row 1) in the Theme Colors area (Fill Color gallery) to change the fill color of the selected range.

5 Click the Font Color arrow (Home tab | Font group) and then click Automatic in the Font Color gallery to change the font color of the selected range.

6 Enter the following data in the indicated cells:

Cell	Data for Durat Theater	Cell	Data for Durat Theater
B5	79207.20	B9	3080.00
B6	15247.39	B10	4295.20
B7	28175.65	B11	3599.64
B8	14400.00	B12	2500.00

7 Click an empty cell to deselect the previous cell (Figure 5–38).

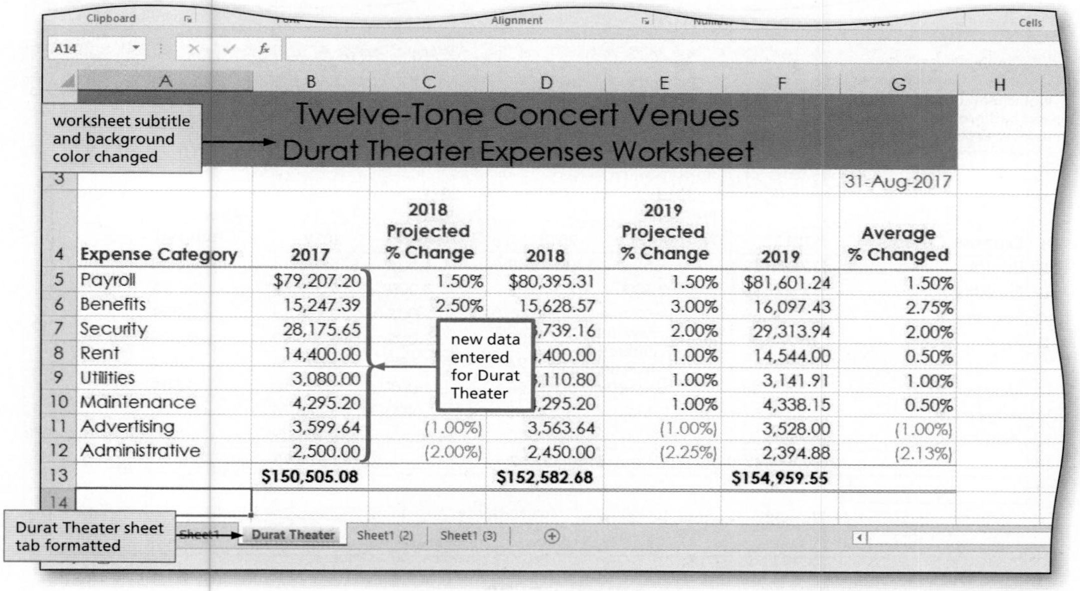

Figure 5–38

To Modify the Truman House Sheet

The following steps modify the Truman House Theater worksheet Sheet1 (2)

1 Double-click the Sheet1 (2) sheet tab to select it. Type **Truman House** and then press the ENTER key to change the worksheet name.

2 Right-click the Truman House sheet tab, point to Tab Color on the shortcut menu, and then click 'Gray - 50%, Accent 1, Lighter 60%' (column 5, row 3) in the Theme Colors area to change the sheet tab color.

3 Double-click cell A2. Drag through the word, Consolidated, to select the text, and then type **Truman House** to change the worksheet subtitle.

4 Select the range A1:A2. Click the Fill Color arrow (Home tab | Font group) and then click 'Gray - 50%, Accent 1, Lighter 60%' (column 5, row 3) in the Theme Colors area (Fill Color gallery) to change the fill color of the selected range.

5 Click the Font Color arrow (Home tab | Font group) and then click Automatic in the Font Color gallery to change the font color of the selected range.

6 Enter the following data in the indicated cells:

Cell	Data for Truman House Theater	Cell	Data for Truman House Theater
B5	72870.62	B9	2833.60
B6	14027.60	B10	3951.58
B7	25921.60	B11	3311.67
B8	13248.00	B12	2250.00

7 Click an empty cell to deselect the previous cell (Figure 5–39).

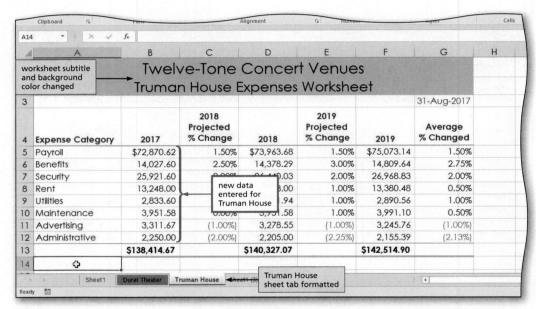

Figure 5–39

To Modify the Stage Xanadu Worksheet

The following steps modify the Stage Xanadu worksheet Sheet1 (3).

1 Double-click the Sheet1 (3) sheet tab to select it. Type **Stage Xanadu** and then press the ENTER key to change the worksheet name.

2 Right-click the Stage Xanadu sheet tab, point to Tab Color on the shortcut menu, and then click Light Blue in the Standard Colors area to change the sheet tab color.

3 Double-click cell A2. Drag through the word, Consolidated, to select the text, and then type **Stage Xanadu** to change the worksheet subtitle.

④ Select the range A1:A2. Click the Fill Color arrow (Home tab | Font group) and then click Light Blue in the Standard Colors area (Fill Color gallery) to change the fill color of the selected range.

⑤ Click the Font Color arrow (Home tab | Font group) and then click Automatic in the Font Color gallery to change the font color of the selected range.

⑥ Enter the following data in the indicated cells:

Cell	Data for Stage Xanadu	Cell	Data for Stage Xanadu
B5	88712.06	B9	3449.60
B6	17077.07	B10	4810.62
B7	31556.73	B11	4031.60
B8	16128.00	B12	2700.00

⑦ Click an empty cell to deselect the previous cell (Figure 5–40).

⑧ Click the Save button on the Quick Access Toolbar.

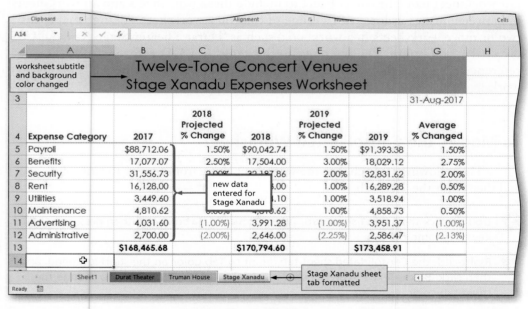

Figure 5–40

Referencing Cells Across Worksheets

With the three location worksheets complete, you now can consolidate the data. Because this consolidation worksheet contains totals of the data, you need to reference cell data from other worksheets.

BTW

Drilling an Entry
Besides drilling a number down through a workbook, you can drill a format, a function, or a formula down through a workbook.

BTW
Importing Data
Expenses, such as those entered into the range B5:B12, often are maintained in another workbook, file, or database. If the expenses are maintained elsewhere, ways exist to link to a workbook or to import data from a file or database into a workbook. Linking to a workbook is discussed later in this module. To see a list of typical sources of outside data, click the `Get Data From Other Sources' button (Data tab | Get External Data group).

BTW
3-D References
If you are summing numbers on noncontiguous sheets, hold down the CTRL key rather than the shift key when selecting the sheets.

To reference cells in other worksheets within a single workbook, you use the worksheet name, which serves as the **worksheet reference**, combined with the cell reference. The worksheet reference must be enclosed within single quotation marks (') when the worksheet name contains a non-alphabetical character such as a space. Excel requires an exclamation point (!) as a delimiter between the worksheet reference and the cell reference. Therefore, the reference to cell B5 on the Durat Theater worksheet would be entered as

= 'Durat Theater'!B5

These worksheet and cell references can be used in formulas, such as

= 'Durat Theater'!B5 + 'Truman House'!B5 + 'Stage Xanadu'!B5

A worksheet reference such as 'Durat Theater' always is absolute, meaning that the worksheet reference remains constant if you were to copy the formula to other locations.

Worksheet references also can be used in functions and range references such as

= SUM('Durat Theater:Stage Xanadu'!B5)

The SUM argument ('Durat Theater:Stage Xanadu'!B5) instructs Excel to sum cell B5 on each of the three worksheets (Durat Theater, Truman House, and Stage Xanadu). The colon (:) delimiter between the first worksheet name and the last worksheet name instructs Excel to include these worksheets and all worksheets in between, just as it does with a range of cells on a worksheet. A range that spans two or more worksheets in a workbook, such as 'Durat Theater:Stage Xanadu'!C6, is called a **3-D range**. The reference to this range is a **3-D reference**. A 3-D reference is also absolute. You can paste the 3-D reference to other cells on the worksheet.

To Modify the Consolidated Worksheet

The following steps change the worksheet name from Sheet1 to Consolidated and then color the sheet tab.

1 Double-click the Sheet1 sheet tab. Type `Consolidated` and then press the ENTER key to rename the tab.

2 Right-click the Consolidated sheet tab, point to Tab Color on the shortcut menu, and then click 'Black, Text 1' (row 1, column 2) in the Theme Colors area to change the sheet tab color.

To Enter a 3-D Reference

1 FORMAT WORKSHEET | 2 FILL LINEAR SERIES | 3 USE DATE & ROUND FUNCTIONS | 4 APPLY CUSTOM FORMAT CODE
5 CREATE CELL STYLES | 6 POPULATE WORKSHEETS | **7 INSERT CHART** | **8 LINK WORKBOOKS**

To consolidate the payroll expenses, the following steps create 3-D references in cells B5, D5, and F5 on the Consolidated worksheet. *Why? Using 3-D references is the most efficient method of referencing cells that reside in the same location on different worksheets.* You can enter a worksheet reference in a cell by typing the worksheet reference or by clicking the appropriate sheet tab while in Point mode. When you click the sheet tab, Excel activates the worksheet and automatically adds the worksheet name and an exclamation point after the insertion point in the formula bar. Then, click the desired cell or drag through the cells you want to reference on the sheet.

If the range of cells to be referenced is located on several worksheets (as when selecting a 3-D range), click the first sheet tab and then select the cell(s). Finally, SHIFT+click the last sheet tab you want to reference. Excel will include the cell(s) on the first worksheet, on the last worksheet, and those on any worksheets in between.

1

- Select cell B5 and then click the Sum button (Home tab | Editing group) to display the SUM function (Figure 5–41).

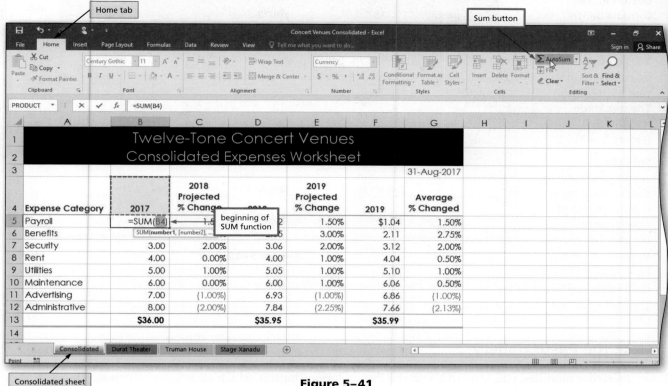

Figure 5–41

2

- Click the Durat Theater tab and then click cell B5 to select the first portion of the argument for the SUM function.

- SHIFT+click the Stage Xanadu tab to select the ending range of the argument for the SUM function (Figure 5–42).

Q&A Could I just type the 3-D reference? Yes, however the Point mode is used in this step, which prevents any errors in typing the reference.

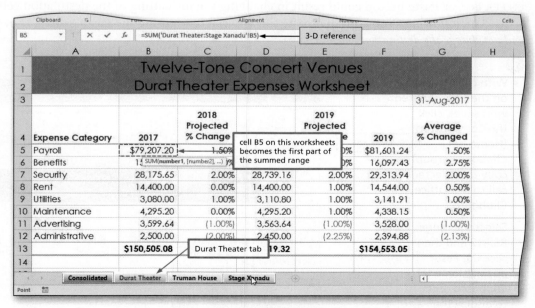

Figure 5–42

3

- Click the Enter button in the formula bar to enter the SUM function with the 3-D references in the selected cell, in this case =SUM('Durat Theater:Stage Xanadu'!B5) (Figure 5–43).

Q&A

Should each worksheet name in the function have individual sets of single quotes?

No, in a 3-D reference that uses a range, Excel requires a single quote before the first worksheet name in the range and an ending single quote after the last worksheet name.

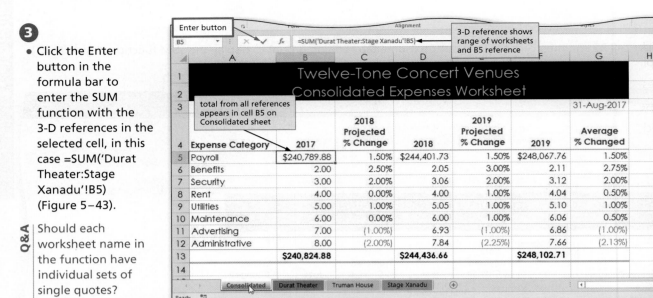

Figure 5–43

To Use the Paste Gallery

In earlier modules, you learned about the Paste Options button, which allows you to choose different ways to paste and copy formulas, values, and functions. The Paste gallery, which displays when you click the Paste arrow (Home tab | Clipboard group), offers many of the same choices, and depending on the type of pasting, many others. When copying a formula that includes a 3-D reference, it is advisable to choose the Formulas button from the Paste gallery to copy without formatting. Using other paste methods such as the fill handle, ENTER key, or Paste button could result in changing the formatting of the destination cells.

The following steps copy and paste the 3-D reference using the Paste gallery. *Why? Using the Paste gallery will not change the destination formatting.*

1

- With cell B5 active on the Consolidated worksheet, click the Copy button (Home tab | Clipboard group) to copy the selected cell to the Office Clipboard.

- Select the range B6:B12 and then click the Paste arrow (Home tab | Clipboard group) to display the Paste gallery (Figure 5–44).

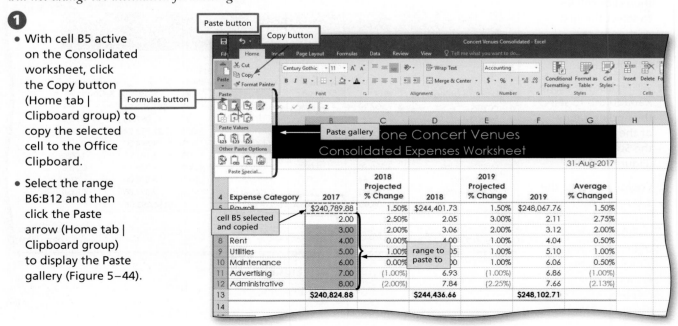

Figure 5–44

2

- Click the Formulas button (column 2, row 1) in the Paste gallery to copy the SUM function to the desired range, replicating the 3-D references.

- Press the ESC key to clear the marquee (Figure 5–45).

- Deselect the previous range.

- Click the Save button on the Quick Access Toolbar to save the workbook.

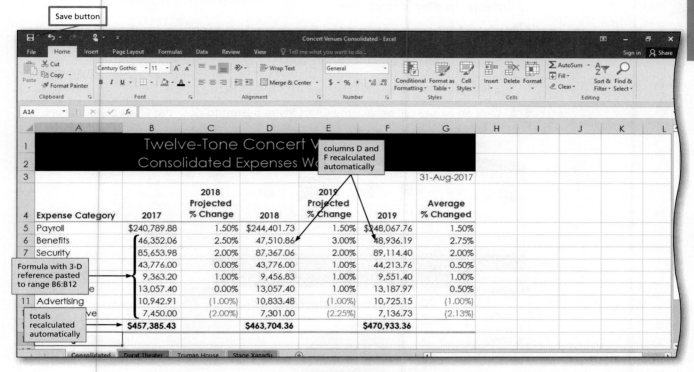

Figure 5–45

Other Ways

1. Right-click selected cell(s), click Copy, right-click destination cell(s), click appropriate Paste button

Break Point: If you wish to take a break, this is a good place to do so. You can exit Excel. To resume at a later time, run Excel, open the file called Concert Venues Consolidated, and continue following the steps from this location forward.

Formatting Pie Charts

In Module 1, you created a pie chart. Pie charts show the contribution of each piece of data to the whole, or total, of the data. You can format a pie chart in many ways including resizing, moving, rotating, adding data labels and leader lines, adding a decorative background, and exploding a slice.

As outlined in the requirements document in Table 5–1, the worksheet should include a pie chart to represent graphically the 2017 expenses totals for all three venues. The pie chart resides at the bottom of the consolidated worksheet, so it will print on the same page.

BTW

Y-Rotation and Perspective
The Y-Rotation arrows tilt the chart toward the back or front, allowing you to control the elevation of the chart. You can tilt the chart toward or away from you in order to enhance the view of the chart. The Perspective value makes close slices appear larger and those further away appear smaller.

To Insert a 3-D Pie Chart on a Worksheet

The following steps insert the 3-D pie chart on the Consolidated worksheet.

1 Select the range A5:B12 to identify the category names and data for the pie chart.

2 Display the Insert tab, click the 'Insert Pie or Doughnut Chart' button (Insert tab | Charts group), and then click 3-D Pie in the Insert Pie or Doughnut Chart gallery to create the desired chart type.

3 Click the chart title, select the text, and then type `2017 Consolidated Expenses` to change the chart title.

4 Deselect the chart title, click the Chart Styles button to display the Chart styles gallery, and then apply Style 3 to the chart (Figure 5–46).

5 Click an empty cell or click the Chart Styles button to close the Chart Styles gallery.

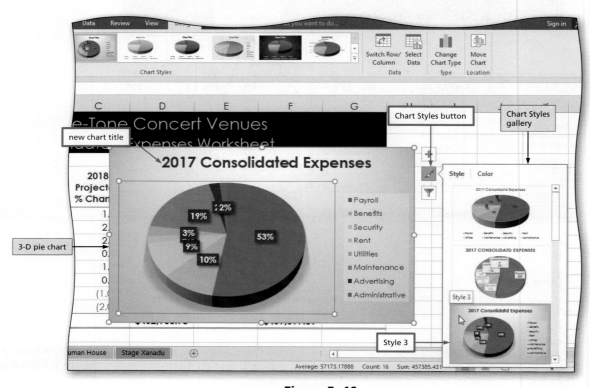

Figure 5–46

To Move a Chart on the Same Worksheet

1 FORMAT WORKSHEET | 2 FILL LINEAR SERIES | 3 USE DATE & ROUND FUNCTIONS | 4 APPLY CUSTOM FORMAT CODE
5 CREATE CELL STYLES | 6 POPULATE WORKSHEETS | 7 INSERT CHART | 8 LINK WORKBOOKS

The following step moves the chart to the space below the data that was used to create the chart. *Why? By default, Excel places charts in the center of the worksheet. You need to move it in order to uncover the data on the worksheet.*

- Point to the border of the chart. When the pointer changes to a four-headed arrow, drag the chart below the worksheet numbers to the desired location (in this case, approximately cell A15) (Figure 5–47).

Experiment

- Point to each of the styles in the Chart Styles group (Design tab) and watch the chart change to reflect each style.

Q&A Could I use the Move Chart button (Chart Tools Design tab | Location group) to move the chart? No. That button moves the chart from sheet to sheet rather than to a new location on the same worksheet.

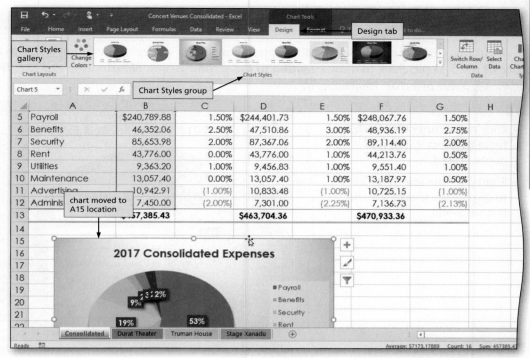

Figure 5–47

To Resize a Chart

1 FORMAT WORKSHEET | 2 FILL LINEAR SERIES | 3 USE DATE & ROUND FUNCTIONS | 4 APPLY CUSTOM FORMAT CODE
5 CREATE CELL STYLES | 6 POPULATE WORKSHEETS | 7 INSERT CHART | 8 LINK WORKBOOKS

The following step resizes the chart to make it larger and more legible. *Why? The chart as created by Excel may not be the optimal size for your worksheet needs.*

①

- If necessary, scroll down until you can see both the bottom of the chart and row 34.

- SHIFT+drag the lower-right resizing handle of the chart until the chart is the desired size (in this case, approximately to cell G34).

- If necessary, zoom out until you can see the entire chart (Figure 5–48).

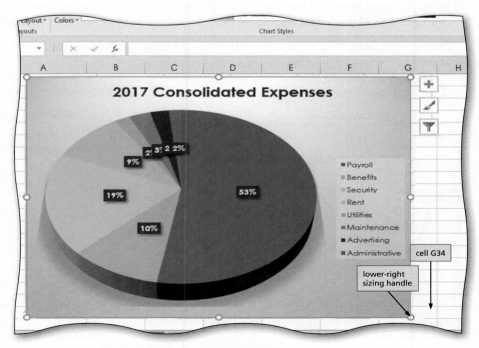

Figure 5–48

To Explode a Slice

In this chart, the Payroll slice dominates because it is so large. The following steps explode the next-largest slice of the 3-D pie chart to draw attention to the second-largest contributing expense. *Why? Exploding, or offsetting, a slice in a chart emphasizes it.*

1

- Click the Security slice (19%) twice to select it. (Do not double-click.)

- Right-click the selected slice to display the shortcut menu (Figure 5–49).

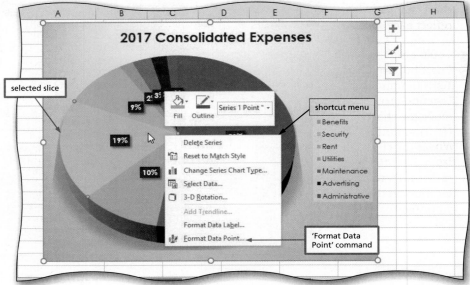

Figure 5–49

2

- Click 'Format Data Point' on the shortcut menu to open the Format Data Point task pane.

- Drag the Point Explosion slider to the right until the Point Explosion box reads 20% to edit the offset distance for the slice (Figure 5–50).

Experiment

- Select different slices and use the Point Explosion slider to offset additional slices and note how the size of the chart changes as you offset additional slices. When done, reset the slices so that the Security slice is the only slice offset, set to 20%.

Q&A | Should I offset more slices?
You can offset as many slices as you want, but remember that the reason for offsetting a slice is to emphasize it. Offsetting multiple slices tends to reduce the impact on the reader and reduces the overall size of the pie chart.

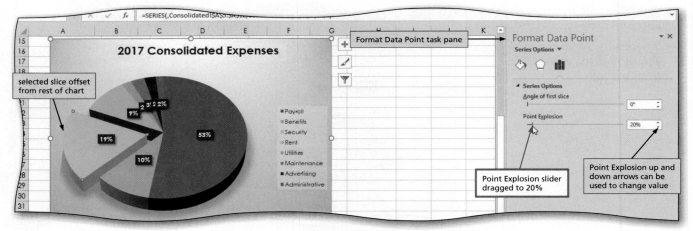

Figure 5–50

Other Ways

1. Click slice twice, drag away from other slices

To Rotate the 3-D Pie Chart

When Excel initially draws a pie chart, it always positions the chart so that one of the dividing lines between two slices is a straight line pointing to 12 o'clock (or 0°). As shown in Figure 5–50, that line that currently divides the Administrative and Payroll slices. This line defines the rotation angle of the 3-D pie chart. Excel allows you to control the rotation angle, elevation, perspective, height, and angle of the axes. The following steps rotate the 3-D pie chart. ***Why?*** *With a three-dimensional chart, you can change the view to better show the section of the chart you are trying to emphasize.*

- Right-click the chart to display the shortcut menu, and then click '3-D Rotation' on the shortcut menu to open the Format Chart Area task pane.

- In the X Rotation box (Format Chart Area dialog box), type 220 to rotate the chart (Figure 5–51).

Q&A
What happens if I click the X Rotation up arrow?
Excel will rotate the chart 10° in a clockwise direction each time you click the X Rotation up arrow.

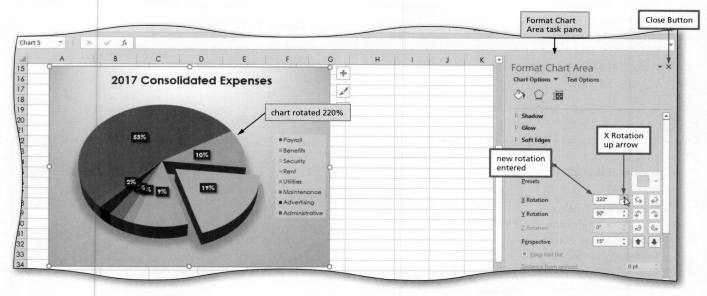

Figure 5–51

- Click the Close button (Format Chart Area task pane) to close the task pane.

Other Ways

1. Click Chart Elements arrow (Chart Tools Format tab | Current Selection group), click Plot Area, click Format Selection button (Chart Tools Format tab | Current Selection group), click Effects button (Format Plot Area dialog box), click up or down arrow in X Rotation box

To Format Data Labels

The following steps format the data labels using the Format Data Labels task pane. You will choose the elements to include in the data label, set the position, choose number formatting and create leader lines. ***Why?*** *A **leader line** connects a data label with its data point helping you identify individual slices.*

1

- Click the Chart Elements button to display the Chart Elements gallery. Point to Data Labels and then click the Data Labels arrow to display the Data Labels submenu (Figure 5–52).

Q&A How does the Legend check box affect the pie chart? If you uncheck the Legend check box, Excel will remove the legend from the chart. If you point to Legend, an arrow will appear. Clicking the arrow displays a list for legend placement.

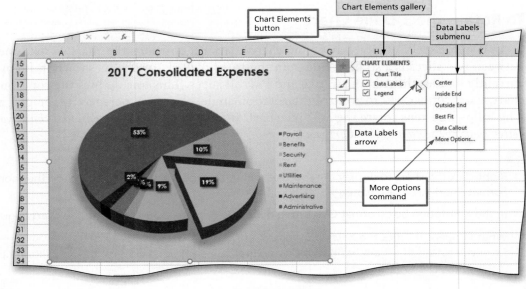

Figure 5–52

2

- Click More Options to display the Format Data Labels task pane.

- In the Label Options area, click to display check marks in the Category Name, Percentage, and 'Show Leader Lines' check boxes. Click to remove check marks in any other check boxes, if necessary (Figure 5–53).

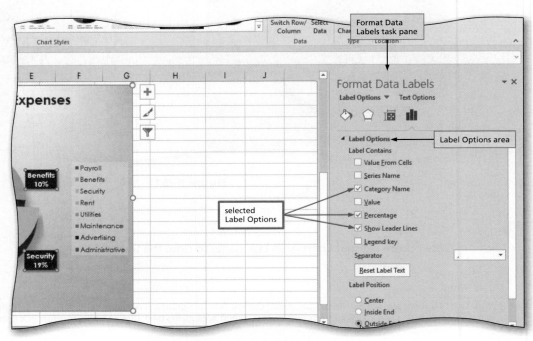

Figure 5–53

3

- In the Label Position area, click Outside End.

- Scroll down in the task pane and click Number to display the Number settings.

- Scroll as necessary to click the Category button and then click Percentage to choose the number style.

- Select any text in the Decimal places text box and then type **1** to format the percentage with one decimal place (Figure 5–54).

Q&A Why did my chart change immediately?
The options in the Format Data Labels task pane use live preview to show you what it will look like.

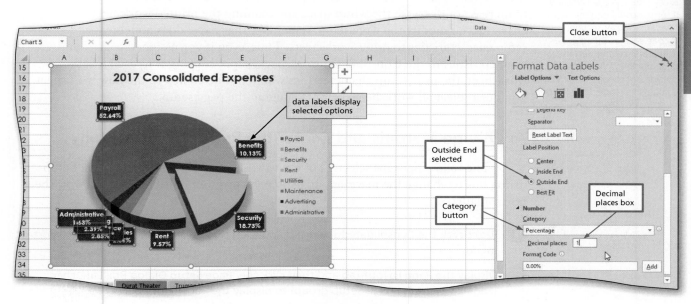

Figure 5–54

4

- Click the Close button on the Format Data Labels task pane to close it.

- One at a time, drag each data label out slightly from the chart to make the leader lines visible (Figure 5–55).

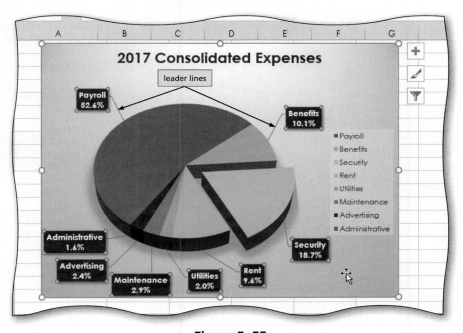

Figure 5–55

Other Ways

1. Click Chart Elements arrow (Chart Tools Format tab | Current Selection group), click Series 1 Data Labels, click Format Selection button (Chart Tools Format tab | Current Selection group), choose settings (Format Data Labels dialog box)

BTW
Header and Footer Codes
When you click a button in the Header & Footer Elements group (Figure 5-58), Excel enters a code (similar to a format code) into the active header or footer section. A code such as &[Page] instructs Excel to insert the page number. When you click outside of the footer box that contains the code, the results of the code are visible.

Printing Multiple Worksheets

Before printing a workbook with multiple worksheets, you should consider the page setup, which defines the appearance and format of a printed worksheet. You can add a header, which appears at the top of every printed page, and a footer, which appears at the bottom of every printed page. You also can change the margins to increase or decrease the white space surrounding the printed worksheet or chart. As you modify the page setup, remember that Excel does not copy page setup characteristics to other worksheets. Thus, even if you assigned page setup characteristics to the Consolidated worksheet before copying it to each location's worksheet, the page setup characteristics would not be copied to the new worksheet. You must select all worksheets before changing the page setup.

To Change Margins and Center the Printout Horizontally

The following steps select all of the worksheets and then use the Page Setup dialog box to change the margins and center the printout of each location's worksheet horizontally.

1 Right-click the Consolidated sheet tab and then click 'Select All Sheets' on the shortcut menu.

2 Display the Page Layout tab and then click the 'Page Setup Dialog Box Launcher' (Page Layout tab | Page Setup group) to display the Page Setup dialog box.

3 If necessary, click the Page tab (Page Setup dialog box) and then click Landscape to set the page orientation to landscape.

4 Click the Margins tab. Enter .5 in both the Left box and Right box to change the left and right margins.

5 Click the Horizontally check box in the Center on page area to center the worksheet on the printed page horizontally (Figure 5–56).

6 Click the OK button (Page Setup dialog box) to close the Page Setup dialog box.

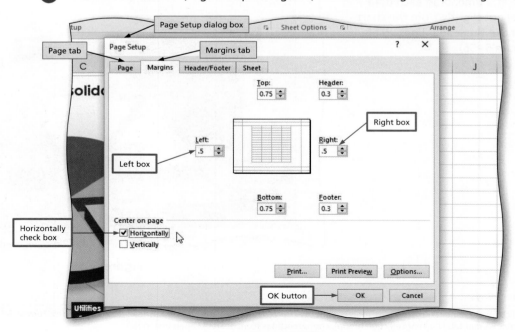

Figure 5–56

To Add a Header

The following steps use Page Layout view to change the headers on the worksheets.

1 With all of the worksheets still selected, click the Page Layout button on the status bar to display the first worksheet in Page Layout view.

2 If necessary, scroll the worksheet up until the Header area is displayed. Click the left header box and then type **Shelly Cashman** (or your name) to enter a page header in the left header box.

If requested by your instructor, add your student ID number to the left header box, below the name entry.

3 Click the center header box and then type **Twelve-Tone Concert Venues** to enter the title.

4 Click the right header box and then click the Current Date button (Header & Footer Tools Design tab | Header & Footer Elements group) to insert the current date (Figure 5–57).

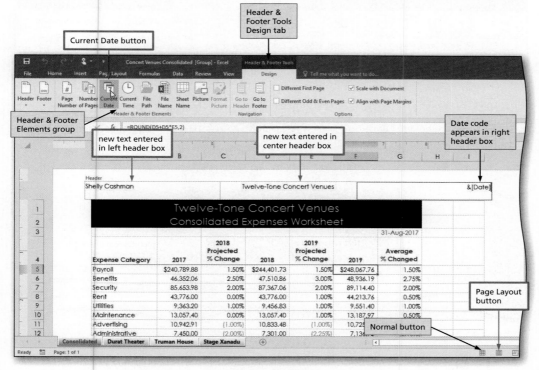

Figure 5–57

To Add a Footer

The following steps change the footers on the worksheets.

1 Scroll the workbook down to view the footer area.

2 Click the middle footer box to select it and then click the Sheet Name button (Header & Footer Tools Design tab | Header & Footer Elements group) to insert the sheet name that appears on the sheet tab as part of the footer.

3 While in the same box, type `Page` as text in the footer. Press the SPACEBAR and then click the Page Number button (Header & Footer Tools Design tab | Header & Footer Elements group) to insert the page number in the footer (Figure 5–58).

Q&A My chart runs over into a new page. What should I do?
Verify that your margin settings match those in Figure 5–56. If the problem remains, change the bottom margin to .5 inches.

Experiment

- Click the left footer box, and then click other buttons in the Header & Footer Elements group on the Header & Footer Tools Design tab. When finished, delete the contents of the left footer box.

4 Click anywhere on the worksheet to deselect the page footer.

5 Click the Normal button on the status bar to return to Normal view.

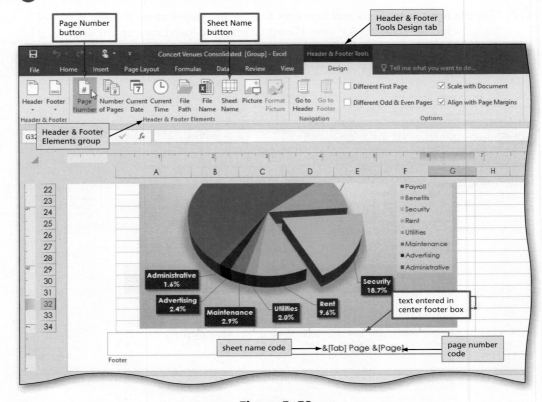

Figure 5–58

To Preview and Print All Worksheets in a Workbook

The following steps print all four worksheets in the workbook.

1 If necessary, right-click any sheet tab and then click 'Select All Sheets' on the shortcut menu.

2 Ready the printer.

3 Open the Backstage view. Click the Print tab (Backstage view) to display the Print gallery.

4 Click the Next Page and Previous Page buttons below the preview to preview the other pages.

5 Click the Print button to print the workbook as shown in Figure 5–59.

6 Right-click the selected tabs and click Ungroup Sheets on the shortcut menu to deselect the four sheets.

7 Save the workbook.

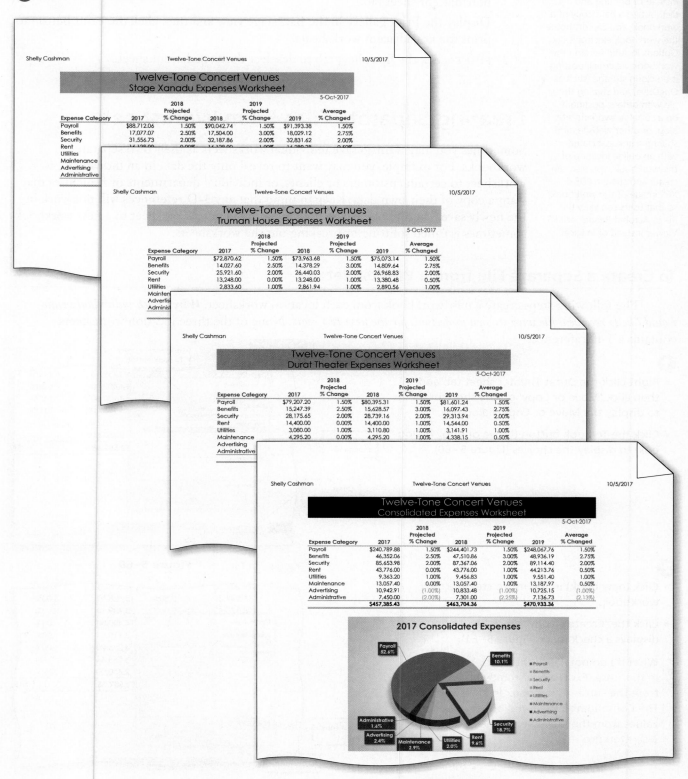

Figure 5–59

TO PRINT NONADJACENT SHEETS IN A WORKBOOK

If you wanted to print nonadjacent sheets in a workbook, you would perform the following steps.

1. With the first sheet active, hold down the CTRL key, and then click the nonadjacent sheet tab.

2. Display the Print gallery in the Backstage view and then click the Print button to print the nonadjacent worksheets.

3 SHIFT+click the first sheet tab to deselect the nonadjacent sheet.

Creating Separate Files From Worksheets

Sometimes you may want to save individual worksheets as their own separate workbooks. For example, you may want to reveal only the data in an individual worksheet to certain customers or clients, or individual departments or franchises may want a copy of their own data. Keep in mind that any 3-D references will not work in the newly saved workbook. Saving, moving, or copying a worksheet to a new workbook sometimes is called splitting or breaking out the worksheets.

To Create a Separate File from a Worksheet

The following steps create a new workbook from each location worksheet. **Why?** *Each individual venue would like to receive a file with its own projections for the next two years*. None of the three location worksheets contains a 3-D reference.

❶

- Right-click the Durat Theater sheet tab and then click 'Move or Copy' on the shortcut menu to display the Move or Copy dialog box

- Click the To book button (Move or Copy dialog box) to display the choices (Figure 5–60).

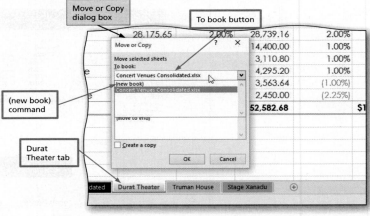

Figure 5–60

❷

- Click (new book) in the list to create a new workbook.

- Click the 'Create a copy' check box to ensure it displays a check mark (Figure 5–61).

Q&A What if I do not check the check box?

In that case, Excel would remove the worksheet from the current workbook in a move function. The Consolidated sheet no longer would display values from the moved worksheet, breaking the 3-D reference.

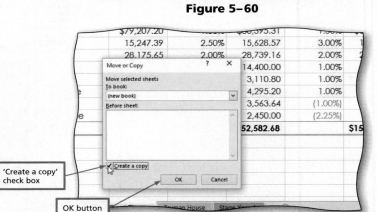

Figure 5–61

❸

- Click the OK button to create the new workbook.

- Save the new file with the name Durat Theater Projected Expenses in the same folder as the Concert Venues Consolidated file.

❹

- Repeat Steps 1 through 3 to save the Truman House and Stage Xanadu worksheets as separate workbooks in the same location. Use the new file names, Truman House Projected Expenses and Stage Xanadu Projected Expenses.

- Close each workbook, including the Concert Venues Consolidated workbook.

Consolidating Data by Linking Separate Workbooks

Earlier in this module, the data from three worksheets was consolidated into a fourth worksheet in the same workbook using 3-D references; however, sometimes the data you need is not in the same workbook. In those cases, it is necessary to consolidate data from separate workbooks, which is also referred to as **linking**. A **link** is a reference to a cell, or range of cells, in another workbook. The consolidated main workbook that contains the links to the separate workbooks is called the **dependent workbook**. The separate, individual workbooks from which you need data are called the **source workbooks**.

You can create a link, using the point mode if both the source workbook and dependent workbook(s) are open. If the source workbook is not open, you have to type the entire drive path, folder, worksheet name, and cell reference into the formula bar. This is known as an **absolute path**. You must include single quotes (') surrounding the drive, folder, workbook name, and worksheet name. You must surround the workbook name with brackets ([ ]). You must include an exclamation point (!) as a delimiter between the sheet name and cell reference. For example, you might type the following:

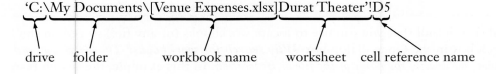

'C:\My Documents\[Venue Expenses.xlsx]Durat Theater'!D5

drive   folder   workbook name   worksheet   cell reference name

Moving Linked Workbooks

Special care should be taken when moving linked workbooks. You should move all of the workbooks together. If you move the dependent workbook without the source workbook(s), all links become absolute—even if you used the point mode to reference them. In addition, if you happen to move the dependent workbook to another computer, without the source workbook(s), the link is broken.

Excel may offer to update or enable your links when you open the dependent workbook independent of the source workbook(s). After moving workbooks, it is best to open the source workbooks first.

The remainder of this module demonstrates how to search for workbooks and how to link separate workbooks, creating a 2018 Consolidated Expenses Worksheet.

CONSIDER THIS

What happens if I update data in one or more of the linked workbooks?
If the source workbooks are open, Excel automatically reads the data in the source workbooks and recalculates formulas in the dependent workbook. Any value changes in the open source workbooks will update in the dependent workbook.

If the source workbooks are not open, then Excel displays a security warning in a pane below the ribbon. If you click the Enable Content button in the warning pane, Excel reads the data in the source workbooks and recalculates the formulas in the dependent workbook, but it does not open the source workbooks.

To Open a Data File and Save it to a New Location

The 2018 Consolidated Expenses workbook is located in the Data Files. Please contact your instructor for information about accessing the Data Files. The file contains headings and formatting and is ready for linking. In the following steps, you will open the workbook and save it to the same location as the files created in the previous steps. For a more complete explanation of opening and saving files, see the Office and Windows module at the beginning of this book. If the Data Files are saved in the same location as your previously saved solution files, you can omit these steps.

1 Run Excel, if necessary, and open the file named 2018 Consolidated Expenses.

2 Display the Backstage view and then click the Save As tab to open the Save As dialog box.

3 Navigate to the location of your previously saved files, and then click the Save button (Save As dialog box) to save the file in a new location.

4 Close the file without exiting Excel.

To Search For and Open Workbooks

Excel has a powerful search tool that you can use to locate workbooks (or any file) stored on the hard drive, using the Search box in the Open dialog box. *Why search for workbooks? The search tool can be used when you cannot remember exactly the name of the file or its location.* In this example, the search text, Expenses, will be used to locate the necessary workbooks. The following steps locate and open the four workbooks of interest.

1
- Display the Backstage view and then click the Open tab to display the Open gallery.
- Click Browse in the left pane and then navigate to the location of your previously saved solution files.
- Type **expenses** in the Search box as the search text.
- One at a time, CTRL+click each of the workbooks that have the word Expenses in the title (Figure 5–62).

Why did the search results include the Concert Venues Consolidated file?
The word, expenses, is in one of the cells in that file. Excel searches through both the file names and file contents.

Figure 5–62

②

- Click the Open button (Open dialog box) to open the selected workbooks.

To Switch to a Different Open Workbook

1 FORMAT WORKSHEET | 2 FILL LINEAR SERIES | 3 USE DATE & ROUND FUNCTIONS | 4 APPLY CUSTOM FORMAT CODE
5 CREATE CELL STYLES | 6 POPULATE WORKSHEETS | 7 INSERT CHART | **8 LINK WORKBOOKS**

The following steps switch to a different open workbook. *Why? You may want to change quickly to another workbook to verify data.*

①

- Display the View tab and then click the Switch Windows button (View tab | Window group) to display the names of the open workbooks (Figure 5–63).

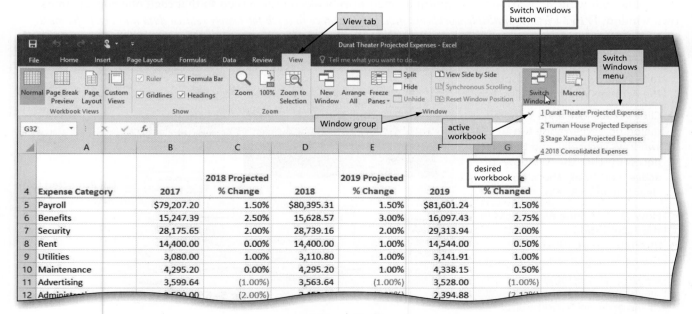

Figure 5–63

2

- Click the name of the desired workbook, in this case, 2018 Consolidated Expenses (Figure 5–64).

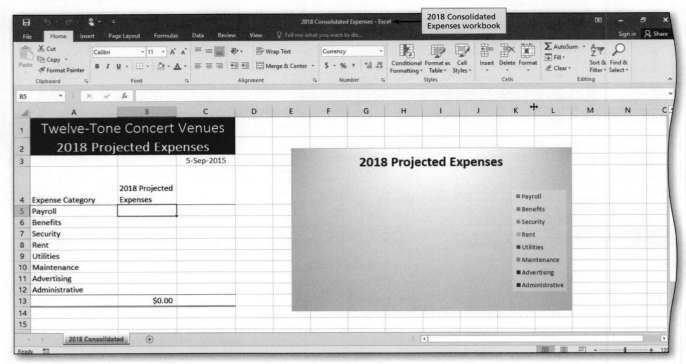

Figure 5–64

Other Ways

1. Point to Excel app button (Windows 10 taskbar), click desired live preview

To Arrange Multiple Workbooks

1 FORMAT WORKSHEET | 2 FILL LINEAR SERIES | 3 USE DATE & ROUND FUNCTIONS | 4 APPLY CUSTOM FORMAT CODE
5 CREATE CELL STYLES | 6 POPULATE WORKSHEETS | 7 INSERT CHART | **8 LINK WORKBOOKS**

The following steps arrange the multiple open workbooks on the screen so that each one appears in its own window. *Why? Viewing multiple workbooks gives you a chance to check for loosely related data and verify formats.*

1

- Click the Arrange All button (View tab | Window group) to display the Arrange Windows dialog box.

- Click Vertical (Arrange Windows dialog box) to arrange the windows vertically, and then, if necessary, click the 'Windows of active workbook' check box to clear it (Figure 5–65).

Q&A How can I arrange workbooks in the Excel window?
Multiple opened workbooks can be arranged in four ways as shown in the Arrange Windows dialog box. You can modify any of the arranged workbooks after first clicking within its window to activate it. To return to showing one workbook, double-click its title bar.

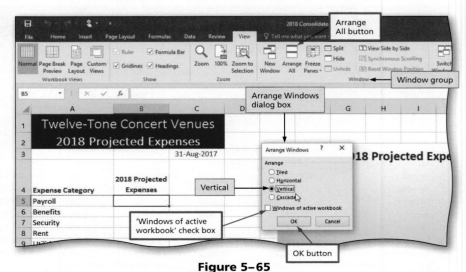

Figure 5–65

2

- Click the OK button (Arrange Windows dialog box) to display the opened workbooks arranged vertically (Figure 5–66).

Q&A Why do the windows display horizontally across the screen, yet the screens were set to Vertical?
The chosen effect determines the change on an individual window, not the group of windows. When you select Vertical, each individual window appears vertically as tall as possible. If you choose Horizontal, the windows appear as wide as possible.

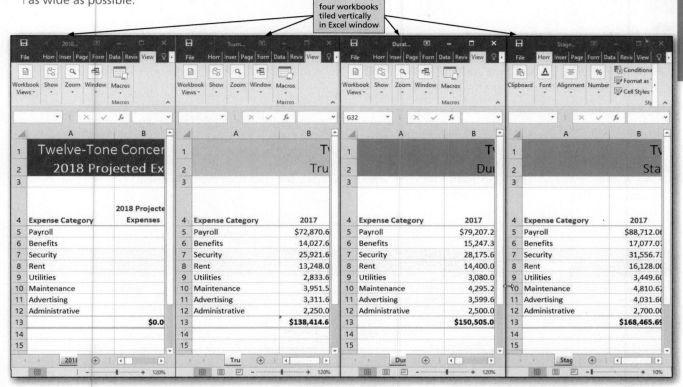

four workbooks
tiled vertically
in Excel window

	A	B			A	B			A	B			A	B
1	Twelve-Tone Concer			1		T		1		T		1		T
2	2018 Projected Ex			2		Tru		2		Du		2		Sta
3				3				3				3		
4	**Expense Category**	2018 Projecte Expenses		4	**Expense Category**	2017		4	**Expense Category**	2017		4	**Expense Category**	2017
5	Payroll			5	Payroll	$72,870.6		5	Payroll	$79,207.2		5	Payroll	$88,712.06
6	Benefits			6	Benefits	14,027.6		6	Benefits	15,247.3		6	Benefits	17,077.07
7	Security			7	Security	25,921.6		7	Security	28,175.6		7	Security	31,556.73
8	Rent			8	Rent	13,248.0		8	Rent	14,400.0		8	Rent	16,128.00
9	Utilities			9	Utilities	2,833.6		9	Utilities	3,080.0		9	Utilities	3,449.60
10	Maintenance			10	Maintenance	3,951.5		10	Maintenance	4,295.2		10	Maintenance	4,810.62
11	Advertising			11	Advertising	3,311.6		11	Advertising	3,599.6		11	Advertising	4,031.60
12	Administrative			12	Administrative	2,250.0		12	Administrative	2,500.0		12	Administrative	2,700.00
13		$0.0		13		$138,414.6		13		$150,505.0		13		$168,465.69
14				14				14				14		
15				15				15				15		

Figure 5–66

To Hide Workbooks

1 FORMAT WORKSHEET | 2 FILL LINEAR SERIES | 3 USE DATE & ROUND FUNCTIONS | 4 APPLY CUSTOM FORMAT CODE
5 CREATE CELL STYLES | 6 POPULATE WORKSHEETS | 7 INSERT CHART | **8 LINK WORKBOOKS**

The following step hides all open workbooks except one. *Why? Hiding is the best way to remove any tiling or arrangement.*

1

- Double-click the title bar of the desired workbook to hide the other opened workbooks. In this case, double-click the 2018 Consolidated Expenses title bar to maximize the window.

- Select cell B5 (Figure 5–67).

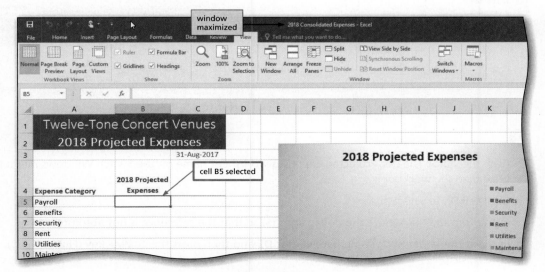

window maximized

2018 Consolidated Expenses - Excel

cell B5 selected

2018 Projected Expenses

Twelve-Tone Concert Venues
2018 Projected Expenses
31-Aug-2017

2018 Projected Expenses

Expense Category
Payroll
Benefits
Security
Rent
Utilities
Mainter

■ Payroll
■ Benefits
■ Security
■ Rent
■ Utilities
■ Maintena

Figure 5–67

To Consolidate Data by Linking Workbooks

The following steps consolidate the data from the three location workbooks into the 2018 Consolidated Expenses workbook. *Why link workbooks? When set up correctly, linking workbooks provides the user with a simple method of consolidating and updating linked data in the original workbook and any workbook with links to the updated data.*

❶

- Click the Sum button (Home tab | Editing group) to begin a SUM function entry in cell B5.

- Display the View tab and then click the Switch Windows button (View tab | Window group) to display the Switch Windows menu (Figure 5–68).

Q&A Does the workbook have to be open to link to it?

Yes, the workbook needs to be open if you want to use point mode. Otherwise, you would have to type the absolute or relative link.

Could I drill cell references in the formula?

No, drilling only applies to selected worksheets within a single workbook, not multiple open workbooks.

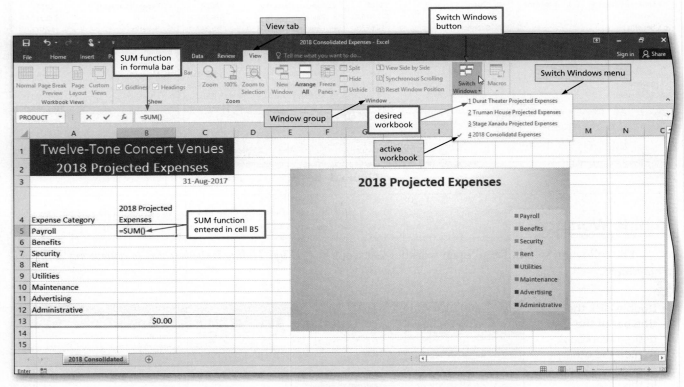

Figure 5–68

❷

- Click the Durat Theater Projected Expenses worksheet name on the Switch Windows menu to select the workbook. Maximize the workbook.

- Click cell D5 to select it.

- In the formula bar, delete the dollar signs ($) so that the reference is not absolute.

- In the formula bar, click immediately after D5 and then press the COMMA key (Figure 5–69).

Q&A
Why do I have to remove the dollar signs ($)?
Linked cell references are absolute ($B$5). You must edit the formula and change these to relative cell references because you plan to copy the SUM function in a later step. If the cell references were left as absolute, then the copied function always would refer to cell B5 in the three workbooks no matter where you copy the SUM function.

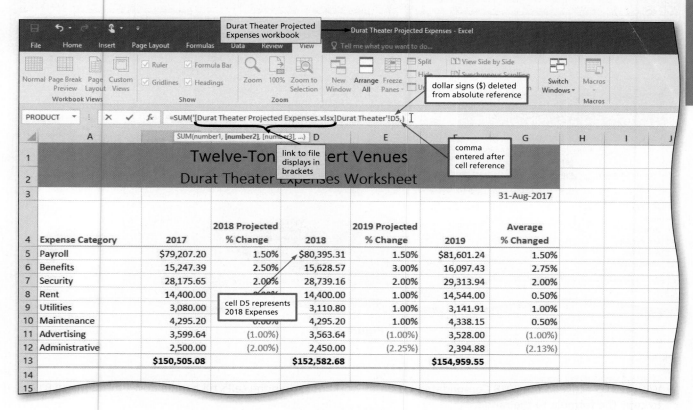

Figure 5–69

3

- Click the Switch Windows button (View tab | Window group) and then click the Truman House Projected Expenses workbook to display the workbook. Maximize the workbook

- Select cell D5 as the next argument in the SUM function.

- If necessary, click the Expand Formula Bar arrow (Formula bar) to display the entire formula. Delete the dollar signs ($) in the reference. Click immediately after D5 in the formula bar and then press the COMMA key.

- Click the Switch Windows button (View tab | Window group), and then click the Stage Xanadu Projected Expenses workbook. Maximize the workbook.

- Select cell D5 as the final argument in the SUM function.

- In the formula bar, delete the dollar signs ($) in the reference.

- Click the Enter button in the formula bar to complete the SUM function and return to the 2018 Consolidated Expenses workbook (Figure 5–70).

Q&A
What if I make a mistake while editing the formula?
If you are still editing, click the Cancel button on the Formula bar, and start again. If you have entered the formula already, click the Undo button. Note that Excel formula error messages do not always indicate the exact location of the error.

Why did the pie chart start filling in?

Excel offers a live preview called **cell animation** that updates as you insert new data. The data file had the pie chart set up to reference the appropriate cells in column B.

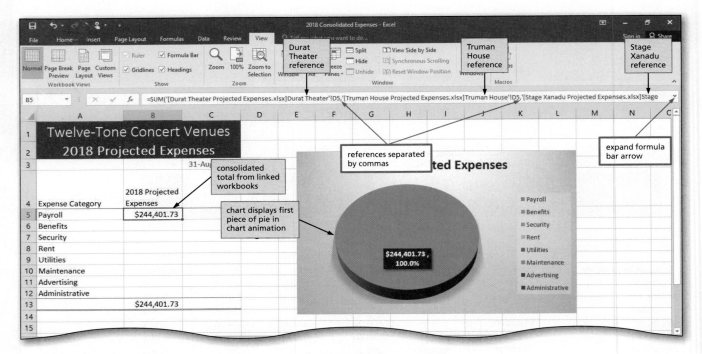

Figure 5–70

4

- With cell B5 active in the 2018 Consolidated Expenses workbook, drag the cell's fill handle down through cell B12 to copy the formula to the range.

- Apply the comma format to cells B6:B12 to remove the floating dollar signs.

- Format the chart as necessary, exploding the Security slice, editing labels, and adding leader lines as shown in Figure 5–71.

Q&A I cannot access the Chart Elements button. What should I do?

Click the Chart Elements arrow (Chart Tools Format tab | Current Selection group) and then choose the area you wish to format. Click the Format Selection button (Chart Tools Format tab | Current Selection group). The same dialog box or task pane will open.

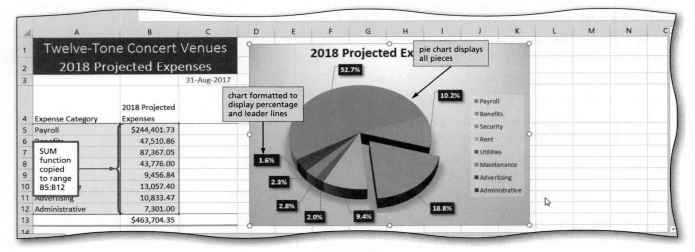

Figure 5–71

- Click the Save button on the Quick Access Toolbar to save the workbook.
- If Excel displays a dialog box, click the OK button (Microsoft Excel dialog box) to save the workbook.

To Close All Workbooks at One Time

To close all four workbooks at one time and exit Excel, complete the following steps.

1 Right-click the Excel app button on the taskbar and then click 'Close all windows' on the shortcut menu to close all open workbooks and exit Excel.

2 If a dialog box appears, click the Save button to save any changes made to the files since the last save.

Summary

In this module, you learned how to create and use a consolidated worksheet. After using the Fill button to create a series, you used the TODAY and ROUND functions to format data. You created a custom format code for a 4-digit year and a custom cell style that used specialized percentage styles for both positive and negative numbers. You learned how to work with multiple worksheets including several ways to copy worksheet data to a new worksheet, and drill an entry through those new worksheets. As you created the consolidated worksheet, you entered a 3-D reference and used the Paste gallery to replicate that reference. You added a pie chart to the consolidated worksheet complete with an exploded slice and formatted data labels with leader lines. You printed the multiple worksheets. Finally, you learned how to break out or split the worksheets into separate workbooks and consolidate the data to a new workbook by linking. With multiple workbooks open, you switched to different worksheets, arranged them in the Excel window, and hid them.

What decisions will you need to make when creating your next workbook to evaluate and analyze data using consolidated worksheets?
Use these guidelines as you complete the assignments in this module and create your own worksheets for evaluating and analyzing data outside of this class.

1. Determine the workbook structure.

 a) Determine how many worksheets and/or workbooks you will need.

 b) Determine the data you will need for your worksheets.

 c) Determine the layout of your data on the consolidated worksheet.

2. Create and format the consolidated worksheet.

 a) Enter titles, subtitles, and headings.

 b) Enter placeholder data, functions, and formulas.

3. Format the worksheet.

 a) Format the titles, subtitles, and headings.

 b) Format the numbers as necessary.

 c) Create and use custom format codes and styles.

4. Create the additional worksheets.

 a) Determine the best method for adding additional worksheets, based on the data in the consolidated worksheet.

CONSIDER THIS: PLAN AHEAD

b) Add the new worksheets to the workbook.

c) Add data and formatting to the new worksheets.

d) Create 3-D references where necessary to replace placeholders in the consolidated sheet with calculated values.

5. Create and use charts.

a) Select the data to chart.

b) Select a chart type for selected data.

c) Format the chart elements.

6. Consolidate workbooks.

a) Create separate workbooks from worksheets if necessary.

b) Link multiple workbooks to facilitate easy updating of data across workbooks.

Apply Your Knowledge

Reinforce the skills and apply the concepts you learned in this module.

Consolidating Payroll Worksheets

Note: To complete this assignment, you will be required to use the Data Files. Please contact your instructor for information about accessing the Data Files.

Instructions: Run Excel. Open the workbook Apply 5–1 Annual Payroll. Follow the steps below to consolidate the payroll figures for a small company. At the conclusion of the instructions, the Annual Totals sheet should resemble the worksheet shown in Figure 5–72.

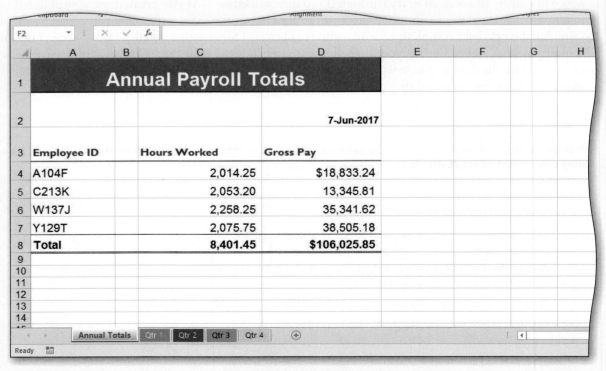

Employee ID	Hours Worked	Gross Pay
A104F	2,014.25	$18,833.24
C213K	2,053.20	13,345.81
W137J	2,258.25	35,341.62
Y129T	2,075.75	38,505.18
Total	8,401.45	$106,025.85

Annual Payroll Totals

7-Jun-2017

Figure 5–72

Perform the following tasks:

1. One by one, click each of the tabs and review the quarterly totals and formats. Change each tab color to match the background color of cell A1 on the corresponding worksheet.

2. Right-click the Annual Totals tab and then click Select All Sheets on the shortcut menu. Perform the following steps.

   a. Insert the date in cell D2 using the TODAY function. Create the 4-Digit Year cell style created earlier in this module. Change the font color to black, if necessary. Right-justify the new style. Apply the cell style to cell D2.

   b. Format the column headings in the range A3:D3 using Heading 3 cell style. Format the range A8:D8 with the Total cell style.

   c. Select the range C5:D7 and format it with the comma style (Home tab | Number group).

   d. Use the SUM function to total columns C and D.

   e. Switch to Page Layout view. Add a worksheet header with file name in the center of the header, and the date in the right header. Add the sheet name and page number to the center of the footer.

   f. If requested by your instructor, add a dash followed by your name to the worksheet left header.

   g. Click outside the header area. Click the 'Page Setup Dialog Box Launcher' (Page Layout tab, Page Setup group) to display the Page Setup dialog box. Center all worksheets horizontally on the page (Margins tab). Close the Page Setup dialog box. Return to Normal view.

3. Click the Qtr 1 sheet tab to select it. SHIFT+click the Q4 sheet tab to select all four quarters without the Annual Totals worksheet. Perform the following steps.

   a. Select cell D4. Use the ROUND function with two decimal places to calculate the gross pay by multiplying B4 by C4.

   b. Use the fill handle to replicate the function to cells D5:D7.

   c. Select the range, C4:C8 and format it with the comma style (Home tab | Number group).

   d. CTRL+click cells D4 and D8 to select them. Format the cells using the currency format (Format Cells dialog box), with a floating dollar sign and parentheses for negative numbers.

4. To consolidate the worksheets, click the Annual Totals sheet tab to select only the Annual Totals worksheet. To create a SUM function with a 3-D reference, select cell C4, and then click the Sum button (Home tab | Editing group). Click the Qtr 1 sheet tab to display the worksheet, and then click cell C4 to select the first portion of the argument for the SUM function. SHIFT+click the Qtr 4 sheet tab to select the ending range of the argument for the SUM function. Click the Enter button in the formula bar to enter the SUM function with the 3-D references in the selected cell.

5. On the Annual Totals sheet, copy the function in cell C4. Paste to the range C5:C7 using the Formulas button in the Paste gallery.

6. Repeat steps 4 and 5 to create a 3-D reference in cell D4 and copy it to the range D5:D7.

7. Preview the five worksheets and print them if instructed to do so.

8. Click the Annual Totals sheet tab to select the sheet. Save the workbook as Apply 5–1 Annual Payroll Complete. Submit the workbook as requested by your instructor.

9. ✺ What would have been the effect if you had consolidated the workbook before rounding the gross pays for each quarter? If you then rounded all of the numbers, would the answers have been the same? Why or why not?

Continued >

In the Labs

Design, create, modify, and/or use a workbook following the guidelines, concepts, and skills presented in this module. Labs 1 and 2, which increase in difficulty, require you to create solutions based on what you learned in the module; Lab 3 requires you to apply your creative thinking and problem-solving skills to design and implement a solution.

Lab 1: Using a Master Sheet to Create a Multiple-Sheet Workbook

Note: To complete this assignment, you will be required to use the Data Files. Please contact your instructor for information about accessing the Data Files.

Problem: You are part of a task force assessing the classroom capacities of the middle schools in your district. You have been charged with creating a master worksheet for the district and separate worksheets for each of the two middle schools. The middle school worksheets should be based on the district worksheet. Once the worksheets have been created, the middle school data can be entered into the appropriate worksheets, and the district worksheet will reflect district-wide information. The district worksheet appears as shown in Figure 5–74.

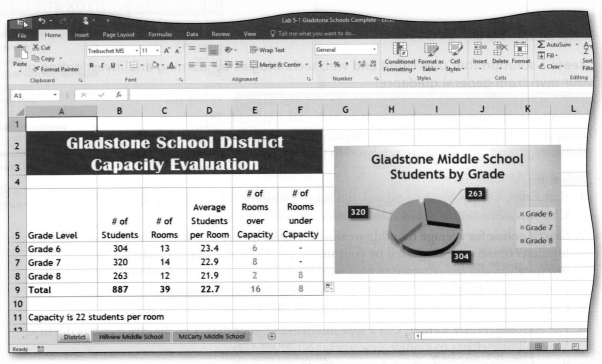

Figure 5–74

Perform the following tasks:

1. Run Excel. Open the workbook Lab 5–1 Gladstone Schools from the Data Files. Save the workbook using the file name Lab 5–1 Gladstone Schools Complete.

2. Add two worksheets to the workbook after Sheet1 and then paste the contents of Sheet1 to the two empty worksheets.

3. From left to right, rename the sheet tabs District, Hillview Middle School, and McCarty Middle School. Color the tabs as shown in Figure 5–74. On each of the school worksheets,

change the title in cell B2 to match the sheet tab name. On each worksheet, fill the range A2:F3 to match the color of its sheet tab. Enter the data in Table 5–8 into the school worksheets.

Table 5–8 Middle School Classroom Capacity Figures

School	Grade	# of Students	# of Rooms	# of Rooms over Capacity	# of Rooms under Capacity
Hillview Middle School	6	180	8	2	0
	7	188	8	8	0
	8	145	7	0	7
McCarty Middle School	6	124	5	4	0
	7	132	6	0	0
	8	118	5	2	1

4. On the two school worksheets, calculate Average Students per Room in column D and totals in row 9.

5. On the District worksheet, use the SUM function, 3-D references, and copy-and-paste capabilities of Excel to populate the ranges B6:C8 and E6:F8. First, compute the sum in cells B6:C6 and E6:F6, and then copy the ranges B6:D6 and E6:F6 through ranges B7:C8 and E7:F8 respectively. Finally, calculate average students per room for the district for each grade level, and for the district as a whole.

6. Select the range E6:E9 on the District worksheet. Select all the worksheets and then use the Format Cells dialog box to apply a custom format of [Red]#,###;;"-".

7. Select the range F6:F9 on the District worksheet. Select all the worksheets and then use the Format Cells dialog box to apply a custom format that will format all nonzero numbers similar to the format applied in Step 6 but with green for nonzero entries.

8. Use the Cell Styles button (Home tab | Styles group) to create a new cell style named My Title. Use the Format button (Styles dialog box) to create a format. Use the Font sheet (Format Cells dialog box) to select the Britannic Bold font, a font size of 22, and a white font color. Check only the Alignment and Font check boxes in the Style dialog box.

9. Select cells A2:A3 on the District worksheet. Select all the worksheets. Apply the My Title style to the cell.

10. Using Figure 5–74 as a guide, add borders to the worksheets. The borders should be the same on all worksheets.

11. Select the District worksheet. Create a 3-D pie chart using the range A6:B8. Edit the title to match Figure 5–74. Apply the Chart Style 3 to the chart.

12. Move the chart to the right of the data. Right-click the pie to display the shortcut menu and then click 'Format Data Series' to open the Format Data Series task pane. Set the Pie Explosion to 10% to offset all of the slices.

13. Select the chart area and display the Format Chart Area task pane. Set the X rotation to 100°.

14. Use the Chart Elements button to display the Data Labels submenu. Click More Options. Select only the Value and 'Show Leader Lines' options. Choose the Outside End label position and adjust the labels as necessary to display the leader lines.

15. If requested by your instructor, enter the text **Prepared by** followed by your name in the header, on the left side.

16. Save the workbook. Submit the revised workbook as specified by your instructor.

17. ✸ Did you calculate an average in cell D9 using the data in column D or the data in row 9? Explain the reasoning for your choice.

In the Labs *continued*

Lab 2: Consolidating Data by Linking Workbooks

Note: To complete this assignment, you will be required to use the Data Files. Please contact your instructor for information about accessing the Data Files.

Problem: The Apply Your Knowledge exercise in this module calls for consolidating the payroll data from four worksheets to a fifth worksheet in the same workbook. This exercise takes the same data, this time stored in four separate workbooks, and then consolidates the total sales and total commission by linking to a fifth workbook.

Part 1: *Perform the following tasks:*

1. If necessary, copy the following five files from the Data Files to the location at which you save your solution files. Lab 5–2 Commission Annual, Lab 5–2 Commission Quarter 1, Lab 5–2 Commission Quarter 2, Lab 5–2 Commission Quarter 3, and Lab 5–2 Commission Quarter 4. Run Excel. Using the Search box with the term, commission, open the five files.

2. Use the Switch Windows button (View tab | Window group) to make Lab 5–2 Commission Annual the active workbook. Save the workbook in the same location, using the file name, Lab 5–2 Commission Annual Complete.

3. Select cell C9. Click the Sum button (Home tab | Editing group) and then switch to the Lab 5–2 Commission Quarter 1 workbook. When the workbook is displayed, click cell D9, change the absolute cell reference $D$9 in the formula bar to the relative cell reference by deleting the dollar signs. Click immediately after D9 in the formula bar and then press the COMMA key.

4. Switch to the Lab 5–2 Commission Quarter 2 workbook. When the workbook is displayed, click cell D9, change the absolute cell reference $D$9 to D9, click immediately after D9 in the formula bar, and then press the COMMA key.

5. Repeat Step 3 for the Quarter 3 and Quarter 4 workbooks. After adding the Quarter 4 workbook reference, press the ENTER key rather than the COMMA key to sum the four quarter sales figures. The annual total sales for employee DK52 should be $221,500.00 as shown in Figure 5–75.

6. With the workbook Lab 5–2 Commission Annual Complete window active, select cell C9 and drag the fill handle through D9 to display total commission for employee DK52.

7. Select cells D9 and C9. Drag the fill handle through cell D13 to display the total sales and total commission for all employees, and as annual totals. When the Auto Fill Options button is displayed next to cell D14, click the Auto Fill Options button and then click 'Fill Without Formatting'.

8. Save and close all workbooks. Submit the solution as specified by your instructor.

Part 2: *Perform the following tasks to update the total sales for Quarter 3 and Quarter 4.*

1. If necessary, run Excel and open Lab 5–2 Commission Quarter 3. Change the quarterly sales for employee LM33 in row 10 from 34,000.00 to 39,500.00. Save and close the workbook.

2. Open Lab 5–2 Commission Quarter 4. Change the Quarterly Sales for employee TZ98 in row 12 from 32,000.00 to 29,000.00. Save and close the workbook.

3. Open Lab 5–2 Commission Annual Complete workbook saved earlier in Part 1 of this exercise. If Excel displays a security warning, click the Enable Content button. Save the workbook using the file name, Lab 5–2 Commission Annual Complete Revised. Click the Edit Links button (Data tab | Connections group). Select each file in the Edit Links dialog box and then click the Update Values button (Edit Links dialog box) to instruct Excel to apply the current values in the four source workbooks to the consolidated workbook (Figure 5–75).

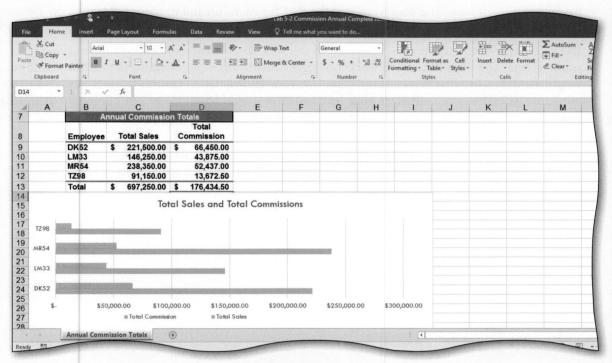

Figure 5–75

4. If requested by your instructor, enter the text **Prepared by** followed by your name in the header, on the left side.

5. Create a chart based on the data in cells you have B8:D12, using the recommended chart feature. Format the chart using techniques learned in this module and others. Move the chart below the sales and commission information. Resize the chart to a size that you think best suits the content and formatting.

6. Save the workbook. Submit the revised workbook as specified by your instructor.

7. ✳ Assess the relative strengths and weaknesses of the two approaches to building a consolidated worksheet, from four separate quarterly workbooks as used in this exercise, and using internal worksheets as you did in the Apply Your Knowledge exercise.

In the Labs *continued*

Lab 3: **Consider This: Your Turn**

Apply your creative thinking and problem-solving skills to design and implement a solution.

Tracking Fitness Data

Note: To complete this assignment, you will be required to use the Data Files. Please contact your instructor for information about accessing the Data Files.

Part 1: You have just started a new running regimen. You decide to track your progress so that you can evaluate your workouts. You decide to use Excel to track information about time, distance, and frequency of your runs. You plan to record the data for each run and to consolidate data on a weekly basis so that you can see how you are progressing from week to week.

Use the concepts and techniques presented in this module to create a workbook for tracking your running data. You want to create a workbook that contains multiple worksheets to allow you to re-view daily data, as well as consolidated data. Use your knowledge of consolidation to design a work-book that will allow you to analyze your progress. You should have at least one computed field, such as average miles per run, in your worksheets. You should include at least one chart presenting fitness data. Submit your assignment in the format specified by the instructor.

Part 2: ✹ This exercise had you create a chart presenting fitness data. List two other ways you could chart the data in Excel. What are the strengths and weaknesses of each of the three chart types for the data you are presenting?

6 Creating, Sorting, and Querying a Table

Objectives

You will have mastered the material in this module when you can:

- Create and manipulate a table
- Delete duplicate records
- Add calculated columns to a table with structured references
- Use the VLOOKUP function to look up a value in a table
- Use icon sets with conditional formatting
- Insert a total row
- Sort a table on one field or multiple fields
- Sort, query, and search a table using AutoFilter

- Remove filters
- Create criteria and extract ranges
- Apply database and statistical functions
- Use the MATCH and INDEX functions to find a value in a table
- Display automatic subtotals
- Use outline features to group, hide, and unhide data
- Create a treemap chart

Introduction

A **table**, also called a **database**, is an organized collection of data. For example, a list of friends, a group of students registered for a class, an inventory list, a club membership roster, or an instructor's grade book — all can be arranged as tables in a worksheet. In these cases, the data related to each person or item is called a **record**, and the individual data items that make up a record are called **fields**. For example, in a table of clients, each client would have a separate record; each record might include several fields, such as name, address, phone number, current balance, billing rate, and status. A record also can include fields that contain references, formulas, and functions.

You can use a worksheet's row-and-column structure to organize and store a table. Each row of a worksheet can store a record, and each column can store one field for each record. Additionally, a row of column headings at the top of the worksheet can store field names that identify each field.

After you enter a table onto a worksheet, you can use Excel to (1) add and delete records, (2) change the values of fields in records, (3) sort the records so that Excel presents them in a different order, (4) determine subtotals for numeric fields, (5) display records that meet comparison criteria, and (6) analyze data using database functions. This module illustrates all six of these table capabilities.

Project — Coffee Craft Daily Services

The project in this module follows proper design guidelines and uses Excel to create the worksheet shown in Figures 6–1a and 6–1b, and the chart (Figure 6–1c). The Coffee Craft company repairs industrial coffee makers, brewers, and espresso machines for restaurants, hotels, coffee shops, and QSRs (Quick Service Restaurants). The company has asked for a workbook that lists their daily service calls and then summarizes key information about technicians and their performance. The data in the workbook should be easy to summarize, sort, edit, and query.

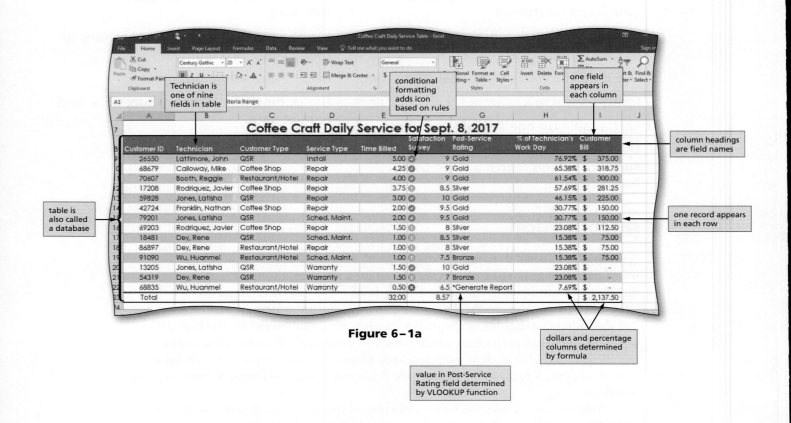

Figure 6–1a

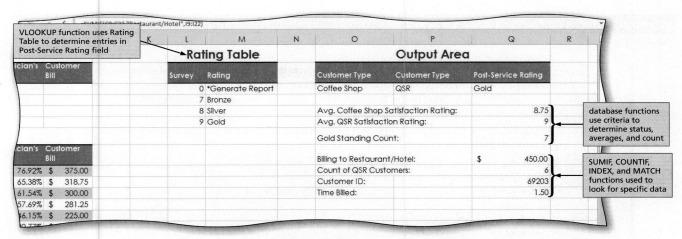

VLOOKUP function uses Rating Table to determine entries in Post-Service Rating field

Rating Table

Survey	Rating
0	*Generate Report
7	Bronze
8	Silver
9	Gold

Output Area

Customer Type	Customer Type	Post-Service Rating
Coffee Shop	QSR	Gold

Avg. Coffee Shop Satisfaction Rating:	8.75
Avg. QSR Satisfaction Rating:	9
Gold Standing Count:	7

database functions use criteria to determine status, averages, and count

Billing to Restaurant/Hotel:	$	450.00
Count of QSR Customers:		6
Customer ID:		69203
Time Billed:		1.50

SUMIF, COUNTIF, INDEX, and MATCH functions used to look for specific data

cian's	Customer Bill
76.92%	$ 375.00
65.38%	$ 318.75
61.54%	$ 300.00
57.69%	$ 281.25
46.15%	$ 225.00

Figure 6–1b

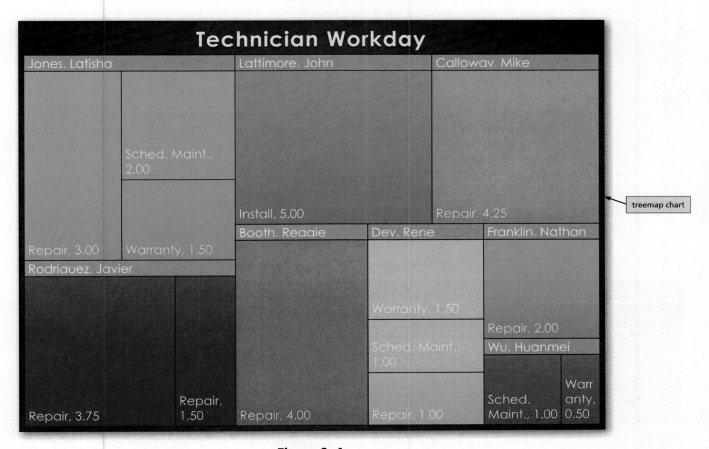

treemap chart

Figure 6–1c

Figure 6–2 shows a sample requirements document for the Coffee Craft Daily Service Table. It includes the needs, source of data, calculations, special requirements, and other facts about its development.

Worksheet Title	Coffee Craft Daily Services Table
Needs	• A worksheet table that lists daily service calls with the customer ID, technician, customer type, service type, and time billed. • The worksheet also should assign a Gold, Silver, or Bronze standing based on the Satisfaction Survey number. Low ratings should present a message, *Generate Report. • The worksheet should calculate the % of Technician's Work Day and also the Customer Bill. • The worksheet should be easy for management to sort, search, filter, and total.
Source of Data	Data supplied by the business owner includes the information in bullet 1 above (see Table 6-1). Remaining numbers in the worksheet are based on calculations.

Calculations	The following calculations are needed:
	• the % of Technician's Work Day = Time billed/6.5
	• Customer Bill = Time Billed * 75, only for non-warranty work (IF function)
	• Standing that is determined as follows:
	    o Gold = a high score of 9 to 10
	    o Silver = an adequate score of 8 to 8.99
	    o Bronze = a low score of 7 to 7.99
	    o *Generate Report = an unacceptable score below 7
	• Average Coffee Shop Satisfaction Rating = DAVERAGE function
	• Average QSR Satisfaction Rating = DAVERAGE function
	• Gold Standing Count = DCOUNT function
	• Total of bills to Restaurants/Hotels = SUMIF function
	• Count of QSR customers = COUNTIF function
	• Look up Time Billed by Customer ID

Other Requirements	• Provide a way to search, sort, and select data based on certain criteria. • Provide an area to ascertain statistics about technicians, such as averages, counts, and totals based on specific factors. • A criteria area will be created above the table to store criteria for use in a query. An extract area will be created below the table to display records that meet the criteria. • Provide a hierarchical and visual chart to display all of the technicians and their work day.

Figure 6–2

Table 6–1 describes the field names, columns, types of data, and descriptions that you can refer to when creating the table.

Table 6–1 Column Information for Coffee Craft Daily Service Table			
Column Headings (Field Names)	**Column in Worksheet**	**Type of Data**	**Description**
Customer ID	A	Numeric	6-digit whole number, previously assigned by service provider
Technician	B	Text	Last name, first name
Customer Type	C	Text	Coffee Shop, Restaurant/Hotel, or QSR
Service Type	D	Text	Repair, Sched. Maint., or Warranty
Time Billed	E	Numeric	Time measured in decimal hours with two decimal places
Satisfaction Survey	F	Numeric	Decimal number with one decimal place, calculated by service provider
Post-Service Rating	G	Text calculation (VLOOKUP function)	Standing of Gold, Silver, Bronze, or *Generate Report based on Satisfaction Survey
% of Technician's Work Day	H	Percentage calculation (Time Billed / 6.5)	Billed time displayed as a percentage of 6.5 hour work day (8 hours minus allowance for travel)
Customer Bill	I	Numeric calculation (Time Billed * 75)	Customer billing at $75 per hour for non-warranty work

Using a sketch of the worksheet can help you visualize its design. The sketch of the service call table consists of the title, column headings, location of data values, and an idea of the desired formatting (Figure 6–3a). (The sketch does not show the criteria area above the table and the extract area below the table.) The general layout of the rating table, output area, and required statistics and query are shown in Figure 6–3b.

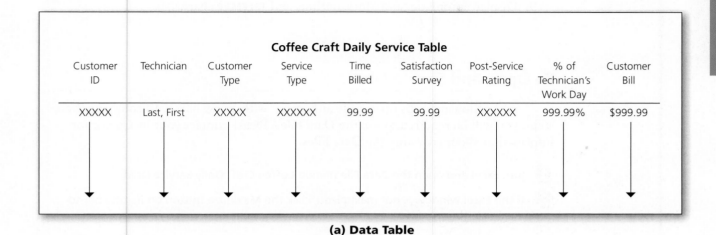

Coffee Craft Daily Service Table

Customer ID	Technician	Customer Type	Service Type	Time Billed	Satisfaction Survey	Post-Service Rating	% of Technician's Work Day	Customer Bill
XXXXX	Last, First	XXXXX	XXXXXX	99.99	99.99	XXXXXX	999.99%	$999.99

(a) Data Table

Rating Table		Output Area		
Survey	**Rating**	**Customer Type**	**Customer Type**	**Post-Service Rating**
0	*Generate Report	Coffee Shop	QSR	Gold
7	Bronze			
8	Silver	Average Coffee Shop Satisfaction Rating:		99.99
9	Gold	Average QSR Satisfaction Rating:		99.99
		Gold Standing Count:		99
		Billing to Restaurant/Hotel:		$ 999,999
		Count of QSR Customers:		99
		Customer ID:		99999
		Time Billed:		99.99

(b) Rating Table and Output Area

Figure 6–3

With a good understanding of the requirements document, a clear list of the necessary decisions, and a sketch of the worksheet, the next step is to use Excel to create the worksheet.

The following roadmap identifies general activities you will perform as you progress through this module:

1. CREATE and format a TABLE.

2. Use LOOKUP TABLES in the worksheet.

3. Insert CALCULATED FIELDS using structured references.

4. Apply CONDITIONAL FORMATTING and icon sets.

5. SORT TABLES.

6. QUERY a TABLE.

7. Extract records with CRITERIA RANGES.

8. Use DATABASE functions and CONDITIONAL FUNCTIONS.

9. Display automatic SUBTOTALS, outline, and TREEMAP chart.

To Open and Save a File

The following steps open a file and save it with a new name. To complete these steps, you will be required to use the Data Files. Please contact your instructor for information about accessing the Data Files.

1 Run Excel and open the Data File named Coffee Craft Daily Service Data.

2 If the Excel window is not maximized, click the Maximize button on its title bar to maximize the window.

3 Click the Themes button (Page Layout tab | Themes group) and then click the Vapor Trail theme.

4 Save the workbook on your hard drive, OneDrive, or other storage location using Coffee Craft Daily Service Table as the file name.

5 If necessary, click cell A1 (Figure 6–4).

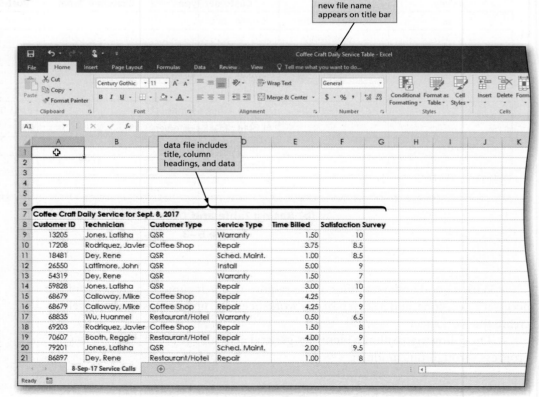

Figure 6–4

Table Guidelines

When you create a table in Excel, you should follow some basic guidelines, as listed in Table 6–2.

Table 6–2 Guidelines for Creating a Table in Excel
Table Size and Workbook Location
1. Do not enter more than one table per worksheet.
2. Maintain at least one blank row between a table and other worksheet entries.
3. A table can have a maximum of 16,384 fields and 1,048,576 records on a worksheet.
Column Headings (Field Names)
1. Place column headings (field names) in the first row of the table.
2. Do not use blank rows or rows with repeating characters, such as dashes or underscores, to separate the column headings (field names) from the data.
3. Apply a different format to the column headings than to the data. For example, bold the column headings and format the data below the column headings using a regular style. Most table styles follow these guidelines.
4. Column headings (field names) can be up to 32,767 characters in length. The column headings should be meaningful.
Contents of Table
1. Each cell in any given column should have similar data. For example, Customer Type entries should use the company standard wording for the types of customers, such as QSR for Quick Service Restaurant.
2. Format the data to improve readability, but do not vary the format of the data within the cells of a column.

Creating a Table

When you create a table in Excel, you can manage and analyze the data in that table, independently from the rest of the data on the worksheet. The advantages of creating a table include:

- Automatic expansion of the table to accommodate data
- Header row remains visible while scrolling
- Automatic reformatting
- Integrated filter and sort functionality
- Automatic fill and calculated fields
- Easy access to structured references
- Automatic adjustment of associated charts and ranges

How should you format a table?

Format a table so that the records are distinguished easily. The data in the worksheet should start several rows from the top in order to leave room for a criteria area. Using banded rows (background colors varying between rows) to format the table provides greater readability. Some columns require calculations that can be created by using the column headings or cell references within formulas. In some cases, calculated columns in tables require looking up values outside of the table. You can use Excel's special lookup functions in such cases. Totals also can be added to the table for averages, sums, and other types of calculations.

CONSIDER THIS

To Format a Range as a Table

The easiest way to create a table is to apply a table style. *Why? Excel automatically creates the table when applying a table style to a range.* You can create a table before or after entering column headings and data. The following steps format a range as a table.

- Zoom to 120% and then scroll down until cell A7 is at the top of the workspace.

- Select the range A8:F22.

- Click the 'Format as Table' button (Home tab | Styles group) to display the Format as Table gallery (Figure 6–5).

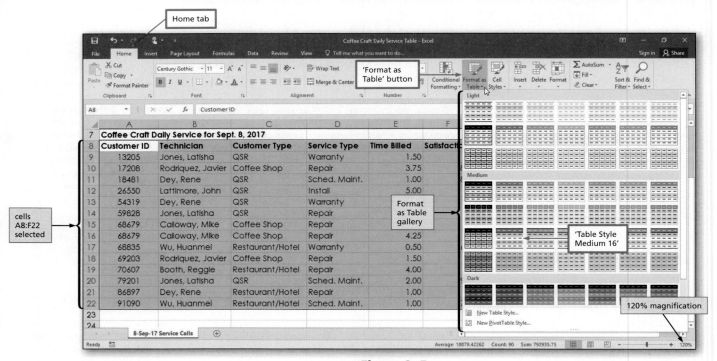

Figure 6–5

- Click 'Table Style Medium 16' in the Format as Table gallery to display the Format As Table dialog box.

- If necessary, click the 'My table has headers' check box to select the option to format the table with headers (Figure 6–6).

Q&A What is a header?
A table header is the column heading that appears above the data. In this case, you want to create the table and include the column headings.

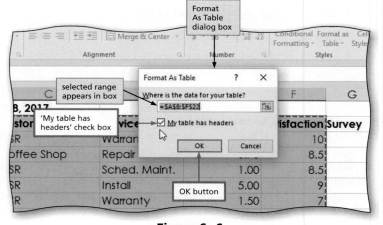

Figure 6–6

3

- Click the OK button (Format As Table dialog box) to create a table from the selected range.
- Click outside the table to deselect it (Figure 6–7).

Q&A What are the buttons with the arrows beside the column headings? The buttons are part of the AutoFilter that you will learn about later in the module.

data range becomes table

each column heading displays filter button

	Customer ID	Technician	Customer Type	Service Type	Time Billed	Satisfaction Surv
7	Coffee Craft Daily Service for Sept. 8, 2017					
9	13205	Jones, Latisha	QSR	Warranty	1.50	
10	17208	Rodriquez, Javier	Coffee Shop	Repair	3.75	
11	18481	Dey, Rene	QSR	Sched. Maint.	1.00	
12	26550	Lattimore, John	QSR	Install	5.00	
13	54319	Dey, Rene	QSR	Warranty	1.50	
14	59828	Jones, Latisha	QSR	Repair	3.00	
15	68679	Calloway, Mike	Coffee Shop	Repair	4.25	
16	68679	Calloway, Mike	Coffee Shop	Repair	4.25	
17	68835	Wu, Huanmei	Restaurant/Hotel	Warranty	0.50	
18	69203	Rodriquez, Javier	Coffee Shop	Repair	1.50	
19	70607	Booth, Reggie	Restaurant/Hotel	Repair	4.00	
20	79201	Jones, Latisha	QSR	Sched. Maint.	2.00	
21	86897	Dey, Rene	Restaurant/Hotel	Repair	1.00	
22	91090	Wu, Huanmei	Restaurant/Hotel	Sched. Maint.	1.00	

Figure 6–7

Other Ways

1. Select range, click Table button (Insert tab | Tables group), click OK button, choose table style (Table Tools Design tab | Table Styles group)

To Wrap Text

The following steps wrap the text in cell F8 to make the heading easier to read.

1 Change the width of column F to 11.

2 Select cell F8, and then click the Wrap Text button (Home tab | Alignment group) (Figure 6–8).

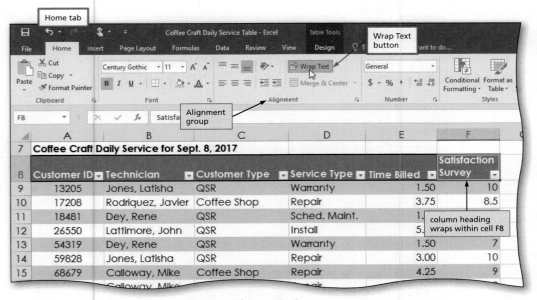

Figure 6–8

BTW
Ranges to Tables
If you select a range before clicking the 'Format as Table' button (Home tab | Styles group), Excel will fill in the range for you in the Format As Table dialog box.

BTW
Banded Columns
Banded columns offer alternating colors every other column. You also can include a different color for the first and/or last column in a table. The style that you choose for a table must have these colors defined in the style. The style used in this module does not include special formatting for banded columns or the first and last columns.

To Name the Table

The following step gives a name to the table. ***Why?*** *Referring to the table by name rather than by range reference will save time.*

1

- Click anywhere in the table and then display the Table Tools Design tab.

- Click the Table Name text box (Table Tools Design tab | Properties group).

- Type `Service_Calls` and then press the ENTER key to name the table (Figure 6–9).

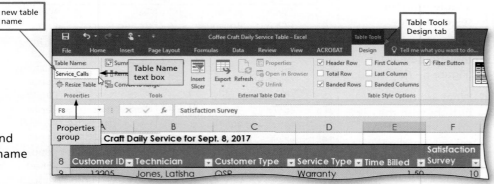

Figure 6–9

Q&A
Why should I use an underscore in the table name?

Excel does not allow spaces in table names. Excel also requires that table names begin with a letter or underscore.

Other Ways

1. Select range, click Name Manager button (Formulas tab | Defined Names group), click New button (Name Manager dialog box), enter name (New Name dialog box), click OK button, click Close button

To Remove Duplicates

Duplicate entries may appear in tables. ***Why?*** *Duplicates sometimes happen when data is entered incorrectly, by more than one person, or from more than one source.* The following steps remove duplicate records in the table. In this particular table, the service call for customer 68679 was entered twice by mistake.

1

- Click anywhere in the table.

- Click the Remove Duplicates button (Table Tools Design tab | Tools group) to display the Remove Duplicates dialog box.

- Click the Select All button (Remove Duplicates dialog box) to select all columns (Figure 6–10).

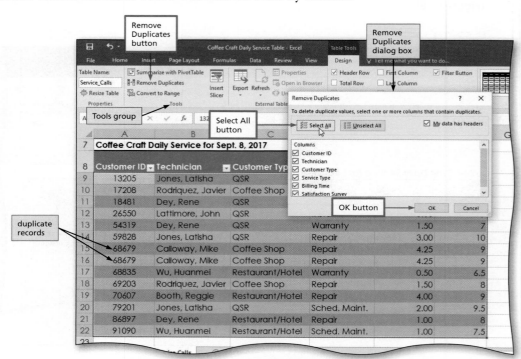

Figure 6–10

- Click the OK button (Remove Duplicates dialog box) to remove duplicate records from the table (Figure 6–11).

Q&A

Did Excel reformat the table?

Yes. The Banded Rows check box (Table Tools Design tab | Table Style Options group) is checked automatically when you selected the table format. **Row banding** causes adjacent rows to have different formatting; each row in the table is distinguishable from surrounding rows.

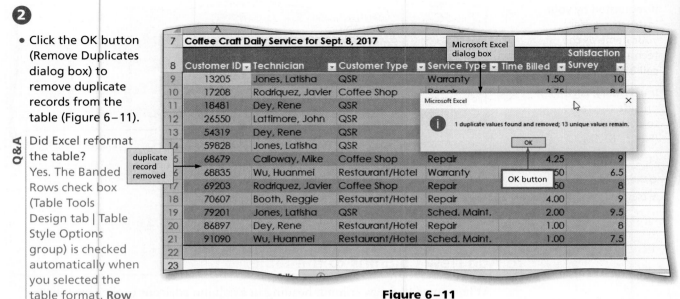

Figure 6–11

- Click the OK button (Microsoft Excel dialog box) to finish the process.

Experiment

- Examine the table to verify removal of the duplicate record for customer 68679.

Other Ways

1. Select range, click Remove Duplicates button (Data tab | Data Tools group)

To Enter a New Record into a Table

1 CREATE TABLE | 2 LOOKUP TABLES | 3 CALCULATED FIELDS | 4 CONDITIONAL FORMATTING | 5 SORT TABLES
6 QUERY TABLES | 7 CRITERIA RANGES | 8 DATABASE & CONDITIONAL FUNCTIONS | 9 SUBTOTALS & TREEMAP

The following step enters a new service call record into the table. You will insert the information just below the table. **Why?** *Data entered in rows or columns adjacent to the table becomes part of the table.* Excel will format the new table data automatically.

1

- Select cell A22.
- Type the new entries below.

Experiment

- As you enter the data, notice that Excel tries to complete your fields based on previous common entries.

A22	42724
B22	Franklin, Nathan
C22	Coffee Shop
D22	Repair
E22	2.00
F22	9.5

If requested by your instructor, enter your name as the technician in cell B22.

- If necessary, click outside the table to deselect it (Figure 6–12).

12	26550			Install		9
13	54319	Dey, Rene	QSR	Warranty	1.50	7
14	59828	Jones, Latisha	QSR	Repair	3.00	10
15	68679	Calloway, Mike	Coffee Shop	Repair	4.25	9
16	68835	Wu, Huanmei	Restaurant/Hotel	Warranty	0.50	6.5
17	69203	Rodriquez, Javier	Coffee Shop	Repair	1.50	8
18	70607	Booth, Reggie	Restaurant/Hotel	Repair	4.00	9
19	79201	Jones, Latisha	QSR	Sched. Maint.	2.00	9.5
20	86897	Dey, Rene	Restaurant/Hotel	Repair	1.00	8
21	91090	Wu, Huanmei	Restaurant/Hotel	Sched. Maint.	1.00	7.5
22	42724	Franklin, Nathan	Coffee Shop	Repair	2.00	9.5
23						

row 22 displays new data

Figure 6–12

Other Ways

1. Drag table sizing handle down to add new row, enter data

To Add New Columns to the Table

When you add a new column heading in a column adjacent to the current column headings in the table, Excel automatically adds the adjacent column to the table's range and copies the font format of the existing table heading to the new column heading. The following steps insert column headings for three new columns in the table.

1 Change the column width of column G to 16.00. Click cell G8. Type **Post-Service Rating** and then click the Enter button to enter the heading. Click the Wrap Text button (Home tab | Alignment group) to wrap the text.

2 Change the column width of column H to 16.50. Click cell H8. Type **% of Technician's Work Day** and then click the Enter button to enter the heading. Wrap the text in the cell.

3 Change the column width of column I to 11.00. Click cell I8. Type **Customer Bill** and then click the Enter button to enter the heading. Wrap the text in the cell (Figure 6–13).

new columns

	D	E	F	G	H	I
Row 8	Service Type	Time Billed	Satisfaction Survey	Post-Service Rating	% of Technician's Work Day	Customer Bill
	Warranty	1.50	10			
	Repair	3.75	8.5			
	Sched. Maint.	1.00	8.5			
	Install	5.00	9			
	Warranty	1.50	7			
	Repair	3.00	10			
	Repair	4.25	9			
el	Warranty	0.50	6.5			
	Repair	1.50	8			
tel	Repair	4.00	9			
	Sched. Maint.	2.00	9.5			
tel	Repair	1.00	8			
el	Sched. Maint.	1.00	7.5			
	Repair	2.00	9.5			

Figure 6–13

To Center Across Selection

The following steps center the title in cell A7 across a selection using the Format Cells dialog box. In earlier modules, recall you used the 'Merge & Center' button (Home tab | Alignment group) to center text across a range. *Why? This earlier technique centered the title, but it removed access to individual cells, because the cells were merged.* The Center Across Selection format centers text across multiple cells but does not merge the selected cell range into one cell.

- Select the range A7:I7. Right-click the selected range to display the shortcut menu (Figure 6–14).

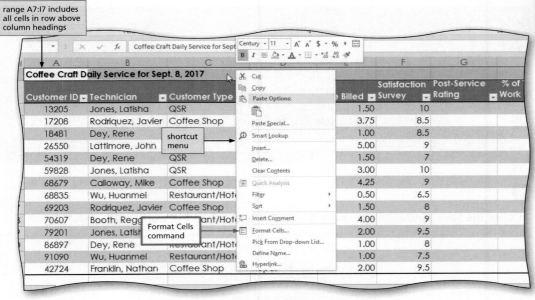

Figure 6–14

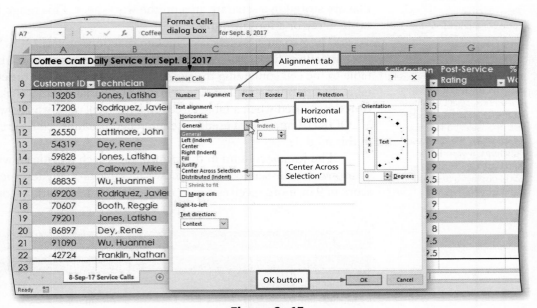

- Click Format Cells on the shortcut menu to display the Format Cells dialog box.

- Click the Alignment tab (Format Cells dialog box) and then click the Horizontal button in the Text alignment area to display a list of horizontal alignments (Figure 6–15).

Figure 6–15

- Click 'Center Across Selection' in the Horizontal list (Format Cells dialog box) to select the option to center the title across the selection.

- Click the OK button (Format Cells dialog box) to apply the settings.

- Click the Cell Styles button (Home tab | Styles group), and then apply the Title style to cell A7. Bold the cell, and then change the font size to 20 (Figure 6–16).

Figure 6–16

- Click the Save button on the Quick Access Toolbar to save the workbook again.

Using a Lookup Table

BTW

Other Database Functions

For a complete list of the database functions available for use with a table, click the Insert Function button in the formula bar. When Excel displays the Insert Function dialog box, select Database in the 'Or select a category' list. The 'Select a function' box displays the database functions. If you click a database function name, Excel displays a description of the function.

The entries in the Satisfaction Survey column give the user a numerical evaluation of the customer feedback for each technician. Some people, however, prefer simple ratings or letter grades, which, when used properly, group the technicians in the same way sports teams award their medals or instructors group student grades. Excel contains functions that allow you to assign such rankings based on a range of values that are stored in a separate area on the worksheet. This range is sometimes called a **table array** or a **lookup table**.

The two most widely used lookup functions are HLOOKUP and VLOOKUP. Both functions find a value in a lookup table and return a corresponding value from the table to the cell containing the function. The **HLOOKUP function** is used when the table direction for a field of data is horizontal, or across the worksheet. The **VLOOKUP function** is used when a table direction is vertical, or down the worksheet. The VLOOKUP function is used more often because most tables are vertical, as is the table in this module.

The Rating column in this project rates each technician with a value of gold, silver, or bronze for the service call. As shown in Table 6–3, any technician receiving an average score of 9 or more receives a gold rating. A technician with a score of 8 or more receives

Table 6–3 How the Ratings Are Determined	
Survey	**Rating**
0 to 6.99	*Generate Report
7 to 7.99	Bronze
8 to 8.99	Silver
9 and higher	Gold

a silver rating. A technician with a score of 7 or more receives a bronze rating. An average score of less than 7 will cause the table to relay a message that the office should generate a report and get back in touch with the customer to help remedy the situation.

To facilitate the display of each technician's rating, you will use the VLOOKUP function. The general form of the VLOOKUP function is

=VLOOKUP(lookup_value, table_array, col_index_num)

The three arguments of the VLOOKUP function represent the data that the function needs to do its job. The first argument is the **lookup value**, which is the data, or the location of the data, that you wish to look up. In the case of the service call table, that data is located in column F, the Satisfaction Survey. You only need to enter the first occurrence of the data, cell F9; because it is a relative reference in a table, Excel will fill in the rest.

The second argument is the location of the lookup table (represented as table_array in the syntax of the function). The location is a contiguous set of rows and columns with the numeric rating in the left column and the corresponding rating, letter grade, or text value in the other columns. The left column values in a table array are called **table arguments**, and they must be in sequence from lowest to highest. In this project, the table arguments are 0, 7, 8, and 9 — the lowest value in each rating. One or more columns to the right of the table arguments are the return values. The **return value** is the answer you want to appear as a result of the VLOOKUP function. In the service call table, the return value will be *Generate Report, Bronze, Silver, or Gold.

The third argument of the function is the **column index number** (represented as col_index_num in the syntax of the function), which represents the column location of the return value within the table array. In this project, that is column 2.

A fourth, optional argument allows you to enter a logical value that specifies whether you want VLOOKUP to find an exact match or an approximate match.

To Create a Table Array Area

Before using the VLOOKUP function, you must create the table array. The following steps create a table array in the range L1:M7.

① Change the width of column M to 16.5.

② Click cell L1. Type **Rating Table** as the table array title and then click the Enter button on the formula bar.

③ Apply the Title style and bold formatting to cell L1.

④ Select the range L1:M1. Right-click the selection and then click Format Cells on the shortcut menu to display the Format Cells dialog box. On the Alignment tab (Format Cells dialog box), click the Horizontal button, and then click 'Center Across Selection'. Click the OK button to apply the settings.

⑤ In cell L2, type **Survey** to enter the column heading.

⑥ In cell M2, type **Rating** to enter the column heading.

⑦ Select cell I8. Click the Format Painter button (Home tab | Clipboard group) and then drag through cells L2:M2 to copy the format of the selected cell to the column headings.

8 Enter the data shown below (Figure 6–17).

Cell	Data	Cell	Data
L3	0	M3	*Generate Report
L4	7	M4	Bronze
L5	8	M5	Silver
L6	9	M6	Gold

Q&A Why do the table arguments contain single digits instead of a range?
You only have to enter the least value for each argument. Excel will evaluate all values in the range.

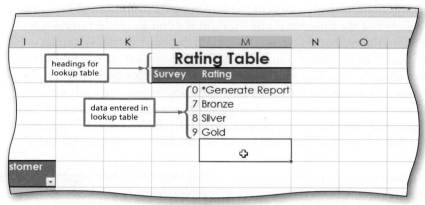

Figure 6–17

To Use the VLOOKUP Function

1 CREATE TABLE | 2 LOOKUP TABLES | 3 CALCULATED FIELDS | 4 CONDITIONAL FORMATTING | 5 SORT TABLES
6 QUERY TABLES | 7 CRITERIA RANGES | 8 DATABASE & CONDITIONAL FUNCTIONS | 9 SUBTOTALS & TREEMAP

The following steps use the VLOOKUP function and the table array to determine the Post-Service Rating for each technician. *Why? Using the VLOOKUP function with a table allows Excel to display the ratings, rather than the user typing them in individually.*

1

- Click cell G9. Type =vlookup(f9, $L$3:$M$6,2) as the cell entry (Figure 6–18).

Q&A Why should I use absolute cell references in the function?
You need to use absolute cell references, indicated by the dollar signs, so that Excel will not adjust the table array location when it creates the calculated column in the next step. If Excel adjusted the cell references, you would see unexpected results in column G.

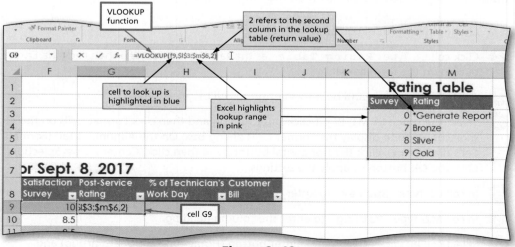

Figure 6–18

- Click the Enter button to create a calculated column for the selected field, the Post-Service Rating field in this case.

- Scroll the worksheet to show the completed table (Figure 6–19).

Q&A

What happens when you click the Enter button?
Because cell G9 is the first record in a table, Excel continues the calculated column by replicating the VLOOKUP function through row 22.

How does the VLOOKUP function determine the ratings?
The LOOKUP function is not searching for a table argument that matches the lookup value exactly. The VLOOKUP function begins the search at the top of the table and works downward. As soon as it finds the first table argument greater than the lookup value, it stops, and the function returns the previous row's corresponding value from column M.

	Service Type	Time Billed	Satisfaction Survey	Post-Service Rating	% of Technician's Cur... Work Day	Bill
	Warranty	1.50	10	Gold		
	Repair	3.75	8.5	Silver		
	Sched. Maint.	1.00	8.5	Silver		
	Install	5.00	9	Gold		
	Warranty	1.50	7	Bronze		
	Repair	3.00	10	Gold		
	Repair	4.25	9	Gold		
el	Warranty	0.50	6.5	*Generate Report		
	Repair	1.50	8	Silver		
tel	Repair	4.00	9	Gold		
	Sched. Maint.	2.00	9.5	Gold		
tel	Repair	1.00	8	Silver		
tel	Sched. Maint.	1.00	7.5	Bronze		
	Repair	2.00	9.5	Gold		

Excel fills in column with data from lookup table

Figure 6–19

Other Ways

1. Click Insert Function box in formula bar, click 'Or select a category' button, click 'Lookup & Reference', click VLOOKUP in 'Select a function' list, enter arguments

2. Click 'Lookup & Reference' button (Formulas tab | Function Library group), click VLOOKUP, enter arguments

Adding Calculated Fields to the Table

A **calculated field** or **computational field** is a field (column) in a table that contains a formula, function, cell reference, structured reference, or condition. When you create a calculated field, Excel automatically fills in the column without the use of a fill or copy command; you do not have to use the fill handle to replicate formulas in a calculated field.

Table 6–4 contains the three calculated fields used in this project. You created the first one in the previous steps.

Table 6–4 Calculated Fields		
Column Heading	**Column**	**Calculated Field**
Post-Service Rating	G	Uses the VLOOKUP function to determine a rating based upon the Satisfaction Survey (column F).
% of Technician's Work Day	H	Divide the Time Billed by 6.5 hours
Customer Bill	I	Multiply the Time Billed by 75

To Create Calculated Fields

1 CREATE TABLE | 2 LOOKUP TABLES | 3 CALCULATED FIELDS | 4 CONDITIONAL FORMATTING | 5 SORT TABLES
6 QUERY TABLES | 7 CRITERIA RANGES | 8 DATABASE & CONDITIONAL FUNCTIONS | 9 SUBTOTALS & TREEMAP

Another advantage of using a table is in how you type formulas in a calculated field. Rather than using normal cell references, Excel allows you to type a structured reference. A **structured reference** uses some combination of the table name (such as Service_Calls), the column heading (such as Time Billed), or any named or special rows, rather than the usual column letter and row number references (such as F10). Named rows use a

sign before the row name (such as #Totals). If the column heading contains any spaces between words, its name must be enclosed in brackets (such as [Satisfaction Survey] for column F).

Using structured references has several advantages. *Why? Excel updates structured references automatically when any column heading changes or when you add new data to the table. Using this notation also makes formulas easier to read.* If you have multiple tables, you can include the table name in the structured reference, making it easier to locate data in large workbooks. The following steps enter structured references for the last two columns of data in the table.

1

- Click cell H9 to select it.

- Click the Percent Style button (Home tab | Number group) and then click the Increase Decimal button (Home tab | Number group) twice so that data is formatted with two decimal places.

- Type = [to display the list of available fields in the table (Figure 6–20).

Q&A What is the purpose of the [(left bracket)?
The [begins a structured reference and causes Excel to display the list of table fields (column headings).

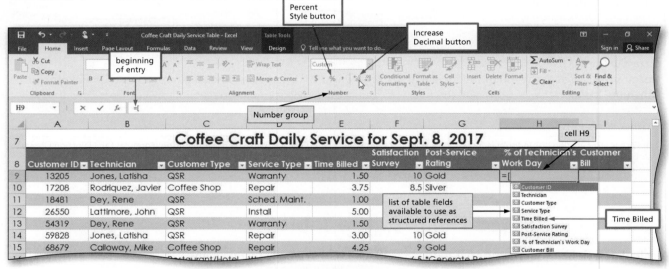

Figure 6–20

2

- Double-click Time Billed to select the field to use for the structured reference.

- Type] /6.5 to complete the formula and then click the Enter button to create the calculated column (Figure 6–21).

Figure 6–21

Do I have to set the formatting before I enter the structured reference formula?

No, you do not have to; however, applying formatting before entering the formula prompts Excel to generate the calculated column with your desired formatting. Otherwise, you would have to format the column manually after it generates.

Why am I dividing by 6.5?

The company uses a 6.5-hour workday, allowing some time for technician travel.

3

- Click cell I9 to select it.

- Click the 'Accounting Number Format' button (Home tab | Number group) so that data in the selected column is displayed as a dollar amount with two decimal places.

- Type `=if(d9="Warranty",0,[Time Billed]*75)` and then click the Enter button to create a calculated column (Figure 6–22).

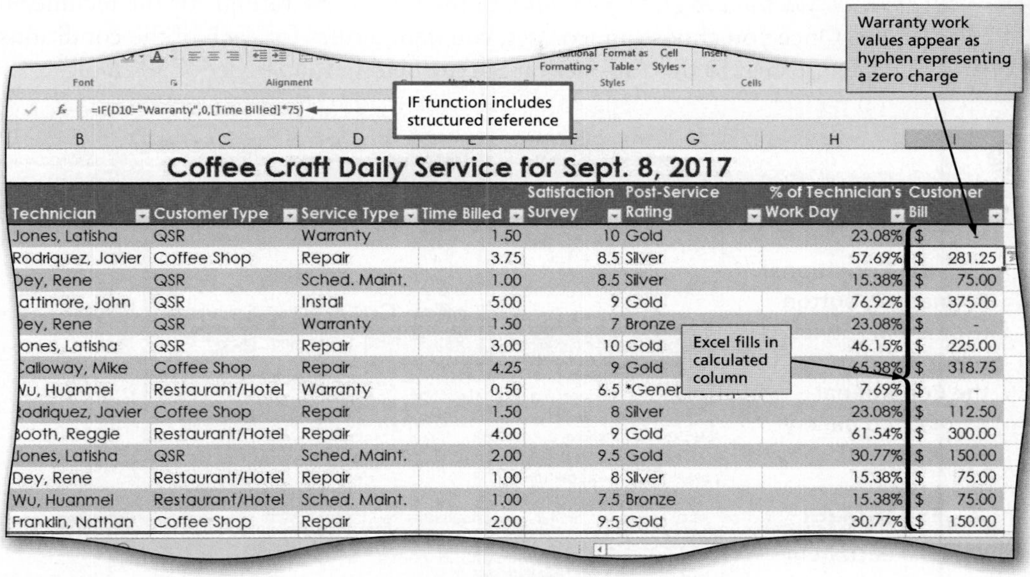

Figure 6–22

What does the IF function do in the formula?

The IF function looks for service calls related to warranty (the condition in the function); in those cases the customer is billed zero (the first argument). The company charges other customers $75 per hour for repair services (the second argument in the function).

Conditional Formatting

Conditional formatting allows you to create rules that change the formatting of a cell based on its value. For example, you might want negative values to appear highlighted in red. Excel includes five preset types of conditional formats: highlight, top and bottom rules, data bars, color scales, and icon sets, as well as the ability to create your own conditional formats. You can combine different types of formats on any cell or range. For example, based on a cell's value, you can format it to include both an icon and a specific background color. You also can apply multiple conditional formatting rules to a cell or range.

The Conditional Formatting Rules Manager dialog box allows you to view all of the rules for the current selection or for an entire worksheet and change the order in which the rules are applied to a cell or range. In addition, you can stop applying subsequent rules after one rule is found to be true. For example, if the first rule specifies that a negative value should appear in red, then you may not want to apply any other conditional formats to the cell.

To Add a Conditional Formatting Rule with an Icon Set

The Post-Service Rating field provides succinct feedback to the user about performance of the technician on each service call. Another method to present the information visually is to display an icon next to the Satisfaction Survey number. Conditional formatting provides a variety of icons, including traffic signals, circles, flags, bars, and arrows. Icon sets include sets of three, four, or five icons. *Why? You choose an icon set depending on how many ways you want to group your data.* In the case of the ratings for the technicians, you will use three different icons. Once you choose an icon set, you define rules for each of the conditions. The following steps add a conditional format to the Satisfaction Survey field in the Service_Calls table.

- Select the range F9:F22 and then click the Conditional Formatting button (Home tab | Styles group) to display the Conditional Formatting gallery (Figure 6–23).

 Experiment

- Point to each item in the Conditional Formatting gallery and then point to various items in the sub galleries to watch how the table changes.

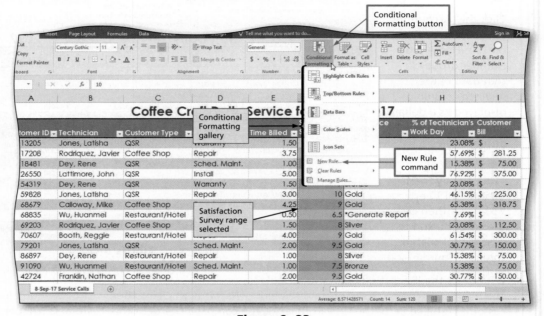

Figure 6–23

2

- Click New Rule in the Conditional Formatting gallery to display the New Formatting Rule dialog box.

- Click the Format Style button (New Formatting Rule dialog box) to display the Format Style list (Figure 6–24).

Q&A What do the color scale formats do?
You can choose between two or three values and apply different color backgrounds. Excel graduates the shading from one value to the next.

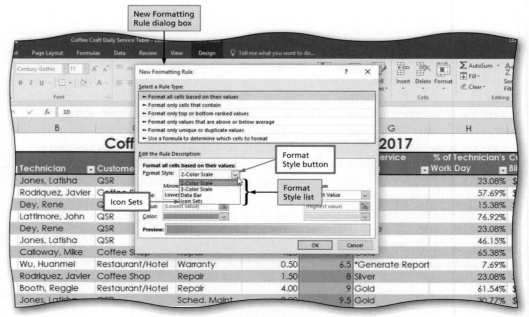

Figure 6–24

- Click Icon Sets in the Format Style list (New Formatting Rule dialog box) to display the Icon Style area.

- Click the Icon Style button to display the Icon Style list and then scroll as necessary to display the '3 Symbols (Circled)' icon style in the list (Figure 6–25).

Experiment

- Click a variety of icon styles in the Icon Styles list to view the options for each style.

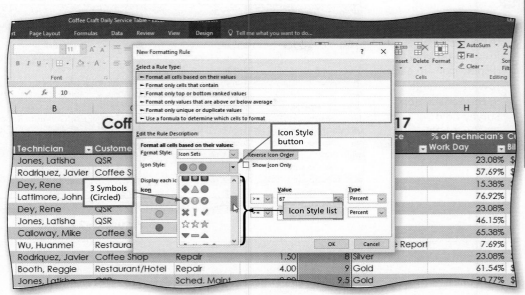

Figure 6–25

- Click the '3 Symbols (Circled)' icon style in the Icon Style list (New Formatting Rule dialog box) to select an icon style that includes three different circles.

- Click the first Type button and then click Number in the list to select a numeric value.

- Click the second Type button and then click Number in the list to select a numeric value.

- Type 9 in the first Value box. Type 7 in the second Value box and then press the TAB key to complete the conditions (Figure 6–26).

Q&A
Why do the numbers next to each icon change as I type?
Excel automatically updates this area as you change the conditions. Use this area as an easy-to-read status of the conditions that you are creating.

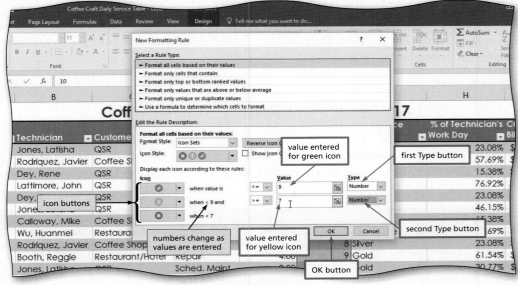

Figure 6–26

- Click the OK button (New Formatting Rule dialog box) to display icons in each row of the table in the Satisfaction Survey field (Figure 6–27).

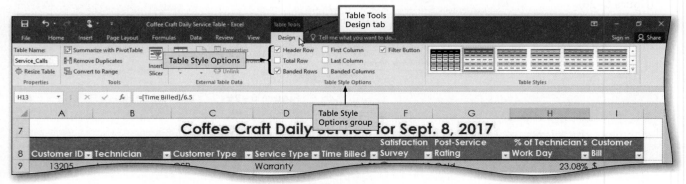

	Customer Type	Service Type	Time Billed	Satisfaction Survey	Post-Service Rating	% of Technician's Work Day	Customer Bill
ha	QSR	Warranty	150	✓	10 Gold	23.08%	$ -
Javier	Coffee Shop	Repair	375	ⓘ	8.5 Silver	57.69%	$ 281.25
	QSR	Sched. Maint.	100	ⓘ	8.5 Silver	15.38%	$ 75.00
ohn	QSR	Install	500	✓	9 Gold	76.92%	$ 375.00
	QSR	Warranty	150	ⓘ	7 Bronze	23.08%	$ -
a	QSR		300	✓	10 Gold	46.15%	$ 225.00
ike	Coffee Shop		425	✓	9 Gold	65.38%	$ 318.75
ei	Restaurant/Hotel		50	✕	6.5 *Generate Report	7.69%	$ -
Javier	Coffee Shop	Repair	150	ⓘ	8 Silver	23.08%	$ 112.50
gie	Restaurant/Hotel	Repair	400	✓	9 Gold	61.54%	$ 300.00
ha	QSR	Sched. Maint.	200	✓	9.5 Gold	30.77%	$ 150.00
	Restaurant/Hotel	Repair	100	ⓘ	8 Silver	15.38%	$ 75.00
ei	Restaurant/Hotel	Sched. Maint.	100	ⓘ	7.5 Bronze	15.38%	$ 75.00
han	Coffee Shop	Repair	200	✓	9.5 Gold	30.77%	$ 150.00

conditional format displays icons in column F

Figure 6–27

Working with Tables in Excel

When a table is active, the Table Tools Design tab on the ribbon provides powerful commands that allow you to alter the appearance and contents of a table quickly. For example, you quickly can add and remove header and total rows in a table. You also can change the style of the first or last column. Other commands that you will learn in later modules include inserting slices, exporting tables, and summarizing the data with a PivotTable.

To Insert a Total Row

1 CREATE TABLE | 2 LOOKUP TABLES | 3 CALCULATED FIELDS | 4 CONDITIONAL FORMATTING | 5 SORT TABLES
6 QUERY TABLES | 7 CRITERIA RANGES | 8 DATABASE & CONDITIONAL FUNCTIONS | 9 SUBTOTALS & TREEMAP

The Total Row check box (Table Tools Design tab | Table Style Options group) inserts a total row at the bottom of the table, summing the values in the last column. *Why? The default setting creates a total in the last column; however, total rows display a button beside each cell to create other totals and functions.* If the values are nonnumeric, then Excel counts the number of records and puts that number in the total row. The following steps create a total row.

- Click anywhere in the table and then display the Table Tools Design tab (Figure 6–28).

🔍 Experiment

- Select a variety of combinations of check boxes in the Table Style Options group on the Table Tools Design tab to see their effect on the table. When finished, make sure that the check boxes are set as shown in Figure 6–28.

Figure 6–28

- Click the Total Row check box (Table Tools Design tab | Table Style Options group) to display the total row and display the sum in the last column of the table, cell I23 in this case.

- Select cell E23 in the total row and then click the button on the right side of the cell to display a list of available functions (Figure 6–29).

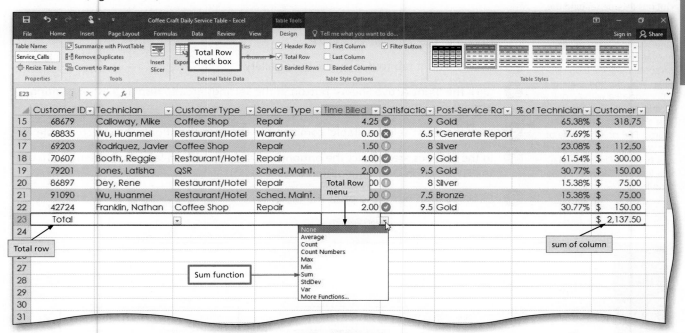

Figure 6–29

- Click Sum in the list to select the Sum function for the selected cell in the total row, thus totaling the billable hours for the day.

- Repeat the process to create an average in cell F23, thus averaging the satisfaction surveys. Format the cell by decreasing the decimals to two decimal places (Figure 6–30).

Ⓟ **Experiment**

- Choose other cells in the total row and experiment with the different kinds of statistical functions, such as using the MAX function in cell H23 or the COUNT function in cell D23.

Figure 6–30

④

- Click the Save button on the Quick Access Toolbar to save the workbook again.

Other Ways
1. Right-click table, point to Table on shortcut menu, click Totals Row on submenu

Break Point: If you wish to take a break, this is a good place to do so. You can exit Excel. To resume at a later time, run Excel, open the file called Coffee Craft Daily Service Table, and continue following the steps from this location forward.

To Print the Table

When a table is selected and you display the Print tab in the Backstage view, an option in the Settings area allows you to print the contents of just the active, or selected, table. The following steps print the table in landscape orientation using the Fit Sheet on One Page option.

1 If necessary, click anywhere in the table to make it active, and then click File on the ribbon to open the Backstage view.

2 Click the Print tab to display the Print gallery.

3 Click the 'Print Active Sheets' button in the Settings area to display a list of printing options.

4 Click the 'Print Selected Table' command to choose to print only the selected table.

5 In the Settings area, select the options to print the table in landscape orientation. Use the Fit Sheet on One Page option (Figure 6–31).

6 Click the Print button to print the table.

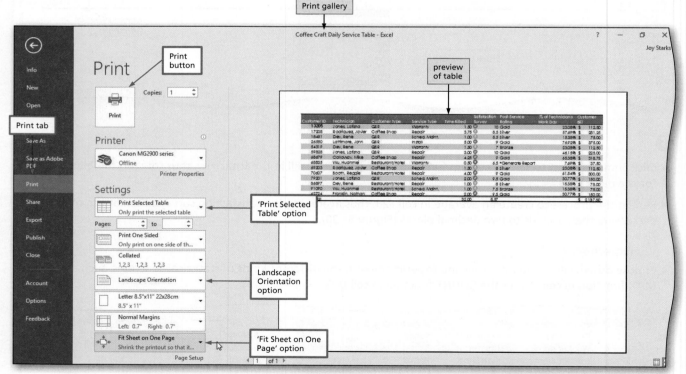

Figure 6–31

Sorting a table

The data in a table is easier to work with and more meaningful if the records appear sequentially based on one or more fields. Arranging records in a specific sequence is called **sorting**. Data is in **ascending order** if it is sorted from lowest to highest, earliest to most recent, or alphabetically from A to Z. Data is in **descending order** if it is sorted from highest to lowest, most recent to earliest, or alphabetically from Z to A.

The field or fields you select to sort are called **sort keys**. When you sort a table, all of the records in each row move together; so even if the selected cell is in the last name column, for example, the first name and all data in the row will be moved when the table is sorted by last name.

You can sort data in a table by using one of the following techniques:

- Select a cell in the field on which to sort, click the 'Sort & Filter' button (Home tab | Editing group), and then click one of the sorting options on the Sort & Filter menu.

- With the table active, click the filter button in the column on which to sort and then click one of the sorting options in the table.

- Use the Sort button (Data tab | Sort & Filter group).

- Use the 'Sort A to Z' or 'Sort Z to A' button (Data tab | Sort & Filter group).

- Right-click anywhere in a table and then point to Sort on the shortcut menu to display the Sort submenu.

BTW

Sorting Dates
When you use AutoFilter to sort date fields, the filter menu will list commands such as 'Sort Newest to Oldest' and 'Sort Oldest to Newest'.

Which field is best for sorting?

Ideally, the user of the worksheet should be able to sort the table on any field using a variety of methods and sort using multiple fields at the same time. Depending on what you want to show, you may sort by a name field or list value, by a numeric field, or by date. You also can sort a table in ascending or descending order.

CONSIDER THIS

To Sort Ascending

1 CREATE TABLE | 2 LOOKUP TABLES | 3 CALCULATED FIELDS | 4 CONDITIONAL FORMATTING | **5 SORT TABLES**
6 QUERY TABLES | 7 CRITERIA RANGES | 8 DATABASE & CONDITIONAL FUNCTIONS | 9 SUBTOTALS & TREEMAP

The following steps sort the table in ascending order by the Technician field using the 'Sort & Filter' button (Home tab | Editing group). *Why? Names commonly display in alphabetical order.*

- Scroll to display the entire table. If necessary, display the Home tab.

- Click cell B9 and then click the 'Sort & Filter' button (Home tab | Editing group) to display the Sort & Filter menu (Figure 6–32).

Q&A What if the column I choose includes numeric or date data?

If the column you choose includes numeric data, then the Sort & Filter menu shows the 'Sort Smallest to Largest' and 'Sort Largest to Smallest' commands. If the column you choose includes date data, then the Sort & Filter menu shows the 'Sort Oldest to Newest' and 'Sort Newest to Oldest' commands.

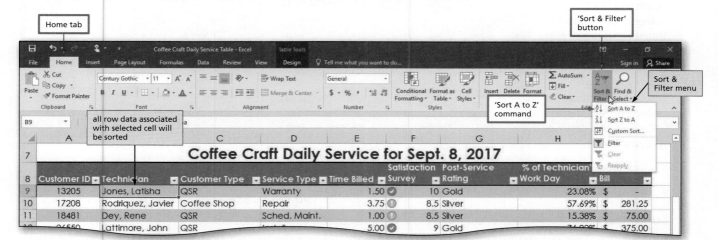

Figure 6–32

2

- Click 'Sort A to Z' to sort the table in ascending order by the selected field, Technician in this case (Figure 6–33).

🔍 **Experiment**

- Select other fields in the table and use the same procedure to sort on the fields you choose. When you are finished, remove any sorting, select cell A9, and repeat the two steps above.

Q&A Can I undo the sort?
Yes, you can click the Undo button (Quick Access Toolbar) or press CTRL+Z; however, if you close your file, the original order will be lost. If you want to undo a sort, it is a good practice to do so before continuing with other commands.

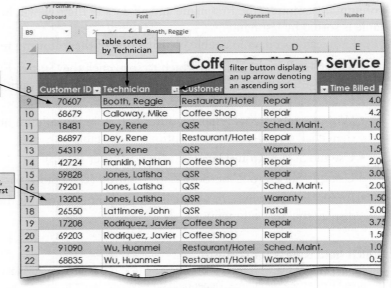

Figure 6–33

Other Ways

1. Select field in table, click 'Sort A to Z' button (Data tab | Sort & Filter group)
2. Click filter button of field on which to sort, click 'Sort A to Z'
3. Right-click column to sort, point to Sort on shortcut menu, click 'Sort A to Z'

To Sort Descending

1 CREATE TABLE | 2 LOOKUP TABLES | 3 CALCULATED FIELDS | 4 CONDITIONAL FORMATTING | 5 SORT TABLES
6 QUERY TABLES | 7 CRITERIA RANGES | 8 DATABASE & CONDITIONAL FUNCTIONS | 9 SUBTOTALS & TREEMAP

The following step sorts the records in descending order by Time Billed using the 'Sort Largest to Smallest' button on the Data tab. *Why? Sometimes it is more convenient to use the Data tab and sort with a single click.*

1

- Click cell E9 to position the sort in the Time Billed column.
- Display the Data tab.
- Click the 'Sort Largest to Smallest' button (Data tab | Sort & Filter group) to sort the table in descending sequence by the selected field, Time Billed, in this case (Figure 6–34).

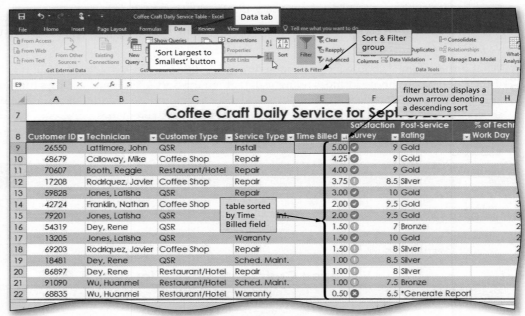

Figure 6–34

Other Ways

1. Select field in table, click 'Sort and Filter' button (Home tab | Editing group), click 'Sort Largest to Smallest'
2. Click filter button of field on which to sort, click 'Sort Largest to Smallest'
3. Right-click column to sort, point to Sort on shortcut menu, click 'Sort Largest to Smallest'

To Custom Sort a Table

While Excel allows you to sort on a maximum of 256 fields in a single sort operation, in these steps you will use the Custom Sort command to sort the Coffee Craft Daily Service Table using three fields. You will sort by Satisfaction Survey within Service Type within Customer Type. *Why? That phrase means that the records within the table first are arranged by Customer Type (Coffee Shop, QSR, or Restaurant/Hotel). Then, within Customer Type, the records are arranged alphabetically by Service Type (Repair, Sched. Maint., Warranty). Finally, within Service Type, the records are arranged from largest to smallest by the Satisfaction Survey number.* In this case, Customer Type is the major sort key, Service Type is the intermediate sort key, and Satisfaction Survey is the minor sort key. You can sort any field in ascending or descending order, depending on how you want the data to look. The following steps sort the Service_Calls table on multiple fields.

- Display the Home tab.
- With a cell in the table active, click the 'Sort & Filter' button (Home tab | Editing group) to display the Sort & Filter menu.
- Click Custom Sort on the Sort & Filter menu to display the Sort dialog box.
- Click the 'Column Sort by' button (Sort dialog box) to display the field names in the table (Figure 6–35).

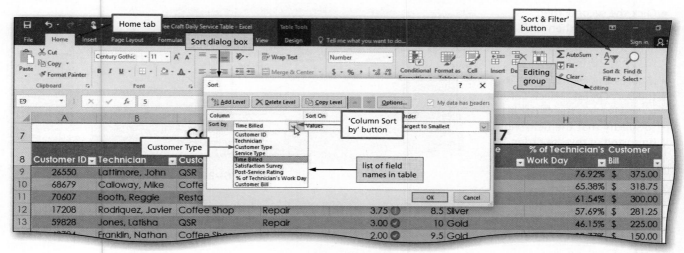

Figure 6–35

- Click Customer Type to select the first sort level, or major sort key.
- If necessary, click the Sort on button (Sort dialog box) and then click Values in the Sort On list.
- If necessary, click the Order button and then click 'A to Z' to sort the field alphabetically (Figure 6–36).

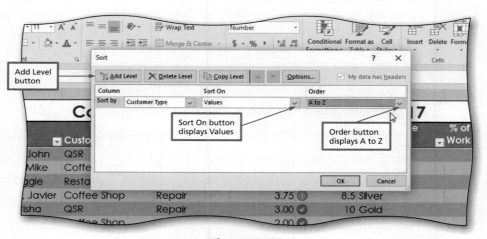

Figure 6–36

- Click the Add Level button (Sort dialog box) to add a second sort level.

- Click the Then by button and then click Service Type in the Then by list to select an intermediate sort key.

- If necessary, select Values in the Sort On list.

- If necessary, select 'A to Z' in the Order list to sort the field alphabetically (Figure 6–37).

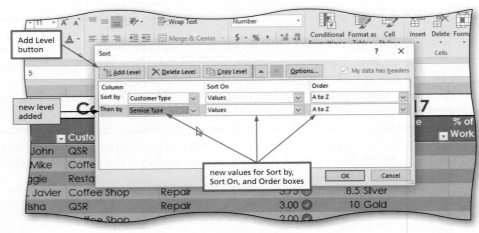

Figure 6–37

- Click the Add Level button to add a new sort level.

- Click the second Then by button and then click Satisfaction Survey to select a minor sort key.

- If necessary, select Values in the Sort On list. Select 'Largest to Smallest' in the Order list to specify that the field should be sorted in reverse order (Figure 6–38).

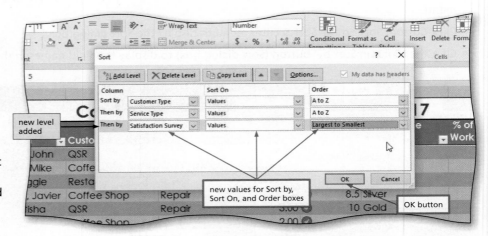

Figure 6–38

- Click the OK button to sort the table, in this case by Satisfaction Survey (descending) within Service Type (ascending) within Customer Type (ascending) (Figure 6–39).

Q&A What should I do if I make a sorting error?

If you make a mistake in a sort operation, you can return the records to their original order by clicking the Undo button on the Quick Access Toolbar or by pressing CTRL+Z. You can undo all steps back to when you originally opened the file — even if you have saved multiple times. Once you close the file however, there is no way to undo a sorting error.

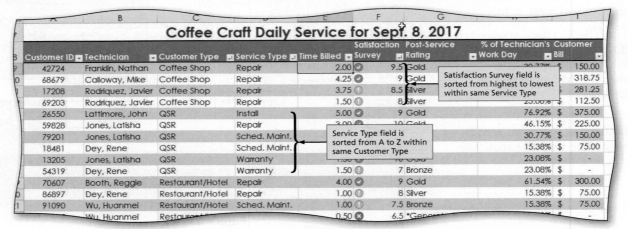

Figure 6–39

Querying a Table Using AutoFilter

When you first create a table, Excel automatically enables AutoFilter, a tool used to sort, query, and filter the records in a table. While using AutoFilter, filter buttons appear to the right of the column headings. Clicking a button displays the filter menu for the column with various commands and a list of all items in the field (shown in Figure 6–40).

The sort commands work the same way as the sort buttons that you learned about earlier. The filter commands let you choose to display only those records that meet specified criteria such as color, number, or text. In this context, **criteria** means a logical rule by which data is tested and chosen. For example, you can filter the table to display a specific name or item by typing it in a Search box. The name you selected acts as the criteria for filtering the table, which results in Excel displaying only those records that match the criteria. The selected check boxes indicate which items will appear in the table. By default, all of the items are selected. If you deselect an item from the filter menu, it is called the filter criterion. Excel will not display any record that contains the unchecked item.

As with the previous sort techniques, you can include more than one column when you filter, by clicking a second filter button and making choices. The process of filtering activity based on one or more filter criteria is called a **query**. After you filter data, you can copy, find, edit, format, chart, or print the filtered data without rearranging or moving it.

To Sort a Table Using AutoFilter

1 CREATE TABLE | 2 LOOKUP TABLES | 3 CALCULATED FIELDS | 4 CONDITIONAL FORMATTING | 5 SORT TABLES

6 QUERY TABLES | 7 CRITERIA RANGES | 8 DATABASE & CONDITIONAL FUNCTIONS | 9 SUBTOTALS & TREEMAP

The following steps sort the table by Customer Bill using the 'Sort Largest to Smallest' command on the filter menu. *Why? Using the filter menu sometimes is easier than other sort methods; you do not have to leave the table area and move to the ribbon to perform the sort.*

• Click the filter button in the Customer Bill column to display the filter menu (Figure 6–40).

🔍 **Experiment**

• Click various filter buttons. Notice that the filter menu is context sensitive, which means it changes depending on what you are trying to filter. When you are finished, again click the Filter button in the Customer Bill column.

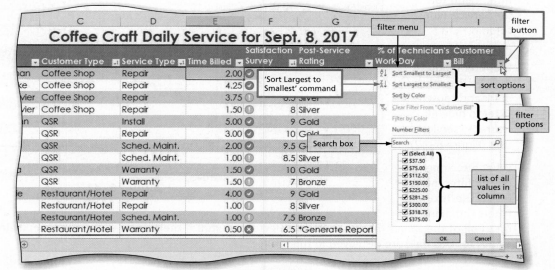

Figure 6–40

- Click 'Sort Largest to Smallest' on the filter menu to sort the table in descending sequence by the selected field (Figure 6–41).

Q&A

Does performing a new sort overwrite the previous sort? Yes. A new sort undoes the previous sort, even if it is a custom sort or a sort based on multiple sort keys.

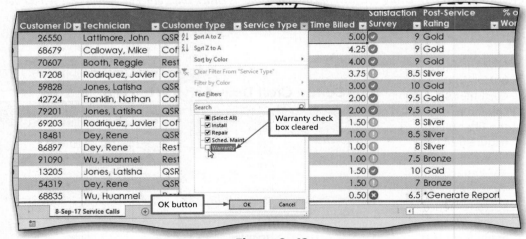

table is sorted by Customer Bill

Coffee Craft Daily Service for Sept. 8, 2017

	Customer Type	Service Type	Time Billed	Satisfaction Survey	Post-Service Rating	% of Technician's Work Day	Customer Bill
ohn	QSR	Install	5.00 ✓	9	Gold	76.92%	$ 375.00
ike	Coffee Shop	Repair	4.25 ✓	9	Gold	65.38%	$ 318.75
e	Restaurant/Hotel	Repair	4.00 ✓	9	Gold	61.54%	$ 300.00
vier	Coffee Shop	Repair	3.75 ◑	8.5	Silver	57.69%	$ 281.25
ı	QSR	Repair	3.00 ✓	10	Gold	46.15%	$ 225.00
an	Coffee Shop	Repair	2.00 ✓	9.5	Gold	30.77%	$ 150.00
a	QSR	Sched. Maint.	2.00 ✓	9.5	Gold	30.77%	$ 150.00
avier	Coffee Shop	Repair	1.50 ◑	8	Silver	23.08%	$ 112.50
	QSR	Sched. Maint.	1.00 ◑	8.5	Silver	15.38%	$ 75.00
	Restaurant/Hotel	Repair	1.00 ◑	8	Silver	15.38%	$ 75.00
ei	Restaurant/Hotel	Sched. Maint.	1.00 ◑	7.5	Bronze	15.38%	$ 75.00
na	QSR	Warranty	1.50 ✓	10	Gold	23.08%	$ -
	QSR	Warranty	1.50 ◑	7	Bronze	23.08%	$ -
el	Restaurant/Hotel	Warranty	0.50 ✗	6.5	*Generate Report	7.69%	$ -

Figure 6–41

To Query a Table Using AutoFilter

1 CREATE TABLE | 2 LOOKUP TABLES | 3 CALCULATED FIELDS | 4 CONDITIONAL FORMATTING | 5 SORT TABLES
6 QUERY TABLES | **7 CRITERIA RANGES** | 8 DATABASE & CONDITIONAL FUNCTIONS | 9 SUBTOTALS & TREEMAP

The following steps query the Coffee Craft Daily Service Table using AutoFilter. *Why? The AutoFilter will cause the table to display only specific records, which may be helpful in very large tables.* In this case, using the check boxes on the filter menu, you will choose those records with a Service Type not equal to Warranty and whose Post-Service Rating is equal to Gold.

- Click the filter button in cell D8 to display the filter menu for the Service Type column.

- Click Warranty in the filter menu to remove the check mark and cause Excel to hide all warranty service calls (Figure 6–42).

Q&A

What else appears on the filter menu? Below the Text Filters command is a list of all of the values that occur in the selected column. A check mark in the top item, (Select All), indicates that all values for this field are displayed in the table.

Customer ID	Technician	Customer Type	Service Type	Time Billed	Satisfaction Survey	Post-Service Rating	% o Wor
26550	Lattimore, John	QSR		5.00 ✓	9	Gold	
68679	Calloway, Mike	Cof		4.25 ✓	9	Gold	
70607	Booth, Reggie	Rest		4.00 ✓	9	Gold	
17208	Rodriquez, Javier	Cof		3.75 ◑	8.5	Silver	
59828	Jones, Latisha	QSR		3.00 ✓	10	Gold	
42724	Franklin, Nathan	Cof		2.00 ✓	9.5	Gold	
79201	Jones, Latisha	QSR		2.00 ✓	9.5	Gold	
69203	Rodriquez, Javier	Cof		1.50 ◑	8	Silver	
18481	Dey, Rene	QSR		1.00 ◑	8.5	Silver	
86897	Dey, Rene	Rest		1.00 ◑	8	Silver	
91090	Wu, Huanmei	Rest		1.00 ◑	7.5	Bronze	
13205	Jones, Latisha	QSR		1.50 ✓	10	Gold	
54319	Dey, Rene	QSR		1.50 ◑	7	Bronze	
68835	Wu, Huanmei	Rest		0.50 ✗	6.5	*Generate Report	

Filter menu items: Sort A to Z, Sort Z to A, Sort by Color, Clear Filter From "Service Type", Filter by Color, Text Filters, Search, (Select All), ✓ Install, ✓ Repair, ✓ Sched. Maint., ☐ Warranty

Warranty check box cleared

OK button — OK — Cancel

8-Sep-17 Service Calls

Figure 6–42

2

- Click the OK button to apply the AutoFilter criterion.
- Click the filter button in cell G8 to display the filter menu for the selected column.

- Click to remove the check marks beside Bronze and Silver, so that only the Gold check box contains a check mark (Figure 6–43).

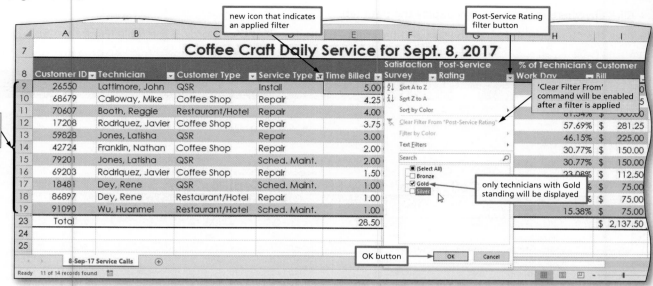

Figure 6–43

❸

- Click the OK button to apply the AutoFilter criterion (Figure 6–44).

Q&A

Are both filters now applied to the table?

Yes. When you select a second filter criterion, Excel adds it to the first; hence, each record must pass two tests to appear as part of the final subset of the table.

Did the filter remove the previous sort?

No. Notice in Figure 6–44 that the records still are sorted in descending order by Customer Bill.

Figure 6–44

Other Ways

1. Click filter button, enter desired data in Search box (filter menu), click OK button

To Remove Filters

1 CREATE TABLE | 2 LOOKUP TABLES | 3 CALCULATED FIELDS | 4 CONDITIONAL FORMATTING | 5 SORT TABLES
6 QUERY TABLES | 7 CRITERIA RANGES | 8 DATABASE & CONDITIONAL FUNCTIONS | 9 SUBTOTALS & TREEMAP

You can remove a filter from a specific column or remove all of the filters in a table at once. Each filter menu has a 'Clear Filter From' command that removes the column filter (shown in Figure 6–43). The Clear button (Data tab | Sort & Filter group) removes all of the filters. The following step removes all filters at once, to show all records in the table. *Why? The filters, or query, hid some of the records in the previous steps.*

1

- Click anywhere in the table and display the Data tab.

- Click the Clear button (Data tab | Sort & Filter group) to display all of the records in the table (Figure 6–45).

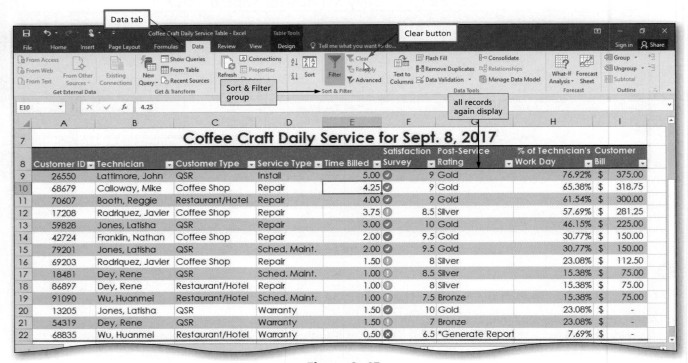

Figure 6–45

Other Ways

1. Click desired filter button, click (Select All) on filter menu

2. Right-click filtered column, point to Filter on shortcut menu, click 'Clear Filter From' command

---

To Search a Table Using AutoFilter

1 CREATE TABLE | 2 LOOKUP TABLES | 3 CALCULATED FIELDS | 4 CONDITIONAL FORMATTING | 5 SORT TABLES
6 QUERY TABLES | **7 CRITERIA RANGES | 8 DATABASE & CONDITIONAL FUNCTIONS | 9 SUBTOTALS & TREEMAP**

Using AutoFilter, you can search for specific records by entering data in the Search box. The data you enter is called the **search string**. For example, in a student table, you might want to search for a specific student ID number that might be difficult to locate in a large set of records. If an exact match exists, the value appears in the filter menu; then, if you click the OK button, the entire record appears in the table. Table searches are not case sensitive.

Alternately, you can search for similar or related data. In the Search box, you can type **?** (question mark) to represent any single character. For example in a quiz table, if you wanted to find answer1, answer2, and answer3, you could type **answer?** as the search string. Another way to search includes using an * (asterisk) to represent a series of characters. For example, in an inventory table, to find all of the items that relate to drive, you could type ***drive*** in the Search box. The filter would display results such as flash drives, CD-R drive, and drivers. The ? and * are called **wildcard characters**.

The following steps search for a specific record in a table using the filter menu. **Why?** *When tables are large, searching for individual records using the filter menu is quick and easy.*

1

- Click the filter button in the Technician column to display the filter menu.

- Click the Search box, and then type **jones** as the search string (Figure 6–46).

Q&A

Is this search the same as using the Find command? No. This command searches for data within the table only and then displays all records that match the search string. Three records matching the search appear in Figure 6–47. The Find command looks over the entire worksheet and highlights one cell.

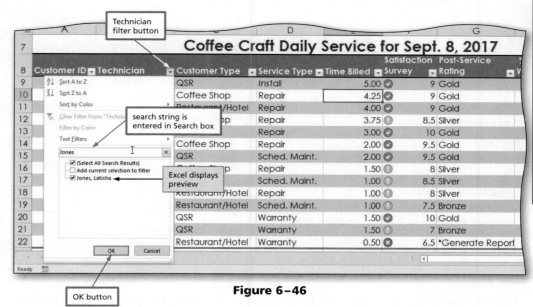

Figure 6–46

2

- Click the OK button to perform the search (Figure 6–47).

🔎 **Experiment**

- Search other columns for different kinds of data. Note that the total row reflects only the records displayed by the filter.

Figure 6–47

3

- Click the Clear button (Data tab | Sort & Filter group) to display all of the records in the table.

To Enter Custom Criteria Using AutoFilter

1 CREATE TABLE | 2 LOOKUP TABLES | 3 CALCULATED FIELDS | 4 CONDITIONAL FORMATTING | 5 SORT TABLES
6 QUERY TABLES | 7 CRITERIA RANGES | 8 DATABASE & CONDITIONAL FUNCTIONS | 9 SUBTOTALS & TREEMAP

Another way to query a table is to use the Custom Filter command. The Custom Filter command allows you to enter custom criteria, such as multiple options or ranges of numbers. *Why? Not all queries are exact numbers; many times a range of numbers is required.* The following steps enter custom criteria to display records that represent service calls whose Satisfaction Survey number is between 7 and 9, inclusive; that is, the number is greater than or equal to 7 and less than or equal to 9 ($7 \leq$ Satisfaction Survey ≤ 9).

1

- Click the filter button in cell F8 to display the filter menu for the Satisfaction Survey column.

- Point to Number Filters to display the Number Filters submenu (Figure 6–48).

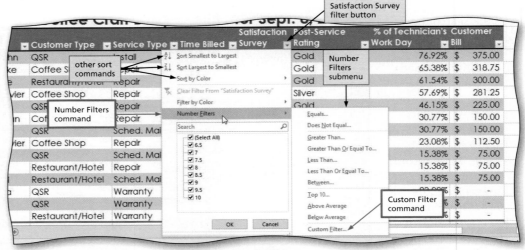

Figure 6–48

2

- Click Custom Filter on the Number Filters submenu to display the Custom AutoFilter dialog box.

- Click the first Satisfaction Survey button (Custom AutoFilter dialog box), click 'is greater than or equal to' in the list, and then type 7 in the first value box.

- Click the second Satisfaction Survey button. Scroll as necessary, and then click 'is less than or equal to' in the list. Type 9 in the second value box (Figure 6–49).

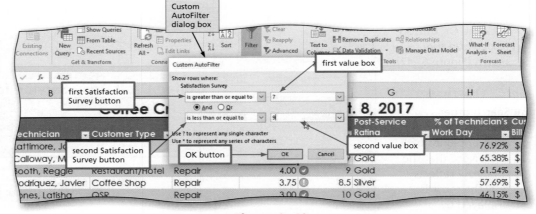

Figure 6–49

How are the And and Or option buttons used?

You can click options button to select the appropriate operator. The AND operator indicates that both parts of the criteria must be true; the OR operator indicates that only one of the two must be true.

3

- Click the OK button (Custom AutoFilter dialog box) to display records in the table that match the custom AutoFilter criteria, in this case, service calls in which the Satisfaction Survey number is between 7 and 9, inclusive (Figure 6–50).

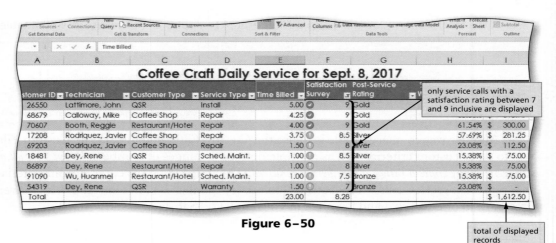

Figure 6–50

4

- Click the Clear button (Data tab | Sort & Filter group) to display all of the records in the table.

More about AutoFilters

Other important points regarding AutoFilter include the following:

- When you query a table to display some records and hide others, Excel displays a filter icon on the filter buttons used to establish the filter. Excel also displays the row headings of the selected records in blue.
- Excel does not sort hidden records.
- If the filter buttons do not appear, then you must manually enable AutoFilter by clicking the Filter button (Data tab | Sort & Filter group).
- To remove a filter criterion for a single piece of data in a field, click the Select All check box on the filter menu for that field.
- When you create a formula in the total row of a table, the formula automatically recalculates the values even when you filter the list. For example, the results shown in the Total row in Figure 6–50 update automatically if you apply a filter to the table.
- You can filter and sort a column by color or conditional formatting using the 'Sort by Color' and 'Filter by Color' commands on the filter menu (shown in Figure 6–48).

To Turn Off AutoFilter

You can turn off and on the AutoFilter feature by hiding or showing the filter buttons. ***Why?*** *Sometimes you may want to view the table without the distraction of the buttons.* The following steps hide and then redisplay the AutoFilter.

- Click the Filter button (Data tab | Sort & Filter group) to hide the filter buttons in the table (Figure 6–51).

- Click the Filter button (Data tab | Sort & Filter group) again to display the filter buttons in the table.

3

- Click the Save button on the Quick Access Toolbar to save the workbook.

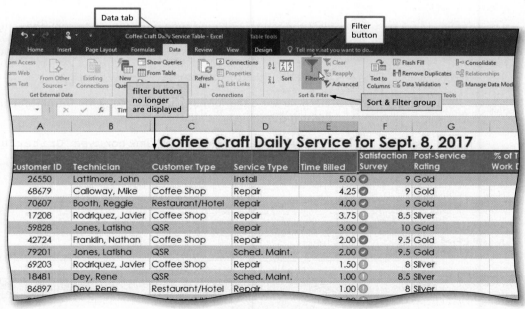

Figure 6–51

Other Ways

1. Click 'Sort & Filter' button (Home tab | Editing group), click Filter command in 'Sort & Filter' list
2. CTRL+SHIFT+L

Using Criteria and Extract Ranges

Another advanced filter technique called a criteria range manipulates records that pass comparison criteria. A **criteria range** is a location separate from the table used to list specific search specifications. Like a custom filter, a criteria range compares entered data with a list or table, based on column headings. Using a criteria range sometimes is faster than entering criteria through the AutoFilter system because once the range is established, you do not have to access any menus or dialog boxes to perform the query. You also can create an **extract range** in which Excel copies the records that meet the comparison criteria in the criteria range to another part of the worksheet.

CONSIDER THIS

Does Excel provide another way to pull data out of a table?

Yes. You can create a criteria area and extract area on the worksheet. The criteria area can be used to enter rules regarding which records to extract, without having to change the AutoFilter settings. For example, the criteria area might ask for all full-time students with a grade of A from the table. The extract area can be used to store the records that meet the criteria. Extracting records allows you to pull data from a table so that you can analyze or manipulate the data further. For example, you may want to know which customers are delinquent on their payments. Extracting records that meet this criterion allows you then to use the records to create a mailing to such customers.

To Create a Criteria Range

When creating a criteria range, it is important to place it away from the table itself. Commonly, criteria ranges are located directly above the table. That way, if the table grows downward or to the right in the future, the criteria range will not interfere. It also is a good practice to copy the necessary column headings rather than type them, to prevent errors. The following steps create a criteria range and copy the column headings.

1 Select the range A7:I8 and then press CTRL+C to copy the range.

2 Select cell A1 and then press the ENTER key to paste the clipboard contents.

3 Change the title to `Criteria Range` in cell A1.

4 If necessary, use the format painter to copy the formatting and wrap column headings to match the table headings.

5 Select the range A2:I3, click the Name box, type `Criteria` as the range name, and then press the ENTER key (Figure 6–52).

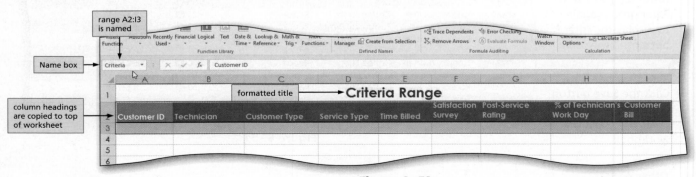

Figure 6–52

To Query Using a Criteria Range

The following steps use the criteria range and the Advanced Filter dialog box to query the table and display only the records that pass the test: Service Type = Repair AND Time Billed > 2 AND Satisfaction Survey >= 8. The criteria data is entered directly below the criteria range headings. *Why? Because the Advanced Filter dialog box searches for a match using column headings and adjacent rows.*

1

- In cell D3, enter the criteria **Repair**, in cell E3 type **>2**, and in cell F3 type **>=8** (Figure 6–53).

Figure 6–53

2

- Click the table to make it active.

- Click the Advanced button (Data tab | Sort & Filter group) to display the Advanced Filter dialog box (Figure 6–54).

Q&A What are the default values in the Advanced Filter dialog box?
In the Action area, the 'Filter the list, in-place' option button is the default selection. Excel automatically selects the table (range $A$8:$I$23) in the List range box. Excel also automatically selects the criteria range ($A$2:$I$3) in the Criteria range box, because the name Criteria was assigned to the range A2:I3 earlier.

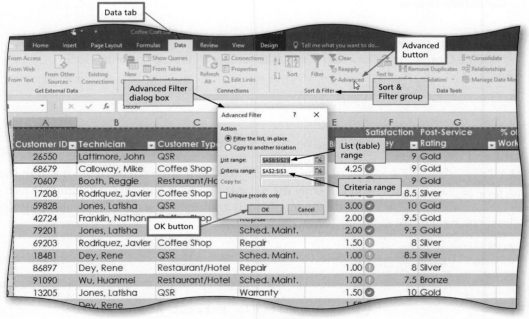

Figure 6–54

3

- Click the OK button (Advanced Filter dialog box) to hide all records that do not meet the comparison criteria. If necessary, scroll up to display the criteria range (Figure 6–55).

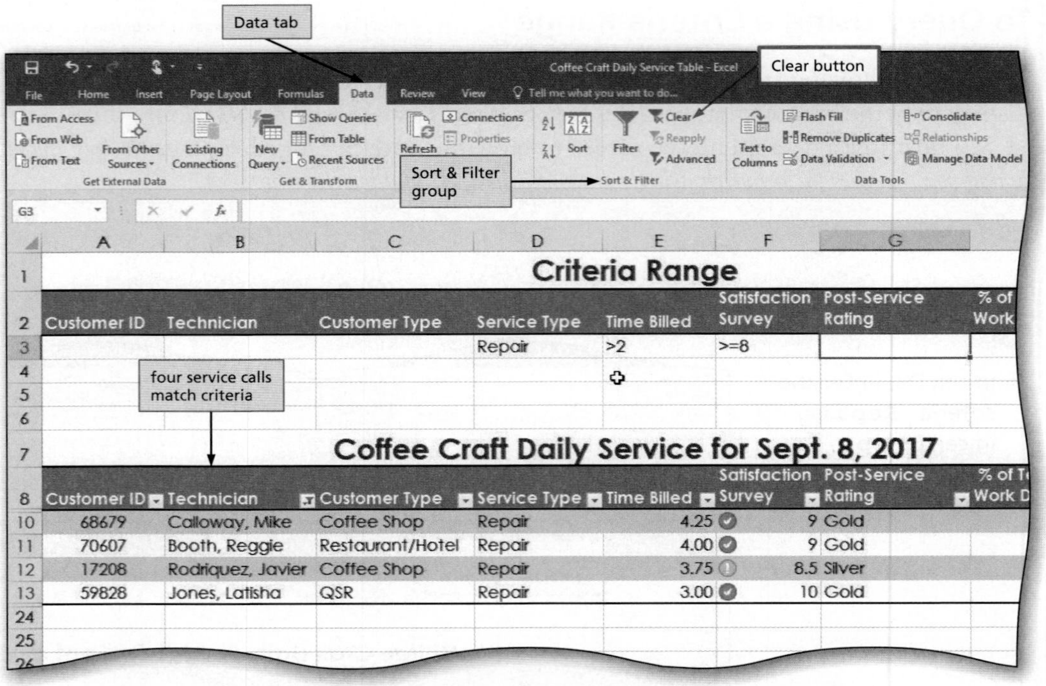

 Q&A What is the main difference between using the AutoFilter query technique and using the Advanced Filter dialog box with a criteria range?

Like the AutoFilter query technique, the Advanced Filter command displays a subset of the table. The primary difference between the two is that the Advanced Filter command allows you to create more complex comparison criteria, because the criteria range can be as many rows long as necessary, allowing for many sets of comparison criteria.

Figure 6–55

4

- Click the Clear button (Data tab | Sort & Filter group) to show all records.

BTW

AND and OR Queries
If you want to create a query that includes searches on two fields, you enter the data across the same row in the criteria range. If you want to search for one piece of data OR another, enter the second piece of data on the next row.

To Create an Extract Range

In the previous steps, you filtered data in place within the table itself; however, you can copy the records that meet the criteria to another part of the worksheet, rather than displaying them as a subset of the table. The following steps create an extract range below the table.

1 Select the range A7:I8 and then press CTRL+C to copy the range.

2 Select cell A25 and then press the ENTER key to paste the contents.

3 Change the title to **Extract Area** in cell A25.

4 Select the range A26:I45, click the Name box, type **Extract** as the range name, and then press the ENTER key.

Q&A Why am I including so many rows in the extraction range?
The table has many records; you want to make sure you have enough room for any search that the company might desire.

5 If necessary, use the format painter to copy the formatting and wrap column headings to match the table headings (Figure 6–56).

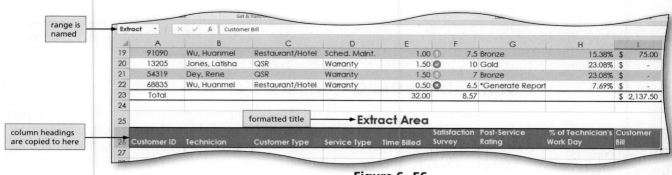

Figure 6–56

To Extract Records

1 CREATE TABLE | 2 LOOKUP TABLES | 3 CALCULATED FIELDS | 4 CONDITIONAL FORMATTING | 5 SORT TABLES
6 QUERY TABLES | 7 CRITERIA RANGES | 8 DATABASE & CONDITIONAL FUNCTIONS | 9 SUBTOTALS & TREEMAP

The following steps extract records that meet the previous criteria, using the Advanced Filter dialog box. **Why?** *The Advanced Filter dialog box allows you to use the complex criteria from a criteria range on the worksheet and send the results to a third location, leaving the table undisturbed.*

1

- Click the table to make it active.

- Click the Advanced button (Data tab | Sort & Filter group) to display the Advanced Filter dialog box.

- Click 'Copy to another location' in the Action area (Advanced Filter dialog box) to cause the records that meet the criteria to be copied to a different location on the worksheet (Figure 6–57).

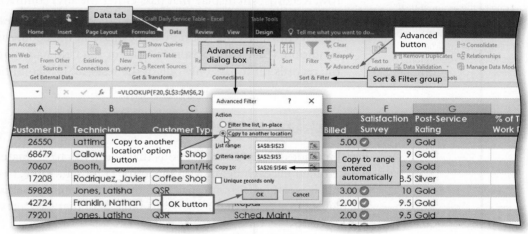

Figure 6–57

2

- Click the OK button to copy any records that meet the comparison criteria in the criteria range from the table to the extract range. Scroll to display the entire extraction area (Figure 6–58).

Figure 6–58

Q&A What happens to the rows in the extract range if I perform another advanced filter operation?

Each time you use the Advanced Filter dialog box with the 'Copy to another location' option, Excel clears cells below the field names in the extract range before it copies a new set of records that pass the new test.

3

- Click the Save button on the Quick Access Toolbar to save the workbook again.

Break Point: If you wish to take a break, this is a good place to do so. You can exit Excel. To resume at a later time, run Excel, open the file called Coffee Craft Daily Service Table, and continue following the steps from this location forward.

More about the Criteria Range

The comparison criteria in the criteria range determine the records that will pass the test when the Advanced Filter dialog box is used. As you have seen, multiple entries in a single data row of the criteria range create an AND condition. The following examples describe different comparison criteria.

- If the criteria range contains a blank row, it means that no comparison criteria have been defined. Thus, all records in the table pass the test and will be displayed.
- If you want an OR operator in the same field, your criteria range must contain two (or more) data rows. Enter the criteria data on separate rows. Records that pass either (or any) comparison criterion will be displayed.
- If you want an AND operator in the same field name, you must add a column in the criteria range and duplicate the column heading.
- If you want an OR operator on two different fields, your criteria range must contain two (or more) data rows. Enter the criteria for each field on a separate row. Records will display that pass either (or any) comparison criterion.
- When the comparison criteria below different field names are in the same row, then records pass the test only if they pass all the comparison criteria, an AND condition. If the comparison criteria for the field names are in different rows, then the records must pass only one of the tests, an OR condition.

BTW
Keeping Data in Order
If you want to perform various sorts, but need to have a way to return to the original order, you might consider adding a column that numbers the entries before sorting.

BTW
Using Quotation Marks
Many of the database functions require a field name as one of the arguments. If your field name is text, rather than a cell reference, number, or range, the argument must be enclosed in quotation marks.

Using Database Functions

Excel includes 12 database functions that allow you to evaluate numeric data in a table. These functions each begin with the letter D for data table, to differentiate them from their worksheet counterparts. As the name implies, the **DAVERAGE function** calculates the average of numbers in a table field that pass a test. The general form of the DAVERAGE function is

=DAVERAGE(table range, "field name", criteria range)

Another often-used table function is the DCOUNT function. The **DCOUNT function** counts the number of numeric entries in a table field that pass a test. The general form of the DCOUNT function is

=DCOUNT(table range, "field name", criteria range)

In both functions, table range is the location of the table, field name is the name of the field in the table, and criteria range is the comparison criteria or test to pass. Note that Excel requires that you surround field names with quotation marks unless you previously named the field.

Other database functions that are similar to the functions described in previous modules include the DMAX, DMIN, and DSUM functions. See Excel Help for a complete list of database functions.

BTW
Functions and Ranges
When using a function such as DAVERAGE or DCOUNT, Excel automatically adjusts the first argument if the table grows or shrinks. With functions such as SUMIF and COUNTIF, you have to correct the function argument to reflect the new range if the range grows or shrinks.

To Create an Output Area

The following steps set up an output area in preparation for using the database functions. Cells O2:Q3 will be used as criteria. Cells O5:O11 will be labels for the output.

1 Change the width of columns O, P, and Q to 18.00.

2 Select cell O1 and then type **Output Area** to enter a criteria area title. Center the title across the selection O1:Q1. If necessary, copy the formatting from cell L1 to cell O1.

3 In cell O2, type **Customer Type**. In cell P2, type **Customer Type**. In cell Q2, type **Post-Service Rating** to create the column headings. Use the format painter to copy the formatting from cell L2 to cells O2:Q2.

4 Enter other labels as shown below (Figure 6–59).

Cell	Text
O3	Coffee Shop
P3	QSR
Q3	Gold
O5	Avg. Coffee Shop Satisfaction Rating:
O6	Avg. QSR Satisfaction Rating:
O7	Gold Standing Count:
O8	Billing to Restaurant/Hotel:
O9	Count of QSR Customers:
O10	Customer ID:
O11	Time Billed:

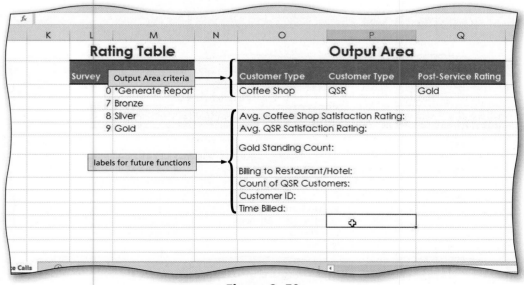

Figure 6–59

To Use the DAVERAGE and DCOUNT Database Functions

The following steps use the DAVERAGE function to find the average Coffee Shop Satisfaction rating. You will use the DCOUNT function to count the number of service calls that have a Gold rating. *Why? The DAVERAGE and DCOUNT functions allow you to enter a range to average, and criteria with which to filter the table.* The DAVERAGE function requires a numeric field from the table range; therefore, you will use "Satisfaction Survey" as the second argument. Field names used as numeric arguments in these functions should be surrounded with quotation marks, unless previously named.

- Select cell Q5 and then type `=daverage (a8:i22, "Satisfaction Survey",o2:o3)` to enter a database function (Figure 6–60).

Q&A
My function does not wrap as shown in the figure. Did I do something wrong?
No, it depends on how far to the right you are scrolled. If there is not enough room on the screen, Excel will wrap long cell entries.

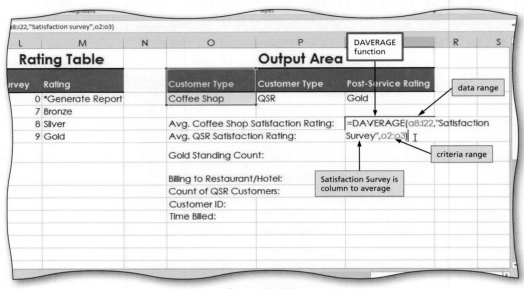

Figure 6–60

- Click the Enter button to finish the function and display the answer.
- Select cell Q6 and then type `=daverage (a8:i22, "Satisfaction Survey",p2:p3)` to enter a second database function (Figure 6–61).

Q&A
Why do the two DAVERAGE functions, which both use the Satisfaction Survey field, generate different answers?
The criteria range differentiates the two entries. The range O2:O3 averages the satisfaction survey results for Coffee Shop customers. The range P2:P3 averages the survey results related to QSR customers.

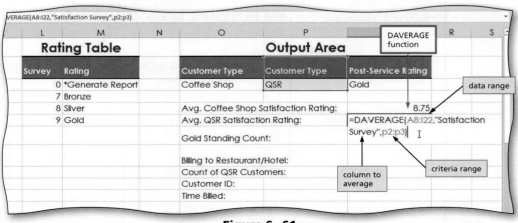

Figure 6–61

- Click the Enter button to finish the function.

- Select cell Q7 and then type `=dcount(a8:i22, "Satisfaction Survey",q2:q3)` to enter a database function.

- Click the Enter button to finish the function (Figure 6–62).

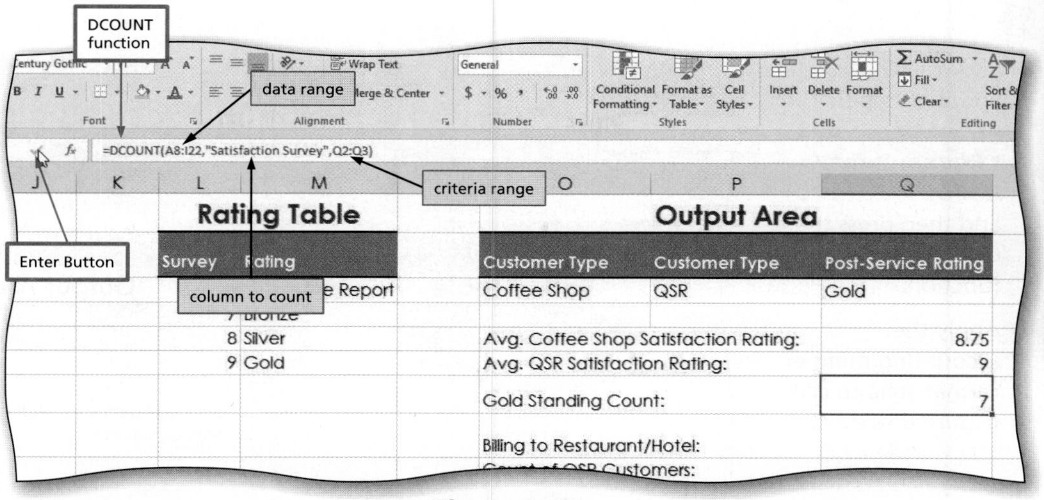

Figure 6–62

Q&A What is the DCOUNT function actually counting?
The DCOUNT function is counting the number of Gold ratings in the table, as referenced by the Q2:Q3 criteria.

Other Ways

1. Click Insert Function box in formula bar, click 'Or select a category' button, click 'Database', click DAVERAGE or DCOUNT in 'Select a function' list, enter arguments

Using the Sumif, Countif, Match, and Index Functions

Four other functions are useful when querying a table and analyzing its data. The SUMIF and COUNTIF functions sum values in a range, or count values in a range, only if they meet a criteria. The MATCH function returns the position number of an item in a range or table. For example, if you search for a specific student name, the MATCH function might find it in position 3 (or the third column in the table). You then can use that number with other functions, cell references, or searches. The INDEX function returns the value of a cell at the intersection of a particular row position and column position within a table or range. For example, you might want to know the age of the fifth student in a table, where ages are stored in the second column. Using the numbers 5 and 2 would eliminate the need to know the exact cell reference because the positions are relative to the table or range. Unlike the database functions, the range for these functions need not be a table.

To Use the SUMIF Function

1 CREATE TABLE | 2 LOOKUP TABLES | 3 CALCULATED FIELDS | 4 CONDITIONAL FORMATTING | 5 SORT TABLES
6 QUERY TABLES | 7 CRITERIA RANGES | **8 DATABASE & CONDITIONAL FUNCTIONS** | **9 SUBTOTALS & TREEMAP**

The following step uses the SUMIF function to ascertain the sum of the billings to Restaurants and Hotels. **Why?** *The SUMIF function allows you to sum a range based on criteria.* The general format of the SUMIF function is

=SUMIF(criteria_range, data, sum_range)

The first argument is the criteria range, or the range you want to search. The second argument is the desired piece of data in that range; it must be enclosed in quotes if the data is alphanumeric. The third argument is the location of the values you want summed. In this case, you are searching column C for "Restaurant/Hotel", and then summing Column I.

- Click cell Q8 and then type `=sumif(c9:c22, "Restaurant/ Hotel",i9:i22)` and then press the ENTER key to enter a function.
- Apply the accounting number format style to cell (Figure 6–63).

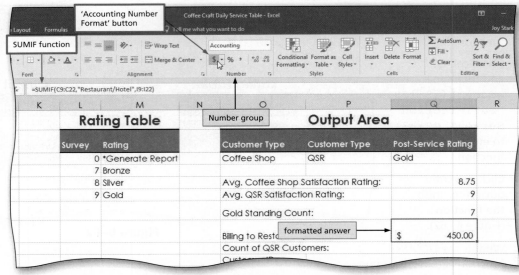

Figure 6–63

Other Ways

1. Click Insert Function box in formula bar, click 'Or select a category' button, click 'Math & Trig', click SUMIF in 'Select a function' list, enter arguments
2. Click 'Math & Trig' button (Formulas tab | Function Library group), click SUMIF, enter arguments

To Use the COUNTIF Functions

1 CREATE TABLE | 2 LOOKUP TABLES | 3 CALCULATED FIELDS | 4 CONDITIONAL FORMATTING | 5 SORT TABLES
6 QUERY TABLES | 7 CRITERIA RANGES | 8 DATABASE & CONDITIONAL FUNCTIONS | 9 SUBTOTALS & TREEMAP

The following step uses the COUNTIF to ascertain the number of QSR customers. *Why? In large tables, counting the number of records that match certain conditions provides useful data for analysis.* The general format of the COUNTIF function is

$$=COUNTIF(count\_range, data)$$

The first argument is the range containing the cells with which to compare the data in the second argument. Again, if the data is text rather than numbers, the data must be enclosed in quotes. In this case, you are counting the number of QSR service calls in Column C.

- In cell Q9, type `=countif (c9:c22,"QSR")`, and then click the Enter button to enter the function (Figure 6–64).

Figure 6–64

Other Ways

1. Click Insert Function box in formula bar, click 'Or select a category' button, click 'Statistical', click COUNTIF in 'Select a function' list, enter arguments
2. Click 'More Functions' button (Formulas tab | Function Library group), point to 'Statistical', click COUNTIF, enter arguments

To Use the MATCH and INDEX Functions

1 CREATE TABLE | 2 LOOKUP TABLES | 3 CALCULATED FIELDS | 4 CONDITIONAL FORMATTING | 5 SORT TABLES
6 QUERY TABLES | 7 CRITERIA RANGES | 8 DATABASE & CONDITIONAL FUNCTIONS | 9 SUBTOTALS & TREEMAP

The MATCH function can be used to find the position number using the general format

$$=MATCH(lookup\_value, lookup\_array, match\_type)$$

The first argument is the cell reference for the search data. The second argument is the range to search. The range must be a group of cells in a row or column. The third argument specifies the type of search: –1 for matches less than the lookup value, 0 (zero) for an exact match, and 1 for matches higher than the lookup value.

The INDEX function finds a value in a table or range based on a relative row and column. The general format is

$$=INDEX(range, row, column)$$

When used together, the MATCH and INDEX function provide the ability to look up a particular value in a table based on criteria. Because the MATCH function returns the row location in this case, you can use it as the second argument in the INDEX function. For example, to find the Time Billed for a specific customer in the table, the format would be

$$=INDEX(A9:I22, MATCH(Q10, A9:A22, 0), 5).$$

Within the INDEX function, A9:I22 is the table range, the MATCH function becomes the row, and 5 refers to column E, the time billed data. That final argument must be an integer rather than an alphabetic reference to the column. Within the MATCH function, Q10 is the location of the customer number you wish to search for, followed by the range of customer numbers in A9:A22, followed by a designation of 0 for an exact match. Sometimes called nesting, the inner function is performed first.

The following steps assume you want to look up the Time Billed for any given customer by using the customer number. *Why? The table is not sorted by customer number; this method makes it easier for the company to find the time billed for a specific customer.*

- Click cell Q10 and then type **69203** to enter a lookup value.

- In cell Q11, type **=index(a9:i22, match(q10, a9:a22, 0), 5)**, and then press the ENTER key to enter a function.

- Display the data with two decimal places (Figure 6–65).

- Click the Save button on the Quick Access Toolbar to save the workbook again.

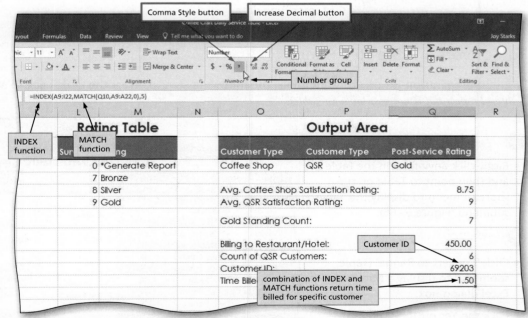

Figure 6–65

Other Ways

1. Click Insert Function box in formula bar, click 'Or select a category' button, click 'Lookup & Reference', click MATCH or INDEX in 'Select a function' list, enter arguments

2. Click 'Lookup & Reference' button (Formulas tab | Function Library group), click MATCH or INDEX, enter arguments

Summarizing Data

Another way to summarize data is by using subtotals. A subtotal is the sum of a subset of data while a grand total sums all of the data in a row or column. You can create sub totals automatically, as long as the data is sorted. For subtotals, the field on which you sort is called the **control field**. For example, if you choose the Customer type field as your control field, all of the Coffee Shop, QSR, and Restaurants/Hotel entries will be together within the data range. You then might request subtotals for the Time Billed and Customer Bill fields. Excel calculates and displays the subtotal each time the Customer Type field changes. A grand total displays at the bottom of the range. The most common subtotal uses the SUM function, although you can use other functions. If you change the control field, Excel updates the subtotal automatically. Note that the subtotal feature cannot be used with the table feature, only with normal ranges of data.

The Subtotal command displays outline symbols beside the rows or above the columns of the data you wish to group. The **outline symbols** include plus and minus signs for showing and hiding portions of the spreadsheet, as well as brackets identifying the groups. For example, you might want to minimize the display of technicians who have a bronze rating and show only those with silver and gold ratings. Outlining is extremely useful for making large tables more manageable in size and appearance.

To Sort the Data

Subtotals can only be performed on sorted data. The following step sorts the table by Customer Type.

1 Click the filter button in cell C8 and then click the 'Sort A to Z' command to sort the Customer Type data.

To Convert a Table to a Range

1 CREATE TABLE | 2 LOOKUP TABLES | 3 CALCULATED FIELDS | 4 CONDITIONAL FORMATTING | 5 SORT TABLES
6 QUERY TABLES | 7 CRITERIA RANGES | 8 DATABASE & CONDITIONAL FUNCTIONS | 9 SUBTOTALS & TREEMAP

In preparation for creating subtotals, the following steps convert the table back to a range. *Why? The Subtotal command is not available for tables.*

1

• Right-click anywhere in the table and then point to Table on the shortcut menu to display the Table submenu (Figure 6–66).

2

• Click 'Convert to Range' (Table submenu) to display a Microsoft Excel dialog box.

• Click the Yes button (Microsoft Excel dialog box) to convert the table to a range.

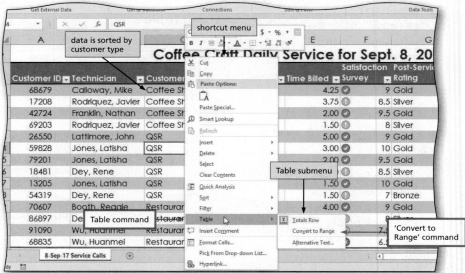

Figure 6–66

Other Ways

1. Click 'Convert to Range' button (Table Tools Design tab | Tools group), click Yes button (Microsoft Excel dialog box)

To Display Subtotals

The following steps display subtotals for the Time Billed and Customer Bill based on Customer Type. *Why?* *Subtotals are useful pieces of data for comparisons and analysis.*

- Click in one of the numeric fields you wish to subtotal (in this case, column I).

- Click the Subtotal button (Data tab | Outline group) to display the Subtotal dialog box.

- Click the 'At each change in' button (Subtotal dialog box) and then click Customer Type to select the control field.

- If necessary, click the Use function button and then select Sum in the Use function list.

- In the 'Add subtotal to' list (Subtotal dialog box), click Time Billed and Customer Bill to select values to subtotal. Clear any other check boxes (Figure 6–67).

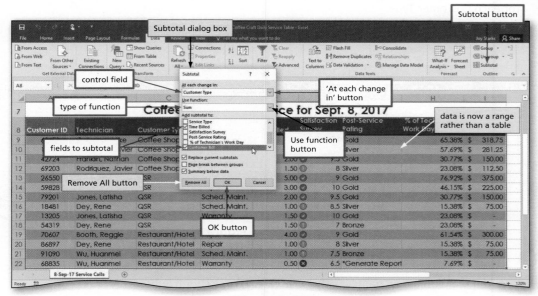

Figure 6–67

- Click the OK button to add subtotals to the range. Deselect the range.

- Zoom to 100% magnification.

- Scroll so that cell A8 is at the top of the worksheet, so that you can see the entire subtotal and outline area (Figure 6–68).

Q&A What changes does Excel make to the worksheet?
Excel adds three subtotal rows — one

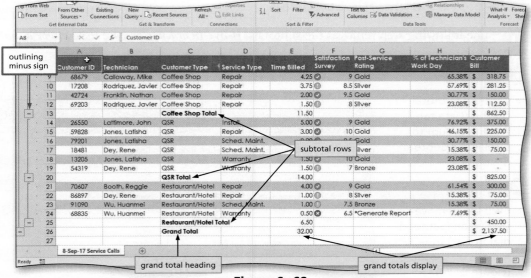

Figure 6–68

subtotal for each different Customer Type — and one grand total row for the entire table. The names for each subtotal row come from the sorted controls field and appear in bold. Thus, the text, Coffee Shop Total, in cell C13 identifies the row that contains subtotals for Time Billed and Customer Bill for the Coffee Shop customer type. Excel also displays the outlining feature.

To Use the Outline Feature

Excel turns on the outline feature automatically when you create subtotals. The following steps use the outline feature of Excel. *Why? The outline feature allows you to hide and show data and totals.*

- Click the second outlining column header to collapse the outline and hide the data (Figure 6–69).

Experiment

- One at a time, click each of the plus signs (+) in column two on the left side of the window to display detail records for each Customer Type.

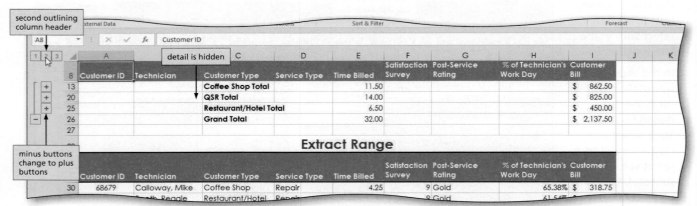

Figure 6–69

- Save the file with a new name, Coffee Craft Daily Service with Subtotals.

To Remove Automatic Subtotals

The following step removes the subtotals. *Why? In order to prepare the data for a chart, you want to remove subtotals.*

- Click the Subtotal button (Data tab | Outline group) to display the Subtotal dialog box.

- Click the Remove All button (Subtotal dialog box) to remove all subtotals (Figure 6–70).

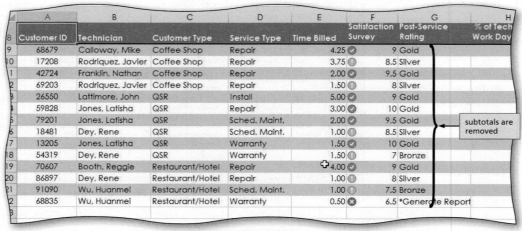

- Close the file without quitting

Figure 6–70

Excel. If you are prompted to save the file, click the No button (Microsoft Excel dialog box).

Treemap Charts

A **treemap chart** provides a hierarchical, visual view of data, making it easy to spot patterns and trends. Instead of hierarchical levels, treemap charts use rectangles to represent each branch and sub branch (or data category) by size, enabling users to display categories by color and proximity and to compare proportions. One of the fields in a treemap chart must be numeric, in order to generate the size of each rectangle. As with other types of charts, you can format fonts, colors, shape, and text effects, as well as add data fields and adjust data labels. Treemap charts compare values and proportions among large amounts of data that might be difficult to show with other types of charts.

To Create a Treemap Chart

1 CREATE TABLE | 2 LOOKUP TABLES | 3 CALCULATED FIELDS | 4 CONDITIONAL FORMATTING | 5 SORT TABLES
6 QUERY TABLES | 7 CRITERIA RANGES | 8 DATABASE & CONDITIONAL FUNCTIONS | **9 SUBTOTALS & TREEMAP**

The following steps create a treemap chart to compare technicians. *Why? The company would like to see how the technicians are spending their day using the Technician as the branch and the Repair Type as the sub branch. The Time billed will be reflected by the size of the rectangles.*

- Open the file named Coffee Craft Daily Service Table.
- If necessary, click the Filter button (Data tab | Sort & Filter group) to display the filter buttons. Sort the data in ascending order by Technician.
- Drag to select cells B8: E22 to select them.
- Display the Insert tab and then click the 'Insert Hierarchy Chart' button to display the gallery (Figure 6–71).

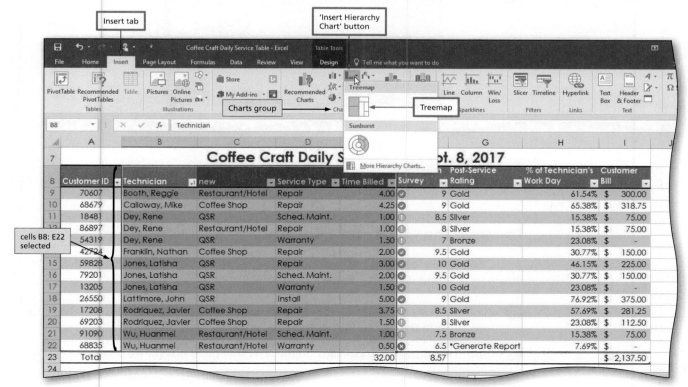

Figure 6–71

Q&A Do I have to use the table file rather than the file with subtotals?

Recall that you removed the table formatting in the file with subtotals. It is easier to start with the data stored as a table.

2

- Click Treemap (Insert Hierarchy Chart gallery) to insert the chart.

- Click the sixth chart style (Chart Tools Design tab | Chart Styles group) to select the style.

- Click the Chart Elements button located to the right of the chart and then click the Legend check box to remove the check mark (Figure 6–72).

Experiment

- Point to each rectangle in the chart to see a ScreenTip showing from which data points the rectangle was created.

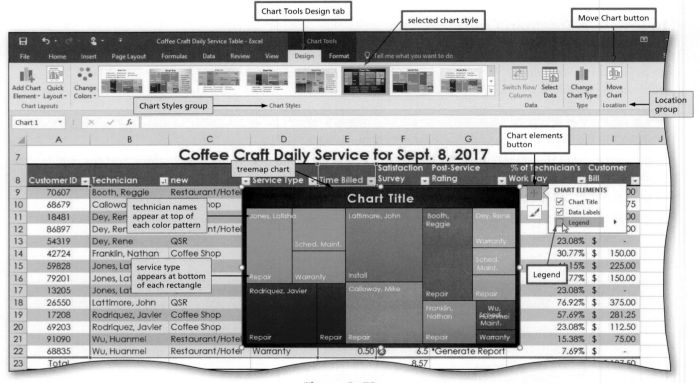

Figure 6–72

Other Ways

1. Select data, click the Recommended Charts button (Insert tab | Charts group), click All Charts tab (Recommended Charts dialog box), click Treemap, click OK button

To Move the Chart and Edit Fonts

The following steps move the chart to its own named worksheet and then edit the chart title and data label fonts.

1 Click the Move Chart button (Chart Tools Design tab | Location group) and then click New sheet in the Move Chart dialog box.

2 Type **Technician Treemap** in the New sheet text box (Move Chart dialog box) and then click the OK button.

3 Right-click the Chart Title and then click Edit Text on the shortcut menu. On the Home tab, change the font size to 24. Type **Technician Workday** to change the title.

4 Click any of the data labels in the chart. Change the font size to 14 (Figure 6–73).

Q&A How is the data presented in this chart?

The treemap allows you to compare each technician's day with other technicians: how much time they spent (size of color block) and how many service calls they completed during that time (number of subdivisions within each color block).

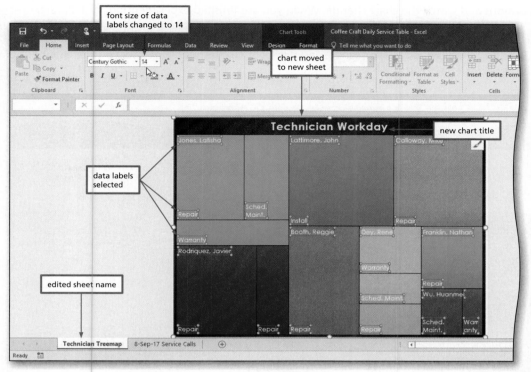

Figure 6–73

To Edit Treemap Settings

1 CREATE TABLE | 2 LOOKUP TABLES | 3 CALCULATED FIELDS | 4 CONDITIONAL FORMATTING | 5 SORT TABLES
6 QUERY TABLES | 7 CRITERIA RANGES | 8 DATABASE & CONDITIONAL FUNCTIONS | 9 SUBTOTALS & TREEMAP

The following steps format the chart with settings that are unique to treemaps. *Why? Changing some of the settings will make the branches stand out and make the chart more user-friendly.*

1

- Right-click any of the rectangles to display the shortcut menu. Do not right-click a data label (Figure 6–74).

Figure 6–74

②

- Click 'Format Data Series' on the shortcut menu to display the Format Data Series task pane.
- Click Banner in the Label Options area (Figure 6–75).

Experiment

- Click each of the label options and watch the chart change. When you are finished experimenting, click Banner.

Q&A | What other choices can I make in the Format Data Series task pane?
On the Effects tab, you can add shadows, a glow, or other special effects. On the Fill & Line tab, you can change the color of the fill and the borders for each rectangle.

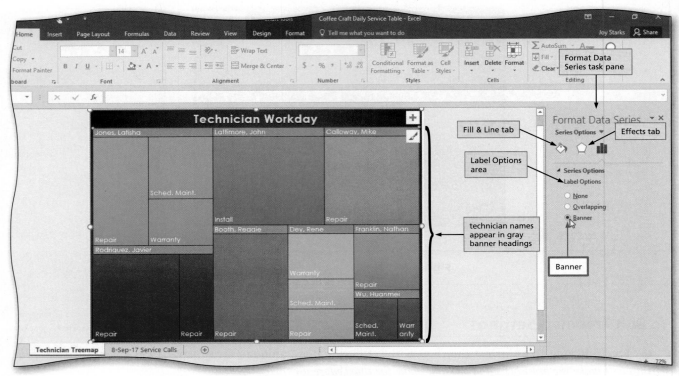

Figure 6–75

③

- Right-click any of the data labels, and then click 'Format Data Labels' on the shortcut menu to display the Format Data Labels task pane.
- Click to display a check mark in the Value check box. The Category Name check box should contain a check mark already (Figure 6–76).

Experiment

- Click various combinations of the check marks and watch the chart change. When you are finished experimenting, select only Category Name and Value.

Q&A | Why did the task pane display only three choices of labels?
You selected four fields in the data. The first field displays in the banner. The Series Name is the name of the numeric field, in this case Time Billed. Category represents the Service Type. Value is the numeric data, which also dictates the size of the rectangle.

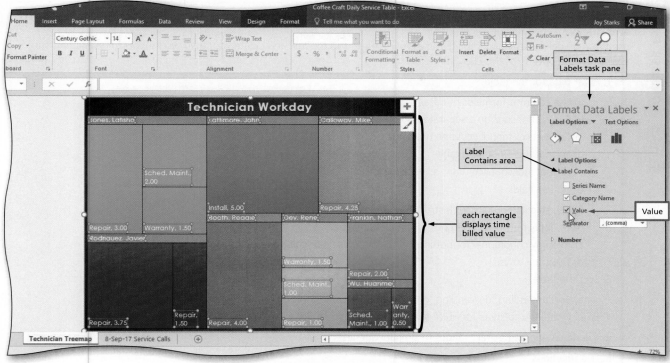

Figure 6–76

4 Save the file with the name **Coffee Craft Daily Service with Treemap** as the file name.

5 Click the Close button on the right side of the title bar to close the file and exit Excel.

6 If the Microsoft Office Excel dialog box is displayed, click the Don't Save button.

Summary

In this module, you learned how to create, sort, format, and filter a table (also called a database). You created calculated fields using structured references. Using conditional formatting, you applied an icon set to a field in the table. As you queried the table, you used AutoFilters with customized criteria. In a separate area of the worksheet, you created criteria and extract ranges to quickly search for and display specific data. You also created an output area using database functions such as SUMIF, COUNTIF, MATCH, and INDEX. After converting the table back to a range, you summarized data with subtotals. Finally, you created a treemap chart to display the technician workday in a visual format.

What decisions will you need to make when creating your next worksheet with a table to create, sort, and query?

Use these guidelines as you complete the assignments in this module and create your own worksheets for evaluating and analyzing data outside of this class.

1. Enter data for the table.

    a) Use columns for fields of data.

    b) Put each record on a separate row.

    c) Create user-friendly column headings.

    d) Format the range as a table.

    e) Format individual columns as necessary.

2. Create other fields.

    a) Use calculated fields with structured references.

    b) To apply rankings or settings, use a lookup table.

    c) To apply conditional formatting, consider icon sets or color groupings.

    d) Use total rows.

3. Sort the table.

    a) Sort ascending, descending, or combinations using tools on the Home tab and the Data tab.

4. Employ table AutoFilters for quick searches and sorts.

5. Create criteria and extract ranges to simplify queries.

6. Use functions.

    a) Use DAVERAGE and DCOUNT for database functions analyzing table data.

    b) Use SUMIF, COUNTIF, MATCH, and INDEX to find answers based on conditions.

7. Summarize data with subtotals and use outlining.

8. Create a treemap chart.

Apply Your Knowledge

Reinforce the skills and apply the concepts you learned in this module.

Creating a Table with Conditional Formatting

Note: To complete this assignment, you will be required to use the Data Files. Please contact your instructor for information about accessing the Data Files.

Instructions: The Dean's office has provided a list of student scholarship recipients and their current grade point averages. You are to create a table to include letter grades and summary data as shown in Figure 6–77. The conditional formatting is based on a green circle for 3.0 GPA or above, yellow for 2.0 or above, and red for students below 2.0 that are in danger of losing their scholarships.

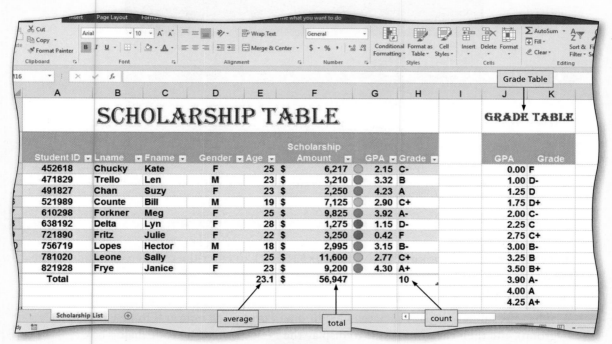

Figure 6–77

Perform the following tasks:

1. Run Excel and open the file named Apply 6–1 Scholarship Table. Save the file on your storage device with the name, Apply 6–1 Scholarship Table Complete.

2. Select the range, A2:G13. Click the 'Format as Table' button (Home tab | Styles group) and then click 'Table Style Medium 7' in the Format as Table gallery. When Excel displays the Format As Table dialog box, if necessary, click the 'My table has headers' check box to select the option to format the table with headers.

3. Name the table, Scholarships, by using the Table Name text box (Table Tools Design tab | Properties group).

4. Remove duplicates in the table by clicking the Remove Duplicates button (Table Tools Design tab | Tools group). When Excel displays the Remove Duplicates dialog box, click the Select All button and then click the OK button.

5. If requested to do so by your instructor, add your name as a scholarship winner and fill in the corresponding fields of data.

6. Insert a new column in the table (column H), with the column heading, Grade.

Continued >

Apply Your Knowledge *continued*

7. Change the row height of row 1 to 39. Click cell A1. Apply the Title cell formatting, the Algerian font, and a font size of 28. Center the title across the selection, A1:H1, using the Format Cells dialog box.

8. Add dollar signs with no decimal places to the scholarship amounts and format column widths as necessary. Wrap the text in cell F2. Format the GPA figures to have two decimal places.

9. To create the lookup table, enter the data from Table 6–5, beginning with Grade Table in cell J1. Format cell J1 with the Algerian font at size 14. Use the format painter to copy the table column heading format to cells J2 and K2. Right-align the GPA amounts and format with two decimal places. Left-align the grades.

Table 6–5 Scholarship Grade Table	
Grade Table	
GPA	**Grade**
0.00	F
1.00	D–
1.25	D
1.75	D+
2.00	C–
2.25	C
2.75	C+
3.00	B–
3.25	B
3.50	B+
3.90	A–
4.00	A
4.25	A+

10. In cell H3, type `= vlookup(g3, $j$3:$k$15, 2)` to enter the calculated column in the main table.

11. To apply conditional formatting:

   a. Select the range G3:G12, click the Conditional Formatting button (Home tab | Styles group), and then click New Rule to display the New Formatting Rule dialog box.

   b. Click the Format Style button (New Formatting Rule dialog box) to display the Format Style list.

   c. Click Icon Sets in the Format Style list (New Formatting Rule dialog box) to display the Icon area.

   d. Click the Icon Style button and then click '3 Traffic Lights (Unrimmed)' in the Icon Style list (New Formatting Rule dialog box) to select an icon style that includes three different colored circles.

   e Click the first Type button and then click Number in the list to select a numeric value. Click the second Type button and then click Number in the list to select a numeric value.

   f. Type **3** in the first Value box, type **2** in the second Value box, and then press the TAB key to complete the conditions.

   g. Click the OK button (New Formatting Rule dialog box) to display icons in each row of the table.

12. Display the total row by clicking the Total Row check box (Table Tools Design tab | Table Style Options group). Average the Age column, and sum the Scholarship Amount column.

13. Save the file again.

14. Use the Sort button on the Data tab to sort in ascending order by last name.

15. Use the 'Sort & Filter' button on the Home tab to sort in descending order by scholarship amount.

16. Use the Sort command on the filter menu to sort by grade point, with the highest grade point first.

17. Submit the workbook in the format specified by your instructor.

18. ✳ What other kind of criteria, filter, or output might be helpful if the table were larger? When might you use some of the database and statistical functions on this kind of data? Why?

Extend Your Knowledge

Extend the skills you learned in this module and experiment with new skills. You may need to use Help to complete the assignment.

Using Functions

Note: To complete this assignment, you will be required to use the Data Files. Please contact your instructor for information about accessing the Data Files.

Instructions: Run Excel. Open the workbook Extend 6–1 Business Analyst Table. You have been asked to summarize the data in a variety of ways as shown in Figure 6–78. Complete the following tasks to summarize the data.

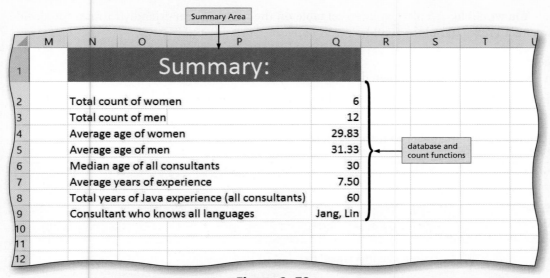

Figure 6–78

Perform the following tasks:

1. Save the workbook using the file name, Extend 6–1 Business Analyst Table Complete.

2. Create a new column called Count in column L. Use the COUNTIF function in cell L11 to count all of the Y entries in the row — indicating the number of languages in which the consultant is proficient.

3. If requested to do so by your instructor, insert your name and programming language experience as an additional row in the table.

4. Name the table, BA_Table.

Continued >

Extend Your Knowledge *continued*

5. Beside the table, create Summary title and row headings as shown in Figure 6–78.

6. Use the COUNTIF function for males and females. Use the AVERAGEIF function for the average ages. (*Hint*: Use Help to learn about the AVERAGEIF function.)

7. Use the MEDIAN function to find the median age of all consultants. (*Hint*: If necessary, use Help to learn about the MEDIAN function.)

8. Use the AVERAGE function to average the years of experience.

9. Use the SUMIF function to find the total years of Java experience in the company.

10. Use the MATCH function wrapped inside the INDEX function, as you did in the module, to find the one technician who is proficient in all seven languages.

11. Round off the averages to two decimal places, if necessary.

12. Save the file again and submit the assignment as requested by your instructor.

13. ✸ Which functions used structured references? Why?

Expand Your World

Create a solution that uses cloud and web technologies by learning and investigating on your own from general guidance.

Converting Files

Problem: You would like to place your Excel table on the web in a user-friendly format. You decide to investigate a Web 2.0 tool that will help you convert your table to HTML.

Instructions:

1. Run Excel and open any completed exercise from this module.

2. Drag through the table and column headings to select them. Press CTRL+C to copy the table cells.

3. Run a browser and navigate to http://tableizer.journalistopia.com/ (Figure 6–79).

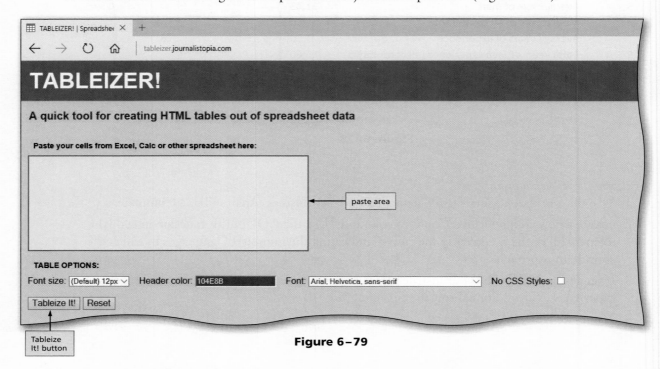

Figure 6–79

4. Click inside the gray paste area, and then press CTRL+V to paste the cells.

5. Click the Tableize It! button and wait a few seconds.

6. If you want to create an HTML page, copy the HTML code generated by Tableizer into a text editor such as Notepad. Save the Notepad file with the file name, MyTable.html. Display the file in a browser.

7. ✳ Many websites use tables to compare products, services, and pricing plans. Research HTML tables and web accessibility. What kinds of issues do screen readers have with HTML tables? Is it the best way to present information on the web?

In the Labs

Design, create, modify, and/or use a workbook following the guidelines, concepts, and skills presented in this module. Labs 1 and 2, which increase in difficulty, require you to create solutions based on what you learned in the module; Lab 3 requires you to apply your creative thinking and problem-solving skills to design and implement a solution.

Lab 1: **Creating Structured References, a Lookup Table, and a Treemap**

Problem: The City Market wants an easier way to keep track of the shelf life of fresh vegetables. You will format and summarize the data as shown in Figure 6–80a, and create the treemap shown in Figure 6–80b.

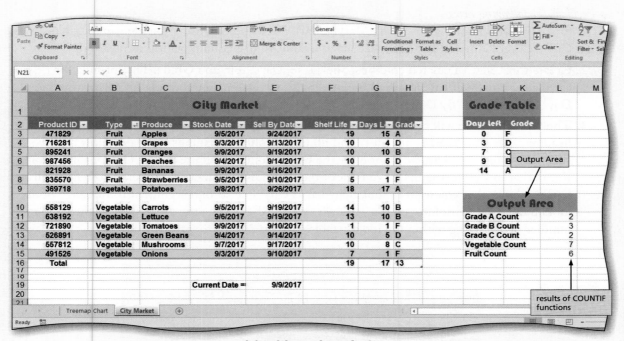

(a) Table and Analysis

Continued >

In the Labs *continued*

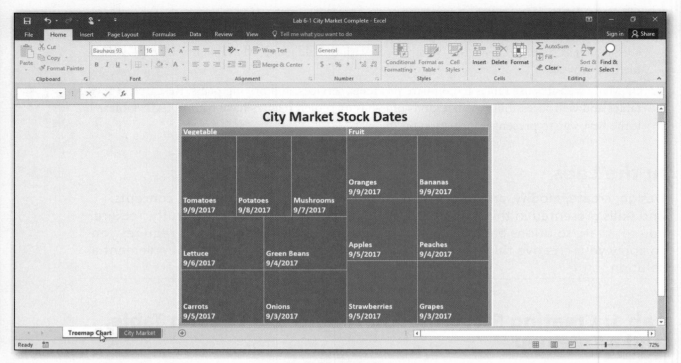

(b) Treemap Chart
Figure 6–80

Perform the following tasks:

1. Open the workbook Lab 6–1 City Market. Save the workbook using the file name, Lab 6–1 City Market Complete. Format the data as a table. Adjust column widths as necessary.

2. Create three new calculated columns, Shelf Life, Days Left, and Grade. The formula for calculating the Shelf Life is = [Sell By Date] – [Stock Date]. The formula for calculating the Days Left is = [Sell By Date] – currentDate. (*Hint:* currentDate is a named cell, E19.)

3. The Grade column will require you to create a lookup table area, shown in Table 6–6. Type the heading, **Grade Table** in cell J1 and fill in the column headings and data below that, as shown in Table 6–6. The calculation for the Grade column will use the VLOOKUP function. Recall that in a table, the first argument of the VLOOKUP function references the first cell in the column that you want to look up (such as G3). The second argument is the range of the lookup table with absolute references (such as $J$3:$K$7). The third argument is the column number of the rating within the lookup table (such as 2).

Table 6–6 Grade Table

Grade Table	
Days Left	Grade
0	F
3	D
7	C
9	B
14	A

4. Create an output area, as shown in Figure 6–80a, using several COUNTIF functions to total the grades, fruits, and vegetables. Recall that the first argument of the COUNTIF function is the range of data (for instance, the grade ratings in H3:H15, or the type of produce in B3:B15) and the second argument is the desired data (such as "A" or "Vegetable").

5. To create the treemap:

   a. Sort the table by Type and then select the range B2:F15.

   b. Select the Treemap chart and apply the second chart style.

   c. Remove the legend.

   d. Move the Chart to a new worksheet, named, Treemap Chart.

   e. Change the font size of the chart title to 32 and type `City Market Stock Dates` as the new title. Change the font size of the data labels to 18.

   f. Apply the Banner label option to the data series.

   g. Display the Category name and Value data labels, and separate the labels by placing Value on a new line.

6. If requested to do so by your instructor, on the City Market tab, add one more item to the Output Area to display the count of your favorite fruit or vegetable. (*Hint:* If you use the correct function and arguments, the count should equal 1.)

7. Save the file again and submit the assignment as requested by your instructor.

8. ✳ If you were to add a criteria range, or filtering technique, to the worksheet, for what kinds of data and conditions would you search? Why? What criteria would be most important to the owner of the City Market?

Lab 2: **Creating and Querying a Table**

Note: To complete this assignment, you will be required to use the Data Files. Please contact your instructor for information about accessing the Data Files.

Problem: Vacation Rentals would like the answers to the questions listed below about rental units. Run Excel. Open the workbook Lab 6–2 Rental Units Data. Save the workbook using the file name, Lab 6–2 Rental Units Table Complete.

Perform the following tasks:

1. Format the data as a table using your choice of Table styles. Adjust column widths and wrap text in the headings as necessary. Remove any duplicates from the table. Name the table Rental_ Units.

2. Create a heading in cell A7 that says Vacation Rentals. Center the title across the selection, A7:L7. Format the heading.

3. Copy the headings from the table to create both a criteria range (above) and an extract area (below) the table. Name the ranges.

Continued >

In the Labs *continued*

4. Fill in the comparison criteria to select records from the list to solve each of the problems in the following steps. So that you better understand what is required for this assignment, the answer is given for the first problem.

   a. Select records of units with at least 2 bedrooms and a pool. The criteria displays in Figure 6–81a. The extracted records display in Figure 6–81b.

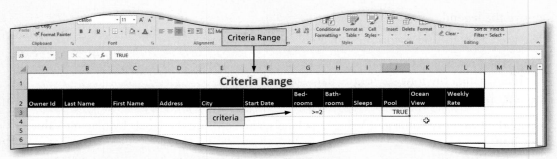

Figure 6–81a

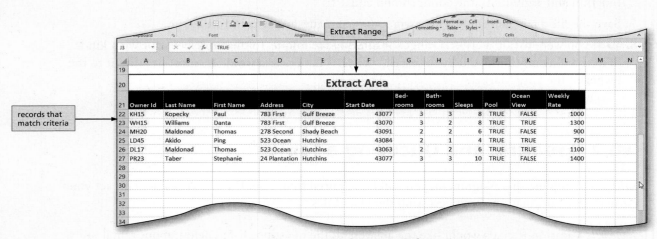

Figure 6–81b

   b. Select records that are located in the city of Gulf Breeze and have an ocean view.

   c. Select records that have only 1 bathroom.

   d. Select rental locations that are available in November and are less than $1000 per week.

   e. Select all locations owned by Thomas Maldonad.

   f. Select locations that can sleep 6 or 8 and are located on First street.

5. Save the file again and submit the assignment as requested by your instructor.

6. ✳ Do you think a treemap chart would work with the data in this exercises? Why or why not? What fields would you include?

Lab 3: **Consider This: Your Turn**

Apply your creative thinking and problem-solving skills to design and implement a solution.

Querying an Inventory

Part 1:   A local company would like to be able to search their inventory in an easy manner. They have given you sample data shown in Table 6–7.

Table 6–7 Inventory Data				
Inventory Number	Description	Manufacturer	List Price	Quantity in Stock
AX1D1	projector	Aldus	$595.00	2
CD7XL	coder	Boles	$195.00	4
R562W	stylus	Indirection	$49.00	14
TP45L	touch pad	Gladstone	$180.00	2
BC30W	card reader	Boles	$199.00	11
MX550	scanner/fax	Menem	$295.00	2
QR123	bar code scanner	Boles	$375.00	5

Create the criteria range, the table, and the extract range with formatted headings and data.

Save the worksheet. Perform the following extractions.
  a) all inventory items with more than 10 in stock

  b) all inventory items from the manufacturer, Boles

  c) all inventory items under $100

  d) all inventory items with 5 or less in stock and a list price of less than $300

Part 2:   ✳ Do you think small companies without extensive database experience might use tables such as this every day? What would be some advantages and disadvantages? What calculated fields might you add to the table?

7 Creating Templates, Importing Data, and Working with SmartArt, Images, and Screenshots

Objectives

You will have mastered the material in this module when you can:

- Create and use a template
- Import data from a text file, an Access database, a webpage, and a Word document
- Use text functions
- Paste values and paste text
- Transpose data while pasting it
- Convert text to columns
- Replicate formulas

- Use the Quick Analysis gallery
- Find and replace data
- Insert and format a bar chart
- Insert and modify a SmartArt graphic
- Add pictures to a SmartArt Graphic
- Apply text effects
- Include a hyperlinked screenshot

Introduction

In today's business environment, you often find that you need to create multiple worksheets or workbooks that follow the same basic format. A **template** is a special-purpose workbook you can create and use as a pattern for new, similar workbooks or worksheets. A template usually consists of a general format (worksheet title, column and row titles, and numeric formatting) and formulas that are common to all the worksheets. Templates can be saved to a common storage location so that everyone in a company can use them to create standardized documents.

Another important concept to understand is Excel's capability to use and analyze data from a wide variety of sources. In this module, you will learn how to **import**, or bring in, data from various external sources into an Excel worksheet and then analyze that data. Excel allows you to import data from a number of types of sources, including text files, webpages, database tables, data stored in Word documents, and XML files.

Finally, a chart, graphic, image, or screenshot often conveys information or an idea better than words or numbers. You can insert and modify graphics, images, and screenshots to enhance the visual appeal of an Excel workbook and illustrate its contents. Many of the skills you learn when working with graphics in Excel will be similar when working in other Office programs, such as Word, Publisher, or PowerPoint.

Project — Home Security Systems

Home Security Systems (HSS) is a retail and online outlet for hardware used in securing homes and small businesses. The company owner has requested that the in-store and online sales results for the last two years be compared among its four stores. One of the stores provides the requested data in a plain text format (Figure 7–1a) rather than in an Excel workbook. To make use of that data in Excel, the data must be imported before it can be formatted and manipulated. The same is true of formats in which the other locations store data, such as Microsoft Access tables (Figure 7–1b), webpages (Figure 7–1c), or Microsoft Word documents (Figure 7–1d). Excel provides the tools necessary to import and manipulate the data from these sources into a single worksheet (Figure 7–1e). Using the data from the worksheet, you will create a bar chart to summarize total sales by category (Figure 7–1f). Finally, you will add SmartArt graphics that include images (Figure 7–1g) and a hyperlinked screenshot to support your work (Figure 7–1h).

Figure 7–2 illustrates the requirements document for the HSS Sales Analysis workbook. It includes the needs, sources of data, calculations, charts, and other facts about the workbook's development.

In addition, using a sketch of the main worksheet can help you visualize its design. The sketch of the worksheet consists of titles, column and cell headings, the location of data values, and a general idea of the desired formatting in the worksheet. The data will include 2016 and 2017 data, with a summary on the right (Figure 7–3a). Figure 7–3b displays a basic sketch of the requested graph, a bar chart, showing the 2017 totals by category.

With a good understanding of the requirements document, an understanding of the necessary decisions, and a sketch of the worksheet and graph, the next step is to use Excel to create the workbook.

The following roadmap identifies general activities you will perform as you progress through this module:

1. CREATE a TEMPLATE with sample data and formulas.

2. USE a TEMPLATE to create a new workbook.

3. IMPORT and format outside DATA into an Excel workbook.

4. USE the QUICK ANALYSIS gallery to create totals and charts easily.

5. FIND and REPLACE data.

6. INSERT and format a BAR CHART.

7. CREATE and format a SMARTART graphic to display pictures and text.

8. ADD a hyperlinked SCREENSHOT.

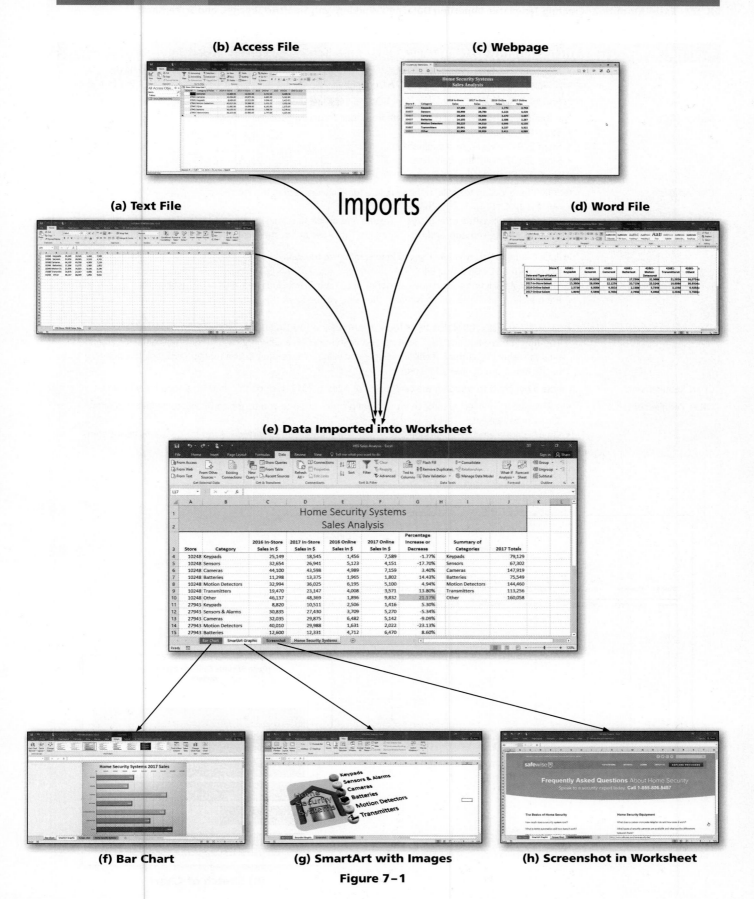

(b) Access File

(c) Webpage

(a) Text File

Imports

(d) Word File

(e) Data Imported into Worksheet

(f) Bar Chart

(g) SmartArt with Images

(h) Screenshot in Worksheet

Figure 7–1

Worksheet Title	Home Security Systems Sales Analysis
Needs	• A template with headings, sample data, and formulas than can be used to create similar worksheets • A workbook, made from the template, containing a worksheet that combines sales data from the four stores • A chart that compares the 2017 total sales for each category of products that the store sells
Source of Data	The four sales managers will submit data from their respective stores as follows: • Store 10248 saves data in a text file. • Store 27943 uses an Access database. • Store 33607 maintains web data. • Store 42681 uses Word to store data in a table.
Calculations	Include the following formula in the template for each line item in the inventory: • =((D4+F4)/(C4+E4))-1 This formula takes the total of 2017 in-store and online sales minus the total of 2016 in-store and online sales to arrive at a percentage, and then subtracts 1 to arrive at just the increase or decrease. Include the following two functions to help summarize the data: • IF(COUNTIF($B$4:B4,B4)=1,B4,"") This formula will find the unique categories in column B. It includes the COUNTIF function that will return true if a match occurs. If no match is made, the value will be false; then, the IF function will display the value from column B. • =SUMIF($B$4:$B$100,I4,$D$4:$D$100)+SUMIF($B$4:$B$100,I4,$F$4:$F$100) This function will add the 2017 in-store and online sales on a category basis. It adds the value in column D plus the value in column F, if cell I4 matches the value from column B. The function will look through row 100 as the maximum number of records.
Chart Requirements	Create a bar chart to compare the categories for sales in 2017. Include the chart on a separate worksheet.
Other Requirements	• Investigate a SmartArt graphic to include the pictures given to you by the company, to be included on a separate worksheet. • On a separate worksheet, include a screenshot of the website they recommend for questions about home security systems (http://safewise.com/home-security-faq).

Figure 7–2

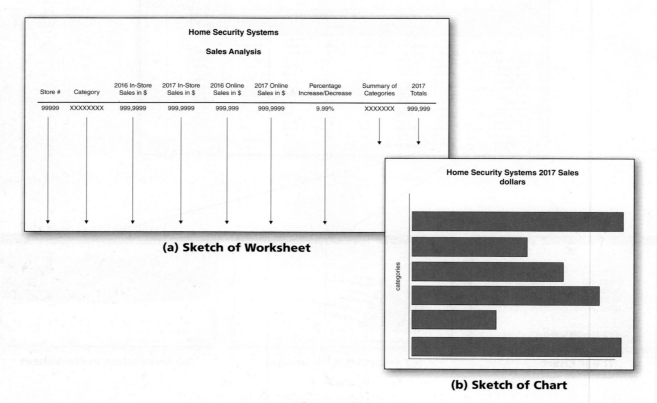

(a) Sketch of Worksheet

(b) Sketch of Chart

Figure 7–3

Creating Templates

The first step in building the project in this module is to create and save a template that contains the titles, column and row headings, formulas, and formats. After the template is saved, it can be used every time a similar workbook is developed. Because templates help speed and simplify their work, many Excel users create a template for each project on which they work. Templates can be simple — possibly using a special font or worksheet title; or they can be more complex — perhaps using specific formulas and format styles, such as the template for the HSS Sales Analysis workbook.

What factors should you keep in mind when building a template?

A template usually contains data and formatting that will appear in every workbook created from that template. Because the template will be used to create a number of other worksheets, make sure you consider the layout, cell formatting, and contents of the workbook as you design the template. Set row heights and column widths. Use placeholders for data when possible and use dummy data to verify formulas. Format the cells in the template.

Creating a template, such as the one shown in Figure 7–4, follows the same basic steps used to create a workbook. The only difference between developing a workbook and a template is the file type used when saving the template.

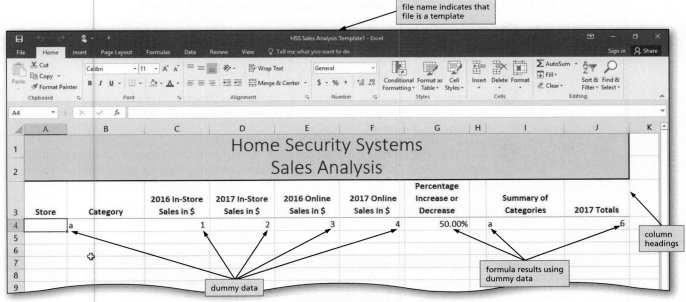

Figure 7–4

To Open a Blank Workbook and Format the Rows and Columns

The following steps open a blank workbook and set the row height and column widths.

1 Run Excel.

2 Click the Blank workbook thumbnail on the Excel start screen to create a blank workbook and display it in the Excel window.

3 If the Excel window is not maximized, click the Maximize button on its title bar to maximize the window.

4 CTRL+click rows 1 and 2 to select them. Using the row heading area, drag the bottom boundary of row 2 down, until the ScreenTip displays 'Height 28.50 (38 pixels)' to change the height of the rows. For row 3, drag the bottom boundary down until the ScreenTip displays Height 45.75 (61 pixels) to change the height of the row.

5 Set the column widths as follows: A = 9.00 (68 pixels), B = 17.00 (124 pixels), C = 14.00 (103 pixels), D = 14.00 (103 pixels), E = 14.00 (103 pixels), F = 14.00 (103 pixels), G = 14.00 (103 pixels), H = 3.00 (26 pixels), I = 17.00 (124 pixels), and J = 14.00 (103 pixels).

To Enter Titles in the Template

The following steps enter and format the titles in cells A1 and A2.

1 In cell A1, type **Home Security Systems** to enter the worksheet title.

2 In cell A2, type **Sales Analysis** to enter the worksheet subtitle.

3 Display the Page Layout tab. Click the Theme Colors button (Page Layout tab | Themes group) and then click Blue Green in the Colors gallery to apply the Blue Green colors to the worksheet.

4 Select the range A1:A2. Click the Cell Styles button (Home tab | Styles group) and then apply the Title cell style to the range. Change the font size to 24.

5 Select the range A1:J1. Click the 'Merge & Center' button (Home tab | Alignment group) to merge and center the selected cells.

6 Repeat Step 5 to merge and center the range A2:J2.

7 Select the range A1:A2, click the Fill Color arrow (Home tab | Font group), and then click 'Aqua, Accent 2, Lighter 60%' (column 6, row 3) in the Fill Color gallery to set the fill color for the range.

8 With the range A1:A2 still selected, click the Borders arrow (Home tab | Font group), and then click 'Thick Outside Borders' in the Borders gallery to apply a border to the range.

9 Select cell A3 and zoom to 130% (Figure 7–5).

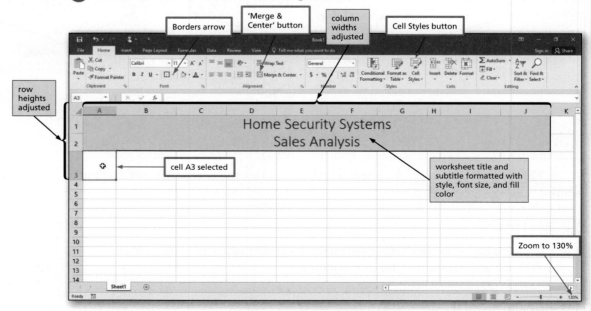

Figure 7–5

To Enter Column Titles in the Template

The following steps enter and format the column titles in row 3.

1 Select cells A3:J3 and then click the Wrap Text button (Home tab | Alignment group) to apply the formatting. Click the Center button (Home tab | Alignment group) and then apply the Heading 3 cell style to the range.

2 Type the following column titles into the appropriate cells (Figure 7–6).

A3	Store
B3	Category
C3	2016 In-Store Sales in $
D3	2017 In-Store Sales in $
E3	2016 Online Sales in $
F3	2017 Online Sales in $
G3	Percentage Increase or Decrease
H3	<blank>
I3	Summary of Categories
J3	2017 Totals

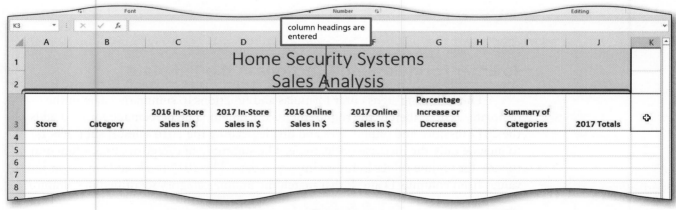

Figure 7–6

To Enter Sample Data in the Template

When a template is created, sample data or dummy data is used in place of actual data to verify the formulas in the template. Selecting simple text, such as a, b, or c, and numbers, such as 1, 2, and 3, allows you to check quickly to see if the formulas are generating the proper results. In templates with more complex formulas, you may want to use numbers that test the extreme boundaries of valid data, such as the lowest or highest possible number, or a maximum number of records.

The following steps enter sample data in the template.

1 Select cell B4. Type **a** to enter the first piece of sample data.

2 Select cell C4. Type **1** to enter the first number in the series.

3 Enter the other dummy data as shown in Figure 7–7.

4 Select the range C4:F4. Apply the comma style with no decimal places to the selected range.

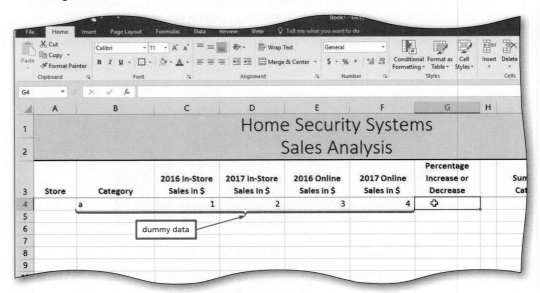

Figure 7–7

To Enter Formulas and Functions in the Template

The following steps enter formulas and functions to summarize data in the template, as described in the requirements document. The percentage formula adds the 2017 in-store and online sales and divides that by the 2016 sales. It subtracts 1 to include only the increase or decrease. The summary of categories uses a function to look for unique values in future imported data. The 2017 totals add any imported values from columns D and F that match the unique category identified in column I.

1 Select cell G4. Type `=((d4+f4)/(c4+e4))-1` as the formula for calculating the percentage increase or decrease from 2016 to 2017 and then click the Enter button.

2 Format cell G4 with a percent sign and two decimal places.

3 Select cell I4. Type = `if(countif($b$4:b4,b4)=1,b4,"")` to enter a function that displays a value from the Category list if it is unique. Click the Enter button.

4 Select cell J4. Type `=sumif($b$4:$b$100,i4,$d$4:$d$100) + sumif($b$4:$b$100,i4,$f$4:$f$100)` to enter a function that adds columns d and f, if the value returned in cell I4 matches the data in the Category list in column B. The function will look through row 100 as the maximum number of records. Click the Enter button.

5 Format cell J4 with a comma and no decimal places.

6 Change the sheet tab name to Home Security Systems to provide a descriptive name for the worksheet.

7 Change the sheet tab color to Aqua, Accent 2 to format the tab (Figure 7–8).

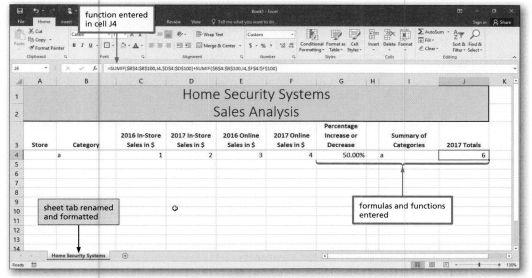

Figure 7–8

To Save the Template

1 CREATE TEMPLATE | 2 USE TEMPLATE | 3 IMPORT DATA | 4 USE QUICK ANALYSIS
5 FIND & REPLACE | 6 INSERT BAR CHART | 7 CREATE SMARTART | 8 ADD SCREENSHOT

Saving a template is similar to saving a workbook, except that the file type, Excel Template, is selected in the 'Save as type' box (Save As dialog box). Excel saves the file with the extension, .xltx, to denote its template status. Saving in that format prevents users from accidentally saving over the template file and causes Excel to open new workbooks based on the template with the proper format. In business situations, it is a good idea to save the template in the default Templates folder location. *Why? Company templates saved in the Templates folder appear with other templates when users need to find them.* In lab situations, however, you should save templates on your personal storage device. The following steps save the template using the file name, HSS Sales Analysis Template on your storage device.

1

- Click cell A4 to position the current cell.

- Click the Save button on the Quick Access Toolbar to display the Save As gallery and then click the Browse button to display the Save As dialog box.

- Type **HSS Sales Analysis Template** in the File name box to enter a name for the file.

- Click the 'Save as type' arrow and then click Excel Template in the list to specify that this workbook should be saved as a template.

- Navigate to your storage device and desired folder, if any (Figure 7–9).

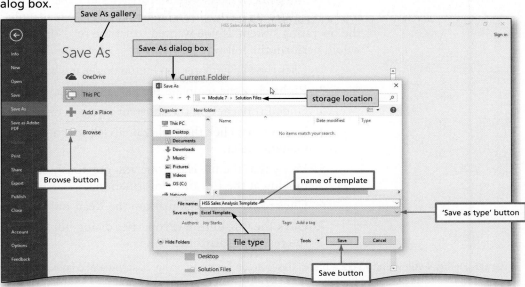

Figure 7–9

Q&A Why does Excel change the folder location when the Excel Template file type is chosen?

When the Excel Template file type is chosen in the 'Save as type' box, Excel automatically changes the location to the Templates folder created when Office 2016 was installed. In a production environment — that is, when you are creating a template for a business, a school, or an application — the template typically would be saved in the Templates folder, not on your personal storage device.

- Click the Save button (Save As dialog box) to save the template in the selected folder on the selected save location with the entered file name.

- Exit Excel.

Other Ways

1. Press CTRL+S, click Browse button (Save As gallery), type file name (Save As dialog box), select Excel Template in 'Save as type' box, select drive or folder, click Save button

TO CHANGE THE DEFAULT LOCATION OF TEMPLATES

If you wanted to change the default location where templates are stored, you would perform the following steps. Once this option is set, all templates you save will appear automatically under Personal in the New gallery.

1. Click File on the ribbon to open the Backstage view.
2. Click Options to display the Excel Options dialog box.
3. Click Save in the left pane (Excel Options dialog box) and then in the Save workbooks area, enter the path to the personal templates location in the 'Default personal templates location' box. This path typically is C:\Users\ UserName\Documents\Custom Office Templates\.
4. Click the OK button (Excel Options dialog box).

TO SET THE READ-ONLY ATTRIBUTE

Once a template is created, you may want to change the file's attribute, or classification, to read-only. With a **read-only file**, you can open and access the file normally, but you cannot make permanent changes to it. That way, users will be forced to save changes to the template with a new file name, keeping the original template intact and unchanged for the next user.

While you can view system properties in Excel 2016, you cannot change the read-only attribute from within Excel. Setting the read-only attribute is a function of the operating system. If you wanted to set the read-only property of the template, you would perform the following steps.

1. Click the File Explorer app button on the taskbar. Navigate to your storage location.
2. Right-click the template file name to display the shortcut menu.
3. Click Properties on the shortcut menu to display the Properties dialog box.
4. If necessary, click the General tab (Properties dialog box) to display the General sheet.
5. Verify that the file is the one you previously saved on your storage device by looking at the Location information.
6. Click to place a check mark in the Read-only check box in the Attributes area.
7. Click the OK button (Properties dialog box) to close the dialog box and apply the read-only attribute.

Break Point: If you wish to take a break, this is a good place to do so. To resume at a later time, continue following the steps from this location forward.

To Open a Template and Save It as a Workbook

As with other Office apps, you can open an Excel template in one of several ways:

- If you use the Open gallery in the Backstage view, you will open the template file itself for editing.

- If you have stored the template in the default template storage location, you can click the New tab in the Backstage view and then click Personal. Clicking the template file in the Personal gallery will open a new file based on the template.

- If you stored the template in another location, you must double-click the file in the File Explorer window to create a new file based on the template.

When you open a file based on a template, Excel names the new workbook using the template name with an appended digit 1 (e.g., Monthly Budget Template1). **Why?** *Adding a 1 to the file name delineates it from the template; it is similar to what Excel does when you first run Excel and it assigns the name Book1 to the new workbook.* You can save the file with a new file name if you want.

The following steps open a file based on the template. You then will save it in the .xlsx format with a new file name in order to proceed with data entry.

- Click the File Explorer app button on the taskbar to run the File Explorer app.

- Navigate to your storage location (Figure 7–10).

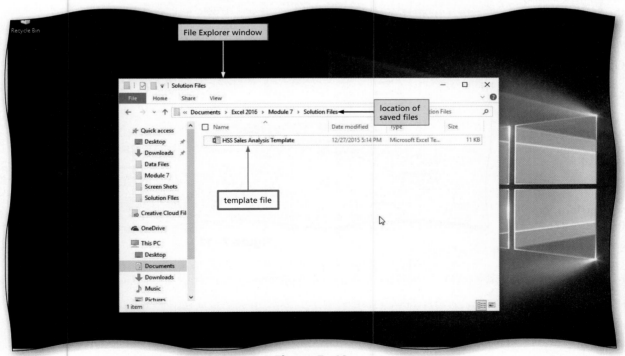

Figure 7–10

- Double-click the file named HSS Sales Analysis Template to open a new file based on the template (Figure 7–11).

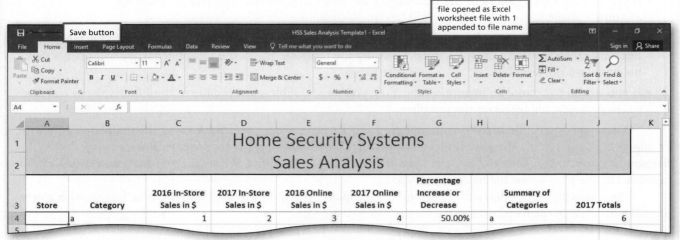

Figure 7–11

- Click the Save button (Quick Access Toolbar) to display the Save As gallery in the Backstage view.

- Click the Browse button to display the Save As dialog box.

- Type **HSS Sales Analysis** in the File name box (Save As dialog box) and then navigate to your storage location (Figure 7–12).

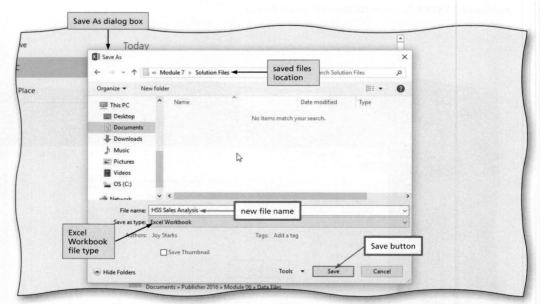

Figure 7–12

Q&A Should I change the file type?

No. Excel automatically selects Excel Workbook as the file type when you attempt to save a file based on a template.

- Click the Save button (Save As dialog box) to save the file with the new file name.

Importing Data

Data may come from a variety of sources and in a range of formats. Even though many users keep data in databases, such as Microsoft Access, it is common to receive text files with fields of data separated by commas. More and more companies are creating HTML files and posting data on the web. Word documents, especially those including tables of data, often are used in business as a source of data for workbooks. **XML (Extensible Markup Language)**, a popular format for data exchange, is a set of encoding rules that formats data to be readable by both humans and devices. Excel allows you to import data made available in all of those formats and more. Importing data into Excel can create a link that can be used to update data whenever the original file changes.

CONSIDER THIS

How should you plan for importing data?

Before importing data, become familiar with the layout of the data, so that you can anticipate how each data element will be arranged in the worksheet. In some cases, the data will need to be transposed, meaning that the rows and columns need to be switched. You also might need to format the data, move it, or convert it from or to a table.

In the following sections, you will import data from four different stores and in four different formats. You will look for data inconsistencies, format the data as necessary, and replicate the formulas to create the consolidated worksheet shown as a printout in Figure 7–13.

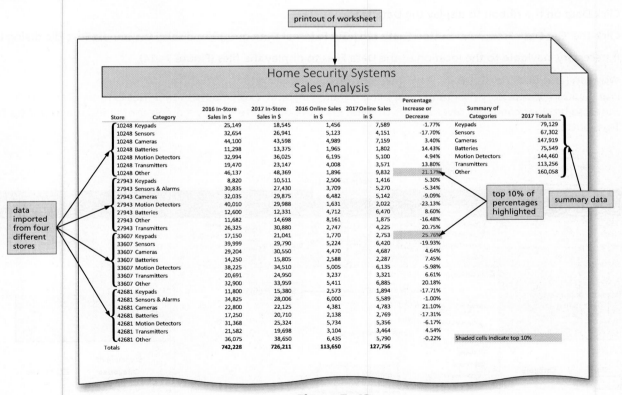

Figure 7–13

Text Files

A **text file** contains data with little or no formatting. Many programs, including Excel, offer an option to import data from a text file. Text files may have a file extension such as .txt, .csv, .asc, or .cdl, among others. Companies sometimes generate these text files from input fields via proprietary business applications.

In text files, commas, tabs, or other characters often separate the fields. Alternately, the text file may have fields of equal length in columnar format. Each record usually exists on a separate line. A **delimited file** contains data fields separated by a selected character, such as a comma. Such a file is called a **comma-delimited text file**. A **fixed-width file** contains data fields of equal length with spaces between the fields. In the case of a fixed-width file, a special character need not separate the data fields. During the import process, Excel provides a preview to help identify the type of text file being imported.

To Import Data from a Text File

The following steps import a comma-delimited text file into the HSS Sales Analysis workbook using the Text Import Wizard. *Why? The wizard helps you make sure the data is imported correctly.* To complete these steps, you will be required to use the Data Files. Please contact your instructor for information about accessing the Data Files. The text file contains data about sales for Store #10248 (shown in Figure 7–1a).

- With the HSS Sales Analysis workbook active, if necessary, select cell A4.
- Click Data on the ribbon to display the Data tab.
- Click the 'Get Data From Text' button (Data tab | Get External Data group) to display the Import Text File dialog box.
- If necessary, navigate to the location of the Data Files to display the files (Figure 7–14).

Q&A Why can I not find the 'Get Data From Text' button?
If any add-in or accessory programs have been installed in Excel, Excel may display a 'Get External Data' button on the Data tab that combines several types of data. Click the button to display a menu containing the 'Get Data From Text' button.

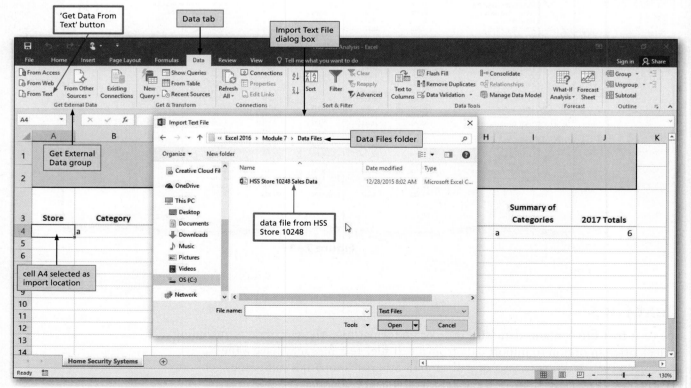

Figure 7–14

2

- Double-click the file name 'HSS Store 10248 Sales Data' to start the Text Import Wizard and display the Text Import Wizard - Step 1 of 3 dialog box (Figure 7–15).

What is the purpose of the Text Import Wizard?
The Text Import Wizard provides step-by-step instructions for importing data from a text file into an Excel worksheet. The Preview box shows that the text file contains one record per line and the fields are separated by commas. The Delimited option button is selected in the Original data type area.

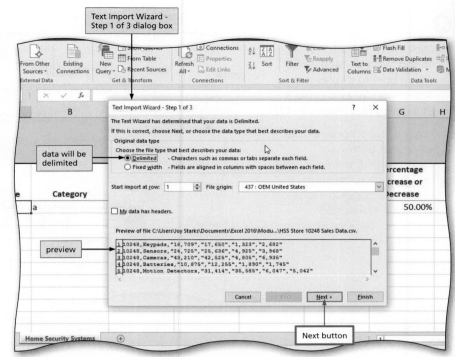

Figure 7–15

3

- Click the Next button (Text Import Wizard - Step 1 of 3 dialog box) to display the Text Import Wizard - Step 2 of 3 dialog box.

- Click Tab to remove the check mark.

- Click Comma to place a check mark in the Comma check box and to display the data fields correctly in the Data preview area (Figure 7–16).

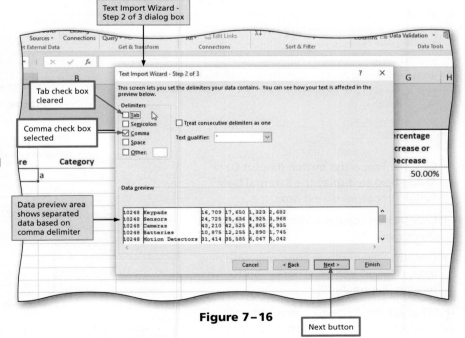

Figure 7–16

4

- Click the Next button (Text Import Wizard - Step 2 of 3 dialog box) to display the Text Import Wizard - Step 3 of 3 dialog box (Figure 7–17).

Q&A What is the purpose of the Advanced button?
When clicked, the Advanced button displays settings related to numerical data such as decimals and thousands separators.

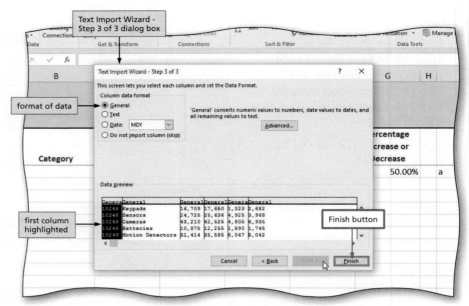

Figure 7–17

5

- Click the Finish button (Text Import Wizard - Step 3 of 3 dialog box) to complete the Text Import Wizard and display the Import Data dialog box (Figure 7–18).

Q&A What is shown in the Import Data dialog box when importing text?
The Import Data dialog box allows you to choose in which cell to import the text and to specify properties of the imported text.

Figure 7–18

6

- Click the Properties button (Import Data dialog box) to display the External Data Range Properties dialog box.

- Click 'Adjust column width' to remove the check mark.

- Click the 'Overwrite existing cells with new data, clear unused cells' option button to select it (Figure 7–19).

Q&A What are the Refresh control options?
The Refresh control options allow you to receive updated data from the text file based on a manual refresh, a specific time interval, or every time the workbook is opened, thus linking the text file to the current workbook.

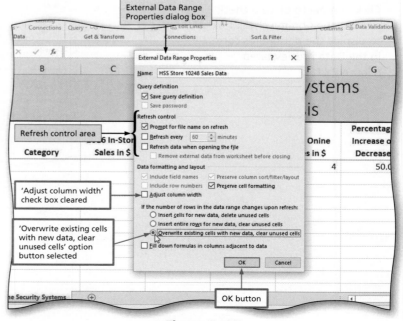

Figure 7–19

7

- Click the OK button (External Data Range Properties dialog box) to accept the settings and display the Import Data dialog box again.

- Click the OK button (Import Data dialog box) to import the data from the text file into the worksheet beginning at cell A4 (Figure 7–20).

- Select cell C4 and then display the Home tab.

- Click the Format Painter button (Home tab | Clipboard group) and then drag through the range C5:F10 to copy the formatting to the range (Figure 7–20).

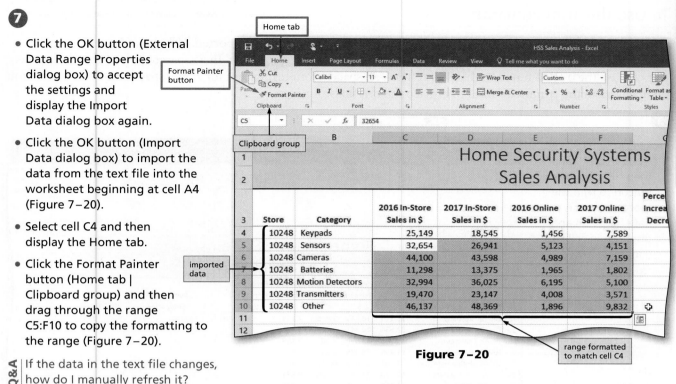

Figure 7–20

Q&A If the data in the text file changes, how do I manually refresh it?
After the text file is imported, Excel can refresh, or update, the data whenever the original text file changes using the Refresh All button (Data tab | Connections group).

Text Formatting

Sometimes data imported from various sources will have some input inconsistencies and will need to be reformatted. It is important to check imported data closely and make corrections as necessary, without changing any values. Excel has a series of text functions to help you convert numbers to text, correct inconsistencies in capitalization, and trim off excess spaces, as well as functions to retain only parts of a cell contents or join pieces of text together. Table 7–1 displays some of the available text functions.

Table 7–1 Text Functions				
Function	**Purpose**	**Syntax**	**Example**	**Result**
TEXT	Converts a numeric value to text and lets you specify the display formatting by using special format strings (Once converted, you cannot use it in calculations.)	TEXT(value, format_text)	=TEXT(42.5, "$0.00")	$42.50
TRIM	Removes all spaces from text except for single spaces between words	TRIM(text)	TRIM(" Roy S. Lyle ")	Roy S. Lyle
RIGHT	Returns the rightmost characters from a text value	RIGHT(text,[num_chars])	RIGHT("Joyce",1)	e
LEFT	Returns the leftmost characters from a text value	LEFT(text,[num_chars])	LEFT ("Joyce",2)	Jo
MID	Returns a specific number of characters starting at a specified position	MID(text, start_num, num_chars)	MID("Joyce",2,3)	oyc
UPPER	Converts text to uppercase	UPPER(text)	UPPER("Joyce")	JOYCE
LOWER	Converts text to lowercase	LOWER(text)	LOWER("Joyce")	joyce
CONCATENATE	Joins several text items into one text item	CONCATENATE(text1, [text2], ...)	CONCATENATE ("Mari","lyn")	Marilyn

To Use the Trim Function

The following steps trim extra spaces from the category data you imported. **Why?** *You notice that the data was stored with extra spaces, making it impossible to align the words in the column.* In a separate part of the workspace, you will use the TRIM function that will remove all spaces from text except for single spaces between words. You then will paste the trimmed values to replace the originals.

1

- Select cell B12, type `=trim(b4)` and then click the Enter button to trim the spaces from the data in cell B4 and display it in cell B12 (Figure 7–21).

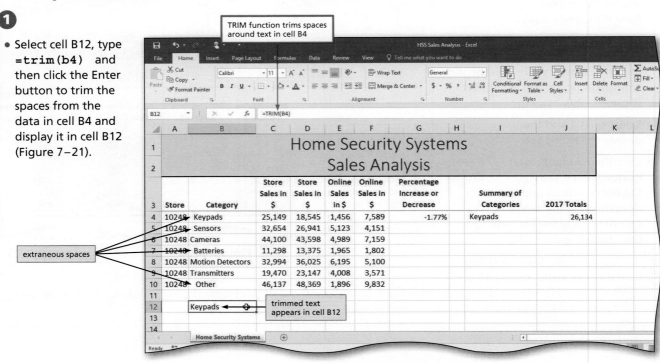

Figure 7–21

2

- Drag the fill handle of cell B12 down through cell B18 to display the trimmed data for all categories.

- Do not deselect (Figure 7–22).

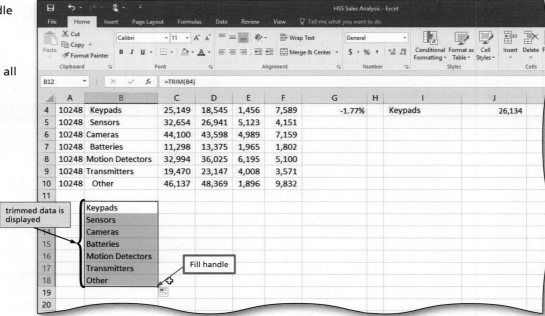

Figure 7–22

To Paste Values Only

The following steps cut the data from cells B12 through B18 and paste only the trimmed values back to cells B4 through B10. *Why? If you simply paste the contents of the clipboard using CTRL+V, you will retain the trim function notation. You want only the trimmed values.* To paste values, you will use Paste Options.

1

- With the range B12:B18 still selected, press CTRL+C to copy the data.

- Right-click cell B4 to display the shortcut menu (Figure 7–23).

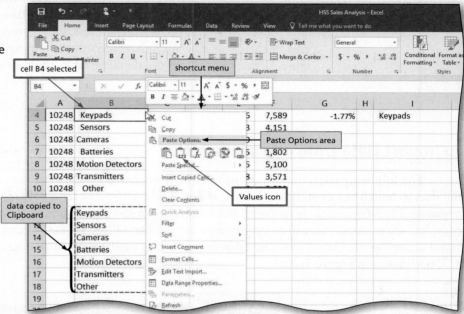

Figure 7–23

2

- In the Paste Options area, click the Values icon to paste only the values.

- Delete the data in the B12:B18 because you have already pasted it to the correct location and no longer need it (Figure 7–24).

Experiment

- Click various cells in the range B4:B10 to verify that the values were posted, rather than the trim function.

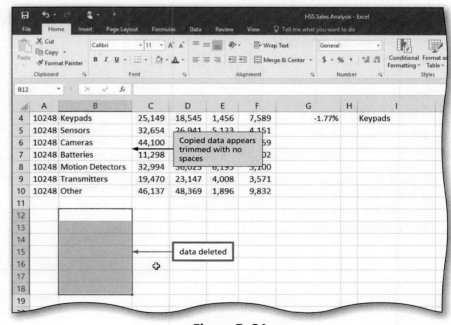

Figure 7–24

Access Files

Data from Microsoft Access files are stored in tabular format. Each row is a record; columns indicate fields. When you import Access files, you commonly import an entire table, which includes column headings. Sometimes you may need to make a query of the data. A **query** is a way to qualify the data to import by specifying a matching condition or asking a question of a database. For example, a query can identify only those records that pass a certain test, such as records containing numeric fields greater than a specific amount or records containing text fields matching a specific value. When Excel imports a database table, the data is placed in an Excel table.

To Import Data from an Access Table

1 CREATE TEMPLATE | 2 USE TEMPLATE | 3 IMPORT DATA | 4 USE QUICK ANALYSIS
5 FIND & REPLACE | 6 INSERT BAR CHART | 7 CREATE SMARTART | 8 ADD SCREENSHOT

The following steps import an entire table from an Access database into an Excel table and then reformat the data to match the existing worksheet. *Why? A table inserted in the middle of a longer list like this one would be confusing. The table needs to be converted to a range; the cells then should be reformatted after Excel imports the data.* To complete these steps, you will be required to use the Data Files. Please contact your instructor for information about accessing the Data Files. The table in the Access database contains data about sales revenue for Store #27943 (shown in Figure 7–1b).

- Select cell A11 so that the Access table is imported starting in cell A11.

- Click the 'Get Data From Access' button (Data tab | Get External Data group) to display the Select Data Source dialog box.

- Navigate to the location of the Data Files (Figure 7–25).

Q&A
What if the database contains more than one table?
If more than one table is in the database, then Excel allows you to choose which table to import.

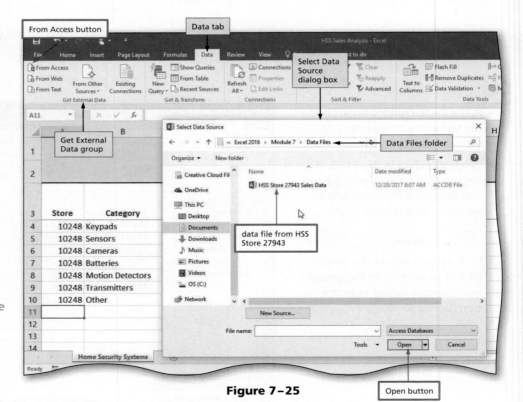

Figure 7–25

2

- Click the file 'HSS Store 27943 Sales Data' to select the file.

- Click the Open button (Select Data Source dialog box) to display the Import Data dialog box (Figure 7–26).

Q&A | What is shown in the Import Data dialog box when importing from an Access database?
The Import Data dialog box allows you to choose whether to import the data into a table, a PivotTable Report, a PivotChart and associated PivotTable Report, or only create a connection to the data. You also can choose to import the data to an existing worksheet or a new worksheet.

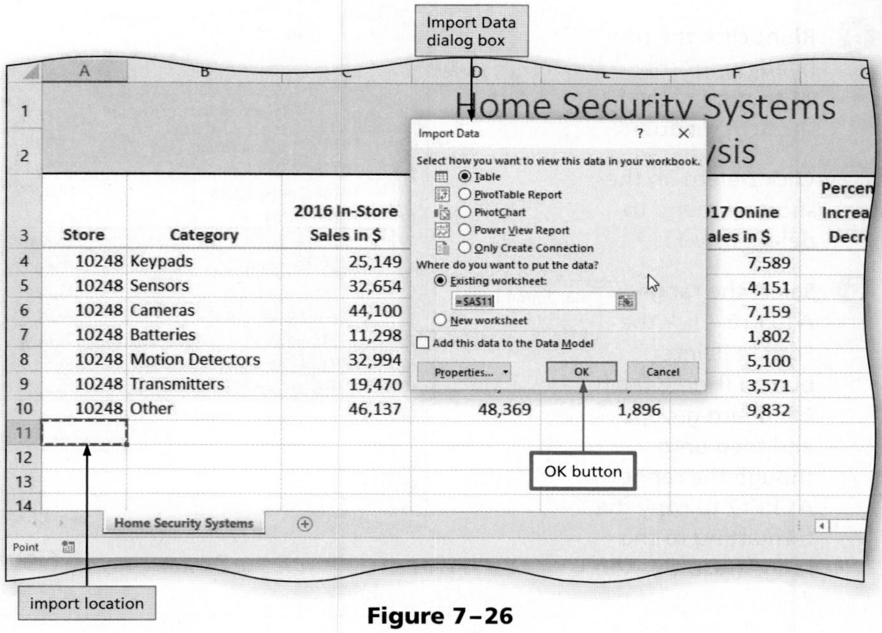

Figure 7–26

3

- Click the OK button (Import Data dialog box) to import the table data in the database beginning at cell A11.

- Scroll as necessary to display rows 11-18 (Figure 7–27).

Q&A | What happened to the layout of the worksheet when Excel imported the data?
Excel created a table using the data from the database. The names of the fields in the Access database appear in row 11. The table is formatted with the default table style for the worksheet's theme.

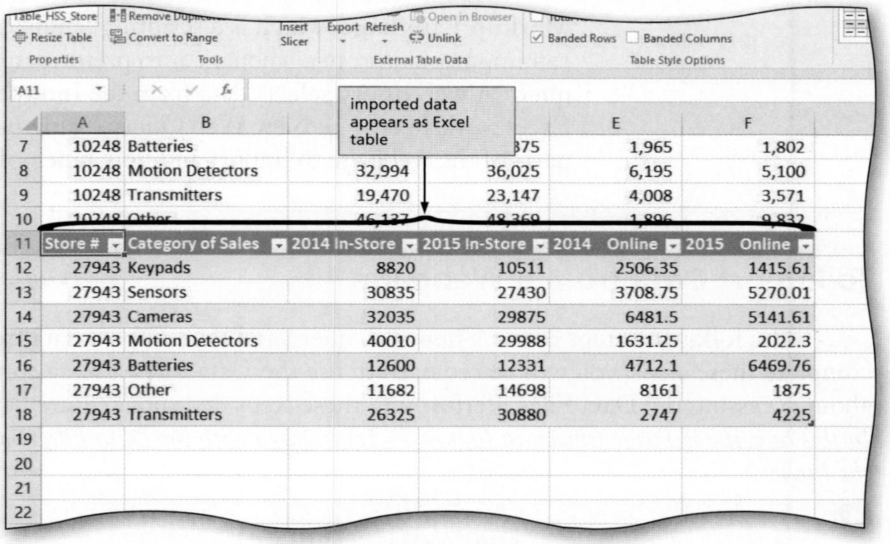

Figure 7–27

To Format the Access Data

The following steps convert the Access data table to a range and format it. Recall that you have converted tables to ranges in a previous module.

1 Right-click cell A11 and then point to Table on the shortcut menu.

2 Click 'Convert to Range' on the Table submenu to display a Microsoft Excel dialog box.

3 Click the OK button (Microsoft Excel dialog box) to convert the table to a range.

④ Right-click the row heading for row 11 to display the shortcut menu.

⑤ Click Delete on the shortcut menu to delete row 11.

⑥ Select the range A10:F10. Click the Format Painter button (Home tab | Clipboard group) and then drag though the range A11:F17 to copy the formatting to the range (Figure 7–28).

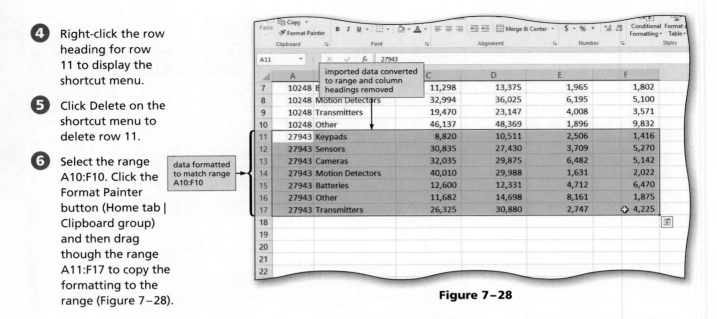

Figure 7–28

Web Data

Webpages use a file format called HTML. **HTML** stands for **Hypertext Markup Language**, which is a scripting language that browsers can interpret. Excel can import data from a webpage into preformatted areas of the worksheet using a web query. A **web query** selects data from the Internet or from an HTML file to add to the Excel worksheet. The New Web Query dialog box includes options to specify which parts of the webpage to import and how much of the HTML formatting to keep.

To Import Data from a Webpage

1 CREATE TEMPLATE | 2 USE TEMPLATE | 3 IMPORT DATA | 4 USE QUICK ANALYSIS
5 FIND & REPLACE | 6 INSERT BAR CHART | 7 CREATE SMARTART | 8 ADD SCREENSHOT

The following steps create a new web query and then import data from a webpage into the worksheet. To complete these steps, you will be required to use the Data Files. Please contact your instructor for information about accessing the Data Files. Performing these steps does not require being connected to the Internet. *Why? In this case, the webpage (shown in Figure 7–1c) is stored with the Data Files; normally you would have to be connected to the Internet.*

①

- Select cell A18 to specify the destination location and then display the Data tab.

- Click the 'Get Data From Web' button (Data tab | Get External Data group) to display the New Web Query dialog box.

- In the address bar, type the drive letter followed by a COLON (:), the path location of the Data Files, followed by the name of the desired file. Separate the name of each folder with a SLASH (/). For example, type `c:/users/username/documents/cis 101/data files/HSS Store 33607 Sales Data.htm` to insert the file name. Your file path will differ.

- Click the Go button (New Web Query dialog box) to display the webpage in the preview area.

- Resize the New Web Query dialog box as necessary (Figure 7–29).

Q&A | Could I navigate to the file and double-click?
No, double-clicking the file would open it in a browser, rather than creating a query. You must type in the location, just as you would for a URL. Contact your instructor for the exact path and location.

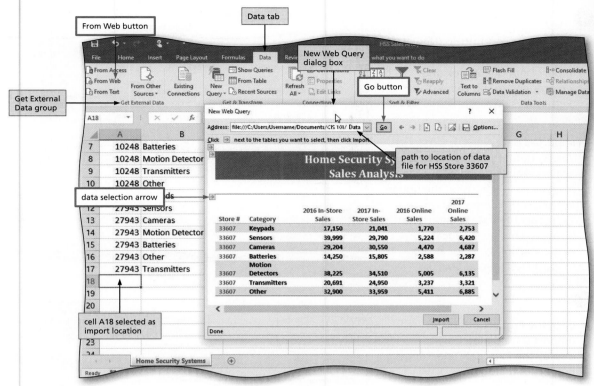

Figure 7–29

2

- Click the data selection arrow button near the data in the HTML table to select it (Figure 7–30).

 Why did Excel add file:/// at the beginning of the address in the address bar?
Excel appends file:/// to the beginning of the address to indicate that the address points to a file saved on disk rather than a file on the web.

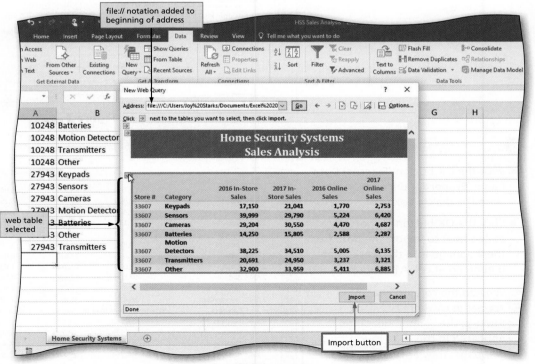

Figure 7–30

- Click the Import button (New Web Query dialog box) to display the Import Data dialog box and a marquee around cell A18 (Figure 7–31).

Q&A Can I change the location of the imported data?
Yes. By default, the cell that is active when the web query is performed will become the upper-left cell of the imported range. To import the data to a different location, change the location in the Existing worksheet box (Import Data dialog box).

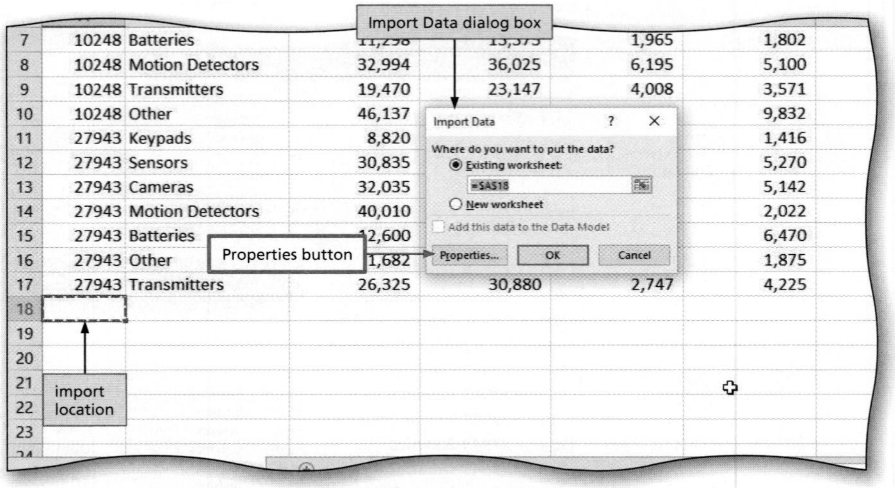

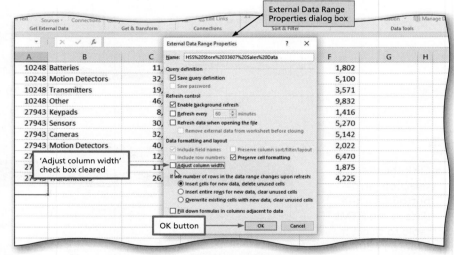

Figure 7–31

- Click the Properties button (Import Data dialog box) to display the External Data Range Properties dialog box.

- Click 'Adjust column width' to remove the check mark (Figure 7–32).

Figure 7–32

- Click the OK button (External Data Range Properties dialog box) to close the dialog box.

- Click the OK button (Import Data dialog box) to import the data from the webpage into the worksheet beginning at cell A18 (Figure 7–33).

Q&A Why do the column headings appear in row 18?
Because the column headings appeared in the webpage, they are imported with the other data and are displayed in row 18. The extra column headings must be deleted.

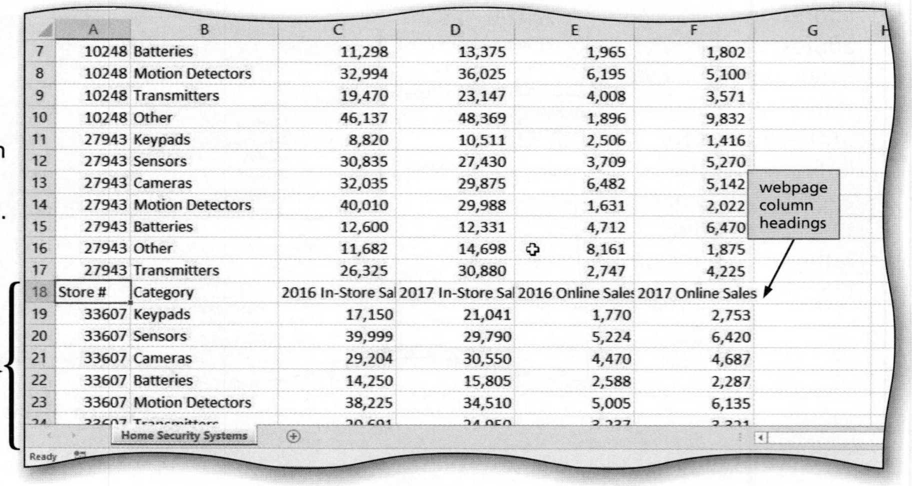

Figure 7–33

- Delete row 18 to remove the imported headings.

- Use the format painter to copy the format of cells A17:F17 to the range A18:F24 (Figure 7–34).

Q&A Why should I use a web query instead of copying and pasting from a webpage?

Using a web query has advantages over other methods of importing data from a webpage. For example, copying data from webpages to the Office Clipboard and then pasting it into Excel does not maintain all of the webpage formatting. In addition, copying only the desired data from a webpage can be tedious. Finally, copying and pasting does not create a link to the webpage for future updating.

13	27943	Cameras		29,875	5,142
14	27943	Motion Detectors	40,010	29,988	1,631	2,022
15	27943	Batteries	12,600	12,331	4,712	6,470
16	27943	Other	11,682	14,698	8,161	1,875
17	27943	Transmitters	26,325	30,880	2,747	4,225
18	33607	Keypads	17,150	21,041	1,770	2,753
19	33607	Sensors	39,999	29,790	5,224	6,420
20	33607	Cameras	29,204	30,550	4,470	4,687
21	33607	Batteries	14,250	15,805	2,588	2,287
22	33607	Motion Detectors	38,225	34,510	5,005	6,135
23	33607	Transmitters	20,691	24,950	3,237	3,321
24	33607	Other	32,900	33,959	5,411	6,885

Home Security Systems

range A18:F24 formatted to match range A17:F17

Ready   Average: 19384.7

Figure 7–34

Using Word Data

A Word document often contains data stored in a table. While you could save your Word data in a text format such as .txt and import it as you did earlier, you can copy and paste directly from Word to Excel. A few things should be taken into consideration, however. On some occasions, Word data requires some manipulation once you paste it into Excel. For example, the Word data may be easier to work with if the rows and columns were switched, and, thus, you will need to transpose the data. In other situations, you may find that Excel did not paste the data into separate columns, and, thus, you will need to split the data or convert the text into columns. Finally, some text to column conversions need extra space or columns when the data is split, requiring you to move other data out of the way. An example of each will occur in the following sections, as you copy, paste, transpose, move, and split data from Word to Excel.

To Paste Text without Formatting

1 CREATE TEMPLATE | 2 USE TEMPLATE | 3 IMPORT DATA | 4 USE QUICK ANALYSIS
5 FIND & REPLACE | 6 INSERT BAR CHART | 7 CREATE SMARTART | 8 ADD SCREENSHOT

The Word document that contains data from Store # 42681 (Figure 7–1d) includes a Word table with rows and columns. The following steps copy and paste that data from Word into Excel. *Why? The manipulations that you will need to make on the Word data are performed more easily in Excel.* The Paste Special command allows you to choose to paste text only without any kind of formatting from the source or the destination locations; it also provides options for pasting HTML, pictures, and hyperlinks. To complete these steps, you will be required to use the Data Files. Please contact your instructor for information about accessing the Data Files.

- Scroll as necessary to select cell A34.

- Run Word and then open the Word document named, HSS Store 42681 Sales Data, from the Data Files.

- In the Word document, drag through all of the cells in the second through last columns in the table to select the table cells.

- Press CTRL+C to copy the contents of the table to the Office Clipboard (Figure 7–35).

Q&A Why did I select cell A34 in Excel?

You will paste the data to that location, out of the way, in order to manipulate it.

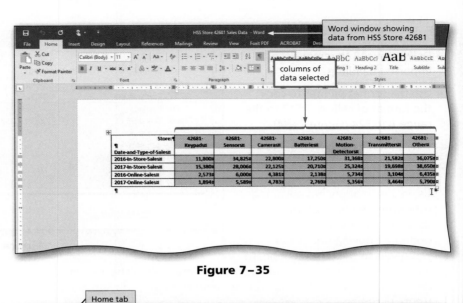

Figure 7–35

- Exit Word and, if necessary, click the Excel app button on the taskbar to make Excel the active window.

- With cell A34 active, click the Paste arrow (Home tab | Clipboard group) to display the Paste gallery (Figure 7–36).

Q&A Could I use the 'Keep Source Formatting' or 'Match Destination Formatting' buttons in the Paste gallery?

No. Both of those paste options include formatting information that you do not want to use while importing the data.

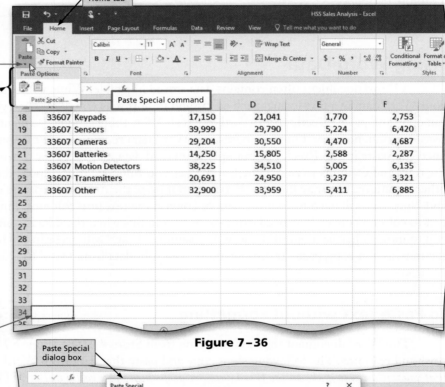

Figure 7–36

❸

- Click the Paste Special command in the Paste gallery to display the Paste Special dialog box.

- Click Text in the As list (Figure 7–37).

Q&A Why do I select the Text format in the As list?

The Text format brings in only text that has not been processed, formatted, or manipulated, also known as **raw data**. Importing raw data provides greater flexibility to manipulate the text in Excel.

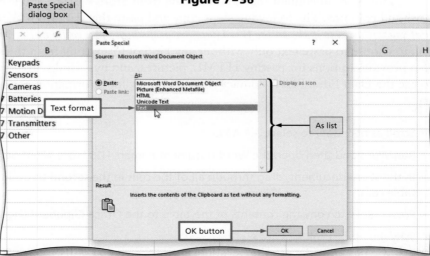

Figure 7–37

4

- Click the OK button (Paste Special dialog box) to paste the contents of the Office Clipboard as raw data.

- Scroll as necessary to display the data, but do not select any other cells (Figure 7–38).

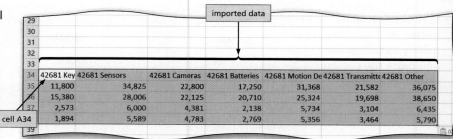

	imported data

	42681 Key	42681 Sensors	42681 Cameras	42681 Batteries	42681 Motion De	42681 Transmitte	42681 Other
35	11,800	34,825	22,800	17,250	31,368	21,582	36,075
36	15,380	28,006	22,125	20,710	25,324	19,698	38,650
37	2,573	6,000	4,381	2,138	5,734	3,104	6,435
38	1,894	5,589	4,783	2,769	5,356	3,464	5,790

cell A34

Figure 7–38

To Transpose Columns and Rows

1 CREATE TEMPLATE | 2 USE TEMPLATE | 3 IMPORT DATA | **4 USE QUICK ANALYSIS**
5 FIND & REPLACE | 6 INSERT BAR CHART | 7 CREATE SMARTART | 8 ADD SCREENSHOT

Recall that the Paste gallery may display many different kinds of paste options, depending upon the data on the Office Clipboard and the paste location. When you copy and paste within Excel (rather than across apps), the Paste gallery displays many more options for pasting, such as pasting only the formulas, pasting only the values, pasting as a picture, and pasting transposed data, among others. The Transpose option in the Paste gallery automatically flips the rows and columns during the paste. In other words, the row headings become column headings or vice versa. All pasted data is switched as well. The following steps copy the data and paste it, transposed. *Why? The original Word data had category titles across the top; the spreadsheet template expects titles down the left side.*

1

- With the range A34:G38 still selected, press CTRL+C to copy the selection to the Office Clipboard.

- Scroll as necessary, and then select cell A25 to prepare for pasting the data to that location.

- Click the Paste arrow (Home tab | Clipboard group) to display the Paste gallery (Figure 7–39).

Experiment

- Using live preview, point to each of the paste options in the Paste gallery to see how the pasted format changes.

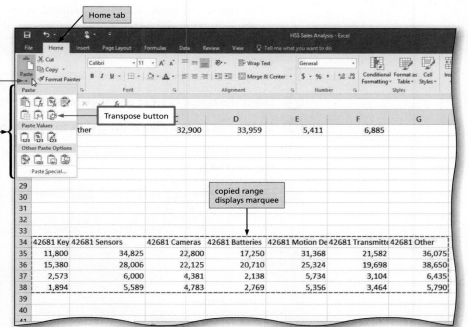

Figure 7–39

Q&A Why do I have to copy the data to the clipboard again?

The Transpose paste command is available only when Excel recognizes the cell format. You cannot transpose directly from copied Word tables.

2

- Click the Transpose button in the Paste gallery to transpose and paste the copied cells to the range beginning with cell A25 (Figure 7–40).

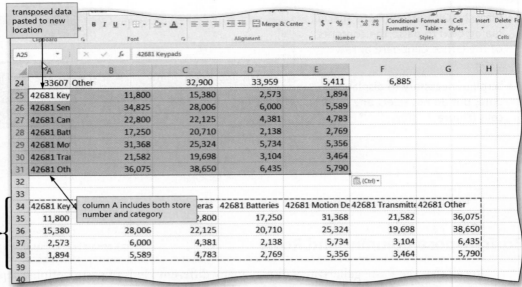
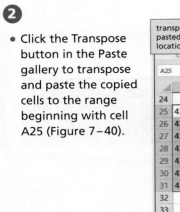

Figure 7–40

To Delete, Cut, Paste, and Format Data

The following steps delete the original Word data from range A34:G38 because you no longer need it. The steps also move some of the transposed data to make room for splitting column A into two columns.

1 Delete the data in the range A34:G38.

2 Select the range B25:E31 and then press CTRL+X to cut the data.

3 Select cell C25 and then press CTRL+V to paste the data.

4 Use the format painter to copy the formatting of cell C24 to the range C25:F31 (Figure 7–41).

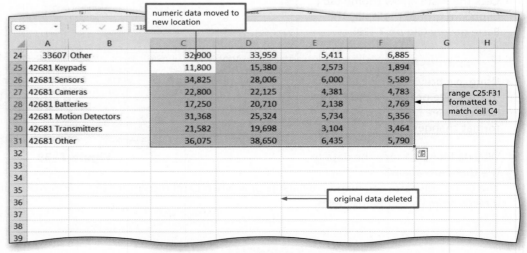

Figure 7–41

To Convert Text to Columns

Column A of the imported data from Store #42681 includes both the store and category in the same cell. The following steps split the data. *Why? The data must be separated using Excel's 'Text to Columns' command so that the category information is in column B.* You have two choices when splitting the column. You can have Excel split the data based on a specific character, such as a space or comma; or, you can have Excel split the data based on a certain number of characters or fixed width. In this case, because the data from HSS includes multiple spaces, it is better to use a fixed width to separate the store number from the inventory category.

1

- Select the range A25:A31 to prepare for converting the text to columns.

- Display the Data tab.

- Click the 'Text to Columns' button (Data tab | Data Tools group) to display the Convert Text to Columns Wizard - Step 1 of 3 dialog box.

- Click the Fixed width option button (Figure 7–42).

◄ What other tasks can
Q&A be accomplished using the Convert Text to Columns Wizard?
With the Delimited option, you can split the data into separate columns by specifying a break at a specific character.

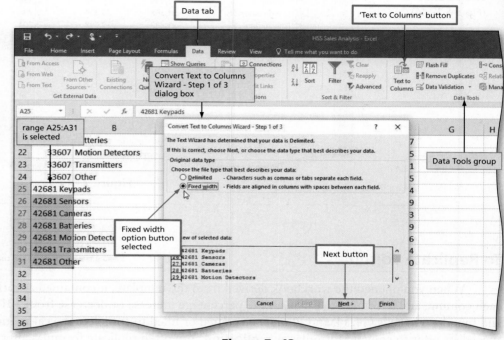

Figure 7–42

2

- Click the Next button (Convert Text to Columns Wizard - Step 1 of 3 dialog box) to accept a fixed width column and to display the Convert Text to Columns Wizard - Step 2 of 3 dialog box.

- In the Data preview area, drag the arrow line to the right one space to specify the width for the first column (Figure 7–43).

 Experiment

- Click the Next button to view options related to formatting or skipping parts of the data before splitting it. Do not make any changes.

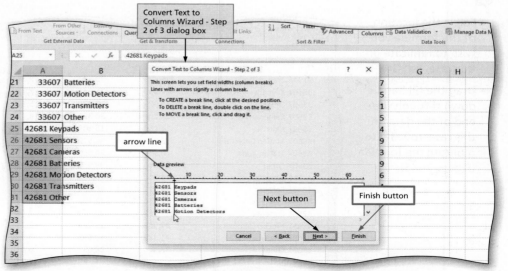

Figure 7–43

3

- Click the Finish button (Convert Text to Columns Wizard dialog box) to close the dialog box and separate the data in column A into two columns (Figure 7–44).

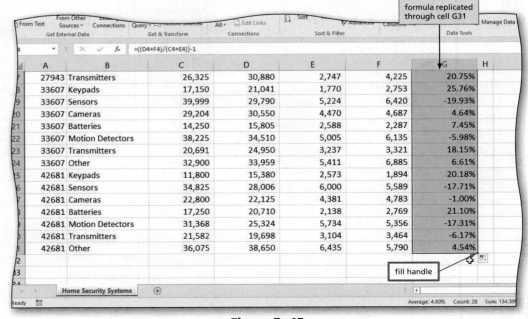

Figure 7–44

To Replicate Formulas

1 CREATE TEMPLATE | 2 USE TEMPLATE | 3 IMPORT DATA | 4 USE QUICK ANALYSIS
5 FIND & REPLACE | 6 INSERT BAR CHART | 7 CREATE SMARTART | 8 ADD SCREENSHOT

When you opened the workbook derived from the template, it contained a worksheet title, headings for each column, and a formula to calculate the percentage increase or decrease from 2016 to 2017. The formula and functions in cells G4, I4, and J4 must be copied or filled to complete the calculations. Some spreadsheet specialists refer to copying formulas as **replication**. You often replicate formulas after completing an import. *Why?* *Usually, the total number of records to be imported is unknown when you first begin a workbook.* The following steps use the fill handle to replicate the formulas.

- Select the location of the formula you wish to replicate (in this case, cell G4).

- Drag the fill handle down through the end of the data (in this case, row 31) to replicate the formula (Figure 7–45).

Figure 7–45

- Select cells I4:J4.

- Drag the fill handle down through row 10 to replicate the formulas and functions (Figure 7–46).

Q&A

Why did I stop the replication of the summary at row 10?
Only seven categories are used for the stores; however, you can replicate further if more categories are added. If you were to copy the formulas to row 11, you would see that cell I11 remains blank and cell J11 does not display a value.

| | | | Percentage | | |
In-Store Sales in $	2016 Online Sales in $	2017 Onine Sales in $	Increase or Decrease	Summary of Categories	2017 Totals
18,545	1,456	7,589	-1.77%	Keypads	79,129
26,941	5,123	4,151	-17.70%	Sensors	133,597
43,598	4,989	7,159	3.40%	Cameras	147,919
13,375	1,965	1,802	14.43%	Batteries	75,549
36,025	6,195	5,100	4.94%	Motion Detectors	144,460
23,147	4,008	3,571	13.80%	Transmitters	113,256
48,369	1,896	9,832	21.17%	Other	160,058
10,511	2,506	1,416	5.30%		
27,430	3,709	5,270	5.34%		

Home Security Systems
Sales Analysis

functions replicated through cell J10

Figure 7–46

③

- Click the Save button (Quick Access Toolbar) to save the workbook with the same name in the same location.

Break Point: If you wish to take a break, this is a good place to do so. You can exit Excel now. To resume at a later time, run Excel, open the file called HSS Sales Analysis, and continue following the steps from this location forward.

Using the Quick Analysis Gallery

Recall that in a previous module you used the status bar shortcut menu to provide an easy analysis of selected data. Another tool for analyzing data quickly is the Quick Analysis gallery. Quick Analysis first appears as a button below and to the right of selected data. When clicked, Excel displays the Quick Analysis gallery (Figure 7–47).

Each tab at the top of the gallery displays its own set of buttons to help you complete a task easily. For example, notice in Figure 7–47 that the Formatting tab displays conditional formatting options. The tabs always apply to the previously selected area of the worksheet. In addition, the Quick Analysis gallery uses live preview — in other words, you can preview how the feature will affect your data by pointing to the button in the gallery.

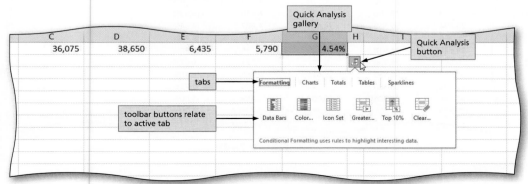

Figure 7–47

To Format Using the Quick Analysis Gallery

The following steps use the Quick Analysis gallery to format the top 10% of column G, the percentage increase or decrease in sales. *Why? The company executives want to see the stores and products with the highest increase in sales.* Formatting using the Quick Analysis gallery is much faster than using the ribbon to apply conditional formatting.

- Select the range you want to analyze, in this case G4:G31.

- Click the Quick Analysis button to display the Quick Analysis gallery.

- If necessary, click the Formatting tab to display the Quick Analysis gallery related to formatting (Figure 7–48).

 Experiment

- Point to each of the buttons on the Quick Analysis gallery to display a live preview.

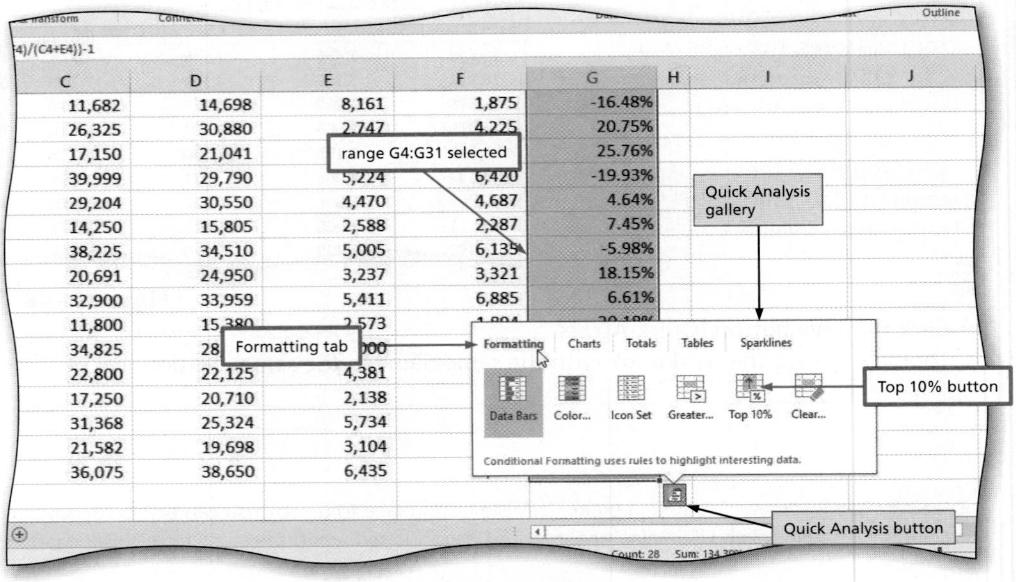

Figure 7–48

2

- Click the Top 10% button (Quick Analysis gallery).

- Click outside the selection and scroll as necessary to display the cells highlighted by the conditional formatting (Figure 7–49).

Q&A Why did Excel highlight the numbers in pink?
The default value for conditional formatting is pink.

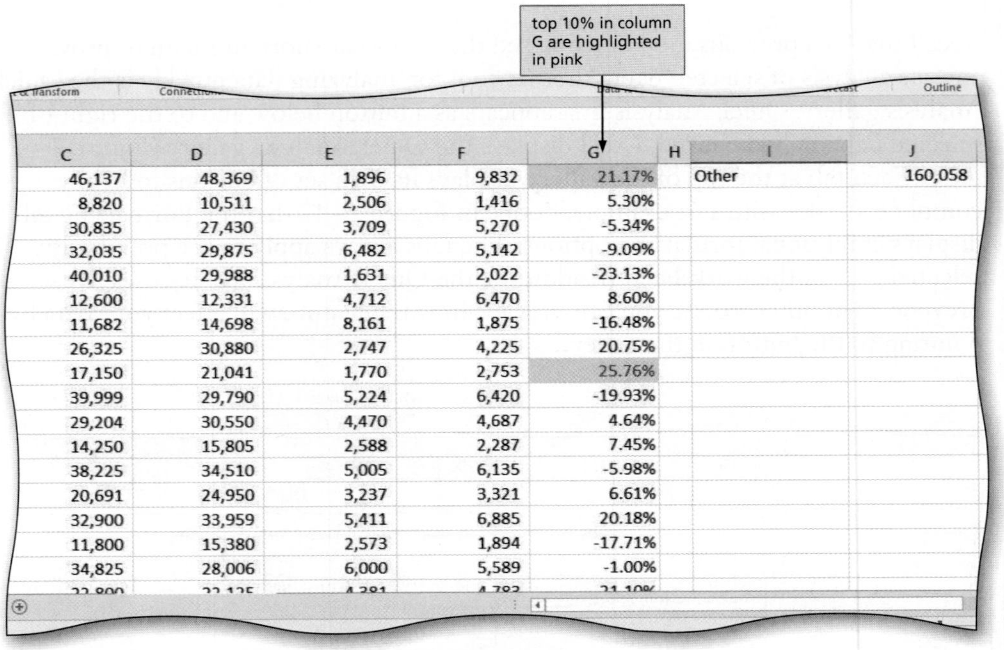

Figure 7–49

- Click cell I32. Type
  **Shaded cells
  indicate top
  10%** and then press
  the ENTER key to
  create a legend for
  the formatting.

- Drag through cells
  I32:J32 and display
  the Home tab.

32,900	33,959	5,411	6,885	6.61%
11,800	15,380	2,573	1,894	20.18%
34,825	28,006	6,000	5,589	-17.71%
22,800	22,125	4,381	4,783	-1.00%
17,250	20,710	2,138	2,769	21.10%
31,368	25,324	5,734	5,356	-17.31%
21,582	19,698	3,104	3,464	-6.17%
36,075	38,650	6,435	5,790	4.54%

formatted legend in cell I32

Shaded cells indicate top 10%

Figure 7–50

- Click the Fill Color arrow (Home tab | Font Group) and then More Colors to display the Colors dialog box. Double-click a pink color to format the cell.

- Click outside the selection to view the formatting (Figure 7–50).

  If instructed to do so, select cell I33, type **Prepared by** and then type your name.

Q&A | How would I clear the formatting?
You can highlight the cell or cells, click the Quick Analysis button, click the Formatting tab, and then click the Clear button (Quick Analysis gallery).

To Total Data Using the Quick Analysis Gallery

1 CREATE TEMPLATE | 2 USE TEMPLATE | 3 IMPORT DATA | 4 USE QUICK ANALYSIS
5 FIND & REPLACE | 6 INSERT BAR CHART | 7 CREATE SMARTART | 8 ADD SCREENSHOT

The following steps use the Quick Analysis gallery to total the sales data from the four stores. *Why? Companies routinely want to examine grand totals for all stores.*

- Select the range you
  want to analyze, in
  this case C4:F31.

- Click the Quick
  Analysis button to
  display the Quick
  Analysis gallery
  and then click the
  Totals tab to display
  the Quick Analysis
  gallery related to
  totals (Figure 7–51).

  Experiment
- Point to each of the
  buttons on the Totals
  tab to display a live
  preview.

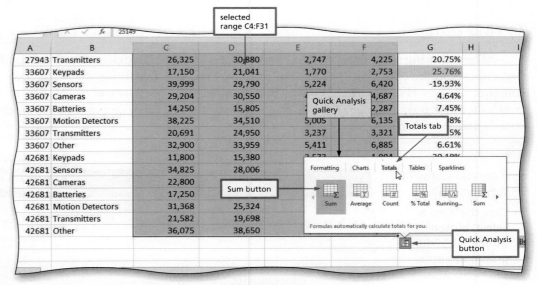

Figure 7–51

- Click the Sum button (Quick Analysis gallery).

- Select cell A32 and then type `Totals` to enter a row heading.

- Replicate cell G31 down to G32 to indicate the total percentage increase or decrease (Figure 7–52).

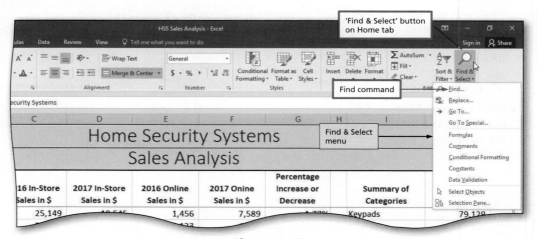

Figure 7–52

Using the Find and Replace Commands

To locate a specific piece of data in a worksheet, you can use the Find command on the Find & Select menu. The data you search for sometimes is called the **search string**. To locate and replace the data, you can use the Replace command on the Find & Select menu. If you have a cell range selected, the Find and Replace commands search only the range; otherwise, the Find and Replace commands begin at cell A1, regardless of the location of the active cell. The Find and Replace commands are not available for charts.

Selecting either the Find or Replace command displays the Find and Replace dialog box. The Find and Replace dialog box has two variations. One version displays minimal options, while the other version displays all of the available options. When you select the Find or Replace command, Excel displays the dialog box variation that was used the last time either command was selected.

To Find Data

1 CREATE TEMPLATE | 2 USE TEMPLATE | 3 IMPORT DATA | 4 USE QUICK ANALYSIS
5 FIND & REPLACE | 6 INSERT BAR CHART | 7 CREATE SMARTART | 8 ADD SCREENSHOT

The following steps show how to locate the search string, Batteries. The Find and Replace dialog box that displays all the options will be used to customize the search by using the Match case and 'Match entire cell contents' options. **Why?** *Match case means that the search is case sensitive and the cell contents must match the data exactly the way it is typed. 'Match entire cell contents' means that the data cannot be part of another word or phrase and must be unique in the cell.*

- If necessary, display the Home tab.

- Click the 'Find & Select' button (Home tab | Editing group) to display the Find & Select menu (Figure 7–53).

Figure 7–53

②

- Click Find on the Find & Select menu to display the Find and Replace dialog box.

- Click the Options button (Find and Replace dialog box) to expand the dialog box so that it appears as shown in Figure 7–54.

- Type **Batteries** in the Find what box to enter the search string.

- Click Match case and then click 'Match entire cell contents' to place check marks in those check boxes (Figure 7–54).

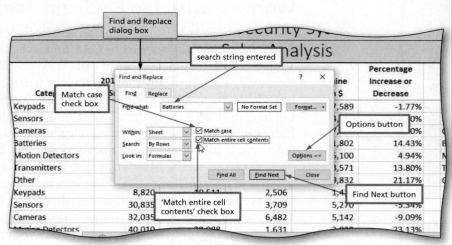

Figure 7–54

Q&A Why does the appearance of the Options button change?
The two less than signs pointing to the left on the Options button indicate that the more comprehensive Find and Replace dialog box is active.

③

- Click the Find Next button (Find and Replace dialog box) to cause Excel to begin the search and locate an occurrence of the search string (Figure 7–55).

Q&A What if Excel does not find any occurrences of the search string?
If the Find command does not find the string for which you are searching, Excel displays a dialog box indicating it searched the selected worksheets and cannot find the search string.

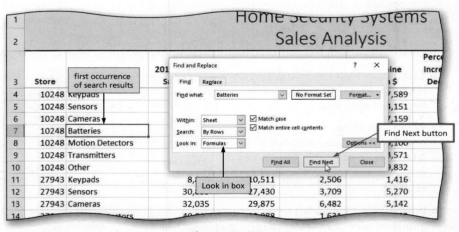

Figure 7–55

④

- Continue clicking the Find Next button (Find and Replace dialog box) to find the string, Batteries, in three other cells on the worksheet.

- Click the Close button (Find and Replace dialog box) to stop searching and close the Find and Replace dialog box.

Q&A What happens if you continue clicking the Find Next button?
Excel will cycle through the cells again. You have to watch the row and column references to determine if you have found them all.

Why did Excel not find the word Batteries in cell I7?
The default value in the Look in box (shown in Figure 7–55) was to search for formulas, which includes cells with entered text, but does not include the result of functions such as the one from the template, replicated in cell I7.

Other Ways

1. Press CTRL+F, enter search string, click Find Next button (Find and Replace dialog box)

Working with the Find and Replace Dialog Box

The Format button in the Find and Replace dialog box allows you to fine-tune the search by adding formats, such as bold, font style, and font size, to the search string. The Within box options include Sheet and Workbook. The Search box indicates whether Excel will search vertically through rows or horizontally across columns. The Look in box allows you to select Formulas, Values, or Comments. If you select Formulas, Excel will look in all cells except those containing functions or comments. If you select Values, Excel will look for the search string in cells that do not contain formulas, such as text or functions. If you select Comments, Excel will look only in comments.

If you select the Match case check box, Excel will locate only cells in which the string is in the same case. For example, when matching the case, accessories is not the same as Accessories. If you select the 'Match entire cell contents' check box, Excel will locate only the cells that contain the search string and no other characters. For example, Excel will find a cell entry of Other, but not Others.

To Find and Replace

1 CREATE TEMPLATE | 2 USE TEMPLATE | 3 IMPORT DATA | 4 USE QUICK ANALYSIS
5 FIND & REPLACE | 6 INSERT BAR CHART | 7 CREATE SMARTART | 8 ADD SCREENSHOT

The Replace command replaces the found search string with new data. You can use it to find and replace one occurrence at a time, or you can use the Replace All button to replace the data in all locations at once. The following steps show how to use the Replace All button. **Why?** *You want to replace the string, Sensors, with the string, Sensors & Alarms.*

- Click the Find & Select button (Home tab | Editing group) to display the Find & Select menu.

- Click Replace on the Find & Select menu to display the Find and Replace dialog box.

- Type **Sensors** in the Find what box and then type **Sensors & Alarms** in the Replace with box to specify the text to find and to replace.

- If necessary, click Match case and then click 'Match entire cell contents' to place check marks in those check boxes (Figure 7–56).

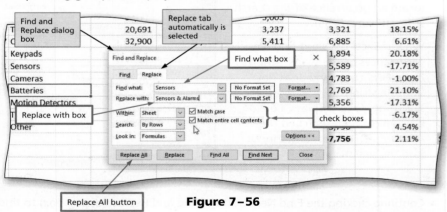

Figure 7–56

- Click the Replace All button (Find and Replace dialog box) to replace the string (Figure 7–57).

Q&A | What happens when Excel replaces the string?
Excel replaces the string, Sensors, with the replacement string, Sensors & Alarms, throughout the entire worksheet. If other worksheets contain matching cells, Excel replaces those cells as well. Excel displays the Microsoft Excel dialog box indicating four replacements were made.

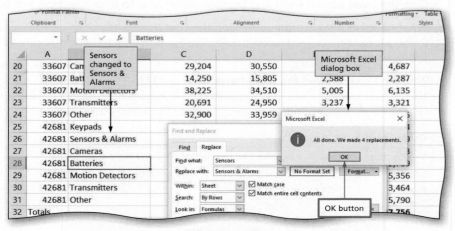

Figure 7–57

3

- Click the OK button (Microsoft Excel dialog box).

- Click the Close button (Find and Replace dialog box).

Q&A Why did Excel change the function value in cell I5?

Even though this cell is a function and therefore would not be changed because of the Formula designation in the Find and Replace dialog box, cell I5 searches column B. So, when Excel changed column B, the function itself changed cell I5.

Other Ways

1. Press CTRL+H, enter search string, enter replace string, click Replace All button (Find and Replace dialog box)

Inserting a Bar Chart

The requirements document shown in Figure 7–2 specifies that the workbook should include a bar chart, sometimes called a bar graph. A bar chart uses parallel, horizontal bars of varying lengths to measure and compare categories of data or amounts, such as sales, counts, or rates. The bars can be all one color, or each bar may be a different color.

When should you use a bar chart?

You should use a bar graph when you want to compare different groups of data. Because bar charts plot numerical data in rectangular blocks against a scale, viewers can develop a clear mental image of comparisons by distinguishing the relative lengths of the bars. You also can use a bar graph to display numerical data when you want to present distributions of data. Bar charts tend to be better than column charts for positive numbers, larger numbers of categories, and longer data labels.

CONSIDER THIS

If you are comparing more than one piece of data per category, the chart becomes a clustered bar chart. The only differences between a bar chart and a column chart are in orientation and the amount of room for data labels. Longer data labels display better using bar charts. If you have any negative values, the bars appear pointing left; columns would appear pointing down. You will create the bar chart shown in Figure 7–58 by using the Quick Analysis gallery and formatting the data, axes, and title.

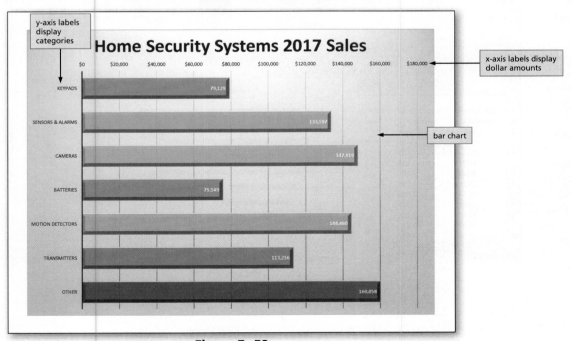

Figure 7–58

To Insert a Chart Using the Quick Analysis Gallery

The following steps insert a chart using the Quick Analysis gallery. *Why? The Quick Analysis gallery is near the data and provides an easy way to access charts.*

1

- Select the range I4:J10 to select the data to include in the chart.
- Click the Quick Analysis button to display the Quick Analysis gallery.
- Click the Charts tab to display the buttons related to working with charts on the toolbar (Figure 7–59).

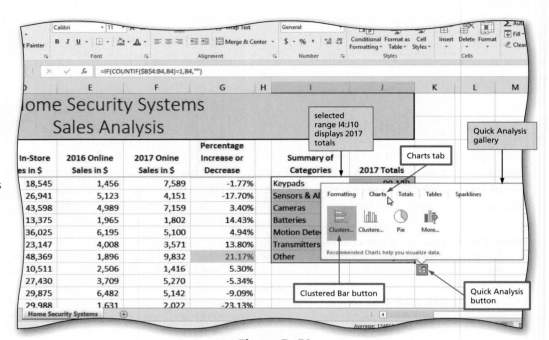

Figure 7–59

2

- Click the Clustered Bar button (Quick Analysis gallery) to insert the chart (Figure 7–60).

Q&A

Why are only three charts displayed?
Excel lists the charts that it recommends for your data. You can click the More button (Quick Analysis gallery) to open the Insert Chart dialog box and choose another style. (The cone chart shape is no longer available in Excel 2016.)

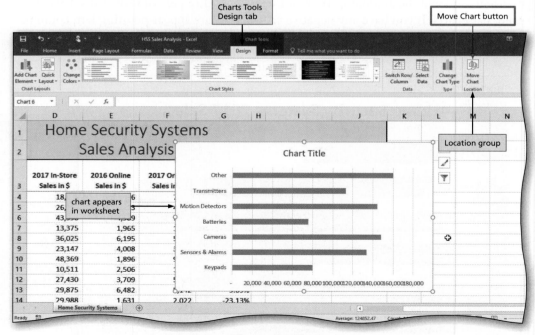

Figure 7–60

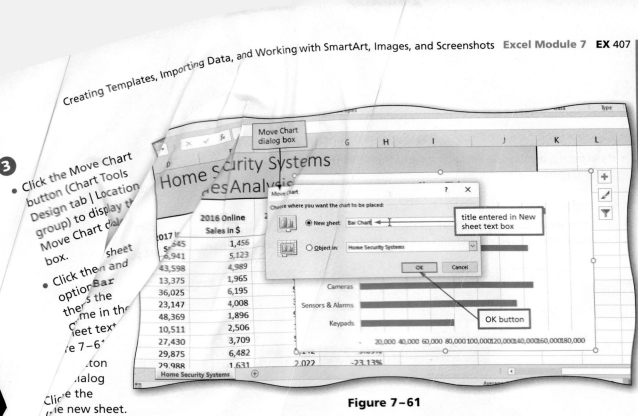

3

- Click the Move Chart button (Chart Tools Design tab | Location group) to display the Move Chart dialog box.

  - Click the New sheet option button and type Bar Chart as the name in the New sheet text box (Figure 7–61).

  - Click the OK button (Move Chart dialog box) to create the new sheet.

- Change the sheet tab color to blue.

Figure 7–61

---

1 CREATE TEMPLATE | 2 USE TEMPLATE | 3 IMPORT DATA | 4 USE QUICK ANALYSIS
5 FIND & REPLACE | 6 INSERT BAR CHART | 7 CREATE SMARTART | 8 ADD SCREENSHOT

To Format the Chart

The following steps change the style of the chart; change the color, order, and bevel of the category bars; and then edit the number format of the x-axis or horizontal labels. **Why?** *You always should customize the chart with formatting that applies to the data and the concept you are trying to portray.* You also will reverse the order of categories to display the longest bar across the bottom.

1

- Click the Style 3 button (Chart Tools Design tab | Chart Styles group) to change the style of the chart.

- Right-click any of the data bars on the chart to display the shortcut menu (Figure 7–62).

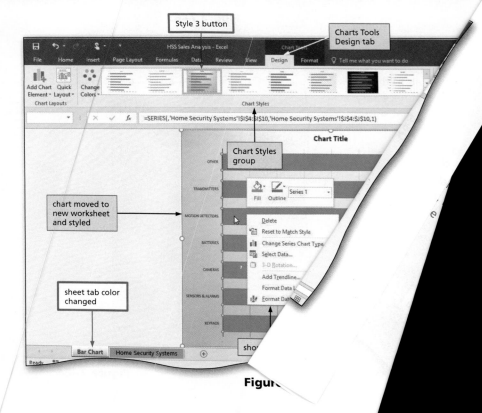

Figure

②

- Click 'Format Data Series' on the shortcut menu to display the Format Data Series task pane.

- Click the Fill & Line tab (Format Data Series task pane) to display the Fill & Line sheet.

- If necessary, display the Fill settings and then click the 'Vary colors by point' check box to display the bars in various colors (Figure 7–63).

Experiment

- Click the Series Options tab (Format Data Series task pane) to view the settings. Note that you can set the Overlap (for clustered charts) and the Gap Width (the interval between bars).

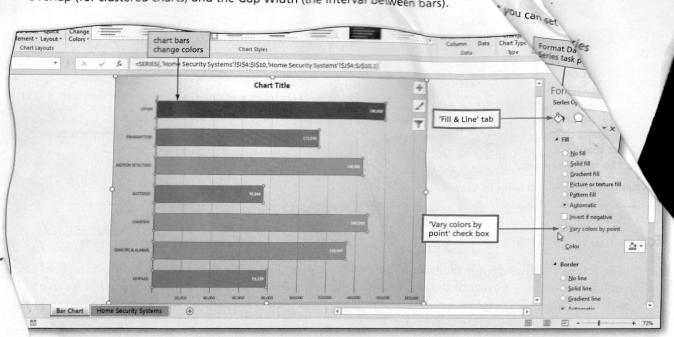

Figure 7–63

...he Effects tab to display
...ects sheet. If necessary,
...he 3-D Format settings
...–64).

...s of effects can I
...he Effects sheet?
...nge the shadow,
...bevel, and 3-D
...bars.

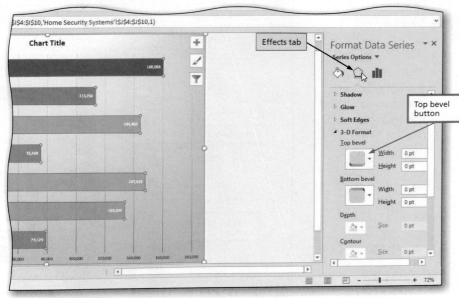

Figure 7–64

- Click the Top bevel
  button to display
  the Top bevel gallery
  (Figure 7–65).

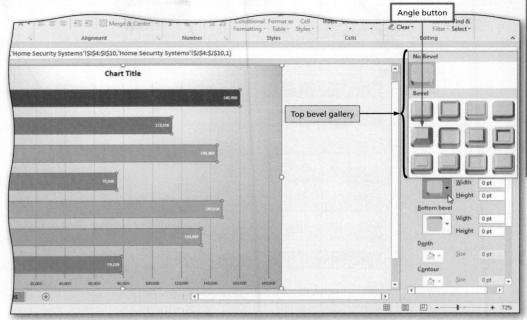

Figure 7–65

- Click the Angle button (Top bevel gallery) to apply an angle bevel to the bars in the chart.

- Right-click the y-axis or vertical category labels and then click Format Axis on the shortcut menu to display the Format Axis task pane.

- If necessary, click the Axis Options tab (Format Axis task pane) to display the sheet.

- In the Axis position area, click the 'Categories in reverse order' check box (Figure 7–66).

Q&A What other options
can I set using the
Format Axis task
pane?
You can change
how tick marks,
labels, and numbers
display. On the
Size & Properties
tab, you can set
the alignment,
text direction, and
margins of the axes.
The Fill & Line tab
and the Effects tab
are similar to the
Format Data Series
task pane that you
used earlier.

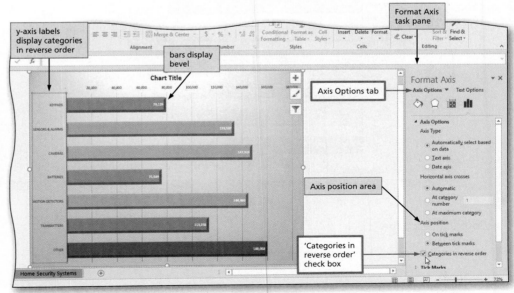

Figure 7–66

- Right-click the x-axis or horizontal labels across the top of the chart and then click Format Axis on the shortcut menu to display the Format Axis task pane.

- If necessary, click the Axis Options tab (Format Axis task pane) to display the sheet.

● Scroll down as necessary in the Format Axis task pane and then click Number to display the settings related to numbers (Figure 7–67).

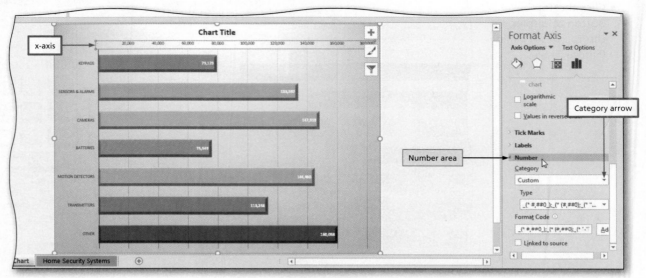

Figure 7–67

7

● Click the Category arrow to display its menu and then click Currency in the list (Figure 7–68).

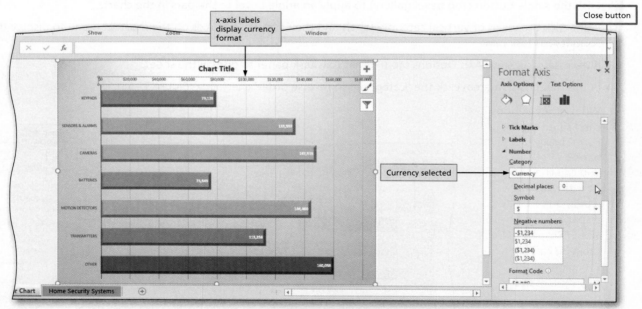

Figure 7–68

8

● Close the task pane.

To Format the Chart Title

The following steps format the chart title.

1 Click the chart title and then press CTRL+A to select all of the text.

2 Display the Home tab and change the font size to 32.

③ Type **Home Security Systems 2017 Sales** to change the title (Figure 7–69).

④ Click the Save button (Quick Access Toolbar) to save the workbook with the same name in the same location.

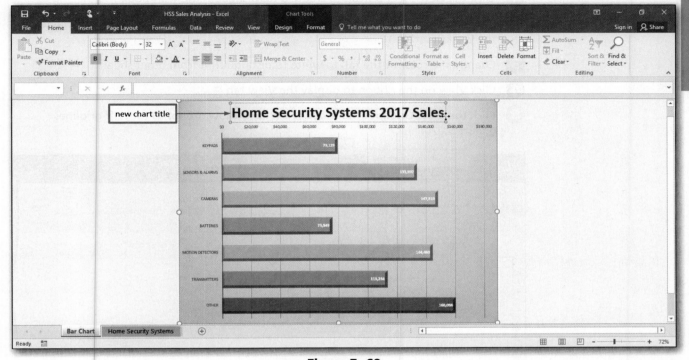

Figure 7–69

Break Point: If you wish to take a break, this is a good place to do so. You can exit Excel now. To resume at a later time, run Excel, open the file called HSS Sales Analysis, and continue following the steps from this location forward.

Working with SmartArt Graphics

A **SmartArt graphic** is a customizable diagram that you use to pictorially present lists, processes, and relationships. For example, you can use a SmartArt graphic to illustrate the manufacturing process to produce an item. Excel includes nine types of SmartArt graphics: List, Process, Cycle, Hierarchy, Relationship, Matrix, Pyramid, Picture, and Office.com. Each type of graphic includes several layouts, or templates, from which to choose. After selecting a SmartArt graphic type and layout, you customize the graphic to meet your needs and present your information and ideas in a compelling manner.

How do you choose the type of SmartArt graphics to add?
Consider what you want to illustrate in the SmartArt graphic. For example, if you are showing nonsequential or grouped blocks of information, select a SmartArt graphic in the List category. To show progression or sequential steps in a process or task, select a Process diagram. After inserting a SmartArt graphic, increase its visual appeal by formatting the graphic, for example, with 3-D effects and coordinated colors.

CONSIDER THIS

In the following sections, you will create a SmartArt graphic with shapes, pictures, and text. You then will add a style to the SmartArt graphic.

To Create a New Sheet

In preparation for inserting a SmartArt graphic, the following steps create a new sheet and hide gridlines.

1 Click the New sheet button to create a third sheet in the workbook.

2 Rename the worksheet `SmartArt Graphic` to provide a descriptive name for the worksheet.

3 Change the color of the tab to white to distinguish it from other sheets.

4 Click View on the ribbon to display the View tab.

5 Click the View Gridlines check box (View tab | Show group) to turn off gridlines (Figure 7–70).

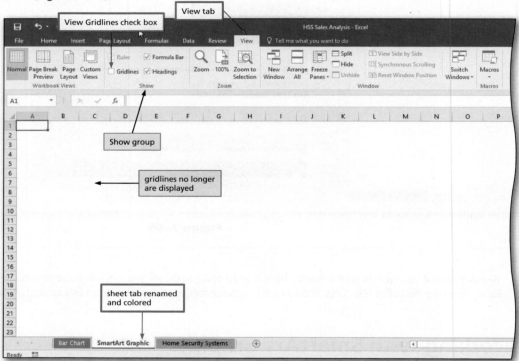

Figure 7–70

To Insert a SmartArt Graphic

1 CREATE TEMPLATE | 2 USE TEMPLATE | 3 IMPORT DATA | 4 USE QUICK ANALYSIS
5 FIND & REPLACE | 6 INSERT BAR CHART | 7 CREATE SMARTART | **8 ADD SCREENSHOT**

To illustrate the categories of products sold by HSS, you decide to use a SmartArt graphic. *Why? A SmartArt graphic with pictures can be used in marketing and promotional material for the company.* The following steps insert a SmartArt graphic named Accented Picture.

1

- Display the Insert tab.
- Click the 'Insert a SmartArt Graphic' button (Insert tab | Illustrations group) to display the Choose a SmartArt Graphic dialog box.
- Click the desired type of SmartArt in the left pane; in this case, click Picture to display the available SmartArt layouts in the middle pane (Choose a SmartArt Graphic dialog box).
- Click the desired layout in the gallery, in this case, the Accented Picture layout, to see a preview of the chart in the preview area (Figure 7–71).

Q&A What do the middle and right panes of the dialog box display?
The middle pane of the dialog box (the layout gallery) displays available types of picture charts, and the right pane (the preview area) displays a preview of the selected SmartArt graphic.

Experiment

- Click the various SmartArt graphics to see a preview of each in the preview area. When you are finished, click Accented Picture in the middle pane.

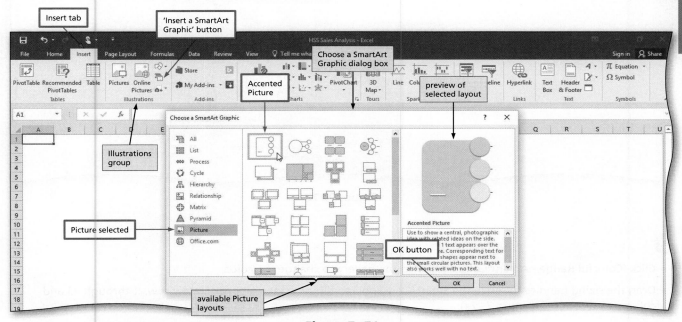

Figure 7–71

2

- Click the OK button (Choose a SmartArt Graphic dialog box) to insert an Accented Picture SmartArt graphic in the worksheet (Figure 7–72).

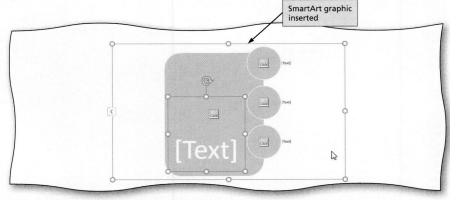

Figure 7–72

To Color and Resize the SmartArt Graphic

1 CREATE TEMPLATE | 2 USE TEMPLATE | 3 IMPORT DATA | 4 USE QUICK ANALYSIS
5 FIND & REPLACE | 6 INSERT BAR CHART | **7 CREATE SMARTART** | **8 ADD SCREENSHOT**

The following steps change the color of the SmartArt graphic and then resize it. *Why? You want the graphic to appear visually pleasing and as large as possible in the given space.*

1

- Click the Change Colors button (SmartArt Tools Design tab | SmartArt Styles group) to display the Change Colors gallery (Figure 7–73).

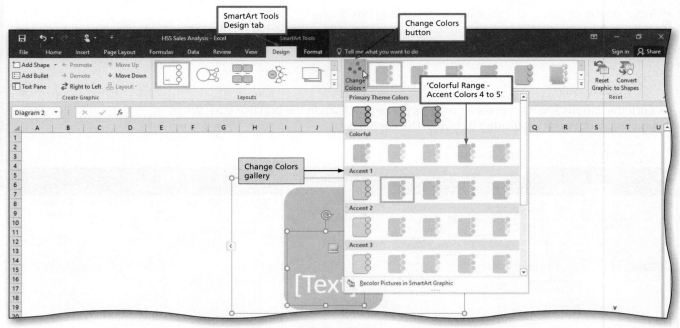

Figure 7–73

2

- Click 'Colorful Range - Accent Colors 4 to 5' in the gallery to change the color.
- Drag the sizing handles to resize the SmartArt graphic to fill the screen, approximately rows 1 through 23 and columns F through Q (Figure 7–74).

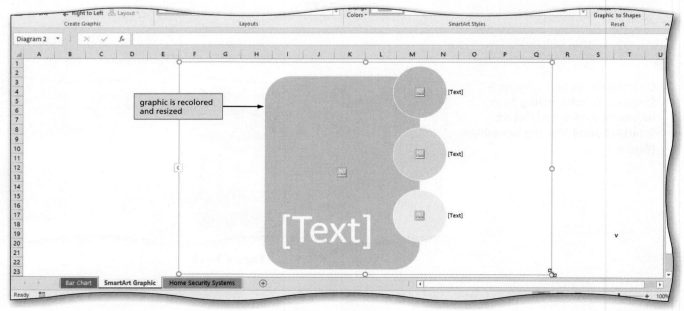

Figure 7–74

Experiment

- Click the SmartArt Tools Format tab and look at the various groups, buttons, and galleries available to format SmartArt graphics.

To Add Shapes to a SmartArt Graphic

Many SmartArt graphics include more than one shape, such as a picture, text box, or combinations, grouped in levels. Level 1 is considered the largest object or main level. Level 2 is a sublevel and may display one to three shapes when first created. You can add a shape or text box to each level. You also can **demote** or **promote** a shape, which means you can move the shape to a lower level or an upper level, respectively.

The default Accented Picture SmartArt graphic layout includes a large shape for level 1 and three smaller shapes at level 2. The following step adds three new shapes to the SmartArt graphic. *Why? You decide to show six categories in the SmartArt graphic.*

- Click the Add Shape button (SmartArt Tools Design tab | Create Graphic group) three times to add three more level 2 shapes (Figure 7–75).

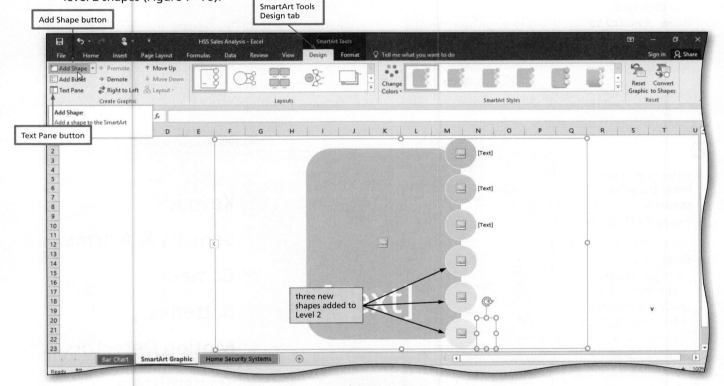

Figure 7–75

Q&A Why does Excel change the layout of the chart?
When you add a new shape to a SmartArt graphic, Excel rearranges the shapes in the graphic to fit in the same area. As shown in Figure 7–75, Excel reduces the size of each circle and the font size of the text to accommodate the added circles.

Other Ways

1. Right-click SmartArt graphic, point to Add Shape on shortcut menu, click 'Add Shape After' or 'Add Shape Before' on Add Shape submenu

To Add Text to a SmartArt Graphic

The following steps add text to the SmartArt graphic. You can type text directly in the text boxes of the SmartArt graphic, or you can display a Text Pane and add text to the shape through the Text Pane. The Text Pane displays a bulleted outline corresponding to each of the shapes in the SmartArt graphic. *Why? You may find it easier to enter text in the Text Pane because you do not have to select any object to replace the default text.*

- If the Text Pane does not appear, click the Text Pane button (SmartArt Tools Design tab | Create Graphic group) to display the Text Pane.

- Click the first bulleted item in the Text Pane and then type **Home Security Systems** to replace the default text (Figure 7–76).

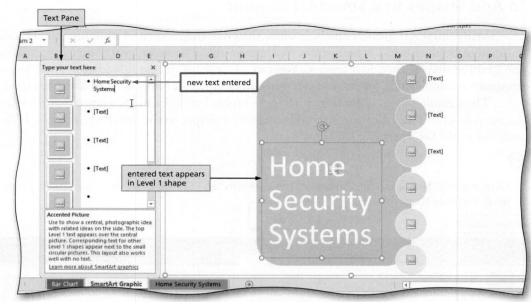

Figure 7–76

- Enter text in the other boxes as shown in Figure 7–77.

Q&A Did Excel resize my font?
Yes. Excel resizes all of the level 2 fonts to autofit the text in the graphic. Thus, it is important to resize the graphic before adding text.

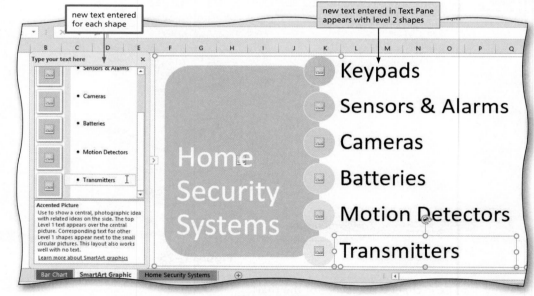

Figure 7–77

Other Ways

1. Click left arrow on edge of SmartArt graphic border to open Text Pane, insert text

2. Click individual text box in SmartArt graphic, type text

To Add Pictures to a SmartArt Graphic

1 CREATE TEMPLATE | 2 USE TEMPLATE | 3 IMPORT DATA | 4 USE QUICK ANALYSIS
5 FIND & REPLACE | 6 INSERT BAR CHART | 7 CREATE SMARTART | 8 ADD SCREENSHOT

The following steps add pictures to the SmartArt graphic. *Why? The CEO wants to highlight the kinds of products the company sells.* Other times, you may want to locate images or clip art from the web, also called online pictures. Excel 2016 uses a Bing Image Search to help you locate images licensed under Creative Commons. The resulting images may or may not be royalty and copyright free. You must read the specific license for any image you plan to use, even for educational purposes. In this module, you will add pictures from the Data Files. Please contact your instructor for information about accessing the Data Files.

- Scroll to the top of the Text Pane and then click the first Insert Picture icon to display the Insert Pictures dialog box (Figure 7–78).

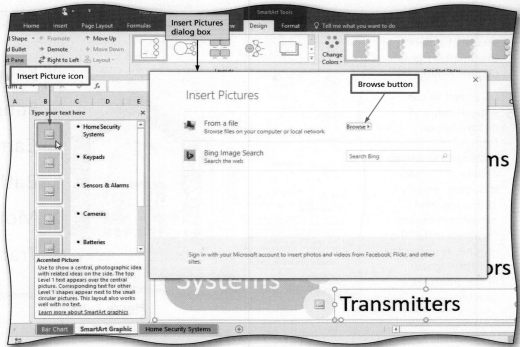

Figure 7–78

- Click the Browse button to display the Insert Picture dialog box and then browse to the Data Files (Figure 7–79).

Q&A Why do the files in my dialog box appear differently? Your system may display a different view. If you want to match the display in Figure 7–79, click the 'Change your view' arrow and then click Large Icons.

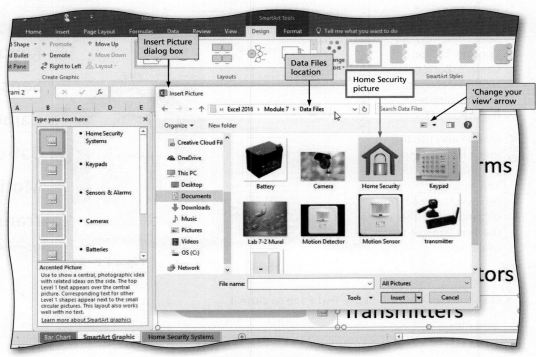

Figure 7–79

- Double-click the file named Home Security to place it in the SmartArt graphic (Figure 7–80).

Q&A Do I need to use a special type of picture file or format?

Excel accepts a wide variety of formats including .png, .gif, .bmp, .jpg, and .tif, among others. Excel will resize the graphic as necessary to fit the space in the SmartArt graphic.

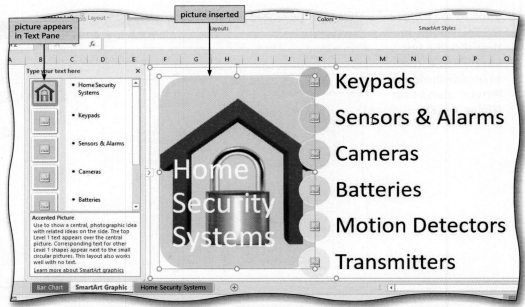

Figure 7–80

- One at a time, click each of the Insert Picture icons in the Text Pane to insert the appropriate picture from the Data Files: Keypad, Window Sensor, Camera, Battery, Motion Detector, and Transmitter (Figure 7–81).

Q&A Could I also use the Insert Picture icon in the shape?

Yes, as with the text, you can add a picture from either the Text Pane or the shape itself.

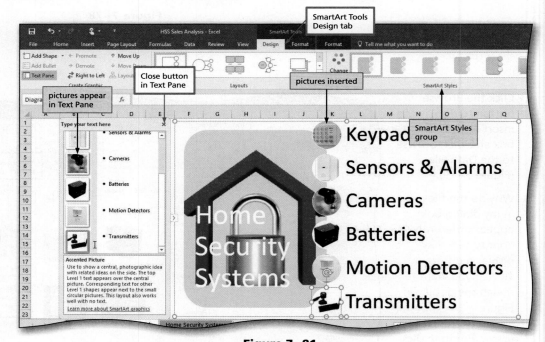

Figure 7–81

5

- Click the Close button in the Text Pane to close it.

Other Ways

1. Click Insert Picture icon in SmartArt graphic, select location (Insert Pictures dialog box), double-click picture

To Format Text Effects

The following steps format the text, Home Security Systems, with an outline text effect. *Why? Outlining, also called stroking the letters, will make them easier to read with the picture background.* You also will move the text box.

- Select the text, Home Security Systems.

- Right-click the text and then click Format Text Effects on the shortcut menu to display the Format Shape task pane.

- If necessary, click the 'Text Fill & Outline' tab (Format Shape task pane) and then click Text Outline to display the choices.

- In the Text Outline area, click the Solid line option button and then click the Outline color arrow to display the color gallery (Figure 7–82).

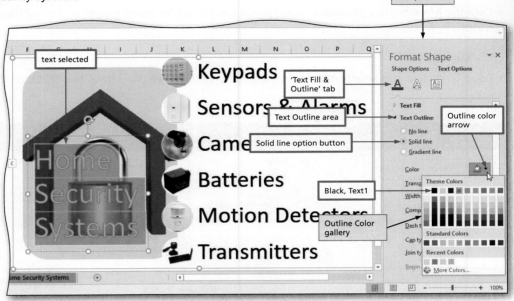

Figure 7–82

- Click 'Black, Text 1' in the Outline color gallery to add an outline to the text.

- Click outside of the SmartArt graphic to remove the selection and then drag the text box up as shown in Figure 7–83.

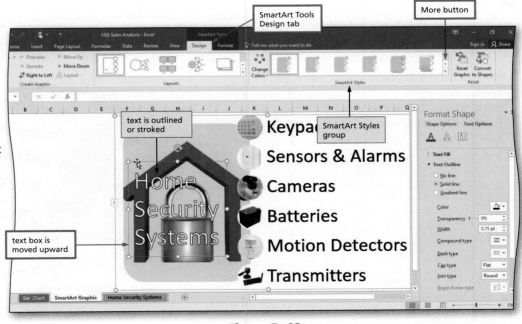

Figure 7–83

❸

- Close the Format Shape task pane.

Other Ways

1. Click Text Outline button (SmartArt Tools Format tab | WordArt Styles group), select color (Text Outline gallery)

To Add a Style to a SmartArt Graphic

Excel allows you to change the style of your SmartArt graphic. *Why? The SmartArt styles create different special effects for added emphasis or flair.* The following steps change the style of the SmartArt graphic.

①

- If necessary, display the SmartArt Tools Design tab.
- Click the More button (SmartArt Tools Design tab | SmartArt Styles group) to display the SmartArt Styles gallery (Figure 7–84).

Experiment

- Point to each of the SmartArt styles in the gallery to see a live preview of the effect on the worksheet.

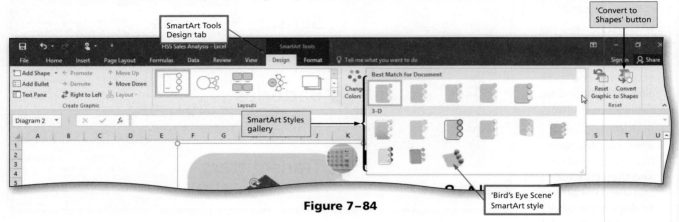

Figure 7–84

②

- Click the 'Bird's Eye Scene' style to apply it to the SmartArt graphic (Figure 7–85).

Q&A What does the 'Convert to Shapes' button do?

Clicking the 'Convert to Shapes' button (SmartArt Tools Design tab | Reset group) converts the SmartArt graphic to individual shapes that can be resized, moved, or deleted independently of the others.

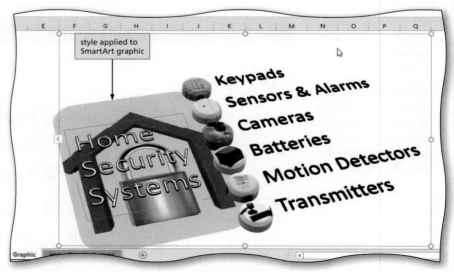

Figure 7–85

③

- Click the Save button (Quick Access Toolbar) to save the workbook with the same name in the same location.

TO INSERT AN INDIVIDUAL IMAGE INTO A WORKBOOK

If you wanted to insert an individual image into your workbook, you would perform the following steps.

1. Select the cell at which you wish the image to display.
2. Display the Insert tab.
3. Click the From File button (Insert tab | Illustrations group) to display the Insert Picture dialog box.
4. Navigate to the location of the picture to insert and then double-click the file to insert the picture in the worksheet.
5. Resize the picture as necessary.
6. To format the picture, display the Picture Tools Format tab.
7. Click the Picture Styles More button (Picture Tools Format tab | Picture Styles group) to display the Picture Styles gallery.
8. Click the desired picture style to apply the style to the image.

Break Point: If you wish to take a break, this is a good place to do so. You can exit Excel now. To resume at a later time, run Excel, open the file called HSS Sales Analysis, and continue following the steps from this location forward.

Using Screenshots on a Worksheet

Excel allows you to take a screenshot of any open window and add it to a workbook. Using the screenshot feature, you can capture whole windows or only part of a window. For example, if your company has a webpage, you can take a screenshot of the page and insert it into a workbook before presenting the workbook at a meeting. In addition, you can capture a screen clipping to include in your Excel workbook. A **screen clipping** is a portion of the screen, usually of one object or a section of a window. You first will create a new worksheet in the workbook to hold the screenshot and then insert a screenshot of a webpage.

To Create Another New Sheet

In preparation for inserting the screenshot, the following steps create another new sheet.

1 Click the New sheet button to create a fourth sheet in the workbook.

2 Rename the worksheet **Screenshot** to provide a descriptive name for the worksheet.

3 Change the color of the tab to orange and hide the gridlines on the worksheet.

4 If necessary, click cell A1 to make it the active cell (Figure 7–86).

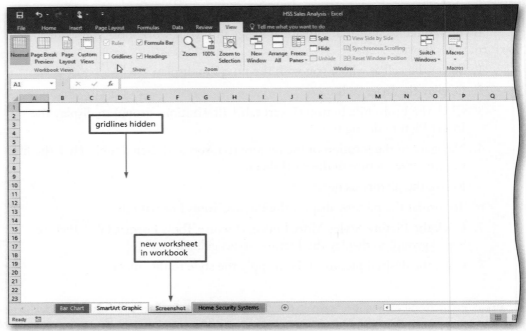

Figure 7–86

To Insert a Screenshot on a Worksheet

1 CREATE TEMPLATE | 2 USE TEMPLATE | 3 IMPORT DATA | 4 USE QUICK ANALYSIS
5 FIND & REPLACE | 6 INSERT BAR CHART | 7 CREATE SMARTART | **8 ADD SCREENSHOT**

The staff at HSS often shares helpful home security websites with customers. The following steps add a screenshot to a worksheet. *Why? In anticipation of an upcoming meeting where the sales analysis will be reviewed, the CEO requests a screenshot of a popular website that answers typical home security questions.*

1

- Run Internet Explorer or a similar browser.

- Type **http://safewise.com/home-security-faq** in the address bar and then press the ENTER key to display the webpage (Figure 7–87).

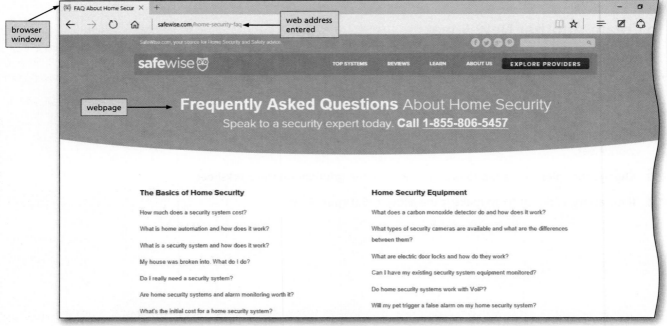

Figure 7–87

- Click the Excel app button on the taskbar to return to Excel.

- Display the Insert tab.

- Click the 'Take a Screenshot' button (Insert tab | Illustrations group) to display the Take a Screenshot menu (Figure 7–88).

Q&A My browser window is not displayed in the gallery. Did I do something wrong?
If Excel cannot link to your browser, you may have to insert a screen clipping instead of a screenshot. To do so, click Screen Clipping (Take a Screenshot gallery), navigate to the desired window, and then draw a rectangle over the portion of the screen you want to insert into the Excel workbook. Note that this process inserts a picture rather than a hyperlinked screenshot and displays the Picture Tools Format tab.

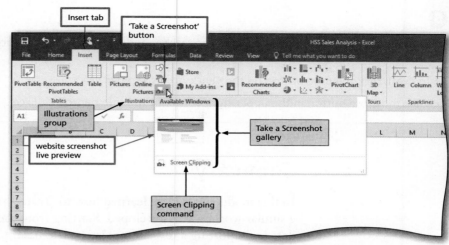

Figure 7–88

- Click the 'Frequently Asked Questions About Home Security' live preview to start the process of inserting a screenshot (Figure 7–89).

Q&A Should I include the hyperlink?
If you plan to present your workbook to an audience and wish to view the updated website in a browser, you should insert the screenshot with a hyperlink. Inserting the hyperlink also gives you access to the link at a later time, without retyping it.

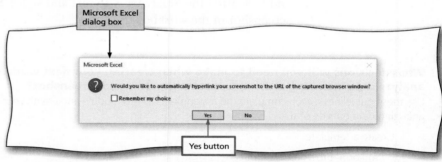

Figure 7–89

- Click the Yes button (Microsoft Excel dialog box) to insert the screenshot with a hyperlink (Figure 7–90).

🔎 **Experiment**

- Scroll to view the entire screenshot. Note that the screenshot displays only the part of the webpage displayed in the browser.

Q&A How do you use the hyperlink?
You can right-click the screenshot and then click Open Hyperlink on the shortcut menu. Clicking Open Hyperlink opens a browser and displays the website.

Figure 7–90

5

- Right-click the browser app button on the taskbar and then click Close window on the shortcut menu to exit the browser.

- In Excel, click the Save button on the Quick Access Toolbar.

- Click the Close button in the upper-right corner of the title bar to exit Excel.

Summary

In this module, you have learned how to create a template that can be used every time a similar workbook is developed. Starting from the template, you gathered external data by importing a text file, an Access database, a Word document, and a website. You formatted the data and transposed it when necessary. You replicated the formulas and functions, and then used Quick Analysis to display specific formatting. Then, you created a bar chart, formatting the bars with a style, color, and bevel. After reversing the order of the categories, you edited the number format of the horizontal labels. While creating a SmartArt graphic, you inserted pictures relevant to the spreadsheet and formatted the SmartArt with text and styles. Finally, you inserted a hyperlinked screenshot in the workbook.

CONSIDER THIS: PLAN AHEAD

What decisions will you need to make when creating your next workbook based on a template to analyze data including a chart, SmartArt graphic, and screenshot?
Use these guidelines as you complete the assignments in this module and create your own worksheets for evaluating and analyzing data outside of this class.

1. Create a template.

    a) Format rows and columns.

    b) Enter titles and headings.

    c) Enter sample or dummy data.

    d) Enter formulas and functions.

    e) Save as a template file type.

2. Create a new workbook based on the template and import data.

    a) Open a template file and save it as a workbook file.

    b) Import data corresponding to type of data.

    c) Format imported data.

    d) Paste special and transpose data when necessary.

3. Format using the Quick Analysis gallery.

    a) Apply formatting or totals using the Quick Analysis gallery.

4. Create new sheets for each part of your analysis workbook.

5. Use SmartArt graphics to illustrate data.

    a) Gather appropriate pictures.

    b) Use text effects to enhance graphic.

6. Use screenshots to aid in presenting analysis.

    a) Hyperlink screenshots from the web, if necessary.

Apply Your Knowledge

Reinforce the skills and apply the concepts you learned in this module.

Using a Template to Create a Consolidated Workbook

Note: To complete these steps, you will be required to use the Data Files. Please contact your instructor for information about accessing the Data Files.

Instructions: You will create the 2016-2017 consolidated workbook and SmartArt graphic for Prototype Labs shown in Figure 7–91.

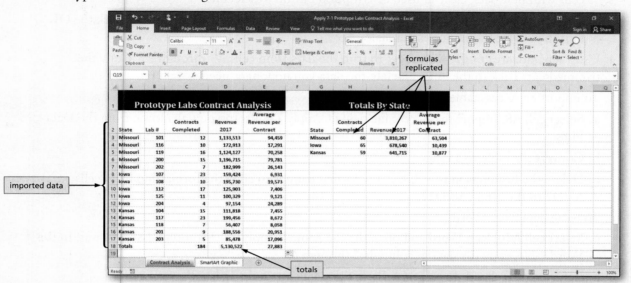

a) Imported Data in Worksheet

b) SmartArt Graphic

Figure 7–91

Perform the following tasks:

1. Open a File Explorer window and double-click the file named Apply 7-1 Prototype Labs Template from the Data Files. Save the template as a workbook using the file name, Apply 7-1 Prototype Labs Contract Analysis.

2. Add a second sheet to the workbook, named SmartArt Graphic. Color the tab white.

Continued >

Apply Your Knowledge *continued*

3. To import a text file:

a. With the Contract Analysis worksheet active, select cell A3. Import the text file named, Apply 7-1 Prototype Labs Missouri from the Data Files.

b. In the wizard dialog boxes, choose the Delimited format with commas.

c. When Excel displays the Import Data dialog box, click the Properties button to display the External Data Range Properties dialog box. Remove the check mark in the 'Adjust column width' check box (External Data Range Properties dialog box). Click the 'Overwrite existing cells with new data, clear unused cells' option button to select it.

d. Click the OK button to close the External Data Range Properties dialog box. Click the OK button to close the Import Data dialog box.

4. Use a separate area of the worksheet to trim the data from cells A3 through A7. Copy the trimmed data back to the range. Delete the data you no longer need.

5. To import an Access table:

a. Select cell A8. Import the Access file named, Apply 7-1 Prototype Labs Iowa, from the Data Files.

b. Convert the table to a range.

c. Delete the headings in row 8. Use the format painter to copy the formatting from cells A7:D7 to the range A8:D12.

6. To paste data from Word:

a. Select cell A20. Run Word and open the file named, Apply 7-1 Prototype Labs Kansas. In the Word table, copy the data in columns 2 through 6.

b. Return to Excel and then use the Paste Special command to paste the data as text.

c. Copy the Excel range, A20:E22. Click cell A13 and transpose the data while pasting it.

d. Delete the original imported data in cells A20:E22.

e. Cut the data in cells B13:C17 and paste it to cell C13 to move it one column to the right.

f. Select cells A13:A17. Click the 'Text to Columns' button (Data tab | Data Tools group). In the wizard dialog boxes, choose the Delimited format with commas.

g. Use the format painter to copy the formatting from cells A12:D12 to the range A13:D17.

7. Use the fill handle to replicate cells H3:J3 to H4:J5.

8. Enter the word, **Totals**, in cell A18. Use the Quick Analysis gallery to sum the range C3:D17.

9. Replicate the formula in cell E3 down through cell E18.

10. Insert your name and course number in cell A21.

11. Go to the SmartArt Graphic sheet. Remove the gridlines. Insert the Continuous Picture list SmartArt graphic. Resize the SmartArt graphic as necessary.

12. One at a time, replace the word, Text, with the words, Missouri, Iowa, and Kansas, respectively.

13. Change the color scheme to 'Colorful - Accent Colors' in the Change Colors gallery.

14. One at a time, click the picture icon in each part of the graphic, and search the web for a graphic related to the state. Make sure you review the license to ensure you can comply with any copyright restrictions.

15. Save the file again.

16. Submit the publication in the format specified by your instructor.

17. ✳ In what format do you think most companies submit data? Why? If the data changes, how do the consolidated workbooks with imported data adjust? Do all the formats lend themselves to recalculating? Why or why not?

Extend Your Knowledge

Extend the skills you learned in this module and experiment with new skills. You may need to use Help to complete the assignment.

Inserting a SmartArt Organization Chart and Image on a Worksheet

Note: To complete these steps, you will be required to use the Data Files. Please contact your instructor for information about accessing the Data Files.

Instructions: Run Excel. Open the workbook Extend 7-1 Highsmith Investment from the Data Files and then save the workbook as Extend 7-1 Highsmith Investment Complete. You will add a SmartArt graphic and an image to the workbook and then format both graphics as shown in Figure 7–92.

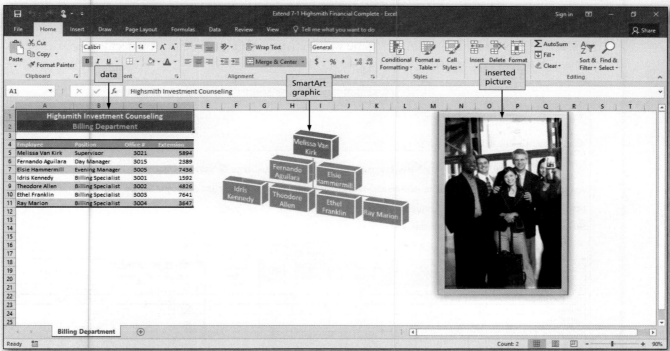

Figure 7–92

Perform the following tasks:

1. Insert a SmartArt graphic using the Hierarchy type and the Organization Chart layout.

2. Select the shape in the second row of the chart and then add a shape.

3. Add a shape in the third row. If necessary, promote the shape to be level with the other three.

4. Display the Text Pane and drag its border to the right side of the chart. Use cutting and pasting techniques to insert the names from column A into the graphic, as shown in Figure 7–92. Insert your name in place of the Evening Manager.

5. Change the color scheme of the hierarchy chart to Gradient Loop - Accent 2 in the Change Colors gallery.

6. Use the SmartArt Styles gallery to change the style to Brick Scene.

7. Move the SmartArt Graphic to the right of the data.

8. Use Help to read about formatting pictures. Insert an online picture related to the search term, people, similar to the one shown in Figure 7–92. Format the picture using a Picture style (Picture Tools Format tab | Picture Styles group) with a wide gray border.

Continued >

Extend Your Knowledge *continued*

9. Move and resize the picture so that it fits beside the SmartArt graphic.

10. Add your name and course number to the worksheet.

11. Save the workbook. Submit the assignment as requested by your instructor.

12. ✸ When do you think a company would use a spreadsheet like this? What formatting and changes might make it even more useful?

Expand Your World

Create a solution that uses cloud and web technologies by learning and investigating on your own from general guidance.

Using Web Data

Problem: You would like to import some web statistics about your state. You decide to retrieve U.S. census data from the web (Figure 7–93).

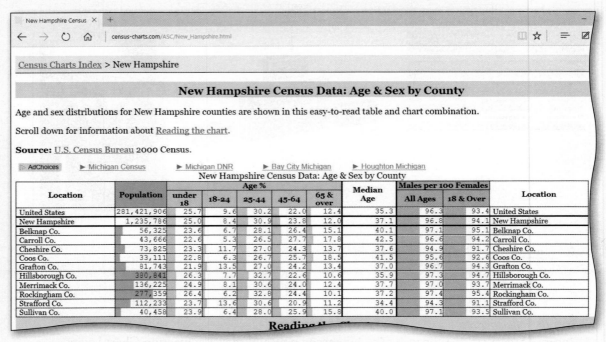

Figure 7–93

Instructions:

1. Run a browser and navigate to http://www.census-charts.com/.

2. In the Data by State and County area, click 'Age and Sex' and then click your state.

3. When the website presents the data, copy the URL address.

4. Run Excel and open a blank workbook.

5. Hide the grid lines and rename the sheet Screenshot. Use the 'Take a Screenshot' button (Insert tab | Illustrations group) to insert a screenshot of your data. Close the browser.

6. Add a new sheet to the workbook, named Web Data.

7. Select cell B2. Click the 'Get Data From Web' button (Data tab | Get External Data group). Paste the URL into the address text box in the New Web Query dialog box. Click the Go button (New Web Query dialog box).

8. When the webpage appears, double-click its title bar to maximize the window. Click the table selection arrows to select the table with the numeric data. Click the Import button (New Web Query dialog box).

9. When Excel displays the Import Data dialog box, click the OK button.

10. When Excel displays the data, format the title and column headings, as well as the column widths. Save the file and submit it in the format specified by your instructor.

11. ✸ What kinds of analysis could you perform in Excel on the data you downloaded from the census website? What would make the data more meaningful and useful? Why?

In the Labs

Design, create, modify, and/or use a workbook following the guidelines, concepts, and skills presented in this module. Labs 1 and 2, which increase in difficulty, require you to create solutions based on what you learned in the module; Lab 3 requires you to apply your creative thinking and problem-solving skills to design and implement a solution.

Lab 1: Using the Quick Analysis Gallery and Formatting a Bar Chart

Note: To complete these steps, you will be required to use the Data Files. Please contact your instructor for information about accessing the Data Files.

Problem: Custom Fragrances has prepared an annual sales analysis but would like to show the data in a more visual way, along with grand totals (Figure 7–94).

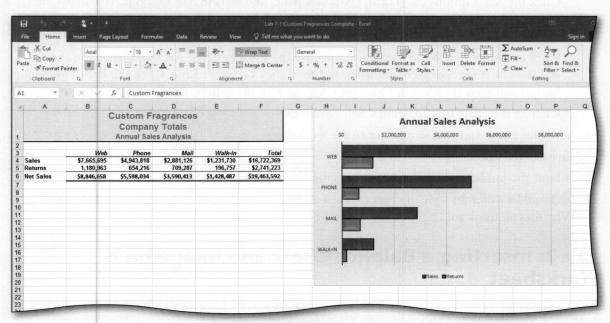

Figure 7–94

Instructions Part 1: Perform the following tasks:

1. Open the workbook, Lab 7–1 Custom Fragrances from the Data Files. Save the file with file name Lab 7–1 Custom Fragrances Complete.

2. In cell A6, type **Net Sales** to enter a row heading.

Continued >

3. Select the range B4:E5. Click the Quick Analysis button, click Totals, and then click Sum. Use a Cell Style to create a double-underline below the totals.

4. In cell F3, type `Total` to enter a column heading. Copy the formatting from cell E3 to F3.

5. Select the range B4:E6. Click the Quick Analysis button, click Totals, and then click the second Sum button to create row totals. Copy other formatting as necessary.

6. Drag through the range A3:E5. Use the Quick Analysis gallery to insert a Clustered Bar Chart. Move the Chart beside the data.

7. Format the chart as follows:

   a. With the chart selected, click the Change Colors button (Chart Tools Design tab | Chart Styles group), and then click Color 4 in the gallery.

   b. Change the chart style to Style 3 (Chart Tools Design tab | Chart Styles group).

   c. Click any of the data labels (the numbers on the bars themselves), and press the DELETE key to delete the data labels.

   d. Right-click the y-axes or vertical labels. Click Format Axis on the shortcut menu. In the Axis position area, reverse the order of the categories.

   e. With the task pane still displayed, click any of the data bars that represent Sales to display the Format Data Series task pane. On the Fill & Line tab, add a black, solid line border to the series. On the Effects tab, click the 3-D format area, and then click the Top bevel button. In the gallery, click the Soft Round style.

   f. Repeat step 7e for the data bars representing the Returns.

   g. Click the x-axis or horizontal labels at the top of the chart to display the Format Axis task pane. Click the Axis Options tab (Format Axis task pane) and expand Axis Options. To narrow the range in the chart area and thus make the bars seem larger, in the Bounds area, type `8000000` in the Maximum text box. In the Units area, type `2000000` in the Major text box.

   h. Click an empty portion of the chart to display the Format Chart Area task pane. On the Fill & Line tab, if necessary, click Border, and then click Gradient Line. Click the Preset gradients button and then click 'Light Gradient - Accent 3' in the gallery. Close the task pane.

   i. Change the chart title to Annual Sales Analysis.

8. Add your name and course number to the worksheet.

9. Save the file again.

10. Submit the publication in the format specified by your instructor.

11. ❋ Would a different style of chart create a more effective visual representation of the data? Why do you think so?

Lab 2: Inserting a Balance Chart and Image on a Worksheet

Note: To complete these steps, you will be required to use the Data Files. Please contact your instructor for information about accessing the Data Files.

Problem: The Joy of Art, a local company, is considering having a mural painted on the side of its building. You have been asked to create a worksheet with a high-level overview of the pros and cons regarding the mural. The finished worksheet should look like Figure 7–95.

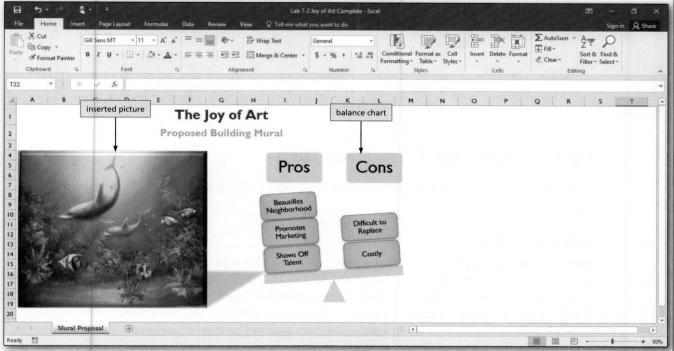

Figure 7–95

Perform the following tasks:

1. Run Excel. Open the workbook Lab 7–2 Joy of Art from the Data Files. Save it as Lab 7–2 Joy of Art Complete.

2. Insert the Lab 7–2 Mural image file from the Data Files in the worksheet.

3. Move and resize the image so that its upper-left corner is aligned with the upper-left corner of cell A4 and the lower-right corner of the image is aligned with the lower-right corner of cell F19.

4. Format the image as follows:

   a. Click the Picture Effects button (Picture Tools Format tab | Picture Styles group), click Shadow, and then click 'Perspective Diagonal Upper Right'.

   b. Click the Picture Effects button (Picture Tools Format tab | Picture Styles group), click Bevel, and then click Art Deco.

5. Insert a SmartArt graphic using the Relationship type and the Balance layout.

6. Move and resize the SmartArt graphic so that its upper-left corner is aligned with the upper-left corner of H4 and the lower-right corner of the graphic is aligned with the lower-right corner of cell M19.

7. Use the Text Pane to enter three Pros: Shows Off Talent, Promotes Marketing, and Beautifies Neighborhood; and two Cons: Costly and Difficult to Replace. Make certain that the Pros column appears on the left of the chart. Be sure to delete the unused shape on the right side of the balance chart. The upper-left shape in the chart should read Pros, and the upper-right shape in the chart should read Cons. Note that the direction of the tilt of the balance changes when more pros than cons are entered in the chart.

8. Format the Balance SmartArt as follows:

   a. Change the color scheme to 'Colored Fill - Accent 3' in the Change Colors gallery.

   b. Apply the Subtle Effect SmartArt style.

Continued >

In the Labs *continued*

9. Add your name to cell N1.

10. Save the workbook. Submit the assignment as requested by your instructor.

11. ✳ In what other kinds of situations might you use a balance chart, other than for pros and cons? Would a table listing the pros and cons be as effective? Why or why not?

Lab 3: **Consider This: Your Turn**

Apply your creative thinking and problem-solving skills to design and implement a solution.

Create a Cover Sheet

Part 1:   You are competing to design a cover sheet for an academic department at your school to include in their workbooks when they send out statistics. Run a browser and view the webpage for your chosen department at your school. Create a workbook and turn off the viewing of gridlines for the first sheet. Insert a screenshot of the department webpage and size it appropriately. Insert a SmartArt list to highlight three or four of the best qualities of your department. Use text effects to enhance the text. Change the colors to match more closely your school colors. Choose an appropriate SmartArt style. Below the SmartArt graphic, add a screen clipping of the school's logo. Finally, next to the logo add your name and format it so that it appears as a title. Below your name, in a smaller font, insert the name of your department.

Part 2:   ✳ How did you decide on which SmartArt layout and style to use?

4 | Creating Reports and Forms

Objectives

You will have mastered the material in this module when you can:

- Create reports and forms using wizards
- Modify reports and forms in Layout view
- Group and sort data in a report
- Add totals and subtotals to a report
- Conditionally format controls
- Resize columns
- Filter records in reports and forms

- Print reports and forms
- Apply themes
- Add a field to a report or form
- Add a date
- Change the format of a control
- Move controls
- Create and print mailing labels

Introduction

One of the advantages to maintaining data in a database is the ability to present the data in attractive reports and forms that highlight certain information. Reports present data in an organized format that is usually printed. The data can come from one or more tables. On the other hand, you usually view forms on the screen, although you can print them. In addition to viewing data, you can also use forms to update data. That is, you can use forms to add records, delete records, or change records. Like reports, the data in the form can come from one or more tables. This module shows how to create reports and forms by creating two reports and a form. There are several ways to create both reports and forms. One approach is to use the Report or Form Wizard. You can also use either Layout view or Design view to create or modify a report or form. In this module, you will use Layout view for this purpose. In later modules, you will learn how to use Design view. You will also use the Label Wizard to produce mailing labels.

Project — Reports and Forms

PrattLast Associates is now able to better keep track of its account information and to target account needs by using the database of accounts and managers. PrattLast hopes to improve their decision-making capability further by using two custom reports that meet their specific needs. Figure 4–1 shows the Account Financial report, which is a modified version of an existing report. The report features

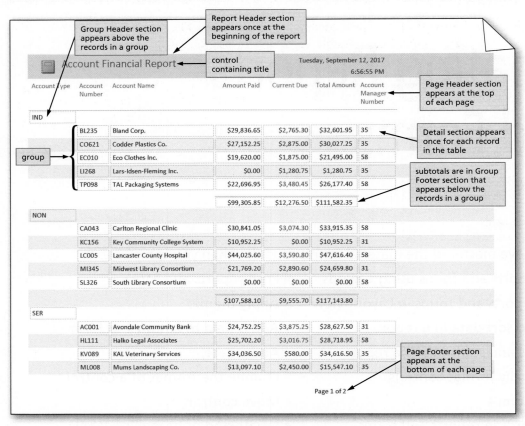

Figure 4–1a

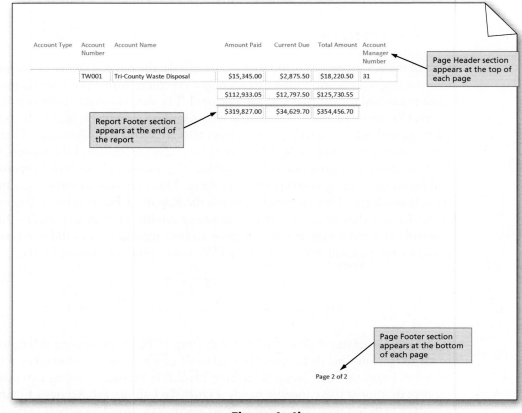

Figure 4–1b

Microsoft Access 2016

File   Home   Create   External Data   Database Tools   Tell me what you want to do...

PrattLast Associates : Database- C:\Users\Owner\Documents\CIS

grouping. The report shown in Figure 4–1 groups records by account types. There are three separate groups, one each for the three possible account types: IND, NON, and SER. The appropriate type appears before each group. The totals of the Amount Paid, Current Due, and Total Amount fields for the accounts in the group (called a **subtotal**) appear after the group. At the end of the report are grand totals of the same fields.

Figure 4–2 shows the second report. This report encompasses data from both the Account Manager table and the Account table. Like the report in Figure 4–1, the data is grouped, although this time it is grouped by account manager number. Not only does the manager number appear before each group, but the first name and last name of the manager appear as well. Like the first report, this report contains subtotals.

BTW
Consider Your Audience
Always design reports and forms with your audience in mind. Make your reports and forms accessible to individuals who may have problems with colorblindness or reduced vision.

Accounts by Account Manager

AM #	First Name	Last Name	AC #	Account Name	Amount Paid	Current Due
31	Haydee	Rivera				
			AC001	Avondale Community Bank	$24,752.25	$3,875.25
			KC156	Key Community College System	$10,952.25	$0.00
			MI345	Midwest Library Consortium	$21,769.20	$2,890.60
			TW001	Tri-County Waste Disposal	$15,345.00	$2,875.50
Summary for 'Account Manager Number' = 31 (4 detail records)						
Sum					$72,818.70	$9,641.35
35	Mark	Simson				
			BL235	Bland Corp.	$29,836.65	$2,765.30
			CO621	Codder Plastics Co.	$27,152.25	$2,875.00
			KV089	KAL Veterinary Services	$34,036.50	$580.00
			LI268	Lars-Idsen-Fleming Inc.	$0.00	$1,280.75
			ML008	Mums Landscaping Co.	$13,097.10	$2,450.00
Summary for 'Account Manager Number' = 35 (5 detail records)						
Sum					$104,122.50	$9,951.05
58	Karen	Murowski				
			CA043	Carlton Regional Clinic	$30,841.05	$3,074.30
			EC010	Eco Clothes Inc.	$19,620.00	$1,875.00
			HL111	Halko Legal Associates	$25,702.20	$3,016.75
			LC005	Lancaster County Hospital	$44,025.60	$3,590.80
			SL326	South Library Consortium	$0.00	$0.00
			TP098	TAL Packaging Systems	$22,696.95	$3,480.45
Summary for 'Account Manager Number' = 58 (6 detail records)						
Sum					$142,885.80	$15,037.30
Grand Total					$319,827.00	$34,629.70

Tuesday, September 12, 2017   Page 1 of 1

Figure 4–2

PrattLast also wants to improve the process of updating data by using a custom form, as shown in Figure 4–3. The form has a title and a date. Unlike the form you can create by clicking the Form button, this form does not contain all the fields in the Account table. In addition, the fields are in a different order than in the table. For this form, PrattLast likes the appearance of including the fields in a stacked layout.

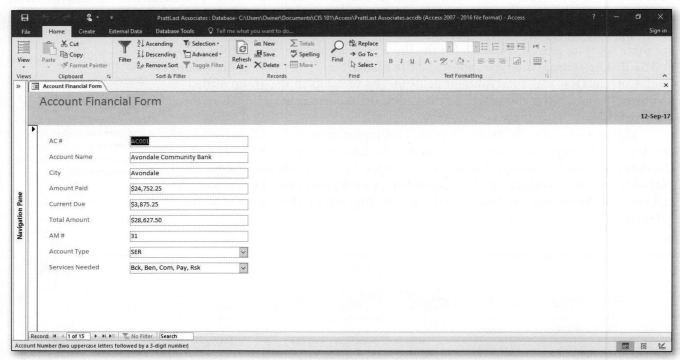

Figure 4–3

PrattLast also wants to be able to produce mailing labels for its accounts. These labels must align correctly with the particular labels PrattLast uses and must be sorted by postal code (Figure 4–4).

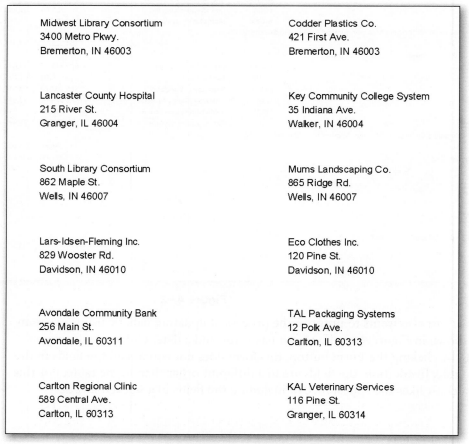

Figure 4–4

In this module, you will learn how to create the reports, forms, and labels shown in Figures 4–1 through 4–4. The following roadmap identifies general activities you will perform as you progress through this module:

1. GROUP, SORT, and TOTAL in a report.
2. CONDITIONALLY FORMAT CONTROLS in a report.
3. FILTER REPORT RECORDS.
4. Create a MULTIPLE-TABLE REPORT.
5. Create a form using the FORM WIZARD.
6. MODIFY CONTROLS in a control layout on a form.
7. FILTER FORM RECORDS.
8. Create MAILING LABELS.

Report Creation

When working with a report in Access, there are four different ways to view the report: Report view, Print Preview, Layout view, and Design view. Report view shows the report on the screen. Print Preview shows the report as it will appear when printed. Layout view is similar to Report view in that it shows the report on the screen, but it also allows you to make changes to the report. Using Layout view is usually the easiest way to make such changes. Design view also allows you to make changes, but it does not show you the actual report. It is most useful when the changes you need to make are complex. In this module, you will use Layout view to modify the report.

Report Sections

A report is divided into various sections to help clarify the presentation of data. A typical report consists of a Report Header section, Page Header section, Detail section, Page Footer section, and Report Footer section (see Figure 4–1). In Design view, which you will use in later modules, you can see the names for each section on the screen. Even though the names of the sections are not visible in Layout view, it is still useful to understand the purpose of the various sections.

The contents of the Report Header section appear once at the beginning of the report. In the Account Financial Report, the report title is in the Report Header section. The contents of the Report Footer section appear once at the end of the report. In the Account Financial Report, the Report Footer section contains the grand totals of Amount Paid, Current Due, and Total Amount. The contents of the Page Header section appear once at the top of each page and typically contain the column headers. The contents of the Page Footer section appear once at the bottom of each page; Page Footer sections often contain a date and a page number. The contents of the Detail section appear once for each record in the table; for example, once for Bland Corp., once for Codder Plastics Co., and so on. In this report, the detail records contain the account number, account name, amount paid, current due, total amount, and account manager number.

When the data in a report is grouped, there are two additional sections. The contents of the Group Header section are printed above the records in a particular group, and the contents of the Group Footer section are printed below the group. In the Account Financial Report, the Group Header section contains the Account Type, and the Group Footer section contains the subtotals of Amount Paid, Current Due, and Total Amount.

BTW

The Ribbon and Screen Resolution
Access may change how the groups and buttons within the groups appear on the ribbon, depending on the computer's screen resolution. Thus, your ribbon may look different from the ones in this book if you are using a screen resolution other than 1366 x 768.

BTW

Touch Screen Differences
The Office and Windows interfaces may vary if you are using a touch screen. For this reason, you might notice that the function or appearance of your touch screen differs slightly from this module's presentation.

BTW

Enabling the Content
For each of the databases you use in this module, you will need to enable the content.

To Group and Sort in a Report

In Layout view of the report, you can specify both grouping and sorting by using the Group & Sort button on the Design tab. The following steps open the Account Financial Report in Layout view and then specify both grouping and sorting in the report. *Why? PrattLast has determined that the records in the report should be grouped by account type. That is, all the accounts of a given type should appear together immediately after the type. Within the accounts in a given type, accounts are to be ordered by account number.*

1

- Run Access and open the database named PrattLast Associates from your hard disk, OneDrive, or other storage location. If you do not have the PrattLast Associates database, see your instructor.
- Right-click the Account Financial Report in the Navigation Pane to produce a shortcut menu.
- Click Layout View on the shortcut menu to open the report in Layout view.
- Close the Navigation Pane.
- If a field list appears, close the field list by clicking the 'Add Existing Fields' button (Report Layout Tools Design tab | Tools group).
- Click the Group & Sort button (Report Layout Tools Design tab | Grouping & Totals group) to display the Group, Sort, and Total pane (Figure 4–5).

Q&A | My report is in a different order. Do I need to change it?

No. You will change the order of the records in the following steps.

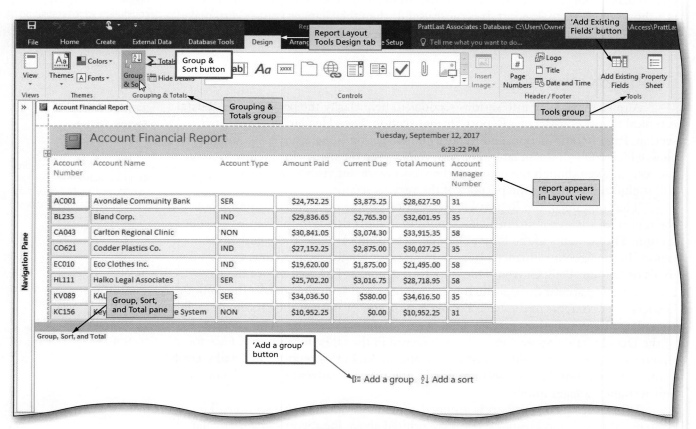

Figure 4–5

2

- Click the 'Add a group' button to add a group (Figure 4–6).

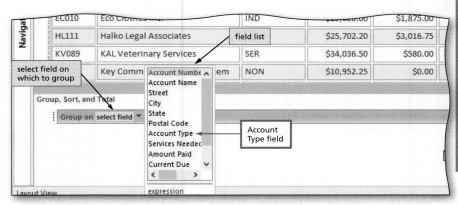

Figure 4–6

3

- Click the Account Type field in the field list to select a field for grouping and group the records on the selected field (Figure 4–7).

Q&A

Does the field on which I group have to be the first field?
No. If you select a field other than the first field, Access will move the field you select into the first position.

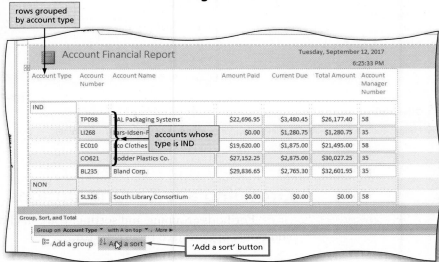

Figure 4–7

4

- Click the 'Add a sort' button to add a sort (Figure 4–8).

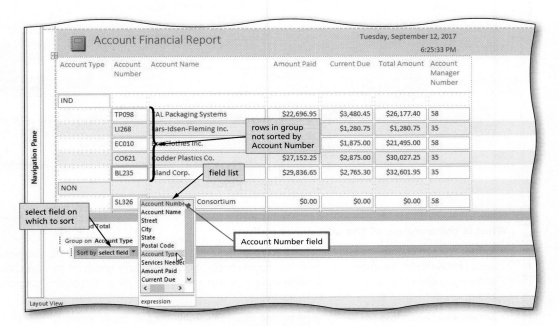

Figure 4–8

5

- Click the Account Number field in the field list to specify the field on which the records in each group will be sorted (Figure 4–9).

Q&A

I thought the report would be sorted by Account Type, because I chose to group on that field. What is the effect of choosing to sort by Account Number?

This sort takes place within groups. You are specifying that within the list of accounts of the same type, the accounts will be ordered by account number.

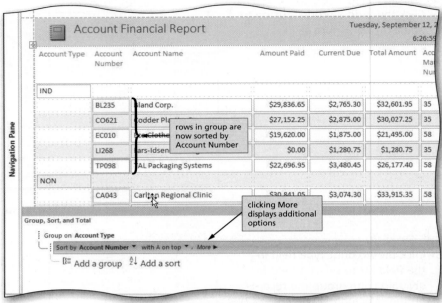

Figure 4–9

Other Ways

1. Right-click column header for field on which to group, click Group On (field name)

Grouping and Sorting Options

For both grouping and sorting, you can click the More button to specify additional options (see Figure 4–10).

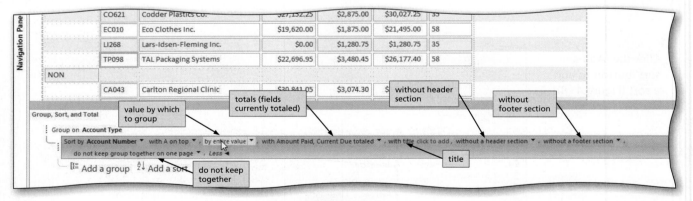

Figure 4–10

CONSIDER THIS

What is the purpose of the additional options?

- **Value.** You can choose the number of characters of the value on which to group. Typically, you would group by the entire value, for example, the entire city name. You could choose, however, to only group on the first character, in which case all accounts in cities that begin with the same letter would be considered a group. You could also group by the first two characters or by a custom number of characters.

- **Totals.** You can choose the values to be totaled. You can specify whether the totals are to appear in the group header or in the group footer and whether to include a grand total. You can also choose whether to show group totals as a percentage of the grand total.

- **Title.** You can customize the group title.

- **Header section.** You can include or omit a header section for the group.

- **Footer section.** You can include or omit a footer section for the group.

- **Keep together.** You can indicate whether Access should attempt to keep portions of a group together on the same page. The default setting does not keep portions of a group together, but you can specify that Access should keep a whole group together on one page, when possible. If the group will not fit on the remainder of the page, Access will move the group header and the records in a group to the next page. Finally, you can choose to have Access keep the header and the first record together on one page. If the header would fit at the bottom of a page, but there would not be room for the first record, Access will move the header to the next page.

Report Controls

The various objects on a report are called **controls**. You can manipulate these controls to modify their location and appearance. The report title, column headers, contents of various fields, subtotals, and so on are all contained in controls. When working in Layout view, as you will do in this module, Access handles details concerning placement, sizing, and format of these controls for you automatically. When working in Design view, you will see and manipulate the controls. Even when working in Layout view, however, it is useful to understand the concepts of controls.

The report shown in Figure 4–1 has a control containing the title, Account Financial Report. The report also includes controls containing each column header (Account Type, Account Number, Account Name, Amount Paid, Current Due, Total Amount, and Account Manager Number). A control in the Group Header section displays the account type.

There are three controls in the Group Footer section: One control displays the subtotal of Amount Paid, a second displays the subtotal of Current Due, and a third displays the subtotal of Total Amount. The Detail section has controls containing the account number, account name, amount paid, current due, total amount, and account manager number.

Access has three types of controls: bound controls, unbound controls, and calculated controls. **Bound controls** are used to display data that comes from the database, such as the account number and name. **Unbound controls** are not associated with data from the database and are used to display such things as the report's title. Finally, **calculated controls** are used to display data that is calculated from other data, such as a total.

BTW
Grouping
You should allow sufficient white space between groups. If you feel the amount is insufficient, you can add more space by enlarging the group header or group footer.

BTW
Report Design Considerations
The purpose of any report is to present specific information. Make sure that the meaning of the row and column headings is clear. You can use different fonts and sizes by changing the appropriate properties, but do not overuse them. Finally, be consistent when creating reports. Once you decide on a general report style or theme, stick with it throughout your database.

To Add Totals and Subtotals

1 GROUP, SORT, & TOTAL | 2 CONDITIONALLY FORMAT CONTROLS | 3 FILTER REPORT RECORDS | 4 MULTIPLE-TABLE REPORT
5 FORM WIZARD | 6 MODIFY CONTROLS | 7 FILTER FORM RECORDS | 8 MAILING LABELS

To add totals or other statistics, use the Totals button on the Design tab. You then select from a menu of aggregate functions, which are functions that perform some mathematical function against a group of records. The available aggregate functions, or calculations, are Sum (total), Average, Count Records, Count Values, Max (largest value), Min (smallest value), Standard Deviation, and Variance. Because the report is grouped, each group will have a **subtotal**, that is, a total for just the records in the group. At the end of the report, there will be a **grand total**, that is, a total for all records.

The following steps specify totals for three of the fields. *Why?* *Along with determining to group data in this report, PrattLast has also determined that subtotals and grand totals of the Amount Paid, Current Due, and Total Amount fields should be included.* Even though totals were previously specified for the Amount Paid and Current Due fields, you need to do so again because of the grouping.

1

- Click the Amount Paid column header to select the field.

Does it have to be the column header? No, you could click the Amount Paid field on any record.

- Click the Totals button (Report Layout Tools Design tab | Grouping & Totals group) to display the list of available calculations (Figure 4–11).

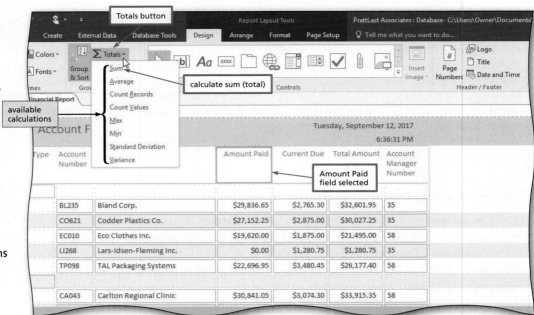

Figure 4–11

2

- Click Sum to calculate the sum of the Amount Paid values.

- If the subtotal does not appear completely, click the subtotal and then drag the lower boundary of the control for the subtotal to the approximate position shown in Figure 4–12.

I moved the control rather than resizing it. What did I do wrong? You dragged the control rather than dragging its lower boundary. Click the Undo button on the Quick Access Toolbar to undo your change and then drag again, making sure you are pointing to the lower boundary.

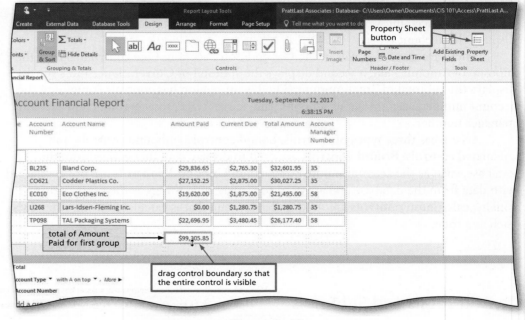

Figure 4–12

3

- Using the same technique as in Steps 1 and 2, add subtotals for the Current Due and Total Amount fields.

- Click the subtotal of the Total Amount field to select it.

- Click the Property Sheet button (Report Layout Tools Design tab | Tools group) to display the property sheet for the subtotal control.

- Click the Format box to produce an arrow, and then click the Format arrow.

- Click Currency to apply the Currency style to the subtotal of the total amount.

- Click the Property Sheet button (Report Layout Tools Design tab | Tools group) to close the property sheet.

- Scroll to the bottom of the report and use the same technique to change the format for the grand total of Total Amount to Currency.

- If necessary, drag the lower boundaries of the controls for the grand totals so that the numbers appear completely (Figure 4–13).

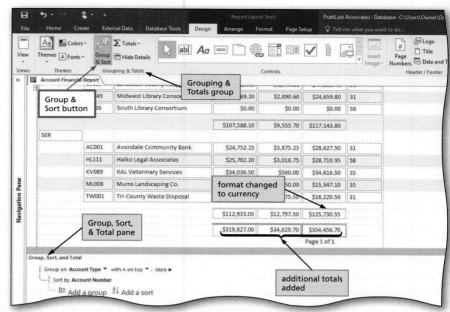

Figure 4–13

Other Ways

1. Right-click column header for field on which to total, click Total (field name)

To Remove the Group, Sort, and Total Pane

1 GROUP, SORT, & TOTAL | 2 CONDITIONALLY FORMAT CONTROLS | 3 FILTER REPORT RECORDS | 4 MULTIPLE-TABLE REPORT
5 FORM WIZARD | 6 MODIFY CONTROLS | 7 FILTER FORM RECORDS | 8 MAILING LABELS

The following step removes the Group, Sort, and Total pane from the screen. *Why? Because you have specified the required grouping and sorting for the report, you no longer need to use the Group, Sort, and Total pane.*

1

- Click the Group & Sort button (Report Layout Tools Design tab | Grouping & Totals group) to remove the Group, Sort, and Total pane (Figure 4–14).

Q&A
Do I need to remove the Group, Sort, and Total pane?
No. Doing so provides more room on the screen for the report, however. You can easily display the pane whenever you need it by clicking the Group & Sort button again.

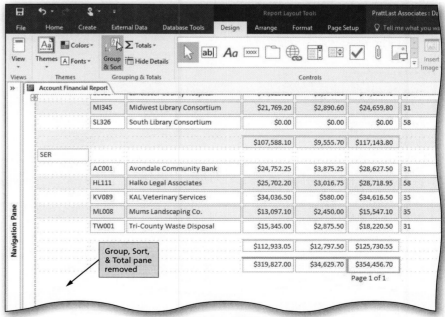

Figure 4–14

Other Ways

1. Click 'Close Grouping Dialog Box' button

How do you determine the organization of the report or form?
Determine various details concerning how the data in your report or form is to be organized.

Determine sort order. Is there a special order in which the records should appear?

Determine grouping. Should the records be grouped in some fashion? If so, what should appear before the records in a group? If, for example, accounts are grouped by city, the name of the city should probably appear before the group. What should appear after the group? For example, does the report include some fields for which subtotals should be calculated? If so, the subtotals would come after the group. Determine whether you need multiple levels of grouping.

To Conditionally Format Controls

1 GROUP, SORT, & TOTAL | **2 CONDITIONALLY FORMAT CONTROLS** | 3 FILTER REPORT RECORDS | 4 MULTIPLE-TABLE REPORT
5 FORM WIZARD | 6 MODIFY CONTROLS | 7 FILTER FORM RECORDS | 8 MAILING LABELS

Conditional formatting is special formatting that is applied to values that satisfy some criterion. PrattLast management has decided to apply conditional formatting to the Current Due field. *Why? They would like to emphasize values in the Current Due field that are greater than or equal to $3,000 by changing the font color to red.* The following steps conditionally format the Current Due field by specifying a **rule** that states that if the values in the field are greater than or equal to $3,000, such values will be formatted in red.

1

- Scroll to the top of the report.
- Click Format on the ribbon to display the Report Layout Tools Format tab.
- Click the Current Due field on the first record to select the field (Figure 4–15).

Q&A Does it have to be the first record?
No. You could click the field on any record.

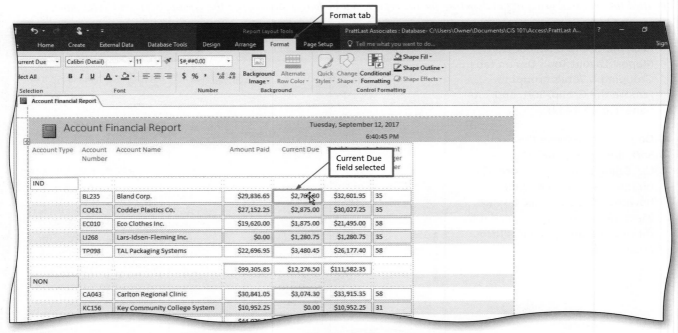

Figure 4–15

2

- Click the Conditional Formatting button (Report Layout Tools Format tab | Control Formatting group) to display the Conditional Formatting Rules Manager dialog box (Figure 4–16).

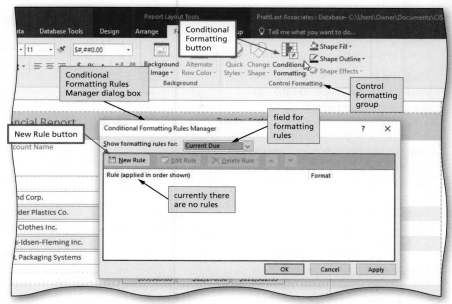

Figure 4–16

3

- Click the New Rule button (Conditional Formatting Rules Manager dialog box) to display the New Formatting Rule dialog box (Figure 4–17).

Q&A I see that there are two boxes to enter numbers. I only have one number to enter, 3000. Am I on the right screen?
Yes. Next, you will change the comparison operator from 'between' to 'greater than or equal to.' Once you have done so, Access will only display one box for entering a number.

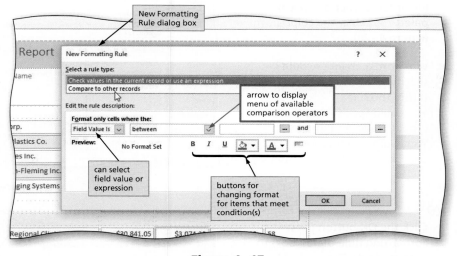

Figure 4–17

4

- Click the arrow to display the list of available comparison operators (New Formatting Rule dialog box) (Figure 4–18).

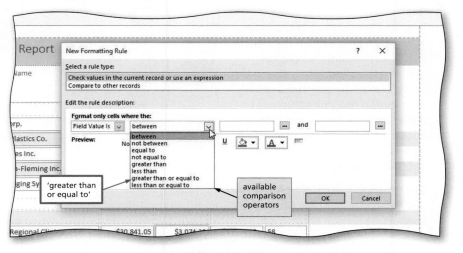

Figure 4–18

5

- Click 'greater than or equal to' to select the comparison operator.

- Click the box for the comparison value, and then type 3000 as the comparison value.

Q&A What is the effect of selecting this comparison operator and entering this number?
Values in the field that are greater than or equal to 3000 satisfy this rule. Any formatting that you now specify will apply to those values and no others.

- Click the Font Color arrow (New Formatting Rule dialog box) to display a color palette (Figure 4–19).

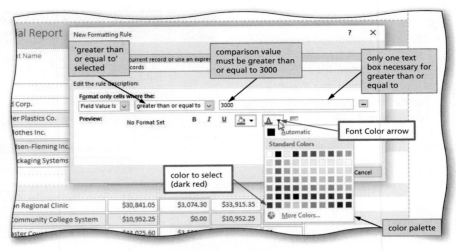

Figure 4–19

6

- Click the dark red color in the lower-left corner of the color palette to select the color (Figure 4–20).

Q&A What other changes could I specify for those values that satisfy the rule?
You could specify that the value is bold, italic, and/or underlined. You could also specify a background color.

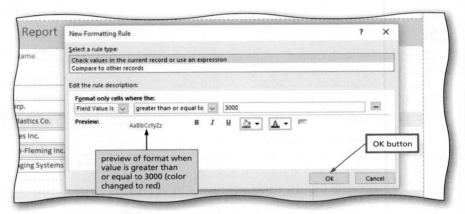

Figure 4–20

7

- Click the OK button (New Formatting Rule dialog box) to enter the rule (Figure 4–21).

Q&A What if I have more than one rule?
The rules are applied in the order in which they appear in the dialog box. If a value satisfies the first rule, the specified formatting will apply, and no further rules will be tested. If not, the value will be tested against the second rule. If it satisfies the rule, the formatting for the second rule would apply. If not, the value would be tested against the third rule, and so on.

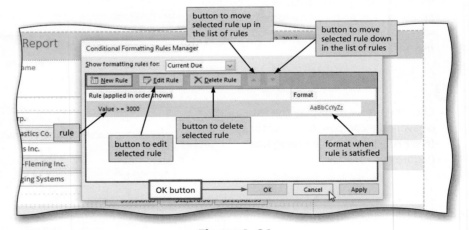

Figure 4–21

Can I change this conditional formatting later?
Yes. Select the field for which you had applied conditional formatting on any record, click the Conditional Formatting button (Report Layout Tools Format tab | Control Formatting group), click the rule you want to change, click the Edit Rule button, and then make the necessary changes. You can also delete the selected rule by clicking the Delete Rule button, or move the selected rule by clicking the Move Up or Move Down buttons.

8

- Click the OK button (Conditional Formatting Rules Manager dialog box) to complete the entry of the conditional formatting rules and apply the rule (Figure 4–22).

9

- Save your changes by clicking the Save button on the Quick Access Toolbar.

Experiment

- After saving your changes, experiment with different rules. Add a second rule that changes the format for any current due amount that is greater than or equal to $500 to a different color to see the effect of multiple rules. Change the order of rules to see the effect of a different order. When you have finished, delete any additional rules you have added so that the report contains only the one rule that you created earlier.

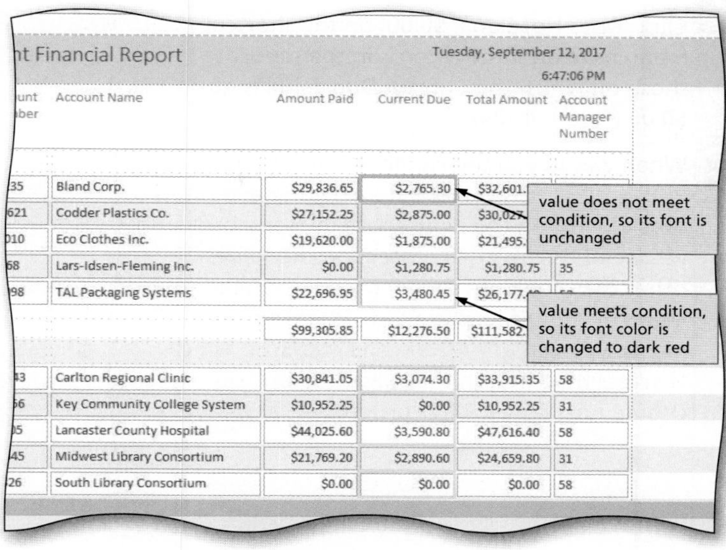

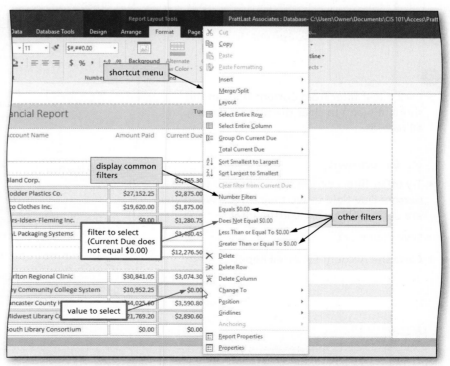

Figure 4–22

To Filter Records in a Report

1 GROUP, SORT, & TOTAL | 2 CONDITIONALLY FORMAT CONTROLS | 3 FILTER REPORT RECORDS | 4 **MULTIPLE-TABLE REPORT**
5 FORM WIZARD | 6 MODIFY CONTROLS | 7 FILTER FORM RECORDS | 8 MAILING LABELS

You sometimes might want to filter records in a report. *Why? You may want to include in a report only those records that satisfy some criterion and be able to change that criterion easily.* To filter records in a report, you can use the filter buttons in the Sort & Filter group on the Home tab. If the filter involves only one field, however, right-clicking the field provides a simple way to filter. The following steps filter the records in the report to include only those records on which the current due amount is not $0.00.

1

- Right-click the Current Due field on the first record where Current Due is 0 to display the shortcut menu (Figure 4–23).

Q&A Did I have to pick the first record where the value is $0.00?
No. You could pick any record on which the Current Due value is $0.00.

Figure 4–23

2

- Click 'Does Not Equal $0.00' on the shortcut menu to restrict the records in the report to those on which the Current Due value is not $0.00 (Figure 4–24).

Q&A

When would you use Number Filters?
You would use Number Filters if you need filters that are not on the main shortcut menu or if you need the ability to enter specific values other than the ones shown on the shortcut menu. If those filters are insufficient for your needs, you can use Advanced Filter/Sort, which is accessible through the Advanced button (Home tab | Sort & Filter group).

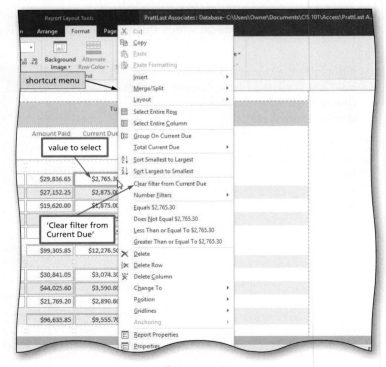

Amount Paid	Current Due	Total Amount	Account Manager Number
$29,836.65	$2,765.30	$32,601.95	35
$27,152.25	$2,875.00	$30,027.25	35
$19,620.00	$1,875.00	$21,495.00	58
$0.00	$1,280.75	$1,280.75	35
$22,696.95	$3,480.45	$26,177.40	58
$99,305.85	$12,276.50	$111,582.35	
$30,841.05	$3,074.30	$33,915.35	58
$44,025.60	$3,590.80	$47,616.40	58
$21,769.20	$2,890.60	$24,659.80	31
$96,635.85	$9,555.70	$106,191.55	

only Current Due values that are not $0.00 are included

Figure 4–24

Other Ways

1. Click Selection button (Home tab | Sort & Filter group)

To Clear a Report Filter

1 GROUP, SORT, & TOTAL | 2 CONDITIONALLY FORMAT CONTROLS | 3 FILTER REPORT RECORDS | 4 MULTIPLE-TABLE REPORT
5 FORM WIZARD | 6 MODIFY CONTROLS | 7 FILTER FORM RECORDS | 8 MAILING LABELS

The following steps clear the filter on the Current Due field. *Why? When you no longer want the records to be filtered, you clear the filter so that all records are again included.*

1

- Right-click the Current Due field on the first record to display the shortcut menu (Figure 4–25).

Q&A

Did I have to pick the first record?
No. You could pick the Current Due field on any record.

2

- Click 'Clear filter from Current Due' on the shortcut menu to clear the filter and redisplay all records.

Experiment

- Try other filters on the shortcut menu for the Current Due field to see their effect. When you are done with each, clear the filter.

- Save your work.

- Close the Account Financial Report.

Figure 4–25

Other Ways

1. Click Advanced button (Home tab | Sort & Filter group)

The Arrange and Page Setup Tabs

When working on a report in Layout view, you can make additional layout changes by using the Report Layout Tools Arrange and/or Page Setup tabs. The Arrange tab is shown in Figure 4–26. Table 4–1 shows the buttons on the Arrange tab along with the Enhanced ScreenTips that describe their function.

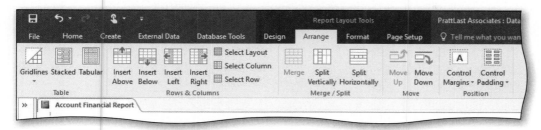

Figure 4–26

Table 4–1 Arrange Tab	
Button	**Enhanced ScreenTip**
Gridlines	Gridlines.
Stacked	Create a layout similar to a paper form, with labels to the left of each field.
Tabular	Create a layout similar to a spreadsheet, with labels across the top and data in columns below the labels.
Insert Above	Insert above.
Insert Below	Insert below.
Insert Left	Insert left.
Insert Right	Insert right.
Select Layout	Select layout.
Select Column	Select column.
Select Row	Select row.
Merge	Merge cells.
Split Vertically	Split the selected control into two rows.
Split Horizontally	Split the selected control into two columns.
Move Up	Move up.
Move Down	Move down.
Control Margins	Specify the location of information displayed within the control.
Control Padding	Set the amount of spacing between controls and the gridlines of a layout.

BTW

Using the Arrange Tab

Because the commands located on the Arrange tab are actions associated with previously selected controls, be sure to select the desired control or controls first.

BTW

Searching for Records in a Report

You can use the Find button to search for records in a report. To do so, open the report in Report view or Layout view and select the field in the report on which to search. Click the Find button (Home tab | Find group) to display the Find and Replace dialog box. Type the desired value on which to search in the Find What text box (Find and Replace dialog box), and then click the Find Next button.

The Report Layout Tools Page Setup tab is shown in Figure 4–27. Table 4–2 shows the buttons on the Page Setup tab along with the Enhanced ScreenTips that describe their function.

Figure 4–27

Table 4–2 Page Setup Tab	
Button	**Enhanced ScreenTip**
Size	Choose a paper size for the current document.
Margins	Select the margin sizes for the entire document or the current section.
Show Margins	Show margins.
Print Data Only	Print data only.
Portrait	Change to portrait orientation.
Landscape	Change to landscape orientation.
Columns	Columns.
Page Setup	Show the Page Setup dialog box.

BTW
Distributing a Document
Instead of printing and distributing a hard copy of a document, you can distribute the document electronically. Options include sending the document via email; posting it on cloud storage (such as OneDrive) and sharing the file with others; posting it on a social networking site, blog, or other website; and sharing a link associated with an online location of the document. You can also create and share a PDF or XPS image of the document, so that users can view the file in Acrobat Reader or XPS Viewer instead of in Access.

To PRINT A REPORT

If you want to print your report, you would use the following steps.

1. With the report selected in the Navigation Pane, click File on the ribbon to open the Backstage view.
2. Click the Print tab in the Backstage view to display the Print gallery.
3. Click the Quick Print button to print the report.

Q&A How can I print multiple copies of my report?

Click File on the ribbon to open the Backstage view. Click the Print tab, click Print in the Print gallery to display the Print dialog box, increase the number in the Number of Copies box, and then click the OK button (Print dialog box).

Multiple-Table Reports

Sometimes you will create reports that require data from more than one table. You can use the Report Wizard to create a report based on multiple tables just as you can use it to create reports based on single tables or queries.

To Create a Report that Involves Multiple Tables

1 GROUP, SORT, & TOTAL | 2 CONDITIONALLY FORMAT CONTROLS | 3 FILTER REPORT RECORDS | **4 MULTIPLE-TABLE REPORT**
5 FORM WIZARD | 6 MODIFY CONTROLS | 7 FILTER FORM RECORDS | 8 MAILING LABELS

Why? PrattLast needs a report that includes the Account Manager Number, First Name, and Last Name fields from the Account Manager table. In addition, for each account of the manager, they need the Account Number, Account Name, Amount Paid, and Current Due fields from the Account table. The following steps use the Report Wizard to create a report that includes fields from both the Account Manager and Account tables.

- Open the Navigation Pane if it is currently closed.
- Click the Account Manager table in the Navigation Pane to select it.
- Click Create on the ribbon to display the Create tab.

- Click the Report Wizard button (Create tab | Reports group) to start the Report Wizard (Figure 4–28).

Q&A
My Navigation Pane does not look like the one in this screen. Is that a problem? How do I change it?
No, this is not a problem, but you should change the Navigation Pane so it matches the screens in this module. To do so, click the Navigation Pane arrow and then click Object Type.

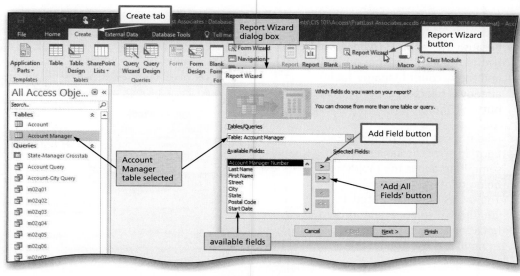

Figure 4–28

2

- Click the Add Field button to add the Account Manager Number field to the report.
- Add the First Name field by clicking it and then clicking the Add Field button.
- Add the Last Name field in the same manner.
- Click the Tables/Queries arrow, scroll if necessary so that the Account table appears, and then click Table: Account in the Tables/Queries list box (Figure 4–29).

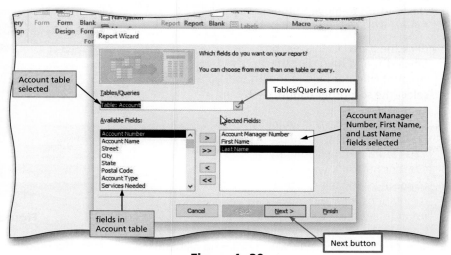

Figure 4–29

3

- Add the Account Number, Account Name, Amount Paid, and Current Due fields by clicking the field and then clicking the Add Field button.
- Click the Next button (Figure 4–30).

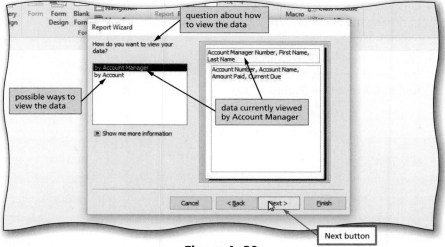

Figure 4–30

4

- Because the report is to be viewed by the Account Manager table, and the Account Manager table already is selected, click the Next button (Figure 4–31).

Q&A
I did not get this screen. Instead, I got an error message that said something about the tables not being related.

The tables must be related. If you did not create a relationship between these tables earlier, do so now, and then begin these steps again.

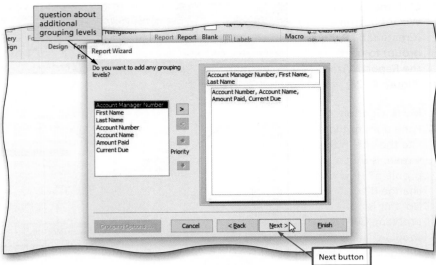

Figure 4–31

5

- Because you do not need to add any grouping levels, click the Next button to move to the next Report Wizard screen.

- Click the arrow in the text box labeled 1, and then click the Account Number field in the list to select the sort order (Figure 4–32).

Q&A
When would I use the Summary Options button?

You would use the Summary Options button if you want to specify subtotals or other calculations for the report while using the wizard. You can also use it to produce a summary report by selecting Summary Only, which will omit all detail records from the report.

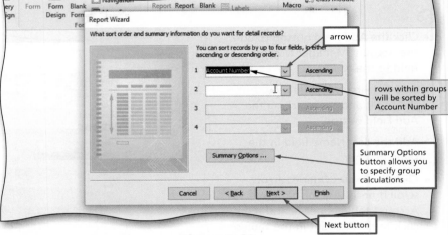

Figure 4–32

6

- Click the Summary Options button to display the Summary Options dialog box.

- Click the check boxes to calculate the sum of Amount Paid and the sum of Current Due (Figure 4–33).

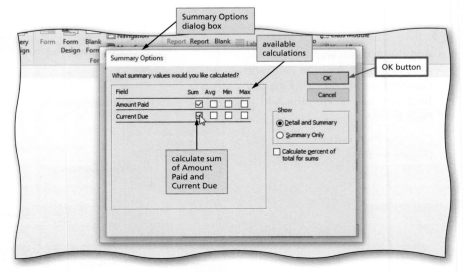

Figure 4–33

7

- Click the OK button (Summary Options dialog box).

- Click the Next button, be sure the Stepped layout is selected, and then click the Landscape option button to select the orientation (Figure 4–34).

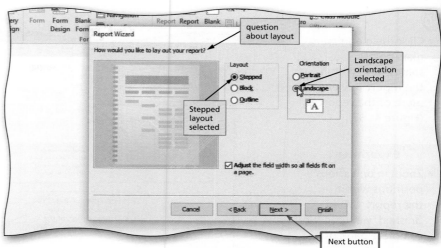

Figure 4–34

8

- Click the Next button to move to the next Report Wizard screen, and then type **Accounts by Account Manager** as the report title (Figure 4–35).

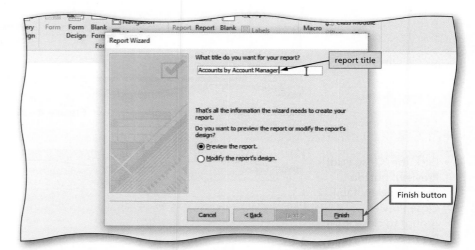

Figure 4–35

9

- Click the Finish button to produce the report (Figure 4–36).

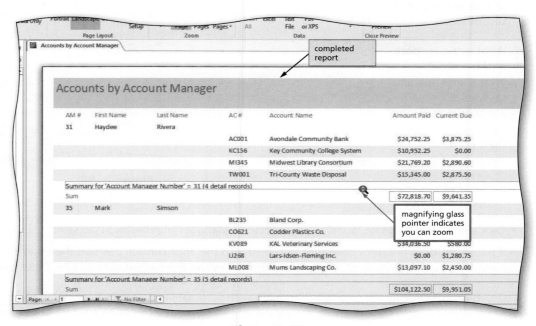

Figure 4–36

- Click the magnifying glass pointer somewhere within the report to view more of the report (Figure 4–37).

Experiment

- Zoom in on various positions within the report. When finished, view a complete page of the report.

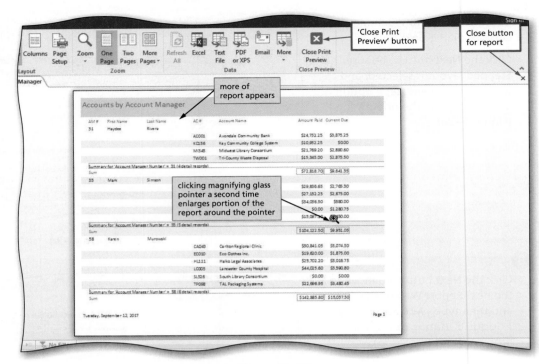

Figure 4–37

- Click the 'Close Print Preview' button (Print Preview tab | Close Preview group) to close Print Preview.

- Click the View arrow (Design tab | Views group), and then click Layout View.

Q&A What is the purpose of the dashed vertical line near the right edge of the screen?
The line shows the right border of the amount of the report that will print on one page. If any portion of the report extends beyond the line, the report may not print correctly.

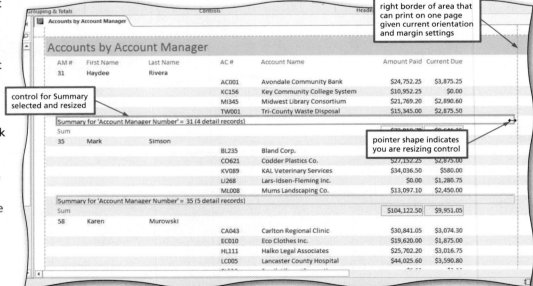

Figure 4–38

- Click the control that says 'Summary for 'Account Manager Number' = 31' to select the control.

- If necessary, drag the right border of the control to the approximate position shown in Figure 4–38 to resize the control so that no portion of the control extends beyond the dashed vertical line. Close the field list, if necessary.

Q&A Do I have to resize all the controls that begin with Summary individually?
No. When you resize one of them, the others will all be resized the same amount automatically.

• Ensure that the control for the Page Number is visible, click the Page number to select it, and then drag it to the left, if necessary, so that no portion of the control extends beyond the dashed line.

• Save your work.

• Click the Close button for the report to close the report and remove it from the screen.

How do you determine the tables and fields that contain the data needed for the report?
First you need to know the requirements for the report. Precisely what data is the report intended to convey? Once you understand those requirements, follow these guidelines:

Examine the requirements for the report to determine the tables. Do the requirements only relate to data in a single table, or does the data come from multiple tables? What is the relationship between the tables?

Examine the requirements for the report to determine the fields necessary. Look for all the data items specified for the report. Each should correspond to a field in a table or be able to be computed from fields in a table. This information gives you the list of fields to include.

Determine the order of the fields. Examine the requirements to determine the order in which the fields should appear. Be logical and consistent in your ordering. For example, in an address, the city should come before the state and the state should come before the postal code, unless there is some compelling reason for another order.

Creating a Report in Layout View

You can use the Report button initially to create a report containing all the fields in a table. You can then delete the unwanted fields so that the resulting report contains only the desired fields. At that point you can use Layout view to modify the report and produce the report you want.

You can also use Layout view to create single- or multiple-table reports from scratch. To do so, you would first create a blank report and display a field list for the table containing the first fields you want to include on the report (Figure 4–39).

BTW
Multicolumn Reports
There are times when you might want to create a report that has multiple columns. For example, a telephone list with employee name and phone number could print in multiple columns. To do so, create the report using Layout view or Design view and then click the Page Setup tab, click the Columns button, enter the number of columns, select the desired column layout, and then click the OK button.

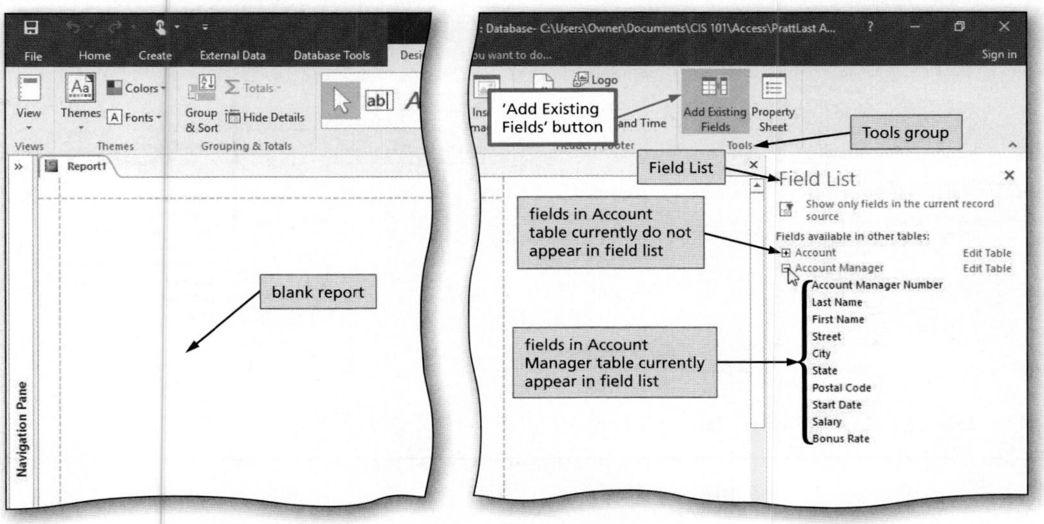

Figure 4–39

You then would drag any fields you want from the table onto the report in the order you want them to appear (Figure 4–40).

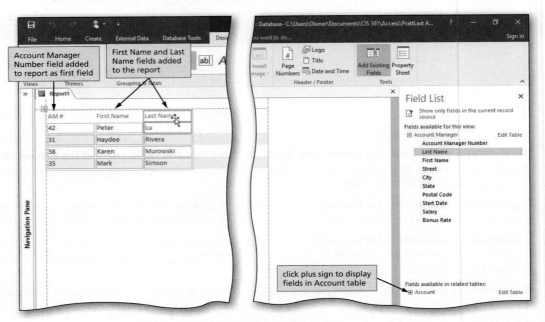

Figure 4–40

If the report involves a second table, you display the fields from the second table in the field list and then drag the fields from the second table onto the report in the desired order (Figure 4–41).

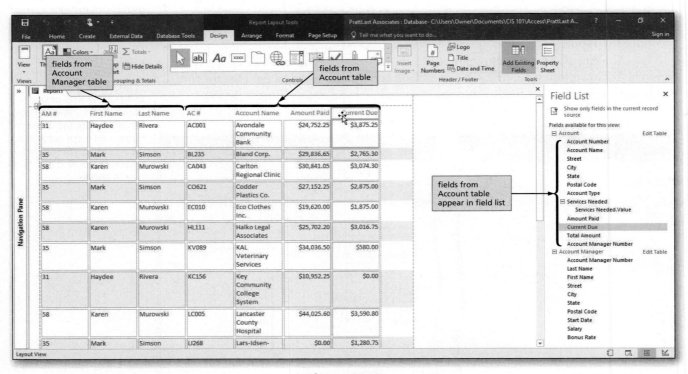

Figure 4–41

When you create a report in Layout view, the report does not automatically contain a title, but you can add one by clicking the Title button (Report Layout Tools Design tab | Header/Footer group) (Figure 4–42).

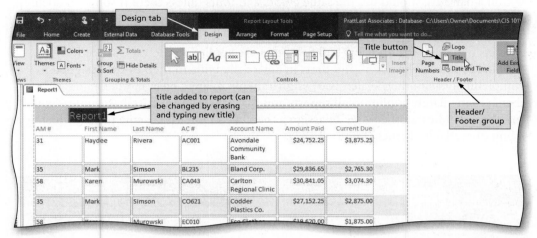

Figure 4–42

Once you have added the title, you can type whatever title you want for the report.

To Create a Report in Layout View by Creating a Blank Report

If you wanted to create a report in Layout view, you would use the following steps.

1. Click Create on the ribbon to display the Create tab.
2. Click the Blank Report button (Create tab | Reports group) to create a blank report.
3. If a field list does not appear, display a field list by clicking the 'Add Existing Fields' button (Report Layout Tools Design tab | Tools group).
4. If the tables do not appear in the field list, click 'Show all tables'.
5. If the fields in a table do not appear, click the plus sign in front of the name of the table.
6. Drag the fields from the field list onto the report in the desired order.
7. If the report involves a second table, be sure the fields in the second table appear, and then drag the fields from the second table onto the report in the desired order. (If the field list covers the portion of the report where you want to drag the fields, move the field list to a different position by dragging its title bar.)
8. To add a title to the report, click the Title button (Report Layout Tools Design tab | Header/Footer group) and then type the desired title.

Using Themes

The most important characteristic of a report or form is that it presents the desired data in a useful arrangement. Another important characteristic, however, is the general appearance of the form. The colors and fonts that you use in the various sections of a report or form contribute to this look. You should keep in mind two important goals when assigning colors and fonts. First, the various colors and fonts

BTW
Using Themes
Office themes are designed to enhance an organization's brand identity. Many organizations consistently use themes, styles, and color schemes to visually assist in identifying their products and/or services.

should complement each other. A clash of colors or two fonts that do not go well together can produce a report that looks unprofessional or is difficult to read. Second, the choice of colors and fonts should be consistent. That is, all the reports and forms within a database should use the same colors and fonts unless there is some compelling reason for a report or form to look different from the others.

Fortunately, Access themes provide an easy way to achieve both goals. A **theme** consists of a selection of colors and fonts that are applied to the various sections in a report or form. The colors and fonts in any of the built-in themes are designed to complement each other. When you assign a theme to any object in the database, the theme immediately applies to all reports and forms in the same database, unless you specifically indicate otherwise. To assign a theme, you use the Theme picker, which is a menu of available themes (Figure 4–43).

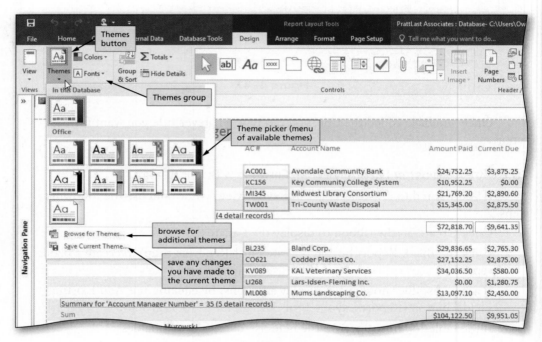

Figure 4–43

If you point to any theme in the Theme picker, you will see a ScreenTip giving the name of the theme. When you select a theme, the colors and fonts represented by that theme will immediately apply to all reports and forms. If you later decide that you would prefer a different theme, you can change the theme for all of the objects in the database by repeating the process with a different theme.

You can also use the Browse for Themes command to browse for themes that are not listed as part of a standard Access installation, but which are available for download. You can also create your own customized theme by specifying a combination of fonts and colors and using the Save Current Theme command to save your combination. If, after selecting a theme using the Themes button, you do not like the colors in the current theme, you can change the theme's colors. Click the Colors button (Report Layout Tools Design tab | Themes group) (Figure 4–44), and then select an alternative color scheme.

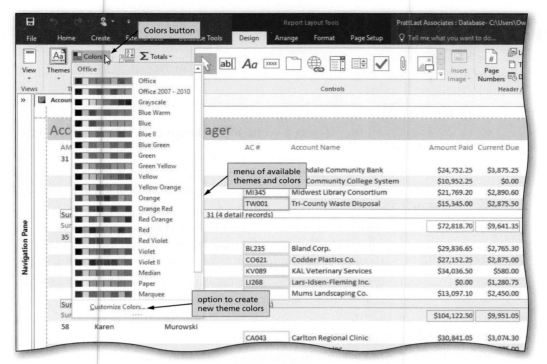

Figure 4–44

Similarly, if you do not like the fonts in the current theme, you can click the Fonts button (Report Layout Tools Design tab | Themes group) (Figure 4–45). You can then select an alternative font for the theme.

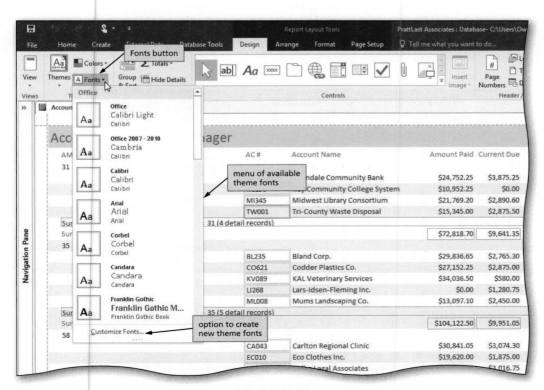

Figure 4–45

TO ASSIGN A THEME TO ALL OBJECTS

To assign a theme, it is easiest to use Layout view. You can use Design view as well, but it is easier to see the result of picking a theme when you are viewing the report or form in Layout view. To assign a theme to all reports and forms, you would use the following steps.

1. Open any report or form in Layout view.
2. Click the Themes button (Report Layout Tools Design tab | Themes group) to display the Theme picker.
3. Click the desired theme.

TO ASSIGN A THEME TO A SINGLE OBJECT

In some cases, you might only want to apply a theme to the current report or form, while all other reports and forms would retain the characteristics from the original theme. To assign a theme to a single object, you would use the following steps.

1. Open the specific report or form to which you want to assign a theme in Layout view.
2. Click the Themes button (Report Layout Tools Design tab | Themes group) to display the Theme picker.
3. Right-click the desired theme to produce a shortcut menu.
4. Click the 'Apply Theme to This Object Only' command on the shortcut menu to apply the theme to the single object on which you are working.

Live Preview for Themes

When selecting themes, Access provides a **live preview** of what the report or form will look like with the theme before you actually select and apply the theme. The report or form will appear as it would in the theme to which you are currently pointing (Figure 4–46). If you like that theme, you then can select the theme by clicking the left mouse button.

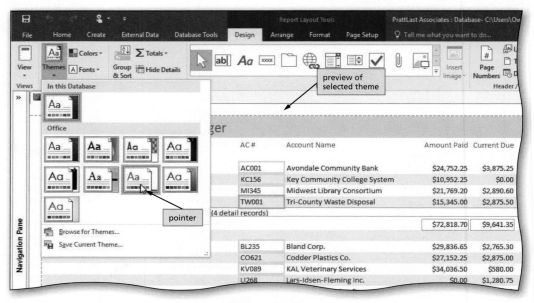

Figure 4–46

To Create a Summary Report

A report that includes group calculations such as subtotals, but does not include the individual detail lines, is called a **summary report**. *Why? You might need a report that only shows the overall group calculations, but not all the records.* The following steps hide the detail lines in the Accounts by Account Manager report, thus creating a summary report.

- Open the Accounts by Account Manager report in Layout view and close the Navigation Pane.

- Click the Hide Details button (Report Layout Tools Design tab | Grouping & Totals group) to hide the details in the report (Figure 4–47).

Q&A
How can I see the details once I have hidden them?
Click the Hide Details button a second time.

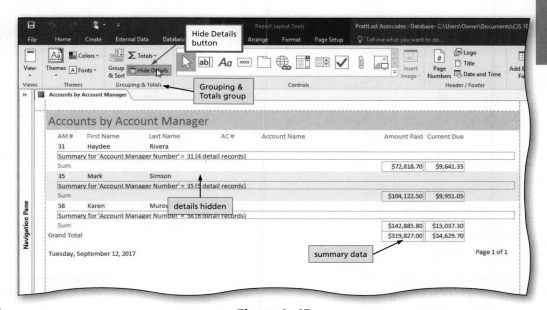

Figure 4–47

- Close the report without saving your changes.

Q&A
What would happen if I saved the report?
The next time you view the report, the details would still be hidden. If that happened and you wanted to show all the details, just click the Hide Details button a second time.

Break Point: If you wish to take a break, this is a good place to do so. You can quit Access now. To resume at a later time, run Access, open the database called PrattLast Associates, and continue following the steps from this location forward.

Form Creation

You can create a simple form consisting of all the fields in the Account table using the Form button (Create tab | Forms group). To create more customized forms, you can use the Form Wizard. Once you have used the Form Wizard to create a form, you can modify that form in either Layout view or Design view.

BTW
Summary Reports
You can create a summary report in either Layout view or Design view.

To Use the Form Wizard to Create a Form

The following steps use the Form Wizard to create an initial version of the Account Financial Form. *Why? Using the Form Wizard is the easiest way to create this form.* The initial version will contain the Account Number, Account Name, Account Type, Services Needed, Amount Paid, Current Due, Total Amount, and Account Manager Number fields.

1

- Open the Navigation Pane and select the Account table.

- Click Create on the ribbon to display the Create tab.

- Click the Form Wizard button (Create tab | Forms group) to start the Form Wizard (Figure 4–48).

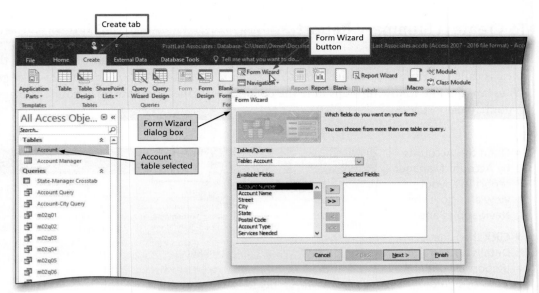

Figure 4–48

2

- Add the Account Number, Account Name, Account Type, Services Needed, Amount Paid, Current Due, Total Amount, and Account Manager Number fields to the form (Figure 4–49).

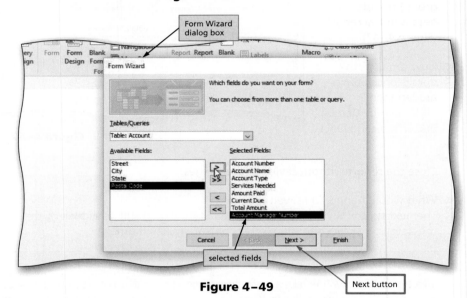

Figure 4–49

3

- Click the Next button to display the next Form Wizard screen (Figure 4–50).

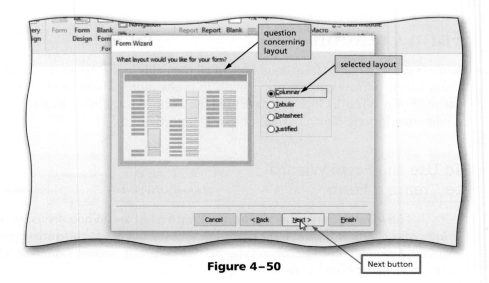

Figure 4–50

4

- Be sure the Columnar layout is selected, click the Next button to display the next Form Wizard screen, and then type **Account Financial Form** as the title for the form (Figure 4–51).

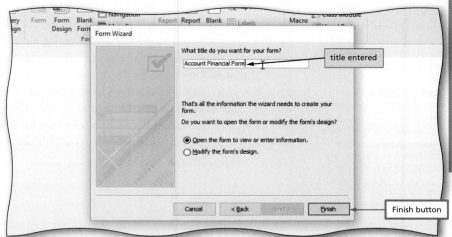

Figure 4–51

5

- Click the Finish button to complete and display the form (Figure 4–52).

6

- Click the Close button for the Account Financial Form to close the form.

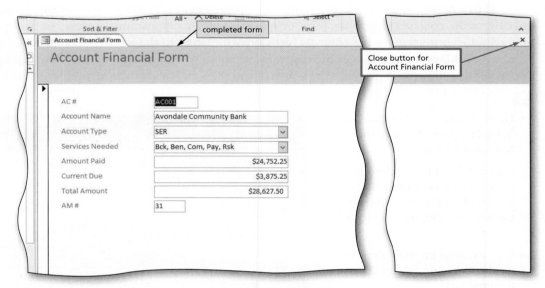

Figure 4–52

Form Sections

A form typically has only three sections. The Form Header section appears at the top of the form and usually contains the form title. It may also contain a logo and/ or a date. The body of the form is in the Detail section. The Form Footer section appears at the bottom of the form and is often empty.

Form Controls

Just as with reports, the various items on a form are called controls. Forms include the same three types of controls: bound controls, unbound controls, and calculated controls. Bound controls have attached labels that typically display the name of the field that supplies the data for the control. The **attached label** for the Account Number field, for example, is the portion of the screen immediately to the left of the field. It contains the words, Account Number (AC#).

BTW
Form Design Considerations
Forms should be appealing visually and present data logically and clearly. Properly designed forms improve both the speed and accuracy of data entry. Forms that are too cluttered or contain too many different effects can be hard on the eyes. Some colors are more difficult than others for individuals to see. Be consistent when creating forms. Once you decide on a general style or theme for forms, stick with it throughout your database.

BTW
Conditional Formatting
Conditional formatting is available for forms as well as reports. To conditionally format controls on a form, open the Form in Layout view or Design view, select the control to format, click the Conditional Formatting button, and then follow the steps found within the To Conditionally Format Controls section (pages AC 188 through AC 191).

Views Available for Forms

When working with a form in Access, there are three different ways to view the form: Form view, Layout view, and Design view. Form view shows the form on the screen and allows you to use the form to update data. Layout view is similar to Form view in that it shows the form on the screen. In Layout view, you cannot update the data, but you can make changes to the layout of the form, and it is usually the easiest way to make such changes. Design view also allows you to make changes, but it does not show you the actual form. It is most useful when the changes you need to make are especially complex. In this module, you will use Layout view to modify the form.

To Place Controls in a Control Layout

1 GROUP, SORT, & TOTAL | 2 CONDITIONALLY FORMAT CONTROLS | 3 FILTER REPORT RECORDS | 4 MULTIPLE-TABLE REPORT
5 FORM WIZARD | 6 MODIFY CONTROLS | 7 FILTER FORM RECORDS | 8 MAILING LABELS

Why? *To use Layout view with a form, the controls must be placed in a control layout.* A **control layout** is a guide that aligns the controls to give the form or report a uniform appearance. Access has two types of control layouts. A **stacked layout** arranges the controls vertically with labels to the left of the control and is commonly used in forms. A **tabular layout** arranges the controls horizontally with the labels across the top and is typically used in reports. The following steps place the controls and their attached labels in a stacked control layout.

1

- Open the Account Financial Form in Layout view and close the Navigation Pane.

- If a field list appears, close the field list by clicking the 'Add Existing Fields' button (Report Layout Tools Design tab | Tools group).

- Click Arrange on the ribbon to display the Form Layout Tools Arrange tab.

- Click the attached label for the Account Number control to select the control.

- While holding the SHIFT key down, click the remaining attached labels and all the controls (Figure 4–53).

Q&A
Did I have to select the attached labels and controls in that order?
No. As long as you select all of them, the order in which you selected them does not matter.

When I clicked some of the controls, they moved so they are no longer aligned as well as they are in the figure. What should I do?
You do not have to worry about it. Once you complete the next step, they will once again be aligned properly.

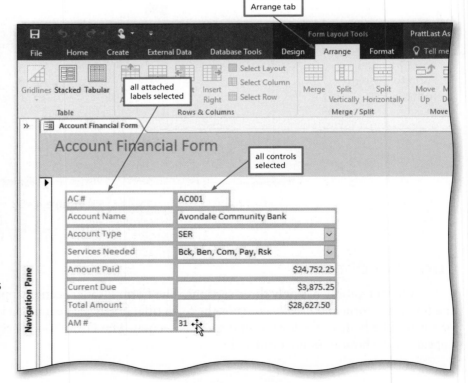

Figure 4–53

2

- Click the Stacked button (Form Layout Tools Arrange tab | Table group) to place the controls in a stacked layout (Figure 4–54).

Q&A How can I tell whether the controls are in a control layout? Look for the Control Layout indicator in the upper-left corner of the control layout.

What is the difference between stacked layout and tabular layout? In a stacked layout, which is more often used in forms, the controls are placed vertically with the labels to the left of the controls. In a tabular layout, which is more often used in reports, the controls are placed horizontally with the labels above the controls.

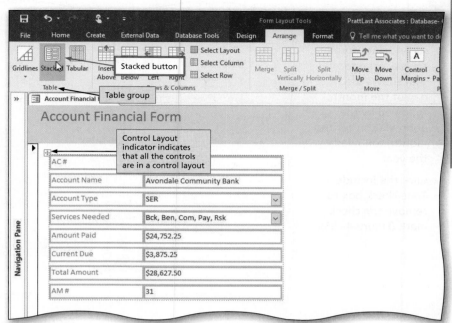

Figure 4–54

To Enhance a Form by Adding a Date

1 GROUP, SORT, & TOTAL | 2 CONDITIONALLY FORMAT CONTROLS | 3 FILTER REPORT RECORDS | 4 MULTIPLE-TABLE REPORT
5 FORM WIZARD | 6 MODIFY CONTROLS | **7 FILTER FORM RECORDS** | 8 MAILING LABELS

Why? *To enhance the look or usability of a report or form, you can add special items, such as a logo or title. You can also add the date and/or the time. In the case of reports, you can add a page number as well.* To add any of these items, you use the appropriate button in the Header/Footer group of the Design tab. The following steps use the 'Date and Time' button to add a date to the Account Financial Form.

1

- Click Design on the ribbon to display the Form Layout Tools Design tab.
- Click the 'Date and Time' button (Form Layout Tools Design tab | Header/Footer group) to display the Date and Time dialog box (Figure 4–55).

Q&A What is the purpose of the various check boxes and option buttons? If the Include Date check box is checked, you must pick a date format from the three option buttons underneath the check box. If it is not checked, the option buttons will be dimmed. If the Include Time check box is checked, you must pick a time format from the three option buttons underneath the check box. If it is not checked, the option buttons will be dimmed.

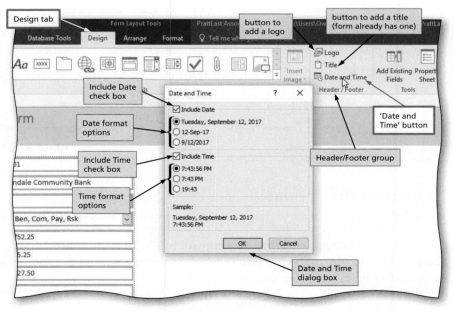

Figure 4–55

2

- Click the option button for the second date format to select the format that shows the day of the month, followed by the abbreviation for the month, followed by the year.

- Click the Include Time check box to remove the check mark (Figure 4–56).

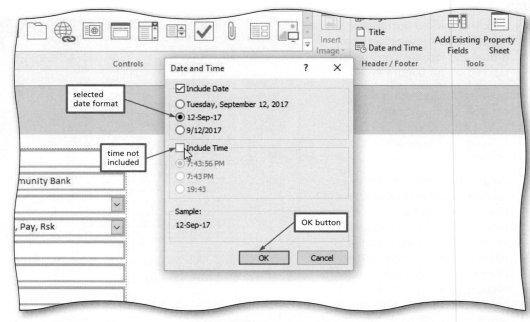

Figure 4–56

3

- Click the OK button (Date and Time dialog box) to add the date to the form (Figure 4–57).

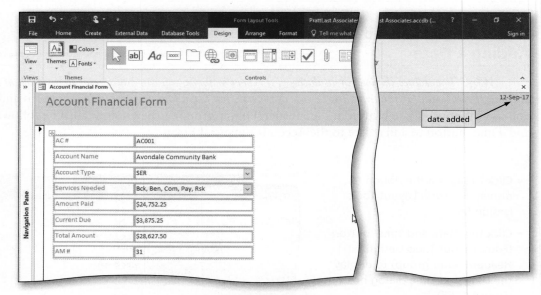

Figure 4–57

To Change the Format of a Control

1 GROUP, SORT, & TOTAL | 2 CONDITIONALLY FORMAT CONTROLS | 3 FILTER REPORT RECORDS | 4 MULTIPLE-TABLE REPORT
5 FORM WIZARD | 6 MODIFY CONTROLS | 7 FILTER FORM RECORDS | 8 MAILING LABELS

You can change the format of a control by clicking the control and then clicking the appropriate button on the Format tab. The following step uses this technique to bold the date. *Why? Formatting controls on a form lets you visually emphasize certain controls.*

- Click the Date control to select it.
- Click Format on the ribbon to display the Form Layout Tools Format tab.
- Click the Bold button (Form Layout Tools Format tab | Font group) to bold the date (Figure 4–58).

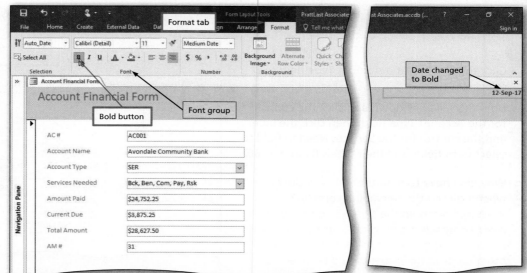

Figure 4–58

To Move a Control

1 GROUP, SORT, & TOTAL | 2 CONDITIONALLY FORMAT CONTROLS | 3 FILTER REPORT RECORDS | 4 MULTIPLE-TABLE REPORT
5 FORM WIZARD | 6 MODIFY CONTROLS | 7 FILTER FORM RECORDS | 8 MAILING LABELS

You can move a control by dragging the control. The following step moves the Date control to the lower edge of the form header. *Why? The default location of some controls might not be ideal; moving controls lets you adjust the design to your specifications.*

- Point to the Date control so that the pointer changes to a four-headed arrow, and then drag the Date control to the lower boundary of the form header in the approximate position shown in Figure 4–59.

Q&A I moved my pointer a little bit and it became a two-headed arrow. Can I still drag the pointer?
If you drag when the pointer is a two-headed arrow, you will resize the control. To move the control, it must be a four-headed arrow.

Could I drag other objects as well? For example, could I drag the title to the center of the form header?
Yes. Just be sure you are pointing at the object and the pointer is a four-headed arrow. You can then drag the object to the desired location.

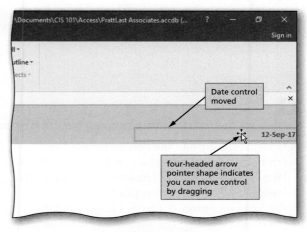

Figure 4–59

To Move Controls in a Control Layout

1 GROUP, SORT, & TOTAL | 2 CONDITIONALLY FORMAT CONTROLS | 3 FILTER REPORT RECORDS | 4 MULTIPLE-TABLE REPORT
5 FORM WIZARD | 6 MODIFY CONTROLS | 7 FILTER FORM RECORDS | 8 MAILING LABELS

Just as you moved the Date control in the previous section, you can move any control within a control layout by dragging the control to the location you want. As you move it, a line will indicate the position where the control will be placed when you release the mouse button or your finger. You can move more than one control in the same operation by selecting multiple controls prior to moving them.

The following steps move the Account Type and Services Needed fields so that they follow the Account Manager Number field. **Why?** *The requirements for the form place these two fields after the Account Manager Number field.*

1

- Click the label for the Account Type field to select it.

- Hold the SHIFT key down and click the control for the Account Type field, then click the label and the control for the Services Needed field to select both fields and their labels (Figure 4–60).

Q&A Why did I have to hold the SHIFT key down when I clicked the remaining controls?
If you did not hold the SHIFT key down, you would only select the control for the Services Needed field (the last control selected). The other controls no longer would be selected.

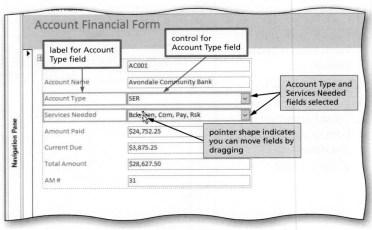

Figure 4–60

2

- Drag the fields straight down to the position shown in Figure 4–61, making sure that the line by the pointer is under the data. (For illustration purposes, do not release the mouse button yet.)

Q&A What is the purpose of the line by the pointer?
It shows you where the fields will be positioned.

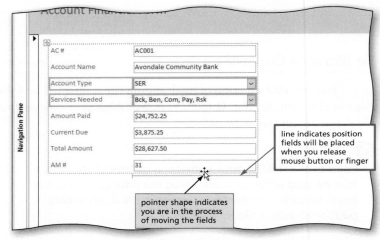

Figure 4–61

3

- Release the mouse button to complete the movement of the fields (Figure 4–62).

Q&A I inadvertently had the line under the label rather than the data when I released the mouse button. The data that I moved is now under the field names. How do I fix this?
You can try to move it back where it was, but that can be tricky. The easiest way is to use the Undo button on the Quick Access Toolbar to undo your change.

I inadvertently moved my pointer so that the line became vertical and was located between a label and the corresponding data when I released the mouse button. It seemed to split the form. The data I moved appears right where the line was. It is between a label and the corresponding data. How do I fix this?
Use the Undo button on the Quick Access Toolbar to undo your change.

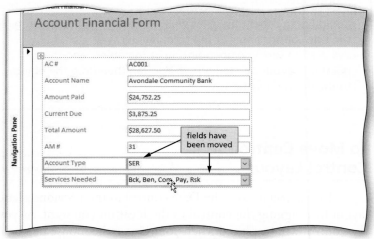

Figure 4–62

To Add a Field

Why? Just as with a report, once you have created an initial form, you might decide that the form should contain an additional field. The following steps use a field list to add the City field to the Account Financial Form.

1

- Click Design on the ribbon to display the Form Layout Tools Design tab.

- Click the 'Add Existing Fields' button (Form Layout Tools Design tab | Tools group) to display a field list (Figure 4–63).

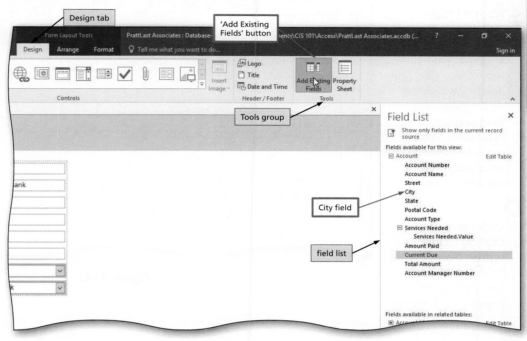

Figure 4–63

2

- Point to the City field in the field list, and then drag the pointer to the position shown in Figure 4–64. For illustration purposes do not release the mouse button yet.

Q&A Does it have to be exact?
The exact pointer position is not critical as long as the line is in the position shown in the figure.

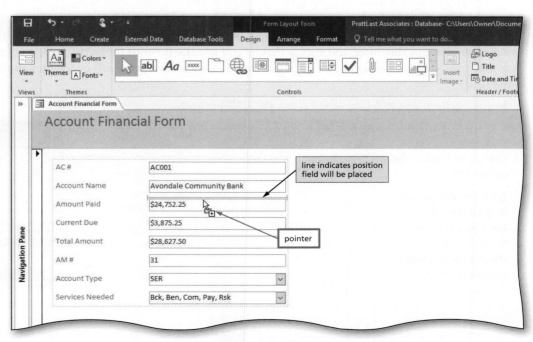

Figure 4–64

3

- Release the mouse button to place the field (Figure 4–65).

Q&A

What if I make a mistake?

Just as when you are modifying a report, you can delete the field by clicking the field and then pressing the DELETE key. You can move the field by dragging it to the correct position.

4

- Click the 'Add Existing Fields' button (Form Layout Tools Design tab | Tools group) to remove the field list.

- Save your work.

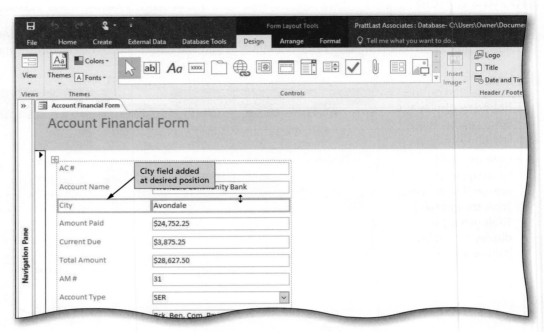

Figure 4–65

To Filter and Sort Using a Form

1 GROUP, SORT, & TOTAL | 2 CONDITIONALLY FORMAT CONTROLS | 3 FILTER REPORT RECORDS | 4 MULTIPLE-TABLE REPORT
5 FORM WIZARD | 6 MODIFY CONTROLS | 7 FILTER FORM RECORDS | 8 MAILING LABELS

Why? Just as in a datasheet, you often need to filter and sort data when using a form. You can do so using Advanced Filter/Sort, which is a command on the Advanced menu. The following steps use Advanced Filter/Sort to filter the records to those records whose city begins with the letter, G. They also sort the records by account name. The effect of this filter and sort is that as you use the form to move through accounts, you will only encounter those accounts whose cities begin with G. In addition, you will encounter those accounts in account name order.

1

- Click Home on the ribbon to display the Home tab.

- Click the Advanced button (Home tab | Sort & Filter group) to display the Advanced menu (Figure 4–66).

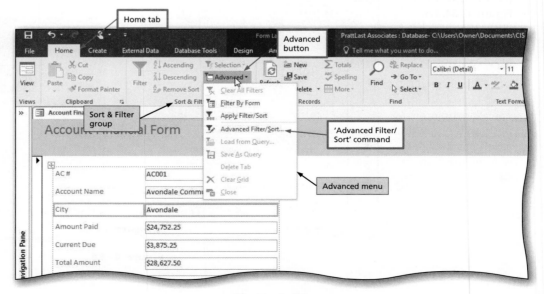

Figure 4–66

2

- Click 'Advanced Filter/Sort' on the Advanced menu.

- If necessary, resize the field list so that the Account Name and City fields appear.

- Add the Account Name field to the design grid and select Ascending sort order.

- Add the City field and type **G*** as the criterion for the City field (Figure 4–67).

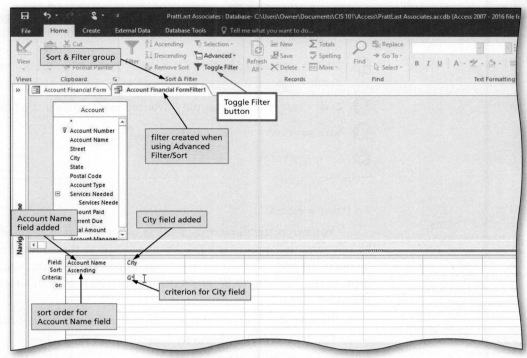

Figure 4–67

3

- Click the Toggle Filter button (Home tab | Sort & Filter group) to filter the records (Figure 4–68).

 I can only see one record at a time in the form. How can I see which records are included?
You need to scroll through the records using the arrows in the Navigation bar.

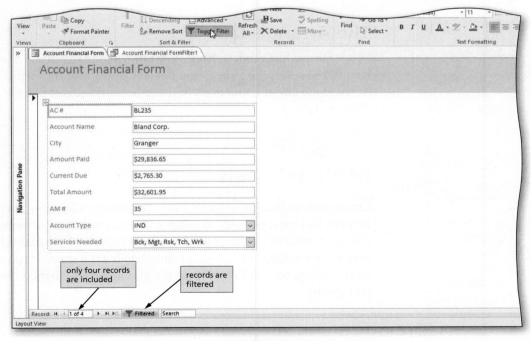

Figure 4–68

To Clear a Form Filter

When you no longer want the records to be filtered, you clear the filter. The following steps clear the current filter for the Account Financial Form.

1 Click the Advanced button (Home tab | Sort & Filter group) to display the Advanced menu.

2 Click 'Clear All Filters' on the Advanced menu to clear the filter.

3 Save your work.

4 Close the Form.

BTW
Printing Forms
To change the page setup and page layout options, such as adjusting margins and changing the orientation, for a form, use the Print Preview window. To open the Print Preview window for a form, click File on the ribbon, click Print, and then click Print Preview.

To Print a Form

You can print all records, a range of records, or a selected record of a form by selecting the appropriate print range. To print the selected record, the form must be open. To print all records or a range of records, you can simply highlight the form in the Navigation Pane. To print a specific record in a form, you would use the following steps.

1. Be sure the desired form is open and the desired record is selected.
2. Click File on the ribbon to open the Backstage view.
3. Click the Print tab in the Backstage view to display the Print gallery.
4. Click the Print button to display the Print dialog box.
5. Click the Selected Record(s) option button in the Print Range section, and then click the OK button.

The Arrange Tab

Forms, like reports, have an Arrange tab that you can use to modify the form's layout. However, the Page Setup tab is not available for forms. The buttons on the Arrange tab and the functions of those buttons are just like the ones described in Table 4–1.

Mailing Labels

Organizations need to send all kinds of correspondence — such as invoices, letters, reports, and surveys — to accounts and other business partners on a regular basis. Using preprinted mailing labels eliminates much of the manual labor involved in preparing mailings. In Access, mailing labels are a special type of report. When this report prints, the data appears on the mailing labels aligned correctly and in the order you specify.

To Create Labels

To create labels, you will typically use the Label wizard. ***Why?*** *Using the wizard, you can specify the type and dimensions, the font, and the content of the label.* The following steps create the labels.

- If necessary, open the Navigation Pane and select the Account table.
- Click Create on the ribbon to display the Create tab.
- Click the Labels button (Create tab | Reports group) to display the Label Wizard dialog box.
- Ensure that English is selected as the Unit of Measure and that Avery is selected in the 'Filter by manufacturer' box.
- If necessary, scroll through the product numbers until C2163 appears, and then click C2163 in the Product number list to select the specific type of labels (Figure 4–69).

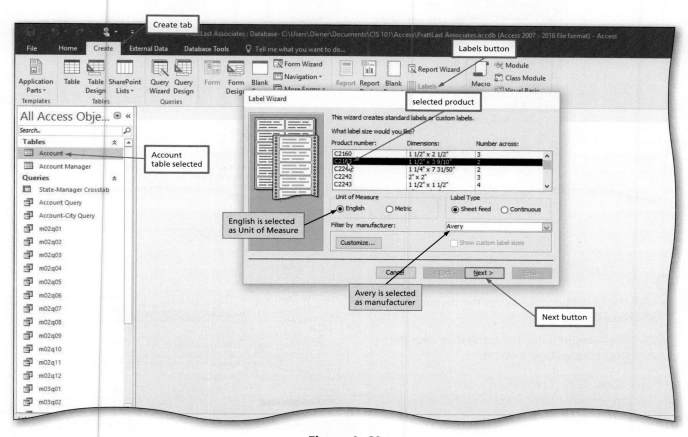

Figure 4–69

2

- Click the Next button (Figure 4–70).

Q&A What font characteristics could I change with this screen?
You could change the font, the font size, the font weight, and/or the font color. You could also specify italic or underline.

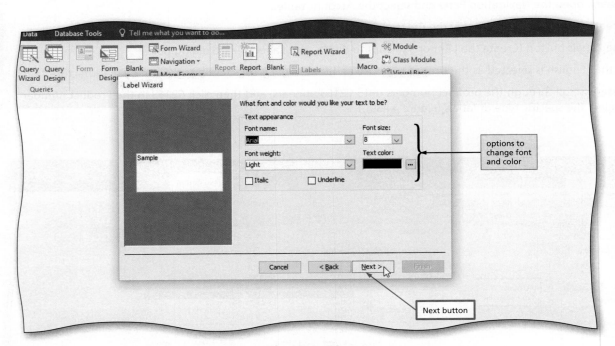

Figure 4–70

3

- Click the Next button to accept the default font and color settings.

- Click the Account Name field, and then click the Add Field button (Figure 4–71).

Q&A What should I do if I make a mistake?
You can erase the contents of any line in the label by clicking in the line to produce an insertion point and then using the DELETE or BACKSPACE key to erase the current contents. You then can add the correct field by clicking the field and then clicking the Add Field button.

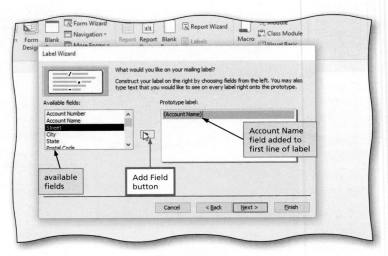

Figure 4–71

- Click the second line of the label, and then add the Street field.
- Click the third line of the label.
- Add the City field, type **,** (a comma), press the SPACEBAR, add the State field, press the SPACEBAR, and then add the Postal Code field (Figure 4–72).

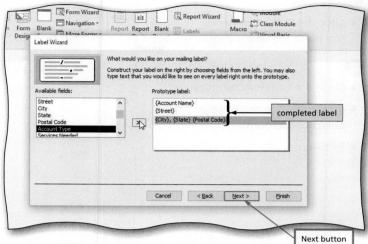

Figure 4–72

- Because you have now added all the necessary fields to the label, click the Next button.
- Select the Postal Code field as the field to sort by, and then click the Add Field button (Figure 4–73).

Q&A Why am I sorting by postal code?
When you need to do a bulk mailing, that is, send a large number of items using a special postage rate, businesses that provide mailing services often require that the mail be sorted in postal code order.

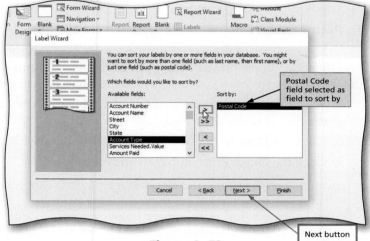

Figure 4–73

6

- Click the Next button.
- Ensure the name for the report (that is, the labels) is Labels Account (Figure 4–74).

If requested to do so by your instructor, name the labels report as Labels FirstName LastName where FirstName and LastName are your first and last names.

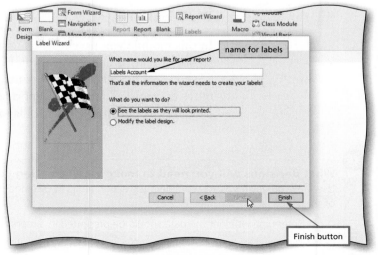

Figure 4–74

7

• Click the Finish button to complete the labels (Figure 4–75).

8

• Close the Labels Account report.

• If desired, sign out of your Microsoft account.

• Exit Access.

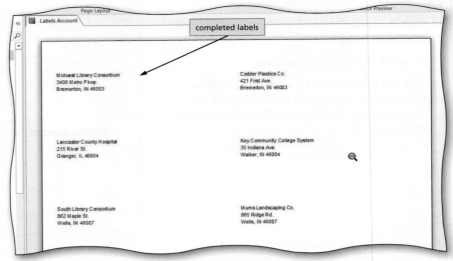

completed labels

Figure 4–75

To Print Labels

You print labels just as you print a report. The only difference is that you must load the labels in the printer before printing. If you want to print labels, you would use the following steps once you have loaded the labels in your printer.

1. With the labels you wish to print selected in the Navigation Pane, click File on the ribbon to open the Backstage view.

2. Click the Print tab in the Backstage view to display the Print gallery.

3. Click the Quick Print button to print the report.

Q&A I want to load the correct number of labels. How do I know how many pages of labels will print?

If you are unsure how many pages of labels will print, open the label report in Print Preview first. Use the Navigation buttons in the status bar of the Print Preview window to determine how many pages of labels will print.

BTW

Customizing Mailing Labels

Once you create mailing labels, you can customize them just as you can customize other reports. In Design view, you can add a picture to the label, change the font size, adjust the spacing between controls, or make any other desired changes.

Summary

In this module you have learned to use wizards to create reports and forms, modify the layout of reports and forms using Layout view, group and sort in a report, add totals to a report, conditionally format controls, filter records in reports and forms, resize and move controls, add fields to reports and forms, create a stacked layout for a form, add a date, move controls in a control layout, apply themes, and create mailing labels.

CONSIDER THIS

What decisions will you need to make when creating your own reports and forms?

Use these guidelines as you complete the assignments in this module and create your own reports and forms outside of this class.

1. Determine whether the data should be presented in a report or a form.

   a. Do you intend to print the data? If so, a report would be the appropriate choice.

   b. Do you intend to view the data on the screen, or will the user update data? If so, a form would be the appropriate choice.

2. Determine the intended audience for the report or form.

   a. Who will use the report or form?

   b. Will the report or form be used by individuals external to the organization? For example, many government agencies require reports from organizations. If so, government regulations will dictate the report requirements. If the report is for internal use, the user will have specific requirements based on the intended use.

   c. Adding unnecessary data to a report or form can make the form or report unreadable. Include only data necessary for the intended use.

   d. What level of detail should the report or form contain? Reports used in day-to-day operations need more detail than weekly or monthly reports requested by management.

3. Determine the tables that contain the data needed for the report or form.

   a. Is all the data found in a single table?

   b. Does the data come from multiple related tables?

4. Determine the fields that should appear on the report or form.

5. Determine the organization of the report or form.

   a. In what order should the fields appear?

   b. How should they be arranged?

   c. Should the records in a report be grouped in some way?

   d. Are any calculations required?

   e. Should the report be used to simply summarize data?

   f. Should the data for the report or form be filtered in some way?

6. Determine the format of the report or form.

   a. What information should be in the report or form header?

   b. Do you want a title and date?

   c. Do you want a logo?

   d. What information should be in the body of the report or form?

   e. Is any conditional formatting required?

   f. What style should be applied to the report or form? In other words, determine the visual characteristics that the various portions of the report or form should have.

   g. Is it appropriate to apply a theme to the reports, forms, and other objects in the database?

7. Review the report or form after it has been in operation to determine whether any changes are necessary.

   a. Is the order of the fields still appropriate?

   b. Are any additional fields required?

8. For mailing labels, determine the contents, order, and type of label.

   a. What fields should appear on the label?

   b. How should the fields be arranged?

   c. Is there a certain order (for example, by postal code) in which the labels should be printed?

   d. Who is the manufacturer of the labels and what is the style number for the labels?

   e. What are the dimensions for each label?

   f. How many labels print across a page?

How should you submit solutions to questions in the assignments identified with a symbol?

Every assignment in this book contains one or more questions identified with a symbol. These questions require you to think beyond the assigned database. Present your solutions to the questions in the format required by your instructor. Possible formats may include one or more of these options: write the answer; create a document that contains the answer; present your answer to the class; discuss your answer in a group; record the answer as audio or video using a webcam, smartphone, or portable media player; or post answers on a blog, wiki, or website.

CONSIDER THIS

Apply Your Knowledge

Reinforce the skills and apply the concepts you learned in this module.

Creating Two Reports and a Form

Note: To complete this assignment, you will be required to use the Data Files. Please contact your instructor for information about accessing the Data Files.

Instructions: Run Access. Open the Apply NicelyNeat Services database from the Data Files and enable the content. NicelyNeat Services provides janitorial services to local businesses. The company uses a team-based approach and each team has a team leader or supervisor. You will create two reports and a form for the company's owner.

Perform the following tasks:

1. Open the Client Financial Report in Layout view and modify the report to create the report shown in Figure 4–76. The report is grouped by Client Type and sorted by Client Number. Include subtotals and grand totals for the Amount Paid and Current Due fields. Apply conditional formatting to the Current Due field by changing the font color to dark red for all records where the Current Due is greater than or equal to $2,000.00. Save the changes to the report.

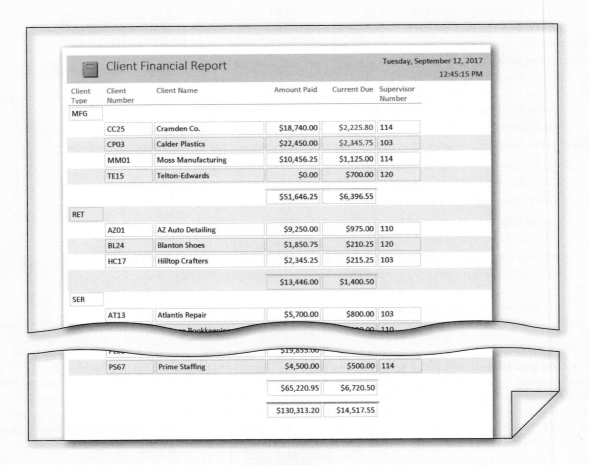

Figure 4–76

2. Create the Clients by Supervisor report shown in Figure 4–77. The report is grouped by supervisor number and sorted by client number. Include a total for the Total Amount field. Be sure to apply the Currency format to the Total Amount subtotals and grand total. Resize the total controls, if necessary. Decrease the size of the total controls so the report prints on one page. Save the report.

Clients by Supervisor

SU #	Last Name	CL #	Client Name	Total Amount
103	Estevez			
		AT13	Atlantis Repair	$6,500.00
		CP03	Calder Plastics	$24,795.75
		HC17	Hilltop Crafters	$2,560.50
		KD15	Klean n Dri	$2,100.50
Summary for 'Supervisor Number' = 103 (4 detail records)				
Sum				$35,956.75
110	Hillsdale			
		AZ01	AZ Auto Detailing	$10,225.00

			Prime Staffing	~~,~~000.00
Summary for 'Supervisor Number' = 114 (3 detail records)				
Sum				$37,547.05
120	Short			
		BL24	Blanton Shoes	$2,061.00
		KC12	Kady Regional Clinic	$9,910.50
		TE15	Telton-Edwards	$700.00
Summary for 'Supervisor Number' = 120 (3 detail records)				
Sum				$12,671.50
Grand Total				$144,830.75

Figure 4–77

3. Create the Client Financial Form shown in Figure 4–78. The form has a stacked layout and includes the current date. Bold the date control. Save the form.

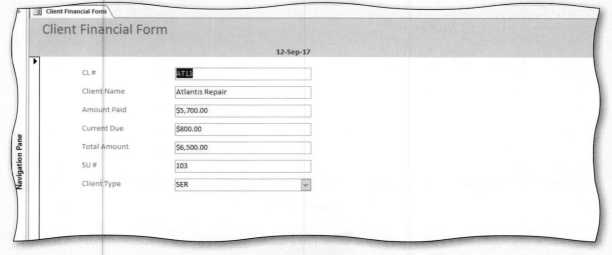

Figure 4–78

Continued >

Apply Your Knowledge *continued*

4. If requested to do so by your instructor, rename the Clients by Supervisor report as Clients by LastName where LastName is your last name.

5. Submit the revised database in the format specified by your instructor.

6. ✹ How would you add the City field to the Client Financial Form so that the field appears below the Client Name field?

Extend Your Knowledge

Extend the skills you learned in this module and experiment with new skills. You may need to use Help to complete the assignment.

Creating a Summary Report and Assigning Themes to Reports and Forms

Note: To complete this assignment, you will be required to use the Data Files. Please contact your instructor for information about accessing the Data Files.

Instructions: Run Access. Open the Extend PowerWashers database from the Data Files. PowerWashers is a company that does power washing of residential properties. You will create a summary report for the PowerWashers database, assign a theme to an existing report, and create a form.

Perform the following tasks:

1. Open the Customer Financial Report in Layout view. Change the theme for the report to Integral and the Theme Colors to Red Violet. Save your changes to the report.

2. Use the Report Wizard to create the summary report shown in Figure 4–79. Name the report Customers by Worker Summary. Group the report by Worker ID and sort by Customer Number within Worker ID. Sum the Amount Owed field. Change the orientation to landscape. Delete the Page control and resize the summary lines so that the report prints on one page. Save your changes to the report. *Note*: The theme you applied in Step 1 will also apply to this report.

Figure 4–79

3. Create the Customer Financial Form shown in Figure 4–80. The form has a stacked control layout. Apply the Organic theme to this form only. Save the changes to the form.

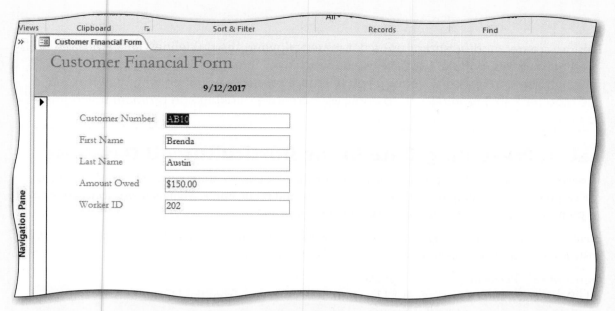

Figure 4–80

4. If requested to do so by your instructor, open the Customer Financial Form in Form view and change the first name and last name for Customer AB10 to your first and last names.

5. Submit the revised database in the format specified by your instructor.

6. ✳ How would you change the theme font for the Customer Financial Form to Arial?

Expand Your World

Create a solution, which uses cloud and web technologies, by learning and investigating on your own from general guidance.

Problem: Reports are often used to present data to individuals outside an organization. Forms are often used to input data and to display data retrieved from a query. When you create reports and forms, it is important to follow certain design guidelines. For example, there are certain fonts that you should use for a title and certain colors that you should avoid because they are harder for individuals to see.

Instructions:

1. Save the PrattLast Associates database as First Name Last Name Associates, where First Name Last Name is your first and last name, to a storage location of your choice.

2. Use a web search engine to research report and form guidelines. Document your research and cite your references in a blog or shared document. For example, the online OneNote or the Word apps.

3. Modify the Account Financial Report to illustrate poor design features for a printed report. In your blog or document explain what design principles were violated.

4. Modify the Account Financial Form to illustrate poor design features for an online form. In your blog or document explain what design principles were violated.

5. Submit the revised database and the blog or document in the format specified by your instructor. Be sure to turn in the document that contains your research references.

6. ✳ Should all reports and forms for a particular company use the same basic design and themes? Why or why not?

In the Labs

Design, create, modify, and/or use a database following the guidelines, concepts, and skills presented in this module. Labs are listed in order of increasing difficulty. Labs 1 and 2, which increase in difficulty, require you to create solutions based on what you learned in the module; Lab 3 requires you to apply your creative thinking and problem solving skills to design and implement a solution.

Lab 1: Presenting Data in the Horticulture4U Database

Problem: Horticulture4U provides products for the gardening community. Sales representatives are responsible for selling to wholesalers, nurseries, and retail stores. Management needs your help in preparing reports and forms to present data for decision making.

Note: To complete this assignment, you will be required to use the Data Files. Please contact your instructor for information about accessing the Data Files.

Instructions: Perform the following tasks:
1. Run Access and open the Lab 1 Horticulture4U database from the Data Files.

2. Open the Customer Financial Report in Layout view and modify the report to create the report shown in Figure 4–81. Add the Total Amount field to the report. Group the report by State and sort by Customer Name within State. Include totals for the Amount Paid, Balance Due, and Total Amount fields. Change the orientation to landscape. Make sure the total controls appear completely and that the Total Amount subtotals and grand total have the currency format.

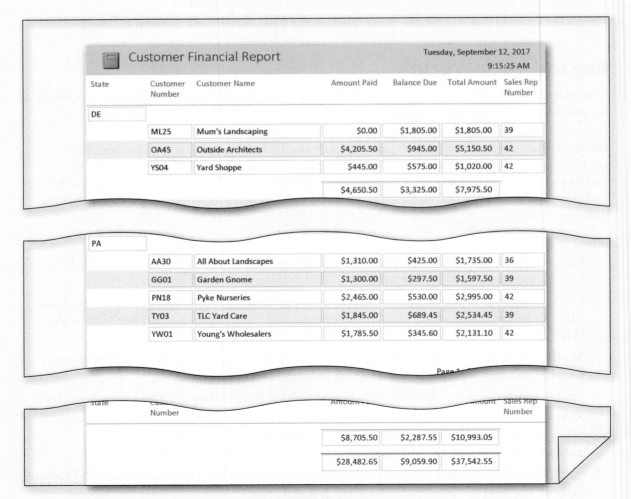

Figure 4–81

3. Create the Customers by Sales Rep report shown in Figure 4–82. Sort by Customer Number and include the average for the Balance Due field. Change the orientation to landscape. If necessary, open the report in Layout view and decrease the size of the summary line so that the report prints on one page. Save the report.

Customers by Sales Rep

SR #	Last Name	First Name	CU #	Customer Name	Balance Due
36	Fitzmyer	Patti			
			AA30	All About Landscapes	$425.00
			LH15	Lawn & Home Stores	$515.25
			PL10	Pat's Landscaping	$180.75
			SL25	Summit Lawn Service	$675.50
			TW34	TAL Wholesalers	$350.00

Summary for 'Sales Rep Number' = 36 (5 detail records)

Avg					$429.30
39	Gupta	Rudy			
			CT02	Christmas Tree Growers	$860.35
			GG01	Garden Gnome	$297.50
			ML25	Mum's Landscaping	$1,805.00
			TY03	TLC Yard Care	$689.45

Summary for 'Sales Rep Number' = 39 (4 detail records)

Avg					$913.08
42	Ortega	Gloria			
			GT34	Green Thumb Growers	$865.50
			OA45	Outside Architects	$945.00
			PN18	Pyke Nurseries	$530.00
			YS04	Yard Shoppe	$575.00
			YW01	Young's Wholesalers	$345.60

Summary for 'Sales Rep Number' = 42 (5 detail records)

Avg					$652.22

Figure 4–82

4. Create the Customer Financial Form shown in Figure 4–83. The form includes the date. Bold the date control. Apply the Slice theme for this form only. Save the form.

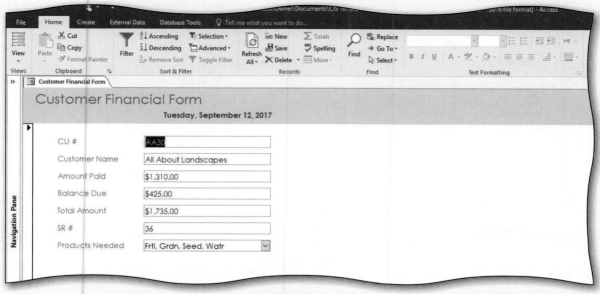

Figure 4–83

Continued >

In the Labs continued

5. Create mailing labels for the Customer table. Use Avery labels C2163 and format the labels with customer name on the first line, street on the second line, and city, state, and postal code on the third line. Include a comma and a space after the city and a space between state and postal code. Sort the labels by postal code.

6. If requested to do so by your instructor, rename the mailing labels as Labels First Name Last Name where First Name and Last Name are your first and last names.

7. Submit the revised database in the format specified by your instructor.

8. ✹ How could you display only the records of sales rep 42 in the Customer Financial Form?

Lab 2: **Presenting Data in the SciTech Sundries Database**

Problem: The local discovery place operates a gift shop that sells science and technology merchandise. The gift shop manager would like to prepare reports and forms for the database.

Note: To complete this assignment, you will be required to use the Data Files. Please contact your instructor for information about accessing the Data Files.

Instructions: Perform the following tasks:

1. Run Access and open the Lab 2 SciTech Sundries database from the Data Files.

2. Open the Item Status Form in Layout view and create the form shown in Figure 4–84. Be sure to place the controls in a stacked control layout. (*Hint:* Place the controls in a control layout before adding the Wholesale Cost field.) If there are fewer than 10 items on hand, the on hand value should appear in a red bold font. Save the changes to the form.

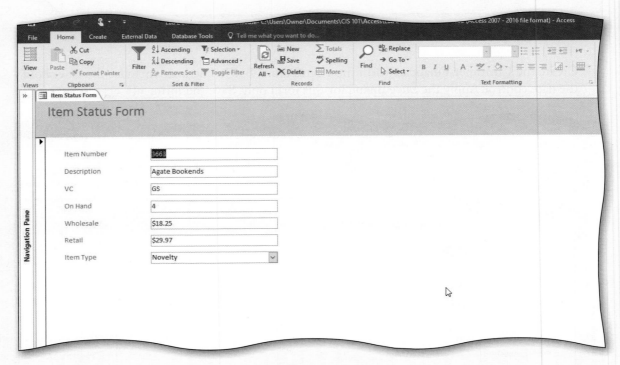

Figure 4–84

3. Open the Item Status Report in Layout view and create the report shown in Figure 4–85. Group the report by Item Type and sort by Description within Item Type. Display the average wholesale cost. If there are 5 or fewer items on hand, the value should appear in a red bold font. Save the changes to the report.

| | Item Status Report | | | Tuesday, September 12, 2017 12:58:03 PM |

Item Type	Item Number	Description	On Hand	Wholesale Price
Activity				
	3673	Amazing Math Fun	8	$12.50
	4553	Cosmos Explained	9	$8.95
	4573	Crystal Growing Kit	7	$6.75
	5923	Discovery Dinosaurs	3	$12.35
	6325	Fun Straws	20	$4.55
	7934	Gyrobot	24	$27.99
	8590	Paper Airplanes	22	$7.10
	9201	Sidewalk Art and More	15	$9.35
	9458	Slime Time Fun	15	$15.35
				$11.65

Item Type	Item Number	Description	On Hand	Wholesale Price
Novelty				
	3663	Agate Bookends	4	$18.25
	4583	Dinosaur Ornament	12	$7.50
	6185	Fibonacci Necklace	5	$16.75
	8344	Onyx Jar	2	$7.50
				$12.50
				$11.20

Figure 4–85

4. Filter the report for all items where the number on hand is less than 10. Save the filtered report as Filtered Item Status Report.

5. Use the Report Wizard to create the Items by Vendor report shown in Figure 4–86. The report is grouped by Vendor Name and sorted by Description within Vendor Name. There are no subtotals or totals.

6. If requested to do so by your instructor, rename the Items by Vendor report as Items by First Name Last Name where First Name and Last Name are your first and last names.

7. Submit the revised database in the format specified by your instructor.

8. ✸ How could you modify the Items by Vendor report to display the average wholesale cost?

Continued >

In the Labs *continued*

Items by Vendor

Vendor Name	Description	Item Number	Wholesale
Atherton Wholesalers			
	Amazing Math Fun	3673	$12.50
	Big Book of Why	3873	$7.99
	Crystal Growing Kit	4573	$6.75
	Discovery Dinosaurs	5923	$12.35
	Gem Nature Guide	7123	$9.50
	Onyx Jar	8344	$7.50
Gift Sundries			
	Agate Bookends	3663	$18.25
	Dinosaur Ornament	4583	$7.50
	Fibonacci Necklace	6185	$16.75
	Gyrobot	7934	$27.99
	Sidewalk Art and More	9201	$9.35
Sinz Distributors			
	Cosmos Explained	4553	$8.95
	Fun Straws	6325	$4.55
	Fun with Science	6234	$12.95
	Geek Guide	6345	$5.10
	Paper Airplanes	8590	$7.10
	Slime Time Fun	9458	$15.35

Figure 4–86

Lab 3: Consider This: Your Turn

Presenting Data in the JSP Analysis Database

Note: To complete this assignment, you will be required to use the Data Files. Please contact your instructor for information about accessing the Data Files.

Instructions: Open the Lab 3 JSP Analysis database from the Data Files. Then, use the concepts and techniques presented in this module to perform each of the following tasks:

Part 1: JSP Analysis is a small company that provides marketing research services to the nonprofit, service, and retail sectors. You are doing an internship at JSP and the owner has asked you to create two reports and a form.

    a. Modify the Client Financial Report so that the report is grouped by marketing analyst number. Sort the report by client number within marketing analyst number. Use conditional formatting to highlight any values in the Current Due field that are greater than $5,000.00. Include subtotals and totals for the currency fields.

b. Create a report that includes data from both the Marketing Analyst table and the Client table. Include the Marketing Analyst Number, First Name, and Last Name from the Marketing Analyst table. Include the Client Number, Client Name, Amount Paid, and Current Due fields from the Client table. Group the report by marketing analyst number and sort by client number. Include subtotals for the two currency fields. Change the orientation to landscape. Adjust the size of the summary controls and move the page number control so the report prints on one page.

c. Create a form for the Client table. Include the Client Number, Client Name, Amount Paid, Current Due, Total Amount, Marketing Analyst Number, and Client Type fields on the form.

d. Filter the form you created in Step c for all accounts where the Amount Paid is greater than $4,000.00 and sort the results in descending order by amount paid. Save the form as Filtered Form.

e. Create mailing labels for the Client table that are similar to the labels shown in Figure 4–75. Sort the labels by postal code.

f. Submit your assignment in the format specified by your instructor.

Part 2: You made several decisions while creating these reports and forms, including conditionally formatting values. What was the rationale behind your decisions? Which formatting option did you choose for the conditional formatting? Why? What other options are available?

PrattLast Associates : Database- C:\Users\Owner\Documents\CIS

Microsoft Access 2016

File   Home   Create   External Data   Database Tools   ♀ Tell me what you want to do...

5 | Multiple-Table Forms

Objectives

You will have mastered the material in this module when you can:

- Add Yes/No, Long Text, OLE Object, and Attachment fields
- Use the Input Mask Wizard
- Update fields and enter data
- Change row and column size
- Create a form with a subform in Design view
- Modify a subform and form design

- Enhance the form title
- Change tab stops and tab order
- Use the form to view data and attachments
- View object dependencies
- Use Date/Time, Long Text, and Yes/No fields in a query
- Create a form with a datasheet

Introduction

This module adds to the PrattLast database several new fields that require special data types. It then creates a form incorporating data from two tables. Recall that the two tables, Account Manager and Account, are related in a one-to-many relationship, with one account manager being related to many accounts, but each account being related to only one account manager. The form that you create will show one account manager at a time, but also will include the many accounts of that account manager. This module also creates queries that use the added fields.

Project — Multiple-Table Forms

PrattLast Associates uses its database to keep records about accounts and account managers. After using the database for several months, however, PrattLast has found that it needs to maintain additional data on its account managers. The company wants to identify those account managers who have reached their Professional in Human Resources (PHR) certification. They also want to include each account manager's special skills as well as the account manager's picture. Additionally, account managers now maintain files about current and potential accounts. These files are separate from the database; some are maintained in Word and others in Excel. PrattLast would like a way to attach these files to the corresponding account manager's record in the

BTW
Touch Screen Differences
The Office and Windows interfaces may vary if you are using a touch screen. For this reason, you might notice that the function or appearance of your touch screen differs slightly from this module's presentation.

BTW
Touch and Pointers
Remember that if you are using your finger on a touch screen, you will not see the pointer.

database. Finally, PrattLast wants to add the Phone Number field to the Account Manager table. Users should type only the digits in the telephone number and then have Access format the number appropriately. If the user enters 8255553455, for example, Access will format the number as (825) 555–3455.

After the proposed fields have been added to the database, PrattLast wants users to be able to use a form that incorporates the Account and Account Manager tables and includes the newly added fields as well as some of the existing fields in the Account Manager table. The form should also include the account number, name, amount paid, and current due amount for the accounts of each account manager. PrattLast would like to see multiple accounts for each account manager on the screen at the same time (Figure 5–1). The database should allow users to scroll through all the accounts of an account manager and to open any of the attachments concerning the account manager's account notes. Finally, PrattLast requires queries that use the PHR Certification, Start Date, and Special Skills fields.

Figure 5–1

Microsoft Access 2016

File   Home   Create   External Data   Database Tools   Tell me what you want to do...

PrattLast Associates : Database- C:\Users\Owner\Documents\CIS

In this module, you will learn how to create and use the form shown in Figure 5–1. The following roadmap identifies general activities you will perform as you progress through this module:

1. ADD FIELDS to the Account Manager table.
2. ENTER DATA into the new fields.
3. CREATE a FORM for the Account Manager table.
4. ADD CONTROLS to the form.
5. ADD a SUBFORM to the form.
6. MODIFY the SUBFORM.
7. ENHANCE the FORM.
8. CREATE QUERIES with the new fields.

Adding Special Fields

Having analyzed its requirements, the management of PrattLast has identified a need for some new fields for the Account Manager table. They need a Phone Number field and they want to assist users in entering the correct format for a phone number, so the field will use an input mask. An **input mask** specifies how data is to be entered and how it will appear. For example, an input mask can indicate that a phone number has parentheses around the first three digits and a hyphen between the sixth and seventh digits.

PrattLast also needs a PHR Certification field, which uses a value of Yes or No to indicate whether an account manager has attained the Professional in Human Resources certification; this field's data type will be Yes/No. They need a Special Skills field that identifies each manager's unique abilities, which will be a Long Text field. The Account Notes field, which must be able to contain multiple attachments for each account manager, will be an Attachment field. The Picture field is the only field whose data type is uncertain — it could be either OLE Object, which can contain objects created by a variety of applications, or Attachment.

Certainly, OLE Object is an appropriate data type for a picture, because when you store an image as an OLE object, the image becomes a part of the database. On the other hand, if an Attachment field contains picture, the field will display an icon indicating that there is a picture as an attachment. Other types of attachments, such as Word documents and Excel workbooks, would also appear in the Attachment field as an icon representing the type of attachment. You can then open the attachment. In the case of a picture, this action will display the picture. In the case of a Word document, it will open the file in Word. PrattLast Associates has decided to use OLE Object as the Picture field data type for two reasons. First, the form shown in Figure 5–1 contains another field that must be an Attachment field, the Account Notes field. In Datasheet view, an Attachment field appears as a paper clip rather than the field name. Thus, if the Picture field were also an Attachment field, the form would display two paper clips, leading to potential confusion. A second potential problem with using an Attachment field for pictures occurs when you have multiple attachments to a record. Only the first attachment routinely appears in the field on either a datasheet or form. Thus, if the picture were not the first attachment, it would not appear.

BTW

The Ribbon and Screen Resolution
Access may change how the groups and buttons within the groups appear on the ribbon, depending on the computer's screen resolution. Thus, your ribbon may look different from the ones in this book if you are using a screen resolution other than 1366 × 768.

BTW

OLE Object Fields
OLE Object Fields can store video clips, sound, and other objects from Windows-based apps.

BTW

Long Text Fields
Long Text fields can store up to a gigabyte of text. If you need to keep a historical record of changes to a Long Text field, set the value for the Append Only property to Yes. To use formatting such as bold and underline in a Long Text field, set the value for the Text Format property to Rich Text.

BTW

Adding Captions to Attachment Fields
You can add a caption to an Attachment field. To add a caption in Design view, use the Caption property box.

To Add Fields with New Data Types to a Table

1 ADD FIELDS | 2 ENTER DATA | 3 CREATE FORM | 4 ADD CONTROLS | 5 ADD SUBFORM
6 MODIFY SUBFORM | 7 ENHANCE FORM | 8 CREATE QUERIES

You add the new fields to the Account Manager table by modifying the design of the table and inserting the fields at the appropriate position in the table structure. The following steps add the PHR Certification, Special Skills, Picture, and Account Notes fields to the Account Manager table. *Why? PrattLast has determined that they need these fields added to the table.*

- Run Access and open the database named PrattLast Associates from your hard disk, OneDrive, or other storage location. If you do not have the PrattLast Associates database, contact your instructor for the required file.

- If necessary, enable the content and open the Navigation Pane.

- Right-click the Account Manager table to display a shortcut menu (Figure 5–2).

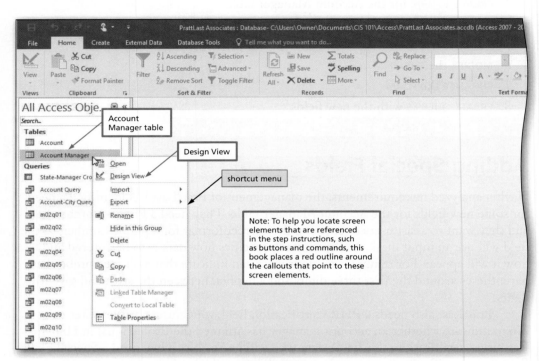

Figure 5–2

- Click Design View on the shortcut menu to open the table in Design view (Figure 5–3).

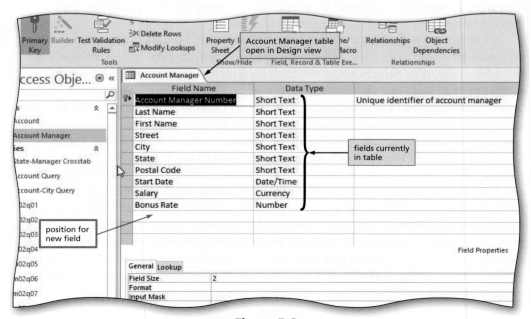

Figure 5–3

- Click the first open field to select the position for the first additional field.

- Type **PHR Certification** as the field name, press the TAB key, click the Data Type arrow, select Yes/No as the data type, and then press the TAB key twice to move to the next field.

- Use the same technique to add a field with Special Skills as the field name and Long Text as the data type, a field with Picture as the field name and OLE Object as the data type, and a field with Account Notes as the field name and Attachment as the data type (Figure 5–4).

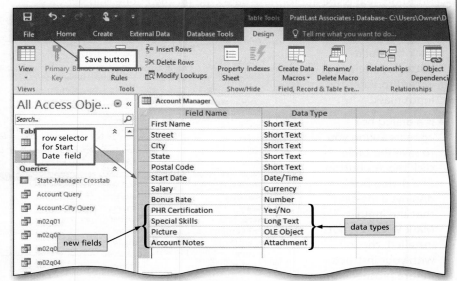

Figure 5–4

- Click the Save button on the Quick Access Toolbar to save your changes.

To Use the Input Mask Wizard

1 ADD FIELDS | 2 ENTER DATA | 3 CREATE FORM | 4 ADD CONTROLS | 5 ADD SUBFORM
6 MODIFY SUBFORM | 7 ENHANCE FORM | 8 CREATE QUERIES

As mentioned previously, an input mask specifies how data, such as a phone number, is to be entered and how it will appear. You can enter an input mask directly, but you usually will use the Input Mask Wizard. **Why?** *The wizard assists you in the creation of the input mask by allowing you to select from a list of the most frequently used input masks.*

To use the Input Mask Wizard, select the Input Mask property in the field's property sheet and then select the Build button. The following steps add the Phone Number field and then specify how the telephone number is to appear by using the Input Mask Wizard.

- Right-click the row selector for the Start Date field (shown in Figure 5–4) to produce a shortcut menu, and then click Insert Rows to insert a blank row above Start Date.

- Click the Field Name column for the new field.

- Type **Phone Number** as the field name, and then press the TAB key to enter the field.

- Click the Input Mask property box (Figure 5–5).

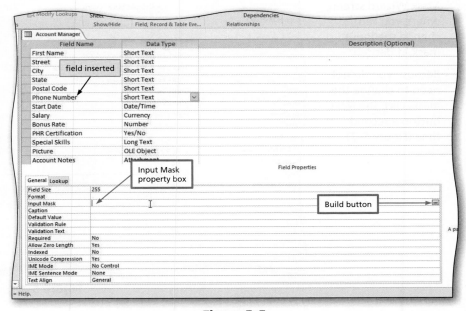

Figure 5–5

Q&A Do I need to change the data type?

No. Short Text is the appropriate data type for the Phone Number field.

2

- Click the Build button to use a wizard to enter the input mask.

- If a dialog box appears asking you to save the table, click the Yes button. (If a dialog box displays a message that the Input Mask Wizard is not installed, check with your instructor before proceeding with the following steps.)

- Ensure that Phone Number is selected (Figure 5–6).

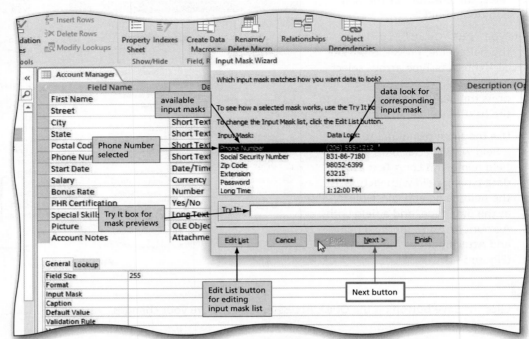

Figure 5–6

Experiment

- Click different input masks and enter data in the Try It text box to see the effect of the input mask. When you are done, click the Phone Number input mask.

3

- Click the Next button to move to the next Input Mask Wizard screen, where you can change the input mask, if desired.

- Because you do not need to change the mask, click the Next button a second time (Figure 5–7).

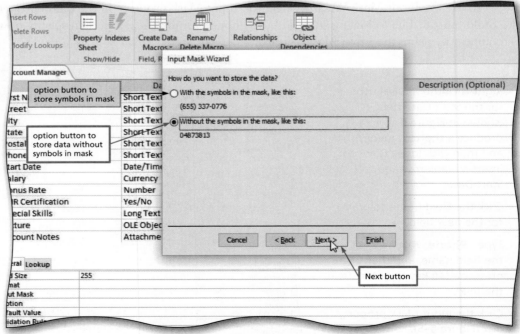

Figure 5–7

4

- Be sure the 'Without the symbols in the mask, like this' option button is selected, click the Next button to move to the next Input Mask Wizard screen, and then click the Finish button (Figure 5–8).

Why does the data type not change to Input Mask?

The data type of the Phone Number field is still Short Text. The only thing that changed is one of the field properties, the Input Mask property.

Could I have typed the value in the Input Mask property myself, rather than using the wizard?

Yes. Input masks can be complex, however, so it is usually easier and safer to use the wizard.

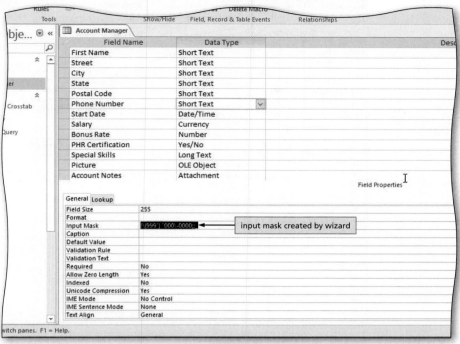

Figure 5–8

5

- Click the Save button on the Quick Access Toolbar to save your changes.
- Close the Account Manager table.

Adding Fields in Datasheet View

Previously you added fields to a table using Design view. You can also add fields in Datasheet view. One way to do so is to use the Add & Delete group on the Table Tools Fields tab (Figure 5–9). Select the field that precedes the position where you want to add the new field and then click the appropriate button. You can click the Short Text button to add a Short Text field, the Number button to add a Number field, the Currency button to add a Currency field, and so on. Alternatively, you can click the More Fields button as shown in the figure to display the Data Type gallery. You then can click a data type in the gallery to add a field with that type.

The gallery provides more options for ways to display various types of data. For example, if you click the Check Box version of a Yes/No field, the field will be displayed as a check box, which is the common way to display such a field. If instead you click the Yes/No version of a Yes/No field, the value in the field will be displayed as either the word, Yes, or the word, No.

If you scroll down in the Data Type gallery, you will find a Quick Start section. The commands in this section give you quick ways of adding some common types of fields. For example, clicking Address in the Quick Start section immediately adds several fields: Address, City, State Province, Zip Postal, and Country Region. Clicking Start and End Dates immediately adds both a Start Date field and an End Date field.

BTW

Input Mask Characters
When you create an input mask, Access adds several characters. These characters control the literal values that appear when you enter data. For example, the first backslash in the input mask in Figure 5 -8 displays the opening parenthesis. The double quotes force Access to display the closing parenthesis and a space. The second backslash forces Access to display the hyphen that separates the first and second part of the phone number.

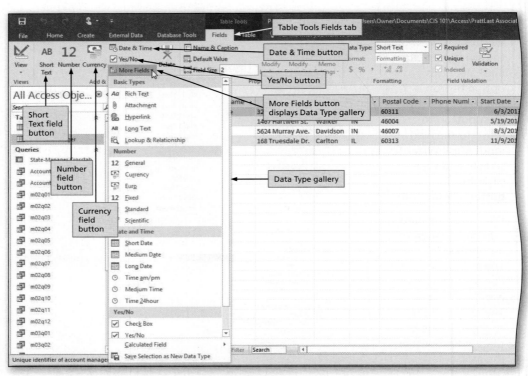

Figure 5–9

In Datasheet view, you can rename fields by right-clicking the field name, clicking Rename Field on the shortcut menu, and then typing the new name. Delete a field by clicking the field and then clicking the Delete button (Table Tools Fields tab | Add & Delete group). Move a field from one location to another by dragging the field.

CONSIDER THIS

How do you determine if fields need special data types or an input mask?

Determine whether an input mask is appropriate. Sometimes the data in the field should be displayed in a special way, for example, with parentheses and a hyphen like a phone number, or separated into three groups of digits like a Social Security number. If so, should Access assist the user in entering the data in the right format? For example, by including an input mask in a field, Access can automatically insert the parentheses and a hyphen when a user enters phone number digits.

Determine whether the Yes/No data type is appropriate. A field is a good candidate for the Yes/No data type if the only possible field values are Yes or No, True or False, or On or Off.

Determine whether the Long Text data type is appropriate. A field that contains text that is variable in length and potentially very long is an appropriate use of the Long Text data type. If you want to use special text effects, such as bold and italic, you can assign the field the Long Text data type and change the value of the field's Text Format property from Plain Text to Rich Text. You can also collect history on the changes to a Long Text field by changing the value of the field's Append Only property from No to Yes. If you do so, when you right-click the field and click Show Column History on the shortcut menu, you will see a record of all changes made to the field.

Determine whether the OLE Object data type is appropriate. Does the field contain a picture? Does it contain an object created by other applications that support **OLE (Object Linking and Embedding)?**

Determine whether the Attachment data type is appropriate. Will the field contain one or more attachments that were created in other applications? If so, the Attachment data type is appropriate. It allows you to store multiple attachments on each record. You can view and manipulate these attachments in their original application.

Determine whether the Hyperlink data type is appropriate. A field with the hyperlink data type contains a hyperlink, that is, a link to another location such as a webpage or a file. Will the field contain an email address, links to other Office documents, or links to webpages? If so, Hyperlink is appropriate.

Updating the New Fields

After adding the new fields to the table, the next task is to enter data into the fields. The data type determines the manner in which this is accomplished. The following sections cover the methods for updating fields with an input mask, Yes/No fields, Long Text fields, OLE fields, and Attachment fields. They also show how you would enter data in Hyperlink fields.

To Enter Data Using an Input Mask

1 ADD FIELDS | 2 ENTER DATA | 3 CREATE FORM | 4 ADD CONTROLS | 5 ADD SUBFORM
6 MODIFY SUBFORM | 7 ENHANCE FORM | 8 CREATE QUERIES

Why? *When you are entering data in a field that has an input mask, Access will insert the appropriate special characters in the proper positions. This means Access will automatically insert the parentheses around the area code, the space following the second parenthesis, and the hyphen in the Phone Number field.* The following steps use the input mask to add the telephone numbers.

- Open the Account Manager table and close the Navigation Pane.

- Click at the beginning of the Phone Number field on the first record to display an insertion point in the field (Figure 5–10).

Q&A
I do not see the parentheses and hyphen as shown in the figure. Did I do something wrong?
Depending on exactly where you click, you might not see the symbols. Regardless, as soon as you start typing in the field, the symbols should appear.

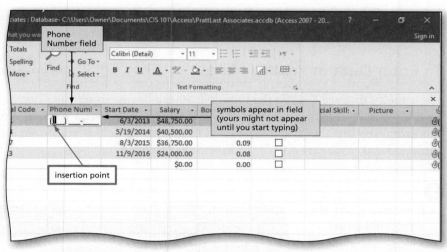

Figure 5–10

2

- Type **8255553455** as the telephone number (Figure 5–11).

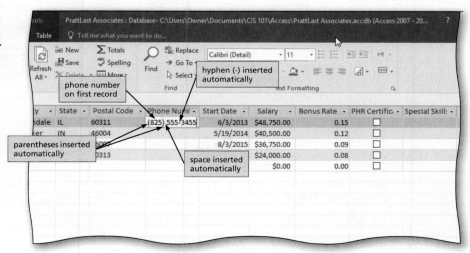

Figure 5–11

- Use the same technique to enter the remaining telephone numbers, as shown in Figure 5–12.
- If requested to do so by your instructor, change the phone number for account manager 42 to your phone number.

Q&A

Do I need to click at the beginning of the field?

Yes. If you do not, the data will not be entered correctly.

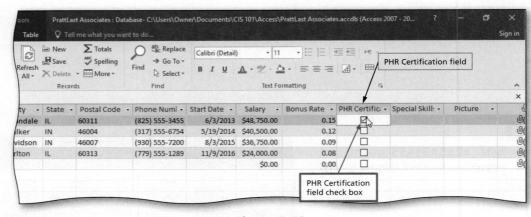

Figure 5–12

1 ADD FIELDS | 2 ENTER DATA | 3 CREATE FORM | 4 ADD CONTROLS | 5 ADD SUBFORM
6 MODIFY SUBFORM | 7 ENHANCE FORM | 8 CREATE QUERIES

To Enter Data in Yes/No Fields

Fields that are Yes/No fields contain check boxes. To set the value to Yes, place a check mark in the check box. *Why? A check mark indicates the value is Yes or True.* To set a value to No, leave the check box blank. The following step sets the value of the PHR Certification field, a Yes/No field, to Yes for the first record. The other three account managers do not yet have their certification.

- If necessary, click the right scroll arrow (shown in Figure 5–15) until the new fields appear.
- Click the check box in the PHR Certification field on the first record to place a check mark in the box (Figure 5–13).

Figure 5–13

1 ADD FIELDS | 2 ENTER DATA | 3 CREATE FORM | 4 ADD CONTROLS | 5 ADD SUBFORM
6 MODIFY SUBFORM | 7 ENHANCE FORM | 8 CREATE QUERIES

To Enter Data in Long Text Fields

To update a long text field, simply type the data in the field. You will later change the spacing to allow more room for the text. *Why? With the current row and column spacing on the screen, only a small portion of the text will appear.* The following steps enter each account manager's special skills.

1

- If necessary, click the right scroll arrow so the Special Skills field appears.
- Click the Special Skills field on the first record, and then type **Fluent in Spanish. Excellent organizational and communi- cation skills. Mentors new employees.** as the entry (Figure 5–14).

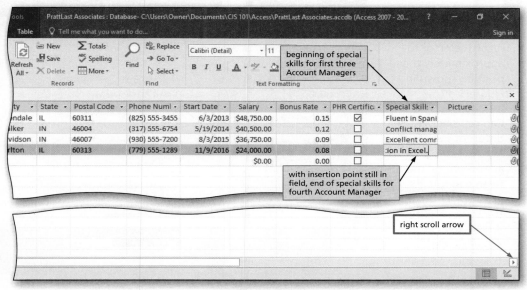

Figure 5–14

2

- Click the Special Skills field on the second record, and then type **Conflict management and negotiation skills. Excels at labor relations.** as the entry.
- Click the Special Skills field on the third record, and then type **Excellent communication skills. Previous IT experience. Familiar with human resources management software.** as the entry.
- Click the Special Skills field on the fourth record, and then type **Accounting background. Microsoft certification in Excel.** as the entry (Figure 5–15).

Figure 5–15

To Change the Row and Column Size

1 ADD FIELDS | 2 ENTER DATA | 3 CREATE FORM | 4 ADD CONTROLS | 5 ADD SUBFORM
6 MODIFY SUBFORM | 7 ENHANCE FORM | 8 CREATE QUERIES

Only a small portion of the special skills data appears in the datasheet. To allow more of the information to appear, you can expand the size of the rows and the columns. You can change the size of a column by using the field selector. The **field selector** is the bar containing the field name. To change the size of a row, you use a record's record selector.

The following steps resize the column containing the Special Skills field and the rows of the table. *Why? Resizing the column and the rows allows the entire Special Skills field text to appear.*

● Use the right scroll
arrow shown in
Figure 5–15 to
scroll the fields to
the position shown
in Figure 5–16,
and then drag the
right edge of the
field selector for
the Special Skills
field to the right to
resize the Special
Skills column to the
approximate
size shown in
Figure 5–16.

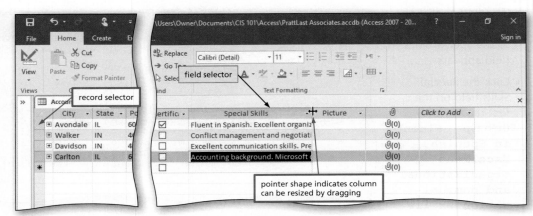

Figure 5–16

● Drag the lower
edge of the
record selector to
approximately the
position shown in
Figure 5–17.

◀ | Can rows be
Q&A | different sizes?
No. Access formats
all rows to be the
same size.

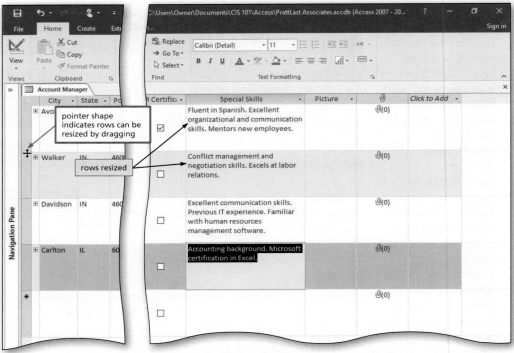

Figure 5–17

Other Ways

1. Right-click record selector, click Row Height to change row
   spacing

2. Right-click field selector, click Field Width to change column size

BTW

**Entering Data in
Long Text Fields**

You also can enter data in
a long text field using the
Zoom dialog box. To do so,
click the long text field and
then press SHIFT+F2 to open
the Zoom dialog box.

Undoing Changes to Row Height and Column Width

If you later find that the changes you made to the row height or the column
width are no longer appropriate, you can undo them. To undo changes to the row
height, right-click the row selector, click Row Height on the shortcut menu, and then
click the Standard Height check box in the Row Height dialog box. To undo changes
to the column width, right-click the field selector, click Field Width on the shortcut
menu, and then click the Standard Width check box in the Column Width dialog box.

To Enter Data in OLE Object Fields

1 ADD FIELDS | 2 ENTER DATA | 3 CREATE FORM | 4 ADD CONTROLS | 5 ADD SUBFORM
6 MODIFY SUBFORM | 7 ENHANCE FORM | 8 CREATE QUERIES

To insert data into an OLE Object field, you use the Insert Object command on the OLE field's shortcut menu. If the object is already created and stored in a file, you could choose to insert it directly from the file. The Insert Object command presents a list of the various types of objects that can be inserted, and it often is better to use one of these types rather than simply inserting from a file. ***Why?*** *Depending on your installation of Access, you might be limited to certain types of graphics files.* When you select a type of object to insert, Access will open the corresponding application to create the object. For example, if you select a Bitmap Image object type, Access will open Paint. You then can use that application to create the picture. In the case of Paint, you easily can create the picture by pasting the picture from a file.

The following steps insert pictures into the Picture field. The pictures will be visible as photographs in the form; however, the table will display the text, Bitmap Image, in the Picture field in the datasheet. The steps assume that the pictures are located in the same folder as your database.

1

- Ensure the Picture field appears on your screen, and then right-click the Picture field on the first record to produce a shortcut menu (Figure 5–18).

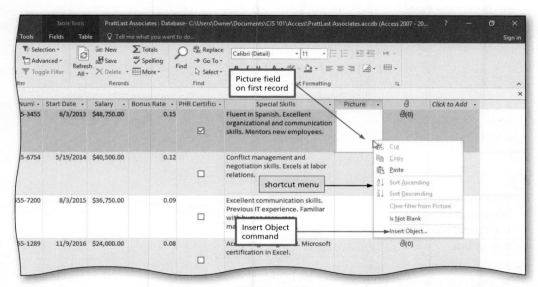

Figure 5–18

2

- Click Insert Object on the shortcut menu to display the Microsoft Access dialog box (Figure 5–19).

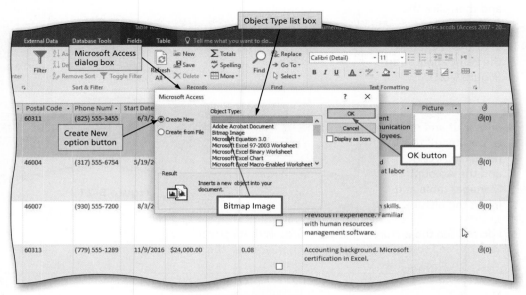

Figure 5–19

❸

- Select the Bitmap Image object type from the Object Type list.

- Click the OK button to open the Paint application.

 Q&A Unlike the figure, my window is maximized. Does that make a difference?
No. The same steps will work in either case.

- Click the Paste button arrow (Home tab | Clipboard group) in the Paint application to display the Paste menu (Figure 5–20).

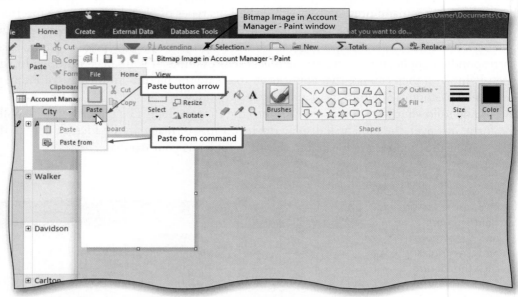

Figure 5–20

❹

- Click the Paste from command to display the Paste From dialog box.

- Navigate to the location for the .jpg file named haydee_rivera, select the file, and then click the Open button.

- Click the File tab in the Paint application (Figure 5–21).

❺

- Click 'Exit and return to document' to return to Access and the Account Manager table and insert the picture.

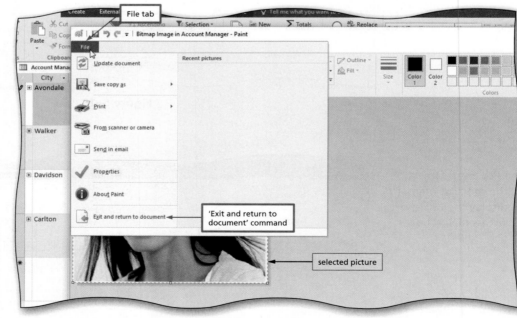

Figure 5–21

 Q&A I do not see the picture. I just see words. Is that correct?
Yes. You will see the actual picture when you use this field in a form.

How can you insert a picture using the 'Create from File' option button?

If your installation of Access supports adding files of the type you want to insert, you would use the following steps:

1. Click the 'Create from File' option button (Figure 5–19), and then click the Browse button to display the Browse dialog box.

2. Navigate to the folder containing the picture you want to insert.

3. Click the file containing the desired picture, and then click the OK button (Browse dialog box) to select the appropriate picture.

4. Click the OK button to complete the addition of the picture.

If the entries do not change to the words, Bitmap Image, after you move to a different record, your installation does not support the addition of your type of files. In that case, use the steps given under To Enter Data in OLE Object Fields.

To Insert the Remaining Pictures

The following step adds the remaining pictures.

 Insert the pictures into the second, third, and fourth records using the techniques illustrated in the previous set of steps. For the second record, select the picture named mark_simson. For the third record, select the picture named peter_lu. For the fourth record, select karen_murowski.

Q&A I see Paintbrush Picture rather than Bitmap Image. Did I do something wrong?

The entries will initially be Paintbrush Picture, but they should change to the words, Bitmap Image, after you move to another record. They should also change after you close and reopen the table.

To Enter Data in Attachment Fields

1 ADD FIELDS | 2 ENTER DATA | 3 CREATE FORM | 4 ADD CONTROLS | 5 ADD SUBFORM
6 MODIFY SUBFORM | 7 ENHANCE FORM | 8 CREATE QUERIES

To insert data into an Attachment field, you use the Manage Attachments command on the Attachment field's shortcut menu. *Why? The Manage Attachments command displays the Attachments dialog box, which you can use to attach as many files as necessary to the field.* The following steps attach two files to the first account manager and one file to the third account manager. The second and fourth account managers currently have no attachments.

1

- Ensure the Account Notes field, which has a paper clip in the field selector, appears on your screen, and then right-click the Account Notes field on the first record to produce a shortcut menu (Figure 5–22).

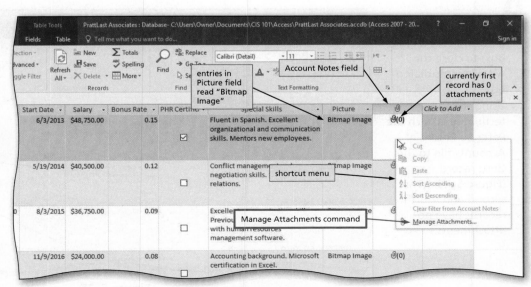

Figure 5–22

2

- Click Manage Attachments on the shortcut menu to display the Attachments dialog box (Figure 5–23).

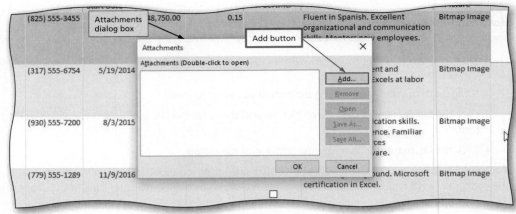

Figure 5–23

3

- Click the Add button (Attachments dialog box) to display the Choose File dialog box, where you can add an attachment.

- Navigate to the location containing your attachment files.

- Click Haydee Rivera Accounts, a Word file, and then click the Open button (Choose File dialog box) to attach the file.

- Click the Add button (Attachments dialog box).

- Click Haydee Rivera Potential Accounts, an Excel file, and then click the Open button to attach the second file (Figure 5–24).

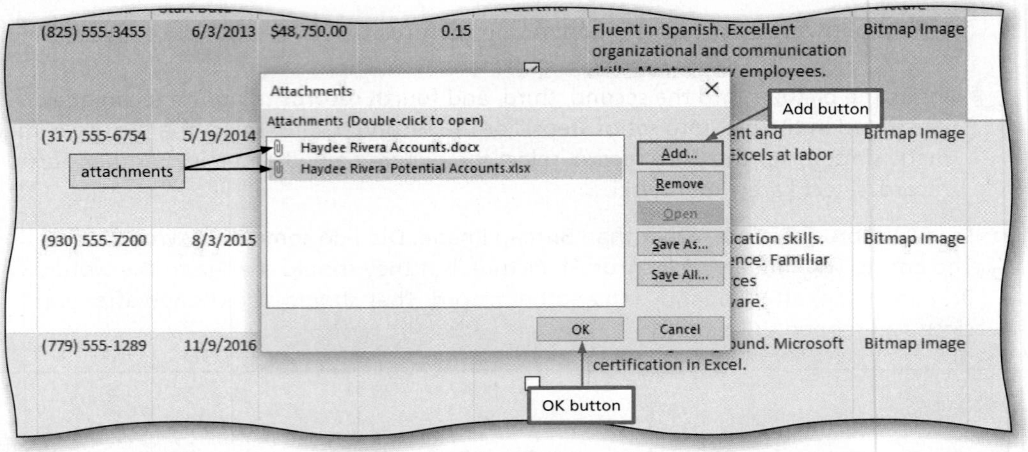

Figure 5–24

4

- Click the OK button (Attachments dialog box) to close the Attachments dialog box.

- Using the same technique, attach the Peter Lu Potential Accounts file to the third record (Figure 5–25). (The second and fourth records have no attachments.)

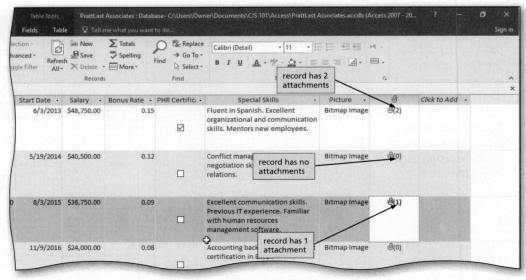

Figure 5–25

TO ENTER DATA IN HYPERLINK FIELDS

If your database contained a Hyperlink field, you would insert data by using the following steps.

1. Right-click the Hyperlink field in which you want to enter data to display a shortcut menu.
2. Point to Hyperlink on the shortcut menu to display the Hyperlink submenu.
3. Click Edit Hyperlink on the Hyperlink submenu to display the Insert Hyperlink dialog box.
4. Type the desired web address in the Address text box.
5. Click the OK button (Insert Hyperlink dialog box).

To Save the Properties

The row and column spacing are table properties. When changing any table properties, the changes apply only as long as the table is active *unless they are saved*. Once you have saved them, they will apply every time you open the table.

The following steps first save the properties and then close the table.

1 Click the Save button on the Quick Access Toolbar to save the changes to the table properties.

2 Close the table.

Viewing Pictures and Attachments in Datasheet View

Although the pictures do not appear on the screen, you can view them within the table. To view the picture of a particular account manager, right-click the Picture field for the account manager. Point to Bitmap Image Object on the shortcut menu, and then click Open. The picture will appear. Once you have finished viewing the picture, close the window containing the picture by clicking its Close button.

You can view the attachments in the Account Notes field by right-clicking the field and then clicking Manage Attachments on the shortcut menu. The attachments then appear in the Attachments dialog box. To view an attachment, click the attachment and then click the Open button (Attachments dialog box). The attachment will appear in its original application. After you have finished viewing the attachment, close the original application and close the dialog box.

Break Point: If you wish to stop working through the module at this point, you can resume the project at a later time by running Access, opening the database called PrattLast Associates, and continuing to follow the steps from this location forward.

Multiple-Table Form Techniques

With the additional fields in place, PrattLast Associates management is ready to incorporate data from both the Account Manager and Account tables in a single form. The form will display data concerning one account manager at a time. It will also display data concerning the many accounts assigned to the account manager. The relationship between account managers and accounts is a one-to-many relationship in which the Account Manager table is the "one" table and the Account table is the "many" table.

BTW
Hyperlink Fields
Hyperlink fields are used to store web or other Internet addresses and email addresses. Hyperlinks can find webpages, intranet servers, database objects (reports, forms, and such), and even documents on your computer or another networked mobile device.

BTW
Converting OLE Object Fields
OLE Object fields can occupy a great deal of space. To save space in your database, you can convert a picture from Bitmap Image to Picture (Device Independent Bitmap). To make the conversion, right-click the field, point to Bitmap Image Object, click Convert, and then select Picture (Device Independent Bitmap) in the Convert dialog box.

BTW
Viewing Attachments
To view attachments, you must have the application that created the attachment file installed on your computer.

To include the data for the many accounts of an account manager on the form, the account data will appear in a **subform**, which is a form that is contained within another form. The form in which the subform is contained is called the **main form**. Thus, the main form will contain account manager data, and the subform will contain account data.

CONSIDER THIS

When a form includes data from multiple tables, how do you relate the tables?
Once you determine that you need data from more than one table, you need to determine the main table and its relationship to any other table.

Determine the main table the form is intended to view and/or update. You need to identify the purpose of the form and the table it is really intended to show, which is the *main* table.

Determine how the additional table should fit into the form. If the additional table is the "many" part of the relationship, the data should probably be in a subform or datasheet. If the additional table is the "one" part of the relationship, the data should probably simply appear as fields on the form.

To Create a Form in Design View

1 ADD FIELDS | 2 ENTER DATA | 3 CREATE FORM | 4 ADD CONTROLS | 5 ADD SUBFORM
6 MODIFY SUBFORM | 7 ENHANCE FORM | 8 CREATE QUERIES

You can create a form in Design view. *Why? Design view gives you increased flexibility in laying out a form by using a blank design on which you place objects in the precise locations you want.* The following steps create a form in Design view.

• If necessary, open the Navigation Pane and be sure the Account Manager table is selected.

• Click Create on the ribbon to display the Create tab (Figure 5–26).

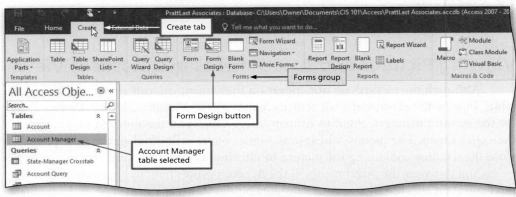

Figure 5–26

• Click the Form Design button (Create tab | Forms group) to create a new form in Design view.

• Close the Navigation Pane.

• If a field list does not appear, click the 'Add Existing Fields' button (Form Design Tools Design tab | Tools group) to

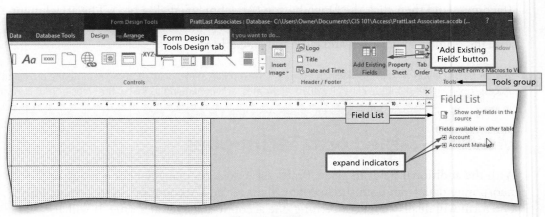

Figure 5–27

display a field list (Figure 5–27). If you do not see the tables listed, click, 'Show all tables'. (Your list might show all fields in the Account table.)

To Add a Control for a Field to the Form

To place a control for a field on a form, drag the field from the field list to the desired position. The following steps place the Account Manager Number field on the form. *Why? Dragging is the easiest way to place a field on a form.*

- If necessary, click the expand indicator for the Account Manager table to display the fields in the table. Drag the Account Manager Number field in the field list for the Account Manager table to the approximate position shown in Figure 5–28. (For illustration purposes, do not release the mouse button yet.)

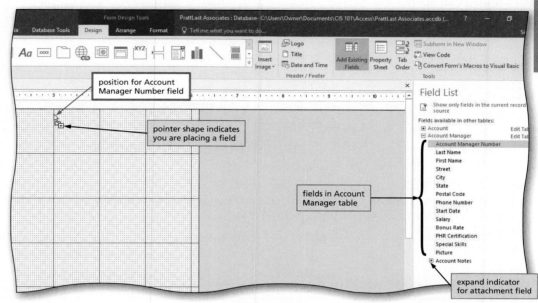

Figure 5–28

Q&A Do I have to be exact?

No. Just be sure you are in the same general location.

- Release the mouse button to place a control for the field (Figure 5–29).

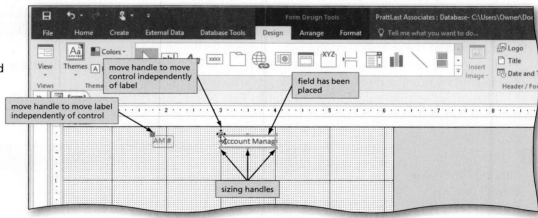

Figure 5–29

To Add Controls for Additional Fields

The following step places controls for the First Name, Last Name, Phone Number, Salary, Bonus Rate, Start Date, and PHR Certification fields on the form by dragging the fields from the field list. *Why? These fields all need to be included in the form.*

1

- Drag the First Name, Last Name, Phone Number, Salary, Bonus Rate, Start Date, and PHR Certification fields and their labels to the approximate positions shown in Figure 5–30.

Q&A

Do I have to align them precisely?
You can, but you do not need to. In the next steps, you will instruct Access to align the fields properly.

What if I drag the wrong field from the field list? Can I delete the control?
Yes. With the control selected, press the DELETE key.

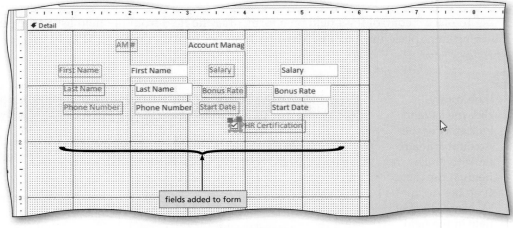

Figure 5–30

To Align Controls on the Left

1 ADD FIELDS | 2 ENTER DATA | 3 CREATE FORM | 4 ADD CONTROLS | 5 ADD SUBFORM
6 MODIFY SUBFORM | 7 ENHANCE FORM | 8 CREATE QUERIES

Why? *Often, you will want form controls to be aligned in some fashion. For example, the controls might be aligned so their right edges are even with each other. In another case, controls might be aligned so their top edges are even.* To ensure that a group of controls is aligned properly with each other, select all of the affected controls, and then use the appropriate alignment button on the Form Design Tools Arrange tab.

You can use one of two methods to select multiple controls. One way is to use a ruler. If you click a position on the horizontal ruler, you will select all the controls for which a portion of the control is under that position on the ruler. Similarly, if you click a position on the vertical ruler, you will select all the controls for which a portion of the control is to the right of that position on the ruler.

The second way to select multiple controls is to select the first control by clicking it. Then, select all the other controls by holding down the SHIFT key while clicking the control.

The following steps select the First Name, Last Name, and Phone Number controls and then align them so their left edges line up.

1

- Click the First Name control (the white space, not the label) to select the control.

- Hold the SHIFT key down and click the Last Name control to select an additional control. Do not release the SHIFT key.

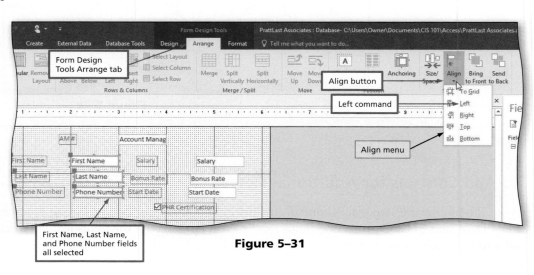

Figure 5–31

- Click the Phone Number control to select a third control, and then release the SHIFT key.

Q&A | I selected the wrong collection of fields. How can I start over?
Simply begin the process again, making sure you do not hold the SHIFT key down when you select the first field.

- Click Arrange on the ribbon to display the Form Design Tools Arrange tab.

- Click the Align button (Form Design Tools Arrange tab | Sizing & Ordering group) to display the Align menu (Figure 5–31).

2
- Click the Left command on the Align menu to align the controls on the left (Figure 5–32).

3
- Click outside any of the selected controls to deselect the controls.

- Using the same technique, align the labels for the First Name, Last Name, and Phone Number fields on the left.

- Using the same technique, align the Salary, Bonus Rate, and Start Date fields on the left.

- If necessary, align the labels for the Salary, Bonus Rate, and Start Date fields on the left.

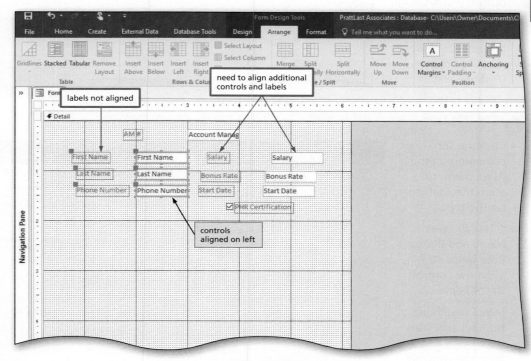

Figure 5–32

Other Ways

1. Right-click selected controls, point to Align

To Align Controls on the Top and Adjust Vertical Spacing

1 ADD FIELDS | 2 ENTER DATA | 3 CREATE FORM | 4 ADD CONTROLS | **5 ADD SUBFORM**
6 MODIFY SUBFORM | 7 ENHANCE FORM | 8 CREATE QUERIES

Why? Aligning the top edges of controls improves the neatness and appearance of a form. In addition, you might want the vertical spacing between controls to be the same. The following steps align the First Name and Salary controls so that they are aligned on the top. Once these controls are aligned, you adjust the vertical spacing so that the same amount of space separates each row of controls.

- Select the label for the First Name control, the First Name control, the label for the Salary control, and the Salary control.

- Click the Align button (Form Design Tools Arrange tab | Sizing & Ordering group) to display the Align menu (Figure 5–33).

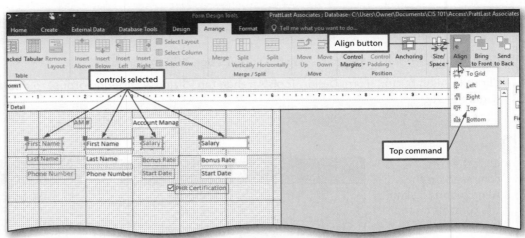

Figure 5–33

②

- Click the Top command on the Align menu to align the controls on the top.

- Select the Last Name and Bonus Rate fields and align the controls to the top.

- Select the Phone Number and Start Date fields and align the controls to the top.

- Click outside any of the selected controls to deselect the controls.

- Select the First Name, Last Name, Phone Number, Salary, Bonus Rate, and Start Date fields.

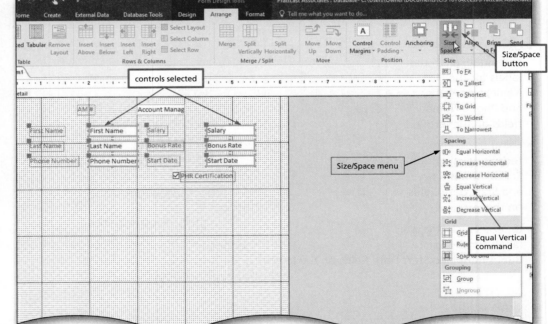

Figure 5–34

- Click the Size/Space button (Form Design Tools Arrange tab | Sizing & Ordering group) to display the Size/Space menu (Figure 5–34).

  Do I need to select the labels too?
No. If you select the control, its label also is selected.

③

- Click Equal Vertical on the Size/Space menu to specify the spacing.

  What is the purpose of the other commands on the Size/Space menu?
You can adjust the spacing to fit the available space. You can adjust the space to match the tallest, shortest, widest, or narrowest section. You can adjust the space to match the closest grid points. You can specify equal horizontal spacing. Finally, you can increase or decrease either the vertical or the horizontal spacing.

Q&A What do you do if the field list obscures part of the form, making it difficult to place fields in the desired locations?
You can move the field list to a different location by dragging its title bar. You can also resize the field list by pointing to the border of the field list so that the mouse pointer changes to a double-headed arrow. You then can drag to adjust the size.

- Because it is a good idea to save the form before continuing, click the Save button on the Quick Access Toolbar.

- Type `Account Manager Master Form` as the name of the form, and then click the OK button to save the form.

To Add Controls for the Remaining Fields

1 ADD FIELDS | 2 ENTER DATA | 3 CREATE FORM | 4 ADD CONTROLS | 5 ADD SUBFORM
6 MODIFY SUBFORM | 7 ENHANCE FORM | 8 CREATE QUERIES

The following steps place controls for the Special Skills, Picture, and Account Notes fields and also move their attached labels to the desired position. *Why? Controls for these fields are to be included in the completed form.*

1

- Drag the control for the Special Skills field from the field list to the approximate position shown in Figure 5–35.

Q&A Is there enough space on the form to add the Special Skills field?
Yes. The size of the form will expand as you drag the field to the form.

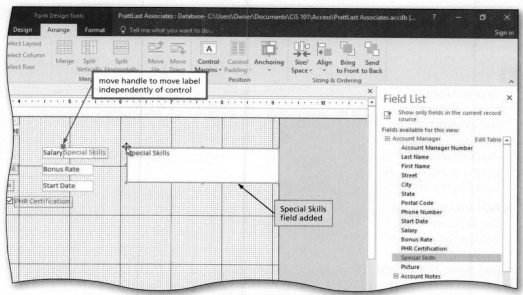

Figure 5–35

2

- Move the label for the Special Skills field to the position shown in Figure 5–36 by dragging its move handle.

Q&A I started to move the label and the control moved along with it. What did I do?
You were not pointing at the handle to move the label independently of the control.
Make sure you are pointing to the little box in the upper-left corner of the label.

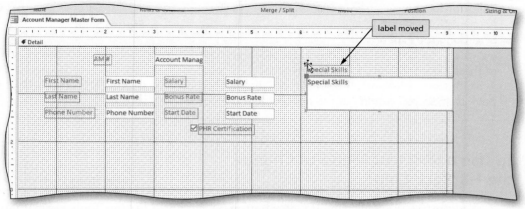

Figure 5–36

- Using the same techniques, move the control for the Picture field to the approximate position shown in Figure 5–37 and move its label to the position shown in the figure.

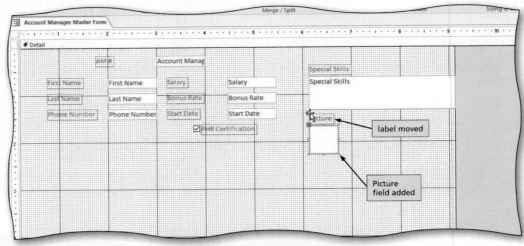

Figure 5–37

- Click the control for the Picture field and drag the lower-right corner to the approximate position shown in Figure 5–38 to resize the control.

- Add the control for the Account Notes field in the position shown in the figure and move its attached label to the position shown in the figure.

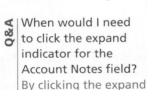

When would I need to click the expand indicator for the Account Notes field?

By clicking the expand indicator, you have access to three special properties of the field: FileData, FileName, and FileType. If you drag one of these onto the form, you will only get the corresponding information in the control. For example, if you drag Account Notes.FileName, the control will display the file name for the attachment. Most of the time, you want the field itself, so you would not use any of these properties.

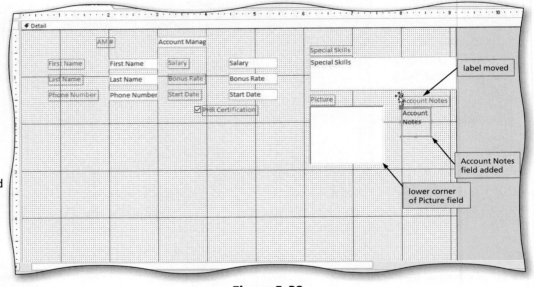

Figure 5–38

To Use a Shortcut Menu to Change the Fill/Back Color

1 ADD FIELDS | 2 ENTER DATA | 3 CREATE FORM | 4 ADD CONTROLS | 5 ADD SUBFORM
6 MODIFY SUBFORM | 7 ENHANCE FORM | 8 CREATE QUERIES

You can use the Background Color button on the Form Design Tools Format tab to change the background color of a form. You can also use a shortcut menu. The following steps use a shortcut menu to change the background color of the form to gray. **Why?** *Using a shortcut menu is a simple way to change the background color.*

1

• Right-click in the approximate position shown in Figure 5–39 to produce a shortcut menu.

Q&A

Does it matter where I right-click? You can right-click anywhere on the form as long as you are outside of all the controls.

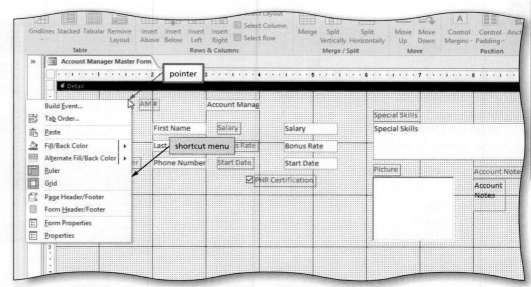

Figure 5–39

2

• Point to the 'Fill/ Back Color' arrow on the shortcut menu to display a color palette (Figure 5–40).

3

• Click the gray color (row 3, column 1) shown in Figure 5–40 to change the fill/ back color to gray.

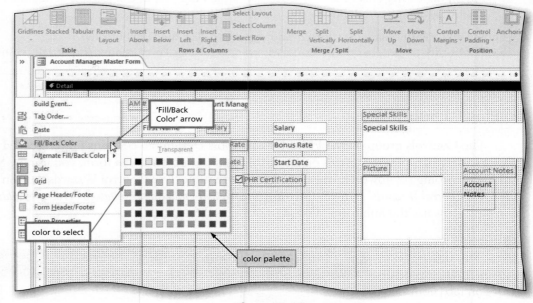

Figure 5–40

To Add a Title

1 ADD FIELDS | 2 ENTER DATA | 3 CREATE FORM | 4 ADD CONTROLS | **5 ADD SUBFORM**
6 MODIFY SUBFORM | 7 ENHANCE FORM | 8 CREATE QUERIES

A form should have a descriptive title. **Why?** *The title gives a concise visual description of the purpose of the form.* The following step adds a title to the form.

• Click Design on the ribbon to select the Form Design Tools Design tab.

• Click the Title button (Form Design Tools Design tab | Header/ Footer group) to add a title to the form (Figure 5–41).

Q&A

Could I change this title if I want something different?
Yes. Change it just like you change any other text.

Why is there a new section?
The form title belongs in the Form Header section. When you clicked the Title button, Access added the Form Header section automatically and placed the title in it.

Could I add a Form Header section without having to click the Title button?
Yes. Right-click anywhere on the form background and click Form Header/Footer on the shortcut menu.

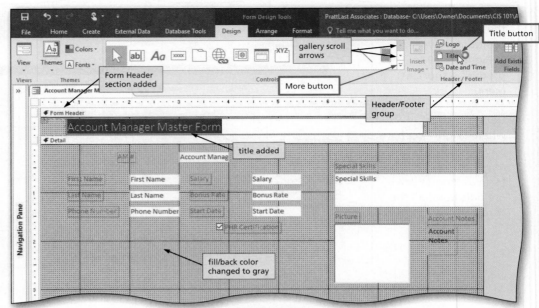

Figure 5–41

To Place a Subform

1 ADD FIELDS | 2 ENTER DATA | 3 CREATE FORM | 4 ADD CONTROLS | **5 ADD SUBFORM**
6 MODIFY SUBFORM | **7 ENHANCE FORM** | **8 CREATE QUERIES**

The Controls group on the Form Design Tools Design tab contains buttons called tools that you use to place a variety of types of controls on a form. To place a subform on a form, you use the Subform/Subreport tool. Before doing so, however, you should ensure that the 'Use Control Wizards' button is selected. *Why?* *If the 'Use Control Wizards' button is selected, a wizard will guide you through the process of adding the subform.* The following steps use the SubForm Wizard to place a subform.

1

• Click the More button (Form Design Tools Design tab | Controls group) (shown in Figure 5–41) to display a gallery of available tools (Figure 5–42).

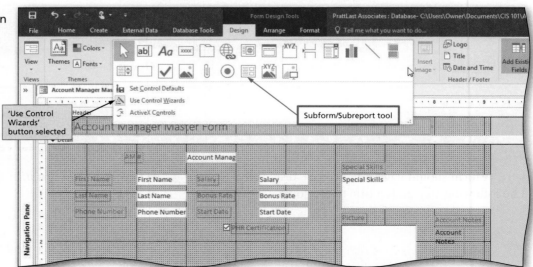

Figure 5–42

2

- Be sure the 'Use Control Wizards' button is selected, click the Subform/Subreport tool on the Form Design Tools Design tab, and then move the pointer to the approximate position shown in Figure 5–43.

Q&A How can I tell whether the 'Use Control Wizards' button is selected? The icon for the 'Use Control Wizards' button will be highlighted, as shown in Figure 5–42. If it is not, click the 'Use Control Wizards' button to select it, click the More button, and then click the Subform/Subreport tool.

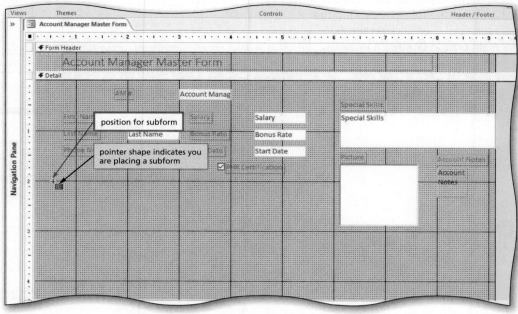

Figure 5–43

3

- Click the position shown in Figure 5–43 and then ensure the 'Use existing Tables and Queries' option button is selected (SubForm Wizard dialog box) (Figure 5–44).

Q&A My control is placed on the screen, but no wizard appeared. What should I do? Press the DELETE key to delete the control you placed. Ensure that the 'Use Control Wizards' button is selected, as described previously.

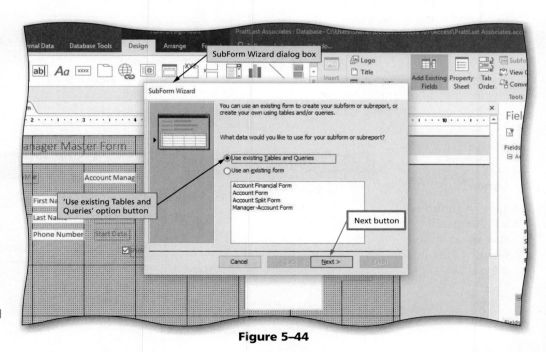

Figure 5–44

4

- Click the Next button.

- If the Account table is not already selected, click the Tables/Queries arrow, and then click the Account table to select it as the table that contains the fields for the subform.

- Add the Account Number, Account Name, Amount Paid, and Current Due fields by clicking the field, and then clicking the Add Field button (SubForm Wizard dialog box) (Figure 5–45).

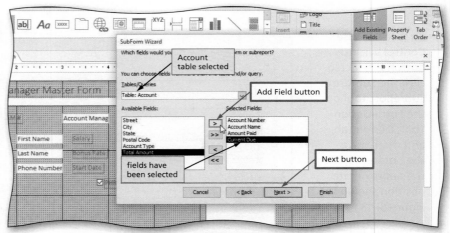

Figure 5–45

- Click the Next button to move to the next SubForm Wizard dialog box.
- Be sure the 'Choose from a list.' option button is selected (Figure 5–46).

Q&A

Why do I use this option?
Most of the time, Access will have determined the appropriate fields to link the subform and the main form and placed an entry specifying those fields in the list. By choosing from the list, you can take advantage of the information that Access has created for you. The other option is to define your own, in which case you would need to specify the appropriate fields.

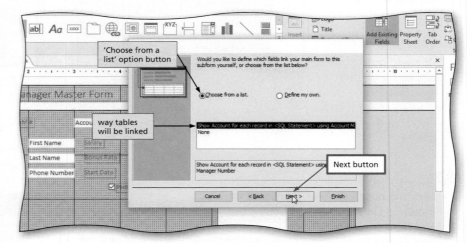

Figure 5–46

- Click the Next button.
- Type **Accounts of Account Manager** as the name of the subform (Figure 5–47).

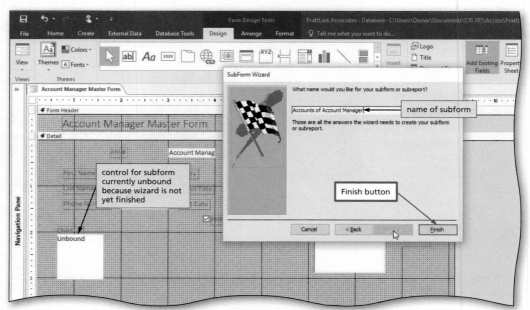

Figure 5–47

7

- Click the Finish button to place the subform.

- If necessary, move the subform control so that it does not overlap any other controls on the form (Figure 5–48).

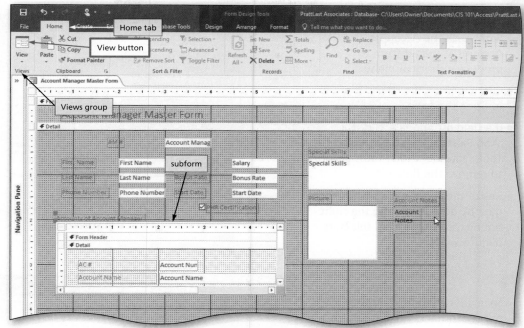

Figure 5–48

8

- Click the View button (Home tab | Views group) to view the form in Form view (Figure 5–49).

Q&A Everything looks good except the subform. I do not see all the fields I should see. What should I do?
You need to modify the subform, which you will do in the upcoming steps.

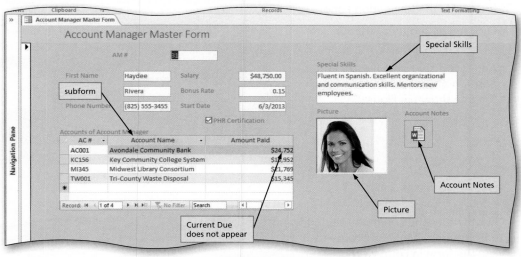

Figure 5–49

9

- Save and then close the form.

Break Point: If you wish to stop working through the module at this point, you can resume the project at a later time by running Access, opening the database called PrattLast Associates, and continuing to follow the steps from this location forward.

To Modify a Subform and Move the Picture

1 ADD FIELDS | 2 ENTER DATA | 3 CREATE FORM | 4 ADD CONTROLS | 5 ADD SUBFORM
6 MODIFY SUBFORM | 7 ENHANCE FORM | 8 CREATE QUERIES

The next task is to resize the columns in the subform, which appears on the form in Datasheet view. The subform exists as a separate object in the database; it is stored independently of the main form. The following steps open the subform and then resize the columns. *Why? The column sizes need to be adjusted so that the data is displayed correctly.* The steps then view the form and finally move and resize the picture.

- Open the Navigation Pane.

- Right-click the Accounts of Account Manager form to produce a shortcut menu.

- Click Open on the shortcut menu to open the form.

- If a field list appears, click the 'Add Existing Fields' button (Form Tools Datasheet tab | Tools group) to remove the field list.

- Resize the columns to best fit the data by double-clicking the right boundaries of the field selectors (Figure 5–50).

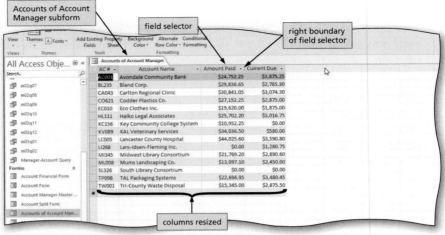

Figure 5–50

- Save your changes, and then close the subform.

- Open the Account Manager Master Form in Design view, and then close the Navigation Pane.

- Click the boundary of the subform to select it.

- Adjust the approximate size and position of your subform to match the one shown in Figure 5–51.

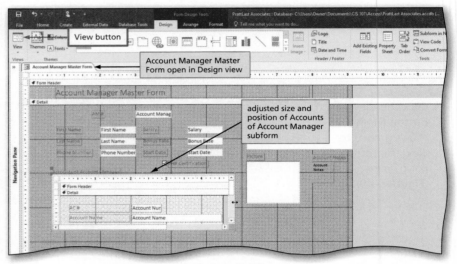

Figure 5–51

- Click the View button (Form Design Tools Design tab | Views group) to view the form in Form view (Figure 5–52).

Q&A
Could I have clicked the View arrow and then clicked Form View?
Yes. You can always use the arrow. If the icon for the view you want appears on the face of the View button, however, you can just click the button.

The picture seems to be a slightly different size from the one in Figure 5–1. How do I fix this?
You can move and also resize the picture, which you will do in the next step.

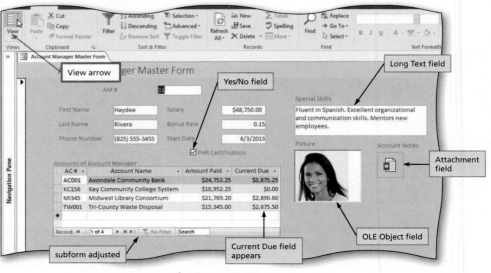

Figure 5–52

4

- Return to Design view, and then move and resize your picture to the approximate size and location shown in Figure 5–53.

Q&A

How can I tell if the new size and location is correct? View the form. If you are not satisfied with the size or location, return to Design view and make the necessary adjustments. Repeat the process until you are satisfied. You may have to allow a small amount of white on one of the borders of the picture. You will learn about some options you can use to adjust the specific look of the picture later in this module.

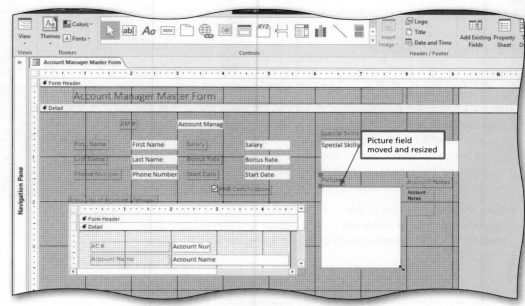

Figure 5–53

To Change a Label

1 ADD FIELDS | 2 ENTER DATA | 3 CREATE FORM | 4 ADD CONTROLS | 5 ADD SUBFORM
6 MODIFY SUBFORM | 7 ENHANCE FORM | 8 CREATE QUERIES

In Datasheet view, shortening the heading for the Account Manager Number column to AM # made sense to save room. Such a change is not necessary in the form. *Why? The form has enough room to display the entire field name, so adding the account manager label adds clarity.* In the form, there is plenty of room for the full field name to appear in the label. The following steps change the contents of the label from AM # to Account Manager Number.

1

- If necessary, return to Design view.

- Click the label for the Account Manager Number to select the label.

- Click the label a second time to produce an insertion point.

- Erase the current label (AM #), and then type **Account Manager Number** as the new label (Figure 5–54).

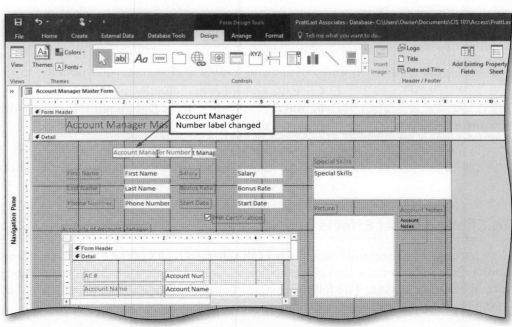

Figure 5–54

2

- Click outside the label to deselect it.

- Click the label to select it.

Q&A

Why did I need to deselect the label and then select it again? With the insertion point appearing in the label, you could not move the label. By deselecting it and then selecting it again, the label will be selected, but there will be no insertion point.

- Drag the move handle in the upper-left corner to move the label to the approximate position shown in Figure 5–55.

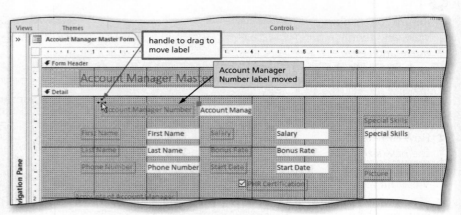

Figure 5–55

3

- Save your changes.

CONSIDER THIS

Is there any way to determine the way pictures fit within the control?
Yes. Access determines the portion of a picture that appears as well as the way it appears using the **size mode** property. The three size modes are as follows:

Clip — This size mode displays only a portion of the picture that will fit in the space allocated to it.

Stretch — This size mode expands or shrinks the picture to fit the precise space allocated on the screen. For photographs, usually this is not a good choice because fitting a photograph to the allocated space can distort the picture, giving it a stretched appearance.

Zoom — This size mode does the best job of fitting the picture to the allocated space without changing the look of the picture. The entire picture will appear and be proportioned correctly. Some white space may be visible either above or to the right of the picture, however.

BTW

Moving Controls
When you are dragging a label or control, you might need to make very small movements. You can use the arrow keys on the keyboard to make fine adjustments to control placement.

TO CHANGE THE SIZE MODE

Currently, the size mode for the picture should be Zoom, which is appropriate. If it were not and you wanted to change it, you would use the following steps.

1. Click the control containing the picture, and then click the Property Sheet button (Form Design Tools Design tab | Tools group) to display the control's property sheet.

2. Click the Size Mode property, and then click the Size Mode property arrow.

3. Click Zoom, and then close the property sheet by clicking its Close button.

To Change Label Effects and Colors

1 ADD FIELDS | 2 ENTER DATA | 3 CREATE FORM | 4 ADD CONTROLS | 5 ADD SUBFORM
6 MODIFY SUBFORM | 7 ENHANCE FORM | 8 CREATE QUERIES

Access allows you to change many of the characteristics of the labels in the form. You can change the border style and color, the background color, the font, and the font size. You can also apply special label effects, such as raised or sunken. The following steps change the font color of the labels and add special effects. *Why? Modifying the appearance of the labels improves the appearance of the form.*

1

- Click the Account Manager Number label to select it, if necessary.

- Select each of the remaining labels by holding down the SHIFT key while clicking the label. Be sure to include the label for the subform (Figure 5–56).

Q&A Does the order in which I select the labels make a difference?

No. The only thing that is important is that they are all selected when you are done.

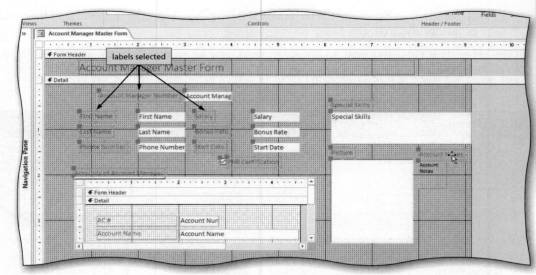

Figure 5–56

2

- Display the Form Design Tools Format tab.

- Click the Font Color arrow (Form Design Tools Format tab | Font group) to display a color palette (Figure 5–57).

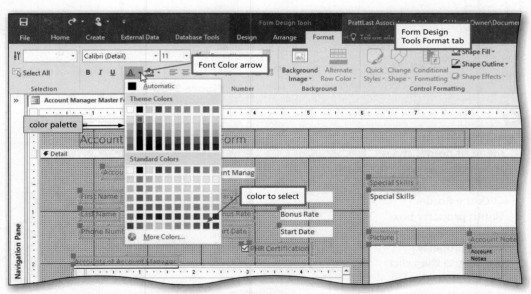

Figure 5–57

3

- Click the blue color in the second position from the right in the bottom row of Standard Colors to change the font color for the labels.

Experiment

- Try other colors by clicking the Font Color arrow and then clicking the other color to see which colors you think would be good choices for the font. View the form to see the effect of your choice, and then return to Design view. When done, select the blue color.

- Display the Form Design Tools Design tab.

- Click the Property Sheet button (Form Design Tools Design tab | Tools group) to produce the property sheet for the selected labels. If your property sheet appears on the left side of the screen, drag it to the right. Make sure the All tab is selected.

- Click the Border Style property box to display the Border Style property arrow, and then click the arrow to display a menu of border styles (Figure 5–58).

 Q&A The property sheet is too small to display the property arrow. Can I change the size of the property sheet?
Yes. Point to the border of the property sheet so that the pointer changes to a two-headed arrow. You then can drag to adjust the size.

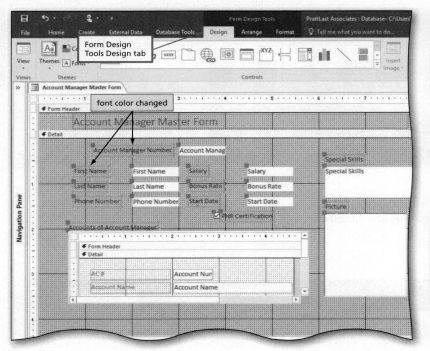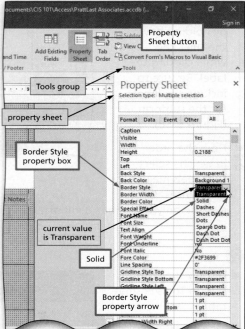

Figure 5–58

❹

- Click Solid in the menu of border styles to select a border style.

- Click the Border Width property box to display the Border Width property arrow, and then click the arrow to display a menu of border widths.

- Click 3 pt to change the border width to 3 pt.

- Click the Special Effect property box to display the Special Effect property arrow, and then click the arrow to display a menu of special effects (Figure 5–59).

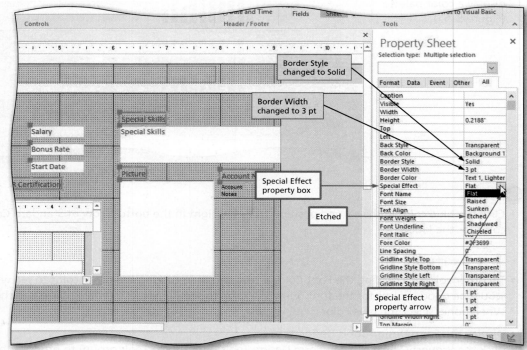

Figure 5–59

5

- Click Etched in the menu of special effects to select a special effect.

 Experiment

- Try other special effects. In each case, view the form to see the special effect you selected and then return to Design view. When you are done, select Etched.

- Click the Account Manager Number control (the white space, not the label) to select it.

- Select each of the remaining controls by holding down the SHIFT key while clicking the control. Do not include the subform.

- Select Sunken for the special effect (Figure 5–60).

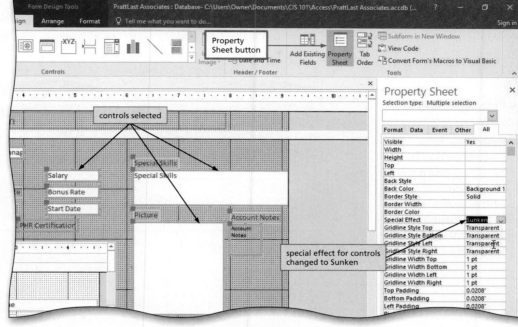

Figure 5–60

6

- Close the property sheet by clicking the Property Sheet button (Form Design Tools Design tab | Tools group).

- Click the View button to view the form in Form view (Figure 5–61).

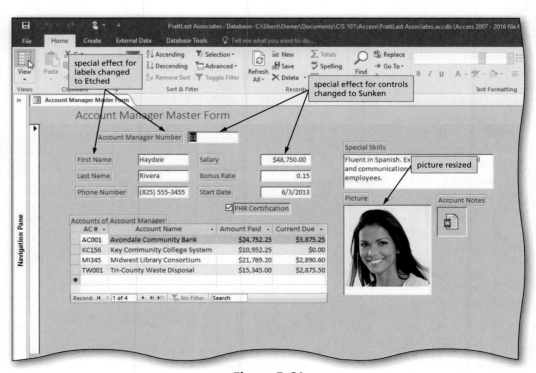

Figure 5–61

To Modify the Appearance of a Form Title

Why? You can enhance the title in a variety of ways by changing its appearance. These options include moving it, resizing it, changing the font size, changing the font weight, and changing the alignment. The following steps enhance the form title.

- Return to Design view.
- Resize the Form Header section by dragging down the lower boundary of the section to the approximate position shown in Figure 5–62.

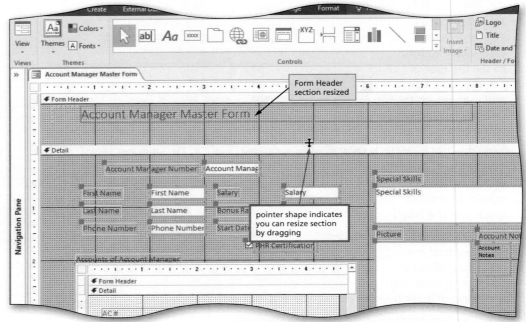

Figure 5–62

- Click the control containing the form title to select the control.
- Drag the lower-right sizing handle to resize the control to the approximate size shown in Figure 5–63.

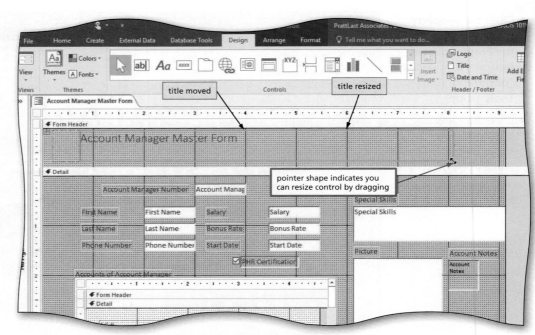

Figure 5–63

- Click the Property Sheet button (Form Design Tools Design tab | Tools group) to display the control's property sheet.

- Click the Font Size property box, click the Font Size property arrow, and then click 28 to change the font size.

- In a similar fashion, change the Text Align property value to Distribute and the Font Weight property value to Semi-bold (Figure 5–64).

- Close the property sheet by clicking the Property Sheet button (Form Design Tools Design tab | Tools group).

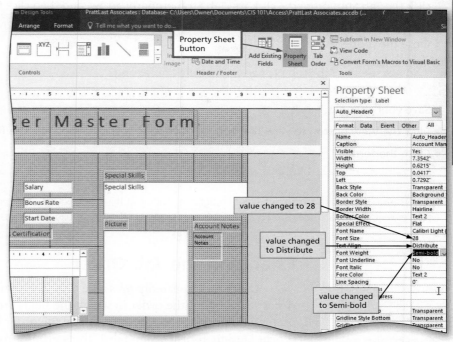

Figure 5–64

Other Ways

1. Enter font size value in Font Size box

To Change a Tab Stop

1 ADD FIELDS | 2 ENTER DATA | 3 CREATE FORM | 4 ADD CONTROLS | 5 ADD SUBFORM
6 MODIFY SUBFORM | **7 ENHANCE FORM** | **8 CREATE QUERIES**

Users can repeatedly press the TAB key to move through the controls on the form; however, they should bypass the Picture and Account Notes controls because users do not enter data into these fields. To omit these controls from the tab stop sequence, the following steps change the value of the Tab Stop property for the controls from Yes to No. *Why? Changing the Tab Stop property for these fields to No removes them from the Tab Stop sequence.*

- Click the Picture control to select it.

- Hold down the SHIFT key while clicking the Account Notes control to select it as well (Figure 5–65).

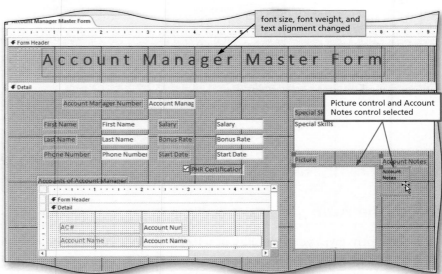

- Click the Property Sheet button (Form Design Tools Design tab | Tools group) to display the property sheet.

Figure 5–65

- Make sure the All tab (Property Sheet) is selected, click the down scroll arrow until the Tab Stop property appears, click the Tab Stop property, click the Tab Stop property arrow, and then click No to instruct Access to skip the Picture and Account Notes fields in the tab sequence.

- Close the property sheet.

Q&A

I do not see the Tab Stop property. What did I do wrong?
You clicked the labels for the controls, not the controls.

- Save your changes.

- Click the View button to view the form in Form view. It should look like the form shown in Figure 5–1.

- Close the form.

Break Point: If you wish to stop working through the module at this point, you can resume the project at a later time by running Access, opening the database called PrattLast Associates, and continuing to follow the steps from this location forward.

BTW
Auto Order Button
If you click the Auto Order button in the Tab Order dialog box, Access will create a top-to-bottom and left-to-right tab order.

Changing the Tab Order

Users can repeatedly press the TAB key to move through the fields on a form. Access determines the order in which the fields are encountered in this process. If you prefer a different order, you can change the order by clicking the Tab Order button (Form Design Tools Design tab | Tools group). You then can use the Tab Order dialog box (Figure 5–66) to change the order by dragging rows (fields) to their desired order as indicated in the dialog box.

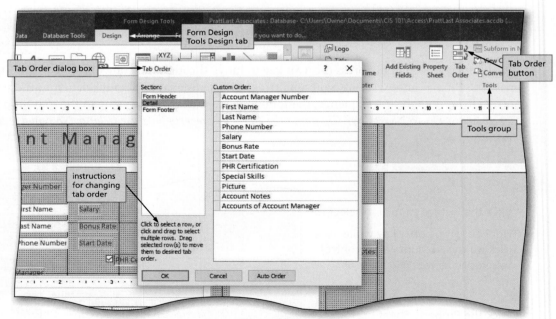

Figure 5–66

To Use the Form

1 ADD FIELDS | 2 ENTER DATA | 3 CREATE FORM | 4 ADD CONTROLS | 5 ADD SUBFORM
6 MODIFY SUBFORM | 7 ENHANCE FORM | **8 CREATE QUERIES**

The form gives you flexibility in selecting both account managers and the accounts of the account manager. *Why? You can use the Navigation buttons at the bottom of the screen to move among account managers. You can use the Navigation buttons in the subform to move among the accounts of the account manager currently shown on the screen.* The following steps use the form to display desired data.

1

- Open the Navigation Pane if it is currently closed.
- Right-click the Account Manager Master Form, and then click Open on the shortcut menu.
- Close the Navigation Pane.
- Right-click the Account Notes field to display a shortcut menu (Figure 5–67).

Figure 5–67

2

- Click the Manage Attachments command on the shortcut menu to display the Attachments dialog box (Figure 5–68).

Q&A How do I use this dialog box? Select an attachment and click the Open button to view the attachment in its original application. Click the Add button to add a new attachment or the Remove button to remove the selected attachment. By clicking the Save As button, you can save the selected attachment as a file in whatever location you specify. You can save all attachments at once by clicking the Save All button.

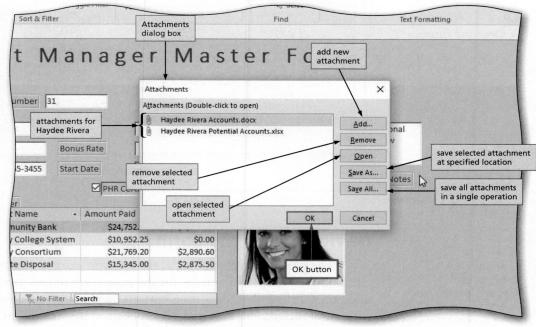

Figure 5–68

Experiment

- Open both attachments to see how they look in the original applications. When finished, close each original application.

- Click the OK button to close the Attachments dialog box.
- Click the form's Next record button three times to display the data for account manager 58 (Figure 5–69).

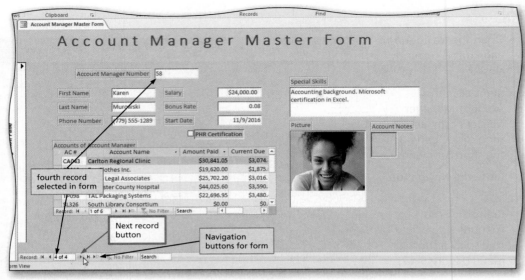

Figure 5–69

- Click the subform's Next record button twice to highlight the third account of account manager 58 (Figure 5–70).

- Close the form.

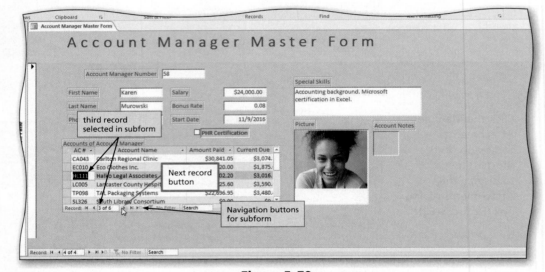

Figure 5–70

Other Ways

1. Double-click Attachments control

Navigation in the Form

BTW

Navigation
To go to a specific record in the main form, enter the record number in the Current Record box for the main form. To go to a specific record in the subform, enter the record number in the Current Record box for the subform.

The previous steps illustrated the way you work with a main form and subform. Clicking the Navigation buttons for the main form moves to a different account manager. Clicking the Navigation buttons for the subform moves to a different account of the account manager who appears in the main form. The following are other actions you can take within the form:

1. To move from the last field in the main form to the first field in the subform, press the TAB key. To move back to the last field in the main form, press SHIFT+TAB.

2. To move from any field in the subform to the first field in the next record's main form, press CTRL+TAB.

3. To switch from the main form to the subform using touch or the mouse, click anywhere in the subform. To switch back to the main form, click any control in the main form. Clicking the background of the main form will not cause the switch to occur.

Object Dependencies

In Access, objects can depend on other objects. For example, a report depends on the table or query on which it is based. A change to the structure of the table or query could affect the report. For example, if you delete a field from a table, any report based on that table that uses the deleted field would no longer be valid.

You can view information on dependencies between database objects. Viewing a list of objects that use a specific object helps in the maintenance of a database and avoids errors when changes are made to the objects involved in the dependency. For example, many items, such as queries and forms, use data from the Account table and thus depend on the Account table. By clicking the Object Dependencies button, you can see what items are based on the object. You also can see the items on which the object depends.

If you are unfamiliar with a database, viewing object dependencies can help you better understand the structure of the database. Viewing object dependencies is especially useful after you have made changes to the structure of tables. If you know which reports, forms, and queries depend on a table, you will be better able to make changes to a table without negatively affecting the related database objects.

To View Object Dependencies

1 ADD FIELDS | 2 ENTER DATA | 3 CREATE FORM | 4 ADD CONTROLS | 5 ADD SUBFORM

6 MODIFY SUBFORM | 7 ENHANCE FORM | **8 CREATE QUERIES**

The following steps view the objects that depend on the Account table. *Why? The objects that depend on the Account might be affected by any change you make to the Account table.*

- Open the Navigation Pane and click the Account table.
- Display the Database Tools tab.
- Click the Object Dependencies button (Database Tools tab | Relationships group) to display the Object Dependencies pane.
- If necessary, click the 'Objects that depend on me' option button to select it (Figure 5–71).

Experiment

- Click the 'Objects that I depend on' option button to see the objects on which the Account table depends. Then try both options for other objects in the database.

- Close the Object Dependencies pane by clicking the Object Dependencies button (Database Tools tab | Relationships group) a second time.

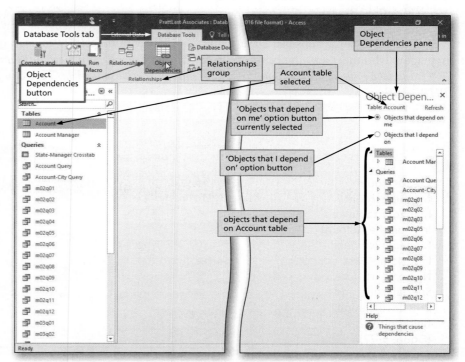

Figure 5–71

BTW
Long Text Fields in Queries
When you query long text fields, consider alternative spellings and phrases. For example, Computer Science also can be referenced as CS.

BTW
Date Fields in Queries
To test for the current date in a query, type Date() in the Criteria row of the appropriate column. Typing <Date() in the Criteria row for the Start Date, for example, finds those account managers who started any time before the date on which you run the query.

Date/Time, Long Text, and Yes/No Fields in Queries

By specifying account manager start dates using Date/Time fields, PrattLast Associates can run queries to find account managers hired before or after a certain date. Another use of the date field might be calculating a rep's length of service by subtracting the start date from the current date. Similarly, management can search for account managers with specific qualifications by adding Long Text and Yes/No fields.

To use Date/Time fields in queries, you simply type the dates, including the slashes. To search for records with a specific date, you must type the date. You can also use comparison operators. To find all the account managers whose start date is after January 5, 2015, for example, you type >1/15/2015 as the criterion.

You can also use Long Text fields in queries by searching for records that contain a specific word or phrase in the Long Text field. To do so, you use wildcards. For example, to find all the account managers who have the word, communication, somewhere in the Special Skills field, you type *communication* as the criterion. The asterisk at the beginning indicates that any characters can appear before the word, communication. The asterisk at the end indicates that any characters can appear after the word, communication.

To use Yes/No fields in queries, type the word, Yes, or the word, No, as the criterion. The following steps create and run queries that use Date/Time, Long Text, and Yes/No fields.

To Use Date/Time, Long Text, and Yes/No Fields in a Query

1 ADD FIELDS | 2 ENTER DATA | 3 CREATE FORM | 4 ADD CONTROLS | 5 ADD SUBFORM
6 MODIFY SUBFORM | 7 ENHANCE FORM | **8 CREATE QUERIES**

The following steps use Date/Time, Long Text, and Yes/No fields in queries to search for account managers who meet specific criteria. *Why? PrattLast wants to find account managers who started after January 1, 2015 and who have the word, communication, in their special skills field. They also want to find reps who have met their PHR certification.*

- Create a query for the Account Manager table and include the Account Manager Number, Last Name, First Name, Start Date, Special Skills, and PHR Certification fields in the query (Figure 5–72).

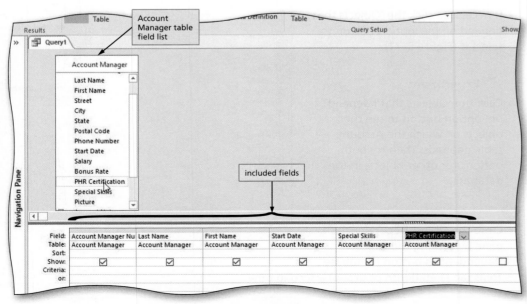

Figure 5–72

Access Module 5

2

- Click the Criteria row under the Start Date field, and then type **>1/01/2015** as the criterion.

- Click the Criteria row under the Special Skills field, and then type ***communication*** as the criterion (Figure 5–73).

Q&A
Why does the date have number signs (#) around it?
This is the date format in Access. Access reformatted the date appropriately as soon as you selected the Criteria row for the Special Skills field.

Are wild card searches in long text fields case-sensitive?
No.

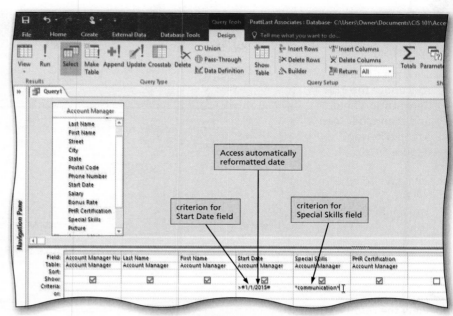

Figure 5–73

3

- View the results (Figure 5–74).

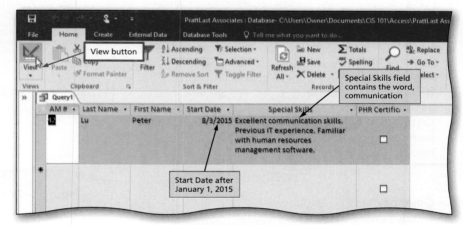

Figure 5–74

4

- Click the View button to return to Design view (Figure 5–75).

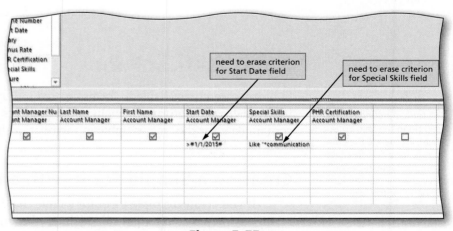

Figure 5–75

5

- Erase the criteria in the Start Date and Special Skills fields.

- Click the Criteria row under the PHR Certification field, and then type **Yes** as the criterion (Figure 5–76).

Q&A Do I have to type Yes?
You could also type True.

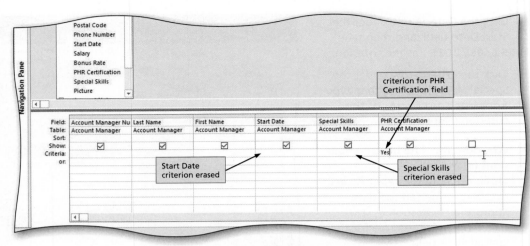

Figure 5–76

6

- View the results (Figure 5–77).

 Experiment

- Try other combinations of values in the Start Date field, the Special Skills field, and/or the PHR Certification field. In each case, view the results.

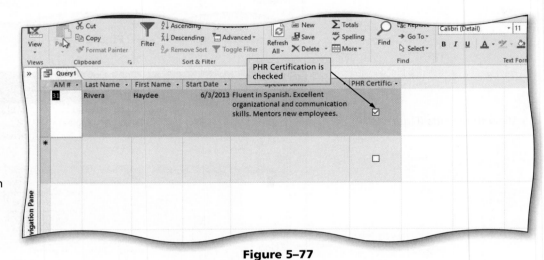

Figure 5–77

7

- Close the query without saving the results.

- If desired, sign out of your Microsoft account.

- Exit Access.

BTW
Date Formats
To change the date format for a date in a query, change the format property for the field using the field's property sheet. To change the date format for a field in a table, open the table in Design view and change the format property for the field.

Datasheets in Forms

Subforms are not available in forms created in Layout view, but you can achieve similar functionality to subforms by including datasheets. Like subforms, the datasheets contain data for the "many" table in the relationship.

Creating a Simple Form with a Datasheet

If you create a simple form for a table that is the "one" table in a one-to-many relationship, Access automatically includes the "many" table in a datasheet within the form. If you create a simple form for the Account Manager table, for example, Access will include the Account table in a datasheet within the form, as in Figure 5–78. The accounts in the datasheet will be the accounts of the account manager currently on the screen, in this case, Haydee Rivera.

Figure 5–78

TO CREATE A SIMPLE FORM WITH A DATASHEET

To create a simple form with a datasheet, you would use the following steps.

1. Select the table in the Navigation Pane that is the "one" part of a one-to-many relationship.
2. Display the Create tab.
3. Click the Form button (Create tab | Forms group).

Creating a Form with a Datasheet in Layout View

You can create a form with a datasheet in Layout view. To create a form based on the Account Manager table that includes the account number, which is stored in the Account table, you would first use the field list to add the required fields from the "one" table. In Figure 5–79, fields from the Account Manager table have been added to the form.

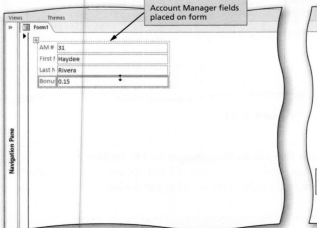

Figure 5–79

Next, you would use the field list to add a single field from the "many" table, as shown in Figure 5–80, in which the Account Number field has been added. Access will automatically create a datasheet containing this field.

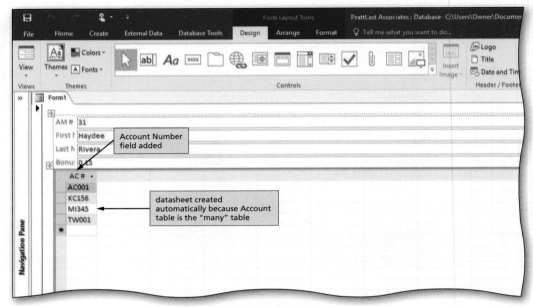

Figure 5–80

Finally, you would click the datasheet to select it and then use the field list to add the other fields from the "many" table that you want to include in the form, as shown in Figure 5–81.

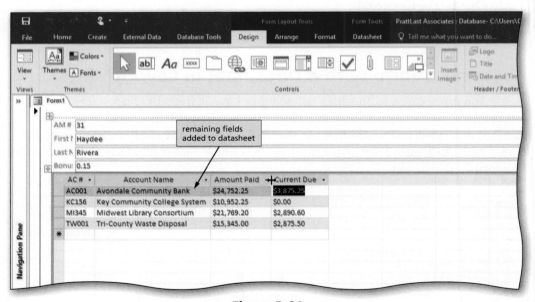

Figure 5–81

CONSIDER THIS

Can you modify the form so that the complete labels for the account manager fields appear?

Yes. Click any of the labels for the account manager fields to select the label, and then click the Select Column button (Arrange tab | Rows & Columns group) to select all the labels. You can then drag the right boundary of any of the labels to resize all the labels simultaneously.

TO CREATE A FORM WITH A DATASHEET IN LAYOUT VIEW

Specifically, to create a form with a datasheet in Layout view, you would use the following steps.

1. Display the Create tab.
2. Click the Blank Form button (Create tab | Forms group) to create a form in Layout view.
3. If a field list does not appear, click the 'Add Existing Fields' button (Form Layout Tools Design tab | Tools group) to display a field list.
4. If necessary, click 'Show all tables' to display the available tables.
5. Click the expand indicator (the plus sign) for the "one" table to display the fields in the table, and then drag the fields to the desired positions.
6. Click the expand indicator for the "many" table and drag the first field for the datasheet onto the form to create the datasheet.
7. Select the datasheet and drag the remaining fields for the datasheet from the field list to the desired locations in the datasheet.

Creating a Multiple-Table Form Based on the Many Table

All the forms discussed so far in this module were based on the "one" table, in this case, the Account Manager table. The records from the "many" table were included in a subform. You can also create a multiple-table form based on the "many" table, in this case, the Account table. Such a form is shown in Figure 5–82.

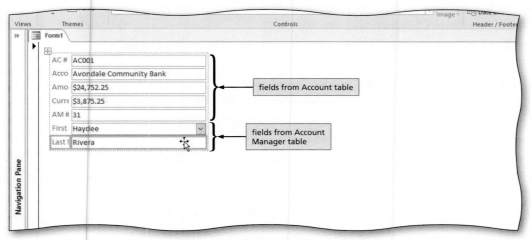

Figure 5–82

In this form, the Account Number, Account Name, Amount Paid, Current Due, and Account Manager Number fields are in the Account table. The First Name and Last Name fields are found in the Account Manager table and are included in the form to help to identify the account manager whose number appears in the Account Manager Number field.

BTW
Distributing a Document
Instead of printing and distributing a hard copy of a document, you can distribute the document electronically. Options include sending the document via email; posting it on cloud storage (such as OneDrive) and sharing the file with others; posting it on a social networking site, blog, or other website; and sharing a link associated with an online location of the document. You also can create and share a PDF or XPS image of the document, so that users can view the file in Acrobat Reader or XPS Viewer instead of in Access.

TO CREATE A MULTIPLE-TABLE FORM BASED ON THE MANY TABLE

To create a multiple-table form based on the "many" table, you would use the following steps.

1. Click the Blank Form button (Create tab | Forms group) to create a form in Layout view.
2. If a field list does not appear, click the 'Add Existing Fields' button on the Design tab to display a field list.
3. Drag the fields for the "many" table to the desired positions.
4. Drag the fields for the "one" table to the desired positions.

Summary

In this module you have learned to use Yes/No, Long Text, OLE Object, and Attachment data types; create and use an input mask; create a form and add a subform; enhance the look of the controls on a form; change tab order and stops; use a form with a subform; create queries involving Yes/No, Date/Time, and Long Text fields; view object dependencies; and create forms containing datasheets in Layout view.

CONSIDER THIS

What decisions will you need to make when creating your own forms?
Use these guidelines as you complete the assignments in this module and create your own forms outside of this class.

1. Determine the purpose of the fields to see if they need special data types.

    a. If the field only contains values such as Yes and No or True and False, it should have Yes/No as the data type.
    b. If the field contains an extended description, it should have Long Text as the data type.
    c. If the field contains a picture or other special object, its data type should be OLE Object.
    d. If the field contains attachments, its data type should be Attachment.

2. Determine whether the form requires data from more than one table.

3. If the form requires data from more than one table, determine the relationship between the tables.

    a. Identify one-to-many relationships.
    b. For each relationship, identify the "one" table and the "many" table.

4. If the form requires data from more than one table, determine on which of the tables the form is to be based.

    a. Which table contains data that is the focus of the form, that is, which table is the main table?

5. Determine the fields from each table that need to be on the form.

    a. Decide exactly how the form will be used, and identify the fields that are necessary to support this use.
    b. Determine whether there are any additional fields that, while not strictly necessary, would make the form more functional.

6. When changing the structure of a table or query, examine object dependencies to see if any report or form might be impacted by the change.

7. Determine the tab order for form controls.

    a. Change the tab order if the form requires a certain progression from one control to the next.
    b. Remove tab stops for those controls for which form navigation is not required.

8. Review the form to determine whether any changes are necessary.

    a. Are there visual changes, such as different colors or a larger font, that would make the form easier to use?
    b. Does the form have a similar look to other forms in the database?
    c. Does the form conform to the organization's standards?

How should you submit solutions to questions in the assignments identified with a symbol?
Every assignment in this book contains one or more questions identified with a symbol. These questions require you to think beyond the assigned database. Present your solutions to the questions in the format required by your instructor. Possible formats may include one or more of these options: write the answer; create a document that contains the answer; present your answer to the class; discuss your answer in a group; record the answer as audio or video using a webcam, smartphone, or portable media player; or post answers on a blog, wiki, or website.

Apply Your Knowledge

Reinforce the skills and apply the concepts you learned in this module.

Adding Phone Number, Yes/No, Long Text, and OLE Object Fields, Using an Input Mask Wizard, and Querying Long Text Fields

Note: To complete this assignment, you will be required to use the Data Files. Please contact your instructor for information about accessing the Data Files.

Instructions: Run Access, and then open the Apply NicelyNeat Services database that you used in Module 4. If you did not use this database, see your instructor about accessing the required files.

Perform the following tasks:
1. Open the Supervisor table in Design view.
2. Add the Phone Number, Safety Training, Other Skills, and Picture fields to the Supervisor table structure, as shown in Figure 5–83. Be sure the Phone Number field appears after the Postal Code field and create an input mask for the new field. Store the phone number data without symbols. Safety Training is a field that indicates whether the supervisor has completed all required safety courses.

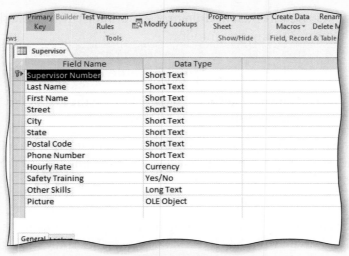

Figure 5–83

Continued >

Apply Your Knowledge *continued*

3. Add the data shown in Table 5–1 to the Supervisor table. Adjust the row and column spacing to best fit the data. Save the changes to the layout of the table.

Table 5–1 Data for Supervisor Table

Supervisor Number	Phone Number	Safety Training	Other Skills	Picture
103	615-555-2222	Yes	Has construction experience. Helps to train new employees.	Pict2.jpg
110	931-555-4433	Yes	Has an Associate's degree. Previous experience as a school custodian.	Pict1.jpg
114	423-555-8877	No	Has construction experience. Excellent mechanical skills.	Pict3.jpg
120	931-555-5498	No	Working on an Associate's degree in supervisory management.	Pict4.jpg

4. If requested to do so by your instructor, change the phone number for supervisor number 103 to your phone number.

5. Query the Supervisor table to find all supervisors who have construction experience. Include the Supervisor Number, Last Name, First Name, and Phone Number fields in the query result. Save the query as Apply 5 Step 5 Query.

6. Query the Supervisor table to find all supervisors with construction experience who have completed all safety courses. Include the Supervisor Number, Last Name, First Name, and Other Skills fields in the query result. Save the query as Apply 5 Step 6 Query.

7. Submit the revised database in the format specified by your instructor.

8. ✸ What value did you enter in the criteria row for the Safety Training field in the query in Step 6 above? Could you have entered the criteria differently? If yes, then how would you enter the criteria?

Extend Your Knowledge

Extend the skills you learned in this module and experiment with new skills. You may need to use Help to complete the assignment.

Adding Hyperlink Fields and Creating Multiple-Table Forms Using Layout View

Note: To complete this assignment, you will be required to use the Data Files. Please contact your instructor for information about accessing the Data Files.

Instructions: Extend Software Engineering is a recruiting company that recruits employees for positions in the software engineering field. You will add a Hyperlink field to the Client table. You will also create the form shown in Figure 5–84.

Perform the following tasks:
1. Run Access and open the Extend Software Engineering database. Open the Client table in Design view and add a field with the Hyperlink data type. Insert the field after the Postal Code field. Use Website as the name of the field.

2. Open the Client table in Datasheet view and add data for the Website field to the first record. Use your school website as the URL. If necessary, resize the column so the complete URL is displayed.

3. If requested to do so by your instructor, enter your name as the client name for the first record of the Client table.

4. Use Layout view to create the multiple-table form shown in Figure 5–84. The Client table appears as a subform in the form. The Recruiter table is the "one" table in the form. Use Clients by Recruiter Form as the form name.

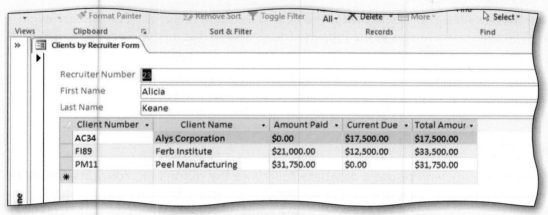

Figure 5–84

5. Submit the revised database in the format specified by your instructor.

6. ✳ How would you add a field for an email address to the Recruiter table?

Expand Your World

Create a solution, which uses cloud and web technologies, by learning and investigating on your own from general guidance.

Problem: Beach Vacations is a database of vacation rentals at a resort beach location. To understand the difference between Attachment and OLE Object data types, you will add those fields to the Rental Unit table. Then, you will insert images that you download from the Internet. Finally, you will create a multiple-table form for the database.

Note: To complete this assignment, you will be required to use the Data Files. Please contact your instructor for information about accessing the Data Files.

Instructions: Perform the following tasks:

1. Access any website containing royalty-free images and search the images to find four different pictures of beach properties for rent.

2. Save these images to a storage location of your choice.

3. Open the Expand Beach Vacations database and open the Rental Unit table in Design view. Add a Property Image field with an OLE Object data type. Add a Picture field with an Attachment data type. Assign the caption, Picture, to the Picture field. The fields should appear before the Owner Code field.

4. Use the techniques shown in the module to add the images to the Property Image field. Add the same images as attachments to the Picture field.

Continued >

Expand Your World *continued*

5. Create a multiple-table form based on the Rental Unit table. Include the Unit Number, Bedrooms, Weekly Rate, and For Sale fields from the Rental Unit table. Include the owner code, and the owner's first and last name on the form.

6. Include a title for the form and the current date. Save the form as Rental Unit Form, and then open the form in Design view.

7. Add the Property Image field and the Picture field to the form. If necessary, use the size mode property to adjust your images in the Property Image field so that they appear appropriately.

8. Submit the revised database in the format specified by your instructor.

9. ✹ In this assignment you stored images as OLE Object and Attachment fields. What differences did you notice on the form? Which storage method do you prefer and why?

In the Labs

Design, create, modify, and/or use a database following the guidelines, concepts, and skills presented in this module. Labs are listed in order of increasing difficulty. Labs 1 and 2, which increase in difficulty, require you to create solutions based on what you learned in the module. Lab 3 requires you to apply your creative thinking and problem solving skills to design and implement a solution.

Lab 1: Adding Fields and Creating Multiple-Table Forms for the Horticulture4U Database

Problem: Horticulture4U needs to maintain additional data on sales reps. Management needs to store notes about each sales rep, indicate whether the sales rep is eligible for a bonus, and display a picture of the sales rep. They also need to store the phone number of each sales rep. Management wants a form that displays sales rep information and the customers for whom they are responsible.

Note: To complete this assignment, you will be required to use the Data Files. Please contact your instructor for information about accessing the Data Files.

Instructions: Perform the following tasks:
1. Run Access and open the Lab 1 Horticulture4U database you used in Module 4. If you did not use this database, see your instructor about accessing the required files.

2. Add the Eligibility, Special Skills, and Picture fields to the end of the Sales Rep table. Eligibility is Yes/No field; Special Skills is a Long Text field; and Picture is an OLE Object Type field. Insert the Phone Number field after the Postal Code field and create the input mask shown in Figure 5–85 for the Phone Number field. Save the changes to the structure of the table.

3. Add the data shown in Table 5–2 to the Sales Rep table. Adjust the row and column spacing to best fit the data. Save the changes to the layout of the table.

Table 5–2 Data for Sales Rep Table

Sales Rep Number	Phone Number	Eligibility	Special Skills	Picture
36	610-555-2212	Yes	Certified Master Gardener. President of local gardening club.	Pict1.jpg
39	215-555-4343	Yes	Previously owned a plant nursery. Has many contacts in business community.	Pict2.jpg
42	201-555-8787	No	Has a BS in Horticulture. Provides volunteer landscaping services to local library.	Pict4.jpg
45	302-555-9854	No	Lectures on organic gardening to local organizations.	Pict3.jpg

4. If requested to do so by your instructor, change the phone number for sales rep 36 to your phone number.

5. Create the form shown in Figure 5–85. Use Sales Rep Master Form as the name of the form, and Customers of Sales Rep as the name of the subform. The form has a background color of gray. The labels have a solid 3 pt border style with a raised special effect and blue font color. All controls except the subform control are sunken. Users should not be able to tab through the Picture control. The title is centered with a font weight of bold and a font size of 24.

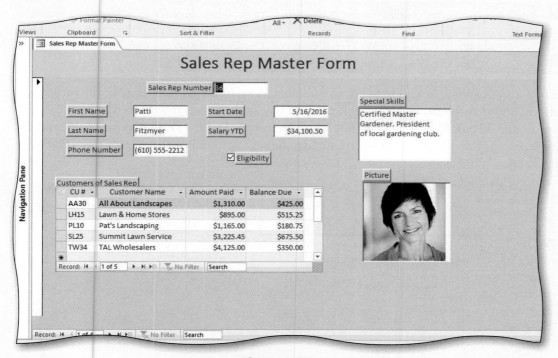

Figure 5–85

6. Query the Sales Rep table to find all sales reps who started before January 1, 2016 and who are eligible for a bonus. Include the Sales Rep Number, Last Name, and First Name in the query results. Save the query as Lab 5–1 Step 6 Query.

7. Submit the revised database in the format specified by your instructor.

8. ✻ The Sales Rep table includes a Start Date field in the format, mm/dd/yyyy. How could you add an input mask for the Start Date field?

Continued >

In the Labs *continued*

Lab 2: Adding Fields and Creating Multiple-Table Forms for the SciTech Sundries Database

Problem: The management of SciTech Sundries has found that they need to maintain additional data on vendors. Management needs to keep track of whether the vendor accepts returns, and whether the vendor allows online ordering. Management would also like to attach to each vendor's record Excel files that contain historical cost data. SciTech Sundries requires a form that displays information about the vendors as well as the items that are purchased from vendors.

Note: To complete this assignment, you will be required to use the Data Files. Please contact your instructor for information about accessing the Data Files.

Instructions: Perform the following tasks:
1. Run Access and open the Lab 2 SciTech Sundries database you used in Module 4. If you did not use this database, see your instructor about accessing the required files.
2. Add the Returns, Online Ordering, and Cost History fields to the end of the Vendor table structure.
3. Add the data shown in Table 5–3 to the Vendor table.

Table 5–3 Data for Vendor Table			
Vendor Code	**Returns**	**Online Ordering**	**Cost History**
AW	Yes	No	AW_History.xlsx
GS	No	Yes	GS_History.xlsx
SD	Yes	Yes	SD_History.xlsx

4. Create the form shown in Figure 5–86. Use Vendor Master Form as the name of the form and Items of Vendor as the name of the subform. The title is shadowed and centered with a font size of 24 and a Dark Red font color. The labels are chiseled with a Dark Red font color and the controls, except the subform control, are sunken. Be sure the entire title appears and that the entire Vendor Name is visible.

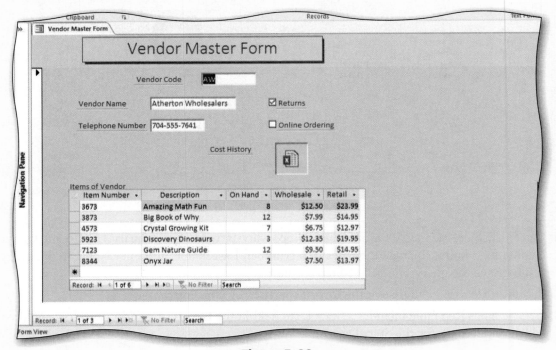

Figure 5–86

5. If requested to do so by your instructor, change the name for Vendor Code AW to your first and last name.

6. Open the Vendor Master Form and then open the cost history for Gift Sundries. Change the previous cost for item 7934 to $24.50. Save the change to the workbook.

7. Query the Vendor table to find all vendors that accept returns and allow online ordering. Include the Vendor Code and Vendor Name in the query results. Save the query as Lab 5–2 Step 7 Query.

8. Submit the revised database in the format specified by your instructor.

9. ✸ What additional field(s) would you add to the Vendor table to assist with online ordering?

Lab 3: **Consider This: Your Turn**

Adding Fields and Creating Multiple-Table Forms for the JSP Analysis Database

Instructions: Open the Lab 3 JSP Analysis database that you used in Module 4. If you did not create this database, see your instructor about accessing the required files.

Part 1: The management of JSP Analysis would like you to add some fields to the Marketing Analyst table. They would also like to create a form for the Marketing Analyst table that shows the clients of each analyst. Use the concepts and techniques presented in this module to perform each of the following tasks:

a. Add a phone number field, a picture field, and a notes field to the Marketing Analyst table. The phone number field should have an input mask.

b. Add the data for these fields to the Marketing Analyst table. Create phone numbers to store in the phone number field. For the pictures, select pictures from the Data Files or use your own photos. For the Notes field, add the notes shown in Table 5–4. Make sure all data appears in the datasheet.

Table 5–4 Data for Marketing Analyst Table	
Marketing Analyst Number	**Notes**
31	Master's degree in Marketing Research; treasurer of a national marketing association.
34	Bachelor's degree in Business Administration; veteran; has database experience.
47	Working on a Master's degree in Management Information Systems.
54	Bachelor's degree in Marketing.

c. Create a Marketing Analyst Master Form for the Marketing Analyst table that is similar in design to the form shown in Figure 5–1. Include the Marketing Analyst Number, First Name, Last Name, Phone Number, Salary YTD, Incentive YTD, Start Date, Picture, and Notes fields from the Marketing Analyst table on the form. The subform should display the Client

Continued >

In the Labs *continued*

Number, Client Name, Amount Paid, and Current Due fields from the Client table. Customize the form by adding special effects to controls and labels and by changing the background color of the form. Add a title and the current date to the form header.

d. Create a query that finds all marketing analysts who started before January 1, 2016 and have a degree in information systems.

Submit your assignment in the format specified by your instructor.

Part 2: You made several decisions while adding the fields and creating the form for this assignment. What was the rationale behind your decisions? Would you add any additional fields to the Marketing Analyst table?

6 | Advanced Report Techniques

Objectives

You will have mastered the material in this module when you can:

- Create and relate additional tables
- Create queries for reports
- Create reports in Design view
- Add fields and text boxes to a report
- Format report controls
- Group and ungroup report controls
- Update multiple report controls

- Add and modify a subreport
- Modify section properties
- Add a title, page number, and date to a report
- Preview, print, and publish a report
- Add totals and subtotals to a report
- Include a conditional value in a report

Introduction

In Module 5, you created forms in Design view. In this module, you will create two reports in Design view. Both reports feature grouping and sorting. The first report contains a subreport, which is a report that is contained within another report. The subreport contains data from a query and is related to data in the main report. The second report uses aggregate functions to calculate subtotals and grand totals. It also uses a function to calculate a value where the actual calculation will vary from record to record depending on whether a given criterion is true.

Project — Creating Detailed Reports

PrattLast Associates wants a master list of account managers. This list should be available as an Access report and will have the name, Account Manager Master List. For each account manager, the report will include full details for all the accounts assigned to the account manager. In addition to offering its human resource services, PrattLast offers workshops designed to educate organizations on various aspects of human resource laws as well as ways to better manage employees. Data on workshop participation is stored in the database. For accounts who are participating in workshops, the report should list the specific workshops being offered to the account.

The Account Manager Master List report is shown in Figure 6–1a. The report is organized by account manager, with the data for each manager beginning on a new page. For each account manager, the report lists the account manager number, first name, and last name; the report then lists data for each account served by that account manager. The account data includes the number, name, street, city, state, postal code, account type, services needed, amount paid, current due, and total

Microsoft Access 2016
File   Home   Create   External Data   Database Tools   ♀ Tell me what you want to do...

PrattLast Associates : Database- C:\Users\Owner\Documents\CIS

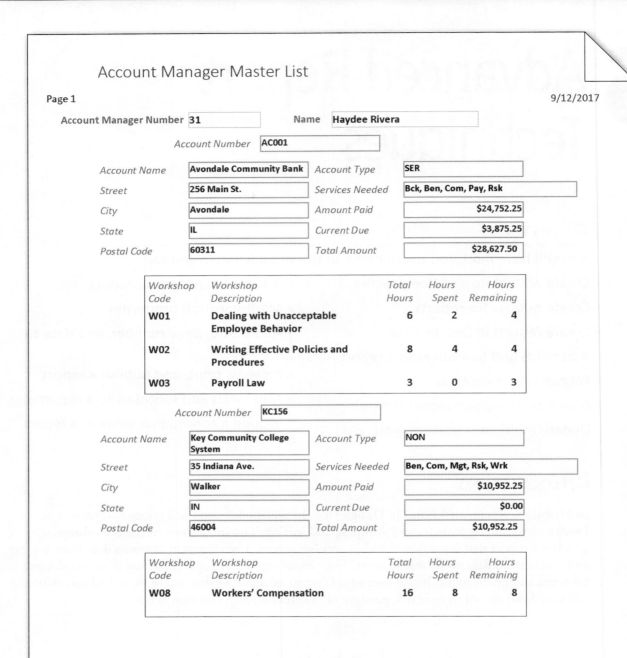

Account Manager Master List

Page 1   9/12/2017

Account Manager Number 31   Name   **Haydee Rivera**

Account Number   **AC001**

Account Name	**Avondale Community Bank**	*Account Type*	**SER**
Street	**256 Main St.**	*Services Needed*	**Bck, Ben, Com, Pay, Rsk**
City	**Avondale**	*Amount Paid*	**$24,752.25**
State	**IL**	*Current Due*	**$3,875.25**
Postal Code	**60311**	*Total Amount*	**$28,627.50**

Workshop Code	Workshop Description	Total Hours	Hours Spent	Hours Remaining
W01	**Dealing with Unacceptable Employee Behavior**	6	2	4
W02	**Writing Effective Policies and Procedures**	8	4	4
W03	**Payroll Law**	3	0	3

Account Number   **KC156**

Account Name	**Key Community College System**	*Account Type*	**NON**
Street	**35 Indiana Ave.**	*Services Needed*	**Ben, Com, Mgt, Rsk, Wrk**
City	**Walker**	*Amount Paid*	**$10,952.25**
State	**IN**	*Current Due*	**$0.00**
Postal Code	**46004**	*Total Amount*	**$10,952.25**

Workshop Code	Workshop Description	Total Hours	Hours Spent	Hours Remaining
W08	**Workers' Compensation**	16	8	8

Figure 6–1a Account Manager Master List

PrattLast Associates : Database- C:\Users\Owner\Documents\CIS

Microsoft Access 2016

File   Home   Create   External Data   Database Tools   ♀ Tell me what you want to do...

D i s c o u n t   R e p o r t

Manager Number	First Name	Last Name	Account Number	Account Name	Amount Paid	Current Due	Discount
31	Haydee	Rivera					
			AC001	Avondale Community Bank	$24,752.25	$3,875.25	$155.01
			KC156	Key Community College System	$10,952.25	$0.00	$0.00
			MI345	Midwest Library Consortium	$21,769.20	$2,890.60	$115.62
			TW001	Tri-County Waste Disposal	$15,345.00	$2,875.50	$115.02
				Subtotals	$72,818.70	$9,641.35	
35	Mark	Simson					
			BL235	Bland Corp.	$29,836.65	$2,765.30	$110.61
			CO621	Codder Plastics Co.	$27,152.25	$2,875.00	$115.00
			KV089	KAL Veterinary Services	$34,036.50	$580.00	$23.20
			LI268	Lars-Idsen-Fleming Inc.	$0.00	$1,280.75	$25.62
			ML008	Mums Landscaping Co.	$13,097.10	$2,450.00	$98.00
				Subtotals	$104,122.50	$9,951.05	
58	Karen	Murowski					
			CA043	Carlton Regional Clinic	$30,841.05	$3,074.30	$122.97
			EC010	Eco Clothes Inc.	$19,620.00	$1,875.00	$75.00
			HL111	Halko Legal Associates	$25,702.20	$3,016.75	$120.67
			LC005	Lancaster County Hospital	$44,025.60	$3,590.80	$143.63
			SL326	South Library Consortium	$0.00	$0.00	$0.00
			TP098	TAL Packaging Systems	$22,696.95	$3,480.45	$139.22

Page 1   9/12/2017

Figure 6–1b Discount Report

amount. For each workshop the account is taking, the report lists the workshop code, description, total hours the workshop requires, hours already spent, and hours remaining.

To attract new accounts and reward current accounts, many companies offer discounts. PrattLast is considering the effect of offering a discount on the current due amount to its current accounts. The exact amount of the discount depends on how much the account has already paid. If the amount paid is more than $20,000, the discount will be 4 percent of the current due amount. If the amount paid is $20,000 or less, then the discount will be 2 percent of the current due amount. To assist in determining the discount, PrattLast needs a report like the one shown in Figure 6–1b. The report groups accounts by account manager. It includes subtotals of both the Amount Paid and Current Due fields. In addition, although not visible in the figure, it includes grand totals of both fields at the end of the report. Finally, it shows the discount amount, which is calculated by multiplying the current due amount by .04 (4 percent) for those accounts for whom the amount paid is more than $20,000.00 and by .02 (2 percent) for all others.

In this module, you will learn how to create the reports shown in Figure 6–1. The following roadmap identifies general activities you will perform as you progress through this module:

1. CREATE and relate additional TABLES.
2. CREATE QUERIES for a report.
3. CREATE a REPORT.
4. SPECIFY GROUPING AND SORTING.
5. Add fields and TEXT BOXES to the report.
6. ADD a SUBREPORT to the report.
7. ADD a TITLE, PAGE NUMBER, AND DATE to the report.
8. CREATE a SECOND REPORT.

Additional Tables

PrattLast managers are frequently asked to present workshops on various aspects of human resources law as well as ways to better manage employees. PrattLast would like to incorporate the workshop data into the PrattLast Associates database.

Before creating the reports, you need to create two additional tables for the PrattLast Associates database. The first table, Workshop, is shown in Tables 6–1a and 6–1b. As described in Table 6–1a, each workshop has a code and a description. The table also includes the total hours for which the workshop is usually offered and its increments; that is, the standard time blocks in which the workshop is usually offered. Table 6–1b contains the specific workshops that the account managers at PrattLast Associates offer to their accounts. The first row, for example, indicates that workshop W01 is called Dealing with Unacceptable Employee Behavior. It is typically offered in two-hour increments for a total of four hours.

Table 6–1a Structure of Workshop Table			
Field Name	**Data Type**	**Field Size**	**Description**
Workshop Code	Short Text	3	Primary Key
Workshop Description	Short Text	50	
Hours	Number	Integer	
Increments	Number	Integer	

Table 6–1b Workshop Table

Workshop Code	Workshop Description	Hours	Increments
W01	Dealing with Unacceptable Employee Behavior	4	2
W02	Writing Effective Policies and Procedures	8	4
W03	Payroll Law	3	1
W04	Workplace Safety	16	4
W05	The Recruitment Process	24	4
W06	Diversity in the Workplace	12	3
W07	Americans with Disabilities Act (ADA)	4	2
W08	Workers' Compensation	16	4

The second table, Workshop Offerings, is described in Table 6–2a and contains an account number, a workshop code, the total number of hours that the workshop is scheduled for the account, and the number of hours already spent in the workshop. The primary key of the Workshop Offerings table is a combination of the Account Number and Workshop Code fields.

Table 6–2a Structure of Workshop Offerings Table

Field Name	Data Type	Field Size	Description
Account Number	Short Text	5	Part of Primary Key
Workshop Code	Short Text	3	Part of Primary Key
Total Hours	Number	Integer	
Hours Spent	Number	Integer	

Table 6–2b gives the data for the Workshop Offerings table. For example, the first record shows that account number AC001 currently has scheduled workshop W01 (Dealing with Unacceptable Employee Behavior). The workshop is scheduled for six hours, and they have so far spent two hours in class.

Table 6–2b Workshop Offerings Table

Account Number	Workshop Code	Total Hours	Hours Spent
AC001	W01	6	2
AC001	W02	8	4
AC001	W03	3	0
EC010	W05	24	12
KC156	W08	16	8
KV089	W07	4	0
LC005	W02	8	4
LC005	W06	12	6
ML008	W03	3	1
ML008	W04	16	4
SL326	W05	24	16
SL326	W06	12	3
SL326	W07	4	2
TP098	W03	3	0
TP098	W08	16	4
TW001	W01	4	2

BTW
Enabling the Content
For each of the databases you use in this module, you will need to enable the content.

BTW
AutoNumber Field as Primary Key
When you create a table in Datasheet view, Access automatically creates an ID field with the AutoNumber data type as the primary key field. As you add records to the table, Access increments the ID field so that each record will have a unique value in the field. AutoNumber fields are useful when there is no data field in a table that is a suitable primary key.

BTW
Copying the Structure of a Table
If you want to create a table that has a structure similar to an existing table, you can copy the structure of the table only. Select the table in the Navigation Pane and click Copy, then click Paste. In the Paste Table As dialog box, type the new table name and click the Structure Only option button. Then, click the OK button. To modify the new table, open it in Design view.

If you examine the data in Table 6–2b, you see that the Account Number field cannot be the primary key for the Workshop Offerings table. The first and second records, for example, both have an account number of AC001. The Workshop Code field also cannot be the primary key. The second and seventh records, for example, both have workshop code W02. Rather, the primary key is the combination of both Account Number and Workshop Code.

To Create the New Tables

1 CREATE TABLES | 2 CREATE QUERIES | 3 CREATE REPORT | 4 SPECIFY GROUPING & SORTING | 5 ADD FIELDS
6 ADD SUBREPORT | 7 ADD TITLE, PAGE NUMBER, & DATE | 8 CREATE SECOND REPORT

You will use Design view to create the new tables. The steps to create the new tables are similar to the steps you used previously to add fields to an existing table and to define primary keys. The only difference is the way you specify a primary key. **Why?** *In the Workshop Offerings table, the primary key consists of more than one field, which requires a slightly different process.* To specify a primary key containing more than one field, you must select both fields that make up the primary key by clicking the row selector for the first field, and then hold down the SHIFT key while clicking the row selector for the second field. Once the fields are selected, you can use the Primary Key button to indicate that the primary key consists of both fields.

The following steps create the tables in Design view.

1
- Run Access and open the database named PrattLast Associates from your hard disk, OneDrive, or other storage location.
- If necessary, close the Navigation Pane.
- Display the Create tab (Figure 6–2).

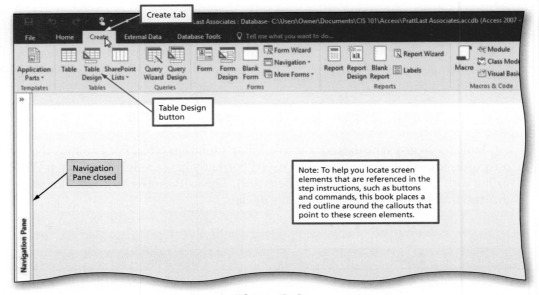

Figure 6–2

2
- Click the Table Design button (Create tab | Tables group) to create a table in Design view.
- Enter the information for the fields in the Workshop table as indicated in Table 6–1a, selecting Workshop Code as the primary key, and selecting the indicated field sizes.
- Save the table using the name **Workshop** and close the table.
- Display the Create tab and then click the Table Design button (Create tab | Tables group) to create a second table in Design view.
- Enter the information for the fields in the Workshop Offerings table as indicated in Table 6–2a.
- Click the row selector for the Account Number field.
- Hold down the SHIFT key and then click the row selector for the Workshop Code field so both fields are selected.

- Click the Primary Key button (Table Tools Design tab | Tools group) to select the combination of the two fields as the primary key (Figure 6–3).

- Save the table using the name Workshop Offerings and close the table.

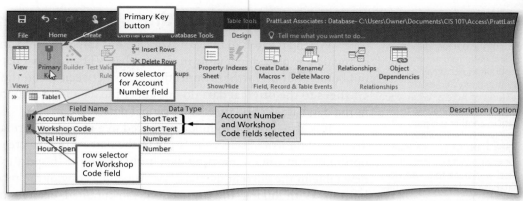

Figure 6–3

I realized I designated the wrong fields as the primary key. How can I correct the primary key?

Click any field that currently participates in the primary key, and click the Primary Key button to remove the primary key. You can then specify the correct primary key.

To Import the Data

Now that the tables have been created, you need to add data to them. You could enter the data manually, or if the data is already in electronic form, you could import the data. The data for the Workshop and Workshop Offerings tables is included in the Data Files. The files are text files formatted as delimited files. The Workshop data is in a tab-delimited text (.txt) file, and the Workshop Offerings data is in a comma-separated values (.csv) file, which is also a delimited text file. The following steps import the data.

1 With the PrattLast Associates database open, display the External Data tab and then click the Text File button (External Data tab | Import & Link group) to display the Get External Data - Text File dialog box.

2 Click the Browse button (Get External Data - Text File dialog box) and then navigate to the location containing the text file (for example, the Access folder in the CIS 101 folder).

3 Select the Workshop file and click the Open button.

4 Select the 'Append a copy of the records to the table' option button, select the Workshop table from the drop-down list, and then click the OK button. With the Delimited option button selected, click the Next button.

5 With the Tab option button selected, click the 'First Row Contains Field Names' check box, click the Next button, and then click the Finish button.

6 Click the Close button to close the Get External Data - Text Box dialog box without saving the import steps.

7 Use the technique shown in Steps 1 through 6 to import the Workshop Offerings.csv file into the Workshop Offerings table. Be sure the Comma option button is selected and there is a check mark in the 'First Row Contains Field Names' check box.

I got an error message after I clicked the Finish button that indicated there were errors. The data was not imported. What should I do?

First, click the Cancel button to terminate the process. Then, review the structure of the table in Design view to ensure that the field names are all spelled correctly and that the data types are correct. Correct any errors you find, save your work, and then redo the steps to import the data.

BTW
Many-to-Many Relationships
There is a many-to-many relationship between the Account table and the Workshop table. To implement a many-to-many relationship in a relational database management system such as Access, you create a third table, often called a junction or intersection table, that has as its primary key the combination of the primary keys of each of the tables involved in the many-to-many relationship. The primary key of the Workshop Offerings table is the combination of the Account Number and the Workshop Code fields.

BTW
Linking
Two of the primary reasons
to link data from another
program to Access are to
use the query and report
features of Access. When you
link an Access database to
data in another program, all
changes to the data must be
made in the source program.
For example, if you link an
Excel workbook to an Access
database, you cannot edit the
linked table in Access. You
must make all changes to the
data in Excel.

Linking versus Importing

When an external table or worksheet is imported into an Access database, a copy of the data is placed in a table in the database. The original data still exists, just as it did before, but no further connection exists between it and the data in the database. Changes to the original data do not affect the data in the database. Likewise, changes in the database do not affect the original data.

It is also possible to link data stored in a variety of formats to Access databases. To do so, you would select the 'Link to the data source by creating a linked table' option button when importing data, rather than the 'Import the source data into a new table in the current database' or 'Append a copy of the records to the table' option buttons. With linking, the connection is maintained; changes made to the data in the external table or worksheet affect the Access table.

To identify that a table is linked to other data, Access displays an arrow in front of the table in the Navigation Pane. In addition, an icon is displayed in front of the name that indicates the type of file to which the data is linked. For example, an Excel icon in front of the name indicates that the table is linked to an Excel worksheet.

To Modify Linked Tables

After you link tables between a worksheet and a database or between two databases, you can modify many of the linked table's features. To rename the linked table, set view properties, and set links between tables in queries, you would use the following steps.

1. Click the 'Linked Table Manager' button (External Data tab | Import & Link group) to update the links.
2. Select the linked table for which you want to update the links.
3. Click the OK button.

To Relate the New Tables

1 CREATE TABLES | 2 CREATE QUERIES | 3 CREATE REPORT | 4 SPECIFY GROUPING & SORTING | 5 ADD FIELDS
6 ADD SUBREPORT | 7 ADD TITLE, PAGE NUMBER, & DATE | 8 CREATE SECOND REPORT

The following steps relate, or create a relationship between, the tables. *Why? The new tables need to be related to the existing tables in the PrattLast Associates database. The Account and Workshop Offerings tables are related through the Account Number field that exists in both tables. The Workshop and Workshop Offerings tables are related through the Workshop Code fields in both tables.*

1
- If necessary, close any open datasheet on the screen by clicking its Close button, and then display the Database Tools tab.
- Click the Relationships button (Database Tools tab | Relationships group) to open the Relationships window (Figure 6–4).

Q&A
I only see one table, did I do something wrong?
Click the All Relationships button to display all the tables in relationships.

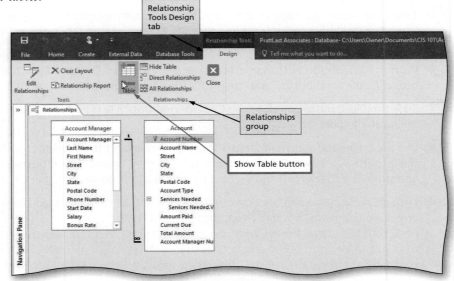

Figure 6–4

2

- Click the Show Table button (Relationship Tools Design tab | Relationships group) to display the Show Table dialog box (Figure 6–5).

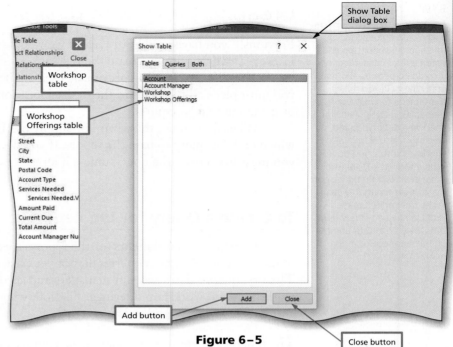

Figure 6–5

3

- Click the Workshop Offerings table, click the Add button (Show Table dialog box), click the Workshop table, click the Add button again, and then click the Close button to add the tables to the Relationships window.

Q&A I cannot see the Workshop Offerings table. Should I repeat the step?
If you cannot see the table, it is behind the dialog box. You do not need to repeat the step.

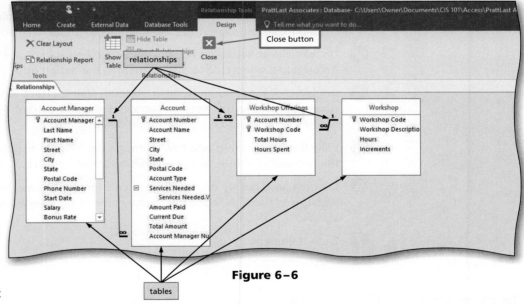

Figure 6–6

- Drag the Account Number field in the Account table to the Account Number field in the Workshop Offerings table to display the Edit Relationships dialog box. Click the 'Enforce Referential Integrity' check box (Edit Relationships dialog box) and then click the Create button to create the relationship.

- Drag the Workshop Code field from the Workshop table to the Workshop Code field in the Workshop Offerings table. Click the 'Enforce Referential Integrity' check box (Edit Relationships dialog box) and then click the Create button to create the relationship (Figure 6–6).

4

- Save the changes and then click the Close button (Relationship Tools Design tab | Relationships group).

Creating Reports in Design View

Previously, you have used both Layout view and the Report Wizard to create reports. However, you can simply create the report in Design view. You can also use Design view to modify a report you previously created. If you create a report in Design view, you must place all the fields in the desired locations. You must also specify any sorting or grouping that is required.

Whether you use the wizard or simply use Design view, you must determine on which table or query to base the report. If you decide to base the report on a query, you must first create the query, unless it already exists.

To Create a Query for the Report

PrattLast's requirements for the reports specify that it would be convenient to use two queries. These queries do not yet exist, so you will need to create them. The first query relates account managers and accounts, and the second query relates workshops and workshop offerings. The following steps create the Account Managers and Accounts query.

1 If necessary, close the Navigation Pane, display the Create tab, and then click the Query Design button (Create tab | Queries group) to create a new query.

2 Click the Account Manager table, click the Add button (Show Table dialog box), click the Account table, click the Add button, close the Show Table dialog box by clicking its Close button, and then resize the field lists to display as many fields as possible.

3 Double-click the Account Manager Number, First Name, and Last Name fields from the Account Manager table to display them in the design grid.

4 Double-click the Account Number, Account Name, Street, City, State, Postal Code, Account Type, Services Needed, Amount Paid, and Current Due fields from the Account table to add the fields to the design grid.

5 View the query results and scroll through the fields to make sure you have included all the necessary fields. If you have omitted a field, return to Design view and add it.

6 Click the Save button on the Quick Access Toolbar to save the query, type `Account Managers and Accounts` as the name of the query, and then click the OK button.

7 Close the query.

To Create an Additional Query for the Report Using Expression Builder

1 CREATE TABLES | 2 CREATE QUERIES | **3 CREATE REPORT** | 4 SPECIFY GROUPING & SORTING | 5 ADD FIELDS
6 ADD SUBREPORT | 7 ADD TITLE, PAGE NUMBER, & DATE | 8 CREATE SECOND REPORT

The following steps create the Workshop Offerings and Workshops query, which includes a calculated field for hours remaining, that is, the total number of hours minus the hours spent. *Why? PrattLast Associates needs to include in the Account Manager Master List the number of hours that remain in a workshop offering.*

1
- Display the Create tab and then click the Query Design button (Create tab | Queries group) to create a new query.

- Click the Workshop table, click the Add button (Show Table dialog box), click the Workshop Offerings table, click the Add button, and then click the Close button to close the Show Table dialog box.

- Double-click the Account Number and Workshop Code fields from the Workshop Offerings table to add the fields to the design grid.

- Double-click the Workshop Description field from the Workshop table.

- Double-click the Total Hours and Hours Spent fields from the Workshop Offerings table to add the fields to the design grid.

- Click the Field row in the first open column in the design grid to select it.

- Click the Builder button (Query Tools Design tab | Query Setup group) to display the Expression Builder dialog box (Figure 6–7).

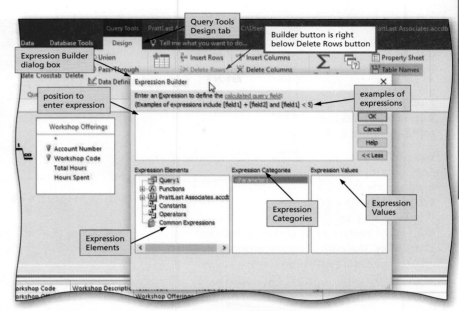

Figure 6–7

- Double-click PrattLast Associates in the Expression Elements section to display the categories of objects within the PrattLast Associates database, and then double-click Tables to display a list of tables.

- Click the Workshop Offerings table to select it.

- Double-click the Total Hours field to add it to the expression.

- Type a minus sign (–) to add it to the expression.

- Double-click the Hours Spent field to add it to the expression (Figure 6–8).

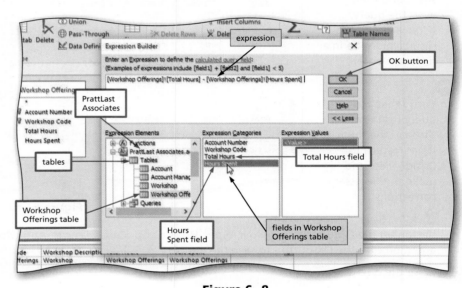

Figure 6–8

Q&A

Why are the fields preceded by a table name and an exclamation point?
This notation qualifies the field; that is, it indicates to which table the field belongs.

Could I type the expression instead of using the Expression Builder?
Yes. You could type it directly into the design grid. You could also right-click the column and click Zoom to allow you to type the expression in the Zoom dialog box. Finally, you could use the Expression Builder, but simply type the expression rather than clicking any buttons. Use whichever method you find most convenient.

- Click the OK button (Expression Builder dialog box) to close the dialog box and add the expression you entered to the design grid.

- With the field in the grid containing the expression selected, click the Property Sheet button (Query Tools Design tab | Show/Hide group) to display the property sheet for the new field.

- Ensure that the General tab is selected, click the Caption property box and type **Hours Remaining** as the caption (Figure 6–9).

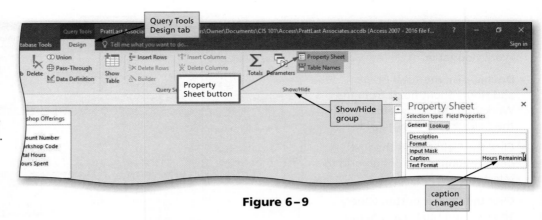

Figure 6–9

 Q&A I do not have a Caption property in my property sheet. What went wrong? What should I do?

You either inadvertently clicked a different location in the grid, or you have not yet completed entering the expression. The easiest way to ensure you have done both is to click any other column in the grid and then click the column with the expression.

- Close the property sheet and then view the query (Figure 6–10). (Your results might be in a different order.)

- Verify that your query results match those in the figure. If not, return to Design view and make the necessary corrections.

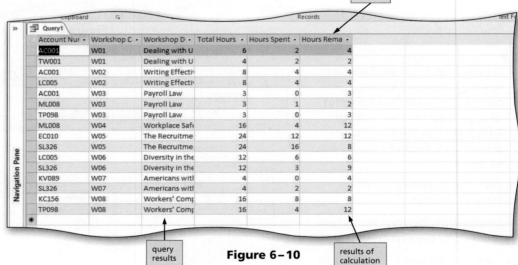

Figure 6–10

- Click the Save button on the Quick Access Toolbar, type **Workshop Offerings and Workshops** as the name of the query, and then click the OK button to save the query.

- Close the query.

Other Ways

1. Right-click field in grid, click Build

How do you determine the tables and fields for the report?

If you determine that data should be presented as a report, you need to then determine what tables and fields contain the data for the report.

Examine the requirements for the report in general to determine the tables. Do the requirements only relate to data in a single table, or does the data come from multiple tables? Is the data in a query, or could you create a query that contains some or all of the fields necessary for the report?

Examine the specific requirements for the report to determine the fields necessary. Look for all the data items that are specified for the report. Each item should correspond to a field in a table, or it should be able to be computed from a field or fields in a table. This information gives you the list of fields to include in the query.

Determine the order of the fields. Examine the requirements to determine the order in which the fields should appear. Be logical and consistent in your ordering. For example, in an address, the city should come before the state, and the state should come before the postal code, unless there is some compelling reason for another order.

What decisions do you make in determining the organization of the report?

Determine sort order. Is there a special order in which the records should appear?

Determine grouping. Should the records be grouped in some fashion? If so, what information should appear before the records in a group? If, for example, accounts are grouped by account manager number, the number of the account manager should probably appear before the group. Should the account manager name also appear? What should appear after the group? For example, are there some fields for which subtotals should be calculated? If so, the subtotals would come after the group.

Determine whether to include a subreport. Rather than use grouping, you can include a subreport, as shown in the Account Manager Master List shown in Figure 6–1a. The data concerning workshop offerings for the account could have been presented by grouping the workshop offerings' data by account number. The headings currently in the subreport would have appeared in the group header. Instead, it is presented in a subreport. Subreports, which are reports in their own right, offer more flexibility in formatting than group headers and footers. More importantly, in the Account Manager Master List, some accounts do not have any workshop offerings. If this information were presented using grouping, the group header will still appear for these accounts. With a subreport, accounts that have no workshop offerings do not appear.

To Create an Initial Report in Design View

1 CREATE TABLES | 2 CREATE QUERIES | 3 CREATE REPORT | 4 SPECIFY GROUPING & SORTING | 5 ADD FIELDS
6 ADD SUBREPORT | 7 ADD TITLE, PAGE NUMBER, & DATE | 8 CREATE SECOND REPORT

Creating the report shown in Figure 6–1a from scratch involves creating the initial report in Design view, adding the subreport, modifying the subreport separately from the main report, and then making the final modifications to the main report.

When you want to create a report from scratch, you use Design view rather than the Report Wizard. *Why? The Report Wizard is suitable for simple, customized reports. With Report Design, you can make advanced design changes, such as adding subreports.*

The following steps create the initial version of the Account Manager Master List and select the **record source** for the report; that is, the table or query that will furnish the data for the report. The steps then specify sorting and grouping for the report.

1

- Display the Create tab.

- Click the Report Design button (Create tab | Reports group) to create a report in Design view.

- Ensure the selector for the entire report, the box in the upper-left corner of the report, contains a small black square, which indicates that the report is selected.

- Click the Property Sheet button (Report Design Tools Design tab | Tools group) to display a property sheet.

Q&A Can I make the property sheet box wider so I can see more of the items in the Record Source list?

Yes, you can make the property sheet wider by dragging its left or right border.

- Drag the left border, if necessary, to increase the width of the property sheet.

- With the All tab (Property Sheet) selected, click the Record Source property box arrow to display the list of available tables and queries (Figure 6–11).

Q&A Can I move the property sheet?

Yes, you can move the property sheet by dragging its title bar.

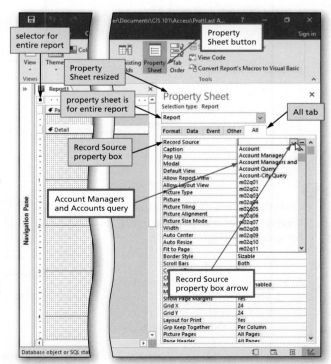

Figure 6–11

2

- Click the Account Managers and Accounts query to select the query as the record source for the report.
- Close the property sheet by clicking the Property Sheet button (Report Design Tools Design tab | Tools group).

Other Ways

1. Right-click report selector, click Properties

To Group and Sort

1 CREATE TABLES | 2 CREATE QUERIES | 3 CREATE REPORT | 4 SPECIFY GROUPING & SORTING | 5 ADD FIELDS
6 ADD SUBREPORT | 7 ADD TITLE, PAGE NUMBER, & DATE | 8 CREATE SECOND REPORT

In Design view of the report, you can specify both grouping and sorting by using the Group & Sort button on the Design tab, just as you did in Layout view. The following steps specify both grouping and sorting in the report. *Why? PrattLast has determined that the records in the report should be grouped by account manager number. That is, all the accounts of a given account manager should appear together. Within the accounts of a given account manager, they have determined that accounts are to be ordered by account number.*

1

- Click the Group & Sort button (Report Design Tools Design tab | Grouping & Totals group) to display the Group, Sort, and Total pane (Figure 6–12).

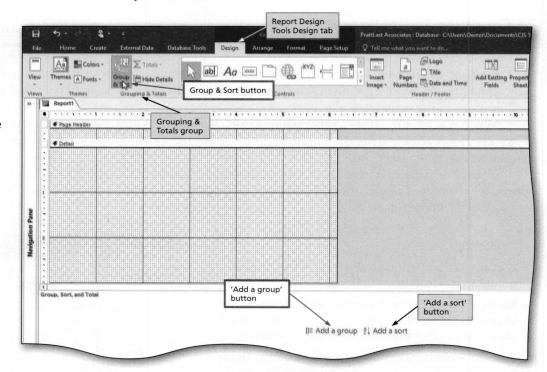

Figure 6–12

2

- Click the 'Add a group' button to display the list of available fields for grouping (Figure 6–13).

Q&A The list of fields disappeared before I had a chance to select a field. What should I do?
Click the select field arrow to once again display the list of fields.

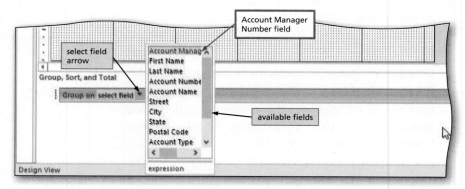

Figure 6–13

3

- Click the 'Account Manager Number' field to group by account manager number (Figure 6–14).

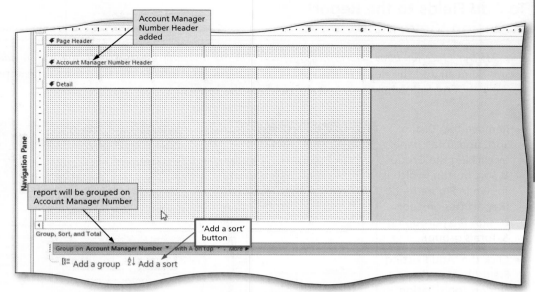

Figure 6–14

4

- Click the 'Add a sort' button to display the list of available fields for sorting (Figure 6–15).

5

- Click the Account Number field to sort by account number.

- Save the report, using **Account Manager Master List** as the report name.

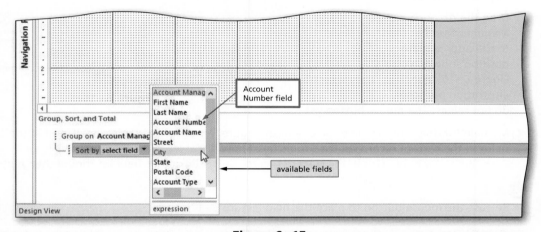

Figure 6–15

Other Ways

1. Right-click any open area of the report, click Sorting & Grouping

---

Controls and Sections

Recall from Module 4 that a report contains three types of controls: bound controls, unbound controls, and calculated controls. As you learned previously, reports contain standard sections, including the Report Header, Report Footer, Page Header, Page Footer, and Detail sections. When the data in a report is grouped, there are two additional possible sections. The contents of the **Group Header section** are printed before the records in a particular group, and the contents of the **Group Footer section** are printed after the group. In the Discount Report (Figure 6–1b), for example, which is grouped by account manager number, the Group Header section contains the account manager number and name, and the Group Footer section contains subtotals of the Amount Paid and Current Due fields.

To Add Fields to the Report in Design View

Why? *Once you have determined the fields that are necessary for the report, you need to add them to the report design.* You can add the fields to the report by dragging them from the field list to the appropriate position on the report. The following steps add the fields to the report.

❶

- Remove the 'Group, Sort, and Total' pane by clicking the Group & Sort button, which is shown in Figure 6–12 (Report Design Tools Design tab | Grouping & Totals group).

- Click the 'Add Existing Fields' button (Report Design Tools Design tab | Tools group) to display a field list.

- Drag the Account Manager Number field to the approximate position shown in Figure 6–16. (For illustration purposes, do not release the mouse button yet.)

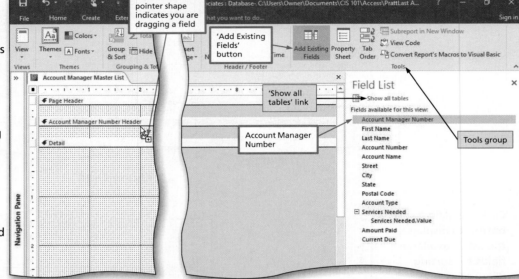

Figure 6–16

Q&A My field list does not look like the one in the figure. It has several tables listed, and at the top it has 'Show only fields in the current record source.' Yours has 'Show all tables.' What should I do?

Click the 'Show only fields in the current record source' link. Your field list should then match the one in the figure.

❷

- Release the mouse button to place the field (Figure 6–17).

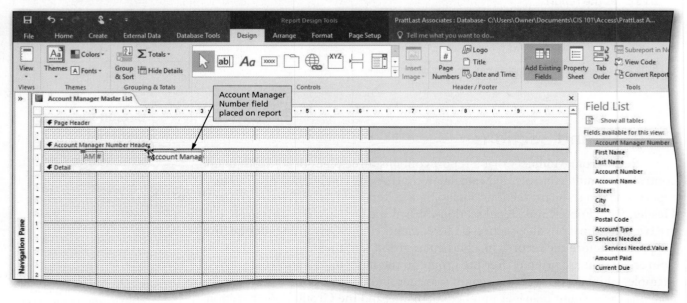

Figure 6–17

❸

- Place the remaining fields in the positions shown in Figure 6–18.

- Adjust the positions of the labels to those shown in the figure. If any field is not in the correct position, drag it to its correct location. To move the control or the attached label separately, drag the large handle in the upper-left corner of the control or label. You can align controls using the Align button (Report Design Tools Arrange tab | Sizing & Ordering group) or adjust spacing by using the Size/Space button (Report Design Tools Arrange tab | Sizing & Ordering group).

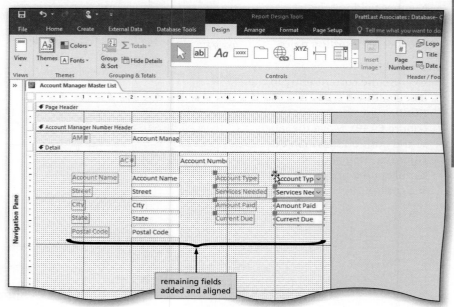

Figure 6–18

Q&A

Sometimes I find it hard to move a control a very small amount. Is there a simpler way to do this other than dragging it with a mouse?

Yes. Once you have selected the control, you can use the arrow keys to move the control a very small amount in the desired direction.

Could I drag several fields from the field list at once?

Yes. You can select multiple fields by selecting the first field, holding down the CTRL key and selecting the additional fields. Once you have selected multiple fields, you can drag them all at once. How you choose to select fields and drag them onto the report is a matter of personal preference.

Experiment

- Select more than one control and then experiment with the Size/Space and the Align buttons (Report Design Tools Arrange tab | Sizing & Ordering group) to see their effects. After trying each one, click the Undo button to undo the change. If you used the Arrange tab, redisplay the Design tab.

To Change Labels

1 CREATE TABLES | 2 CREATE QUERIES | 3 CREATE REPORT | 4 SPECIFY GROUPING & SORTING | 5 ADD FIELDS
6 ADD SUBREPORT | 7 ADD TITLE, PAGE NUMBER, & DATE | 8 CREATE SECOND REPORT

The labels for the Account Manager Number and Account Number fields currently contain the captions AM # and AC # for the fields. The following step changes the contents of the label for the Account Manager Number field from AM # to Account Manager Number. It also changes the contents of the label for the Account Number field from AC # to Account Number. *Why? Because there is plenty of room on the report to display longer names for both fields, you can make the report more descriptive by changing the labels.*

❶

- Click the label for the Account Manager Number field to select the label.

- Click the label for the Account Manager Number field a second time to produce an insertion point.

- Use the BACKSPACE or DELETE key to erase the current entry in the label, and then type **Account Manager Number** as the new entry.

- Click outside the label to deselect the label and then click the label a second time to select it.

- Move the label to the position indicated in Figure 6–19 by dragging the move handle in the upper-left corner of the label.

- Click the label for the Account Number field to select it.

- Click the label a second time to produce an insertion point.

- Use the BACKSPACE or DELETE key to erase the current entry in the label and then type **Account Number** as the new entry (Figure 6–19). Move the label to the position shown in the Figure by dragging the move handle in the upper-left corner of the control.

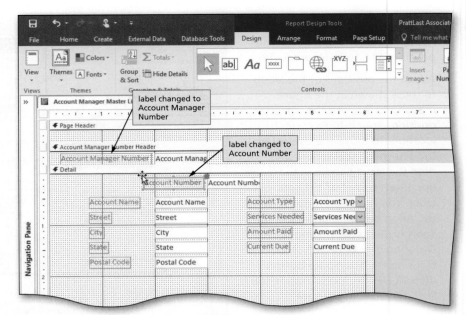

Figure 6–19

Using Other Tools in the Controls Group

Previously, you used the Subform/Subreport tool within the Controls group on the Design tab to place special controls on a form. The Controls group has additional tools available that can be used with forms and reports. A description of the additional tools appears in Table 6–3.

Table 6–3 Additional Tools in the Controls Group	
Tool	**Description**
Select	Select to be able to size, move, or edit existing controls. If you click another tool and want to cancel the effect of the tool before using it, you can click the Select tool.
Text Box	Create a text box for entering, editing, and displaying data. You can also bind the text box to a field in the underlying table or query.
Label	Create a label, a box containing text that cannot be edited and is independent of other controls, such as a title.
Button	Create a command button.
Tab Control	Create a tab control, which contains a series of tabbed pages. Each tabbed page can contain its own controls.
Hyperlink	Inserts a hyperlink to an existing file, Web page, database object, or email address.
Option Group	Create an option group, which is a rectangle containing a collection of option buttons. To select an option, you click the corresponding option button.
Insert or Remove Page Break	Insert or remove a physical page break (typically in a report).
Combo Box	Create a combo box, which is a combination of a text box and a list box.
Chart	Create a chart.
Line	Draw a line on a form or report.
Toggle Button	Add a toggle button. With a toggle button, a user can make a Yes/No selection by clicking the button. The button either appears to be pressed (for Yes) or not pressed (for No).
List Box	Create a list box, a box that allows the user to select from a list of options.
Rectangle	Create a rectangle.
Check Box	Insert a check box. With a check box a user can make multiple Yes/No selections.
Unbound Object Frame	Insert an OLE object (for example, a graph, picture, sound file, or video) that is not contained in a field in a table within the database.

Attachment	Insert an Attachment field.
Option Button	Insert an option button. With an option button, a user can make a single Yes/No selection from among a collection of at least two choices.
Subform/Subreport	Create a subform (a form contained within another form) or a subreport (a report contained within another report).
Bound Object Frame	Insert an OLE object (for example, a graph, picture, sound file, or video) that is contained in a field in a table within the database.
Image	Insert a frame into which you can insert a graphic. The graphic will be the same for all records.

1 CREATE TABLES | 2 CREATE QUERIES | 3 CREATE REPORT | 4 SPECIFY GROUPING & SORTING | 5 ADD FIELDS
6 ADD SUBREPORT | 7 ADD TITLE, PAGE NUMBER, & DATE | 8 CREATE SECOND REPORT

To Add Text Boxes

You can place a text box on a report or form by using the Text Box tool in the Controls group on the Design tab. The text box consists of a control that is initially unbound and an attached label. The next step is to update the **control source**, which is the source of data for the control. You can do so by entering the appropriate expression in the text box or by updating the Control Source property in the property sheet with the expression.

Once you have updated the control source property with the expression, the control becomes a **calculated control**. If the expression is just a single field (for example, =[Amount Paid]), the control would be a **bound control**. *Why? The control is bound (tied) to the corresponding field.* The process of converting an unbound control to a bound control is called **binding**. Expressions can also be arithmetic operations: for example, calculating the sum of amount paid and current due. Many times, you need to **concatenate**, or combine, two or more text data items into a single expression; the process is called **concatenation**. To concatenate text data, you use the **ampersand (&)** operator. For example, [First Name]& ' '&[Last Name] indicates the concatenation of a first name, a single blank space, and a last name.

The following steps add text boxes and create calculated controls.

1

• Click the Text Box tool (Report Design Tools Design tab | Controls group) and move the pointer to the approximate position shown in Figure 6–20.

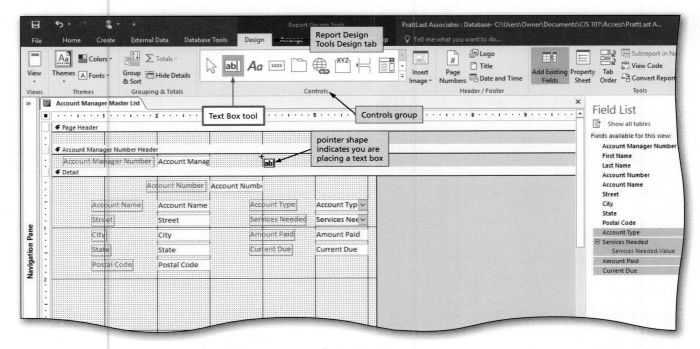

Figure 6–20

❷

- Click the position shown in Figure 6–20 to place a text box on the report (Figure 6–21).

Q&A My text box overlapped an object already on the screen. Is that a problem?

No. You can always move and/or resize your text box to the desired location and size later.

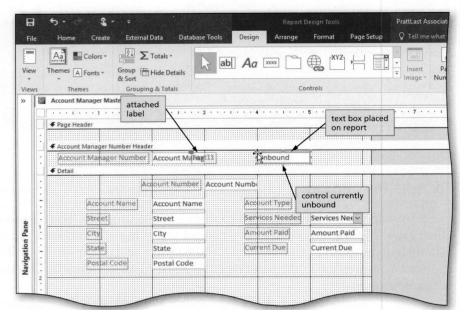

Figure 6–21

❸

- Click in the text box to produce an insertion point (Figure 6–22).

Q&A I inadvertently clicked somewhere else, so the text box was no longer selected. When I clicked the text box a second time, it was selected, but there was no insertion point. What should I do?

Simply click another time.

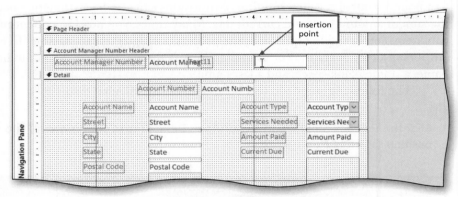

Figure 6–22

❹

- In the text box, type `=[First Name]&' '&[Last Name]` to display the first name of the account manager, followed by a space, and then the last name of the account manager.

Q&A Could I use the Expression Builder instead of typing the expression?

Yes. Click the Property Sheet button and then click the Build button, which contains three dots, next to the Control Source property.

Do I need to use single quotes (')?

No. You could also use double quotes (").

- Click in the text box label to select the label and then click the label a second time to produce an insertion point (Figure 6–23).

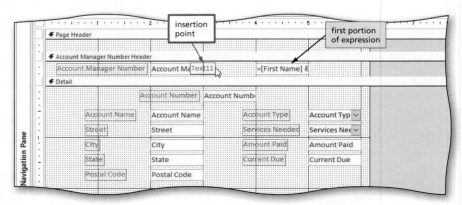

Figure 6–23

5
- Use the BACKSPACE or DELETE key to erase the current entry in the label and then type **Name** as the new entry.
- Click outside the label to deselect it and then drag the label to the position shown in the Figure by dragging the Move handle in the upper-left corner of the label (Figure 6–24).

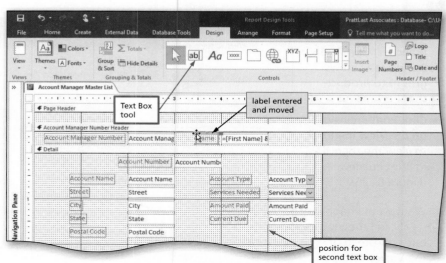

Figure 6–24

6
- Use the techniques in Steps 1 through 5 to place a second text box in the position indicated in Figure 6–24. Type **= [Amount Paid]+[Current Due]** as the expression in the text box, drag the label to the position shown in the figure, erase the contents of the label, and type **Total Amount** in the label (Figure 6–25).

Q&A My label is not in the correct position. What should I do?
Click outside the label to deselect it, click the label, and then drag it to the desired position.

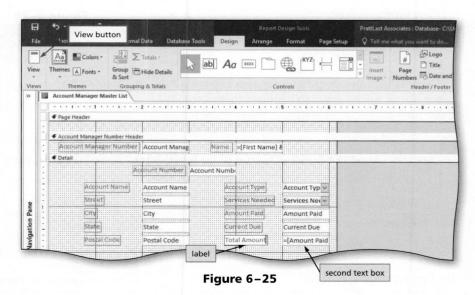

Figure 6–25

Total Amount is already a calculated field in the Account table. Why would you add the calculation to the report rather than just using the calculated field?
One reason is that if you later decide to move this database to another database management system, such as a SQL Server, the new DBMS may not allow calculated fields.

CONSIDER THIS

1 CREATE TABLES | 2 CREATE QUERIES | 3 CREATE REPORT | 4 SPECIFY GROUPING & SORTING | **5 ADD FIELDS**
6 ADD SUBREPORT | 7 ADD TITLE, PAGE NUMBER, & DATE | 8 CREATE SECOND REPORT

To View the Report in Print Preview

The following steps view the report in Print Preview. ***Why?*** *As you are working on a report in Design view, it is useful to periodically view the report to gauge how it will look containing data. One way to do so is to use Print Preview.*

- Click the View button arrow (Report Design Tools Design tab | Views group) to produce the View menu.

- Click Print Preview on the View menu to view the report in Print Preview (Figure 6–26).

What would happen if I clicked the View button instead of the View button arrow?

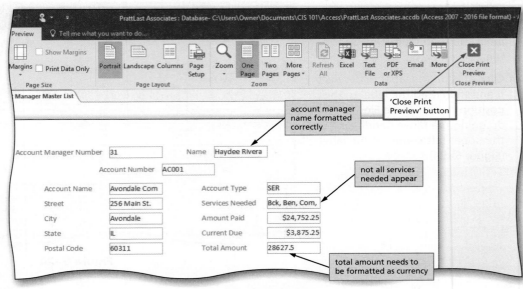

Figure 6–26

The icon on the View button is the icon for Report View, so you would view the results in Report view. This is another useful way to view a report, but compared with Print Preview, Report View does not give as accurate a picture of how the final printed report will look.

The total amount does not appear as currency. Also, the Account Name and Services Needed fields do not display the entire value. How can I address these issues?
You will address these issues in the next sections.

- Click the 'Close Print Preview' button (Print Preview tab | Close Preview group) to return to Design view.

Other Ways

1. Click Print Preview button on status bar

---

1 CREATE TABLES | 2 CREATE QUERIES | 3 CREATE REPORT | 4 SPECIFY GROUPING & SORTING | 5 ADD FIELDS
6 ADD SUBREPORT | 7 ADD TITLE, PAGE NUMBER, & DATE | 8 CREATE SECOND REPORT

To Format a Control

Why? *When you add a calculated control to a report, you often need to format the control, for example, to display a currency value with a dollar sign, decimal point, and two decimal places.* You can use a control's property sheet to change the value in the appropriate property. If a property does not appear on the screen, you have two choices. You can click the tab on which the property is located. For example, if it were a control related to data, you would click the Data tab to show only data-related properties. Many people, however, prefer to click the All tab, which shows all properties, and then simply scroll through the properties, if necessary, until locating the appropriate property. The following steps change the format of the Total Amount control to Currency by changing the value of the Format property and the Decimal Places property.

1

- Because you will not be using the field list, remove it by clicking the 'Add Existing Fields' button (Report Design Tools Design tab | Tools group).

- Click the control containing the expression for Total Amount to select it, and then click the Property Sheet button (Report Design Tools Design tab | Tools group) to display the property sheet.

- If necessary, click the All tab (Figure 6–27).

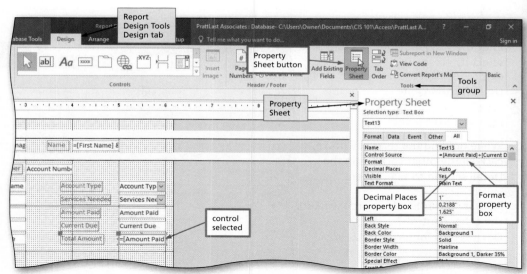

Figure 6–27

 Experiment

- Click the other tabs in the property sheet to see the types of properties on each tab. When finished, once again click the All tab.

2

- Click the Format property box, click the arrow that appears, and then click Currency to select Currency as the format.

- Click the Decimal Places property box, click the arrow that appears, and then click 2 to select two decimal places.

- Remove the property sheet by clicking the Property Sheet button (Report Design Tools Design tab | Tools group) a second time.

- Preview the report using Print Preview to see the effect of the property changes.

- Click the 'Close Print Preview' button (Print Preview tab | Close Preview group) to return to Design view.

Other Ways

1. Right-click control, click Properties

To Group Controls

1 CREATE TABLES | 2 CREATE QUERIES | 3 CREATE REPORT | 4 SPECIFY GROUPING & SORTING | 5 ADD FIELDS
6 ADD SUBREPORT | 7 ADD TITLE, PAGE NUMBER, & DATE | 8 CREATE SECOND REPORT

The following steps group the controls within the Detail section. *Why? If your report contains a collection of controls that you will frequently want to format in the same way, you can simplify the process of selecting all the controls by grouping them. Once they are grouped, selecting any control in the group automatically selects all of the controls in the group. You can then apply the desired change to all the controls.*

1

- Click the Account Number control to select it.

Q&A Do I click the white space or the label?

Click the white space.

- While holding the SHIFT key down, click all the other controls in the Detail section to select them.

Q&A Does it matter in which order I select the other controls?

No. It is only important that you ultimately select all the controls.

- Release the SHIFT key.
- Display the Report Design Tools Arrange tab.
- Click the Size/Space button (Report Design Tools Arrange tab | Sizing & Ordering group) to display the Size/Space menu (Figure 6–28).

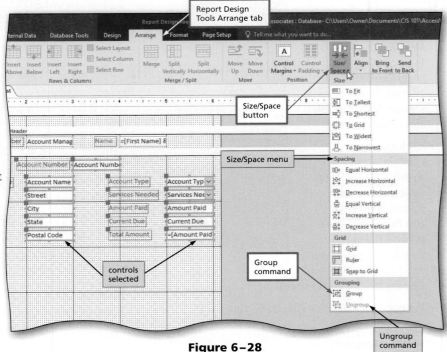

Figure 6–28

2

- Click Group on the Size/Space button menu to group the controls.

Q&A What if I make a mistake and group the wrong collection of controls?

Ungroup the controls using the following steps, and then group the correct collection of controls.

TO UNGROUP CONTROLS

If you no longer need to simultaneously modify all the controls you have placed in a group, you can ungroup the controls. To do so, you would use the following steps.

1. Click any of the controls in a group to select the entire group.
2. Display the Report Design Tools Arrange tab.
3. Click the Size/Space button (Report Design Tools Arrange tab | Sizing & Ordering group) to display the Size/Space button menu.
4. Click the Ungroup button on the Size/Space button menu to ungroup the controls.

CONSIDER THIS

Can you group controls in forms?

Yes. The process is identical to the process of grouping controls in reports.

To Modify Grouped Controls

1 CREATE TABLES | 2 CREATE QUERIES | 3 CREATE REPORT | 4 SPECIFY GROUPING & SORTING | 5 ADD FIELDS
6 ADD SUBREPORT | 7 ADD TITLE, PAGE NUMBER, & DATE | 8 CREATE SECOND REPORT

To modify grouped controls, click any control in the group to select the entire group. *Why? Any change you make then affects all controls in the group.* The following steps bold the controls in the group, resize them, and then change the border style.

1

- If necessary, click any one of the grouped controls to select the group.

- Display the Report Design Tools Format tab.

- Click the Bold button (Report Design Tools Format tab | Font group) to bold all the controls in the group (Figure 6–29).

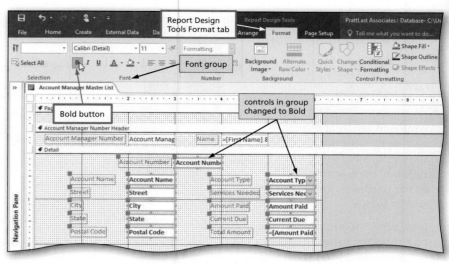

Figure 6–29

2

- Display the Report Design Tools Design tab.

- Drag the right sizing handle of the Services Needed control to the approximate position shown in Figure 6–30 to resize all the controls in the group.

 Do I need to use the Services Needed field or could I use another field?
Any field in the group will work.

How do I change only one control in the group?
Double-click the control to select just the one control and not the entire group. You then can make any change you want to that control.

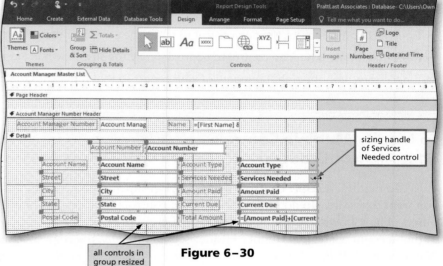

Figure 6–30

3

- Click the Property Sheet button (Report Design Tools Design tab | Tools group) to display the property sheet for the grouped controls.

- With the All tab (Property Sheet) selected, ensure the Border Style property is set to Solid. If it is not, click the Border Style property box to display an arrow, click the arrow to display the list of available border styles, and click Solid.

- Click the Border Width property box to display an arrow and then click the arrow to display the list of available border widths (Figure 6–31).

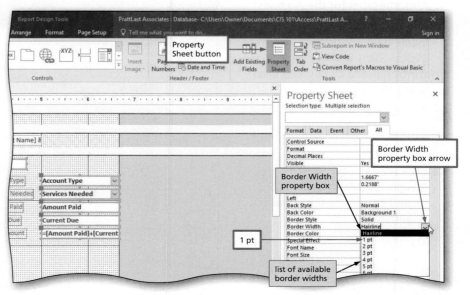

Figure 6–31

4

- Click 1 pt to select the border width.

🔍 **Experiment**

- Try the other border styles and widths to see their effects. In each case, view the report and then return to Design view. When finished, once again select Solid as the border style and 1 pt as the border width.

- Click the Font Size property box to display an arrow and then click the arrow to display the list of available font sizes.

- Click 10 to change the font size to 10.

- Close the property sheet.

- Double-click the Services Needed control to select the control without selecting the entire group.

- Resize the Services Needed control to approximately the size shown in Figure 6–32.

- If necessary, drag the right boundary of your report so that it matches the one shown in Figure 6–32.

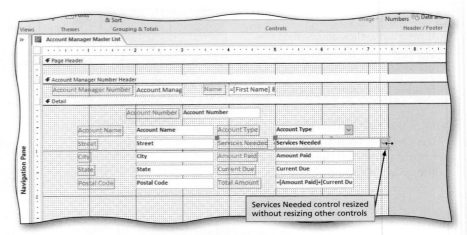

Figure 6–32

To Modify Multiple Controls That Are Not Grouped

1 CREATE TABLES | 2 CREATE QUERIES | 3 CREATE REPORT | 4 SPECIFY GROUPING & SORTING | 5 ADD FIELDS
6 ADD SUBREPORT | 7 ADD TITLE, PAGE NUMBER, & DATE | 8 CREATE SECOND REPORT

To modify multiple controls that are not grouped together, you must simultaneously select all the controls you want to modify. To do so, click one of the controls and then hold the SHIFT key down while selecting the others. The following steps italicize all the labels in the Detail section and then bold all the controls and labels in the Account Manager Number Header section. Finally, the steps increase the size of the Account Manager Name control. **Why?** *With the current size, some names are not displayed completely.*

1

- Click the label for the Account Number control to select it.

- While holding the SHIFT key down, click the labels for all the other controls in the Detail section to select them.

- Release the SHIFT key.

- Display the Report Design Tools Format tab.

- Click the Italic button (Report Design Tools Format tab | Font group) to italicize the labels (Figure 6–33).

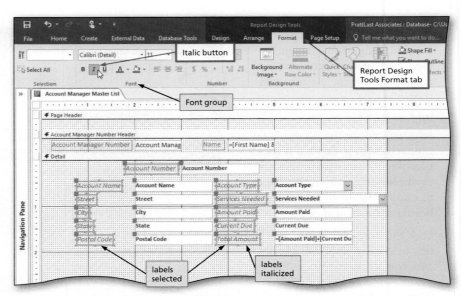

Figure 6–33

2

- Click in the vertical ruler to the left of the Account Manager Number control to select all the controls in the section.

What exactly is selected when I click in the vertical ruler?
If you picture a horizontal line through the point you clicked, any control that intersects that horizontal line would be selected.

- Use the buttons on the Report Design Tools Arrange tab to align the controls on the top, if necessary.

- Display the Report Design Tools Format tab, if necessary, and then click the Bold button (Report Design Tools Format tab | Font group) to bold all the selected controls (Figure 6–34).

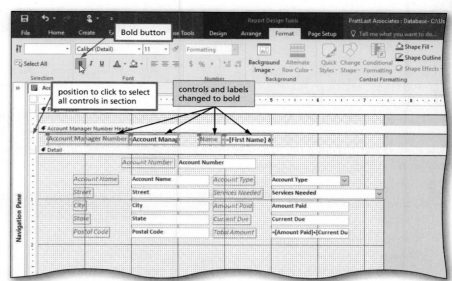

Figure 6–34

3

- Click outside the selected controls to deselect them. Click the control containing the expression for the account manager's name to select it.

Why do I have to deselect the controls and then select one of them a second time?
If you do not do so, any action you take would apply to all the selected controls rather than just the one you want.

- Drag the right sizing handle of the selected control to the approximate position shown in Figure 6–35.

- View the report in Print Preview and then make any necessary adjustments.

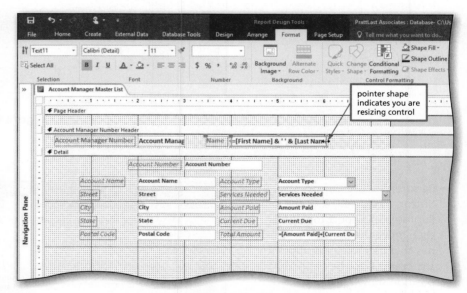

Figure 6–35

Undoing and Saving

Remember that if you make a mistake, you can often correct it by clicking the Undo button on the Quick Access Toolbar. Clicking the Undo button will reverse your most recent change. You can also click the Undo button more than once to reverse multiple changes.

You should save your work frequently. That way, if you have problems that the Undo button will not fix, you can close the report without saving it and open it again. The report will be in exactly the state it was in the last time you saved it.

To Add a Subreport

To add a subreport to a report, you use the Subform/Subreport tool on the Design tab. The following steps add a subreport to display the workshop data, after first ensuring the 'Use Control Wizards' button is selected. *Why? Provided the 'Use Control Wizards' button is selected, a wizard will guide you through the process of adding the subreport.*

1

- Display the Report Design Tools Design tab.

- Click the More button, which is shown below in Figure 6–37 (Report Design Tools Design tab | Controls group), to display a gallery of available tools (Figure 6–36).

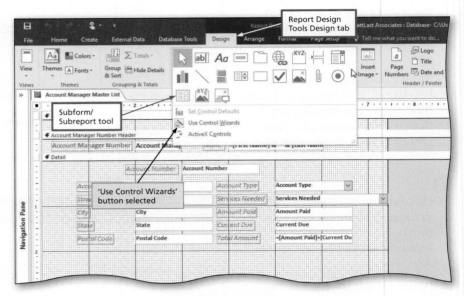

Figure 6–36

2

- Be sure the 'Use Control Wizards' button is selected, click the Subform/Subreport tool, and then move the pointer, which has changed to a plus sign with a subreport, to the approximate position shown in Figure 6–37.

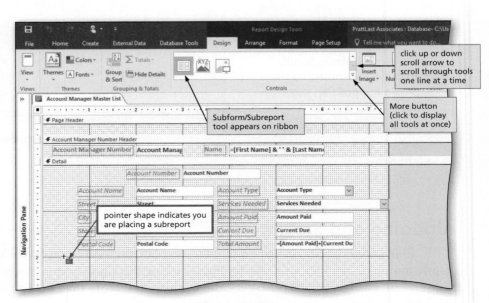

Figure 6–37

3

- Click the position shown in Figure 6–37 to place the subreport and display the SubReport Wizard dialog box. Be sure the 'Use existing Tables and Queries' option button is selected (Figure 6–38).

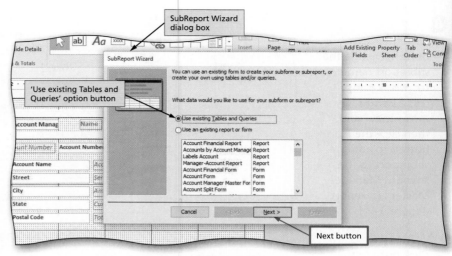

Figure 6–38

4

- Click the Next button.
- Click the Tables/Queries box arrow.
- Scroll down until Query: Workshop Offerings and Workshops is visible, click 'Query: Workshop Offerings and Workshops,' and then click the 'Add All Fields' button to select all the fields in the query (Figure 6–39).

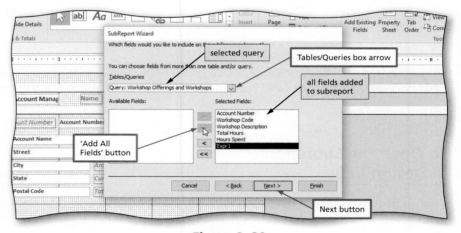

Figure 6–39

5

- Click the Next button and then ensure the 'Choose from a list.' option button is selected (Figure 6–40).

Q&A What is the purpose of this dialog box?
You use this dialog box to indicate the fields that link the main report (referred to as a "form") to the subreport (referred to as a "subform"). If the fields have the same name, as they often will, you can simply select 'Choose from a list' and then accept the selection Access already has made.

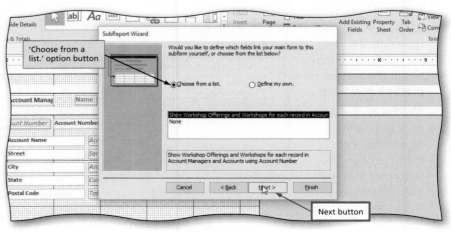

Figure 6–40

6

- Click the Next button, change the subreport name to `Workshop Offerings by Account`, and then click the Finish button to add the subreport to the Account Manager Master List report (Figure 6–41).

7

- Click outside the subreport to deselect the subreport.
- Save your changes.
- Close the report.

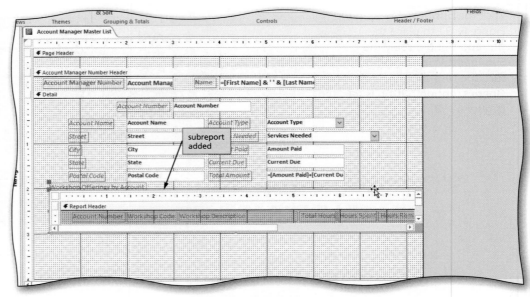

Figure 6–41

Break Point: If you wish to stop working through the module at this point, you can resume the project at a later time by running Access, opening the database called PrattLast Associates, and continuing to follow the steps from this location forward.

To Open the Subreport in Design View

1 CREATE TABLES | 2 CREATE QUERIES | 3 CREATE REPORT | 4 SPECIFY GROUPING & SORTING | 5 ADD FIELDS
6 ADD SUBREPORT | 7 ADD TITLE, PAGE NUMBER, & DATE | 8 CREATE SECOND REPORT

The following step opens the subreport in Design view so it can be modified. *Why? The subreport appears as a separate report in the Navigation Pane. You can modify it just as you modify any other report.*

1

- Open the Navigation Pane, scroll down so that the Workshop Offerings by Account report appears, and then right-click the Workshop Offerings by Account report to produce a shortcut menu.
- Click Design View on the shortcut menu to open the subreport in Design view (Figure 6–42).

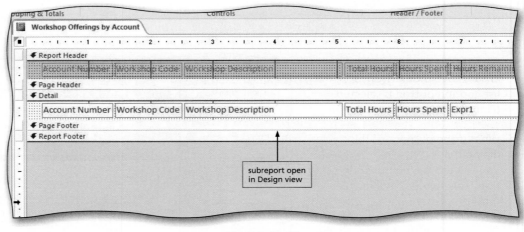

Figure 6–42

Print Layout Issues

If there is a problem with your report, for example, a report that is too wide for the printed page, the report will display a green triangular symbol in the upper-left corner. The green triangle is called an **error indicator**. Clicking it displays an 'Error Checking Options' button. Clicking the 'Error Checking Options' button produces the 'Error Checking Options menu,' as shown in Figure 6–43.

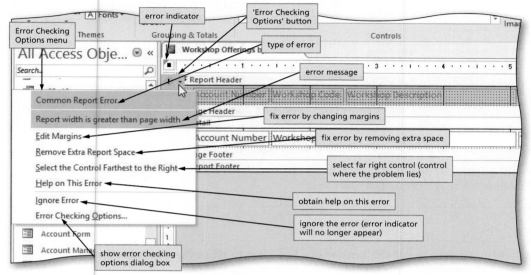

Figure 6–43

The first line in the menu is simply a statement of the type of error that occurred. The second is a description of the specific error, in this case, the fact that the report width is greater than the page width. This situation could lead to data not appearing where you expect it to, as well as the printing of some blank pages.

The next three lines provide potential solutions to the error. You could change the margins to allow more space for the report. You could remove some extra space. You could select the control farthest to the right and move it. The fourth line gives more detailed help on the error. The Ignore Error command instructs Access to not consider this situation an error. Selecting Ignore Error would cause the error indicator to disappear without making any changes. The final line displays the Error Checking Options dialog box, where you can make other changes.

Later in this module, you will fix the problem by changing the width of the report, so you do not need to take any action at this time.

BTW
Subreports
Subreports provide more control in presenting data effectively than multiple levels of grouping can. Because grouping places headers in columns, it often can be difficult to determine the relationship between the group header and the detail. Also, you might want to present subreports side by side. You cannot do that with grouping.

To Modify the Controls in the Subreport

1 CREATE TABLES | 2 CREATE QUERIES | 3 CREATE REPORT | 4 SPECIFY GROUPING & SORTING | 5 ADD FIELDS
6 ADD SUBREPORT | 7 ADD TITLE, PAGE NUMBER, & DATE | 8 CREATE SECOND REPORT

The following step modifies the subreport by deleting the Account Number control and revising the appearance of the column headings. *Why? Because the account number appears in the main report, it does not need to be duplicated in the subreport. In addition, the column headers in the subreport should extend over two lines, as shown in Figure 6–1a.*

- Close the Navigation Pane.

- Click the Account Number control in the Detail section to select the control. Hold the SHIFT key down and click the Account Number control in the Report Header section to select both controls.

- With both controls selected, press the DELETE key to delete the controls.

- Adjust the labels in the Report Header section to match those shown in Figure 6–44. To extend a heading over two lines, click in front of the second word to produce an insertion point and then press SHIFT+ENTER to move the second word to a second line.

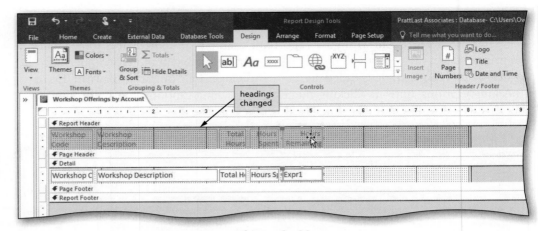

Figure 6–44

- Change the sizes and positions of the controls to match those in the figure by selecting the controls and dragging the sizing handles.

Q&A
Why does Expr1 appear in the Detail section under the Hours Remaining label?
Expr1 indicates that Hours Remaining is a calculated control.

CONSIDER THIS

How can you adjust fields where some of the entries are too long to fit in the available space?
This problem can be addressed in several ways.

1. Move the controls to allow more space between controls. Then, drag the appropriate handles on the controls that need to be expanded to enlarge them.

2. Use the Font Size property to select a smaller font size. This will allow more data to fit in the same space.

3. Use the Can Grow property. By changing the value of this property from No to Yes, the data can be spread over two lines, thus allowing all the data to print. Access will split data at natural break points, such as commas, spaces, and hyphens.

To Change the Can Grow Property

1 CREATE TABLES | 2 CREATE QUERIES | 3 CREATE REPORT | 4 SPECIFY GROUPING & SORTING | 5 ADD FIELDS
6 ADD SUBREPORT | 7 ADD TITLE, PAGE NUMBER, & DATE | 8 CREATE SECOND REPORT

The third approach to handling entries that are too long is the easiest to use and also produces a very readable report. The following steps change the Can Grow property for the Workshop Description field. *Why? Changing the Can Grow property allows Access to optimize the size of fields in reports.*

1

- Click the View button arrow and then click Print Preview to preview the report (Figure 6–45). If an error message appears, indicating the report is too wide, click the OK button.

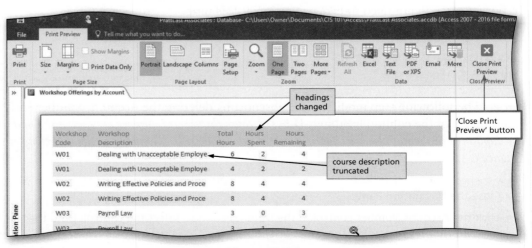

Figure 6–45

2

- Click the 'Close Print Preview' button (Print Preview tab | Close Preview group) to return to Design view.

- Click outside all of the selected controls to deselect the controls.

- Click the Workshop Description control in the Detail section to select it.

- Click the Property Sheet button (Report Design Tools Design tab | Tools group) to display the property sheet.

- With the All tab selected, scroll down until the Can Grow property appears, and then click the Can Grow property box arrow to display the list of possible values for the Can Grow property (Figure 6–46).

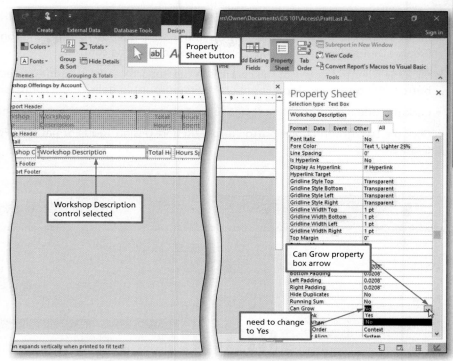

Q&A What is the effect of the Can Shrink property?

If the value of the Can Shrink property is set to Yes, Access will remove blank lines that occur when the field is empty.

Figure 6–46

3

- Click Yes in the list to allow the Workshop Description control to grow as needed.

- Close the property sheet.

To Change the Appearance of the Controls in the Subreport

1 CREATE TABLES | 2 CREATE QUERIES | 3 CREATE REPORT | 4 SPECIFY GROUPING & SORTING | 5 ADD FIELDS
6 ADD SUBREPORT | 7 ADD TITLE, PAGE NUMBER, & DATE | 8 CREATE SECOND REPORT

Why? *PrattLast Associates prefers certain formatting for the subreport controls.* The following steps change the controls in the Detail section to bold and the controls in the Report Header section to italic. They also change the background color in the Report Header section to white.

1

- Drag the right boundary of the subreport to the approximate position shown in Figure 6–47.

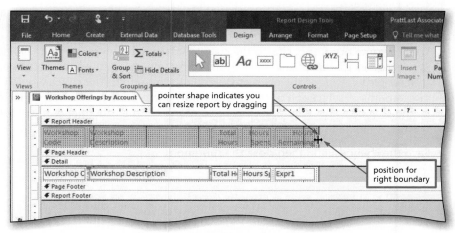

Figure 6–47

2

- Display the Report Design Tools Format tab.

- Click the ruler to the left of the controls in the Detail section to select the controls, and then click the Bold button (Report Design Tools Format tab | Font group) to bold the controls.

- Click the ruler to the left of the controls in the Report Header section to select the controls, and then click the Italic button (Report Design Tools Format tab | Font group) to italicize the controls.

- Click the title bar for the Report Header to select the header without selecting any of the controls in the header.

- Click the Background Color button arrow (Report Design Tools Format tab | Font group) to display a color palette (Figure 6–48).

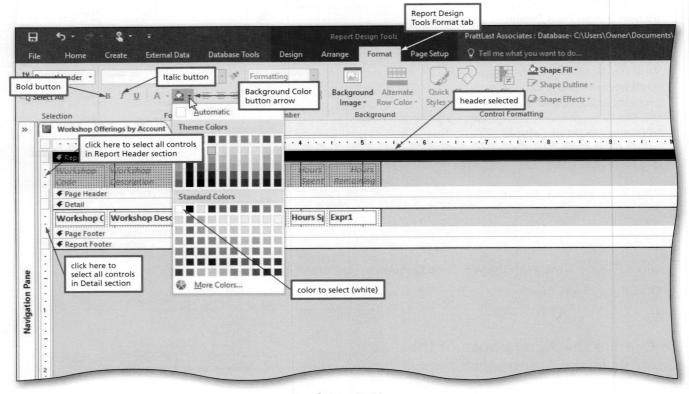

Figure 6–48

3

- Click White in the first row, first column of the Standard Colors to change the background color to white.

Q&A What is the difference between clicking a color in the Theme colors and clicking a color in the Standard Colors?
The theme colors are specific to the currently selected theme. The first column, for example, represents "background 1," one of the selected background colors in the theme. The various entries in the column represent different intensities of the color at the top of the column. The colors would be different if a different theme were selected. If you select one of the theme colors and a different theme is selected in the future, the color you selected would change to the color in the same location. On the other hand, if you select a standard color, a change of theme would have no effect on the color.

- Save the changes, and then close the subreport.

To Resize the Subreport and the Report in Design View

The following steps resize the subreport control in the main report. They then reduce the height of the detail section. *Why? Any additional white space at the bottom of the detail section appears as extra space at the end of each detail line in the final report.* Finally, the steps reduce the width of the main report.

1

- Open the Navigation Pane.

- Open the Account Manager Master List in Design view.

- Close the Navigation Pane.

- Click the subreport and drag the right sizing handle to change the size to the approximate size shown in Figure 6–49, and then drag the subreport to the approximate position shown in the figure.

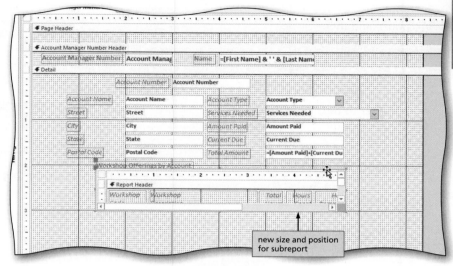

Figure 6–49

2

- Scroll down in the main report so that the lower boundary of the Detail section appears, and then drag the lower boundary of the section so that the amount of space below the subreport resembles that shown in Figure 6–50.

Q&A | I scrolled down to see the lower boundary of the Detail section, and the controls are no longer on the screen. What is the easiest way to drag the boundary when the position to which I want to drag it is not visible?

You do not need to see the location to drag to it. As you get close to the top of the visible portion of the screen, Access will automatically scroll. You might find it easier, however, to drag the boundary near the top of the visible portion of the report, use the scroll bar to scroll up, and then drag some more. You might have to scroll a couple of times.

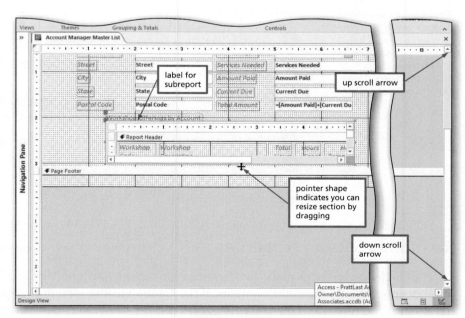

Figure 6–50

3

- If necessary, scroll back up to the top of the report, click the label for the subreport (the label that reads Workshop Offerings by Account), and then press the DELETE key to delete the label.

- Resize the report by dragging its right border to the location shown in Figure 6–51.

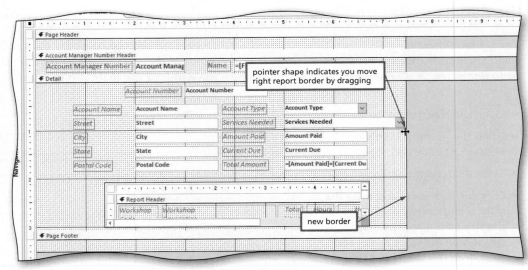

Figure 6–51

To Change the Can Grow Property

The following steps change the Can Grow property for the Account Name control so that names that are too long to fit in the available space will extend to additional lines.

1 Double-click the Account Name control.

2 If necessary, display the property sheet and scroll down until the Can Grow property appears.

3 Click the Can Grow property box and then click the Can Grow property box arrow to display the menu of available values for the Can Grow property.

4 Click Yes to change the value for the Can Grow property.

5 Close the property sheet.

To Modify Section Properties

1 CREATE TABLES | 2 CREATE QUERIES | 3 CREATE REPORT | 4 SPECIFY GROUPING & SORTING | 5 ADD FIELDS
6 ADD SUBREPORT | **7 ADD TITLE, PAGE NUMBER, & DATE** | 8 CREATE SECOND REPORT

The following steps make two modifications to the Account Manager Number Header section. The first modification, which causes the contents of the Group Header section to appear at the top of each page, changes the Repeat Section property to Yes. **Why?** *Without this change, the account manager number and name would only appear at the beginning of the group of accounts of that account manager. If the list of accounts occupies more than one page, it would not be apparent on subsequent pages which account manager is associated with those accounts.* The second modification changes the Force New Page property to Before Section, causing each section to begin at the top of a page.

- Click the Account Manager Number Header bar to select the header, and then click the Property Sheet button (Report Design Tools Design tab | Tools group) to display the property sheet.

- With the All tab selected, click the Repeat Section property box, click the arrow that appears, and then click Yes to cause the contents of the group header to appear at the top of each page of the report.

- Click the Force New Page property box, and then click the arrow that appears to display the menu of possible values (Figure 6–52).

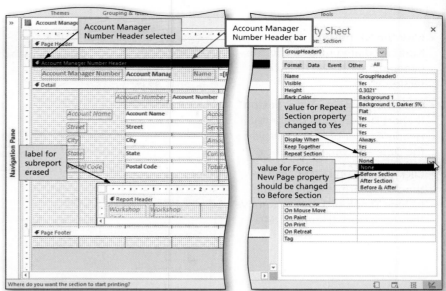

Figure 6–52

②

- Click Before Section to cause a new group to begin at the top of the next page.

- Close the property sheet.

To Add a Title, Page Number, and Date

1 CREATE TABLES | 2 CREATE QUERIES | 3 CREATE REPORT | 4 SPECIFY GROUPING & SORTING | 5 ADD FIELDS
6 ADD SUBREPORT | **7 ADD TITLE, PAGE NUMBER, & DATE** | 8 CREATE SECOND REPORT

You can add a title, page number, and date to a report using buttons on the Design tab. The following steps add a title, page number, and date to the Account Manager Master List report. The steps move the date to the page header by first cutting the date from its original position and then pasting it into the page header. *Why? The date is automatically added to the report header, which means it only would appear once at the beginning of the report. If it is in the page header, the date will appear at the top of each page.*

①

- Display the Report Design Tools Design tab, if necessary, and then click the Title button (Report Design Tools Design tab | Header/Footer group) to add a title.

Q&A The title is the same as the name of the report object. Can I change the report title without changing the name of the report object in the database?
Yes. The report title is a label, and you can change it using any of the techniques that you used for changing column headings and other labels.

- Click the Page Numbers button (Report Design Tools Design tab | Header/Footer group) to display the Page Numbers dialog box.

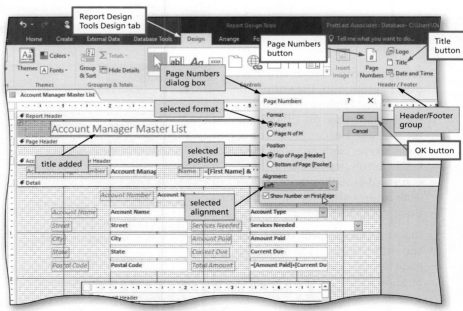

Figure 6–53

- Be sure the Page N and 'Top of Page [Header]' option buttons are selected.

- If necessary, click the Alignment arrow and select Left (Figure 6–53).

- Click the OK button (Page Numbers dialog box) to add the page number to the Header section.

- Click the 'Date and Time' button (Report Design Tools Design tab | Header/Footer group) to display the Date and Time dialog box.

- Click the option button for the third date format and click the Include Time check box to remove the check mark (Figure 6–54).

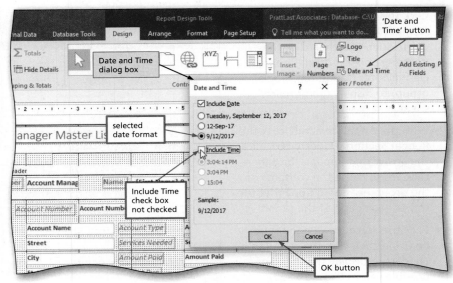

Figure 6–54

- Click the OK button (Date and Time dialog box) to add the date to the Report Header.

- Display the Home tab.

- If the Date control is no longer selected, click the Date control to select it (Figure 6–55).

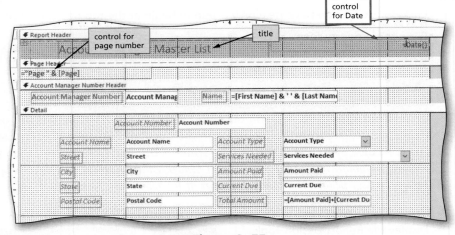

Figure 6–55

- With the control containing the date selected, click the Cut button (Home tab | Clipboard group) to cut the date, click the title bar for the Page Header to select the page header, and then click the Paste button (Home tab | Clipboard group) to paste the Date control at the beginning of the page header.

- Drag the Date control, which is currently sitting on top of the Page Number control, to the position shown in Figure 6–56.

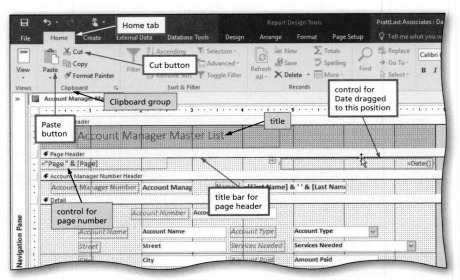

Figure 6–56

To Remove the Header Background Color and the Alternate Color

The report header currently has a blue background, whereas the desired report does not have such a background. In addition, the report has alternate colors. An **alternate color** is a color different from the main color that appears on every other line in a datasheet or report. Using alternate colors can sometimes make a datasheet or report more readable.

The following steps first remove the color from the report header. They then remove the alternate colors from the various sections in the report, starting with the Detail section. *Why? Access automatically assigns alternate colors within the report. In reports with multiple sections, the alternate colors can be confusing. If you do not want these alternate colors, you must remove them.*

1
- Right-click the title bar for the Report Header to select the header without selecting any of the controls in the header.
- Point to the 'Fill/Back Color' arrow to display a color palette (Figure 6–57).

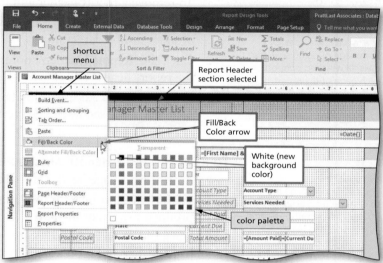

Figure 6–57

2
- Click White in the first row, first column of the color palette.
- Right-click a blank area of the Detail section to produce a shortcut menu.
- Point to the 'Alternate Fill/Back Color' arrow to produce a color palette (Figure 6–58).

3
- Click None on the color palette to remove the alternate color for the selected section.
- Using the same techniques, remove the alternate color from all other sections. (For some sections, the command may be dimmed, in which case you need take no further action.)
- Save and then close the report.
- Open the subreport in Design view.
- Remove the header background color and the alternate color from the subreport, just as you removed them from the main report.
- Save and then close the subreport.

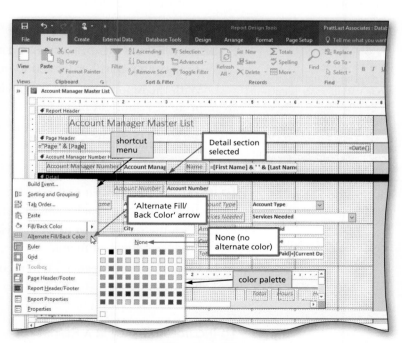

Figure 6–58

Q&A How can I be sure I removed all the background colors?
Open the report in Print Preview to check that all color has been removed from the report.

Headers and Footers

Access gives you some options for including or omitting headers and footers in your reports. They go together, so if you have a report header, you will also have a report footer. If you do not want one of the sections to appear, you can shrink its size so there is no room for any content, or you can remove the header or footer from your report altogether. If you later decide you want to include them, you once again can add them. You have similar options with page headers and page footers.

TO REMOVE A REPORT HEADER AND FOOTER

To remove a report header and footer, you would use the following steps.

1. With the report open in Design view, right-click any open area of the report to produce a shortcut menu.
2. Click the 'Report Header/Footer' command on the shortcut menu to remove the report header and footer.
3. If the Microsoft Access dialog box appears, asking if it is acceptable to delete any controls in the section, click the Yes button.

TO REMOVE A PAGE HEADER AND FOOTER

To remove a page header and footer, you would use the following steps.

1. With the report open in Design view, right-click any open area of the report to produce a shortcut menu.
2. Click the 'Page Header/Footer' command on the shortcut menu to remove the page header and footer.
3. If the Microsoft Access dialog box appears, asking if it is acceptable to delete any controls in the section, click the Yes button.

TO INSERT A REPORT HEADER AND FOOTER

To insert a report header and footer, you would use the following steps.

1. With the report open in Design view, right-click any open area of the report to produce a shortcut menu.
2. Click the 'Report Header/Footer' command on the shortcut menu to insert a report header and footer.

TO INSERT A PAGE HEADER AND FOOTER

To insert a page header and footer, you would use the following steps.

1. With the report open in Design view, right-click any open area of the report to produce a shortcut menu.
2. Click the 'Page Header/Footer' command on the shortcut menu to insert a page header and footer.

TO INCLUDE AN IMAGE IN A REPORT

You can include a picture (image) in a report. You can also use a picture (image) as the background on a report. To include an image in a report, you would use the following steps.

1. Open the report in Design view or Layout view.
2. Click the Insert Image button (Report Design Tools Design tab | Controls group), and then click the Browse command.
3. Select the desired image.
4. Click the desired location to add the image to the report.

TO USE AN IMAGE AS BACKGROUND FOR A REPORT

To include an image as a background for a report, you would use the following steps.

1. Open the report in Design view or Layout view.
2. Click anywhere in the report, click the Background Image button (Report Design Tools Format tab | Background group), and then click the Browse command.
3. Select the desired image for the background.

TO PUBLISH A REPORT

You can make a report available as an external document by publishing the report as either a PDF or XPS file. If you wanted to do so, you would use the following steps.

1. Select the report to be published in the Navigation Pane.
2. Display the External Data tab.
3. Click the PDF or XPS button (External Data tab | Export group) to display the Publish as PDF or XPS dialog box.
4. Select the appropriate Save as type (either PDF or XPS).
5. Select either 'Standard (publishing online and printing)' or 'Minimum size (publishing online).'
6. If you want to publish only a range of pages, click the Options button and select the desired range.
7. Click the Publish button to publish the report in the desired format.
8. If you want to save the export steps, click the 'Save export steps' check box, then click the Save Export button. If not, click the Close button.

> **BTW**
> **Distributing a Document**
> Instead of printing and distributing a hard copy of a document, you can distribute the document electronically. Options include sending the document via email; posting it on cloud storage (such as OneDrive) and sharing the file with others; posting it on a social networking site, blog, or other website; and sharing a link associated with an online location of the document. You also can create and share a PDF or XPS image of the document, so that users can view the file in Acrobat Reader or XPS Viewer instead of in Access.

> **Break Point:** If you wish to stop working through the module at this point, you can resume the project at a later time by running Access, opening the database called PrattLast Associates, and continuing to follow the steps from this location forward.

Creating a Second Report

PrattLast Associates would also like a report that groups accounts by account manager. The report should include subtotals and grand totals. Finally, it should show the discount amount for each account. The discount amount is based on the current due amount. Accounts that owe more than $20,000 will receive a 4 percent discount, and accounts that owe $20,000 or less will receive a 2 percent discount.

To Create a Second Report

The following steps create the Discount Report, select the record source, and specify grouping and sorting options.

BTW
Graphs
You can add graphs (charts) to a report using the Chart tool. To add a graph (chart) to a report, click the Chart tool, move the pointer to the desired location, and click the position to place the graph. Follow the directions in the Chart Wizard dialog box to specify the data source for the chart, the values for the chart, and the chart type.

1 If necessary, close the Navigation Pane.

2 Display the Create tab and then click the Report Design button (Create tab | Reports group) to create a report in Design view.

3 Ensure the selector for the entire report, which is the box in the upper-left corner of the report, contains a small black square indicating it is selected, and then click the Property Sheet button (Report Design Tools Design tab | Tools group) to display a property sheet.

4 With the All tab selected, click the Record Source property box arrow, and then click the Account Managers and Accounts query to select the query as the record source for the report.

5 Close the property sheet.

6 Click the Group & Sort button (Report Design Tools Design tab | Grouping & Totals group) to display the 'Group, Sort, and Total' pane.

7 Click the 'Add a group' button to display the list of available fields for grouping, and then click the Account Manager Number field to group by account manager number.

8 Click the 'Add a sort' button to display the list of available fields for sorting, and then click the Account Number field to sort by account number.

9 Remove the 'Group, Sort, and Total' pane by clicking the Group & Sort button (Report Design Tools Design tab | Grouping & Totals group).

10 Click the Save button on the Quick Access Toolbar, type **Discount Report** as the report name, and click the OK button to save the report.

Q&A Why save it at this point?
You do not have to save it at this point. It is a good idea to save it often, however. Doing so will give you a convenient point from which to restart if you have problems. If you have problems, you could close the report without saving it. When you reopen the report, it will be in the state it was in when you last saved it.

To Add and Move Fields in a Report

1 CREATE TABLES | 2 CREATE QUERIES | 3 CREATE REPORT | 4 SPECIFY GROUPING & SORTING | 5 ADD FIELDS
6 ADD SUBREPORT | 7 ADD TITLE, PAGE NUMBER, & DATE | **8 CREATE SECOND REPORT**

As with the previous report, you can add a field to the report by dragging the field from the field list. After adding a field to a report, you can adjust the placement of the field's label, separating it from the control to which it is attached by dragging the move handle in its upper-left corner. This technique does not work, however, if you want to drag the attached label to a section different from the control's section. If you want the label to be in a different section, you must select the label, cut the label, select the section to which you want to move the label, and then paste the label. You then can move the label to the desired location.

The following steps add the Account Manager Number field to the Account Manager Number Header section and then move the label to the Page Header section. *Why? The label should appear at the top of each page, rather than in the group header.*

1

• Click the 'Add Existing Fields' button (Report Design Tools Design tab | Tools group) to display a field list. (Figure 6–59).

Q&A My field list displays 'Show only fields in the current record source,' not 'Show all tables,' as in the figure. What should I do?
Click the 'Show only fields in the current record source' link at the top of the field list to display only those fields in the Account Managers and Accounts query.

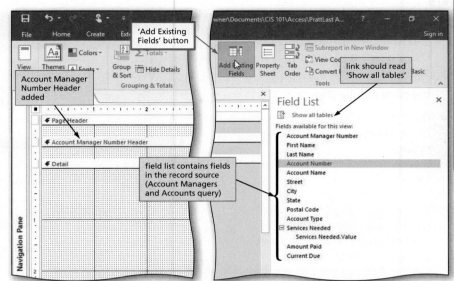

Figure 6–59

2

• Drag the Account Manager Number field to the approximate position shown in Figure 6–60.

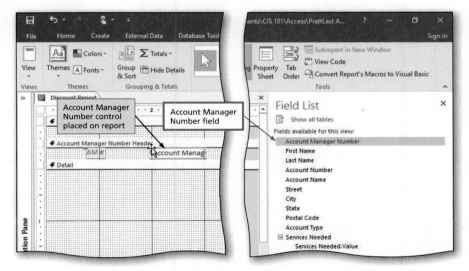

Figure 6–60

3

• Click the label for the Account Manager Number control to select it (Figure 6–61).

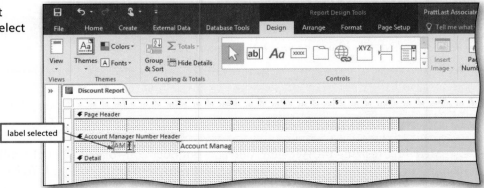

Figure 6–61

● Display the Home tab.

● Click the Cut button (Home tab | Clipboard group) to cut the label.

● Click the Page Header bar to select the page header (Figure 6–62).

Q&A Do I have to click the bar, or could I click somewhere else within the section?

You could also click within the section. Clicking the bar is usually safer, however. If you click in a section intending to select the section, but click within one of the controls in the section, you will select the control rather than the section. Clicking the bar always selects the section.

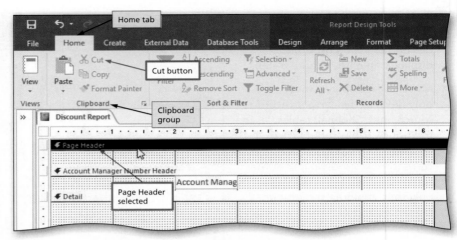

Figure 6–62

● Click the Paste button (Home tab | Clipboard group) to paste the label in the Page Header section (Figure 6–63).

Q&A When would I want to click the Paste button arrow rather than just the button?

Clicking the arrow displays the Paste button menu, which includes the Paste command and two additional commands. Paste Special allows you to paste data into different formats. Paste Append, which is available if you have cut or copied a record, allows you to paste the record to a table with a similar structure. If you want the simple Paste command, you can just click the button.

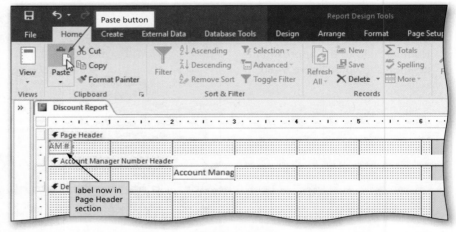

Figure 6–63

● Click in the label to produce an insertion point, use the BACKSPACE or DELETE key to erase the current entry in the label, and then type **Manager Number** as the new entry.

● Click in the label in front of the word, Number, to produce an insertion point.

● Press SHIFT+ENTER to move the word, Number, to a second line.

To Add the Remaining Fields

1 CREATE TABLES | 2 CREATE QUERIES | 3 CREATE REPORT | 4 SPECIFY GROUPING & SORTING | 5 ADD FIELDS
6 ADD SUBREPORT | 7 ADD TITLE, PAGE NUMBER, & DATE | **8 CREATE SECOND REPORT**

After first resizing the Account Manager Number control and label, the following steps add all the remaining fields for the report by dragging them into the Detail section. *Why? Dragging them gets them onto the report, where you can now move the controls and labels individually to the desired locations.* The next steps move the labels into the Page Header section, and move the controls containing the fields to the appropriate locations.

①

- Resize and move the Account Manager Number control to the approximate size and position shown in Figure 6–64.

- If necessary, resize the Account Manager Number label to the size shown in the figure.

- Drag the First Name, Last Name, Account Number, Account Name, Amount Paid, and Current Due fields into the Detail section, as shown in the figure.

Q&A Could I drag them all at once?
Yes. You can select multiple fields by selecting the first field, holding down the SHIFT key, and then selecting other adjacent fields. To select fields that are not adjacent to each other, hold down the CTRL key and select the additional fields. Once you have selected multiple fields, you can drag them all at once. How you choose to select fields and drag them onto the report is a matter of personal preference.

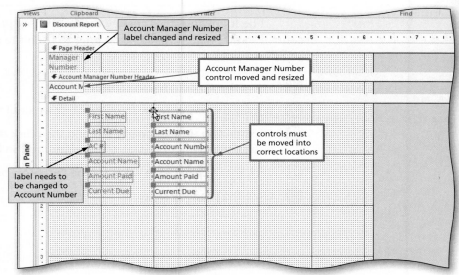

Figure 6–64

②

- Close the field list.

- One at a time, cut each of the labels, paste the label into the Page Header section, and then resize, reformat, and move the labels to the approximate positions shown in Figure 6–65.

Q&A When I paste the label, it is always placed at the left edge, superimposing the Account Manager Number control. Can I change where Access places it?
Unfortunately, when you paste to a different section, Access places the control at the left edge. You will need to drag each control to its proper location after pasting it into the Page Header section.

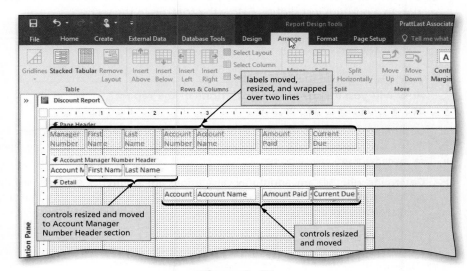

Figure 6–65

- One at a time, resize and move the First Name and Last Name controls to the approximate positions in the Account Manager Number Header section shown in the figure.

- One at a time, resize and move the Account Number, Account Name, Amount Paid, and Current Due controls to the approximate positions in the Detail section shown in the figure.

- Display the Report Design Tools Arrange tab.

- Use the Align button (Report Design Tools Arrange tab | Sizing & Ordering group) as necessary to align all the controls as shown in Figure 6–65.

To Change the Can Grow Property

The following steps change the Can Grow property for the Account Name control so that names that are too long to fit in the available space will extend to additional lines.

① Select the Account Name control.

② Display the property sheet and scroll down until the Can Grow property appears.

③ Click the Can Grow property box and then click the Can Grow property box arrow to display the menu of available values for the Can Grow property.

④ Click Yes to change the value for the Can Grow property.

⑤ Close the property sheet.

To Resize the Detail Section

1 CREATE TABLES | 2 CREATE QUERIES | 3 CREATE REPORT | 4 SPECIFY GROUPING & SORTING | 5 ADD FIELDS
6 ADD SUBREPORT | 7 ADD TITLE, PAGE NUMBER, & DATE | 8 CREATE SECOND REPORT

The following step resizes the Detail section of the Discount Report to remove most of the extra space below the controls in the section. *Why? The extra space would appear after each detail line in the report, which adds unnecessary length to the report. The desired report (Figure 6–1b) does not include such space.*

①

- Scroll down so that the lower boundary of the Detail section appears, and then drag the lower boundary of the section to a position just slightly below the controls in the section.

CONSIDER THIS

How will you incorporate calculations in the report?
Determine details concerning any calculations required for the report.

Determine whether to include calculations in the group and report footers. The group footers or report footers might require calculated data such as subtotals or grand totals. Determine whether the report needs other statistics that must be calculated (for example, average).

Determine whether any additional calculations are required. If so, determine the fields that are involved and how they are to be combined. Determine whether any of the calculations depend on a true or false state for a criterion, in which case the calculations are conditional.

BTW

Arguments
An argument is a piece of data on which a function operates. For example, in the expression = SUM ([Amount Paid]), Amount Paid is the argument because the SUM function will calculate the total of Amount Paid.

Totals and Subtotals

To add totals or other statistics to a footer, add a text box control. You can use any of the aggregate functions in a text box: COUNT, SUM, AVG (average), MAX (largest value), MIN (smallest value), STDEV (standard deviation), VAR (variance), FIRST, and LAST. To use a function, type an equal (=) sign, followed by the function name. You then include a set of parentheses containing the item for which you want to perform the calculation. If the item name contains spaces, such as Amount Paid, you must enclose it in square brackets. For example, to calculate the sum of the amount paid values, the expression would be =SUM([Amount Paid]).

Access will perform the calculation for the appropriate collection of records. If you enter this expression in the Account Manager Number Footer section, Access will only calculate the total for accounts with the given account manager; that is, it will calculate the appropriate subtotal. If you enter the expression in the Report Footer section, Access will calculate the total for all accounts.

Grouping and Sorting Options

As you learned in Module 4, clicking the More button in the Group, Sort, and Total pane allows you to specify additional options for grouping and sorting. The additional options are: Value, which lets you choose the amount of the value on which to group; Totals, which lets you choose the values to be totaled; Title, which lets you customize the group title; Header section, which lets you include or omit a header section for the group; Footer section, which lets you include or omit a footer section for the group; and Keep together, which lets you specify whether Access is to attempt to keep portions of a group together on a page.

To Add Totals and Subtotals

1 CREATE TABLES | 2 CREATE QUERIES | 3 CREATE REPORT | 4 SPECIFY GROUPING & SORTING | 5 ADD FIELDS
6 ADD SUBREPORT | 7 ADD TITLE, PAGE NUMBER, & DATE | **8 CREATE SECOND REPORT**

The following steps first display the Account Manager Number Footer section and then add the total of amount paid and current due to both the Account Manager Number Footer section and the Report Footer section. The steps label the totals in the Account Manager Number Footer section as subtotals and the totals in the Report Footer section as grand totals. The steps change the format of the new controls to currency and the number of decimal places to 2. *Why? The requirements at PrattLast indicate that the Discount Report should contain subtotals and grand totals of amounts paid and current due.*

1

- If necessary, display the Report Design Tools Design tab.

- Click the Group & Sort button (Report Design Tools Design tab | Grouping & Totals group) to display the Group, Sort, and Total pane.

- If necessary, click 'Group on Account Manager Number' to select Group on Account Manager Number (Figure 6–66).

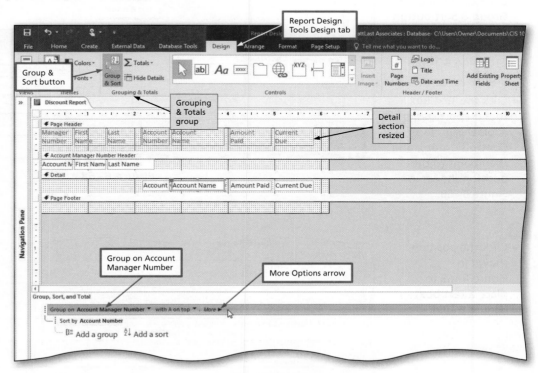

Figure 6–66

2

- Click the More arrow to display additional options for grouping.
- Click the 'without a footer section' arrow to display the available options (Figure 6–67).

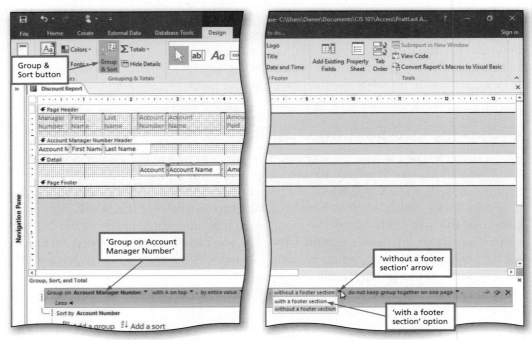

Figure 6–67

3

- Click 'with a footer section' to add a footer.
- Close the Group, Sort, and Total pane by clicking the Group & Sort button (Report Design Tools Design tab | Grouping & Totals group).
- Click the Text Box tool (Report Design Tools Design tab | Controls group), and then point to the position shown in Figure 6–68.

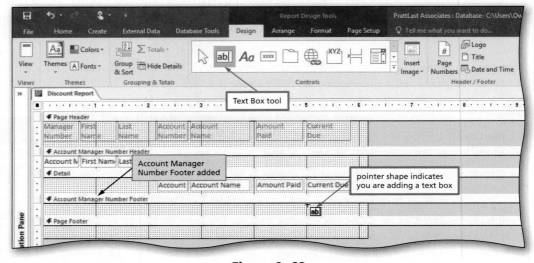

Figure 6–68

4

- Click the position shown in Figure 6–68 to place a text box (Figure 6–69).

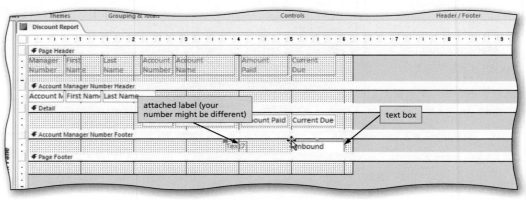

Figure 6–69

5

- Click the text box to produce an insertion point.

- Type **=Sum([Current Due])** in the control to enter the expression calculation, and then press the ENTER key.

- Click the text box label to select it.

- Click the label a second time to produce an insertion point.

- Use the DELETE or BACKSPACE key to delete the Text7 label (your number might be different).

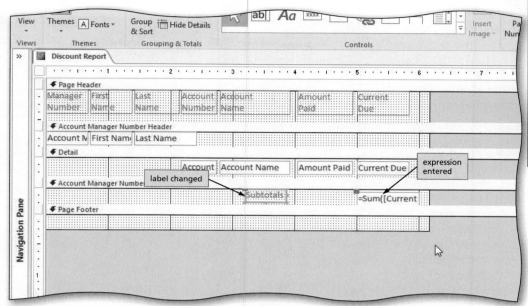

Figure 6–70

- Type **Subtotals** as the label. Click outside the label to deselect it and then drag the label to the position shown in the Figure 6–70.

6

- Click the Text Box tool (Report Design Tools Design tab | Controls group), and then click in the Account Manager Number Footer section just to the left of the control for the sum of Current Due to place another text box.

- Click the text box to produce an insertion point, type **=Sum([Amount Paid])** in the control, and then press the ENTER key to enter the expression (Figure 6–71).

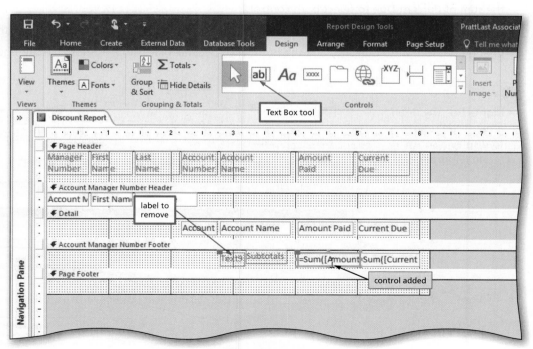

Figure 6–71

Q&A Could I add the controls in the other order?

Yes. The only problem is that the label of the second control overlaps the first control. Adding the controls in the order shown in the steps reduces the overlap. It is not a major difference, however.

- Click the label to select it, and then press the DELETE key to delete the label.

Q&A

I inadvertently deleted the other control rather than the label. What should I do?

First, click the Undo button on the Quick Access Toolbar to reverse your deletion. You can then delete the correct control. If that does not work, you can simply delete the remaining control or controls in the section and start these steps over.

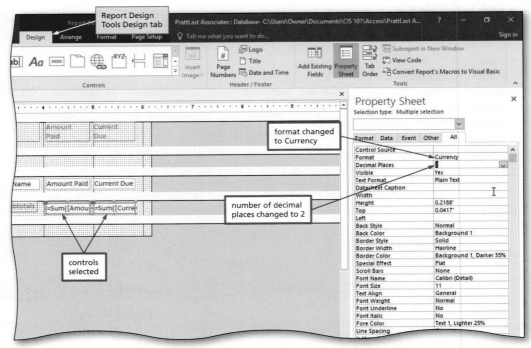

Figure 6–72

- Resize and align the Amount Paid and Current Due controls in the Detail section and the Account Manager Number Footer section to the positions shown in Figure 6–72.

- Click the control for the sum of Amount Paid to select it, and then hold down the SHIFT key and click the control for the sum of Current Due to select both controls.

- Click the Property Sheet button (Report Design Tools Design tab | Tools group) to display the property sheet.

- Change the format to Currency and the number of decimal places to 2 as shown in the figure.

- Right-click any open area of the report to display a shortcut menu (Figure 6–73).

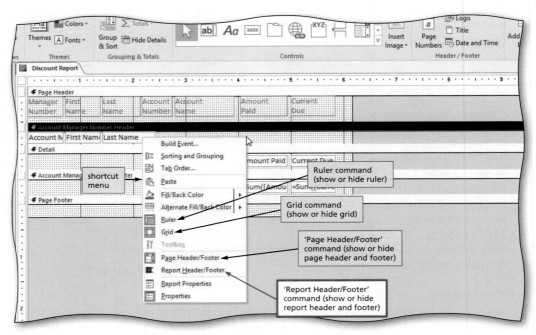

Figure 6–73

9
- Click 'Report Header/ Footer' to display the Report Header and Footer sections.
- Click the ruler in the Account Manager Number Footer to the left of the controls in the section to select the controls.
- Display the Home tab.
- Click the Copy button (Home tab | Clipboard group) to copy the selected controls to the Clipboard (Figure 6–74).

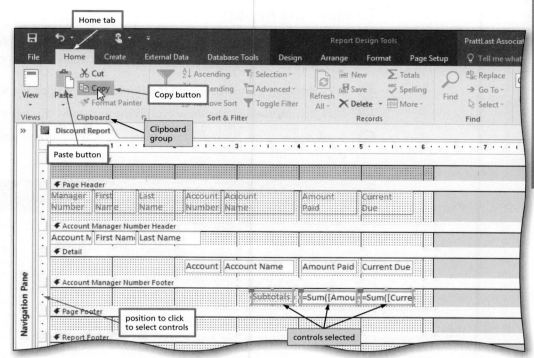

Figure 6–74

10
- Click the Report Footer bar to select the footer, and then click the Paste button (Home tab | Clipboard group) to paste a copy of the controls into the report footer.
- Move the controls to the positions shown in Figure 6–75.
- Click the label in the Report Footer section to select the label, and then click a second time to produce an insertion point.

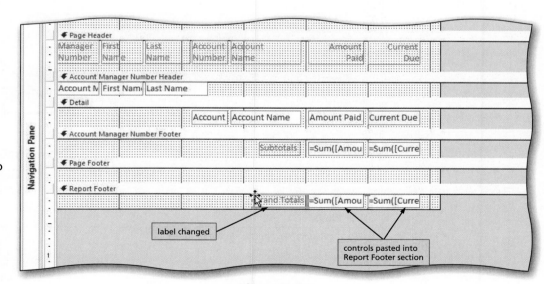

Figure 6–75

- Use the BACKSPACE or DELETE key to erase the current contents, type **Grand Totals** to change the label, and then move the label to the position shown in Figure 6–75.

Q&A Could I enter the controls just as I did earlier, rather than copying and pasting?
Yes. Copying and pasting is simpler, but it is a matter of personal preference.

To View the Report

The following steps view the report in Report view, which is sometimes more convenient when you want to view the lower portion of the report.

① Click the View button arrow on the Home tab to display the View button menu.

② Click Report View on the View button menu to view the report in Report view.

③ Scroll down to the bottom of the report so that the grand totals appear on the screen (Figure 6–76).

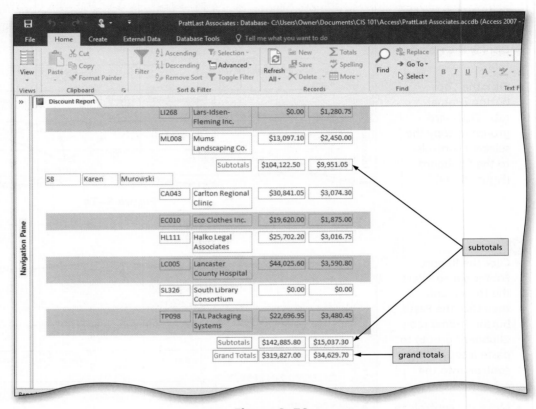

Figure 6–76

Other Ways

1. Click the Report View button on the status bar

To Remove the Color from the Report Header

The following steps remove the color from the Report Header section by changing the background color for the header to white.

① Click the View button arrow and then click Design View to return to Design view.

② Right-click the report header to produce a shortcut menu.

③ Point to the 'Fill/Back Color' arrow on the shortcut menu to display a color palette.

④ Click White in the first row, first column to change the background color to white.

To Assign a Conditional Value

The PrattLast requirements for this report also involved a conditional value related to the amount of an account's discount. *Why? PrattLast has determined that the amount of the discount depends on the amount paid. If the amount paid is greater than $20,000, the discount on the current due amount is 4 percent. If not, the discount is 2 percent.*

To assign a conditional value, you will use the IIf function. The IIf function consists of the letters IIf followed by three items, called **arguments**, in parentheses. The first argument is a criterion; the second and third arguments are expressions. If the criterion is true, the function assigns the value of the expression in the second argument. If the criterion is false, the function assigns the value of the expression in the third argument. The IIf function you will use is IIf([Amount Paid]>20000, .04*[Current Due], .02*[Current Due]). This function applies the following rules: If the amount paid is greater than $20,000, the value assigned is .04*[Current Due], that is, 4 percent of the current due amount. If the amount paid is not greater than $20,000, the value assigned is .02*[Current Due], that is, 2 percent of the current due amount.

The following steps add a text box and then use the Expression Builder to enter the appropriate IIf function in the text box. The steps then change the format of the text box and modify and move the label for the text box. They also add a title, page number, and date, and then change the alignment of the title. The steps then change the size of the report.

- If necessary, display the Report Design Tools Design tab.

- Click the Text Box tool (Report Design Tools Design tab | Controls group) and point to the approximate position shown in Figure 6–77.

Q&A

How can I place the control accurately when there are no gridlines?
When you click the position for the control, Access will automatically expand the grid. You can then adjust the control using the grid.

Can I automatically cause controls to be aligned to the grid?
Yes. Click the Size/Space button (Report Design Tools Arrange tab | Sizing & Ordering group) and then click Snap to Grid on the Size/Space menu. From that point on, any controls you add will be automatically aligned to the grid.

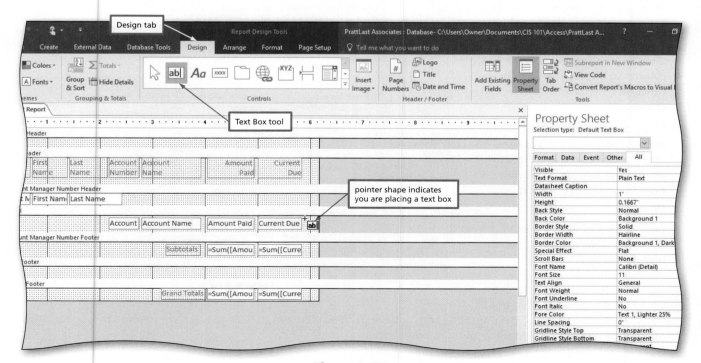

Figure 6–77

2

- Click the position shown in Figure 6–77 to place a text box.

- Click the attached label to select it, and then press the DELETE key to delete the attached label.

- Click the text box to select it, and then click the Property Sheet button (Report Design Tools Design tab | Tools group), if necessary, to display a property sheet.

- If necessary, display the All tab, and then click the Control Source property to select it (Figure 6–78).

Q&A Why did I choose Control Source instead of Record Source?

You use Record Source to select the source of the records in a report, usually a table or a query. You use the Control Source property to specify the source of data for the control. This allows you to bind an expression or field to a control.

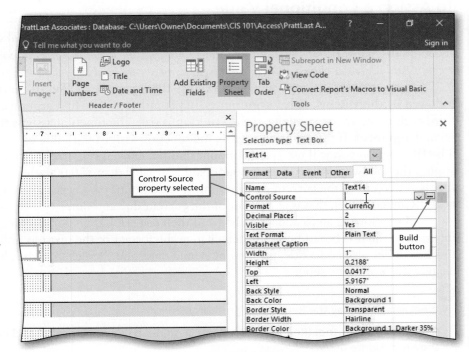

Figure 6–78

3

- Click the Build button to display the Expression Builder dialog box.

- Double-click Functions in the first column to display the function subfolders.

- Click Built-In Functions in the first column to display the various function categories in the second column.

- Scroll down in the second column so that Program Flow appears, and then click Program Flow to display the available program flow functions in the third column.

- Double-click IIf in the third column to select the IIf function (Figure 6–79).

Q&A Do I have to select Program Flow? Could I not just scroll down to IIf?

You do not have to select Program Flow. You could indeed scroll down to IIf. You will have to scroll through a large number of functions in order to get to IIf, however.

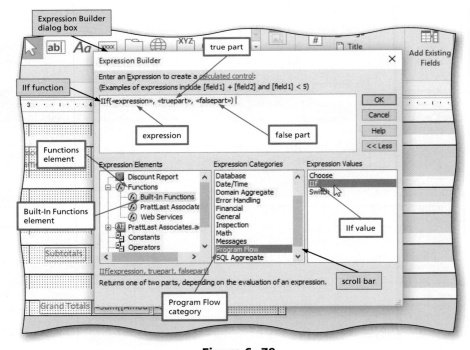

Figure 6–79

4

- Click the
  <<expression>>
  argument to select it
  and type **[Amount
  Paid]>20000** as
  the expression.

- Click the
  <<truepart>>
  argument to
  select it and type
  **0.04*[Current
  Due]** as the true
  part.

- Click the
  <<falsepart>>
  argument to
  select it and type
  **0.02*[Current
  Due]** as the false
  part (Figure 6−80).

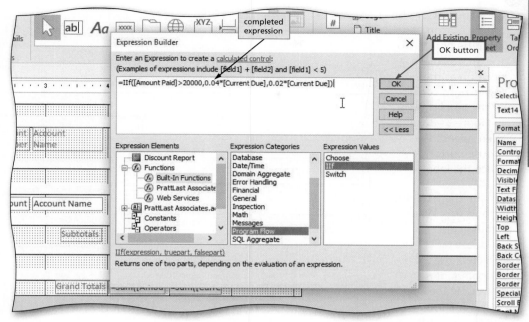

Figure 6−80

Q&A Are there other ways
I could enter the expression?

Yes. You could just type the whole expression. On the other hand, you could select the function just as in these
steps, and, when entering each argument, you could select the fields from the list of fields and click the desired
operators.

5

- Click the OK
  button (Expression
  Builder dialog
  box) to specify the
  expression as the
  control source for
  the text box.

Q&A My property sheet
is covering my OK
button. What should
I do?

Click in the
Expression Builder
dialog box to bring
the entire dialog
box in front of the
property sheet.

- Change the Format
  to Currency.

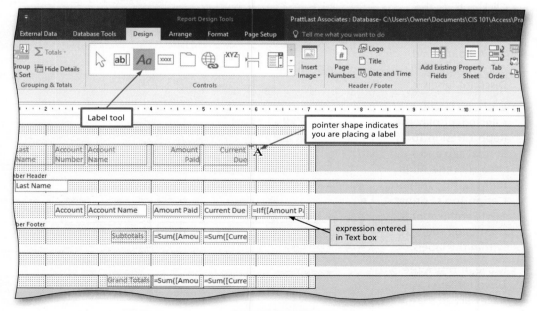

Figure 6−81

- Change the number of decimal places to 2.

- Close the property sheet by clicking the Property Sheet button.

- Click the Label tool on the Report Design Tools Design tab and point to the approximate position shown in
  Figure 6−81.

6

- Press the left mouse button, drag the pointer to the approximate position at the lower-right corner of the label shown in Figure 6–82, and then release the mouse button to place the label.

Q&A

I made the label the wrong size. What should I do?

With the label selected, drag the sizing handles to resize the label as needed. Drag the control in a position away from the sizing handles if you need to move the label.

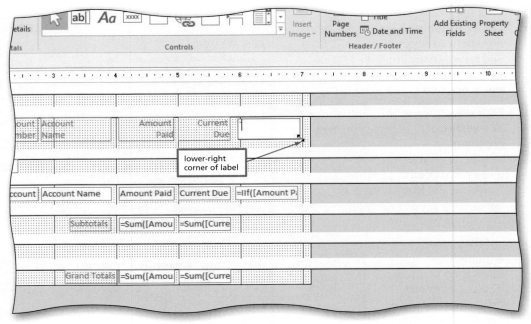

Figure 6–82

7

- Type **Discount** to enter the name of the label.

- Click outside the label to deselect the label and then select the Amount Paid, Current Due, and Discount labels.

- With the labels selected, display the Report Design Tools Format tab and then click the Align Right button (Report Design Tools Format tab | Font group) to right-align the text within the labels.

- Move or resize the Discount label as necessary so that it aligns with the text box containing the IIf statement and with the other controls in the Page Header section.

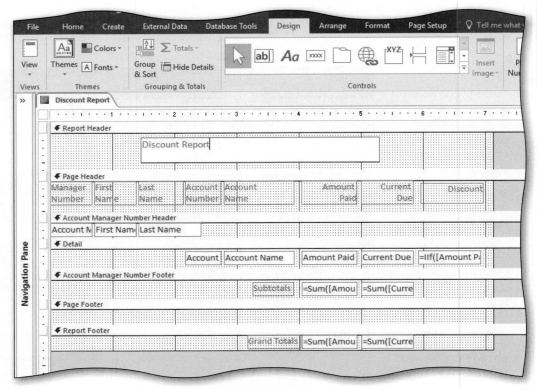

Figure 6–83

- Expand the Report Header section to the approximate size shown in Figure 6–83, place a label in the approximate position shown in the figure, and then type **Discount Report** in the label.

8

- Click outside the label to deselect it and then click the label in the report header to select the entire label.

- Display the property sheet, change the font size to 20 and the text align property to Distribute, which spreads the letters evenly throughout the label. Change the font weight to Semi-bold, and then close the property sheet.

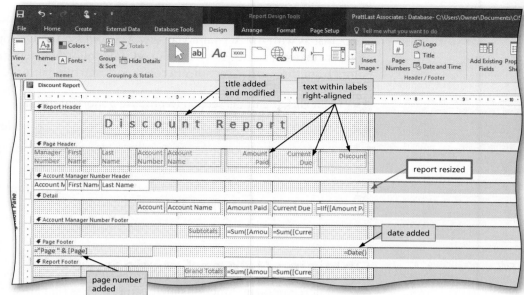

Figure 6–84

- If necessary, increase the size of the Discount Report label so that the entire title is displayed.

- Using the Report Design Tools Design tab, add a page number on the left side of the page footer, then add a date (use the same format you have used previously in this module).

- Cut the date, and then paste it into the page footer. Drag the date so that the date is positioned in the approximate position shown in Figure 6–84.

- Drag the right boundary of the report to the position shown in the Figure to reduce the width of the report, if necessary.

Q&A

The report size was correct before. Why would I need to resize it?

When you move a control and a portion of the control extends into the area to the right of the right boundary of the report, the report will be resized. The new larger size will remain even if you move the control back to the left. Thus, it is possible that your report has a larger size than it did before. If this is the case, you need to drag the right boundary to resize the report.

To Change the Border Style

If you print or preview the report, you will notice that all the controls have boxes around them. The box is the border, which you can select and modify if desired. The following steps remove the boxes around the controls by changing the border style to transparent.

1 Select all controls in the report. You can click the first one, and then hold the SHIFT key down while clicking all the others. Alternatively, you can click in the ruler to the left of the Report Header section and then hold the SHIFT key down while clicking to the left of all the other sections.

2 Display the Report Design Tools Design tab.

3 Click the Property Sheet button (Report Design Tools Design tab | Tools group) to display the property sheet.

4 Click the Border Style property box and then click the Border Style property box arrow to display the menu of available border styles.

5 Click Transparent to change the border style. Close the property sheet.

To Remove the Alternate Color

Just as with the Account Manager Master List, the Discount Report also has alternate colors that need to be removed. The following steps remove the alternate colors from the various sections in the report, starting with the Detail section.

1 Right-click the Detail section to produce a shortcut menu.

2 Point to the Alternate Fill/Back Color arrow to produce a color palette.

3 Click None on the color palette to specify that there is to be no alternate color for the selected section.

4 Using the same techniques, remove the alternate color from all other sections. (For some sections, the command may be dimmed.)

Obtaining Help on Functions

There are many functions included in Access that are available for a variety of purposes. To see the list of functions, display the Expression Builder. (See Figure 6–78 for one way to display the Expression Builder.) Double-click Functions in the first column and then click Built-In Functions. You can then scroll through the entire list of functions in the third column. Alternatively, you can click a function category in the second column, in which case the third column will only contain the functions in that category. To obtain detailed help on a function, highlight the function in the third column and click the Help button. The Help presented will show the syntax of the function, that is, the specific rule for how you must type the function and any arguments. It will give you general comments on the function as well as examples illustrating the use of the function.

Report Design Tools Page Setup Tab

You can use the buttons on the Report Design Tools Page Setup tab to change margins, orientation, and other page setup characteristics of the report (Figure 6–85a). If you click the Margins button, you can choose from among some predefined margins or set your own custom margins (Figure 6–85b). If you click the Columns button, you will see the Page Setup dialog box with the Columns tab selected (Figure 6–85c). You can use this tab to specify multiple columns in a report as well as the column spacing. If you click the Page Setup button, you will see the Page Setup dialog box with the Print Options tab selected (Figure 6–85d). You can use this tab to specify custom margins. You can specify orientation by clicking the Page tab (Figure 6–85e). You can also select paper size, paper source, and printer using this tab.

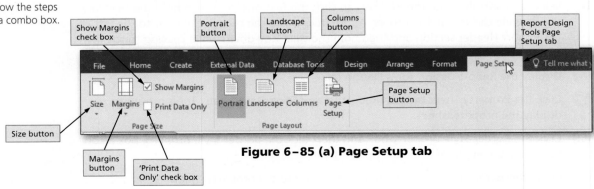

Figure 6–85 (a) Page Setup tab

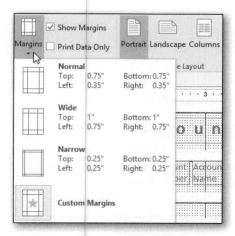

Figure 6–85 (b) Margins menu

Figure 6–85 (c) Columns tab

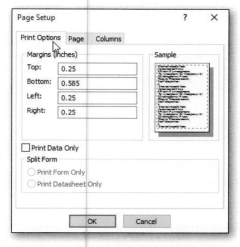

Figure 6–85 (d) Print Options tab

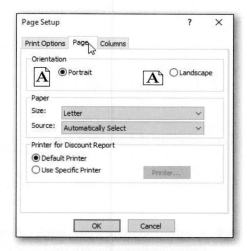

Figure 6–85 (e) Page tab

To Change the Report Margins

If you look at the horizontal ruler in Figure 6–84, you will notice that the report width is slightly over 7 inches. Because the report will probably print on standard 8½" x 11" paper, a 7-inch report with 1-inch margins on the left and right, which would result in a 9-inch width, will not fit. To allow the report to fit on the page, you could change the orientation from Portrait to Landscape or you could reduce the margins. There are two ways to change the margins. You can click the Margins button on the Report Design Tools Page Setup tab and then select from some predefined options. If you want more control, you can click the Page Setup button to display the Page Setup dialog box. You can then specify your own margins, change the orientation, and also specify multiple columns if you want a multicolumn report.

The following steps use the Margins button to select Narrow margins.

1 Display the Report Design Tools Page Setup tab.

2 Click the Margins button (Report Design Tools Page Setup tab | Page Size group).

3 If necessary, click Narrow to specify the Narrow margin option.

Fine-Tuning a Report

When you have finished a report, you should review several of its pages in Print Preview to make sure the layout is precisely what you want. You may find that you need to increase the size of a control, which you can do by selecting the control and dragging the appropriate sizing handle. You may decide to add a control, which you could do by using the appropriate tool in the Controls group or by dragging a field from the field list.

In both cases, if the control is between other controls, you have a potential problem. You may not have enough space between the other controls to increase the size or to add an additional control. If the control is part of a control layout that you had when you modified earlier reports in Layout view, you can resize controls or add new fields, and the remaining fields automatically adjust for the change. In Design view with individual controls, you must make any necessary adjustments manually.

TO MAKE ROOM FOR RESIZING OR ADDING CONTROLS

To make room for resizing a control or for adding controls, you would use the following steps.

1. Select all controls to the right of the control you want to resize, or to the right of the position where you want to add another control.
2. Drag any of the selected controls to the right to make room for the change.

To Save and Close a Report

Now that you have completed your work on your report, you should save the report and close it. The following steps first save your work on the report and then close the report.

1 If instructed to do so by your instructor, change the title of the Discount Report to LastName Report where LastName is your last name.

2 Click the Save button on the Quick Access Toolbar to save your work.

3 Close the Discount Report.

4 Preview and then print the report.

5 If desired, sign out of your Microsoft account.

6 Exit Access.

Summary

In this module you have learned to create and relate additional tables; create queries for a report; create reports in Design view; add fields and text boxes to a report; format controls; group and ungroup controls; modify multiple controls; add and modify a subreport; modify section properties; add a title, page number, and date; add totals and subtotals; use a function in a text box; and publish a report.

What decisions will you need to make when creating your own reports?
Use these guidelines as you complete the assignments in this module and create your own reports outside of this class.

1. Determine the intended audience and purpose of the report.

    a. Identify the user or users of the report and determine how they will use it.

    b. Specify the necessary data and level of detail to include in the report.

2. Determine the source of data for the report.

    a. Determine whether all the data is in a single table or whether it comes from multiple related tables.

3. Determine whether the data is stored in a query.

    a. You might need to create multiple versions of a report for a query where the criterion for a field changes, in which case, you would use a parameter query and enter the criterion when you run the report.

    b. If the data comes from multiple related tables, you might want to create a query and use the query as a source of data.

4. Determine the fields that belong on the report.

    a. Identify the data items that are needed by the user of the report.

5. Determine the organization of the report.

    a. The report might be enhanced by displaying the fields in a particular order and arranged in a certain way.

    b. Should the records in the report be grouped in some way?

    c. Should the report contain any subreports?

6. Determine any calculations required for the report.

    a. Should the report contain totals or subtotals?

    b. Are there any special calculations?

    c. Are there any calculations that involve criteria?

7. Determine the format and style of the report.

    a. What information should be in the report heading?

    b. Do you want a title and date?

    c. Do you want special background colors or alternate colors?

    d. Should the report contain an image?

    e. What should be in the body of the report?

How should you submit solutions to questions in the assignments identified with a symbol?
Every assignment in this book contains one or more questions identified with a symbol. These questions require you to think beyond the assigned database. Present your solutions to the questions in the format required by your instructor. Possible formats may include one or more of these options: write the answer; create a document that contains the answer; present your answer to the class; discuss your answer in a group; record the answer as audio or video using a webcam, smartphone, or portable media player; or post answers on a blog, wiki, or website.

Apply Your Knowledge

Reinforce the skills and apply the concepts you learned in this module.

Adding a Table and Creating a Report with a Subreport

Note: To complete this assignment, you will be required to use the Data Files. Please contact your instructor for information about accessing the Data Files

Instructions: Run Access. Open the Apply NicelyNeat Services database that you modified in Module 5. (If you did not complete the exercise, see your instructor for a copy of the modified database.)

Perform the following tasks:

1. Create a table in which to store data about cleaning services performed for clients. Use Services as the name of the table. The Services table has the structure shown in Table 6–4.

Table 6–4 Structure of Services Table			
Field Name	**Data Type**	**Field Size**	**Description**
Client Number	Short Text	4	Part of Primary Key
Service Date	Date/Time (Change Format property to Short Date)		Part of Primary Key
Hours Worked	Number (Change Format property to Fixed and Decimal Places to 2)	Single	

2. Import the Cleaning Services.txt file into the Services table. The file is delimited by tabs and the first row contains the field names. Do not save the import steps.

3. Create a one-to-many relationship (enforce referential integrity) between the Client table and the Services table. Save the relationship and close the Relationships window.

4. Create a query that joins the Supervisor and Client tables. Include the Supervisor Number, First Name, and Last Name fields from the Supervisor table. Include all fields except Total Amount and Supervisor Number from the Client table. Save the query as Supervisors and Clients.

5. Create the report shown in Figure 6–86. The report uses the Supervisors and Clients query as the basis for the main report and the Services table as the basis for the subreport. Use the name Supervisor Master List for the report. The report title has a Text Align property value of Center. The Border Width property for the detail controls is 1 pt and the subreport name is Services by Client. The report is similar in style to the Account Manager Master List shown in Figure 6–1a.

6. If requested to do so by your instructor, change the title for the report to First Name Last Name Master List where First Name and Last Name are your first and last names.

7. Submit the revised database in the format specified by your instructor.

8. ✺ How would you change the font weight of the report title to bold?

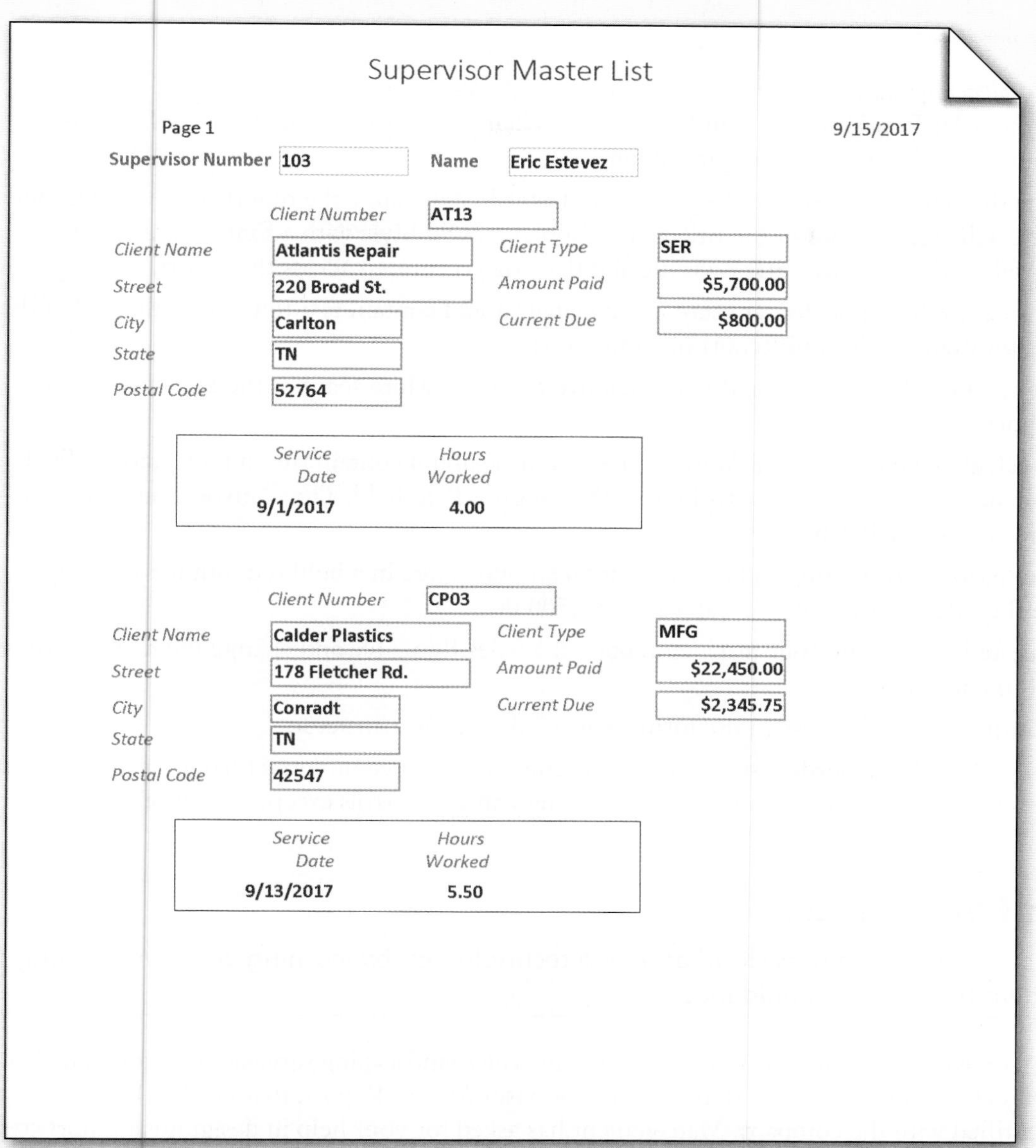

Supervisor Master List

Page 1   9/15/2017

Supervisor Number 103   Name   Eric Estevez

        Client Number   AT13

Client Name   Atlantis Repair   Client Type   SER

Street   220 Broad St.   Amount Paid $5,700.00

City   Carlton   Current Due $800.00

State   TN

Postal Code   52764

Service Date	Hours Worked
9/1/2017	4.00

        Client Number   CP03

Client Name   Calder Plastics   Client Type   MFG

Street   178 Fletcher Rd.   Amount Paid $22,450.00

City   Conradt   Current Due $2,345.75

State   TN

Postal Code   42547

Service Date	Hours Worked
9/13/2017	5.50

Figure 6–86

Extend Your Knowledge

Extend the skills you learned in this module and experiment with new skills.
You may need to use Help to complete the assignment.

Modifying Reports

Note: To complete this assignment, you will be required to use the Data Files. Please
contact your instructor for information about accessing the Data Files.

Instructions: Run Access. Open the Extend Earth Clothes database. Earth Clothes is a
company that manufactures and sells casual clothes made from earth-friendly fabrics.

Continued >

Extend Your Knowledge *continued*

Perform the following tasks:

1. Open the Sales Rep Master List in Design view. Change the date format to Long Date. Move the Date control to the page footer section.

2. Change the report title to Sales Rep/Orders Master List. Change the report header background to white. Change the font of the title text to Bookman Old Style with a font weight of semi-bold. Make sure the entire title is visible and the title is centered across the report.

3. Add a label to the report footer section. The label should contain text to indicate the end of the report, for example, End of Report or similar text.

4. Delete the Postal Code label and field. Remove any extra white space in the Detail section of the report.

5. Add a calculated control, Total Amount. The control should contain the sum of Amount Paid and Balance. Place this new control under the Amount Paid field. The control should have the same format as the Balance field.

6. Use conditional formatting to format the total amount value in a bold red font for all records where the value is equal to or greater than $1,500.00.

7. If requested to do so by your instructor, open the Sales Rep table and change the name of sales rep 44 to your name.

8. Submit the revised database in the format specified by your instructor.

9. ✷ Do you think the borders surrounding the controls enhance or detract from the appearance of the report? How would you remove the borders on all controls except the subreport?

Expand Your World

Create a solution, which uses cloud and web technologies, by learning and investigating on your own from general guidance.

Problem: You work part-time for a company that provides landscaping services. The company has two reports, a Customer Financial Report and Supervisor Master Report, that need to be more clearly identified with the company. Management has asked for your help in designing a report style that they can use.

Perform the following tasks:

1. Run Access and open the Expand Local Landscaping database from the Data Files.

2. Link the Landscape Rates Excel workbook to the database.

3. Search the web to find a suitable royalty-free background image the company can use for its reports, or create your own background image.

4. Open the Customer Financial Report in Design view and delete any alternate background color in the report. Add the background image to the report.

5. Search the web to find a suitable royalty-free logo or image the company can use for its reports, or create your own logo or image.

6. Add the logo or image to the Supervisor Master Report.

7. Add a hyperlink to the Supervisor Master Report that takes the user to a landscaping company website in your local area.

8. Submit the revised database in the format specified by your instructor.

9. ✷ What did you select as a background image and as a logo? What website did you use or did you create your own? Justify your selection.

In the Labs

Design, create, modify, and/or use a database following the guidelines, concepts, and skills presented in this module. Labs are listed in order of increasing difficulty. Labs 1 and 2, which increase in difficulty, require you to create solutions based on what you learned in the module; Lab 3 requires you to apply your creative thinking and problem solving skills to design and implement a solution.

Lab 1: Adding Tables and Creating Reports for the Horticulture4U Database

Problem: The management of Horticulture4U needs to maintain data on a weekly basis on the open orders for its customers. These are orders that have not yet been delivered. To track this information, the company requires a new table – an Open Orders table. The company also needs a report that displays sales rep information as well as information about customers and any open orders that the customer has. The company would like to show its appreciation to current customers by discounting the amount customers currently owe.

Note: To complete this assignment, you will be required to use the Data Files. Please contact your instructor for information about accessing the Data Files.

Instructions: Perform the following tasks:
1. Run Access and open the Lab 1 Horticulture4U database you used in Module 5. If you did not use this database, see your instructor about accessing the required files.
2. Create the Open Orders table using the structure shown in Table 6-5.

Table 6–5 Structure of Open Orders Table			
Field Name	**Data Type**	**Field Size**	**Description**
Order Number	Short Text	6	Primary Key
Amount	Currency		
Customer Number	Short Text	4	Foreign Key; matches primary key of Customer table

3. Import the Open Orders.txt file into the Open Orders table. The file is delimited by tabs and the first row contains the field names. Do not save the import steps.
4. Create a one-to-many relationship between the Customer table and the Open Orders table. Save the relationship.
5. Create a query that joins the Sales Rep table and the Customer table. Include the Sales Rep Number, First Name, and Last Name from the Sales Rep table. Include all fields except Total Amount and Sales Rep Number from the Customer table. Save the query as Sales Reps and Customers.

Continued >

In the Labs *continued*

6. Create the report shown in Figure 6–87. The report uses the Sales Reps and Customers query as the basis for the main report and the Open Orders table as the basis for the subreport. Use Open Orders as the name for the subreport. Change the Can Grow property for the Products Needed field to Yes. The Date control uses the Medium Date format, the title uses Distribute as the Text Align property, and there are no borders around the controls in the Detail section. The report is similar to the Account Manager Master List shown in Figure 6–1a.

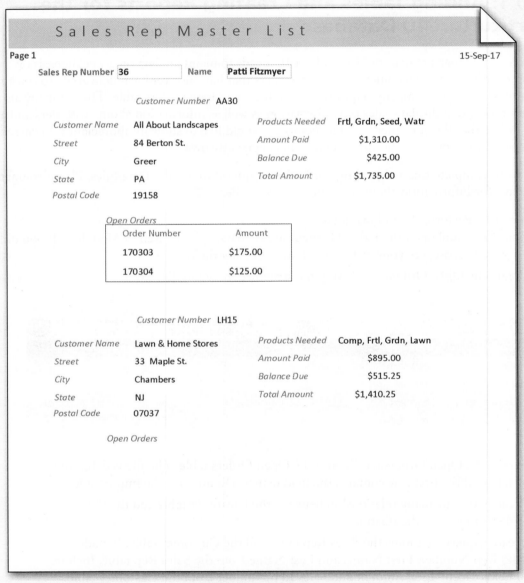

Figure 6–87

7. Create the Customer Discount Report shown in Figure 6–88. The report uses the Sales Reps and Customers query. Customers who have paid $2,000.00 or more will receive a 2 percent discount on the remaining balance, and clients who have paid less than $2,000.00 will receive a 1 percent discount on the remaining balance. The report includes subtotals and grand totals for the Amount Paid and Balance Due fields and is similar in style to the Discount Report shown in Figure 6–1b.

Customer Discount Report

Sales Rep Number	First Name	Last Name	Customer Number	Customer Name	Amount Paid	Balance Due	Discount
36	Patti	Fitzmyer					
			AA30	All About Landscapes	$1,310.00	$425.00	$4.25
			LH15	Lawn & Home Stores	$895.00	$515.25	$5.15
			PL10	Pat's Landscaping	$1,165.00	$180.75	$1.81
			SL25	Summit Lawn Service	$3,225.45	$675.50	$13.51
			TW34	TAL Wholesalers	$4,125.00	$350.00	$7.00
				Subtotals	$10,720.45	$2,146.50	
39	Rudy	Gupta					
			CT02	Christmas Tree Growers	$2,390.75	$860.35	$17.21
			GG01	Garden Gnome	$1,300.00	$297.50	$2.98
			ML25	Mum's Landscaping	$0.00	$1,805.00	$18.05
			TY03	TLC Yard Care	$1,845.00	$689.45	$6.89
				Subtotals	$5,535.75	$3,652.30	
42	Gloria	Ortega					
			GT34	Green Thumb Growers	$3,325.45	$865.50	$17.31
			OA45	Outside Architects	$4,205.50	$945.00	$18.90
			PN18	Pyke Nurseries	$2,465.00	$530.00	$10.60
			YS04	Yard Shoppe	$445.00	$575.00	$5.75
			YW01	Young's Wholesalers	$1,785.50	$345.60	$3.46
				Subtotals	$12,226.45	$3,261.10	
				Grand Totals	$28,482.65	$9,059.90	

Page 1   9/15/2017

Figure 6–88

8. If instructed to do so by your instructor, change the title for the Customer Discount Report to First Name Last Name Report where First Name and Last Name are your first and last name.

9. Submit the revised database in the format specified by your instructor.

10. ✳ How could you concatenate the Street, City, State, and Postal Code fields to display the complete address on one line?

Continued >

In the Labs *continued*

Lab 2: **Adding Tables and Creating Reports for the SciTech Sundries Database**

Problem: The gift shop manager of SciTech Sundries needs to track items that are being reordered from vendors. The report should indicate the date an item was ordered and the quantity ordered. She also needs a report that displays vendor information as well as information about items and the order status of items. SciTech Sundries is considering running a sale of items within the store; the sale price will be determined by the item's original retail price. The manager would like a report that shows the retail price as well as the sale price of all items.

Note: To complete this assignment, you will be required to use the Data Files. Please contact your instructor for information about accessing the Data Files.

Instructions: Perform the following tasks:
1. Run Access and open the Lab 2 SciTech Sundries database you used in Module 5. If you did not use this database, see your instructor about accessing the required files.
2. Create a table in which to store the item reorder information using the structure shown in Table 6–6. Use Reorder as the name of the table.

Table 6–6 Structure of Reorder Table

Field Name	Data Type	Field Size	Description
Item Number	Short Text	4	Part of Primary Key
Date Ordered	Date/Time (Use Short Date format)		Part of Primary Key
Number Ordered	Number	Integer	

3. Import the data from the Reorder.xlsx workbook to the Reorder table.
4. Add the Reorder table to the Relationships window and establish a one-to-many relationship between the Item table and the Reorder table. Save the relationship.
5. Create a query that joins the Vendor table and the Item table. Include the Vendor Code and Vendor Name from the Vendor table. Include all fields except the Vendor Code from the Item table. Save the query as Vendors and Items.
6. Create the report shown in Figure 6–89. The report uses the Vendors and Items query as the basis for the main report and the Reorder table as the basis for the subreport. Use the name Vendor Master List as the name for the report and the name Items on Order as the name for the subreport. The report uses the same style as that demonstrated in the module project. Use conditional formatting to display the on-hand value in bold red font color for all items with fewer than 10 items on hand. Change the Border Style property to Transparent. Change the Text Align property for the title to Center.

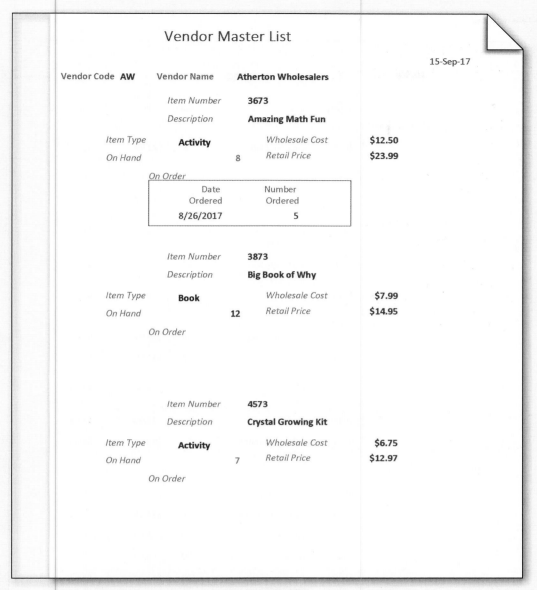

Figure 6–89

7. Create the Item Discount Report shown in Figure 6–90. The report uses the Vendors and Items Query and calculates the sale price for each item. Items with a retail price of more than $20 have a 4 percent discount; otherwise, the discount is 2 percent. Note that the report shows the sale price, not the discount. The report is similar to the Discount Report shown in Figure 6–1b. However, there are no group subtotals or report grand totals. The page number and current date appear in the page footer section. Change the Can Grow property for the Description field to Yes.

Continued >

In the Labs *continued*

Item Discount Report

Vendor Code	Vendor Name	Item Number	Description	On Hand	Retail Price	Sale Price
AW	Atherton Wholesalers					
		3673	Amazing Math Fun	8	$23.99	$23.03
		3873	Big Book of Why	12	$14.95	$14.65
		4573	Crystal Growing Kit	7	$12.97	$12.71
		5923	Discovery Dinosaurs	3	$19.95	$19.55
		7123	Gem Nature Guide	12	$14.95	$14.65
		8344	Onyx Jar	2	$13.97	$13.69
GS	Gift Sundries					
		3663	Agate Bookends	4	$29.97	$28.77
		4583	Dinosaur Ornament	12	$14.99	$14.69
		6185	Fibonacci Necklace	5	$29.99	$28.79
		7934	Gyrobot	24	$49.99	$47.99
		9201	Sidewalk Art and More	15	$16.95	$16.61
SD	Sinz Distributors					
		4553	Cosmos Explained	9	$15.00	$14.70
		6234	Fun with Science	16	$24.95	$23.95
		6325	Fun Straws	20	$8.99	$8.81
		6345	Geek Guide	20	$9.99	$9.79
		8590	Paper Airplanes	22	$13.99	$13.71
		9458	Slime Time Fun	15	$24.99	$23.99

Page 1   9/15/2017

Figure 6–90

8. If instructed to do so by your instructor, add a label to the report footer with your first and last name.

9. Submit the revised database in the format specified by your instructor.

10. ❋ What expression did you use to create the Sale Price calculated field?

Lab 3: **Consider This: Your Turn**

Adding Tables and Creating Reports for the JSP Analysis Database

Note: To complete this assignment, you will be required to use the Data Files. Please contact your instructor for information about accessing the Data Files.

Instructions: Open the Lab 3 JSP Analysis database you used in Module 5. If you did not use this database, contact your instructor for information about accessing the required files.

Part 1:   JSP Analysis offers seminars to its clients to explain applications of data mining. Management needs to maintain data on these seminars. They need a report that lists market analysts as well as the clients they serve and any seminar offerings the client is currently taking. Use the concepts and techniques presented in this module to perform each of the following tasks:

    a. Create two tables in which to store data about the seminars requested by clients. The Seminar table contains data about the seminars that JSP Analysis offers. The structure of the table is similar to the Workshop table shown in in Table 6–1a. Replace Workshop with Seminar, name the table Seminar, and import the Seminar.txt file. The Seminar Offerings table has the same structure as the Workshop Offerings table shown in Table 6–2a except that the Account Number field is Client Number with a field size of 4 and Workshop Code is Seminar Code. Create the Seminar Offerings table and import the Seminar Offerings. csv file. Determine the relationships between the Seminar table, the Seminar Offerings table, and the Client table. Enforce referential integrity between the appropriate tables.

    b. Create a query that joins the Marketing Analyst and the Client tables. Include the Marketing Analyst Number, First Name, and Last Name fields from the Marketing Analyst table. Include all fields from the Client table except Total Amount and Marketing Analyst Number. Save the query.

    c. Create a query that joins the Seminar and Seminar Offerings tables. Include the Client Number and Seminar Code fields from the Seminar Offerings table, the Seminar Description from the Seminar table, and the Total Hours and Hours Spent fields from the Seminar Offerings table. Add a calculated field that contains the difference between Total Hours and Hours Spent. Save the query.

    d. Create a Marketing Analyst Master Report that uses the query from Step b above as the basis for the main report and the query from Step c above as the basis for the subreport. The report should be similar in style to that shown in Figure 6–1a. Add a total amount field to the main report that sums the Amount Paid and Current Due fields for each record.

Submit your assignment in the format specified by your instructor.

Part 2:   You made several decisions, such as adding new relationships, creating and modifying a subreport, and adding a calculated control, while adding these tables and creating the report. What was the rationale behind your decisions? How could you add a logo to the report?

PrattLast Associates : Database- C:\Users\Owner\Documents\CIS

Microsoft Access 2016

File   Home   Create   External Data   Database Tools   ♀ Tell me what you want to do...

7 | Advanced Form Techniques

Objectives

You will have mastered the material in this module when you can:

- Add combo boxes that include selection lists
- Add combo boxes for searching
- Format and resize controls
- Apply formatting characteristics with the Format Painter
- Add command buttons
- Modify buttons and combo boxes

- Add a calculated field
- Use tab controls to create a multipage form
- Add and modify a subform
- Insert charts
- Modify a chart type
- Format a chart

Introduction

In previous modules, you created basic forms using the Form Wizard and you created more complex forms using Design view. In this module, you will create two new forms that feature more advanced form elements. The first form contains two combo boxes, one for selecting data from a related table and one for finding a record on the form. It also contains command buttons to accomplish various tasks.

The second form you will create is a **multipage form**, a form that contains more than one page of information. The form contains a tab control that allows you to access two different pages. Clicking the first tab displays a page containing a subform. Clicking the second tab displays a page containing two charts.

Project — Advanced Form Techniques

PrattLast Associates wants two additional forms to use with its Account and Account Manager tables. The first form, Account View and Update Form (Figure 7–1a), contains the fields in the Account table. The form has five command buttons: Next Record, Previous Record, Add Record, Delete Record, and Close Form. Clicking any of these buttons causes the action indicated on the button to occur.

The form also contains a combo box for the Account Manager Number field that assists users in selecting the correct manager (Figure 7–1b).

To assist users in finding an account when they know the account's name, the form also includes a combo box they can use for this purpose (Figure 7–1c).

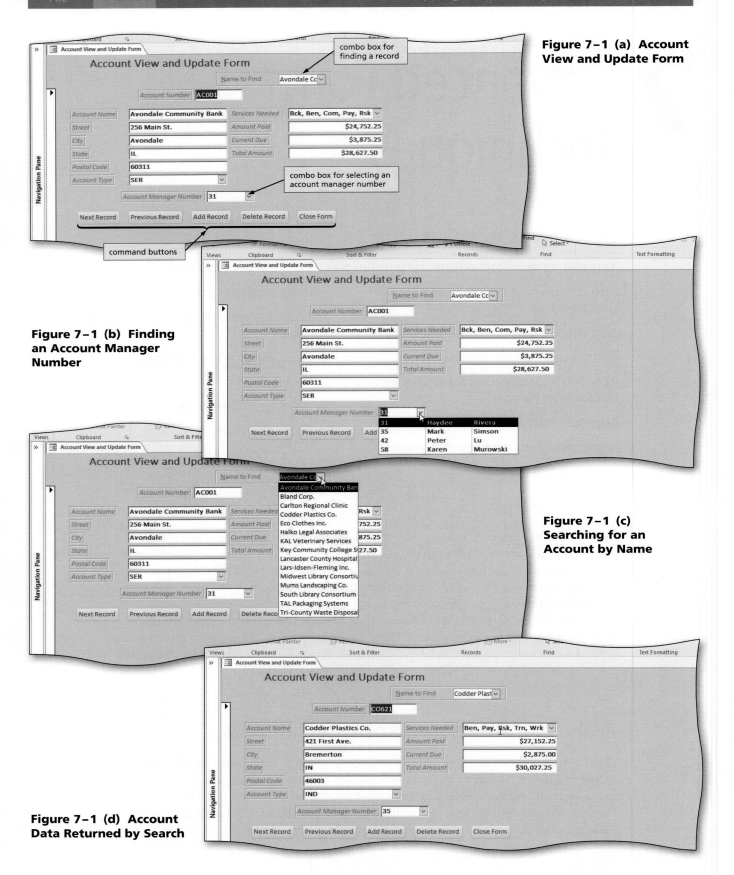

Figure 7–1 (a) Account View and Update Form

combo box for finding a record

Figure 7–1 (b) Finding an Account Manager Number

command buttons

Figure 7–1 (c) Searching for an Account by Name

Figure 7–1 (d) Account Data Returned by Search

Microsoft Access 2016

File   Home   Create   External Data   Database Tools   ♀ Tell me what you want to do...

After displaying the list of accounts by clicking the arrow, the user can simply select the account they want to find; Access will then locate the account and display that account's data in the form (Figure 7–1d).

For the second new form, PrattLast Associates needs a multipage form that lists the numbers and names of managers. Each of the two pages that make up the form is displayed in its own tab page. Selecting the first tab, the one labeled Datasheet, displays a subform listing information about the workshop offerings for accounts of the selected manager (Figure 7–2a).

Selecting the other tab, the one labeled Charts, displays two charts that illustrate the total hours spent and hours remaining by the manager for the various workshops (Figure 7–2b). In both charts, the slices of the pie represent the various workshops. They are color-coded and the legend at the bottom indicates the meaning of the various colors. The size of the pie slice gives a visual representation of the portion of the hours spent or hours remaining by the manager for that particular workshop. The chart also includes specific percentages. If you look at the purple slice in the Hours Spent by Workshop Offering chart, for example, you see that the color represents workshop W02. It signifies 25 percent of the total. Thus, for all the hours already spent on the various workshop offerings by manager 31, 25 percent have been spent on workshop W02.

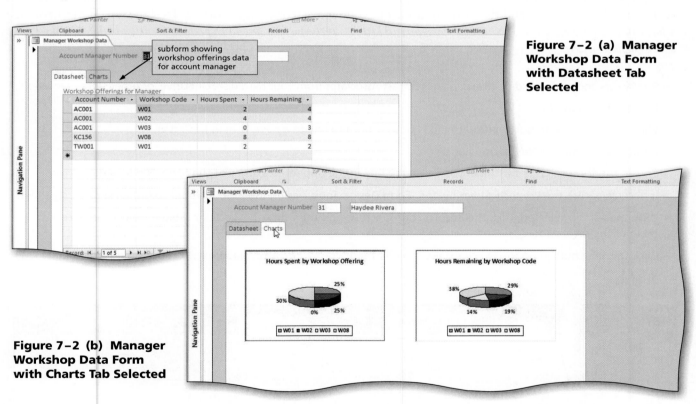

Figure 7–2 (a) Manager Workshop Data Form with Datasheet Tab Selected

Figure 7–2 (b) Manager Workshop Data Form with Charts Tab Selected

In this module, you will learn how to create the forms shown in Figures 7–1 and 7–2. The following roadmap identifies general activities you will perform as you progress through this module:

1. CREATE FORM containing a calculated field.

2. ADD COMBO BOXES, one for selecting data from a related table and one for finding a record on the form.

3. Add **COMMAND BUTTONS** to the form.

4. **MODIFY** a **MACRO** for one of the buttons so that the button works correctly.

5. **MODIFY** the **COMBO BOX** for finding a record so that the combo box works correctly.

6. **CREATE** a **SECOND FORM**, one that contains a tab control.

7. **ADD** a **SUBFORM** to one of the tabbed pages.

8. **ADD** a **CHART** to the other tabbed page.

Creating a Form with Combo Boxes and Command Buttons

After planning a form, you might decide that including features such as combo boxes and command buttons will make the form easier to use. You can include such items while modifying the form in Design view.

To Create a Form in Design View

1 CREATE FORM | 2 ADD COMBO BOXES | 3 COMMAND BUTTONS | 4 MODIFY MACRO
5 MODIFY COMBO BOX | 6 CREATE SECOND FORM | 7 ADD SUBFORM | 8 ADD CHART

As you have previously learned, Access provides several differing ways to create a form, including tools such as the Form Wizard and the Form button. The following steps create a form in Design view. *Why? Creating a form in Design view gives you the most flexibility in laying out the form. You will be presented with a blank design on which to place objects.*

- Run Access and open the database named PrattLast Associates from your hard disk, OneDrive, or other storage location.

- Display the Create tab.

- Click the Form Design button (Create tab | Forms group) to create a new form in Design view.

- If necessary, close the Navigation Pane.

- Ensure the form selector for the entire form, the box in the upper-left corner of the form, is selected.

- If necessary, click the Property Sheet button (Form Design Tools Design tab | Tools group) to display a property sheet.

- With the All tab selected, click the Record Source arrow, and then click the Account table to select the Account table as the record source.

- Click the Save button on the Quick Access Toolbar, then type **Account Master Form** as the form name (Figure 7–3).

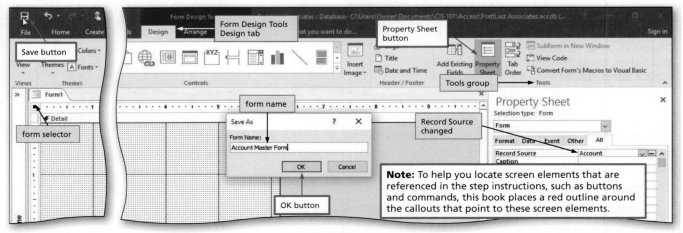

Figure 7–3

2

- Click the OK button (Save As dialog box) to save the form.

- Click the Caption property in the property sheet, and then type **Account View and Update Form** as the new caption.

- Close the property sheet by clicking the Property Sheet button on the Form Design Tools Design tab.

- Click the 'Add Existing Fields' button (Form Design Tools Design tab | Tools group) to display the field list (Figure 7–4).

Q&A Why does the name on the tab not change to the new caption, Account View and Update Form? The name on the tab will change to the new caption in Form view. In Design view, you still see the name of the form object.

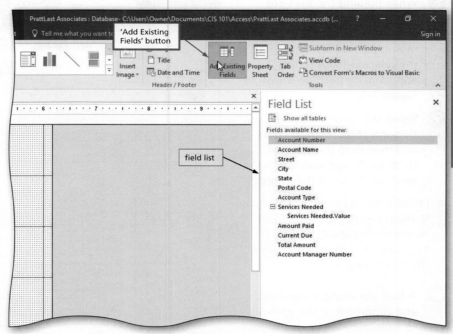

Figure 7–4

To Add Fields to the Form Design

After deciding which fields to add to the Account View and Update Form, you can place them on the form by dragging the fields from the field list to the desired position. The following steps first display only the fields in the Account table in the field list, and then place the appropriate fields on the form.

1 If necessary, click the 'Show only fields in the current record source' link at the top of the field list to change the link to 'Show all tables' and display only the fields in the Account table.

2 Drag the Account Number field from the field list to the top-center area of the form.

3 Click the label once to select it and then click it a second time to produce an insertion point, use the BACKSPACE or DELETE key as necessary to erase the current entry (AC #), and then type **Account Number** as the new label.

4 Click outside the label to deselect it, click the label to select it a second time, and then drag the sizing handle in the upper-left corner of the label to move it to the approximate position shown Figure 7–5.

Q&A I thought the caption for Account Number was changed to AC # so that this short caption would appear in datasheets, on forms, and on reports. Why am I now changing it back?
In these forms, there is plenty of room for the entire field name. Thus, there is no need for the short captions.

5 Click the Account Name field in the field list.

6 While holding the SHIFT key down, click the Account Type field in the field list to select multiple fields, and then drag the selected fields to the approximate position shown in Figure 7–5.

7 Select the Services Needed through Total Amount fields and then drag the selected fields to the approximate position shown in the figure.

Q&A I added the Account Manager Number field by mistake. Can I delete the control?

Yes, select the control and press the DELETE key.

8 Adjust the sizing, placement, and alignment of the controls to approximately match those in the figure. If controls for any of the fields are not aligned properly, align them by dragging them to the desired location or by using the alignment buttons on the Form Design Tools Arrange tab.

9 Close the field list.

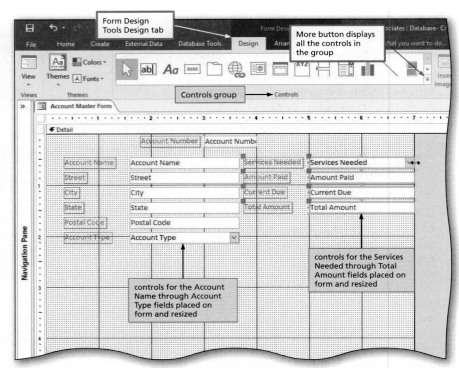

Figure 7–5

✳ **CONSIDER THIS**

How do you decide on the contents of a form?

To design and create forms, follow these general guidelines:

Determine the fields that belong on the form. If you determine that data should be presented as a form, you then need to determine what tables and fields contain the data for the form.

Examine the requirements for the form in general to determine the tables. Do the requirements only relate to data in a single table, or does the data come from multiple tables? How are the tables related?

Examine the specific requirements for the form to determine the fields necessary. Look for all the data items that are specified for the form. Each item should correspond to a field in a table or be able to be computed from a field in a table. This information gives you the list of fields.

Determine whether there are any special calculations required, such as adding the values in two fields or combining the contents of two text fields. If special calculations are needed, what are they? What fields are involved and how are they to be combined?

Combo Boxes

When entering a manager number, the value must match the number of a manager currently in the Account Manager table. To assist users in entering this data, the form will contain a combo box. A **combo box** combines the properties of a **text box**, which is a box into which you can type an entry, and a **list box**, which is a box you can use to display a list from which to select a value. With a combo box, the user can either type the data or click the combo box arrow to display a list of possible values and then select an item from the list.

BTW

Combo Boxes

You also can create combo boxes for reports.

To Add a Combo Box That Selects Values

If you have determined that a combo box displaying values from a related table would be useful on your form, you can add the combo box to a form using the Combo Box tool in the Controls group on the Form Design Tools Design tab. Before doing so, you should make sure the 'Use Control Wizards' button is selected. *Why? A combo box that allows the user to select a value from a list is a convenient way to enter data.* The following steps place on the form a combo box that displays values from a related table for the Account Manager Number field.

1

- Click the Form Design Tools Design tab and then click the More button (Form Design Tools Design tab | Controls group) (see Figure 7–5) to display all the available tools in the Controls group (Figure 7–6).

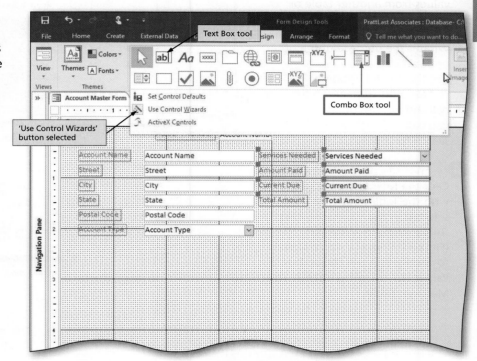

Figure 7–6

2

- With the 'Use Control Wizards' button in the Controls group on the Form Design Tools Design tab selected, click the Combo Box tool (Form Design Tools Design tab | Controls group), and then move the pointer, whose shape has changed to a small plus symbol accompanied by a combo box, to the position shown in Figure 7–7.

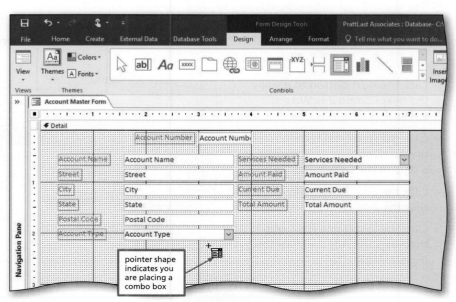

Figure 7–7

● Click the position shown in Figure 7–7 to place a combo box and display the Combo Box Wizard dialog box.

● If necessary, in the Combo Box Wizard dialog box, click the 'I want the combo box to get the values from another table or query.' option button (Figure 7–8).

Q&A | What is the purpose of the other options?
Use the second option if you want to type a list from which the user will choose. Use the third option if you want to use the combo box to search for a record.

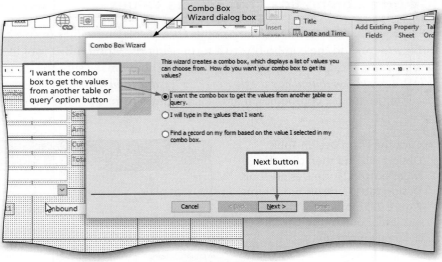

Figure 7–8

● Click the Next button, and then, with the Tables option button selected in the View area, click 'Table: Account Manager' (Figure 7–9) in the list of tables to specify that the combo box values will come from the Account Manager table.

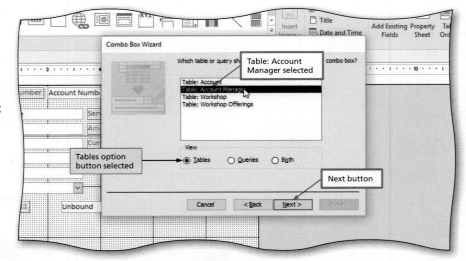

Figure 7–9

● Click the Next button to display the next Combo Box Wizard screen.

● Click the Add Field button to add the Account Manager Number as a field in the combo box.

● Click the First Name field and then click the Add Field button.

● Click the Last Name field and then click the Add Field button (Figure 7–10).

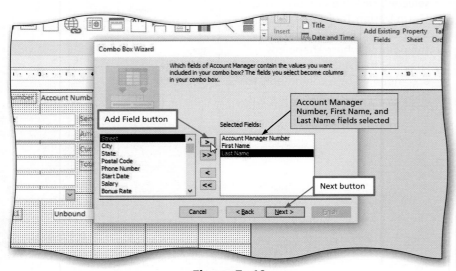

Figure 7–10

6

- Click the Next button to display the next Combo Box Wizard screen.

- Click the arrow in the first text box, and then select the Account Manager Number field to sort the data by account manager number (Figure 7–11).

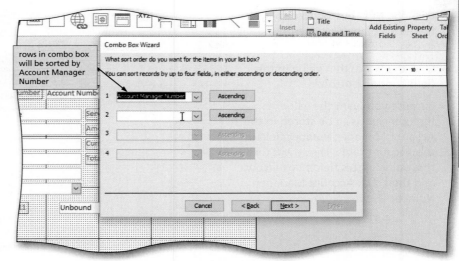

Figure 7–11

7

- Click the Next button to display the next Combo Box Wizard screen (Figure 7–12).

Q&A What is the key column? Do I want to hide it?

The key column would be the Account Manager Number, which is the column that identifies both a first name and a last name. Because the purpose of this combo box is to update manager numbers, you want the account manager numbers to be visible.

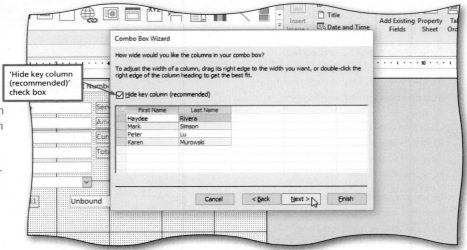

Figure 7–12

8

- Click the 'Hide key column (recommended)' check box to remove the check mark so that the Account Manager Number field will appear along with the First Name and Last Name fields.

- Click the Next button to display the next Combo Box Wizard screen (Figure 7–13).

Q&A Do I need to make any changes here?

No. The Account Manager Number field, which is the field you want to store, is already selected.

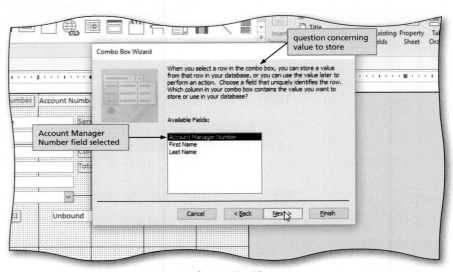

Figure 7–13

9

- Click the Next button to display the next Combo Box Wizard screen.

- Click the 'Store that value in this field:' option button.

- Because you want the value the user selects to be stored in the Account Manager Number field in the Account table, click the 'Store that value in this field:' box arrow, and then click Account Manager Number (Figure 7–14).

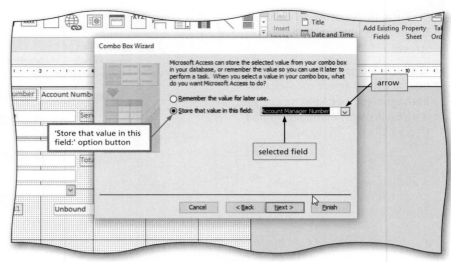

Figure 7–14

10

- Click the Next button to display the next Combo Box Wizard screen.

- Type **Account Manager Number** as the label for the combo box, and then click the Finish button to place the combo box.

Q&A

Could I change the label to something else?

Yes. If you prefer a different label, you could change it.

- Move the Account Manager Number label by dragging its Move handle to the position shown in Figure 7–15. Resize the label, if necessary, to match the figure.

11

- Save your changes to the form.

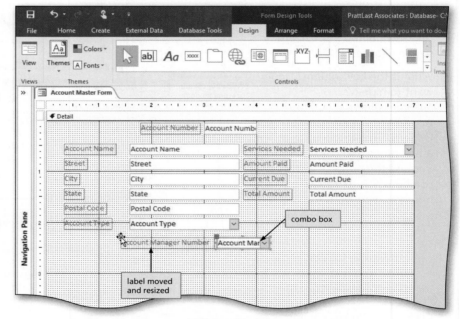

Figure 7–15

To Use the Background Color Button

As you learned in a previous module, you can use the Background Color button on the Form Design Tools Format tab to change the background color of a form. The following steps change the background color of the form to a light gray.

BTW

Touch and Pointers
Remember that if you are using your finger on a touch screen, you will not see the pointer.

1 Click anywhere in the Detail section but outside all the controls to select the section.

2 Display the Form Design Tools Format tab, click the Background Color button arrow (Form Design Tools Format tab | Font group) to display a color palette, and then click the Light Gray 2 color, the first color in the third row under Standard Colors, to change the background color.

Advanced Form Techniques   **Access Module 7**   **AC** 371

Access Module 7

1 CREATE FORM | 2 ADD COMBO BOXES | 3 COMMAND BUTTONS | 4 MODIFY MACRO
5 MODIFY COMBO BOX | 6 CREATE SECOND FORM | 7 ADD SUBFORM | 8 ADD CHART

To Format a Control

You can use buttons on the Form Design Tools Design tab to format a control in a variety of ways. The following steps use the property sheet, however, to make a variety of changes to the format of the Account Number control. *Why? Using the property sheet gives you more choices over the types of changes you can make to the form controls than you have with simply using the buttons.*

- Display the Form Design Tools Design tab.

- Click the Account Number control (the white space, not the label) to select it.

- Click the Property Sheet button (Form Design Tools Design tab | Tools group) to display the property sheet.

- Change the value of the Font Weight property to Semi-bold.

- Change the value of the Special Effect property to Sunken.

- Click the Fore Color property box to select it, and then click the Build button (the three dots) to display a color palette (Figure 7–16).

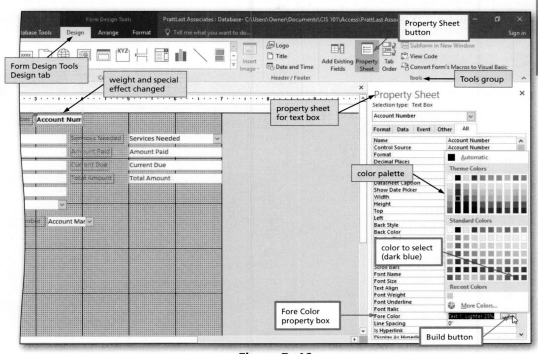

Figure 7–16

- Click the Dark Blue color (the second color from the right in the bottom row under Standard Colors) to select it as the foreground color, which is the font color.

- Click the label for the Account Number field to select it.

- Change the value of the Font Italic property to Yes.

- Change the Special Effect property to Etched (Figure 7–17).

3

- Close the property sheet.

Q&A

Should I not have closed the property sheet before selecting different control?
You could have, but it is not necessary. The property sheet displayed on the screen always applies to the currently selected control or group of controls.

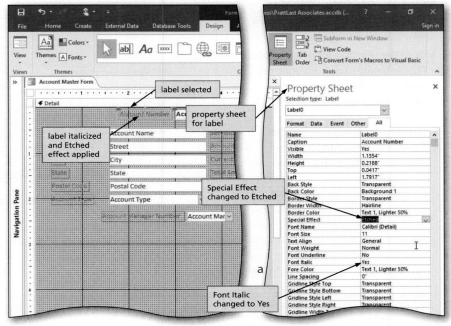

Figure 7–17

To Use the Format Painter

1 CREATE FORM | 2 ADD COMBO BOXES | 3 COMMAND BUTTONS | 4 MODIFY MACRO
5 MODIFY COMBO BOX | 6 CREATE SECOND FORM | 7 ADD SUBFORM | 8 ADD CHART

Once you have formatted a control and its label the way you want, you can format other controls in exactly the same way by using the format painter. *Why? If you click the control whose format you want to copy, click the Format Painter button on the Format tab, and then click another control, Access will automatically apply the characteristics of the first control to the second one.* If you want to copy the format to more than one other control, double-click the Format Painter button instead of simply clicking the button, and then click each of the controls that you want to change. The following steps copy the formatting of the Account Number control and label to the other controls.

1

- Display the Form Design Tools Format tab.

- Click the Account Number control to select it, and then double-click the Format Painter button (Form Design Tools Format tab | Font group) to select the Format Painter.

- Point to the Account Name control (Figure 7–18).

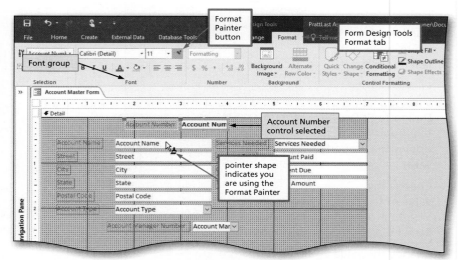

Figure 7–18

2

- Click the Account Name control to assign to it the same formatting as the Account Number control.

- Click all the other controls on the form to assign the same formatting to them.

- Click the Format Painter button (Form Design Tools Format tab | Font group) to deselect the Format Painter (Figure 7–19).

Q&A Do I always have to click the Format Painter button when I have finished copying the formatting?
If you double-clicked the Format Painter button to enable you to copy the formatting to multiple controls, you need to click the

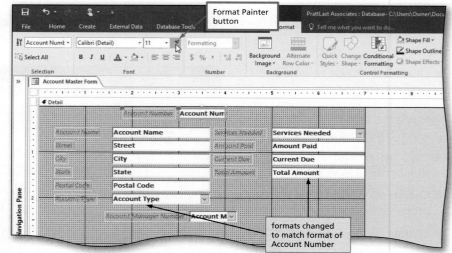

Figure 7–19

Format Painter button again to turn off the copying. If you single-clicked the Format Painter button to enable you to copy the formatting to a single control, you do not need to click the button again. As soon as you copy the formatting to the single control, the copying will be turned off.

Does the order in which I click the other controls matter?
No. The only thing that is important is that you ultimately click all the controls whose formatting you want to change.

3

- Save your changes to the form.

To View the Form

The following steps view the form in Form view and then return to Design view. ***Why?*** *As you are working on the design of a form, it is a good idea to periodically view the form in Form view to see the effects of your changes.*

1
- Display the Form Design Tools Design tab.

- Click the View button (Form Design Tools Design tab | Views group) to view the form in Form view (Figure 7–20).

Q&A Why did I have to change from the Format tab to the Design tab?
The Format tab does not have a View button.

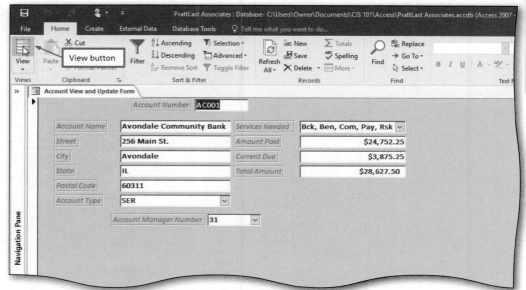

Figure 7–20

2
- Click the View button arrow (Home tab | Views group) to produce the View button menu.

- Click Design View on the View menu to return to Design view.

Q&A Could I simply click the View button?
No. The icon on the View button is the one for Layout view. Clicking the button would show you the form in Layout view, but you are working on the form in Design view.

Other Ways

1. Click Form View button on status bar   2. Click Design View button on status bar

To Add a Title and Expand the Form Header Section

The following steps insert the Form Header and Form Footer sections, and then add a title to the Form Header section. They also expand the Form Header section.

1 Click the Title button (Form Design Tools Design tab | Header/Footer group) to add a Form Header section and to add a control for the title to the Form Header section.

2 Drag the lower boundary of the Form Header section down to the approximate position shown in Figure 7–21.

3 Select the title control, display the Form Design Tools Format tab, and then click the Bold button (Form Design Tools Format tab | Font group) to make the title bold.

4 Drag the right sizing handle to the approximate position shown in the figure to resize the control to the appropriate size for the title.

BTW

Font versus Foreground Color
The font color also is called the foreground color. When you change the font color using the ribbon, you click the Font Color button. If you use the property sheet to change the color, you click the Fore Color property, click the Build button, and then click the desired color.

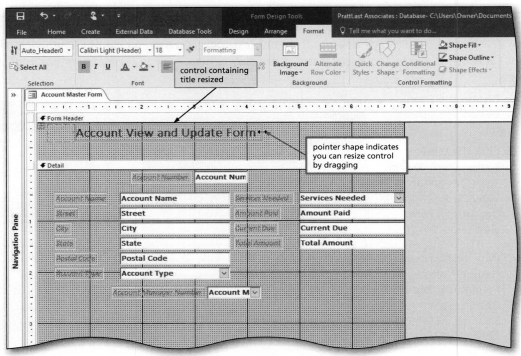

Figure 7–21

To Change the Background Color of the Form Header

The background color of the form header in the form in Figure 7–1 is the same as the rest of the form. The following steps change the background color of the form header appropriately.

① Click anywhere in the Form Header section but outside all the controls to select the section.

② If necessary, display the Form Design Tools Format tab.

③ Click the Background Color button arrow (Form Design Tools Format tab | Font group) to display a color palette.

④ Click the Light Gray 2 color, the first color in the third row under Standard Colors, to change the background color.

⑤ Save your changes to the form.

Headers and Footers

Just like with reports, you have control over whether your forms contain a form header and footer. They go together, so if you have a form header, you will also have a form footer. If you do not want the sections to appear, you can shrink the size so there is no room for any content. You can also remove the sections from your form altogether. If you later decide you want to include them, you can once again add them. You have similar options with page headers and page footers, although typically page headers and page footers are only used with reports. If you had a very long form that spanned several pages on the screen, you might choose to use page headers and footers, but it is not common to do so.

TO REMOVE A FORM HEADER AND FOOTER

To remove a form header and footer, you would use the following steps.

1. With the form open in Design view, right-click any open area of the form to produce a shortcut menu.
2. Click the Form Header/Footer command on the shortcut menu to remove the form header and footer.
3. If the Microsoft Access dialog box appears, asking if it is acceptable to delete any controls in the section, click the Yes button.

TO REMOVE A PAGE HEADER AND FOOTER

To remove a page header and footer, you would use the following steps.

1. With the form open in Design view, right-click any open area of the form to produce a shortcut menu.
2. Click the Page Header/Footer command on the shortcut menu to remove the page header and footer.
3. If the Microsoft Access dialog box appears, asking if it is acceptable to delete any controls in the section, click the Yes button.

TO INSERT A FORM HEADER AND FOOTER

To insert a form header and footer, you would use the following steps.

1. With the form open in Design view, right-click any open area of the form to produce a shortcut menu.
2. Click the Form Header/Footer command on the shortcut menu to insert a form header and footer.

TO INSERT A PAGE HEADER AND FOOTER

To insert a page header and footer, you would use the following steps.

1. With the form open in Design view, right-click any open area of the form to produce a shortcut menu.
2. Click the Page Header/Footer command on the shortcut menu to insert a page header and footer.

BTW

Hyperlink Controls
You can add a hyperlink to forms. To add a hyperlink, click the Hyperlink tool, enter the hyperlink in the Address text box (Insert Hyperlink dialog box) and click the OK button. If necessary, move the hyperlink control to the desired location on the form.

Images

You can include a picture (image) in a form. You can also use a picture (image) as the background for a form.

TO INCLUDE AN IMAGE IN A FORM

To include an image in a form, you would use the following steps.

1. Open the form in Design view or Layout view.
2. Click the Insert Image button (Form Design Tools Design tab | Controls group) and then click the Browse command.
3. Select the desired image.
4. Click the desired location to add the image to the form.

TO USE AN IMAGE AS BACKGROUND FOR A FORM

To include an image as background for a form, you would use the following steps.

1. Open the form in Design view or Layout view.

2. Click anywhere in the form, click the Background Image button (Form Design Tools Format tab | Background group), and then click the Browse command.

3. Select the desired image for the background.

Break Point: If you wish to stop working through the module at this point, you can quit Access now. You can resume the project later by running Access, opening the database called PrattLast Associates, opening the Account Master Form in Design view, and continuing to follow the steps from this location forward.

BTW

Record Order
When you use the Next Record button to move through the records, recall that the records are in order by Account Number, which is the primary key, and not alphabetical order.

Command Buttons

Command buttons are buttons placed on a form that users can click to carry out specific actions. To add command buttons, you use the Button tool in the Controls group on the Form Design Tools Design tab. When using the series of Command Button Wizard dialog boxes, you indicate the action that should be taken when the command button is clicked, for example, go to the next record. Within the Command Button Wizard, Access includes several categories of commonly used actions.

CONSIDER THIS

When would you include command buttons in your form?
You can make certain actions more convenient for users by including command buttons. Buttons can carry out record navigation actions (for example, go to the next record), record operation actions (for example, add a record), form operation actions (for example, close a form), report operation actions (for example, print a report), application actions (for example, quit application), and some miscellaneous actions (for example, run a macro).

To Add Command Buttons to a Form

1 CREATE FORM | 2 ADD COMBO BOXES | 3 COMMAND BUTTONS | 4 MODIFY MACRO
5 MODIFY COMBO BOX | 6 CREATE SECOND FORM | 7 ADD SUBFORM | 8 ADD CHART

You may find that you can improve the functionality of your form by adding command buttons. *Why? Command buttons enable users to accomplish tasks with a single click.* Before adding the buttons, you should make sure the 'Use Control Wizards' button is selected.

In the Record Navigation action category, you will select the 'Go To Next Record' action for one of the command buttons. From the same category, you will select the 'Go To Previous Record' action for another. Other buttons will use the 'Add New Record' and the Delete Record actions from the Record Operations category. The Close Form button will use the Close Form action from the Form Operations category.

The following steps add command buttons to move to the next record, move to the previous record, add a record, delete a record, and close the form.

- Display the Form Design Tools Design tab, click the More button in the control gallery, and then ensure the 'Use Control Wizards' button is selected.

- Click the Button tool (Form Design Tools Design tab | Controls group) and then move the pointer to the approximate position shown in Figure 7–22.

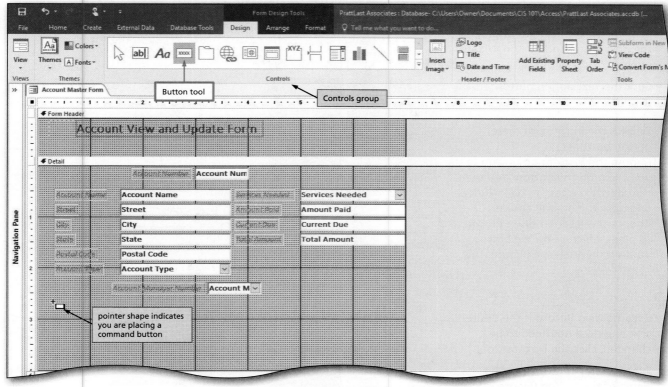

Figure 7–22

2

- Click the position shown in Figure 7–22 to display the Command Button Wizard dialog box.
- With Record Navigation selected in the Categories box, click 'Go To Next Record' in the Actions box (Figure 7–23).

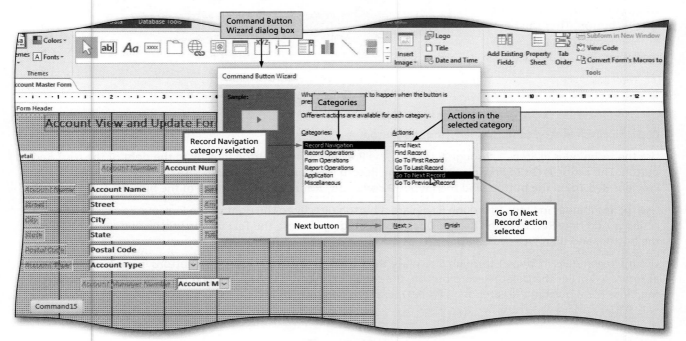

Figure 7–23

● Click the Next button to display the next Command Button Wizard screen.

● Click the Text option button (Figure 7–24).

Q&A What is the purpose of these option buttons?

Choose the first option button to place text on the button. You then can specify the text to be included or accept the default choice. Choose the second option button to place a picture on the button. You can then select a picture.

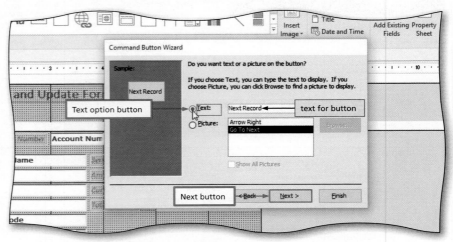

Figure 7–24

● Because Next Record is the desired text and does not need to be changed, click the Next button.

● Type **Next Record** as the name of the button (Figure 7–25).

Q&A Does the name of the button have to be the same as the text that appears on the face of the button?

No. The text is what will appear on the screen. You use the name when you need to refer to the specific button. They can be different, but this can lead to confusion. Thus, many people will typically make them the same.

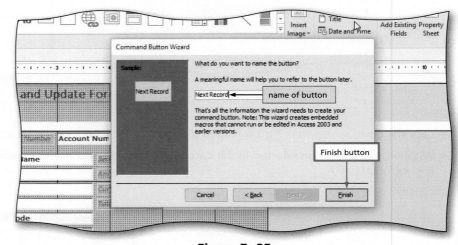

Figure 7–25

5

● Click the Finish button to finish specifying the button.

● Use the techniques in Steps 1 through 5 to place the Previous Record button directly to the right of the Next Record button. The action is Go To Previous Record in the Record Navigation category. Choose the Text option button and Previous Record on the button, and then type **Previous Record** as the name of the button.

● Use the techniques in Steps 1 through 5 to place a button directly to the right of the Previous Record button. The action is Add New Record in the Record Operations category. Choose the Text option button and Add Record on the button, and then type **Add Record** as the name of the button.

● Use the techniques in Steps 1 through 5 to place the Delete Record and Close Form buttons in the positions shown in Figure 7–26. For the Delete Record button, the category is Record Operations and the action is Delete Record. For the Close Form button, the category is Form Operations and the action is Close Form.

Q&A My buttons are not aligned like yours are. What should I do?
If your buttons are not aligned properly, you can drag them to the correct positions. You can also use the buttons in the Sizing & Ordering group on the Form Design Tools Arrange tab.

• Save the changes to the form.

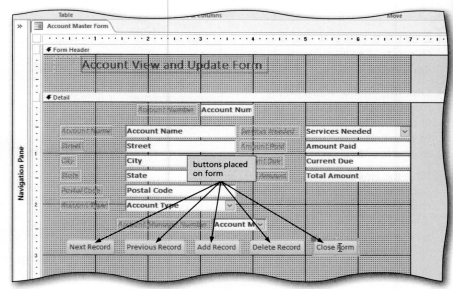

Figure 7–26

To Add a Combo Box for Finding a Record

1 CREATE FORM | 2 ADD COMBO BOXES | 3 COMMAND BUTTONS | 4 MODIFY MACRO
5 MODIFY COMBO BOX | 6 CREATE SECOND FORM | 7 ADD SUBFORM | 8 ADD CHART

Although you can use the Find button (Home tab | Find group) to locate records on a form or a report, it is often more convenient to use a combo box. **Why?** *You can type the account's name directly into the box. Alternatively, you can click the combo box arrow to display a list and then select the desired entry from the list.*

To create a combo box, use the Combo Box tool in the Controls group on the Design tab. The Combo Box Wizard then will guide you through the steps of adding the combo box. The following steps place a combo box for names on the form.

1

• Click the More button (Form Design Tools Design tab | Controls group) to display all the controls.

• With the 'Use Control Wizards' button selected, click the Combo Box tool (Form Design Tools Design tab | Controls group) and then move the pointer, whose shape has changed to a small plus sign with a combo box, to the position shown in Figure 7–27.

Q&A Why is the combo box located in the Form Header section?
Including the combo box in the Form Header section rather than in the Detail section indicates that the contents of the combo box are not changed or updated by the user.

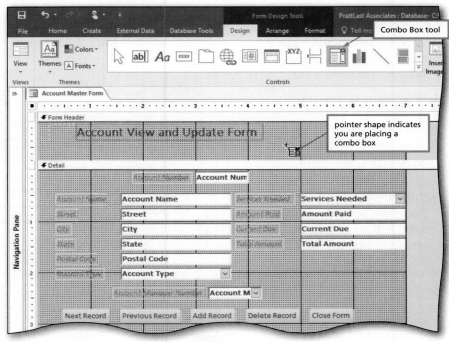

Figure 7–27

● Click the position shown in Figure 7–27 to display the Combo Box Wizard.

● Click the 'Find a record on my form based on the value I selected in my combo box.' option button to specify that the user will select from a list of values.

● Click the Next button, click the Account Name field, and then click the Add Field button to select the Account Name field for the combo box (Figure 7–28).

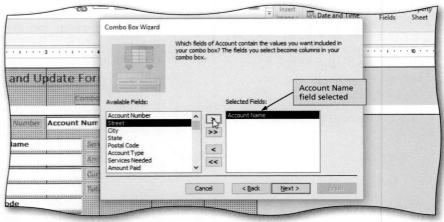

Figure 7–28

● Click the Next button.

● Drag the right boundary of the column heading to the approximate size shown in Figure 7–29.

Q&A Can I also resize the column to best fit the data by double-clicking the right boundary of the column heading?
Yes.

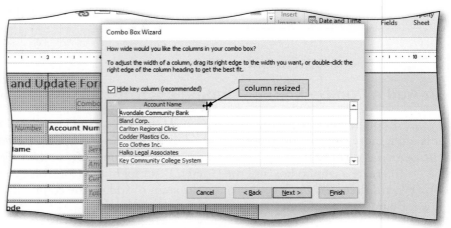

Figure 7–29

● Click the Next button, and then type **&Name to Find** as the label for the combo box.

Q&A What is the purpose of the ampersand in front of the letter, N? The ampersand (&) in front of the letter, N, indicates that users can select the combo box by pressing ALT+N.

● Click the Finish button, and, if necessary, position the control and label in the approximate position shown in Figure 7–30.

Q&A Why is the letter, N, underlined? The underlined letter, N, in the word, Name, indicates that you can press ALT+N to select the combo box. It is underlined because you preceded the letter, N, with the ampersand.

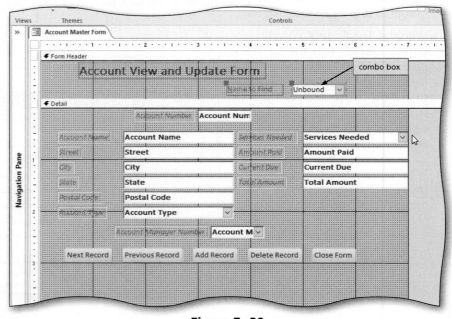

Figure 7–30

When would you include a combo box in your form?

A combo box is a combination of a text box, where users can type data, and a list box, where users can click an arrow to display a list. Would a combo box improve the functionality of the form? Is there a place where it would be convenient for users to enter data by selecting the data from a list, either a list of predefined items or a list of values from a related table? If users need to search for records, including a combo box can assist in the process.

To Place a Rectangle

1 CREATE FORM | 2 ADD COMBO BOXES | 3 COMMAND BUTTONS | 4 MODIFY MACRO

5 MODIFY COMBO BOX | 6 CREATE SECOND FORM | 7 ADD SUBFORM | 8 ADD CHART

The following steps use the Rectangle tool to place a rectangle. *Why? To emphasize an area of a form, you can place a rectangle around it as a visual cue.*

- Click the More button (Form Design Tools Design tab | Controls group) to display all the controls (Figure 7–31).

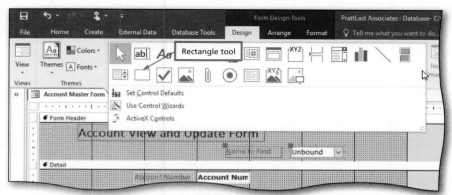

Figure 7–31

- Click the Rectangle tool, which is the second tool in the second row, point to the position for the upper-left corner of the rectangle shown in Figure 7–32, and drag to the lower-right corner of the rectangle to place the rectangle.

3

- Click the Property Sheet button (Form Design Tools Design tab | Tools group) to display the property sheet for the rectangle.

- If necessary, change the value of the Special Effect property to Etched.

- Make sure the value of the Back Style property is Transparent, so the combo box will appear within the rectangle.

Q&A What if the value is not Transparent?

If the value is not Transparent, the rectangle would cover the combo box completely and the combo box would not be visible.

- Close the property sheet.

- Save and then close the form.

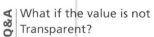

Figure 7–32

To Open the Account View and Update Form

Once you have created the form, you can use it at any time by opening it. The following steps open the Account View and Update Form.

1 Open the Navigation Pane, and then right-click the Account Master Form to display the shortcut menu.

2 Click Open on the shortcut menu to open the form.

3 Close the Navigation Pane (Figure 7–33).

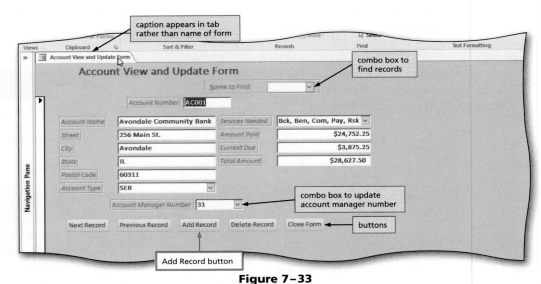

Figure 7–33

Using the Buttons

To move from record to record on the form, you can use the buttons to perform the actions you specify. To move forward to the next record, click the Next Record button. Click the Previous Record button to move back to the previous record. Clicking the Delete Record button will delete the record currently on the screen. Access will display a message requesting that you verify the deletion before the record is actually deleted. Clicking the Close Form button will remove the form from the screen.

To Test the Add Record Button

The following step uses the Add Record button. **Why?** *Clicking the Add Record button will clear the contents of the form so you can add a new record.*

1
• Click the Add Record button (Figure 7–34).

Q&A There is no insertion point in the Account Number field. How would I begin entering a new record?
To begin entering a record, you would have to click the Account Number field before you can start typing.

Why does SER appear in the Account Type field?
The value SER is the default value assigned to the Account Type field.

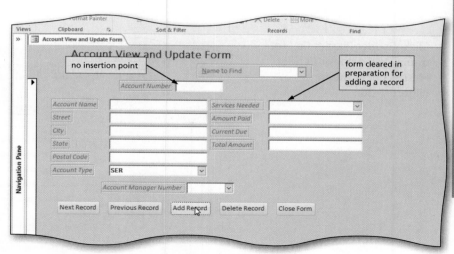

Experiment

- Try each of the other buttons to see their effects. Do not delete any records. After clicking the Close Form button, open the form once again and close the Navigation Pane.

Figure 7–34

To Use the Combo Box

1 CREATE FORM | 2 ADD COMBO BOXES | 3 COMMAND BUTTONS | 4 MODIFY MACRO
5 MODIFY COMBO BOX | 6 CREATE SECOND FORM | 7 ADD SUBFORM | 8 ADD CHART

Using the combo box, you can search for an account in two ways. First, you can click the combo box arrow to display a list of account names, and then select the name from the list by clicking it. It is also easy to search by typing the name. *Why? As you type, Access will automatically display the name that begins with the letters you have typed. Once the correct name is displayed, you can select the name by pressing the TAB key.* Regardless of the method you use, the data for the selected account appears on the form once the selection is made.

The following steps first locate the account whose name is Codder Plastics Co., and then use the Next Record button to move to the next account.

1

- Click the 'Name to Find' arrow to display a list of account names (Figure 7–35).

Q&A — Why does the list not appear in alphabetical order? It would be more useful and easier to use if it were alphabetized.
You will change the combo box later so that the names appear in alphabetical order.

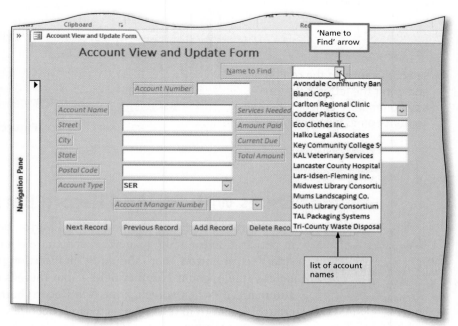

Figure 7–35

2

• Click 'Codder Plastics Co.' to display the data for Codder Plastics Co. in the form (Figure 7–36).

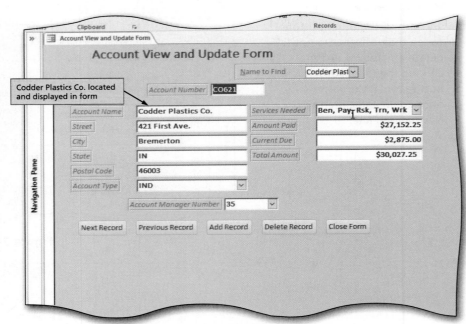

Figure 7–36

3

• Click the Next Record button to display the next record (Figure 7–37).

Q&A
Why does the combo box still contain Codder Plastics Co., rather than Eco Clothes Inc.?
This is a problem with the combo box. You will address this issue later.

Experiment

• Select the entry in the combo box and enter the letter, k, to find Key Community College. Try other account names in the combo box.

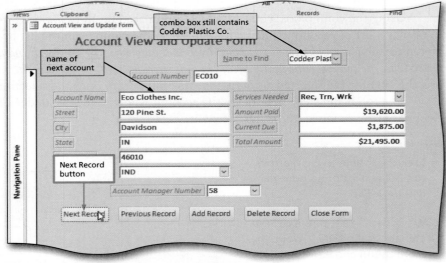

Figure 7–37

Issues with the Add Record Button

BTW
Focus
Sometimes it is difficult to determine which object on the screen has the focus. If a field has the focus, an insertion point appears in the field. If a button has the focus, a small rectangle appears inside the button.

Although clicking the Add Record button does erase the contents of the form in preparation for adding a new record, there is a problem with it. After clicking the Add Record button, there should be an insertion point in the control for the first field — the Account Number field — but there is not. To display an insertion point automatically when you click the Add Record button, you need to change the focus. A control is said to have the **focus** when it becomes active; that is, when it becomes able to receive user input through mouse, touch, or keyboard actions. At any point in time, only one item on the form has the focus. In addition to adding a new record, clicking the Add Record button needs to update the focus to the Account Number field.

Issues with the Combo Box

The combo box has the following issues. First, if you examine the list of names in Figure 7–35, you will see that they are not in alphabetical order (for example, Key Community College comes before KAL Veterinary Services). Second, when you move to a record without using the combo box, such as when navigating using the buttons, the name in the combo box does not change to reflect the name of the account currently on the screen. Third, you should not be able to use the TAB key to change the focus to the combo box, because that does not represent a field to be updated.

Macros

To correct the problem with the Add Record button not displaying an insertion point, you will update a **macro**, which is a series of actions that Access performs when a particular event occurs, in this case when the Add Record button is clicked. (In the next module, you will create macros on your own. In this case, Access has already created the macro; you just need to add a single action to it.)

Specifically, you need to add an action to the macro that will move the focus to the control for the Account Number field. The appropriate action is GoToControl. Like many actions, the GoToControl action requires additional information, called arguments. The argument for the GoToControl action is the name of the control, in this case, the Account Number control.

BTW

Events
Events are actions that have happened or are happening at the present time. An event can result from a user action. For example, one of the events associated with a button on a form is clicking the button. The corresponding event property is On Click. If you associate VBA code or a macro with the On Click event property, the code or macro will execute any time you click the button. Using properties associated with events, you can tell Access to run a macro, call a Visual Basic function, or run an event procedure in response to an event.

To Modify the Macro for the Add Record Button

1 CREATE FORM | 2 ADD COMBO BOXES | 3 COMMAND BUTTONS | **4 MODIFY MACRO**
5 MODIFY COMBO BOX | 6 CREATE SECOND FORM | 7 ADD SUBFORM | 8 ADD CHART

The following steps first change the name of the control to remove spaces (a requirement in VBA, which you will use later), and then modify the macro that is associated with the Add Record button. *Why? Modifying the macro lets you add an action that changes the focus to the Account Number field.* You can use different methods of changing control names so that they do not contain spaces. One approach is to simply remove the space. This approach would change Account Number to AccountNumber, for example. The approach you will use is to insert an underscore (_) in place of the space. For example, you will change Account Number to Account_Number.

After changing the name of the control, you will complete an action that changes the focus to the control for the Account Number field.

1

- Click the View button arrow and then click Design View to return to Design view.

- Click the control for the Account Number field (the white space, not the label), and then click the Property Sheet button (Form Design Tools Design tab | Tools group) to display the property sheet.

- If necessary, click the All tab. Ensure the Name property is selected, click immediately following the word, Account, press the DELETE key to delete the space, and then type an underscore (_) to change the name to Account _Number (Figure 7–38).

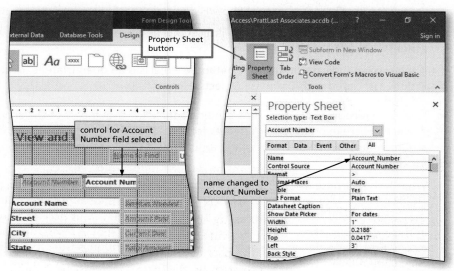

Figure 7–38

Q&A Could I just erase the old name and type Account_Number?
Yes. Use whichever method you find most convenient.

- Close the property sheet and then right-click the Add Record button to display a shortcut menu (Figure 7–39).

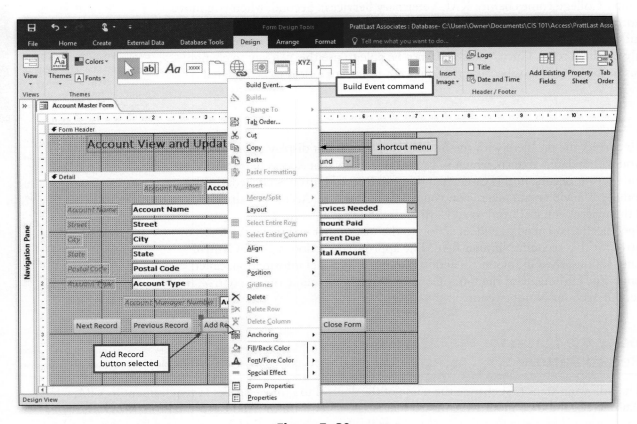

Figure 7–39

2

- Click Build Event on the shortcut menu to display the macro associated with the On Click event that Access created automatically.

- If the Action Catalog, the catalog that lists all of the available actions, does not appear, click the Action Catalog button (Macro Tools Design tab | Show/Hide group) to display the Action Catalog.

- In the Action Catalog, if the expand indicator is an open triangle in front of Actions, click the triangle to display all actions.

- If the expand indicator in front of Database Objects is an open triangle, click the expand indicator to display all actions associated with Database Objects (Figure 7–40).

Q&A How can I recognize actions? How can I recognize the arguments of the actions?
The actions are in bold. The arguments for the action follow the action and are not bold. The value for an argument appears to the right of the argument. The value for the 'Go to' argument of the OnError action is Next, for example.

What is the purpose of the actions currently in the macro?
The first action indicates that, if there is an error, Access should proceed to the next action in the macro rather than immediately stopping the macro. The second action causes Access to go to the record indicated by the values in the arguments. The value, New, indicates that Access should to go to a new record. Because the final action has a condition, the action will be executed only if the condition is true, that is, the error code contains a value other than 0. In that case, the MsgBox action will display a description of the error.

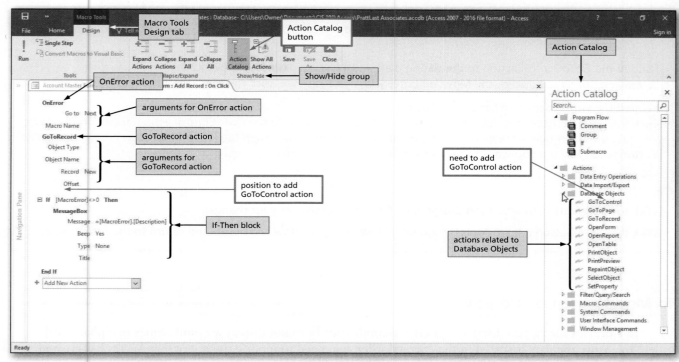

Figure 7–40

3

- Drag the GoToControl action from the Action Catalog to the position shown in Figure 7–40.

- Type `Account_Number` as the Control Name argument (Figure 7–41).

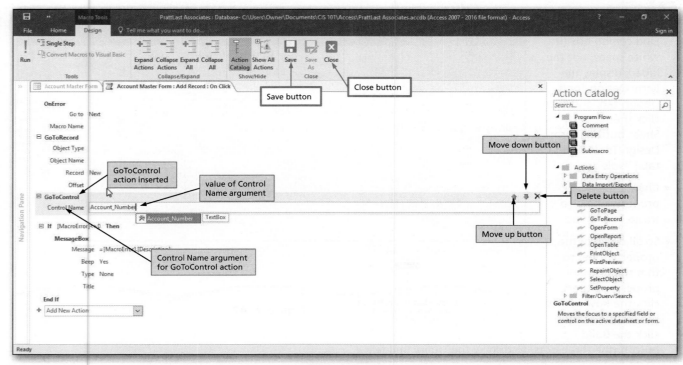

Figure 7–41

Q&A What is the effect of the GoToControl action?

When Access executes this action, the focus will move to the control indicated in the Control Name argument, in this case, the Account_Number control.

I added the GoToControl action to the wrong place in the macro. How do I move it?

To move it up in the list, click the Move up button. To move it down, click the Move down button.

I added the wrong action. What should I do?

Click the Delete button to delete the action you added, and then add the GoToControl action. If you decide you would rather start over instead, click the Close button (Macro Tools Design tab | Close group) and then click the No button when asked if you want to save your changes. You can then begin again from Step 2.

4

- Click the Save button (Macro Tools Design tab | Close group) to save your changes.
- Click the Close button (Macro Tools Design tab | Close group) to close the macro and return to the form design.

To Modify the Combo Box

1 CREATE FORM | 2 ADD COMBO BOXES | 3 COMMAND BUTTONS | 4 MODIFY MACRO
5 MODIFY COMBO BOX | 6 CREATE SECOND FORM | 7 ADD SUBFORM | 8 ADD CHART

In a previous step, you discovered that the combo box does not display account names in alphabetical order. To ensure the data is sorted in the correct order, you need to modify the query that Access has created for the combo box so the data is sorted by account name. Also, the combo box does not update the name in the combo box to reflect the name of accounts currently on the screen, which will require you to modify the VBA (Visual Basic for Applications) code associated with what is termed the On Current event property of the entire form. *Why? The modification to the On Current event property will ensure that the combo box remains current with the rest of the form; that is, it contains the name of the account whose number currently appears in the Account Number field.* The following steps modify the query and then the code associated with the On Current event property appropriately. The final step changes the Tab Stop property for the combo box from Yes to No.

1

- Click the Name to Find combo box (the white space, not the label), display the Form Design Tools Design tab, and then click the Property Sheet button (Form Design Tools Design tab | Tools group).

- Change the property name to **Name_to_Find**.

- Scroll down in the property sheet so that the Row Source property appears, click the Row Source property, and then click the Build button (the three dots) to display the Query Builder.

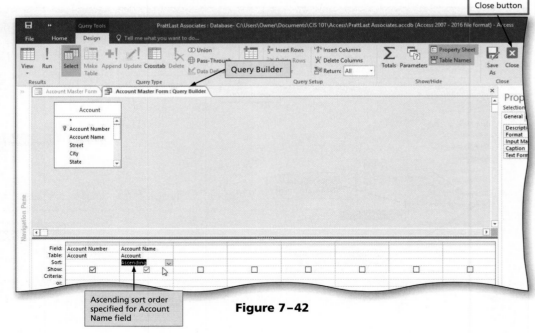

Figure 7–42

- Click the Sort row in the Account Name field, click the arrow that appears, and then click Ascending to change the order and display account names in alphabetical order in the combo box (Figure 7–42).

2

- Click the Save button on the Quick Access Toolbar to save your changes.

- Close the Query Builder window by clicking the Close button on the Design tab.

- Click the form selector (the box in the upper-left corner of the form) to select the form.

- Click the Property Sheet button (Form Design Tools Design tab | Tools group), scroll down until the On Current property appears, and then click the On Current property.

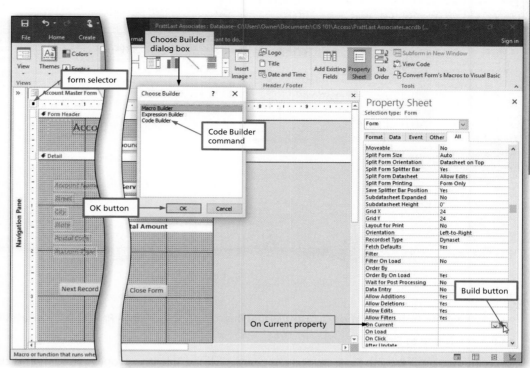

Figure 7–43

- Click the Build button (the three dots) to display the Choose Builder dialog box (Figure 7–43).

3

- Click Code Builder in the Choose Builder dialog box, and then click the OK button to display the VBA code generated for the form's On Current event property (Figure 7–44).

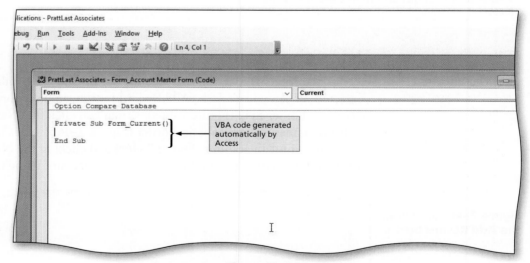

Figure 7–44

4

- Press the TAB key and then type **Name_to_Find = Account_Number ' Update the combo box** as shown in Figure 7–45, to create the command and a comment that describes the effect of the command.

 Q&A

How would I construct a command like this in my own form?

Begin with the name you assigned to the combo box, followed by an equal sign, and then the name of the control containing the primary key of the table. The portion of the statement following the single quotation mark is a comment describing the purpose of the command. You could simply type the same thing that you see in this command.

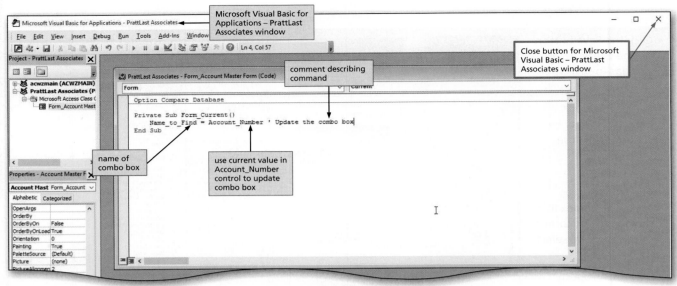

Figure 7–45

- Click the Close button for the Microsoft Visual Basic for Applications - PrattLast Associates window.

- Click the Name to Find combo box.

- Scroll down until the Tab Stop property appears, click the Tab Stop property, and then click the Tab Stop property box arrow.

- Click No to change the value of the Tab Stop property, which skips over the combo box in the tab sequence, and then close the property sheet.

- Save your changes and then close the form.

BTW
Comments in Macros
You can use the Comment action in the Action Catalog to place comments in macros.

Using the Modified Form

The problems with the Add Record button and the combo box are now corrected. When you click the Add Record button, an insertion point appears in the Account Number field (Figure 7–46a). When you click the 'Name to Find' box arrow, the list of names is in alphabetical order (Figure 7–46b). After using the 'Name to Find' box to find an account (Figure 7–46c) and clicking the Next Record button, the 'Name to Find' box is updated with the correct account name (Figure 7–46d).

Figure 7–46 (a) Using the Add Record button

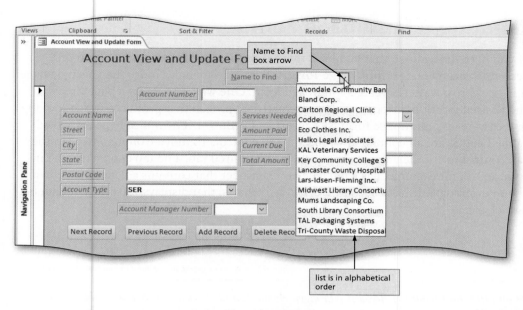

Figure 7–46 (b) Using the Name to Find box

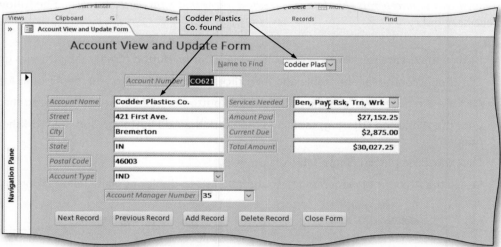

Figure 7–46 (c) Results of using the Name to Find box

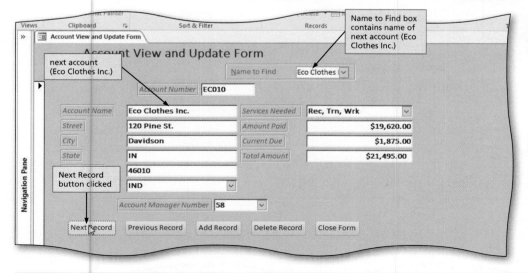

Figure 7–46 (d) Using the Next Record button

Break Point: If you wish to stop working through the module at this point, you can quit Access now. You can resume the project later by running Access, opening the database called PrattLast Associates, and continuing to follow the steps from this location forward.

BTW
Tab Controls
By default, Access places two tabbed pages in a tab control. To add additional tabbed pages, right-click any tab control and click Insert Pages on the shortcut menu.

Creating a Multipage Form

If you have determined that you have more data than will fit conveniently on one screen, you can create a **multipage form**, a form that includes more than a single page. There are two ways to create a multipage form. One way is to insert a page break at the desired location or locations. An alternative approach that produces a nice-looking and easy-to-use multipage form is to insert a tab control. The multiple pages, called tabbed pages, are all contained within the tab control. To move from one page in the tab control to another, a user simply clicks the desired tab. The tab control shown in Figure 7–2, for example, has a tab labeled Datasheet that contains a datasheet showing the relevant data. It has a second tab, labeled Charts, that displays the relevant data in two charts.

To Create a Query

1 CREATE FORM | 2 ADD COMBO BOXES | 3 COMMAND BUTTONS | 4 MODIFY MACRO

5 MODIFY COMBO BOX | 6 CREATE SECOND FORM | **7 ADD SUBFORM** | 8 ADD CHART

Why? *The second form contains data from the Account Manager, Account, and Workshop Offerings tables. The simplest way to incorporate this data is to create a query that joins all three tables.* The following steps create the necessary query.

- Display the Create tab, and then click the Query Design button (Create tab | Queries group) to create a query.
- Click the Account Manager table and then click the Add button to add the Account Manager table to the query.
- Click the Account table and then click the Add button to add the Account table to the query.
- Click the Workshop Offerings table and then click the Add button to add the Workshop Offerings table to the query.
- Click the Close button (Show Table dialog box).
- Resize the Account Manager and Account field lists to display as many fields as possible (Figure 7–47).

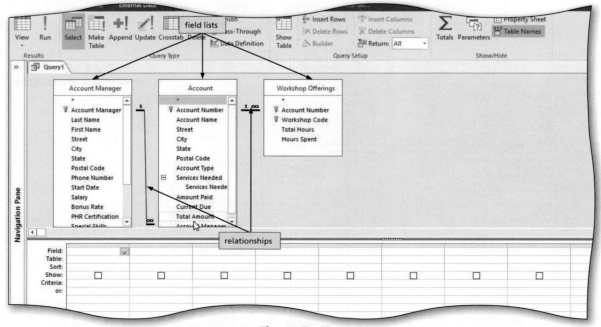

Figure 7–47

- Double-click the Account Manager Number field from the Account Manager table and the Account Number field from the Account table.

- Double-click the Workshop Code and Hours Spent fields from the Workshop Offerings table.

- Right-click the Field row in the first open column of the design grid to produce a shortcut menu.

- Click Zoom on the shortcut menu to display the Zoom dialog box and then type **Hours Remaining:[Total Hours]-[Hours Spent]** in the Zoom dialog box to enter the expression for the field (Figure 7–48).

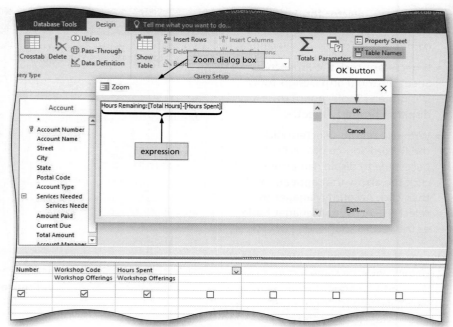

Figure 7–48

- Click the OK button and then view the results to ensure they are correct. The order of your records may differ.

- Click the Save button on the Quick Access Toolbar and type **Managers and Workshop Offerings** as the name of the query (Figure 7–49).

- Click the OK button to save the query.

- Close the query.

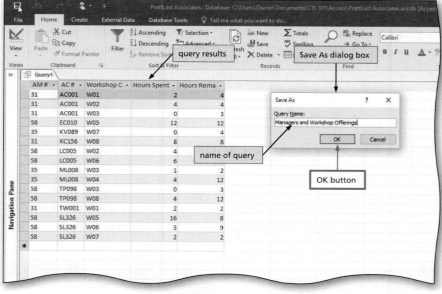

Figure 7–49

To Create a Second Form in Design View

1 CREATE FORM | 2 ADD COMBO BOXES | 3 COMMAND BUTTONS | 4 MODIFY MACRO
5 MODIFY COMBO BOX | 6 CREATE SECOND FORM | 7 ADD SUBFORM | 8 ADD CHART

Why? *The second form will contain the tab control including two tabs: one that displays a datasheet and another that displays two charts.* The following step begins the process by creating a form for the Account Manager table in Design view.

- If necessary, close the Navigation Pane.

- Display the Create tab.

- Click the Form Design button (Create tab | Forms group) to create a new form in Design view.

- Ensure the selector for the entire form — the box in the upper-left corner of the form — is selected.

- If necessary, click the Property Sheet button (Form Design Tools Design tab | Tools group) to display a property sheet.

- With the All tab selected, click the Record Source property, if necessary, to display an arrow, click the arrow that appears, and then click Account Manager to select the Account Manager table as the record source.

Q&A I see more than one choice that begins with the same letters as Account Manager. How do I know I am selecting the right one?
There are two ways to find out if you are selecting the right choice. You could click one of them to produce an insertion point and then repeatedly press or hold down the RIGHT ARROW key to see the remainder of the name. If it is not the correct one, select another. The other way is to expand the width of the property sheet so that more of the property name is visible. You do so by dragging the left border further to the left.

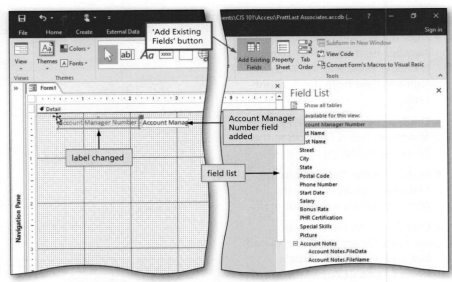

Figure 7–50

- Close the property sheet.

- Click the 'Add Existing Fields' button (Form Design Tools Design tab | Tools group) to display a field list and then drag the Account Manager Number field to the approximate position shown in Figure 7–50.

- Change the label for the Account Manager Number field from AM # to Account Manager Number. Resize and move the label to the position shown in the figure.

To Use the Text Box Tool with Concatenation

1 CREATE FORM | 2 ADD COMBO BOXES | 3 COMMAND BUTTONS | 4 MODIFY MACRO
5 MODIFY COMBO BOX | 6 CREATE SECOND FORM | **7 ADD SUBFORM** | 8 ADD CHART

Why? *If you have determined that* **concatenation,** *which simply means combining objects together in a series, is appropriate for a form, you can create a concatenated field by using the Text Box tool in the Controls group on the Design tab and then indicating the concatenation that is to be performed.* The following steps add a concatenated field, involving two text fields, First Name and Last Name. Specifically, you will concatenate the first name, a single space, and the last name.

1

- Click the Text Box tool (Form Design Tools Design tab | Controls group) and then move the pointer, whose shape has changed to a small plus symbol accompanied by a text box, to the position shown in Figure 7–51.

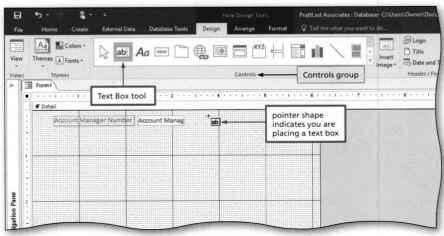

Figure 7–51

- Click the position shown in Figure 7–51 to place a text box on the report.
- Click in the text box to produce an insertion point.
- Type `=[First Name]&' '&[Last Name]` as the entry in the text box.
- Click the attached label to select it (Figure 7–52).

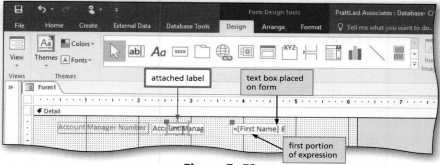

Figure 7–52

- Press the DELETE key to delete the attached label.
- Resize the Account Manager Number control to the approximate size shown in Figure 7–53.
- Click the text box to select it, drag it to the position shown in Figure 7–53, and then drag the right sizing handle to the approximate position shown in the figure.

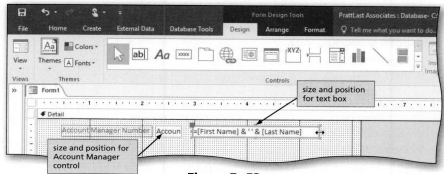

Figure 7–53

- Close the field list by clicking the 'Add Existing Fields' button (Form Design Tools Design tab | Tools group).
- Save the form using the name, Manager Workshop Data.

To Use Tab Controls to Create a Multipage Form

1 CREATE FORM | 2 ADD COMBO BOXES | 3 COMMAND BUTTONS | 4 MODIFY MACRO
5 MODIFY COMBO BOX | 6 CREATE SECOND FORM | **7 ADD SUBFORM** | 8 ADD CHART

Why? *To use tabs on a form, you need to insert a tab control.* The following steps insert a tab control with two tabs: Datasheet and Charts. Users will be able to click the Datasheet tab in the completed form to view workshop offerings in Datasheet view. Clicking the Charts tab will display two charts representing the same workshop data as in the Datasheet tab.

- Click the Tab Control tool (Form Design Tools Design Tab | Controls group) and move the pointer to the approximate location shown in Figure 7–54.

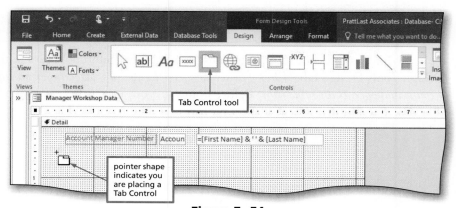

Figure 7–54

2

- Click the position shown in Figure 7–54 to place a tab control on the form.

- Click the far left tab and then click the Property Sheet button (Form Design Tools Design tab | Tools group) to display a property sheet.

- Change the value for the Caption property to **Datasheet** (Figure 7–55).

Q&A

My property sheet looks different. What should I do?
Be sure you clicked the far left tab before displaying the property sheet. The highlight should be within the border of the tab, as shown in the figure.

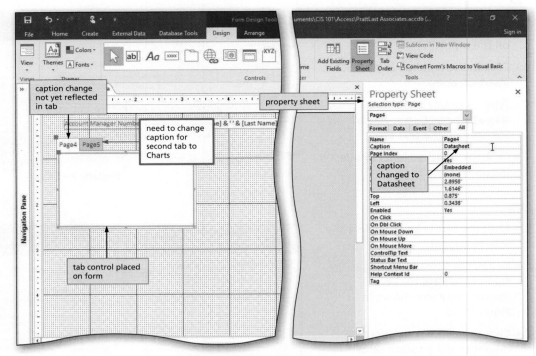

Figure 7–55

3

- Click the second tab without closing the property sheet.
- Change the value for the Caption property to **Charts**.
- Close the property sheet.

CONSIDER THIS

When would you include a tab control in your form?
If the form contains more information than will conveniently fit on the screen at a time, consider adding a tab control. With a tab control, you can organize the information within a collection of tabbed pages. To access any of the tabbed pages, users need only click the corresponding tab.

To Add a Subform

1 CREATE FORM | 2 ADD COMBO BOXES | 3 COMMAND BUTTONS | 4 MODIFY MACRO
5 MODIFY COMBO BOX | 6 CREATE SECOND FORM | **7 ADD SUBFORM** | **8 ADD CHART**

To add a subform to a form, you use the Subform/Subreport tool in the Controls group on the Form Design Tools Design tab. **Why?** *The subform enables you to show data for multiple workshop offerings for a given account manager at the same time.* Before doing so, you should make sure the 'Use Control Wizards' button is selected. The following steps place a subform on the Datasheet tab.

1

- Click the Datasheet tab.

- Resize the tab control to the approximate size shown in Figure 7–56 by dragging the appropriate sizing handles.

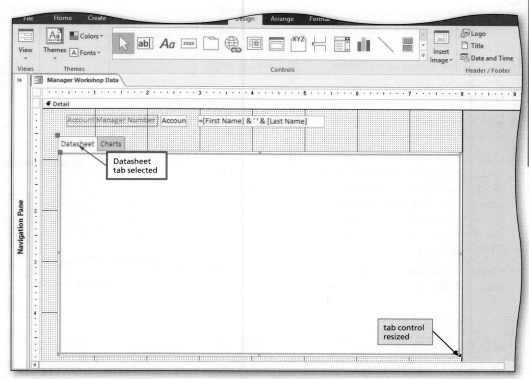

Figure 7–56

2

- Click the More button (Form Design Tools Design tab | Controls group).

- With the 'Use Control Wizards' button selected, click the Subform /Subreport tool (Form Design Tools Design tab | Controls group) and then move the pointer to the approximate position shown in Figure 7–57.

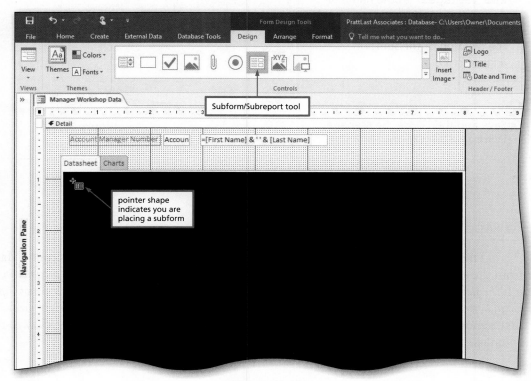

Figure 7–57

- Click the position shown in Figure 7–57 to open the SubForm Wizard.

- Be sure the 'Use existing Tables and Queries' option button is selected.

- Click the Next button to display the next SubForm Wizard screen.

- Click the Tables/Queries arrow and then click the Managers and Workshop Offerings query to indicate that the fields for the subform will be selected from the Managers and Workshop Offerings query.

- Click the 'Add All Fields' button (Figure 7–58).

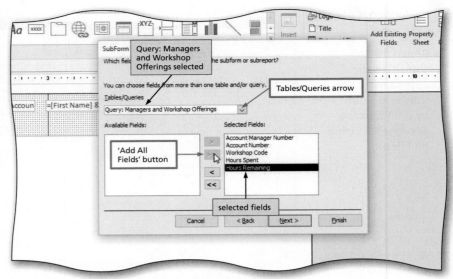

Figure 7–58

- Click the Next button.

- Be sure the 'Choose from a list' option button is selected.

- Click the Next button.

- Type **Workshop Offerings for Manager** as the name of the subform and then click the Finish button to complete the creation of the subform (Figure 7–59).

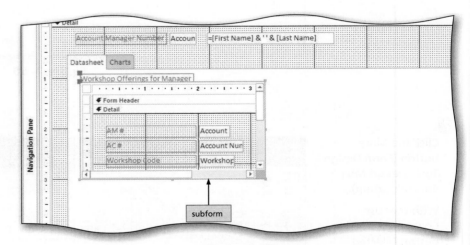

Figure 7–59

⑤

- Save and then close the Manager Workshop Data form.

To Modify a Subform

1 CREATE FORM | 2 ADD COMBO BOXES | 3 COMMAND BUTTONS | 4 MODIFY MACRO
5 MODIFY COMBO BOX | 6 CREATE SECOND FORM | 7 ADD SUBFORM | **8 ADD CHART**

The next task is to modify the subform. The first step is to remove the Account Manager Number field from the subform. *Why? The Account Manager Number field needed to be included initially in the subform because it is the field that is used to link the data in the subform to the data in the main form. It is not supposed to appear in the form, however.* In addition, the remaining columns need to be resized to appropriate sizes. The following step first removes the Account Manager Number field. You then switch to Datasheet view to resize the remaining columns.

1

- Open the Navigation Pane, right-click the Workshop Offerings for Manager form, and then click Design View on the shortcut menu.

- Click the Account Manager Number control, and then press the DELETE key to delete the control.

- Change the label for the Account Number control from AC # to Account Number.

- Save the subform and close it.

- Right-click the subform in the Navigation Pane and click Open on the shortcut menu.

- Resize each column to best fit the data by double-clicking the right boundary of the column's field selector (Figure 7–60).

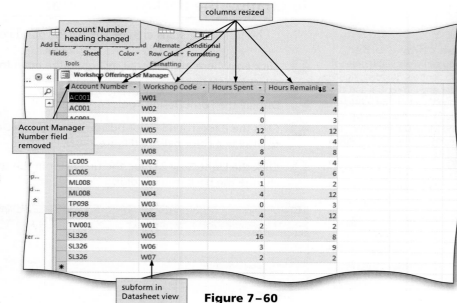

Figure 7–60

2

- Save the subform and then close it.

To Resize the Subform

1 CREATE FORM | 2 ADD COMBO BOXES | 3 COMMAND BUTTONS | 4 MODIFY MACRO
5 MODIFY COMBO BOX | 6 CREATE SECOND FORM | 7 ADD SUBFORM | 8 ADD CHART

The following step resizes the subform. *Why? The size should match the size shown in Figure 7–2a.*

1

- If necessary, open the Navigation Pane, right-click the Manager Workshop Data form and then click Design View on the shortcut menu.

- Close the Navigation Pane.

- Resize the subform to the size shown in Figure 7–61 by dragging the right sizing handle.

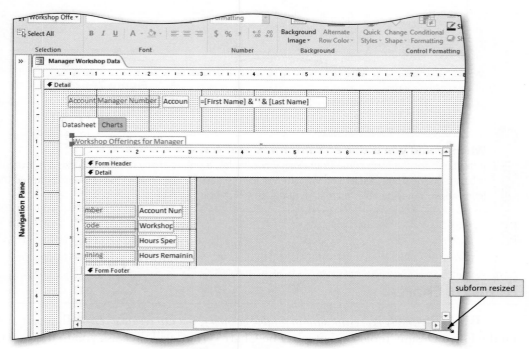

Figure 7–61

To Change the Background Color

The following steps change the background color of the form to a light gray.

1. Click anywhere in the Detail section in the main form but outside all the controls to select the section.

2. Display the Form Design Tools Format tab.

3. Click the Background Color button arrow (Form Design Tools Format tab | Font group) to display a color palette (Figure 7–62).

4. Click the Light Gray 2 color, the first color in the third row under Standard Colors, to change the background color.

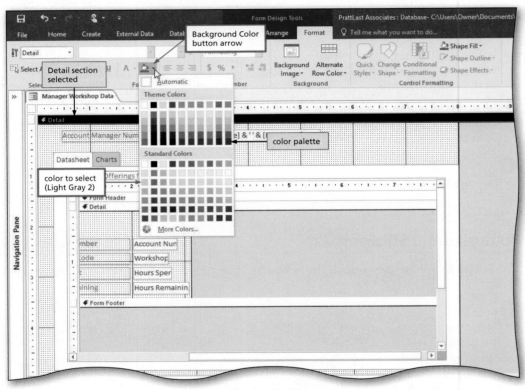

Figure 7–62

When would you include a subform in your form?

If the fields for the form come from exactly two tables, a one-to-many relationship exists between the two tables, and the form is based on the "one" table, you will often place the data for the "many" table in a subform. If there are more than two tables involved, you may be able to create a query on which you can base the subform.

---

1 CREATE FORM | 2 ADD COMBO BOXES | 3 COMMAND BUTTONS | 4 MODIFY MACRO
5 MODIFY COMBO BOX | 6 CREATE SECOND FORM | 7 ADD SUBFORM | **8 ADD CHART**

To Insert Charts

Why? *To visually represent data in a table or query, you can create a chart.* To insert a chart, use the Chart tool on the Form Design Tools Design tab. The Chart Wizard will then ask you to indicate the fields to be included on the chart and the type of chart you want to insert. The following steps insert a chart that visually represents the amount of time managers have spent in their various workshops.

1

- Display the Form Design Tools Design tab.
- Click the Charts tab on the tab control.
- Click the More button (Form Design Tools Design tab | Controls group).
- Click the Chart tool.
- Move the pointer to the approximate position shown in Figure 7–63.

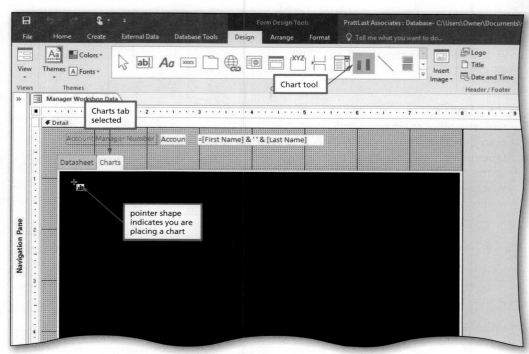

Figure 7–63

2

- Click the position shown in Figure 7–63 to display the Chart Wizard dialog box.
- Click the Queries option button in the Chart Wizard dialog box to indicate that the data will come from a query, scroll down so that the Managers and Workshop Offerings query appears, and then click the Managers and Workshop Offerings query to indicate the specific query containing the desired fields.
- Click the Next button.
- Select the Workshop Code and Hours Spent fields by clicking them and then clicking the Add Field button (Figure 7–64).

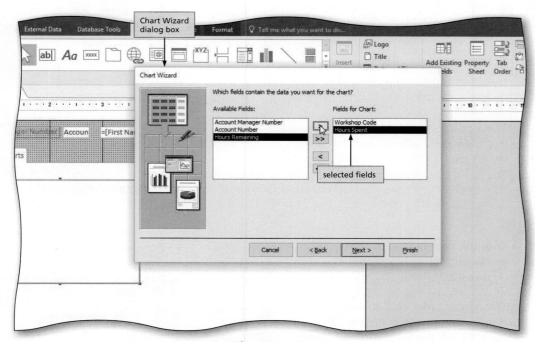

Figure 7–64

3

- Click the Next button.

- Click the Pie Chart, the chart in the lower-left corner (Figure 7–65).

🔍 **Experiment**

- Click the other chart types and read the descriptions of chart types in the lower-right corner of the Chart Wizard dialog box. When finished, click the Pie Chart in the lower-left corner.

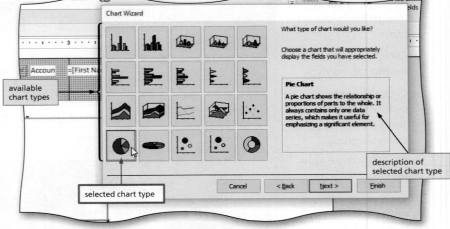

Figure 7–65

4

- Click the Next button to create the chart (Figure 7–66). Your screen might take several seconds to refresh.

Q&A What do these positions represent? Can I change them?
The field under the chart represents the data that will be summarized by slices of the pie. The other field is used to indicate the series. In this example, the field for the series is the workshop code, and the sizes of the slices of the pie will represent the sum of the number of hours spent. You can change these by dragging the fields to the desired locations.

These positions make sense for a pie chart. What if I selected a different chart type?
The items on this screen will be relevant to the particular chart type you select. Just as with the pie chart, the correct fields will often be selected automatically. If not, you can drag the fields to the correct locations.

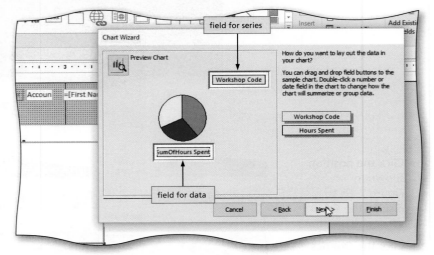

Figure 7–66

5

- Click the Next button to select the layout Access has proposed (Figure 7–67).

Q&A The Account Manager Number field does not appear in my chart. Can I still use it to link the form and the chart?
Yes. Even though the Account Manager Number does not appear, it is still included in the query on which the chart is based. In fact, it is essential that it is included so that you can link the document (that is, the form) and the chart. Linking the document and the chart ensures that the chart will accurately reflect the data for the correct manager, that is, the manager who currently appears in the form.

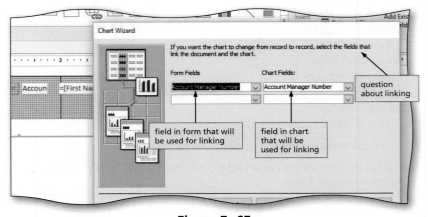

Figure 7–67

6

- Click the Next button, type **Hours Spent by Workshop Offering** as the title, and then click the Finish button (Figure 7–68).

Q&A The data does not look right. What is wrong and what do I need to do to fix it?
The data in your chart might be fictitious, as in Figure 7–68. In that case, the data simply represents the general way the chart will look. When you view the actual form, the data represented in the chart should be correct.

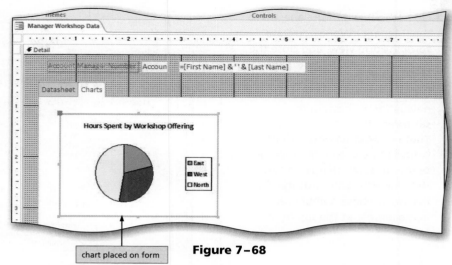

chart placed on form

Figure 7–68

7

- Use the techniques shown in Steps 1 through 6 to add a second chart at the position shown in Figure 7–69. In this chart, which is also based on the Managers and Workshop Offerings query, select Hours Remaining instead of Hours Spent and type **Hours Remaining by Workshop Code** as the title of the chart instead of Hours Spent by Workshop Offering.

- Resize the two charts to the size shown in the figure, if necessary, by clicking the chart and then dragging an appropriate sizing handle.

- If requested to do so by your instructor, add a title with your first and last name to the form.

- Save your changes and close the form.

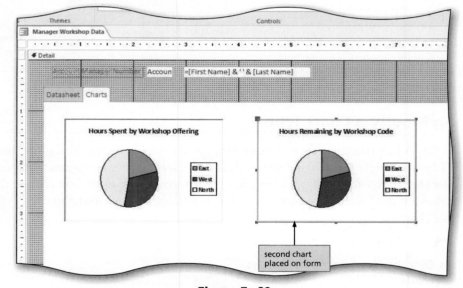

second chart placed on form

Figure 7–69

To Use the Form

1 CREATE FORM | 2 ADD COMBO BOXES | 3 COMMAND BUTTONS | 4 MODIFY MACRO
5 MODIFY COMBO BOX | 6 CREATE SECOND FORM | 7 ADD SUBFORM | 8 ADD CHART

You use this form just like the other forms you have created and used. When using the form, it is easy to move from one tabbed page to another. *Why? All you have to do is to click the tab for the desired tabbed page.* The following step uses the form to view the workshop data.

1

- Open the Navigation Pane, open the 'Manager Workshop Data' form in Form view, and close the Navigation Pane (Figure 7–70).

Q&A What is the purpose of the navigation buttons in the subform?

These navigation buttons allow you to move within the records in the subform, that is, within the workshop offerings for the manager whose number and name appear at the top of the form.

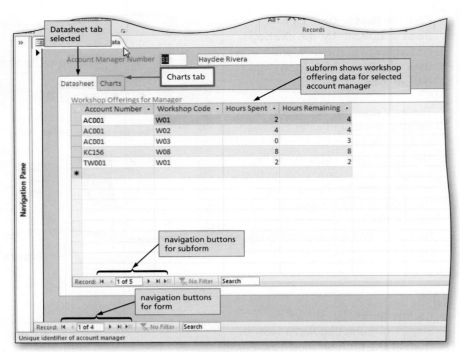

Figure 7–70

1 CREATE FORM | 2 ADD COMBO BOXES | 3 COMMAND BUTTONS | 4 MODIFY MACRO
5 MODIFY COMBO BOX | 6 CREATE SECOND FORM | 7 ADD SUBFORM | **8 ADD CHART**

To Modify a Chart Type

When you first create a chart, you specify the chart type. You sometimes will later want to change the type. *Why? You might find that a different chart type is a better way to represent data. In addition, you have more options when you later change the chart type than when you first created the chart.* You change the type by editing the chart and selecting the Chart Type command. The following steps change the chart type by selecting a different style of pie chart.

1

- Click the Charts tab to display the charts.

- Return to Design view.

- Click the Charts tab, if necessary, to display the charts in Design view (Figure 7–71).

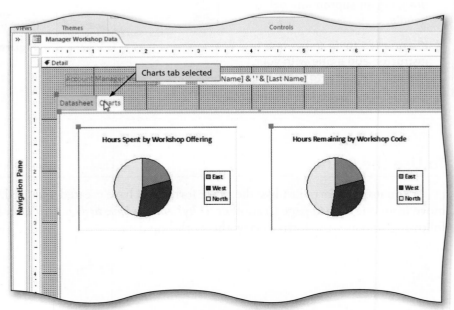

Figure 7–71

2

- Click the 'Hours Spent by Workshop Offering' chart to select it, and then right-click the chart to display a shortcut menu (Figure 7–72).

Q&A Does it matter where I right-click? You should right-click within the rectangle but outside any of the items within the rectangle, in other words, in the white space.

My shortcut menu is very different. What should I do? Click the View button arrow, then click Design View to ensure that you are viewing the form in Design view, and then try again.

- Point to Chart Object on the shortcut menu to display the Chart Object submenu (Figure 7–72).

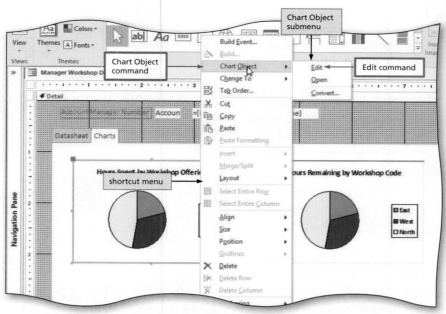

Figure 7–72

3

- Click Edit on the Chart Object submenu to edit the chart. Access will automatically display the underlying chart data in Datasheet view (Figure 7–73).

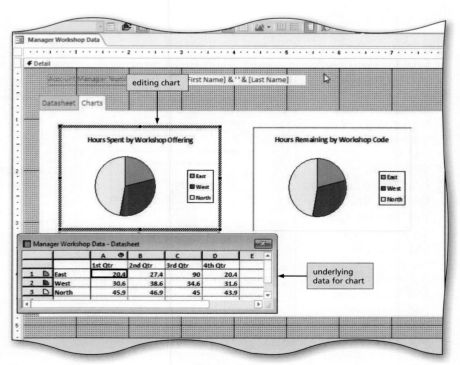

Figure 7–73

4

• Right-click the chart to display the shortcut menu for editing the chart (Figure 7–74).

Q&A Does it matter where I right-click?
You should right-click within the rectangle but outside any of the items within the rectangle, in other words, in the white space.

What types of changes can I make if I select Format Chart Area?
You can change things such as border style, color, fill effects, and fonts.

How do I make other changes?
By clicking Chart Options on the shortcut menu, you can change titles, legends, and labels. For 3-D charts, by clicking 3-D View on the shortcut menu, you can change the elevation and rotation of the chart. You can also format specific items on the chart, as you will see in the next section.

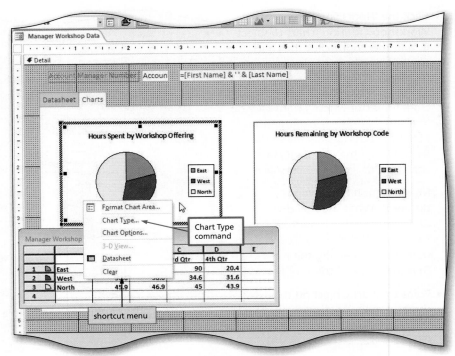

Figure 7–74

5

• Click the Chart Type command on the shortcut menu to display the Chart Type dialog box (Figure 7–75).

Q&A What is the relationship between the Chart type and the Chart sub-type?
You can think of Chart types as categories of charts. There are column charts, bar charts, line charts, and so on. Once you have selected a category, the chart sub-types are those charts in that category. If you have selected the Pie chart category, for example, the charts within the category are the ones shown in the list of chart sub-types in Figure 7–75.

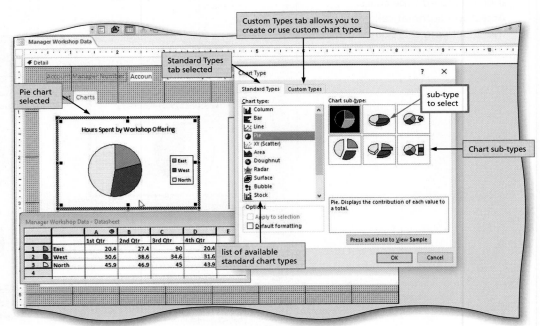

Figure 7–75

6

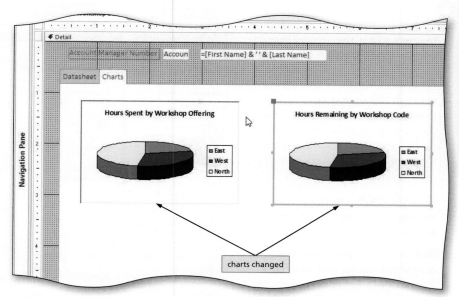

- Click the chart sub-type in the middle of the first row of chart sub-types to select it as the chart sub-type.

🔎 **Experiment**

- Click each of the chart types and examine the chart sub-types associated with that chart type. When finished, select Pie as the chart type and the sub-type in the middle of the first row as the chart sub-type.

- Click the OK button to change the chart sub-type.

- Click outside the chart and the datasheet to deselect the chart.

- Make the same change to the other chart (Figure 7–76).

Figure 7–76

To Format a Chart

1 CREATE FORM | 2 ADD COMBO BOXES | 3 COMMAND BUTTONS | 4 MODIFY MACRO
5 MODIFY COMBO BOX | 6 CREATE SECOND FORM | 7 ADD SUBFORM | 8 ADD CHART

By right-clicking a chart, pointing to Chart Object, and then clicking Edit, you have many formatting options available. You can change the border style, color, fill effects, and fonts by using the Format Chart Area command. You can change titles, legends, and labels by using the Chart Options command. You can also format specific portions of a chart by right-clicking the portion you want to format and then clicking the appropriate command on the shortcut menu. The following steps use this technique to move the legend so that it is at the bottom of the chart. They also include percentages in the chart. *Why? Percentages provide valuable information in a pie chart.*

1

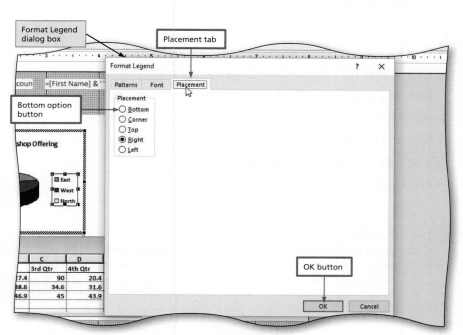

- Right-click the 'Hours Spent by Workshop Offering' chart to display a shortcut menu, point to Chart Object on the shortcut menu to display the Chart Object submenu, and then click Edit on the Chart Object submenu.

- Right-click the legend to display a shortcut menu, and then click Format Legend on the shortcut menu to display the Format Legend dialog box.

- Click the Placement tab (Figure 7–77).

Figure 7–77

2

- Click the Bottom option button to specify that the legend should appear at the bottom of the chart.

Q&A What other types of changes can I make in this dialog box?
Click the Patterns tab to change such things as border style, color, and fill effects. Click the Font tab to change the font and/or font characteristics.

- Click the OK button to place the legend at the location you selected.

- Right-click the pie chart to display a shortcut menu, and then click Format Data Series on the shortcut menu to display the Format Data Series dialog box.

- Click the Data Labels tab.

- Click the Percentage check box to specify that percentages are to be included (Figure 7–78).

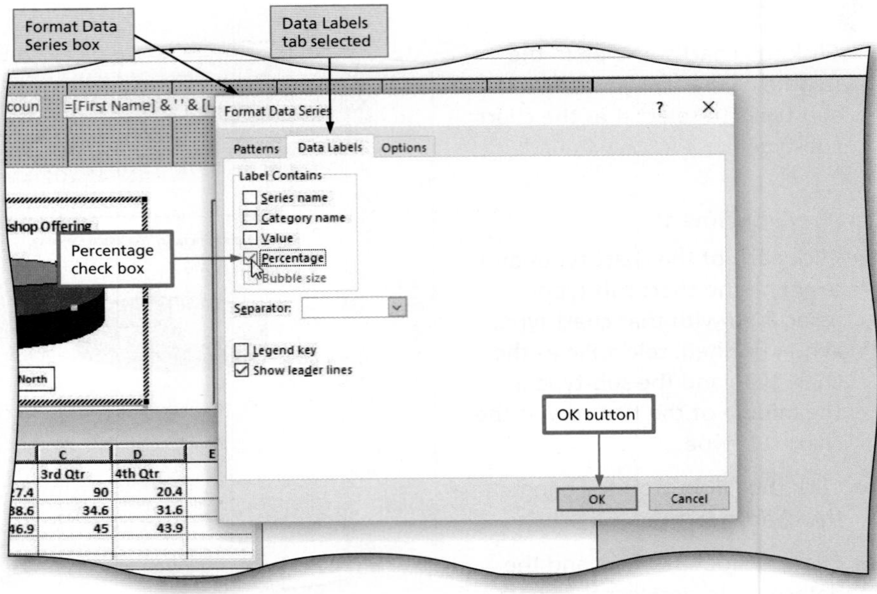

Figure 7–78

Q&A I see a Patterns tab just as with the legend, but how would I use the Options tab? Also, does the fact that these are check boxes rather than option buttons mean that I can select more than one?
Use the Options tab to indicate whether the color is to vary by slice and to specify the angle of the first slice in the pie. Because these are check boxes, you can select as many as you want. Selecting too many can clutter the chart, however.

These options make sense for a pie chart, but what about other chart types?
The options that you see will vary from one chart type to another. They will be relevant for the selected chart type.

3

- Click the OK button to include percentages on the chart.

- Click outside the chart and the datasheet to deselect the chart.

- Make the same change to the other chart.

- View the form in Form view to see the effect of your changes.

- Save and then close the form.

- If desired, sign out of your Microsoft account.

- Exit Access.

BTW
Distributing a Document
Instead of printing and distributing a hard copy of a document, you can distribute the document electronically. Options include sending the document via email; posting it on cloud storage (such as OneDrive) and sharing the file with others; posting it on a social networking site, blog, or other website; and sharing a link associated with an online location of the document. You also can create and share a PDF or XPS image of the document, so that users can view the file in Acrobat Reader or XPS Viewer instead of in Access.

What type of decisions should you make when considering whether to use a chart?
Do you want to represent data in a visual manner? If so, you can include a chart. If you decide to use a chart, you must determine which type of chart would best represent the data. If you want to represent total amounts, for example, a bar chart may be appropriate. If instead you want to represent portions of the whole, a pie chart may be better.

CONSIDER THIS

Summary

In this module you have learned how to create a form in Design view, add a combo box that displays information from a related table as well as a combo box that is used to find records on a form, format controls and use the Format Painter, add command buttons to a form, modify a button and a combo box, add a calculated field to a form, use a tab control to create a multipage form, add and modify a subform, insert charts, change chart types, and format charts.

CONSIDER THIS

What decisions will you need to make when creating your own forms?
Use these guidelines as you complete the assignments in this module and create your own forms outside of this class.

1. Determine the intended audience and the purpose of the form.

   a. Who will use the form?
   b. How will they use it?
   c. What data do they need?
   d. What level of detail do they need?

2. Determine the source of data for the form.

   a. Determine whether data comes from a single table or from multiple related tables.
   b. Which table or tables contain the data?

3. Determine the fields that belong on the form.

   a. What data items are needed by the user of the form?

4. Determine any calculations required for the form.

   a. Decide whether the form should contain any special calculations, such as adding two fields.
   b. Determine whether the form should contain any calculations involving text fields, such as concatenating (combining) the fields.

5. Determine the organization of the form.

   a. In what order should the fields appear?
   b. How should they be arranged?
   c. Does the form need multiple pages?

6. Determine any additional controls that should be on the form.

   a. Should the form contain a subform?
   b. Should the form contain a chart?
   c. Should the form contain command buttons to assist the user in performing various functions?
   d. Should the form contain a combo box to assist the user in searching for a record?

7. Determine the format and style of the form.

   a. What should be in the form heading?
   b. Do you want a title?
   c. Do you want an image?
   d. What should be in the body of the form?
   e. What visual characteristics, such as background color and special effects, should the various portions of the form have?

CONSIDER THIS

How should you submit solutions to questions in the assignments identified with a symbol?
Every assignment in this book contains one or more questions identified with a symbol. These questions require you to think beyond the assigned database. Present your solutions to the questions in the format required by your instructor. Possible formats may include one or more of these options: write the answer; create a document that contains the answer; present your answer to the class; discuss your answer in a group; record the answer as audio or video using a webcam, smartphone, or portable media player; or post answers on a blog, wiki, or website.

Expand Your World *continued*

Perform the following tasks:

1. Open the Expand Crafts database from the Data Files.

2. Open the Item Master Form in Design view. Add a combo box for the Student Code field.

3. Access any website containing royalty-free images to find a suitable background image the college can use for its forms that emphasizes arts and crafts or create your own background image.

4. Add the background image to the form.

5. Add a hyperlink for your school's website to the Form Header.

6. Access any website containing royalty-free images and search for an image suitable to use on a Close Form command button; for example, a Stop sign or a door. Save the image to a storage location of your choice.

7. Add a Close Form command button to the form using the image you downloaded.

8. Save your changes to the Item Master Form.

9. Submit the revised database in the format specified by your instructor.

10. ✷ What image did you choose as the background for your form? What image did you choose for the command button? Why did you make those choices?

In the Labs

Design, create, modify, and/or use a database following the guidelines, concepts, and skills presented in this module. Labs are listed in order of increasing difficulty. Labs 1 and 2, which increase in difficulty, require you to create solutions based on what you learned in the module; Lab 3 requires you to apply your creative thinking and problem solving skills to design and implement a solution.

Lab 1: Applying Advanced Form Techniques to the Horticulture4U Database

Problem: The management of Horticulture4U needs a form for the Customer table that allows users to update data in the table. Horticulture4U also needs a form to display open orders data for sales reps.

Note: Use the database modified in the Lab 1 of Module 6 for this assignment. If you did not use the database, contact your instructor for information on accessing the database required for this exercise.

Instructions: Perform the following tasks:

1. Create the Customer View and Update Form shown in Figure 7–80. Save the form with the name, Customer Master Form. The form includes a title, command buttons, a combo box for the Sales Rep Number field, and a combo box to search for customers by name. Be sure to sort the customer names in alphabetical order, place a rectangle around the combo box, and update the combo box. The user should not be able to tab to the combo box. When the Add Record

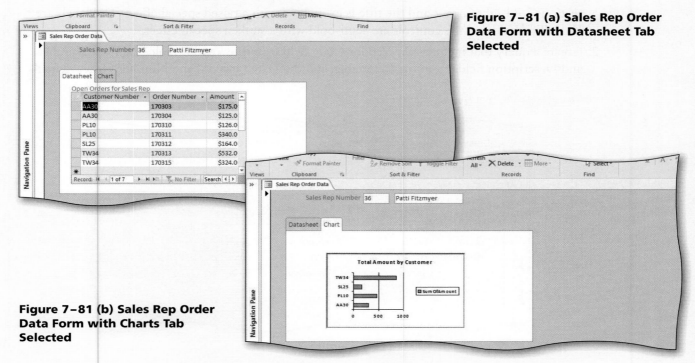

Figure 7–80

button is clicked, the insertion point should be in the Customer Number field. The title is bold. The background of the Detail section of the form is Light Gray 1 (Standard colors). The controls have a semi-bold font weight and a sunken special effect. The labels are italicized with a chiseled special effect. The form is similar in style to that shown in Figure 7–1.

2. Create a query that includes the Sales Rep Number from the Sales Rep table, the Customer Number from the Customer table, and the Order Number and Amount fields from the Open Orders table. Sort the query in ascending order by Sales Rep Number, Customer Number, and Order Number. Save the query as Sales Reps and Open Orders.

3. Create the Sales Rep Order Data form shown in Figure 7–81. The subform that appears in the Datasheet tab uses the Sales Reps and Open Orders query (Figure 7–81a). The chart in the Charts tab uses the same query (Figure 7–81b). Be sure to concatenate the first and last names of the sales rep. Change the background color to Light Gray 2. The form is similar in style to that shown in Figure 7–2.

4. If instructed to do so by your instructor, open the Sales Rep table and change the first and last name of sales rep 39 to your first and last name.

Figure 7–81 (a) Sales Rep Order Data Form with Datasheet Tab Selected

Figure 7–81 (b) Sales Rep Order Data Form with Charts Tab Selected

Continued >

In the Labs *continued*

5. Submit the revised database in the format specified by your instructor.

6. ✳ Could you use a list box instead of a combo box for the Sales Rep Number field in the form? Why or why not?

Lab 2: Applying Advanced Form Techniques to the SciTech Sundries Database

Problem: The gift shop manager of SciTech Sundries needs a form that displays item information. The form should display the total cost of items on hand. It should also include command buttons to perform common operations, a combo box to search for items by description, and a combo box for vendor code. Management also needs a form that displays vendor information as well as items on order and all items associated with a vendor.

Note: Use the database you used in Lab 2 of Module 6 for this assignment. If you did not use this database, contact your instructor for information on accessing the database required for this exercise.

Instructions: Perform the following tasks:

1. Create the Item Master Form shown in Figure 7–82. Use the caption Item View and Update Form for the form. The form includes command buttons, a drop-down box (combo box) for the Vendor Code field, and combo box to search for items by name. Inventory Value is the result of multiplying On Hand by Wholesale Cost. Format Inventory Value as currency with two decimal places. Change the tab order for the controls in the Detail section so that Vendor Code follows Item Type. Be sure to sort the item names alphabetically, place a rectangle around the combo box, and update the combo box. The user should not be able to tab to the combo box. When the Add Record button is clicked, the insertion point should be in the Item Number field. The form is similar in style to that shown in Figure 7–1. The form header and detail sections are Light Gray 2 and the title is extra-bold with a raised special effect. The labels are Dark Blue bold and the controls are semi-bold with a sunken special effect.

2. Create a query that includes the Vendor Code field from the Vendor table, the Item Number and Description fields from the Item table, and the Date Ordered and Number Ordered fields

Figure 7–82

from the Reorder table. Sort the query in ascending order by Vendor Code, Item Number, and Date Ordered. Save the query as Vendors and Orders.

3. Create the Vendor Orders Data form shown in Figure 7–83. The In Stock tab uses the Item table for the subform (Figure 7–83a). The On Order tab (Figure 7–83b) uses the Vendors and Orders query for the subform. Note that the labels for Vendor Code and Vendor Name have been removed and that there is a title on the form. The form title and the labels in the Detail section are bold and have the raised special effect. The controls have the sunken special effect. You can use the Format Painter to copy formatting for controls and labels.

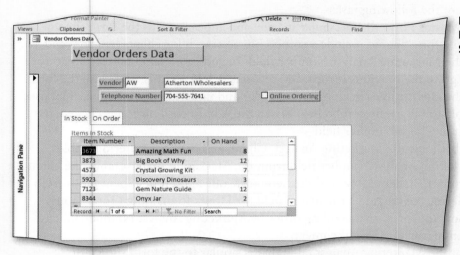

Figure 7–83 (a) Vendor Orders Data Form with In Stock Tab Selected

Figure 7–83 (b) Vendor Orders Data Form with On Order Tab Selected

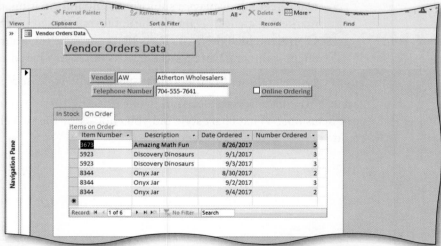

4. If instructed to do so by your instructor, change the phone number for vendor GS to your phone number.

5. Submit the revised database in the format specified by your instructor.

6. ✺ How could you rearrange the tab controls for the Vendor Orders Data form so that the On Order tab appears before the In Stock tab?

Continued >

In the Labs *continued*

Lab 3: **Consider This: Your Turn**

Applying Advanced Form Techniques to the JSP Analysis Database

Part 1:   The management of JSP Analysis needs a form to use to update client data. They also need a form to track seminar offerings by marketing analyst. Open the Lab 3 JSP Analysis database that you modified in Module 6. If you did not modify this database, contact your instructor for information about accessing the required database. Then, use the concepts and techniques presented in this module to perform each of the following tasks:

a. Create a Client Master Form that is similar in style and appearance to the form shown in Figure 7–1. The form should include a combo box to search for clients by name and a combo box for the Marketing Analyst Number field. Include command buttons to go to the next record, go to the previous record, add records, delete records, and close the form. Be sure to sort the client names in alphabetical order and update the combo box. The user should not be able to tab to the combo box. When the Add Record button is clicked, the focus should be the Client Number field.

b. Create a query that joins the Marketing Analyst, Client, and Seminar Offerings tables. Include the Marketing Analyst Number field from the Marketing Analyst table, the Client Number field from the Client table, and the Seminar Code and Hours Spent fields from the Seminar Offerings table. Add a calculated field for Hours Remaining (Total Hours – Hours Spent). Sort the query in ascending order by Marketing Analyst Number, Client Number, and Seminar Code. Save the query.

c. Create a form for the Marketing Analyst table that is similar to the form shown in Figure 7–2a. The form should have two tabs, a Datasheet tab and a Charts tab. The Datasheet tab displays a subform listing information about seminars for clients of the marketing analyst. Data for the subform is based on the query you created in Step b. The Charts tab includes two charts that represent the hours spent and hours remaining for client seminars. Data for the Charts tab is also based on the query created in Step b.

Submit your assignment in the format specified by your instructor.

Part 2:   You made several decisions while creating these two forms. What was the rationale behind your decisions? What chart style did you choose for the two charts? Why? What other chart styles could you use to represent the data?

3 Managing Contacts and Personal Contact Information with Outlook

Objectives

You will have mastered the material in this module when you can:

- Create a new contact
- Create a contact from an email message
- Modify a contact
- Add a contact photo
- Delete a contact
- Manipulate attachments to contacts
- Display contacts in different views
- Sort a contact list

- Find contacts using complete or partial information
- Find contacts from any Outlook folder
- Create a contact group
- Modify a contact group
- Add and remove names in a contact group
- Preview a contact list
- Print a contact list

Managing Contacts and Personal Contact Information with Outlook

This introductory module covers features and functions common to managing contacts in Outlook 2016.

Roadmap

In this module, you will learn how to perform basic contact management tasks. The following roadmap identifies general activities you will perform as you progress through this module:

1. CREATE a NEW CONTACT
2. MODIFY a CONTACT

3. CHANGE the VIEW OF CONTACTS

4. FIND a CONTACT

5. CREATE a CONTACT GROUP

6. PRINT the CONTACT LIST

At the beginning of the step instructions throughout each module, you will see an abbreviated form of this roadmap. The abbreviated roadmap uses colors to indicate module progress: gray means the module is beyond that activity, blue means the task being shown is covered in that activity, and black means that activity is yet to be covered. For example, the following abbreviated roadmap indicates the module would be showing a task in the Change View of Contacts activity.

1 CREATE NEW CONTACT | 2 MODIFY CONTACT | 3 CHANGE VIEW OF CONTACTS
4 FIND CONTACT | 5 CREATE CONTACT GROUP | 6 PRINT CONTACT LIST

Use the abbreviated roadmap as a progress guide while you read or step through the instructions in this module.

Introduction to Outlook Contacts

To keep track of your friends, business partners, family, and others with whom you communicate, you can use Outlook to create contact lists and contact groups. A **contact list** lets you record information about people, such as their email address, phone number, birthday, physical address, and photo. Each person's information is stored in a **contact record** in the contact list. If you have several colleagues at work whom you email frequently, you can add them to a **contact group**. You then can send email messages to all of your colleagues using the contact group rather than having to select each contact individually.

Project — Contact List with Groups

People and businesses create contact lists to keep track of people who are important to them or their business. A contact list may contain groups so that several contacts can be identified with a group name rather than individual contact names. Managing your contacts using a contact list can increase productivity greatly.

The project in this module follows general guidelines and uses Outlook to create the contact list shown in Figure 3–1. This contact list displays individual contacts and contact groups by name. A photograph of each contact helps you associate a face to a name. The contact groups display the name of the group, have a group label, and include a different graphic from the individual contacts.

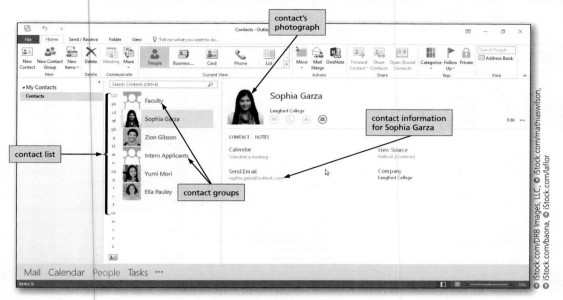

Figure 3–1

Creating a Contact List

The first step in creating a contact list is to enter information such as names, email addresses, and phone numbers for the people you communicate with regularly. After you enter and save contact information, that information is available as you compose email messages. You can type the first few letters of a contact's name into an email message, and Outlook will fill in the rest of the email address for you. If you are working on a mobile device that can make and receive phone calls, you also can use contact information to call someone on your contact list.

What advantages does an Outlook contact list provide for marketing a new business such as a gym?

Creating a contact list of your customer contacts lets you reach more people who can help your business grow by becoming repeat customers and spreading the word about your business. A gym can provide an email sign-up form on its website so that customers can choose to keep up with the latest schedule and deals. For example, a gym might send monthly email messages to advertise specials such as 50 percent off kickboxing classes on a certain date.

CONSIDER THIS

Contacts – Outlook Window

The Contacts – Outlook window shown in Figure 3–2 includes a variety of features to help you work efficiently with a contact list. The Contacts – Outlook window contains many elements similar to the windows in other Office programs, as well as some elements that are unique to Outlook. The main elements of the Contacts window are the My Contacts pane, the contact list, and the People pane.

For an introduction to Windows and instructions about how to perform basic Windows tasks, read the Office and Windows module at the beginning of this book, where you can learn how to resize windows, change screen resolution, create folders, move and rename files, use Windows Help, and much more.

For an introduction to Office and instructions about how to perform basic tasks in Office apps, read the Office and Windows module at the beginning of this book, where you can learn how to run an application, use the ribbon, save a file, open a file, print a file, exit an application, use Help, and much more.

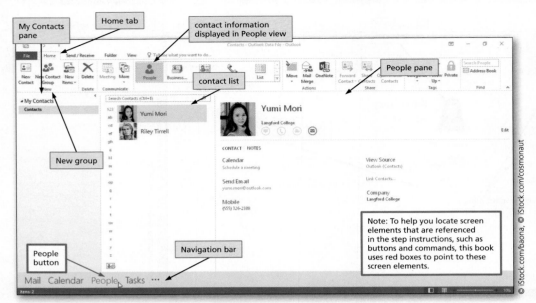

Figure 3–2

BTW

Using More Than One Outlook Data File
If you have multiple email accounts or data files set up in Outlook, you may need to remove the email accounts or data files to practice the steps in this module. To remove an account, click the File tab, click Account Settings, and then click the Account Settings option. Select the email account and click the Remove button to remove the email account.

1 CREATE NEW CONTACT | 2 MODIFY CONTACT | 3 CHANGE VIEW OF CONTACTS
4 FIND CONTACT | 5 CREATE CONTACT GROUP | 6 PRINT CONTACT LIST

To Create a New Contact

To create the contact list in this module, you start by adding Sophia Garza as the first contact. In Modules 1 and 2, you set up Sophia's email account and calendar in Outlook. When you create or update a contact, you add the contact's name, company name, email address, and other information, such as a Twitter username. The following steps create a new contact in the People view. *Why? To organize the contact information of your friends, clients, and colleagues, you should keep an Outlook contact list to communicate efficiently without having to search for information in multiple locations. Sophia is adding herself to her contact list to organize her contact information in a central place.*

1

• Run Outlook and open the Sophia Module 3.pst Outlook Data File from the Data Files.

• Click People (shown in Figure 3–2) on the Navigation bar to display the Outlook Contacts.

• Click the New Contact button (Home tab | New group) to display the Untitled – Contact window (Figure 3–3).

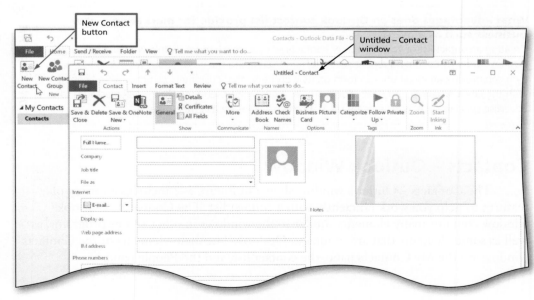

Figure 3–3

Q&A
What should I do if I have more than one Outlook data file open in the Navigation Pane?
Open only the Sophia Module 3.pst Outlook data file, which appears as outlook data file in the Navigation Pane. Close any other Outlook data files open in the Navigation Pane, and then repeat Step 1.

2

- Type **Sophia Garza** in the Full Name text box to enter a name for the contact.
- Type **Langford College** in the Company text box to enter a company (or in this case, a school) for the contact.
- Type **sophia.garza@outlook.com** in the E-mail text box, and then press the TAB key to enter an email address for the contact (Figure 3–4).

Q&A Why did the title of the Contact window change after I entered the name?

As soon as you enter the name, Outlook updates the Contact window title to reflect the information you have entered. Outlook also displays the name in the File as text box. The contact is not saved, however; only the window title and File as text boxes are updated.

Can I add information to other fields for a contact?

Yes. As long as you have the information, you can fill out the fields accordingly. You even can add fields besides those listed by clicking the All Fields button (Contact tab | Show group).

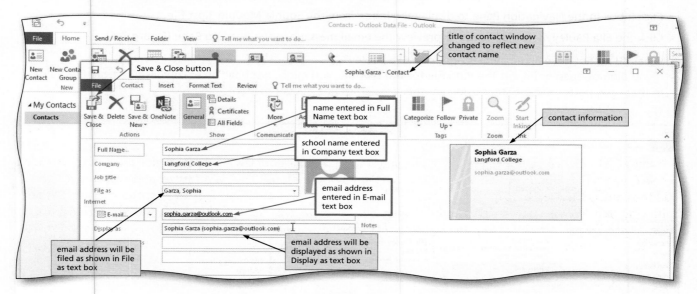

Figure 3–4

3

- Click the Save & Close button (Contact tab | Actions group) (shown in Figure 3–4) to save the contact record and close the Contact window (Figure 3–5).

Figure 3–5

Other Ways

1. Right-click contact list, click New Contact

2. Press CTRL+SHIFT+C

To Create Contacts from Email Messages

Sophia frequently emails Ella Pauley, the director of the Pathways Internship Office. In addition, as a student worker in the Internship Office, Sophia contacts another student named Zion Gibson, who is actively applying for an internship. Creating contacts for Ella and Zion will simplify communications for Sophia. Outlook can create a contact based on the information located within email messages. The following steps create contacts from email messages. *Why? You can quickly add a contact from an email message to better keep track of the sender's information. If you type the first few letters of a contact's name into a new email message, Outlook fills in the email address for you.*

1

- Click the Mail button in the Navigation bar to display your mailbox from the Sophia Module 3.pst file.
- Click Inbox in the Navigation Pane to display the Inbox from the Sophia Module 3.pst file.
- Click the Ella Pauley message header to preview the email message in the Reading Pane (Figure 3–6).

Q&A What if I do not have an email message from Ella Pauley?
If you did not open or import the data file for this module, you might not have an email message from Ella Pauley. In that case, perform these steps using another email message in your mailbox.

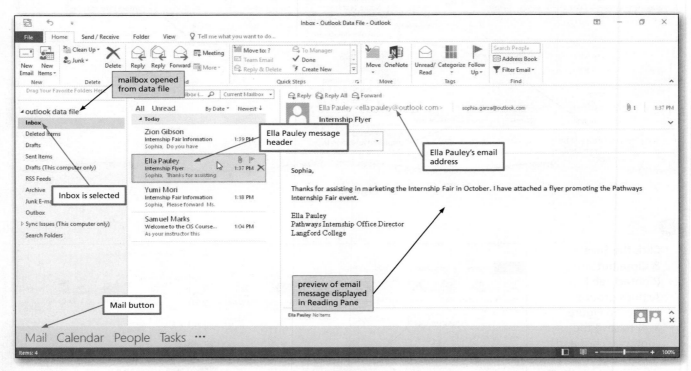

Figure 3–6

BTW
Contacts Window
By default, clicking the People button in the Navigation bar displays the contacts in the Microsoft Outlook window. To display the contacts in a new window, right-click the People button in the Navigation bar, and then click Open in New Window on the shortcut menu.

2

- Right-click Ella Pauley's email address (shown in Figure 3–6) in the message header of the Reading Pane to display a shortcut menu (Figure 3–7).

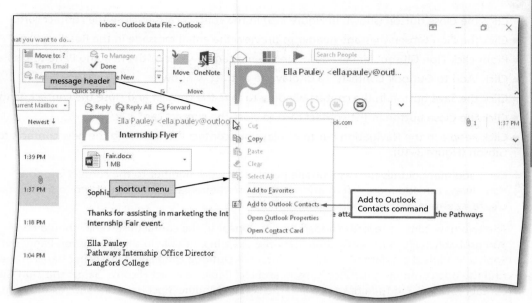

Figure 3–7

3

- Click Add to Outlook Contacts (shown in Figure 3–7) to display the contact window (Figure 3–8).

Q&A Why does the contact window already have Ella's Pauley's name and email address entered into the Name and Email text boxes? Outlook automatically detects the name and the email address for the contact from the existing email message.

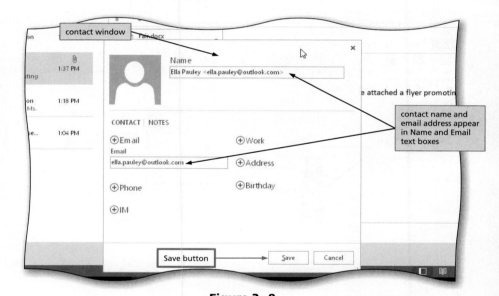

Figure 3–8

4

- Click the Save button (shown in Figure 3–8) in the contact window to save the contact and open the contact card for Ella Pauley (Figure 3–9).

Q&A What can you do with the contact card? The contact card includes shortcuts to tasks typically performed with contacts, such as scheduling a meeting, sending an email message, and editing contact information.

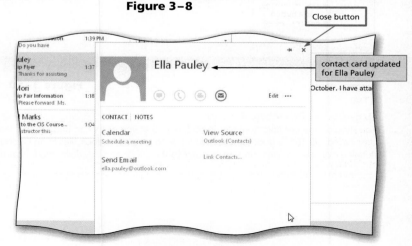

Figure 3–9

- Click the Close button (shown in Figure 3–9) in the contact card to close the contact card.
- Click the Zion Gibson message header to preview the email message in the Reading Pane.
- Right-click Zion Gibson's email address in the message header of the Reading Pane to display a shortcut menu.
- Click 'Add to Outlook Contacts' to display the contact window.
- Click the Save button in the contact window to save the contact and close the contact window.
- Click the Close button in the contact card to close the contact card.
- Click People in the Navigation bar to display your contact list, including the new contacts for Ella Pauley and Zion Gibson (Figure 3–10).

Q&A

Can I add more details such as a phone number or work number to the contact window?
You always can add more information such as another email address or photo to the contact window when you create a contact or later when you have more time.

The two new contact records I added do not appear in the contact list. What should I do?
You probably have another Outlook data file open in Outlook. In the Navigation Pane, note the name of the Sophia Module 3.pst data file, such as Contacts – Outlook Data File. Click other items in the Navigation pane to find the one containing the Zion Gibson and Ella Pauley contact records. Select the Zion Gibson and Ella Pauley contact records, and then drag them to the Sophia Module 3.pst data file, such as the Contacts – Outlook Data File in the Navigation Pane.

Figure 3–10

BTW

Organizing Files and Folders
You should organize and store files in folders so that you easily can find the files later. For example, if you are taking an introductory technology class called CIS 101, a good practice would be to save all Outlook files in an Outlook folder in a CIS 101 folder. For a discussion of folders and detailed examples of creating folders, refer to the Office and Windows module at the beginning of this book.

How can I import contacts from an external source such as an iPhone or Android smartphone?

To create a master list of all your contacts in one location in Outlook, you can import your contacts from your smartphone's address book, Internet-based email addresses such as your Gmail contacts, or from within another program such as an Access database. To import your contacts from an external address book:

1. Click the Address Book button (Home tab | Find group) to open the Address Book: Contacts dialog box.

2. Click the Address Book arrow to view a list of Other Address Books.

3. Click Other Address Books, such as Contacts (Mobile), to display a list of external contacts.

4. Click the first contact, press the SHIFT key, and click the last contact to select the entire list of contacts.

5. Click File to display the File menu. Click Add to Contacts to add the selected contacts to your Outlook contact list.

6. Click the Close button to close the Address Book: Contacts dialog box.

Editing a Contact

After setting up your contact list, you need to keep the information current and add new information, such as a new work phone number, Twitter account username, or picture, to help you interact with your contact. You can attach one or more files to a contact to store documents, tables, pictures, or clip art, for example, along with their contact information. If your colleagues transfer to other companies, remove contact information that you no longer need unless you will continue to interact with them on a regular basis.

BTW
Importing Contacts from External Sources
If you need to copy an existing contact list into Outlook, click the File tab and then click Open & Export. Next, click Import/Export to open the Import and Export Wizard. Based on the type of contact file, select the import file type and follow the steps for the appropriate import type.

When I maximize the Contact window, I noticed a Map It button next to addresses. What is the purpose of the Map It button?

The Map It button opens a Bing map within a browser to show the address listed in the Addresses text box. You could use the map to find directions to the address.

BTW
Touch Screen Differences
The Office and Windows interfaces may vary if you are using a touch screen. For this reason, you might notice that the function or appearance of your touch screen differs slightly from this module's presentation.

To Edit a Contact

1 CREATE NEW CONTACT | 2 MODIFY CONTACT | 3 CHANGE VIEW OF CONTACTS
4 FIND CONTACT | 5 CREATE CONTACT GROUP | 6 PRINT CONTACT LIST

When you created a contact record for Ella Pauley, it did not include her job title, work phone number, or picture. Ms. Pauley has given you the name of her school, proper title, work phone number, and photo, and you want to edit her contact record to include the new information. In addition, you need to include contact pictures for Sophia and Zion. The following steps edit a contact by entering additional information including pictures. To perform the steps, you will be required to use the Data Files. Please contact your instructor for information about accessing the Data Files. *Why? The more information you have about a business contact, the better you can provide personalized service. For example, including a business photo of your contact associates a name with a face. A company logo also could be used instead of a professional photo.*

1

- Click the Ella Pauley contact to display Ella Pauley's contact information in the People pane (Figure 3–11).

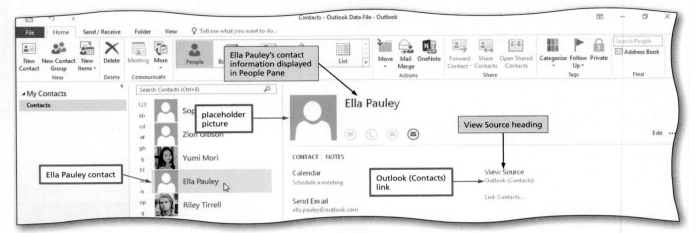

Figure 3–11

2

- Click Outlook (Contacts) below the View Source heading (shown in Figure 3–11) to display the Ella Pauley – Contact window.

- Type `Langford College` in the Company text box to enter a company or school name for the contact.

- In the Phone numbers section, type `(954) 555-1890` in the Business text box, and then press the ENTER key to enter a business phone number for the contact (Figure 3–12).

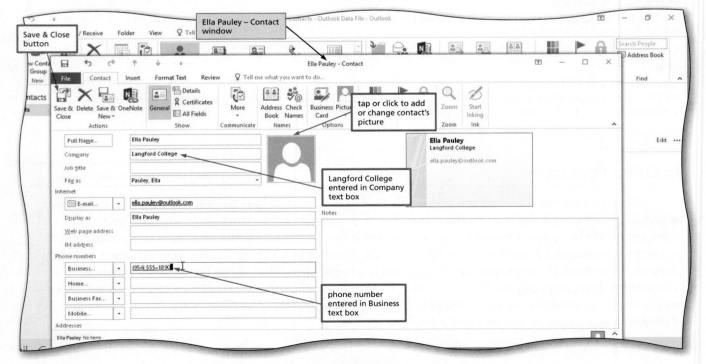

Figure 3–12

- Click the placeholder picture to open the Add Contact Picture dialog box.

- Navigate to the file location, in this case, the Module 03 folder in the Outlook folder provided with the Data Files.

- Click Ella to select the photo of Ella (Figure 3–13).

Q&A Why do I only see filenames and not actual pictures of the contacts?
An image is displayed if the Large icons option is set in your Windows settings.

Figure 3–13

- Click the OK button (shown in Figure 3–13) to add an image to the contact record.

- Click the Save & Close button (Contact tab | Actions group) to save the contact and close the Contact window (Figure 3–14).

Figure 3–14

5

- Click the Sophia Garza contact to display Sophia Garza in the People pane.

- Click Outlook (Contacts) below the View Source heading to display the Sophia Garza – Contact window.

- Click the placeholder picture to open the Add Contact Picture dialog box.

- Click Sophia to select the photo of Sophia.

- Click the OK button to add an image to the contact record.

Figure 3–15

- Click the Save & Close button (Contact tab | Actions group) to save the contact and close the Contact window.

- Repeat these steps to add the contact photograph named Zion for the Zion Gibson contact (Figure 3–15).

Do I have to add actual pictures of every client?

You may not have access to images of every client, but consider adding at least a company logo, which could assist you in making a mental note of where the client is employed.

1 CREATE NEW CONTACT | 2 MODIFY CONTACT | 3 CHANGE VIEW OF CONTACTS
4 FIND CONTACT | 5 CREATE CONTACT GROUP | 6 PRINT CONTACT LIST

To Delete a Contact

Outlook allows you to store a lifetime list of contacts, but keeping a contact list current involves deleting contacts that you no longer need. In addition to deleting old contacts, you may have duplicate contacts that have the same contact information. Duplicate contacts might be created when you import contacts into Outlook. In this case, you can delete the unwanted duplicates. An intern named Riley Tirrell has transferred to another college and Sophia no longer needs his contact information. The following step deletes a contact. *Why? Keeping a contact list current makes your activities with email, phone calls, and social networks more efficient.*

1

- Click the Riley Tirrell contact (shown in Figure 3–15) to select the contact.

- Press the DELETE key to delete the contact information for Riley Tirrell (Figure 3–16).

Figure 3–16

Other Ways

1. Click contact, click Delete (Home tab | Delete group)
2. Right-click contact, click Delete

1 CREATE NEW CONTACT | 2 MODIFY CONTACT | 3 CHANGE VIEW OF CONTACTS
4 FIND CONTACT | 5 CREATE CONTACT GROUP | 6 PRINT CONTACT LIST

To Add an Attachment to a Contact

Zion Gibson sent you his resume, which he plans to send to apply to a marketing internship position at the Kennedy Center. You want to attach the resume document to his contact record. *Why? Including this document as part of his contact record will help you find the document easily.* Any files you attach to a contact are displayed in the Notes section of the Contact window. You also can insert items such as financial spreadsheets, pictures, and meeting slides to the Notes section. The following steps add an attachment to a contact.

1

- Click the Zion Gibson contact to display Zion Gibson in the People pane.

- Click Outlook (Contacts) below View Source to display the Zion Gibson – Contact window (Figure 3–17).

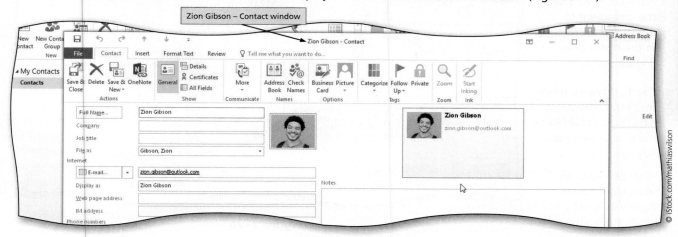

Zion Gibson – Contact window

Figure 3–17

2

- Click Insert on the ribbon to display the Insert tab (Figure 3–18).

Attach File button

Insert tab

Include group

Figure 3–18

3

- Click the Attach File button (Insert tab | Include group) to display a list of Recent Items.

- Click Browse This PC to display the Insert File dialog box.

- If necessary, navigate to the file location, in this case, the Module 03 folder in the Outlook folder provided with the Data Files.

- Click Zion Gibson Resume to select the Word document (Figure 3–19).

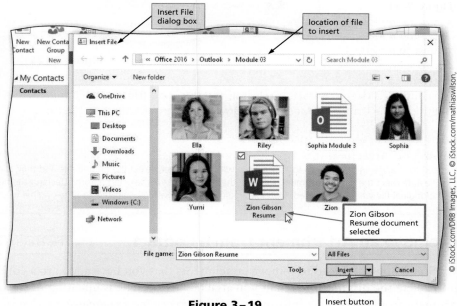

Insert File dialog box

location of file to insert

Zion Gibson Resume document selected

Insert button

Figure 3–19

4

- Click the Insert button (Insert File dialog box) to attach the document to the contact record in the Notes area (Figure 3–20).

Q&A Can I add more than one attachment?
Yes; you can add as many attachments as you want.

How do I view an attachment after I have added it?
Open the contact and then double-click the attachment to open it.

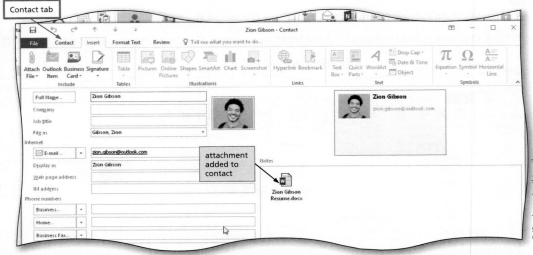

Figure 3–20

5

- Click Contact on the ribbon to display the Contact tab.
- Click the Save & Close button (Contact tab | Actions group) to save the contact record and close the Contact window (Figure 3–21).

Q&A Can I send a meeting request to a contact?
Yes. To send a meeting request to a contact, click the contact to select it, click Meeting (Home tab | Communicate group), enter the details of the meeting in the Untitled – Meeting window, and then click the Send button.

Figure 3–21

BTW

Changing an Attachment

If you need to change an attachment to another file within a contact, select the original file and then click the Insert tab on the ribbon. Click Attach File and select the new attachment. Because the original file was selected before attaching the new file, the new file replaces the original file. If the original file were not selected, Outlook would add the new file while keeping the original file.

---

1 CREATE NEW CONTACT | 2 MODIFY CONTACT | 3 CHANGE VIEW OF CONTACTS
4 FIND CONTACT | 5 CREATE CONTACT GROUP | 6 PRINT CONTACT LIST

To Remove an Attachment from a Contact

Sometimes you need to remove attachments that you have added to a contact. Zion Gibson has asked you to delete the original document you attached because he is updating his resume. You need to remove the attachment from his contact information. *Why? Removing an outdated attachment is important to keep your contact information current.* The following steps remove the attachment from a contact.

1

- If necessary, click the Zion Gibson contact to display Zion Gibson in the People pane.
- Click Outlook (Contacts) below View Source to display the Zion Gibson – Contact window.
- Click the Zion Gibson Resume document to select it (Figure 3–22).

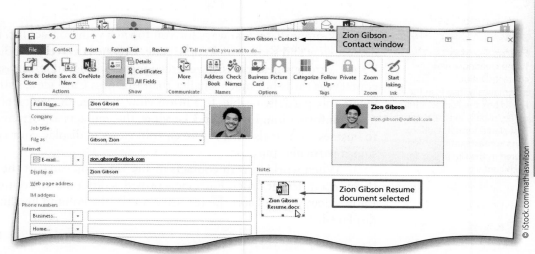

Figure 3–22

2

- Press the DELETE key to remove the attachment (Figure 3–23).

3

- Click the Save & Close button (Contact tab | Actions group) to save the contact and close the Contact window.

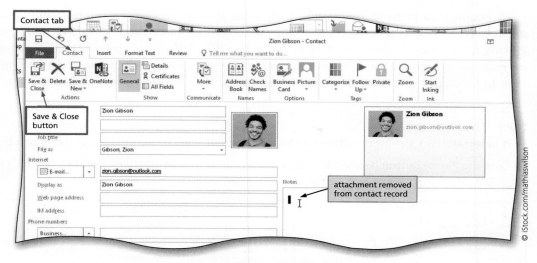

Figure 3–23

Other Ways

1. Click file icon, click Delete (Contact tab | Actions group)

© iStock.com/mathiaswilson

How can I tag a contact to include a color-coded category or follow-up flag to remind me to follow up with a contact later?

To search through your contacts more efficiently, add color-coded categories such as a green tag to remind you of a new intern in the Pathways Internship program, for example. You may want to tag a contact with a Follow Up Tomorrow flag to remind you to email that person in the next day. To add a tag to a contact:

1. Click a contact to display the contact in the People pane.

2. Click Outlook (Contacts) below View Source to display the Contact window.

3. Click Categorize or Follow Up (Contact tab | Tags group) to display a list of color-coded categories or follow-up flags.

4. Click the color-coded category or follow-up flag that you want to use. You can use multiple tags on each contact if needed.

CONSIDER THIS

Viewing and Sorting a Contact List

Outlook supports several ways for you to view your contact list. **People view** is the default view and shows the People pane. **Business Card view** displays the contacts as if they were business cards, a well-recognized format in business. **Card view** shows the contacts as cards but much smaller than Business Card view, with most information being only partially visible. In **Phone view**, you see the contacts in a list displaying phone information. Finally, in **List view**, the contacts are arranged in a list according to businesses. You also can create custom views to display your contacts in a way that suits a particular purpose.

When working with contacts in any view, you can sort the contacts to display them in a different order. Each view provides different sort options. For example, in Phone view, you can sort the list using any of the column heading buttons that are displayed.

To Change the Current View

1 CREATE NEW CONTACT | 2 MODIFY CONTACT | 3 CHANGE VIEW OF CONTACTS
4 FIND CONTACT | 5 CREATE CONTACT GROUP | 6 PRINT CONTACT LIST

People view provides useful information, but the other views also can be helpful. Changing the view sometimes can help you find a contact's information more quickly. Use Phone view, for example, when you are looking for a contact's phone number in a long list. *Why? Phone view provides a tabular layout with each contact in one row, and each column containing one contact's information.* The following steps change the current view to Phone view and then to Business card view to display the contact information on digital business cards.

1
- If necessary, click the More button (Home tab | Current View group) to display the Phone button.
- Click the Phone button (Home tab | Current View group) to switch to Phone view (Figure 3–24).

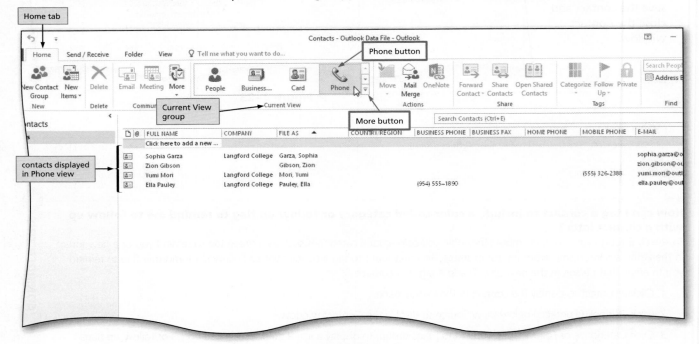

Figure 3–24

2

- If necessary, click the More button (Home tab | Current View group), and then click Business Card to switch to Business Card view (Figure 3–25).

Q&A What if the More button is not displayed in the Current View group?

You likely are using a lower resolution than 1366 × 768, so the ribbon hides additional buttons. Click the Business Card button in the Current View group to switch to Business Card view.

Experiment

- Click the other views in the Current View group to view the contacts in other arrangements. When you are finished, click Business Card to return to Business Card view.

Figure 3–25

To Sort Contacts

1 CREATE NEW CONTACT | 2 MODIFY CONTACT | 3 CHANGE VIEW OF CONTACTS
4 FIND CONTACT | 5 CREATE CONTACT GROUP | 6 PRINT CONTACT LIST

Business Card view lists contacts in alphabetical order by default; however, you can sort the contacts to view them in reverse order. *Why? Reverse order is especially helpful if you want to quickly open a record for a contact at the end of a long contact list.* The following steps sort the contact list in reverse order, and then switch back to alphabetical order.

1

- Click View on the ribbon to display the View tab.

- Click the Reverse Sort button (View tab | Arrangement group) to display the contact list in reverse alphabetical order (Figure 3–26).

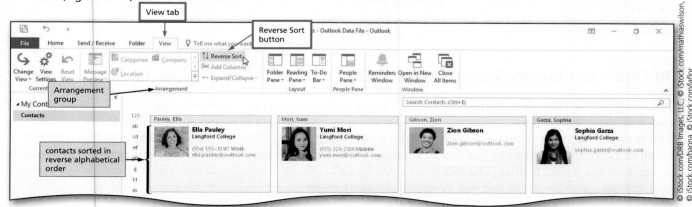

Figure 3–26

2
- Click the Reverse Sort button (View tab | Arrangement group) to display the contact list in the original order (Figure 3–27).

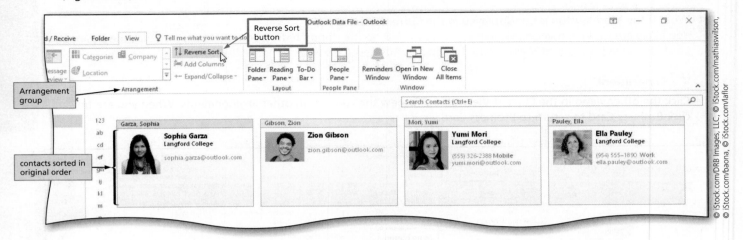

Figure 3–27

Break Point: If you wish to take a break, this is a good place to do so. To resume at a later time, continue to follow the steps from this location forward.

BTW
Outlook Help
At any time while using Outlook, you can find answers to questions and display information about various topics through Outlook Help. Used properly, this form of assistance can increase your productivity and reduce your frustrations by minimizing the time you spend learning how to use Outlook. For instructions about Outlook Help and exercises that will help you gain confidence in using it, read the Office and Windows module at the beginning of this book.

Using Search to Find a Contact

Over time, contact lists can grow quite large, making them difficult to navigate. In addition, you sometimes may not remember details about a contact you want to find. For example, you may remember that someone works for a particular company, but not their name. Alternatively, you may remember a phone number but nothing else. If this happens, you can use the Search People text box to search your contact list.

You also can find contacts using the Search People search box in the Find group on the Home tab. This works no matter which folder you are using (such as Mail, Calendar, People, or Tasks). This means that anytime you need to find your contacts, you can look them up quickly.

You can maximize your search efforts if you create a list of keywords that you can assign to contacts. The more general the keyword, the more results you will find. Using more specific keywords will reduce the number of results.

1 CREATE NEW CONTACT | 2 MODIFY CONTACT | 3 CHANGE VIEW OF CONTACTS
4 FIND CONTACT | 5 CREATE CONTACT GROUP | 6 PRINT CONTACT LIST

To Find a Contact by Searching for Text

If you only know partial information such as the area code in a phone number, the first word in a school name, or the domain name in an email address, you can use it to find matching contacts. Note that you might find many contacts that contain the text for which you are searching. The text you are using as the search term could be part of an email address, a school name, or a Twitter username, for example. Therefore, you may have to examine the results further. The following steps find all contacts that contain the text, langford. **Why?** *To save time, you can search for text or tags such as the college name Langford to locate the correct contact(s) quickly.*

1

- Click the Search Contacts text box to display the Search Tools Search tab (Figure 3–28).

Q&A Why is the Search Tools Search tab displayed when I click the Search Contacts text box?
The Search Tools Search tab contains buttons and commands that can help you search contacts.

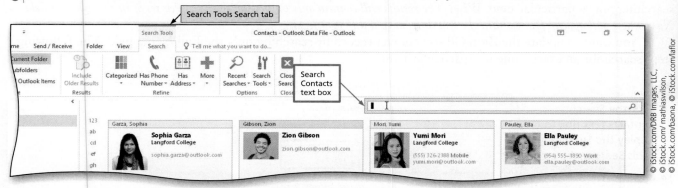

Figure 3–28

2

- Type **langford** in the Search Contacts text box to search for all contacts containing the text, langford (Figure 3–29).

Q&A Can I modify a search further after getting the initial results?
Certainly. You can use the Search Tools Search tab to refine your search by specifying a name or phone number, for example. You also can expand the search to include all of the Outlook folders.

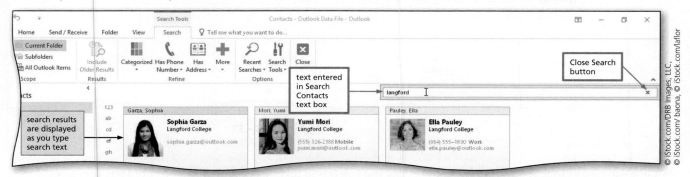

Figure 3–29

3

- Click the Close Search button (shown in Figure 3–29) in the Search Contacts text box to close the search and return to the Contacts – Outlook Data File – Outlook window (Figure 3–30).

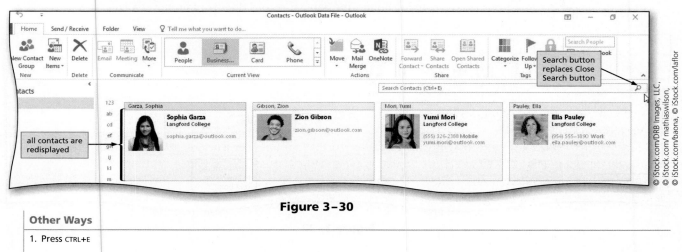

Figure 3–30

Other Ways

1. Press CTRL+E

To Refine a Search

If you type a full name or email address in the Search Contacts text box, you will find your contact, but the information need not be only in the E-mail field or the Company field. The results might contain contacts where the name or email address is part of the Notes field, for example. In that case, you can find a contact by searching only a particular field. *Why? The results will contain only contacts with the search term in the specified field. No contacts will appear that contain the search term in a different field.*

You want to update the Zion Gibson contact record by searching only the Full Name field. The following steps search for an exact name in a particular field.

1

- Click the Search Contacts text box to display the Search Tools Search tab.

- Click the More button (Search Tools Search tab | Refine group) to display a list of common properties for refining a search (Figure 3–31).

Figure 3–31

2

- Click Full Name (shown in Figure 3–31) to display the Full Name text box below the Search Contacts text box.

- Type **Zion Gibson** in the Full Name text box to search for the Zion Gibson contact (Figure 3–32).

Q&A Why might Outlook display search results that do not seem to contain the search text?
When you perform a search, Outlook searches all specified fields for a match. However, the matching fields might not be displayed in the list of search results, although the contact record does contain the search text.

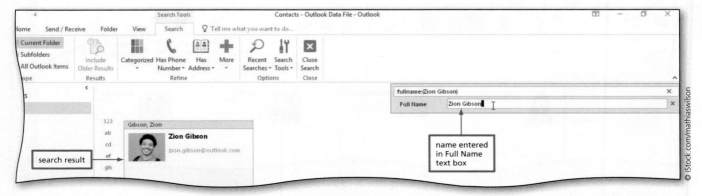

Figure 3–32

3

- Double-click the Zion Gibson contact to open it.

- Type `Interested in the Kennedy Center internship` in the Notes field to update the contact (Figure 3–33).

Figure 3–33

4

- Click the Save & Close button (Contact tab | Actions group) (shown in Figure 3–33) to save the contact and close the Contact window.

- Click the Close Search button in the Search Contacts text box to close the search and return to the Contacts – Outlook Data File – Outlook window.

To Find a Contact from Any Outlook Window

1 CREATE NEW CONTACT | 2 MODIFY CONTACT | 3 CHANGE VIEW OF CONTACTS
4 FIND CONTACT | 5 CREATE CONTACT GROUP | 6 PRINT CONTACT LIST

You do not have to be working in the Contacts – Outlook window to search for contacts. You can use the Search People text box in the Find group on the Home tab to search for contacts when you are working with email or performing other Outlook tasks. If what you type in the search box matches a single contact, that entry will be displayed in a contact window. If what you type matches more than one entry, you will be asked to select the contact that you want to view. **Why?** *For example, if you search for a contact using part of the company name, more than one contact may appear in the search results. You then can select a single contact from the results.*

The following steps search for a contact from the Inbox – Outlook Data File – Outlook window using only part of the company name, college. In this case, you are searching through your college contacts for the information about Yumi Mori.

1

- Click the Mail button on the Navigation bar to display the Sophia Module 3.pst mailbox.

- Click the Inbox folder to display the Inbox from the Sophia Module 3.pst file (Figure 3–34).

Figure 3–34

2

- Type `college` in the Search People text box (Home tab | Find group) to search for contacts containing the search text (Figure 3–35).

Q&A

Outlook searched a different Outlook data file instead of the Sophia Module 3.pst file. What should I do? Open only the Sophia Module 3.pst Outlook data file, which appears as outlook data file in the Navigation Pane. Close any other Outlook data file open in the Navigation Pane, and then repeat the steps. To make an Outlook data file the default, click the File tab, the Account Settings button, Account Settings, and then the Data Files tab, select the appropriate Outlook data file, click Set as Default, and then restart Outlook.

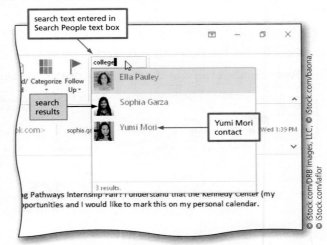

Figure 3–35

3

- Click Yumi Mori to select the contact and display her contact card (Figure 3–36).

Figure 3–36

4

- Click the Close button to close the window.

- Click the People button on the Navigation bar to return to the Contacts – Outlook Data File – Outlook window (Figure 3–37).

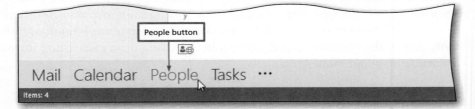

Figure 3–37

Creating and Editing a Contact Group

When you have several contacts that you frequently email or work with as a group, you can create a contact group and add contacts to it. A **contact group**, also called a **distribution list**, provides a single name for you to use when working with two or more contacts. You are not creating subfolders for contacts, but rather another way to reference multiple contacts at one time. For example, you could create a group called Inner Circle and then add all your closest family and friends to the group. Whenever you want to send an email message to your closest family and friends at one time, you could enter the contact group name, Inner Circle, as the recipient of the email message — and every contact in the group would receive the email message.

To Create a Contact Group from Existing Contacts

Why? *A message sent to a contact group goes to all recipients listed in the group. If your contact list gets too cluttered, you can use a contact group to communicate with friends, family, and coworkers more quickly.* When creating contact groups, you choose the name for your contact group and then add the contacts you want to have in the group. To quickly send an email to all the members of the Student Internship Club, you want to create a group of all the members who are part of your contact list and name the group Intern Applicants. The following steps create a contact group and then add the related contacts to the group.

1
- Click the New Contact Group button (Home tab | New group) to display the Untitled – Contact Group window (Figure 3–38).

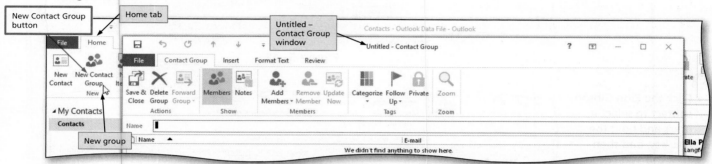

Figure 3–38

2
- Type **Intern Applicants** in the Name text box to enter a name for the group (Figure 3–39).

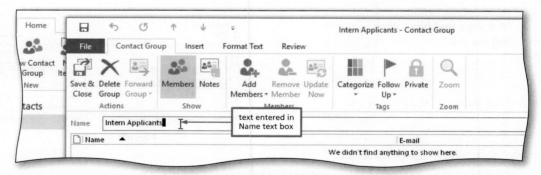

Figure 3–39

3
- Click the Add Members button (Contact Group tab | Members group) to display the Add Members menu (Figure 3–40).

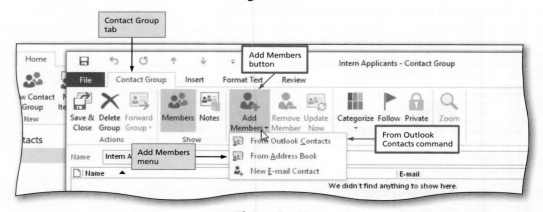

Figure 3–40

4

- Click From Outlook Contacts to display the Select Members: Contacts dialog box (Figure 3–41).

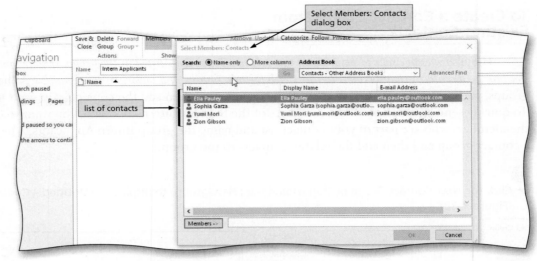

Figure 3–41

5

- Click the Zion Gibson contact to select it, press and hold the CTRL key, and then click the Yumi Mori contact to select both contacts.
- Click the Members button to move the information to the Members text box (Figure 3–42).

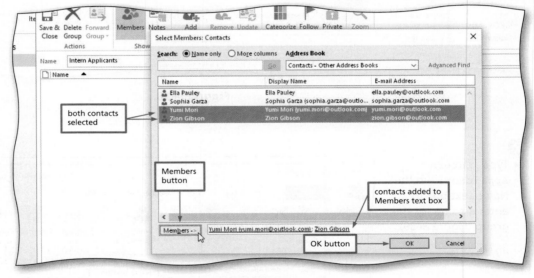

Figure 3–42

6

- Click the OK button to add the contacts to the group (Figure 3–43).

Q&A What if I add the wrong member(s) to the contact group?
In the Contact Group window, select the member you want to remove, and then click the Remove Member button (Contact Group tab | Members group). Next, repeat Steps 3–6 to add any missing members.

Figure 3–43

7

- Click the Save & Close button (Contact Group tab | Actions group) to save the contact group and close th
(Figure 3–44).

Q&A Why are the contacts and the group displayed in the Contacts window?
You use a contact group to send email messages to a set of contacts using the group name; it does not rep
move the existing contacts.

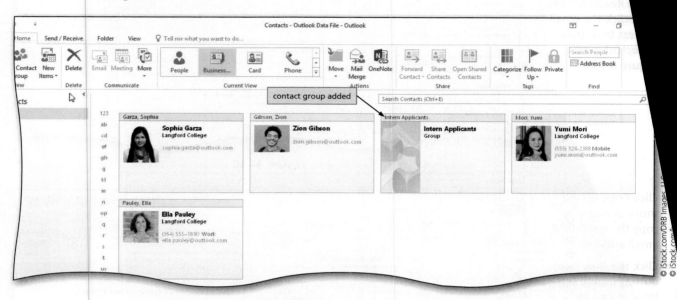

Figure 3–44

To Create a Contact Group from an Existing Email Message

1 CREATE NEW CONTACT | 2 MODIFY CONTACT | 3 CHANGE VIEW OF CONTACTS
4 FIND CONTACT | 5 CREATE CONTACT GROUP | 6 PRINT CONTACT LIST

Outlook allows you to create a group for individuals who are not in your contact list but have sent you an email message. To do this, you copy a name from an email message and then paste the name in the Select Members dialog box when creating the group. The following steps create a contact group named Faculty and then add a member by using information in an email message from Samuel Marks. *Why? You can create a group and add a new contact right after reading an email.*

1

- Click the Mail button on the Navigation bar to display your mailbox (Figure 3–45).

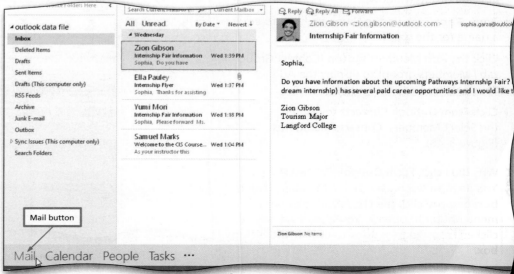

Figure 3–45

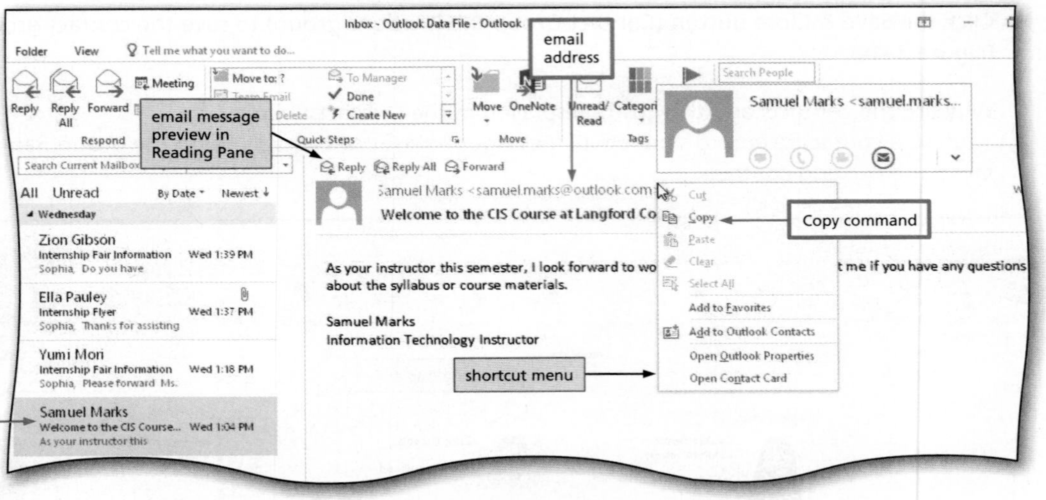

Figure 3–46

on the
menu to
name and
ddress.

e New Items
on (Home tab |
w group) to
play the New
ems menu.

Click More Items to
display the More
Items submenu
(Figure 3–47).

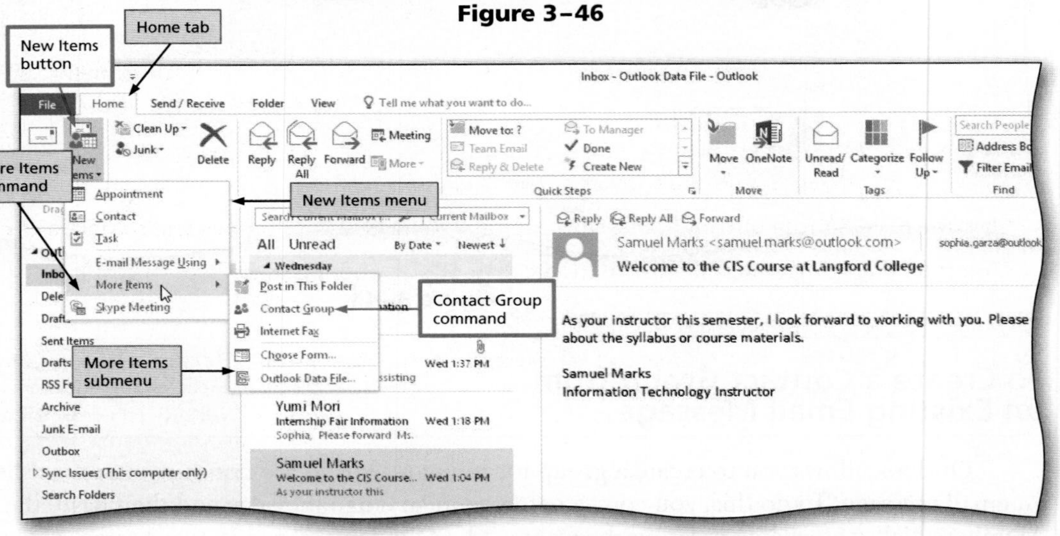

Figure 3–47

4

- Click Contact Group to display the Untitled – Contact Group window.

- Type **Faculty** in the Name text box to enter a name for the group.

- Click the Add Members button (Contact Group tab | Members group) to display the Add Members menu.

- Click From Outlook Contacts to display the Select Members: Contacts dialog box (Figure 3–48).

  Why did I click From Outlook Contacts?
  u need to display the Select Members dialog
  and you click the From Outlook Contacts
  option to open it. You also could have
  From Address Book to display the dialog

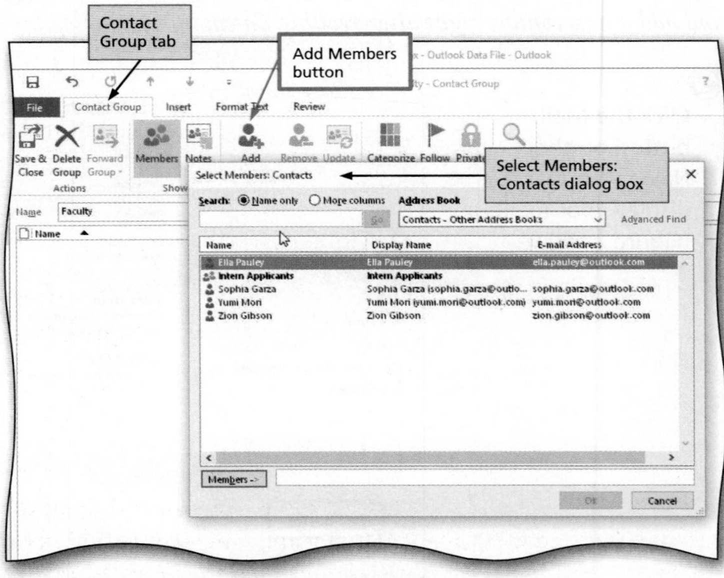

Figure 3–48

- Right-click the Members text box to display a shortcut menu.

- Click Paste on the shortcut menu to paste the copied name and email address (Figure 3–49).

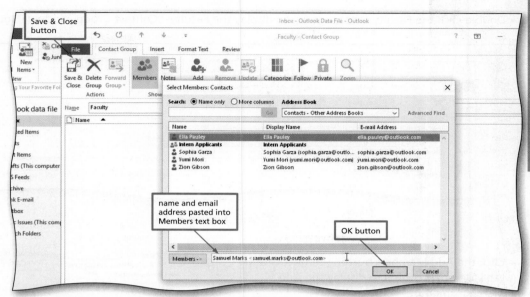

Figure 3–49

- Click the OK button to add the contact to the group.

- Click the Save & Close button (Contact Group tab | Actions group) to save the contact and close the window.

- Click the People button on the Navigation bar to display your contacts (Figure 3–50).

Q&A Can I forward a contact group to someone else?
Yes. You can forward a contact group by selecting the contact group, clicking Forward Contact (Home tab | Share group), and then selecting the option you want to use to forward the contact group.

Figure 3–50

To Add a Name to a Contact Group

1 CREATE NEW CONTACT | 2 MODIFY CONTACT | 3 CHANGE VIEW OF CONTACTS
4 FIND CONTACT | 5 CREATE CONTACT GROUP | 6 PRINT CONTACT LIST

As you meet and work with people, you can add them to one or more contact groups. You have been contacting the instructor Ella Pauley and you want to add her to the Faculty contact group. *Why? By adding people to a group, you can send email messages and meeting invitations to groups of people that you contact frequently without having to enter each individual email address.* The following steps add a new contact to the Faculty contact group.

1

- Double-click the Faculty contact group to display the Faculty – Contact Group window (Figure 3–51).

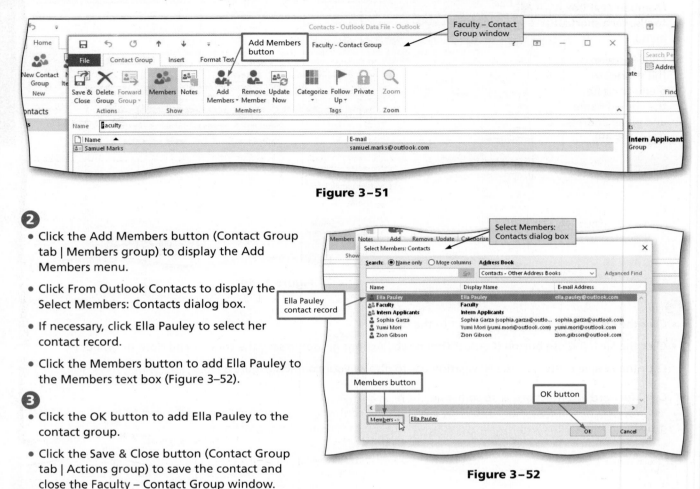

Figure 3–51

2

- Click the Add Members button (Contact Group tab | Members group) to display the Add Members menu.

- Click From Outlook Contacts to display the Select Members: Contacts dialog box.

- If necessary, click Ella Pauley to select her contact record.

- Click the Members button to add Ella Pauley to the Members text box (Figure 3–52).

3

- Click the OK button to add Ella Pauley to the contact group.

- Click the Save & Close button (Contact Group tab | Actions group) to save the contact and close the Faculty – Contact Group window.

Figure 3–52

To Add Notes to a Contact Group

1 CREATE NEW CONTACT | 2 MODIFY CONTACT | 3 CHANGE VIEW OF CONTACTS
4 FIND CONTACT | 5 CREATE CONTACT GROUP | 6 PRINT CONTACT LIST

You can add reminder notes to a contact group. *Why? As you create groups, you may have trouble remembering who is part of the group and why.* The contact group notes are only displayed in the Contacts list when Card view is selected. You would like to add a note to the Intern Applicants contact group that their internship placements must be assigned by November 1. The following steps add a note to a contact group and display the note in the Card view.

1

- Double-click the Intern Applicants contact group to display the Intern Applicants – Contact Group window (Figure 3–53).

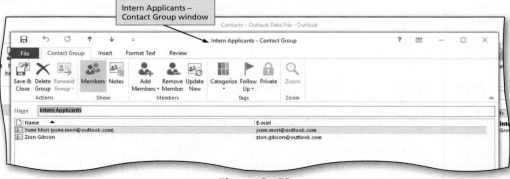

Figure 3–53

2

- Click the Notes button (Contact Group tab | Show group) to display the Notes page.

- Type **The internship placements must be assigned by November 1.** in the Notes page to create a reminder (Figure 3–54).

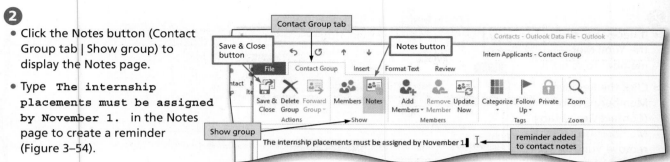

Figure 3–54

3

- Click the Save & Close button on the Notes page to close the Intern Applicants – Contact Group window.

- Click the Card button (Home tab | Current View group) to display the contact list in Card view, which in this case includes the contact group note for the Intern Applicants (Figure 3–55).

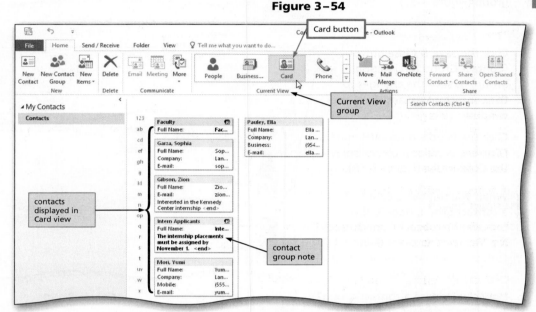

Figure 3–55

To Remove a Name from a Contact Group

1 CREATE NEW CONTACT | 2 MODIFY CONTACT | 3 CHANGE VIEW OF CONTACTS
4 FIND CONTACT | 5 CREATE CONTACT GROUP | 6 PRINT CONTACT LIST

Why? *Periodically, you may need to remove someone from a contact group. For example, contacts may switch jobs or ask to be removed from your list because they no longer are working on or participating in a club or project.* Yumi Mori has decided to transfer and will no longer be participating in the Pathways Internship program. You have decided to remove her from the Intern Applicants contact group so that she will not receive email messages sent to the group. The following steps remove a contact from a group.

1

- If necessary, scroll in the Contacts window until the Intern Applicants contact group is visible.

- Double-click the Intern Applicants contact group to display the Intern Applicants – Contact Group window (Figure 3–56).

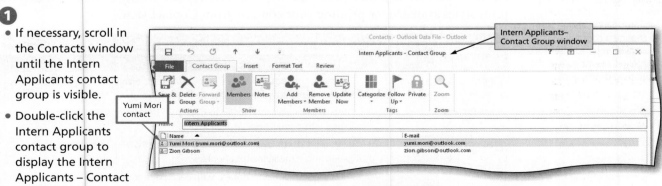

Figure 3–56

2

- If necessary, click the Yumi Mori member to select it.

- Click the Remove Member button (Contact Group tab | Members group) to remove Yumi Mori from the contact group (Figure 3–57).

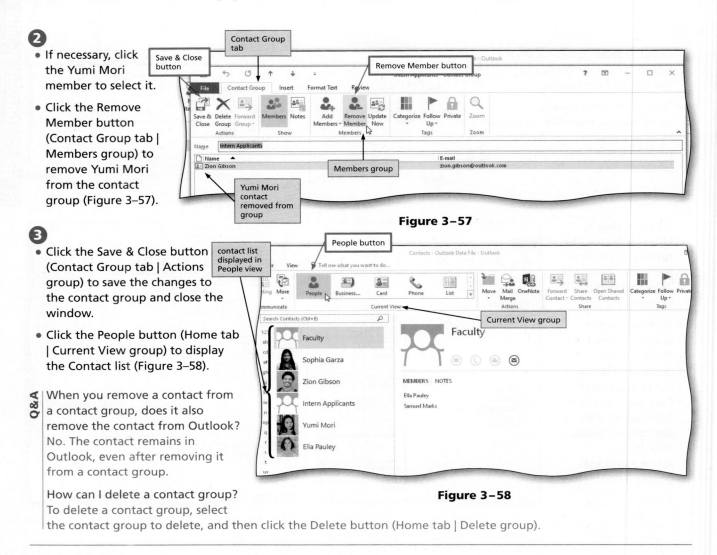

Figure 3–57

3

- Click the Save & Close button (Contact Group tab | Actions group) to save the changes to the contact group and close the window.

- Click the People button (Home tab | Current View group) to display the Contact list (Figure 3–58).

Q&A

When you remove a contact from a contact group, does it also remove the contact from Outlook?
No. The contact remains in Outlook, even after removing it from a contact group.

How can I delete a contact group?
To delete a contact group, select the contact group to delete, and then click the Delete button (Home tab | Delete group).

Figure 3–58

BTW
Outlook Screen Resolution
If you are using a computer or mobile device to step through the project in this module and you want your screens to match the figures in this book, you should change your screen's resolution to 1366 x 768. For information about how to change a computer's resolution, refer to the Office and Windows module at the beginning of this book.

Printing Your Contacts

All or part of your contacts can be printed in a number of different views, or **print styles**. You can distribute a printed contact or contact list to others in a form that can be read or viewed, but cannot be edited. You can choose to print only one contact or the entire list. To print only part of your contacts, select one or more contacts and then change the print options so that you print your selection. This section previews the entire contact list and then prints the selected contacts in Card style. Table 3–1 lists the print styles available for printing your contacts from Contact view.

Table 3–1 Print Styles for Contact View	
Print Style	**Description**
Card	Prints a list of contacts separated by alphabetic dividers and provides a sheet for adding more contact information
Small Booklet	Prints a list of contacts similar to Card style but designed so that it can be folded into a small booklet
Medium Booklet	Prints a list of contacts similar to Card style but designed so that it can be folded into a medium-sized booklet
Memo	Prints a page for each contact, with each page formatted to look like a memo
Phone Directory	Prints a list of contacts showing phone numbers only

To Preview a Contact List

You can print preview a single contact or multiple pages of contacts displayed as cards or in phone lists. The following steps preview the contact list in various print styles. *Why? Unless you change the print options, you will see all your contacts when you preview the list before printing.*

①

● In the Contacts window, select the Zion Gibson and Ella Pauley contacts (Figure 3–59).

Figure 3–59

②

● Click the File tab on the ribbon (shown in Figure 3–59) to open the Backstage view.

● Click the Print tab in the Backstage view to display the Print gallery.

● Click Small Booklet Style in the Settings area to change the print style (Figure 3–60).

Q&A Why are all the contacts displayed when I selected only two contacts?
By default, the print range is set for all items to display and print. You can change the Print Options to print only the selected items.

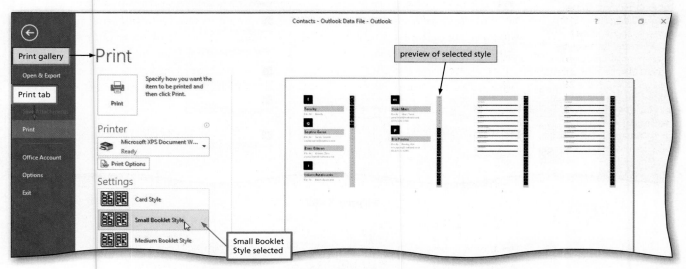

Figure 3–60

3

- Click Phone Directory Style in the Settings area to change to Phone Directory Style (Figure 3–61).

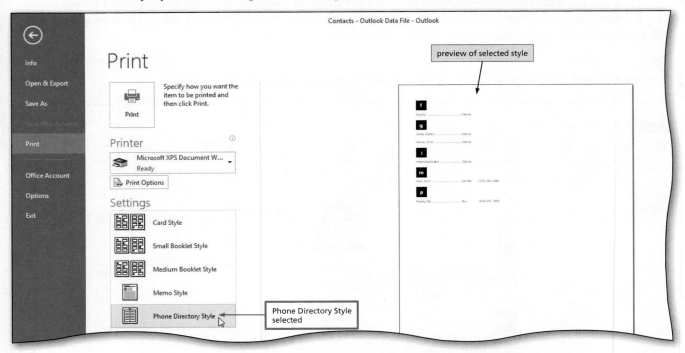

Figure 3–61

4

- Click Card Style in the Settings area to change to Card Style (Figure 3–62).

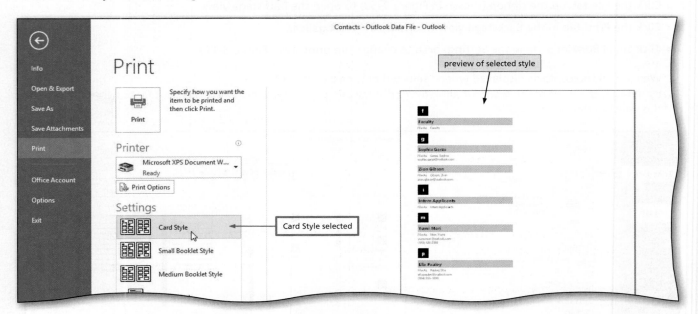

Figure 3–62

5

- Click the Print Options button to display the Print dialog box.

- Click the 'Only selected items' option button (Print dialog box) to preview only the selected contacts (Figure 3–63).

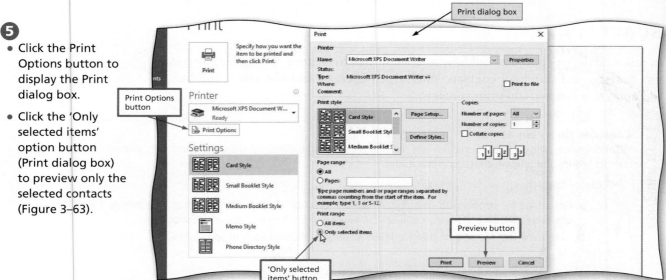

Figure 3–63

6

- Click the Preview button (Print dialog box) to close the dialog box and preview only the selected contacts.

- Click the print preview to zoom in to view the selected contacts (Figure 3–64).

Q&A If I click the other styles, will they only show selected contacts?
No. If you change the style, the preview returns to showing all contacts. To see the selected contacts in a particular style, you select the style and then change the print options.

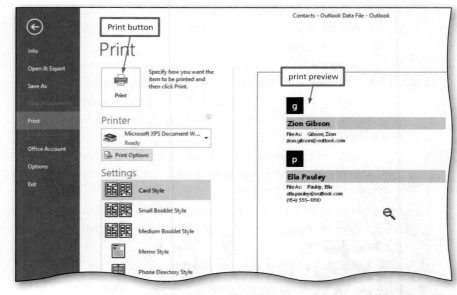

Figure 3–64

BTW
Printing Contacts
Contacts can be printed directly to paper, saved as a PDF file, or sent to OneNote using the Printer button arrow.

To Print a Contact List

1 CREATE NEW CONTACT | 2 MODIFY CONTACT | 3 CHANGE VIEW OF CONTACTS
4 FIND CONTACT | 5 CREATE CONTACT GROUP | 6 PRINT CONTACT LIST

Why? Before heading to a meeting, you may want a printed list of contacts for reference. The following steps print the selected contacts in Card style, and then exit Outlook.

1 Click the Print button to print the selected contacts (Figure 3–65).

2 If you have a contact open, click the Close button on the right side of the title bar to close the Contact window.

3 Click the Close button on the right side of the title bar to exit Outlook.

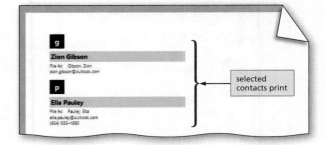

Figure 3–65

Summary

In this module, you have learned how to use Outlook to create a contact list, view and sort contacts, and search for contacts. You learned to create and edit a contact group, add notes to a contact, and print contacts.

CONSIDER THIS

Consider This: Plan Ahead

What decisions will you need to make when creating contacts from friends, family, and coworkers, editing contacts, creating a contact group, and printing contacts in the future?

1. Create contacts.

   a. Determine the people with whom you plan to interact on a regular basis, such as your friends, family, and coworkers. Adding too many contacts can make it difficult to manage your contact list.

   b. Determine the information that would be most helpful about each of your contacts.

2. Edit contacts.

   a. Determine if any additional contact information should be added to a contact.

   b. Determine which contacts should be deleted, such as those with whom you no longer have regular communication.

   c. Request pictures of your contacts to add to their contact information.

   d. Add file attachments as needed to contacts.

3. View and sort contact lists.

   a. Select a view that displays the information you need in a contact list.

   b. Switch views as necessary to have quick access to people's information.

   c. Create a custom view if none of the built-in views is suitable for you.

   d. Sort contacts to display them in a different order.

4. Use Search to find contacts.

   a. Determine the preferred way to view the contacts to find the information you are seeking.

   b. Determine the sort order to use for your contacts, considering what information you are trying to find.

5. Create and edit contact groups.

   a. Plan the relationship of the contacts that are organized under the group name.

   b. Consider a good name for a contact group that will make it easier for you to remember the purpose of the group.

6. Print your contacts.

   a. Plan how best to display your contacts.

CONSIDER THIS

How should you submit solutions to questions in the assignments identified with a ✳ symbol?

Every assignment in this book contains one or more questions with a ✳ symbol. These questions require you to think beyond the assigned file. Present your solutions to the question in the format required by your instructor. Possible formats may include one or more of these options: write the answer; create a document that contains the answer; present your answer to the class; discuss your answer in a group; record the answer as audio or video using a webcam, smartphone, or portable media player; or post answers on a blog, wiki, or website.

Apply Your Knowledge

Reinforce the skills and apply the concepts you learned in this module.

Note: To complete this assignment, you will be required to use the Data Files. Please contact your instructor for information about accessing the Data Files.

Updating a Contact List

Instructions: Run Outlook. Edit the contact list provided in the file called Apply Your Knowledge 3-1 Contacts, located on the Data Files for Students. The Apply Your Knowledge 3-1 Contacts file contains five contacts and a contact group. Many of the contacts have changed and some are incomplete. You now need to revise these contacts and print them in Card view (Figure 3–66).

Perform the following tasks:

1. Import the Apply Your Knowledge 3-1 Contacts file into Outlook.

2. Change Kelly Updike's company to **Adventure Tours**. Move Kelly's Business phone number to the Mobile text box. Change her job title to **Sales Manager**. Add an email address of **kelly.updike@ email.com**.

3. Change Hugo Arenas' company to **Whitewater Rafting Tours**. Type **hugo.arenas@email.com** as his new email address, and change his phone number to **555-0610**. Add the following as his webpage address: **http://www.hugorafting.com/whitewater**.

4. Change Chelsea Nash's email address to **cnash@ adventure.com**. Add a Home phone of **555-9965**.

5. Change the job title for Hansen Jacobs to **Tour Guide**.

6. Change the Adventure contact group name to Adventure Tours. Add the Kelly Updike contact to the contact group and remove the Lauren Mariel contact from the contact group.

7. Add a new contact using your name, email address, and photo.

8. Print the final contact list in Card Style, as shown in Figure 3–66, and then submit the printout to your instructor.

9. Export the Apply Your Knowledge 3-1 Contacts file to a USB flash drive, and then delete the file from the hard disk.

10. ✳ Outlook can display your contacts in a variety of views. Which view do you prefer, and why?

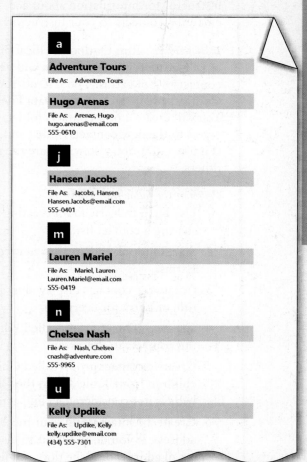

Figure 3–66

Extend Your Knowledge

Extend the skills you learned in this module and experiment with new skills. You may need to use Help to complete the assignment.

Creating a Contact Folder

Note: To complete this assignment, you will be required to use the Data Files. Please contact your instructor for information about accessing the Data Files. An active email account is necessary to email the contacts to your instructor.

Instructions: Run Outlook. A local filmmaker is creating a feature film in your town and needs to create a contacts list of extras. The Extend Your Knowledge 3-1 Contacts file located on the Data Files has no contacts. You will create a new contacts folder, add the names of extras to the new contacts folder, and print the contact list (Figure 3–67). You also will share the contacts folder with others.

Perform the following tasks:

1. Use Help to learn about creating a contacts folder and sharing a contact list.
2. Start Outlook and create a new contacts folder named Extras.
3. Create the contacts displayed in Table 3–2. Add the job title of Extra for everyone.
4. Create a contact group called Film Extras. Add all of the contacts to this group.
5. Create a contact group called Child Actors. Add the children from Table 3–2 to the Child Actors group. A baby is not considered a child actor.
6. Create a contact using your mother's name and email address. If you do not want to disclose your mother's email address or if she does not have one, replace it with your email address.
7. Print the contact list in Phone Directory view, as shown in Figure 3–67, and then submit the printout to your instructor.

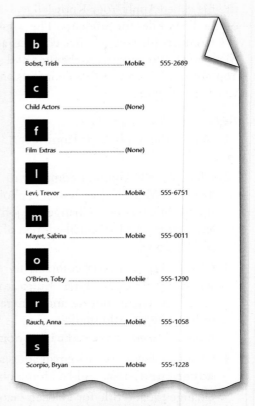

Figure 3–67

Table 3–2 Film Extras Information			
Full Name	**Notes**	**Email Address**	**Mobile Phone**
Bryan Scorpio	College-Aged Male	bryan.scorpio@email.com	555-1228
Toby O'Brien	Middle-Aged Male	mrobrien@world.net	555-1290
Anna Rauch	Girl, Age 10	anna.rauch@earth.com	555-1058
Trevor Levi	Boy, Age 12	tlevi@agent.com	555-6751
Sabina Mayet	Mother with Baby	sabinam@earth.net	555-0011
Trish Bobst	Dog Handler	trish@pupactors.com	555-2689

8. Select all the contacts. Use the Forward Contact button (Home tab | Share group) and click As an Outlook Contact to email the contact list to your instructor.
9. ✳ Why might it be advantageous to create separate folders within your contacts?

Expand Your World: Cloud and Web Technologies

Create a solution that uses cloud or web technologies by learning and investigating on your own from general guidance.

Opening Contacts in Microsoft OneNote 2016

Note: To complete this assignment, you will be required to use the completed Module 3 files from this text.

Instructions: A program named OneNote is part of the Microsoft Office 2016 suite that gathers users' digital notes (handwritten or typed), contacts, drawings, screen clippings, and audio/video commentaries. In this assignment, you will set up a OneNote notebook and copy contacts from Outlook into a OneNote notebook to add contact references that will allow you to take detailed notes about each contact (Figure 3–68).

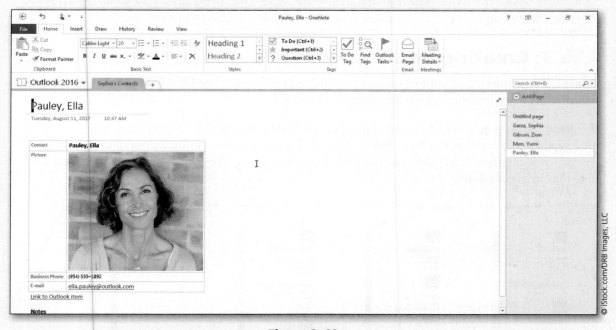

Figure 3–68

Perform the following tasks:

1. Open Outlook with the completed Sophia contacts for Module 3 displayed and then open OneNote.

2. In OneNote, create a notebook named Outlook 2016 and then create a OneNote section named Sophia's Contacts.

3. In Outlook, click People on the Navigation bar to display Sophia's contacts. Select the four individual contacts including Sophia, Zion, Yumi, and Ella.

4. Open Microsoft OneNote if you have never opened the program before to confirm that Microsoft OneNote is set up. Close Microsoft OneNote.

5. Click OneNote (Home tab | Actions group) to open the Select Location in OneNote dialog box.

6. In the Select Location in OneNote dialog box, click the plus sign in front of Outlook 2016 and then click Sophia's Contacts.

7. Click the OK button in the Select Location in OneNote dialog box to copy the contacts into four separate pages in OneNote (Figure 3–68).

Continued >

Expand Your World *continued*

8. Click the Sophia Garza page in the right pane, press the SHIFT key and click Ella Pauley to select all four contact pages.

9. Click the File tab and click Send. Next, click Send to Word to open Microsoft Word, which displays all four contacts.

10. Submit the Microsoft Word document in the format specified by your instructor.

11. ✸ Why would you copy contacts into OneNote? Write at least three ideas in sentence format.

In the Labs

Design, create, modify, and/or use files following the guidelines, concepts, and skills presented in this module. Labs 1 and 2, which increase in difficulty, require you to create solutions based on what you learned in the module; Lab 3 requires you to apply your creative thinking and problem-solving skills to design and implement a solution.

Lab 1: Creating Reunion Contacts

Note: To complete this assignment, you will be required to use the Data Files. Please contact your instructor for information about accessing the Data Files.

Problem: You have agreed to create a contact list of your senior class of your high school in which you graduated for an upcoming reunion. Table 3–3 provides a beginning listing of the classmates' contact information. Enter the contacts into the contacts list. The contact list you create will look like that in Figure 3–69.

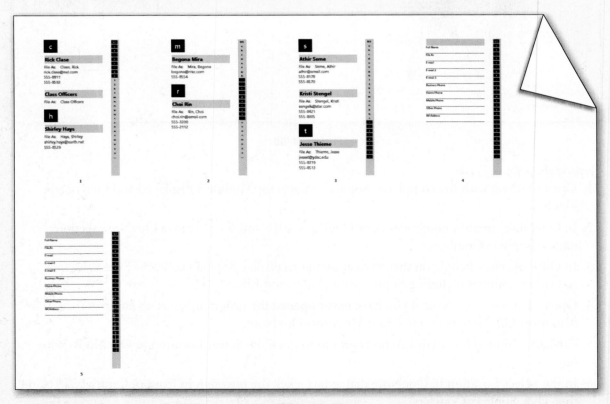

Figure 3–69

Perform the following tasks:

1. Create a new Outlook Data File named Lab 3-1 Reunion Contacts.

2. Create the contacts in the Contacts window, using the information listed in Table 3–3.

Table 3–3 Reunion Contact Information			
Classmate	**Email Address**	**Business**	**Mobile**
Jesse Thieme	jesset@ydac.edu	555-8319	555-8513
Shirley Hays	shirley.hays@earth.net		555-8529
Athir Seme	athir@email.com	555-8178	555-8570
Kristi Stengel	stengelk@star.com	555-8421	555-8005
Begona Mira	begona@nlsc.com		555-8554
Rick Clase	rick.clase@net.com	555-8111	555-8593
Choi Rin	choi.rin@email.com	555-3200	555-2112

3. For each contact, list the webpage address as http://www.classmate.com/rhs.

4. Create a group named Class Officers. Add Athir, Rick, and Choi.

5. Add the following note to Kristi's contact information — `Owns an event coordination company.`

6. Create a contact for yourself with your email address and mobile phone number.

7. Print the contacts list using Small Booklet Style as shown in Figure 3–69, and submit it in a format specified by your instructor.

8. ✹ What other information might be useful to include in the reunion contact list if you plan to share this with the rest of your classmates at the reunion?

Lab 2: Creating an Employee Contact List

Problem: You are the owner of Rock Salt Seafood Supply, a local fresh seafood store. Your store has decided to email reminders to their best customers about weekly specials. You need to create a contacts list and add contact groups so that you send specific information for local restaurant owners and regular customers (Figure 3–70).

Perform the following tasks:

1. Create a new Outlook Data File named Lab 3-2 Rock Salt Contacts.

2. Create two contact groups called Restaurant Owners and Regular Customers.

3. Enter the contacts in the Contacts list, using the information listed in Table 3–4.

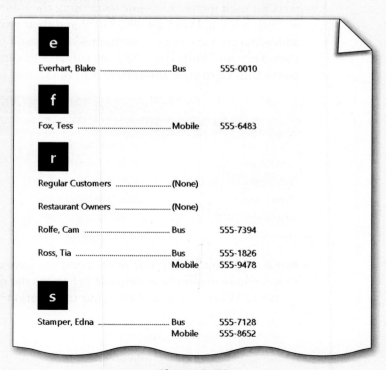

Figure 3–70

Continued >

In the Labs *continued*

4. Add the contacts to the appropriate contact group.

5. Add the following note to Edna's contact information: **Give us a call if Rock Point Oysters available.**

Table 3–4 Rock Salt Seafood Supply Mailing List

Name/Business Name	Email Address	Business Phone	Mobile Phone	Customer Type
Cam Rolfe (Company: Blue Marlin)	bluemarlin@blue.com	555-7394		Restaurant Owner
Tia Ross	tia.ross@email.com	555-1826	555-9478	Regular Customer
Tess Fox	tess09@earth.com		555-6483	Regular Customer
Edna Stamper (Company: Sea Mist)	seamist@email.com	555-7128	555-8652	Restaurant Owner
Blake Everhart (Company: Hard Shell)	hardshell@earth.net	555-0010		Restaurant Owner

6. Add the title of owner to the restaurant owner contacts.

7. Print the contacts list in Phone Directory style as a PDF file and save the Outlook data file as a .pst file. Submit both files in the format specified by your instructor.

8. ✸ What additional information about your customers might be useful to add to your contacts folder?

Lab 3: Scheduling Employees for the Gelato Shop

Professional

Part 1: At the Dolce Gelato Shop, you are in charge of scheduling your team of employees. You need a contact list of all part-time and full-time employees. Using the contacts and techniques presented in this module, create an Outlook Data File named Lab 3-3 Dolce Gelato and add contacts for each member of your team using the information in Table 3–5. The gelato shop is located at 75 Beach Dr., Westlake, FL, 33022 and their website is http://dolcegelatoshop.com. Add three additional contacts using your friends' names and information. Create two contact groups called Part-Time and Full-Time. Add the contacts to appropriate group. Save the contact list and print the contacts in Card style and submit it in the format specified by your instructor.

Table 3–5 Team List Contacts

Full Name	Email Address	Mobile Phone	Part/Full Time
Titus Angel	titus@dolcegelato.com	555-6667	Part Time
Ben Cohen	ben@dolcegelato.com	555-8221	Full Time
Rob Ruiz	rob@dolcegelato.com	555-9856	Part Time
Nina Inwood	nina@dolcegelato.com	555-3846	Full Time
Stan Silver	stan@dolcegelato.com	555-2877	Full Time
Aiko Kuro	aiko@dolcegelato.com	555-8745	Part Time

Part 2: ✸ Should everyone in the company have access to all contact information, or should access to some information be restricted? What was the rationale behind each of these decisions and suggestions? Where did you obtain your information?

Index

Note: **Boldfaced** page numbers indicate key terms